Hangingout.
in
spain

Hangingout™

in

spain

First Edition

A Balliett & Fitzgerald Book

Hungry Minds, Inc.

Balliett & Fitzgerald, Inc.
Project Editor: Kristen Couse
Production Managers: Maria Fernandez, Mike Walters
Production Editor: Paul Paddock
Map Artist: Darshan Bhagat
Line Editors: Carrie Chase, Kim Wyatt, Amy Leibrock
Copy Editors: Carolyn Keubler, Christopher Tinney, Kevin McLain
Proofreaders: Jodi Brandon, Donna Stonecipher, Shoshanna Wingate
Associate Editors: Nathaniel Knaebel, Chris Varmus, Alix McNamara
Editorial Intern: Joanna Cupano

Published by
Hungry Minds, Inc.
909 Third Avenue
New York, NY 10022

ISBN: 0-7645-6245-2
ISSN: 1531-1570

Book design: Sue Canavan and Mike Walters

Special Sales: For general information on Hungry Minds' products and
services please contact our Customer Care Department within the U.S.
at Tel 800-762-2974, outside the U.S. at Tel 317-572-3993 or Fax 317-
572-4002.

For sales inquires and reseller information, including discounts, premium
and bulk quantity sales, and foreign-language translations, please contact
our Customer Care Department at Tel 1-800-434-3422 or Fax 317-572-
4002.

Manufactured in the United States of America

5   4   3   2   1

CONTENTS

spain

contents

backmatter

spain

maps

a disclaimer

Please note that prices fluctuate over the course of time, and travel information changes under the impact of the many factors that influence the travel industry. We therefore suggest that you write or call ahead for confirmation when making your travel plans. Every effort has been made to ensure the accuracy of information throughout this book, and the contents of this publication are believed correct at the time of printing. Nevertheless, the publishers cannot accept responsibility for errors or omissions or for changes in details given in this guide or for the consequences of any reliance on the information provided by the same. Assessments of attractions and so forth are based upon the author's own experience and therefore, descriptions given in this guide necessarily contain an element of subjective opinion, which may not reflect the publisher's opinion or dictate a reader's own experience on another occasion. Readers are invited to write the publisher with ideas, comments, and suggestions for future editions.

Your safety is important to us, however, so we encourage you to stay alert and be aware of your surroundings. Keep a close eye on cameras, purses, and wallets, all favorite targets of thieves and pickpockets.

an invitation to the reader

In researching this book, we discovered many wonderful places—hotels, restaurants, shops, and more. We're sure you'll find others. Please tell us about them, so we can share the information with your fellow travelers in upcoming editions. If you were disappointed with a recommendation, we'd love to know that, too.

Please write to:
Hanging Out in Spain, 1st Edition
Hungry Minds, Inc.
909 Third Ave.
New York, NY 10022

foreword

ost of us have had the experience of going to a new school or moving to a new neighborhood and not knowing a soul there, not knowing the laws of the land, feeling lost and uncool. But if you're lucky, someone comes along who invites you in and shows you where the action is. The same can be said for travel: Unless you're committed to seeing Europe through the moving tinted window of a tour bus, pretty soon you're going to want to get past the initial strangeness and get with it. And to really be able to do that, you need someone or something to help you along, so that what could have been just another cute postcard turns into a new chapter in your life.

Going to Europe is infinitely more complicated—and ultimately more rewarding—than just going on a road trip. Without some help, you may repeatedly find yourself surrounded by a numbed-out tour group, scratching your head and wondering what all the fuss is about. We sent out our teams of writers with just that in mind. Go to where the action is, we instructed them, and tell us how to find it.

Of course we tell you how to see all the cultural and historical goodies you've read about in art history class and heard about from your folks, but we also tell you where to find the party, shake your butt, and make friends with the locals. We've tried to find the hottest scenes in Europe—where traditions are being reinvented daily—and make these guides into the equivalent of a hip friend to show you the ropes.

So, welcome to the new Europe, on the verge of mighty unification. The European Union (EU)—and the euro's arrival as a common currency—is already making many happy, others nervous, and setting the entire continent abuzz with a different kind of energy. As the grand tour of Europe meets the Info Age, the old ways are having to adjust to a faster tempo.

But even as the globe is shrinking to the size of a dot com, Europe remains a vast vast place with enough history and art and monuments to fill endless guides. So we had to make a choice. We wanted the *Hanging Out* guides to live up to their title, so we decided to specialize and not only show you the best spots to eat, shop, sightsee, party, and crash, but also give you a real feeling for each place, and unique but do-able ways to get to know it better. So we don't cover *every single* town, village, and mountaintop—instead, we picked what we felt were the best and serve them up with plenty of detail. We felt it was crucial to have the room to go deeper, and to tip you off as to how to do the same, so that after you see the sights, you'll almost certainly end up in a place where you'll get to know the secret to the best travel: the locals.

Aside from the basics—neighborhoods, eats, crashing, stuff (shopping), culture zoo (sightseeing stuff), and need to know (the essentials)—we cover the bar scene, the live music scene, the club scene, the gay scene, the visual arts scene, and the performing arts scene, always giving you the scoop on where to chill out and where to get wild. We take you on some beautiful walks and show you great places to hang (sometimes for no money). Things to Talk to a Local About actually gives you some fun conversation openers. Fashion tells you what people are wearing. Wired lists websites for each city—some general, some cool, some out-of-the-way—so you can start checking things out immediately. It also takes you to the best cybercafes in each place. Rules of the Game lays out local liquor and substance laws and also gives you the vibe on the street. Five-0 does a quick sketch of cops in each city. Boy meets Girl dares to speculate on that most mysterious of travel adventures. And Festivals & Events lists just that. We also take you out to all the best outdoor spots, where you can hike, bike, swim, jump, ski, snorkel, or surf till you've had enough.

Our adventurous team of writers (average age 24) and editors let you in on the ongoing party. We want to make sure that your time abroad is punctuated by moments when you've sunk deep enough into the mix (or danced long enough to it), so that you suddenly get it, you have that flash of knowing what it's like to actually *be* somewhere else, to live there—to hang out in Europe.

introduction

When was the last time you took a mid-day nap, walked barefoot along the beach, ate fish as fresh as today's catch, literally danced all night, heard flamenco guitar, rode on a moped, watched a local soccer game, wandered around a castle, saw people juggling fire in the streets, felt like it was appropriate to wear tight turquoise pants, didn't mind being lost on narrow streets, drank sangria, or fell in love at first sight? If the answer is "can't remember the last time" or "never" to one or more of these questions, you should seriously consider spending some time in Spain.

Yes, Spain might just be the place to fulfill your fantasies. Fabulous beaches, nights that don't end, colors that burst, streets that echo with history, extravagant festivals that are perfectly scripted—It's a sensory and sensual, experience you won't forget. Spain is not too discovered (yet), but it does have enough of a tourist-friendly infrastructure to make traveling easy.

There is more to this place then meets the eye. Spain is a collection of cultures, languages, landscapes, foods, dances, jokes, and songs. It will call to you. It will draw you near, then push you away in a sexy dance, two steps forward, a brief glance, then a sudden turn.

Few other places feel as rooted in the past while simultaneously racing to embrace the future as Spain, and this combination makes a visit here an exhilarating, enriching experience. History here reaches back indefi-

spain

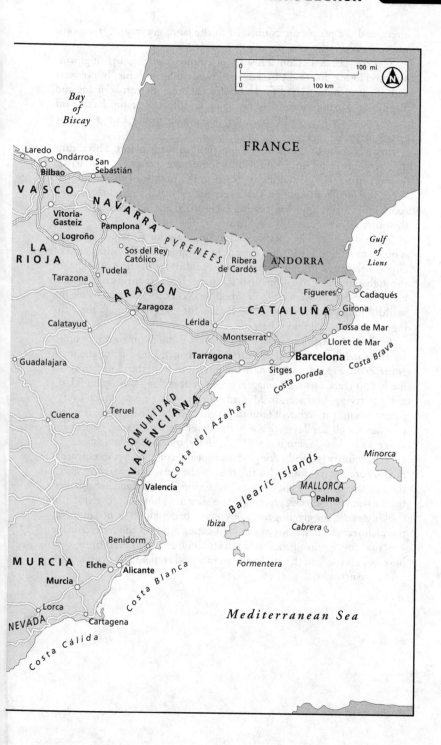

nitely, and the people are connected to the land, geography, traditions, and folkways.

The complicated colonial history of cultures clashing, fighting, winning and losing, forms the backdrop of modern Spanish life. It intersects with the post-modern and the technological present creating insane and inspirational juxtapositions. Today Spain is still working on shaking off the conservative legacy of Franco, but you get the feeling things are only getting better.

Spain is home of the *siesta*, still practiced in many places. This means that between 1 and 4pm, you will be wandering the streets, wondering how it can be that everything is closed in the middle of the afternoon. What the Spaniards know is that everyone is sitting around the dining room table, drinking wine, teasing each other, and telling stories. And then they all take a nap! *This* is Spain.

Spain is also art. The epicenter is bustling Barcelona—which everyone is quick to remind is the most European (as opposed to Spanish) kind of city—with museums and crazy Gaudí buildings, but the quake shakes through the fabric of all Spanish culture. Here, art meets life, shakes hands, and doesn't ask for a Cosmopolitan. Whether you want to see the world through the vision of Goya, Picasso, or Dali, or through the writings of Lorca, you'll find it here.

Spain is also a quiet *pueblo* that you walk through on your way up to an ancient Moorish castle. Spain is fresh-baked bread from the local *panería* where grandmothers have bought bread from the same family for the last 50 years. Spain is teenagers on mopeds making-out. Spain is late-night partying, best seen in Madrid, but pumping pretty much everywhere. Spain is stretches of famous beaches on the Mediterranean where you can lay all day long. Spain is the Pyrenees mountains, perfect for skiing and hiking. Spain is Sevilla and all the romance of Andalusia.

This country is breathtakingly beautiful and complex, yet its moments of glory are always simple. It's the turn of the curve on a winding street, the easy friendliness of your bartender, the simple smiles and handshakes, the kiss-on-two-cheeks greetings, the slammed blue sky, the smell of cooking *paella*, the giggling teenagers on the back of loud-as-hell mopeds, the architecture as various as the landscapes. And it's the indescribable way that the Spanish peoples, languages, cultures, and everything they have built settle into the land with an ease and contentment you cannot find anywhere else.

the best of spain

party spots

Sevilla [Andalucía Region]: Street party central. Bring your own bottle to Plaza Salvador, barhop along the river on Calle Betis, or straight chill in the stony Alameda de Hércules.

Plaza Nueva [Granada]: A funky international crowd congregates here for the multitude of *tapas* bars. Buy a drink, get free tapas—that's how it works here.

Las Fallas [Valencia]: In this festival, held every March 12-19, over 300 giant papier-mâché sculptures are built and displayed in the city's plazas, then ceremoniously set on fire and burnt to the ground. Giant bonfires, fireworks, *paella,* beer, and general anarchy ensue.

Malasaña [Madrid]: Smokey songs of scents and color fill the air in this worthy neighborhood, the site of the best down-to-earth *borracheros* in Spain. Drinking and hanging out in the square Plaza Dos de Mayo before heading to a sticky-floored bar or artsy cafe can't do you wrong on a Friday night.

San Fermin [Pamplona]: This is it, kids: the famous running of the bulls. But you don't have to risk your ass (literally...) against angry he-cows to enjoy one of the world's most outrageous parties. The week of the festival (in early July) is packed full of not only bulls, but plenty of bands and booze. If you think you can survive it, get there early—the first couple days are the best.

End of semester [Salamanca]: If you can, plan your time in Salamanca to coincide with the end of the school year (May). A weekend in Salamanca can get pretty wild, as students attending the countries oldest university blow off some steam as only the Spanish can. It all ends up dancing from dawn to noon the next day on El Barco, the infamous party barge, as DJs spin hard house to a crowd that lost their sobriety long ago, the night before....

La Devesa [Girona]: During the peak season (the warm months), the party at this little residential/park area lasts till 5am. Join the throngs of drinkers at this combination high-school keg party/sophisticated professor toke-a-thon.

CULTURE

La Carbonería [Sevilla]: Some places will always be cool, no matter how many tourists tramp through them, and this flamenco bar is one of them. Built into an old coal yard, there are authentic flamenco shows free-of-charge every night, as well as local jazz and folk in the front room.

Alhambra [Granada]: This Muslim palace/fortress, which dominates the city from its hilltop position, is one of the most sublime examples of Islamic architecture west of Mecca. Everything from lush gardens and fountains to intricately detailed tiling and hand-carved wooden ceilings. Plan ahead.

Toledo: First there's the ancient *Catedral,* which can make you literally step back in awe, with it's stunning architecture and the fantastically eclectic French, Arabic, and Gothic artwork inside. But even if you never make it to the *Catedral,* you can get just as good a show by simply losing yourself in Toledo's labyrinth of mysterious medieval streets for a day.

Paseo del Prado [Madrid]: The concentrated triangle of museums on this famed square is the best art show in the country. The Prado, Reina Sofía, and the Thyssen-Bornemisza are all practically right on top of each other and offer you anything and everything from El Bosco, Velazquez, and Rubens to Picasso, Dalí, and Chillida. You may explode from cultural overload if you atempt them all in an afternoon.

Guggenheim [Bilbao]: Frank Gehry has given the world one of the best new museums of the century. The Guggenheim is not only a world class museum, but it stands as testimony to what forward thinking can bring to a struggling city.

Jazz Festival [San Sebastian]: In mid-July, all of San Sebastian turns into a stage as the world's premier jazz musicians gather in this elegant Basque city to create one of the hottest festivals in Europe. Reserve a room waaaay in advance....

Barcelona: Whether it be new, underground, and hyper-hip Catalán-speaking post-punk, neo-grunge, livin' la vida moda, Piccaso, or Gaudi buildings that look like melting ice cream, Barcelona has more culture than you'll know what to do with. Just go there, open your eyes, ears, and whatever other orifice you want, and have a good old time in the city where culture still has a pulse.

outdoors

Sierra Nevada [Andalucía Region]: These mountains, only 30 minutes from the city of Granada, offer the sunniest and most happening ski/snowboard resort in Spain. Or, you can hike or bike to the top of Spain's highest peak, Mulhacén, from unbelievably green and mysterious river valleys of Las Alpujarras.

Cabo de Gata [Andalucía Region]: Where the desert meets the beach, this promontory offers Spain's wildest beaches with red volcanic cliffs, hidden coves, and the mellowest, least-dressed crowd.

Tarifa [Andalucía Region]: The windsurfing capital of Europe, and for good reason: The wind is blowing all the time here, where the Mediterranean meets the Atlantic, and the green hills of Africa loom in the distance.

Royal Gardens [Aranjuez]: These splendid gardens, just beyond the Palacio Real, are some of the most dignified walks in the Madrid region. If you're looking for an oasis from the dry air and brown-grassed countryside surrounding the oven of a capital city, this is it.

Cangas de Onis [Cantabria]: Want to be thrown off a bridge with only an oversized rubber band tied to your feet? Call the friendly folks at this deluxe outdoor outfitter, and you could be flying through the air in no time. If bungee jumping is too passé for you (or if that's just your excuse, you wuss) it also offers canyoning trips, caving tours, canoeing, horseback riding, and quad tours.

The Pyrenees: If you want to check out some awesome, awesome, awesome mountains, streams, and geography where you can hike, backpack, kayak, or just run, jump and play on some of the must striking natural beauty in Spain, then get thee to the Pyrenees! The two best spots to enter from are Jaca and Benasque, in the community of Aragon. While the transportation can be bumpy, and of course the nightlife is a suffering redheaded stepchild, but you're tough, and you're here to climb, not to drink!

Costa Brava beaches: Co-ed naked sunbathing! If you're a girl, taking your top off on any beach is the thing to do. If you're a gentleman, you'll have to search out an all-nude beach—but they aren't that hard to find, just slightly rarer. Who knew that getting a sunburn on your ass could be so fun?

weird and bizarre

Museo del Bandolero [Ronda]: This museum celebrates the bandits and outlaws who took refuge in the hills here, some of whom were regular Robin Hoods and some of whom were just plain evil.

La Ciudad de Artes y Sciences [Valencia]: This bold new step into the twenty-first century already includes **L'Hemispheric,** an IMAX theater and planetarium housed in a stunning metal and glass eyeball-shaped building. When completed, the complex will also include *L'Oceangrafic,* an aquarium with man-made bodies of water simulating all of the world's oceans.

Convento de Santa Teresa [Avila]: I've wondered about freezing my brain so I could be resuscitated in the future. Well, apparently saving body parts isn't a new concept: Go see Saint Teresa's finger wrapped up at the convent where she spent most of her years. It's not in a huge attention-attracting display, and you can't rub it for luck, but you can feel the saintly vibes through the glass case.

Stone Frog [Salamanca]: We've all heard how the princess kissing a frog got her prince, right? Well, if you can find the stone frog on the façade of Salamanca's University building, rumor has it you're guaranteed good fortune and marriage within the year (if that's considered good fortune...).

The Human Towers [Tarragona]: Every two years, a bunch of guys dress up in black and red and pour into the central square to build huge body buildings that can be over a couple of stories high. Take pictures if you want your friends back home to believe it really happened.

madrid and
environs

madrid and environs

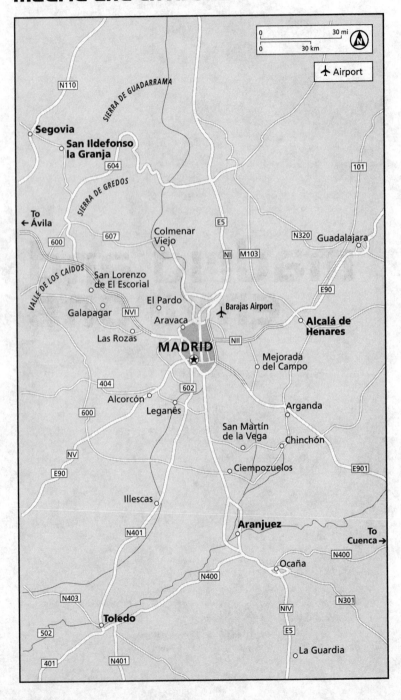

deer and rabbits skitter about on hunting land that stretches between small mountain ranges, and golden grasses sprout up from rocky soil on the plateau. West-central Spain may seem like a rough, maybe even colorless setting, but the towns and their people are anything but dry. The region's best—and, without a doubt, the true heart of the country, culturally as well as geographically—is **Madrid,** a nonstop party and social magnet that simply can't be missed. (Barcelona fans may contest the greatness and superlatives of Madrid, but that's for you to judge.) You can see most of Madrid, the monuments, architecture, museums, park, etc., in about five days comfortably, three if you're the type who likes to zip through on dizzying tours of Europe. To really feel Madrid though, you ought to spend a week...or even up to a lifetime, because it's the people who make this place, and you'll need time to absorb their flavor.

Like any great metropolis, Madrid offers something to do every minute of the day and night, so you will see the streets of the city center full of people most of the time. Between 2 and 4pm, of course, one of the major activities includes a long lunch and perhaps a siesta, which temporarily calms the pedestrian commotion, but freshens everyone up for nighttime activity. Madrileños hit the streets often—to stroll, shop, drink a beer, eat, see a show or movie, or listen to live music. The life is very social, even in the cold of the rainy winters and the heat of the stifling summers. The city's vibrancy can sometimes become overwhelming—the inescapable cacophony of traffic, crowds, and culture—but as soon as you leave you may very well feel a hollow ache for Madrid's commotion, the movement of the masses, and the thousand and one things to do.

If you do spend a week doing a thousand and one things, you should seize the opportunity to visit the surrounding towns of **Aranjuez** and **San Lorenzo de El Escorial,** once among the favorite getaways for royals and royal wannabes. Nowadays, even commoners like us can sample the luxurious lifestyle at either spot, both of which are a hop, skip, and a jump from the big city, perfect for day trips. Where your day in Aranjuez may be spent strolling arm in arm with your honey past trickling fountains, you'll spend time in San Lorenzo de El Escorial below the surface looking at tombs of long-gone kings and contemplating Spain's past. Madrid has spent the last 25 years recovering from Franco, who took power in 1936 after the nation's bloody civil war. Following his death in 1975, Madrid—indeed, the entire country, but most notably its capital—began to open up. "La Movida," as this widespread release of repressed emotions and liberation has been called, finally bestowed upon the Spanish the freedom to express themselves in cinema, on the dance floor, and in the streets. One of the few things that casts a pall over this vibrant city, and a few other regions in Spain, is the specter of ETA, the militant Basque separatist group. ETA was especially active in the 1980's, and resurfaced with deadly force in the year 2000, when a few of its attacks hit home in central Madrid. Although the subject of ETA is discussed more and more openly, it continues to be a sensitive topic that is not casually brought up at any old dinner table.

Ummm...speaking of dinner...let's move on to the really important subject: food. As far as Spanish cuisine goes, you'll find eating out here often involves lots of fried foods, especially if you're carousing in the *tapas* scene. Down your *cerveza* with these small portions of nibbles like calamares, home fries, croquettes, and cheeses. And get ready for that ham! Central Spain is all about the porky pork, and you'll find it in more forms than you ever thought possible. *Chorizo* sausage, *Jamón Serrano* or *Jamón Jabugo* (ham sliced thin, straight off the pig leg and frequently on display in bars), *morcilla* (blood sausage stuffed with rice or onions), *lomo* (pork loin), and so much more. Don't be shy with the stuff like blood sausage—it's actually quite good, in moderation of course. The winter specialty *Cocido Madrileño*, a stew pressure-cooked with all of those pork products, chick peas, and small noodles called *fideos*, is served in courses, separating the broth, meats, and chick peas. It's perfect to fatten you up for the cold weather. Finally, to top things off for the sweet tooth, and I mean *sweet*, a morning or late-night snack of *chocolate con churros* will make even the most confirmed chocoholic say "when." Delicious rings of fried dough are dipped in a thick chocolate pudding that locals insist on actually drinking between bites of the churros. I personally can never finish the whole cup, but it does miracles for the oncoming hangover after a night out, coating your stomach with enough grease and sugar to subdue the queasies.

art and architecture

Madrid's art museums definitely make it onto the European Top 10 in my book. Some of the big timers hanging on the walls here are Velázquez, Goya, Dalí, Miró, and good ol' Pablo P. There are paintings here that you really have to see before skipping town, and not just on the museum postcards, mind you. In the **Prado** [see **madrid,** below], *Las Meninas* by Diego de Velázquez (1599-1660) portrays the artist painting the king and queen, while little ladies of the court look on. The really cool thing is how Velázquez plays with visual perception: His self-portrait and the young women appear to be looking at you, despite the fact that they are actually watching the royal couple, who are the subject of the painting within the painting, who are seen in a distant mirror in the background....

Also in the Prado are Francisco de Goya's (1746-1828) mysterious *Majas*, a pair of paintings that depict the same woman stretched on a couch; in one, she is naked, and in the other one, dressed. (It's like one of those magic pens that you turn upside down to make the girl's dress disappear.) Goya was a pretty frustrated guy all around, and after years of painting pastel-colored religious and courtly canvases, he eventually turned to making dark political statements about the revolutionary times. Witness his *War for Independence* series, or his last *Pinturas Negras* ("Black Paintings"), painted by an aging and ailing Goya on the walls of his house. Some of these last paintings, like *The Witches Sabbath* and *Saturn Devouring One of His Sons,* are downright ghoulish and even get a little trippy, though not as trippy as Salvador Dalí's (1904-1989) melting clocks in the *Reina Sofía* [see **madrid,** below]. The Dalí collection here is surprisingly small, but worth visiting for his first foray into surrealism, *El Gran Masturbador* ("The Great Masturbator"). The Reina Sofía more than makes up for its Dalí shortage with its number of works by Picasso (1882-1973) and Miró (1893-1983) in large rooms brimming over with cubism, random lines and points, and distorted images. Follow the tour groups up to Picasso's 1937 *Guernica* or, if you're too cheap to pay the entrance fee, have the man at the door of the museum explain its controversial themes of the Spanish Civil War. Joan Miró's works go with the surrealist flow, though technically he came 10 years after the movement; his paintings have a sort of connect-the-dots quality, scattered all over with simple lines and points of color.

As for architecture styles in the region, you'll find all the usual suspects (Romanesque, Gothic, Baroque, Neoclassic, and Modernist), but Spain throws an interesting jolt of Muslim and Islamic influences into the mix. These mudéjar elements include features such as exterior brick and horseshoe arches, and highly detailed wooden ceilings with geometrical designs. Once you start looking for them, you'll see them all over town.

Unlike Barcelona with its Gaudí buildings, or Seville with its ancient monuments (some dating from the Moorish occupation), nobody visits Madrid for its architecture. The city grew haphazardly and virtually all styles are incorporated, including garish and impersonal blocks of apartment houses that evoke the suburban ghettos around Moscow. The one exception to that is the **Plaza Mayor** and the network of narrow old streets that branch off from it. This famous square, which was known during the Middle Ages as Plaza de Arrabal, forms the core of old Madrid. Its original designer was the architect Juan Gómez de Mora, who labored under the commissions of Philip III.

Three major fires have swept over the square. After 1790, the Plaza Mayor was designed by Juan de Villanueva, and his architecture is essentially what you see today. Slate spires are the most obvious architectural feature. The square contains Madrid's most graceful arcades, spindly towers, and open-air verandahs, combinations of which became the hallmark of the Madrid style of architecture. Later, parts of the city that expanded outward from the inner core around the Plaza Mayor were designed by architects during the 19th century.

getting around the region

Tooling about in west-central Spain is quite easy because the buses and trains establish their main routes out of Madrid. The big city serves as a starting point for the country's highways at *kilometro zero* in the **Puerta del Sol**, and the two train stations, **Atocha** and **Chamartín**, have frequent, well-networked regional and international lines, making it a perfect home base for travelers on day or weekend trips. The *Renfe* train system runs smoothly and generally on time—surprising for a country full of people who run on a clock that's at least 15 minutes behind yours. Train schedules are often quite easy to figure out, but riding the rails isn't always the quickest way to get from point A to point B. Buses can be faster—although you'll have to put up with cramped legs and smelly feet (I don't mean yours, of course)—and on busy holidays, they're often the best bet for finding an open seat at the last minute.

▶▶ROUTES

Our suggested route leads you in a circle around Madrid. These towns are best visited as individual day trips from Madrid. You should plan on returning to the city as a stop in between so you can leave your hefty bags in the train station or a hostel in Madrid to make travel lighter and more carefree:

Madrid to Avila, Avila to San Lorenzo El Escorial, San Lorenzo El Escorial to Madrid (by Cercanías Renfe train),

Madrid to Aranjuez (by Cercanías Renfe train)

TRAVEL TIMES

All times are by road unless indicated by a star:

	Madrid	Aranjuez	San Lorenzo de el Escorial
Madrid	-	:40	:40
Aranjuez	:40	-	1:15
San Lorenzo de el Escorial	:40	1:15	-

madrid

Folks in Madrid toss down little cups of coffee like muscle cars guzzle gas, smoke cigarettes like it was their last day on Earth, eat nothing but fried foods, and drink till—at (the very) least—three in the morning. This town is one of the true world-class capitals of late, late night fun. In fact, there are more bars and pubs here than in the other western European capitals combined. On most nights, seemingly the whole city is drinking and dancing at an untold number of venues until the sun comes up. You can even drink in the streets. But these are just the bare facts; the actual experience of a weekend in Madrid is kind of like a 72-hour (don't forget about Sunday) bungee jump: Just give into the gravity and know that somehow you'll bounce back by Monday morning. After all, everyone else seems to be able to....

With all these vices, you would think that the average resident of this sprawling capital would have Homer Simpson's body and Keith Richards' face, but, remarkably, it isn't so. The locals are thin, healthy, and happy, smoking and drinking until a ripe old age. How do they do it? Well, if you ask a group of Madrileños, they'll tell you that their health is the result of *una vida más tranquila:* a more easy-going way of life. "Enjoy yourself here," they'll tell you, "nobody wants problems." Even though you'll have more fun in Madrid than Marilyn Manson in a latex factory, to these Spaniards the party is genuinely fueled by the desire to spend just a little more time with their friends and family.

Not surprisingly, the sunny inhabitants of this city are tolerant of all sorts. Still, young global travelers traveling in flocks are sometimes perceived here as odd birds: swooping down with baseball hats and big running shoes, demanding Internet access and rollerblades. The natives might chuckle at this sight, but mostly they're curious. Madrileños are also happy to know that visitors are interested in learning more about their language and culture, especially since an open relationship has been difficult in the past—it's only in the last 20 years or so (since the end of Franco's reign) that Spain has emerged as a significant First World nation. This is great in certain ways, but it also means that the country has opened itself up to Hollywood, Levi's, and nearly every fast-food chain that America has spawned. The result is that younger people dig Sharon Stone and Keanu Reeves; they listen to Eminem; they have cell phones; they rave. Still, even though young people are more likely than their parents to speak English, this ain't Holland or Sweden, amigo. Chances are that you won't be playing Scrabble anytime soon with any of your new Spanish friends who speak "ah leetul" English.

No matter what language you speak, with so much going on, it's hard to figure out what you're gonna do in the next five minutes, much less the next few days. Don't freak out, just get your hands on the all-knowing, all-powerful Buddha of nightlife, *Guía del Ocio.* This weekly magazine has got everything, man: live music, movies, performing arts, bars, clubs, and more. Buy it for 125 pesetas at any kiosk, and kneel down and worship (or read). Other good sources of info are the fliers and employees at hipster and club clothing stores (such as those on Calle Fuencarral) and also the millions of posters around town.

Finally, remember, Madrileños like to get close—really close. At first it's a little frightening when people keep putting their cheerful faces right up to yours when they're speaking, but try and stifle the urge to shove the natives back. If you look around, you'll see that Spanish guys often have a hand on their buddy's shoulders and that many women walk arm in arm with their good friends. Spanish closeness, of course, also has its own etiquette. Although men simply shake hands when meeting for the first time, women kiss each other—and men—on both cheeks when first introduced. Does this imply some lovin' later on? Absolutely not. The tradition of *dos besos* (two kisses) is as old as the culture itself, and you'll seem cold and standoffish if you don't give out *dos besos* to a woman to whom you've been introduced. So don't sweat all the Spanish physical contact. Strangers will bump into you hard without apologizing, and new friends will be holding onto you like you just saved their lives. Go with it, you'll like it.

neighborhoods

A few areas seem to stand out for a young and hopelessly cool traveler such as yourself...**Sol** is the very center of downtown Madrid. Most buses and the busiest Metro lines converge here, as do the thousands of travelers who come to gawk at the impressive **Plaza Mayor.** Good shopping (at El Calle de Preciados) and good drinking (at bar haven Plaza Santa Ana) are also in this general area. The two hundred or so bars in **Bilbao** and **Alonso Martínez** *(three Metro stops to the north and northeast of Sol)* tend to be somewhat white-bread by Spanish standards, but that's by Spanish stan-

FiVE THiNGS TO TALK TO a LOCAL aBOUT

1. Bullfighting: Cruel and unusual or merely unusual? Pretend to be a baby Hemingway with blood lust or a tree-hugger insisting on the use of a tofu bull and see what arguments develop. If you want to check it out first, go to the Plaza Monumental de Toros de las Ventas *(Metro Ventas)* for listings. Seats in the sun cost less.

2. Madrileños love to diss their counterparts up in Barcelona. They'll tell you that the folks in Barcelona are *más cerrado* (close minded), *separartístas* (separatists), and *más europeos* (more European, less Spanish). Challenge them to explain how they produced so many great artists.

3. The current political party in power is El Partido Popular, which is seeking to close bars at the ungodly hour of 2am! In freakin' Madrid! Ask your local *camarero* (bartender) what he thinks about that, and you'll get an earful. Agree with him and you'll probably get a shot on the house.

4. Most young people will have at least some opinions on the ECU (which becomes "real" money in 2002) and the European Union. Some are thrilled to be able to travel more freely, others are less thrilled about the prospect of all those Europeans traveling freely here.

5. When all else fails, nothing beats an old fashioned hash vs. marijuana symposium. Most Spanish have never smoked the green and many travelers are newcomers to the cosmically obliterating powers of *el chocolate.*

dards. **Malasaña** *(Metro Tribunal, four stops north of Sol)* is full of artists and musicians, along with the associated poetry readings, great coffee houses, vegetarian restaurants, and down-home drinking holes. The famed, funky, and fabulous **Calle Fuencarral** begins in this neighborhood and continues right out to the Gran Vía Metro stops. Walking down **Gran Vía,** though, is kinda like eating snails: Experience the slime, excessive panhandling, and decayed greatness of this tired road at least once, just so that you can say you tried it. **Chueca** *(a few blocks south of Gran Vía and west of Calle de Fuencarral)* is the epicenter of Madrid's gay and lesbian communities. This groovy neighborhood has great coffee and shopping by day and perhaps some of the wildest bar scenes in Madrid by night. **Atocha** *(Metro stop of the same name and home of the Atocha Renfe train station),* features some cheap hostels and easy walking to **El Retiro** and **El Prado** [see *culture zoo,* below, for both], but it's special for both its

only here

You'll only have to be in Madrid for a day or two before it will dawn on you that everyone here makes out anywhere and at anytime. You'll be amazed at the, um, vigor with which young lovers express their affection for each other in public places such as street corners and the Metro. While walking in any of the parks (particularly El Parque del Oeste, which is right near the Complutense University), you'll see couples rolling around together in a way that will make you feel like you're on a certain street in Amsterdam. So what's with the truckloads of PDA? Well, some of it can be attributed to the more open ways of the Spanish in general, but the real reason is more likely to be the fact that most Spanish live with their parents until they get married, at age thirty or so. You'd be getting into your lover's pants in the park too, if Mom was home in the little apartment all day. Besides, as one bright Spaniard put it, it's too bad that Americans think it's okay to walk around the streets with guns but feel it's weird to hug and kiss each other in public.

Uniqueness of a slightly less physically intimate nature can be found in the sprawling, crowded weekend market, El Rastro [see *stuff*, below]. It's really not to be missed. Everything from old telephones to beautiful dresses to random squares of foam—yes, foam—can be bought here. Although a lot of the stuff here is standard (the t-shirts don't change that much from booth to booth) some of the trinkets here are more rare than Saint Stephen at a Dead show. Finally, you don't want to miss Madrid's **Teleférico (cable car)** ride *(Paseo del Pintor Rosales; Tel 91/541-74-50; Metro Argüelles; 11am-10:30pm daily, weekends only from Oct through March; www.ddnet.es/teleferico-Madrid; 515ptas round trip)*, which connects Casa de Campo and the Parque de Oeste. The slow-moving and mellow gondolas are perfect for seeing and learning more about your host city from a bird's eye view. In your 11-minute ride, you'll get particularly good views of El Palacio Real, its regal gardens, and the taller buildings of downtown Madrid.

blue-collar bars and its freaky youth bars. **Moncloa** and **Argüelles** (near the university, at the western end of the city) are infested with bars whose clientele all seem to take their partying cues from 1980s college frat-party movies. Definitely check out the low-rent neighborhoods of **La Latina** *(west of Sol)* and **Embajadores** *(south of Sol)*, home of the El Rastro outdoor weekend market [see *stuff*, below], and then head over to the terraced, high-profile bars of the **Santiago Bernabeu** area (at the northern end of the city) to see the flip side. All of these neighborhoods have Metro stops that bear their names.

Walking between these distinct neighborhoods is easy. You'll be amazed again and again at how close they are to each other. When asking for directions, most people will guide you via one of the many glorietas (traffic circles) or plazas. The most common points of reference, though, are Metro stops. They're easy to see and are often named after the neighborhoods in which they're located. If you tire of walking, you might want to actually hop on the Metro, which is cheaper than candy (680ptas for 10 trips), quick, and easy to use. The **E.M.T.**, Madrid's public bus system, has the advantage of being above ground but is a whole lot more confusing and much slower. Unless you're gonna be in Madrid for several months and have an advanced degree in Busology, stick to the Metro. All lines are the same price, transfers are free, and you can pick up a pocket-sized map at the ticket booths.

As in most places that aren't the United States, it is very difficult to buy a gun in Spain. There's still crime here, obviously, but the perps are out for your wallet rather than your blood. Watch for pickpockets, especially in the crowded parts of Sol and the weekend market, El Rastro. If you can handle big North American cities, though, most parts of Madrid won't cause you any trouble: Walk in pairs or groups (especially women, although the threat is more like harrassment from dirty old men than phyical harm), keep track of your stuff, and use common sense. As you already guessed, there isn't a curfew in Madrid. In fact, it's rare that you'll ever hear the word "no" here.

hanging out

If your goal is to meet some actual Spanish people, you're sure to have good luck at the **Plaza Dos de Mayo** (*Metro Tribunal*). The plaza is the focal point of Malasaña, the most artsy and with-it area in Madrid; a lot of poetry readings, skits, and live music go down here. The smallish plaza with a standard European freestanding arch, surrounded by benches and a little playground, plays host to the occasional drum circle, and young people have been known to score their hash here. Similar activities can also take place at **El Retiro** (*Metro Retiro*). The locals enjoy running and rollerblading through this enormous park with its tall trees, peaceful lawns, and ornate fountains. It becomes a real spectacle on the weekends when the streets swell up with families, musicians, performers, and vendors. A great attraction here are the rowboats that you can rent for use in the huge man-made pond (it's a small lake, really) located in the center of the park (520ptas for unlimited time; 10:30am-8:30pm). Although the parks in Madrid are fun, they're not a place to be at night if you are alone.

Starting at about 1am, many street vendors line up on **Gran Vía** with beer, candy, and often hot food like chicken and rice (about 300ptas). There's always groups of people around the vendors catching their breath before hitting the next disco, and since it's quieter out here, you'll usually have an easier time communicating with Juan/Juanita de España than you would in the 300-beats-per-minute din of the clubs. We're not sug-

¿donde esta el tabaco?

"How the hell am I supposed to get some stamps for Mom's postcard? And man, could I use a Snickers bar right now...." If this is you or perhaps a collective "you" of friends, head on down to the nearest *estanco,* or tobacco shop. The *estancos* are those little brown stands that you see on most major streets in Madrid. Most of them even say TABACO right on them with big yellow letters. These great little places will sell you stamps, postcards, phone cards, cigars, lighters, and assorted snacks. The only way they could be better is if they sold ice cream—but the ice cream stands are usually right next door.

Smoking, by the way, is an integral part of Spanish life. They love it! Unlike California (where apparently it's now illegal to even think about cigarettes while in a public place), smoking here is allowed in the food markets, stores, and hospital waiting rooms. The postal workers smoke while toting around the mail, university students smoke in class, and there is no such thing as a non-smoking section anywhere. You just have to deal with it.

gesting that you'll make friends for life while eating rice on a street corner at 3 in the morning, but you could find some amigos for the next few hours if you *habla* a little. And you shouldn't have too much trouble getting a little info on the next club (or person) that you want to check out.

What's a *guiri?* Well, you are. Guiri is Spanish slang for anyone who is foreign—and doesn't necessarily understand the finer points of Spanish culture. The word doesn't have bad connotations, really, it's just what they call you and your Nike-wearing friends. If you've got the urge to talk with some other guiris (maybe you're tired of people laughing at how you pronounce *torero*), check out one of the 15 or so Irish pubs in Madrid. **Finbar's** *(Marqués de Urquijo 10; Tel 91/548-37-93; Metro Argüelles; 10am-3am daily; No credit cards),* for example, upholds the proud tradition of Guinness (575ptas per pint), Jameson, and dark wood decor. It also features live Celtic music on Fridays and Saturdays at 10pm and English Premier League soccer on a large-screen TV during the week.

If the barstool scene isn't quite what you're looking for, however, put on something nice (the atmosphere is a little swank) and head over to the Fiesta de Intercambio that is held at the **Palacio Gaviria** *(Arenal 9; No phone; Metro Sol; 10:30pm-3am Thur only; V, AE, MC)* on Thursday nights. The Palacio is a stately club, and the place where you might meet that French (or Italian or Greek or Spanish...) girl/guy that you've always dreamed of (lovin' is definitely on the menu here). Entrance is 1,600ptas for two people and includes two free drinks. Also pay a visit to La Plaza Santa Ana (Metro: Sol), where foreign students (and the Spaniards who want to meet them) crawl all over each other like ants as they try to get to the next bar via the narrow cobblestone streets. The area has bars and clubs to suit almost any taste; **La Comedia Bar** [see *bar scene*, below] is definitely a good choice if you're feeling overwhelmed.

bar scene

Madrileños call their nightlife *la marcha* (the march), because they typically prefer to have a single drink in a bar before moving on to the next (and the next, and the next...). So, trying to sum up Madrid's bar scene by describing only a few bars is like trying to tell someone about a beach by showing them only a few grains of sand. Add to the nearly limitless possibilities the fact that there are thousands of people in the streets and the bars don't close until 4am, and it's easy to see why Madrid is the undisputed champion of European nightlife. Use the following bars as highlights and marcha your butt off—it's the only way to get the full effect. All of these bars have a similar primetime of around 1am on the weekends. The only exception is El Viajero, which usually sees action by 11 at night. Also, unless noted, these bars take pesetas only, no credit cards.

Although **Angie** *(San Vicente Ferrer 4; Tel 91/940-61-26; Metro Tribunal; 10pm-5am daily)* is located in Malasaña with about 2,000 other bars, it stands out because it's got a lot of literature on other cool places. Julio, the bartender and DJ, leans towards Lou Reed, the Pixies, Nirvana, and-of course-los Rolling Stones. A no-frills bar filled with great local people. Beers cost about 250ptas. **El Viajero** *(Plaza de la Cebada 11; Tel 91/366-90-64, Fax 91/366-91-53; Metro La Latina; Bar Hours: 7:30pm-3am daily, Terrace Hours: 12:30pm-1:30am daily, Restaurant Hours: 12:30pm-midnight daily; V, MC, AE)* is a great bar and restaurant in the very cool La Latina district of Madrid. Get an aerial view of this artist's community while eating in the third-floor terrace or relax on the second floor, which is lit almost entirely by candles—both are potentially very romantic. A little more expensive than average, but so worth it.

There's plenty of room to shake your money maker to the hip-hop playing at **La Comedia Bar** *(Príncipe 16; No phone; Metro Sol; 8pm-4am daily)*. Of course you'll want to check out the entire international lovefest that is the Plaza de Santa Ana scene, but the warmth and soul of La Comedia is a step above the rest. The crowd is a little heavy on the travelers (it goes with the neighborhood), but that doesn't detract from the heat in the back dance room or the fun, hey-baby attitude that swings in the large, see-and-be-seen front room. Drinks are 900ptas. **Carda Momo** *(Echegarry 15; No phone; Metro Sol; 8pm-4am daily)* is another Santa Ana bar that has got a lot of dance to it: Flamenco-pop and salsa, to be precise. The grown-up crowd here (25 and up) certainly likes to get down, and with about 300 people, it's easy to get swept up in the moment. The men favor the suit-without-tie mafioso look, while a lot of the women have got

madrid

BARS/CLUBS ▲
900 Pub **2**
Angie **11**
Bulevar **13**
Café la Palma **5**
Carda Momo **17**
Deep **9**
ES3 **1**
El Viajero **8**
La Comedia Bar **15**
Long Play **12**
Maravillas **10**
Nature **6**
Populart **16**
Siroco **4**
Soma **7**
Taberna La de Elisa **18**

CULTURE ZOO ●
Centro de Arte
  Reina Sofia **19**
Museo de la Real
  Academia de Bellas
  Artes de San Fernando **14**
Museo del Prado **21**
Palacio Real **3**
Thyssen-Bornemisza
  Museum **20**

boozing in madrid

You may be disappointed at first to find that mixed drinks in Madrid are about the same price as at home. But on closer inspection you'll find that the Spanish really know how to mix a drink. Keep your eye on the bartender, and you'll be psyched to see that your rum-and-coke will almost always be 1/2 to 2/3 good stuff. None of that Puritan, one-shot crap! "Good" bartenders will give you a glass full of rum and top it off with coke, so watch out. Mixed drinks are often served in two parts—a tall glass with ice and the liquor, and the mixer in a separate glass bottle—so that you can mix the drink to your liking. Nearly all bars will give some sort of rudimentary tapas plate, such as peanuts, chips, or olives. You usually have to pay for more elaborate sorts of snacks. Although a gratuity is included in prices you pay at bars, it's okay to give a small tip (25ptas or so) if you're happy with the service. Keep in mind that many Spanish don't drink to get drunk, at least not right away. If you want to sit at the bar and slam a pint glass against your head, that's all well and fine, but remember that the real party isn't even gonna get started till 2am or so. If you want to get the most Madrid for your money, do like the Spanish do; drink light and eat the tapas they give you until about one in the morning. From there on out, it's more acceptable to be drunker, if that's your thing, as long as you don't get too sloppy. Remember, it's life-*affirming* here.

this Manhattan/Gypsy thing going on (sleek urban black clothes accessorized with tons of gypsy bangles and baubles). Located in Plaza de Santa Ana, but unique in that few foreigners come here. The drinks are 850ptas. One final recommendation for dance is **Bulevar** *(Corner of Horteleza and Santa Theresa; No phone; Metro Antón Martín; Noon-3:30am daily)*, which has perhaps one of the greatest DJs in any bar anywhere. On Fridays and Saturdays, DJ Antonio spins an extra-smooth mix of soul, R&B, and funk that will absolutely put you in the mood to groove. The room has several intimate booths, dark, dark wood, dim lights behind a big bar, and the feeling that Humphrey Bogart might walk in at any moment. If he doesn't, you'll still be happy to stare at the crew of good-looking twentysomethings who do come around on a regular basis. If you don't feel like dancing, try **Pub 900** *(Benito Gutiérrez 30; Tel 91/543-14-51; Metro Argüelles; 4pm-3:30am daily)*, which caters mainly to Spanish university students. Sit in a booth here with friends and play one of the many board games that 900 has to offer (and learn some more Español in the process...). Music is Smashing Pumpkins, Lauryn Hill, and Motown, and drinks are only 500ptas. Mood ranges from Very Chill to Super-Crowded.

In addition to *la marcha* (or maybe *el staggero* by the end of it) listed above, the following neighborhoods are definitely worth your carousing time. Alonso Martínez is the home of college bars for cool college students who aren't freaks or artists. Yes, many of them might be jocks, but the smart, cool, well-dressed kind of jocks. Don't confuse the bars and people here with the rowdy mayhem that frequently erupts in Moncloa and Argüelles. Santiago Bernabéu (along the Avenida de Brasil) features a fantastic, bustling terrace bar scene. The crowd is similar to the Alonso Martínez set, but more like 30- rather than 20-year olds. Sit outside with friends, drink, and watch the (well-dressed) Spanish world talk, gesture, and dance on by. The best people-watching nights here are often right after a futbol (soccer) match at the nearby Estadio Santiago Bernabéu.

LIVE MUSIC SCENE

Yeah, the Spanish dance their flamenco, they fight their bulls, and they have their Goyas and Dalís...but they don't do rock 'n' roll very well. It's usually uninspired, unoriginal, high-school level musicianship. The Blues scene doesn't bring much more to the table—many of the acts have an American frontman and a barely acceptable local backing group. But the

chico meets chica

Maybe we can describe relations between el and ella by saying that being sexy is fundamental to the Spanish. Take the words *guapa* and *guapo* for example, which translate to "good-looking in a sexy way." Watching the locals in action will continuously remind you that "in a sexy way" applies to almost everything in this country. Women really are beautiful and feminine and men really are tall, dark, and handsome. The Spanish touch and talk to each other nonstop anyway, so opening conversations can contain a strong sexual charge without implying a threat or a promise. (Of course your average Spaniard could fry an egg or dial a phone with their strong sexual charge; it's what fuels the flair for which they're known.) When you get down to it, though, the general rules are more or less the same here as at home: A guy will buy a girl a drink because he digs her, and if a girl dwells on your eyes, go buy her a drink! Also remember that Spanish men are second only to the Italians when it comes to chasing bootie. If you're looking good, baby, expect the whistles and come-ons. And if you're a girl of the tall and blonde variety? Brace yourself.

Jazz scene is a lot better, and reggae, salsa, and other world beat-style bands usually have it together. And, of course, big-name tours stop in Madrid often. R.E.M., Sugar Ray, and Maceo Parker are just a few of the big acts that have recently played in one of the football stadiums around Madrid. As always, consult the entertainment bible, *Guía del Ocio* (and the thousands of posters around the city) to see who's playing and where. For the most part, the clubs here open at about 9:30pm, the live music starts between 10 and 11 and ends at around 2am, and—in the traditional Madrid style—the clubs remain open till 6am with a DJ. Keep in mind, though, that the Spanish invented arriving fashionably late. Midnight is when things are hottest for live music in this town. You can also skip the live music and just swing by around three for the DJ session. These clubs also do not accept plastic unless noted otherwise.

If you're still hell-bent on seeing some Spanish rock 'n' roll, go to **Siroco** *(San Dimas 3; Tel 91/593-30-70; Metro San Bernardo; Open Thur-Sat; siroco@siroco.es)* At least the venue is small, dark, and loud—the way a rock club should be. The upper floor adds some space, but the stage—and most of the action—is crammed into the basement. The 18-30 clientele is dressed in 1976 AC/DC (Back In) Black, the preferred attire of Spain's rock 'n' rollers. This is a very popular venue on weekends, and the men's room has one of the few condom machines in Madrid. Cover is anywhere from 800-2,000ptas, depending on the act.

Like Siroco, **Maravillas** *(San Vicente Ferrer, 35; Tel 91/52-33-07-11; Metro Tribunal or San Bernardo; Fri-Sat)* is a stepping stone for many soon-to-be-bigger acts, the difference being that many of these rising stars aren't from Spain. The modest use of black lights and pink trim in this otherwise dark basement club gives it a burnt-out 1985 California feel, but the drugs aren't as heavy and not many of the 300 or so people that fit in here would recognize anything off of Jane's Addiction's first album besides "Jane Says." The Pixies, however, played here during their first European tour, and more recent FM groups that have visited here include Blur and Kula Shaker. When the occasional DJ spins, this is one of the few non-American bars where you can hear the Beastie Boys.

fIVE-O

The Spanish philosophy of shunning complications often applies to the law, too. Cops in Madrid (like their civilian counterparts) are, for the most part, smiling (imagine that in New York!), helpful people. It probably has something to do with the fact that you can't buy a gun in Spain.... It's not uncommon to see officers in the local pubs, taking a short break from their rounds and chatting with the neighbors. As many a Spaniard will tell you, the police rarely care what you're doing if it's not bothering anyone else.

Cover ranges from 800 to 1,500ptas, but does not include a drink because the door is the bands' pay.

Cafe Jazz Populart *(Huertas 22; Tel 91/429-84-07; Metro Tribunal; 6:30pm-3am daily)* is the place for Madrid's lukewarm blues. But its small stage is also graced by "live music of all types," including swing, salsa, reggae, and flamenco. Decorated with old horns and photos of American blues and jazz heavyweights, this midsized bar attracts a mix of 25-to-40-year-old yuppie types and college-aged Spanish artists and musicians (many of whom can speak a little English). Upcoming acts are listed by the entrance. *Raciones* (snacks) are served, and a beer costs 450ptas. Because it's a smaller venue here, you'll want to get a good seat by showing up on time (more or less), usually about 10pm. A lot of Spain was Celtic at one time, which explains why there are at least 15 Irish pubs in downtown Madrid, and there's even a Musica Celta section in the Guía del Ocio.

La Taberna de Elisa *(Santa Maria 42; Tel 91/429-54-15; Metro Antón Martín; 6:30pm-3am Tues-Sun; V, MC, AE)* opened its doors in 1989 and features live traditional music every Friday and Saturday and open jam sessions on Tuesday at 10:30 (Celtic) and Sunday at 9:30 (general European folk). Although it's true that you'll meet some Irish here, it turns out that the locals (usually young professionals) stop by because they dig the ambience at Elisa, which is almost Disney-like in its meticulous recreation of an Irish streetcorner and pub: The bar is crammed with tarnished Irish knicknacks (including a streetlamp in the middle of the pub) and, well, many merry people (maximum of about 150).

Café La Palma *(La Palma 62; Tel 91/522-50-31; Metro Noviciado; 4pm-3am daily; lapalma62@hotmail.com; V, MC)* is one of the epicenters of young artist culture in Madrid. Live music is played Thursday-Sunday nights at about 10pm and is oftentimes folk or Cuban. Cover is 1,000ptas, including one drink. This kickin' venue features four separate rooms: a Moroccan style 'chill-out' with cushions on the ground for seats, the actual stage room (holds about 250 people when they push the small tables to the back), the bar room, and the cafe room (which has beat-up comfortable booths and the bulk of the artwork). Storytelling, [see *arts scene*, below] takes place on Tuesdays at 9:30 (300ptas entrance), and the eclectic artwork, which rotates every 15 days, is by local artists and is for sale.

club scene

Clubs in Madrid always have a schedule that begins at midnight, but nothing happens in any of them before 2:30am. Just accept it, like you accept lying politicians and Jesse on MTV. Although entrance prices *(entradas)* are usually 1,000ptas (or so), they always include a free drink *(consumición)*, and you can pay a little less by picking up door passes at hip clothing stores [see *stuff*, below]. The following clubs are offered as alternatives to Madrid's standard-dance-club scene. If you want to get on the good foot at places like **Kapital** *(Atocha 125; Metro Atocha)*, **Pachá** *(Barceló 11; Metro Tribunal)*, and **Joy Eslava** *(Arenal 11; Metro Sol)* then go for it. They're always crowded and sexy, and sometimes fun, but have dress codes (i.e., no sneakers), cost more, and are usually full of ugly tourists (we can't help it!). The venues below are more real: The clientele speaks Spanish and the doorman won't be wearing a freaking headset. Except for the more styled ES3 and Deep [see below for both], these clubs will not turn anyone away unless they're bleeding from the forehead or foaming at the mouth. Also, all clubs have a coatcheck, and unless noted, don't accept credit cards, don't have phones, and are open from midnight till 6am.

Nature *(MidDay) (Amaniel 13; Metro San Bernardo; Open Thur-Sat as Nature; 1pm-8pm on Sundays as MidDay)* (pronounced 'nah-two-ray') is absolutely worth a visit, especially on Thursdays. Unlike the normal club scene, this place is laid-back and dreddy, with a very open, hole-in-the-wall atmosphere, and DJs spinning mostly house and the occasional (relatively good) techno. The metallic decor and low red lighting makes it seem like Han Solo might show up later on. Little TVs show Japanese anime; wear your old t-shirts, sunglasses, and comfortable sneakers. Entrance is 1,000ptas, and drinks are 900ptas after that.

Although praised by many a local, **Long Play** *(Plaza Vázquez de Mella 2; Metro Gran Vía; Open Fri-Sat)* turns out to be an average club with even more average techno blaring at the white-bread clientele (aged in the low 20s). The first floor is a lot better, though, with a black and cushy salon feel and more soulful music. Sit back in one of the large semi-circular booths here and take in the rich smoke and smell of about 20 purros (hash and tobacco joints) being smoked all at once. This club can

rules of the game

The legal drinking age in Madrid is 18, but the police certainly don't enforce that law with the same weird vigor as they can in some places. Although all other drugs are illegal, the entire city smokes purros like they were chewing gum. Purros are tobacco rolled together with hash, and it's pretty much the only way that Spaniards get high. In a small bar, use your judgment before sparking one up—if you're not sure, ask. No matter what the response, it won't include the shocked, you-must-be-a-heroin-addict look that you might get elsewhere. Hash, or chocolate, is legal to possess in small amounts for personal use only (a half gram or less). Smoking and drinking on the streets or in parks is fine with the law. As long as you're cool and in control, Jose Law has got better things to do than to give someone a hard time for enjoying themselves. Be forewarned, friends. There's a reason that the hash here is always smoked with tobacco: To smoke it solo in a bowl will take you to Planet WhupAss in approximately five minutes. The return flight, however, usually doesn't leave until the following morning. (We're totally serious, by the way.)

be fun, but not mind-blowing. Entrance is 1,200ptas (free on Fridays between midnight and 3am), drinks are 900ptas.

If **Soma** *(Leganitos 25; Tel 609/300-163; soma2@mx2. redestb.es; Metro Santo Domingo; Open Thur-Sun)* were in the U.S.A., its license plates would read 'Live Techno or Die.' Soma hosts big name DJs like Stacey Pullen (Detroit), but the main dance floor is a glorified hallway that gets too crowded too quick. The two smoky 'chill-out' rooms actually live up to their name, though, and there is pinball, pool, and foos in the recroom. Hardcore ravers hang here, few of whom are older than 22. The club goes by the Superfly moniker on Thursdays, when the crowd and the music both have more soul. Entrance varies from 1,000-1,500ptas.

ES3 *(Ferraz 38; Metro Argüelles; 11pm-4am Wed-Thur, 11pm-5:30am Fri-Sat; AE, V, MC)* is a salsa discotheque, baby! The girls are guapa (goodlooking/sexy), the fellas are smooth, and everyone (aged 18 to low 30s) is dancing. Even if your clunky feet can't quite get with it, you can still have a great time watching the smooth and sexy regulars. ES3 has a midsized dance floor with a subdued (but effective) lighting system. This place hops on Wednesdays (and weekends), and you oughta get dressed up in your seductive best for the event. Entrance is 1,000-1,500ptas. Drinks are 950ptas.

With great house spinning in a big, beautiful venue, it's no wonder **Deep** *(Ronda de Toledo 1; Tel 902/49-99-94; Metro Puerta de Toledo; Open Thur-Sun)* is so popular. A little more expensive than other clubs, but, hey, you're paying to hang with a lot of beautiful people and possibly the best electronica house DJs in town. Killer sound system, killer lights, excellent floor. Dress with taste because looking good is essential to feeling good here. Free entrance 12-3am on Fridays and 12-2am on Saturday (the hardcore disco locals make a point of showing up during the last hour of these free entrance times). Although weekend nights are most popular, weeknight options are just as cool, with less crowd: Da Place plays it funky on Wednesdays, and Studio1 gives you 70s Disco on Thursdays. 1,500ptas entrance; 1,000ptas drinks.

arts scene

▶▶VISUAL ARTS

El Mercado Fuencarral mall [see *stuff*, below] and the nearby Malasaña neighborhood are the epicenters of Madrid's young and happening subcultures. The overall attitude at El Mercado Fuencarral is metallic, 21st century, and "who-the-f—k-are-you," but if you can dig—or at least get past—all that, it's a fantastic source of info on Madrid's art and club scenes. Art shows and dance parties often go down here and there's a great community bulletin board that has signs for everything from Reiki for Healing to Bass Player Wanted to Rooms for Rent. Malasaña, on the other hand, is more of a soul shakedown party, mon. This area is the young artists' neighborhood of choice, because it is the home of a fine arts college and a music school. Dreds and artist-types like to congregate in cafes surrounding the Plaza Dos de Mayo, the center of the Malasaña district. Malasaña features more vegetarian restaurants and literary events than any other neighborhood in Madrid [see *eats and stuff,* below].

Café La Palma [see *live music scene,* above] is so good we had to write it up twice. Check out this warm and buzzing place to integrate yourself with Madrid's young art scene. It's one of the preferred venues for students at El Colegio de Bellas Artes, and not only can you meet cool artists while enjoying great music or storytelling [see below], you can also buy their work. The walls of the cafe are decorated by a different artist every fifteen days. A price list tells you what's what.

The **Escuela de Fotografía y Centro de Imagen** *(Fuentearrabia 4-6; Tel 91/552-99-99; Metro Menéndez Pelayo; 10am-2pm / 5-10pm Mon-Fri, 11am-2pm Sat; www.efti.es; No entrance fee)* is half school and half gallery. The featured work is occasionally by students, but prize-winning photography is also often on display (such as winners from the recent Hasselblad Open, an international contest sponsored by the Swedish camera manufacturer). Displays throughout the first floor inter-mingle with studios, students, and a common room with some exotic image, photography, design, and style magazines that you may not have seen back home. A great way to spend an hour or two, and also a very likely place to strike up a conversation with a local art student. Set in a pleasant neighborhood with tranquil streetside cafes.

Garaje Pemasa *(General Díaz Porlier 35; No phone; Metro Lista; 6-9pm Mon-Sat, also noon-2 on Sat; Occasionally shut down for new exhibitions, check the Guía del Ocio for updates)* is no Reina Sofía [see *culture zoo,* below], and that's the way they like it. Unlike the antiseptic feel of many galleries in Madrid, the space here is an actual work of art in itself. You almost feel like you're walking into a painting when you step into this former auto-repair garage, with its high ceilings and metal walls. The physical trippiness of the building lends a sharp and biting edge to the exhibitions of sculpture, paint-ings, and other mediums. Plus the curators are very friendly.

The **Facultad de Bellas Artes** *(El Greco 2; Tel 91/394-36-26; Metro Moncloa and then Bus 46 to Avenida de Juan de Herrera; 9am-10:30pm Mon-Sat;)* is the school for fine arts at Madrid's huge Com-plutense University. You can only get here by bus, but it's not too bad, and the reward is that you will be right smack in the middle of the Madrid student art scene! The big, ever-changing gallery here displays paintings, sculptures, and interactive works by students. A second smaller room hosts plays, discussions, and occasional films. In addition to a lot of books, the library here is home to nearly 300 drawings from students who studied here in the 18th and 19th centuries.

▶▶**PERFORMING ARTS**

Sometimes it seems like Madrid's theater and other performing arts get over-shadowed by its world-class museums and 200 proof nightlife, but the per-forming arts scene here is alive and well, running the gamut from classical ballet to avant-garde film and theater. Meanwhile, if you want to see the latest Sandra Bullock or Mel Gibson flick dubbed into Spanish, head down to any one of the huge, old theaters at the Callao Metro stop on Gran Vía

festivals and events

Madrid has a bunch of festivals that correspond with Christian holidays including the **Entierro de la Sardina,** in which a sardine is placed in a small casket, paraded about Madrid, and then buried at Paseo de la Florida. This all takes place on Ash Wednesday (mid-March), for some reason, and thousands participate in the adventure. Despite the lack of ceremonial fish, however, the best festivals take place in the summertime, particularly in May.

The time of the **San Isidro festival** is when Madrid is at its very best. San Isidro is the patron saint of the city, and man do they love him. The week-long event in his honor takes place during the third week of May (more or less) and is like New Year's, Fourth of July, and Halloween all rolled together! There are kids in costumes, a tremendous amount of hoopla (including live music, carnival food, street markets, dance performances, and more), and the drinking and dancing in the streets (particularly in the Las Vistillas neighborhood) is probably unlike anything you've ever seen. Be sure to check out the fireworks at Las Vistillas. The local tourist offices and the Guía del Ocio will have all the info. Also noteworthy, though not as insane, is **Festimad** *(Usually for two days in the middle of June; www.festimad.es),* an alternative arts festival highlighting everything from literature to photography to music and dance. Most venues listed in this chapter will have posters with all the info, but contact **Círculo de Bellas Artes** *(Marqués de Casa Riera 2; Tel 91/531-77-00; Metro Banco de España)* if for some reason you don't come across one. If you've got at least one tattoo or more than two earrings, you won't want to miss the **Dos de Mayo** celebration in the Plaza Dos de Mayo in Malasaña. This holiday commemorates Madrid's rebellion against Napoleon's occupation of Spain, but the only people who bother to celebrate are those who live in the plaza of the same name. It's a neighborhood party kind of thing (with food, bands, etc.), but what a neighborhood! We've written enough about Malasaña already—bring your drums and a doobie.

(hey, it's a great way to learn Spanish). Movies are 700-800ptas (often half price on Wed), and the price for snacks is not ridiculous. As always, check the Guía del Ocio for a complete listing of what's happening and when.

Cine Dore/Filmoteca *(Santa Isabel 3; Tel 91/369-11-25; Metro Antón Martín; 4pm-10:45pm for movies-check the Guía del Ocio, 1:30pm-3:30pm/4pm-midnight, closed Mon; No credit cards)* is to the movies what DJs who play the Velvet Underground are to rock 'n' roll. Filmoteca specializes in classic or off-beat films from any director at any time and for only 225ptas a flick. Especially cool in the summer months, when they screen movies out on the terraza (patio). All films are original versions (subtitled), and often conform to a theme or director of the week (such as Movies about Trains or Roman Polanski Week). The entire building, including the great cafe and bookstore, has a "golden era of Hollywood" feeling with marble floors and tables, large indoor plants, and subtle turquoise neon highlights. Show up early, as most showings sell out. Pick up the monthly schedule in the foyer.

The movies at **Alphaville Cinema** *(Martín de los Heros 14; Tel 91/559-38-36; Metro Ventura Rodriquez; 4:30pm-10:45pm Mon-Sat, opens at 12:30pm Fri-Sat; 800ptas a show, 500ptas on Mon)* are a step more commercial than those at Filmoteca, but in a good, indie, sort of way. Features here are usually new independent films. All movies here are shown in their original versions. The largest of the four rooms has new, comfy seating (including two-person lovers seats). It's cool to sit—and be seen sitting—in the coffee shop while reading over one of the free handouts printed for each movie. Cine de Renoir, a very similar theater, is right next door.

Ensayo 100 *(Ramundo Lulio 20; Tel 91/447-79-05; Metro Iglesia, Bilbao, Alonso Martinez; Shows start at 8:30pm Fri-Sun; No credit cards)* is half acting school and half theater. The small-but-with-it theater stages acts that range from Isaac Chocrón's La Revolución to Anton Chejov's Uncle Vanya. The (sometimes English) productions are frequented by young actors, and it's a favorite in the Madrid alternative arts scene. Entrance is 2,000ptas, 1,000ptas if you've got a student card. The small pop-art bar here can be a great place to make connections and new friends after a show. Some say that you can't see the real-deal Flamenco in a heartless slab of stone like Madrid, but **Casa Patas** *(Cañizares, 10; Tel 91/369-04-96; Metro Tirso de Molina; Restaurant Hours noon-5pm/8pm-3am daily; Show Hours: 10:30pm Mon-Thur, midnight Fri-Sat; www.visualware.es/guíamad/anct/patas.htm; V)* sure comes close. Skilled and heart-wrenching classical guitar will impress you even before the dancers come out. When they do come out, you'll realize that any Flamenco dancer worth her salt is at least as tough as Ice T (but obviously a lot more graceful). The locals come here, and they all know that the delicous meals are definitely secondary when compared to the show. Entrance is 2,000ptas (but very worth it).

There's no confusing what **Madrid en Danza** *(Various venues; Telephone 012 — that's it!; Approx May 15th-June 15th; www.comadrid.es; No credit cards)* is all about. For nearly fifteen years, this month-long festival has brought the world's best dance to Madrid, including Flamenco, ballet, modern...you name it, and they're dancing it. Over 150 performances in more than 20 different venues. Fliers and posters come out about the middle of April, and all of the events are also listed in the *Guía del Ocio*.

▶▶**CUENTA CUENTOS**
Cuenta cuentos, the traditional Spanish art of storytelling, currently has the coolness equivalent that poetry slams had in Manhattan in their heydey. The Malasaña District (Metro Tribunal) easily has the largest concentration

of cafes that host these events; Pepe Botella, Café La Palma [see *live music scene,* above], and nänai [see *gay scene,* below] are just three examples of with-it, smart hangouts in the area that host cuenta cuentos sessions once a week. The stories told are by a single performer and usually end as a joke or moral lesson or both. These events are often free and are a definite must-see if you want to meet thoughtful Spaniards or have a truly rich cultural experience. The physical expressions of the performers will lessen the language gap as you listen uninterrupted to true orators with great voices and accents. Most sessions last for an hour or so with about three performers.

If you like *Whose Line Is It Anyway?* (the British version, of course), then you'll love **Libertad 8** *(Libertad 8; Tel 91/532-11-50; Metro Banco de España; Noon-2am daily; No credit cards),* which hosts grupo cuentacuentos, putting a twist on storytelling by having the audience select the topics for the performers' stories. Plus they play awesome classic Argentine tango between performances. This happening little spot also hosts live folk music acts, normal cuenta cuentos sessions, and even a young artists' connection night (once a month). Stop by and pick up the monthly schedule to see what's happening next at this old-time intellectuals' and artists' hangout. **Pepe Botella** *(San Andrés 12; Tel 91/522-43-09; Metro Tribunal or Bilbao; 11pm-2am daily, till 3am weekends; No credit cards)* is a similar establishment in Malasaña, but with a less revolutionary look and feel. Thursday nights are reserved for poetry reading/story telling (9:30pm, free), and other events come and go on a less-strict schedule. Check the bulletin board to see what's coming up. This big, ornate coffeehouse and bar has several rooms and many little corners and cubbies to sit quietly in. It's full of sexy bookish types who like to drink.

gay scene

The zona Chueca (chew-ey-ka) is the center of the Madrid gay scene, playing home to femme and butch alike, male or female. The Metro stop of the same name opens right in the middle of a little plaza that becomes a party dynamo at night with happening bars, dance clubs, and drag shows. Many establishments here carry solid literature on the gay community, including free magazines such as *Shangay Express. Entiendes,* a magazine with more local info, can be bought at newsstands local to the area and Gran Vía. The articles in these zines are in Spanish, but the advertisements for clubs and bars are occasionaly in English. Chueca is more than just gay bars, of course. The bookstores, clothing stores, and many outdoor coffee houses merit a stroll during business hours. FYI: The verb *entender* (to understand) has special significance in the gay community. If you say that you *entiendo,* you're saying that you're gay. It's kind of like saying that you "really understand."

Café Aquarela *(Gravina 10; Tel 91/522-21-43; Metro Chueca; 3pm-3am daily; No credit cards)* is fabulous. Relax in the warm ambiance and contemplate how they decorated it like grandma's living room and still made it work. Ample old chairs and little dark tables are pleasantly jumbled together, yet the cafe still exudes openess. It can become too crowded at prime-time (from 10:30pm on, later on weekends) better to come during daylight hours. Breakfast is served on holidays, Saturday, and Sunday beginning at 11am. Mostly young-and-beautiful gay clientele, but it also caters to a mixed crowd, too. From 250ptas for "café solo" (black) to 800ptas if you want Bailey's in it.

nänai *(Barco 26; No phone; 9am-10:30pm/1am on weekends; No credit cards)* is a quiet little cafe that has great info on the lesbian scene and women's issues in general. The big open place has old couches, tables, and floor lamps. Hang out for hours undisturbed after you buy a snack or drink (the milkshakes are awesome) and check out (and even buy, if you like) the work of local artists. Plays host to skits, readings, etc., on Wednesdays and Thursdays at 8:30pm. A free movie is shown every Sunday at 5:30pm. Lots of stuff is always going on here; check their bulletin board to see what's up.

Chueca's Friends *(Plaza de Chueca; No phone; Metro Chueca; 5pm-4am daily; No credit cards)* is just one of the many bars in the Chueca area, but is noteworthy because it has a countertop piled high with flyers and neighborhood newspapers giving you the dope, as well as foosball and electronic darts. Despite these amenities, the spare latex black walls give the big room a slightly cold feeling. The generally mixed gay/lesbian crowd adds its own warmth, though, talking and dancing to a good combination of modern rock and electronica (though you might hear k.d. lang a little more often than you'd like ...). Drinks are about 500ptas.

If you don't understand already that **Olvas** *(Augusto Figueroa 1; Tel 91/522-73-27; Metro Gran Vía; 10:30am-2pm/5pm-9pm Mon-Sat; V, AE, MC)* is a clothing store for the gay male, the TVs embedded in the floor playing male stripshows will clue you in pretty quickly. You can buy an anatomically correct "Carlos" doll here along with your standard array of dance-club clothes. It also has a small leather section. Olvas carries a lot of info on the gay community including local newsletters, club, and bar info.

Although it's not as outrageous as some of the queen clubs, **Ohm** *(Plaza de Callao 4; No phone; Metro Callao; Midnight-6am Thur-Sat; www.interocio.es/ ohm; No credit card)* spins good House and Trance, and certainly sees it's share of boys in dresses. The single-floor venue is big, with good lights, good sound, and red velour everywhere. On Sundays, the name changes to *Weekend,* and is the preferred hangout for Madrid's bar and club staff (of any orientation) that had to work all weekend. Sunday nights are unbelievably crowded and fun from about 2:30am until when most people are getting ready to start the work week. 1,000ptas entrance, with little trouble from the doorman, unless your pants are on your head or something. 1,000ptas drinks.

CULTURE ZOO

Madrid's art museums are awesome, and they're half-off if you have a Spanish student card (anything from a foreign school—particularly if it doesn't have a date on it—usually won't fly). But even at full price most venues are only about 500ptas. The following days are free for all museums:

May 18 (International Day of Museums), October 12 (Fiesta Nacional de España), and December 6 (Día de Constitución Española). If you're walking everywhere, you may want to do the three biggies (Prado, Reina Sofía, Thyssen) together because they form a surprisingly small triangle with each other. The Palacio Real and the Museo de la Real Academia de Bellas Artes de San Fernando are also relatively close to each other. The other museums listed here are a little further out and may not be worth your time if you don't have a lot of it. It depends on how much of an art-fiend you really are.

Museo del Prado *(Paseo del Prado; Tel 91/330-28-00; Metro Banco de España or Atocha; 9am-7pm Tue-Sat, 9am-2pm Sun; 500ptas, 200ptas students, free under 18, free Sat and Sun 2:30pm-7pm):* Where does an 800 pound Museo del Prado sit? Anywhere it wants. Miss the enormous collection of medieval and Renaissance work in this top-notch museum, and your parents will never send you anywhere again. Miss the moody Goyas and trippy Boschs and you only cheat yourself.

Thyssen-Bornemisza Museum *(Palacio de Villahermosa, Paseo del Prado 8; Tel 91/420-39-44; Metro Banco de España; 10am-7pm Tue-Sun):* If you were going to be stranded on a desert island for the rest of your life, which museum would you want with you? Well, the Thyssen would make good company because it's got a little bit of everything: from Renaissance to Realism and Cubism to Pop Art.

Museo Nacional Centro de Arte Reina Sofía *(Santa Isabel 52; Tel 91/467-50-62; Metro Atocha; 10am-9pm Tue-Sat, 10am-2:30pm Sun):* With a whole lot of Picasso, Dalí, and Miró, it's like a modern art supermarket. Price check on the Guernica at register 6....

Palacio Real *(Plaza de Oriente; Bailén 2; Tel 91/542-00-59; Metro Opera or Plaza de España; Oct-March: 9:30am-5pm Mon-Fri; Apr-Sept: 9am-6pm Mon-Fri):* Real? Royal? No matter how you spell it, it means splendor and opulence on a level you never thought possible. The nifty clocks alone make it worth a visit, but the official tour can make it all seem big, beautiful, and boring.

Museo de la Real Academia de Bellas Artes de San Fernando *(Alcalá 13; Tel 91/522-14-91; Metro Sol or Sevilla; 9-7pm Tue-Fri, 9-2:30pm Sat-Mon)* If it's Spanish, they've got it here. Sculpture, 18th-century painting, and photography are only a few steps away from Puerta del Sol.

Panteón de Goya *(Glorieta de San António de la Florida; Tel 91/542-07-02; Tue-Fri: 10am-2pm, 4pm-8pm, Sat-Sun: 10am-2pm, Closed Mondays; Metro Príncipe Pío):* Goya painted the ceiling of this church shortly before his death. Although considered his finest moment, it is, after all, only one moment. Unless Goya is your God, if your time is limited, best stick to the museums downtown.

Museo Lázaro Galdiano *(Seranno, 122; Tel 91/561-60-84; 10-2pm Tue-Sun, Closed Mondays; Metro Rubén Darío—Castellana Exit):* Financier José Lázaro Galdiano collected nearly 15,000 works of art in his life—including two of Goya's goulish black paintings—making his personal collection a lot bigger than yours. There are also as many artifacts as art, including sculpture, furniture, and jewelry.

by foot

To get a whole lot of angry young Madrid in your eye, it's hard to beat a stroll down Calle de Fuencarral. Start at the McDonald's on **Gran Vía** *(Metro Gran Vía)* (for God's sake don't go in!), cross the street, and never look back at that horrible place. The turbulent sights, smells, and fashions of Fuencarral await you on the other side of Gran Vía, and so begins your walk on the wild side. We mention this street often in other sections of this chapter, but we swear that it's sub-Madrid at its best. In the first block or so, you'll pass cramped stores selling everything from wristwatches and walkmans to pornography, but the street quickly transforms itself into a hipster's wet dream. You'll first come across clothing stores of all shapes and sizes. Many of the windows have gallery-style displays, including mannequins with TV-heads and far-out latex fantasies. As you continue, the stores will be joined by restuarants and bars where the fashions being sported by the clientele transform them into living mannequins. Both the stores and the cafes come to a climax at the plaza right next to **Mercado Fuencarral,** which is full of cafe tables, more stores, and a whole lot of people just hanging out.

A few more blocks will bring you to the **Metro Tribunal.** Located here is the **Museo Municipal,** an ugly building whose haunting facade you will not forget anytime soon. Taking a left on any of the streets across from the museum will bring you into Malasaña, our favorite part of the city. Proceeding forward will bring you to a handful more restuarants, and finally, **La Glorieta de Bilbao,** where you can sit at the sidewalk tables of **Café Comercial** [see *wired,* below] and enjoy a small cup of good coffee.

Twenty minutes southwest of Bilbao is **Plaza de España,** the starting point of your second walk. Before beginning, though, you might want to check out some modern—decidedly unhip—Madrid consumer culture: Plaza de España borders **Calle de Princesa** (whose name changes to Gran Vía as you get closer to Sol), which is full of fast food, movie theaters, a VIPS, and—about two minutes east of the plaza—one of Madrid's best arcades (featuring the newest pinball

modification

You certainly could get a few extra holes in your body while running with the bulls, but you're less likely to get an infection if you go to a professional. **El Rastrillo** *(Montera 17; Tel 91/532-28-48; Metro Sol; 11am-9pm Mon-Sat; V, MC, AE)* has a tattoo and piercing parlor above and a headshop/used clothing store below. The good folks upstairs are licensed, sterile, and will

machines, virtual racing, pool tables, and a general level of cleanliness that you won't find elsewhere in this city). Once you get to the Plaza de España proper, take it slow. The beautiful fountains and trees offer a welcome place to sit and relax a few moments. There's often hordes of young people here, too, playing soccer, smoking cigarettes, and otherwise letting time pass by. Continue walking through the plaza lengthwise, towards the southwest, until you come to **Calle de Ferraz.** Think of this busy street as a commercial during your favorite TV show.... Walk two minutes to the right (NW), cross the street, and climb up to **El Templo de Debod.** The Egyptian artifacts here were given to Spain and other countries in exchange for financial assistance in the building of Egypt's Aswan Dam. You can pay to go into the small museum at the top of the hill, but you'll have just as much fun taking in the view of the city below including El Palacio Real and its gardens. There are also pay telescopes to check out the details. If it's a hot day (and it often is in Madrid in the summer) you'll be particularly happy let the wind cool you down with droplets from the small fountain here. Now that you've been refreshed, walk down the steps on the opposite side of the hill that you climbed up (the western side) and take a right onto the **Paseo del Pintor Rosales.** This shady, windy pathway runs through the end of **El Parque del Oeste** and is a great place to hold hands with a new "friend." Now that you're in the mood, you will be happy to notice that Marid's **Teleférico** [see *only here,* below] is right in front of you. Climb into one of the cable cars and relax. You'll be dropped off at the eerily bare **Casa de Campo,** which is supposed to be a nature reserve, but don't let the scrub brushes and dirt paths drag you down. Go to the cafetería and have a drink; you've earned it. Walk around a bit more if you like, and then return via the gondolas. When you return, cross Calle de Ferraz again and walk down **Calle de Marqués de Urquijo,** where most of the trendy little pubs accept credit cards and serve authentic Spanish cuisine.

pierce anything (You can point at the pictures if you don't know the word for clitoris...). They charge 2,000ptas to add some weight to your ears or nose, but the jewelry itself begins at 2,400ptas. **Mao & Cathy** *(Corredera Alta de San Pablo 6; Tel 91/523-13-33; Fax 91/531-19-73; Metro Tribunal; 3:30pm-8pm Mon, 11am-2pm /3:30pm-8pm, Tue-Sat; No credit cards)* is Madrid's oldest and, according to many, best tattoo parlor. The place just has

12 hours in madrid

1. **Rastro Weekend Market:** The constant physical contact with the crowds, the hawking of bizarre goods, and the various smells make this a must. Buy a can of beer from one of the shops and walk, baby [see *stuff,* below].
2. **Retiro Park on the weekend:** Promenade along the main pool and check out the dozens of musicians, puppeteers, mimes, and other freaks[see *hanging out,* above].
3. **Plaza Mayor lunch:** Lunch doesn't begin in Spain till about 2pm, but if you show up a little earlier, you'll be sure to get a ringside seat at one of the several restaurants that keep shop in the Plaza Mayor. Tourists? Oh yeah. But also the most toothless, rowdiest, weirdest, panhandlers in all of Madrid. It's a freakin circus.
4. **Disco nite till dawn:** Madrid cannot be messed with in the world of the Late Night. Choose from any one of our fine selection of nightclubs [see *club scene,* above], or seek out something new, but whatever you do, make it last till dawn. The whole rest of the city will be dancing and drinking right there with you.
5. **Malasaña dinner and drinks:** Malasaña is distinctly young, artsy, and bohemian—and distinctly Spanish. Enjoy authentic Spanish cuisine and atmosphere at Albur [see *eats,* below] before hitting the Plaza Dos de Mayo [see *hanging out,* above] and the bottle.
6. **Las Vistillas:** Metro Opera will bring you within a few minutes walk of this lovely little neighborhood that happens to have a spectacular view of El Palacio Real. Pleasant gardens with fountains

the right feel to it: you know you're in good hands the moment you walk in. A tattoo will cost you 5,000ptas and up. Piercing costs about 5,500ptas for your ear or nose, but the jewelry costs a lot less: starting from 600ptas. Mao & Cathy will also pierce anything in your pants, starting at 10,000ptas.

great outdoors

Of course the easiest place to go running is the huge city park, El Retiro (Metro El Retiro). The only problem is that you might be running from pickpockets and panhandlers as much as for your health. The Calle de Moyano is the best entrance for running and rollerblading, because it is far from all of the pond-related hype that goes down in the central part of the park. The high altitude of the **Parque Juan Carlos I** *(Metro Campo de las Naciones; 9am-11:30pm daily),* and its removal from the city makes it worth the half-hour Metro ride from downtown. A weird mix of nature and huge modern statues and bridges give the park a postapocalyptic, *Planet of the Apes* vibe that is somehow very calming. Without a doubt, this is Madrid's

and great outdoor seating under shady trees (and on real grass) make this little place an island of tranquility in the otherwise loud and paved sea of Madrid. Directions: Get yo ass to the Royal Palace. Walk south along Calle de Bailén. Cross the big bridge. Turn right immediately after the bridge and you're there.

7. **Walk on the wild side at Calle de Fuencarral:** This street begins at Gran Vía with all the grime, heavy traffic, and lost souls that you'd expect from a city of 5 million. From there it becomes starving artist and club chic.[see *by foot,* below]

8. **One floor of the Thyssen-Bornemisza Museum:** Although it's probably the least known of Madrid's big three museums, the Thyssen easily has the best variety. Get in the mood, maybe bring a walkman, and enjoy the show. [see *culture zoo,* below].

9. **Sol Survivor:** You'll probably wind up in Puerta del Sol whether you like it or not. It's the epicenter of downtown Madrid. There's a political demonstration of some sort most days of the week here. Be sure to check out the military guys with the wacky hats on the south end of the plaza (opposite Gran Vía).

10. **Get some PDA, baby!:** Yes, that's right. We're suggesting that a higlight of Madrid is to make out on a streetcorner while surrounded by strangers. It's liberating, it's a rush, and it feels right. [see *only here,* above].

best location for biking, running, rollerblading, skateboarding, kite flying, frisbee throwing, and day tripping [see *need to know,* below, for bike rental info]. You might even enjoy the espectáculos on Thursday-Sunday nights at 10:30pm; they include music, fireworks and synchronized fountains. As with most things, consult the Guía del Ocio for specific times and prices. FYI: Parque Juan Carlos I is completely safe for single women during the day. Nobody hangs out here unless they've come for one of the specific activities listed above. The weirdness/sliminess factor is zero.

The bulletin board at **Central Vegetariana** [see *eats,* below] has great information on acupuncture, yoga, and other healthy activities in the Madrid area, and the friendly staff is more than happy to chat with you about the holisitc happenings in Madrid. If you actually want to interact with nature, it's best that you hop on the magic bus *(Bus 724 from Plaza de Castilla, 130ptas)* and travel north for an hour towards the village of **Manzares el Real.** This small village is the base point for the enormous **Pedriza National Park.** On weekends, the main road becomes polluted with

Madrileños driving their cars to a central area of the park for a picnic, but they're clearly missing the point. You'll be much happier with the fantastic hiking trails (over 1,000 of them), lush and green scenic views, and fresh air.

STUFF

What are you going to bring home to your folks and friends? A flamenco dancer doll? A little keychain that says "I ♥ España?" An unabridged Don Quixote? If you're looking for gifts, your friends might dig one of those infamous "Italian recordings" of a favorite band in concert. Or if it's fashion you want, whip out your plastic and get on down to Puerta del Sol, where stores such as **Zara,** and even **El Corte Inglés** (both on Calle de Preciados) will be more than happy to help you spend you money fast. Only slightly less expensive, but a lot more club-oriented, are the nearly 30 clothing stores on Calle Fuencarral between Gran Vía and the Tribunal Metro Stops. This street has also got plenty of information on which clubs you want to see tonight. At its epicenter is the three-story high mall, **Mercado Fuencarral** *(Fuencarral 45; Tel 91/521-59-85; Metro Tribunal, Gran Vía, Chueca; Stores open from 10am-9pm Mon-Sat; Cybercafé and bar open till 3am on weekends; www.ttcom.com/fuencarral; A few stores take plastic),* a must-see for those who wanna get with it in Madrid. This throbbing core of coolness features nearly 50 stores that sell clothes, jewelry, smoking equipment, music and other (sub)culturally relevant items. Also has a (sometimes free) movie theater, two bars (one of them with internet a la Net Café—see *wired,* below) and a hair stylist, all of them named a variation of Fuencarral.

▶▶BOUND

The huge, corporate-feeling, **Casa Del Libro** *(Gran Vía 29; Tel 91/521-22-19; Fax 91/522-77-58; 9:30am-9:30pm Mon-Sat; www.casa dellibro.com)* will have any book that you could ever want, especially maps and dictionaries. They have some titles in English, too. Much like Borders or Barnes and Noble, you can sit and read for as long as you want without anyone bothering you. Large posters in the stairwell quote famous people from the Marx Brothers to Einstein to Cervantes; reading them is a great way to practice your Español.

Calle de los Libreros *(Off of Gran Vía; Metro Callao; Most stores open from 9am-12:30/4-8pm Mon-Sat; Most don't accept credit cards)* is more than just a name. Yup, it really is a street that's full of booksellers. Makes for a great stroll, but many of these stores cater to university courses, meaning that a few of the librerias here only have chemistry or biology books. The majority, however, carry cool philosophy titles and the usual assortment of literary greats. If you want to get *The Iliad* or *The Sun Also Rises* in Spanish, this is the place. (If you want something in English, though, you best head back to Casa Del Libro or wait till you get home). Most stores also have a small used book section.

Cuesta de Moyano *(Outdoor vendors on Calle de Moyano; Metro Atocha; 10-2/6-9pm Mon-Fri, 9-3pm Sat-Sun; No credit cards)* is the emotional, silly Stimpy to the academic, loveless Calle de los Libreros' Ren. More than 30 vendors line up along this tree-lined slope of a street to buy and sell any book you can imagine. Romances, kids titles, and popular novels fill

moda

If you're *de moda*, you're in style, and in Madrid, like in any other city that has publicly elected officials and Lenny Kravitz on the radio, moda is what you make of it: hippie, chic, metal, whatever. Although they're always well dressed (i.e. prep), the run-of-the-mill Madrileños are clearly not in touch with the edgy fashion scene from Paris or New York. One distinguising characteristic, though, seems to be that the fashion here is tighter, particularly—but not exclusively—for the girls. Of course, women from all over will wear little tanktops and dresses in the summer, but Madrid women really go for the "butt" look. Really. The attitude here is that any butt, from "too-flat-to-pedal-a-bike" and all the way to "juicy fruit," is looking good when wrapped up in black stretch pants or small jeans. And the club gear? Well...it's club gear, friends. The Spanish sorority-girl types will wear the international S.P. (sorority pants) and white tops until they die, and as in the rest of the world, fellas in the know are currently wearing the Adidas running pants with a t-shirt or tanktop that's clean.

each vendor's booth to the brim with possibilities. If chance is on your side (bring your lucky rubber nipples), you might find some real treasures here.

▶▶PAYING RETAIL

No Comment *(Fuencarral 39; Tel 91/531-19-57; Metro Gran Vía; 10:30am-2:30pm/5pm-9pm Mon-Fri, 11am-3pm/4pm-9pm Sat; nocomment@nc-f39.es; V, MC, AE)* is one of literally dozens of cool clothing shops on Calle de Fuencarral and Calle de Hortaleza between the Gran Vía and Tribunal Metro stops. All-new, all-hip clothing and accessories for guys and girls. Very friendly staff and lots of club information.

Get wedding gifts and things for grandma at **Casa Talavera** *(Isabel Católica 2; Tel 91/547-34-17; Metro Santo Domingo; 10am-1:30pm/5pm-8pm Mon-Fri, 10am-1:30pm Sat; No credit cards)*. One thing that Spain does well is ceramics, and Casa Talavera sells only the best. The small store is stuffed with soup bowls, vases, tiles, lamp shades, etc. Take your time looking because many treasures are semi-hidden throughout the store's clutter. From 800ptas for a single tile to 14,000ptas or higher for enormous, ornate vases that could hide a monkey.

▶▶TUNES

Club Amigos del Disco *(Fernandez de los Ríos 93; Tel 91/543-05-03; 10-2pm/5-8pm Mon-Fri, 10am-2pm Sat; No credit cards)* is also amigos with vinyl, cassettes, and posters. They buy and sell CDs. This place is not exactly downtown, but is worth checking out because it's loaded with those legal-only-in-Italy live recordings of your favorite bands. The atmosphere here is exactly like your favorite local record store back home: posters covering the walls, Beck on the stereo, and scruffy musician-types flipping through the records for their find-of-the-week.

If, by some remarkable twist of fate, you cannot find what you're looking for here, you can always head over to **FNAC** *(Preciados 28; Tel 91/595-61-00; Metro Callao; Bus 44, 75, 133, 146, 147; 10am-9:30pm Mon-Sat, noon-9:30pm Sun; AE, MC, V)*, located in Sol's Calle de Preciados. FNAC is the musical equivilant of Casa del Libro: very corporate, very big selection (featuring too much top 40 and a good selection of world music), and very many listening centers. They also carry a huge selection of videos, magazines, software, and international newspapers.

▶▶**THRIFT**

El Banco de la Ropa *(Ruiz 14, Tel 91/593-32-13; Metro Tribunal; Noon-9 Mon-Fri, 12-3:30/4:30-9 Sat; V)* Buy and sell used clothes here! Although more expensive than the Salvation Army, you'll find lots of great stuff. Owners Pilar and Conchita speak English. They carry some new clothes; more stuff for girls than boys. Selling your clothes is on consignment only. What doesn't sell goes to local charities.

The infamous **El Rastro** *(Various streets; Metro La Latina and Tirso de Molina; 10:30am-2:30pm Fri-Sun; Credit cards? Yeah, right.)* outdoor market is a seething concoction of bootlegged t-shirts, questionable antiques, and won't-find-anywhere gifts for friends back home. It's one of the most fun things you'll see in Madrid. There are some true artisans mixed in with the homeless people selling a few rusty nuts and bolts, and there's also plenty of bars to have a bite to eat and maybe a small caña of beer. Watch your pockets here, and try and check out the scene on Sundays before noon. Friday and Saturday are only half as much fun, as the place become unbearably crowded by 12:30.

Eats

Madrid is well known for the richness of its nightlife, but the cuisine is surprisingly bland in comparison. In general, your options are 1) Something that came from a pig; 2) Spanish tortilla (a tasty, thick omelet kind of thing made of eggs and potatoes); and 3) Fast food (like everywhere). Even the mighty Spanish paella (yellow rice topped with meat and seafood in a spicy, brothy sauce) is less common than one would think. If you want something cheap, take three steps in any direction and walk into the nearest...pub! Nearly all pubs are open from about 7am till 2am and serve tapas (small sandwiches or portions of food) like tortilla, calamari, olives, or something with bacon. Tortilla is always a safe bet for breakfast or a snack; it's served with bread and costs only 250-350ptas. In the afternoon, usually from around 1-4pm, the larger of these pubs will serve El Menu del Día (about 1,000ptas), which consists of bread, an appetizer (usually a vegetable), two main plates (usually pasta or soup and a meat dish), dessert, and a drink (beer, water, or wine). Other inexpensive options are the alimentación stores (what they call bodegas in

Spain), outdoor markets, and even supermarkets. **Día** *(San Bernardo 83; Metro San Bernardo)* is a particularly low-cost chain with several locations. If you aren't finding a whole lot of vegetarian options in the restaurants and your protein count is running low, try the cozy **Central Vegetariana** *(La Palma 15; Tel 91/447-80-13; Metro Tribunal; 10am-2pm/5-8pm Mon-Fri, 10-1:30pm Sat)*. The friendly staff at this market is happy to answer your questions about soy chorizo or any other vegetarian/vegan food, supplement, or drink that they sell.

A handful of restaurants at **Plaza Emperador Carlos V** *(Metro: Atocha)* stay open for 24 hours on the weekends, but other than that, you will have to settle for a 7-11 or the Spanish equivalent, VIPS, after you've sampled the local chocolate and are red-eyed and starving. Also remember that you can drink in any restaurant in Spain; even Burger King and KFC serve beer!

▶▶**CHEAP**

La Cafetería Reina Sofía *(Atocha 110; Metro Atocha or Alónso Martín; 9am-3am Sun-Wed, 24hrs Thur-Sat; No credit cards)* is one of a handful of restaurants at Metro Atocha that stays open 24 hours. 'Nuff said. La Reina is here for your drunken needs with food (250ptas for a Spanish tortilla sandwich) and beer. If you're experiencing Madrid properly, you'll arrive at this otherwise average corner bar too late at night for the flourescent lights and typically dirty floors to make an impact. Besides, this place is really nothing more than a human gas station; it's best to get your food and get out. If you want atmoshpere, hit the bars and clubs.

Ali-Baba *(Velarde 8; Tel 91/448-55-20; Metro Tribunal; 12:30pm-4pm/8pm-12 Mon-Thur, Open till 2am Fri-Sat, 8pm-midnight Sun; No credit cards.)* is located in another drinking district, Malasaña. Yes, you came to Spain to experience Spanish culture and cuisine, but how much pig can you eat? Ali-Baba's got the Middle Eastern flava, so get a falafel or some hummus. The simple restaurant is too small to offer anything more than standup counters and a few posters of Israel, but the music is always fun Middle Eastern pop, and—at only 350ptas—the food is delicious and authentic.

▶▶**DO-ABLE**

Maravillas Pizza *(Plaza 2 de Mayo 9; Tel 91/523-19-73; 12:30pm-2am/3:30am on weekends, evenings only (from 5pm) Oct -May; pepitilla @olemail.com; No credit cards)* offers great pizza, casseroles, and several vegetarian dishes as well as huge salads from 700ptas. The outdoor seating opens up onto the plaza and offers fantastic people watching (including the other patrons). This is one of the best hangouts for young artists and people who just want to look that way.

If you're feeling a little New World, try **Las Mañanitas** *(Fuencarral 82; Tel 91/522-45-89; Metro Bilbao or Tribunal; Noon-4/8-Midnight Mon-Fri, 1pm-4pm/8pm-Midnight Sat-Sun; V, MC)*. Despite the common language, many Mexican restaurants in Spain are, well, crappy. Las Mañanitas, however, is *muy bueno.* The maize-colored floor tiles, mariachi music, and simple (but comfortable) furniture—along with great nachos, quesadillas, and margaritas—will make you happy to be there. 800-1,500 ptas for a meal.

madrid

EATS ◆
Albur **3**
Ali-Baba **6**
Cafetería
  Reina Sofía **11**
Día **2**
Las Mañanitas **7**
Maldeamore **1**
Maravillas Pizza **5**

CRASHING ■
Hostal Palma **4**
Hostel Greco **8**
Hostel Residencia
  Zamora **9**
Pensión Mollo **10**

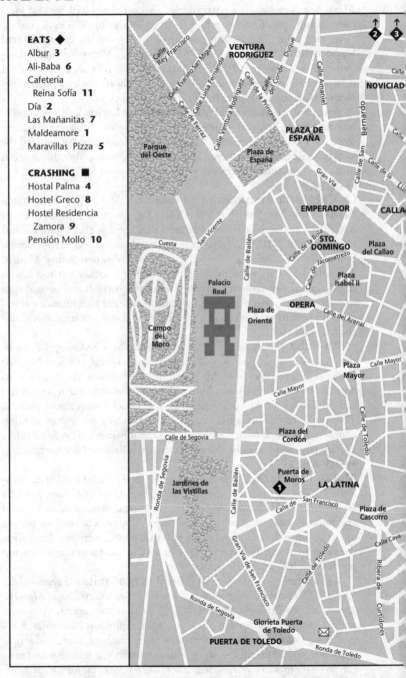

For local tastes, check out **Albur** *(Manuela Malasaña 15; Tel 91/594-27-33; Metro Bilbao; Noon-5:30pm/7:30pm-Midnight Sun-Thur, till 1am on weekends; V, AE, MC).* They serve their fantastic paella on weekends only, but the traditional Spanish cuisine served the rest of the week is also right on the money. Albur has a fun, neighborhood-restaurant atmosphere, Spanish style: small tables crammed together (be prepared to make friends with some fellow diners), a staff that's truly *gracioso* (witty, funny), and wine that flows as quickly as the locals' animated Spanish chatter. Plus you get a free shot of cider liquor at the end of your meal. 1,100ptas for the Plato del Día.

▶▶**SPLURGE**

A perfect atmosphere with a beautiful menu and...sushi!! **Maldeamore** *(Don Pedro 6; Metro La Latina; Noon-2am Tue-Sun, Dinner 9pm-12:30 only; AE, V, MC, D)* also offers you many fantastic salads, Gil Gilberto on the stereo, and the coolest bar stools you ever saw. It's all very uptown: Hardwood floors and old, old brick walls sit agreeably with fresh flowers and the stainless-steel bar. The building is historically protected; it's lower level is created from arches and walls that were built in Moorish times. 1,200 to 2,500ptas for an entrée; the sushi combo platter is 3,000ptas.

crashing

Don't sweat trying to find a hostel in the "right" area. Yeah, Madrid's a big city, but it's physically squished. The various zones are surprisingly close together, and if you're centrally located you'll never have to walk for more than 20 minutes to get to your destination (five or ten is usually more like it). If you're a big lazy-ass who doesn't feel like walking, the Metro will obviously make any trip a lot shorter. If all else fails, cabs breed like flies in Madrid and are safe, honest, and very cheap, especially if you're traveling with a few people. Although imposter cabs are extremely rare, be sure that your cab is white with the little green light on top. Your ride will be metered with extra charges for luggage, of course, and you can tip a little (5%) if you like; tipping for any service is not a big part of Spanish culture.

Most hostels in Madrid keep their main doors locked and buzz their tenants in. Although totally annoying and inconvenient, it's true that your backpack is a lot safer this way. So, even though most hostels will tell you that they don't have a curfew, be patient when you are ringing the bell to be let in at 6am!

Though we think the places we've picked are the best, if they're all booked and you need more choices, go to any bookstore and pick up the **Guia Oficiale de Hotels,** which is a comprehensive list of all the hotels in Madrid. It's in Sapnish, but addresses and phone numbers are the same in any language. Or, if you're the plan-ahead type, log on to ***www.hotelsearch.com*** or ***http://madrid.hotels.ru/spain/madrid/hotall/asp,*** either of which will give you a list of Madrid hotels and let you book a room on line at no charge.

▶▶CHEAP

The small, pleasant **Hostel Palma** *(Palma 17, 1st floor; Tel 91/447-54-88; Metro Tribunal or San Bernardo; 1,500-1,700ptas singles; 2,700 doubles; No credit cards.)* is right where the action is: Malasaña. Because it is clean, accesible, and on a relatively quiet street, you get much more than your money's worth here. Each room has a sink and a simple desk, chair, and closet. Many rooms also have balconies. The common bathroom is clean. The best thing about this hostel is that they give you a key to the building, allowing you to come and go whenever (and with whomever) you please.

The building and main hallway at **Pensión Mollo** *(Atocha 104, 4th floor; Tel 91/528-71-76; Metro Atocha; 1,800ptas singles; 3,300ptas doubles, 4,000ptas triples; No credit cards.)* are dark and dingy, but the rooms are very bright and pleasant. Along with a basic chair, desk, and closet, many rooms also have a small balcony. All triples and some doubles have private bath, singles only have a sink. For 300-800ptas, the staff'll do your laundry. Close to the **Prado** [see *culture zoo*, above], Atocha Renfe train station, and the Atocha bar district.

These two all full-up? Never fear, there are a couple other good, cheap options: **Albergue Santa Cruz de Marcenado** *(Calle de Santa Cruz de Marcenado 28; Tel 91/547-45-32; Dorm bed 1200ptas under 26, 1820ptas over 26, no private baths, breakfast included; 1:30am curfew; No credit cards)*, with 72 beds; and **Hostal-Residencia Mondragon** *(Calle San Jeronimo 32, 4th floor; Tel 91/429-68-16; Single 2000ptas, double 3000ptas, triple 3900ptas, no private baths; No credit cards)*. Cool fact: the first Spanish motion picture ever, *Ría en un Café*, was filmed in the Residencia Mondragon!

▶▶DO-ABLE

Hostel Residencia Zamora *(Plaza Vázquez de Mella 1, 4th floor; Tel 91/521-70-31; Metro Gran Vía; 3,500ptas singles, 5,000-6,000ptas doubles, 6,900ptas triples, 2,000ptas per person in rooms of 4 or 6 people; No credit cards)* was renovated only a few years ago, and all the rooms now have private bath, television, heat, and air conditioning. Really nice patterned hardwood floors, too. Because the rooms overlook the Plaza Vázquez de Mella, all the rooms are bright as well as quiet. If you don't have a reservation and are worried about getting stranded, check out this hostel first because there are several others in the same building. Convenient to Gran Vía, Sol, and Calle de Fuencarral.

All rooms at **Hostel Greco** *(Infantas 3, 2nd floor; Tel 91/532-46-32; Metro Gran Vía; 3,800-4,500ptas Singles, 5,600-6,500ptas doubles, 7,800ptas triples; V, MC)* have private baths, phones, TVs, and closets. Most have a safe deposit box. One of about 25 hostels in the area, but most rooms here are big and sunny with ornate mirrors and simple desks and chairs. Very close to Gran Vía, Sol, Chueca, and the cool parts of Fuencarral and Hortaleza streets. The husband's kind of grumpy; save your questions for the wife.

Other reasonable options include **Hostal Cervantes** *(Cervantes 34, 2nd floor; Tel 91/429-27-45; Double 6500ptas, private bath; No credit cards),* near Retiro Park; the sunny and newly renovated **Hostal-Residencia Luz** *(Calle Fuentes 10, 3rd floor; Tel 91/542-07-59; Single 2500ptas, double 3700ptas, triple 5500ptas, 1000ptas extra for*

wired

Most of us know that using e-mail is the best way to keep up with latest gossip back home, but who knew that the Internet cafes in Madrid would be prime locations to create some gossip of your own? When you walk into an e-mail center, be prepared to get checked out. Not like a quick-turn-of-the-head look, but more of a "mmm, mmm, mmm..." look. Seriously, forget the bars and discos, and never mind all those small cafes and museums; 90 percent of the people in Internet cafes are foreigners between 20 and 30 years old. Add the fact that—like with everything else in Spain—you can smoke and drink at these locations, and you've got yourself a regular little scene. Common lines include "Do you know how to use hotmail?", "Did your computer stop working, too?", and "Where'd you learn to type like that?". Perhaps the best place for said lines is the **Net Café** *(San Bernardo 81; Tel 91/594-09-99; Metro San Bernardo; 10am-2am daily, till 3am Fri, Sat; www.net-café.es; No credit cards),* which plays loud modern rock, displays random movies on a projector screen, and mixes stiff drinks. It's a dark bar first and Internet station second, with eight computers ingeniously recessed into Star Wars-style bar tables that function as computer screens and, well, bar tables. Internet use is free for 45 minutes if you buy one drink worth 500ptas or more. Although **Café Comercial** *(Glorieta de Bilbao 7; Metro Bilbao; 8am-1:30am Sun-Thur, 8am-2:30am Fri-Sat; No credit cards)* is a lot quieter, you can still buy drinks and food from the cafeteria downstairs. Computer use is a mere 500ptas per hour, but, because the computers are coin-op(!), there is no technical support here. Café Commercial is also a great place to study in general, as there are huge windows and always many vacant tables here. If you've got actual work to do, you best head down to **Gopher Web** *(Cea Bermúdez 66; Tel 91/399-34-39; Metro Islas Filipinas; 7:30am-12:30am daily; información@www.gopherweb.com, www.gopherweb.com; No credit cards.).* The rates here are nearly double the other places (700ptas for an hour—although there are bulk-time discounts), but you can use Word and its MS Office brethren, save to floppy disks, and print. Plus, they have 20 machines, and the staff know what they're talking about.

down and out

Diving for butts? Tumbleweed blowing through your wallet? Well...if **Filmoteca** [see *arts scene*, above] has already sold out it's 225ptas shows, and you've gotten all you can out of the **Thyssen museum** [see *culture zoo*, above], then maybe you ought to hop on the city bus, route Circular, and get a 50 cent tour of the city. This route can be picked up at the bus stops in Sol, and will last about an hour and 15 minutes.

private bath in any room, laundry 1000ptas; No credit cards), in the center of town; and **Hostal-Residencia Rober** *(Calle Arenal 26, 5th floor; Tel 91/541-91-75; Single 3600ptas w/shower, 4500ptas w/ bath, double 5700ptas w/bath, triple 7000ptas w/bath, all rooms have TV and A/C; No credit cards)*, which offers non-smoking rooms.

▶▶SPLURGE

The rooms at **Casón de Tormes** *(Río 7; Tel 91/541-97-46; Metro Plaza de España; 12,500ptas doubles, 15,800ptas triples; V, MC)* have private baths, air conditioning, TVs, and telephones, but it might be the laundry service that you appreciate most. Located near the start of one of our two walks at the **Plaza de España** [see *by foot*, above]. This hotel also offers a bar for your traveling pleasure....

If you're looking for something with a little more spice (wink, wink), check yourself into the funky **Hotel Monaco** *(Calle Barbieri 5; Tel 91/552-46-30, Fax 91/521-16-01; Single 7500ptas, double 10,700ptas, triple 13,500ptas, quad 15,000ptas, private baths; V, MC, AE)*. This swanky hotel is housed in a former bordello and the owners have parlayed that fact into a whole theme, with R-rated frescoes and big ol' mirrors everywhere. Even if you don't have the bucks to stay here, stop by their hip lounge, bar, or cafe.

need to know

Currency You can exchange money in the airport and in Cambio booths around the Sol neighborhood, but a bank, ATM, or credit card will always get you the best rates and the lowest service charge.

Tourist Offices It's not the main Tourist Office, but the one located in the **Plaza Mayor** *(Tel 91/588-16-36; Metro Sol; 10am-8pm Mon-Fri, 10am-2pm Sat)*, is by far the easiest to get to and has adequate information on the city of Madrid. They won't book a hotel room for you.

Public Transportation It all boils down to the **Metro** (subway) and the **EMT** (buses). Both use the same tickets, but the Metro is infinitely easier to use. Plus, it's (usually) fast, safe, and clean. Buy your 10 trip MetroBus pass in the subways for only 680ptas (about 50 cents a ride). Metro system planos (maps) are located at the ticket windows. The subways are closed from 1am till 6am.

American Express (Tel 91/572-03-20, Plaza de las Cortes 2; Metro Banco de España or Sevilla).

Health/Emergency Emergency: 112. The two main hospitals in Madrid are **Ciudad Sanitaria la Paz** *(Paseo de la Castellana 261; Tel 91/358-28-31; Metro Begoña)* and **Hospital General Gregorio Marañón** *(Doctor Esquerdo 46; Metro Ibiza or O'Donnell).*

Pharmacies Every little neighborhood in Madrid has at least one *farmacia,* marked by big **green neon crosses**. No single one is open 24 hours a day; instead, farmacias rotate the all-night responsibility. Each one posts a schedule of who will be open on which night, as do the major newspapers like *El País.*

Telephones City code: *91;* operator: *1003;* International operator: *1005.* Note that recent changes in Spain's phone system now require that all local calls within Madrid be dialed with the 91 prefix.

Airport Barajas International Airport *(Tel 91/393-60-00)* is about 13km northeast of the city. Metro service runs directly from the airport via line 8. A bus runs about every 15 minutes from the airport to **Plaza de Colón** (350ptas); you can switch to the Metro or a taxi from there.

Trains Renfe *(Tel 91/328-90-20)* is Spain's national train line. The two main stations are **Atocha** (Metro Atocha Renfe) and **Chamartín** (Metro Chamartín). Both are adorned with easy-to-read signs that will direct you to the Metro. Going to a hostel near Chamartín isn't the best idea; it's nearly 20 minutes from downtown. Instead, get on the Metro and get off at Tribunal, Antón Martín, Sol, or Gran Vía to put yourself in the center of town. Although you can walk to a few places from Atocha Station (exit to Rhonda de Atocha), you might as well use the cheap, fun Metro to get to those same stops.

Out-Of-Town Buses The main station is **Estación Sur de Autobuses** *(Mendéz Alvaro; Tel 91/468-42-00; Metro Mendéz Alvaro).*

Bike, Moped, and Car Rental If you're thinking about moving around on wheels, remember that gas is expensive and hard to find in the city, parking is scarce, and the roads are as crammed and disorienting. Okay, having said that, call **Europcar** *(Tel 91/721-12-22)* for a car, and **Motoalquiler** *(Tel 91/542-06-57)* for a cycle or scooter. Good luck....

Internet See *wired,* above.

everywhere else

aranjuez

Spanish royalty didn't summer in the Hamptons; they summered in lovely Aranjuez, building their **Palacio Real** [see *culture zoo,* below] strong and sturdy here, just 45 minutes from Madrid. If you're based in Madrid or are on your way there, it's best to visit Aranjuez's Palacio before the capital's—although the one in Aranjuez is decked, it's really no comparison to the splendor of Madrid's. (Keep in mind Aranjuez was their *vacation* home.) When the folks of the royal court needed a holiday (from what I don't know), they loved to step out of their city shoes to wander through the gardens and breathe fresh air along the Tajo river. Aranjuez's rose- and gray-colored stone palace may appear cold and barren as you walk in the main entrance, but it's all in the facade—the colorful gardens behind the structure, as well as the gold and riches found inside the king's quarters, are quite dazzling.

Nowadays, with faster and more convenient trains, Aranjuez is a magnet for non-royal day-trippers. Arriving at the Palacio or in the main square of Aranjuez in the summer, you'll find quite a few tourists passing through for the afternoon, drooling over the stands that sell the region's famous strawberries and cream, *fresones con nata,* at high prices. (Locals say the bigger the berry, the greater the possibility that it's not the real thing. Beware of these genetically altered, shipped-in imitators.) The town is geared for visitors with a sweet tooth, but somehow has escaped having useless tourist junk shops blocking the view.

Aranjuez is a peaceful refuge for those who need a break from the big city. Come here for the relaxing walks and the chance to get near or on the water, which is nowhere in sight in Madrid. Follow the Tajo's shore, promenading in the royal gardens or paddling in a kayak [see *great outdoors,* below].

Apart from the tourist flow, the town is quiet and goes about its business. No building stands more than five stories, and the center consists of a few streets lined with shops and cafeterías. Everything is within easy

only here

When springtime strawberries burst into season, a steam train chugs mid-morning out of Madrid's Atocha Renfe station [see **madrid**] to Aranjuez. It's just like the days of yore; the choo-choo carries strawberries and sun-beaten tourists on the **Tren de Fresas** excursion *(Atocha Renfe station; Tel 902/22-88-22; Metro Atocha Renfe; Sat-Sun late Apr-mid Oct; www.ffe.es/delicias, www.aranjuez-realsitio.com; 3250ptas Adults; No credit cards)*, which only has one departure per day at 10:05am and returns at 6pm. Sitting in wooden seats that make your neck stiff, you'll feel every movement of the old machinery, and that's if it's running well that day. When I say steam train, I mean billowing black clouds of steam that drift in the window and make it hard for you to breathe (you should be used to that by now from the number of smokers in this country). Don't let that stop you from going on this lovely trip to what used to be the countryside far outside Madrid, now only about an hour by train if the old steam engine is running smoothly.

Although traipsing around a city in an organized group, complete with a tour guide holding an umbrella in the air, isn't normally my piece of strawberry shortcake, this tour is unique and worthy. After you get off the train, the guide takes you to the **Palacio Real,** the **Jardín de la Isla,** and the **Museo de Falúas** *(Jardín del Príncipe, Puerta Embarcado—a gate on Calle de la Reina; Tel 91/891-24-53; 10am-5:15pm, closed Mon; 150ptas Adults)*, a maritime museum. You get some free time to break loose from the gang before heading back to the big city around six in the evening. If you plan to go, don't wear white: they give you samples of ripe strawberries on the train. And don't be shy when going for the fat juicy ones on the tray—they only come around once or twice. It's best to reserve a place a few days in advance if you travel between May and July.

walking distance; you won't find any metro here. Maybe that's what keeps most of the locals from shipping off to Madrid. Of course the kids get stir crazy and happily escape off to a night in a neighboring club with rhythms that beat faster than the ambling pace of the average Aranjuez pedestrian.

hanging out

The main thing on the agenda here is strolling through the shade of the well-manicured shrubs and kicking back in the palace gardens, the backyard of the palace. The gardens are the most picturesque part of town, and though walking through the commercial streets is pleasant and peaceful, you won't feel particularly royal. If it's cold out and you need a spot to warm up, the Jamaican coffees spiked with rum, cream, and chocolate at the **Café la Farnesina** *(Infantas 25; Tel 91/891-36-82; 9am-2am daily; Snacks 450-600ptas; No credit cards)* are choice. Against a backdrop of frosted windows and brick walls, you also can revive your spirits with a *caña* (little beer), perhaps shamefully humming along to "Come on Irene" or "Walk Like an Egyptian." This joint is about it for socializing late at night, and so it attracts some *touristas* from the few hotels nearby. The cafe also offers morning toast, pastry treats, and mini sandwiches to go with a plain *cafe con leche* (175ptas). As the day progresses, women pull up chairs to chat and friends meet for a relaxing cup of joe in the morning, or wine and beer for an evening rendezvous.

green space

Before city planners were required to include green space in the works, royalty couldn't live without it. They extended their cottage, the **Palacio Real,** into impressive gardens called **Jardín de la Isla** *(No phone; 8am-8:30pm daily Apr-Sept; 8am-6:30pm daily Oct-Mar; Free).* The Tajo river and a man-made canal surround it, creating an island of well kept grounds northwest of the Palacio, close enough for Queen Isabel's afternoon distractions. When I think of a garden, I think tomato plants or a few begonias. Here, we're talking park-sized "gardens" with walkways along the river, and fountains, fountains, fountains—at every turn you hear water burbling in the peaceful corners of the *jardines.* (Plentiful trees and shade provide cover, just in case all that tinkling water reminds you of the bathroom. **The Jardín Paterre** *(No phone; 8am-6:30pm daily; Free)* behind the Palacio, is less shady, but on a hot day you'll appreciate the refreshing mist spraying in the wind from the fountains. Bordered by the Calle de la Reina, down the way from Paterre, is the **Jardín del Príncipe** *(No phone; 8am-6:30pm daily; Free)* which is another lovely meandering garden, edged by the river and canal. All three are impressive, from the maintenance crew shuffling around in knee-high green boots, constantly manicuring the plants, to the fat statue of Bacchus toasting with some good wine from his perch on top of a fountain.

aranjuez

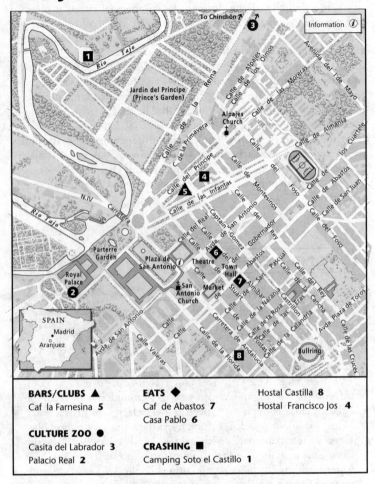

BARS/CLUBS ▲	EATS ◆	Hostal Castilla **8**
Caf la Farnesina **5**	Caf de Abastos **7**	Hostal Francisco Jos **4**
	Casa Pablo **6**	
CULTURE ZOO ●		
Casita del Labrador **3**	**CRASHING** ■	
Palacio Real **2**	Camping Soto el Castillo **1**	

CULTURE ZOO

Palacio Real *(Plaza Palacio; Tel 91/891-13-44; 10am-6:15pm, closed Tues, Apr-Sept, 10am-5:15pm, closed Tues, Oct-Mar; 700ptas Adults, 300ptas Students):* The palace is about the only thing to see here, and it's more than enough to fill your plate. They won't let you in without a guide, and you have to keep your hands behind your back like you did in the fancy store your mom took you to as a kid. Of course, you know you're not supposed to touch, though you may long to fondle the antiques or stroke the walls in the porcelain room. After seeing a few rooms, you'll feel the grandeur of days past.

Casita del Labrador *(Calle Reina; Tel 91/891-03-05; Appointment only: 10am-5:15pm fall-winter, 10am-6:15pm spring-summer; 700ptas* adults, 300ptas students; No credit cards): In one of the gardens set off from the palace, Jardín del Príncipe, this "little house of the laborer" sounds like modest servants' quarters. If this were really how workers lived back in 1803, I'd be game. From the looks of it, though, my bet is that this is simply where they stuck all the marble, china, antiques, and clutter that didn't fit in the palace. It's said that Carlos IV's queen had a few rolls in the hay here with Godoy, the prime minister. *Call ahead* to set up a visit.

great outdoors

Far above the Tajo river stands the **Estación de Turismo Náutico** *(Carretera de Madrid N IV #6; Tel (mobile) 696/315-111; 1,200-1,600ptas day trip, 3,500-4,000ptas initiation course; No credit cards),* a perfect starting point for kayaking down the long stretches of the river. This club runs 3- to 5-hour daily guided trips, leading off with an orientation and get-to-know-your-paddle session around 10am. You must know how to swim and how to get wet—the recreational boats are open, without the fitted skirt. For the longer tours, bring a sandwich so you can picnic at midpoint to recharge your batteries for the return. Even though it's not too strenuous a journey, everyone could use a little energy to push them through the afternoon. If you get hooked, the club also teaches an 8-hour initiation course over a couple of weeks, an arrangement which makes it entirely feasible to wet your oars by day in Aranjuez country, then wet your whistle back in the bars and clubs in Madrid at night. To nose around for information or to talk with the staff, it's best to come by late afternoon when everyone has gotten back from excursions and lunch. (Don't forget, Spanish lunchtime starts around 2pm!) Other outfits, like the **Camping del Soto** *(Soto del Rebollo s/n; Tel 91/891-13-95, Fax 91/891-41-97; May-Sept; www.aranjuez.org)* know about the Tajo's 10 kilometers of calm curves and rent similar open kayaks to paddle on your own. If you don't want to get wet, you can rent a bike here (500ptas per hour), or come to Aranjuez the second week of June for the regional championship *piragüismo* (kayak) races to watch scads of kids and adults take laps around the course.

eats

Come springtime, as soon as you step off the Jardín del Parterre, right behind the Palacio, huge signs yelling *FRESA CON NATA* lead you to the famous strawberries with cream. If you're on the palace tour, you check out the juicy berries on your own time. Around the corner, across the river, down the Carretera de Madrid N IV, there's a row of *fresa* stalls too. Another local specialty that always gets mixed reviews from the tourists is white asparagus, which is plentiful almost all year round. You either love them or you're completely turned off by their texture and the mayo that's dumped over them 98 percent of the time. Restaurants and cafeterias are scattered through the town's commercial area, especially along the roads Almibar and Príncipe, but there's no defined concentration of eateries.

▶▶CHEAP

Café de Abastos (*Abastos 56; Tel 91/891-65-37; 8am-11:30pm Mon-Fri, till midnight or 1am Sat; 550-700ptas combo plates; No credit cards*) looks like the owner went to Pier One and Ikea to create the clean, not typical grunge, Spanish bar. The food, however, is your basic Spanish style, and very fresh—you won't see the tapas-like *ensaladilla rusa,* a cousin of potato salad, form that telltale yellow mayo crust here. The *platos combinados* are more substantial dishes made up of a few tapas, for example: a small beef filet, two eggs, potatoes, and croquettes. It's also a fun hangout to grab a cappuccino, a milk shake, or a snack of a crêpe filled with ham and cheese.

▶▶SPLURGE

Try those white asparagus at **Casa Pablo** (*Almibar 42; Tel 91/891-14-51; 1-4:30pm/8pm-midnight daily, closed Aug; 1,900-2,500ptas per entree, 3,000ptas menu; V, MC, AE*). The roast chicken, shrimp omelet, and grilled whitefish are tasty, too. Walk into the old-fashioned bar decorated in wood and wrought iron, and as you enter the dining room, take notes from the photo display on *torero* (bullfighting) culture. Not a soul is around in August, but during the other summer months, dine outside on the colorful, geranium-filled *terraza.*

crashing

Folks normally don't stay the night in Aranjuez, simply because it's so small and so close to Madrid. There are a handful of *hostales* listed by the **tourist office** (see *need to know,* below) with numbers and addresses you can choose from.

▶▶CHEAP

Despite sitting on a desolate-looking street, the four-story brick building **Hostal Francisco José** (*Príncipe 26; Tel 91/891-11-40; Bus 1, 2 to third block of Calle Príncipe; 3,500ptas single, 5,000ptas double; V, MC*) is rather centrally located. It's only a few blocks away from the Palacio gardens, and a short walk to a cute little church, Alpajés (worth a glance but nothing special). The hostel's faded curtains flap in the breeze in the basic rooms, all equipped with bathrooms.

There's a campground on the other side of the river, north of the center and across from the Jardín del Príncipe, about a kilometer (.62 miles) away from the Palacio and only reachable by car or on foot. **Camping Soto el Castillo** (*Soto del Rebollo s/n; Tel 91/891-13-95, Fax 91/891-41-97; May-Sept; www.aranjuez.org; 4,000-6,000ptas double; No credit cards*) is no rough-and-tumble campsite—more like a well-equipped rec center. It has its own pool and is right on the water—perfect for a day in a kayak or on a bike. They rent both [see *great outdoors,* above].

For another comfortable, cheap option try **Hostal Rusiñol** (*Calle De San Antonio 76; Tel 918/910-155; Single with bath 3,800ptas, single without bath 1,975ptas, Doubles with bath 5,600 ptas; doubles without bath 3,800ptas; V, MC*), right in the city center.

▶▶DO-ABLE

Walk through the courtyard patio of **Hostal Castilla** *(Carretera Andalucia; Tel 91/891-26-27; 6,200ptas double, 7,500ptas triple, 8,900ptas quad, 400ptas breakfast; AE, V, MC, Din)* as sunlight filters down onto the colorfully tiled walls that give advice like *"Con el vino viejo y jamón no se padece del corazón,"* which more or less means "Old wine and ham keep the heart strong." Good advice to follow while in Spain, I say. Another says *"La mujer y la sardina cuanto más chica más fina,"* which is a curious comparison of a woman to a sardine. Most rooms look onto this patio and all have a bathroom and a tele.

need to know

Currency Exchange Deplete your account from banks and ATMs around town, especially in the **shopping area centered around Calle Almibar.**

Tourist Info The folks at the **tourist office** *(Plaza de San Antonio 9; Tel 91/891-04-27; 10am-2pm/4pm-6pm Mon-Fri)* are helpful and speak some English.

Public Transportation A **bus urbano** spins around the little town, but isn't really necessary considering the short distances you have to cover. From the train station to town, take Bus 1 or 2. You can also call **taxis** *(Tel 91/891-11-39)* to come pick you up.

Health and Emergency Emergency: *112;* Police: *091, 092;* Red Cross *(Sol 5; Tel 91/891-02-52);* Ambulance *(Gobernador 82; Tel 91/891-14-30)*

Pharmacies Pharmacies are marked by the **lit-up green crosses.** For night needs, check the local paper or the window of a pharmacy for the one that is currently open on the rotating night duty schedule.

Telephone City code: *91;* international operator: *1005.* International calls dial *00* then area code, and so on. You can use either coins or ***tarjetas telefónicas*** (telephone cards) that you buy at tobacco shops.

Trains Cercanías commuter trains are the easiest means of getting from Aranjuez to Madrid's **Atocha Renfe** [see **Madrid,** *need to know*] and take about 45 minutes to an hour. They leave frequently from the **Renfe station** *(Calle Estación; Tel. 91/891-02-02)* which is an easy five- to 10-minute walk down the Avenida Palacio to the Palacio and center, or a quick hop on Bus 1 or 2.

Bus Lines Out of the City Buses with **AISA** *(Tel 91/891-01-83)* leave from **Avenida Infantas 16** and go to Madrid's **Estación Sur de Autobuses** *(Madrid ticket windows 54-57; Tel 91/527-12-94).*

Laundry Laundromats in Spain are virtually nonexistent in small historic towns like Aranjuez. You'll be washing your undies in the sink till you get to a bigger city.

Postal You may get the wild urge to ship strawberries home from **Correos** *(Peñarredonda 3; 91/891-11-32),* but they may be a disappointment when they arrive: The berries are much better fresh, eaten at the source.

san Lorenzo
de el escorial

At first sight, the massive **palace** and **monastery** [see *culture zoo,* below] make the town of San Lorenzo de El Escorial feel bigger than it actually is. When it comes right down to it, though, the streets of interest are few, and they all border the monastery, which is virtually a city in itself (look and you'll see it takes up half the town map). Since 1557, when King Philipe built the monument to commemorate a victory over France, San Lorenzo de El Escorial has been a royal playground for hunting, vacationing, and escaping from Madrid's hustle and bustle. It continues to be a day or weekend jaunt for *madrileños,* and people like you. If you're not used to "summering" in Spain in a coastal villa, prepare to adjust your budget—there will be a noticeable hike in the prices of lodging and food. Buyer, beware: Sometimes these royal prices are just a cover for sucking in tourist dollars, rather than delivering royal treatment.

It's hard to tell if the town's present wealth is a holdover from the royal past, but even if this is new money living it up, there's still evidently an upper-crust mentality. Attitudes are frivolous and appearances meticulous. The children wear crinoline jumpers and mom's acrylic nails match her sandal straps.

Money is definitely poured into the town's maintenance, making for more than pleasant strolling grounds. The main street, **Calle del Rey,** extends parallel to the northern edge of the monastery. A few shops, restaurants, and bars are located on the blocks around it, with **Calle Floridablanca** the loveliest, though most touristy, of the lot. On clear days, sunlight filters through the branches of the trees lining Floridablanca and casts lacy shadows upon the sidewalk, slowing down even the most frantic tourist. It's by far the best people-watching street—day or night—and there are a few stairways leading from here up to the monastery, where views of the buildings and mountains are photo-worthy.

Another surprising place to kick back is the **Whistle-stop cafe** by the tracks. It's in the station itself and serves just ordinary bar fare, but in warm weather the few outdoor tables along the railways are actually quite relaxing. You might want to miss your train on purpose and find a new friend or two while waiting to head back to Madrid together.

bar scene

Surprisingly, San Lorenzo de El Escorial has a fairly decent nightlife, centered on an area stretching along the Calle Floridablanca and dwindling off onto the Calle del Rey. In the summer and pleasant weather, it's almost impossible to resist enjoying one of the outdoor cafes. Most of the bars are your typical Spanish watering holes, where you can pack on a few pounds downing *tapas* and beer galore. Bars tend to stay open till the demand or the tap runs dry. On the weekends, things can carry on till

5am or later. There's no need to recommend any one Spanish bar over the next, unless it's this garden of pleasures and tropical drinks: **El Jardín de las Delicias** *(Floridablanca 34; Tel 91/890-01-28; 8pm-undetermined Mon-Fri, noon-undetermined Sat-Sun; No credit cards)*, a worldly choice owned by a worldly woman. She's lived in L.A. (where she probably learned how to make the sushi she serves) and Mexico (where the art of daiquiri mixing was perfected). In the short time El Jardín has been open, it's become a fave of the international crowd, who turn up every night around 11-11:30 and on Saturday nights at midnight to gawk and jiggle with the belly dancer. A tropical fruit drink varies in price with the season and, accompanied by reggae, Arabic, or world music, might just bring out the belly dancer in you.

CULTURE ZOO

One comprehensive ticket *(purchased on-site; 800ptas)* includes admission into the two San Lorenzo sights: **Real Monasterio de San Lorenzo de El Escorial** *(San Lorenzo de El Escorial 1; Tel 91/890-59-03; 10am-7pm, closed Mon Apr-Sept; 10am-6pm, closed Mon Oct-Mar; 800ptas adults; No credit cards):* This complex houses a church, mausoleum, monastery, palace, library, and museum. Believe me, 3 hours here is a one-stop cultural overload. The patient visitor and museum nerd will love it; for the rest of us, there are so many sections, you may well want to skip from one to the next to prevent having everything start to run together in your mind. The one bit you don't want to skip is the eerily elaborate **Panteón de los Reyes** (Royal Pantheon), where Spanish rulers forever rest (from Carlos I to Alfonso XII). Only Philip V, Ferdinand VI, and Amadeus of Savoy are buried at the summer palace of La Granja. The **Panteón de los Infantes** (Children's Pantheon) is a sort of catch-all grave not just for royal kids but also royal offspring who did not succeed to the Spanish throne.

Other highlights of a visit to the monastery include the **church** designed by master architect Juan de Herrera, who was commissioned by King Philip II in the 16th century. The church interior was inspired by St. Peter's in Rome, and was designed with a Greek cross plan. Its stunning attraction, created by Herrera, is a 100-foot tall retable crafted from red marble, onyx, and jasper. The richly decorated library, also by Herrera, is made of exotic woods shipped in from various parts of the Spanish empire, with a ceiling painted by Tibaldi.

The **Nuevos Museos** is a treasure trove of art depicting religious themes, with some of the biggest Old Masters in Europe represented, including Veronese, Titian, Tintoretto, Van Dyck, Rogier Van der Weyden, Ribera, and Zubáran.

Casa de Príncipe *(Reina; Tel 91/891-03-05; 10am-5:45pm Sat, Sun, holidays Apr-Jul, Sept, till 6:45pm Oct-Mar; 10am-5:45pm, closed Mon Aug):* Carlos III and his buddies took hunting trips out to the "country" house , which you'll find decorated with clocks, china, chandeliers...only the bare necessities. A visit to see where the boys spent their r&r can be left

san lorenzo de el escorial

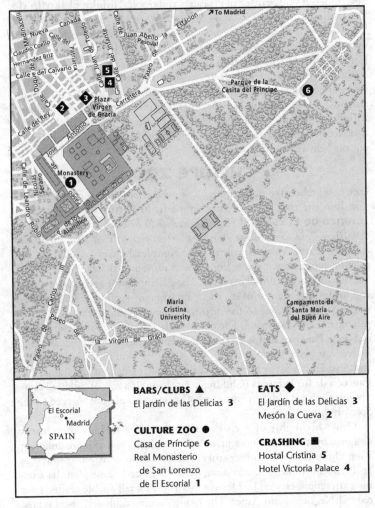

BARS/CLUBS ▲
El Jardín de las Delicias **3**

CULTURE ZOO ●
Casa de Príncipe **6**
Real Monasterio
de San Lorenzo
de El Escorial **1**

EATS ◆
El Jardín de las Delicias **3**
Mesón la Cueva **2**

CRASHING ■
Hostal Cristina **5**
Hotel Victoria Palace **4**

for an afternoon. After the monstrous overload of El Escorial, Casa de Principe comes as a refreshing break. The kings were hardly roughing it here, as the pavilion is like a miniature jewel of a palace, with painted Pompeian ceilings, silk hangings, almost priceless porcelain, rare marbles, chandeliers, and art work by major masters, including Luca Giordano.

EATS

Plenty of day visitors means plenty of low-quality meals. If you see an eatery or a *cafeteria* displaying full-color posters of paella, don't be fooled—this paella is most certainly not fresh and most definitely mass-produced, not cooked with love and care as it should be. Also, anywhere that says *cordero* (lamb), ready-to-eat or take-out, has to be questionable. For cheap sandwiches of Spanish omelet or ham, the Calle Floridablanca is lined with stands during the warm weather—one differs very little from the next.

How 'bout a big plate of beans and pork sausage for that train ride home? Try the *Fabada Asturiana,* if you dare, at **Mesón la Cueva** *(San Antón 4; Tel 91/890-15-16; 1-4pm/8:30-11:30pm, closed Mon; Menu 1,800-3,500ptas; No credit cards).* Other dishes include Spanish special-ties like Segoviano piggies and lamb, and the paella Valenciana (a better bet here than at the places with the posters). Although touristy, this restaurant, decorated with antiques, stained glass windows, and iron-work, has more character than the others. For dinner, **El Jardín de las Delicias** [see *bar scene,* above] tosses some crispy salads with spinach, corn, basil, and tomato, stir-fries up a rice, veggie, and shrimp dish *(1,000ptas each),* and rolls the sushi *(950-1,200ptas).* With luck, you'll find a free table and some low stools so that you can sit down and dip into the wasabi while deciding which tropical fruit drink to order. Belly dancing comes much more naturally on a full stomach of light food than it does after chorizo and fries.

If you want to pack a picnic or stock up on snacks, there's a grocery store inside the main market house at the end of Calle del Rey number 7.

crashing

Since most travelers can cover the sights in a morning or afternoon, there's not much of a need to stay here overnight. Budget beds are scarce-to-none in the historic zone, narrowing the options to two hotels that are next to each other, across the street from the out-of-town bus station and the stop for the train station shuttle bus, where you can get dropped off or picked up.

▶▶DO-ABLE
You'll sleep tight in the clean and basic rooms—with showers and TVs—at **Hostal Cristina** *(Juan de Toledo 6; Tel 91/890-19-61, Fax 91/890-12-04; 6,200ptas double; V, MC).* Stop and talk to the Spanish guests in the little garden, or hop over to the monastery a couple blocks away—you can't miss it. There's a restaurant below the hostal as well.

Other do-able options in town include **Albergue El Escorial** *(Calle De La Residencia 14; Tel 918/905-924, Fax 918/902-412; Singles/doubles 2,000-3,000ptas/person);* **Hostal Vasco** *(Plaza De Santiago; Tel 918/901-619; Double w/bath 4,900ptas; No credit cards);* and **Miranda & Suizo** *(Calle Floridablanca 20; Tel 918/904-711; Fax 918/904-358; Singles 8,500ptas, doubles 10,500ptas; All rooms with private bath; V, MC),* in the center of town.

▶▶SPLURGE
Hotel Victoria Palace *(Juan de Toledo 4; Tel 91/890-15-11, Fax 91/896-98-96; 11,900-17,900ptas double; AE, V, MC, Din)* might look faded from the outside, but that's just its cover. The hotel isn't as old as the monastery, but mimics its architectural style. The pool in the gardens

shimmers suggestively, and the lure of a dip here makes the hotel one of *the* in places to escape to for the weekend from stifling Madrid. Of course, rooms have bathrooms and bouncy mattresses, not to mention a parking lot. After all, it *is* a four-star hotel—who's going to be taking a bus here?

within 30 minutes

The looming presence of Francisco Franco remains at **El Valle de los Caídos (The Valley of the Fallen Ones)** *(Tel 91/890-56-11; 9:30am-7pm, closed Mon Apr-Sept; 10am-6pm, closed Mon Oct-Mar; 650ptas adults, 250ptas students; No credit cards)*, a basilica set down in the rocks of the Sierra Guadarrama, topped with a 150-meter-tall cross. This monument to Spanish Civil War heroes—the Nationalists, not the Republicans—towers 13 kilometers (8 miles) north of El Escorial. The soldiers' tombs—many of whom died during construciton when they were being used as slave labor—are embedded in the walls of the chapel, 9 corpses deep. On the surface, you'll see ancient tapestries depicting the apocalypse. Franco is among those resting in peace (or, in his case, maybe burning in hell...). Even if you're not learned in Franco lore, this place is worth a trip to soak in the macabre splendor. To get there, leave from **Autocares Herranz, S.L.** station in El Escorial [see *need to know,* below] on the once-daily bus to El Valle de los Caídos at 3:15pm, returning at 5:30pm, Tuesday to Sunday. Tickets cost 870ptas round-trip.

need to know

Currency Exchange On the Calle del Rey number 26, a **Caja Madrid** bank will exchange money and also has a 24-hour ATM.

Tourist Info The tourist office is on **Floridablanca 10** *(Tel 91/890-15-54; 10am-2pm, 3-5pm Mon-Friday, 10am-2pm Sat)*.

Public Transportation For 130ptas, a special city **bus** picks up passengers from the train station and stops at the out-of-town bus station near the monastery. Take the bus; otherwise, it's an uphill walk. **Taxis,** whose fares are more expensive than in Madrid, line up at the foot of **Calle Floridablanca** *(Tel 91/890-17-17)*.

Health and Emergency Red Cross: *91/890-41-41;* Ambulance: *91/896-11-11;* Fire: *080;* Police: *091, 092,* or *91/890-52-23*

Pharmacies Look for the **green flashing crosses** scattered around town. The pharmacies rotate night shifts, so check the local paper for the *Farmacia de guardia* of the day.

Telephone City code: *91;* info: *1003;* international operator: *1005.* For international calls dial *00,* then area code, and so on. You can use either coins or *tarjetas telefónicas* (phonecards) that you buy at tobacco shops.

Trains The **Renfe station** *(Crta Estacion; Tel 91/890-07-14)* is a mile away from town. The walk is pleasant and tree-lined for part of the way, but if you decide to hoof it, do so on your way back to the station when you'll be heading downhill.

Bus Lines Out of the City The bus company serving Madrid, el Valle de los Caídos, and a few other local destinations is **Autocares Herranz, S.L.** *(Main office: Del Rey, 27, 1ª Dcha; Tel 91/896-90-28).* Buses from Madrid to Escorial leave from Calle Princesa *(Metro Moncloa at the Intercambiador de Moncloa platform 3; Tel 91/580-19-80, a public transport info line).* Check the timetables at the bus station info counter, which is at the top of the stairs you come up if you get to the station on the metro. The trip takes about one hour.

Postal Correos is on Calle Juan de Toledo 2 *(Tel 91/890-26-85).*

extremadura & castilla la mancha

extremadura
& castilla
la mancha

extremadura & castilla la mancha

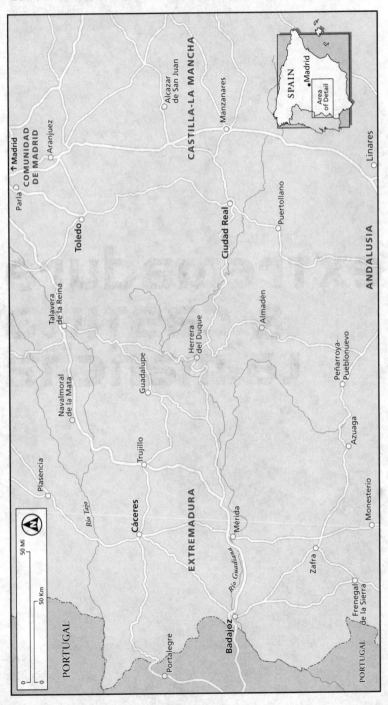

getting caught up in *la vida loca* of Madrid doesn't give you much of a chance to think about what's outside the city's walls and its blocks of bars, but the area beyond the city limits is definitely worth exploring. Castilla La Mancha (an area once known as New Castile) and Extremadura, the regions south and west of Madrid, respectively, offer a totally different experience than you'll find in the city hubbub. They are worlds apart culturally and historically. As a matter of fact, the only thing they really have in common is ham, cheese, and wine—the three unifying elements in all of Spain. (And if you've been in this country for even one day, you know that eating and drinking are the focus of daily activity.) Very few people leave either region without plowing through slices of a pig's leg, a *tabla de quesos* (plate of cheeses), and a bottle or two of wine.

Whether they've read all 1,000 pages or not, almost everyone trekking through Spain knows of *Don Quixote*, the Man of La Mancha. The epic tale takes place in Castilla La Mancha, and that in itself makes the region—just one hour south of Madrid—a necessary stop on any traveler's itinerary. The region is also one of the two strongholds of Castilian culture (the other is its northern neighbor, Castilla y León), and central to Spanish identity. Castilian is a way of being. Imagine someone asking you to describe what it means to be a Chicagoan. They'll watch as you grope at trying to explain that feeling of sitting in the bleachers at Wrigley Field, or walking along Lake Michigan. It's a feeling you know from experience. Being Castilian is being Spanish. It combines culinary, musical, historical, linguistic, and everyday elements of life. Castilians also proudly claim to speak the purest form of *castellano,* Iberian Spanish. To achieve a better understanding of what Castilian means, you as the traveler must practice your keenest sense of observation. You must watch the people hanging out in the streets, note the way they speak with their hands (although not as much as the Italians), observe their hospitality. You must eat their food, see their history in the cathedrals and monuments, listen to the lisp-like accent. Then from interacting with the culture you can create a feeling of what it is to be in Castilla, the heart of Spain.

If you're looking to capture this essence in photos, locals will appear in almost every shot, because even in the smallest *pueblos,* they socialize and dwell outside their homes, giving vibrant life to what could otherwise be just fruitless land and still monuments. **Toledo** alone, where a jambalaya of civilizations has touched down over the centuries, gives you a good sense of the history from which the Castilian culture has arisen. The monuments that paint this town's picture reflect the varied peoples who have made this area their home over the centuries. Visigoths, Romans, Moors, Jews, and Christians have all come and gone and come again, leaving their tread marks both next to and on top of one another. You see art and architecture styles overlapping, with the horseshoe arches in Gothic cathedrals right next door to Baroque pinnacles and stained-glass stars of David. Toledo was also home to El Greco, "the Greek"—who spent so much time here that he's almost considered Spanish. After leaving the tutelage of Titian in Venice, he became a pioneer of Spanish mysticism in art. Most of his work is now in the Prado, but the real gold mine of long-faced, foreboding paintings is in Toledo.

Extremadura, on the other hand, isn't the setting for any famous novels or home to any classic painters. The only time most travelers pass through it is on the night train from Madrid to Lisbon. Don't be one of those people—get off that train and explore! Though the oft-ignored Extremadura region rarely makes the cut on a four-day blast through Spain, it actually has a lot to offer. Life here is fairly slow-paced, which is probably due to the fact that its biggest cities, Badajoz and Cáceres, aren't that big, with populations of 150,000 and 72,000, respectively. Although most people in the area live in Badajoz, you should skip this industrial wasteland. It lacks the character and history—and the nightlife—of **Cáceres.** Cáceres's Plaza Mayor is the party hotspot of central Extremadura—you can't miss parking yourself here for a few hours of debauchery with the masses of swashbuckling youth who attend the local Extremaduran university. Nearly all of them are studying English and are anxious to try out their new sounds on foreigners visiting their city. In American terms, the students of Cáceres would be like those found in West Texas as opposed to Ivy League colleges. Most of them come from families who grew up in a land of cruel extremes—arid plains that bake in intense summer heat, and chill the bone in midwinter. They tend to be less cosmopolitan than the students of Madrid, and more rugged out-doorsman (and woman) types, at home on a horse or out in the woods with a tent. Many of the students are descended from proud aristocratic families, and even though much of their former wealth is long gone, the offspring of the conquistadors are still proud of their noble heritage—some are quick to offend if you don't agree that Extremadura is the greatest place on earth...and the noblest.

Smaller pueblos worthy of a trek are **Trujillo,** with its castles and conquistadors, and **Guadalupe,** oft visited by pilgrims hoping to catch a glimpse of the Virgin Mary.

The word "Extremadura" sounds like it could mean "extra hard." It'd make sense, too, since most of the landscape is hard, dry, and rocky. But the name actually refers to the location of the region, as the "land beyond the River Duoro." (Sounds like Brad Pitt will come running out of the woods any minute, brushing back his golden locks....) As in much of central Spain, a ride through the countryside takes you over flat, golden fields that roll out to touch small mountain ranges and the silvery-gray olive orchards that sits beneath them. You'll see more shades of brown and green than you ever thought possible, all filtered through the warm, amber sunlight.

Today Extremadura is a relatively poor part of Spain, although around the first and second century it was attractive enough for the Romans to trek over and plant some roots. You can see the remains of their ruins to the north in Merida. After the Romans left, Extremadura became famous as a departure point rather than a destination—it was from here that medieval upstarts who couldn't sit still in their hometowns ventured off to the New World. The Romans (and the ruins they left behind), the conquistadors, and the explorers are the area's claim to fame; sheep and pig farmers, and cork, olive, and fruit gatherers. The dry climate and rough landscape hasn't drawn Spanish youth to the area, with the exception of Cáceres.

As in the rest of Spain, Extremeño cuisine uses every edible part of the pig, and even some parts you wouldn't think were edible. The little piggies here are fattened up on acorn diets, which makes the local *jamón ibérico* (Spanish ham) some of best in the country. The *cordero* (lamb) and *perdiz* (partridge) that roam the region often don't make it to old age either, meeting their end in casseroles and stews. *Chanfaina* is a typical stew made with lamb liver, lung, heart, and kidney with tomato, garlic, white wine, and hot pepper. Plenty of Extremaduran dishes are spiced with hot pepper, which was first brought to the region by explorers returning from the New World. If you're just going to be ordering tapas, try the cheese made with sheep's milk, *torta de casar,* which comes from just north of Cáceres. Complement the cheese with one of the local wines from "Ribera del Guadiana." Vineyards produce traditional varieties from grapes such as *pardina, cayetana,* and *montúa,* which usually create fresh, aromatic, and light whites. The region is also branching out into other white varieties like the *white macabeo* (another smooth, fresh white) as well as the reds *cencibel* (wild and fruity) and *garnacha* (a dark rich red).

GETTING AROUND

Toledo is one of the best day trips from Madrid. You can get there by bus or train with equal ease because it's one of the hot tourist attractions from the capital. Spending the night can be fun too, and it will give you the chance to see the town with fewer camera-laden dawdlers.

It's not quite as easy hopping about Extremadura as other parts of Spain. Trains run in and around the region's larger towns, but sometimes pretty infrequently. It's best to keep an eye on the schedules and make sure you know them inside and out *before* you leave the station. Compared to a stuffy bus, the space and comfort levels are definitely higher on the trains, but you'll usually pay for it. Taking buses can be a cheaper and faster option, and unlike the trains, they also make it to some of the small *Extremeño pueblos* that are well worth a visit.

▶▶ROUTES

Spend a day in Toledo while overnighting in Madrid. After that, about three or four days in Extremadura should be sufficient, with one night each in Cáceres, Trujillo, and Guadalupe. If you have a car, you can stop in Guadalupe for the afternoon, but if you're busing it, the schedules may force you to stay the night. The most sensible route is in a line, starting from **Cáceres,** busing it east to **Trujillo,** then farther east to **Guadalupe,** especially if you plan to go back to **Madrid**; or in reverse if you plan to head out to Portugal.

TRAVEL TIMES

All times are by road
unless indicated by a star
 * = time by train
** = time by fast train

	Caceras	Guadalupe	Trujillo	Toledo	Madrid
Caceras	-	2:30	:45	2:00	4:00** 5:00*
Guadalupe	2:30	-	1:20	3:05	3:10
Trujillo	:45	1:20	-	2:20	2:30
Toledo	2:00	3:05	2:20	-	1:15*

extremedura

Cáceres

It's a bird, it's a plane, it's a STORK! Not only is Cáceres known for being a UNESCO World Heritage City and the second most populous city in Extremadura, it's prime baby delivery zone as well. No, toddlers aren't screaming around every corner, but storks nest on any high flat surface they can find in this town, and they make a sound like a kid running down the street, clacking a stick on a picket fence. The spindly-legged birds fly in from Africa in February, and are permanent features until the end of the summer. Why here? They must have heard the gaggles of students at the region's central university, **Universidad Extremeña,** and decided Cáceres was as good a place as any. A "World Heritage City" sounds as if the place ought to be a dead town full of old folks from the Extremeño historical society collecting antiques and old maps. The truth is, Cáceres fares well with the young population, which is ready to learn, but mostly to party on any high, flat surface—think stairs, curbs, or car-roof tops—at the **Plaza Mayor,** the social center of town.

If you flew over Cáceres in a helicopter, looking down at the tile-roofed stone constructions, you'd see the walls containing the lovely historic section called **Ciudad Monumental** and think it was perfectly laid out, like a miniature model in an anthropology museum. The old center hasn't been penetrated much by the modern world, and little else outside it has any cultural significance. You'll see a lot of churches and old mansions built with riches amassed from the pillaging of New World explorers and conquistadors. Today, the mansions remain private homes that have been passed down the family line, or are occupied by government bureaucrats.

The west wall of the Ciudad Monumental forms the border of the **Plaza Mayor.** Every old Spanish town has a Plaza Mayor where, at one time, the town's central activities—markets, social life, meetings, and so on—took place. In many towns, the Plaza Mayor has lost its true meaning, and has become a spot on the historic map—not so in Cáceres. The Plaza here continues to breathe with life, especially young life, engaging in all the essential activities: eating, sleeping, drinking a beer with a friend, and any other pursuits you might imagine. Much of the social life starts and ends here.

Plaza Mayor (it is equally known as Plaza General Mola) opens onto the whitewashed new town, home of the region's university, 4 kilometers east of Plaza Mayor. To the north, all the narrow streets lead into **Plaza de Santa Maria,** with its fine Gothic church. To the southwest, the broad **Avenida de España** leads you to the modern town as it borders the eastern Parque Calvo Sotelo. Once you pass the roundabout near the park, Avenida de España becomes the straight-as-an-arrow Avenida de Alemania, going southwest for another kilometer to the transportation hub of the city. Both the bus depot and the train station front each other at the junction of **Avenida Alemania** and **Avenida de la Hispanidad,** 3 kilometers southwest of Plaza Mayor.

hanging out

If you're from a small town, you know what it's like to have to make your own fun. The uniting power of alcohol never fails to bring on the good times and bridge the cultural gaps. In the '60s and '70s, kids here would have riotous house parties called *guateques,* which kept a lid on things indoors, confining the damage to within four walls. A fiesta is a fiesta, but some things have changed now that the parties have moved outdoors. Today, you take part in the phenomenon called *botellón,* which literally means "big bottle" and is a crucial ingredient to the party. It's like a big Fourth of July picnic without the barbeque, fireworks, or stars and stripes. There's an oddly liberating feel to this *Animal House*-style of socializing, getting sloshed in the middle of Plaza Mayor, loitering around with lots of open containers in the fresh air. Twentysomethings on down let loose here; young women in tight shirts belt out songs at the top of their lungs as beer bottles crash down the 13th-century stone stairs. During prime botellón season—usually for a few weeks during the university's fall term, but it could go down any time students abound—the plaza isn't used as a parking lot, nor is there room for a bottle to fall in this sea of bodies. Once the semester begins, and before exams get in full swing, the Plaza Mayor is flooded with kids, booze, and bloodshot eyes, while cars get the boot. (Firing up right there on the square is illegal, but it can be an exhilarating cultural exchange with your new Spanish friends.) Rain, sleet, snow, or shine, the parties are as reliable as the postal carrier. During the summer, though, they simmer down a tad when the students and young people take off on vacation, and cars fill the lot. Thursday, Friday, and Saturday all see a different mix in the crowd. The university crowd skips

cáceres

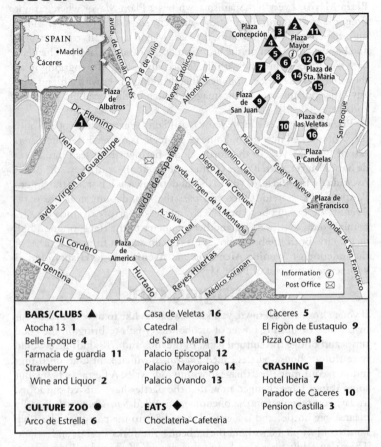

BARS/CLUBS ▲

Atocha 13 **1**

Belle Epoque **4**

Farmacia de guardia **11**

Strawberry
  Wine and Liquor **2**

CULTURE ZOO ●

Arco de Estrella **6**

Casa de Veletas **16**

Catedral
  de Santa Marìa **15**

Palacio Episcopal **12**

Palacio Mayoraigo **14**

Palacio Ovando **13**

EATS ◆

Choclaterìa-Cafeterìa

Càceres **5**

El Figòn de Eustaquio **9**

Pizza Queen **8**

CRASHING ■

Hotel Iberia **7**

Parador de Càceres **10**

Pension Castilla **3**

class early, starting the weekend on Thursday nights; Cáceres locals hit it on Fridays; and Saturdays are by far the best when *everyone* comes out of the woodwork for a grand old time. Everyone that is, except for ma and pa, who stir in their beds at the noise, but think back to their days of *guateques* and roll over.

bars, live music, clubs

To do as the locals do, follow this progression....

Step one is **Strawberry Wine and Liquors** *(Plaza Mayor; Tel 927/246-128; 9:30pm-2am Thur-Sat; Box wine 200ptas, liter beer 250ptas; No credit cards)*, a store that seems to exist only to provide a cheap means to the state of drunkenness. Go straight for the shelves lined with low-cost box wine and bottles of cola. Their recipe for a hangover: a large plastic cup, two "bricks" of wine, one two-liter Coca-Cola, and a couple of buddies to hold your hair back. There's also an icebox of Mahou or

Aguila brewskies to hug tight to your chest. As Vincent Vaga noticed with the Quarter Pounder with Cheese ("They call it a *Royale with cheese!*"), the metric system changes names and dimensions. There's no 40-ounce Coors. Beer comes in liters, and is drunk like Coca-Cola. Second, proceed with *botellón* activities [see *hanging out,* above].

After warming up, step three is venturing into one of the bars lining the square. Don't worry, steps two and three are flexible. You can pop into a bar for a beer that lasts only a song or two, then pop back out to the plaza for the fast, furious, and frivolous.

Café Cáceres *(Plaza Mayor 16; Tel 927/249-763; Daily 7am-midnight; Fixed price menus 1,700ptas; Main courses 500-700ptas; MC, V)* is the town's most central cafe and bar, a hangout place from early morning until late at night. They have one of the largest selections of wine in town, with many bottles costing only 400ptas. If you sit out at a table on the terrace, you'll be able to check out the local scene better than anywhere else. It is said that all visitors to Cáceres pass through this square several times a day. If you stick around to eat, the chef makes the town's best paella (with seafood). For something really local, order *migas Estremenas* (pork sausage and fried bread flavored with lots of garlic and paprika).

Nearby is the chief rival to the above cafe and bar, **Café & Restaurant El Puchero** *(Plaza Mayor 7-9; Tel 927/245-497; 9am-11pm Sun-Thur; 9am-1am Fri-Sat; V, MC)*. It's much the same as Café Cáceres, except that, as the waiter at El Puchero confided to us, it's customers are much prettier. This bar also has tables spilling out onto the plaza. You can have lunch here, return for an early evening cocktail, or else hit it around midnight for a final nightcap. They prepare sandwiches all afternoon, and their *platos combinados* are reasonably priced, costing 750 to 1,000ptas. If you want something more formal, you can go into their dining room which is known for serving some of the best value fixed priced meals in the city, costing 1,200 to 1,800ptas. Try the roast pork with Russian salad or the beefsteak with potatoes. You can also order a bottle of wine (starting at 800ptas) and spend virtually all night hanging out on the square, watching the passing scene.

Finally, after the bars close and the liquor shops run dry (around 3-3:30am), it's time to head to another area of town: La Madrila. The clubs, pubs, and bars here don't even *begin* to open until around 3:30 or 4am, and they're going strong until 7 or 8 in the morning—or later if things are on a roll. La Madrila is west of the old town, just west of Avenida de España. La Madrila is defined in two sections: the *alta,* the "upper," on Dr. Fleming, or the *baja,* the "lower," on Plaza de Albatros. Don't worry if you're indecisive; the *alta* and *baja* are within a short walk of each other, so you can hit them both. If you like to stay up 'til at least 5 on weekends, the most fun bar is **Acuario** *(Avenida España; Tel 927/220-614; 8am-midnight daily; Tapas 600-1,000ptas.; MC, V),* which is the hottest discoteca in town but only on Thursday, Friday, and Saturday when the joint jumps until the wee hours have become not-so-wee. Students from Cuenca dance alongside various foreign young people on three levels.

These fun-loving patrons swig down *cuchimollo* (red wine and Coca-Cola to keep their engines fueled).

Remember, you're never committed in Spain. Going out means keeping it moving. Try not to plant yourself in one place too long. When you realize that the music is really bad, or that you dipped the cuffs of your jeans in a puddle on the trip to the TP-less ladies room, or that the hot girl in the corner wasn't offering to give you language lessons, she was telling you to beat it, it's time to move on.

Two suggestions on and by the Plaza Mayor: At first glance, the two entrances of **Farmacia de Guardia** *(Plaza Mayor 1; No phone; Bus 1 to Avda España; 6pm-3am; Mixed drinks 600ptas; No credit cards)* make you think there are two different bars flooding the air with noise, but all of the volume is actually coming from just one place. Under the vaulted ceilings that hold in the heat like a brick oven, twentysomethings break out the stiff dance moves here and there. Everyone sings along to the Spanish music—not folk music or anything, and not much *bakalao* (techno), just a go at American-style rock 'n' roll, and some chart-topping tunes. It's quite cozy: You can bump into the chosen one, or their cigarette cherry, when things get going around 11pm.

Down Calle General Ezponda, about a two-minute walk southeast of Plaza Mayor, are more bars, including the ever-fun **Belle Epoque** *(General Ezponda; Tel 927/223-093; Bus 1 to Avda España; 10pm-3am Wed-Sat; belleepoque@hotmail.com; Show cover 500-1,000ptas; No credit cards),* where the counters are covered with old 45s, retro plastic furniture lines the walls, and the crowd always welcomes the short, tall, gay, straight, and not-so-sure. The owner sets up live music gigs on Fridays, sticking mostly to lots of Spanish music—flamenco, Gallego, and Basque—but he also throws in some techno, funk, and soul. Shows start around 10:30-11pm. This kitschy dream technically closes its doors at 3, but it doesn't really stop kicking till 6 or 7am.

CULTURE ZOO

Walking through the streets and squares of the Ciudad Monumental is the best way to see those attractions that aren't related to hanging out and drinking. Actually, Cáceres has some of the most diverse examples of historic architecture in the entire country. The architecture, from church facades to palace doors, is a blend of Roman, Arabic, Gothic, and Renaissance influences. And since this was a conquistador outpost, some New World styles have seeped into the mix.

The 11th- and 12th-century *murillas* (walls) box in the old town, which has remained surprisingly free of tourist junk shops, leaving only a few restaurants and a handful of baking nuns [see *get thee to a nunnery,* below]. Begin by entering the walls and ramparts through the **Arco de Estrella** (the Arch of the Star), from the Plaza Mayor. It's the one with the iron star and a statue of a virgin at the point of the arch. The Arco de Estrella leads you to the road going to the Plaza de Santa María. From

Since 1992, the **WOMAD (World of Music & Dance)** festival has drawn more than 200,000 people annually to Cáceres to groove to the beats of world music. The concerts and dance performances start in early May and go on for a couple of weeks. The program is different each year, but you can always count on African, Indian, and Celtic notes to drift up above the medieval walls in the open air. Performers take the stage in the Plaza Mayor, and all around the old center. This citywide groovefest is free and fun, but totally crowded, so make sure you reserve a room beforehand. Check with the tourist office for performance listings, or e-mail to request a schedule *(granteatro@bme.es)*.

there, the sound of a kid playing flamenco-style guitar may call you right up to the **Catedral de Santa María,** the token Gothic cathedral displaying a *Cristo Negro,* a black Christ, an example of the Moorish influence. Also on the Plaza de Santa María are a few 16th- and 17th-century *palacios* of interest: **Palacio Episcopal, Palacio de Mayoraigo,** and the **Palacio de Ovando.** There are facades on almost every corner, bedecked with a silvery, *plateresque* (which means "resembling silver plate") design (a style known for elaborate and overwhelming ornamentation) and floorless balconies where townspeople used to throw hot oil onto invaders.

Casa de las Veletas *(Plaza de las Veletas; Tel 927/247-234; 9:30am-2pm Tue-Sat, 10:15am-2:30pm Sun, closed holidays; 200ptas adults, free for students, EU citizens, & Sundays to all; No credit cards):* This archaeological museum holds some Roman artifacts. The main "attraction" is the *aljibe,* the Arabic water well. Toss a few pesetas in for good luck. If you know Spanish, the tourist office's *visita guiada* (guided tour) is well worth it. If you're lucky, the guy who looks like Cheech, smokes 15 Ducados (black tobacco cigs) in the course of an hour, and chews gum like it's going out of style, will be your guide. Start on the Plaza Mayor, shell out the 500ptas, and put on the sticker identifying you as part of the herd. Unless you're 14 and worried about looking cool and being bored, you'll learn something and see more of Cáceres than you would on your own. You could probably figure out some of the stops by yourself, but the tour takes you through some doors you wouldn't think are open to visitors. Cheech takes the group around to look at all the mansions, churches, and convents, bringing them to life with anecdotes, jokes, and legends. Tour times vary, but the hour of the next scheduled one is posted in the window of the tourist office, even if it's closed. During pleasant weather, they'll sometimes arrange night visits [see *need to know,* below].

eats

Sitting around the Plaza Mayor, you're bound to end up hungry. Good thing this is where most of the eating is concentrated. Food in Extremadura includes a lot of game, like partridge, which in Cáceres is prepared with honey and sugar, making for a rich dish. Cheeses are also rich and delicious in this region; the most typical are made from goat *(cabra)* and sheep *(oveja)* milk, and range from mild *semicurado* to sharper aged *curado*. An interesting popular side dish is *migas extremeñas,* bits of bread fried in oil with *chorizo,* the spicy Iberian sausage.

▶▶CHEAP

When the late-night munchies strike, **Pizza Queen** *(Plaza Mayor 36; Tel 927/225-253; Bus 1 to Avda España; Noon-4pm/7pm-1:30am Mon-Thur, till 2-4am Fri-Sun; Avg. large pizza 2,200ptas; No credit cards)* fits the bill. Just what you need to add to your post-midnight, empty calorie intake—a few cheesy slices. Take-out, sit down inside, or haul your pizza to one of the outside tables they set up in warm weather. The tuna pizza tastes good on a beer buzz—bet Domino's never thought of that!

Speaking of munchies, don't be deceived by the **24 horas** mini-mart on Calle General Ezpronda by the Plaza Mayor. It's not reliable like the 7-Eleven. They decide which 24 hours they want to be open—if you're lucky, it'll be the 24 you're in town.

For a cheap meal that offers a bit more sustenance, try the basic pasta, salad, chicken, pork loin, or trout on the *menu del día* (menu of the day) at **Chocolatería-Cafetería Cáceres** *(Plaza Mayor 16; Tel 927/249*

get thee to a nunnery!

In the old center, where cars and buses are prohibited, you'll have to walk to the Plaza San Mateo to visit the **Convento de San Pablo,** *(Plaza San Mateo; No phone; 9am-1pm/5-8pm Mon-Sat; No credit cards),* where *monjas* (nuns) do more than pray—they sell baked goods! Stepping up to the wooden turnstile window, where the nuns hide behind a screen, is like stepping back in time. Place your order through the slit in the wood. The list of treats includes *pastas almendras* (almond tea cookies), *yemas* (sugared egg yolks), *galletas* (cookies), and more. Wait for the women to wrap up a dozen with care—they've got an eternity, unlike us sinners. Then they spin the sweets around and you put down 500ptas to be spun back to them in exchange. Nice doin' business with you, sistah!

763; Bus 1 to Avda España; 7:30am-1:30am Sun-Thur, till 2-3am Fri-Sat). At night pick on tapas like calamares and cheeses; or nosh on hamburgers, sandwiches, or *migas* (breadcrumbs fried and mixed with sausage). The outdoor tables under the arched walkway, bordering the Plaza Mayor, are also a good spot to read your guidebook over a coffee and *churros.*

▶▶DO-ABLE

Ask any local for advice on where to eat and they'll direct you 100 meters southeast of the Plaza Mayor to **El Figón de Eustaquio** *(Plaza San Juan 12; Tel 927/248-194; Bus 1 to Avda España; 1:30-4pm/8pm-12:30am; Menu 1,700-2,800ptas; AE, V, MC, DC).* It's been around for over 50 years, serving up typical Extremadura cuisine to tourists and locals alike. What's that, you ask? Why, partridge, ham, and hake, of course! You can also order a tasty slab of beef, the *solomillo.* The atmosphere is cozy, with its old-fashioned rustic decor. The a/c is a cool welcome on those hot Extremeño days, so eating a two-course meal won't be too heavy—till you get back outside.

crashing

Most budget and moderate *hostales* and *pensiones* are around the Plaza Mayor; if the following places are full, get your hands on a Cáceres tourist map (at the tourist office), which has *Alojamiento* (lodging) listings of places to stay in all ranges.

▶▶CHEAP

Pensión Castilla *(Ríos Verdes 3; Tel 927/244-404; Bus 1 to Avda España; 2,200ptas per person; No credit cards)* is a no-frills, straightforward pensión. There's not a toilet or a shower in any of the rooms, which provide not much more than a crash pad for one to five people, a sink, and a mini towel (don't worry, everyone gets their own towel). The fact that this place has 24 rooms and 40 beds may help you compete with the other Brit, French, and American guidebook-users calling for reservations. The best deal is the young townie sitting watch all night to let you in, so you don't have to embarrass yourself stumbling and slurring up the stairs in front of a little old lady. He's seen all the nightlife in town—if you want local insight on which side of the Plaza Mayor is cooler, ask him.

Other options on the cheap side include **Pension Carretero** *(Plaza Mayor 22; Tel 927/24-74-82; Singles 2,000ptas, doubles 3,500ptas, shared baths; V, MC, AE)* and **Hostal Residencia Almonte** *(C. Gil Cordero 6; Tel 927/24-09-25; Fax 927/248-602; Singles 2,900ptas, doubles 4,500ptas, all rooms with private bath; No credit cards).*

▶▶DO-ABLE

Spending a night at the **Hotel Iberia** *(Pintores 2; Tel 927/247-634, Fax 927/248-200; Bus 1 to Avda España; 5,000ptas single, 7,000ptas double, 8-10,000ptas suite, 400ptas breakfast; V, MC),* a three-minute walk west of Plaza Mayor, is like staying in a museum. Each *habitación,* with new, full baths and antique furniture, has its own style. One wing of the place doesn't have room numbers; they are identified by the *azul, rojo,* or *verde* color themes. The owner loves this place—she probably spends more money and time on decorating and caring for it than she does on anything else. There's even a dollhouse-sized Hotel Iberia in the breakfast room! The only problem is that the place is so cool, you run the risk of hanging out in your room all day, instead of walking around town.

Other do-able options include **Hostal Goya** *(Plaza Mayor 31; Tel 927/249-950; Fax 927/213-758; Singles 5,000ptas, doubles 8,500ptas, all rooms with private bath; V, MC, AE);* **Hotel Alfonso IX** *(Calle Moret 22; Tel 927/246-400; Fax 927 24 78 11; Singles 5,200ptas, doubles 8,800ptas, all rooms wih private bath; V);* and **Hostal Plaza De Italia** *(Calle Constancia 12; Tel/Fax 927/247-760; Singles 4,000ptas, doubles 6,500ptas, all rooms with private bath; V, MC).*

▶▶**SPLURGE**

Bounce on the big luxe beds at **Parador de Cáceres** *(Ancha 6; Tel 927/211-759, Fax 927/211-729; Bus 1 to Avda España, but if you can afford to stay here, you can afford a taxi; 16,500ptas double, 25,000ptas suite; AE, V, MC, DC).* It's a former 15th-century palace that the state has taken over and reformed into a plush hotel. Don't worry about bumping into one of the suits of armor in the hallways on the way to the toilet in the middle of the night. Not only do you get your own full bath, but also hair dryers and little packets of soaps, shower caps, and stuff to take home to prove you stayed here!

need to know

Currency Exchange Almost all banks will change your money at approximately the same rate. **Banks** and **ATMs** line the **Calle Pintores,** a two-minute walk southwest of Plaza Mayor.

Tourist Info The **tourist office** is at Plaza Mayor 20 *(Tel 927/246-347)* and is open 9:30am-2pm/5-7:30pm Monday to Friday, 9:45am-2pm Saturdays, Sundays, and holidays. They offer guided tours for 500ptas.

Public Transportation Eight city **bus** routes traverse the new city streets from 8am to 10pm; in summer, about a half-hour later. Bus maps are available at the tourist office. **Taxis** line up on the Plaza Mayor and at the bus and train stations. To call one, dial 927/212-121.

Health and Emergency Emergency: *112;* Police: *091, 092;* Red Cross: *Tel 927/247-858.* On the north end of Avenida de España you will find the main **Hospital Provincial** *(Tel 927/256-800).*

Pharmacies On the Plaza Mayor and the Calle Pintores there are pharmacies, which are marked by **lit green crosses.** For night needs, check the local paper or the window of a pharmacy for the rotating night duty schedule.

Telephone City code: *927;* international operator: *1005.* International calls dial *00* then area code and so on. You can use either coins or ***tarjetas telefónicas*** (phonecards) that you buy at tobacco shops.

Trains To motor from the **Renfe** station on Avenida Alemania *(Tel 927/233-761)* to the center of town, get on city buses 1 or 4, or take a taxi. The walk is only about 20 minutes. Start up Avenida de Alemania to a large roundabout called Plaza de America, and turn northeast on Avenida de España, which runs along the east side of Parque Calvo Sotelo. At the end of this road, follow Calle Parras northeast about 10 minutes to Plaza Mayor.

Bus Lines Out of the City The **Empresa Mirat** bus station is across the street from the train station on **Ctra Sevilla** *(Tel 927/232-550; Information window open 7:30am-11pm Mon-Fri; 8:30am-11pm Sat-Sun)*. City bus 4 goes from the station to town. To hoof it into town, see *trains*, above.

Postal Central post, **Correos,** is on Paseo Primo de Rivera 2 *(Tel 927/225-071; 8:30am-8:30pm Mon-Fri; 9:30am-2pm Sat)*.

Internet See *wired*, below.

wired

Around the corner from the 11th-century towers is an air-conditioned, freshly painted room with 22 computers, ready to serve your Internet needs. Ahhh...**Ciberjust:-)** *(Diego María Creguet 7; Tel 927/627-274; Bus 1 or 2 to Avda España; 10am-2am Mon-Sat, noon-2am Sunday; ciberjust@arrakis.es; 500ptas/hour; No credit cards)* faces the Policia Nacional. Students and foreigners clack at e-mail en masse between 6 and 10pm, but surprisingly, the wait to get online isn't much more than 10-15 minutes. That is, unless the users are local kids playing Net games with the employee on duty, furiously trying to reach the next level. Chips, lollipops, and cola are available to add sugar to the cyber equation.

guadalupe

A monastery, built to honor the Virgin of Guadalupe, is the only thing to see in this humble, out-of-the-way, mountainous town. Ironically, though, the original apparition of the Virgin wasn't seen here in Guadalupe, España, but thousands of miles away, in the hills of what is now Mexico, way back in 1531. According to legend, she spoke to a young Aztec man, and identified herself, curiously, as the Virgin of Guadalupe. (Imagine that.) The young Aztec immediately converted to Catholicism—surprise, surprise—and word of the miracle traveled all the way back to the hills of Extremadura, home of many of the conquistadors, and inspired construction of the **Real Monasterio de Santa María de Guadalupe** *(Plaza de Juan Carlos 1; Tel 927/367-000; 9:30am-1pm/3:30-7pm daily Apr-Oct; 9:30am-1pm/3:30-6:30pm daily Nov-Mar; 300ptas Adults; No credit cards)*. Thousands come here each year to visit the Virgin, who is forever immortalized in the altar's centerpiece. The virgin, with rays of light emanating from behind her robes, has acted as a symbol of religious inspiration and a cultural bridge between the old world and the new. She is everywhere here, on family and church altars, even on dashboards.

For centuries, believers have traveled here to kiss the Virgin—in the hopes of a miracle, to test their faith, or just for luck. You have to take a tour as a pre-requisite for a kiss. The guides will explain the history of the church, the *mudéjar* cloister, the 16th-century this, the 17th-century that.... When the guide finally wraps things up and you think, "What's the story? Where's the lady? When do I get to kiss the Virgin?", a monk arrives on the scene, pulls out a plate embossed with the Virgin's likeness. The plate is attached to the altar with a string, and the monk wipes it with a hankie after each kiss (How thoughtful). That's it. You kiss a plate.

The village of Guadalupe sits up in the mountains, outside the confines of the monastery. It would be the perfect place to hide away after retirement, when you don't have much more to do than water your plant-lined patio on one of the narrow streets off the Plaza Mayor, and take care of your goat. Before retirement, take advantage of the fact that while tourists do frequent Guadalupe, they don't come in hordes because it's a pain in the ass to get to without a car. Though it's only about a 3-hour trip from Madrid, the limiting bus schedules keep it small and quaint. If you plan your travel times ahead, Guadalupe's charm and its monastery's religious inspiration may convert you and bring you back for another visit.

eats

Weren't those lambies you saw in the countryside on the way here so cute? Add garlic, thyme, throw 'em in a hot wood-fired oven and they're even cuter! The "Lamb Inn," **Mesón el Cordero** *(Alfonso Onceno 27; Tel 927/367-131; 1-4pm/7-11pm, closed Mon, closed Feb 1-15; Menu del día 1,500ptas; AE, V, MC, Din),* cooks up its specialty dish, *asado de cordero*—your fuzzy friend on a plate, minus the fuzz. Delicious and best finished off with *flan,* the famous Spanish custard dessert.

An unheralded little budget restaurant, **Cerezo II** *(Plaza Santa Maria de Guadalupe 33; Tel 927/154-177; Main courses 600 to 1,500ptas, fixed price menu 1,200ptas; 8:30am-1:30pm daily; AE, DC, MC, V)* shares the square with the tourist office in the center of town. This typical old *bodega,* or canteen, rests under arches and is decorated with rustic artifacts of Extramadura. The place attracts a devoted following who enjoy the countryside's robust flavors. In the fall that means game such as partridge. Year-round, expect pork sausage, platters of spare ribs, and lamb baked aromatically with fresh thyme. The chef also prepares the famous *cocido España,* or stew (don't ask what goes in the pot). The typical dessert is a fig and nut biscuit.

crashing

Get even closer to the Virgin's residence by staying in the **Hospedería Real Monasterio** *(Plaza Juan Carlos 1; Tel 927/367-000, Fax 927/367-177; Closed Jan 12-Feb 12; 7,750ptas double; V, MC),* the former cloister of the monastery, now one of the fines hotels in the entire region. Pretend you're one of the pilgrims who used to lodge here when they finally reached their destination—except you get a few more luxuries, like a/c and a beautifully tiled bathroom all to yourself. The spacious rooms are tastefully decorated with antique reproductions of Iberian furniture. The on-site restaurant and bar offers one of the best meals in the district. It's traditional to order the local brew, *licor de Guadalupe,* to finish off your meal. Don't bother asking how it's made—no one will tell.

Other options on the cheap side include **Hostal Cerezo** *(Gregorio Lopez 12; Tel 927/367-379; Singles 3,500ptas, doubles 5,300ptas, all rooms with private bath; V, MC, AE),* **Pension Tena** *(Calle Ventilla 1; Tel 927/367-104; Singles 2,500ptas, doubles 3,500ptas, all rooms with private bath; No credit cards),* **Meson Tipico Isabel** *(Plaza De Santa Maria De Guadalupe; Tel 927/367-126; Singles 3,000ptas, doubles 4,000ptas, all* *roms with private baths; No credit cards)*, and **Hostal Lujuan** *(C/ Gregorio Lopez 19; Tel 927/367-170; Singles 3,000ptas; Doubles 4,000ptas, all rooms with private bath; V, MC)*, in the city center.

If you're really after the royal treatment, you can't get much better than **Parador Nacional Zurbaran** *(Marques De La Romana 12; Tel 927/367-075, Fax 927/367-076; Doubles 16,000ptas, suites 17,500ptas, all with private bath; V, MC, AE)*, located in a beautiful spot in the village center.

need to know

Currency Exchange The **banks** around the center (and the monastery), will trade your bucks for pesetas, and some have **ATMs** for those of you living off plastic.

Tourist Info The **tourist office** is on the Plaza Santa María, also known as the Plaza Mayor *(Tel 927/154-128; 10am-2:30pm/5-7pm Tue-Fri, 10am-2:30pm Sat-Sun summer, 10am-2:30pm/4-6pm Tue-Fri 10am-2:30pm Sat-Sun winter)*.

Bus Lines Out Of City There's no **bus station** here in Guadalupe. Buses drop you off in town, and you buy tickets from the driver on the way. Buses run here from both Trujillo and Cáceres twice daily on weekdays. There is only one bus per day going to and from Madrid. Buses to Cáceres seem to follow no writ-in-stone schedule, so it's better to call **Empresa Mirat** *(Tel 927/232-550)* for exact schedules. The tourist office also keeps a list of bus schedules.

TRUJILLO

Sitting in the Plaza Mayor at a cafe on a Friday night, I asked some idle youth what there was to do around here. They told me I was looking at it. Hmm...there's not even a movie theater. With nothing to do, people live at a slower pace. Next door in Cáceres, there may be more fiestas, but Trujillo is *precioso* (precious)—that's how a chatty Spanish friend will describe the town if you tell them you're coming here. You feel like you stepped into the guidebook glossy photo the second you enter Plaza Mayor: The big guy and native son, Francisco Pizarro, rides the horse wearing a suit of armor, arches border the entire plaza, and a Moorish castle backdrops the scene. Famed for being the birthplace of a guy who went over to America in search of fame and fortune, found it, and proceeded to steal it out from under the natives, Trujillo is packed with history at every turn.

If you weren't paying attention in that Latin American history class, think "P" for Pizarro and Peru. Pizarro is a hero here for opening up the door to New World riches for little Trujillo, but he's far from a hero to indigenous Peruvians. The rumor is that the sculptor originally designed Trujillo's Pizarro statue as a likeness of Hernán Cortés, a Mexican conquistador. But Mexico was quite unappreciative of any such gift, so it was passed on to Trujillo, and passed off as Pizarro. If you want to investigate the truth of this rumor, the tourist office sure won't admit to anything, so whip out a thousand *peseta* note from your wallet (if you still have any dinero left) and compare Pizarro's shining face on paper money to the three-dimensional one in bronze.

The lay of the land is typical—the old **Plaza Mayor,** where most of the eating and lolling about takes place, is outside the walled upper town, with its historic labyrinth of streets. Trujillo is a perfectly preserved, quaint little town, and the old center doesn't get too complicated. The castle sits up to the northeast, and churches and palaces are scattered throughout the enclosed rectangular *casco antiguo*.

CULTUrE ZOO

The tourist office offers a guided tour for 800ptas, which, if you do the math, is a bit cheaper than if you were to go to each site on your own. But the tour is only offered in Spanish, and the guide never looks anyone in the eye as he gives lengthy explanations over a squeaky microphone in a monotone Spanish for what seems like an eternity. You're better off checking out the sites on your own. The souvenir guidebook from the tourist office (400ptas) makes for a better visit.

The Plaza Mayor fronts scads of palaces and the town hall. Many of the palaces were built with loot that the Pizarro clan brought back from the New World. In the **Palacio de la Conquista**, on the south side of Plaza Mayor, Francisco Pizarro's half-brother, Hernando, lived with his wife, who was Francisco's half-Inca daughter. Cozy, eh? The balconies on their palace, and on the **Palacio San Carlos** (a 16th-century ducal residence directly across the plaza), are bedecked with family coats of arms, and are the most visible and elaborate of the *balcones de esquina*. A mainstay on the corners of buildings, these balconies were the old version of keeping up with the Joneses.

Iglesia Santa María *(Ballesteros; No phone; 10am-2pm/4:30-7:30pm daily; 100ptas admission):* You can tell the restorers recently made a stop at this Gothic cathedral, which is nice and scrubbed up on the inside. Open space and stained-glass windows brighten things up so that you can see its big wooden altarpiece.

Castillo *(Trujillo's hilltop; Free; Daylight hours):* Run around the castle grounds and play knight in shining armor, leaping from rampart to rampart. Built by the Moors in the 10th century and "improved" upon by the Christians, the castle offers one of the best views in town.

EATS

▶▶CHEAP

If you're getting into town at an odd hour, your bags weighing you down and your stomach growling, the **Restaurante Nuria** *(Plaza Mayor 27; Tel 927/320-907; 8am-midnight or 1am daily; Menu 1,300ptas, sandwiches and raciones 300-2,000ptas; V, MC)* is your oasis. This basic and casual restaurant serves food all day long to groups of families and friends,

Trujillo

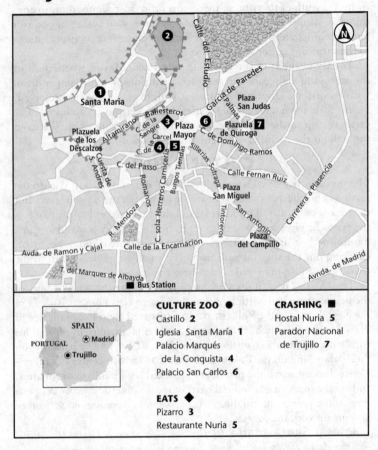

SPAIN
PORTUGAL ⊕ Madrid
⊙ Trujillo

CULTURE ZOO ●
Castillo **2**
Iglesia Santa María **1**
Palacio Marqués
de la Conquista **4**
Palacio San Carlos **6**

EATS ◆
Pizarro **3**
Restaurante Nuria **5**

CRASHING ■
Hostal Nuria **5**
Parador Nacional
de Trujillo **7**

and has outdoor tables on the square, where you can enjoy the weight lifted off your back and the *cordonices al tomillo* (cornish game hens) sticking their little legs up off the plate. The tasty little buggers in rosemary sauce are recommended items on the *menu del día* lunch main course choices. For snacky appetites, there are sandwiches and *raciones,* plates of croquettes, ham, cheese, and more. Summer is the best time to try a lemon slushy (called *granizado de limon*) for 250ptas.

La Emilia *(Plaza del Campillo 28 or General Mola 28; Tel 927-320-083; Fixed price menu 1,000ptas, main courses 1,500-2,000ptas; 7am to 1am daily; No credit cards)* is the cheapie of town. Although its regular à la carte menu is comparably priced with that of many other Trujillo eateries, the fixed price menu is the best deal all around. Regional cuisine is quite savory here, at least to carnivores who dig into the *caldereta* (lamb with potatoes). There is some fish on the menu, too. The chef is known for his well-seasoned potatoes which appear on the menu as *criadillas de tierra.*

Café Bar El Escudo *(Plazuela Santiago 2; Tel 927/322-966; Tapas from 350ptas; Fixed price menu 1,600ptas; Daily 9:30am-10pm; No credit cards),* in the center of town, is cheap and good. It's like a local tavern and hangout for all ages, with simple regional decorations of wood and ceramics. It is said that more wine is consumed with the tapas served here than at any other place in town. If you don't fill up on them, opt for *filet de terna* (veal filet) or *morga* (porks spareribs). Despite this city's inland location, the hake arrives fresh from the waters of Cádiz every day.

▶▶**DO-ABLE**

If you're standing facing the statue in the Plaza Mayor, the big awnings scream PIZARRO—you never forget who you're dealing with in this town. The restaurant **Pizarro** *(Plaza Mayor 13; Tel 927/320-255; 1:30-4pm/8:30-10:30pm Wed-Sun; Entrees 1,200-2,100ptas; AE, V, MC, Din)* hasn't been around since Francisco set out on his adventure, but it's been around longer than you or I. Since 1864, it's been an inn and since 1919, it's been what it is today. Go upstairs to the little dining room (downstairs is someone's home) to be served Extremeño cuisine— goodies like partridge casserole and ham from fat pigs fed on only the best acorns.

Mesón Restaurante La Troya *(Plaza Mayor 10; Tel 927/321-364; 1pm-midnight daily; V),* in the exact center of town, serves the hearty, rugged fare of the dusty plains. They offer only one fixed price menu, but at 2,500ptas, it's hailed as one of the best food values in Trujillo. Specialties include a local favorite, *migas Extremenas* (bread fried in olive oil with pork sausages) and *caldereta de cordero,* the regional lamb dish, usually served fried in a savory sauce. You can also order spareribs with zesty dashings of paprika. The place is decorated in traditional Extremaduran style, with red brick walls and provincial wooden tables and chairs, and regional ceramics hanging on the wall.

crashing

▶▶**DO-ABLE**

Snuggles the detergent bear must have gone on a cultural exchange to Trujillo and left fabric softener at **Hostal Nuria** *(Plaza Mayor 27; Tel 927/320-907; Reception at bar 8am-midnight or 1am daily; 3,300ptas single, 5,500ptas double, 6,500ptas triple; V, MC).* The plush, sweet-smelling towels haven't been line dried as they are in most places in Spain, and make the stay ever-so-cushy, as do the clean bathrooms, TV, and a/c. Some of the rooms overlook the Plaza Mayor, and even those that don't still get the sun shining in. The staff works so hard to leave rooms spic and span, they don't have time to finish their snacks. Amid the cleanliness, we found a piece of cheese in the closet!

Other reasonable options include **Pension Boni** *(C. Mingo De Ramos 11; Tel 927/321-604; Double without bath 3,500ptas, small double with bath 4,000ptas, large double with bath 5,000ptas, single without bath 2,000ptas; No credit cards),* 100 meters from the Plaza Mayor; **Pension Emilia** *(Calle General Mola 28; Tel 927/320-083; Singles 2,600ptas, dou-*

bles 3,900ptas, all rooms with private baths; No credit cards); and **Hostal Trujillo** *(C. De Francisco Pizarro 4-6; Tel 927/322-274; Singles 3,200ptas, doubles 4,500ptas, all rooms with private baths; V, MC),* a block east of plaza de la Merced.

▶▶**SPLURGE**

Signs all over town lead you to the old Santa Clara convent, **Parador Nacional de Trujillo** *(Santa Beatriz de Silva; Tel 927/321-350, Fax 927/321-366; 15,500ptas double, 17,500ptas suite; AE, V, MC, Din).* The nuns got the boot in the eighties when it was transformed into this elegant hotel with cloisters, chapels, and vaulted ceilings. The medieval rooms are decked out with marble, an extravagance the sisters would have raged about. If you're not going to stay the night, at least roam through the lobby and courtyard.

need to know

Currency Exchange You can exchange money in any **bank** around town, some of which have **ATMs** attached.

Tourist Info The **tourist office** *(Plaza Mayor s/n; Tel 927/322-677; 9am-2pm/5-7pm daily Apr-Oct, 9am-2pm/4-6pm daily rest of the year)* gives out brochures and organizes tours on the west side of the Plaza Mayor, where you will also see some stores with knickknacks and postcard stands.

Public Transport The town is small enough that you should be able to get wherever you're going on foot. If you need to take a taxi, call *927/321-822, 927/320-661,* or *927/320-274.*

Health and Emergency Emergency: *112;* Police: *091, 092;* Fire: *085;* Red Cross: *Tel 927/321 177.* The region's hospital, **Centro de Salud** *(Tel 927/322 016)* is near the bus station, around the point where Calle de la Encarnación turns into Calle Ramón y Cajal.

Pharmacies Pharmacies are marked by **lit green crosses.** For night needs check the local paper or the window of a pharmacy for the one on a rotating duty schedule.

Telephone City code: *927;* international operator: *1005.* International calls dial 00 then area code and so on. You can use either coins or *tarjetas telefónicas* (phonecards) that you buy at tobacco shops.

Bus Lines Out of the City The Auto Res *estación de autobuses* at **Avenida Miajadas** *(Tel 927/301-202; www.auto-res.es, auto-res@auto-res.es)* serves Cáceres and Madrid.

Postal The local **Correos** *(Calle de la Encarnación, 28 Tel 927/320-533; 9am-2:30pm Mon-Fri, 9:30am-1pm Sat)* is between the bus station and the old center.

castilla la mancha

TOLEDO

Arrive early in the morning and you just might catch the fog rolling off the bridges that cross the Tajo river to Toledo. This mysterious, medieval fortress town seems straight out of a fairy tale, and is absolutely one of the best day trips out of Madrid. Unfortunately, the sight of postcard racks and shelves of cheap pottery drains some of the magic out of the *casco antiguo,* like a "South of the Border" bumper sticker stuck on a Studebaker. The earlier you arrive, the better chance you have at an honest look past the tourist attractions to the wonders of this village from the Middle Ages. While the monuments, synagogues, monasteries, and museums are fascinating (and mostly closed on Monday), half the fun of passing through Toledo is getting lost in the labyrinth of narrow streets. You can have a map, or even a tiny man who asks for directions tucked in your pocket, but no miracle will lead you directly to your destination. [Warning: Keep your arms and legs on the narrow sidewalks at all times. Motorists don't yield to pedestrians, especially not the map-holding kind.] You can run, but there's really no place to hide here, so plaster yourself against the buildings lining the streets of the old center and give in to the awe.

The town, encircled by the **Tajo river** and boosted up on a rocky foundation, reminds one of Mont Saint Michel in France; it's a small island of a town that you can reach by land only when the tide is low. Toledo crowns land that was once a melting pot of cultures. It was capital and home to the Visigoths as early as the sixth century; then around about the Middle Ages, Christian, Muslim, and Jewish cultures started fusing together here. The result is architecture and art that's as much of a melting pot as the people who have occupied it. One of the bragging rights of Toledoans is El Greco (see *el greco,* below), the famous painter, who lived here from 1577 until his death in 1614.

The major cultural sights are contained in the old city and, on a map, form a line with just a slight curve. But don't be deceived—trace a walk from the first to the last and you'll come up with a big squiggly doodle. The square where the most social activity takes place is surprisingly not the **Plaza Mayor,** but the **Plaza Zocodover,** toward the northeast edge of town next to the bus station. The rest of the town branches out in a serpentine weave of narrow streets where you'll randomly bump into glorious monuments that are forever immortalized on postcards to send cousin Fred in Toledo, Ohio.

El greco

Works by El Greco, "the Greek," look as if someone forgot them on the dashboard of their Chevy in the blaring summer sun. You'll recognize his paintings by the religious characters with long, almost distorted fingers, faces, and body parts that seem way more experimental than anything else being painted at the time (late 16th century). So why's he famous here if he's Greek? El Greco picked up and left the island of Crete to study art in Italy, and after being called to Toledo in 1577 to work on an altarpiece, he not only decided Toledo was one of the best day trips, he ended up calling it home. Painting up quite a collection until he died in 1614, El Greco has writ his name large on the top of the Toledo guest book—his masterpieces are scattered around town. The famed *Asunción* from 1613 is in the **Museo de Santa Cruz** *(Miguel de Cervantes 3; Tel 925/221-036; Bus 5,6 to Zocodover; 10am-2pm/4-6:30pm Mon, 10am-6:30pm Tue-Sat, 10am-2pm Sun; 200ptas Adults; No credit cards),* which also houses master painters such as Ribera and Goya, along with plenty of furniture and artifacts. Other El Greco paintings hang in the **Hospital de Tavera** *(Hospital de Tavera 2; Tel 925/220-451; 10:30am-1:30pm/3:30-6pm daily; 500ptas Adults; No credit cards),* near the bus station, and the **Catedral** (see *culture zoo,* above). To take a more personal peek at the man, go to **Casa de El Greco** *(Samuel Levi s/n; Tel 925/224-046; 10am-2pm/4-6pm Tue-Sat, 10am-2pm Sun; 200ptas adults; No credit cards),* which wasn't really his home—can you say *tourist trap?* Actually, they've got one of his paintings, which they've set up in a mock studio, complete with all the El Greco tidbits and factoids you'll ever need to win a game of Trivial Pursuit.

toledo

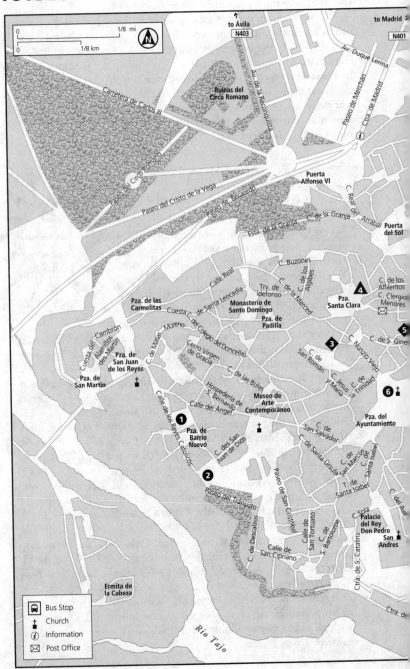

0 —————— 1/8 mi
0 —————— 1/8 km

to Ávila
N403

to Madrid
N401

Av. Duque Lerma

Paseo de Merchán
Ctra. de Madrid

Carretera de Carlos III

Ruinas del
Circo Romano

Av. de la Reconquista

Paseo del Circo Romano

Puerta
Alfonso VI

Paseo del Cristo de la Vega

Paseo de Recaredo

C. Real del Arrabal

Puerta
del Sol

Esta. de la Granja

C. de la Granja

C. de la Granja

C. Buzones

C. de los Algibes

C. de la Merced

Calle Real

Trv. de S. Idefonso

Pza. de las
Carmelitas

Cuesta C. de Santa Leocadia

Monasterio de
Santo Domingo

Pza. de
Padilla

4 Pza.
Santa Clara

C. de los
Alfileritos

C. Clergio
Menores

⊠

C. de Matías Moreno

Cuesta del Colegio del Doncellas

Cerro Virgen
de Gracia

3

C. de
San Román

C. de Nunzio Viejo

C. de S. Gines

5

Cuesta del Cambrón

Alavillos des Martín

Pza. de
San Juan
de los Reyes

C. de las Bulas

C. Jesús y María

C. de la Trinidad

6 ✝

Pza. de
San Martín

✝

Hospedería de
S. Bernardo

Calle del Ángel

**Museo de
Arte
Contemporáneo**

Pza. del
Ayuntamiento

1

Pza. de
Barrio
Nuevo

Calle de los Reyes Católicos

C. des San Juan de Dios

✝

C. de
San Salvador

C. de Santa Úrsula

C. de
San Marcos

C. de
Santa Isabel

2

Paseo del Tránsito

Paseo de San Cristóbal

C. de Descalzos

Calle de
San Cipriano

Calle de
San Tortuato

C. de
S. Bartolomé

Ctra. de S. Catalina

T. de
Santa Isabel

S. Sola

**Palacio
del Rey
Don Pedro**

San
Andrés ✝

C. del Ave

Ermita de
la Cabeza

Ctra. de

Río Tajo

🚌	Bus Stop
✝	Church
ⓘ	Information
⊠	Post Office

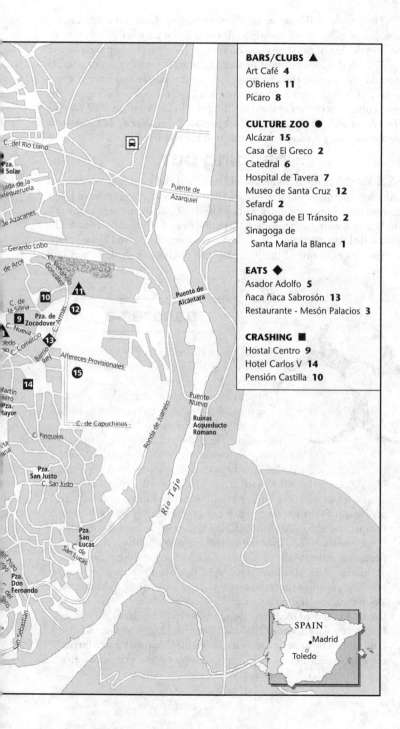

BARS/CLUBS ▲
Art Café **4**
O'Briens **11**
Pícaro **8**

CULTURE ZOO ●
Alcázar **15**
Casa de El Greco **2**
Catedral **6**
Hospital de Tavera **7**
Museo de Santa Cruz **12**
Sefardí **2**
Sinagoga de El Tránsito **2**
Sinagoga de
  Santa Maria la Blanca **1**

EATS ◆
Asador Adolfo **5**
ñaca ñaca Sabrosón **13**
Restaurante - Mesón Palacios **3**

CRASHING ■
Hostal Centro **9**
Hotel Carlos V **14**
Pensión Castilla **10**

The people of Toledo are slowly migrating to the suburbs. During the day, lots of tourists and townspeople come in for a stroll through history, to work in one of the shops, restaurants, or hotels, or to stop for a bite to eat. But in the evening most of them head back home or on to another destination, leaving the charming city center quieter and quieter every year, which makes it a nice place to spend the night. For listings of current cultural activities and events, buy the local newspaper, *El Déa de Toledo,* or pick up the bulletin *Delegación Provincial de la Consejería de Educación y Cultura* (in Spanish) at the tourist office.

hanging out

Since Toledo's main draws are the old buildings and seemingly hundreds of churches, mosques, and synagogues, there's plenty of opportunity to find a compatriot to compare notes with. Outside of just about every site, you'll find groups, young and old, decompressing from the cultural overload. The **Plaza del Ayuntamiento,** at the foot of the cathedral and by one of the tourist offices, is one of the best places to catch some shade or run into

panorama

Losing yourself in the maze of streets, it's hard to view Toledo in its entirety. The cathedral, museums, and architectural highlights are almost impossible to snap pictures of because there's no space to back up and get a wide-angle shot. To get a panoramic perspective of the whole island-of-a-town, you have a couple of options. One: Take the dinky little tour train that leaves from the main Plaza Zocodover. All aboard from 11am till 10pm for 600ptas. Trains leave on the hour and tour for 50 minutes around the perimeter of the old center. They cross the Tajo river via the bridges Alcántara and San Martín, offering a view of the city from a distance, then go back into the center through the Plaza del Ayuntamiento, and near the cathedral. If you're here on Friday, Saturday, or Sunday, the trains after dusk wind through the city, now lit-up for an even more spectacular view. Two: Use your *pies* and walk around Toledo. It'll take you about 2 hours to cover the 4 kilometers (2.5 miles) or so. If you decide to trek it, start from the bridge **Puente de Alcantara** to the northeast, working your way around until you come back into the city across the **Puente de San Martín,** the southwestern entrance. Keep your eyes on the prize and you'll stay more on track than you did in the center of town.

someone you haven't seen since elementary school. In the **Plaza Zocodover,** locals and tourists flock to the outdoor cafes, where groups of both tend to keep to themselves over drinks and conversation. (The proud, at times arrogant, people of Toledo have never been viewed as particularly welcoming to strangers in their midst. But don't feel that their lack of friendliness is a reflection on you, the visiting foreigner. Many Toledans view visiting *Madreleños* driving down for the day with the same contempt.) Food, on the other hand, brings people together in every corner of the world. No exception in Toledo, where the local sandwich shop **ñaca ñaca Sabroson** [see *eats,* below], on this very plaza, calls to one and all. During the day, the conversation and bridging of cultures is limited, but at midnight Saturday or 4am Sunday, things warm up and friends are easily made as the common goal of stuffing your face unites you. The shop is open nonstop from Saturday night till Sunday morning, and is packed the entire time with kids whiling away the wee hours of the weekend.

bar scene

Everyone has something different to say about nightlife here. A young guy at the hostel says it's a dead town, the couple passing by on the narrow street say *"Tenemos más bares que iglesias"* (We have more bars than churches). But even if this couple is right, going out is minimal, especially if compared to neighboring Madrid. During the summer, most notably in August, the townies take flight and the students haven't arrived back on campus yet, so the scene is really dead. To see all that Toledo bars have to offer, winter 'tis the season when there's nothing better than a drink inside to ward off the chills, as the students come out of their cubbyholes to socialize. A few concentrated areas of bars stretch along the **Calle Alfileritos,** off the **Plaza Zocodover,** and on the streets surrounding the **Iglesia Santo Tomé** in the old town, about a 15-minute walk southwest. In the summer, the best you can do is head to the **Miradero,** a scenic overlook with a view of the northern edge of the old town and the countryside. The spot has been converted into a few outdoor bars, where you kick up dirt and pee in an outdoor toilet that's a notch above a port-a-potty. Walk to the end of Calle las Armas for these views and brews.

On the Calle las Armas, **O'Briens** *(Armas 16; No phone; Bus 5,6 to Zocodover; Noon-2:30am daily, till 4am Thur-Sat; 500ptas pint; No credit cards)* is a more civilized, proper Irish pub run by a fine Irishman named Brian—don't worry, his name isn't Brian O'Brien. Everything is truly Irish here: Decor, quotes, memorabilia, and maps on the ceiling are freshly painted because the place just opened summer 2000. Only the music veers from the theme, and then only on weekends, when it changes from Irish to popular; even so, they sneak in some U2, the Corrs, etc. Crowds filter in around 11-11:30pm to warm up their fist with a Guinness. Major football matches are projected on the big screen, and a home team victory (or simple beer drinking) has been known to provoke dancing on tables, which the locals find quite hilarious. Basic pub fare is served before 8pm [see *eats,* below].

Right around the corner from the Calle Alfileritos, the **Pícaro** *(Cadenas 6; Tel 925/221-301; Bus 5,6 to Zocodover; 4pm-as late as 4am daily; Shows 11pm; Show admission 1,000ptas; AE, V, MC)* is hard to squeeze into one category. Walking into the mod loft-like decor and the open space at 8pm, it feels like entering the latest chic New York bar, but around 11pm once or twice a week, usually on Fridays, the downstairs converts into a theater stage. Cool cats watch performances of flamenco, comedy, dance, and you-name-it skits from above. Again, the winter months are more happening, but they're still drinking beer for 250ptas. Drop by the Pícaro for a program of the scheduled shows.

During the day, after lunch or early evening, time gets warped in the **Art Café** *(Plaza San Vicente 6; Tel 925/257-682; Bus 5,6 to Zocodover; Noon-11pm minimum; No credit cards)*, where the hours slip away into a cup of perfect cappuccino dusted with cinnamon. The unbelievable attention to detail here turns every aspect of the moment into art. The owner has an inimitable way of making guests—from giggling teenagers to hip thirtysomethings to cigar-smoking old men—feel at home. He personally imports special beers, wines, and champagnes, and the food, which sounds like typical tapas (600-1500ptas), has an added touch of something memorable. One German beer was so surprisingly rare that we saw a German visitor do a double take (925ptas)! Someone said coming here was like strolling through a painting. Be careful not to forget about the rest of the world as you zone into the classic and modern art blending together on the walls—you may miss your train.

CULTURE ZOO

If you can visit only one place outside Madrid, make it Toledo, even if it means you have to confine your visit to Madrid to only one day. Tinged with drama and mysticism, Toledo is a virtual living museum, hailed as both the spiritual and intellectual capital of the country. What the Medici did for Florence, a string of cardinals—notably Cisneros, Tavera, and Mendoza—did for Toledo. They were great patrons of the arts, and they filled Toledo with Renaissance monuments before its decline in the 16th century.

Most museums and other attractions with admission fees are closed Mondays, and ticket offices close shop 15-30 minutes before museum closing hours to hurry out the crowds, so plan your day in Toledo wisely. There are no special discounts for students. One last useful budget tidbit: Freebie days are May 18 and 31, October 12, and December 6.

Catedral *(Arco de Palacio 2; Tel 925/222-241; Bus 5,6 to Zocodover; 10am-6:30pm Mon-Sat, 2-6:30pm Sun; Museum admission 700ptas; No credit cards):* Unlike many Gothic cathedrals, impressive from the exterior and carbon copies of each other on the inside, here in Toledo three centuries of interior decorators have worked up a distinct treasure trove of goodies. Over the years, they've touched the cathedral up with intricate wood-worked French- and Arabic-style altars and a choir, finishing it off with El Greco paintings. The most renowned is *El Expolio (The Disrobing*

only here

Back in the old days, the measure of a man's power was not the size of his sword, but how it was made. Such is still true in Toledo, where the surprisingly graceful art of sword-making continues. Other lasting trades and crafts include the weaving of wool textiles, and the delicate technique of inlaying gold, copper, and silver threads on a blackened piece of steel, called *damasquinado*. You can buy swords and all the damasquinado stuff hand-crafted at **Simón Artesania** (*Cardenal Lorenzana 8, Plaza San Vicente 1; Tel 925/222-132; Bus 5,6 to Zocodover; 9:30am-2pm/4-8pm Mon-Sat; AE, V, MC, Din*) from Simon himself. With all the junk shops in town, he's one of the few honest guys left.

of Christ), painted specifically for the cathedral. This work is located in the sacristy alongside other big-time art by Raphael, Rubens, Velázquez, and Titian. There are two sections to the cathedral—the church and the sacristy, and the chapel of San Juan; the sacristy and chapel are part of the museum. The cathedral lies right in the heart of the old town, directly west of Plaza Mayor.

Alcázar (*General Moscardzó 4; Tel 925/223-038; Bus 5,6 to Zocodover; 10am-2:30pm/4-6pm, till 7pm summer, closed Mon; 125ptas adults; No credit cards):* This fortress on the eastern edge of the old town once housed royalty, and now houses their guns as an army museum. It was the target of many a siege up until the Spanish Civil War in 1936. See the phone that a colonel used to say good riddance to his kin when he allowed his kidnapped son to be shot in the name of the Republic.

Sefardí/Sinagoga de El Tránsito (*Samuel Leví; Tel 925/223-665; Bus 2; 10am-1:45pm/4-5:45pm Tue-Sat, 10am-1:45pm Sun, closed Mon, as well as Jan 1, May 1, Dec 24-25, 31; 400ptas adults; No credit cards):* Built in the 14th century, and now one of two remaining synagogues in Toledo, El Tránsito, on the far western edge of the old town, contains a wealth of Sephardic history. Historic Jewish tombstones, wedding outfits, sacred objects, and Hebrew manuscripts are all on display. The synagogue's interior gives you some of the world's best stucco work, with Gothic, Islamic, and Hebrew motifs. **Sinagoga de Santa María la Blanca** (*Reyes Católicos 4; Tel 925/227-257; Bus 2; 10am-2pm/3:30-6pm daily till 7pm summer; 200ptas adults; No credit cards):* Out of Spain's original eight synagogues, this is the oldest and largest left standing. Its rows of horseshoe arches and columns will look familiar after a stroll in the souvenir shops. It's located just north of El Transito.

EATS

Are you game? Menus in Toledo are all about the wild catch of the day—partridge, pheasant, quail, venison, and other animals you have to shoot. But the real catch is that you'll pay higher prices than a local ever will. Most of the restaurants near the main attractions offer overpriced tourist menus, so avoid them and eat on the fringes of town unless you have *pesetas* to burn. Try the regional specialties a la carte, especially *manchego* cheese; it's particularly tasty, and comes *semicurado* (soft and mild) to *curado* (harder and sharper or more tangy). For dessert, top it off with the almond paste *mazapán* treat in different shapes and sizes [see *sweet tooth*, below].

▶▶CHEAP

For something other than partridge or ham, try **O'Briens** [see *bars*, above], the Irish pub in town, for hamburgers, baked potatoes, club sandwiches, tuna melts, or meals like Irish steak, pastas, and meatballs in a Guinness sauce (450-1,200ptas). The kitchen closes at 8pm, so you won't be eating at Spanish hours.

Say it 20 times fast: ñaca, ñaca, ñaca. Try it when you're hungry: **ñaca ñaca Sabroson** *(Plaza Zocodover 7; Tel 925/253-559; 9am-midnight Mon-Fri, 9am-8pm/9pm-9am Sat-Sun; Bus 1,5,6 to Zocodover; 400-500ptas sandwich; No credit cards)*. Hot or cold *bocadillos* (sandwiches) attract the late-night owls and the thin wallets. Reading the lit menu on the wall is a Subway-esque (the low-brow sandwich chain) experience, with a scraggly-looking kid smoking behind the counter included. They

SWEET TOOTh

You either like marzipan—the regional specialty that's spelled *mazapán* in Spanish—or you don't. Made from an almond and sugar paste, it comes in cookie form and is sometimes rolled in whole almonds or pine nuts before being baked. This cookie-like marzipan is a Toledo specialty, and it's probably different from the sweet animal- or fruit-shaped marzipan you may have eaten. The most famous and delicious shop for tasting and buying is **Santo Tomé** *(Plaza Zocodover; Tel 925/254-302; Bus 1,5,6 to Zocodover; 9am-10pm daily; V, MC)*. Professional pastry women wearing white smocks take a minute from their phone conversations to package up a variety box (740-2,950ptas), or to give you a single cookie. Try the *Imperiales* rolled in whole almonds.

seem too nice to spit in your food, though, and the ingredients are Spanish-a-fied. Choose from Iberian ham, cheeses, and the famous *tortilla* omelet. It's on the central square of Toledo, with meals to take out and snack in the sun, or cool off and eat indoors.

El Catavinos *(Avenida Reconquita 10; Tel 925/224-342; Main courses 1,500-2,600ptas; Fixed price menu 2,200ptas; 7:30am to 11pm daily; MC, V)* lies a 10-minute walk from the Puerta de Bisagra at the north of the old town. Go here for reasonable prices and to escape the tourist hordes. The name of the restaurant translates as "wine taster" and, appropriately enough, the bistro started life as a wine cellar. You can actually fill up at a reasonable price at the wine and tapas bar downstairs, though you should go upstairs for a more formal meal which can be enjoyed outside on the terrace. The chef specializes in game, including such delicacies as a partridge salad or bell peppers stuffed with hare. In autumn he's rightly proud of his grilled venison and veal meatballs in a zesty tomato sauce.

The one place in the tourist zone that charges reasonable prices is **La Tatasca** *(Calle Hombre de Palo 6; Tel 925/224-342; Main courses 1,500-2,600ptas; Fixed price menu 2,200ptas; 7:30am to 11:pm daily; MC, V)*. Perhaps that's because it is a bit hidden on a small side street two blocks north of the cathedral. This is the domain of the Martin brothers, whose two dining rooms and cafeteria carry the look of 19th-century Toledo. Here the hearty, robust fare of the Toledan kitchen is celebrated, including the most frequently ordered appetizer, *sopa castella,* a hearty regional soup made with various beans and meats and practically a meal unto itself. If you're really hungry, opt for a generous portion of grilled steak and potatoes, though we prefer the locally caught trout or roast quail in a savory game sauce.

▶▶DO-ABLE

Your first clue to authenticity is the whole cured hams hanging from the foyer ceiling. You'll find ham throughout Spain, of course; here, it's thinly sliced for an appetizer, but you won't need one with the *menu del dia*.... People flood into the dimly lit dining room for a substantial meal with two courses, dessert, and wine at **Restaurante-Mesón Palacios** *(Alfonso X El Sabio 3; Tel 925/215-972; Noon-4pm/7-11pm Mon-Sat, noon-4pm Sun; Menu 1,000-1,700ptas; V, MC, AE, DC)*. You can choose from lots of typical dishes like paella, gazpacho, and tortilla, which are good and filling. For the price you pay, don't expect the absolute best you've ever had. It's basic, but the locals come here. The fact that the menu is translated into German and English tells you about the rest of the clientele.

▶▶SPLURGE

To sink your teeth into a little partridge in a pear tree, try **Asador Adolfo** *(La Granada 6; Tel 925/227-321; Bus 5,6 to Zocodover; 1-4pm/8pm-midnight Mon-Sat 1-4pm Sun; Menu 5,550-6,500ptas; AE, V, MC, DC)*. Right near the cathedral, it's convenient for those sightseers who aren't yet used to midday closing time. The place is a classic that you might not notice from the spruced-up entrance, but some of the building includes wall paintings dating back 600 years. The menu originates from that day, too, with lots of rustic animal fare. Take your pick of venison, lamb, beef, birds, or hake fish—these are substantial portions and good quality. Top it off with house *mazapán* for dessert.

crashing

As small as it is, Toledo packs in about 50 hotels, hostales, and pensions. That said, arrival without making any reservations is not recommended. Planning ahead is essential when the summer visitors come in hordes. To help you find a place to rest your head, the tourist office will print out a full, updated list of accommodations, but will not reserve for you.

▶▶CHEAP

Right off the central Plaza Zocodover, **Pensión Castilla** *(Recoletos 6; Tel 925/256-318; Bus 1,5,6 to Zocodover; 2,200ptas single, 3,900ptas double; No credit cards)* only has two singles, which share a bathroom, and four doubles, each with their own. You can turn the doubles into triples for 5,400ptas total, so it's wise to call ahead and reserve. It's an old building with wooden rafters, but the fact that it has heat, ceiling fans, and the best, most airtight windows around makes it comfortable in any season. The windows are also soundproofed to keep the street noise down. The house shuts down at 1am, unless you talk to the friendly owner ahead of time.

Another excellent low-cost option is the youth-centric **Juvenil San Servando (HI)** *(Castillo San Servando; Tel 925/224-554, Fax 925/267-760; 1,400ptas/per person under 26, 1,800ptas/per person over 26; No credit cards)*, a 10-minute walk from the city center just across the Puente de Alcantará.

▶▶DO-ABLE

In the centro, you will find the appropriately named **Hostal Centro** *(Nueva 13; Tel 925/257-091; Bus 1,5,6 to Zocodover; www.aplinet.com/ toledoguia/cl/centrolabrador; 4,500ptas single, 6,500ptas double; V, MC)*, a blink of an eye from the Plaza Zocodover. Spanish and foreign travelers fill the 23 freshly renovated and painted rooms. The cool A/C in the summer adds to the list of amenities not to be taken for granted, and the young guy at the desk isn't too bad to look at. This one isn't in the other guidebooks yet, so there's still a chance to score a room, even if you call for tonight.

Other do-able options include **Hotel Maravilla** *(Plaza De Barrio Rey 7; Tel 925/228-317, Fax 925/228-155; Singles 4,500ptas with private bath outside the room, doubles with bath 6,500ptas; V, MC)*, in the city center a short walk from Plaza de la Magdalena; **Hotel Imperio** *(Calle De Las Cadenas 7; Tel 925/227-650, Fax 925/224-900; Singles 4,400ptas, doubles 6,400ptas; V, MC)*, a few blocks from the Alcázar; and **Hotel El Diamantista** *(Plaza De Retama 5; Tel 925/251-427; Singles 4,000ptas; doubles 6,500ptas; 1,000ptas extra in summer, all rooms with private bath; V, MC)*, at the south end of town, overlooking the beautiful Rio Tajo.

▶▶SPLURGE

While **Hotel Carlos V** *(Trastamara 1; Tel 925/222-105; alfonsovi@ macom.es; Bus 5,6 to Zocodover; 10,600ptas single, 15,525ptas double; AE,*

Cortez the Killer

Born in the small Extremadura town of
Medellin in 1485, Hernando Cortez began
his explorations and exploits at the early age
of sixteen. Like his counterparts Pizzaro and
de Leon, Cortez was enthralled by the prospects
of fame and destiny offered by the undiscovered
lands of the Americas.

In a ruthless and brutal manner, Cortez realized the glory he
sought via the capture and destruction of the Aztec empire (6th
grade social studies ringing any bells?).

In 1518, Cortez and roughly 700 troops made contact with the
Aztec empire in Tenochtitlan. Despite the warm welcome offered by
Emperor Montzuma and his subjects, Cortez imprisoned the Aztec
leader and became the oppressive tyrant one has come to expect
from those drunk on power. The Aztec's one attempt at revolution
resulted in a slaughter of the entire community, subsequently obliterating an entire civilization.

A much loved figure in his era for his intrepid attempts to take
Spain world wide, Cortez became the Governor of New Spain; however, the atrocities he committed against natives of the region were,
even then, deemed appalling and Cortez was eventually asked to
relinquish his authority.

A shipwreck and an unsuccessful attempt to conquer Algiers left
Cortez embittered and relatively poor in his old age, he died in
Sevilla in 1574. His legacy: Mexico, genocide, and a really great Neil
Young song.

V, MC) is fit for a king, the decor here certainly isn't princess-style. You
won't find any Laura Ashley prints amidst all this dark, wooden furniture.
In fact, you may feel the need to pull out a cigar and have a brandy. There
are plenty of rooms, but they're widely diverse. A phone call ahead can get
you one of the larger rooms with a view. Lounge around the lobby, or sip
a drink at the bar out on the summer terrace before eating at the restaurant *(2,800ptas for set menu)*.

need to know

Currency Exchange There's a strange **money machine** for exchanging
currency in front of the **Caja Rural** on the Plaza Zocodover—use at
your own risk. Otherwise, you can depend on the **ATMs,** many of
which lie along Calle El Commercio between the cathedral and Plaza
Zocodover—or change cash before arrival.

Tourist Info One of the **tourist offices** is at Puerta de Bisagra *(Tel 925/220-843; Bus 5,6 to Puerta de Bisagra; 9am-6pm Mon-Fri, till 7pm Sat, and till 3pm Sun; www.jccm.es)*, where info is limited to the regular ho-hum of brochures and maps. There's another office on Plaza del Ayuntamiento 1 *(Tel 925/254-030; Bus 5,6 to Zocodover; 10:30am-2:30pm/4:30-7pm Tue-Sat, 10:30am-2:30pm Mon)* where one of those little trains [see *panorama*, above] leaves every hour for the 50-minute grand tour of the town. Hide your head in the sand all you want, it's still a walk-free way to enjoy panoramic views of Toledo.

Public Transport The **city buses** run every 15-20 minutes until 11pm, on the hour between midnight and 3am, but *only through the new section* of Toledo. Fare is 120ptas. You'll mostly be taking buses **1, 5,** and **6,** which run to the bus and train stations.

Health and Emergency Emergency (Red Cross): *Tel 925/222-222;* Fire: *062* or *Tel 925/269-717;* Police: *092, 091* or *925/250-412;* Ambulance: *925/221-522.* The main hospital, **Virgen de la Salud** *(Avenida Barber, s/n; Tel 925/269-200; Bus 4)*, is in the new part of town, 2 km northwest of the cathedral.

Pharmacies Look for the **green flashing crosses** scattered around town. There is a nighttime pharmacy in the new part of town, **Farmacia Elena Castro Sierra** *(Barcelona 1; Tel 925/228-098; 9:30am-2pm, 5pm-8pm Mon-Fri, 9:30am-2pm every other Sat)*.

Telephone City code: *925;* international operator: *1005.* International calls dial *00* then area code, and so on. You can use either coins or *tarjetas telefónicas* (phonecards) that you buy at tobacco shops.

Trains The **Renfe** train station *(Paseo Rosa; Tel 925/223-099; Bus 1,5,6)*, right across the Azarquiel bridge outside the old town, is a short bus ride and a bit of a hike to the center. Trains to Madrid run on a fixed schedule about every half hour between around 6:30am-8:30am and 8-9pm depending on the day of the week.

Bus Lines Out of the City Buses to Madrid, Talavera, and Cuenca leave from the station *(Tel 925/215-850)*, just north of the old town off the Ronda del Granada. Bus 5 takes you to and from the center and to the train station in a jiff. Buses leave every half hour to and from Madrid between 6:30am-10pm weekdays and 8:30am-11:30pm Sundays and holidays.

Laundry It's surprising that a town as big as Toledo does not have a public self-service laundromat. Laundry and dry cleaning can be done by the staff at **Tintel Pascual** *(Calle Sierpe 8; Tel 925/222-138; 9am-1:45pm Mon-Fri)*, fifty meters southwest of Plaza Zocodover.

Postal The **Correos** *(Tel 925/251-066; 8:30am-8:30pm Mon-Fri, 9am-2pm Sat)* in the old town is on Calle la Plata.

CASTILLA Y LEÓN

castilla y léon

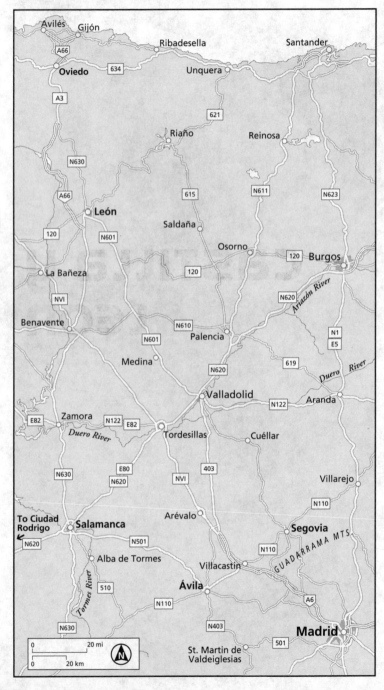

a s you head northwest out of Madrid and the city fades from sight, you will soon find yourself surrounded by the vast plains of Castilla y León (Old Castille and León). The region's great cities—and there are many—seem to rise like islands in the sea of wheat. Three of them—**Salamanca, Ávila,** and **Segovia**—are UNESCO World Heritage Sites, which is simply another way of saying that they're un-missable. Salamanca, one of the larger cities of the region, is home to Spain's oldest university, which in its day was one of the top intellectual centers in the world. Today its students fuel a thriving nightlife in this ancient town. Elsewhere in the region, medieval walls protect the beautiful city of Ávila, where Saint Teresa, one of the most important women in Spanish (and Catholic) history, was born in 1515. In Segovia, water flows down a stunning Roman aqueduct, its old streets twist and turn, and you can drink in the flavor of the golden age of Spain (Queen Isabella, probably the most important woman in Spanish history, was crowned in a church here). To the north, cathedral spires soar to the sky in the lively cities of **León** and **Burgos;** the debate over which of these cities has the more glorious cathedral is something you need to decide for yourself.

These are the lands that gave birth to modern Spain. Castile and Aragón bonded when Isabella of Castile married Ferdinand of Aragón in 1469; five years later, she became queen of the ancient kingdom of León as well. Isabella and Ferdinand forced the Muslims out of Spain after hundreds of years of Moorish domination, then took it upon themselves to unite all the kingdoms of Spain, with *Castellano* being the dominant language. They also knew a guy named Christopher Columbus, but that's another story.

Castilla y León fulfills a visitor's image of Spain, with its ancient cathedrals, plentiful tapas, and authentic Spanish culture. People still gather in town squares every evening around 7-8pm to socialize and meet friends and family. Castles from the days of knights in shining armor still dot the countryside, and of course some of Spain's grandest cathedrals are within the region's borders. The Camino de Santiago, which is one of the largest Christian pilgrimages in the world, made its way through the northern part of the region to Santiago de Compostela, bringing believers from around the world to this land.

There is a tangible sense of history to this region. The old towns remain the center of activity in most of its cities (that nasty urban sprawl you loved to hate in France won't be found here), so daily living takes place in many a Gothic and Baroque building. The past feels really close but somehow it's not oppressive. As you walk down the ancient cobblestone streets of the old towns it is easy to imagine what life must have been like hundreds of years ago. And in Castilla y León, which kind of peaked in the 1500s, life was pretty magnificent. It's a heady experience to get a taste of it now.

getting around the region

RENFE train lines run from Madrid and make for an effortless trip into the region. Once there, it's easy to get from one city to the next, although because of the area's size, travel times can eat into your schedule. Trains run west from Madrid to Ávila and Salamanca and on to Portugal; and other lines head north to the cities of León, Segovia, and Burgos. From there the trains go on to the coast. Buses also present a viable option, and in some cases can cut travel times in half. Every city has a main bus station, and lines run frequently. Local service is inexpensive as well.

TRAVEL TIMES

All times are by road unless indicated by a star
 * = time by train
 ** = time by fast train

	Salamanca	Ávila	Segovia	León	Burgos	Madrid
Salamanca	-	1:15*	2:30	4:40	2:30*	2:40
Ávila	1:10*	-	1:10	2:30** 4:20*	2:20*	1:30*
Segovia	2:30	1:10	-	5:20	2:20	1:40*
León	4:40	2:30** 4:20*	5:20	-	1:40*	4:30*
Burgos	2:30*	2:20** 4:20	2:20	1:40*	-	4:00

Ávila and Segovia both make for excellent weekend or day trips from Madrid. If you can't spend the night, make sure to get up early to give yourself enough time to explore these fascinating ancient cities. Salamanca is easily reached by trains from Madrid and is within perfect distance for a weekend jaunt. Once there, unless you're heading back to Madrid or continuing on to Portugal, you'll be busing it to your next destination. The northern cities of León and Burgos sit on the train line that connects Galicia with Barcelona. This makes it a breeze to get anywhere from either of these two cities. Both are also easily accessible from Madrid.

▶▶ROUTES

The northwest tour: From Madrid hop a train to Ávila and spend a day admiring this walled city at the foot of the mountains. From there continue by train to Salamanca. Try to time your trip for a weekend when the city's *marcha* is in full swing. Hop on an early bus for Segovia where a cathedral, castle, and Roman aqueduct all deserve exploration. Return to Madrid.

The pilgrims' route north: Take a train from Madrid to Burgos. Enjoy its cathedral, billed as one of the country's most spectacular. From there, continue by train to León to see if its claims to a greater cathedral hold true. Hit it on a weekend to enjoy the city's wild *marcha*. Both cities lie on the pilgrims' path so there are many religious monuments. Continue on to Galicia and end your pilgrimage in the city of Santiago de Compostela, which has drawn thousands of pilgrims over hundreds of years. A pilgrimage here is said to cut your time in purgatory in half.

salamanca

It's not the sheer number of historical buildings that gives this ancient city its richness, nor is it the copper hue of the buildings, which has moved some people to call it "the golden city." Even the rowdy clubs and wild *discotecas* can't take credit for energizing the scene. The thing that gives Salamanca its life, diversity, and atmosphere is its university.

Salamanca is an old city with a modern university and a brutal past. Hannibal (the one who crossed the Alps with his armies and elephants, not Dr. Lecter) laid siege to the town during Roman times. It was conquered and liberated several times during the Muslim occupation of Spain, and in the mid-1400's there was a bitter War-of-the-Roses-type feud that split the city in half (one mother whose sons were killed even followed the killers into Portugal and didn't return until she had their heads to lay on her sons' graves). Salamanca took part in the War of the Spanish Succession (between a French Bourbon monarch and an Austrian Hapsburg...go figure) in the early 1700s. With only 100 years to recover, the city found itself unwillingly involved in the Peninsular War between the British and the French, which ended at the Battle of Arapiles, right outside Salamanca. Here Wellington defeated Napoleon's army, finally driving it from the country. But through it all Salamanca not only survived, it also thrived.

The **Universidad de Salamanca** was established in 1218, and became one of the world's leading educational centers during medieval times. By the 15th century, it had become so highly regarded that the Pope called Salamanca one of the four leading lights of the world, along with Oxford, Paris, and Bologna. Although the university's reputation has diminished over the years, the life that the students bring to the city certainly hasn't.

Today the university is on the upswing, with language programs that are turning the world's head. During the school year Salamanca not only attracts thousands of Spanish students, but also lots of international students spending time in this lovely city to work on their...language skills (yeah, right!).

What makes Salamanca so distinct is that it has a very modern, cosmopolitan feel, yet you are surrounded by buildings hundreds of years old. You'd think that this contradiction would screw with things a bit, but somehow in Salamanca it all makes perfect sense, as if that's the only way it could be.

Although the clubs do provide an outlet for all the free-floating energy around town, it is the students who fill them and channel that energy into wild nights that can't be forgotten (or maybe even remembered). Since this is Spain's number one college city, the weekends are always a blast. Even during the week it's not hard to find a small party going on. Most venues are geared to the students: student-friendly atmosphere, student-friendly hours, and best of all, student-friendly prices. The locals have had almost 800 years to get used to the student population, so by now the two fit together well. Old and young sit next to one another on benches and bar stools, allowing themselves to be enchanted by the city.

The best source for finding out what's going on in Salamanca is *Lugares,* a small magazine that can be picked up in most of the bars around town. It's loaded with details about the party scene as well as live music events, theater, and other cultural affairs. There are also two university papers, ***Tribuno Universitario*** and ***Campus,*** which list similar activities. The locals who are into the scene, however, don't recommend planning your weekends by either of the college papers....

neighborhoods

Everything of interest lies conveniently within the heart of the old town, whose center is the **Plaza Mayor.** This is one of the grandest original plazas in Spain. Its ornate Baroque architecture seems to shine just as brightly today as it must have the day it was created. While some central plazas in Europe have lost their appeal and are largely left vacant, Salamanca's is as alive today as it ever was. People gather in the late afternoon to socialize, groups rendezvous here before hitting the bars and clubs at night, and young lovers sit with arms locked around each other...well, you get the point. Plaza Mayor is the center of Salamanca's world.

The university and most of the historic monuments lie to the south of the Plaza Mayor, so expect to find yourself surrounded by students and tourists. To reach this area, follow the less-than-scenic **Rua Mayor** south out of the Plaza; it will take you right down the center of this historic district. If you take your time and just wander around some of the narrow side streets, you'll feel yourself pulled back hundreds of years. The peacfeul **Rio Tormes** runs along the southern edge of this district.

The commercial section of town extends north of the Plaza Mayor. If it's shopping you want, just stroll down **Calle de Toro** or **Calle de**

salamanca

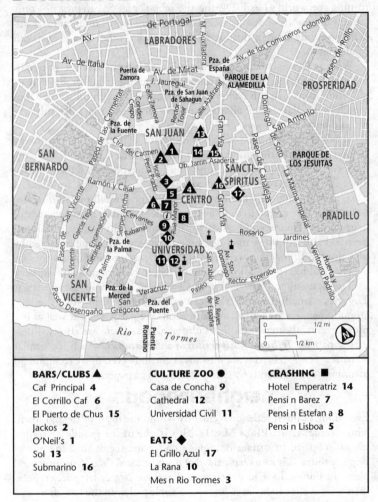

BARS/CLUBS ▲
Caf Principal **4**
El Corrillo Caf **6**
El Puerto de Chus **15**
Jackos **2**
O'Neil's **1**
Sol **13**
Submarino **16**

CULTURE ZOO ●
Casa de Concha **9**
Cathedral **12**
Universidad Civil **11**

EATS ◆
El Grillo Azul **17**
La Rana **10**
Mes n Rio Tormes **3**

CRASHING ■
Hotel Emperatriz **14**
Pensi n Barez **7**
Pensi n Estefan a **8**
Pensi n Lisboa **5**

Zamora to find everything from club gear to vintage guitars. The pace of life is a little more 21st century in this part of town, but with all the old buildings, there's still a strong medieval feel. **Calle Gran Via de España** runs north to south, dividing the eastern part of the commercial section, and is also home to many shops and, particularly on the streets just off it, bars.

Just east of Gran Via, around **Calle San Justo** (another great spot to find excitement at night), you'll find **Breton.** This little neighborhood is the down-and-out artistic area in town. The scene here is small, but it does have a couple of popular modern relics such as the art cinema.

Salamanca is best explored on foot. With the exception of the train station and the bus station (which are both about a 20-minute walk from the Plaza Mayor), everywhere you'll want to go is an easy and engrossing walk away. Most of the smaller streets in the old town are closed to cars anyway. So come prepared with a good pair of shoes and a yen to explore.

hanging out

Finding a lively spot to meet and chill with some of the locals shouldn't pose any difficulty in this friendly city. The streets are usually pretty active, no matter where you are, and the area around the university is always swarming with students. Salamanca also attracts lots of travelers, so you'll find making friends from all over the world as easy as sitting on a park bench.

It all begins at the **Plaza Mayor.** Here the old, the young, the restless, insiders, outsiders, and out-of-towners congregate. Without question the social center of the city, the Plaza Mayor is a great place to relax with a cup of coffee in the morning. There are lots of cafes to choose from, all with tables outside in the warmer months so you can sit and watch the scene unfold in front of you. Come back in the late afternoon or early evening, when people fill the plaza, socializing as only the Spanish know how to do. As you take it all in, surrounded by beautiful Baroque architecture, you'll understand why this is one of the greatest plazas in Spain.

During the day, students gather between and after classes on the **Plaza de Anayo,** on the north side of the **Catedral** [see *culture zoo,* below] right by many of the university buildings. It's another easy place to meet students and other tourists.

rules of the game

The rules here are like the rules in most of the country. You're allowed to carry a drink with you on the street (How do you think the Spanish manage to make it to so many places in one night?). It's legal to own marijuana for personal consumption (until about eight years ago you were also allowed small amounts of cocaine too, but José Law is cracking down). As in the rest of the country, the green stuff is next to nonexistent; *El chocolate* (hash) is prevalent. In most of the big clubs it isn't unusual to see people puffing, and asking around for it. **Sol** [see *club scene,* below] has become known as the unofficial hash bar, although Amsterdam it is certainly not. The scene is still mellow and what people are rolling is what they brought in with them.

wired

With a constant stream of students and back-packers coming through the city, it is no surprise that Salamanca has perfected the Internet experience. **Internet Bar** *(Zamora 7; Tel 923/261-589; 9:30am-2am daily; 150ptas/15min., 300ptas/30min., 500ptas/hr., from 9pm-2am prices cut in half)* is the best spot in town to plug in. It's just north of the Plaza Mayor, making it oh so easy to get to. There are enough terminals here that you won't drain your drink while waiting for your password to clear on Hotmail. It's a great place to meet people, too; most people here are travelers passing through town who are just as eager to make friends as you are. Rumor has it they have some of the best sangria in town, too. Make it one of your first stops of the evening. Settle into one of the terminals with a tall drink, tell your friends what a blast you're having, assure your mom you're eating well and being safe, tell your significant other you miss her or him or it, and then take some time to get acquainted with the person sitting next to you. It's always more fun to hit the scene with others.

bar scene

There is no such thing as a world-renowned university without a couple of world-renowned bars; Salamanca is no exception to this rule. While **Camelot** [see *live music,* below] has spent many years as the visitors' darling, locals will tell you **Sol** [see *club scene,* below] is where the real scene is happening. The variety of bars, lounges, and clubs is pretty impressive, and most cater to a young generation....Friday and Saturday nights are the wildest nights of the week, with the party lasting until noon the next day. That doesn't mean people stay in all week to rest up for the weekend, though. Thursdays are usually pretty lively, with most of the clubs getting big crowds. It might be tougher to find an all-night party the rest of the week, but you can certainly find a bar with something going on. A lot of places have drink specials and games (yes, games—this is a college town, not Paris) Monday through Thursday. A popular one is the "coin flip special": Call it heads or tails in the air and you could win yourself a free drink.

The scene is scattered in Salamanca, but since the city center is pretty compact, it's easy to jump from place to place. Nocturnal activities unfold on San Justo around Gran Via, where there's a bunch of unique bars and lounges to choose from. One student bar, **Potemkin** *(Calle Consuelo),* draws an alternative/intellectual crowd. They come for the creative vibe of the place and stay to enjoy good Spanish rock (yes, I did put those three words together in the same sentence...) and hip-hop. It also brings in the occasional live band.

Just north of the Plaza Mayor near the town clock you'll find **O'Neill's** *(Zamora 14; Tel 923/210-397; Noon-midnight daily; No credit cards)*, the best Irish pub in town. This dark wooden tavern attracts a mix of American and Spanish students. Guinness is on tap, but at 550ptas a pint it's on the expensive side. Or if you so desire, fill up on the small meals and sandwiches served here; most will cost you about 700ptas.

One of the stranger theme bars in the city (theme bars seem to be one of the "in" things here) is **Jackos** *(Calle Iscar Peyra 22; No phone; Noon-midnight daily)*, a shrine to, you guessed it, Michael Jackson. Pictures and memorabilia line the walls, which sounds more terrifying than it is. This is actually a pretty fun place where a lot of American students start their nights in Salamanca. A big beer (big as in liter—this is the measurement Europeans use to buy gas!) is only 375ptas, so get your buzz going here before you hit the town. Jackos is in the center of town, a three-minute walk west of Plaza Mayor.

Cum Laude *(Prior 7; No phone; 11am-3am daily)* lies right off the Plaza Mayor and seems to be so taken by this fact that it has decorated its

COLLEGE KIDS ARE EASY

What better place to find true love than in a university city, right? Well, maybe love isn't the right word. With popular club song lyrics blaring, "You and me baby, we ain't nothing but mammals, so let's do it like they do on the Discovery channel," animal lust is more like it. Whatever it is, finding a mate here is easier than finding that damn frog at the university [see *the great frog hunt,* below].

First, the bad news. Hundreds of students come here every semester from the U.S. to study, so you're about as unique here as a Canadian in New York City. But even if you can't play the exotic card, you can expect more patience from the Spaniards in Salamanca, who are used to dumb-witted foreigners by now. And let us repeat, hundreds of students come here from the U.S. every semester to study ... so guys, you won't have to translate your best pick-up lines into Spanish, and ladies, you can actually understand what some guy who's been following you around all night is saying (or maybe it was better when you didn't know!). The one bad thing is that a lot of the visiting students live with host families, so having someone invite you home isn't too likely.

interior to resemble the famous plaza. Downstairs is the "plaza," otherwise known as the dance floor, which on weekends can get pretty packed. Upstairs, you can watch all the action from the "balcony," made to look like the second-floor windows surrounding the Plaza Mayor. Cum Laude usually attracts a hip, fairly well-dressed crowd, with the hottest times being from 1-3am on weekends.

By far the most unique theme bar in town is **El Puerto de Chus** *(Plaza de San Julian 6)*, a four-minute walk east of Plaza Mayor. Walk inside and you'll feel like you've stumbled into a Disney World exhibit. The inside is a wild mockup of an entire small city block, complete with cobblestone street, arched balconies, and sidewalk. It's a little corner of New Orleans, right here in northern Spain. Besides the main bar, which runs next to the "street," there's another bar off to the side, so you can barhop without ever leaving. On the weekends this 20- to 30-year-old crowd gets pretty lively between 1 and 3am. The dress is typical Spanish "I look good, I'm going out" attire. It's a fun spot to hit, but with beers running 400ptas and mixed drinks 600ptas, not where you want to spend the entire night.

LIVE MUSIC SCENE

There's no shortage of bands in this town, as is the case in most college towns. Quality bands, that's another story. Some of the groups here are really talented and can jam with the best of 'em, others need beer bottles thrown at them to get the hint (sometimes it's just one of those nights). But whether you're looking for it or not, you're bound to hear someone playing a six-string in a bar if you stay in town for any amount of time. A lot of bars will book a blues, rock, or folk band to pull in more people during the week.

About a one-minute stroll north of Casa de Las Conchas in the center of town, **Bruin Café Erasmus** *(Melendez 7; Tel 923/265-742; 9am-3am daily; Fixed price menu 1,500 ptas)* books decent local talent, nothing spectacular, but perfect for sitting and listening to while drinking a cold one. The bars post signs out front advertising weekly shows; *Lugares* will also list most of them.

To catch the best acts in town, there's only one name you need to know about: The centrally located **El Corrillo Café** *(Melendez 18; Tel 923/271-917; 9:30am-4am daily summer; 9:30am-2:30am off-season; Fixed price lunch 1,500 ptas)* is by far the best place to hear some quality music. Thursdays and Fridays are the nights for music here. The stage is downstairs and the cover for big-name acts never exceeds 1,000ptas including drink; most of the time it's only 500ptas. The owner has done a great job in booking bands from all over the world, including Spain, the U.S., Brazil, Cuba, and Africa. These are mainly jazz and blues bands, but some world music shows up here, too. During the week when bands aren't on stage, theater companies sometimes give performances here. Swing by during the day and talk to the bartender over a drink; he'll let you know what's going on. Posters out front also list the upcoming schedule. Actually, checking out El Corrillo Café during the day is a good idea—it's a friendly, quintessential college town cafe that attracts a young, hip, artistic crowd, here to enjoy food even students can afford. There's seating in the street behind the cafe, but if you sit inside you can look at the art on the walls.

One other place worth mentioning, not in the same category as El Carrillo but better than most other places in town, is **Café Principal** *(Rua Mayor 9; Tel 923/211-379; www.mmteam.interbook.net/principal)*. Bands of all kinds and colors come through here from around the country. Call or swing by to get the exact info on who's playing—usually the sets are downstairs on Wednesday and Thursday nights around 11pm. It's a real friendly place with art by local artists gracing the walls. During the day the cafe serves tapas and a good selection of beer, wine, and tea. You can also get a small breakfast if you're up early enough; or at the other end of the day, it's a good early evening spot to start the night off. The cafe is a one-minute walk north of the cathedral.

club scene

Hours of alcoholic pre-gaming, blaring dance music, sexy outfits, hypnotic lights, and maybe even a little hashish fuel the club scene here. In other words, it's the normal Spanish affair. The students keep the energy pumping well into dawn. Like most places, the clubs really don't get

fashion

If you're having trouble communicating with people and you're getting frustrated, relax. You're forgetting that words are just one form of communication. What you wear also says a lot. Fashion in Salamanca works like it does many places in Spain. It isn't cool to look casual. The university students dress prep, and you won't see too many guys walking around in T-shirts. They usually have something with a collar to say to the women, "I'm serious. I'll rock your world." The women don't wear tank tops and shorts. Skirts and blouses call out to the guys, "I'm sophisticated. I'll rock *your* world." When people are going out to the clubs, you can bet the skirts get shorter and tighter while the guys' shirts get...well, fancier—no translation necessary to know what's going on here. But if you find that in your rush to pack you left all your nice stuff at home, there are enough American students around who understand that a simple T-shirt says "I'm from outta town, too—wanna go get a drink?"

going until 4am; show up before then and you'll be on the dance floor by yourself. There is a mix of different styles of clubs here. Some you go to for the atmosphere, others it's all about dancing your butt off until 8am. Whatever your pleasure, it won't be too hard to keep yourself entertained—the only question is, how long can you hang?

Although not your normal Spanish *discoteca* by any means, **Irish Rover** *(Rue Antigue 11; Tel 923/281-074; Noon-12:30am daily; Beer 375ptas, mixed drinks 600ptas, main courses 875-1,500ptas)* is a wild scene that's definitely worth checking out, and with no dress code and no cover charge, there's no excuse not to. Part of what creates this crazy scene is the club's setting in a lavish old opera house where chandeliers hang from the ceiling (apparently during the day it's a reputable restaurant, which you'd never guess after spending a night here). Let's just get one thing straight, though: This is not the best place to meet locals. The crowd is probably 80 percent students studying in Salamanca from other countries (especially the U.S.). While this may make getting to the real Salamanca a little harder, it also makes meeting and talking to people a breeze. Wednesday through Saturday nights are the Rover's wildest nights. The old stage is covered with people moving like they're getting ready for MTV's "The Grind." Wednesday is hip-hop and reggae night, while weekends are a mix of everything from Top-40 to salsa and merengue. Keep an eye open for people handing out two-for-one drink tickets, good Monday through Thursday nights. It's a four-minute walk southwest of Plaza Mayor, next to Casa de Las Conchas.

Another unique place to check out is **Camelot** *(Bordadores 3; Tel 923/212-182; 7pm-5am daily)*, a five-minute walk south of Plaza Mayor. Although locals don't speak too highly of it, years of entertaining travelers with its untraditional setting has earned it some props. It's located in an old monastery where you really do feel like you've been transported back to medieval times (well, except for the lights and the loud music). Dancing around stone pillars that 400 years ago only heard the prayers of monks can really get that little devil in you going.

When you've hit high gear and are ready to get to the real party, head for **Garamond** *(Calle Toro 62-66; Beer 400ptas, mixed 700ptas)*, one of the best discos in town. Everyone converges here after about 4am. The highly energized crowd keeps the party going strong past 7am, and if the people ever flag, the music sure doesn't.... A real mix of stuff gets played here, from hard house to James Brown—basically anything with a strong beat that will keep the bodies moving. To help you keep going, there are two bars, so you don't have to wait to quench your thirst, and leather couches off to the side where you can rest up if you need a break. There's no cover to get in, but if you're wearing sneakers you're out of luck. Other than that the dress code is really light. Girls won't have a problem getting through the door, but guys will usually get a second once-over. **Versus** *(Calle Correhuala 11; Tel 923/264-040)* and **Cotton Club** *(Calle Bermejeros 18; Tel 923/266-591)* also host late-night parties. Versus is a four-minute walk northeast of Plaza Mayor; Cotton Club is a three-minute walk northeast of Plaza Santa Eulalia.

Not really a club, but so much more than a bar, **Sol** *(Pozo Amarillo 26-28; Tel 923/239-925; 7am-11pm Mon-Sat)* has become known as the unofficial hash bar in town. The best time to hit it is around 2 or 3am. Head through the blue doors on the street, down the blazing red and yellow hallway to the big blue sun, then down the stairs to enter this mellow, chilled-out lounge. Everything about this place is loungy, from the soft lighting to the plush sofas and chairs. There is usually a dj spinning trance for the twentysomething crowd. People blaze in here (and have been known to purchase the goods on-site). It's a 20-minute walk northeast of Plaza Mayor.

If you've survived the night and are still looking for action as the discos close down around 7am, then what you need is a healthy dose of after-hours action. The best place in town for such a thing is **El Barco** *(Paseo Fluvial s/n; No phone; Noon-4:30pm/8:30pm-midnight daily food service; 11pm-8am Thur-Sun disco; Main courses 900-2,000ptas; No cover; MC, V)*. In this case it's more than just a name. El Barco hosts the after-hours wildness on a boat in the river down by the Roman Bridge. To get there, just walk past the cathedral toward the river and follow the road around to the right—you won't miss the music. Things have been known to get way out of hand here at times, with people ending up in the river. A dj usually spins some great house and trance, though, so do your best to stay on board to enjoy that.

arts scene

For a city with such a storied intellectual history, the art scene is surprisingly weak here. Not nonexistent, just weak. A few places try to breath a little art into everyone's lives, but they are small in number, and their appearance sporadic. Beyond the architectural wonders of the city, there are few things to feast your eyes on.

A couple of cafes in town do their best to provide the world with a little light. **Café Principal** and **El Corrillo Café** [see *live music,* above, for both] use their walls as informal galleries. Café Principal mostly highlights local talent, while El Corrillo showcases artists from all over the world, some as far away as Japan. Both places host an artist's exhibit for four to six weeks before letting someone else strut their stuff. El Corrillo Café also opens up its stage downstairs for theater performances during the week. Usually drama and comedy performances are given; stop by for dates and times.

There is one highlight to the art scene. Salamanca has one of the best art cinemas in the country. **Teatro Breton** *(Plaza de Breton 12; Tel 923/269-844; 640ptas, 450ptas on Wednesday; Show times vary, usually 5:30pm-1am)* is the perfect place to go if you want to see a German movie made by an Italian director with Spanish subtitles. The theater gets films from all over the world, including the U.S., Japan, the U.K., and Ger-

THE GREAT FROG HUNT

For reasons that nobody agrees about, the frog has become the symbol of Salamanca. You'll see it everywhere in the tourist shops, on T-shirts, keychains, and shot glasses. But the big question is, why a frog? Depending on whom you ask, you'll receive wildly differing accounts. We heard everything, from one person who said it represents the evils of prison to a wild tale about how the city was once overrun by the amphibious croakers. How a frog relates to prison life, and how a city that survived Hannibal (again, the one Livy, not Thomas Harris, wrote about) was almost taken out by a swarm of overgrown tadpoles, remains a mystery to us. Some claim that the frog represents earthly pleasures. We've heard of the princess kissing a frog, but isn't this taking things a little too far?! Whatever the frog may represent, it is everywhere here. One obligatory task while you're here: Try to spot the frog on the facade of the *Universidad Civil* building. Custom has it that anyone who spots it without aid is guaranteed good fortune and marriage within the year (hey, what happened to good fortune!). If you believe this (and you're ready to get hitched), take some time and try to find the little guy; he's there. For those of you not wanting a spouse in the next year, here's the secret. Find the big column on the right-hand side and follow it about a third of the way up, to the three skulls. On the top of the left skull you'll find the little amphibian staring back at you. Whatever the frog may represent, he or she sure doesn't look very friendly sitting up on that memento mori.

many, as well as Spain. If foreign language films aren't your thing and you don't want to have to worry about reading Spanish subtitles, don't write this place off. Some of the movies from the U.S. and U.K. are still in English; they don't dub them all. With four screens running simultaneously, there's always something good showing. A small adjacent cafe serves food and coffee, and you can pick up a pint too if you want a little something to wet your whistle during the flick. The theater is a four-minute walk southwest of Plaza Mayor.

GAY SCENE

Although it's a college town, Salamanca is still fairly conservative. Most of the kids dress prep; you won't see many tattoos and body piercings, and there is not a large openly gay scene. But since a good percentage of the city's population is students, people are not close-minded. The gay scene here is just not the most happening one around.

A five-minute walk east of Plaza Mayor, **Submarino** *(San Justo 27; Tel 923/260-265; Beer 350ptas, mixed 550ptas)* is one of the better-known gay-friendly bars. Submarino opens nightly at 9pm, and there's no set closing time. It's a really cool place that puts you in the belly of a ship. With pipes running all over the walls and the ceiling, and one wall completely decked out to look like the side of a ship, all one can ask is, "Permission to come aboard, Captain." More than just a bar, this place plays some house music to provide the beat for anyone interested in dancing. Most of the time the crowd here is evenly mixed between gay and straight, so it's a fun place for everyone. It's been said that sometimes people buy bags of hash on the street out front.

CULTURE ZOO

Salamanca's true cultural treasures are its architectural wonders. Most of the buildings in the old town are constructed from tan sandstone, which gives them a golden copper hue. In the early evening, when the sun is low in the sky, the buildings almost seem to have a 24-karat glow, which is why some have dubbed Salamanca "the golden city." Just strolling around and enjoying the building facades is one of the true delights of being here. And no trip to Salamanca is complete without spending some time searching for the frog on the facade of the Universidad Civil building [see *the great frog hunt,* above].

Catedral *(Plaza Juan XXII; Tel 923/217-476; 9am-1pm/4-6pm daily Oct-March; 9am-2pm/4-8pm daily April-Sept):* When you're ready to head inside, this is the place to go. Everybody visits this building, or rather buildings, a few blocks south of Plaza Mayor. This is the only place in Spain where you will find a new cathedral built right next to an old cathedral. The new cathedral dwarfs its older sibling in size and style. Finished in the 1700s, it took over 200 years to build, incorporating Gothic and Baroque styles. Twentieth-century restorers couldn't resist adding their little touch to the building, so even though the Spanish have never landed a man on the moon, they have put an astronaut into the building's facade near the side entrance. The old cathedral is much plainer, constructed in the Romanesque style of the 13th century. Beautiful frescos from 1242, which can be found in the small *Capilla de San Martin,* are the highlight of a trip inside. The organ here is one of the oldest in Europe.

Museo de Salamanca *(Patio de las Escuelas 2; Tel 923/212-235; 10am-2pm/4:30-7:30pm Tues-Sat, 10am-2pm Sat; 200ptas):* Housed in a beautiful 15th-century building a few blocks west of the university, this local branch of the nation's Museo de Bellas Artes has a permanent collection that includes paintings from as far back as the 1600s and some more recent ones from the early 1900s. A couple of sculptures are included for variety. The museum is worth a stop while you're in the city.

Casa de Conchas *(Calle de Libreros, s/n; Tel 923/269-317; Open 9am-9pm Mon-Fri, 10am-2pm/5-8pm Sat and Sun; Free):* This famous building a few blocks south of the Plaza Mayor is probably the most photographed building in town. What makes it so unique are the more than four hundred scallop shells carved into the facade. What are they doing there? The creator was a member of the order of Santiago, whose symbol is the scallop shell. He built this in celebration of the great pilgrimage to the Spanish city of Santiago de Compostela. One story about this building is that there came a time when it was going to be torn down. In order to save it, word spread that pearls were hidden behind some of the shells. Since those tearing the building down didn't know which shells hid the pearls, the structure was spared, and it's now one of the great landmarks of Salamanca. Believe the story or not, but check out the building. Inside there's a little library and an information kiosk.

Torre de Clavero *(Plaza de Colon):* One of the city's old defensive structures dating back to the 15th century, this is sure to grab your attention as you walk down Gran Via. The octagonal tower is all that remains of a castle that was built here in 1450. You can't go inside, but you can check out the distinctive Mudéjar trelliswork that decorates the sentry turrets.

CITY SPORTS

We thought the pub crawl was just about as much exercise as most people could handle, but if your legs aren't shot from dancing until noon and your vision is returning from blurry, there are a couple of good places around town where you can get your body in shape while enjoying the surroundings. Most Salamancans head to **Parque Fluvial** for their exercise. The park stretches out in a really nice spot in the southeast corner of the city along the Río Tormes. Besides great paths for walking and jogging, the park also has soccer fields and basketball and tennis courts. On the weekends it comes alive with people of all ages out enjoying themselves.

If you had something a little grander in mind, **Alquiler** [see *need to know,* below] will outfit you with camping and kayaking gear as well as mountain bikes and ten-speeds. Rates here are more than reasonable, and the very friendly staff can point you to the best spots. If you're interested in biking, they'll suggest a peaceful, scenic ride over the river and out of the city. The kayaks they rent are basic plastic ones; a lifejacket and paddle are included. On Thursdays, Alquiler organizes guided excursions of the river. The price is only 2,400ptas and includes kayak rental, transport to and from the river, and some knowledgeable company.

The countryside around Salamanca isn't exactly the wilderness, but there are some nice spots for camping close by. Alquiler rents out tents, backpacks, sacks, stoves, and fuel for anyone who wants to get out and explore. They'll also give you details about good camping grounds and the best way to reach them.

STUFF

If it's shopping you seek, Salamanca can deliver. There are tons of stores selling the latest fashionable threads to make you look like a million bucks, there are plenty of music stores where you can find your band's latest release or discover a hot new act, and your friends back home will be thrilled when you bring them one of the many souvenirs the tourist shops peddle. Give in to frog fever and pick up something with an amphibian on it—this symbol of the city is plastered on everything from T-shirts to keychains.

The best place to start your quest is Calle Toro, north of the Plaza Mayor. Partly a pedestrian mall, this is where most of the fashionable clothes, beauty, and shoe stores are, as well as plenty of ATMs to refill your wallet. One block over is Zamora, which offers more of the same. South of the Plaza Mayor, Rua Mayor is the main commercial center. Also closed to everything but pedestrian traffic, it's fun to wander down. If you need to stock up on small, cheesy gifts, you'll find most of the tourist shops here.

▶▶DUDS/CLUB GEAR

Is your wardrobe getting a little old? You'll find no shortage of clothes here for hitting the town, from basic black to the wild latex look. People around town do their best to look good when they go out at night, so if you don't want to be "that guy/girl," you might want to consider wearing something a little nicer than your favorite tattered T-shirt.

7A Avenida (*Corner of Monroy and Las Franciscas; Tel 923/212-815; 9:45am-2pm/4:30-8:30pm Mon-Fri; MC, V, AE*) is a good, not too wild, place to start. The clothes here, for men and women, are hip but not too fancy or over-the-top. Girls can pick up a tank top or shirt for 2-3,000ptas, pants start around 3,000ptas. For guys, shirts start at 2,000ptas, but most are more in the 3,000ptas range. It's a seven-minute walk northwest of Plaza Mayor, en route to Plaza de España.

A two-minute walk south of Plaza de España between Calle Toro and Calle Azafranal is **Los Vaqueros** (*Monroy 16, Tel 923/212-815; 9:45am-2pm/4:30-8pm Mon-Fri*), a small boutique that specializes in *ropa de moda* for women. You'll find lots of sexy tank tops, skirts, and shirts running 2,000ptas and up.

For women wanting to attract more stares than they're already getting, **Stradivarius** (*Toro 39; Tel 923/210-674; 10am-2:30pm/4:30-8pm daily; V, MC*) has rack after rack of outfits that demand attention. The store plays house music so you can check out how your new look will work on the dance floor. There's also good info here on parties and upcoming events. It's just north of the Plaza Mayor.

▶▶TUNES

You won't find yourself losing touch with the music scene during your time in Salamanca. The latest music is played everywhere—clubs, bars, even stores. And if you actually want to buy some music instead of just freeloading, **Compac** (*Rua Mayor 30; Tel and Fax 923/265-013; 10am-12:15pm/4:30-8:30pm Mon-Sat, 11:30am-2pm Sun*) is a great bet. Although it's a small place, it stocks a little of everything, from punk to salsa, house to hip-hop. You'll find Spanish and international groups and lots of underground and alternative selections. The staff here is super-friendly and will point you toward the best places to hear good live music, and clue you into the best djs around town. Compac is a three-minute walk north of the cathedral.

▶▶BOUND

Given the large population of English-speaking students in the city, finding a read printed in English isn't too difficult. A four-minute walk south of Plaza Mayor, **Libreria de Nunes** *(Rua Mayor 13-15; Tel 923/212-052; 10am-2pm/4-8pm daily)* has a good selection, with Charles Dickens novels next to trashy romance paperbacks. You can also pick up travel guides, the latest papers, and magazines.

EATS

One of the joys of Salamanca is that there are so many good places to grab a bite, very few of which will put a big dent in your wallet. The best tapas strip lies a bit out of the center on Calle Van Dyck northeast of the Plaza de Espana. The streets around the Plaza Mayor are also loaded with restaurants eager to dish out their treats to tired and hungry travelers. Just wandering around looking at the menus out front is enough to get you salivating like Pavlov's dog.

▶▶CHEAP

Most of the eating establishments in the city are on the inexpensive side. The really cheap deals can be had at the small cafeterias and fast-food joints (yes, the Evil Empire has reached this historic place—a McDonald's is just off the Plaza Mayor). **Leonardo** *(Gran Via 83; Tel 923/215-307; 1-4pm/6:30pm-2:30am Sun-Wed, 1-4pm/6pm-5am Thurs-Sat; 500ptas average meal; MC, V)*, also right off the plaza on Calle del Prior, is a Spanish fast-food joint; stop here during a night of boozing to fuel up on a greasy burger, or order *bocadillos* (sandwiches) if you want to keep the grease intake to a minimum.

For lunch, check out **La Rana** *(Calle de San Francisco de Victoria 39; Tel 923/123-447; 8am-2am daily; Fixed price menu 1,200ptas, sandwich and soda 700ptas; No credit cards)*, a university hangout with a good selection of sandwiches and other things for a few hundred pesetas. If the rock music inside is too much for you, you can escape to one of the outdoor tables.

Vegetarians should swing by **El Grillo Azul** *(Calle El Grille 1; Tel 923/219-233; 1-4pm daily; 775ptas-1000ptas)*, a seven-minute walk southeast of Plaza Mayor. It's only open for lunch, so plan accordingly. The menu is typical vegetarian eats, and has scored lots of surprisingly good reviews in this nation of meat-eaters. The dining room is small and cozy, with a bright blue decor. You can tell people here are dedicated to healthy living not only from the bulletin board covered with info on holistic study, but also because this is one of the few places in the *country* that's smoke-free.

▶▶DO-ABLE

Unless you're here on the company's expense account, the do-able range of restaurants covers pretty much everything else in town. This includes nice sit-down restaurants with plenty of atmosphere. Right off the Plaza del Corrillo is **Meson Rio Tormes** *(Plaza del Corrillo 20; Tel 923/211-323; 8am-1am daily; Fixed price menu 1,500ptas, main courses 1,000-2,500ptas; AE, MC, V)*, which serves an extensive menu of typical Castilian cuisine—hearty dishes like paella and rice and, of course, lots of different ham to choose from. The real deal here is the *menu de dia:* For 1,300ptas you get two dishes, both with huge portions, bread, drink, and dessert. Stone walls, wooden beams, and old photos and paintings of Salamanca hanging on the walls give the place the feel of an old tavern. The crowd here is really mixed. It's popular with students and older adults alike. Up front, a bar serves a good selection of tapas.

crashing

Enough hotels, hostels, and *pensiones* cram themselves into the center of the city that it's a buyer's market. Whether you're in the market for a dirt-cheap room or luxury digs, finding it won't be hard. Most places are ideally located within a couple blocks of the Plaza Mayor.

▶▶CHEAP

Most *pensiones* here fall into the cheap category. What you will get for your money is an adequate room; some even come with a private shower. The luxury of a window is not a given. If this satisfies you, start looking on Melendez, which has a number of cheap *pensiones* in an unbeatable location, just steps away from some of the hottest action in town.

One such place, **Pension Barez** *(Melendez 19; Tel 923/217-495; 1400ptas single, 2600ptas double, triple 1300ptas per person, prices rise 100-200ptas July-Sept; No credit cards)* offers decent rooms at rock-bottom prices. The triples in particular are spacious and airy, although some of the singles lack any direct sunlight. The owners are nice and provide a common lounge with a TV, although they will charge you 150ptas for a 10-minute hot shower. (The cold shower is free, probably because you won't linger in it for too long.) They will also do a load of laundry for you for 500-1,000ptas (the price depends on how long it's been since you cleaned anything).

Pension Estefania *(Calle Jesus 3-5; Tel 923/217-372; 2,000ptas single, 3,500ptas double, 4,800ptas triple; No credit cards)*, in the city center, is a great deal considering that all the rooms have a small private shower and sink. Beyond that, the appeal of the rooms varies—some have terraces, while others don't even have a window. But the management is nice and does its best to make you feel comfortable.

Another cheap option is **Pension Villanueva** *(C. San Justo 8, 1st Fl; Tel 923/268-8-33; Singles without bath 1,600ptas, doubles with bath 3,600ptas; No credit cards)*.

If you've got the gear, there are some nice campgrounds around these parts. The best are **Regio Camping, Carretera Salamanca** *(Tel 923/138-888; MC, V)*, which lies 4 km east of town on the highway toward Madrid. This is a first-class campsite that's like an inexpensive little resort, with two tennis courts and a swimming pool. There's also a good restaurant. The campgrounds abut an expensive tourist complex. You can spend the night for 475ptas, or rent a tent for 850ptas. Count on hot showers.

A much less desirable campsite is **Don Quijote, Carretera Salamanca** *(Tel 923/209-052; No credit cards),* 4 km from town along the road to Aldealengua. This is a second-rate camping joint with few facilities. But the price is the cheapest in the area; it costs only 400ptas per person to sleep under one of the on-site tents.

▶▶**DO-ABLE**

Not much falls in the in-between price range in Salamanca. If you want a little more luxury than just four walls and a bed, you have to move up to the splurge price range. If you're just after a place where you can have your own bathroom, **Pension Lisboa** *(Calle de Mélendez 1; Tel 923/274-333; 1,800ptas single, 3,400ptas with bath, 2,800ptas double, 3,800ptas with bath; No credit cards),* just south of Plaza Mayor, has a few rooms with small, private baths; the rest share one down the hall. The rooms on the street in particular are very bright here at night.

Other do-able options are **Hotel El Toboso** *(Calle Del Clavel 7; Tel 923/271-462, Fax 923/271-462; Singles 4,700ptas, doubles 7,000ptas, all rooms with private bath, breakfast 300 ptas; V, MC, AE),* in the city center a few minutes from Museo Taurino; **Hostal Laguna** *(Calle Del Consuelo 19; Tel 923/218-706, Fax Tel 923/218-706; Singles w/bath 3,500ptas, singles without bath 3,000ptas, doubles with bath 5,300ptas, doubles without bath 4,280ptas; V, MC),* in the city center a few minutes from plaza de Colon; and **Le Petit Hotel** *(Cuesta Sanctuspiritus 39; Tel 923/265-567; jcdir@teleline.es; Singles 4,000ptas, doubles 6,500ptas, all rooms with private baths; No credit cards),* a short walk from Plaza San Cristóbal.

▶▶**SPLURGE**

You can get a taste of the high life at a price that is not entirely out of the question in Salamanca. One place to pamper yourself is **Hotel Emperatriz** *(Rua Mayor 18; Tel 923/219-156; 5,500ptas single, 8,000ptas double, 10,800ptas triple, 12,800ptas quad; V, MC, AE),* a modern hotel on a street brimming with life. Each of the very comfortable rooms comes complete with full bathroom, TV, phone, and minibar. Every morning, the hotel serves a continental breakfast downstairs for 300ptas. You can also change money at the front desk, where there is an attendant 24 hours a day.

NEED TO KNOW

Currency Exchange Nowhere in Salamanca will you find yourself far from an **ATM.** There is one in the Plaza Mayor, a bunch on Rua Mayor and Toro, and others scattered around town; most are accessible 24 hours. During the day, Toro has a lot of banks open if you need to change money or cash travelers' checks.

Tourist Information The **main tourist office** *(Plaza Mayor 14; Tel 923/218-342; 9am-2pm/4:30-6:30pm daily)* is the best place to start for info about the city. It has details on everything from lodging options to upcoming cultural events. There is also an **information kiosk** *(Tel 923/268-571; 10am-2pm/5-8pm Mon-Fri)* in the Casa de Conchas. This office has more regional information, while the office in the Plaza Mayor has more information on the city.

Public Transportation The historic core of Salamanca can be covered on foot, although there is **bus service** *(Tel 923/236-717)*, with buses leaving from the station at Plaza del Mercado. The cost of a typical fare is 500ptas, but you'll spend half that if you purchase 10 tickets at the bus station for a combined price of 2,500ptas. Buses serving the center of Salamanca are numbers 1, 23, 3, 4, 6, 8, and 9.

American Express Viajes Salamanca *(Plaza Mayor 24; Tel 923/215-215)* is the city's American Express representative. It offers travel services, sells and refunds travelers' checks, and has emergency check cashing. It will also organize tours, book hotels and flights, and hold a client's mail.

Health and Emergency In the event of a medical emergency, a **Red Cross Ambulance** can be reached by calling *923/222-222*. The office is located on San Benito. The **National Health Office** *(Avda. De Mirat 28; Tel 923/291-100)* is another source for medical services. The **Police Station** is in the center of the city at Ronda de Sancti Spiritus 8. They can be reached in the event of an emergency at *092*.

Pharmacies There are *farmacias* all over the city marked by **neon green crosses.** *Farmacias* rotate the responsibility of being open all night, and each one posts a schedule indicating who will be open on what night. One pharmacy right off the Plaza Mayor is **Farmacia** *(Plaza del Corrillo 18; Tel 923/213-410; V, MC, AE)*

Telephone City code: *923*. Payphones take coins as well as *tarjetas téléphones,* which you can buy at any tobacco shop.

Trains The **train station** *(Paseo de la Estacion; Tel 923/120-202)* is about a 20-minute walk northeast of the city center. There are cabs at the station, but the walk into town isn't bad. Take a left when you hit the main road, Paseo de la Estacion, in front of the station. Follow that until you come to Plaza Espana; from there, take Gran Via to the center. There are three trains daily to Madrid as well as connections to Ávila, Cuidad Rodrigo, and Valladolid.

Bus Lines Out of the City The **main bus station** *(Filiberto Villalobos 71; Tel 923/236-717)* is also about a 20-minute walk west of the city center. There are frequent connections to Zamora and other nearby towns, as well as Madrid, Ávila, Leon, and Cacéres.

Laundry Lavanderia *(Pasaje Azafranal 18; Tel 923/260-216; 9:30am-2pm/4-8pm Mon-Fri, 9:30am-2pm Sun; 500ptas wash/dry)* is in a mini-mall; the entrance is at Calle Azafranal 3-9. It's got plenty of washers and dryers to wash all those dank clothes in your pack.

The nice woman in charge will even transfer your things for you if you ask nicely.

Postal The **main post office** is on Gran Via *(Gran Via 25-29, Tel 923/260-607; 8:30am-8:30pm Mon-Fri, 9:30am-2pm Sat).*

Internet See *wired,* above.

everywhere else

ávila

The lack of a youth vibe is visible the moment you step off the bus in Ávila. Take a spin around town to confirm: You'll see old women who love to strike up conversations under their breath, and families—or couples working on a family—running errands, buying bread, and tending shops and restaurants. One of Ávila's biggest attractions—a medieval wall with 88 turret towers—surrounds the historic center, making the town look like a LEGO castle set. The rectangular medieval construction is a handy reference point, dividing the town into *dentro de las murillas* and *fuera de las murillas*—inside and outside the walls, respectively. Life is *tranquilo* within the walls, and few people are out and about during the week. The summer is the only time you'll run into someone during the dead lunch hours—and he or she will most likely be a tourist.

The other big attraction in town? Santa Teresa, the Catholic nun who was born here in 1515 [see *only here*, below] and went on to reform the Carmelites. She's one of Spain's two patron saints (the other is Santiago), and Spanish schoolgirls adore her; you might see busloads of them arriving to pay homage to her during your stay.

Map in hand, Ávila is an easily navigable town. The town's chief square is **Plaza de la Victoria,** or Plaza Mayor, a small enclosed square set to the west of the cathedral and surrounded by arcades. You can take **Calle San Segundo** along the eastern side of the walls, leading to **Puerta de Alcazar,** the main gate of the old town. At the narrow west end, you'll see ancient bridges still spanning the Adaja River. If you want to go along the top of the walls, the only way to access them is through the garden of the **Ávila Parador,** built just inside the northern edge of the city walls. Two old Jewish neighborhoods still stand, though the Jews are long gone. One is in the northern sector of town, around the **Puerta de San Vicente.** The other is in the southwestern corner, between **Puerta del Puente** and **Puerta de la Mala Dicha.**

ávila

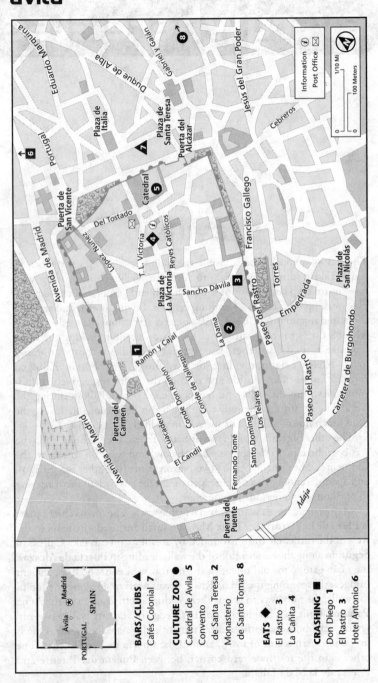

SPAIN
PORTUGAL
Madrid
Avila

BARS/CLUBS ▲
Cafés Colonial 7

CULTURE ZOO ●
Catedral de Ávila 5
Convento
de Santa Teresa 2
Monasterio
de Santo Tomas 8

EATS ◆
El Rastro 3
La Cañita 4

CRASHING ■
Don Diego 1
El Rastro 3
Hotel Antonio 6

Modern Ávila, of course, has long outgrown its old walls. The bus depot and train station lie in the eastern and modern section of town. Other than those transport hubs, the only part of town outside the walls that might interest you is the neighborhood of **Los Verracos,** lying to the east of the walls. This sector of Ávila, centered around **Plaza de Italia,** is about as old as anything within the walls. Two blocks to the south, lying outside Puerta de Alcazar, stands one of the most beautiful and evocative corners of Ávila, **Plaza de Santa Teresa,** well worth the stroll outside the walls.

You can ask for directions at the tourist office, but it's more fun to ask a local, who might just accompany you to your destination. Every corner turned in the old town isn't necessarily a newfound discovery or hidden photo opportunity, but plenty of religious buildings and **Las Murillas** [see *culture zoo,* below]—Ávila's version of the Great Wall—help create a panoramic postcard. Before the wall went up, Ávila saw the usual power struggle between Celts, Romans, and later, Muslims and Christians. The Christians and Alfonso VI won in the end, and they figured that the plateau that sets old Ávila up at 1130 meters (3,707 feet) gave them quite a defensive advantage. The wall construction began in 1090, but the major part of the work was carried out during the 12th century.

Ávila's elevated geography means chilly winter winds that bite into the warmest of jackets and cool summer breezes that warrant wearing long sleeves even in July—summer garb that's unheard of in sweltering Madrid. If you come in on the train from the capital, a summer information stand awaits you at the station with maps and booklets on Ávila's history and sights; the folks at the **main tourist office** [see *need to know,* below] will provide a few more details if you're really nice. If you can't get enough information there, check ***www.Avila.net*** (written in Spanish, but, *si usted no habla españoles,* you can get the gist of it using AltaVista's Babel Fish) or grab the local newspaper (also in Spanish) from a kiosk to find out what's going on.

hanging out

After spending the morning strolling around the wall in Ávila's historic center, pack a picnic and head for the **Parque del Rastro** to sit under the trees and look up at the turrets. This small relaxing park is just outside the eastern gate, Puerta del Rastro. There's a shortage of bars and vampire activity in Ávila, and the cafe crowd doesn't exactly flood the sidewalks either. In the summer, though, the main square (which also serves as a part-time parking lot), **Plaza del Mercado Chico,** and a square to the north that's outside the walls, **Plaza de Santa Teresa,** have tables for weary walkers.

The locals call the Plaza de Santa Teresa *La Grande,* and probably the newest place here is **Cafés Colonial** (*Estrada 1 Tel 920/253-981; 8:30am-1am daily; No credit cards*), a coffee-lover's dream—especially for those with frozen toes on a cold day. The cafe has flavored syrups, plenty of drinks topped with whipped cream or ice cream, and coffees that'll

ONLY HERE

The finger, I want to see the finger! Step right up, ladies and gentlemen, and see the wrapped finger of the ever-so-popular Santa Teresa on display, *now*, at the *Sala de Reliquias* of the **Convento de Santa Teresa** *(Plaza de la Santa; Tel 920/211-030; Bus 1 Arco del Rastro; 9:30am-1:30pm/3:30-8:30pm daily Oct-Apr, till 9pm May-Sept; Free).*

Saint Teresa de Jesus, a scribe of religious writings, reformed the convent system by making all the nuns wear sandals, and later beat herself up over it, taking part in the mysticism fad in which nuns made a fashion of flagellation (in Teresa's case, she snipped off her own finger). She probably wouldn't appreciate the Baroque grandeur, the statue of her wearing an ornate golden crown or the sight of her finger, covered with rings, preserved as a relic in the sacristy. The finger and flagellating rope are a sideshow to the birthplace of Ávila's patron saint. The convent/church that sits on a crypt is the only construction of its kind in Spain, and one of the nearly 20 convents the sis founded.

warm you up in the winter or get you chatting on the outdoor terrace in the summer. The spiked coffees are well worth the 500ptas, and so are the syrup-flavored ones, at 300ptas. Bookworms who don't need a caffeine buzz to lose themselves in a story can linger long over a cup of exotic herbal tea—the only distraction is the elevator-esque music trickling through the speakers.

In the center of town, just one minute's walk from the cathedral, is **La Canselas** *(Cruz Viejo 6; Tel 920/212-249; 9am-11pm daily; V, MC, AE, DC),* the most convenient bar in the old town. This is a tavern for all ages, attracting both young and old, visitors and locals. Although many come just to drink wine or beer, one of the tavern's main attractions is its 2,000ptas menu, one of the best food values in Ávila. If you don't want that, hang out in the bustling tapas bar where the range of tapas begins at 185ptas. The homemade bread is excellent, as is the roasted chicken with French fries. The habitués often order a *caña*, a small shot of beer served with a tapas.

A lot of Ávila youth head to **Copa Cabaña** *(Calle Cristo de la Luz; Tel 920/223-508; 9am-midnight daily, summer, 9am-midnight weekends, winter; No credit cards),* which sounds like a Forties nightclub, the kind that would attract Barbara Walters. Although we spotted two young women on our last visit who looked like modern-day clones of Saint

Teresa, most of the crowd here is hip and far from saintly. They come for the robust red wine and the tapas, which range in price from 200 to 600ptas. One student fills up every night on a dinner of French fries alone. The waitstaff doesn't go out of their way with courtesy, and the noise can be a bit deafening, but it's a fun spot nonetheless. Count yourself lucky if the chef decides to prepare *judias del Baro* (the famous beans from Barco de Ávila, traditionally served with sausage).

CULTURE ZOO

If you're the devotional type, or someone who gets inspired by the sight of a church at mass time, you'll be praying in Ávila's convents, monasteries, chapels, and churches as much as the patron Saint Teresa did. Of the 60 sights that the tourist map highlights, maybe 10 at most aren't related to religion. If you feel overwhelmed by all the choices, a private tour company offers guided tours of the Cathedral, Santa Teresa's house, and the main square, pointing out architectural details and historical notes along the way. The **Turávila tours** *(José Bachiller 14; Tel 920/250-962; 11:30am and 4:30pm Mon-Fri; 800ptas includes entrance fees; No credit cards)* leave from Plaza de la Catedral in front of the tourist office. Turávila tours are led in Spanish and last two to three hours. For the Spanish-impaired, try the English option with guide **Elena Borchers** *(Tel 920/214-413 or 667/510-332; 10:30am Mon-Sat, noon Sun; 2500ptas in groups of five; No credit cards)*. This tour also meets at the tourist office and lasts two to three hours. The bigger your group gets, the cheaper the tour.

Las Murillas *(surrounding the city):* If you can't find these walls, you're not in Ávila. The 11th-century medieval walls, built in only nine years and stretching 2.5 kilometers (1.5 miles), aren't visible from the space shuttle, but they are particularly impressive under the spotlights of Ávila at night. Within the Alcázar Gate, off the Plaza de Santa Teresa, an entrance leads to a walkway on the wall where you can check out views of the dry land spreading out from Ávila. The best views, however, are of the stone walls themselves, from the ground along their perimeter.

Catedral de Ávila *(Plaza Catedral; Tel 920/211-641; Bus 1 to Plaza Catedral; 9am-7pm Mon-Sat, noon-7pm Sun; Cloisters 250ptas adults; No credit cards):* A church and fortress in one? Isn't that a tad contradictory? Religion isn't often distinguished by physical boundaries, but this Romanesque and Gothic cathedral is actually built into the perimeter of a wall. Begun in 1099, the exact year the city's walls were completed, the cathedral was constructed directly into the ramparts. The interior is a stunning peppermint candy-like blend of mottled red and white stone. Over the years, several Renaissance chapels were added, disrupting the cathedral's originally purity of design. Of the many tombs, the best-known is that of noted 15th-century bishop Alfonso de Madrigal, who was called "El Tostado" because of his swarthy complexion. His tomb is found behind the chapel. A small museum on site contains some treasures including an old copy of an El Greco painting and a 15th-century triptych.

FESTIVALS

Since this *is* the village of **Santa Teresa,** a day of fiestas is dedicated to the old gal. Apart from the somber mass in the cathedral, the festivities are like the Fourth of July. People parade through the streets, concerts are held in the main squares, bulls challenge men in tight pants, and the bombs bursting in air give proof through the night that Santa Teresa's finger is still here. The annual activities *(October 8-15)* coincide with *Semana de Flamenco,* a week of Flamenco music, making Ávila a travel brochure for how Spain is typically pictured.

In the first days of September, Avila transforms its market space on the **Plaza Mercado del Chico** into a medieval market that brings back aromas of incense and rosemary from the days when showering once a year was common practice. Puppet shows, jugglers, mock slave auctions, and costumed clergymen entertain the crowds.

Monasterio de Santo Tomas *(Plaza Granada 1; Tel 920/220-400; Bus 1,2,3; Museum 11am-12:45pm/4-6pm daily, Cloisters 10am-1pm/4-8pm Mon-Sun; Museum 200ptas adults, Cloisters 100ptas adults; No credit cards):* The icing on the cake in this Gothic monastery just southeast of the town center are the cloisters. The swirling plant vines and spheres dotting the arches could have been designed by a perfectionist pastry chef. The history here is just as rich—thieves emptied the tombs of Tomás de Torquemada, First Grand Inquisitor of Spain (1420-98), and Prince Juan, the only son of Ferdinand II & Isabella, who died at 19.

EATS

During the Inquisition, the food of the Islamic and Jewish cultures in Ávila was Christianized. Veal, sausages, bacon, and other piggy bits were added to staples like white beans and potatoes. Today, piglet carcasses sprawl out in many restaurant windows, which indicates that it's hard to find a dish that doesn't squeal. Desserts, on the other hand, maintain Islamic and Jewish flavors in almond-based pastries that sometimes contain pine nuts. The most renowned sweet, and perhaps the most rejected by visitors, is the *yema de Santa Teresa,* a sugared egg yolk that looks like it could be yummy, but can be pretty hard to swallow. Go for it anyway—you only live once.

▶▶CHEAP

Among the *menus turisticas* you'll find plenty of overpriced basic meals that you could throw together at home. **La Cañita** *(Enrique Larreta 3; Tel 920/255-307; Bus 1 to Mercado Chico; Bar 10am-11pm, Restaurant 1-4pm daily; Menu 1,100ptas; V, MC)* is an exception only in price. At night the bar serves up tapas and nibbles, but the kitchen is open for full meals at lunchtime, with wine, bread, and dessert part of the deal. Pasta with a tomato and chorizo sauce and a thin beef filet with home-cut fries and topped off with fresh melon satisfies the wanderer who's weary from menu hunting. The fluorescent-lit restaurant, like the food, is no frills, but you'll pay another 800ptas for the same basic meal at the tourist restaurants just a block away.

▶▶**DO-ABLE**

If you're going the porcine route, try the more traditional dishes at **El Rastro** *(Plaza del Rastro; Tel 920/211-219; Bus 1 to Arco del Rastro; 1-4pm/9-11pm daily; Menu 1,700-2,500ptas; AE, V, MC, Din)*. Castilian cuisine tends to include a lot of young critters, so roast baby lamb and veal are a couple of the many meaty house specialties...and what typical Ávila restaurant would be complete without the *yema de Santa Teresa* dessert? This old tavern, which is adjacent to a hostel, would feel authentically medieval if it weren't for the other tourists soaking it up.

crashing

The tourist office map handed out at the train station or on the Plaza de la Catedral has a short list with phone numbers of all the lodgings in Ávila, but they won't reserve for you. Dig out that phrase book and give the hotels a call to make sure you have a bed for the night, but don't worry about making reservations days or weeks in advance.

▶▶**CHEAP**

The nationally run **Parador Hotel** pales in comparison to its neighbor, the **Don Diego**—just kidding. Jokes aside, Don Diego *(Marqués de Canales y Chozas 5; Tel 920/255-475, Fax 920/254-549; Bus 1 to Mercado Chico; 3,000-4,000ptas single, 4,800-5,800ptas double; AE, V, MC)* is a good option if you can't afford the upscale Parador, which is a 15th-century palace-cum-luxury hotel. If you paid Don Diego prices at the

TO MARKET

Every week since the days of the Catholic Ferdinand II and Isabella, Ávila has been home to colorful open-air markets. On Fridays, people make the rounds to three different markets, each selling something different. Produce and ceramics are sold in the **Plaza Mercado del Chico,** an odd mix, but you gotta have a bowl to put the salad in. Handbags, clothing, and fabric are up for grabs in the **Atrio de San Isidro,** and farmers bring livestock to the **Mercado Grande,** just in case you want to bring home a real live bull.

Parador, they'd stick you in the broom closet, so you'll do well coming across the street where the rooms have bathrooms and all that jazz. You don't get a key for the street door, which is annoying (even though there's no curfew), but really doesn't matter since the town goes to bed early.

Other options on the cheap end of things are **Pension Continental** *(Plaza Catedral 6; Tel 920/211-502; Fax 920/251-691; Singles without bath 2,500ptas; Doubles without baths 4,300ptas; Doubles with bath 5,500ptas; V, MC, AE);* **Hostal Casa Felipe** *(Plaza Victoria 12; Tel 920/213-924; Singles without bath 2,800ptas; doubles with bath 5,800ptas; V, MC);* and **Hostal Las Cancelas** *(Calle De La Cruz Vieja 6; Tel 920/212-249; Fax 920/212-230; Singles 5,500ptas, doubles 8,500ptas, all rooms with private bath; V, MC, AE).*

▶▶DO-ABLE

Walk through the city gate and stay at the former Palacio Abrantes, now called **El Rastro** *(Plaza del Rastro 4; Tel 920/211-218, Fax 920/251-626; Bus 1 to Arco del Rastro; Doubles 6,350ptas; No credit cards).* It sounds romantic and extravagant, but the rooms are basic with a lot of character. They only have 10 (with bathrooms and TVs), so this old inn built into the city wall is often *completo* during the summer and festival season. A typical *meson,* the old-fashioned, family-style restaurant El Rastro draws people downstairs to eat so much they can't move and have to spend the night (see *eats,* above).

The welcome at **Hotel Antonio** *(Avda José Antonio 27; Tel 920/227-689, Fax 920/222-979; Bus 1 to Renfe; 6,000-8,500ptas double; V, MC)* is less than friendly, but it is convenient: Stepping off the train, you'll practically fall into their door, and a bus to the old center leaves from the same corner for an easy commute to the sights. You may be inspired to pull your hair into a side ponytail and sing Duran Duran while you skip down the halls (the decor is horridly '80s and pink) but the rooms aren't bad. You can veg out on late-night TV when the town shuts down, and enjoy not having to wait in line for the shower for a change—each room has its own!

Other do-able options are **Gran Hostal San Segundo** *(Calle De San Segundo 28; Tel 920/252-690; Rooms off season 5,000-6,000ptas, Summer 7,000-8,000ptas, all rooms with private bath; V, MC),* located just outside the eastern walls of the old city; and **Hostal San Juan** *(Calle De Los Comuneros De Castillo; Tel 920/213-198;),* in the old city center a few blocks from Inglesia San Juan.

If you simply must stay in a deluxe hotel, **Gran Hotel Palacio De Valderrabanos** *(Plaza Catedral 9; Tel 800/528-12-34, 920/255-200, Fax 920/251-691, doubles 15,000ptas, suite 25,000ptas, all rooms with private bath; V, MC, AE),* is right next to the entrance of the Catedral de Ávila.

NEED TO KNOW

Currency Exchange There are a few banks in the historic center with **ATM** access, which often gives a better exchange rate than the bank itself.

Tourist Information Right outside the train station, a summer tourist information stand has maps and colorful brochures you can cut apart for your scrapbook. The moody women at the **tourist office** *(Plaza Catedral; Tel 920/211-387; Bus 1 to Plaza Catedral; 10am-2pm/4-7pm Mon-Fri, 9:30am-2pm/4-7pm Sat, 9:30am-2pm/4:30-8:30pm Sun Apr-Oct, 10am-2pm/5-8pm Mon-Fri, 9:30am-2pm Sat Nov-Mar)* in front of the Catedral will throw flyers at you and point you in the right direction.

Public Transportation **Ávila Buses** run through the new and old parts of town inside and outside of the walls (we're hard pressed to imagine why you'd want to go to the new town, however). Pay the driver 90ptas a ride *(Tel 920/252-411).*

Health and Emergency Emergency: *Tel 920/222-222;* Fire: *080;* National police: *091,* City police: *092;* local hospital: **Hospital Provincial** *(Jesús del Gran Poder 42; Tel 920/357-200)*

Pharmacies Look for the **green flashing crosses** scattered around town. The pharmacies rotate night shifts, so check the local paper for the *Farmacia de guardia* of the day.

Trains Trains to Madrid leave about every 60 minutes from 6:15am-8:30pm daily from the **Renfe** train station *(Avenida de José Antonio 40; Tel 920/250-202; Bus 1 Renfe),* about a half mile northeast of the city center.

Bus Lines Out of the City Buses to Madrid, Segovia, Salamanca, Valladolid, Cuenca, and Sevilla leave from **Avenida de Madrid 2** *(Tel 920/220-154; Bus 1),* about halfway between the city center and the train station.

Telephone Country Code: *34;* city code: *920;* info: *1003;* international operator: *1005.* International calls dial *00* then area code and so on. You can use either coins or *tarjetas telefónicas* (phonecards) that you buy at tobacco shops.

Postal The most convenient post office Correos y Telégrafos is on the Plaza de la Catedral 2 *(Tel 920/211-354).*

segovia

If you come to Segovia on the weekend or in the summer, expect to run into tourists tied up in camera straps, daytrippers from Madrid, and students from the local university avoiding their studies. And for good reason: It's a great place to escape the shoving and pickpocketing of Madrid, to relax by the two rivers, Eresma and Clamores, and to gaze at the Guadarrama mountain range from the top of the town. Quite a few Segovians live off the tourist trade, so they don't mind the thousands passing through, and thankfully, none of that city grime or stress seems to have rubbed off on them. People take it easy in this town and don't rush life.

The old center, *el casco antiguo,* is the most interesting part of Segovia, and it sits like an island between the rivers, up on a rocky pedestal. Per-

segovia

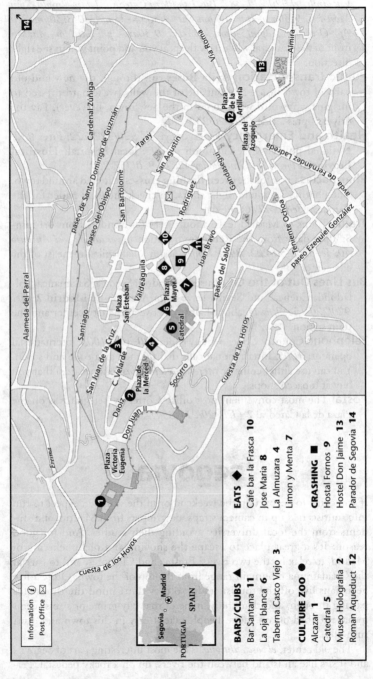

EATS ◆
Cafe bar la Frasca **10**
Jose Maria **8**
La Almuzara **4**
Limon y Menta **7**

CRASHING ■
Hostal Fornos **9**
Hostel Don Jaime **13**
Parador de Segovia **14**

BARS/CLUBS ▲
Bar Santana **11**
La oja blanca **6**
Taberna Casco Viejo **3**

CULTURE ZOO ●
Alcazar **1**
Catedral **5**
Museo Holografia **2**
Roman Aqueduct **12**

Information ℹ
Post Office ✉

PORTUGAL
SPAIN
Segovia ○ ⊛ Madrid

haps it's this unforgettable setting that has attracted crowds throughout the years, or maybe it's the incredibly blue sky that often stretches over the town. Whatever the reason or the season, the changing backdrop of snow-topped mountains, blossoming springs, golden summers, and rainbow autumns has made Segovia a worthy stop for centuries.

This town has seen many faces and passed through many hands, and everyone left an impression, changing, replacing, or amplifying the art, architecture, and culture. Before 100 B.C. the Romans had a military presence here. Then the Arabs came to establish a wool and textile industry until the Christians booted them out in 1085 B.C. After that, the Spanish set up camp, and Segovia became a seat for royalty. Queen Isabel the Catholic was crowned here, and you can go check out her throne room in the big Disney World-looking castle, the **Alcázar** [see *culture zoo,* below]. (The similarity is no coincidence—Walt Disney used the place as his model in California.)

From the arching Roman aqueducts to the towering Gothic cathedral, you'll find yourself unsuspectingly carried up and down the streets **Calle Cervantes, Juan Bravo, Plaza del Corpus,** and **Isabel la Católica,** which lead you to the **Plaza Mayor,** again and again. Plaza Mayor stands at the very heart of the historic old city; there you'll find a string of hotels, tapas bars, and eateries. The main pedestrian street is known by various names, but most often **Calle Real.** It's lined with clothing shops, postcard and camera stores, restaurants, and gaggles of pedestrians. Reaching the Plaza Mayor, where the town's social life stirs, you may want to stop in the square to sip a coffee or beer when the sun warms the wheat-colored Gothic, Romanesque, and Baroque buildings. Right off the Plaza is the **Calle de la Infanta Isabel,** which you'll soon discover is also known as the *Calle de Los Bares,* or "Street of Bars." A five minute walk south from the Plaza Mayor leads to the **Paseo de Salon,** a promenade at the city's southern walls which is worth visiting for the panorama alone. Another major pedestrian shopping street is **Calle Cervantes,** which runs through the southern section of Segovia east to **Plaza del Azoguejo,** which used to be the town center and chief marketplace.

Segovia is rather small, so you don't have to go too far to get to where you need to be. Not that you *need* to be anywhere at any particular time here; Segovians set their own pace, slowly strolling through the streets with their families, amicably rubbing shoulders with packs of frenzied tourists. Ah, the lessons to be learned.

hanging OUT

You won't be smashing a beer can on your head or chanting home team anthems in Segovia. The bar scene here is *tranquilo,* just like the way of life. People really enjoy going out, and you'll see them eating and drinking all over town. Warmer weather brings 'em out of the woodwork to the *terrazas* in the fresh air. You can casually sip and snack in the Plazas San Martín and Mayor, or mosey over to the Calle de la Infanta Isabel for a drink.

wired

Ludos-la truncolorum *(José Zorrilla 26; Tel 921/444-469; 1pm-2:30am Sun-Thurs, till 3:30am Fri-Sat; No credit cards)* isn't exactly a convenient Internet connection, since it's a 10-15 minute walk from the center of town—but hey, it's also a bar. From the aqueduct, take San Francisco to Muerte y Vida, and pass through Plaza de Somorrostro to Puente de Muerte y Vida, a street that takes you to José Zorrilla. Grab a beer, play darts, or sing karaoke (fortunately only on the weekends). The computers are in little booths that match the art deco look of the place, and are coin-operated for 300ptas per half hour. There's no food here besides chips and olives.

On the Plaza Mayor, where you can tapas-hop in circles if you choose, make sure to include **la oja blanca** [see *eats*, below] in your circuit. The old-fashioned, classic-looking bar stops serving monster tapas around 11:30pm, when it dims the lights and turns off the daytime soft oldies tunes. But don't be deceived by the low lights; locals and tourists who know best grab at least one round here—unofficial closing is around 3:30 in the morning.

bar scene

While Segovia's nightlife is pretty mellow, there's also the aptly nick-named Calle de Los Bares (Calle Infanta Isabel), a street full of bars that give Segovia's nightlife a bit more oomph. On this narrow little street, you'll bump into Spanish and foreign students consuming time, tapas, *cañas* (little beers), and perhaps a puff or two. It's also not out of the ordi-nary to spot folks discreetly rolling and passing a (hash) joint.

Start off and end up at **Bar Santana-Galería/Cervecería** *(Calle Infanta Isabel 18; Tel 921/463-564; 10:30am-between 3am and 5am daily; Beer with tapas 140ptas; No credit cards)* on Calle Infanta Isabel. The tapas are homemade (try the potatoes!), and the scene is like family. Two brothers own this bar/art gallery, and they live by the motto "Rock and tapas." Show up on Thursdays for the free concerts (rock, funk, and the like) starting at 10pm.

From the Plaza Mayor, follow the streets Escuderos and Covarrubias right by the Plaza San Esteban and you'll find **Taberna Casco Viejo** *(Calle Vallejo; Tel 921/461-031; Beer 150ptas, mixed drinks 550ptas; No credit cards)*, a place with a lot of history. Painter Mauricio Fromques used to live here, if you know who he is. It was a bar way back in the 1870s, and it re-opened as one again about 10 years ago. Wander up the warped wooden stairs, take a seat at one of the tables near the ivy-covered wrought iron window, and chill out with friends over a beer and a game of Parcheesi.

In the center of town, **Bar Plato** *(Corner of Calle Hermano Baral and Calle Fernand de la Vereda; Tel 921/46-93-18; Mon-Fri noon-4am; No credit cards)* fills up early in the evening with tapas-devouring locals and a mixture of international tourists, and is taken over later by the heavy wine drinkers. Although this is not a dinner place, it's easy to fill up on the tapas, especially if the local specialty, *cochinillo asado* (roast suckling pig), is being dished out.

CuLTurE ZOO

There's no avoiding a cultural tour of Segovia: You'll keep running into monuments, churches, and palaces at every turn. The three things that you really can't miss (and that end up on postcards the most) are the aqueduct, the cathedral, and the Alcázar, which form a line right through the center of town. Strolling from one point to the next up the Calle Real, you'll encounter other photo-worthy churches, plazas, and architectural highlights.

Roman aqueduct: The aqueduct borders the Plaza Azoguejo, but you can't miss the long bridge of arches that transported water in the first century. Pulling out one of the stones (don't you even think about it!) would be like playing a giant game of Jenga—there's no mortar or cement holding them together!

Catedral de Segovia *(Plaza Mayor, Calle Marqués del Arco; Tel 921/462-205; 9am-7pm Sun-Fri, 9:30am-6pm Sat and holidays; Cathedral free; Cloisters, museum, and chapel room 250ptas):* It's easy to see why she's known as *"la dama de las catedrales."* Built in the 16th century, the Lady of Cathedrals is the last Gothic cathedral constructed in Spain, and she was adorned with even more curves and feminine characteristics than those that came before her. The monument is filled with treasures, including some stunning stained-glass windows, exquisitely carved choir stalls, and, its chief treasure, the flamboyant Blessed Sacrament Chapel. On site is a cathedral museum with a collection of rare antique manuscripts, jewelry, and more religious art.

El Alcázar *(Plaza de La Reina Victoria Eugenia; Tel 921/460-759; 10am-7pm daily Apr-Sept; 10am-6pm daily Oct-Mar; 375ptas admission):* The palace for Spanish royalty, not Tinkerbell, sits high on its perch, making for an awesome panoramic view—if you're willing to climb the old prisoners' tower. On the far western promontory of the old city, the Alcázar may even predate Roman times, although what you see today is an architectural pile created betwen the 14th and 16th centuries. Gutted by a monstrous fire in 1862, it was massively restored and now looks a bit like a faux-medieval chateau. The only really authentic element is the keep from the original structure which forms the entrance today. It was at this castle that the terrible Isabella of Castile met the even more terrible Ferdinand of Aragón. In the throne room, the two throne replicas are on equal landings, as Isabella insisted on retaining her royal rights after mar-

FESTIVALS

The festivals of **San Juan** and **San Pedro** *(June 24-29)* bring on the bulls, parades, music, and fiestas. "La Noche de San Juan" kicks things off on June 24, with bands, theater performances, and swarms of people in the Plaza San Nicolas.

During the first or second week of May, **Titirimundi,** *(www.titirimundi.com),* a marionette and puppet festival, takes place all over the city. International performers hide behind curtains, set up flea circuses, raise the pitch of their voices, and get kids bug-eyed and laughing at their slapstick humor. When the puppets are in town, it's hard not to revert to age five.

riage. More fascinating than the castle's interior is a walk along its battlements where former residents tossed boiling oil onto any invaders trying to scale the castle from below.

EATS

If you've eaten in Spain at least once, you can probably guess what Segovia's specialty is. Yup, another pig product—actually the *whole* pig: *Cochinillo asado* (roast suckling pig). Whole, not-yet-roasted little piggies sit in restaurant windows to entice you to come in. Other than that, there's a big white bean stew called *judiones de la Granja* that warms you in the winter and is sure to add a little extra padding on the hips. It expands fourfold in your stomach 10 minutes after you stand up from the table, and you'll thank God or whomever for the siesta. Although it's a little strange, you may be compelled to try Segovia's specialty dessert, *yemas* (egg yolks loaded with sugar), which are best downed with a cup of coffee. You can find these, other pastries, and *violetas imperials* (hard candies) at **Limon y menta** *(Calle Isabel la Católica 2; Tel 921/462-141; 9:30am-9:30pm daily; No credit cards)* on a corner right near the Plaza Mayor. There are restaurants and bars everywhere, but the ones around the Plaza Mayor are always choice for the scenery and people watching.

▶▶CHEAP

Right on the Plaza Mayor, the atmosphere is old-fashioned, polite, and family-style at **la oja blanca** *(Plaza Mayor 7; Tel 921/460-894; 7am-3am Wed-Mon; Sandwiches 800ptas, tapas 150ptas; No credit cards)*. You can get sandwiches at the bar, but the real reason to come here is the huge tapas they slide over to you with your beer. You can choose from paella, tortillas, sardines, soup (in winter), or any other nibble that's on display.

Cleaner and newer than your typical corner tapas bar, **Café-Bar La Frasca** *(Plaza de la Rubia 6; Tel 921/461-038; 9am-2am Mon-Fri, 10am-2am Sat-Sun, hot food till 1am; Raciones 1,000ptas, sandwiches 400-750ptas;*

No credit cards) is just a few steps behind Plaza Mayor. Their fresh baguette sandwiches and *raciones* (portions) of shrimp, omelet, and croquettes are key for the munchies. There's a full bar, with vermouth from the barrel and spiked or flavored coffee to savor while looking at the old poster art.

▶▶**DO-ABLE**

Vegetarians who get a little squeamish at the sight of those baby pigs and unidentifiable animals displayed in restaurant windows, have no fear—**La Almuzara** *(Marqués del Arco 3; Tel 921/460-622; 1-5pm/8pm-midnight Wed-Sun, 8pm-midnight Tue; Entrees 1,000 ptas; V)* is here. You can see the cathedral out of the corner of your eye from one of the tables (it's located just west of Plaza Mayor), and you'll have plenty of time to gaze at it: The wait for salads, crepes, lasagna, tofu, pizza, or whatever you order can be long, so don't come famished. If you're hurried and few in number, sit at the small barstools for faster service.

▶▶**SPLURGE**

Go for the rustic, go for the suckling pig at **José María** *(Cronista Lecea 11; Tel 921/461-111; Bar 10am-1am, restaurant 1-4pm/8-11:30pm Daily; Entrees 1,500-2,000ptas; AE, V, MC, DC)*. This is a super-typical Spanish spot with regional specialties and no-nonsense decor, located just east of Plaza Mayor. The fixed-price menu is 4,000-6,000ptas, and from the a la carte menu you can choose ham, salmon, shrimp, eel, or hake, to name a few.

crashing

You can find cheaper accommodation in Madrid and make Segovia a day trip, but that's what thousands do. You'll want to sleep over and have the evening, and town, more to yourself. The waves of tourists dissipate later in the day, and the locals take to wandering the streets and enjoying the extra elbowroom. You'll find a few hotels and *hostales* to lay your weary head on Calle Juan Bravo and around the Plaza Mayor in the *casco antiguo*.

▶▶**CHEAP**

Near the aqueduct, you'll find **Hostal Don Jaime** *(Ochoa Ondátegui 8; Tel 921/444-787; 3,000-3,200ptas single, 5,300-5,600ptas double, 6,500-7,000ptas triple; V, MC)*. Here you have the option of walking down the hall to the bath or not, depending on how much you want to pay, but all rooms have a little sink, TV, and phone. The building is old (like, what isn't in these Euro towns?) but the rooms are clean and in good shape.

Other cheap options are **Pension Ferri** *(C. Escuderos 10; Tel 921/460-957; Singles 1,750ptas, doubles 2,500ptas, 325ptas for use of shared bath; No credit cards)* and **Hostal Juan Bravo** *(C. Juan Bravo 12, 2nd Fl; Tel 921/463-413; Doubles without bath, low season 4,300ptas; Doubles without bath, high season 4,600ptas; doubles with bath, low season 4,700ptas, doubles with bath, high season 5,200ptas; V, MC, AE)*.

▶▶**DO-ABLE**

This site used to be an historical hotel way back when, and has recently reopened as **Hostal Fornos** *(Calle Infanta Isabel 13, reception at Bar*

Santana [see *bars*, above]; *Tel 921/460-198; 6,000-8,000ptas doubles; V, MC).* Walk through the front door and into the room with the white curtains blowing in from the balcony, and you'll feel like you're on a honeymoon. Each room has stencils painted on the headboard in cool pastels. All rooms have full baths and TVs. It's a little lap of luxury, right on the Calle Infanta Isabel.

Other do-able options are **Hostal El Hidalgo** *(Calle De Jose Canalejas 3-5; Tel 921/463-529; Private baths; Singles, low season 3,975ptas, summer 4,975ptas; doubles, low season 4,975ptas, summer 5,975ptas, all with private bath; V, MC),* right in the city center two minutes from Plaza Mayor; **Hotel Las Sirenas** *(Calle De Juan Bravo 30; Tel 921/462-663; Fax 921/462-657; Singles 5,500ptas, doubles 8,500ptas, all rooms with private baths; V, MC);* and **Hostal Plaza** *(Calle Cronista Lecea 11; Tel 921 460-303; Singles 4,500ptas, doubles 5,600ptas, all rooms with private bath; V, MC),* a few blocks southeast of the cathedral.

▶▶SPLURGE

A para-who? A *parador* is usually an old palace or church that the state has converted into a lux hotel. In some cases, however, the hotel is a newer construction, as is the grandiose **Parador de Segovia** *(Carretera Valladolid, s/n; Tel 921/443-737, Fax 921/437-362; 14,000ptas single, 19,795ptas double, from 29,425ptas suite; AE, V, MC, DC).* It's so cushy that you may never get around to visiting Segovia's other sights: Pools, gardens, and a panoramic view of that famous Segoviano sky will keep you on the premises for hours. It's also 3 kilometers (1.8 miles) from the town's center, and unfortunately, the only way to get here without your own car is on foot or by taxi [see *need to know,* below].

need to know

Currency Exchange Most banks change foreign money. You'll have the most luck finding one on or around **Avenida de Fernández Ladreda, Calle Cervantes,** and **Calle Juan Bravo.** ATMs are also a good way to get low current rates and are attached to the banks.

Tourist Info There are two main **tourist offices,** one on the **Plaza Mayor** *(Plaza Mayor 10, Tel 921/460-334; 10am-2pm/5-8pm daily)* and the other down by the Roman aqueducts on the **Plaza del Azoguejo** *(Plaza del Azoguejo 1, Tel 921/462-906; 10am-2pm/5-8pm daily).* You can get maps and general brochure stuff at the Plaza Mayor, and if there are any events on, they've usually got the schedules. But though they will give you info on local hotels, they won't actually make the reservations for you.

Public Transportation There are **city buses,** but you won't really need them. In the center of the old town, it's not that far from one end to the other. The only bus ride you may want to take is from the train station to the center on Bus 3. Find bus info at **Transportes Urbanos de Segovia** *(Plaza Mayor 8; Tel 921/460-329).* Twenty-four-hour **taxis** *(Tel 921/445-000)* are the only other way around. Call or try flagging one in the Plaza Mayor.

Health and Emergency Medical emergency (ambulances): *Tel 921/460 000.* There Are Two Hospitals, **Hospital Policlínico** *(San Agustín 13; Tel 921/419-298)* and **Hospital General** *(Crta. de Soria; Tel 921/419-100 or 921/419-065).*

Pharmacies Look for the **green flashing crosses** scattered around town. There's at least one on the **Calle Juan Bravo** near the Plaza Mayor.

Telephone City code: *921;* local operator: *010;* international operator: *1005.* International calls dial *00* then the area code, and so on. You can use either coins or *tarjetas telefónicas* (phonecards) that you buy at tobacco shops.

Trains The **Renfe** station *(Plaza del Obispo Quesada, s/n; Tel 921/420-774),* is either a 20-minute walk northwest to town, or a short ride on Bus 3. You can catch a train to Madrid here.

Bus Lines Out of the City Estacionamiento Municipal de Autobuses *(Po. Ezequiel González 10; Tel 921/427-725)* is where 10 to 15 Madrid buses come in and depart each day. Walking to the center from the station, take Avenida Fernandez Ladreda, which will lead you straight to the Roman aqueducts and Plaza Azoguejo—it's about a 3m walk. The ride is 825ptas one-way to Madrid. **La Sepulvedana** is the bus company in Madrid serving Segovia *(Paseo de la Florida 11; Metro to Principe Pio; Tel 915/304-800).*

Postal Postcards and telegrams can be sent from the **main post office** *(Plaza del Docoter Laguna 5, Tel 921/461-616).*

Internet See *wired,* above.

LEÓN

Set between the plains and the mountains in northern Castilla y León, León is a city with a storied past and a prosperous present. It fuses the old and new together into a seamless, very appealing entity. León got its name not from 'lion'—although that has become a symbol of the city—but from the Latin *legio,* meaning "legion"; the city got its start as a barracks for a Roman legion that was sent here to protect a gold mine in 70 A.D. León served as the capital of the Asturian kingdom in the 10th century as the Christians were chasing the Moors from their lands. During this time the city flourished as both a religious and commercial center, with rich agricultural lands outside the city and precious metals mined from the nearby mountains. A main stop along the pilgrim's route to Santiago de Compostela, León also enjoyed a steady stream of travelers.

Then in 1230 León merged with the Castile kingdom and soon the city began to fade from glory, a downward spiral that continued until the 19th century, when the city's economy was restored largely by mining. In the 20th century, more industry moved in, the university grew, and the restoration of historic monuments such as the cathedral led to a boom in tourism.

león

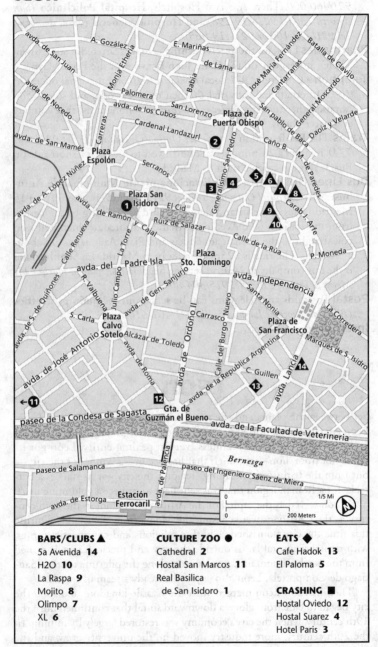

BARS/CLUBS ▲
5a Avenida **14**
H2O **10**
La Raspa **9**
Mojito **8**
Olimpo **7**
XL **6**

CULTURE ZOO ●
Cathedral **2**
Hostal San Marcos **11**
Real Basilica
  de San Isidoro **1**

EATS ◆
Cafe Hadok **13**
El Paloma **5**

CRASHING ■
Hostal Oviedo **12**
Hostal Suarez **4**
Hotel Paris **3**

León has long been a favorite with student travelers from abroad because of its *chocolaterias* where you can meet fellow students; for the narrow, twisting streets of the old town with its copious bars; for its antique bookstores and boutique-lined boulevards; and for its great monuments, none more notable than its soaring Gothic **cathedral,** famous for its stained-glass windows. It's fun to spend a day or two here checking out the monuments in the morning and spending the late afternoon and evening at one of the popular student hangouts clustered around old town's **Plaza Mayor** or **Plaza San Martin.** These squares are packed with tapas bars, and you can go on a bar crawl, sampling the local wine and enjoying a pinchito (tidbit) as you stroll from one haunt to the other. On the weekends the bars in the **Húmedo** district explode in a lively *marcha* that seems to be enjoyed by everyone between the ages of 16 and 60. Clubs keep people moving until early in the morning.

The people of León—the *Leones*—are relaxed and casual, as most people in Spain are. They enjoy long meals and plenty of wine with friends. They talk about their city with pride and are more than willing to offer advice to visitors so they can enjoy the city, too. The people of León are by far the best resource to find out what's going on in town. Ask them what bars are hot and half the time they'll bring you there and party with you. Another option is to check out the local paper, *El Diario de León,* which has some listings of upcoming cultural events, movies, music, and recreational schedules.

neighborhoods

The center of León is not that big, so getting around is easy. The train and bus stations are on the western side of the **Río Bernesga.** To reach the center of town, cross the bridge near the stations and walk 15 minutes east, along **Avenida de Ordoño II.** This major thoroughfare is lined with banks and shops as well as some hotels as it makes it way through **San Marcelo,** the modern commercial center of León. There are plenty of restaurants and shops on the side streets as well as a bunch of budget *hostales* on the northeast bank of the river off **Glorieta Guzman el Bueno.** This is the traffic circle on the east side of the bridge you'll cross on your way into town from the train and bus station.

As you continue east through San Marcelo, Avda de Ordoño II changes into **Calle Ancha** (sometimes referred to by its former name, Generalisimo Franco, by those nostalgic for the good ol' days of fascism) as it bisects the city's old town. To the north is where the cathedral, basilica, and old city walls can be found. To the south stretches a neighborhood known as **Barrio Húmedo** (the "Wet Quarter"...the name will make sense after you spend an evening imbibing here), the social center of León. The twisting streets of this medieval quarter hide many great restaurants and bars. During the weekends the city's *marcha* is centered here and people crowd the streets until well past 3am. The heart of Húmedo is **Plaza San Martín** [see *hanging out,* below], a block west of the Plaza Mayor.

four things to talk to a local about

1. **Lions**—Ask locals where the symbol came from and why it's appropriate. Tell them they don't deserve it and you may just hear a mighty roar.
2. **The Cathedral**—Lots of cities in Spain claim to be home to the greatest cathedral, and not everyone in León agrees that theirs is the best. Ask them where they think the greatest one lies.
3. **León's connection to Asturias**—As it was once a part of Asturias, some people believe León's ties are still closer to its neighbor to the north than to Castilla y León.
4. **Madrid vs. Barcelona**—Get an unbiased opinion on the age-old question of which is the greatest Spanish city.

The public transportation system of León is very limited so your best option for getting around is your own two feet. In the older neighborhoods many streets are open only to pedestrians anyway, so buses can't be of much service there.

hanging out

Plaza de San Martín serves as a social center at any time of day or night. On the weekends—be it 2pm, with groups gathering at one of the many cafes, or 2am, with people hanging out between bar visits—people are always here maxin' and relaxin'. This is one of the best places in the city to come and meet the locals. Needless to say, getting a seat at one of the outdoor cafes here puts you in a great position to people-watch.

A more relaxed place to hang out is **Jardines Papalaguinda,** which runs along the eastern bank of the Río Bernesga. This a pleasant park with paths lined with benches overlooking the river. Here families and friends come to enjoy a little solitude, away from the bustling city.

If you want to meet other travelers, the best places to start looking are near the city's major attractions. **Plaza Regla,** right in front of the cathedral, is usally filled with slack-jawed foreigners staring in awe at the cathedral. You're bound to hear many languages spoken. Make a pithy comment about the cathedral (compare the weightlessness of its medieval interior with the modern work of Mies van der Rohe, for example) and in no time at all you should know a couple of other people in town. Another spot is **Plaza San Marcos** right outside the **Hostal San Marcos** [see *cultural zoo,* below]. Although the tourists here tend to be older, it's a great place to share travel tips and destinations and find out about some other "must-see" attractions close by.

bar scene

The bar scene in León is a lively one that attracts Leones of all ages. The weekend is without a doubt the undisputed king of the week when it comes to partying, but often people can't wait to get started and Thursday nights see a moderate crowd. In general, during the week most bars close around 3-4am, depending largely on how full they are. During the weekend, though, bars don't really think of closing their doors before 5am and most will stay open as long as there is a crowd, until 6 or 7am—which all makes sense when you realize nobody hits the bars till at least 11 (most of them open around 9). The general style among people is to dress prep. Although none of the bars have any kind of a dress code, Spaniards like to look good (if prep is your idea of good, of course...).

The nightlife revolves around two areas in León—one in the old town, one in the new. The largest is the **Húmedo** neighborhood, where bars line the twisting streets and the plazas become just as crowded as the bars. **H20** (c/ Zapaterias 14) is a good place to start a night off. People usually make it one of their first stops, to take advantage of the free pinchos that are served with drinks. They're nothing special, usually just a small

wired

León will take good care of all you partying Internet addicts. There are several fun bars around town where you can get a drink, play some pool, do some dancing, and check your Hotmail all at the same time. How's that for complete entertainment? The king of them all is **Café Hadok** (c/ Santisteban y Osorio 9; 1pm-4am daily), at the south end of Avenida Republica Argentina. This bar has three pool tables, darts, and seven coin-operated Internet hook-ups. The monitors are recessed and placed under glass so they become great tables, too; just try not to spill your drink. Downstairs there is a large dance floor where at night a dj spins house and dance music. It's a popular spot with young people in the city and draws a lot of university students conducting, ummm... research. The fashion sketches decorating the walls bear evidence that this is one stylish joint.

If mere computing is all you want to do, right around the corner is the much more functional **Lokura** (Avda Luncia 7; 10am-when-ever the crowd dwindles, except Sun nights when it closes at midnight). This place has lots of computers with decent Internet connections. Although not as wild as Hadok, Lokura can be a good spot to meet people from the city as you catch up on affairs back home.

by foot

After a long night of overindulgence in the bars in Húmedo, there's only one way to shake off that groggy feeling—a peaceful, culturally stimulating walk. Start out in **Plaza Regla** facing the cathedral. Stare up at the cathedral in wonderment. Aren't you a little jealous of all those storks that have set up permanent residence within the spires of the cathedral? Turn to your left and head north along **Calle Florez.** This is a quiet residential street where you can start to get your brain in gear. When the street ends you should head into the **Fundacion Vela Zanetti** [see *visual arts,* below] and see the amazing *Mural de los Derechos Humanos.* Come out of the museum and continue along **Calle Pablo** (pretty much your only option to continue without backtracking when Calle Florez ends). Take the time as you walk to ponder exactly what the rights of humans are. Before you get lost in that thought you will come upon the **Puerta Castilla.** Built into the old city walls, this was one of the entrance gates into the old city. What remains of the wall is best seen from this point, as it stretches above the apartments in both directions. Head through the gate and take your first left, following the outside of the old wall. Continue a block or so until you reach the end of the street. From here take a left onto **Ramón y Cajal.** Walk one block along the western wall of the city's basilica. Take a right into the Plaza San Isidoro, enter the basilica, and check out the Pantéon, considered by some the best remaining example of Romanesque art in Europe. Pretty, isn't it? Head straight out of the basilica south along **El Cid.** Grab a quiet seat in the **Jardines el Cid** a block south, sit down with your trusty guidebook, and figure out how you're going to spend the rest of the day now that you're awake and functioning.

sandwich, but they're free until the supply runs out sometime around 1am. The crowd is well mixed and fairly casual.

Calle Zapaterias has a lot of bars on it, including **El Chupito** *(Calle Zapaterias 11).* This is a tiny, walk-up shot bar with a ton of exotic concoctions to choose from. Most shots cost around 400ptas. If you're just passing by and want to add a little edge to your buzz, they have a 'walk-through' window opening onto the street.

Plaza San Martín always sees crowds spilling into it from all the bars. It's a great central spot with lots of options nearby. **Mojito** *(c/ Misericordia 7),* right off the plaza, brings an air of the tropics to northern Spain, with exotic mixed drinks, palm fronds swaying overhead, and salsa/afro-flavored dance music. Just around the corner from the Plaza

San Martín is the popular *puff,* **XL** *(c/ Ramiro III 9; Beer 300ptas, mixed drinks 550ptas).* This place is bigger than it first appears—two rooms upstairs and two down below provide patrons with four bars, which eliminates any waiting around for a drink. Upstairs is more of a traditional bar scene; downstairs has disco lights and plenty of room to dance. A lot of Spanish pop and dance music is played, much to the delight of the twenty- and thirtysomething crowd. If you show up here and it seems beat, give it a little time. Some groups save this for the last stop of the night, while others make it the pre-disco spot. It's pretty much always happening, with different crowds coming and going.

The other place to find bars in León is along **Calle del Conde Guillen** and **Avda de Lancia** in the southern part of town. The bars here seem to appeal most to the university crowds and are usually at their peak both early in the night and very late. One of the more popular places is **Café 5a Avenida** *(Avda Lancia 9).* With a DJ spinning trance and hip-hop under the black lights, you could easily get lost in the atmosphere here if it weren't for the foosball table that always seems to have a heated game in process. Two bars here to make sure everyone is served in a timely fashion.

LIVE MUSIC

When it comes to live music, the options become limited and the quality questionable. There are no venues in León that specialize in bringing in bands for concerts, and most of the bars here seem content with offering their crowds recorded music, or maybe they'll go as far as to have a dj. The scene is more geared to drinking and dancing than standing around and watching a live band perform. So if you want to hear live music, your options are few.

Your best bet for some quality live music is **El Gran Café** *(Calle Cervantes s/n; Tel 987/272-301; 3:30pm-5am daily; 500-1,000ptas cover for shows, starting 11pm Wed, Thurs; V, MC),* a block north of Calle Ancha. This popular, posh bar hosts occasional jazz performances. On these nights, the notes flow over the velvet seats and slide around the chic, martini-sipping crowd. This is also a nice spot to enjoy a drink during the week when some of the other bars in town are slow.

Just north of Plaza de San Martín, **Pub Asi-Tabli** *(c/ Sta Maria del Paramo s/n),* also hosts some live music with the random punk or rock show. However, the bands here are to be enjoyed more for their performance style than their talent, so consider yourself forewarned. The bar posts a schedule of upcoming events in the front window. When bands do play it's usually on a weeknight so as not to interfere with the wild weekend *marcha.*

CLUB SCENE

The clubs of León are not on the scale of those in Madrid or Barcelona. No velvet ropes out front to rein the crowds in, no doormen to look you up and down before giving you either a nod or a "no way" shake of the head. You're not going to find anyone handing out reduced admissions or drink tickets on the street, either. Although all this may sound like a failing club scene, it's actually pretty refreshing, and makes going out in León fun and relaxed.

The clubs and the bars tend to blend a little in León. Basically what distinguishes the clubs is their size and the power of their amps. What also distinguishes the club scene here is that unlike the scene in other Spanish cities—where you go to the bars until 4 or 5am and then head to the clubs—the clubs in León draw crowds a little earlier, but everyone wanders in and out of them as they would a bunch of bars. Here, people will go to a club for a little dancing from 2 to 3am, then head to a neighboring bar for a drink or two, before heading back to one of the clubs.

Most of the clubs are in the Húmedo neighborhood, mixed in with the bars. Partiers are a little more relaxed in dress here than in other areas of Spain, but looking sharp is still the norm. Two principal clubs get people revved up. **Olimpo** (c/ Misericordia 13; Beer 350ptas, mixed drinks 600ptas; No cover) is right on Plaza San Martín. The entrance is in a building with three doors, each leading to different bars. You want to take the door that leads upstairs. The crowds start building in this large open club (with two long bars to keep everyone happy) as early as 2am. A dj spins a lot of house music for all the dancing revelers who pack the place. Basically the whole room becomes a dance floor. The party here is pretty active from 2 to 6am so you have plenty of time to check it out.

The other big club nearby is **La Raspa** (c/ Zapaterias 10; Beer 350ptas, mixed drinks 600ptas; No cover). A young crowd of 18-30 year-olds dances, spins, and grinds on the spacious dance floor. The mainstay music is Spanish club hits, but the djs mix it up with U.S. hits and a little techno. The party at La Raspa usually carries on a little longer than at Olimpo, with things not winding down until after 7am.

ART SCENE

León doesn't exactly have the most cutting-edge art scene in the country. In fact, it doesn't have much of an art scene at all. There are not many galleries that showcase local artists and few theaters where acting troupes are able to perform. This is somewhat surprising considering León's progressive attitude toward other cultural expressions.

▶▶VISUAL ARTS

The one notable gallery in León's otherwise bleak art scene is **Fundacion Vela Zanetti** (Plazuela Villaperez 3; 10am-1pm/5-8pm Tues-Fri, 5-8pm Sat and Sun; Free). The museum houses a collection of Zanetti's works from 1949-68. The top floor is dedicated to his masterpiece, *Mural de los Derechos Humanos* ("Mural of Human Rights"), which is on display at the United Nations. This exhibit includes a full-size replica of the mural as well as many of the sketches and ideas Zanetti worked from during its creation. The second floor has works by Diego Rivera, Orozco, and Siqueiros. Although little on display is original, this is still a really interesting place to visit. It can be found by heading down Calle Florez off to the right of the cathedral. When the road opens onto a little plaza, it is the orange building on the right.

▶▶PERFORMING ARTS

The performing arts scene in León has even less luster than the visual arts scene. **Teatro Emperador** *(Avenida de la Independencia 14; Tel. 987/250-9210)* sits in the center of town just off Plaza Santo Domingo. Normally this theater functions as a movie theater showing the latest big-name picture, often an import from Hollywood. Once in a while, though, the theater hosts dramatic performances. The only way to find out what's going on is to swing by the place; it has a schedule posted outside the box office, which opens at 4pm.

CULTURE ZOO

León's main cultural attractions are religious relics. It was León, after all, that King Ordoño II named as the seat of the Asturian Kingdom in the 10th century, as the Christians tried to push the Moors from their land. One reason for all the religious monuments built around this time might just have been to prove how mighty the Christian God was.

Catedral *(Plaza Regla s/n; Tel 987/875-770; 8:30am-1:30pm/4-8pm daily; Admission 500 ptas):* If León's cathedral was built to put an end to any doubt in the minds of non-Christian skeptics, it should have worked. This great cathedral stands as one of the most beautiful Gothic cathedrals in the country. Coming around the corner from Calle Ancha, you find yourself facing the huge structure, the sole occupant of a small plaza (whose only purpose, it seems, is to provide a place from which to admire the face of the cathedral). The outside is on a level of grandeur that would give a Disney animator a wet dream. Towers covered with ornate mold-ings dwarf the surrounding buildings. The entrance doors are covered with carvings of saints and angels—far too many to count. Once inside, the first thing that strikes you as your eyes adjust to the light is all the stained glass—beautiful, intricate, and everywhere. On bright days sun-light filters through more than 30 stained-glass windows, bathing the cavernous interior in a magical blue glow. The cathedral does lack much of its original wealth of gold and silver, said to have been melted down to help finance the war against Napoleon. Services are held regularly here; check the entrance for times. The **Cathedral Museum** *(9:30am-1:30pm/4-7pm Mon-Fri, 9:30am-1:30pm Sat; 500ptas)* adjoins the cathe-dral and includes a tour of the cloister. There are also religious artworks and relics on display. A visit to the museum is done by tour guide only, in Spanish. Besides the full tour, which lasts an hour and 15 minutes, there is also a 30-minute tour offered for 300ptas.

Real Basilica de San Isidoro *(Plaza San Isidoro s/n; Open all day):* Not far from the cathedral is the basilica. A sign at the entrance reminds visitors that they are entering an active holy place. In the back, through the main chamber, is a room where people fill the pews in silent prayer. Finished in the 11th century, the basilica was used as the burial grounds for almost 50 kings and queens. The 12th-century frescoes covering the

Pantéon are considered by some to be the best remaining examples of Romanesque art in Europe. Try to time your visit at an off-peak time, though, because this is a stop on the holy bus circuit, where busloads of senior citizens wander, somewhat dazed, around the place. If you're the religious type, who enjoys rosaries and confessions (times posted at entrance)—you'll dig it. If you're a person who gets hot over Romanesque art and architecture—you'll dig it. If you're a person with nothing better to do—you'll dig it. But cover the cathedral first.

Hostal San Marcos and **Museo de León** *(Plaza de San Marcos 7; Tel 987/245-061; 10am-2pm/5-8pm Tues-Sat, 10am-2pm Sun; 200ptas):* Somewhat removed from the center of town is the Plaza de San Marcos, which has an old monastery that once housed pilgrims as they made the pilgrimage to Santiago de Compostela and the knights protected them. It is now home to León's only 5-star hotel. As you stare at this magnificent building you're sure to find yourself thinking thoughts like "Damn those people who're staying in there, while I'm holed up in a room without even so much as a window...." The building really is a piece of art and worth the 10-minute walk northwest from the center. The plaza out front has a bunch of recessed fountains that give the illusion people are walking on water. Also in the same building is the Museo de León, which displays relics from prehistoric, Roman, and Visigoth times. The exhibits are nicely laid out and if you've made the walk down here, you might as well check it out.

modification

So you've been partying since 10pm the previous night, it's now 10am, you have yet to sober up, and you want to tattoo the name of the cute girl/guy you met last night over your heart (whose name, when pressed, you're actually a little fuzzy about ...). No problem! Just scoot your butt over to **Tattoo por Fernando** *(Plaza Torres do Omana 3; Tel 929/876-875; E-mail: fertatoo@jet.es; 11am-2:15/5:30-8:30pm Mon-Fri, noon-2:30pm Sat),* just off Calle Cervantes. Fernando's is a tattoo, piercing, and skate shop. Tattoos and piercings are all done in a very clean and sterile studio. Judging by Fernando's book, he has lots of experience and knows what he's doing. The "skate" shop lacks decks, trucks, or wheels, but it does have *Thrasher* magazine and all the latest skate fashion wear. So once you're inked and pierced, you might as well pick up some baggy shorts and a chain wallet, and complete the look.

city sport

With the Picos de Europa [see below] and all its outdoor adventures not far from León, the people of the city know how to stay active. Within the city, there are many sports facilities that are open to the public for a small fee. South of the bus station, on the western bank of the river, there are two large sports facilities next to each other that, combined, can fill any of your fitness needs. **Polideportivo Saenz de Miera** and **Palacio Municipal de Deportes** collectively occupy several city blocks' worth of modern workout space. Polideportivo Saenz de Miera has several pools, including an Olympic-sized 50-meter pool. Day passes are available for a couple hundred pesetas. Next door is Palacio Municipal de Deportes, which has a huge gym area with indoor ball courts, gym, and workout rooms. Aerobic classes are also offered. A complete list of classes and costs is available at the front desk.

Right across the river from the two sports facilities is **Jardines Papalaguinda.** This park stretches alongside the length of the river and is popular with joggers and cyclists, who get their workouts on a finished path that runs next to the river. Within the park there are also recreation areas with basketball nets (none set up for a full-court game, though) and outdoor ping-pong tables—you'll need to supply your own paddles and balls.

STUFF

The shopping scene in León is nothing to tell your girlfriends about back home. In general, the stores here are Spanish chain stores, with standard stock being sold at standard prices. This isn't to say an afternoon spent wandering around window-shopping can't be a good time; just don't expect to find many unique stores on your expeditions.

Most of the retail outlets set up shop in San Marcelo, the commercial center of the city. The bigger stores can be found along the east/west street Avda Ordoño II, which bisects the district. The side streets offer a mix of clothing stores, outdoor and sporting good stores, and specialty shops.

EATS

There really is nothing better than walking into a restaurant, choosing a dish from many delicious options, enjoying a glass of wine while it is prepared, eating a scrumptious meal, and then leaving without having to clean anything up. The worst part is that when you're on the road, you're forced to endure this pampering daily. These are the hardships of travel. The restaurants and cafes of León are sure to pamper you plenty. The streets of the Húmedo area offer many hidden dining delights, and making your choice for the night is half the fun. Restaurants also crowd the streets of the old town off Calle Ancha. You will never have to search hard for a square meal.

▶▶CHEAP

If you're looking for a good sit-down meal in León at an affordable price, try to take advantage of the set menus offered at most restaurants between 2-4pm. These consist of 4-5 options for a first course, 4-5 options for a second course, and come complete with bread and wine, usually for less than 1,500ptas. During the later dinner hour the same set menu's price will take a significant leap. One budget option for a sit-down meal is **Rocco's Pizzeria** *(Plaza San Martín s/n; 1:30-5pm/8pm-midnight nightly)*, which serves good Italian cuisine, including pastas, pizzas, and main-dish entrees, most for under 1,000ptas. The place is small and relaxed and draws a wide variety of people from university students to families. Right next door is a popular tapas bar, **La Bicha.** This place can often get so crowded that the customers spill out into the plaza. The tapas are delicious and the atmosphere very social.

▶▶DO-ABLE

For those willing to spend a little more, the dining possibilities increase significantly. **El Paloma** (*Calle Escalerilla s/n; Tel 987/254-225; Menú de día 1,300ptas*) offers fine dining at a price that is easy on your budget. The elegant dining room is set with white tablecloths, but is not overly stuffy. Most of the dishes are regional specialties that include a lot of meats and take advantage of fresh trout and other fish caught in nearby rivers.

For dining with real atmosphere check out **Mesón Leones del Racimo de Oro** (*Cano Badillo 2; Tel 987/257-575; 1:45-4pm/9pm-midnight Wed-Sat, 1:45-4pm Sun; 1,500-2,500ptas entrees; AE, V, MC*). Housed in a building older than the U.S.A., this is a great place to try some regional specialties such as roast meats and stews or trout cooked over an open flame. The setting provides a lot of the charm of the place, but the food draws people in as well. The service is friendly and the atmosphere relaxed, and the dining room overlooks a pleasant patio.

▶▶SPLURGE

When it comes to fine dining in León, those in the know will tell you, **Casa Pozo** (*Plaza San Marcelo 15; Tel 987/223-039; 1-4pm/8:30-11:30pm, closed Sun evenings; Menú de día 3,500ptas*) is among the best in the city. It's known for using only the freshest ingredients and making everything from scratch, with a lot of heart. Some of the finest dishes here are delicate trout and salmon meals. Pozo also serves roast meats such as suckling lamb, made with the same TLC. The service is almost as good as the meals, and that's saying a lot.

crashing

With its place along the famed pilgrims' path, León has been hosting travelers for centuries and has learned all the tricks of the trade. The lions of the city know that there are those who come through town who are impoverished and need affordable, low-frills lodging. They know that there will be traveling royalty seeking rooms with as many amenities, if not more, as they have in their castle back home. They also realize that the majority of visitors will fall somewhere in between these two, and so they offer the entire range of lodging options. Whatever your budget, whatever level of comfort you seek, you can find it here without a hassle.

Hotels and *hostales* are scattered throughout the city center. Since the center is fairly compact, location is not a principal concern when choosing where to stay. Generally, most places are within a block north or south of the major arteries of the city, Avda Ordoño II and Calle Ancha. There are also several budget places just over the bridge on the way into town from both the train and bus station.

▶▶CHEAP

Cheap *hostales* and boardinghouses abound in León. Rarely does there seem to be a shortage of budget rooms. Best of all, the city's budget lodging is not just located on the outskirts of town, but is mixed in side by side with all the other places. If you're heading into town from the bus station or train station, **Hostal Oviedo** (*Avda Roma 26; Tel 987/222-236; 2,000ptas single, 3,500ptas double; No CC*) is just over the bridge on your way in. Close to both stations and no more than a 15-minute walk to the cathedral, Oviedo's location isn't far removed from the center. The owners are very friendly and helpful and maintain a clean hostal. The eight rooms here share two full baths. The only drawback is that some rooms lack any outside windows. There are also several other budget *hostales* in the same building.

Right in the center of town is **Hostal Suarez** (*c/ Ancha 60; Tel 987/254-288; 2,000ptas single, 3,000ptas double, 3,600ptas triple; No reservations; No CC*). The rooms are basic here, but nice. They all share a couple of baths down the hall. The real joy of this place is its location. With the Húmedo section of town as your backyard and the cathedral a block away, it really can't be beat. The woman that runs the place is a little curt, but in a nice kind of way.

▶▶DO-ABLE

A few more pesetas will give you a slightly higher level of comfort. Firmer mattress and more pillows are just some of the amenities these places will provide. **Hotel Reina** (*Puerto de la Reina 2; Tel 987/205-212; 1,870ptas single without bath, 4,000ptas with bath, 3,365ptas double without bath, 5,000ptas with bath; V, MC*) offers both budget and moderate rooms to its guests. The budget rooms all share a couple of bathrooms down the hall and most lack a TV, while the moderate rooms come complete with full private bath and TV hooked up to a satellite dish. If you can accept these gross inequalities in the rooms, you'll enjoy the friendly service. To get to the hotel walk two blocks south on Avda de la Independencia from Avda Ordoño II. The Húmedo district is a stone's throw to the east of the hotel doors.

Another nice lodging option is **Guzman el Bueno** (*Lopez Castrillon 6; Tel 987/236-412; 3,500ptas single, 5,500ptas double; V, MC*). Located in the center of town on a quiet side street, Guzman el Bueno is a well-kept former boardinghouse. All rooms enjoy private bathrooms, TV, and phones. This is a popular place for foreign students to stay while studying in León. To get here, simply walk north one block on El Cid from c/Ancha. Take your first right and the place will be just ahead on this pedestrian-only street.

Other cheap to moderate options include **Pension Berta** (*Plaza Mayor 8, Tel 987/257-039; Singles 1,800ptas, doubles 3,200ptas; Shared baths; No credit cards*); **Hostal Bayon** (*Calle del Alcazar de Toledo 6, Tel 987/231-446; Doubles 2,000ptas; Sinks in rooms; No credit cards*); and **Hostal Orejas** (*Calle de Villafranca 8, Tel/Fax 987/252-909; Singles 6,100ptas, doubles 7,500ptas; Private baths; V, MC, AE*), in the center of town.

▶▶SPLURGE

Those wanting to add a little swank to their vacation should look into the **Hotel París** (*c/ Anacha 18; Tel 987/238-600; Fax 987/271-572;*

E-mail: hparis@lesein.es; 7,000ptas single, 10,000ptas double; AE, V, MC). As centrally located as any place in town—only a block away from the cathedral—the Hotel Paris offers its guests comfortable rooms complete with private bath, TV, and phone. The rooms are pleasantly decorated with desks, chairs, and a very comfortable beds. The hotel also has a restaurant and cafe where guests can enjoy breakfast, lunch, and dinner. The staff is extremely helpful and will go out of their way to ensure your stay is as pleasant as possible.

NEED TO KNOW

Currency Exchange Avenida de Ordoño II is lined with banks; in fact, there is one representing every major city in the country. Most all of them have 24-hour ATMs. Normal bank hours are 8:30am-2pm Mon-Fri if you have traveler's checks you need to exchange.

Tourist Information The **main tourist office** *(Plaza de Regla 3; Tel 987/237-082; Fax 987/273-391; 10am-2pm/5-8pm Mon-Fri, 9am-2:30pm/4:30-8:30pm Sat, 11am-2pm Sun)* is directly across from the cathedral. This office can set you up with a good city map, accommodation guides, and regional guides. The helpful staff speaks broken English.

Public Transportation Public buses run throughout the city from 7am-10pm (midnight on weekends). Service is limited. For info call Tel 987/259-271.

Health and Emergency For any medical problems, there is a *Cruz Roja* Hospital on Avda. Alvaro Lopez Nunez. In the event of a medical emergency, call Tel 987/222-222. The **Police** can be reached at either Tel 091 for *policía nacional* or Tel 092 for *del policía local.*

Pharmacies Like everywhere in Spain, pharmacies are designated by a **neon green cross** out front. They are scattered everywhere in town. *El Diario León* has the rotating 24-hour schedule for all night openings.

Telephone City code: *987.* Calling cards are most easily picked up in the tobacco shops that clutter the streets.

Trains The **RENFE** train station *(Avda de Astorga s/n; Tel 987/270-202)* lies across the river in the western extension of the city. From the station it is only a 15-minute walk to the cathedral. León has many connections heading in every direction. Many daily trains head south toward Madrid, about a five-hour trip; a couple run north to Oviedo and Gijón. There are connections running west to A Coruña and Galicia. Heading east you can connect with cities as far away as Barcelona.

Bus Lines Out of the City León's main **bus station** *(Paseo del Ingeniero Saenz de Miera s/n; Tel 987/211-000)* is also across the river in the western part of town. To get into town, exit the station and walk north with the river on your right to the first bridge. Cross over the bridge and head straight into town. The cathedral is about a 20-minute walk from the bus station. There are bus connections to Madrid, Salamanca, Bilbao, and just about any other major city in the north.

Postal The main **post office** *(Jardines de San Francisco s/n; Tel 987/234-290; 8:30am-8:30pm Mon-Fri, 9:30am-2pm Sat)* is located in between Húmedo and San Marcelo just north of Avda de Lucia.

Internet See *wired*, above.

burgos

While the people of León like to think that their cathedral is the greatest in all of Spain, the people of nearby Burgos would beg to differ. They say that without a doubt their city's cathedral is the greatest example of Gothic architecture in the country. There's really only one way to settle this debate; hop on a train and find out for yourself.

Burgos is a proper city, thank you very much, and hasn't strayed too far from its religious roots. Nuns walking the street are a common sight, and there are still two very active monasteries just outside the city. It was probably the city's history as a major stop along the pilgrimage to Santiago de Compostela that led to the city's fervent religious tone.

Burgos was founded as a military garrison in 884 during the rule of Alfonso III, and for five centuries it ruled as the capital of Castile. Small towns, or burgs, began to form around the garrison and soon they all merged into one big Burgos. For centuries it's been known for its fanatical militarism and equally fanatical religious observance. Even today, that legacy hasn't completely vanished; it's likely you'll see more nuns and army officers on the streets of Burgos than anywhere else in the country.

In the 1930s, General Franco made Burgos the seat of his Nationalist forces during their attempt to crush the rebels. After assuming power, Franco brought much industry to Burgos as a reward for its loyalty to him during the Civil War.

Burgos seems to attract a more serious visitor, so you won't have to worry about being besieged by too many day trippers. Drawn to Burgos' pure Castilian history and outstanding architecture left over from the Middle Ages, tourists here are genuinely interested in Iberian culture, history, and politics. The people of Burgos are said to speak the most eloquent Castilian (*"El Theed"* for *"El Cid"*).

Burgos is not known for its great weather since it lies on the *meseta*, or great plain of Spain. That means that it's fiery hot in summer, especially during July and August, and fiercely cold in winter, when harsh winds blow across the Castilian plains.

The **Catedral de Santa María** [see *culture zoo*, below] dominates the old quarter of Burgos, which lies between the Rio Arlalánzon and the mount to the northwest, where you can still view the ruins of the ancient castle that once protected the town. The more modern part of the city lies south of the river, where you'll also find the rail station and bus depot.

The best time to visit Burgos is the last week in June and the first two weeks of July. Locals use the excuse of religious festivals honoring Peter

burgos

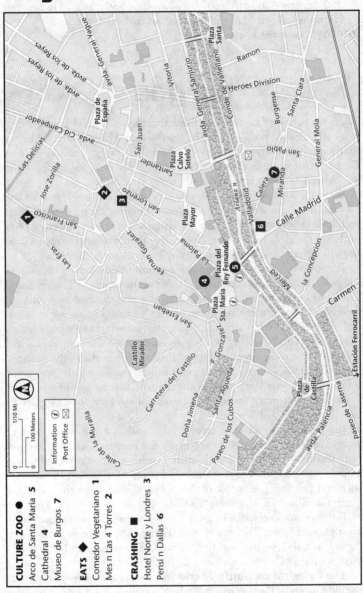

CULTURE ZOO ●
Arco de Santa Maria **5**
Cathedral **4**
Museo de Burgos **7**

EATS ◆
Comedor Vegetariano **1**
Mes n Las 4 Torres **2**

CRASHING ■
Hotel Norte y Londres **3**
Pensi n Dallas **6**

and Paul to go wild, with a series of parades, rock concerts, fireworks, bull-fights, and dancing in the streets. One university student told us, "I stick around until the festivals are over before heading for the beaches to escape the summer heat. The beaches have to wait, because for a short time every year, thanks to the festivals, we're the most fun place to be in all of Spain."

hanging out

The people of Madrid are known as *los gatos* (the cats) because they prowl around late at night. The young people of Burgos, perhaps imitating their Madrileño cousins, are throwing off decades of fascist repression and learning to live again. When all those nuns and military officers disappear from the streets after dark, gaiety prevails in *tasca* after *tasca* dispensing the local wine, Ribera de Duero.

The party begins in several streets near the cathedral. The first street to see action is **Calle Avellanos,** which branches off **Plaza Alonso Martínez.** This street is lined with bars and frequented by young students in search of wine, women (or men, if you prefer), and song. As the night progresses, action shifts to the nearby **Calle del Huerta del Rey** and its side streets. The whole area is nicknamed "las Llanas."

Those who have decided to party all night head for such streets as **Calle San Juan,** which is filled with dance clubs (still called *discotecas* here) where loud music blasts throughout the long night. San Juan runs southeast from Plaza Alonso Martínez. Finally, the **Bernardos** area, to the east side of town around Plaza de España, centering around **Calle de los Calzadas,** is where the last blasts of music are heard after the sun has begun its rapid rise and the street cleaners appear, scrubbing up for Burgos to face another day.

culture zoo

Catedral de Santa María *(Tel 947/204-712; 9:30am-1pm/4-7pm daily; Admission to cathedral free, museum entrance 400ptas adults, 250ptas students):* This is the big event in Burgos. Those who say the cathedral is the greatest example of Gothic architecture just may have hit on something. The grand spires of the 13th-century cathedral can be seen from blocks around and though they may be made of stone, they've been carved to look hollow, giving them an amazingly light and airy feel. The mold-ings and carvings inside the cathedral are no less impressive.

Arco de Santa Maria *(11am-2pm/5-7pm Tues-Sat, 11am-2pm Sun; Free):* Right in front of the cathedral is the most exciting "gateway" into the city. It was once part of the city wall, and the rooms above the arch now host temporary art exhibits that change about every three weeks.

Museo de Burgos *(Calera 25; Tel 947/265-875; 10am-2pm/4-7:30pm Tues-Fri, 10am-2pm/4:45-8:15pm Sat, 10am-2pm Sun; 200ptas adults, students free):* This is another must-see while in town. It houses both the city's Bellas Artes exhibits and archeological exhibits. The art collection includes everything from 8th-century stone carvings up to 20th-century contemporary works. The archeological displays have

El Cid Campeador (1026-1099) was born Rodrigo Díaz de Vivar in the hamlet of Vivar, 5½ miles north of Burgos. So many romantic legends have been woven around this rogue that the actual facts have long been distorted and the events of his life obscured.

El Cid is a part historical, part mythical hero of the Christian Reconquest of Spain. Most Spaniards consider him a great soldier who fought the Moors to liberate Spain from the heretics and bring the Christians into power. While that may be partly true, El Cid was mainly a hot-shot mercenary, and perhaps not as noble as legend would have us believe.

As a brilliant army captain, El Cid supported the ruler, Alfonso VI, who grew obsessively jealous of him after El Cid's success in attacking the Moors in 1081. Alfonso banished El Cid, even though he was a warrior hero, and even though he was married to Alfonso's cousin, Ximena Díaz. After his banishment, this soldier of fortune (whose services were available to anyone with a pot of gold) hired himself out to the Moorish king of Zaragoza and actually fought Christian forces with the same fervor that he'd previously attacked the Moors. Spaniards like to conceal this part of El Cid's story.

El Cid's greatest triumph came in 1094 when, with 7,000 men, he took the city of Valencia after a nine-month siege. Contrary to popular legend, his army was not entirely composed of Christian soldiers, but mostly of Muslims.

His victory at Valencia was not followed by other conquests. El Cid's last battle against the Moors near Cuenca ended in defeat. The conquering hero died shortly thereafter, although his widow held onto the city of Valencia until 1102. When enemies began to overrun the fortifications, she set fire to the city and fled to Burgos with the remains of El Cid, who was eventually buried in a local monastery. In 1921, his bones were transferred to the cathedral at Burgos.

In time, this ruthless warrior of the early Middle Ages became hailed as El Campeador, or "Champion of Castile." He is depicted as a chivalrous knight of exceptional valor. The first great epic in Castilian literature, *El Centar del Mio Cid,* which appeared in 1180, celebrated his exploits. Romantic ballads followed. In 1618, a romantic version of El Cid appeared in *Las Mocedades del Cid,* in which Guillen de Castro relates the warrior's imagined youthful adventures. In 1636, Corneille based his drama *Le Cid* upon this work.

Today, young boys in Burgos climb up to touch the large testicles on El Cid's sculpted horse, which stands in front of the cathedral. Local legend has it that by doing so, these boys will grow into macho Castilians with great sexual prowess. Give it a try, guys!

carvings from 1-3,000 B.C., as well as artifacts gathered up around the region from the Paleolithic era, Bronze and Iron Ages, and Roman era. Really interesting dioramas detail the excavation sites, and mock-ups offer an idea of what the sites looked like when they flourished. Both exhibits are well laid out, and together can take a full afternoon to explore.

eats

Restaurants and cafes abound in and around the old city. Vegetarians will delight in **Comedor Vegetariano** *(Calle San Francisco 31)*, where veggie combo plates run about 1,000ptas. **Mesón las 4 Torres** *(Plaza de Alonso Martinez 5)* is a nice spot where the 1,200ptas *menú del dia* will satisfy the carnivore in anyone.

La Posada *(Plaza Santo Domingo de Guzman 18; Tel 947/203-125; 8am-1am daily; Main courses 1,500-2,500ptas; Fixed price menu 1,800ptas; AE, MC, V)* is the favorite restaurant of all visiting matadors and their fans. It's also the most central restaurant in Burgos, lying next to the cathedral and behind a statue honoring that homegrown hero, El Cid. A hearty regional cuisine is dished out here. For the most authentic dishes, try the *alubias blancas y rojas* (white and red beans), *lechazo al horno* (baby lamb baked to tender perfection in the oven), and *morcilla de Burgos* (the town's famed blood sausage). You can drop in almost any time for a meal; it's open till 1am, when the last of the wine guzzlers have departed, some of them singing, into the Castilian night.

Mesón La Amarilla *(Calle San Lorenzo 26; Tel 947/205-936; 9:30am-4pm/7pm-midnight daily; Main courses 700-1,000ptas, fixed price menu 1,400ptas, tapas 500-950ptas; DC, MC, V)* is extremely central, lying between the landmark squares Plaza Alonso Martin Martinez and Plaza Mayor. The chefs do a good job, but their rugged fare is not for the faint of heart. Start with the delicious *potage de garbanzo* (chickpea soup), and follow perhaps with *bacalao à la Riojana* (dried codfish with tomatoes) or *patatas à la Riojana* (potatoes with the regional sausage of Burgos.) Expect a rustic décor of wood and brick and a crowd of young diners, often students from the university in Salamanca.

crashing

Burgos offers visitors many great places to stay. **Pensión Dallas** *(Plaza de Vega 6; Tel 947/205-457; 2,500ptas single, 4,800ptas double; No credit cards)* is just over the bridge that leads to the Arco de Santa Maria. This is the most centrally located boarding house in Burgos, lying just in front of the cathedral. It's also in the best location if you want to make nightlife the center of much of your fun: The best tascas, bars, and dance clubs lie nearby. None of the rather dark bedrooms has a private bath, although corridor baths are adequate. Mattresses are a bit thin, but the place is decent and tidily kept. No breakfast is served at the pension itself, but there's an inexpensive cafeteria downstairs.

Hotel Norte y Londres *(Plz Alonso Martinez 10; Tel 947/264-125; 5,900-6,800ptas single, 8,500-10,200ptas double; AE, MC, V)* is a little more classy, although the rates have gone up. Deep in the heart of Burgos, the hotel evokes a faded grandeur, with stained glass and leaded glass windows, and crystal chandeliers in the public lobby. Rooms here are well-furnished but a bit on the dowdy side. The number of amenities justifies the price, since each unit comes with a private phone, TV, and a complete bathroom with both tub and shower. Breakfast costs 700ptas.

need to know

Currency Exchange The best and most central banks (each near the cathedral) where you can find ATMs include **Banco Bilbao Vizcaya,** Calle Victoria 7 *(Calle Victoria, Tel 947/202-343),* and **Banco Santander,** *(Paseo del Espolon, Tel 947/477-200).*

Tourist Information The local **Tourist Office** *(Plaza Alonso Martinez 7; Tel 947/203-125; 9am-2pm/5-7pm Mon-Fri, 10am-2pm/5-8pm Sat and Sun)* has a very helpful staff that can supply you with maps of the city, accommodation guides, regional guides, a list of city sites, and answer just about any question you can fire at them.

Trains and Buses The **train station** is a short 5-10 minute walk south of the center of town; the more conveniently located **bus station** is right on Calle Miranda. Trains can take you to the big cities of Madrid and Léon.

galicia

galicia, cantabria & asturias

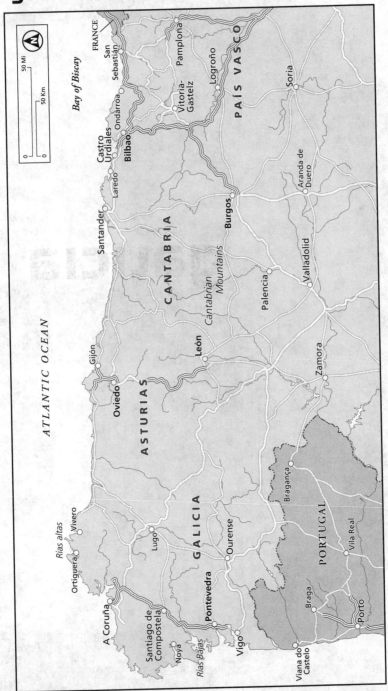

I t will surprise most people to discover that there is a region in Spain where the greatest influence is Celtic, where fjord-like inlets cut into the land, and lush green hills give way to gray slate buildings. Forget sun-drenched earth and castanets. Far from the center of Spain—sitting right above Portugal in the northwest corner of the country—Galicia is also a world away from most people's Iberian stereotype. Galicia is unlike any other region in the country. What this means is basically that if you were blindfolded and dropped here, you would not say, "Gee, looks like Spain." You'd be more likely to think, "Where the hell am I? It looks like Ireland, smells like Nova Scotia, and it sounds like the people are speaking some long-forgotten Celtic dialect." Welcome to Galicia, truly one of Spain's greatest, and most overlooked, regions.

A visit here is like a 2-for-1 offer. You can save on that trip to Dublin, because two things define Galicia more than anything else: the sea and its Celtic roots. Unlike the rest of Spain, the hills here are deep green, they roll, and they end in dramatic cliffs that fall into the seething Atlantic below. Sounds a lot like Ireland, doesn't it? Just wait until you find yourself confronted with street musicians playing bagpipes for change.

Celtic people first inhabited the area over 5,000 years ago, and they left a profound mark still obvious in the region. The Romans followed in the Celts' footsteps a couple of thousand years later and left *their* mark (these guys were like dogs at the park) on the land with such structures as the Tower of Hercules in the coastal city of **A Coruña** and the great city walls around the old town of **Lugo.**

The rest of Spain sort of forgot about Galicia during the *Reconquista,* while the Moors and Christians battled it out, and Galicia never really came back into the fold. It looked to the sea to provide for its people; fishing and shipping are its main industries. All of the larger cities grew up next to, and were supported by, the sea. Independent in spirit, the people here struggled over the years to make a living, until modern tourists discovered Galicia and brought a new prosperity to an area always considered one of the poorest in Spain. Vacationers sunbathe on the beautiful white beaches that line the dramatic coast and delight in the undiscovered treasures the region offers, including the medieval quarter of A Coruña and one of Spain's (perhaps even the world's) most fascinating cities, **Santiago de Compostela.**

TONGUE TWISTER

The Galician language *Gallego* (or *galego*, in Castilian Spanish), which might sound to you like a tongue-twister of a language, full of X's, is actually a living language (not a dialect, but a combination of Spanish and Portuguese) that is taught in schools and still spoken by a vast majority of the population.

A note on all those x's—'x' in *Gallego* generally replaces the Spanish 'g' or 'j' and is pronounced as a soft 'sh'. So don't hesitate to go to the Xeneral Hospital if your 'xaw' is broken. Also, and perhaps most importantly, ask in which direction the *praia* (beach) is and some friendly local will point you in the direction of one of the many beautiful stretches of sand. Fear not, though—everyone also speaks Castilian.

We use the Galician words—for example, the Spanish *plaza* becomes *praza* in Galician; La Coruña in Spanish becomes A Coruña; and, of course, *praia* takes the place of *playa*. We do provide the Castilian version where helpful.

Catholic believers have come to Santiago de Compostela for centuries to see the resting place of the apostle Santiago. It counts as one of the largest Christian pilgrimage destinations in the world. To reach the sacred city, pilgrims traverse the Camino de Santiago on various routes all the way from France, and those who complete it are said to get their purgatory sentence cut in half. Even if you're not a true believer, you'll be pretty impressed by this medieval city.

Galicians speak *Gallego,* which was probably not offered at your local high school, so you're not going to understand a lot. If you're a whiz kid and have Castilian down, you've got a shot, but first you need to get used to some different endings, accents, and flow. *Gallego* has the same roots as Castilian, but it moves a little more smoothly from one word to the next. For many years, you wouldn't have heard *Gallego* spoken in public. Franco banned all local dialects, including *Gallego,* throughout the country in an effort to take away separate cultural identities (despite the fact that he was from Galicia). He believed in a centralized Spain to the core, and one language was mandatory. Now *Gallego* is having a resurgence. Maps are mixed between Castilian and *Gallego,* so ask for one in Castilian if possible.

getting around the region

Getting around the region won't pose any problems to persistent travelers. The RENFE train line connects Aviles, Gijon, and Oviedo in Asturias to the major east-west rails between Galicia and Barcelona, as well as to Madrid. Once in the area, buses are your best bet for getting around. There is also the smaller-gauge FEVE train line that runs along the coast. From Gijon, one line runs east to the Basque country and another line runs west to Ferrol in Galicia. A warning, though: FEVE trains are slow and pass through each town just two or three times a day, so they're not your best option.

Galicia is roughly broken up between the Rías Altas to the north (Santiago de Compostela and A Coruña) and the Rías Bajas (Vigo and Ponteverde) to the south. The *rías* are estuaries that stretch into the land from the coastline. Rich in sea life, they provide many of the ingredients for the region's famed seafood dishes.

The roads in Galicia, though now finally getting some much-needed attention, have long been thought of as the worst in Spain. Do yourself a favor and leave the wheels behind. Getting around by train is easy, anyway. The RENFE rail system has a good series of tracks that connects all of the major cities and runs through many of the smaller towns. Trains are never crowded and are an economical means of getting from point A to point B. A Coruña is pretty much the transportation hub of the region. From its train station you can catch a ride south along the coast to any of the towns in the Rías Bajas or catch one of the long-distance trains that head to Barcelona and Madrid.

Travel Times

All times are by road unless indicated by a star: * = time by train	A Coruña	Santiago de Compostela	Madrid
A Coruña	-	1:00*	8:30*
Santiago de Compostela	1:00	-	7:30*

a coruña

The history of A Coruña (La Coruña in Castilian) rivals that of any other city in Spain, but it's not resting on its laurels. Today, A Coruña is Galicia's biggest and most thriving city, with a population of 250,000. People used to come here because of the port, the largest in the region; now, they come to enjoy the beautiful location of this isthmus, snugly sandwiched between river and ocean.

A quick word about that history. The port here was an important stop on the Roman tin-trading route (which might not sound all that exciting until you imagine all those gladiators without their armor). A bit later, the doomed Spanish Armada set sail from here in 1588, only to get their asses kicked by the Brits. What goes around, comes around, however, and the Brits got the treatment from the French during their Peninsular War: In 1809, the English were forced back to A Coruña and had to hold the French at bay while they loaded onto ships to escape. The English leader, Sir John Moore, however, took a cannonball through the chest and has remained in the city as a permanent fixture ever since.

During the summer months now, A Coruña experiences a storming of another kind. July and August find this city bursting to the gills with Spanish vacationers. The beaches become overrun to the point that you think they'll sink into the sea. To get the maximum enjoyment from this city, visit it right before or after the summer rush. Don't worry that you'll miss out on all the fun, though. Things don't die down much during the off-season when it comes to the city's *marcha*. The nightlife here is one of the region's best, year-round. With plenty of bars and *puffs* (mini discos) spread throughout the isthmus, and a couple of good discos in the new part of town and on the beach, the party scene here marches on into the early dawn hours.

If you do find yourself here during the summer months, be prepared to go hard. Spaniards on vacation seem to party twice as much as they normally do, and that's saying a lot. During the summer the bars and clubs are packed; the streets are, too. The party flows onto the sidewalks and streets, so the whole place really jams. Not just on the weekends, either; it's a weeklong affair. Luckily there are plenty of hours in the day to lie on the beach and recharge.

One small thing to mention about A Coruña, especially if you're thinking about an off-season visit. The city has earned the name "crystal city" from the glassed-in balconies, known as *gallerias,* that dot its facades. The glass is beautiful, but it's got a practical purpose: to shield people's apartments from the rough weather that can roll in off the Atlantic, especially during the late fall and winter. If you can only make it to A Coruña during this time, you shouldn't be discouraged from visiting; these storms are not a regular event. With or without a storm, the *gallerias* themselves are interesting architecturally—the ones in the old town have inspired imitations all over town. A walk through newer sections of the city reveals new buildings with modern *gallerias.*

The people of A Coruña welcome outsiders more graciously than folks in other parts of Galicia, probably because they are so used to people from all over coming to enjoy their city. Like all Spaniards, Galicians are relaxed and good-natured, although they are more reserved. In A Coruña a few broad smiles is all it will take to get a Galician to talk about this place that they take such pride in. If you speak Spanish you'll definitely stand at a huge advantage. Although most people directly related to the tourist trade do know some English, don't expect everyone to understand it. Most people, however, will be more than willing to help you in any way they can, even if all you speak is jive.

Several papers and monthly magazines give the lowdown on what's going on in the city. The tourist office hands out a **Guia del Ocio** during the season that will give you the basics, but not much beyond that. Locals say the best place to really find out about the action is to pick up a copy of the newspaper **La Voice de Galicia** at any newsstand. In the local section you'll find lists of upcoming events around the city, including things in the worlds of music, culture, and leisure. It's obviously not an English-language paper so unless you speak Spanish following it could be a bit tough. **Forum Metropolitano** is a small monthly newsletter that can be found throughout the city in bars like **Picasso** [see *bar scene,* below]. It covers the more offbeat cultural events and while it's also a Spanish-language publication, it's got pictures! So you might actually be able to figure out what's happening.

neighborhoods

One of the features that makes A Coruña such an exciting city is its unique layout. The city center extends onto a peninsula surrounded on

a coruña

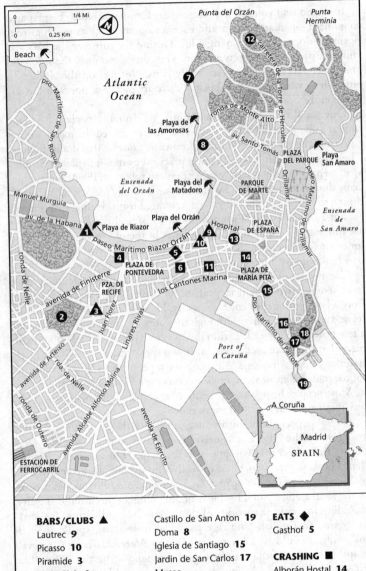

Punta del Orzán

Punta Herminia

Beach

Atlantic Ocean

pso. Marítimo de San Roque

carretera de la Torre de Hércules

ronda de Monte Alto

Playa de las Amorosas

av. Santo Tomás

PLAZA DEL PARQUE

Playa San Amaro

Manuel Murguia

av. de la Habana

Ensenada del Orzán

Playa del Matadoro

PARQUE DE MARTE

Orillamar

paseo Marítimo de Orillamar

Ensenada de San Amaro

Playa de Riazor

Playa del Orzán

Hospital

PLAZA DE ESPAÑA

paseo Marítimo Riazor Orzán

ronda de Nelle

avenida de Finisterre

PLAZA DE PONTEVEDRA

PZA. DE RECIFE

Juan Florez

Linares Rivas

los Cantones Marina

PLAZA DE MARÍA PITA

pso. Marítimo del Parrote

Port of A Caruña

avenida de Arteixo

rda de Nelle

ronda de Outeiro

avenida Alcalde Alfonso Molina

avenida de Ejercito

ESTACIÓN DE FERROCARRIL

A Coruña

Madrid

SPAIN

BARS/CLUBS ▲
Lautrec **9**
Picasso **10**
Piramide **3**
Playa Club **1**

CULTURE ZOO ●
Aquarium **7**
Casa de Ciensias **2**

Castillo de San Anton **19**
Doma **8**
Iglesia de Santiago **15**
Jardin de San Carlos **17**
Museo
 de Arqueológico **19**
Museo de Bellas Artes **13**
Museo Militar **18**
Torre de Hércules **12**

EATS ◆
Gasthof **5**

CRASHING ■
Alborán Hostal **14**
Hostal Centro **6**
Hostal Maria **11**
Hotel Finisterre **16**
Hotel Raizor **4**

three sides by water. The waters squeeze in on the city; at its most narrow, it's no more than a 3-minute walk from one side of town to the other. On the east side of the peninsula is the calm port where large commercial freighters, small fishing boats, and the occasional cruise ships all tie up. The other side opens up onto the Atlantic, where swells off the ocean roll up onto the city's beaches.

The tiny **Ciudad Vieja,** or old town, sits nestled in the bottom southeast corner of the peninsula. During the days of pirates and raiders it offered pretty good cover for the city's inhabitants, who built a wall to protect the one side that wasn't water. The life of the city has long since moved out of the old town onto other parts of the peninsula, leaving behind many undisturbed old churches and a couple of decent museums. Today the old town is quiet and peaceful, and exploring its narrow streets and many "prazas" (that's *plaza* in *gallego*) makes for a pleasant afternoon. The **Praza de María Pita,** which separates the old town from the newer parts, is a nice open plaza where you can enjoy a cold drink at one of the many cafes. Above the *ciudad vieja* to the northwest you'll find mostly residential blocks, which end at the cliffs above the water, by the old Roman lighthouse, **Torre de Hercules.**

The **Centro,** where you'll find most of the hostels and hotels, bars and restaurants, shops and banks, is on the isthmus that connects the bulb to the mainland. Getting around here is easy enough as it's a short walk from side to side. The two main city beaches line this part of town. **Praia do Orzán** and **Praia de Riazor,** although right next to the city, offer a great escape from it. This is also where the local *marcha* spends most of its time. Basically things heat up in the restaurants around **Calle da la Franja** (just west of Plaza de María Pita) and then slowly work their way across town to **Calle del Sol** and **Juan Canalejo,** where there are more than enough bars and *puffs* to accommodate the crowds.

The city is constantly expanding up onto the mainland. The bus and train stations are here, and if you take the 30-minute walk from either one to the peninsula, you'll quickly realize A Coruña is a thriving, modern city. The big shopping malls and businesses are on the mainland, but there isn't much of interest up here beyond a couple of museums and one or two interesting shopping districts. **Juan Florez,** a busy road that acts as an informal border between peninsula and mainland, is a good place to wander around.

Although A Coruña is fairly spread out, things in the center and on the isthmus are within walking distance of one another. The only places that are really out of leg range are the bus and train stations and the Torre de Hercules. For these, you'll have to take one of the good **city buses** [see *need to know,* below]. A tourist trolley operates in the summer; it circles around the peninsula and is the perfect way to get out to the Torre de Hercules. The major drawback, of course, is that you'll be arriving on a bus full of tourists also going to the same spot—not exactly forging your own new path. Save that for another time. When all else fails there are plenty of cabs around town. One of the main cabstands is just past the *correos* on the way to the mainland.

hanging out

Listen, if you've got free time on your hands and you're looking for a place to hang out, don't mess around, just go straight to the beach. A Coruña doesn't have any great parks or groovy plazas with locals hanging out and playing the bongos. Everybody's on the beach in the spring and summer months, so get your butt down there.

The two main city beaches are **Praia de Riazor** and **Praia do Orzán.** They are separated from one another by a lookout that connects to the walkway above. Both beaches curve around the inlet that opens onto the ocean and have plenty of room to stretch out on. The crowd is a mix of all types. Kids kick around soccer balls and gather in groups to chill, families play in the surf, and, because the beach is so accessible, people on their lunch break come down to grab some rays, too. During the day surfers and boogie boarders who enjoy the good-sized swells that roll in from the ocean crowd the waves off Praia do Orzán. You know this place gives its surfers respect when you notice the monument—yes,

wired

Don't expect to find any Internet cafes serving drinks here; people take their bars seriously in A Coruña. "You socialize in bars with people, not machines," they say. Instead, the people here have found other ways to make getting hooked into the Net enjoyable. As if the whole Internet experience—"talking" on-line to someone thousands of miles away—isn't sci-fi enough, **Net & Games** *(Juan Canalejo 63; Tel 981/214-359; 10am-2pm/4pm-2am Mon-Fri, 4pm-2am Sat and Sun; 100ptas for 20 minutes),* near Praia do Orzán, has created a far-out cave environment, with walls that look like rocks and muted lighting, where you can play Net games or log into your e-mail account. Their machines are coin-operated so just walk in, sit down, drop some change in the slot, and you're surfing. Fast connections make catching up with everyone back home a breeze. If you've got nothing better to do and a pocket full of change, play some Network games, like Quake. Mostly a local Spanish crowd uses this place, so it's not a bad place to meet some locals.

A much more functional, no-frills Net experience can be found at **On-line** *(Maria Auxiliadora 2; Tel 981/205-254; 8:45am-2pm/4-8pm Mon-Fri, 10am-2pm Sat; 250ptas an hour),* where it'll be just you and a couple of computers in a copy shop. To make up for the lack of diversions, the owners are really nice and the rates can't be beat. It's right off Rúa Hospital by the Museo de Bellas Artes.

monument!—to surfers in a small plaza right above the beach. Right around the corner from the beach and below the surfer's monument, you'll find the smaller and more hidden **Praia do Matadoro.** Usually a little less crowded, this beach is surrounded by steep rock faces and cliffs. All three of these beaches have some showerheads for washing off the salt water or just cooling down.

If you left your blow-up water wings at home or simply want a place to swim that offers a little more protection, head out to **Praia San Amaro** by the Torre de Hercules [see *cultural zoo,* below]. Popular mostly with families with small children, this small shallow bay offers some relief from the surf that the other beaches often receive.

bar scene

The bar scene is alive and well and living in A Coruña, thank you very much. Most of the bars are located in the Centro between the port and the beaches, and there's something for everyone. So figure out what you're after, or better yet just go out wandering and let yourself stumble upon the perfect match.

It's customary to begin the night sometime between 9 and 11pm in a nice bar where you can enjoy a glass of wine while tasting tapas. Prime hunting grounds for such activities are along Franja and Torreiro on the port side of the center. Most of the restaurants along these streets have a tapas-and-drinks bar for those who don't want to do the sit-down meal thing. **La Traida** *(Torreiro 1; Tel 981/229-321)* is one of the more memorable. It has a good tapas spread and plenty of wines and beers to wash them down. Old bullfighting posters from some of the city's festivals decorate the walls. **L'Abadis** *(Franjal 5),* another lively tapas bar in the area, also attracts a hip crowd.

Once the clock strikes midnight, things begin to cross to the other side of the isthmus, closer to Praia do Orzán. This is where the nightlife—actually, the early-morning life—is centered. Between midnight and 3-4am, especially along Sol and Juan Canalejo, people pack the hopping bars, just waiting until the discos open. Juan Canalejo is loaded with *puffs;* unfortunately, the drink prices are a little steeper in these joints. One of the quieter places on Sol is **Picasso.** The place is kind of a haven for the artistic crowd. Contemporary art hangs on the walls next to pictures of the great man himself. Soul and rock play on the stereo, but the whole thing's pretty mellow. It's a comfortable joint to start the night off.

When you want to step things up a couple notches, head to **Garibaldi** *(Juan Canalejo 33; No phone).* The beers go for 350ptas and it's a lively place with a good-size dance floor. Mostly techno pop fills the large room with a happy vibe; on weekends, a DJ usually spins stuff along the same lines. The lighting is mellow low, and recessed neon red lights add a devilish glow to the place. Two bars help to keep the drink orders moving. The 20-30-year-old crowd that hangs here also makes its way down the street to **Cisco** *(Juan Canalejo 43),* a *puff* that is decked out in a neo-industrial theme. A foos-ball table in the corner entertains revelers while a disco light and DJ keep the main crowd moving on the floor to hip-hop and dance. The one problem here is that the place tries to be a full-on club but just doesn't have the room or the respect. Beers running at 500ptas a piece means most people only stay for one drink.

For a totally different scene check out **Limerick Irish Pub** *(Barrie de la Maza 15; Tel 981/228-164)*. Besides being a great Irish tavern, this is also where members of the local soccer team (who surprised everyone when they won the '99-'00 national title) let loose when they're home. Located right across the street from the beach, it's a popular spot all day long. A pint will run you 475ptas. Try to time a stop here at sunset— you'll get a great view over your pint.

LIVE MUSIC SCENE

Unfortunately, live music does not rank high on A Coruña's list of priorities. Beyond the local rock bands that play in the bars around Sol, there isn't much to the scene. Your best bet for finding out what little is going on is to pick up a copy of *La Voice de Galicia*. During festivals [see *festivals,* below], live bands often count as one of the attractions.

One bar in town that has live music fairly often, particularly on summer weekends, is **Lautrec** *(Sol 12-14)*. Bands—usually the classic rock bands that are barroom staples, but sometimes a world music band drifts in as well—go on earlier in the night. There is never a cover. Once the bands pack up, the place turns into a rocking bar with a dance floor and black lights.

CLUB SCENE

A Coruña has a lively nightlife, although it's limited to a few clubs. But even though the choices aren't that varied, the ones that are here definitely rock. You'll find the most going on at the end of Praia de Riazor by the soccer stadium, and along Juan Florez. The discos along the beach obviously get most of the draw in the summer time for two reasons: One, they're on the beach, and two, the tourists like to go to the clubs that they can easily find. During the off-season, generally the clubs on Juan Florez are the popular ones.

When we were visiting, **Piramide** *(Juan Florez 48; 981/276-157)* was the hot club in town. The loud thumping of the house music seems to draw people into its doors starting around 3am. Inside you'll find plenty of room to shake your body next to the other beautiful people of the city. The musical selection features lots of house along with Euro-dance, and the better music usually gets played later in the night when things are really swinging.

Playa Club is the first building you come to on the beach as you walk along Praia de Riazor toward the soccer stadium. A cafe and restaurant upstairs open onto the street, but you want to go around back and enter from the beach. Location is everything here: With such a beautiful scene right outside the door, it's hard to decide whether you want to be in or out. The pull of the music and furious dancing of the hot bodies will

rules of the game

This is Spain, so the rules are relaxed. The drinking age is 18 but no one's checking. Hash is legal in small quantities for personal use. You may run into some dude peddling harder stuff like coke or E inside or outside the clubs. Galicia is said to be a major entry for drugs flowing into Spain, especially stuff from those friendly South American cartels. Mostly, you won't see it, hear about it, or even be aware of it, and it's best to keep things that way.

Cops here are really mellow. The general rule is, as long as you aren't bothering anyone, they aren't going to bother you. This isn't a frat party at State U., so just be cool. Pacing yourself is the name of the game, with the party lasting into dawn; can you?

quickly make up your mind for you. Beyond the normal weekend parties here, the club sporadically hosts release parties for new albums. If it's not listed in the paper it will be listed on posters outside the club. The release parties usually have a cover charge of about 1,000ptas.

ARTS SCENE

The arts scene in A Coruña is pretty lame (remember, we warned you that this place is about the beach, and nothing but the beach). The cultural strides the city has taken have been more in the direction of science and history than of the arts. But, if you look really carefully, you can uncover a few artistic happenings.

▶▶VISUAL ART

Considering the fact that as a boy Picasso spent five years of his life in A Coruña and had his first show here, at the age of 13, the city does not have a very energetic local art scene. Ask someone where the *gallerias* are and they'll just get a confused look on their face and point up to the glassed-in balconies. Nice, but not quite what we're looking for. **Asociacion de Artistas** *(Riego de Agua 32; Tel 981/225-277)* displays the work of artists from all over the country. It occasionally highlights work from international artists as well. The main goal here seems to be more about selling art than displaying it, but that doesn't mean you can't go in for a look.

▶▶PERFORMING ARTS

At some point in everyone's life, you realize that there is a time to grow up and experience the finer, more sophisticated pleasures in life. What better way than to spend a night at the **Opera** *(Glorieta de America s/n; Tel 981/140-404; 1,000-3,000ptas)?* The opera house is part of the new Palacio de Congresses y Auditorio building, which the tourist board is proud to display on the maps it hands out to visitors. Performance times vary but are usually on Friday and Saturdays nights starting around 8:30pm. This is the opera, so try to make a little effort to look nice.

fEStIVALS and EVEntS

What's more fun than spending time in a summer resort where everyone is out to have a good time? Being there for one of the many festivals, of course. The Spanish have perfected the art of the festival. In this region it is fact that there are more festivals than towns and villages! A Coruña makes its living from giving visitors a memorable trip, which means they put together a summer jammed full of festivals of all shapes and sizes. In the month of August alone, one festival simply leads into the next. It's a month-long party that no one wants to leave.

El Noche de San Juan *(June 23-24):* This festival sort of opens the season, and it's a fun one to catch before things really take off. During the night, people build bonfires on the beach and bands play to the delight of everyone. Sometimes pretty big-name acts appear; The Cars played in '99.

María Pita *(August 1-31):* A month of activities is dedicated to the little girl who supposedly was the first to see Sir Francis Drake invading. She sounded the alarm, saving the city from his English forces. Events include art exhibits, craft fairs, folk shows and music, parades, naval reenactments, and bullfights—the main event.

Patron Saint Day *(Around 7th of October):* Feasts are held in the *ciudad vieja* in honor of the Lady of the Rosary. Parties last well into the night.

If opera isn't your bag (whose bag is it, really?), there is also **Teatro Colon** *(show times vary; 650ptas for movies)* next to the post office. Besides having randomly scheduled theatrical events, the theater also shows movies. There's only one screen here, and it usually is a Hollywood flick. Visit the theater for all the latest info on movies and theatrical events.

gay SCEnE

The Galicians are traditional people, in some ways slower to adapt to the changing world than the rest of the country. Homosexuality hasn't come out as much here as it has in cities like Madrid and Barcelona. When people are asked about gay bars and clubs, they get a little red and say they think there is one somewhere around and then vaguely point at the map to an area encompassing several blocks. The bars keep a low profile and usually don't display much in the way of signs out front. Things are still somewhat underground.

The one place we were able to find (we think) is **La Aberinto** *(Medico Rodriguez 15).* We say "we think" because we were never able to actually get in the door. There isn't much marking this bar from the street, so if you're brave, push in the door, check it out, and let us know what you find.

CULTURE ZOO

An ugly truth lies behind the beauty of A Coruña. As one young Irish woman who was studying here for the year told me, "One of the first Spanish words I learned to say here was umbrella." Unfortunately, it does rain a fair amount here. But fear not—even on a rainy day there is plenty to keep you occupied. The city recently spent a good chunk of money on building a couple of new museums as well as renovating old ones. Add to that a decent number of historical structures that are worth a visit and you will have more than enough to do even when the weather isn't totally agreeable.

Torre de Hercules *(Ctra. de la Torre s/n; Tel 981/202-759; Bus 9 or 13 or tourist trolley in summer; 11am-9pm July-Sept, 10am-7pm Oct-June; 250ptas):* Legend has it that Hercules himself built this tower after defeating a giant. Believe that, or believe that the Romans built it in the second century. Either way, it is the city's oldest structure and the world's oldest functioning lighthouse. Everyone who comes to this city should try to make it out here, but no one makes the trip just to see an old monument (which is in fact hidden under an 18th-century skin). They come to climb over two hundred steps to get an amazing view of the city. I'd recommend packing a picnic and walking out here from town. Start by Praia do Orzán and just follow the coast; it's a beautiful shoreline. You can sit in the grass out by the lighthouse and enjoy your meal after climbing to the top.

Castillo de San Anton and the **Museo Arqueológico** *(Paseo Maritimo s/n; Tel 981/205-994; 10am-9pm Tues-Sat, 10am-2:30pm Sun summer, 10am-7pm Tues-Sat, 10am-2:30pm Sun winter; 300ptas):* On the far opposite end of the peninsula you'll find the castle and museum. The castle still keeps a watchful eye from its position at the port entrance. Built in the 12th century; it has played many roles, from protector to prison. Things are tamer these days, the only thing the castle guards is the Archeology Museum inside. The museum has Stone Age, Bronze Age, Roman, and medieval artifacts from the region. There are also some things left behind, like cannons, from the days when the castle protected this important port. Half the fun of the museum is exploring the castle.

Iglesia de Santiago *(Tel 981/205-696; 10:15am-1pm/6:30-8:30pm daily; free):* While you're near the old town, if you're into old relics, you should swing by this church—dating from the 12th century, it's the oldest one in A Coruña. No pilgrim on his way to Santiago de Compostela would come into town without stopping here first. Today it is pretty quiet, and it just takes a quick peek to get the groove.

Jardín de San Carlos *(10am-sunset daily; free):* Just east of the church along Paseo del Parrote lies this equally peaceful park. Here you'll find an idyllic setting where the remains of General Moore now rest. Lots of benches among the well-kept gardens offer good views over the port.

Museo Militar *(Maestranza s/n; Tel 981/206-791; 10am-2pm/4-7pm daily; free):* Across the street from the gardens is this museum, whose collection of swords, guns, and light artillery from the 18th-20th centuries will appeal to military buffs. The displays of flags and uniforms from the many armies that have fought in this land might humble you—others have indeed come before. A huge diorama brings to life the battle of Eluina, which happened right outside the city during the Peninsular War. It was during this battle that Moore made it possible for his English soldiers to escape the French. He, unfortunately, was not so lucky.

Museo de Bellas Artes *(Zalaeta 2; Tel 981/223-723; 10am-8pm Tues-Fri, 10am-2pm/4:30-8pm Sat, 10am-2pm Sun; 400ptas, 200ptas Students, free Sat afternoons and Sun):* In the Centro, in a new building designed by Gallego Jorreto, for which he won a national architecture award, this museum is itself a work of art. It has an open feel and innovative layout; the rooms flow together in an appealing, organic way. Its collection of fine paintings from the 14th to 20th centuries includes works by such great Spanish artists as Picasso and Goya. The museum also exchanges works with the Prado in Madrid and hosts temporary exhibits. If the artwork doesn't get you, maybe the building will.

Casa de Ciencias *(Parque de Santa Margarita s/n; Tel 981/271-828; 10am-7pm Mon-Fri; 300ptas, 200ptas extra for planetarium):* This is the first of the three new museums that the city recently built devoted to the sciences. Dubbed *Las Tres Casas Coruñesas,* they represent an ambitious project to bolster the city's commitment to science. For 1,200ptas, you can buy a pass at any one of the three museums that will get you into all of them. **Casa de Ciencias** has exhibits dealing with natural science, including plants, animals, and minerals. Although it is hailed as one of the premier new museums, I thought it was rather small and stark. It's definitely geared to a younger crowd. Much more entertaining is **Doma—Casa de Hombre** *(Santa Teresa 1; Tel 981/217-000; 10am-7pm Mon-Fri; 300ptas),* which is dedicated to the human body, and man, is it wild. It starts with the body's basic building blocks and moves on to cover all the major systems. It's full of interactive displays and computers that are a blast to fool around with no matter how old you are. The info is in Spanish but all the computers read out in English as well. My advice would be to hit this place when you're feeling young at heart and want to play. A fun museum, just try not to get run down by the hordes of kids. The last of the three is **Casa de los Peces-Aquarium** *(Paseo Maritimo s/n; Tel 981/217-191; 10am-7pm Mon-Fri; 1,000ptas),* a cool aquarium that has tanks full of fish, of course, but also some interesting displays on the world's oceans and other watery life forms. The aquarium is very modern and well laid-out. Unlike aquariums you might have visited elsewhere, it's more likely that you'll be swarmed here by busloads of foreign tourists than lunchbox-carrying schoolchildren.

▶▶**MODIFICATION**

If you have an overwhelming urge to put holes in your body or decorate your skin in bright colors, head to **Tattoo Urubu** *(Galera 47-2nd floor;*

Tel 981/200-763; 11am-2pm/5-8pm Mon-Fri) in the center of town. With a wide selection of rings, barbells, hoops, and studs, the folks here can hook you up (literally in some cases) in just about any way you'd want. The studio also does a lot of tattoo work, and some of the tattoo artists can regale you with tales of tattooing old sea dogs in the days before the modern body art kick. Just remind them that you don't want an anchor with "Mom" written under it.

CITY SPORTS

This city is all about being outside, and it's got what you need to keep your body looking its best so that you can attract the attention of all those cuties on the beach.

Plenty of athletic facilities in town are open to the public. **Deportiva la Torre** *(Avda. de Navarra s/n; Bus 9 or 13; 10am-8pm Mon-Sat, noon-*

THE RIAS ALTAS

A Coruña is a gateway stopover for many adventure seekers who want to explore **Rias Altas,** which has some of the most dramatic coastal scenery in all of Spain. This is especially true along Cabo Ortegal and Serra de la Capelada. *Rias* are inlets made by the Atlantic Ocean into the Galician coastline (in Scotland they're called lochs; in Norway fjords). The easiest to reach from A Coruña, and the best venue for hiking, camping, and kayaking, is **Ria de Betanzos.** It's centered around Betanzos, the capital of ancient Galicia, and is a 45-minute bus ride away. From Betanzos, you can also hop a bus to Miño, 12 kilometers to the north, home of the finest white sandy beach in the Rias Altas. One note to the wise: It seems to rain every minute along the coast (only a bit of an exaggeration), so dress accordingly.

You can bus it from A Coruña to Ria de Betanzos: JASA buses *(Tel 981/239-001)* leave A Coruña hourly and cost 250 pesetas one way. The trip takes 45 minutes. You can also hop a bus from Betanzos to Miño. Buses leave hourly; the half-hour ride costs 280 pesetas. Once you've arrived in the Rias Altas, getting around by public transportation can be a pain, and precious hours can be wasted in transit. A car is better if you can afford it. If you're going to hang for a few days, you can stay at **Camping Playa de Miño** *(Tel 981/784-212; 500ptas per night; open June-Sept),* which is right off the beach at Miño. Call ahead to make reservations.

6pm Sun; prices vary), out by the Torre de Hercules, has a million and one soccer fields to choose from. Some of the fields are grass while most are sand. This facility also has basketball and jai-lai courts, as well as weight machines and exercise rooms. Some things you have to pay for, but it's totally cool just to walk in and shoot some hoops or play a little soccer.

In the old town you'll find **La Solana** *(Paseo del Parrote 2-4; Tel 981/205-400; 10am-1:30pm/4:30-7:30pm Mon-Thur and Sat, 10am-7:30pm Fri; Day pass 1,700ptas),* located on the grounds of Hotel Finisterre. Besides having four outdoor pools, including an Olympic-sized pool and another with a large twisty water slide leading into it, this place also has tennis courts, basketball courts, ping-pong, and a host of other activities. There's lots of activity in the weight rooms and on the courts, so you might have to be patient. If you just want to relax, though, you can lounge by a pool, get a massage, have a sauna, and take a relaxing bath. The day pass doesn't entitle you to all of the club's facilities—you either have to be a hotel guest or member for that—but it will get you in the door and in some cases that affords all the access you'll need.

Locals like to jog along **Barrie Mazo** and **Pasao Maritimo.** Start behind the beaches and head out around the peninsula. The route is long and the views dramatic enough to keep your mind off the agony you're putting yourself through. The promenade is wide here so walkers and joggers have no problem squeezing by one another.

If you're ready for a little adventure, **Bucea** *(Cantabrico 2; Tel 981/212-206; 10am-2pm/5-9pm Mon-Fri, 10:30am-2pm/5-8pm Sat)* has an office across the street and above Praia do Matadoro. You can sign up here for some world-class scuba diving in the waters around A Coruña. A lot of the dive sites are to ships—or the remains of them—that have foundered off this treacherous coast. A dive including all the rental gear costs 7,000ptas; if you have your own gear it'll only cost you 2,000ptas. You must be a certified diver. If you're not, but you want to learn, Bucea offers courses. The store also stocks a bunch of gear.

Whether or not you're into sports, if you're in the city on a Sunday between September and May, check to see if the soccer team has a home game. As mentioned earlier, A Coruña won the '99-'00 national title, which was pretty amazing given the size, talent, and depth of teams from larger cities like Madrid and Barcelona. The **soccer stadium** is close to the center of town, right at the end of Praia de Riazor. There is no better way to truly understand the locals than to see thousands of them act like maniacs as they try to cheer their team on to another successful season. The best way to get tickets is at the box office in the stadium; scalpers can sometimes be found outside the stadium before matches as well.

STUFF

Ah, consumerism....You gotta love it, and you'll really love it in A Coruña. There are plenty of shops and boutiques here to keep you entertained while you're nursing that sunburn; most of them are in the Centro. Calles Real, Riego de Agua, Galeria, and Franja are all pedestrian-only streets

fashion

Since A Coruña is a summer resort, the dress code is much more lax than it is in the interior of the country. Women can walk around town in tank tops; bikinis are another matter—abundant on but not off the beach. Actually, they're not even that abundant *on* the beach; after all, this is Europe, so topless bathing is an option. Just don't forget the sunscreen. Guys, T-shirts work here more than anywhere else. Yeah, it'll still mark you as a non-native, but no one's going to give you a second look. Since A Coruña is popular with surfers, it doesn't come as a surprise that surf wear is one major trend. I wouldn't recommend the shortie for just hanging out on the beach, though.

At night things heat up in the bars and clubs, and everyone goes all out to dress the part. Looking good and going out are just fundamental in this country no matter where you are. Guys need more than just a T-shirt; for women, short skirts seem to be the norm. For everyone, leave the sandals and sneakers back in the room. Try to look nice, but don't worry too much. What you lack in fashion can easily be made up in attitude.

loaded with shops for clothes, shoes, jewelry, and trinkets. You'll find some American chains mixed in with the local and national stores. If you head up the hill onto the mainland you'll discover lots of shopping areas. Juan Florez and the streets running off it could easily keep a person busy window-shopping for an entire afternoon.

▶▶DUDS

In the center of town near the Plaza de Maria Pita, **Celtic** *(Baileu 2)* sells some hippyish-type clothes, but it's not exclusively a clothing store. It mainly specializes in things that reflect the Celtic roots of the region. Besides clothes, the store also carries stitched bags, wind chimes, and jewelry with Celtic symbols on them. Tucked away in the corner is a small display case of sex toys and kinky things (how this is Celtic, your guess is as good as mine). If you need flavored condoms or KY, check 'em out.

▶▶OUTDOOR SPORTING GOODS

If you're just itching to get off the beach and actually do something—that is, if aliens have taken over your body—then **The Adventure Factory** *(San Andres 14-16; 10:30am-2pm/5-8:30pm)* will outfit you. Even looking around this place gets the heart rate up. There's lots of hiking, camping, and kayaking gear to choose from, and the friendly staff is very knowledgeable.

▶▶MALL RATS

If you don't want to waste too much precious vacation time shopping, head to **Corte Ingles** *(Ramón y Cajal 57-59; Tel 981/290-011; 10am-9:30pm Mon-Fri)*, a huge department store on the mainland that has sections for men, women, and kids. It's also got a travel agent, restaurant, supermarket, and bookstore (English language, too!), as well as services for cutting hair and exchanging money. Although it's a little out of town, close to the bus station, this is one-stop shopping at its easiest.

EATS

With a plethora of choices awaiting visitors to A Coruña, a decent meal is never far away. Galician food is pretty excellent, especially if you like fish. Shellfish from the *Rios* and off the coast is a mainstay of the diet, as are squid and octopus. Lightly grilling seafood seems to be one of the most popular ways of preparing it, and garlic is one of the favorite seasonings. Remember that, if you've got romance on your mind.

Eating schedules follow the standard of Spain, with one exception—dinner. Breakfast is small—coffee and a pastry or the like. Lunch is eaten between 2-4 and is the biggest meal of the day. But at dinnertime, when anywhere else in Spain you'd be out of luck, many of the restaurants here think of us poor, pathetic tourists and do a little more than they normally would. Large sit-down dinners are not out of the question here, so if you're having trouble adjusting to eating a ton around 3pm, fear not; you can hold out until later and still fill up.

TO MARKET

Nothing says Europe like a *plein-air* picnic (thank you, Manet). In A Coruña, take your picnic basket out to the grounds around Torre de Hercules. Stock up on supplies ahead of time at the **Mercado San Agustin,** in the Praza San Augustin near the old town. This huge enclosed market has lots of stalls selling the freshest meats, fish, fruits, and veggies around. Vendors also sell cottage goods like cheeses, jams, and preserves. Ask a butcher for a specific cut of meat and he'll hack it right off the larger piece. You can buy fish, straight from the waters off shore, either gutted or whole. All right, maybe those aren't the best picnic treats, but the fruits and veggies are really fresh and delicious. You can pick up all the other odds and ends you may need at the full-size, modern supermarket downstairs. Don't forget plastic bags, otherwise sand will ruin your sandwich!

Tapas aren't as popular here as they are in other parts of the country, but hell, this is Spain, so they can't be ignored [see *bar scene,* above]. They're sort of an afterthought—a little something to put in your stomach while you socialize and work your way through a couple of drinks.

Begin a restaurant search on the calles west of Praza de María Pita. Franja is particularly loaded with dining options from cheap to expensive. Nearby Real and La Galera can prove fruitful. On the other side of the isthmus, near the beaches, you'll find tons of cafeterias and a couple of restaurants that feed the hungry sunbathers. Most offer outside seating.

▶▶CHEAP

If it's just a quick cheap meal you crave, **Yellow and Green** *(Franja 5; No phone; 1pm-1am Mon-Sat)* is one answer. Nothing more than a small sandwich shop, this place serves up burgers, *bocadillos,* and *platos combinados* costing no more than the change in your pocket. No *bocadillo* runs over 300ptas and the combo plates are all under 800ptas. Don't be put off by the bright yellow and green walls; there had to be some reason for the shop's name.

On the other side of town, overlooking Praia do Orzán, is **Gasthof** *(Barrie de la Maza 4; Tel 981/221-027; 11am-midnight Sun-Thur, 11am-2:30am Fri and Sat),* a modern Spanish diner that serves breakfast, lunch, and dinner. Kind of the Spanish answer to Denny's only with liquor, tapas, and *bocadillos.* You can order just a burger or sandwich (300-600ptas) or an entree or combo plate (775-1,000ptas). If you still can't afford these low prices, try your luck with the slot machine in the corner.

▶▶DO-ABLE

There are plenty of pleasant, sit-down restaurants to choose from that aren't overly expensive. **Sontiso** *(Franja 49)* offers delicious dishes at friendly prices. It specializes in Galician cuisine, cooking up some of the great seafood for which the region is known. Fish entrees run between 675-1,000ptas. If you're really hungry, the *menú del día* is a steal at only 1,100ptas, and includes two courses as well as wine and dessert.

▶▶SPLURGE

Splurge? There's no need here. Even the most acclaimed restaurants in town don't cost all that much. Spend that extra money on another bottle of Galician wine; you'll enjoy it more in the long run.

crashing

The skinny is that there are tons of rooms available in A Coruña. The beautiful beaches have brought in the tourists, and the tourists have brought in the *hostales* and hotels to accommodate them. That said, A Coruña suffers from the old July-August syndrome. You won't ever have a problem finding a room here, unless you're visiting during these two months, when out-of-towners descend on the city. Finding a room then can be difficult unless you've booked one ahead. Travelers looking for a single during this time will have an especially difficult time as most rooms are converted to doubles in the summer. Many places also jack up their rates during the height of the season, so even the economical options become a bit pricey. The simplest way to avoid this is to come to A Coruña in June or September when the weather is still warm, but the hordes have thinned.

Most of the cheaper places in town are in the Centro, which conveniently is exactly where you want to be. From here it is only a couple blocks to the beaches, the port, and most of the major sites. Hotels are spread out a bit more throughout the city. Since A Coruña is a popular destination, expect to pay more for rooms than you're used to.

▶▶CHEAP

Finding a barebones room here for real cheap presents a challenge. There are some very basic *hospedejas* (what are called *pensiones* elsewhere in Spain) on either side of the train station as you come out the front. They are the cheapest options in town, but with a 30-minute walk to the center, hardly worth it if you really want to explore the city. Once you get down to the Centro, start looking for a room along Rúa Nueva.

Hostal Centro Gallego *(Estrella 2; Tel 981/222-236; 2,500ptas single, 3,500ptas June 17-Aug 31; 3,500ptas double, 5,600ptas Jun-Aug; 5,000ptas triple, 6,000ptas Jun-Aug; No credit cards)* counts as one of the cheapest options in the center. The rooms are all nice for the money and come complete with small private bath and TV. Some even have their own little *galleria*. The owners are readily available in their cafe downstairs.

Not far away is **Hostal Maria** *(Galera 49; Tel/Fax 981/221-802; 2,800ptas single, 4,500ptas July and Aug; 4,500ptas double, 6,600ptas July and Aug)*. The rooms here are all spacious, comfortable, and very clean. The doubles can come with either two beds or one. Every room has a large private bath as well as a TV and phone. The staff is really friendly. I'd even recommend this place to my mother.

Another cheap option is **Pension La Alianza** *(C. Riego De Agua 8, 1st Fl; Tel 981 22 81 14; singles 2,000 ptas; doubles 3,500; shared baths; No credit cards)*.

▶▶DO-ABLE

About a block from the beach, **Hostal Sol** *(Sol 10; Tel/Fax 981/210-362; 3,500ptas single, 4,500ptas summer; 7,000ptas double, 9,000ptas summer; 9,000ptas triple, 12,000ptas summer; V, MC)* is a decent choice. The rooms are kind of Euro-Holiday Inn style, very functional and clean, but not very original. All do include a private bath, TV, and phone. The doubles come with either one bed or two, while the triples are doubles with a supplemental bed added. There is a cafeteria on the ground floor, but go out, the city has lots of great places to eat.

In the heart of the food area just west of Praza de María Pita is **Alboran Hostal** *(Riego de Agua 14; Tel 981/226-579; www.meiganet.com/hostalalboran; 3,745ptas single, 4,280ptas Aug; 5,350ptas double, 7,490ptas Aug; 7,223ptas triple, 10,111ptas Aug)*. All the rooms are quite nice with private bath, TV, and phone. They are modern and very comfortable.

A few other do-able options are **Hostal La Provinciana** *(Rua Nueva 7-9; Tel 981/220-400; singles 3,000 ptas, doubles 5,000 ptas; No credit* *cards),* **Hostal Santa Catalina** *(Travesia De Santa Catalina 1; Tel 981/226-609; singles, low season 2,700 ptas; singles, high season 4,200 ptas; doubles, low season 4,800 ptas; doubles, high season 7,000 ptas; all rooms with private bath; V, MC),* and **Hostal Alameda** *(Calle De La Alameda 12; Tel 981/227-074; singles, low season 3,000 ptas; singles, high season 4,000 ptas; doubles, low season 4,500 ptas; doubles, high season 7,000 ptas; all rooms with private bath; No credit cards).*

▶▶**SPLURGE**

For those willing to throw down a few more pesetas, you will find a bunch of luxury hotels vying to cater to you. If location is a key concern, **Hotel Riazor** *(Avda. Barrie de la Maza 29; Tel 981/253-400; hriazor@lander.es; 9,200ptas single, 11,760ptas Aug; 11,500ptas double, 14,700ptas Aug; 15,300ptas triple, 19,600ptas Aug; V, MC, AE)* is the only place you need. Sitting right across the street from the beach of the same name, this hotel knows how to take care of its guests. Most of the rooms face the beach and come with full bath, satellite TV, mini bar, and phone. The hotel also offers its guests parking and fax service.

The true king of all the lodging options here, though, is **Hotel Finisterre** *(Paseo del Parrote 2-4; Tel 981/205-400; www.hotelfinisterre.com; 15,500ptas single, 17,000ptas summer; 18,500ptas double, 20,400ptas summer; V, MC, AE).* Its glitzy lobby leaves no doubt that you are going to be pampered. The comfortable rooms overlook the port and come with a ton of extras: luxury private bath, satellite TV, phone, mini bar, and air conditioning. Guests get full run of La Solana [see *city sports*, above], so you can begin to understand what living the highlife is all about. But come to think of it, the rest of us have a great beach, what more could we want? (Okay, the massage would be nice.)

need to know

Currency Exchange You'll never have a problem finding a bank with a 24-hour accessible ATM here. The **Centro** has banks scattered throughout its streets, as does the **mainland.** One of these banks is on **Rúa Nova 30,** on the corner of San Andres. If you need to exchange money or cash checks, the bank's hours are 8:30am-2pm Mon-Fri. It has a 24-hour ATM.

Tourist Info The main **Tourist Office** *(Darsena de la Marina s/n; Tel 981/222-18-22; 9am-2pm/4:30-6:30pm Mon-Fri, 10:30-1pm Sat, 10-2pm/5-7pm Sat, Sun in summer)* is in the weird spot of occupying the median of the major road that runs next to the port. It's a nice office though, and they have all the info you'd want about the city and region. They won't make hotel reservations for you, but they'll give you a list of all the hotels in town—if you call ahead, they'll even fax or mail it to you. English is spoken.

Public Transportation Once you're in the center, most things are within walking distance. A Coruña is a big city though, so getting some places is more than a 30-minute walk (which often is quite nice). **City buses** *(Tel 981/250-100; 7am-11:30pm; 110ptas)* run throughout the city. Each bus stop posts the route. The tourist office sometimes has maps as well. During the summer there is a **Tourist Trolley** that operates during the day. Its route is simple: Just following the Paseo Maritimo around the bulb of the peninsula.

Health and Emergency Medical Emergencies: *061;* police (national): *091;* there is also the **San Jose Health Center** *(Comandante Fontanes 8; Tel 981/226-335)* to help you with any medical problems. The **National Police** *(Avda. Alferez Provisional 3; Tel 981/122-500)* can be contacted in the event of an emergency.

Pharmacies **Neon green crosses** mark the *farmacias,* which can be found throughout the city. No single one is open 24 hours a day; instead, *farmacias* rotate the all-night responsibility. Each one posts a schedule indicating who will be open on what night. **Farmacia Ossorio** *(San Nicolas 17; Tel 981/223-210; 9:30am-10pm daily)* is in the center.

Telephone City code: *981.* Operator: *1009.* International operator: *1005, 11 or 14.*

Airport **Aeropuerto de Alvedro** *(Tel 981/187-200)* is 9km (5mi) outside the city. There are only five flights a week from Madrid and getting to/from the city requires a cab ride.

Trains The **Estacion de San Cristobal** *(San Cristobal s/n; Tel 981/150-202)* isn't very conveniently located. It's about a 30-minute walk to the center, or you can hop on Bus 5, which will take you down to the port. A Coruña seems to be the rail hub for the region. It has connections to the southern cities of Santiago de Compostela, Ponteverde, and Vigo, as well as to the long-distance lines that run to Madrid through Orense and Zamora. There are also lines that run to Barcelona through Lugo, León, Bilbao, and Zaragoza.

Bus Lines Out of the City The **Estacion de Autobuses** *(Caballeros s/n; Tel 981/239-644)* has service to all the surrounding towns and villages in the region. It also has long-distance lines to Madrid—4 buses daily. The bus station is located out by the train station. Bus 14 runs between the bus station and the city center.

Postal To make friends and family jealous, send postcards from the **main post office** *(Alcalde Manuel Casas s/n; Tel 981/225-175).*

Internet See *wired,* above.

santiago de compostela

Santiago de Compostela's deserved status as a World Heritage City is not what attracts visitors to this city in the northwest corner of Spain (it just confirms what many already know). They come because of its significance as one of the world's top Christian pilgrimage destinations, they come to enjoy one of the most attractive old cities in the country, and they come from all over the world. They've also been coming for a very long time. Santiago de Compostela was one of the first "tourist" destinations in the world, and the first travel guide was written by a monk to help lead pilgrims to this holy city. (We've come a long way, haven't we?) For those of you who are losing track of all the sinful acts committed in the folly of youth, making the pilgrimage is allegedly good to get you out of half your time in purgatory. (Eternity divided by two...what does that work out to?)

Santiago de Compostela was the original field of dreams: "Build it and they will come." The "it" in this case is the legend of St. James, an apostle who had the misfortune of being beheaded. His body went missing until 813, when a shepherd in Galicia claimed to have been led to his tomb by a guiding star. It is said his body was taken to Galicia by boat to be buried. From that the game was afoot. A church gave rise to a cathedral—the *Catedral del Apóstol*—to accommodate and impress the growing number of pilgrims, and the story grew and grew. Believers flocked to Galicia, some to prove their faithfulness, others on a spiritual quest, and still more looking for redemption. In the 1500s, the ashes of the Saint were, ah..."misplaced," to keep them out of the hands of Sir Francis Drake, pirate and Englishman, who frequently raided the coast. But even with

santiago de compostela

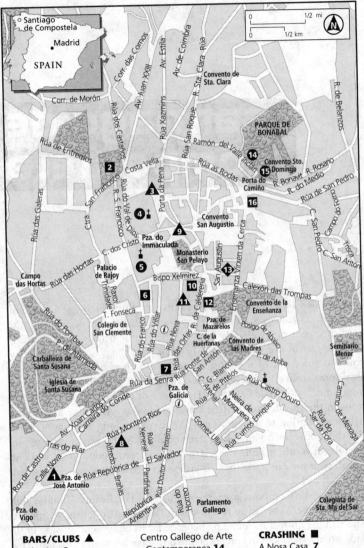

BARS/CLUBS ▲
Atlantico **3**
Casting **8**
Discoteca Apolo
  and Discoteca **1**
Pasajero Perdido **9**
Teatro Principal **11**

CULTURE ZOO ●
Catedral Fontana **5**

Centro Gallego de Arte
  Contemporanea **14**
Monasterio de
  San Martín Pinario **4**
Museo
  de Pobo Gallego **15**

EATS ◆
Mercado **13**
Restaurant Barbantes **6**

CRASHING ■
A Nosa Casa **7**
Hostal Barbantes **6**
Hostal-Reidencia
  "Giadas" **16**
Hostel
  dos Reis Católicos **2**
Hotel Real **12**
Santa Catalina **10**

the saint missing from his tomb, that didn't stop the pilgrims looking for a "get out of hell free" card.

Finally, in 1879, a workman making repairs on the cathedral discovered an urn that contained the remains of the saint. (This was totally unrelated, no doubt, to the fact that the number of visitors to the cathedral had declined.) Rome requested a chip from the skull to test the validity of the claim, and indeed, it was a match.

Today the pilgrimage is as popular as it ever has been. As you wander through this enchanting old city you will see hordes of pilgrims—they're the ones walking around with hand-carved hiking sticks, scallop shells on their hats (the symbol of St. James and the pilgrimage; see *the scallop scoop,* below), and, in more than a few cases, the latest titanium release from Trek mountain bikes. People from all walks of life come to complete the pilgrimage. While many still do it to prove their faithfulness, they are also joined by those looking to prove something to themselves. Several routes actually make up the Camino de Santiago. They all start in southern France and then split when they reach Spain. Some follow the coast, while others wander into cities that have other important cathedrals and religious monuments. When the pilgrims finally reach Santiago, they mingle with the tourists who descend on the city to see the great cathedral, a student crowd that keeps the city lively into the early hours on the weekends, and backpackers curious to find out what all the buzz is about.

Most likely they (and you) will want to check out the city's *Casco antiguo,* or old town, a living museum of antique granite *pazos* (manor houses), churches, convents, and a maze of narrow cobblestone streets opening unexpectedly at times onto little squares. To catch the best architecture, walk along Rúa do Vila, Rúa do Franco, and Rúa Nova. Part of these streets are covered by what locals call *soportales,* or arcaded walkways, giving the city its distinctive look. Poets have long rhapsodized about the "wet stones" of Santiago when the sun strikes them at the right angle, creating a golden glaze that often comes over the city.

Santiago de Compostela feels like an international city. Don't be surprised to hear German, English, French, and even Japanese spoken as well as Spanish and *Gallego.* Although the heart of Santiago beats strongly, the feel of the old town can sometimes get buried beneath the tour buses and groups that clog it during the height of the summer. It's hard to appreciate the cathedral when tour guides and their noisy flocks keep nipping at your heels. But that said, there are still a good nine and a half months when the streets are quiet and the city lives as it has for hundreds of years.

If you're heading to Santiago, or anywhere in Galicia for that matter, make sure you listen to Mom and bring your raincoat. Another of Santiago's great distinctions is that it receives more rain than any other city in Spain. The locals like to play it off, saying that the rain is good for the granite and that it adds to the charm of the old town. This is true—as you'll discover if you throw on your slicker and wander around on a rainy afternoon. There's something about old, rain-soaked, cobblestone streets that makes you feel more alive than the bluest of skies. Stumbling into majestic courtyards with fountains of wild horses, strolling through the arches of the galleries that line some the streets in the old town—you'll feel a sense of time and antiquity resonating in the stone itself. And if that poetry doesn't touch you, then there's plenty else to keep you entertained on a rainy day. Theatrical and musical performances abound in the summer, and it's easy to wile away a few hours in some of the fine museums here.

To find out what is going on around town, pick up a copy of *Compostela Capital.* The tourist office puts out this monthly paper with its listings of local theater, music, and art events. You can get a copy at the tourist office, and most bars in the old town also have a stack lying around. Although the events listings are in Spanish, they're easy to figure out with the most basic understanding of the language. The rest of the articles and listings are written in *Gallego,* Spanish, and English. *Compostelan* is another source to find out what is going on in the restaurants, bars, clubs, theaters, and museums. Grab it in any of the bars around town.

neighborhoods

A map of Santiago doesn't define specific neighborhoods, but it won't take too long to figure out the different moods of the city. You'll want to spend most of your time in the old town, the **Casco Historico.** It's one of the loveliest and best-preserved old towns in the north. One of the best things about it is that nearly the entire area is closed off to traffic, making it one big joyous pedestrian free-for-all. You can lose yourself in its many twisting streets; have no fear, though, the old town is pretty small, so getting lost is just for fun.

You will find most of the *hostales, pensiones,* and hotels in the old town, as well as more restaurants than a pilgrim could hurl his stick at. Many small, comfortable bars also pack themselves into the tiny streets here. On weekends, the *marcha* starts to get its drink on here before moving to the newer part of town.

To the south of the old town lies the commercial center of Santiago. Walking into this part of the city from the old town makes you feel like you're traveling time as well as distance. Here the streets buzz with the hustle and bustle that the 21st century has brought us. If you want to go shopping for the latest threads or pick up the most recent copy of *Maxim* or *Cosmo,* this is where you'll find it. **Praza Roxa** and the streets leading off of it have the most promising stores. In this area of town, you will also find many cafes. The *marcha* makes it way out to these parts sometime between 3-4am, keeping the groove moving at the local *puffs* and discos until the wee, wee hours of morning. The **train station** (RENFE) marks the southern border of the commercial center of town, running along **Avenida de Lugo.** From the train station it is a leisurely 15-minute walk to the old town.

To the west of the old town, across the **Carballeira de Sta. Susana,** is the **University of Santiago South Campus.** Head here if you're missing college friends and the college scene from back home; it's a great place to make new friends who will be willing to show you some of Santiago's lesser-known treasures.

hanging out

Santiago offers weary travelers many places to collapse and catch their breath. It all depends on the mood you're in.

If you just seek a nice place to relax, head for **Carballeira de Santa Susana.** This big park separates the old town from the University of Santiago West Campus, and so it attracts all kinds of people—families out with the little ones, old Spaniards just kinda wondering around, tourists looking to escape all the culture for a bit, students getting a little exercise. There are plenty of gardens, tree-lined walkways, and, best of all, benches. Grab yourself an *helado* (ice cream) from one of the many vendors at the entrance, sit your butt on a bench, and enjoy. Watch the more energetic folk jogging around the soft-surface walkway that rings the entire park, or get up and follow them around until you're looking back toward the cathedral. You'll get a great view of the spires stretching for the sky—plus it's an excellent spot to sit back and finish off that ice cream.

If it's fellow travelers you want to meet, one of the best spots is right behind the cathedral in **Praza Da Galicia.** Here people gather on the

wired

Don't look for any wild bars where you can tie one on as you hook into the Net. There aren't any. But come on, do you really need to drink to enjoy e-mailing? Of course not. Santiago has plenty of fun places to tap in and hook up (to the Internet, that is). **Nova 50** *(Rúa Nova 50; Tel 981/560-100; 9am-midnight daily; 250ptas an hour)* has plenty of computers upstairs to accommodate the many backpackers who use these facilities to stay in the game back home. It's a fun social atmosphere where you can make plenty of friends. The young crowd is a mix of Spaniards and foreigners, so you can practice your Español with the locals and your Australian dialect with those blokes from down under who seem to be everywhere.

One place that stays open later and offers great value is **Works & Games** *(Avda. Rodrigo de Padron 10; Tel 981/580-109; 11-3am daily; 100ptas per half hour)* in the old town. Coin-operated machines mean a pocket full of change will catch you up on all the gossip on the home front. The connections aren't the fastest, though, so don't plan on mailing off your manifesto. They offer Internet connection and network games if you can't stand seeing anymore of those damn historical sites!

large steps or at one of the outdoor cafes. Pilgrims sit here at the end of the day and enjoy the last rays of the sun before it sets behind the cathedral. Ask a couple of them about their adventures in getting here. The pilgrimage for most has become less of a religious passage and more about the journey itself, whether they did it by foot, bike, or even horseback. These people will be more than happy to tell you about the time it rained for four days and they had a gaping hole in their tent. You might find yourself transported as well as you absorb the beauty of this cathedral; there are few buildings in the world that symbolize so much.

bar scene

The bar scene in Santiago de Compostela veers off a bit from the Spanish norm. This isn't to say that bars don't exist or that they close at midnight. The *marcha* is definitely alive here. There are just fewer bars and they tend to be small, but each one is unique. What they do share in common are the hours: The typical bar here is open from 8pm to 3am, while discos open their doors at 11:30pm and close at 5am. (And, like most bars and clubs in Spain, they don't list their phone numbers!)

Given that Santiago is a tourist town, it's pretty tough to find bars off the beaten path; and most of the crowds are international, not local. But if it's a weekend and the game is on, and if you follow the *marcha* until dawn, you'll find that most of those big shots from out of town who talk a lot of game about loving the Spanish nightlife will have fallen to the curb before the night hits its climax. With the riff-raff out of the way, you can meet some pretty cool people. Things usually start out in one of the cozy bars in the old town. The tourist office actually prints—in English!—a guide to the bar scene. It's not bad, but the best way to find out what's going on is just to wander around and keep your ears cocked so that you can hear where the crowd sounds fun.

Early in the night, the liveliest scene is on Rúa Franco, in the old town, and the neighboring streets, where everyone jumps around from

rules of the game

Things are a little more conservative here than elsewhere in Spain. Santiago is, after all, the destination of the third most important Christian pilgrimage in the world. Yeah, people party, but they mainly just stick to booze. You may catch an occasional wisp of hash smoke in the air at some clubs (universities do always lead to higher education). Drinking on the street is legal, but largely not done. Most people keep the drinking to the chill cafes that have tables set up outside. The cops are relaxed, though. They aren't the ones who are going to give you a tough time; it's more likely you'll get dirty looks from the church lady.

one place to another, downing tapas and drinks. Most of the people taking part in this revelry are 30 and over, but that doesn't mean a little young blood can't get into the game. Later in the night, midnight and after, things spread out more in the old city, although finding a crowd is never too hard.

If it's a nice, mellow neighborhood spot you want, **Atlantico** *(Rúa da Troia; Tel 981/577-396)* is the perfect spot in the old town. Locals gather to gossip, play chess, and relax in this very low-key place. The crowd is a mix of old and young, and the music varies just as widely. One second you'll be listening to classical Celtic music and then, before you know it, it's modern punk. With a draft costing only 200ptas, it's not a bad place to get comfortable.

A number of lively spots line Paio de Antealtares, about a block behind the cathedral. They mostly draw in young rowdy crowds. **Pasajero Perdido** *(Calle Antealtares 3, Sotano),* located in a small square off this ancient street, is one of the city's oldest bars. Old age has not slowed this place down at all, though—only given it more character. Scratch your name over the thousands of others on the staircase that goes down to the cellar establishment. Masks from all around the world decorate the walls, testimony—as the bar's name, the Lost Traveler, implies—to the fact that someone was indeed lost for a very long time. After a couple of drinks (beers 250ptas, mixed 500ptas) you may find yourself getting lost in here—especially once Jimi starts playing on the system. The music tends to be a lot of classic rock.

There are a couple of *puffs* on the outskirts of the old town. A *puff* is what the Spaniards call a mini-disco, basically something a little bigger than a bar that is full of disco lights, loud dance music, and a hip crowd. **Abastos** *(Plaza de Abastos 8, Tel 981/560-421)* is right by the market of the same name. It plays a mix of Euro-dance and Top-40 music for a young, hip, weekend crowd that's just warming up around 2-4am before hitting the full-sized clubs. Not far away from the Porta do Camino, the old portal through which the ancient pilgrims entered town, is **Ultramarinos** *(Casas Reais; Tel 981/582-418; 8pm-3am daily),* another *puff* for young hipsters who make their own pilgrimage here around 1-3am. Head downstairs for the real action, to a dance floor where people get down to dance and house music. Drinks aren't that expensive (beers 300ptas, mixed 500ptas), so take advantage of them before heading to the clubs.

live music scene

The live music scene in Santiago is not your normal affair. A handful of pubs book bands some nights of the week, but most of the live music acts in town get showcased in big, fancy auditoriums. Santiago is into providing visitors with a culturally rich visit, and there's no slacking when it comes to the music program. So if you want to see the Galician Philharmonic or hear a great tenor with piano accompaniment, you've hit pay dirt. If you'd rather listen to a good band in an informal setting, your options are limited. The city does sponsor some live music events that are free, so make sure to check the Compostela Capital.

The **Auditorio de Galicia** *(Burgo das Nacions s/n; Tel 981/552-290)* and **Teatro Principal** *(Rúa Nova 21; Tel 981/586-521)* put on a wide variety of upscale, and large-scale, musical performances, from classical orchestras to opera singers. Although the prices of shows vary, neither place is particularly cheap.

It isn't uncommon to come across a band of *Tunas* in front of the Cathedral. These aren't fish that have sprouted feet and lungs, but rather groups of university students dressed in medieval ropes. They sing traditional songs and, after an entertaining performance, sell CDs and tapes. Ducking out before the hat gets past won't make you any friends when the audience is small. When it's bigger, well....

For a totally different kind of music scene, check out **Modus Vivendi** *(Paio Feixoo 1; No phone)*, an intimate jazz bar that's a great place for good conversation and good music. This dark, wood-paneled club (whose walls showcase the work of local artists) hosts live jazz bands certain nights of the week; only trouble is, these nights can vary week to week and there's no phone, so you'll need to drop by to find out about upcoming shows.

club scene

While the club scene is a far cry from the wild times to be had in Madrid and other big cities, the students at the university still make sure things stay lively well into the night and early morning. The one exception is the summer (mid-July to mid-September), when most students take off. Although the city's size limits the number of venues, in most cases quality is not sacrificed. Things tend to get going a little earlier here; the crowds begin to trickle in around 2am, and things really get off the ground by 3am. This is when the *marcha* leaves the confines of the old city and heads out to the newer parts of town where all the big clubs are located. A lot of the clubs here have just a small cover charge and a lax dress code, but that still doesn't mean sneakers and Birkenstocks; leave them in your room, have the sense to wear something more than a T-shirt, and you should be okay. As for the cover, whatever they may lose at the door from low prices, they more than make up for with what they charge for drinks.

In the basement of the Hotel Araguaney, just outside of the old town, **Casting** *(Alfredo Branas, 5; Tel 981/595-900; midnight-6am Wed-Sat; 500ptas cover)* is arguably the city's biggest and best club. This place, laid out on multiple levels, pulls in a crowd of mixed ages from 20-40 ready to get lost in the wild atmosphere. The ceiling of the club has windows into the hotel's swimming pool above; hey, just pretend you're on some James Bond set. Drinks here will suck pesetas out of your pocket at an astonishing rate, with beers costing 500ptas and mixed drinks running 800ptas. Things are at their best here on Fridays and Saturday nights from 2 to 6am. Thursday doesn't see the same packed crowds, but there is still plenty of life in this club.

Before you hit Casting, there are a couple of smaller clubs to check out nearby, in the area around Plaza Roxa, or "Red Square." This is the center of disco life in Santiago. From Plaza Roxa, the adjoining streets are also lined with bars and cafes—try Rúa Nove, Rúa de Frei Rodendo Salvado, and Rúa de Fernando III o Santo. Most places here play recorded music, are open till dawn, and are simple in décor (they rely on their clientele to provide the charm and character). **Discoteca Apolo** and **Discoteca Fontana,** next door to each other on Santiago del Estero, attract a lot of university students who come here in preparation for the bigger clubs. Cover in both places is 500 pesetas, and you can grab a beer for 350 pesetas.

ARTS SCENE

Santiago strives to provide a deep cultural experience for its residents, visitors, and pilgrims alike. Given the city's size of just under 100,000 people, the number of galleries, theaters, and auditoriums is quite impressive. That's probably why Santiago was chosen as a World Heritage City, one of nine European cities that represent the changing cultural face of Europe as it heads into the 21st century. Although deeply connected to its past, Santiago's arts program is as up-to-date as any major city around.

▶▶VISUAL ARTS

Taking their cue from the success of Santiago's art museums [see *culture zoo,* below], small galleries increasingly have been popping up in the city. Most are situated in the old center, so wandering in and out of them is easy, and that's the best way to find out what you dig, anyway. **Galeria de Arte** (*Xelmirez 25; Tel 981/576-239; noon-2pm/6:30-9pm Mon-Fri; palomapintos@mixmail.com*) is a small one-room gallery that hosts contemporary exhibits from regional artists. Nearby, the ancient street Rúa Nova is home to a couple of good contemporary art galleries. **Trinta Arte Contemporineo** (*Rúa Nova 30; Tel 981/584-623; 12:30-2:30pm/5:30-9pm*), one of the city's larger gallery spaces, hosts exhibits by artists from throughout Galicia. Right down the street you'll find **Galeria de Arte Sargadelos** (*Rúa Nova 16; Tel 981/581-905*), which also features regional artists. Both of these galleries hold each exhibiting artist for four to six weeks before highlighting someone else.

A couple of the fancier hotels also use their lobbies as informal gallery spaces. Next to the cathedral, the famous and very swanky **Hotel Reyes Católicos** (*Praza do Obradoiro 1; Tel 981/582-200*) hosts temporary exhibits. Checking out the artwork here will also give you an excellent excuse to get into the hotel, which is the oldest in the world, and one of the nicest! To think, this used to be where poor pilgrims came to sleep after finishing their holy journey. Outside the old town, **Hotel Araguaney** (*Alfredo Branas 5; Tel 981/595-900*), another of the city's luxury hotels, also hosts temporary exhibits in its lobby.

▶▶PERFORMING ARTS

The best place to go if you're in the mood for some theatrical excitement is the **Teatro Principal** (*Rúa Nova 21; Tel 981/586-555*), which puts on a large variety of theatrical events throughout the year. Don't expect any catering specifically to English speakers, though. Besides drama and comedy shows, this theater also gives its stage over for musical concerts, opera, pretty much anything. *Compostela Capital* lists the offerings, as does *Compostelan*. Or you can just stop by the theater during your wanderings; a schedule of events is posted outside. Comedy and drama performances run all week when the troupe is in at **Salon Teatro** *(Rúa Nova 34; Tel 981/563-965)*, a slightly more informal theater. Performances generally start around 9pm and tickets cost about 1,000ptas. It's best to stop by the box office to reserve tickets ahead. Info on current performances is posted on the street in front of the theater.

There are no big Cineplex movie theaters in the old city. **Cine** *(Vilar 51; Tel 981/582-029; Show times vary but usually 6, 8, 11pm; 600ptas weekdays, 675ptas weekend, 500ptas Seniors, students, kids)* is as good as it gets, with one screen that usually shows the latest (i.e., Hollywood) blockbuster. Save a few pesetas and sneak off to the Monday matinee, which costs only 450ptas. On Sunday afternoons this theater sometimes hosts shows for kids (puppet shows and the like), and it also advertises drama courses for adults and kids. Swing by for the full scoop.

CULTUrE ZOO

Santiago de Compostela is a cultural minefield. Every step you take, you're bound to land on the steps of one of its many monuments or museums. It is impossible to come through this city without being changed by it. At the end of your stay you'll be less a poor, intellectually deprived American and more a cultured European (or, at least a more cultured American). The old city is home to many of the most glorious attractions and is a well-preserved relic in its own right. Give yourself plenty of time to make it around to all of the sites. Each would be worth a trip even if it was the only game in town. With all of them collected together as they are, you may find your head spinning at times.

Catedral *(Praza do Obradoiro; Tel 981/584-081, 7am-9pm daily)*: This is Santiago's centerpiece—and what draws everyone to this place. Hailed as the crowning achievement of Romanesque architecture, the majority of this amazing structure was built between 1075-1211. Since then, of course, towers and altars have been added, in every conceivable architectural style. Everyone wanted to put their touch on the destination point of one of the largest Christian pilgrimages in the world. In particular, it is hard to ignore the fancy Baroque "improvements." Even the influence of the Conquistadors from the new world seems to be reflected in what appear to be Mayan, pyramid-like structures built on to one portion. Although any glimpse of the structure will stun you with its beauty, facing it from Praza do Obradoiro gives you a view of the bell towers reaching for heaven that can only be described as breathtaking. Whether you're a deeply religious person or not, your spirit will soar as you gaze upon its many ornate carvings.

Just inside the entrance from Praza do Obradoiro you'll find Master Mateo's treasured *Portico de la Gloria,* which is considered by some to be

the scallop scoop

So what the hell is the deal with the scallop shells you keep seeing everywhere? They're the symbol for the Camino de Santiago. But nobody really knows how this came to be. One story has it that a man riding his horse to meet the boat carrying the body of St. James was washed out to sea. The saint, covered in scallop shells, rose from the sea to rescue him. Another variation says the man's wife prayed to St. James to save her drowned husband, whereupon the man rose from the depths covered in scallop shells. In fact, though, the scallop shell really didn't get hooked to St. James until the 12th century, long after his death. But scallops do thrive in the *rías* near Santiago, so when the pilgrims were looking for a symbol, scallops made a natural choice. Scallops were widely sold to pilgrims in Santiago and the tag may have just stuck. At any rate, the scallop shell became part of the uniform of pilgrims on their way to Santiago. It worked as a passport for crossing boundaries unhindered, it got them free board along the way, and it allegedly offered some sort of divine protection. Robbing—not to mention killing—a pilgrim was considered one of the worst things a person could do.

It even got to the point that the selling of scallop shells was outlawed anywhere along the route except in Santiago. The first thing a pilgrim would do upon entering Santiago would be to buy and eat a scallop, then tie the shell to his brim to indicate that he had completed his journey.

Some say there is more to it than that, though. They draw a link between St. James and Venus, the goddess of love, who is also symbolized by a scallop shell. Apparently, the scallop shell is an emblem of the vagina. Now that certainly puts a whole new spin on this religious experience.

one of the world's finest Romanesque sculptures. It took 20 years to carve, and another 20 years couldn't bring it any closer to perfection. After you've appreciated every detail of this masterpiece, take a stroll past the supposed remains of St. James. They lie in a little silver urn in a passageway beneath the main altar. If you need to get away from tour groups, seek out some of the smaller chapels and sanctuaries that line the outskirts of the nave and main altar. In these peaceful hideaways, people kneel in prayer, true to the *raison d'etre* of the church. These people are the ones who understand what this cathedral is all about.

Sometimes I wondered about everyone else. Things here are a little different from other cathedrals you might have visited. For one thing, there is artificial lighting inside. True, it does bring out a lot of the finer details in the gorgeous carvings that cover almost every square inch of the building, and it does make the altar glow brighter than the city of El Dorado, but it also detracts a little from the spiritual feel. Another thing that's hard to overlook is that instead of lighting a candle after making an offering here, you simply drop a coin in a slot and a little electrical candle lights up for you—anyone feeling holy? It does seem like a lot of the religious splendor has been sold out to tourism. I'm not saying that this isn't a gorgeous and worthy place. I just feel it has fallen a bit victim to its own fame; I mean, there's a gift shop in the damn cathedral that sells *ashtrays* picturing the place.

If, however, you have had a very different experience and can't wait to see more, you should definitely check out the **cloister and museum** *(10am-1:30pm/4-7:30pm Mon-Sat, 10am-1:30pm/4-7pm Sun June-Sept; 11am-1pm/4-6pm Mon-Sat, 10am-1:30pm/4-7pm Sun Oct-May; 500ptas)* that are a part of the cathedral. Inside the museum you will find a couple of large tapestries that have survived from the 16th century and two statues of a pregnant Virgin Mary (come on, the folks are only going to believe the virgin story for so long). There are also archeological findings from some of the digs done in the cathedral as well as a couple of manuscripts of old travel guides written for pilgrims.

Monasterio de San Martín Pinario *(Praza de San Martin; 10am-2pm/5-8:30pm daily):* If you haven't suffered from a religious overdose, leave through the north entrance of the cathedral, cross Praza da Inmaculada, and head into another building whose altars and moldings of unbelievable detail and beauty would have anyone believing God is great. Not surprisingly, given its neighbor, this was once the most powerful monastery in the region.

Museo do Pobo Gallego *(Convento de San Domingos de Bonaval; Tel 981/583-620; 10am-2pm/4-8pm Mon-Sat, Sun 11am-2pm; Free):* If you need to escape the religious world for a bit, Santiago offers lots of great museums to get lost in. In this great regional ethnographic museum, displays of the old agricultural ways, including old farm tools and dioramas, can be found alongside traditional Galician outfits and dress. One very interesting room not only has lots of Galician pottery, but also explains the different ways it was crafted and even how the clay was excavated. The music room features regional instruments like bagpipes, castanets, and a zanfona (you gotta see it to understand it), and another large room explores traditional Galician maritime traditions. One of the highlights of the museum, though, is a staircase. This isn't any ordinary, run-of-the-mill staircase; this thing looks like it belongs at Harry Potter's Hogwarts. Three intertwined, free-floating, spiral staircases carry you to most of the exhibit rooms and are a site in their own right.

Centro Gallego de Arte Contemporaneo *(Valle Inclan s/n; Tel 981/546-621; 11am-8pm Tues-Sun; free):* Opened in 1993, this was Galicia's first major museum devoted to contemporary art and Santiago's first attempt to modernize the city's art collection; they succeeded on both accounts. Besides housing a permanent collection of contemporary works by Galician artists, the museum also plays host to a range of temporary art exhibits.

Museo Eugenio Granell *(Pazo de Bendana, Praza do Tournal; Tel 981/576-394; 11am-9pm Mon-Sat, 11am-2pm Sun; 300ptas, Students 150ptas, Sunday free):* A bit smaller than the Centro Gallego de Arte Contemporanea, but just as interesting, this surreal museum is sure to spin your mind in new directions. Housed in an old country manor, its permanent exhibit includes works by Picasso, Breton, and Granell. Come here for a psychedelic trip after visiting the grand cathedral. What a contrast.

Museo das Peregrinaciones *(Rúa de San Miguel 4; Tel 981/581-558; 10am-8pm Tues-Fri, 10:30am-1:30pm/5-8pm Sat, 10:30am-1:30pm Sun; 400ptas, Students 200ptas):* If you want to learn more about the sacred pilgrimage to Santiago, the best place to find out—shy of buying a pilgrim a beer—is to pay a visit to this museum. The exhibits, including relics of things the pilgrims themselves carried on their journey, are sure to enlighten the curious traveller. With eight well-designed rooms covering every aspect of the pilgrimage, St. James, Santiago de Compostela, and the cathedral itself, you'll leave here with a full understanding of why it was created, and what it's all about.

city sports

Santiago is into brains, not brawn. Its museums, monuments, theaters, and galleries will give the heaviest part of your body, your head, more than enough exercise. But if the rest of your body demands a full workout, too, there are a couple of places to go.

Jogging on the soft path in the **Carballeria de Santa Susana** is popular with the city's university population. Besides offering a place to work off extra energy, the park also has some amazing views looking back toward the old town and the cathedral.

If you continue through the park and onto University Campus South, there are more options for sports and activities. Once on campus, head for the Praza de Rodriguez Cadarso, where you'll find the **campus sports center.** This sports complex is open to the public, although some activities—like using the pool—do cost a small fee. Here there are tennis and basketball courts as well as a pool; outside are the soccer fields. You must sign up for a tennis court ahead of time.

To experience some of the dramatic scenery just outside of Santiago, head for the **Cabo Finisterre,** one of the westernmost points in Europe. According to the Roman poet Horace, the ancients considered the cape "the end of the world." The nightmare of early mariners, this rock-strewn coastline is called the "Coast of Death," or La Costa de la Muerte in Spanish, because of the countless shipwrecks off its shore. Fortunately, it's smoother sailing for visiting landlubbers, who get to enjoy some of the most panoramic views in all of Spain, not to mention amazing sunsets. As our buddy Horace put it, "The brilliant skylight of the sun drags behind it the black night over the fruitful breasts of earth." We couldn't have said it better ourselves.

Once you've drunk in the view, you can head for the beaches, which spread out from the fishing port of Cabo Finisterre along Ría de Corcubión. In summer, boat trips along the coast leave periodically from the harbor. To reserve a ride, call *981/740-375*. Once at the harbor, look for a company called "Pleasure Boats" (yes, in English), which charges a mere 125ptas for a 1-1/2 hour tour.

It's easy to get from Santiago to the cape. In summer there are several daily buses that cost 1,450ptas one way. The ride takes two hours.

STUff

Most of what this town has to offer visitors is connected to the cathedral, pilgrimage, or St. James himself in some way or another. You'll find the area right around the cathedral and Rúa do Franco packed full of tourist shops with the image of the cathedral plastered on T-shirts, plates, clocks, and other things no one in the world needs. The ubiquitous scallop shell can also be found on any number of souvenirs. If you're looking for gifts to bring to people back home that scream, "I was in Santiago!" you'll be overwhelmed with choices.

On the south side of the cathedral you'll also find a cluster of silver stores. Silversmithing was a popular trade in old Santiago, and the tradition has remained. In Roman times, local smiths created pieces of art out of whatever silver didn't get sent south along the *Ruta de Plata* to be shipped back to Italy. Most of the items on sale today are rather grandiose and borderline tacky. But, if you have your heart set on finding a nice piece, it can be done with a little digging.

At the head of Rúa Nova and the area around it, during the late spring and summer, artisans set up stands in the street selling crafts of all kinds, from woven bags to handmade jewelry. Don't be afraid to try a little bargaining here. Most of their prices are set by the tourist dollar.

Most shopping, other than for souvenirs and silver, should take place out of the old town. The streets around Praza Roxa offer plenty of more modern options.

▶▶**DUDS**

If you want to do some clothes shopping you'll have to head out of the old town to **Praza Roxa.** Here you'll find a number of stores that sell the latest fashions. None, however, particularly stick out for their cutting-edge style or alternative look.

▶▶**BOUND**

Unless you want to read about the Camino de Santiago (and Santiago has plenty of such books in just about every language) again, head out of the old city. **Follas Novas** *(Montero Rios 37; Tel 981/594-406; 9am-2pm/4-8pm Mon-Sat),* near Praza Roxa, has three floors full of books. You'll find a decent English section on the bottom floor. The store stocks an odd variety of titles from Danielle Steele to Dante to textbooks, so don't have your heart set on a particular book.

▶▶SPORTS/OUTDOOR

If you find your pack unrepairable after your own long pilgrimage, **Piteira** *(Huerfanas 38; Tel/Fax 981/586-794; 9:30am-1:30pm/4:30-8pm Mon-Fri, 9:30am-2pm/5-8pm Sat)* carries a wide selection of replacements. It's also got lots of sports gear and attire as well as a helpful staff that can point you to the best spots to use 'em.

EATS

No pilgrim has ever gone hungry making a pilgrimage down Rúa Franco or Calle Raina. You'll find both streets packed with restaurants, most with refrigerated display cases showing their choicest-cut meats, fresh lobster, and finest octopus tentacles (a delicacy!). You're bound to find exactly what your stomach craves, from cheap bocadillos to gourmet mollusks. Tapas aren't as central to the dining experience here as they are elsewhere in Spain. Few of the bars have tapas and the selection in those that do is very limited. This is probably because the many foreigners who pass through town are used to more traditional dinners. At any rate, sit-down

in the mood

There's only one thing worse than a nic-fit and that's a choco-fit. It starts out as a little idea in the back of your mind, then gradually becomes more insistent. Before you know it your head is screaming, "Get me some damn chocolate!" If you find this happening to you, do not pass go, do not collect two hundred dollars. Go directly to **Matate** *(Antealtares 12; No phone; 6pm-3am Mon-Sat; No CC)*, a really cool bar in the old town that will satisfy any sweet tooth. One of the glorious discoveries made in the New World was chocolate, which, along with other wonderful new foods, was brought back to Europe by ships returning from the newly discovered land. Galicia was the first stop for most of the boats, and the townspeople happily adopted many of these new delights into their cuisine. Matate uses an old Galician chocolate recipe and makes extremely rich chocolate drinks, most mixed with various liqueurs (about 400ptas). Chocolate mousse (350ptas) is a house specialty. Matate also has a wide selection of beers (including Guinness), coffees, and wines. There is also an upstairs cafe *(entrance around block on Preguntoiro 12, 7am-9pm)* for when the urge strikes earlier in the day.

restaurants and a filling meal are what's on tap for the evening. Considering this is a tourist town, dining isn't that expensive, with few entrees exceeding 2,000ptas.

▶▶**CHEAP**

You don't have to look too far for some good cheap eats here. You can satisfy your hunger without going broke at **Bar Coruna** *(Raina 17; Tel 981/583-968; noon-1am daily; Avg 170-300ptas; No CC)*, a beer and bocadillo joint. Bocadillos, or the local version thereof (called *impañada*), are, of course, the specialty, but they also serve burgers and sandwiches. If you need a little more variety, they also have octopus, salads, and cheese and ham plates for lunch, dinner, or pre-*marcha*.

If you just want to pick up a bite on the move during the day, then grab a sandwich or bocadillo at **Mercado** *(Rúa da Acibecheria 8; 7:30am-2pm Mon-Sat; Avg 500ptas)*. This small market in the old town has a bocadillo counter where you can eat in or have it wrapped to go.

▶▶**DO-ABLE**

One of the more atmospheric places on Calle Raina is **Sant Yago** *(Calle Raina 12; 2-4pm/6pm-midnight Mon-Sat; Avg 1,500ptas)*. As you flip through the menu, with its appetizing selection of seafood and meat, your taste buds will jump to a heightened state of anticipation. Galician dishes such as seafood soup and fresh hake are always delicious in this pretty, stone-walled dining room, and the *menú del día* guarantees you won't walk away hungry or disappointed.

Not far away, **Restaurante Barbantes** *(Franco 3; Tel 981/581-077; 1-4pm/8pm-midnight daily; 1,000-2,000ptas per entree; V, MC)* offers more regional cooking prepared to perfection. It also has outside seating in a pleasant courtyard during warmer weather. At the height of the season, though, things can get a little noisy around here as crowds wander up and down this popular street. If you'd like to dine in peace, the inside room is very pleasant.

▶▶**SPLURGE**

If you have some pesetas to throw around and really want to experience the finest in Galician cooking, **Moncho Vilas** *(Avda. de Villagarcia 21; Tel 981/598-387; 1:30-4:30pm/8:30pm-midnight daily; 2,000-3,800ptas per entree; V, MC, AE)* is one place that even the locals swear by. I'm told they have the best fish soup in town. The atmosphere here is pretty low-key, considering its reputation. It feels more like a tavern than a fine dining establishment.

crashing

Whether you've arrived by a long pilgrimage or a short train ride (relatively speaking, of course), finding a place to call home in Santiago won't pose a problem. The city has been hosting travelers for over 1,700 years, so the locals know how to make you comfortable. The old town, where the action lies, has lots of *hostales* and *pensiones* packed into its twisting streets. The range of accommodations extends from basic to world-class. Some places hike up the price a few hundred pesetas in July and August when rooms are most in demand. Reserve ahead if you can during these months.

▶▶CHEAP

Charming yet affordable **Santa Catalina** *(Rúa de Xelmirez 18; Tel 606/674-017; 2,000ptas single; 4,000ptas double, 5,000ptas with bath; 6,000ptas triple; No credit cards)* is in the center of things in the old town. Rates vary a lot, depending on room size and location. When I asked for a single, I was shown a room with a double bed for 2,500ptas; when I asked for something cheaper I got a cozy, windowless room for 1,000ptas. All the rooms are clean, comfy, and look like they've recently been renovated. They are pleasantly decorated and have a desk and chair. The owner is nice and pretty much leaves you alone. The shared bathroom is modern and clean.

Other cheap options are **Hospedaje Ramos** *(C. Raina 18, 2nd Fl; Tel 981/581-859; single without bath 1,800ptas; single with bath 2,000ptas; double without bath 3,350ptas; double with bath 3,650ptas; No credit cards)*, 100 meters from the cathedral, and **Hospedaje Forest** *(Callejon De Don Abril Ares 7; Tel 981/570-811; double 2,900ptas; single 1,600ptas; shared baths; No credit cards)*.

▶▶DO-ABLE

Just inside the edge of the old town you'll find **A Nosa Casa** *(Entremurallas 9; Tel 981/585-926; anosacasa@bch.navegalia.com, www.navegalia. com/bch/anosacasa; 3,100ptas single, 3,600ptas July-Nov; 4,500ptas double, 5,600ptas July-Nov; 6,000ptas triple, 7,000ptas July-Nov, No credit cards)*, a hostel that occupies a building over one hundred years old, although you'd never guess it from looking at the rooms. They are nice and clean, a little small, but each comes complete with bathroom, TV, and phone. The hostel also offers breakfast, laundry, and fax services for its guests.

Hostal-Residencia "Giadas" *(Plazuelo del Matadero 2; Tel 981/587-071; 3,300ptas single, 5,000ptas double, prices increase 200ptas per room July and Aug; No credit cards)* is right outside the city by the Porta do Camino. The rooms here are large, bright, and very comfortable, some even with a sofa or a couple chairs for lounging around. All the rooms have bathrooms and TVs and look recently redone too. A restaurant on the ground floor, open to the public, serves inexpensive, typical Spanish dishes.

A lot of restaurants here have lodging above them. Above Restaurante Barbantes [see *eats*, above], is **Hostal Barbantes** *(Franco 3; Tel 981/581-793; 4,280ptas single, 5,350ptas double, No credit cards)*, partnered by Barbantes II, which you'll find across a pleasant little plaza from the original. Both operate under the same management, so going to one is the same as going to the other. In both cases, the rooms all have private bathrooms. They are nice and clean, but basic. The doubles come either with one bed or two, depending on how close you want to be to your travel buddy.

Another do-able option is **Hostal Alameda** *(Campo De San Clemente 32; Tel 981/588-100; Fax 981/588-689; single without bath, low season 2,700ptas; single without bath, high season 3,500ptas; single with* *bath, low season 2,800ptas; single with bath, high season 4,500ptas; double with bath, low season 5,800ptas; double with bath, high season 7,500ptas; V, MC, AE).*

▶▶**SPLURGE**

If you plan on spending a lot of time in your room and want pleasant surroundings, and price isn't an issue, **Hotel Real** *(Caldereria 49; Tel 981/569-290; hrealsc@teleline.es, www.hotelreal.com; 6,500ptas single, 7,500ptas April-Oct; 9,500ptas double, 10,500ptas April-Oct; V, MC)* is in the old town and offers its guests top-notch rooms complete with private bath, TV, phone, and breakfast. But if you're going good, why not go all the way to the best and stay at **Hostal dos Reis Católicos** [see *art*, above]. You have a credit card, just charge the 30,000ptas (over $180) starting price. It's one of the best in the world, you know!

need to know

Currency Exchange This is tourist country. The locals have made it very easy, with banks and ATMs all over town for you to change your money into their money so you can spend it in their wonderful city. Lots of larger hotels and places in the old town advertise exchanging, but for the best rate stick to the banks and ATMs. You'll find a number of them on and around the central Praza de Galicia. The most central bank with an ATM is **Banco Central Hispano** *(Rúa Vilar 30, Tel 981/581-612)*. There are many banks and currency exchanges (also ATMs) in the vicinity of the cathedral, along Calle Franco and Rúa Nova.

Tourist Info The main **tourist office** *(Rúa do Vilar 63; Tel 981/555-129; 9am-9pm daily)* is staffed by an extremely knowledgeable and helpful group of people that speaks English as well as many other languages. They have written info on anything you'll want to know about the city from monuments to museums to bars—most of it is in English, too. Ask them about the ghost in the office.

Public Transportation Since most of the old town is open only to pedestrian traffic, walking will be your principal means of transport. Even the sights beyond the old town are not out of walking distance. **City buses** *(Info Tel 981/581-815; 100ptas)* operate everywhere outside of the old town. Most lines pass through Praza de Galicia on the edge of the old town. All bus stops post a map of the different lines.

American Express Ultratur *(Avda. Figueroa 6; Tel 981/587-000; 10am-2pm/4:30-7pm Mon-Fri)* is the city's American Express representative. It's a 2-minute hike south of the cathedral.

Health and Emergency Medical emergencies: *061*. National Police: *091* The **Hospital Xeral de Galicia** *(Vidan-Estrada de Noia; Tel 981/950-000)* lies to the northeast of the center. The **National Police** *(Rodrigo de Padron; Tel 981/581-944)* can be called in the event of an emergency.

Pharmacies Farmacia R. Bescansa *(Praza de Toral 11; Tel 981/585-940; Open 24 hours)* is a 24-hour pharmacy conveniently located in the old town. Like everywhere in Spain, *farmacias* are designated by **neon green crosses.**

Telephone City code: *981*. Phone cards can be picked up at tobacco shops. There is also a **Telephone/Fax Office** *(Rúa das Bautizados 15; Tel 981/575-346)* that has phones for international calling. Their rates aren't that much better than public phones, however. They also exchange money.

Airport **Aeropuerto de Lavacolla** *(Tel 981/547-500)* lies 15-20 minutes outside the city by car on the road to Lugo. It is the region's only international airport. Iberia has daily flights from Madrid and Barcelona. From the airport you can either get to Santiago by taxi or bus. The bus schedule varies.

Trains **Estacion Santiago Apostol** *(Rúa Horreo s/n; Tel 981/520-202)* is about a 15-minute walk south from the center of town. Sixteen trains make the one-hour trip daily to A Coruña, where there are connections to Madrid and Barcelona. From Santiago there are also trains that run to Vigo and Ponteverde, as well as smaller local towns.

Bus Lines Out of the City **Estacion de Autobuses** *(Praza de Camilo Diaz Balino s/n; Tel 981/587-700)* is inconveniently located a good 30 minutes north of the old town. It's hardly worth the trip. Unlike other places in Spain, most of the trains in Galicia are faster and cheaper than the buses.

Bike Rental If you're getting a little jealous of the wheels the poor pilgrims are coasting into town on, head to **Bici Total** *(Tel 981/564-562; 2,500ptas 1-day bike rental)* on Avenida Lugo. Unfortunately, this is a healthy walk from the center of town (it takes about 20 minutes if you take Rúa Trompas south of the cathedral). Just as well, since the tight streets here don't make cruising the best idea anyway. If you really want to stretch your legs, they'll give you a map and point you to the best biking trail. It'll take you to Monte Pedroso, where you'll get a panoramic view of the city.

Postal The **main post office** *(8:30am-8:30pm Mon-Fri, 9:30am-2pm Sat)* sits on the corner of Rúa do Franco and Travesia de Fonseca about a block south of the cathedral.

Internet See *wired*, above.

camino de santiago

The top three reasons to go on the Camino de Santiago are: 1) You need to shed a few pounds and hiking for 30 days through woods and small Spanish towns sounds better than the Slim Fast diet plan; 2) You have done something very naughty and need to be absolved of all of your sins; or 3) You want to take a cheap trip and you love the outdoors, history, wine, and meeting hikers and other cool people from around the world.

The Camino de Santiago is one of the three main pilgrimages of the Catholic Church (after Jerusalem and Rome). It consists of a series of roads that start at different points all over Europe and end in **Santiago de Compestela,** a town in western Spain. Legend has it that the bones of St. James, the apostle who supposedly converted the pagan Spaniards, are kept in Compostela. The pope declared in 1179 that anyone who finished the Camino would be awarded official absolution from their sins; needless to say, this attracted lots of people. The most popular route, called the **Camino Frances,** traverses northern Spain. It begins in a small town in France called **Saint-Jean-Pied-de-Port** and heads up and over the **Pyrenees Mountains** and through some of the most beautiful small towns, quiet hills, empty valleys, and greatest scenery in the world.

It is tough to walk the Camino de Santiago without being transformed. There are many things that will affect you: the friendly helpfulness of the locals; the Spanish countryside; the religious and spiritual undertones that form a constant theme of the journey; the fact that you are walking a route that perhaps millions of other people have walked since the Middle Ages. When you finish the hike and go home, people will definitely see a difference in your behavior. It might be that having received your official "get-out-of-hell-free card" direct from the pope, you will finally be able to forget that mistake you made with Candy, the friendly "woman of the night" in Vegas, and get on with your life. Or maybe you'll come away with a little, quiet place tucked away under the grime and stank that you picked up on your journey, a place you can rely on the next time your train is stuck and you're fifteen minutes late for work. Or hey, maybe you'll just get blistered toes.

Okay, the Camino de Santiago might be a little played. It *has* received millions of visitors over the last 2,000 years. In the Middle Ages, because so many European pilgrims wanted to check out the saint's bones, the Camino became something of a tourist trap, complete with five-star hotels, brothels, churches, and chapels...all the trappings of a 14th-century Disneyland. Fortunately for us, the Camino went out of fashion for a couple hundred years, after the Reformation and other social and political changes whittled away at the prominence of the Catholic Church. The Camino is just beginning to regain popularity today. Some say it is due to a rebirth of spirituality brought on by the millenium, or by the New Age movement, but we just think it is because outdoorsy folks from around the world are starting to hear about it again. And really, who could resist a challenging hike that takes you from the Pyrenees to the western coast of Spain, all the while sampling great Spanish food, drinking wine from the Rioja valley, checking out ancient churches, bridges, paintings, and towns, and meeting all kinds of great Spanish and international people. If you ask us, you don't need to be a New Age crystal lover to dig on the Camino de Santiago.

All told, from door-to-door the Camino is around 774 kilometers, or 300 miles long. That sounds like a ton, but if you take the daily recommended dosage, and pace yourself for 30 days, you only have to hike an average of 10 miles a day—not too bad. You might also want to acquire a walking stick or staff at some point. The traditional stick for a pilgrim is a staff a little taller than head length, with some kind of carving on top. You can buy these in towns along the Camino, or just pick one out of the woods. During the Middle Ages, it was this staff that served to mark the pilgrims for special treatment in town. If you dress the part, people along the way will be extra friendly, yelling out greetings and waving as you pass.

Since the Camino is so long, you'll see a variety of terrain. The most beautiful parts of the trip are at the beginning and the end. The middle half can be boring, with long periods of walking along paved roads, but the first and last quarter of the journey are fantastic. There you'll find country roads that wind through mountains dotted with little farmhouses and staring cows, simple paths that squirm through patches of forest, stone bridges that cross gurgling creeks, as well as roads that look out onto vineyards, city streets, and sometimes major highways. You will be passing through some of the coolest areas of Spain, including the Basque country, Pamplona, Logrono, Burogos, León, and Santiago de Compostela. We know we already mentioned it, but you can walk through the Rioja, where you will taste some of the best wine of your life. The prices are cheap, and it's all good. If you are not an experienced hiker, don't worry: It is all pretty simple, with well-marked paths and no technical work. Remember, this path has been beaten straight by a few million footfalls.

When you do pass people along the way, they are super-friendly (they all think that it is cool to walk the Camino, really). The towns where you sleep and eat are pretty small, but there is always a place to stay in *refugios,* hostel-like buildings built along the road specifically for people walking the Camino. Many local bars and restaurants will also have a special *"menú del peligrino"* for pilgrims. You will pretty much find that people will go out of their way to make a tired pilgrim happy. Because of the cheaper food and accommodations, you'll find that $10 a day is plenty of money. And since the walking isn't too arduous, you have time to do a little sightseeing around these great little villages—checking out the local church, or a quiet brook, or the fountain in the small town plaza.

Depending on what you want, the best time to go is during May and June. Generally considered the best hiking weather, it's not too hot, spring has arrived, and much of northern Spain is lush green. But it's also when most foreign tourists go, so if you want to avoid German über-hikers and hang out with Spanish *peligrinos,* you'll need to wait for their vacations, usually in July and August. It's much, much hotter, but you can practice what Mrs. Johnson taught you in the 10th grade: "Me llamo Jenny."

Lots of people only walk part of the Camino, a day or two, or up to a week. If you decide to only walk part of the route, leave from **Saint-Jean-Pied-de-Port** (a train goes from the Spanish city of Irun, through French Bayonna, to St. Jean daily) on the **Route de Napoleon,** because it is the most beautiful part of the journey (in our humble opinion). You get to follow the actual path that Napoleon used to invade Spain and cross the Pyrenees, all the while eating fantastic Basque cuisine (the *tortilla français,* kind of an omelet with spinach, is great). It takes about three days to walk from Saint-Jean-Pied-de-Port to Pamplona, where the Route de Napolean joins up with the **Camino Aragones** (the other starting point, which we don't recommend because it's boring). From here, there's pretty much just one road to Santiago. The path out of Saint-Jean-Pied-de-Port is very clearly marked with white and red stripes, and you leave town near the fountain that is right by the graveyard. (One thing to watch for: In France the yellow signs lead to another path, so *do not* follow them. The white and red stripes are your friends.) If you have questions, you can call the *refugio* in town *(Rue de la Citadelle 27; 05/59-37-03-79; 9am-10pm daily).*

If you do decide to walk the entire Camino, get a *credencial* at the beginning of the walk so that you will be an official pilgrim, which means you can sleep for cheap or free at the *refugios* and get your note from the pope at the end. You can pick one up at the **Colegiata** *(No address; it is the church, trust me—you will see it; 948/760-067; Open during daylight)* in Roncesvalles, Spain (the first town that you come to after Saint-Jean-Pied-de-Port, about a seven-hour hike), or at any of the *refugios* along the way. If you get the *credencial* stamped at the *refugios* in all your cities, you can be absolved of all your sins, officially, by the pope. No joke. The **Office of the Pilgrim** *(Rua do Vilar 1; 981/562-414; 10am-2pm/4:40-7pm Mon-Sat; 10am-2pm Sun and holidays)* in Santiago de Compestela will give you a certificate when you present the stamped *credencial.* Then, you just need to find a priest and confess all of your sins within 30 days, and you're guaranteed a ticket into heaven (If you believe in that sort of thing).

There aren't really any hours at the *refugios,* but if you don't want to wake the friendly people that run them, you'll want to stop by before dark. Hell, they're letting you sleep there for free. You just need to convince them that you are a serious pilgrim, and perhaps help out with a small donation (500ptas is fine). Most *refugios* have kitchens, and are generally great places to meet people. There is almost always room at a *refugio* in town, and the only stories I've heard of places being full end with a staff person setting pilgrims up at another place. There is also some camping along the Camino, but it is kind of out of the way, and the extra weight of a tent is not recommended. You can talk to the folks at any of the *refugios,* and they'll hook you up with someplace to sleep in your tent.

The Camino is well-marked, with either yellow arrows or—in France—white and red dashes. You'll also see a picture of a shell used to mark the path, or a little drawing of a hiking pilgrim. If you do get off the path for any reason and get lost, you can always ask the locals where it is: *Donde esta el Camino de Santiago?*

If you are going to be in a city on the Camino, like Pamplona or León, you can find the path very easily, and it is a fun trip for a day just to hike out for a while and then head back to your hostel. Just ask the front desk, and they are sure to be able to point you in the right direction.

cantabria
and
asturias

The neighboring northern regions of **Cantabria** and **Asturias** are off the beaten path, especially for non-European visitors, and for this reason alone merit a visit. Both regions share the northern coastline known as the **Costa Verde** (Green Coast), where sheer cliffs alternate with sandy beaches and tiny coves. Many small fishing villages line this rocky coast and make for great exploring. Although Cantabria and Asturias lack the significant historical and architectural wonders of the rest of the country, they are enjoying a boom. And it's not the cities that are the biggest draw, although both regions have appealing ones— **Santander** in Cantabria, **Oviedo** in Asturias. It's nature, Mother Nature, that draws them in, from the **Picos de Europa** national park to the small coastal towns and resorts. In from the coast, both regions remain very rural—beautiful, but rural. Transportation along the coast is easy enough, but for those wishing to explore inland it can be difficult if you are relying solely on public transportation.

One of Spain's newest regions, Cantabria was officially "created" in 1978 (although history here dates back over 38,000 years—the greatest examples of Paleolithic cave art can be found in the caves of Altamira, about an hour outside Santander). Prior to this it was part of Old Castile (Castilla y León) and just thought of as an extension of that region. Despite the fact that the government failed to officially recognize the separate identity of the Cantabrian people for so long, the inhabitants of this area have always been extremely independent—and strong-willed. The Romans had great difficulty subduing the local tribes when they first landed here in 29 B.C. Over the years the fighting spirit didn't wane; the Cantabrian people again showed their strength as they stood strong against Franco's fascists during the Civil War. (It was perhaps for this reason that Franco saw fit to deny them their rightful identity as a separate region.)

Asturias, which really doesn't get the respect it deserves, is also home to a quietly rebellious crowd. As in Cantabria, the independent mindset of the people is abundantly clear: They will eagerly tell you that this is where Spain was born; the rest, they say, is merely conquered land. It was from Asturias, the one part of Spain that the Muslims never occupied, that the Spanish launched the Reconquista, a series of bloody battles waged against the Muslims. A small force of Christians won the first battle at Covadonga in Asturias in 727, although it was centuries before the Spanish were completely successful in their efforts to push the Moors out of the rest of Spain. As the fighting moved down south, and eventually subsided, Asturias was largely forgotten, and the people returned to their fields and herds.

Wedged between the mighty Picos de Europa, Europe's largest national park, and the Bay of Biscay, land-locked Asturias is increasingly leaving behind its agricultural past as tourism grows within its borders. Part of its appeal is its idiosyncratic nature. Along with Galicia, Asturias was Celtic territory before the Romans came to town, and the influence can still be seen—witness the many glasses of hard cider *(sidras)* that are downed nightly. Follow tradition and pour it from high over your head, an unusual if innovative way to get the most carbonation into the drink.

There are plenty of appetizing local dishes in Asturias and Cantabria to fill you up after a long day of hiking. Dairy products are a major export from the area. Don't miss out on the region's cheeses. More varieties of cheese are made here than anywhere else in Europe. If you're used to Kraft singles, however, they may take some getting used to; some are pretty smelly and have a strong bite. Rumor has it that Cantabria is home to the greatest density of cows in all of Europe. See how many you can count.

TRAVEL TIMES

All times are by road unless indicated by a star: *time by train	Santander	Castro Urdiales	Cangas de Onis	Oviedo	Picos de Europa	Madrid
Santander	-	:45	2:05	3:00	1:30	5:30*
Castro Urdiales	:45	-	2:40	3:35	2:00	4:20
Cangas de Onis	2:05	2:40	-	1:05	:10	5:55
Oviedo	3:00	3:35	1:05	-	1:20	5:55*
Picos de Europa	1:30	2:00	:10	1:20	-	6:05

The Sistine Chapel of Paleolithic Art

Located in the small Cantabria town of **Santillana del Mar,** fifteen miles west of Santander, the **Altimara Caves** are some of the finest examples of pre-historic art in existence. Roughly 150 feet long and consisting of a series of winding passages and connecting rooms, the dwellings were discovered in the late 19th century by a local landowner and part-time archeologist named Marcelino de Santuola. Often referred to as the "Sistine Chapel of Paleolithic Art," the main room features a ceiling covered with 15,000 year-old drawings of bison, deer, and other local wildlife. The drawings, believed to be the work of the Magdalenia people of northern Spain, are surprisingly detailed despite being comprised of a mere three colors.

Unfortunately, access to the caves is extremely limited due to the damaging effects of carbon dioxide omitted by humans. Archeologists and historians are able to enter for the purpose of research, but unless you have one heck of a convincing story, you'll have to settle for the startlingly accurate replica that will be opening in early summer. For information on visits and the opening of the museum and replica dwelling, call *34/942-818-005.*

getting around the region

The RENFE train line connects Oviedo in Asturias and Santander in Cantabria to the major east-west rails between Galicia and Bilbao, as well as to Madrid. Once in the area, buses are your best bet for getting around. Oviedo and Santander are the transportation hubs, with bus lines that run just about everywhere. There is also the smaller-gauge FEVE train line that runs along the coast east to the Basque country and west into Galicia. A warning, though: FEVE trains are slow, and pass through each town just two or three times a day, so they're not your best option.

▶▶**ROUTES**

Arriving in Oviedo, hop on a bus out to Cangas de Onis and spend several days exploring the Picos de Europa National Park. Once you're hiked out, return by bus to Oviedo and from there take a train back to Madrid. Or, if you have more time on your hands, take a bus or train to Santander and relax on the beach or in a park. If Santander is too "big city" for you, take a bus to the seaside town of Castro-Urdiales for more serene beach exploration.

cantabria

santander

Competing with San Sebastián as the jewel of the northern coast, Santander has made itself into a classy seaside retreat. With such old European charms as the famous El Sardinero district balanced by an active fisherman's wharf, graceful promenades overlooking beautiful stretches of soft sand beaches, and a wild nightlife that only the Spanish can supply, Santander has certainly earned its place as a popular European summer escape.

First officially conquered by the Romans around 20 B.C., Santander led a fairly tame existence for almost the next 2,000 years. During this time it enjoyed some success as a port, but its true potential was not realized until the early 1900s, when King Alfonso XIII discovered the city and began spending his summers here. The locals were so taken by his attention that they gave him Magdalena Peninsula [see *city sports,* below], on which he built a small summer palace. It didn't take long for Santander to catch on as *the* place to summer—thus the El Sardinero district with its elegant buildings and chi-chi atmosphere.

Today you don't have to be visiting royalty to enjoy the wonders of Santander. Even common folk like ourselves can wander the grounds of the old palace and bask in the sun on one of the many choice beaches. There is, however, one thing to keep in mind: Santander is a summer resort city; it goes from slow speed, with many of the tourist facilities closed or working at half-staff, to full speed in a matter of a month. Probably the best times to visit are during the cusp months of May, June, and September, when things are open, the days are warm, and the streets are not packed to capacity.

In the off-season, the 200,000 or so permanent residents of Santander have the city virtually to themselves and, regardless of the time of year, enjoy it to the fullest. There is also a university here that pumps life into the off-season *marcha* and ensures that the clubs and bars don't operate solely by tourist schedules. The people of Santander will tell you they have one of the best *marchas* around. After experiencing one you may just have to agree with them.

The best way to find out what is going on around town is just to be friendly and ask people. It's amazing how knowledgable the store clerks, cashiers, waiters, and bartenders are about their city. Another, perhaps more reliable source, is the city's local paper, ***El Diaro de las Montañas,*** which can be obtained at any newsstand. It has information regarding upcoming events, music, and movies.

neighborhoods

Santander is an elongated city that stretches out along the northwest side of a bay. This peculiar layout leaves Santander with several distinct neighborhoods. Since things tend to be spread out here, the best way to get

five things to talk to a local about

1. **Santander vs. San Sebastián** Santander and San Sebastián have an unofficial battle over which is the best resort city in the north. Although most outsiders will agree that San Sebastián has the edge, the people here are loyal to their city and might just be able to make you see their side of things.
2. **Where they are from** Most people in Santander are from out of town, just like you. Strike up a conversation and find out where they're from originally—maybe you can score some useful insider tips for your journey ahead.
3. **Cantabria compared to its neighboring regions** Until recently Cantabria was part of Old Castile (Castilla y León). Now it stands alone and proud. Ask people how it differs from Asturias to the west and see what they think of those crazy Basque separatists to the east.
4. **El Sardinero** It's interesting to find out what the locals think of the famed El Sardinero district in their city. Do you think it's an accident it becomes a virtual ghost town when the tourists leave the city?
5. **The best beach in town** Everyone has his or her favorite for one reason or another. Even though they are all so similar, we did see this turn into a heated debate late one night.

santander

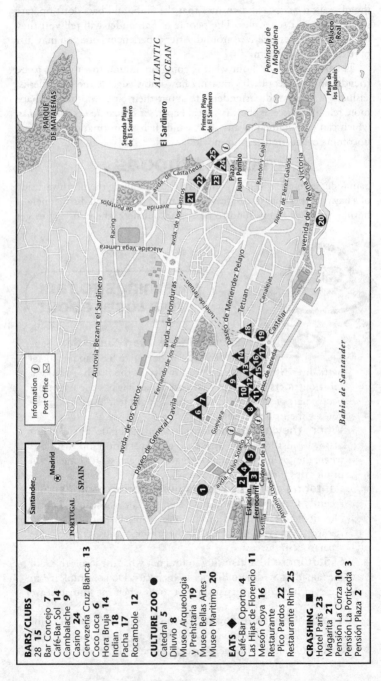

ATLANTIC OCEAN

PARQUE DE MATALEÑAS

Segunda Playa de El Sardinero

El Sardinero

Primera Playa de El Sardinero

Peninsula de la Magdalena

Palacio Real

Playa de los Biquinis

25
24
22 23
21

Plaza Juan Pombo

Ramón y Cajal

paseo de Perez Galdos

avenida de la Reina Victoria

20

avda. de Castañeda

avda. de los Castros

de Pontejos

Racing

Alcalde Vega Lamera

Autovia Bezana el Sardinero

avda. de los Castros

túnel de Tetuan

paseo de Menendez Pelayo

avda. de Honduras

Fernando de los Rios

Tettuan

18

Castelar

Canalejas

19

14

13

9

10 12

11

8

avda. de los Castros

Guevara

paseo de General Davila

1

6 7

Pso. de Pereda

Bahía de Santander

Estación Ferrocarril

Castilla

avda. Calvo Sotelo

Calderón de la Barca

Antonio López

2 4 5

3

SPAIN
PORTUGAL
Madrid
Santander

Information ⓘ
Post Office ✉

LET IT RIDE

Gambling is legal throughout Spain. That's why you'll see slot machines in almost every neighborhood bar you go into. Yet even though most major cities have a casino—or maybe even two in the larger ones—somehow it seems that casino gambling has never really caught on. This doesn't mean gambling isn't popular—you can spend an evening in any quiet bar and there is always some guy sitting at the slot machine, shoveling in fistful after fistful of coins. But with gambling machines so readily available, in lots of places the casinos seem to be just standing idly by. Santander is different: The **Gran Casino** is actually a major draw for many people staying in El Sardinero. Maybe it's the class involved in this operation, which has a Monte Carlo flare that brings out visions of casino gambling from a Bond movie. Whatever it is, whether you're a gambler or not, it's fun to poke around a little. If you do decide to head to the casino, dress formally (tuxedos and gowns aren't a must, but try to make your mother proud) and bring your passport. Inside you'll find all the normal casino games such as craps and roulette. So go on, throw some money down. You never know what's going to hit next.

around is to use the public buses that run from the city center out along the coast to El Sardinero. The numbers 1, 3, 4, 5, and 9 buses make regular runs along this route [see *need to know,* below].

The heart of the city is aptly called the **city center.** This huge chunk of Santander has just about everything you'll need during your time here. As you wander the streets of Santander you'll notice that unlike most other European cities, there is no "old town" here. That's because in 1941 a huge fire devastated the city center, burning up what was the old town. Although Santander looks great today, the blaze did destroy some of the original character of the place.

On the west end of town are the Renfe and Feve train stations and the bus station. Right around the stations you'll find some of Santander's cheaper lodging options. Heading east will bring you through the commercial center of the city, brimming over with shops, especially along **Avenida Burgos.** Continuing east through the city center, everything behind and to the east of the main tourist office falls into the **Zona de Ambiente** (also known as the nightlife area). This extends as far east as **Casimiro Sainz.** Within this zone of the city center you'll find lots of great restaurants, tapas bars, *puffs,* and discos. During the weekends,

Plaza Canadio Bazan fills with people as the bars overflow onto the streets. If you continue heading east from here towards the peninsula you will quickly come upon nice residential homes with manicured lawns and hedges—not much here for the intrepid traveler.

South of the city center is the **Barrio Pesquero,** or the fishermen's wharf, which is not nearly as exciting as it sounds. It's no rough-and-tumble part of town inhabited only by old fishermen who growl and have parrots perched on their shoulders. However, what this part of town does have are seafood restaurants lined up one after another along **Marques de la Ensenada.** The price you pay for this pleasure is a 20-minute walk from the city center.

A bus ride from the city center brings you to the famed **El Sardinero.** This elegant district of manicured gardens and large, classy houses and hotels is known for indulging those used to upscale living. This is the part of town that made Santander a popular resort destination, and after fire destroyed the old city center, El Sardinero carried the burden of giving Santander a sense of character. Walk around here, and look over the area from the promenades above the **Playa El Sardinero,** to get a taste of the high life. This isn't to say backpackers and students aren't welcome in El Sardinero. Quite the contrary, everyone is welcome; just be prepared to pay a little more.

hanging out

There is nothing easier to do while in Santander than to hang out. As a resort city, it was, in fact, designed for this very purpose: to give people a place where they could escape their hectic lives, leave behind their worries and responsibilities, and simply hang out. King Alfonso XIII started it, and now it's up to us to perfect it. My, what a difficult life we lead.

The first thing to consider when deciding where to hang in Santander is the weather. If it's a bright, beautiful, warm day, you have some serious decisions to make. Should you go to the beach or the park, and then which beach or what section of the park? Fear not, fellow traveler. Hanging out, after a little guidance, will be a breeze.

Santander has no fewer than seven (that's right—seven) official beaches within its city limits. Now this may sound a little daunting at first, but the truth of the matter is that Santander's seven beaches are actually two long separate stretches of beach that have been sub-divided (for the purpose of sounding enviable in travel literature, perhaps). **Playa de El Sardinero** (broken down from south to north into **Playa del Camello, Playa de la Concha, Primera Playa de El Sardinero,** and **Segundo Playa de El Sardinero)** is the largest and most dramatic stretch of beaches Santander has to offer at its doorstep. The sand here is incredibly soft, the surf sometimes kicks up enough to support small roving bands of surfers and boogie boarders, and the wind off the ocean cools sunbathers on the hottest days of the summer. In short, this is the beach to be seen on. Unfortunately, during the summer, everyone wants to be seen here and to describe it as "crowded" can be an understatement.

A much calmer and more protected stretch of beach can be found just around the headland, on the bay side of the city. Here **Playa de los**

wired

Surprisingly, Santander is somewhat slim on public Internet connections. Maybe the big Internet boom has yet to hit this city as it has the rest of the world. More likely, perhaps, vacationers want a true escape from the call of the office and outside responsibilities. Whatever the reason, don't expect to find any wild disco bars where you can sip your favorite mixed drink while catching up with friends and family back home. The best Santander has to offer in the city center is **La Copia** *(Calle Lealtadi 13, second floor; 9:30am-1pm/4-8pm Mon-Fri, 10am-1pm Sat; 150ptas for 15 minutes, 500ptas for one hour).* Yes, it's a copy shop. Not a storefront, but head up one flight of stairs, take a left, and follow the scent of fresh Xerox. The staff is friendly and they're not into strictly watching the clock. Since this is one of the few places to check your Hotmail in town, don't be surprised to meet other travelers.

Peligros, Playa de la Magdalena, and **Playa de los Biquinis** wrap around the bay from east to west, almost extending as far as the end of the peninsula. Playa de los Peligros tends to be the family beach, where parents play with their children in the calm bay waters. At the other end of the stretch, Playa de los Biquinis, which lies entirely within the grounds of the park on the peninsula, tends to attract a younger crowd of teenagers (could have something to do with the name). Although the sands of these three beaches aren't as delicately soft as El Sardinero's, these beaches do offer protection from currents, waves, and strong winds.

You might notice, as you sit here on one of the bay-side city beaches where sand is no longer visible because the entire beach is covered in towels and oiled bodies, that there is an unoccupied stretch of beach on the other side of the channel. Enticing, isn't it? However, it is not advised to try to swim across the channel, as many large ships pass through here and odds are a swimmer would not be seen by one of these huge craft and would be quickly turned into propeller food. So the question remains: How do you get to that beach right across the channel without risking your life? All it's going to cost you is a couple hundred pesetas. Behind the main tourist office [see *need to know,* below] at the port you'll find the office of **Los Reginas** *(Tel 942/216-753).* This company not only offers boat tours of the bay, but also runs regular launch service (every half hour in the summer) to **Pedreña** and **Somo,** those gorgeous dunes across the bay. Ride the launch to Somo and you'll find all the space you'll need for your sunbathing.

If you're getting tired of laying on the beaches all day and want something a little different while still enjoying a gorgeous day, head for **Península de la Magdalena.** What was once the King's private palace estate has been opened to the public and is now a huge picturesque park. There are acres of lawns, forest, and beaches to explore. The King's palace still remains in its cliff-top location with a commanding view of the coast. Unfortunately, the palace does not offer tours, but strolling the grounds is amazing enough. Within the park there is even a mini-zoo. The park is open from sunrise to sunset and makes a great place to picnic, relax, or get involved in a pickup soccer game.

bar scene

It probably won't dawn on you until the following morning—when you wake up to blinding sunlight beaming in through your room's window— just how many bars there are in Santander. I mean, there are sections where if you went into each bar on the street for just one drink, the odds are against you that you would make it the length of the block. Yes, Santander has a very lively bar scene, especially on the weekends, when it seems every watering hole is packed and the party flows out onto the streets, surging through the city. Is it a good time? You bet!

The heart of the nightlife lies at the east end of the city center. Plaza Cañadio is always alive on the weekends. The bars around this plaza seem to attract an older crowd in their thirties and forties. But at the same time it lies central to the *marcha* so makes a good reference point. The streets running east from the plaza, such as Hernán Cortés and General Mola, are lined with spots; the scene ends around Casimiro Sainz, which has two of the city's major clubs [see *club scene,* below].

None of the bars have any kind of a dress code, but as you know, to fit in with the Spaniards, dress it up a little. If you are planning on hitting the clubs later on, forego the sneakers and sandals—you won't be allowed in. Generally the bar scene in Santander is laid-back and the goal is simply for people to get out and have a good time.

One great street to start the night on is Río de la Pila, in the city center. Here you will find a largely university crowd hanging out at the numerous small bars. Someone was indeed a little *loco* when they decided to paint the inside of **Coco Loca** *(Rio de la Pila 19)* blue and yellow, but

rules of the game

The rules of the game here in Santander are quite simple: Don't be dumb. The scene in Santander seems conservative compared with that of other parts of the country and relies much more on alcohol than other drugs to get its juices flowing. This isn't to say that you won't catch a hash breeze wafting through the streets or clubs, but it seems much more kept out of view here. Ecstasy and other popular club drugs do not have a large presence in the scene either.

it makes for a fun atmosphere. Fortunately the prices are pretty sane: a beer costs 250ptas and mixed drinks go for 500ptas. There's not much in the way of entertainment here besides a dartboard that sees lots of competitive action. Spanish and U.S. pop hits play from a CD player behind the bar. Across the street is **Bar Concejo**, where you can order a mixed drink for 550ptas or a beer for 225ptas. The music selection here is a little harder, with hits by AC/DC and the Clash getting tossed into the rotation with Clapton and Marley. It only takes a drink or two to befriend the bartender and other patrons at this small, cozy, casual place.

If you crave a beer, and you want something specific, try heading to **Cervecería Cruz Blanco** *(corner of Hernán Cortés and Lope de Vega; Tel 942/364-295)*. Here they have 36 bottled beers to choose from as well as seven more choices on tap, including Guinness and Murphy's. This is another place that should be an early stop on your evening's *marcha* route. It's a nice tavern with a bit of a German influence on the inside. Most ex-pats in town, especially Brits and Germans, seem to end up here. The evening crowd is in the 22 to 40 age range, about an even mix of locals and visitors.

Once the evening progresses, the bars along Santa Lucía tend to draw the crowds. If you walk down this street half a block east of Lope de Vega, you will find Pasadizo Zorrilla, a small side street with a couple of kicking places. Also nearby is **Café-Bar Sol** *(Calle Santa Lucía 32; Tel 942/215-805)*, the theme of which is, as the name implies, the great sun. In fact, suns of all shapes, sizes, and colors decorate the walls here. A large bar makes getting a drink to quench your thirst an easy task. This is mainly a local bar, often attracting young Santander professionals in their twenties and thirties. In summer it gets more foreign visitors, especially from Britain, plus lots of visiting Spaniards—mostly young people—from inland cities such as Madrid.

Rocambole *(Hernán Cortés 35-37)* rates as another great mid-*marcha* bar. This is a dark and moody place whose heart is all jazz, but whose spirit is pure rock 'n' roll. It's a fun place to go for a drink, which will run you about 650 ptas or 350ptas for a beer. If you're alone, the vast array of decorations hanging from the walls is entertainment enough. Brass instruments sidle up to vintage Coca-Cola ads, while newspaper clippings pay homage to great jazz musicians. Although this would make the perfect jazz den, there is a DJ who plays pop and rock. More than other places in town, Rocambole draws a fairly artistic crowd that enjoys its old-style class and elegance.

LIVE MUSIC

If you're looking to see a live show or want to spend a relaxing evening in a smoky jazz bar, Santander is not the place to do it. In fact, tracking down the live music scene here can prove to be a wild goose chase. Someone will tell you they think they heard that such-and-such place has bands every Thursday night, but when you go there you just get blank stares from the bartender. That's what the music scene here is. Try digging through the ever-resourceful *El Diario de las Montañas* to see if it lists any upcoming concerts.

The lack of a solid music scene here is really surprising given the fact that during the month of August, Santander hosts the annual **Festival Internacional de Santander.** The festival covers all kinds of music from jazz to classical, and stages are erected throughout the city.

club scene

As you've guessed, one of the joys of Santander is its thriving nightlife. Days spent relaxing on the beach give way to insane evenings following the *marcha* into the wee hours of the morning. There are plenty of clubs to fit anyone's taste—whether you enjoy clubs filled with people dancing hypnotically to a techno beat or theme clubs that take you to another reality, you can find it here. Just make sure you don't outdo yourself in the bars and that you're ready to hit fifth gear sometime around 5 or 6am on the weekends. This is Spain; you should be getting used to it by now.

Santander isn't into underground rave-style parties. Most of the clubs offer pretty standard fare. This isn't meant to take anything away from them, just to help you understand the scene. The best way to find out what is hot when you are in town is simply to ask the people you meet in bars or in shops. They have their fingers on the pulse and can steer you in the right direction. If you're planning on clubbing, sneakers are generally not allowed and you have to wear something nicer than a T-shirt or tank top. If you look decent, getting in to a club should be no hassle.

Although most of the big clubs don't draw a crowd until after 4am, there are two notable exceptions. **Cambalache** *(Calle Santa Lucía s/n; 11pm-6am Fri and Sat; No cover)* gets the music thumping earlier than most places in town, and those people eager to dance love it. Head down the stairs on the south side of the street to the club door, where you'll have to get a nod from the bouncers. The crowd is generally in their twenties and looking sharp. Two bars flank the dance floor, where disco lights play

boy meets girl

This city is loaded with attractive people— vacationers, university students, backpackers—and everything seems geared toward meeting them. Santander's very social atmosphere means that it's no harder to meet someone new than going up and saying hello. You are surrounded all day by prospective soul mates (or one-night-stands, if you're movin' on real soon), so why waste time? On the beach, ladies, if you see a cute surfer who's turning your sunburn three degrees redder, go up and ask him for a lesson. Guys, in the clubs, don't be shy. Smile at her and then go up and dance with her. People come to Santander to have a good time. Making new friends is all part of the fun.

enchantingly over the crowd. Mixed drinks are 550ptas and the music ranges from house to dance-pop—anything with a solid beat. This club sees most of its action between 2 and 5am.

Another great spot to gear up for the clubs is **28** *(Calle General Mola 28; No cover)*. Mixed drinks are 650ptas and a beer costs 375ptas. By no means a club, but a really hot *puff*, 28 will get your blood flowing between 3-5am. Nobody seems to notice the plain gray walls or the lack of any kind of decoration; they all seem lost in the music, which ranges widely from techno Elvis, to Tone-Loc, to Spanish dance music. No sneakers allowed in here.

Once you've got your groove on and your dance moves down, head right down the street from 28 to Santander's largest disco, **Pacha** *(Calle General Mola 45; No cover)*. With two floors of late-night hedonism, this is the disco you want to end up at, but show up before 4:30-5am and you'll be dancing alone. Shoes and nice dress are required to get in the door, but once inside any rules seem to float out of the room right along with the pumped-in smoke. DJs spin a wide variety of styles here, with their best saved for last. House and trance tend to make it into the mix more frequently as the night draws on and the cheesy dance music is put to bed. Don't expect to leave here before sunrise when the party is hot.

Not far from Pacha is a disco that couldn't be more different. At **Indian** *(Calle Casmiro Sainz 10; No cover)*, you'll take a trip to the Wild West, beginning at the front door where a sign reminds, "Cowboys, please scrape shit from boots before entering." Decorated in a fusion of John Wayne and Harley Davidson, Indian is Disneyland on acid. You are definitely not in Kansas anymore, Toto. Regardless of the whacked-out theme, everyone here is dressed in normal Spanish attire (you may have to scrape shit from your boots before entering, but you're not getting in wearing sneakers). Three bars keep the crowd from going thirsty, and the dance floor manages to draw a swarm. Blues, rock, and country give way to the more usual *discoteca* music as the night wears on and the party heats up. If you're into theme establishments then you have to check this place out. Just don't offend the Harley-clad bouncer at the door.

arts scene

If you thought the cultural scene in Santander was short on content, wait until you see the void in the art scene. Galleries showcasing local talent are so few that the **Museo de Bellas Artes** [see *culture zoo*, below] is forced to showcase local talent. One floor here is also dedicated to temporary exhibits. To find out what is showing, call or swing by the museum. It is pretty much the only place in town to see art. Your only other option is to wander the suburbs around El Sardinero and enjoy the elegant architecture from the *Bella Epoque* era, when King Alfonso XIII and other royalty were turning the area into their summer retreat.

gay scene

If there is a gay scene in Santander, it keeps a very low profile. None of the locals seemed to know of any gay hotspots. We did see a few gay couples who looked right at home in the big discos such as **Pancha** [see *club scene,* above] and in the bars. So if you're looking for a good time, just go along with everyone else and wander around the happening city center.

CULTUre ZOO

Let's get one thing straight right away. If you are looking for a strictly cultural tour of Spain, Santander may not be the ideal destination for you. If, however, you're visiting here and something has gone wrong—it's raining outside or your sunburn is *really* burning—Santander can provide you with some interesting little distractions. A cultural treasure trove, however, it is not.

About an hour outside of Santander are the near-legendary **caves of Altamira.** What makes these particular caves so famous is the fact that prehistoric cave paintings dating from sometime around 12,000 B.C. were discovered on the walls. Before 1977 these cave paintings, some of them 2 meters tall, were open to the public. Hordes of gawking visitors caused the paintings to deteriorate and now only 20 people a day are allowed to view the paintings. Permission to see the caves must be obtained a year in advance. While this will prove a bummer to anyone set on seeing some of the world's earliest art, all is not lost.

Museo Arqueologia y Prehistoria (*Calle Casimiro Sainz 4; Tel 942/207-109; 9am-1pm/4-7pm Tues-Sat, 11am-2pm Sun; Free):* Here you can see photos of the Altamira paintings and some artifacts from Altamira. Although not nearly as interesting as the real thing, I imagine, this is probably as close to the paintings as you'll get without an advanced degree in archeology. Aside from the Altamira exhibits, the museum also has huge engraved tablets and wheels, prehistoric animal bones, Neanderthal and Bronze Age artifacts, and things found from the Roman Age in the region, such as pottery, metal shards, and a full skeleton. Nice, but this is not the most engaging archeological museum in Spain. Accompanying each exhibit is a detailed explanation in Spanish; unfortunately, there are no English brochures to let you in on the details. The museum is easy to get to and free, so it's worth about a half-hour.

Museo Maritimo (*San Martín de Bajamar s/n; Tel 942/274-962; 11am-1pm/4-7pm Tues-Sat June 16-Sept 14, 11am-2pm Sun, rest of the year 10am-1pm/4-6pm Tues-Sat, 11am-2pm Sun; Free):* This fun museum, geared more toward oceanography than Santander's maritime history, is worth a little time. It lies on the bay at the west end of Playa de los Peligros [see *hanging out,* above]. When you enter the museum, you're greeted by a huge skeleton of a whale that hangs over all the exhibits. On the lower floor are lots of fish, most of them in formaldehyde. If you want to see real, live, swimming fish, there is a limited *(limited!!!!)* aquarium with some fish species found in the waters off Santander. On the next floor you'll find a mock-up of a complete marine biologist's laboratory from the turn of the century. This is accompanied by displays of ship models and nautical instruments. The musuem is adding more to its holdings, including several ships, and hopefully all the work will be done by early 2001.

Museo de Bellas Artes *(Calle Rubio 6; Tel 942/239-485; 10:30am-1pm/5-8pm Mon-Fri June 15-Sept 15, 10:30am-1pm Sat, rest of the year open 10am-1pm/5-8pm Mon-Fri, 10am-1pm Sat; Free):* Although we'd heard rumors that the museum's permanent collection contained works by such Spanish legends as Goya and Picasso, we didn't see any sign of them. What the museum does have on display are paintings done by Cantabrian artists from the late 1800s and 1900s, including works by Santanderian artists. Styles include everything from Impressionism to Cubism. The ground floor has contemporary art, including some sculptures. The top floor is dedicated to temporary exhibits, while the rest of the museum is said to be a permanent collection. The museum is not huge, so don't plan on spending more than an hour or so in it, but it is interesting and worth the time.

Catedral: The city's cathedral sits behind the main post office [see *need to know,* below]. Basically it is small and uninspiring and we give you full permission to skip it in favor of lying on the beach guilt-free (just don't tell your mother).

modification

Santander is about old money and class. If you don't believe that, take a walk around El Sardinero. Rumor has it that this is where some of Spain's most successful professionals come to summer. So, if you were planning on having your nipples, tongue, lip, toes, and elbows pierced, this is not the best place to do it. Save it for when you trek east to Bilbao, where they specialize in toe and elbow piercing. If you want to get pierced or pricked specifically to throw a rebellious nod at the aristocratic order, you should probably sober up and think this one through. But if you're still rarin' to go, head to **Cheva Tattoo** *(Calle Marcelino Sanz de Sautuola 12; Tel 942/314-827; www.imedia.es/cheva)* in the city center. Cheva Tattoo is a professional studio where sterile conditions and giving customers exactly what they want are top priorities. The staff is patient and friendly, and flipping through their book proves that they have some good experience behind them. These people are also great at pointing out often overlooked cafes and nightly hot spots.

city sport

Perhaps the best reason to come to Santander is to take some summer classes, to learn something new and leave a smarter, more well-rounded individual. No, we're not suggesting you send away for a catalogue from the city's university; we're talking about courses that won't separate you from the beach. If you have a week or more to spend in Santander, then there is plenty to learn.

Godofredo *(Paseo de Perede 31; Tel 942/215-751; 10am-1:30pm/4-7pm Mon-Fri, 11am-2pm/4-9pm Sat)* is a full-service dive shop that runs trips for those who want to explore the underwater world off Santander's coast. Trips run 2,000ptas a dive (6,000ptas if you rent gear). If you want to get certified as a sport diver, Godofredo also offers PADI courses. Some of their instructors speak English, so make sure to inquire prior to signing up. Godofredo's also sells fishing equipment for people more interested in eating fish than swimming with them.

If diving beneath the waves isn't your idea of a great time, how about learning to ride them? If that sounds ideal to you, hop on a boat across the bay to **Somo** [see *hanging out,* above] and head to **Escuela Cantabra de Surf** *(Playa de Somo s/n; Tel 942/373-573; ecsurf@navegalia.com, www.navegalia.com/personal/ecsurf).* This surf school has been around for the past 10 years and insists that the conditions right outside their front door are ideal for learning as well as for those who already know how to rip. Classes last five days for a total of 10 hours of instruction. Price for the course and all rented gear is 14,000ptas. The school staff will be more than happy to help you find a nice room at an affordable *hostal* in Somo while you're taking a class. If you don't have the time to devote to the classes or have no need for them, the school rents out surfboards and wetsuits for 1,500ptas per hour or 3,000ptas for three hours.

If you have come to Santander to escape classes or just want time to yourself, there are still options for you to enjoy the great outdoors. In the park on **Peninsula de la Magdalena** [see *hanging out,* above], it is easy enough to join in one of many pickup soccer games on the polo grounds. There are also people throwing Frisbees around; all you have to do is make a friend and jump on in. The park also offers joggers lots of trails and paths. Add to this its kilometers worth of swimming beaches, and there's no excuse for not having the perfect beach body for your stay in Santander.

STUFF

When the city center burned in 1941, city planners looked at this as the glass being half full and saw great opportunity. They turned the western half of the center into a commercial district, so that today, a walk through this part of town and along Avenida Burgos reveals a vast number of retail stores. The only problem is that the shops here are unoriginal and overpriced, dominated by Spanish clothing chain stores. Few, if any, small shops sell anything of interest from the region. One would think that with all the tourists, merchants would have targeted their markets, but unfortunately a walk through the retail areas in Santander is just like a walk through the retail areas anywhere else in the country. Santander completely lacks any interesting, independent retail stores worth checking out.

That said, there are more than enough shops if you just want a new pair of shoes or a fancy shirt. The selection is conventional but plentiful, and if you're looking for a specific item, it can probably be found with some dedicated shopping time.

The one store we found that might be of great service to visitors in Santander is **Surf 33** *(Calle Cadiz 19; Tel 942/224-141; 10am-2pm/4-7pm Mon-Fri).* If you forgot to pack a bathing suit or are missing any other beach necessities, one quick stop here will set you straight. The store carries plenty of bathing suits for him and her as well as shades and hats for when the sun is at its hottest. For more ambitious beachgoers, Surf 33 also has a pretty good selection of surfboards, boogie boards, and wetsuits. How you get your surfboard back home with you is your problem.

EATS

Dining out in Santander can be, like so many other things here, nothing shy of a moving experience. We will say unequivocally that the finest tapas we had were in Santander, the most delicious tortilla we ate was in Santander, and the filthiest sandwich we laid eyes on was in Santander. Alright, so maybe not every kitchen in town is graced with a gourmet chef, but there are definitely a couple of places here that stand head and shoulders above your average dining experience.

You'll find a lot of super-fresh fish dishes being served around town. (Cod and anchovies commonly find their end on a dinner plate.) If it's a seafood feast you seek surrounded by a wacky maritime theme, head down to the Barrio Pesquero. A simple stroll down Calle Marqués de la Ensenada will unveil a wealth of seafood restaurants, all admittedly pretty similar. But the fact is you don't have to walk 20 minutes from the city center to enjoy good seafood. Literally every restaurant and bodega in town serves a menu that reflects the sea's bounty.

If you want to fit in and be like the locals come dinnertime, then going out for tapas is a prerequisite. The hot tapas bars tend to come and go as most trendy places do, but some, if their kitchens stay the course, are sure to weather any change in the scene.

▶▶CHEAP

There is little inexpensive dining to be found around the streets of Santander. If you are eating on a budget, then your best bet is to make use of the lunchtime *menú del día* many restaurants offer. This will give you a filling meal for about 1,000-1,600ptas. The same meal would cost at least another 1,000ptas come dinnertime. So fill up if you can midday and try to limit yourself to a couple of tapas at night. That's how the Spanish do it; how do you think they all stay so slender?

But if it's midday and your stomach isn't quite ready for a full meal, than head to **Café/Bar Oporto** *(Calle Lealtad 18-20; 10am-8pm Mon-Fri, noon-4pm Sat).* What's so great about this ordinary looking joint, you may ask as you walk in the door. Well, ask for *"un pincho de tortilla especial"* and you'll find out. Basically a Spanish omelet in pie formation, the tortilla here is a well-known secret to Santander's working force, which often sneaks out for a taste. Home cooked and a little oozy, the tortilla and a *café con leche* will set you back less than 300ptas.

If you want a cheap dinner and something different, check out the Chinese restaurant next to Meson Goya [see *eats, do-able,* below]. Entrees hover around the 1,000ptas mark and the atmosphere is truly Chinese.

▶▶DO-ABLE

As you have no doubt come to realize, tapas always seem like a great way to eat out and save money, but after eating about 10 of them and downing three drinks, you realize your bill isn't all that much less than the cost of a full meal at a restaurant. Once you accept this fact you will find going out for tapas to be great fun. And Santander has two fantastic tapas joints. First, stop at **Las Hijas de Florencio** *(Paseo de Pereda 23).* This is a bustling tapas spot where the well-dressed crowd often spills out onto the plaza behind. If you order the *"rioja de la casa"* (house red wine, 125ptas), you also get a small dish of some tasty cheeses. Larger orders of *raciones* serve several people and run 500-1,000ptas.

To sample the best tapas dining has to offer, a stop at **Diluvio** *(General Mol 14; 150-250ptas tapas)* is a must. What an abundance of tapas to choose from, and all so good looking! You have to walk around the bar once just to see all the choices, and that's if you can get through the crowd. The beers here are 200ptas, and a glass of wine is 150 ptas. Fresh trays of homemade tapas perfection continually emerge from the kitchen and are quickly devoured by the hungry patrons. The homemade tortilla is practically gone before it hits the bar. Yes, these are some of the most delicious tapas you may taste during your time in Spain. Dress nicely to partake. The crowd here covers the spectrum from young to old.

If a sit-down dinner is more your style, **Mesón Goya** *(Calle Daoiz y Verlarde 25; Tel 942/213-066; 1-4pm/8pm-midnight Tues-Sun; menú del día 1,700ptas)* offers a real deal in fine dining. Low light and exposed brick walls lend the two dining rooms here a nice atmosphere. The menu has quite a few choices. Meat and fish entrees all run for under 2,000ptas, while some even drop below 1,000ptas. The food is well-prepared and there is an excellent wine selection to accompany your meal.

In El Sardinero, dining options abound just like everywhere else in the city. For a change of pace, try **Restaurante Pico Pardos** *(Avda. de los Infantes; Tel 942/272-188; 1-4pm/8-11:30pm; menú del día 1,395ptas)*. This Italian pizzeria/restaurant offers lots of pasta (700-1,800ptas), pizza (1,000-1,500ptas), and meat entrees (1,200-1,900ptas) to choose from. Pico Pardos does a good job of providing a comfortable atmosphere for a relaxed dining experience.

▶▶SPLURGE

If you're going to blow a load on dining, why not go all the way and head to the ultra-popular **Restaurante Rhin** *(Avda. de Castaneda s/n; menú del día 2,900ptas; V, AE)* in El Sardinero? Across from the casino, with a huge deck overlooking the beach, Restaurante Rhin offers a commanding view of the Sardinero coast. But dining with such a view does come at a price. Entrees are all priced between 2,000-3,000ptas, and the simple fact is that despite the cost, this kitchen does not put out the finest food in Santander (but no one would turn their noses up at it, either). The view can't be beat, and besides having an elegant indoor dining room, El Rhin also sets up lots of tables on its huge deck space when the weather is nice.

crashing

Santander offers plenty of choices to rest one's weary head, from basic rooms to luxurious suites. During the summer months, however, vacationers descend on the city, and then it's the same old tune: Rooms can be difficult to find if you haven't booked ahead. If you are planning to attend the music and culture festival in August, think about booking a room several months in advance. Don't end up as one of those low-key backpackers left wandering the streets without a bed. Many places also increase their rates during the months of July and August, so those two months are probably not the best for dropping in; Fear not, if your travel schedule allows you no other time to visit this city, just try to call ahead or arrive early and make sure you have a place to stay before spending all day on the beach.

As in many other popular resort cities, single travelers will find that in the summer many places convert their single rooms to doubles, so the only way to get a bed is to fork out the extra loot for an imaginary friend.

Basically the lodging options in Santander are split between the city center and El Sardinero. Although the city center isn't as glamorous as El Sardinero, it does have great eating and drinking spots. The area around El Sardinero is more geared to tourists and there are more than enough services to keep one entertained, usually for a little more money, though. Also, many of the establishments in El Sardinero are open only from July through September. Wherever you end up, make sure you leave time to explore the other area so that you see both sides of Santander.

▶▶CHEAP

Some of the most inexpensive places in Santander lie conveniently in the city center, only a block away from both the train and bus stations. Many backpackers and students stay in these spots when they come to Santander. **Pensión La Porticada** (*Calle Méndez Núñez 6; Tel 942/227-817; 2,000ptas single (winter only), 3,000-5,000ptas double without bath, 4,000-6,000ptas double with bath; No credit cards*) is only half a block from the bus station and offers guests nine airy rooms painted in warm pastel colors. There is a TV lounge where you can gather with other guests and plan your attack on the city.

One of the cheapest options out in El Sardinero is **Pensión Soledad** (*Avda. de los Castros 17; Tel 942/270-936; 2,600-2,700ptas single, 4,400-4,700ptas double; Open July, August, and September only; No credit cards*). Only about a block and a half from the beach, Pensión Soledad offers travelers on a budget a chance to sample the classy lifestyle of El Sardinero. The rooms are basic but the owners are kind. There are shared baths at the end of the halls.

▶▶DO-ABLE

Since Santander is a resort city, it is no huge surprise that prices here are more than what you will pay in other parts of the country. Even so, there are still plenty of affordable places. One such spot is **Pensión La Corza** (*Hernán Cortés 25; Tel 942/212-950; 3,000-4,000ptas single (off-season only), 3,500-5,000ptas double without bath, 4,500-6,000ptas double with half bath; 7,000-8,000ptas triple with half bath; V, MC*). Its location on a quiet plaza in the center of the old town can't be beat. It's within blocks of some of the city's best eating and drinking spots. La Corza offers guests nice big rooms with floor-to-ceiling windows, sink, sofa, comfortable bed, and room to spin and dance. In the summer it is recommended to book a month in advance.

Another option close to the train and bus station is **Pensión Plaza** (*Calle Cádiz 13; Tel 942/212-967; 3,745-5,000ptas single, 6,420-9,095ptas double, 8,000-11,500ptas triple*). There's only one single here, so call ahead if you're traveling alone. All the rooms are nice and modern with full carpeting, private bath, TV, and phone. There are lots of windows, which keep the rooms full of light.

If you want to stay in El Sardinero, check out **Margarita** *(Avda. de los Castros 19; Tel 942/270-973; 2,000-4,100ptas single; 4,000-6,000ptas double; Open May-September),* which has basic rooms with bed and sink; bathrooms are down the hall. It is only a block and a half to the beach and the owners will do their best to make you feel comfortable.

Other reasonably-priced options include **Hostal Cabo Mayor** *(Calle de Cadiz 1, Tel 942/211-181; single 3,500ptas winter, 6,000ptas summer; double 5,000ptas winter, 7,500ptas summer; triple 6,500ptas winter, 9,000ptas summer; private baths; TV; cabomayor@ono.com, www.interhotel.com; V, MC, AE, DC);* **Hospedaje Botin** *(Calle de Isabel II 1, Tel 942/210-094; single 2,200ptas low season, 2,900ptas mid, 3,700ptas high; double 3,400ptas low season, 4,800ptas mid, 6,000ptas high; triple 4,800ptas low season, 6,500ptas mid, 8,000ptas high; quad 6,800ptas low season, 7,500ptas mid, 10,500ptas high; shared baths; No credit cards);* and **Pension Real** *(Plaza de la Esperanza 1, Tel 942/225-787; single 5,000ptas Aug, 2,000ptas rest of year; double 6,000ptas Aug, 3,500ptas rest of year; No credit cards).*

▶▶SPLURGE

Santander offers the explorer with a credit card in someone else's name a plethora of options for wining and dining themselves into the high life. If you want to be pampered and stay in four- and five-star hotels, head straight for El Sardinero. Here you can sip champagne in your room before putting on your tux or dinner gown and heading down to the casino to throw money around like it is nothing more than a plastic chip. If you want to live the European highlife, Santander is one of the best places to deliver on it. The **Hotel Real** *(Paseo Pérez Galdós 28; Tel 942/272-550; 18,550-31,200ptas single, 23,200-39,000ptas double)* is where all the big shots stay when they come to Santander. Its five stars ooze class. If this is a little out of your budget, try up the street a little at **Hotel Paris** *(Avda. de los Hoteles 6; Tel 942/272-350; 8,000-9,500ptas single, 10,000-13,000ptas double; Open June 30-September 30; V, MC),* which offers elegant rooms in the spirit of El Sardinero right near the casino and beach. The owners were doing some refurbishing when we were there in hopes of opening their door year-round starting in 2001.

need to know

Currency Exchange There are banks, many with 24-hour ATMs, all over town, so finding a place to get money should never present a problem. The bank **La Caixa (8:15am-2pm Mon-Fri, 4:30-7:45pm Thur)** is located across the street from the main tourist office. It claims to have the best exchange rate in town, but you'll still do better if you're using a credit card.

Tourist Info The **Main Tourist Office** *(Tel 942/362-054; 9:30am-1:30pm/4:30-7:30pm Mon-Fri, 10am-1pm Sat)* is located in the *Jardines de Pereda* on Paseo de Pereda. Some English is spoken and in general the staff here will go out of their way to help you get acquainted with the city. They won't make hotel reservations for you, but they'll give you an exhaustive list of the hotels in town.

Public Transportation Santander has **City Buses** that run regularly from 6am-10:30pm (midnight during the summer months). Fares are 110ptas per ride and payable to the driver. Buses number 1, 3, 4, 5, and 9 run from the city center out to El Sardinero.

American Express Santander's local American Express representative is the travel agency **Altair Viajes** *(Caldrón de la Barca 11; Tel 942/319-060; Fax 942/319-061; 9:30am-1:30pm/4:30-8pm Mon-Fri, 10am-1:30pm Sat)*. Located in the city center, Altair Viajes will sell traveler's checks (they won't cash them), help with lost/stolen cards, and receive replacement cards. They'll even let you pay your bills here. Beyond all this they are an extremely helpful travel agency.

Health and Emergency Emergency: *092;* ambulance: *112.* There is a **Hospital** *(Marques de Valdecilla 25; Tel 942/205-502)* in town should you need any medical attention during your stay. The **Police** *(Plaza Verlade s/n; Tel 942/337-300)* can easily be reached should you have any problems.

Pharmacies Like everywhere in Spain, *green crosses* placed outside their doors easily identify pharmacies. **Lavin y Camus** *(Hernán Cortés 2; Tel 942/211-269; Open 24 hrs including festivals)* is a 24-hour pharmacy that can be relied on to be open at whatever time you need it.

Telephone City code: *942;* local operator: *05;* international operator: *07.* Calling cards can be bought at tobacco stores.

Airport There is an **airport** out about 5km (3miles) outside of town that has a few regular flights to and from Madrid and Barcelona. The airport can only be reached by taxi.

Trains Santander has two train stations that sit next to each other on Plaza Estaciones off Calle Rodríguez. The **RENFE Station** *(Tel 942/280-202; Info open 7:30am-11pm)* has many trains that run to Valladolid and then onto Madrid or Salamanca. Next door, the **FEVE** *(Tel 942/211-687; Info open 9am-2pm/4-7pm)* runs two daily trains west to Oviedo and three daily trains east to Bilbao.

Bus Lines Out of the City The **Bus Station** *(Pl Estaciones; Tel 942/211-995, info open 8am-10pm Mon-Fri; 9am-9pm Sat and Sun)* is a new facility that offers connections to many surrounding towns and villages as well as long-distance buses to Barcelona, Madrid, A Coruña, Bilbao, and everywhere in between.

Laundry In El Sardinero, **Lavatu** *(Avda. los Castros s/n; 9:30am-1pm/4-7:30pm Mon-Fri, 9:30am-1pm Sat)* has coin-operated washers and dryers. It sits on the south side of the street next to the street M. Prieto Lavín. Soap and dryer sheets can be bought here, so all you need to supply are coins and dirty laundry.

Postal The **Main Post Office** *(Avda. Alfonzo XIII s/n; Tel 942/212-673; 8:30am-8:30pm Mon-Fri, 9:30am-2pm Sat)* is located in the city center at the opposite end of the Jardines de Pereda from the main tourist office.

Internet See *wired*, above.

castro urdiales

It used to be that Castro Urdiales was a well-kept secret along Spain's northern coast. Lying in between Santander and Bilbao, for a long time it remained out of the spotlight. As hordes of tourists flooded Santander every summer, the wise residents of that town quietly slipped away to Castro Urdiales for July and August to enjoy the peace and quiet of this beautiful fishing village.

Castro Urdiales still hasn't quite been discovered...yet. The real estate market has definitely seen a big jump, and not too many locals are probably going to be living in the apartments being built up above town, but the fishing fleet still heads out into the Bay of Biscay, the beautiful Gothic church still looks down on the old town from its bluff above the ocean, and the streets of the old quarter still buzz with friends and neighbors catching up with one another.

Castro Urdiales has a classic small-town feel; it's the kind of place where it seems like everyone has known one another since childhood. It's got a very social atmosphere; people passing on the street will stop and exchange pleasantries, not just rush on by. If you're lucky enough to stay over on a weekend, you'll discover it's no wonder they all know each other. Every weekend, everyone, young and old, seems to come out in force onto the streets of the old town, where they *marcha* together until dawn.

The fortress-like Gothic structure **Iglesia de Santa María de la Asunción** [see *culture zoo,* below] towers over the narrow, cobblestone streets of the historic core, known as **Mediavilla.** The focal point of old town life is the arcaded **Plaza del Ayuntanmiento,** where the locals congregate while visitors are off flaunting their stuff on the beach. Although the buildings in the old town appear old, a lot of them date from 1813, when they were reconstructed after a disastrous fire swept through the quarter. The old quarter is riddled with *tascas* (bars); you'll want to return after dark for a tasca crawl, especially along **Calle de la Rua.** Wander this maze of streets for an hour or two during the day before heading for one of two beaches, **Playa de Ostende,** at the western end of town, or the less desirable **Playa Brazomar,** at the eastern end.

Sandwiched between the beaches is the oldest fishing port along the Cantabrian coast. Dating from the 13th and 14th centuries, when Castro Urdiales was the leading whaling port of Spain, the port is dominated by the ruins of a Templar castle, now the site of a lighthouse. Believe it or not, the town back in those centuries had three times the population of its present count of 15,000. The port looks like a movie set, with weather-beaten old fishermen rubbing elbows with tourists. These fishermen are known for catching *Besugo* or sea bream, which is hailed as one of the tastiest seafood delicacies in Spain. Nearby, facing the port, is **La Plazuela,** site of a significant portion of the bar scene.

The modern part of town lies for the most part behind the beach, Playa de Ostende. Since it lacks character, you'll want to spend little time here unless you use its sports complex or seek lodgings in summer when the old town is vastly overbooked.

hanging out

People don't come to Castro Urdiales to marvel over historical landmarks, and they don't come here to ponder world-class artwork. They come to

rules of the game

Yes, Castro Urdiales can turn into a dangerous place on the weekends as kids, parents, grandma, and grandpa all come down to the streets of the old town to PARTY!!! If you are at all worried about losing your sobriety during this time we recommend you store it in a very safe spot that you will not forget no matter how, um...well...how much you lose it. The rules of engagement are relatively straightforward and simple here. Have a good time and don't do anything stupid. Getting drunk is expected of the young and old. Getting drunk and puking in the street will earn you no friends. Does this mean it doesn't happen? Of course not. Just don't be that guy/girl. Hash happens—it's not something anyone is going to advertise, but don't be shocked if some young person asks you for a paper during your stay. They don't want a sheet of notebook paper. Other than that, other drugs don't figure heavily into the Castro Urdiales scene. This is a small town that has yet to be corrupted by big city values.

castro urdiales

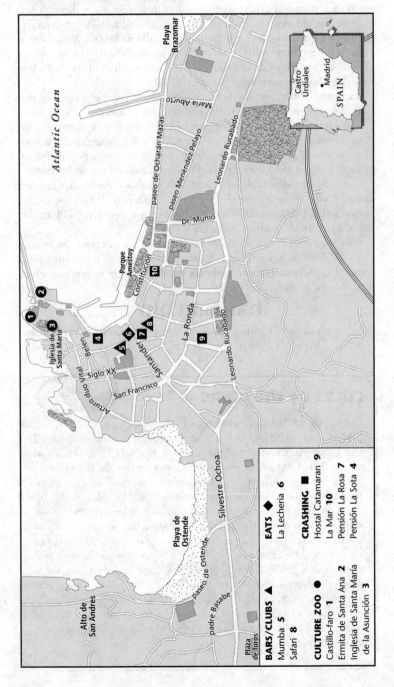

SPAIN
Castro
Urdiales
Madrid

Atlantic Ocean

Playa Brazomar

María Aburto

Leonardo Rucabado

Paseo de Ocharán Mazas

Paseo Menéndez Pelayo

Dr. Munio

Parque Amestoy

Constitución

10

La Ronda

Leonardo Rucabado

2

1

3

Iglesia de Santa María

Belén

4

5 **6** **7** **8**

Arturo Vital

Siglo XX

Santander

San Francisco

9

Alto de San Andrés

Playa de Ostende

Paseo de Ostende

Silvestre Ochoa

padre Basabe

Plaza de Toros

BARS/CLUBS ▲
Mumba **5**
Safari **8**

CULTURE ZOO ●
Castillo-faro **1**
Ermita de Santa Ana **2**
Inglesia de Santa María
de la Asunción **3**

EATS ◆
La Lecheria **6**

CRASHING ■
Hostal Catamaran **9**
La Mar **10**
Pensión La Rosa **7**
Pensión La Sota **4**

Castro because it is a quiet seaside escape—plain and simple. Hanging out is what you're supposed to do here, so when in Rome, right?

Castro has two beaches within its city limits, and that's pretty much all you need to know about hanging out here. On the west side of town, the larger beach, **Playa de Ostende,** stretches around the lower portion of the bay and thus offers a little more protection from the pounding Atlantic. It is popular with locals and families and on a sunny day makes the perfect place to throw down a towel and soak in the atmosphere, not to mention the sun.

On the east side of the town is **Playa Brazomar.** There's a little more wave action here and surfers sometimes frolic in the swells. This beach lies right below the hill where the new tower apartment complexes have been built, so when people start moving into them this could prove to be a popular, perhaps crowded, spot. You can also swim off of **Muella de Don Luis,** the jetty that encloses the east side of the harbor. The side of the jetty facing Playa Brazomar has stairs along its length that are nice to relax on, or swim off.

To the east of Playa Brazomar is a beautiful, peaceful park, **Cotolino.** To reach it, walk past Playa Brazomar away from the town center. The park is out on the point. It may get a bit breezy for a game of ultimate Frisbee, but you'll find lots of open lawns, pathways, and benches to sit on where you can watch as the boats enter and leave the harbor.

If you are seeking some peace and solitude within the center, there is a nice, often overlooked, park west of the old town by the intersection of calle Siglo XX and calle de Arturo Duo. Framed around a natural pool where ocean water comes in through a small cave, this little retreat has benches and a staircase to hang out on and make new friends. For a quiet spot and a great view, venture out to the cliffs beyond the park: Walk over the cave and follow the path through the grass to the cliffs, where wild flowers grow, seagulls swoon, and waves crash against the rocks below, and enjoy the excellent views across the bay back toward Playa Ostende.

bar, club, and live music scene

When you walk the quiet streets of the old town during the day there's no way you could imagine the transformation they make during weekend nights and holidays. The people of Castro like to get wild on the weekends: The streets are more alive at 3am on a Saturday night than at noon on a Tuesday. During the summer, the place rips just about every night. When people are out to party here—watch out!

A compact *marcha* zone means it's easy to wander in and out of all the spots, and you're never going to miss the party. So *marcha* away until you find a scene that's your flavor. Basically, things runs along calle de la Rua in the old town, ending around calle de Nuestra Senora. A lot of the bars turn themselves into *puffs* by putting on flashing lights for the weekend. It's funny and it works. Nowhere in town, including the two discos, sets any kind of dress code, but the locals still do their best to look nice, so try to upgrade from the T-shirt and sandals you wore all day on the beach.

One of the more popular and happening spots along the stretch is **Twist 61** *(Calle de la Rua 16)*. Mixed drinks are priced at 600ptas and beers are 300ptas. Like most places, the age range of the crowd is mixed; 20- to 40-year-olds all have a great time. Twist 61 is the perfect place to start to get your dance on before the clubs. People get down to everything from U.S./Spanish pop to classics from the 50s.

Right across the street is **Bar Meneses** *(Calle de la Rua 17-19)*. The beers here cost 200ptas and mixed drinks run about 550ptas. This is one of those places that during the week is a standard bar where friends gather to share a few drinks. Then for the weekend—presto, the everyday lights go off, blinking lights come on, and all of a sudden it's a raging time. Bar Meneses attracts a slightly older crowd of 25-45, but age makes little difference in Castro. Everyone enjoys dancing to the variety of music from merengue to disco. There's a cool tripped-out mural covering one of the walls of a mythical Cantabria gnome by his gnome home.

The rowdier side of the scene lies right around the corner from Bar Meneses on calle de Artinaro, which is actually more of an alley lined with packed bars. Generally, this is where the younger, 18-25 crowds can be found from about midnight to 4am. **Discobar Robote** is one packed *puff* on the street. It's a fairly casual scene where kids 20-30 squeeze together and seem to dance as one. The system blares out U.S. and Spanish dance music, making this one of the liveliest early evening places in town. Across the street is **Koala.** Don't let the name and the paintings of cute bears on the walls fool you—there's nothing soft and cuddly about this joint. It's popular with 17- to 25-year-old men and the women who love them. Heavy metal and hard rock play at levels almost equal to the amount of angst in the room.

There are two official clubs in Castro Urdiales, a good number considering the town's size, and, amazingly, both are packed come 5am. Don't bother making your way to them before 4am. Stay in the bars and once those clear out, follow the procession to the clubs. As to which of the two is better, all we can say is they're both different.

Mumba *(Calle de la Rua 12-14; No cover)* is where you go if all you want to do is dance. And this is what the entire town seems to want to do. Eighteen to 60-year-olds hang here (although it is mostly the younger people dancing). A DJ spins house and dance and the crowd really gets moving. Sofas line the back wall if you need to take a break and enjoy a beer for 400ptas or a mixed drink for 750ptas. Only a block away you'll find Castro's other club, **Safari** *(Calle Ardigales 16; 400ptas beer, 750ptas mixed; No cover)*. Safari lives up to its name by providing an exotic atmosphere. All the beams of the place resemble tree trunks, and plastic trees and animals are scattered about. Don't let the walls covered in animal hides sketch you out. Safari has an elongated set-up with a dance floor in the middle. The dance floor is small, though, and given the size of the place, not quite as lively as Mumba. While Safari has the atmosphere, it appears Mumba still holds the party.

culture zoo

There are few places of historic relevance in Castro Urdiales. There are no major museums that will leave you a better person for seeing them. But there is one interesting landmark that helps give Castro much of its personality.

Iglesia de Santa María de la Asunción *(Open 4-6pm Mon-Fri):* This 13th-century Gothic church sits on a bluff above the city, looking out over the ocean, and marks the center of the town, which stretches out on either side of the church along the coast. Services are still held at the church.

chico meets chica

Meeting that cute member of the opposite sex here is easier than you think. A small town means a new face is easily and quickly noticed. While you are staring at a roomful of complete strangers, they all know each other quite well and every one of them of the opposite sex has already looked you up and down before you even got in the door. So, if they like what they see, and you know they do because you are such a cutie, be prepared. The women are just as bold as the men here when approaching people. Language can prove a frustrating barrier in situations like these, but relax and have fun with it. Don't be embarrassed to use what little Spanish you know and encourage your counterpart to try the English he or she learned in school. They may be bashful, but they know a bit. Keep this up long enough and you may move to a form of communication that's levels beyond words.

Castillo-faro *(6-8pm Mon-Fri, noon-2pm/4-6pm Sat, noon-2pm Sun; Free):* Next to the church you'll find this present-day lighthouse, which is actually built upon the remains of the city's original fortifications. Although the inside of it holds nothing of great interest, a trip up to the top does offer a great view over the city.

Ermita de Santa Ana: Just down the bluff from the church and the lighthouse, overlooking the port, is this lookout. Alright, there is nothing of great significance about this place, and even the locals aren't too sure about it; one man told me it is a remainder of the city's old fortifications, while someone else told me it was built within the past hundred years. Regardless, it does offer a pretty good view over the port.

CITY SPORTS

If you really want to get your heart rate soaring and blood rushing through your body, my advice is to swim about 50-100 yards out into the ocean. Once there, start humming the theme from *Jaws* and let your mind go. Of course, if this isn't your idea of "proper exercise," Castro can provide a more conventional workout.

For all you masochistic sport types who just can't enjoy relaxing on a beach, Castro has a number of municipal sports centers. **Peru Zaballa** *(Tel 942/891-920; 9am-10pm Mon-Fri, 9am-2:30pm Sat)* lies right behind the western end of Playa Ostende. It is the largest of the sports complexes in town and houses a full-size indoor swimming pool, ball courts, gym, and a sauna. The staff is friendly and will help you get set up with whatever you need for a proper workout. Outside there is a small skate park complete with ramps, kickers, and a mini-half pipe.

If you really want to explore the waters off the coast of Castro Urdiales, head to **Subnorte** *(Calle Victoria Gainza s/n; Tel 942/861-239),* a full dive shop offering lessons and equipment. It also runs trips out along the coast during the summer; the staff promised us that shark attacks are minimal.

EATS

If you're not a fish fan when you get to Castro Urdiales, you'll either leave as one or you'll miss out on some great local dishes. There is no shortage of incredible *mesones* (literally, "houses," used to suggest restaurants or taverns) and restaurants that crowd the old town and serve up fantastic fish dishes brought in from the fleet only hours before.

Most of the evening dining in Castro is done tapas-style, hopping from one place to another. The area right around La Plazuela is literally lined with choices. Most offer just tapas, but even the *restaurantes* here have both a tapas bar and a separate dining room. Most places also offer homemade fish and shellfish soups. The people here have certainly learned to maximize the bounty the sea has provided for them.

If fish isn't your thing or you're on a tight budget, you by no means have to fast during your stay in town. Along Avenida de la Constitución you'll find an assortment of *cafetarias* that offer filling meals for a pocket full of coins. If you're in Castro during the summer, the choices are even more varied.

▶▶CHEAP

There are many options open to the budget-minded traveler. By no means should *dinero* stand between you and the great local cuisine. The best way to get a taste is to try some tapas. Not only are the little tidbits only a couple hundred pesetas apiece, but you'll be bumping elbows with the locals and fitting right in. A brief warning, though: The price of a tapas here, a tapas there, can snowball quickly into the equivalent of a full meal at a nice restaurant, so keep in mind to "just sample."

Cafetarias are a great way to get a filling meal at a friendly price. **Restaurante La Darsena** *(La Plazuela 12)* is devoted to the great Spanish pastime: soccer. Jerseys and pictures cover the walls and a game is usually playing to everyone's delight on the TV. This spot offers typical cafeteria dishes of sandwiches and burgers as well as combo plates, all for between 800-1,500ptas. Downstairs there is a pool hall that's a hangout for late teen/early twentysomething kids.

Another option just down the street is **Cerveceria Serman** *(Avenida de la Constitución 4; 700-1,200ptas per entree)*. Imagine the twisted fusion of a diner and bar and you got this place. Popular with the 20-30 crowd, it can be a fun place for a bite and a beer. The menu is typical diner food with *bocadillos*, burgers, and *platos combinados*. During the warmer months it has tables and chairs set up outside so you can eat while enjoying the view over the harbor. **La Lecheria,** located next to Pensión La Rosa [see *crashing*, below], offers takeout roasted chicken and *bocadillos*, all for under 1,000ptas. Not a bad deal if you want to grab something and then go have a little picnic on the beach.

▶▶DO-ABLE

One of the nicer neighborhood restaurants is **Restaurante Escala** *(Corner of La Rua and Juan la Cosa; 1,000-2,000ptas per entree),* in the old town. It serves some great dishes in a cozy dining room. The specials change daily, and the chef takes pride in them; they can be counted on to make your taste buds hungry for more. Like most places in town, the fish dishes are usually the best.

▶▶SPLURGE

From our investigations—scientifically conducted by talking to people, wandering in and out of places, and tasting all we could get our sticky hands on—a top local favorite seems to be **Mesón Segovia** *(Plazuela 19; No phone; 2000-3000ptas per entree; V).* We have to say that its reputation is well deserved. The majority of the tapas here make use of the day's fresh catch and sit in bite-sized pieces next to octopus arms, shellfish, and, of course, ham, the Spanish favorite. If the tapas get your gastric juices flowing, then try to grab a table to get a full meal. The entrees are prepared with the same devotion as the tapas, but you don't have to share them with everyone else.

crashing

Visitors, tourists, and overnight guests are nothing new to Castro Urdiales. The locals understand that people want a taste of their lovely small town, so they've taken it upon themselves to make people feel comfortable while they're here. All the *hostales* and hotels are very comfortable and accommodating, but be forewarned that during July and August rooms can be difficult to find, so try to book ahead if possible. The rest of the year shouldn't pose much of a problem. Unlike other Spanish coastal towns, the room rates don't vary that greatly between cheap and expensive, but room rates do increase all over town during the summer.

The most convenient place to stay is within the old center. Although not right on the water, it is the heart of town, with restaurants, bars, and shops. And since this is a small town, the beach is no more than a 10-minute walk away.

▶▶**CHEAP**

One of the cheapest places in town lies outside the old center, a couple of blocks back from Playa de Ostende. Conveniently, it is also just a couple of blocks away from where the buses from Santander drop you off. At **Hostal Catamaran** *(Calle Victorina Gainza 2; Tel 942/870-066; No singles July-Aug, 2,000ptas single without bath, 3,210ptas single with bath, 4,000ptas double without bath, 5,350ptas double with bath, 6,000ptas double without bath July-Aug, 7,490ptas double with bath July-Aug),* the rooms are modern and clean but not of particular note. Generally, the rooms with attached baths all have TVs and phones, while rooms without attached baths tend to lack such amenities. For them the owners have a TV lounge where you can witness the hysteria of Spanish game shows. There is also a restaurant that serves typical Spanish food on the ground floor; it's open to the public.

▶▶**DO-ABLE**

The streets of the old town offer several nice lodging options with an affordable price tag. The best place to start is **La Mar** *(Calle La Mar 27; Tel 942/870-524, Fax 942/862-828; 3,500-4,500ptas single; 5,000-7,000ptas double).* La Mar offers guests 16 comfortable, modern rooms, all complete with private bathroom, TV, and phone. The hotel is centrally located, just a block away from the port in the old town. Add to all this the fact that it provides 24-hour service and you might get the feeling that you're a royal visitor.

Another option only a block or two away is **Pensión La Rosa** *(Calle Ardigales 4; Tel 942/872-709; 2,500ptas single without bath, 5,000ptas double without bath, 6,000-7,000ptas double with bath; No credit cards).* This is a cozy, family-run place where the owners will go out of their way to make you feel at home. All of the rooms have TVs and some of the doubles have fold-out sofas that can accommodate up to four people in a room. For only 1,000ptas the owners will do a load of laundry for you. With just four rooms, get here early or call ahead to reserve one.

▶▶**SPLURGE**

Splurging here doesn't bring with it the Ritz or rooms with Jacuzzis; it's not going to make you feel like a rock star or bring you fame and fortune. Splurging here means paying a couple hundred more pesetas and getting a place where maybe the pillows are fluffed one extra time or the toilet paper is that soft, plush kind. It can definitely get you a very comfortable night's sleep at **Pensión La Sota** *(Calle la Correria 1; Tel 942/871-188, Fax 942/871-284; 4,000-6,000ptas single, 7,000-9,000ptas double; V, AE)*. Right by the waterfront in the heart of the old town, La Sota's advantage lies in the fact that it is as central as one can be. It has 20 modern rooms that all come complete with full, private baths, TV, and phone. It offers guests 24-hour service, should you require anything at 5am. For anyone who comes into this tiny hamlet and can't bring themselves to move on, La Sota also rents out apartments.

need to know

Currency Exchange Banks are scattered around Castro, both in the old town and in the newer areas. One that will *cambio* your dinero is **BBV** *(on the corner of Avenida de la Constitución and Melton P. Camino; 8:30am-2:30pm Mon-Fri)*, conveniently right across the street from the tourist office. It also provides 24-hour ATMs.

Tourist Information The **Tourist Office** *(Avda. de la Constitucion 1; Tel 942/871-512; 9am-2pm/5-7pm, 9am-9pm Jun-Aug)* is located on the water by the port. The staff here is very friendly and helpful and will give you bus schedules and departure points, dining and lodging recommendations, and even tell you where the best bars are.

Health and Emergency Emergency (medical): *112;* police: *092.* There is a **Cruz Roja Espanol (Spanish Red Cross)** hospital on Barrera *(Barrera 3 Tel 942/861-640).* The **Police Office** is in the *Plaza del Ayuntamiento (Tel 942/859-009 for non-emergency calls).*

Pharmacies All around town, *farmacias* are easily identified by a **green cross** out front. One with a friendly staff is **Roviralta** *(La Mar 21; Tel 942/861-185).* There are no 24-hour pharmacies in Castro Urdiales.

Bus Lines Out of the City There is no bus station in Castro Urdiales. There are, however, several buses daily heading to both Santander and Bilbao. The tourist office can provide you with the latest schedules and point out exactly where each bus is met.

Postal The **main post office** can be found on Calle Juan de la Cosa 8-10 *(8:30am-8:30pm Mon-Fri, 9:30am-2pm Sat).*

cangas de onis

This small, unassuming town at the base of the mountains in the Picos de Europa has been attracting visitors since before the dawn of time. Paleolithic man wandered his way up from the coast, a mere 25 kilometers (15 miles) away, to hunt deer and lamb (oh-so-dangerous) in the summertime. Today, people are again finding their way to Cangas de Onis to chase adventure and excitement (lambs be warned!).

The big attraction of this tiny town is that it is the gateway to the **Picos de Europa National Park** [see *the great outdoors*, below]. Cangas de Onis makes a great base for adventures into the park. It offers plenty of lodging and eating options as well as stores where you can stock up on last-minute supplies before heading off into the wilderness. A number of adventure tour operators have set up shop in Cangas—where they've have perfected the art of shooting heart rates through the roof [see *great outdoors*, below]. Guides lead unwitting suspects over wild rapids or encourage them to leap from bridges with nothing but an oversized rubber band tied to their ankles. Call them if you dare!

Walking through the small town center, it is hard to believe that this is where Spain was born. It was in Covadonga, 12 kilometers (7 miles) away, that the turning point in the war against the Muslim occupation took its first turn to the Christian advantage in 722. After the victory, led by King Pelayo, the Asturian Kingdom was established, with Cangas de Onis as its first capital. From there the *Reconquista* took off and Spaniards have been bad-mouthing Muslims ever since.

Until recently, the region mainly thrived off of agricultural means; today, people here are quickly discovering the ease with which money rolls in through tourism. The two industries sometimes collide, in the best possible way. Wagons drawn by donkeys still hold up tour buses coming down the main road, so you know things have not been lost completely to the almighty peseta. The town can still provide a quiet,

rules of the game

This is not a big city, so check all your big-city habits at the door. This is a small town, where people tend to notice what goes on. Drinking is a popular pastime here, like everywhere in Spain, but you gotta keep it together more. While drinks are allowed on the street, we by no means recommend walking down the main ave at 5am with a couple brews, getting loud with your friends. The bars in town are not the place where people blaze up. Most folks save it for a nice peaceful overlook while hiking.

peaceful retreat for those looking to escape from the hectic pace of modern life.

If you really want to enjoy this town at its best, stay as far away from it as possible during July and August. Even the locals, who ordinarily welcome visitors with a warm smile, get the hell out of Dodge during this time. Hordes of vacationers descend on the area, swallowing everything that gives it its beauty and character. Come through here in late spring or early fall, however, and you'll see the town in all its splendor. This is also when the Picos de Europa can best be enjoyed without the crowds.

Cangas de Onis has the classic small-town feel to it. Everyone knows each other and will stop and chat as they pass in the plaza or on the street. People are just as relaxed here as they are in other parts of Spain, although we wouldn't recommend burning one down while walking down the main street. The old and young mix easily, and PlayStation is a source of entertainment for kids here as much as it is anywhere.

The town center starts at the Río Sella and runs along Avenida de Covadonga for a couple of kilometers before tapering off. It will take you all of an hour or two before you know it well enough to drink a couple bottles of *sidras* (locally produced cider) and have no problem finding your way home. Everything you'll need is in the center and within easy walking distance.

Two blocks from the river, in the exact center of town along Avenida de Covadonga, locals of all ages gather at **Plaza de Ayuntamiento** to socialize and enjoy the last lingering hours of sunlight. The cafes around the plaza set up outdoor tables, perfect for sitting with a cold drink, people-watching, and trying to make a new friend or two.

bar & club scene

You aren't going to find any wild underground clubs here that host world-renowned parties, or bars that keep on rocking until dawn. Cangas isn't about that. It's small. The scene is small. The *marcha* is small and next to nonexistent on any nights other than Friday and Saturday. If you want to party, head for the big cities. This is a place where you wake up early and hike to a hilltop to greet the rising sun, not stumble out of a club to see it and think, "Oh damn, I missed another night's sleep."

What you will find are a few comfortable bars where you can sit and relax with friends and talk about the day's adventures. You'd have to try real hard to miss the scene in this town. On weekends the center of activity is on calle Bernard Pendas, where you'll find a couple of bars and *sidrerías* [see *eats*, below]. The town's *puff* stands at the end of Bernard Pendas, and since it's the only game in town it attracts a pretty mixed crowd. Basically it's for everyone who's up and wants to get down. It plays a mix of American, Spanish, and Euro dance music. Given the town's size, it's as good as can be expected and with the flashing lights and blaring music you can lose yourself for a little bit. But there's no need to stuff your best duds into your pack. Image isn't as big a deal here as it is elsewhere in Spain. The bars

cangas de onis

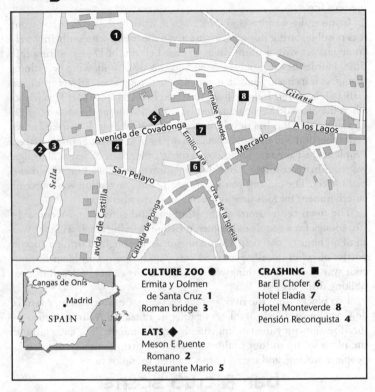

Cangas de Onís
Madrid
SPAIN

CULTURE ZOO ●
Ermita y Dolmen
  de Santa Cruz **1**
Roman bridge **3**

EATS ◆
Meson E Puente
  Romano **2**
Restaurante Mario **5**

CRASHING ■
Bar El Chofer **6**
Hotel Eladia **7**
Hotel Monteverde **8**
Pensión Reconquista **4**

around the *discoteca* are all unremarkable, but with good company and a cold beer, who really cares? One of the more noteworthy bars in town is **Ten De Re Te** *(San Pelayo 10; 5pm-2am Mon-Sun)*, a nice, laidback spot that's popular with the 20-30 crowd. Rock walls give the place a comfortably rustic feel and remind you that you're only a stone's throw from the mountains and gee, you need to get up early in the morning, so you'd better finish off that beer.... The sofa in the back is a huge score if you find it unoccupied. Don't be taken back by the bedpans that hang over the bar, there are *baños*. An interesting collection of 1940s-era ads hang on the wall, and if those don't grab you, there's a dartboard. This is a good place to go and unwind after hiking around all day, and with beers running 250ptas, the price ain't bad either.

CULTURE ZOO

In a place so close to the site of dramatic historical occurrences, and with a history that extends to the dawn of man, it is surprising that Cangas de Onis lacks major cultural sites. There are only two things in town that will interest those looking to get in touch with the history of the region, and neither will hold your attention for more than a half hour. Most of the historical remains from the area have been toted away to museums in larger cities like Oviedo.

Roman bridge: This is not only an attraction, but also a local landmark. The bridge spans the Río Sella by the entrance to town in what would be—if it weren't for the major highway crossing here—an idyllic setting. But despite the noise from the road, many locals still find plenty of peace here as they cast lines into the river, hoping to pull out a trout or salmon. The bridge itself arches high over the river and has a large cross, a copy of the Victory Cross, hanging from the center. Walking across the bridge provides for some good views of the larger hills and mountains surrounding the town. You'll probably hear some know-it-all talking about how the bridge is obviously Medieval and not Roman. Just tell them to piss off, that the Medieval bridge was built to replace the Roman one, which is where the name comes from. If it's hot enough, one of the calmer pools in the river here would make a nice place for a quick dip.

Ermita y Dolmen de Santa Cruz: You'll find this church, the one other interesting site in town, just over the bridge on the street that leads to the **Sports Center** [see *city sports,* below]. Getting in here kinda depends on lucking onto someone unlocking the building, or you can ask for the key at the Ayuntamiento (across the street from the ALSA bus office). From the outside it looks like just another small church. It has been rebuilt many times, most recently after the Spanish Civil War, but it stands on the spot where the first Christian church in Spain was built. The church's true treasure—a dolmen—lies in an underground crypt. And, "what is a dolmen?" you might ask. It's a stone tomb: two stone legs capped by a stone slab. Think Stonehenge. This dolmen is probably of

the art of the pour

You may give your local bartender props back home for drawing a clover in the head of your Guinness with froth, but those guys can't do nothing against the talented *sidras* bartenders. In some ways more difficult than a Jordan dunk, the cider pour is an above-the-head, behind-the-back, no look, nothing-but-glass (sometimes) pour...all in the interest of giving the drink maximum carbonation. Try it yourself and you're bound to stand in a puddle of your own failure. You'll also notice that true *sidras* aficionados down the whole cup in one gulp, enjoying it while the carbonation is at its fullest. Some places even have a trough around the edge of the bar. That is where the true aficionado throws the swill of each cup.

festivals and events

Although a small town, Cangas de Onis *is* still Spanish, so it enjoys a healthy dose of festivals. It shouldn't be a big surprise that many have their roots in the agricultural calendar.

Feria de Primavera *(usually toward the end of April)* celebrates the coming of spring. The *sidras* batches have spent the winter fermenting in dank cellars and are now as hard as the night is long...so there's a lot of pouring going on.

Fiesta Patronal de San Antonio *(mid-June)* pays homage to the town's patron saint. It's a weeklong affair with soccer games, concerts, and moving discos at night, ending in a bang with a fireworks!

Feria de Otono *(mid-October)* is the town's autumn fair. What originally was a day intended to celebrate the harvest is now just another excuse to take the day off and party. Many of the local cheeses are brought to market at this time for tasting.

Celtic origin, dating from 3000 B.C., and is covered with engravings. Rumor has it priests used to hide in this crypt from invading Moors. An etching in one of the pillars of a cross over a crescent moon represents the Christian victory over Islam.

Buxu Cave *(town of Cardes; 10am-2pm/4-6:30pm; 200ptas):* If you are willing to go for a small hike, this is a good destination. Here you can find some of the last remaining traces of early man's existence in these parts. Archeological digs at the cave's entrance have uncovered a few cave drawings, evidence of human inhabitants during the high Paleolithic era 18,000 years ago. Unfortunately, only 25 visitors a day are allowed to enter the cave; turns out respiration is a major contributor to the deterioration of the carvings (try to convince them you'll hold your breath). Arrive early if you can. To get there, follow the road out of Cangas de Onis toward Covadonga for 3km. From there head down the road on your left that leads to Cardes, the town closest to the caves. From the town follow the signs for the *cueva;* it's an easy 15-minute walk through the countryside to the cave.

the great outdoors

With mountains looming up in the distance and beautiful streams running through the town, you immediately know that outside is the only place to be. While the nearby **Picos de Europa National Park** [see below] offers some of the best hiking and outdoor exploration in the area, Cangas de Onis has some good trails if you're tight on time, too. The **main tourist office** [see *need to know,* below] hands out a guide outlining a couple of good local hiking routes. Immediately south of town lies a dramatic 38-kilometer scenic stretch called **Los Beyos Defile,** reachable via N625, the rural highway running along the Sella River. The Sella River's raging waters cut through the 6-mile defile—a thick layer of limestone. Immediately to the south of that is the **Mirador de Oseja de Sajambre,** which offers one of the greatest views in the Picos de Europa, from the center of which the **Pico Niaja** rises 1,732 meters.

If you've made it this far, though, you might as well go all the way and enjoy the full splendor of the national park.

FIVE THINGS TO TALK TO a LOCAL about

1. **The Great Outdoors:** Although not everyone in this town may traverse the mountain passes and gorges right in their backyard, you can bet your bottom dollar that they spend most of their time outside. People here have grown up in rhythm with all the hills and streams that surround them. So while one person might tell you about the time he got caught in the mountains during the biggest storm of the century, someone else may share with you a tip on where the best salmon beds are found.

2. **Cheese:** Cheese here is like bottled beer back home: Everybody knows their cheese is the best and everybody has a favorite. So while they may drone on about all the different varieties, sharpness, and smells (everyone's an expert), just cut to the cheese and ask them what their favorite is and why. This is also closely related to...

3. **Sidras:** Another well-respected product that the area is known for. People grew up drinking this homebrewed cider like we drank Coke. Ask them about the secret to a good *sidras.*

4. **Tourists:** With this one, you'll get lots of different reactions. Some people will say they love 'em, others can't get the hell out of town fast enough during tourist season. Still others will act indifferent, but they're hiding something. No matter what, locals can't ignore tourists, and while they may not give voice to it, everyone has an opinion.

5. **The National Park:** You'd think it would be a great, well-received thing, but the national park was actually contested by people living in the area, especially within the boundaries of the park. While it has definitely brought a lot of money to Cangas, not everyone is totally pleased with restrictions placed on the land.

The best place to get info on the park is **Casa Dago** *(Avda. Covadonga 43; Tel 985/848-614, Fax 985/848-699; www.mma.es; 9am–2pm/4-6:30pm Mon-Sun),* the National Park office in the center of Cangas. Pick up some free brochures (including English) or buy a detailed hiking map or more in-depth literature on the park. The park office is one of the better places to find out the latest conditions around the area. Outside the office, check out the large relief map of the park. It's an excellent way to get yourself oriented and to see what's out there.

If years of ultra-realistic video games have left you numb to the simpler pleasures in life and you need more than a glacier lake to get your spirits up, Cangas can cater to your needs as well. There are no fewer than three major adventure tour companies in Cangas de Onis. All offer very similar outings—generally along Los Beyos Defile or the River Sella—at similar prices; in fact, for horseback riding, everybody goes through the same barn, regardless of operator, so the price is the same no matter who you sign up with (1,700ptas for an hour ride and 3,000ptas for two hours). The only real need to shop around would be to find out which company will throw in a picnic lunch, or if transportation to and from the site is included in the price. But for the most part all the trips are fairly consistent from company to company. So the real question is, what thrill do you seek today?

Your choices are canoeing, canyoning (pioneered in Interlaken, Switzerland, canyoning combines the thrill of descending rapids on foot with climbing techniques to navigate the canyon), spelunking (exploring some of the caves in the area), bungee jumping (jump, bounce, bounce...), horseback riding, and guided quads tours. If that's not enough to keep you interested, some of the operators also offer guided hikes through the National Park.

All the companies have offices in the center of town. During the busy season it's best to reserve a spot a day or two ahead. Sign up at any of the following companies:

Cangas Aventura *(Avda. Covadonga s/n; Tel 985/849-261)* is the oldest operator in town. The staff here will hook you up with whatever your pleasure is. Canoeing trips run 3,000ptas; bring a bathing suit and towel and they'll provide everything else, including a bag lunch. Canyoning trips run from 10am–2pm (5,000ptas); again, they'll supply everything, but it's best to reserve ahead. Spelunking trips run in the afternoon for 2-1/2 hours (3,500ptas); bring a pair of hiking boots, and they'll provide all the gear. Bungee jumps require a minimum of four people. It'll only cost you 3,000ptas for your first jump, and if you survive that, 1,000ptas for each additional jump. An hour guided quad trip costs 3,500ptas; get a buddy on your machine with you and it'll cost 5,000ptas.

Los Cauces *(Avda. Covadonga 23; Tel 985/840-138)* offers the same trips at similar prices, although its spelunking trips are 500ptas less than any of the other operators. Like the others, it'll outfit you in everything you need to journey into the center of the earth. Canoe trips depart at 10:15am, 11am, 11:45am, and 1pm. They are unguided so you have the luxury of taking as much time as you damn well please. Canyoning trips depart at 10:30am, 3:30pm, and 4pm and last 2 to 3 hours. Los Cauces does require that you have a valid driver's license before you hop on their quads; if you don't have one, find a friend who does and jump on with him. The outfit also offers guided hikes in the national park. Fifteen thousand pesetas covers an experienced and all-knowing guide for the day to take a group of any size out to enjoy the park.

The price fixing continues at **Monteverde** *(Sargento Provisional 5; Tel 985/848-079)*, which is not only a hotel, but also a tour operator. The one exception to the uniform prices is that for 5,000ptas, it offers a slightly more challenging canoe trip than the other operators, as well as the relaxing one for 3,000ptas.

Unfortunately, the closest place to town to rent a bike practically requires a bike to get to. **La Casa de la Montana** *(Tel 985/844-189)* is a good 6 to 7 kilometers (about 4 miles) southeast of town on Route 0220 toward Covadonga. If you do make it out there, though, there are some great trails in the area. Even just sticking to the roads, as most Spaniards do, will present you with some amazing scenery. You're given maps and assisted with information about where the best trails are, and which are rated difficult, as the roads are very steep. The most scenic bike trip (allow a day for this type of touring) is the road southeast of Covadonga leading to Lakes Enol and Ercina, which lie at the end of 0220 and form the northern periphery of the **Parque National de la Montand de Covadonga.** The most stunning stop along the trail is at the **Mirador de la Reina,** 8 kilometers southeast of Covadonga, where you are rewarded with a cluster of stunning rock "pyramids" making up the mountain range of **Sierra de Covalierda.** You can then make your descent to two of the most beautiful lakes in the Picos de Europa, Enol and Ercina, both at an altitude of 1,232 meters. If you remembered to stock up on provisions in Covadonga, this is most definitely an idyllic spot for a picnic.

CITY SPORTS

Hundreds of miles of unspoiled wilderness aren't enough to tire you out? You need more than paddling against the river for a couple hours? Who are you, Superman? Well, if all the activity just leaves you hungry for more, there is **Pabellon Municipal de Deportes** *(Avda. Contranquil s/n; Tel 985/848-590; 9am-1:30pm/4:30-11pm Mon-Fri, 10am-2pm/5-8pm Sat, 11am-2pm Sun Oct-June; 10am-1:30pm/5-10pm Mon-Fri, 10am-2pm/5-8pm Sat July-Sept)*, just outside the center. This large, new sports facility has weight machines and basketball and volleyball courts inside, soccer and tennis court outside. There's also a sauna (perfect after long hikes) and a large, well-equipped climbing wall. If you want to perfect your skills before hitting the mountain face, this would be the place to do it. Or take a class, in aerobics, karate, etc. The facilities are open to everyone, though some activities will cost a couple hundred pesetas if you're not a resident. The people working reception are very willing to help out. To get here, follow the sign off Avenida de Covadonga to the sports center. You'll know you've made it when you see a big building surrounded by playing fields. It's about a 5- to 10-minute walk from the center.

STuff

Although no one is going to come to Cangas to buy their spring wardrobe or the latest pirated recording of the Beastie Boys show, there are plenty of shops that specialize in what people do come to Cangas de Onis for: the mountains. Stock up here on all your supplies before heading into the park, as options quickly diminish after this outpost. So grab some grub, maybe an extra flashlight and the latest guidebook, and you'll be ready to hit the trail.

Tunon *(San Pelayo 31; Tel 985/947-061; 10am-2pm/4-7pm Mon-Sat, closed Sat afternoon)* is one of the best places for camping, hiking, and especially climbing gear. It's a great place to grab those odds and ends you'll need, and it has a knowledgeable staff that can clue you into the park. For those of you just looking for something clever to bring the folks back home, there are a number of tourist shops near the ALSA bus stop. They'll sell you anything from genuine *sidra* and cups to hand-carved walking sticks and Asturian wooden shoes. Check out **El Bocau** next to Hotel Eladia [see *crashing*, below]. Yeah it's a tourist shop, but it's also a great place to pick up some Asturian cottage foods. They stock a wide selection of those kick-ass local cheeses, jams, *sidras,* and odd local liqueurs.

EATS

When the main livelihoods of a place are farming and fishing, you know you're in for some good food. Everything here is incredibly fresh and full of flavor. Besides fresh beef and lamb dishes, you can dine on trout and salmon caught in the streams. *Fabes,* Asturian beans, is another popular local dish. Above all, this region is known for two things in particular: cheese and *sidras,* both of which must be sampled before leaving. *Sidrerías* are the Asturian take on a tavern. Aside from selling excellent homemade *sidras,* they serve hearty meals.

Eating well in Cangas is easy, a good thing since you'll soon be venturing off into the wilderness with God knows what kind of provisions. With lots of restaurants, cafes, and *sidrerías* to choose from, the only difficulty can be which to choose. Of the more popular local places, **Restaurante Mario** *(Avda. Covadonga 19; Tel 985/848-105)* scored highly with us. This is a comfortable spot where *sidra* poured on the floor is the rule, not the exception. Big saws and ox yokes hang on the walls, so you won't forget where your meal is coming from. You hardly need the reminder, the dishes are so fresh here. Asturian-influenced starters run between 500-1,200ptas. The cheese plate is a must. Meat and fish entrees cost between 1,200-2,500ptas.

For lunch, **Meson El Puente Romano** *(next to bridge on far bank, Tel 985/848-110)* can't be beat. It sits right next to the Río Sella with tables outside to enjoy the view. The food is good and ranges from 700-2,000ptas, but the location is really this place's biggest attribute.

A bunch of popular spots cluster together on Constantino Gonzalez, right before the bridge that leads to the Dolman of Santa Cruz. They range from sit-down restaurants to drinks and tapas joints. **Sidrería Acebeu** usually collects a healthy crowd enjoying tapas with a glass or three of wine.

If it's provisions you're in need of, there are two supermarkets in the town center. Both are across the street from each other on Avenida de Covadonga, about a block toward the Roman bridge from the tourist office.

crashing

To give you some idea of what this otherwise-peaceful town gets like during the height of the tourist season, the tourist office lists over 30 official lodging options for a town of just 6,000. That's a lot of rooms for a place this size, yet people still have trouble finding a room come August. Reserve ahead if you're hitting town during July or, especially, August. Any other time of the year, you shouldn't have a problem finding a place to lay your weary head.

Lodging options here run the gauntlet from cheap rural houses to luxury five-star affairs. Prices here mimic those places on the shore, with low prices most of the year that skyrocket for the high season. Take the cue and avoid visiting here "in season."

Among the cheaper options in town is **Bar El Chofer** (*Emilio Laria 10; Tel 985/848-305; 2,000ptas single, 3,000ptas double, 5,500ptas triple, rates go up an undisclosed amount July and Aug; No credit cards*). The rooms are adequate and comfortable, with shared bathrooms that are modern and clean and will make you feel like a human being again after a week in the woods. Friendly people run this hotel, and they spend most of their time in the restaurant they manage downstairs (there were some pretty good smells coming out of the kitchen).

Pensión Reconquista (*Avda. de Covadonga 6; Tel 985/848-275; 3,000ptas double*), right on the town's main plaza, sits above the restaurant of the same name and offers nice rooms at an affordable price. Bathrooms are shared. A third supplemental bed can be added to the rooms if needed. Next door is **Principado** (*Tel 985/848-350*), which also has

wired

Yes, even in the mountains you can stay wired. **Inga** (*Avda. Covadonga 13; Tel 985/849-427; 10:30am-1:30pm/4-9pm Mon-Fri, morning hours only Sat and Sun*) has Internet hookups for 500ptas an hour. The entrance is around the back.

economical rooms, although the owners aren't always the best about answering their doorbell.

If you just want to roll out of bed and into adventure, then **Hotel Monteverde** *(Sargento Provisional, 5; Tel 985/848-079; 3,000ptas single, 4,200ptas July, 5,500ptas Aug, 4,500ptas double, 6,075ptas July, 7,850ptas Aug; montever@arrakis.es, www.arrakis.es/~montever; V, MC, AE)* is the place for you. With the adventure tour company of the same name [see *the great outdoors,* above] on the street level, this makes it all so easy. The rooms here are nice and new, too. All come complete with bathroom, TV, and phone. Add to that the cafeteria that the hotel runs and you could spend all your time in Cangas right here, although I don't know why you'd want to.

Another of the slightly more upscale options in town is **Hotel Eladia** *(Avda. Covadonga 14; Tel 985/848-000; 3,500ptas single, 5,000ptas July and Aug, 5,000ptas double, 7,000ptas July and Aug, 6,000ptas triple, 9,000ptas July and Aug; V, AE).* If there is a central location in this small town, I guess this place has it. It's right across the street from the tourist office and no more than three blocks from anywhere else in town. The rooms are all nice and modern with bathroom, TV, and phone. The restaurant on the ground floor is open to the public.

If you find yourself in a bind, one more do-able option is **Hotel Puente Romano** *(Puente Romano 8, Tel 985/849-339/Fax 985/847-284; 8,000ptas single, 9,000ptas double; private baths; V, MC).*

need to know

Currency Exchange Take the time to exchange money here, as banks and ATMs aren't as abundant further into the park. The center of town in Cangas has plenty of banks that will exchange money and travelers checks for you. Most also have 24-hour ATMs.

Tourist Info The **main tourist office** *(Avda. Covadonga s/n; Tel 985/848-005; www.cangasdeonis.com; 10am-2pm/4-7pm Sept-June, 10am-10pm July-Sept)* is across the street from the ALSA bus stop, in the plaza. Aside from that there are several maps of Cangas scattered around town; one is in the main plaza. They show most of the lodging options in the center as well as the locations of other important buildings.

Health and Emergency Emergencies, **call 1006.** The **Centro de Salud** *(Carcel s/n; Tel 985/848-571; 3-8pm Mon-Fri, 10am-1pm/5-7pm Sat and Sun)* is in the center of town for health problems. There is also a **hospital** *(Tel 985/840-032)* for 24-hour care. The **local police** office *(Tel 985/848-558)* is located in the city hall.

Pharmacies There are no 24-hour pharmacies here, so plan accordingly if at all possible. *Farmacias* are marked with a **neon green cross** out front. One is **Farmacia Comas** *(San Pelayo 5; Tel 985/848-028; 9am-9pm daily).*

Telephone City code: *985.*

Bus Lines Out of the City The easiest way into and out of town is **ALSA** bus line *(Avda. Covadonga s/n, Tel 985/848-133).* Its office is almost directly across the street from the tourist office. It offers many connections to Oviedo as well as to Llanes and Valladolid. There is one bus that stops daily on its run between Llanes and Madrid and several that service local towns including Covadonga (which lies inside the national park).

Postal The town's **main post office** is on Constantino Gonzalez between Avenida de Covadonga and the Río Guena.

Internet See *wired*, above.

OViEdO

Situated in the mountains in the middle of Asturias, Oviedo makes a logical regional capital. Maybe that's why the seat of government was moved here from Cangas de Onis way back in 821 A.D. Today, the town is also the commercial center of Asturias. With its pleasant mix of old city and new business, Oviedo makes for a satisfying stop. Although the city itself does not have an overwhelming number of sites and attractions to entice visitors, it is the major transportation hub of the region and a good place to stay if you'll be making trips out into the Asturian countryside.

One thing you may notice while strolling along the streets of Oviedo is that this town has a fountain fetish. Every plaza, traffic circle, and park has some sort of fountain shooting geysers of water into the air. Perhaps it comes from the deeply embedded agricultural roots of Asturias, a reminder to the urbanites of the fresh mountain streams that flow right outside their city. Whatever the reason, the fountains give a nice air to the city. Perhaps also to remind locals of their pastoral roots, the streets of Oviedo are wide, and many in the commercial center are open only to pedestrian traffic, which gives the whole place a pleasant feel.

Okay, Oviedo's a little dull; a little spark certainly wouldn't hurt it. But it's a comforting place to visit, very homey. This is not one of those grand cities that leave visitors with a sense of insignificance. Oviedo instead leaves all that come feeling a part of it. The social scene is relaxed and casual, with no velvet ropes dividing the "in crowd" from everyone else. Instead, everyone enjoys the city together. When heading out here, your best resource to the inside track of what is happening is *Agenda de Oviedo.* It's a free monthly magazine distributed in bars, hotels, and some *hostales.* In its colorful pages you can find out all about what is going on in terms of cultural events, musical showcases, and everything else the city hosts. If nothing inside the pages of this magazine seems to peak your interest, it does have bus schedules for those wanting to move on.

neighborhoods

Oviedo is a small city with a compact center that should pose no difficulty to navigate. There are several major roads that make getting around a breeze. If you arrive at the RENFE train station, **Calle de Uría** will

oviedo

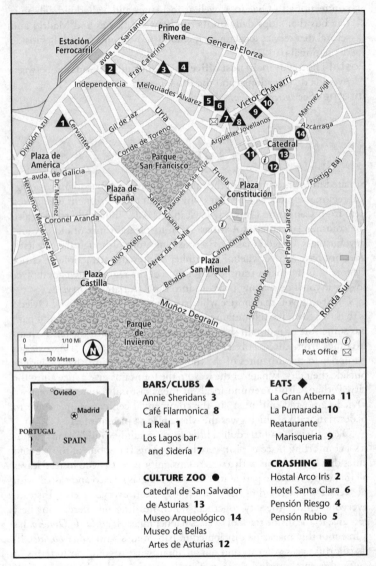

BARS/CLUBS ▲
Annie Sheridans **3**
Café Filarmonica **8**
La Real **1**
Los Lagos bar
and Sidería **7**

CULTURE ZOO ●
Catedral de San Salvador
de Asturias **13**
Museo Arqueológico **14**
Museo de Bellas
Artes de Asturias **12**

EATS ◆
La Gran Atberna **11**
La Pumarada **10**
Reataurante
Marisqueria **9**

CRASHING ■
Hostal Arco Iris **2**
Hotel Santa Clara **6**
Pensión Riesgo **4**
Pensión Rubio **5**

stretch out in front of you, heading southeast into the city. Follow this down until you see a large park, **Campo de San Francisco,** on your right, then take a left and you'll find yourself in the newer, commercial center of town, just north of the old city.

If you arrive by bus, you have about a 10-minute walk west on **Calle de Fray Ceferino** before it meets up with Calle de Uría. Calle de Fray Ceferino marks the northern boundary of the commercial center; the major pedestrian-only streets of the newer part of town are **Palacio Valdez, Calle Campoamor,** and **Calle de Caveda.** All these streets are lined with retail stores, restaurants, and bars and make for relaxed wandering.

To the south of the commercial center is Oviedo's **old town,** where you'll find the cthedral and a number of small plazas. The old quarter stretches out below the cathedral and its square, Plaza Alfonso II. Oviedo's older section isn't as impressive as in some cities, but wandering through it does produce some fun, and uncrowded, discoveries. **Plaza de la Constitición,** one of the larger plazas in the old town, stands as its unofficial center.

Campo de San Francisco is the major park in Oviedo, and is right in the middle of the new section of the city. As far as visitors are concerned, the most interesting things in Oviedo are to be found to the east of the park—in the commercial center and old town. The exception: There are a couple of late-night discos on the streets north of the park.

Getting around Oviedo is best accomplished on foot. Public buses [see *need to know,* below] do run throughout the city, but with many main streets closed to traffic, especially in the old town, buses can't always get you where you want to go. The city is compact and scenic, so walking is enjoyable—and good exercise to get you ready for conquering the mountains outside the city.

hanging out

While not the liveliest city in Spain, Oviedo offers many great spots to just kick back and enjoy the scenery. The plazas of the old town make great places to watch the world pass by while sipping a glass of the house red at an outdoor table. **Plaza de la Constitución** has several cafes with tables and chairs set up outside, ideal for people-watching. Late afternoons and early evenings tend to be when the plazas are busiest, with people out socializing after a day's work.

Perhaps the best place in the city to enjoy some peace and quiet is the city's main park, **Campo de San Francisco.** This is a good-sized park complete with tree-lined walkways, lawns, benches, and, of course, in the great Oviedo style, fountains—several of them, in fact. The park seems to be popular with everyone, and families and lovers mix easily (a little too easily by U.S. standards, perhaps) here. A small pond surrounded by pine trees in one corner of the park serves as a temporary home to some ducks and, more interestingly, a flock of wild peacocks. Although it is a little thrill to see these birds walking freely and spreading their beautiful tails, it seems as if the thrill has worn off for local refreshment vendors, who have to continually shoo the birds away from their stands with brooms.

The youth of the city have no designated hangout spot. They can be found east of the Campo de San Fransisco on the **university campus** during the day. Another popular area is among the shops and boutiques in the commercial center. The pedestrian road of **Palacio Valdes** tends to collect a good crowd, as does **Calle Campoamor.** No one appears to actually shop at any of the surrounding stores; it just seems like a central place where groups of friends meet up before heading off somewhere else.

wired

Oviedo has yet to catch up with the Internet cafe trend, but that doesn't mean you'll have to be disconnected during your visit here. In fact, right in the center of town there is a computer center that is open 24/7 for insomniacs and Internet addicts. This means staying in touch with all the kids back home is easy and can be done at whatever time your crazy travel schedule allows. **Laser Internet Center** *(Calle San Francisco, 9; www.las.es; open 24 hours a day, 7 days a week; 150ptas for 15 minutes)* is located right where the commercial center and the old town meet, just a block from the Campo de San Francisco. It's got plenty of computers with quick Internet connections and a friendly staff that will help you get going in no time.

bar, club, and live music scene

The weekends aren't as outrageous here as they are in Madrid, the parties not as wild as Bilbao's, and the festivals nowhere near as untamed as Pamplona's San Fermin, but Einstein taught the relevance of relativity, and this is still Spain. Yes, if you are here on a weekend you will be hard-pressed not to have a great time. On a weekday, however, you'll have to dig deeply—and even then, you might not come up with anything.

Clubs aren't really the thing here, which is surprising given that Oviedo is a regional capital and a city of over 200,000 people. The couple of clubs that do keep the party going until the wee hours are conventional and offer nothing new or out of the ordinary. The bars are kinda the same; there's no distinct *marcha* district, and *bodegas* play more of a role than bars. So do *sidrerías*—think of them as northern Spain's taverns, where a good meal and plentiful drink are easy to come by. If you don't eat at one you still must stop in to sample a bottle of sidras. You will have a good time here in Oviedo; you may just remember it for a change.

In the center of the city is **Annie Sheridans** *(Calle Campoamor 4; 6pm-2am daily; pints 600ptas),* a genuine Irish pub in all respects, with haunting Celtic music, pints of Guinness, and Jameson paraphernalia decorating the green walls. In fact, a place as Irish as this could only exist far outside the borders of the old country. It's a very comfortable place to go and get a drink and have a conversation, but with prices as high as they are, only casual drinking is recommended in this social atmosphere.

Another good spot for a drink is **Danny's Jazz Café** *(La Luna 11; Tel 985/211-483; beer 300ptas, mixed drinks 500ptas).* Relaxed like all jazz cafes should be, Danny's offers patrons a laid-back atmosphere where great jazz recordings play from the stereo and everyone is made to feel at home.

Right around the corner is **Café Filarmonica** *(Calle Arguelles 8-10)*, a large open space with a gracefully curving bar surrounded by lots of tables. Aside from the usual selection of mixed drinks, wines, and beers, Café Filarmonica also offers a large menu of teas and coffees. The atmosphere is a little classy, but don't be too intimidated to be a big kid and order one of their tasty looking sundaes.

If you are ready to experience the fun of a real *sidrería*, try **Los Lagos bar and Sidrería** *(Plaza del Carbayon 3; Tel 985/201-681; 4pm-midnight daily)* in the city center. Belly up to the bar and order a bottle of hard cider (no glasses, only bottles served), then sit back and have one of the masterful bartenders pour the cider into your glass from three feet up. The reason for this display of pouring virtuosity is to get the maximum carbonation out of the sidras. If you're brave, give it a try yourself—just make sure that when you miss (and you will), you won't be pouring on someone's shoes. Besides great *sidras,* this place also offers tasty eats (most dishes for under 1,500ptas) to munch on while you contemplate the best pouring method.

There are a couple of small clubs on Calle Santa Clara, but if you really want a disco, head west out of the old town to **La Real** *(Calle Cervantes 9; free)*, which is known as one of the best clubs in the city (although I guess that's not saying an incredible amount). Even though this isn't a world-class venue, La Real will give you a fun night. Packed with a well-groomed crowd, the large dance floor here can be a good time as everyone gets down to house, disco, and dance with bumping force.

At the risk of sounding like a broken record...the live music scene here is not exactly thriving. Local bands playing in beer-soaked clubs really doesn't happen much in Oviedo. This, given the talent of most Spanish "rock" groups, is probably for the best. But for those of you who would like to hear some live music, all is not lost. In fact, that's one area where the tourist board seems to be devoting some energy. During the summer months (April-September) bands of all styles and genres play concerts from the gazebo in Campo de San Francisco. They're a whole lot of fun and attract a varied crowd, from families to young lovers who do what the

fIVE-O

You'll be glad to hear that the police (both national and local) in Oviedo are as relaxed as everyone else here. Probably a lot of this is due to the fact that things and people don't get quite as out of control as they do in other cities in the country, and probably a lot of it is due to the fact that things are just more relaxed here. The police presence is something you really don't notice that much, and when you do see a cop he's probably having a friendly chat with someone, just blending into the scene.

Spanish do best with a little PDA. The concerts usually take place on Sundays starting around 12:30pm. Check out the listings at the tourist office for the exact times and bands. Don't expect to see any bands that you've heard of before; these are just casual "music in the park" affairs, and even with the non-involvement of Ticketmaster, Pearl Jam has yet to sign on....

arts scene

While the majestic mountains and dramatic coast surrounding Oviedo may inspire your soul, don't expect to see any art in the capital that will.

▶▶VISUAL ARTS

The visual arts scene is all but dead here. The galleries to wander are the streets of the old town, and the artwork to admire is the centuries-old architecture. Young, ambitious artists have left Oviedo behind as they seek out larger cities where an art culture exists. If you're interested in seeing paintings by Asturian artists you should head to the **Museo de Bellas Artes** [see *culture zoo*, below], where there is a small collection by local artists. There are no other galleries that showcase local talent.

▶▶PERFORMING ARTS

The performing arts scene in the city is definately a step ahead of the visual arts scene, but still could use a jump-start. The major center for performing arts is the **Teatro Campoamor,** which sits across a plaza from the east corner of the Campo de San Francisco, near the post office. This venue hosts a wide variety of events including classical and orchestral music performances as well as theatrical shows. Prices vary per event, but tickets are rarely under 1,000ptas. To find out what is going on, visit the box office at the theater where postings and bulletins detail all upcoming events. Or flip through the pages of the always-handy *Agenda de Oviedo.*

If all you really want is a movie to enjoy for a couple of hours, Oviedo has several theaters scattered about town. Most have the latest Hollywood release showing on their one screen about ten times a day. **Minicines 1,2,3, y 4** *(Calle Caveda s/n; 4pm–midnight nightly; 700ptas)* offers more choices than most other cinemas in town. A little hidden in a small alley off Calle Caveda, it's close to where Calle San Bernabe comes in, off the other side of the street next to the church. Here they show a mix of Spanish and American movies for you to choose from. All show times are posted outside the theater.

culture zoo

Although not loaded with cultural sites, Oviedo has done a good job of making sure the attractions it does offer are of good quality (and all of them are conveniently in the old town, too). There's enough here to keep you occupied and happy on those days when you're not heading out of the city, but to cancel a trip to the mountains for extended sightseeing around Oviedo would be massive overkill. If you wanted, Oviedo's cultural sites could be covered in one leisurely day.

Catedral de San Salvador *(Plz Alfonso II s/n; Tel 985/221-033; 10am-1pm/4-7pm; Admission to cathedral free, museum and cloisters 400ptas; 10am-1pm/4-8pm Mon-Fri, 10am-1pm/4-6:30pm Sat;):* The cathedral has just gone through a major overhaul, giving its thousand-year-old parts a new lease on life. It was started as a chapel to protect Christian relics back in the days when the Spanish were beginning to turn the Moors from Spain, so face-lifts, additions, and replacements are nothing new to this structure. The museum contains numerous religious relics as well as carvings by Maestro Mateo (whose master work graces the cathedral in Santiago de Compostela).

Museo Arqueológico de Asturias *(Calle San Vincente 3; Tel 985/215-405; 10am-1:30pm/4-6pm Tues-Sat, 11am-1pm Sun and festivals; Free):* Housed in the gorgeous old Monostario de San Vincente on a quiet street behind the cathedral, the archeological museum has charm and character and is worth exploring. The museum displays a wide range of artifacts from prehistoric rock tools and carved bone trinkets to exhibits from the Roman occupation, including coins, carvings, and a section of a tiled floor. There are some old Asturian farming tools and furniture that may leave you feeling like you're back in New England. Most of the objects were recovered from Asturias, and maps along the exhibit walls show the many different site locations. The museum offers a great way to get a true understanding of exactly how far history extends in this part of the world and, moreover, just how varied it has been.

Museo de Bellas Artes de Asturias *(Santa Ana 1; Tel 985/213-061; 10:30am-2pm/4:30-8:30pm Tues-Fri, 11:30am-2pm/5-8pm Sat, 11:30am-2:30pm Sun and festivals; Free):* If you walk a couple of blocks into the old town from the cathedral and archeological museum, you will stumble upon this art museum with its large, well laid-out collection. The only thing that this place lacks is a little life. If you're into classical paintings from centuries past, then you will really enjoy wandering through the galleries here. If, however, you prefer more modern artwork, you're out of luck. The museum houses a large collection of works from the 1500s up to the early 1900s. Paintings by such famed Spanish artists as Goya and Melendez can be found here along with lesser-known—but no less stunning—works. Wandering around the halls here is enjoyable, and it's one of the few, if not the only, places to see displays devoted entirely to Asturian artists.

CITY SPORT

With so many people passing through the city on their way to the Picos de Europa [see below], many outdoor sporting good stores and organizations have based themselves in Oviedo. The staffs of these stores are Picos veterans and can offer a wealth of advice on exploring the park. One of the best places to check out is **Oxigeno** *(Calle Manual Pedrecal 4-6; Tel 985/227-975; 10am-1:30pm/4:30-8:30pm Mon-Sat).* If the pro staff can't help you with planning a trip to the park, they can at least sell you an excellent map or the latest gear. This is the perfect place to come for everyone from the serious hiker who wants to get the most out of her time in the park to the first-timer who just wants to have a pleasant outing.

STUFF

Oviedo is not what you'd call a shopper's paradise. Although the commercial center of the city does have streets lined with stores and boutiques, most seem on the level of a Spanish Gap: major retail chains that offer the same stock across the country.

There is a **Corte Ingles** *(Melquia des Alvarez s/n; 10am-9:30pm Mon-Sat)* in the center. This huge staple in Spanish department stores has all anyone would ever need in terms of men's, women's, and kid's clothing and accessories, travel needs (including a travel agency), games, toys, and food. If you need something in a pinch, odds are you can find it on one of the floors of this retail giant.

One retail area Oviedo does excel in is outdoor stores, ready to equip you with all you will need for a National Geographic–sized expedition into the Picos de Europa (no worries, their prices are set with smaller-scale expeditions in mind.) **Deportes Tunon** *(Calle Campoamor 7; Tel 985/214-840; 10am-1:30pm/4:30-8:30pm Mon-Fri; MC, V)* has a huge stock of outdoor gear, including everything from fly fishing rods to skateboards and off-road roller blades. The store has a serious department devoted to hiking, camping, and climbing with books, tents, packs, and whatever else you'd need to survive. The knowledgeable staff can offer a lot of advice if you are planning a trip into the mountains. The people

fashion

If you want to look a part of things here you have to dress like your local peers. So bring it back to the eighties and go prep. Whoa—wait a second, I'm not talking about taking things as far as Duran Duran eighties, just basic prep. As in so many other parts of Spain, university students here do their part to look presentable. Guys wear collared, button-down shirts and actually button them. Even more, they tuck them in! Jeans are totally acceptable and the preferred route to go. Cargo pants are a rarity. It's harder for women, especially when you're living out of a backpack, but if you want to go toe-to-toe with the Spanish women, you're going to have to pack some nice skirts and blouses. Pants are definitely acceptable, but to really fit in, tighter is better. Now just make sure you pack an iron to keep all your duds looking sharp.

here also have info on nearby rafting and canoe trips *(Tel 985/84-16-36)*. Another great outdoor sporting shop is **Oxigeno** [see *city sport,* above].

EATS

Eating in Oviedo can be a truly satisfying experience, given the wide range of flavors the city has to offer. If you just stick to the different specialties of the region, you could enjoy a great fish dish influenced by one of the small fishing villages along the coast or a satisfying country meal at a *sidrería.* Add to the mix the many cafes tucked in among the small hidden plazas of the old town and you can see that finding a place to eat every night is half the fun. Restaurants, *sidrerías,* and cafes are spread out around town so there is no specific "hunting grounds" to head for when your stomach starts to growl.

▶▶CHEAP

The center is liberally doused with fast-food joints, both Spanish and American, if you just want a quick, cheap bite. To be quite honest, other than fast food, there aren't too many cheap eating alternatives in town. Sometimes you can find an inexpensive lunch menu for around 1,000ptas, but once dinnertime rolls around those prices usually double.

▶▶DO-ABLE

Two great, authentic *sidrerías* sit across the street from each other and do constant battle to serve patrons the best they have to offer. **Restaurante Marisqueria** *(Calle Gascona 9; 1:30-4:30pm/7:30pm-1am; entrees 1,400-3,400ptas)* is a great down-home *sidrería,* complete with sawdust on the tiled floor for soaking up all the missed poured cider. The *menú del día* runs 1,100ptas during lunchtime and should be taken full advantage of. The menu offers a wide range of choices of fish and meats, most cooked in traditional Asturian style. To complete the atmosphere, the walls are painted with scenes of fishing villages on Asturias's north coast. Right across the street is **La Pumarada.** Similar to its neighbor in menu and price, the one major difference here is that La Pumarada offers buckets to catch the cider before it washes onto the floor, instead of sawdust. Asking people which is the better method can start a heated but good-natured argument, with waiters screaming back and forth. Our advice is to continue to investigate this rivalry.

One restaurant close to the cathedral that comes well-recommended by the locals is **La Gran Atberna** *(Gonzalez Abascal 5; 1-4pm/8pm-midnight; entrees 1,900-2,400ptas).* The stone walls of this popular dining room and bar create a cozy setting. During siesta hours, a lot of young working professionals from the city make this their hideout. The food here is traditionsl Asturian with a modern twist, which results in some truly delicious dishes.

▶▶SPLURGE

Paying more in Oviedo doesn't mean that the food is significantly better. Like most things, location is key. In the small plazas of the old city, there are several cafes and restaurants that take advantage of their prime locations and set up tables outside during the warmer months. Yes, they are charming, and yes, you do pay a little more. But indulge—it's all in the name of exploration and broadening horizons, right? South of the cathedral, wandering through the twisting streets will produce a lot of these dining options. **Chiquito Plaza** *(Plz de la Constitición 6; 1:30pm-midnight; entrees 1,800-3,300ptas)* is as popular for a late-afternoon drink as it is for an evening feast. The menu is geared to typical Asturian meat or fish dishes, often grilled or cooked over an open flame. I'd recommend perhaps arriving in the early evening and enjoying wine and appetizers (1,100-2,300ptas) while watching the activity of the plaza.

crashing

Whether you want luxurious living or a simple room you should have no problem finding it here. During the summer months, August in particular, there is a fair crowd that descends on the city on their way to enjoy the nearby mountains or beautiful coastline. This doesn't mean you have to book a room months in advance, but calling a couple of days ahead could work to your advantage. Be warned that most places do increase their prices during the summer boom.

The center of Oviedo is fairly compact and is where you'll find ninety percent of the hotels, hostales, and *pensiones.* Close to the train and bus stations there are a number of economical choices on Calle de Uría and Calle de Fray Ceferino. Since most people coming to Oviedo are either just passing through or using it as a base for excursions into the countryside, being near public transportation can be a big selling point.

▶▶CHEAP

Most of the economical choices are conveniently located close to the train station, so getting in and out of town is a breeze. **Hostal Arco Iris** *(Uria 39; Tel 985/245-908; 2,000ptas single, 3,000ptas double; No credit cards)* is right across the street from the RENFE station and offers guests big, pleasantly decorated rooms that have sitting chairs and a table along with a sink in every room. The owner says that prices do increase (an undetermined amount) in the summer and advises calling ahead to reserve a room during these months.

Another economical option is **Pensión Riesgo** *(Nueve de Mayo 16; Tel 985/218-945; 2,000-2,400ptas single without bath, 3,400ptas single with bath, 4,200ptas double without bath, 4,600-5,000ptas double with bath; No credit cards),* situated in the commercial center about a 5-minute walk from the bus station. The rooms are basic, but a fine home for a night. All rooms have sinks and there are two shared baths down the hall.

The centrally located **Pensión Rubio** *(Covadonga 8; Tel 985/215-601; 2,500ptas single, 4,000ptas double, 5,000ptas triple; No credit cards)* is a small family place with just 5 rooms, all complete with TV and sink. There are two bathrooms down the hall. The rooms are cozy, clean, and bright, but nothing terribly memorable.

▶▶DO-ABLE

There is not much in the range between cheap and expensive accommodations here in Oviedo. **San Juan** *(Palacio Valdes 4; Tel 985/330-002;*

4,500-6,000ptas double; No credit cards) does offer guests a central location and a few more amenities at only a small increase in price. The rooms here are clean and pleasant, and all have a private bath and TV. The friendly owners will be more than happy to give you dining tips.

▶▶**SPLURGE**

Most of the traffic the fancier hotels in Oviedo see comes from businesspeople during the week, so some actually drop their prices over the weekend in an attempt to attract guests. But hey, their loss is your gain, and if you're here on the weekend and really just want to indulge yourself, take advantage of it. One hotel that engages in this price slashing is **Hotel Santa Clara** *(Santa Clara 1; Tel 985/222-727; Fax 985/228-737; single 6,200ptas weeknights, 5,000ptas weekends, double 10,100ptas weeknights, 8,000ptas weekends; V, AE).* Its location—surrounded by shops and restaurants in the central commercial area, not far from the old city—makes it ideal. The rooms are not terribly luxurious given the price—they resemble a classy Holiday Inn, with big windows that make them pleasantly bright—but they all have full private baths, TV, and phone. There is a salon/bar on the ground floor where guests can relax.

need to know

Currency Exchange Exchanging whatever currency you carry for some nice Spanish pesetas is never a hassle in Oviedo. Banks are easily found throughout the city; **Calle de Uría** is lined with them. Most have 24-hour ATMs, too. **Caja Madrid** *(Uria 6; 8:15am-2:30pm Mon-Fri)* is right across from the park and will happily change money for you; they have a 24-hour ATM too.

Tourist Information The **main tourist office** *(Plz Alfonso II El Casto 6; Tel 985/213-385; 9am-2pm/4-6:30pm Mon-Fri, 9am-2pm Sat)* overlooks the plaza that the city's cathedral sits on, so finding it should be a snap. It carries a decent amount of information on Oviedo and Asturias and displays posters with information on upcoming events in the city. There is also a small **tourist kiosk** in the eastern corner of the Campo de San Francisco. It doesn't have as much info, but it can provide you with good maps of the city.

Public Transportation Buses *(Info Tel 985/222-422; buses run 8am-10pm; fare is 1110ptas)* run throughout the city, but the center is compact and nothing is more than a 15-minute walk away. With many areas open only to pedestrian traffic, walking really is the best mode of transport around the center.

Health and Emergency Emergency *061;* Police: *091* or *092.* The **Hospital General de Asturias** *(Avda de Julian Claveria s/n; Tel 985/108-000)* is in the western part of the city.

Pharmacies Farmacia Nestares *(Calle Uria 36; Tel 985/223-925)* is open 24 hours a day, 7 days a week, for all of your needs.

Telephone City code: *985.*

Trains There are two train stations in town. The **RENFE** *(at the end of Calle Uria, Tel 985/250-202)* runs trains to Gijon on the coast and trains to León, Madrid, and Barcelona. The **FEVE** *(Avda Santander s/n; Tel 985/284-096)* sits next to the RENFE station and runs trains east as far as Santander and Bilbao, stopping at many villages along the way, and west along the coast as far as Ferrol in Galicia.

Bus Lines Out of the City ALSA *(Pl General Primero de Rivera 1; Tel 985/969-696)* runs buses both regionally and to distant cities. The main bus station handles most local routes (Gijon, Aviles, Luarca, Cangas de Onis, etc.). If you walk out the front of the main station, cross the road on your right and continue around the plaza until the next street, you'll find the station that handles longer routes up that block on the left. Here you can get connections to major cities in the north as well as Madrid and Barcelona.

Postal The **Main Post Office** *(Alonso Quintanilla 1; Tel 985/214-186; 8am-8:30pm Mon-Fri, 9:30am-2pm Sat)* is located in the center of town and can handle all your mailing needs.

Internet See *wired,* above.

picos de europa

Looking out over the sweeping vistas and deep gorges of Picos de Europa National Park, you can't help but wish you'd paid a little more attention in geology class to understand how something so beautiful comes to be. Although the creation of the park started some 300 million years ago, it was only in 1995 that the park was officially set up. Its area extends into three provinces of Spain: Asturias, Cantabria, and Castilla y León. The park is made up of three principal massifs, or *Macizos*. **Andara** is the easternmost area; **Los Urrieles,** the most impressive as well as most forbidding part, lies in the center; and at the western edge of the park is **Cornion,** which is probably the most visited area in the park. It holds Spain's only remaining glacier lakes. Although the Picos de Europa are not the highest mountains in Spain (the highest peak in the park reaches 2,646 meters, or approximately 8,820 feet), outdoor enthusiasts of all sorts will delight in what the park has to offer, including **Torca del Cerro,** the world's fourth-deepest chasm. Hikers will find happiness on the numerous trails of all levels spread throughout the park. Climbers will enjoy conquering some of the challenging peaks. Anglers will want to try their luck in the streams full of salmon and trout. Add to all this canoeing, biking, caving, and a host of other activities, and it becomes difficult to just sit still and enjoy the serenity of it all. A wide range of wildlife makes the park their home. Although visitors rarely see brown bear and wolves, these animals do spend time within the park boundaries. There are also chamois (an odd cross between antelope and goat), foxes, beavers, and deer. Keep an eye to the sky and you might see eagles and vultures. There are also more than seven hundred species of flowering plants in the park. Give the park the respect it deserves. Each year always brings a couple of tragedies, most

spelunker

Sure the Picos de Europa is spectacular above ground, but, believe it or not, it is just as breathtaking a few thousand feet underground.

If you'd like to find out for yourself, you'll have to go spelunking, or caving. Although a rather difficult undertaking at times, this is an opportunity not to be missed. Sporting the **Sima del Trave,** the fifth deepest cave in the world, the Picos de Europa is a notorious and sought after spot amongst the world's spelunkers. If you decide to go for it, you'll definitely be running with the big dogs.

Caving is serious stuff though, so don't under any circumstances try to venture down one of these holes alone. Although quite stunning, the terrain of the park's caves is particularly rocky and jagged, making travel rather tricky, so make sure you are in a large group led by an experienced and certified guide. When you're well over a thousand feet under ground, you're not going to have convenient access to a hospital and there's always a chance you're going to get lost, so save that Indiana Jones fantasy for another time.

For information on how to journey to the center of the earth contact **Cangas Adventura** [see **Cangas de Onis**] they run daily spelunking adventures for a relatively reasonable rate. You can also try the **Los Cauces** [see **Cangas de Onis**] which also offers caving expedition, but at a slightly cheaper price.

that easily could have been avoided. The weather here is highly unpredictable and hikes that start off under bright sun can quickly be taken over by thick fog and storms. Being prepared and not overextending yourself are your best defenses. The best source of information on the park can be found at the main visitors' center, the **Casa Dago,** in Cangas de Onis. There are also a bunch of outdoor outfitters in Cangas that will help you take full advantage of all the cool stuff the Picos have to offer [see **Cangas de Onis,** above, for both].

euskadi

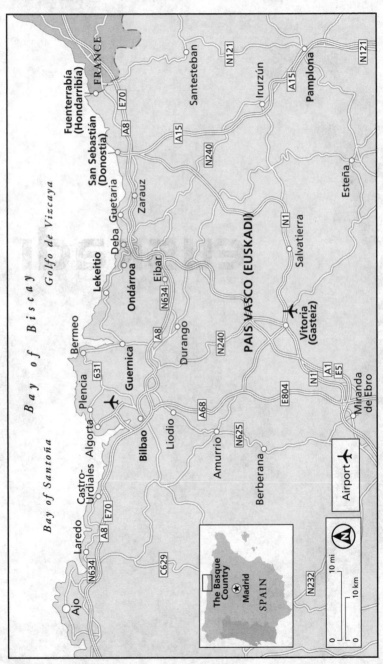

Compared to the rest of Spain (excepting the northwestern parts) Basque country feels positively air-conditioned. During July and August, Madrileños escape in droves to the seaside resort of San Sebastián, other coastal resorts, and the Basque mountains to escape the fierce heat. Indeed, the countryside in this northeast corner of Spain is so enticing that you'll want to escape from the city to have a look at it. Unlike most of Spain, the landscape here is lush and green, crisscrossed with a network of rushing mountain streams that cut through a series of steep and narrow valleys on their way to the sea. The stone houses dotting the countryside may remind you of chalets in the Alps. Once you leave the countryside, however, it will feel far away: Some parts of Basque are the most industrialized in Spain.

The Basque people are among the oldest and most misunderstood people in all of Europe. Their origins are as mysterious as the people themselves. The most popular theory is that they were the original Iberians, pushed up into the Pyrenees from the peninsula by succeeding waves of invaders— Celtic, Roman, Visigoth, and Muslim. Today the Basques live in three regions, two of which—the Basque country and Navarra—are in northeastern Spain. The third is in southern France. Collectively, the Basque refer to Basque country as **Euskadi;** in Castilian, the area is known as Pais Vasco.

Visitors to the **Basque country** and to a lesser degree **Navarra** will immediately be struck by how different the people, attitudes, and language are here from the rest of the country. The younger people dress more informally than elsewhere in Spain; T-shirts are more the norm, and the streets of Bilbao are full of punk rockers and graffiti. It's more than just a fashion statement, though: These kids aren't just copping a 'tude; they're rebelling against traditional Spanish looks and views.

After years of struggling to preserve their culture and identity while having outside influences thrust upon them, the people here will proudly tell you they're not Spanish, they're Basque. This wasn't always the case. Basque nationalism began over a hundred years ago, when their rights were taken away after they sided with the losers during the Carlists Wars. During the Spanish Civil War, Navarra sided with Franco while the Basque country supported the Republicans. Franco was pissed off, to put it mildly, and in exchange for the ingratitude he granted the Nazis permission to test their new air-raid tactics on the small peaceful Basque city of Gernika (Guernica in Castilian). (Picasso was so moved by the mercilessness unleashed on the town that he produced one of his greatest paintings, called *Guernica.*) When the war was over and the smoke cleared, the Basque country found itself tightly under Franco's thumb, while Navarra was allowed some degree of freedom.

you say tomato...

The Basque language—*Euskara*, in Basque—predates just about every language on our planet, but even if you had another million years you probably couldn't figure out how it got to be the way it is. This complex, unfamiliar tongue will not only confuse you, it has also left linguists baffled as to its origins. Every word seems to have at least three "e"s,' "u"s,' and "k"s.' (In essence, "k" takes over the Castilian "c", and "tx" often replaces "ch.") If you think you're ready for the challenge, try to learn some from the locals; it'll humble even the savviest wordsmiths.

In 1961 the world saw the emergence of the ETA—which stands for Euskadi ta Askatasuna and means Basque Fatherland and Liberty in Basque—the Basque nationalist terrorist group whose goal is to create an autonomous Basque nation. Their violent acts have included bombings as far away as Madrid and the Canary Islands and political assassinations carried out in broad daylight within the region. The majority of Basque people feel that it's "Basta ya" (enough already); even though they want a separate Basque nation, most would rather achieve it through peaceful means.

After hundreds of years of people trying to take away their identity, the Basque people have become somewhat xenophobic, and they kept their culture out of view from outsiders for fear of seeing it crushed. Slowly, however, things seem to be changing. *Euskara,* the Basque language, is now proudly displayed on street signs and menus in the region [see *you say tomato...*, below], and more and more of all things Basque are celebrated in the public eye: Berets on the local police force, Basque folklore festivals, and some strange but ancient sporting events (such as log-chopping and grass-cutting). All this and more will reward visitors curious to learn about one of the continent's truly unique cultures.

Visitors should not be dissuaded from visiting the Basque region; in fact, it's one of the greatest regions in Spain for travelers. With top attractions like the elegant beaches of San Sebastián, the new Guggenheim Museum in Bilbao, and the insane annual San Fermín festival in Pamplona, El Pais Vasco should be a stop on everyone's trip through Spain. While proud, the Basque people are also very friendly, and many of them speak at least a little English. They're used to confused and lost foreigners, so don't be timid about asking for help. Just smile a lot; as long as you make an effort, and behave a bit better than Joe Tourist on the go, they'll be willing to help. Carry your map with you if you're looking for directions, because street names pronounced in Basque look nothing like what they sound like. It's easier to have people point.

Many consider Basque food to be the best in the country, and the Basques take their cooking very seriously. There are entire underground male cooking societies in San Sebastián where groups of men gather to...cook! Most dishes come from the abundant marine life living in the waters off the coast. Squid cooked in their own ink and freshly caught cod cooked in garlic sauce are two top regional dishes. The tapas are delicious, too, and are often washed down with a small glass of wine.

getting around the region

Getting around the region is simple enough. Trains to Barcelona and Madrid come though the region, so wherever you're coming from or going to, a stop in the Basque country can be fit in along the way. Once in the area, buses are your fastest and cheapest way of getting around.

▶▶ROUTES

This route can be run in either direction if your final goal is Madrid. If you're heading to Barcelona, end in Pamplona.

Arrive by train in Bilbao. Spend a couple days exploring one of Spain's most rebellious cities. The weekends get pretty wild here, and of course the Guggenheim is a must-see. From Bilbao take a very scenic bus ride to San Sebastián. Spend a couple of relaxing days lounging in one of Spain's best seaside cities. The beaches here aren't the only draw. Next, hop a bus to Pamplona. Whether San Fermín is in full swing or not, Pamplona is one town that rocks year-round.

TRAVEL TIMES

All times are by road unless indicated by a star:
  *time by train
  **time by fast train

	Bilbao	San Sebastián	Pamplona	Madrid
Bilbao	-	1:05	2:00	5:40** 8:40
San Sebastián	1:05	-	2:00*	6:00* 6:20**
Pamplona	2:00	2:00*	-	5:00*

País vasco

bilbao

Ask anyone what they know about Bilbao, and the word "Guggenheim" will come out of even the least astute crackhead's mouth. The **Guggenheim Museum** [see *culture zoo*, below] captured the world's attention when it opened in 1997, and its impact on the city has been tremendous, drawing in waves of excited visitors and encouraging rapid gentrification. With a new subway and international airport, Bilbao is launching itself into the 21st century faster and more energetically than most European cities. Yet the city is more than just one museum: At its core it remains a quintessentially Basque location, which is evident everywhere you look, from the Basque national flags to streets lined with graffiti demanding liberation.

Bilbao was long thought of as the industrial workhorse of the Basque country, its main industries fishing and shipbuilding. Of course, given its prime location along the banks of the Rio de Bilbao, it should come as little surprise that Bilbao is the largest port in Spain, and its sixth largest city. Over one million people now live in what used to be, in the 14th century, a small fishing village. It was the Rio de Bilbao that transformed the sleepy village, which made an ideal port for trading with England and France. As trade blossomed, the city began to expand ever closer to the mouth of the river from whence the riches flowed.

During the industrial revolution, access to the river again blessed Bilbao. Hydropower and nearby iron mines made it possible for factories and steel mills to pop up all over. Soon smokestacks dominated the skyline, covering the city with a layer of grime, and Bilbao became one of Spain's industrial centers. If you think Pittsburgh is ugly, it doesn't hold a candle to what Bilbao was during its industrial heyday.

When the bottom fell out of Bilbao's industrial core in the mid-20th century, some thought the city would crumble alongside its vacant factories. But Bilbao refused to go the way of the dinosaur. With aggressive urban renewal plans fueled by a $1.5 billion grant, Bilbao is again leading the way into the future. Its banking and insurance industries have provided the backbone while the city has invested heavily in its infrastructure and culture to make it a place that tourists can't ignore. The "new" Bilbao is a city of wide boulevards, a fashionable riverwalk promenade, and the greatest concentration of restaurants and bars along the north coast of Spain. Gentrification projects are gradually replacing the gutted-out factories and rails that line the river with gardens and parks, ensuring that Bilbao will thrive well into the 22nd century.

Despite all the efforts by city officials to remove Bilbao's industrial edge, they have not, nor will they ever be able to, remove the edge of its people. The people in Bilbao are Basque to the core. They're proud of their Basque heritage and somewhat resent the fact that their city has given so much to Spain over its long history. Attitudes are more rebellious here than anywhere else in Spain, which is reflected in the style of dress: it's much more casual than anywhere else in Spain, with a little bit of punk thrown in for good measure. Graffiti calling for a separate Basque nation covers walls that the punk rockers cruise by.

If you are privileged enough to be in Bilbao for a weekend, you'll get to experience the wild, no-holds-barred *marcha* that the city has mastered. There are plenty of people wanting to rage till noon the next day in the city's all-night discos. More good news: You'll hear less of that Euro-dance stuff masquerading as music, and more down-and-out trance and house music.

Recreational use of hash is widespread among young people and ecstasy (*pastilles*) can be found at some of the wilder clubs. The law doesn't seem overly concerned with either. What has officials worried here is the rise of heroin use. Drugs aren't just a recreational activity here: Like most big cities, Bilbao has its fair share of addicts and junkies. They won't bother you as long as you stay out of the dodgier parts of town (namely, San Francisco).

The tourist office hands out **Bilbao guia,** which is written in Spanish, Basque, and English. With its listings of cultural events, restaurants, shops, and some bars and clubs, it's a good way to get clued into what is going on in the city. If, however, you're going to be in Bilbao for an extended period of time and really want to find your way into the scene, pick up a copy of **La Ría del Ocio** for a couple hundred pesetas at any newsstand. This goes into a lot more detail, with up-to-date listings of what's happening in the clubs and bars as well as theater and art.

neighborhoods

Although the city limits of Bilbao run for miles along the length of the **Rio de Bilbao,** the city center is much smaller and more compact, nesting against both banks of the river. On the western side of the river

bilbao

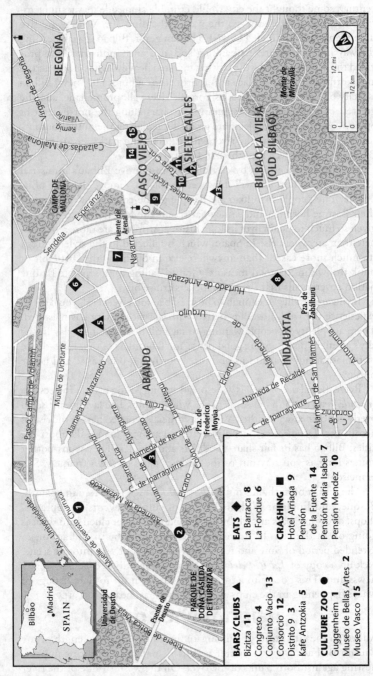

BEGOÑA

Virgen de Begoña

Remig
Vilariño

Calzadas de Mallona

Campo de
Mallona

SIETE CALLES

CASCO VIEJO

BILBAO LA VIEJA
(OLD BILBAO)

Monte de
Miravilla

15
14

Torre Gtk.

Jardines Víctor

11
10
9
12
13

Puente del
Arenal

Navarra

Esperanza

Sendeia

Paseo Campo de Volantín

Muelle de Urbitarte

Alameda de Mazarredo

6
5
4

Hurtado de Améezaga

Urkijo

Pza. de
Zabálburu

INDAUXTA

Automía

ABANDO

Ercilla

Larreategui

Henao

de Barraincúa

Ajuriaguerra

Iturundi

Alameda de Recalde

C. de Iparraguirre

Colón de
Larreátegui

Elcano

Juan de

Pza. de
Frederico
Moyúa

Alameda de Recalde

Alameda

de

C. de Iparraguirre

Alameda de San Mamés

C. de
Gordoniz

3

Muelle de Mazarredo

Alameda de Mazarredo

Ribera de Botica Vieja

Puente de
Deusto

PARQUE DE
DOÑA CASILDA
DE ITURRIZAR

1

2

7

8

Av. Universidades

Muelle de Everso Churruca

Universidad
de Deusto

Puente de
Deusto

Bilbao

Madrid

SPAIN

1/2 mi
1/2 km

BARS/CLUBS ▲
Bizitza **11**
Congreso **4**
Conjunto Vacío **13**
Consorcio **12**
Distrito 9 **3**
Kafe Antzokia **5**

CULTURE ZOO ●
Guggenheim **1**
Museo de Bellas Artes **2**
Museo Vasco **15**

EATS ◆
La Barraca **8**
La Fondue **6**

CRASHING ■
Hotel Arriaga **9**
Pensión
de la Fuente **7**
Pensión María Isabel **14**
Pensión Mendez **10**

is the modern city, well laid out along a grid intersected by diagonal streets. Across the river to the east is the much smaller **Casco Viejo,** or old town.

The Casco Viejo is where most of the cheaper hostels are, and it's also the center of the bar and restaurant scene. South of the cathedral, which sits in the center of the old town, lie the notorious **Siete Calles.** By day, these streets (the area's name refers to the original seven streets of the village that once stood here—there are now hundreds of streets) are home to fashion shops and restaurants. At night they really come alive, offering the kinds of nocturnal adventures that have gained them fame. **Barrena,** one of the streets on the west side of the Siete Calles, is lined with bars and on the weekend this old town gets rowdy enough to raise the dead.

Across the river is the **new town.** Here you'll find the modern sprawl of Bilbao, where high-rises—home to banks and insurance companies— mix with boutiques and restaurants. **Calle de Elcano** runs through the the center and divides the new town in two. The northern half is called **Abando.** Here the streets lining the banks of the river are in the midst of getting a facelift, and gardens are coming to life where factories used to be. The two train stations are in this part of town, right across the river from the old town. This is also where you'll find the **Guggenheim** [see *culture zoo,* below] which everyone coming to Bilbao is sure to visit. A few bars and clubs also give Abando some life at night.

To the south of Gran Via is **Indautxa.** Although not much different from Abando, Indautxa a little bit newer, a little bit shinier, and has a little less character. The main bus station sits on its southwest corner, out by the soccer stadium.

Avoid the area of **San Francisco.** It lies to the south of the old town, across the river. As one local put it, "There are nothing but junkies and whores there." There's a little bit more to it than that, but not much, and it really should be left alone. You may think it is hiding some hip club, but it's really not.

Most things are within easy walking distance of the old town. The notable exceptions are the Guggenheim, the **Museo de Bellas Artes** [see *culture zoo,* below], and the bus station. But conveniently, along with Bilbao's new image came a new metro. Extremely user-friendly and clean, it makes getting around easy and fast. It has only one line, so getting lost is just a matter of heading the wrong way. This also means it may not take you as close to your destination as you'd want, but at 135ptas for a one-zone ride, who's complaining? The metro's main job is ferrying people in and out of the 'burbs, but you can ride it all the way to the ocean beaches if you'd like for only 190ptas. There are also local buses that roam around the city, but stick to the metro; it really is faster and oh so much easier. The metro will take you across the river from the old city to the new, but many people prefer to hoof it and use the bridge instead.

down and out

Begging for change to get into the museums? Street performing act not drawing the crowds you'd hoped for? Fear not. For a city that can suck the life out of your wallet pretty fast, there are still some (well, one at least...) cheap things to keep you sticking around town. A great afternoon can be had *al fresco,* with the best view in the city at your beck and call. Take the **Funicular de Artxanda** *(Tel 944/454-966; 7:15am-10pm Mon-Sat, 8:15am-10pm Sun, during summer till 11pm Sat, Sun, and festivals; Round-trip 220ptas)* to enjoy a spectacular view without all that bothersome physical activity of making your way up a steep winding road. Momma never said anything about chocolates, but she did tell us that the best way to understand a new place was to go to the top of its tallest structure and look down. In Paris there's the Eiffel Tower, in New York City it's the Empire State Building, and, in Bilbao, it's the Funicular. At the top you'll find a pleasant park with walkways and lawns. Add to that the spectacular views and you're in one groovy setting. One side looks down over the city nestled in the valley, while the other side offers a view all the way out to the ocean. There's a restaurant up top, but since you're short on change, stop in the supermarket located in the plaza right outside the entrance to the Funicular at the base. Pick up some picnic supplies to bring with you and enjoy the great outdoor setting.

To get to the Funicular, cross over the Zubizuri bridge from Abando (which is a sight in itself). Cross Paseo Campo Volantin and walk one block left to Mugica y Butron. Follow that straight to its end, where you'll see the base station. And remember, they don't call it FUNicular for nothing.

hanging out

Even with all the hustle and bustle of this big city, Spaniards and Basques alike always find time in the day to sit around the plaza to socialize and relax. Bilbao doesn't offer as many great hangout spots in its center as other, smaller cities do, but there are a couple of places where the crowds tend to congregate late in the afternoon. In the Casco Viejo, it's at a plaza without a name right outside the Casco Viejo metro stop. Here you will find young and old gathering with friends, and young rebellious Basques who will talk your ear off about the need for a separate Basque nation while they chain-smoke cigarettes and get sidetracked talking about their favorite bands. It's a good spot to relax and people-watch as the crowds move through the streets and in and out of the metro station.

If you want to meet other travelers, then go directly to what brings everyone to the city. The plaza in front of the Guggenheim [see *culture zoo,* below] is always teeming with people during museum hours. As you sit listening to languages from all corners of the globe, you can relax and enjoy the sculpture by Jeff Koons that sits at the head of the plaza. *Puppy* is a 25-foot statue of a dog, covered in thousands of multicolored flowers. After looking at it for only a minute you will soon find yourself wondering who got stuck with the gardening duties that go along with this piece of art. We're sure glad we don't have to pick up after it.

Not far away, behind the Museo de Bellas Artes [see *culture zoo,* below], is **Parque de Dona Casilda de Iturrizar,** the largest and most beautiful park in the city. While New York's Central Park it's not, it does have plenty of lawns and trees to let you escape the city for a bit. You'll find young lovers rolling around like dogs in heat, and people just strolling through enjoying the atmosphere. There's a small pond with a couple of fountains as centerpieces. Next to it you'll find a bandstand that periodically hosts small groups of kids gathering around to play drums and maybe pass around a *purro* or two.

bar scene

To say the city's nightlife is centered in the old town is accurate, although it does give short shrift to other areas. Bilbao is a big city and there are bars scattered everywhere throughout it. Wandering around most parts at night will reveal a variety of places that meet anyone's desires, but to find the hottest concentration of places there is only one place to look: the Siete Calles south of the cathedral.

wired

None of Bilbao's Internet spots are as exciting as they are elsewhere in Spain: no bars that will let you get buzzed while surfing the net, no cafes where you can sit and enjoy a bite while getting caught up with the goings-on back home, no peering over the computer screen to eye the night's prospective dates. Bilbao is about business, so you gotta go to copy and computer stores, where it's all about functionality. **Net Center 2000** *(Doctor Areilza15, second floor; Tel 944/418-250; Metro Indautxu; 9am-10pm Mon-Fri, 10am-1pm Sat; 150ptas per 30 min, 250ptas per hour; V, MC)* has great rates. You can scan and print things out, and they'll let you on a computer for a full five hours if you've got something major to do. They also have the distinction of not closing at midday, so while everybody else is snoozing, you can take a break and tell your girlfriend or boyfriend you miss her or him.

rules of the game

Standard Spanish rules apply here. Drinking on the street is standard outside the bars on the weekends. Smoking a little hash here and there isn't going to get anybody deported, executed, or even noticed for that matter. The cops here are relaxed. They have more to worry about than to bust up a good time. So as long as you're cool and keep it under control, people will be cool toward you.

The exceptions: Bilbao is a big city and therefore has big-city problems with crime and drugs. San Francisco is one neighborhood best avoided for these reasons. Heroin is a problem and that is where most of the junkies go to score their smack. There are also a lot more beggars and homeless in Bilbao than in other parts of Spain. They are both visible and invisible: Most of the homeless here stay out of the public eye, but you'll see some cardboard shelters set up under bridges, and you might get asked for change, but nothing more aggressive than that. Generally that's it.

These streets in the old town are more alive at 1am on a Friday or Saturday night than they are all week. Of the seven, the three on the west side (closer to the river) are where most of the action takes place. Walk down these streets during the day and they'll seem pretty quiet and relaxed; walk down them on a Friday night and you'll be squeezing between people just to get to the next bar. A quick stroll up and down the street will quickly clue you in to the different attitudes of the different bars.

Kaixo *(Barrenkale 28; 5-2am Mon-Thur, 4am Fri, Sat; Beer 225ptas; No credit cards)* breathes Bilbao. Don't be fooled by the pink neon lights as you enter: This bar has as much edge as any in the area. With its stickers and signs calling for separation, it's no wonder that it's popular with the young rebellious crowd. The music selection follows the flow with a lot of punk and ska CDs taking turns on the stereo. Beers cost a mere 225ptas, so buy a couple for your bar mates and start finding out what it means to be young and Basque.

On the weekends, **Kasko** [see *eats,* below] switches gears from hip restaurant to mini disco. The party swings to a DJ spinning house and trance for a large crowd. At 600ptas for a mixed cocktail, drinks can be a tad expensive, but this is one of *the* places to be around 2 or 3am.

Outside the old town, the density of bars slacks off, but the quality remains high. In Abando, **Kafe Antzokia** [see *live music scene,* below] becomes a popular *puff* Thursday through Saturday nights, with a good mix of music, from house to Euro-dance. It's the perfect place to get your swing on before heading to **Congreso** [see *club scene,* below] around the corner. Kafe Antzokia attracts the young, the hip, and the artistic.

If you care to venture farther out into Indautxu, the area around Licenciado Poza and Aranzadi is hot. An alley runs south from the intersection of these two streets, and that's where you'll find most of the bars and *puffs*. The crowd is generally younger, with 18- to 26-year-olds making up the majority of the scene. The hot spots of the district are two bars, both of whose names begin with "Z."

Ziripot *(Calle Licenciado Poza 46; Tel 944/270-530; 7am-2:30am Fri; 9:30am-3am Sat; No credit cards)*, serves tapas almost (but not quite) as good as those offered up at Zortzi. Patrons sipping their *txikitos* (small glasses of beer) spill out onto the streets on weekends. "Old" teenagers and drinkers in their early 20s show up here in droves on Friday and Saturday nights for a "walk on the wild (west) side" of town. Tapas cost around 225ptas each.

The tapas are a bit better (the wine the same) at nearby **Zortzi** *(Calle Licenciado Poza 54; Tel 944/424-940; 1-3pm and 9-1pm Mon-Fri; 2-3:30pm and 9pm-1am Sat-Sun; DC, MC, V)*, decorated in a typical macho Basque style. This is a full-fledged restaurant as well as a bar, with tapas costing 250ptas each, main courses going for 1,500 to 2,000ptas. The best and tastiest tapas are *pinco de bacalao* (made with salt cod) and *pincho de salmon ahumado* (made with smoked salmon).

LIVE MUSIC SCENE

Since Bilbao's youth scene is fueled by rebellion and anger, it's not a surprise to see punks sporting mohawks and enough metal in and around their bodies to sink a small ship. Unfortunately, this vigorous punk-rock scene has about as much talent as the punk bands that wash up for open-mic night at CBGB's. It's not that punk necessarily takes talent, but the good ones—like the Ramones, who made a living from three chords and two-minute songs—had something Spanish punk bands lack: indifference. To some degree, these guys just have too much to say.

There are, however, always exceptions. One place that books the better local acts sits south of the Siete Calles, across the river. **Bilborock** *(Muelle de la Merced 1; Tel 944/151-306; Cover 500-1,000ptas; No credit cards)* showcases rock and alternative bands from around the area that like to play with full force. Bands with names like *Superskunk* and *Hot Dogs* make it their duty to rev up the crowd with all the energy they can muster. Showtimes vary widely, so call or stop by the theater for a schedule. Entrance fees won't exceed 1,000ptas unless they have a big-name band, which isn't too often. For smaller local bands it usually won't cost you more than 500ptas.

There are other, less hectic options out there, too. **Kafe Antzokia** *(San Vincent 2; Tel 944/244-625; 1pm-2am Sun-Wed, open till 4am Thur-Sat; info@kafeantzokia.com, www.kafeantzokia.com; Cover free-1,000ptas; No credit cards)* is a really cool place with live music Thursday and Friday nights. The acts, which can be anything from jazz and rock to Basque and international, draw Bilbao's 20- to 30-year-old hipsters and artists. The bands go on sometime between 8 and 10pm so they can be off in time to start the disco later that night. This place also serves set menus for lunch and dinner, and it has a bar that attracts art-minded young bloods. The bar/restaurant is open from 5pm-midnight.

In the old town, **Kasko** [see *eats,* below] has jazz every Sunday night at 9pm. Entrance is free, but unless you're eating dinner there, you're sitting at the bar and you're kinda obligated to buy a drink (oh damn!). The atmosphere is relaxed, the music hot, the drinks chill.

For events on a slightly bigger level, try **Rock Star** *(Gran Via 87; No phone; Cover 2,000ptas and up; No credit cards).* They put on a lot of rock concerts here—some quality, most not. Swing by the club for a listing of shows and times as they vary wildly, or take a peek in *La Ría del Ocio.* Ticket prices begin at 2,000ptas, but could go much higher depending on the show.

In the summer the city puts on free concerts at the bandstand near the tourist office. The events are held on Sunday nights, usually starting around 9pm.

club scene

Bilbao has a wealth of clubs and discos to choose from, and each one caters to a different whim. There are chilled-out lounges, wild transvestite gatherings, and parties that last well into the following afternoon (always popular!). Things generally happen on the weekend, but some spots can't hold back and have smaller parties on Thursday nights. Bilbao is really the party center of the north, but don't let anyone from Pamplona hear you saying that. Still, bigger town means bigger parties; it's

festivals

Like everywhere else in Spain, Bilbao has its fair share of festivals and events where the whole idea is just to give people a reason to celebrate—something the Spaniards have nearly perfected. Most of Bilbao's bigger festivals occur in the summer and early fall; during these times they pack the streets with people making merry.

You can party for 10 days straight at **La Semana Grande,** which begins on the first Saturday after August 15. It is exactly what the name implies—a big week. It's got all the traditional festival fanfare, with one twist: The people take to the river in regattas and flotillas, in reflection of the city's maritime heritage. And to think—all this wildness is in honor of the Virgin of Begona.

On July 25th, the city honors its patron saint, **Santiago.** This just might be the best day of the year in Bilbao. The streets around the Casco Viejo in particular come alive with music and dancing. When the sun sets, things don't cool down—after dark, the party is just starting.

really an easy equation that you can figure out no matter how plowed you are. So whip out that zoot-suit, grab your mojo, and get ready to hit the scene. *La Ría del Ocio* is the best source to find out what parties are going on where, or check out one of the many fashion stores in the old town, as most have flyers for upcoming parties.

Right across the river from the old town, on the fringe of San Francisco (stay outta there!), is one of Bilbao's leading gay dance clubs, **Conjunto Vacio** *(Muelle de la Merced 4; No phone; 10pm-4am Fri-Sun; after-hours 9am-1pm Sat, Sun; No credit cards).* This is the place to kick off the night if the bar scene isn't your thing. A wild collection of club kids and hipsters gather here to dance to Euro-dance, pop, and house. DJs spin the music, although the real talent doesn't come on until after-hours, so you'll want to come back later on, too—much later, like 9am. Normally though, this is a hot spot from midnight to 4am. Prices are 400ptas for beer and 600ptas for mixed drinks. Although it's on the edge of San Francisco, it's fairly safe—just don't walk around the area alone.

Once things begin to break up at Conjunto Vacio, head back across the bridge into the old town to **Consorcio** *(Barrencalle Barrena s/n; Tel 944/169-904; 11pm-8am Fri-Sat; Cover 1,000ptas; No credit cards).* Consorcio collects a lot of the barflies when the bars begin to shut down around 4am, and the barflies mix easily with the clubbers, who continue their all-night party here. More dance and pop music is played at Consorcio than at some of the other clubs, but the crowd is lively, and the music fuels the mood. This *discoteca* is most popular from 4 to 8am. After that, head back across the river (if your feet can stand a little more dancing) to Conjunto Vacio for its after-hours scene.

In Abando, you'll find **Congreso** *(Muelle de Uribitarte 4; Midnight-7am, Fri, Sat; No credit cards),* one of the best clubs in the neighborhood. The party starts late here, with things really getting rolling around 5am. The strobe and colored lights have a hypnotic effect on the mixed crowd. Preps dance next to beats, who swing with clubbers. Mixed drinks run 625ptas and beers go for 400ptas. The only problem with this place is that it closes at the ungodly hour of 7am, just when the party is reaching its climax. To help alleviate the uncomfortable effects of blue feet, there are a couple of great after-hours spots where you can work your dance to a fully satisfying finish.

For those with a spirit for adventure (and a belly full of booze), **Columbus** *(Urazurrutia s/n; Tel 944/472-020; Cover 1,000ptas; No credit cards)* is considered the ultimate in town. Its location, however, doesn't make it terribly accessible. It lies to the west of the center, across the river from the old town, near Canal de Deusto. But if you're willing to make the schlep, you'll be rewarded with two floors of mind-blowing fun and DJs spinning some of the best trance and modern ambience in Spain. It's less like a club and more like a really chill lounge *(sala alternativa)* with a collection of Bilbao's young and hip twenty- to thirtysomethings. It hosts one of the city's best after-hours parties on Saturdays and Sundays from 7am-noon.

ARTS SCENE

The gravity-defying pull of the Guggenheim has jump-started Bilbao's own local arts scene. There is no shortage of drama and dance performances in this town, and there are a host of small galleries highlighting local, regional, and national talent. To find out what's going on, check out either the guide the tourist office hands out, or the *Ría del Ocio*. Both list locations and times with a brief description of most events and exhibits.

▶▶VISUAL ARTS

The best place to gallery hop in Bilbao is Abando, where many have opened in the streets surrounding the museum. Calle Juan de Ajuriaguerra has two galleries in the space of one block, each showcasing a different style of art with individual tweaks and turns, but both sticking to the traditional media of sculpture, photography, and painting.

Windsor Kulturgintza *(Juan de Aljuariaguerra 14; Tel 944/238-989)* likes to highlight unique local talent. It will feature the work of one artist—often someone who's working in new media—in a month-long exhibit.

Right down the street is **AT Amaste** *(Juan de Aljuariaguerra 18; Tel 944/244-902; 10am-2pm/4:30-8:30pm Mon-Fri)*, a gallery that mainly sticks to paintings by regional artists.

One of the larger galleries in the area is **J. M. Lumbreras** *(Henao 3; Tel 944/244-545)*. With three exhibit spaces open at one time, this gallery houses a great variety of different artists and styles. A cartoon exhibit might run next to watercolor paintings, which are set up next to a display of traditional oil paintings. If you like to mix your flavors, this is the best place to start.

▶▶PERFORMING ARTS

A lot of the places that host live music on weekend nights capitalize on their spaces by hosting drama performances on their nights off. **Kafe Antzokia** and **Bilborock** [see *live music scene,* above, for both] have theater performances and the odd poetry reading mixed into their schedules. The shows here tend to be drama or comedy and are usually performed by some of the city's better troupes. Kafe Antzokia in particular gets some hilarious shows. Whether or not you speak Spanish, the laughter is contagious and sometimes it breaks out to near epidemic levels. Most performances run between 500 and 1,800ptas. Call or swing by the clubs for a full schedule. During intermission, interesting, artistic locals wander around, so it's a great place to meet people. Talk about the play, theater—hell, even soccer works. People are a little more open here than they are on the street.

If you crave theater of the higher level, never fear, it's here. **Teatro Social de Basuar** *(Nagusia 2; Tel 944/263-185; 1,000-2,000ptas; No credit cards)* holds classical theater, drama, and dance performances. It's probably best if you show up here in something other than a T-shirt, as the crowd tends to be a little upscale. Nevertheless, these are usually good performances, although Shakespeare is brutally hard to understand in classical Spanish.

gay scene

Bilbao is known as a liberal city, an alternative city, and a rebellious city. It's no wonder then that it has a strong, really out-in-the-open gay scene. Gay bars and stores proudly hang rainbow-colored flags out front, couples walk down the street hand in hand, and some of the best mainly gay discos draw a good number of straights, who go because they've got some of the wilder scenes in town.

The main tourist office has a special pamphlet, *Plano Gay y Lesbico,* which lists more than 30 gay and gay-friendly bars, restaurants, cafes, stores, and organizations in town. Conveniently, the majority of them are located in the old town along with most everything else of interest. Bilbao in some ways is like New York City, where people and things from different worlds tend to mix easily.

Colectivo de Lesbianas Feministas de Bizkaia *(Pelota 3; Tel 944/155-483),* the major lesbian organization in the city, is in the old town, a 5-minute walk southwest of the Museo Vasco; **Aldarte Centro de Atencion** *(Barroeta Aldemar 7; Tel and Fax 944/237-296; aldarte@euskalnet.net),* a 5-minute walk west of Plaza Venezuela, is the primary gay organization. Besides offering legal advice and counseling for Bilbao residents, it also has plenty of information on gay activities, groups, and places to meet. It serves both gay and lesbian crowds.

One of the nicer gay cafes/bars in the heart of the old town is **Bizitza** *(Torre 1; 1pm-2am Mon-Thur, open later Fri, Sat).* Cozy and comfortable, it has brightly painted walls that lend a cheerful atmosphere. You'll hear a wide range of music on the stereo, from Middle Eastern to funk. On weekend nights there's a dance floor in back that gets pretty crowded. The crowd is mainly casual guys in their twenties and early thirties, although ladies are welcome too. During the day Bizitza also serves a limited menu, with nothing expensive on it.

On the weekends, **Distrito 9** *(Alameda Recalde 18; Tel 944/200-056; Midnight-8am Fri,Sat; No credit cards)* hosts one of the wildest parties in the city. These nights of pure narcissism and abandonment attract gays, lesbians, transvestites, bis, and straights all looking to get lost in the crazy atmosphere. The hedonism reaches an apex early in the morning, around 6am, when everyone's been completely hypnotized by the scene. Whether you're gay, curious, or straight, it's a scene like no other.

Culture Zoo

Bilbao is in the process of transforming itself from a grimy, filthy hole (some of its residents still refer to it affectionately as *Botxo,* which apparently means "orifice" in Basque) to a modern, 21st-century, culturally happening city. The metro was a start, and rejuvenating the riverfront was a good idea, too, but at the heart of Bilbao's transformation is a single building. Frank Gehry's awesome design for the Guggenheim Museum has done more for this city than anything else in its recent history, bringing in floods of tourists who stand staring slack-jawed at the museum, com-

only here

No matter how far Bilbao goes to spit and shine its image, some things are indelibly printed on its soul, indeed, its very walls. We're talking graffiti...and the real thing, not Chico tagging the corner wall with his mark or graffiti artworks of Jay-Z puffin' a fatty. We're talking true-to-the-cause, revolutionary graffiti. It's everywhere. Even the cathedral in the Casco Viejo isn't safe from it. Messages of liberation, revolution, and discontent blanket this city. This is Basque nationalism, and it's the ETA, the Basque version of the IRA in Northern Ireland. And while the general population may not agree with the ETA's tactics, they do agree with the cause. And the graffiti—though it may not all be about the ETA—is all about the cause. So while you're walking down the street, take some time and actually look at the writing on the walls. It's both a clue to the general feel of the city, and some pretty powerful stuff. When the 't' in Policia National is replaced by a big red swastika and walls are painted red to represent the spilling of Basque blood, you'll start to realize that passions run deep in this corner of the world.

pletely enthralled by it. And tourists, of course, love to spend money, so with more money Bilbao has made the commitment to further its cultural status. Maybe Bilbao will one day be thought of as one of the great cultural centers of the world, along with New York City, Paris, and Rome. And to think, from what was once just a stinking hole.

The Guggenheim (*Abandoibarra etorbidea 2; Tel 944/359-080; Metro Moyua; 10am-8pm Tue-Sat; Open Mon July and Aug only; www.Guggenheim-bilbao.es; 1,000ptas adults, 500ptas students and seniors, can increase depending on exhibits*): Yes, it's as impressive as everything you've heard. When city planners gave Frank Gehry license to build this structure, he responded with one of the most impressive modern feats of architecture. Some say the building looks like a fish, others say it's a ship ready to set sail down the river next to it. Whatever it may or may not resemble (although we're with the boat school of thought), you gotta see it. The curving glass tower that lies at the center of the building stretches four stories high, running through wildly curving balconies. The harshness of exposed metal beams is offset by graceful curves, while the central hall beckons visitors in with a wall of glass and skylights that make the hall bright, exciting, and alive. Truly the greatest work in this museum is the structure itself. Although the museum has yet to acquire a full permanent collection, it is slowly acquiring world-renowned works. Most of what graces the walls here comes from the Guggenheim Foundation art collection, which consists of over 10,000 works that also rotate to its museums in New York and Venice. Temporary exhibits are the mainstay now, but they are the best around. To give you an idea of the variety, at one time the museum was host to both *The Art of Motorcycles* and *Degas to Picasso.* It goes without saying that if you're in Bilbao, you go to the Guggenheim. Missing it would be like going to Paris and never looking for the Eiffel Tower—even worse, because the museum, these days at least, *is* Bilbao.

Museo de Bellas Artes *(Plaza del Museo 2; Tel 944/396-060; Metro Moyua; 10am-1:30pm/4-7:30pm Tue-Sat, 10am-2pm Sun; 600ptas, 300ptas students, seniors, and unemployed, Wed free):* If, after spending an enchanting couple of hours at the Guggenheim, you're all hyped up on art and need more, head down the river a couple of blocks to the Bellas Artes. The collection is much more old-school here, which might lead to a little retro shock. The main collections consist of Classical art, Contemporary art, and Basque art. The museum also hangs temporary exhibits that are sponsored by major corporations in the city. The collections are well laid-out, and though the museum can't compete with the shine of the Guggenheim (literally—the titanium-sided Guggenheim puts out a mean glare), art lovers will still find it worth the trip.

Museo Vasco *(Cruz 4; Tel 944/155-423; Metro Casco Viejo; 10:30am-1:30pm/4-7pm Tue-Sat, 10:30am-1:30pm Sun; http://euskal-museoa.org; 300ptas adults, 150ptas students, Thur free):* Finally, a museum that is more than just stuff hanging on the walls. This cool museum, in the city center just south of the old town, has life-size dioramas depicting traditional Basque ways of life. Displays include Basque hunting and trapping tools, farming gear, and traditional clothes. There's also a whole room dedicated to the strong Basque maritime tradition. They even play old-time Basque music to really set the mood. Upstairs, an archaeological display features artifacts—including bone carvings, stone tools, and pottery—from the Paleolithic, Neolithic, and Roman eras, all recovered from the region. Photos and maps of the dig sites help you to realize just how far history dates back in this area. All in all, you'll be cheating yourself if you pass on this museum.

modification

There are still places in the world where, if you show up with a pierced eyebrow, the locals will gaze in wonder, touch it, play with it, and wonder what would ever possess a person to do such a strange thing. Some small remote villages in northern Spain are like this. Bilbao, however, is not. You're going to have to put a hell of a lot of metal in your face before you even draw an odd look. Piercings and tattoos are common in the city—it goes with its wild attitude and rebel streak. So if you're ready to try to compete with the locals in the arena of retro punk look, or if you've become so inspired by the Guggenheim that you want to add a little gallery art on your backside, there are definitely places to go. Conveniently enough, they are all located in the Casco Viejo, so you can get your nipples pierced between seeing the sights.

Nebula *(Somera 25; Tel 944/790-601; 10am-1pm/4-8pm Mon-Fri, closed Mon morning)* offers professionally done tattoos and piercings in its modern studios. Its book of art reveals that the artists here have plenty of quality experience. Nebula also sells *ropa de moda* (fashionable clothes) and has flyers on upcoming parties and events. The staff is with it and will be happy to clue you into the local scene.

If you're looking to go a little more risqué with your piercing, **Logan** *(Santa Maria 11; Tel 944/790-874; 10am-1:30pm/4-8pm Mon-Sat , closed Mon morning and Sat afternoon; V, MC)* is the place to go. They tend to get more of the in-the-pants jobs than Nebula. They also offer fashionable haircuts and extensions, and they'll even professionally dread your hair (if there is such a thing as professionally done dreads).

CITY SPORTS

So you're having trouble sitting still. Two hours spent standing around in museums demands four hours of physical activity just to work it off, is that the deal? Well, Bilbao doesn't offer the best in terms of getting out into the great outdoors—this is a pretty big city, after all. But there are always ways to get the blood flowing. Joggers should enjoy the newly renovated riverfront along Abando, where walkways and gardens have taken the place of railroad tracks and decaying factories. It makes for a scenic, mostly uninterrupted jog (there are only one or two streets that you need to cross). Really, either side of the river will do, since they both have walkways. Start at Puente del Aranal, the bridge connecting the new city to the Casco Viejo, and follow the river as it curves around the city. Jog to the Guggenheim or beyond, cross the river on one of the bridges, and head back on the opposite bank.

Every Spanish city has its share of public sports facilities *(polideportivos)*, and Bilbao is no exception. The **tourist office** [see *need to know*, below] can provide you with a complete listing. One of the larger *polideportivos* is **Pabellon de Deportes** *(Next to Plaza de la Casilla at the southern end of Alemeda del Doctor Areilza–Indautxu; Tel 944/448-908; 8am-10pm Mon-Sun, closed Aug; 1,500ptas per day)* in Indautxu. The facility has a couple of ball courts that switch between basketball and volleyball. There's also a weight room and an exercise room where you can take aerobics classes as well as karate and other such things. Call ahead for a full schedule.

STUFF

There are plenty of shops and stores to keep even the most diehard consumer happy in Bilbao. The Casco Viejo alone literally swarms with places that sell all the latest fashions, trendy knickknacks, and unique gifts for those poor saps stuck back home ("Dad—I had a great time in Spain and I bought you this authentic Basque leather canteen that's perfect for bringing out the happy punch!") Clothing and shoe stores line

fashion

Unlike most other parts of Spain, Bilbao is not all hung up on fashion. Well, that's not entirely true, as this *is* Spain and fashion *is* huge, but here you'll see kids and young adults wearing T-shirts around the city. And we're not talking "Spanish T-shirts," which still outclass most things in our closets; we're talking about grungy, worn-out, concert T-shirts. They're the uniform for the young upstarts with attitude in this city. There are also lots of punk rockers and heavy-metal types sporting their gear. At any rate, this is one place in Spain where you won't feel totally low-class and out of place wearing your favorite tee. The club scene is the normal affair, though. Even that kid you saw with the mohawk and ripped shirt earlier is now wearing fashionable club duds to impress the ladies. We all gotta grow up some time.

the Siete Calles, where you can also find many bars and restaurants should you need a break from all the shopping. But don't get stuck just on those seven streets; great tiny shops are hidden throughout the area.

▶▶**DUDS/CLUB GEAR**

Grab some hot duds to hit the club scene in at **Skunk Funk** *(Plaza Nueva 2; Tel and Fax 944/152-859; 10:30-2pm/4:30-8:30pm Mon-Sat, closed Mon and Sat morning; www.skunkfunk.net; V, EC).* You'll find stuff that will practically guarantee more than a passing look from that cute Spanish *chico/chica* you noticed earlier. Take your time picking out the right outfit and enjoy the hip-hop and trance they play. Aside from urban wear and skate wear, they also have a grow section (hence the skunk) for those of you with plants that aren't holding up too well crammed into your packs. The staff is very helpful, and the store has some flyers detailing upcoming parties.

▶▶**BOUND**

Looking for something to read? **Iguma** *(Barrenkale Barrena 9; Tel 944/162-108; 10am-1:30pm/4-8pm Mon-Fri)* stocks a wide assortment of books, 'zines, and comics, although English isn't well represented. They also carry some CDs (mostly punk and alternative), a few random videos, and some weird and wild things—action figures and beyond. It's a store worth poking your head into.

For those of you heading out of Spain into places unknown, **Borda** *(Somera 45; Tel 044/159-465; 10am-2pm/4:30-8:30pm Mon-Sat, closed Mon morning and Sat afternoon; www.bilbaoweb.com/borda; V, MC)* has a wealth of travel guides to choose from. Most titles are familiar English ones, so you won't have to read about Istanbul in Spanish before trying to translate things into Turkish. If you're heading out into the mountains, you can kill two birds with one stone: Borda also carries outdoor gear! Rugged hiking boots, sacks, coats, maps, supplies—it's more than just a bookstore, it's your travel headquarters.

▶▶ART

You might as well face it: After seeing the Guggenheim you're going to want to bring home something that carries its emblem or picture. Well, the **Museum Store at the Guggenheim** [see *culture zoo,* above] has more than enough cheesy products to prostitute this cultural icon. Grab a travel bag with the museum logo on it or a wavy bar of soap "inspired by the forms and shapes of the Guggenheim." Or opt for a less kitschy product, such as a book about a special exhibit or a reproduction of one of the museum's pieces.

▶▶**ONE-STOP SHOP**

Need some new sandals? Some soap? A gift for your sis? Head on down to **El Corte Ingles** *(Gran Via 7-9; 10am-9pm Mon-Sat),* a department store that carries everything you could possibly need.

EATS

We challenge you to find a street corner in Bilbao that doesn't give you a view of at least two restaurants or cafes. Seems like every cuisine in the world is represented here—French, Italian, Thai, you name it.... Add to that a wealth of places specializing in Spanish and Basque cooking and you'll have no problem keeping all your senses happy in this stimulating city. Tapas are still omnipresent (remember, you are still in Spain, despite what some of the locals would have you believe). But Bilbao offers more choices in terms of sit-down restaurants where you can get something other than a couple slices of bread decorated with one of a million variations of ham to fill your stomach.

Like so many other cities in this country, the old town is one of the best places to start your search for a tasty dish. Here you'll find a great selection of both sit-down restaurants and tapas bars. The tapas joints tend to be more concentrated on the Siete Calles, where they're mixed in with actual restaurants.

▶▶**CHEAP**

Aside from some fast-food options (both those nasty American chains and their Spanish rip-off counterparts), Bilbao doesn't offer a whole lot in the way of cheap eating. It does have standard-order cafes and food counters in the business center, which attract the lunchtime business crowd and offer good-sized meals for a fair price. None are overly remarkable, though. Vegetarians and non-vegetarians alike will enjoy **Garibolo** *(Ferandez del Campo 7; Tel 944/223-255; 1-4pm Mon-Sat;.* Menúu diario *1,000ptas).* For some baffling reason, it's open only for lunch, like most strictly vegetarian eateries in Spain. It has some good, green meals, a remarkable feat in this country of ham and meat worshippers. Garibolo offers a set *menúu diario* that runs a mere 1,000ptas. It consists of a couple of choices for your first and second dish as well as a drink, dessert, and bread. Salads, pastas, and soups are usually the choices, along with fruit dishes. There's always something in season here. They also have info on holistic happenings if you feel like your aura's getting unbalanced.

▶▶DO-ABLE

Eating can get a little pricey in this city—why, we don't know. But at least you'll be getting some really tasty dishes for those pesetas you blow. For some quality home-cooked Basque food in the Casco Viejo, **Ariatza Jatetxea Erretegia** *(Somera 1; Tel 944/155-019; 1-3:30pm/8-11:30pm Tue-Sun; Starters 850-1,500ptas, entrees 1,400-2,700ptas; V, MC)* is a great place to start. Don't start tripping over all those 'x's in its name; the menu has been translated into Spanish and English for those of us still getting our Basque down. It's a homey, comfortable atmosphere with a friendly staff. There are lots of inexpensive starter choices if you just want a bite. If you're in the mood to gorge, the fish and meat entrees (including some Basque BBQ) are well worth the higher price.

Outside the Casco Viejo and across the bridge in Abando you'll find some other good spots tucked away. For those craving a break from Spanish food, **La Fondue** *(Acebal Idigoras 6; Tel 944/232-328; 1-10pm daily; Avg. dinner fondue 2,000ptas, avg. dessert fondue 700ptas; V, EC, AE)* offers just what you'd expect, so grab a buddy (two mouths are required on most of these) and your fondue stick. They also serve meat and fish dishes cooked up in the great French tradition. If the meat, cheese, and fish fondues are too pricey for you, consider just swinging by for a chocolate fondue for dessert. The three devilishly good dessert fondues also require a partner, and spooning chocolate into another person's mouth by candlelight has been known to lead in some interesting directions ("Could we get this to go, please?").

If it's atmosphere you're after, check out the slightly upscale **Kasko** *(Santa Maria 16; Tel 944/160-311; 1-4pm/8-11:30pm Mon-Sun, bar open till 2am, open till 4am Fri and Sat, open Sun only for lunch; Avg lunch menu 1,500ptas, avg dinner entree 2,400ptas; V, EC)*. Although Kasko offers only a set menu, each course has three options to choose from, creative fish dishes as well as vegetables and meat. The night menu is pricey, so take advantage of the afternoon menu, which offers almost the same choices for much less. At night someone usually tickles the ivories as you eat, and on Friday and Saturday nights this place actually turns into a happening *puff* that keeps the crowds dancing until the clubs are hot. On Sunday nights, check this place out for live jazz [see *live music scene* and *bar scene,* above].

▶▶SPLURGE

If you're willing to dig deep into your pockets, a world of eating pleasures awaits you in Bilbao. You might be able to end your quest for the perfect paella in this town at **La Barraca** *(Garcia Salazar 12; Tel 944/102-021; Paella 1,200-1,600ptas; V, MC, EC, AE)*. The clientele—and their dress—is a little bit upscale, and reservations are recommended in the summer months. To give you some idea of the place, let's just say you have to buzz to get in the door. Once inside you'll find sharply dressed waiters attending patrons in the sharply appointed dining room, where paella has been elevated to an art form. The paellas themselves aren't too expensive, but it's hard to keep your bill under 3,000ptas a head at this place without making a conscious effort.

crashing

Finding a bed should never present too much of a problem in Bilbao. There are plenty of choices, ranging in price from 2,000ptas past 20,000ptas. It all depends on how much fluff you want in your pillow. Typically things tend to get a little more crowded during July and August when the entire country (and possibly continent for that matter) goes on vacation. Bilbao, however, does not get quite as overrun with people as some of its neighbors on the coast do. Typically, prices do not rise during the summer, though if rooms are in demand you're sure to find an owner willing to earn some extra pesetas at your expense. Most places post their official prices near the door or office, so if you get a price that sounds high, don't be afraid to check their written rates and call them on it.

Most of the *hostales* and *pensiónes* tend to be clustered in, or near, the Casco Viejo, while more expensive hotels can be found anywhere in the city. Paying more doesn't mean you'll find yourself in a better spot, however, since the Casco Viejo really is where you want to be. It's the center of activity, near the metro and within walking distance of most other attractions. The one drawback is it can get rowdy during the weekends, making sleep difficult if you have to call it an early night—but why would you ever want to do that?

▶▶CHEAP

Prices in Bilbao tend to be cheaper than in most of the neighboring cities, so if you're on a really tight budget, you might even want to consider setting yourself up here for a bit and day-tripping it to nearby sights. **Pensión Maria Isabel** *(Amistad 5; Tel 944/248-566; Metro Abando; 2,000ptas single, 4,000ptas double, 6,000ptas triple; No credit cards)* is one of the cheaper options around. It sits right across the bridge from the Casco Viejo, near the train stations in Abando. Its location makes it an easy walk to the old town or the newer business center. There's a crazy system of motion-detecting lights in the hall that makes stumbling in late at night a little easier. But it does make it tough to have a friendly conversation with another traveler, as you'll find yourselves jumping around like idiots just to keep the lights on. The owners are nice enough to have a city map and guide waiting for you in your room (the same ones you'll get at the tourist office). The one drawback is that you don't get a key to the main door, but the owner assured us there is someone there to buzz you in 24 hours a day, and we were never left hanging in the street.

Across the river in the Casco Viejo, **Pensión De la Fuente** *(Sombereria 2; Tel 944/790-001; Metro Casco Viejo; 2,000ptas single with shower, 3,500-4,000ptas double, 5,000ptas with bath, 5,000ptas triple)* offers 12 pleasant rooms right around the corner from the Plaza Nueve. The location is nice, not too far from the metro and a stone's throw from all the activity. For 500ptas they'll put a TV in your room, but odds are there's only crap on, so go spend that coin on a museum.

Another cheap option is **Hostal Roquefer** *(Calle De La Loteria 2; Tel 944/150-755; 3,000ptas singles; 5,000ptas doubles; shared baths; No credit cards).*

▶▶DO-ABLE

Also in the old town, the recently renovated **Pensión Mendez** *(Santa Maria 13, first and fourth floors; Tel 944/160-364; Metro Casco Viejo; 3,000-6,000ptas single, 4,000-7,000ptas double, 6,000-9,000ptas triple; No credit cards)* is within stumbling distance of some of the country's wildest weekend watering holes. The deal: You'll find the cheapest rooms on the unrenovated fourth floor (first quoted price), where the bathrooms are communal and the bedroom decor unexciting. Some rooms have a sink, but not all. The first floor (second quoted price) recently underwent a major facelift and now has nice rooms, all with complete bath and TV in the room. Fresh, new, and spotless, these rooms offer a welcome break from the usual backpacker dens. On either floor ask for a room on the *calle;* they all have a small balcony out the window, which offers a nice place to sit and think while you look out over the rooftops of the city.

If things in town are busy and you're finding a lot of places full, try heading for **Arana** *(Bidebarrieta 2; Tel 944/156-411; Metro Casco Viejo; 4,500ptas single, 5,500ptas with bath, 5,500ptas double, 6,600ptas with bath; No credit cards).* With 69 rooms, it's the biggest non-hotel option in the city. It's not far from the bridge into Abando, so walking to whatever you want will be easy. The rooms are nothing special, but nice enough to come home to after a long day.

Another do-able option is **Hostal Mardones** *(Calle De Jardines 4; Tel 944/153-105; 3,500ptas single without bath; 5,000ptas doubles without bath ; 6,000ptas doubles with bath).*

▶▶SPLURGE

One of the few hotels in the Casco Viejo is **Arriaga** *(Ribera 3; Tel 944/790-001; Metro Casco Viejo; 6,500ptas single, 9,500ptas double, 12,000ptas triple; V, EC, AE),* a small, quaint hotel that sits across the street from the Teatro Arriaga. All the rooms are nicely decorated and come complete with full bathroom, TV, and phone. Reservations are strongly recommended, especially during the summer months when it fills up quickly. When reserving, specify that you want one of the rooms with a view over the river. The hotel also offers parking if you have a set of wheels with you.

Another deluxe option is **Hotel Abando** *(Calle De Colon De Larreategui 7; Tel 944/236-200; Fax 944/245-526; 14,000ptas single, 12,500ptas weekend rate; 19,500ptas doubles, 15,000ptas weekend rate; V, MC, AE).*

need to know

Currency Exchange As Bilbao thrives, so do the banks, so it's never too difficult to find one. There are several right by the train station on the Plaza Circular that will exchange, change, and rearrange your *dinero*. These also have ATMs, as do the tourist offices. The impressively huge department store **El Corte Ingles** [see *stuff,* above] will exchange currency in its travel department.

Tourist Information The main **tourist center** *(Paseo del Arenal 1; Tel 944/795-760; 9am-2pm/4-7:30pm Mon-Fri, 9am-2pm Sat, 10am-2pm Sun)* sits next to the river on the outskirts of the Casco Viejo. The more-than-courteous staff here speaks English, and with the aid of their trusty computers can answer *any* question you can throw at them. There is also an information kiosk outside the Guggenheim *(Abandoibarra Etorbidea 2; No phone; 11am-2pm/4-6pm Tue-Sat, 11am-2pm Sun).*

Public Transportation The *metro (Tel 944/254-025; 6am-2am Mon-Sat, 7am-11pm Sun)* is brand spanking new and easy to use. Most visit-worthy places in Bilbao are within walking distance, but the few that aren't usually are close to a metro stop. There's only one line, and you pay by the zone (135ptas for a one-zone ride, 160ptas for a two-zone ride, and 190ptas for a three-zone ride). Take a look at the map displayed in the station, input your destination in the friendly little ticket machine, and it will spit a ticket back at you. Hang on to it; you'll need this to exit. The **local bus system** *(Tel 944/484-080)* will confuse the hell out of you until you have an understanding of the city layout, so we'd recommend sticking to the subway. Both RENFE and FEVE trains [see *trains,* below] also offer local service within the metropolitan area.

Health and Emergency Emergencies: *112.* **Hospital Civil de Basurto** *(Avda. Montevideo 18; Tel 944/006-000; Metro San Mames)* is near the river past the bus station on the edge of the center of town. The *Municipal Police Station* is by the hospital at Luis Brinas 14 *(Tel 944/205-000, for emergency call Tel 092).*

Pharmacies Bilbao is stocked with pharmacies, all identified by **neon green crosses** out front. You'll find the most in the Casco Viejo. No single one is open 24 hours a day; instead, *farmacias* rotate the all-night responsibility. Each one posts a schedule indicating who will be open on what night. One pharmacy in the Casco Viejo is *Farmacia E. Zubia (Portal de Zamudio 4; Tel 944/152-128).* It's a block below the metro stop there and has the rotating schedule posted in its window.

Telephones Country code: *34;* city code: *94.*

Airport Aeropuerto de Bilbao-Sondika *(Tel 944/869-300)* is 5 miles north of the city. There are flights to places throughout Spain including Madrid, Barcelona, Sevilla, Santiago de Compostela, and Valencia as well as to international cities such as Brussels, Frankfurt, Lisbon, London, Milan, Paris, and Zurich. *Red Bus A3247 (6am-11pm daily;*

140ptas) will take you from the airport to the heart of the city, a block north of the tourist office. Buses depart from the airport for the city, and vice versa, about every 40 minutes.

Trains The two main train stations in Bilbao are located next to each other, right across the river from the Casco Viejo. **Estacion de Abando** *(Plaza Circular 2; Tel 902/204-202; Metro Abando)* handles all the RENFE lines that run both within the city limits and through the country. There are two daily trains to Madrid and two to Barcelona. Other trains head toward Galicia, Valencia, and Malaga. The FEVE station next door *(Bailen 2; Tel 944/232-266; Metro Abando)* runs lines that make their way along the northern coast. Service is usually sluggish—RENFE is always the better bet.

Bus Lines Out of the City Most of the major bus lines have all moved to the new **Garellano Bus Terminal** *(Gurtubay 1; Tel 944/395-205; Metro San Mames),* a short metro ride from the center of town (you *could* walk, but it would take you about half an hour). From here you can get connections to many of the surrounding towns and cities, including San Sebastián and Pamplona, as well as service to Cantabria, Asturias, and Galicia. International service extends to Belgium, France, Germany, Holland, Italy, Morocco, Portugal, Switzerland, and the UK. **Ansa** *(Autonomia 17; Tel 944/443-100)* offers service to Madrid, Barcelona, Leon, and Burgos. The main tourist office can give you a printout of the latest schedules.

Boats Believe it or not, you can catch a ferry, operated by **P&O** *(Tel 944/234-477),* from Bilbao to Portsmouth, England. The trip takes a staggering 30 hours and the price doesn't make it sound any more attractive (lowest walk-on fare is 20,000ptas for fare and cabin). The ferry docks are on the coast, so take the local RENFE line to Santurtzi. Call ahead for reservations.

Laundry Drop-off service is available at **Lavaclin** *(Campo Volantin 15; 9:30am-1:30pm/4-8:30pm Mon-Fri; 1,000-1,500ptas per load).*

Postal The **main post office** is located in the eastern portion of Indautxa *(Alameda Urquijo 19; Tel 944/220-548; 8am-8:30pm Mon-Fri, 9:30am-2pm Sat).*

Internet See *wired,* above.

san sebastián

San Sebastián (Donostia in Basque) is one of Spain's most elegant seaside cities. Carved into the northern coast, wedged between rolling green hills and the angry north Atlantic, it's less than 15 miles from the French border. The highlight of San Sebastián is the beautiful Bahía de la Concha. This spectacular bay, ringed by beaches and protected from the temperamental ocean by the Isla de Santa Clara, sets a mood that can only be described as mesmerizing.

San Sebastián is also one of the many hot spots for Basque nationalism. You'll come across enormous Basque flags and graffiti calling for separatism almost as often as you'll see pasty white foreigners trying to get as tan as the locals. Despite the prominent tourist scene, the heart of San Sebastián is Basque. Although the odds that you'll see it are slim, don't be caught off-guard if you come upon angry youths hurling bottles at the local police force. (P.S. This is probably one local custom that you'd do best to avoid.)

San Sebastián has probably been around as long as the Basque people have been, and no one really knows how long that is. As boats made their way for England, France, and, later, the New World, San Sebastián grew as a trading port. It suffered during the Peninsular War; first Napoleon occupied the city, and then the liberating Portuguese army took their celebrations a bit too far and almost burned the whole place down. Much of what you see today was built after 1814.

San Sebastián has been attracting summer vacationers ever since Queen Isabel II made it fashionable in the 1850s. Today, it is *the* resort town on the northern coast, thanks to its elegance, grace, and charm. Everyone from the Spanish elite to Joe and Jenny Backpacker come here to escape the summer heat, and given the crowds, it's no surprise that the nightlife is just as active as the day-life. Spaniards (and tourists) like to relax on the beach by day, then hit the bars and clubs at night. In the old town, San Sebastián's center of nocturnal delights, people of all ages crowd the bars and the streets and jazz bars keep the live music beat, while people flow in and out of the clubs lining Playa de la Concha until sunrise and beyond.

The best way to get the full scoop on what's going on around town is to pick up a copy of *Donosti Aisia.* It's a small monthly magazine that lists everything from live music to food to the arts: If it's out there, it's in here. The guide is written in both Basque and Spanish, so it's helpful if you know one or the other. (Since Basque is said to be one of the most difficult languages to learn, we'd stick with the Spanish.) You can find the mag at bars, the tourist office, or the Wash 'N Dry [see *need to know,* below]. So if you actually do muster up the energy to get off the beach and do something, you'll actually know what's going on.

Another way to get the inside scoop is by asking around. In fact, this is the best way to really get to know and understand San Sebastián. The beauty of the Basque culture lies within its people and their strong sense of identity, and you'll really feel this in San Sebastián. True, they aren't the most extroverted people in the world, and they can be a little hesitant to open up to strangers. (This can seem strange to those of us who think it's normal to spill our guts to someone sitting next to us on the plane!) But if you're sincerely interested in learning about one of Europe's oldest and most distinct cultures, people will sense that and they'll be very friendly and sharing.

Old and young folks mix easily here. The older generation tends to be a bit more reserved than their younger counterparts, but just about everybody is calm and relaxed (it would be hard not to be, living in a place like this!). Like kids anywhere, the kids in San Sebastián like to have fun. They surf off the Playa de la Zurriola, party in the many bars scattered around the old town, and have even been known to pass around a hash *purro* in one of the clubs. Things are laid-back here; it's kind of like San Diego meets Monterey with a heavy Euro twist.

neighborhoods

San Sebastián's layout only enhances its overall enchantment. Ringed with beaches and promenades and protected by the **Isla Santa Clara,** the beautiful **Bahía de la Concha** is the city's centerpiece. Some hail the bay as one of the most beautiful in Spain, and we didn't hear any arguments otherwise. At both ends of the bay, the land swells up into tall hills. The **Rio Urumea** empties into the bay on the east side, cutting off **Gros,** a residential neighborhood, and the RENFE station from the rest of the city. Four bridges run over the river; **Puente Santa Catalina,** the second one from the ocean, is elaborately decorated and worth a look.

San Sebastián is a city of about 170,000 people, although that number seems to quadruple in July and August. The city center is fairly compact,

san sebastián

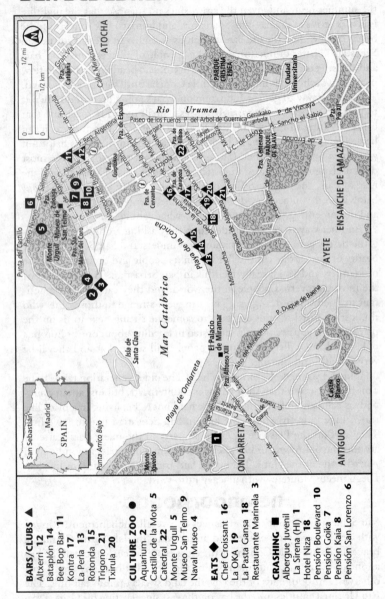

with many smaller neighborhoods spread throughout the hills and surrounding area. Most visitors will want to linger in three principal parts of town, each of which has its own flavor.

You'll spend most of your time away from the beach in the **Parte Vieja,** or old town. Most of the *hostales, pensiónes,* and restaurants are in this area, and there are more bars here than you could *marcha* through in a week. Since it was torched in the early 1800s, the old city doesn't have quite the same antique feel as others do, but that isn't to say it isn't oozing with character. Tucked below the green **Monte Urgull,** which rises over the east end of the peninsula, it's a fab nabe to wander through, whether you're going from bar to bar sucking down octopus tapas or looking for that perfect suit to turn every head on the beach.

by foot

All of its stunning views make San Sebastián perfect for exploring by foot. You'll find some great vistas of the city from the top of Monte Urgull and Monte Igeldo. The latter offers the better view; Monte Urgull has a beautiful park.

Monte Urgull *(8am-9pm summer, 8am-7pm winter):* Start just past the Aquarium and follow the walkway up the hillside. As it starts to cut back and forth through the woods, keep heading whatever direction leads up. Once you get to the top, you'll find Napoleon's battery (which, like Napoleon, once went up in smoke, taking a few casualties with it), an English cemetery from the war, and *Batteria de las mujeres,* which offers a great view over the bay. Sitting on top of the hill is the castle, **Castillo de la Mota,** with its huge statue of Christ on top looking down over the city (did somebody say Rio?). Exploring the castle and grounds can be fun, since there usually aren't too many people up here. Bring a picnic if you'd like and enjoy the great views.

Monte Igeldo: The first key to enjoying this walk is to skip the hard part. Hop in the Funicular *(Bus 16 from Alameda del Boulevard; 7am-10pm summer, 8pm winter; 115ptas one way, 225ptas round-trip)* and ride it to the top. Here you'll be awed by an incredible view of the entire city nestled along the coast. Yeah, this is the postcard shot that you see everywhere. Up top there's a restaurant, hotel, and *Parque de Attractiones*—Six Flags this is not. Instead of a wild roller coaster there's a small toboggan run you slide down on burlap bags. Once you're done taking in the view, begin the walk by heading down the twisty road that leads to the base. Stop frequently to look out over the stunning, rugged northern coast. Once you get down to the bottom, follow the seawall out past Playa de Ondarreta to Spanish sculptor Eduardo Chillida's work, *Wind Combs.* These three odd-looking, twisted metal sculptures that cling to the sides of boulders represent the teeth of a comb to smooth and soothe the fierce winds that blow in off the North Atlantic. Catch your breath and enjoy the scene from the steps of the small plaza here.

South of the old town and across **Alameda del Boulevard,** a small plaza that used to be the site of the town's fortifications, you'll find yourself in the **Centro.** Centro is what happened when San Sebastián spilled over its city walls: It's modern, it's commercial, and it lacks the distinct character of the old town. But what it lacks in character it makes up for in action, including the fancy hotels that line the **Playa de la Concha,** on the neighborhood's west side. After you've been baking on the beach all day, there are great restaurants and cafes just a short walk away. The Centro also has a fair smattering of art galleries [see *arts scene,* below] and the city's cathedral, **Catedral del Buen Pastor** [see *culture zoo,* below]. Though its night scene is not as happening as the old town's, the roads south of the cathedral do offer some *marcha* options [see *bar scene,* below].

Across the Rio Urumea to the east lies **Gros.** A little bit quieter and less crowded than its neighbors to the west, Gros has more of a residential feel. Come here if you're trying to discover the *real* San Sebastián—and to escape the hordes of tourists that keep getting in the way. This is the blue-collar section of town, with a bit of beach bum thrown in for good measure. **Playa de la Zurriola,** or Playa de Gros as it is also called [see *hanging out,* below], keeps the surfers happy with its breakers.

Most of the major spots that you'll want to hit are within walking distance of each other. The majority of the old town is open only to pedestrian traffic anyway (although some Spaniards bend the rules a bit and bring their scooters). For exploring the rest of town, there are 25 public bus lines that circulate throughout the city, with most routes starting or ending at the Alameda del Boulevard on the south side of the old town. All stations post maps of the routes, or you can pick up a map at the tourist office. Most buses run from about 7am-10pm, and each trip will cost you 115ptas.

hanging out

No big surprise: In San Sebastián just about everybody spends his 'n' her leisure time at the beach. There are three public beaches that, given the fact that the city runs them, score high marks for crowd, sand, sun, and fun: **Playa de la Zurriola** in Gros, and **Playa de Ondarreta** and **Playa de la Concha** on Bahía de la Concha. The bay here is calm and protected by Monte Igeldo and Monte Urgull, which makes it a great place for a relaxing swim if you don't mind the chilly temperature. Isla de Santa Clara, at the head of the bay, closes it off to those nasty northern Atlantic swells. The island rises out of the bay like a molehill in the middle of the plain. This ain't no romantic island of palm trees; this thing is all rock and stands tall in the ocean, ready to take a beating from the constant barrage of waves. Picnickers delight in taking a boat out to the island for a scenic look back. Boats leave from the port about every half hour in the summer and cost a couple hundred pesetas. Those feeling their machismo flowing just swim out to the island. But watch out for the boats heading to the same spot—a propeller could bring a quick end to your relaxing vacation.

wired

Since San Sebastián sits on the backpacker's route, there is little wonder that the locals, being good-natured and generous, help to make the travelers feel more at home by giving them quick connections to the Internet, the ability to stay in touch with their mothers, and a comfortable spot to do it all in. So when the weather isn't good or the wind is coming off the coast and ruining the break, head to the old town and you can surf all you want—web we're talking now.

Want to sit back, munch a tapa, sip some wine, and tell your ex-lover how great life is without him or her? **Donosti-NET** *(Embeltran 2; donostinet@hotmail.com; 9:30am-9:30pm daily)* is the perfect spot to do it while you keep an eye open for new romance. It's no secret that the vast majority of people in these places are there for the exact same reason you are. The best time to hit these places is right before dinner, so you can find someone to join you when you check out that great tapas joint you read about in *Hanging Out in Spain.*

Zarr@net *(San Lorenzo 6; Tel 943/433-381; www.zarranet.com; 10am-10pm daily, till midnight during the summer; 250ptas per 15 min, 350ptas per hour, 550ptas if only one hour; No credit cards)* isn't all that wild, but the connections are fast and when the other places start to overflow, this one is less likely to make you wait. Besides, you never know who might walk in.

Playa de Ondarreta is the westernmost stretch of beach, separated from Playa de la Concha by the rocky outcroppings of **Parque de Miramar.** The park is on the grounds of **El Palacio de Miramar** *(Grounds open June-Aug 9am-9pm, 10am-6pm Sept-May),* a palace that has played home to Spanish royalty and Bismarck. A stroll through the grounds offers some nice views of the bay, but nothing so spectacular that it's a must-see.

Playa de Ondarreta hosts a more youthful crowd than its neighbor, but it's still a total mix of people and ages—the old women enjoy topless bathing here as much as the young. This beach is also a little steeper than Playa de La Concha, which means there's more sand to sit on at high tide.

Next door, Playa de la Concha has the distinction of shrinking from the largest to the smallest beach in San Sebastián in the span of half a day. During low tide the beach reaches far out into the bay, offering plenty of room for scantily clad bodies to spread out. But come high tide, the beach shrinks to about a quarter of its morning size, squeezing everyone up against the seawall. Not that this is necessarily a bad thing;

we just recommend that you get to know your neighbor before your towels are on top of each other's. Playa de la Concha is more popular with families, but like everything here, people mix easily: That hottie you saw in the plaza yesterday could make this beach his or her tanning station today.

Playa de la Zurriola (also called Playa de Gros) is a complete change of scene from the other, tamer beaches. This beach offers zero protection from the temperamental ocean. Waves roll into the beach set after set to the delight of the many surfers who float offshore waiting for the perfect break. This is a big beach, and one that's not too affected by the tides. A young crowd, mostly 18- to 30-year-olds, catches the rays here. Lots of tourists don't realize that the city extends past the river, so the ratio of locals to visitors is favorable. The only drawback to this beach is that casual swimming can be a bitch. A pretty strong undertow lurks under those big waves rolling in. And if the waves are crowded, it's best to head out only if you have a board yourself; otherwise, you risk getting run over by someone who didn't see you among the waves.

bar scene

Words you will never hear spoken in San Sebastián? "Where can I go to get a drink around here?" There's probably enough booze in this town to keep all of the EU buzzed for a day. Your biggest challenge will be keeping up with the locals as they drink their way from place to place.

The main concentration of bars is in the Parte Viejo. The nightly *marcha* takes off from here and quickly reaches cruising altitude. People flow out of the bars onto the cobblestone streets, and the place is always hopping. Although you'll see a good joint just about everywhere you turn

rules of the game

What's with all the cops around here, you might ask. Am I in mortal danger? No! Despite the possibility of seeing a riot or two between local youths and the cops, San Sebastián is safe. Basque country has gotten a lot of bad press because of ETA terrorist attacks, but the fact is they've moved their attacks out of their homeland and now strike in faraway places such as Madrid, Seville, and even the Canary Islands. So as long as you're not a local politician working against the ETA (in which case you'd have an extremely bleak life expectancy), you shouldn't worry.

The party scene here is just as liberal as anywhere else in Spain, with the expected amount of hash floating around. Alcohol is not allowed on the beaches in general, but on Playa de la Zurriola sometimes the rules tend to bend a little more.

in the old town, calle Fermin Calbeton and calle San Jeronimo seem to be the two major hotbeds of activity. The bars line up one after another, so it takes zero energy to stumble from place to place. Calle Fermin Calbeton also totally blurs the distinction between dinner and drinks, as most of the bars here serve excellent tapas [see *eats,* below]. This means that the lull that comes between dinner and heading out for the night simply doesn't exist: You go out for tapas, get your buzz on, and things just flow from there. But come prepared with plenty of cash: Most places around town accept credit cards, but that's usually only if you're eating in the restaurant, not just pulling tapas and drinks at the bar. You'll find all the bars listed below in the old town.

San Sebastián has learned to cater to those who flock to it, so you'll find something here that you won't see in most Spanish towns—happy hour. Of course, this is Spain, so happy hour starts at about the time an American bar would be wrapping up the chicken wings and emptying the till. **Bar Tas Tas** *(Calle Fermin Calbeton, between calle San Jeronimo and calle Mayor; Tel 943/430-616; 3pm-2:30am Sun-Thur, till 3:30am Fri, Sat; AE, DC, MC, V)* has a two-for-one happy hour on Sundays through Thursdays from 8:30 to 11:30pm. Given that a bottle of beer runs around 375ptas and mixed drinks cost 625ptas, you definitely want to catch this if you can. During the week this is a great spot to meet other travelers; in fact, you'd be hard-pressed to find a Spaniard here. On the weekends it's a totally different story; the place turns into one of the most happening *puffs* in the old town.

A similar atmosphere holds sway at **Egarri Discobar** *(Calle Inigo 10; Tel 943/270-363; 3pm-2:30am Sun-Wed; till 4am Thur-Sat; No credit cards),* another *puff* that keeps the lights and music on during the week. Funny part is, for all the hype, there's no dance floor to actually get down on. But it's another good spot to run into other English-speaking kids, and on weekends it, too, becomes a hot spot for all. Enjoy the two-for-one happy hour from 10 to 11pm Sunday through Thursday. Drinks run 600ptas for mixed drinks and 400ptas for a beer, so take advantage of the specials and keep an eye out for people handing out two-for-one coupons on the street.

Sariketa *(Calle Fermin Calbeton 23; Tel 943/422-985; 5pm-2am Sun-Thur, till 3:30am Fri-Sat; No credit cards)* draws a more mixed crowd of locals and travelers. It's popular in the early evening and then again later at night. Walls covered in a Scottish tartan surround a casual crowd of 20- to 35-year-olds. Lots of U.S. rock gets played here, and some cheesy old-school dance stuff, but it's all in good fun. On the weekends this place gets too packed for any dancing, though.

If you feel the need to shake your moneymaker, head down Fermin Calbeton to the no-name bar next to Tas Tas. On weekends, 20- to 30-year-old Spaniards descend on this place to shake, rattle, and roll in preparation for the clubs. Under the atmospheric black lights and strobes, the crowd gets down to the Euro-dance music and techno. There's plenty of room to dance and plenty of willing partners to dance with. It's a fun

festivals and events

Everyone knows that San Sebastián has one of Europe's best summer jazz festivals, and they've heard of the film festival held here in late August/early September, but unless you've planned well in advance, odds are the city is full and you're SOL. But fear not, persistent traveler, this city has more events and festivals than days in the week.

Jazz Festival *(Third week in July, www.jazzaldia.com):* Plan around a year ahead, because finding a room at festival time can be next to impossible. But it's well worth it. Founded in 1966, this festival has become one of the best in Europe, and has drawn such legends as B.B. King and the late Dizzy Gillespie. Although the heart of the festival is jazz, it also showcases a variety of bands doing everything from blues to salsa. During this week San Sebastián shines even brighter than usual. Stages are set up throughout the city, so get a program and don't miss a thing.

San Sebastián International Film Festival *(Tel 943/481-212; www.sansebastianfestival.ya.com; Late Aug-early Sept):* It began in 1953 and claims to hold the same distinction as Cannes and Venice. Like those events, tickets to screenings can be next to impossible to come by—even if you're sleeping with the director—and finding a place to crash isn't any easier. But if you can get a room, it's fun to rub elbows with the entertainment world's elite in such an ideal setting. For more information about tickets and availability, call the festival office or visit their website.

San Sebastián Day *(Jan 20; Tel 943/481-166):* This annual event honors the city's patron saint. Festivities start promptly at 12:01am with the hoisting of the city flag to the beat of the Gastro-

scene and a good place to find a friend or two to walk with as you head out to the discos.

While it lacks the old town's concentration of places, the Centro offers a few more options—mostly on calle San Martin and the streets south of the cathedral. A fair number of spots can be found on calle Reyes Católicos south of the cathedral. One of the crazier ones is **Udaberri-berri** *(No phone; 5pm to 1am daily; No credit cards),* right on the corner of Reyes Católicos and Larramendi. (Its name alone is a giveaway.) Upstairs is a nice, normal, unassuming bar; downstairs it's a different scene. Don't be fooled by the foos-ball and the pool table: What really brings people down here is the karaoke. Whether it's at its best (or more likely its worst), it's always fun to listen to Spaniards trying to sing their favorite U.S. tunes.

nomic Society's drum corps, and take place all over the city. Parades, parties, and eating are the main events.

Carnaval *(First week of Mar; Tel 943/481-166):* It's not quite the carnival of Rio, but things have been known to get a little wild. Each year there is a different theme to the citywide festivities.

Beer Fair *(Usually the third week in June; Tel 943/292-393):* This is not a joke. You actually get to sound sort of cultured ("I'll be at the local festival today...") while you wander around the Intxaurrondo section of town, sampling beers from all over the world. Does life get any better than this? Remember, the beers aren't free and they don't accept American Express, so bring your pesetas.

Open Zone *(Early to mid July, Tel 943/322-479):* The surfing extravaganza takes place at the Playa de la Zurriola, drawing boarders from around the globe. There's surfing, skating, beach volleyball competitions, and live music—and the parties ain't too bad, either.

Grand Week *(Mid to late Aug; Tel 943/481-166):* A weeklong, citywide festival made up of exhibitions, concerts, sports, and bullfights. It also coincides with the **International Fireworks Contest,** where for seven nights the best companies in the world light up the sky with fantastic displays of fireworks over Bahía de la Concha.

Basque Festival *(Early Sept; Tel 943/481-166):* This weeklong event celebrates all things Basque, from the berets to the food—lots of food. Sporting events, concerts, and folklore performances are all held in the old town. A group also reenacts the French Army's surrender to the Portuguese and Spanish forces in 1813 (the subsequent burning of the city is left out).

On calle San Martin, one of the more popular spots is **Molly Malone's** *(Calle San Martin 55; Tel 943/469-822; Noon-3 or 4am daily; AE, DC, MC, V),* a big Irish pub that holds the young crowd well. This split-level place sometimes has live folk musicians on Thursday and Friday nights. It's not a bad spot if you're jonesin' for a little English conversation.

LIVE MUSIC SCENE

Like other places in Spain, the local rock scene doesn't have a lot of muscle, but we know you can take heavy metal and thrash for only so long. Your best bet for decent live music is jazz. San Sebastián hosts one of Europe's premiere jazz festivals every summer, so you know they've got the feel. A couple of good jazz bars on the east side of the old town have the occasional session. *Donosti Aisia* carries the full listings, or visit the clubs themselves to find out what they've got going on. There's usually no cover, which is a great deal and definitely one to take advantage of. **Altxerri** *(Reina Regente 2; Tel 943/422-931; Sun-Thur 5pm-1:30am, till 3:30am Fri, Sat; V, MC)* has the most going on, and it's hard to miss: It sits almost directly across the street from the tourist office. Like any jazz spot worth its name, this one is in a basement and has plenty of atmosphere. Stone walls and columns give it a great cave-like feel and actually seem to add to the acoustics of the music, while photos by local artists hang on the walls. Sit down, have a drink, and listen to the music—this is a pretty good listening crowd. Given the size of the corner where the bands set up, we're guessing no big band acts swing through this place. A Thursday jam starts at 11pm every week, and the club also has some acts around midnight on select Fridays and Saturdays. While there's no standard cover, if there's a name band playing you'll have to pay something to enter; there's no cover for the Thursday jam session, but drink prices go up in order to pay the musicians. Band or not, there's always jazz music playing, and you'll enjoy this nice, intimate setting that oozes jazz in all the right ways.

Another option around the block is **Bee Bop Bar** *(On Paseo de Salamanca at corner of Gen. Echague; Tel 943/429-869; 3pm to 5am daily; No cover; No credit cards)*. Although it books live acts less frequently than Altxerri, this place is still all jazz. Jazz memorabilia and photos cover the walls of the good-sized room with a good-sized bar—and a not-so-good-sized stage for the bands. But then again, jazz is all about getting close enough to the musicians to see the sweat on their brows, right? Bee Bop attracts a young, casual crowd, with some older folks as well. It's a great spot to relax, listen to some good music, and sip a drink or café con leche.

San Sebastián also hosts some big-name rock acts, especially during the late spring and summer. You'll see posters up all over town advertising upcoming tours (Pearl Jam and Lou Reed were here recently). The posters will have the ticket information, or you can try calling **Telekutxa** *(Tel 943/411-200)* to order them over the phone. Most of the larger music events are held at **Kursaal Auditorium** *(Avda. Zurriola; Tel 943/481-179; Avg ticket 3,000ptas; V, MC)*, which is the big modern building right on the water in Gros.

CLUB SCENE

Clubbing in San Sebastián can be wild, exciting...and also very costly. Unfortunately, the club owners here have discovered that people on vacation tend to pay more to have a good time. But there is a ray of hope—if you're female, that is. The hefty cover charges at the clubs on the waterfront (some as high as 3,000ptas) apply only to male patrons. Hugh Heffner could try to walk in with his harem of women, and while they all slipped through the door, the old guy would still be held up for 3,000ptas.

Disappointingly, once you've paid the steep cover, you may not feel like you're getting your money's worth: None of the clubs here are all that spectacular. You'll have a good time, but nothing mind-blowing, and def-

fIVE-O

Do you know your José Law? If you've been traveling in Spain, you've probably noticed that each town has its local and national police forces. Generally they do the same job, totally oblivious to the other's existence. But here in the País Vasco, we get to add a third police force to the mix. The autonomous Basque police can be easily identified by their red berets. These guys really don't get along too well with their counterparts, and they're something of an issue with the powers that be in Madrid, who feel they don't do enough investigating of ETA attacks. But Madrid can't disband the Basque police, as it would create even more dissent than is already there. So in this autonomous province, the autonomous police continue to do their best to give the region a little character. You'll usually see them hanging out and chatting with locals in a very casual manner. They're good-natured guys until someone throws a bottle at their heads.

initely not good enough to justify the cover charge. The DJs are run of the mill, and the music is average. So why go? Because the clubs are on the beach, which just about says it all.

The three most accessible clubs are **Rotonda, Batapleón,** and **La Perla.** All three can be found along the Paseo de la Concha, which runs parallel to the beach. Rotunda and Bataplón seemed to be the two more popular clubs when we were there, while La Perla drew a more sophisticated, older crowd. Unfortunately, all three charge a 3,000ptas cover for guys. This includes one drink, but that hardly makes up for it; after the first one, mixed drinks run 700ptas. The DJs in both clubs spin the standard mix of Euro-dance, pop, and techno. As in most places, the better music tends to come on later at night, which could also be considered earlier in the morning since none of the clubs really get going until 3 or 4am. Show up before that and you're dancing alone.

Locals swear by two more clubs, **Disco Ku** *(Calle Igueldo; Tel 943/314-176; 1-6am daily; Cover 1,000ptas; No credit cards)* and **Keops,** but unfortunately both are a cab ride from the center of town. Disco Ku is the better bet, though it's farther away, out past the Funicular. This club rages until the sun rises well above the ocean. **Keops** *(On Plaza Alta Donostia near Estadio de Anoeta; Tel 943/465-722; 1:30-5:30am daily, also 6-10pm Wed, Sat, Sun; No cover; No credit cards)* is in the neighborhood south of the bus station. It might be a good idea to talk to a local before you make the trek to either place, just to make sure that the party will be kicking. On the bright side, if you make the effort—even during the crowded summer months—you'll find yourself breaking new ground, far from your fellow tourists who find happiness only in the most obvious spots.

arts scene

The arts scene in San Sebastián is fairly lively, especially given the city's size. That's probably because the city is more than just a beach resort town; it's also a cultural center for Basque heritage. The fact that San Sebastián sits on one of the most beautiful pieces of land on the whole darn globe seems to inspire plenty of people to create art as well as to consume it. From theater to galleries to movies, there are plenty of ways to stimulate yourself here other than just analyzing (and maintaining) your tan. Pull out that ever-faithful *Donosti Aisia* for a current list of what is up and running.

▶▶VISUAL ARTS

San Sebastián has lots of good galleries spread around town. All have ever-changing exhibits with runs of about a month or two and are open year-round. The tourist office can hook you up with a complete list of galleries and exhibits. The ones mentioned here are all in Centro, unless otherwise indicated.

One of the better galleries in town is **Galeria DV** *(San Martin 5; Tel 943/429-111; 5-9pm Tue-Fri, 11am-1pm/5-9pm Sat)*. The self-stated purpose of this gallery is to promote young artists from the Basque country. It showcases local talent working in all styles, and also periodically shows the latest work of big-name contemporary artists from all over Spain (in part to get the cash needed to run the gallery so it can continue to help lesser-known artists). If you're not sure the art is really your thing, you might be convinced by the free wine and cheese served at the opening parties (a happy tradition at most galleries).

Not too far away on the gallery circuit is **Galeria Dieciseis** *(Plaza Buen Pastor 16; Tel 943/466-916; 5-7pm Tue-Fri, 11am-2pm/6-9pm Sat)*, located in the basement under the Levi's store next to the cathedral. This exciting gallery is home to contemporary artists from around the region.

If you've started to feel guilty about lying on the beach all day and totally missing out on cultural enrichment, you still have a chance to redeem yourself. Once the high tide pushes you off Playa de la Concha, head to **Galeria Echebarria** *(Paseo de la Concha 11; Tel 943/428-923; 10am-1pm/5-8:30pm, closed Mon morning and festivals)*, just steps from the beach. This gallery specializes in figurative works by artists from all over Spain. It also has more works on display than any of the other galleries we visited, although some that were "on display" were simply stacked four-deep against a wall. But all in all, it's not a bad place to check out when the sun gets too hot and you want to escape to an air-conditioned room for a little while.

▶▶PERFORMING ARTS

It's easy to find a good old Hollywood blockbuster, as is the case anywhere in Spain. **Cines Principe** *(Tel 943/411-200; Movies at 5pm, 7:30pm, and 10:30pm; 750ptas; DC, MC, V)* on Plaza de Zuloaga in the old town will give you all the mindless blood, sex, and action your heart desires. It gets major Hollywood flicks not long after their release in the States, so you can keep abreast of American pop culture from across the ocean. You might want to check the movie posters out front first to see if the movie is subtitled or dubbed. In the dubbed versions, the characters have strange voices and look like they're speaking kung fu, if such a thing were possible. It kinda dampens the appeal of those sexy Hollywood stars and starlets.

The **Teatro Principal** *(Calle Mayor s/n; Tel 943/426-112; Box office open 4:30-8:30pm/9:30-11pm daily, show times 8pm and 10:30pm summer, 8pm winter; Tickets 750ptas and up)* hosts most of the performing arts events in the city. Most nights the theater screens a great movie, usually an artistic one, whether Spanish or international. You can catch the latest big deal from the film festivals, including Cannes. The theater also puts on theme nights—such as all classic horror flicks or wild sci-fi. Visit the theater to get the latest schedule; they have it posted out front. In the summer, some live theatrical events also take place here.

During the summer, you can catch a play or live performance in many of the little plazas scattered throughout the city. As always, *Donosti Aisia* is your best resource for getting the inside scoop. Most of the performances in the plazas tend to be a bit amateurish, which can lead to wild laughs or groans, depending on the troupe.

gay scene

The gay scene in San Sebastián is a little more out than in other cities in the area. However, while no one in San Sebastián cares what anyone else's flavor is—because of the laid-back atmosphere, or the sea salt in the air, or who knows why—the gay scene is a bit subdued. It's accepted, but not much is happening, especially compared to the scene elsewhere in town. None of the gay clubs draws that large a crowd and they all seem like dark and lonely places. The weekend breathes a little more life into them, but they're still not as lively as other clubs in town. The gay scene centers mainly around San Martin in the Centro part of town; all the venues listed below are in this district, and they all have similar hours, opening around 5pm and running until 2am on weeknights and 4am on weekends.

The liveliest place we found was **Trigono** *(Calle Lertsund between San Martin and San Bartolome; No phone; 5pm-3am daily),* which is really a gay *puff.* Loud music, black lights, and glowing ceiling stars transport you to another universe. Trigono attracts mostly a younger male crowd that's not afraid to take a turn or two on the dance floor. Expect Euro-dance and pop; mixed drinks run 550ptas, beers 300ptas. There ain't any big signs out front with the name of the place, so keep your eyes peeled for a purple arrow that points down to the door, on the right side of the street walking away from the beach.

A DJ spins jazzy dance and house music at **Txirula** *(San Martin 51; No phone; 4pm-3am daily; No cover; No credit cards)* while a thirtysomething male crowd lounges on large plush sofas opposite the bar. Peel your eyes away from the scene for a minute to check out the really cool contemporary art mural on the ceiling. Beers run 400ptas; mixed drinks will cost you 650ptas.

One other spot that deserves a mention just for its mirrored dance floor is **Kontra** *(Calle Manterola 4-6; No phone; Daily 2pm-3am; No* *cover; No credit cards).* The bar itself is pretty dark and it's not the most upbeat scene in town, but if you ever wanted to see just what an ass you look like trying to dance after a couple of drinks, then this dance floor is great! Unfortunately, the music—mostly rock, although there are some soul songs thrown into the mix—isn't likely to get you in your best groove. Beers cost 400ptas, and it's mostly an older male crowd.

CULTURE ZOO

The true key to San Sebastián's cultural scene doesn't hide within the walls of any museum and it isn't chipped into the side of the cathedral—it's all about the people. If you want to get to know and understand the city, wander through the streets of the old town, enjoy Basque food and drink at one of the many authentic restaurants, and sit on the Playa de la Zurriola and talk with the locals about what they think. That said, if you're not the most outgoing person in the world and you prefer learning in a museum-like setting, there are a couple of places worth checking out.

Museo San Telmo *(Plaza Zuloaga 1; Tel 943/424-970; 10am-1:30pm/4-7:30pm Tue-Sat, 10am-1:30pm Sun; Free):* This convent from the 16th century houses one of the city's most varied collections: If it survived war and fire, you'll probably find it here. At the time of publication, the ground floor was being renovated and turned into a Basque heritage museum. It will include exhibits on Basque ways of life from past to present, including fishing, farming, and carpentry. You'll find regional archaeology (including artifacts from ancient through Roman and medieval times) and ethnography on the first floor; Spanish paintings from the 1500s through the 1800s adorn the second. Finally, you'll find Basque art from the 19th and 20th centuries on the third. The collection is decent and does include an El Greco, as well as the work of some interesting contemporary artists. Some of the works displayed are on loan from the Prado in Madrid.

Museo Naval *(Paseo del Muelle 24; Tel 943/430-051; 10am-1:30pm/5-8:30pm Tue-Sat June 15-Sept 15; 10am-1:30pm/4-7:30pm Tue-Sat rest of the year; 200ptas adults, 100ptas students):* This is a small museum that lies on the waterfront out by the Aquarium and Monte Urgull, the town's highest peak, recognizable by the giant statue of Christ at the top. Learn everything you ever wanted to know about shipbuilding (from cutting down trees to setting sail) from the photos on the ground floor, where you'll also find small handcrafted wooden boats on display. If you've ever had any interest in the history of the anchor (and really, who hasn't?), a thought-provoking display tells all—following its evolution from a rock with a line tied to it to that modern metal claw that we know and love today. Upstairs you'll find some pretty cool model ships, and photos and drawings showing the development of some of the port cities on the north coast, including San Sebastián. Old nautical instruments fill cases on the rest of the floor.

Aquarium *(Plaza Carlos Blasco de Imaz s/n; Tel 943/440-099; 10am-10pm daily June 15-Sept 15; 10am-8pm daily rest of the year; 1,100ptas):* Ever dreamed of being a fish? Fork over the dough: This place is worth it.

Say hello to the humungo whale skeleton near the entrance, then take a gander at the cases around the room displaying exotic collections of shells and coral. There are also exhibits on commercial fishing techniques (where did you think they got all that seafood you've been eating?) and displays on maritime history with lots of drawings and cool models upstairs. Finally, when you've finished all the learning stuff, head into the aquarium for a satisfying immersion in all things fishy. There are tanks holding fish from around the world (some of them traveled even farther than you did to get here!), temporary displays on issues such as sea pollution, and a really, really cool aquarium tunnel—a glassed-in tube that runs through the largest tanks and offers 360-degree views of your fishy friends. It's reassuring to know that the sharks are on the other side of the glass; when you head back to the beach, you're on your own. The aquarium is on the southwestern tip of the same spit of land as Parque Monte Urgull.

Catedral del Buen Pastor *(At the head of calle Loyola on Plaza Del Buen Pastor; Tel 943/464-516; 8:30am-12:30pm/5-8pm daily):* A 2-minute walk southwest of Plaza Bilbao, the cathedral is the only significant cultural site outside the old town. Personally we think it's beautiful 'cause its steeple seems to follow you no matter where you go. Comforting, isn't it? For an especially cool sight, go stand at the head of calle Hernani, just on the edge of the old town, and look down the street, where the buildings along Hernani frame the face of the cathedral. The inside doesn't quite compare to the grand old cathedrals common to Spain, maybe because it was constructed in the 19th century. But on a sunny day it's fun to step inside and see all the stained-glass windows filtering the sunshine and lighting up the interior in a rainbow of colors.

Iglesia de Santa María *(Corner of calle Mayor and calle 31 de Agosto; Tel 943/423-124; 8am-2pm/4:30-8:30pm daily)* and **Iglesia de San Vicente** *(Corner of calle San Vicente and calle 31 de Agosto; Tel 943/420-955; 8am-1pm/6-8pm Mon-Sat; 10am-1:15pm/7-9pm Sun):* If it's religious monuments you crave, head back into the old town to these two churches. Iglesia de Santa María is best appreciated from the outside, as its Baroque facade is one of the most ornate to be found in the city. Iglesia de San Vicente's distinction comes from the fact that it is the oldest religious structure in town, dating back to the 1500s.

modification

San Sebastián is upscale, but that doesn't mean you're out of luck when it comes to getting just the right ornament for that perfect, full-body tan. At **A&T Tattoo** *(Gen. Echague 2; Tel 943/421-885; 4-8pm Mon; 10am-1pm, 4-8pm Tue-Sun; No credit cards)* in the old town, the specialty seems to be very cool Basque nationalist body art, like clenched fists and the like. However, we're sure they won't laugh at that clover or dolphin you've had your heart set on.

If you're looking for a place to get a snazzy haircut, wander down calles Elcano or Garibai between Alameda del Boulevard and Avenida de la Libertad. There's a string of salons in this area that will make you look good for the beach, but they'll put a dent in your wallet. Beauty just doesn't come cheap. Two centrally located salons are **Peluqueria Maiso** *(Avda. Libertad 45; Tel 943/429-811)* and **Peluqueria Marcial Munoz** *(Calle Bergata 5; Tel 943/428-286).*

CITY SPORTS

If sun, sand, swells, swimming, and surfing aren't enough to keep you occupied, then how about some sports? The Basques love sports. True, some of those games they love may be a bit strange in our eyes: The Basques invented jai alai, and they've certainly perfected handball in all of its forms, but they get off on just about any form of competition, including soccer (remember, we're still in Spain, where soccer is king). Beyond these testosterone-driven activities, there are also pleasant hiking trails around San Sebastián. The best hiking trail is the one to the 604-foot summit of Monte Igueldo. The tourist office will give you a free map and point you on your way. At the top you'll be rewarded with one of the most dazzling views along the Cantabrian coast. The walk up isn't that grueling, but if you're a bit lazy you can take the Funicular to the top, then walk back down. It runs daily from 10am to 9pm and costs 175ptas one way.

For bike tours, consider hooking up with **Green Service** *(Calle Ramon Maria Lili 1; Tel 943/277-733),* which offers three-hour jaunts at 4,000ptas per person. You can also rent a bike from **Comet** *(Avda. Libertad 6; Tel 943/422-351; 10am-4pm daily; 3,000ptas per day)* next to the tourist office and cycle around the Playa de la Concha.

Or join the locals down at one of the *polideportivos*—public sports facilities—of which San Sebastián frankly seems to have more than its fair share. A couple of the largest of these are south of the bus station by **Estadio de Anoeta** *(Avda. Sancho El Sabio s/n; Tel 943/481-865; Bus 26 or 28 from Alameda del Boulevard; 8am-8pm daily),* a 10-minute walk south of Plazio Pio XXIII. The stadium itself has a 400-meter running track, a grass soccer field, and seating for a couple thousand. If you feel this might be a bit above your level, there are two sports facilities on either side of the building.

The main one is **Polideportivo "J.A. Gasca"** *(Paseo de Anoeta 8; Tel 943/481-890; Hours vary but usually 9am-10pm Mon-Fri, till 9:30pm Sat, till 1:30pm Sun Sept-June; 9am-1pm/5-9pm Mon-Fri, 9am-1pm Sat July-Aug; Day pass about 2,000ptas).* This whopping modern gym houses, among other things, a pool, weight room, gym, and sauna. The gym is bright and clean and you'll never have to wait long to use any of the equipment.

If you're in the mood for a swim but just can't deal with the ocean (see too many sharks at the aquarium?), then check out the other sports facility by the stadium, **Polideportivo "Piscinas Paco Yoldi"** *(Paseo de Anoeta 16; Tel 943/481-870; 8am-10pm Mon-Sat, 9am-2pm Sun Sept-June; 8am-8pm Mon-Fri, 9am-8:30pm Sun July-Aug; 2,000ptas).* It has a 50-meter Olympic-sized pool, two smaller pools, two weight rooms, and a small gym. Given the size of the place, you'll never really have to deal with crowds.

If flailing around in a chlorinated pool is not exactly your idea of water fun, then stop by the offices of **Atletico San Sebastián C.D.** *(Paseo de la Concha 8; Tel 943/473-723; Usually 10am-2pm/4-7pm)*, conveniently located right on the beach. Here you can rent a small kayak for a couple of thousand pesetas a day. Take one out and cruise the bay. For more advanced paddlers, the staff can hook you up with info about going out of the bay and heading up and down the coastline.

Certified scuba divers, or those interested in learning, should check out **APSAS** *(Aldamar 32-bajo; Tel 943/423-748)*, which has its office in the old town. They'll take certified divers (or teach you how to become one) in the waters off San Sebastián. Eight thousand pesetas will cover the cost of all the rental gear, boat ride, and dive. For those of us who can't afford to eat out every night, APSAS also offers courses in underwater fishing.

If the beach really has you in a lazy mood and you see absolutely no need for sports and exercise, there's still one place that might make you hop off that towel—or roll off it, since you don't have to go far to reach **La Perla** *(Paseo de la Concha s/n; Tel 943/458-856; 8am-10pm; www.la-perla.net; V, MC)*. This spa caters to those who want to be coddled—and who doesn't? Its beach-side setting whispers seductively, "Massage me. Pamper me. Cover me in mud." They offer such rejuvenating services as bathing (in healing, heated seawater, no less), special mud baths, and massage. All you have to do is make it to the door—they'll do all the work once you get there. But these services don't come cheap. A half-hour massage will set you back 3,200ptas (5,500ptas for the full hour); a full bath in special ocean mud to appease your inner child, 4,275ptas (perhaps you'll opt to spend just 1,650ptas for limited applications of the goo). A bio-aroma bath costs 3,500ptas (this might actually be worth it if you've been backpacking a long time without a shower). But there are some bargains at this place. If you're under 25, you can get an hour and 45 minutes in the thermal baths (a small pool with heated seawater and a view overlooking the bay) for 1,400ptas (2,300ptas for those over 25). This is the place to come if you want a taste of the high life, and oh, what a taste.

STUFF

Step in line behind all the other tourists when you go out shopping in San Sebastián. There are clothing stores, and stores selling San Sebastián key chains and T-shirts, and clothing stores, and stores selling San Sebastián key chains and T-shirts, and...you get our drift. As you've probably figured out by now, what the Spaniards don't spend on food and drink, they spend on clothes. Sometimes it seems like one day they ran out of permits for regular clothing stores, which is when they decided that masses of T-shirt stores catering to tourists would be a good idea. You'll find plenty of these in the old town, especially on calle Puerto toward the harbor, on the walk along the port out to the Aquarium, and on Paseo de Muelle. For a cheap thrill, stop in at one of these places and get your mom something that says Donostia on it (remember, that's Basque for your host city). You'll have her in a state of total confusion as to your whereabouts over the past couple of months.

The main commercial center in San Sebastián is in Centro, where most of the fashionable designer clothing and jewelry stores ply their wares. Calles Elcano, Churruca, and Getaria running between Alameda del Boulevard and Alfonso VIII by the cathedral are open only to pedestrian traffic, so window-shopping along these streets can be relaxing.

The old town is not just about clothing stores and T-shirt stores, thank God. Mixed in among all the restaurants and bars you'll find some unique shops selling everything from that Cure record you lost back in the seventh grade to that Big Johnson that you've been dreaming about getting up and riding on all day (I'm talking, of course, about the surfboard).

▶▶SURF

Pukas Surf *(Calle Mayor 5; Tel 943/427-228; 10am-1pm/4-8pm, closed Sun and Mon mornings; pukas@facilnet.es)* in the center of the old town will serve as your center for all the surfing equipment, clothes, and advice you'll need. The kind people here have taken the liberty of stocking up on the best beachwear around: You could go in blindfolded and still find something great. Choose from plenty of swim trunks for him, suits and bikinis for her. Shades and shirts? Yeah, they got that covered too. This place is also loaded with wetsuits and boards for those not wanting to just watch other people ride. The staff knows the scene and the breaks well and will be able to guide you to scoring the ultimate ride. They also have some party flyers for upcoming events by the cash register, so even if you stay out all night and sleep through beach time, this is a store worth stopping in.

▶▶DUDS

Also in the old town is the eclectic **Hermes** *(Fermin Calbeton 33; Noon-1:30pm/4:30-8pm Mon-Sat)*. This small boutique carries *ropa de moda* (hip clothes) for him and her, although there's definitely a larger her section. There's also a section of used and bruised secondhand clothing. The selection depends largely on what's coming into the store, so it's kind of a hit-or-miss thing. In a side room you'll find a wide-ranging collection of old vinyl, CDs, tapes, comics, and videos. If you're willing to take the time to weed through them, you might find something interesting.

▶▶TUNES

Better yet, head across the old town to **Beltza Records** *(San Juan 9; Tel 943/430-609; 10am-1:30pm/4-8pm Mon-Sat)*, which offers an extensive selection of old records, including classic rock, soul, blues, punk, and everything in between. They also sell comics. The owner is very nice and will take the time to try to clue *viajeros perdidos* (lost travelers) into the live music scene in San Sebastián.

EATS

San Sebastián is famous for many things. Its beaches are some of the best city beaches in the country. Its local culture is one of the richest. Now here's one more to add to the list: the food. Some people consider San Sebastián cooking—Basque cooking—to be Spain's finest. People here take their food seriously. Need proof? How about the mostly all-male clubs whose members get together and...cook—dish after succulent dish—for their members. Although the odds of getting invited to one of these shindigs is about as slim as shagging one of the movie stars that call on the film festival, there's always second best: San Sebastián's chefs have perfected the fine art of Basque cooking, which is not haute cuisine but is damn good. Most of the dishes here have something to do with the sea, which the Basques have always relied on for food. And since they've been around practically since the dawn of man, they've had time to figure out how to cook it just right.

Most of the best dining is found in the old town. Take advantage of the *menú del día* offered during lunch hours (1-4pm most places). This combo of two dishes, bread, drink, and dessert will be enough to fill you up, and at 1,100-1,800ptas, it's a great deal. At night you're likely to pay double that for the same food, so once the sun goes down, it's more economical to stick to tapas.

▶▶CHEAP

Even in an elegant city like this, it's possible to find a cheap meal that will leave you with enough money for a couple of drinks later on. **La Pasta Gansa** *(Zubieta 56; Tel 943/426-663; 1:30-3:30pm/8:30pm-midnight Wed-Mon; Avg meal 775-1,000ptas; AE, DC, MC, V),* in the Hotel Niza [see *crashing,* below] in the Centro, offers a big meal that will fill you up for minimal pesetas. This Italian pizzeria offers pastas, lasagnas, pizzas,

TO MARKET

So you want to know where the underground market is? It's located in the old town; you've just got to do a little digging. Seriously, one of the best places for fresh meats, fish, veggies, and fruit is located right underground. Check out the Sunday market at **Azoka Mercado** *(Take the escalator down from the glass-roofed plaza by San Juan and San Lorenzo)*—it's full of stalls where vendors sell delicious fresh food. Cheeses, pastries, peaches, and pike are all available. It's best to go between 7 and 10 in the morning when everything is fresh. There is also a supermarket, **Lidl,** in the underground complex. It's a big modern supermarket, perfect for stocking up on picnic supplies, but buy the meats and fruits outside at the stalls for maximum freshness. You must check your bag to enter the supermarket (100ptas for a locker), so hit the supermarket before anything else.

and more. The helpings are hefty in the great Italian tradition, and with even the splashiest dishes costing no more than 1,100ptas, you will be plenty full for your buck.

Your other choices for inexpensive dining are the cafeterias that run along calle Puerto. Most serve up *platos combinados* for under 1,000ptas. Better to head out for tapas; sure, they can get a little expensive between all the drinks, and they aren't very filling so you've got to chaw a lot of 'em, but it's a cultural thing, and sometimes you just gotta bite the bullet. Besides, these tapas follow the Basque tradition for excellence, so you won't be disappointed.

You can spend all night walking up and down calle Fermin Calbeton, ducking into different places. **Bar Etxaniz** *(Calle Fermin Calbeton 22)* is exclusively a tapas joint and puts its efforts into many fine choices. The bar is completely covered with plates of tasty little tidbits on toothpicks, so order your drink and don't be shy. Grab what looks good and follow the Spanish way when you're done: Just toss your toothpick and napkin on the floor (it's kind of a liberating experience). The eagle-eyed bartenders don't miss a trick, and your bill will reflect every bite you had.

Another good tapas experience is **Munto Jatetxea Taberna** *(Calle Fermin Calbeton17)*. This spot takes great pride in its presentation. A flower or similar decoration garnishes each plate of tapas. The food can stand on its own, though.

For breakfast or a mid-afternoon snack, try **Chef Croissant** *(Easo on corner with San Marzial)* in Centro. This small corner place has a counter and just four tables—two inside, two out—but it's a great spot to sit and enjoy a café con leche and a fresh pastry (we highly recommend the chocolate-filled Napoleon). They also serve up warm *bocadillos* in 4 minutes flat. There's counter seating if the tables are full.

Vegetarians should check out **La OKA** *(San Martin 43, Centro; 1-3:30pm/8:30-11pm)*, part cafeteria, part diner. It's a fun "do-it-yourself" spot; they set the food out and you just go through and pull out whatever looks good, sit down, and munch. There's also a lunch *menú del día* for 1,100ptas.

▶▶DO-ABLE

There are plenty of affordable and good eating options in the city. **Beti-Jai Jatetxea** *(Fermin Calbeton 22; Tel 943/427-737)* is a seafood mecca. It can be hard to get a table here, so it's best to reserve ahead. Fish and meat entrees run between 1,600-2,700ptas. If you just want to sample the excellent cooking, the bar at the front serves excellent tapas. This is your opportunity to finally find out what octopus tastes like—c'mon, it's *nothing* like eating worms on *Survivor!*

A table with a great view can be had at **Restaurante Marinela** *(Paseo del Muelle 14)*. This place sits right alongside the harbor and has outside seating that lets you take in everything. Seafood is the specialty here, with dishes that run between 950-2,800ptas; there are also a couple of meat dishes on the menu for about the same price.

The esplanade is a good place to find any number of restaurants. A simple stroll up and down will let you find one to your liking. The prices at most are the same, though, as are the offerings. These places get packed at lunch (1-3:30pm) and only some are open for dinner.

▶▶SPLURGE

Unfortunately, a taste of the best that Basque cooking has to offer comes with a price...a high price. **Casa Nicolasa** (Aldamar 4; Tel 943/421-762; 1-3:30pm/8:30-11:30pm Mon-Sat; 2,600-4,500ptas per entree; MC, V, AE) is one of the city's finest overall eating establishments, and is said to be the best for Basque cooking. Make a reservation, and dress well. You can get an excellent meal of traditional as well as more innovative Basque dishes. And you'll be treated like visiting royalty—sometimes a little too *much* like visiting royalty.

crashing

If you're unprepared, finding a room in San Sebastián can be an ordeal. During the summer, hotels, *hostales,* and *pensiónes* fill up faster than the prom queen's date book, as Spaniards from the boiling interior flee to the coasts for some cool breeze and R&R. It just so happens that San Sebastián is *the* most popular escape on the north coast, so if you're in town during the summer months, expect large crowds. In July and August, finding a room can be an all-day affair that might end with you settling for an over-priced room far from the center...unless, of course, the jazz or film festival is on, in which case you won't even be that lucky. There are some local travel agencies that will make reservations for you [see *need to know,* below].

Single travelers may also find it difficult getting a single room *any-where* from May through late September. Most owners use their single rooms as doubles during this time, and the only way you'll get a room is to pay for the double. The upside is that because of the demand for lodging, San Sebastián has lots of options; 80 percent of the time, you'll have no problem finding a room right in the part of town you want to be in. Admittedly, the prices here are higher than what you may be used to if you've been traveling around other parts of Spain, and they take a big jump in the summer as well, so be forewarned.

The old town has a lot of *pensiónes* and *hostales* scattered about, and it's a good place to be if you don't have to get up early. Things can get a little noisy at night, making it hard to sleep. The key is just to stay out in the thick of it all.

Outside the old town, you'll find *hostales* and hotels in the Centro. Most of the hotels are more expensive and require reservations. The *hostales* in this part of town are clustered on San Martin and calle Easo.

▶▶CHEAP

You want cheap? Don't come looking for it here. There's only one cheap option in San Sebastián, and it's the **Albergue La Sirena** youth hostel (Paseo de Igueldo 25; Tel 943/310-268; June 1-Sept 15: 2,000ptas for those under 26, 2,255ptas for those over; Rest of year: 1,640ptas for those under 26, 2,000ptas for those over; 400ptas for sheets; V, MC). There are a couple of problems with this place. One, it's kinda out of the way, set back a couple of blocks from the end of Playa de Ondarreta. Yeah, it's not too far from the beach, but it's a 30-minute walk to the old town (Bus 16 goes to and from the hostel, and it's a 10-minute ride). Secondly, for a youth hostel, this place still costs a pretty penny. The worst part is the lockout hours. Summer curfew is 2am; during the rest of the year it's midnight, extended to 2am on weekends. There's also a lockout between 11am-3pm. On the bright side, it is a fairly modern, well-kept place where you can meet other travelers, and breakfast is included. Reservations should be made 15-20 days in advance.

▶▶**DO-ABLE**

If you're willing to spend a little more than you normally would for lodging, San Sebastián will reward you. Not that the quality of the hotel is going to be better than elsewhere, but the location is definitely worth the investment. The old town is probably the best place to be. Of all the places we visited, our number-one pick is **Pensión San Lorenzo** (San Lorenzo 2; Tel 943/425-516; 3,500-5,000ptas double, depending on season; No credit cards). There are only five rooms here, so getting one isn't easy, but if you catch it on the right night, consider it a score. All the rooms are cheerfully painted doubles, and they each come with a private modern bathroom and shower (a luxury considering what you'd have to pay at another place). Each room also has its own mini fridge, perfect for chilling water for the next day. Four of the rooms have two beds, while one has a queen-size bed. A coin-op computer in the hallway lets you connect to the Internet. The woman who runs the place is very kind and helpful, and if her place is full, she'll call around to a couple of other places to check their status. Most of the guests are English speakers. Single travelers might even want to consider paying for a double room here, as it's one of the best values in town.

The same people own **Pensión Boulevard** (Alameda del Boulevard 24; Tel 943/429-505; 3,500-6,500ptas double; No credit cards). It has four double rooms on the edge of the old town that go for a slightly higher rate.

Urgull (Esterlines 10; Tel 943/430-047; 2,000-3,000ptas single, 3,000-5,000ptas double) offers another economical choice. Warning to the solo traveler: This place won't have any single rooms May-September. The rooms are nice enough and the shared bathroom is nothing to complain about. It's in the heart of the old town, and hopefully you won't be spending all your time in your room.

Another option within spitting distance of anywhere you'd want to be in the old town is **Pensión Goika** (Puerto 6; Tel 943/431-114; 4,000-6,000ptas single; 5,000-7,500ptas double; pgoika@airtel.net). Small groups can take advantage of this place, since some of the doubles can be expanded to handle up to four people (generally 2,000-3,000ptas more per head). The six rooms have three very modern bathrooms to share. Stick to the one the owner shows you, as this is a pet peeve of hers. The rooms are nice and should be getting ceiling fans installed any day now.

Just down the street from Pensión Goika, **Pensión Kaia** (Puerto 12; Tel 943/431-342; 4,500-6,000ptas single, 6,900-9,000ptas double, 9,000-

12,000ptas triple, 12,000-16,000ptas quad) can also accommodate larger numbers of people. We can't guarantee these prices, as the husband and wife (who were both very helpful) were still deciding how much to charge when we visited. But we wouldn't be surprised if you see these prices come down some, seeing as some of the rooms lack windows. Other than that, all are clean and pleasant with a private bath and TV.

In the Centro, **Anorga** (*Easo 12; Tel 943/467-945; 3,000-4,000ptas single, 4,000-5,000ptas double without shower, 5,000-6,500ptas double with shower; No credit cards*) is one of the larger *hostales*, with 21 rooms. Doubles come with or without showers; the singles all use the bathroom down the hall. The joy of this place is that it's a block away from Playa de la Concha.

▶▶SPLURGE

In the Centro, right on the Playa de la Concha, is **Hotel Niza** (*Zubieta 56; Tel and Fax 943/426-663; niza@adegi.es, www.adegi.es/hotelniza; 6,650-7,500ptas single, 8,950-13,200ptas double, extra bed 2,750ptas; V, MC, AE*). One look at the elegant sitting room with its dangling chandeliers and you know this place will treat you well. Forty-one rooms, most overlooking the bay, all come complete with TV, phone, and full bath. The rooms are modern, though lacking character, but with a view like that who's going to want to stare at the walls? There's also a coffee shop and restaurant [see *eats*, above] on the premises.

need to know

Currency Exchange There are banks and ATMs all over town. Avenida de Libertad in the Centro has the highest concentration of banks in the city. Most have 24-hour ATMs attached. **Exchange** (*Avda. de Libertad 1; 9am-2pm/4-7pm Mon-Fri, 10am-2pm/4-6pm Sat*) is open longer than the banks, but also charges a higher commission. Cash machine in Basque is **"Kutxa."**

Tourist Information The main **tourist office** is located on the east corner of the main theater (*Reina Regente s/n; Tel 943/481-166; 8am-8pm Mon-Sat, 9am-2pm Sun June 15-Sept 15; 9am-2pm/3:30-7pm Mon-Sat, 9am-2pm Sun rest of the year*). The extremely helpful staff here will be able to provide you with any information on the city that you want (English spoken). They won't make hotel reservations for you, but a local **travel agency** (*General Echague 14; Tel 943/430-927*) will, free of charge.

Public Transportation San Sebastián has a public bus system that operates 25 lines (*Tel 943/287-400*). Most service runs between 7am-10pm, so the buses won't help you out much at night. Each ride costs 115ptas. Maps can be picked up at the tourist office, and there are also maps at all of the bus stations. Most things are within walking distance, though, and the buses are not allowed in the constricted streets of the old town. The closest stop to the old town is Alameda del Boulevard.

Health and Emergency Emergency: *112*. The main **Hospital** is located out of the city center in *Alto de Zorroaga* (*Tel 943/007-000*)

and there's also a **Red Cross,** *Cruz Roja (Matia 7; Tel 943/272-222).*
The **Local Police** *(Easo 41; Tel 943/450-000; Emergency: 092)* and the
National Police *(Emergency: 092)* are also on hand to help you should
you need it.

Pharmacies There are *farmacias* all over the city marked by **neon green
crosses.** No single one is open 24 hours a day; instead, *farmacias* rotate
the all-night responsibility. Each one posts a schedule indicating who
will be open on what night. One pharmacy in the old town is on Nar-
rica 23 *(Tel 943/420-649).*

Telephones City code: *94;* operator: *05;* international operator: *07.*

Airport Aeropuerto de San Sebastián *(Tel 943/641-267)* is 20km away
from the city in Hondarridia. There are two flights daily to Madrid
and one to Barcelona. **Interbus** *(Tel 943/641-302)* runs buses to Hondarridia that stop just outside the airport every 15 minutes from
7:45am-10pm. Buses leave and arrive in Plaza Giluzkoa in the Centro;
the trip costs 210ptas.

Trains The main train station, **Gare du Train** *(Paseo de Francia s/n; Tel
943/283-089),* is across the river in Gros, about a half-mile from the
old town. It serves all the RENFE lines. Here you can get connections
to the Madrid line, the Barcelona line, the La Coruna line, and the
Salamanca line. There are also overnight trains between Madrid and
Paris that stop in San Sebastián.

Bus Lines Out of the City The main bus station for the city is in the
south along the river near Plaza Pio XII, a good mile from the swingin'
part of town. It's really not much of a station, but more of an open
parking lot. The ticket offices are on the street near the station. **PESA**
(Avda. De Sancho El Sabio 33) has connections to most major cities
nearby. In many cases buses tend to be cheaper and faster than the
train. Buses 17, 26, 27, and 28 all stop near the bus station.

Bike Rental Comet *(Avda. de Libertad 6; Tel 943/426-637; 10am-
1pm/4-8pm Tue-Fri, 10am-1:30pm/4-7:30pm Sat, 4-8pm Mon;
2,500ptas half-day rental, 3,000ptas full-day)* is a great place to rent a
bike to explore the outer reaches of the city. Long-term rentals—for a
week or month—are an option here, too.

Laundry Although an Aussie Laundromat may look out of place in this
Basque city, **Wash 'N Dry** *(Iparragirre Kalea 6-Gros; Tel 943/293-150;
Open 7 days a week, 8am-10pm; 700ptas per machine)* is very much at
home here. The best part about this place is that the Aussie owner will
clue you in to all the ins and outs of the city while you wait for your
laundry to be ready. She'll even arrange for a guided night out in the
tapas bars for an inside look at the city. Soap and softener are available
from coin-operated machines, and if you want your stuff ironed,
they'll take care of it.

Postal The **main post office** is located on Urdaneta *(Tel 943/463-417),*
directly behind the cathedral. They'll send your postcards off to your
friends so you can remind them what they're missing.

Internet See *wired,* above.

navarra

pamplona

The lure of Pamplona *(Iruña, Iruñea* in Basque) is irresistible. Hemingway made the city famous with his romantic tales of fiestas and bullfighting, and the romance lives on. People here party hard all year just to ease the wait until the next **Festival de los San Fermínes** [see *san fermin and the great running of the bulls,* below], known to most Americans as "The Running of the Bulls," which begins on July 6 and lasts for one unbelievable week. But Pamplona has a serious side, too. Although it's the capital of the province of Navarra *(Nafarroa* in Basque), its roots are just as Basque as its neighbors in the Basque country, and Pamplona's many Basque flags, signs, and graffiti reveal people's strong support of Basque liberation.

Passing this city by would be a loss at any time of year. Just because San Fermín isn't going 110 miles an hour doesn't mean things stand still here—quite the contrary. The streets of the old town are abuzz day and night, and outside the ancient walls you'll find a modern city that offers the inquisitive traveler just about anything imaginable.

Because of its location near the French border, Pamplona has been dubbed "the gateway to Spain." That and its location along the Camino de Santiago have brought many people to Pamplona over the years, some welcome, some not. The Romans, who founded Pamplona in 75 B.C., named the city after Pompey the Great. In the many years since then, it's been a prime target for invaders, from the Visigoths to the Muslims. During the 8th century, some towns and cities around Pamplona began to band together to defend themselves. Soon one of the first kingdoms of Spain, the kingdom of Navarra, was formed, with Pamplona as the seat of power.

Things today have probably changed a little since then. Forget invaders—the people of Pamplona would rather die partying than fighting! The streets of the old town burst with bars catering to old and young alike, and on the weekends everyone is out enjoying themselves. As the night progresses, there are plenty of clubs outside the old town to keep you rocking well into the afternoon the following day—a feat that's accomplished routinely by the locals.

In fact, the people in Pamplona fancy themselves the hardest partiers in all of Spain. Considering Spain's reputation for going all out, that's a pretty hefty claim. Their great festival obviously does score major props, and after spending a weekend in Pamplona you may just start to agree. Their basic recipe: Drink until you can't drink anymore, smoke some hash, open another pack of cigarettes, and then drink some more.

The most amazing thing about Pamplona is that it is still a very religious city, and come Sunday (no matter how late people stayed up on Saturday night), the church bells echo down the cobblestone streets and the faithful put on their dress clothes and make their way to church.

Most everyone here is very good-natured and friendly, and you'd really have to try hard not to meet people. In the bars you'll be approached by lots of people interested in talking. Most of the younger crowd speaks some English, and they're not afraid to try to speak to you with what little they know. If you know any Spanish, even just stuff you learned in high school, try it out. They'll appreciate it, and if they correct you, they're not being snotty, they just want to help. They love foreigners because they love their city and think it's the best, and love showing it off.

Pamplona draws its youth and vigor from the University of Pamplona, open year-round except during July and August. They also hold a few summer classes (Basque language lessons, anyone?) during those months. While you won't see many students hanging around in the daytime, at night they fill up the bars and taverns with a lively joie de vivre. The students also play a role in the cultural life of the city, staging concerts, art exhibitions, and other cultural activities during the school year.

The best way to get the inside scoop on what's going on around town is to go straight to the source—ask the locals. They love to feel like they can help you out, and they'll reveal whatever they know. In some cases, though, this can take a long time. So for a quick fix, pick up *Disfrutar Pamplona.* It's a monthly guide that can be found at most hostels or the tourist office. It's written mostly in Spanish, but some parts are in English and it's easy to follow. It dishes all the goods on cultural events like theater, dance, art exhibits, movies, live music, restaurants, sports, and, of course, nightlife. Best of all, it's free.

neighborhoods

Pamplona's center is compact and easy to navigate. The **old town** is tucked into the bank of the **Rio Arga,** which slowly flows by to the north and east. City planners were thinking ahead as the town grew, and they preserved open land just west of the old town for parks, known today as

pamplona

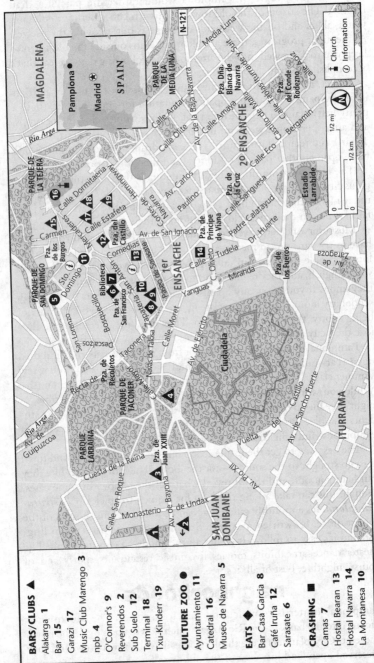

MAGDALENA

SPAIN

Pamplona ●
Madrid ★

BARS/CLUBS ▲
Alakarga **1**
Bar **15**
Garazi **17**
Music Club Marengo **3**
npb **4**
O'Connor's **9**
Reverendos **2**
Sub Suelo **12**
Terminal **18**
Txu-Kinderr **19**

CULTURE ZOO ●
Ayuntamiento **11**
Catedral **16**
Museo de Navarra **5**

EATS ◆
Bar Casa García **8**
Café Iruña **12**
Sarasate **6**

CRASHING ■
Camas **7**
Hostal Bearan **13**
Hostal Navarra **14**
La Montanesa **10**

✝ Church
ⓘ Information

the **green belt.** Here you'll find large expanses of peaceful, open lands where you can go to relax, away from tall buildings and crowded streets. The commercial center is found in the grid of streets that starts to the south of the old town.

The heart and history of the city oozes out of every cobblestone street and cracked building facade in the old town. It's full of life, and yeah, it may be old, but this is where locals and travelers come to find food, drink, and fun. **Plaza del Castillo** stands roughly in the center of the action. The streets off the plaza literally burst with restaurants, bars, and clubs. If you ever slow down during your time here, this area is also the best place to find a bed to collapse in.

Walking south out of the old town along **Avenida Carlos III,** you'll enter the modern center of **Ensanche.** A really weird mix of corporate suits, beat artists, confused foreigners, and dazed university students gives the streets of this district an interesting twist. This is where you'll find some of the city's galleries, a handful of good restaurants, and enough shopping to require a little wallet CPR afterward. The grandiose traffic circles may be hell to navigate by car, but the fountains that sit in the middle of them are pretty spectacular.

Continuing farther south, things gradually mellow out until **Mila-grosa.** This neighborhood, sandwiched between the Public University and the University of Navarra, is not the most happening part of town during the day, but it wakes up at night, when a couple of discos keep things lively. The real club scene, however, is found to the west of the old city, in **San Juan Donibane.** By day it's just another unassuming district without much of interest. At night its streets house the city's biggest clubs, such as **Reverendos** [see *club scene,* below], and man, do the people here party. The one bitch is that it's kind of a hike from the old town, where things get started at night, so get a good buzz on before you start your trek. Most of the city buses stop running after 10pm, but as one local put it, "If you can dance, you can walk."

During the day, Pamplona has an efficient system of **city buses** [see *need to know,* below]. They'll take you just about anywhere you want to go in the city—or out of it—for nothing more than pocket change. If you're just sticking to the old town where most of the major sites are, all you'll need is a comfortable pair of shoes. There are cabs around, although they're not out in force as in bigger cities. Generally they're expensive and unless it's night—and even then it's safe to walk—stick to the buses if you need to travel any distance.

hanging out

The best place to relax after spending time wandering through the old town is **Plaza del Castillo.** Even though it's in the center of town, this big plaza is relatively calm. There are plenty of benches where you can just sit back and watch the city move around you. It gets busiest in the late afternoon and early evening, when people gather to socialize, and it's also popular on weekends for a quick break between the bars.

san fermin and the great running of the bulls

Anyone who has ever heard of Pamplona equates it with one thing more than anything else, and that is the Running of the Bulls, *El encierro*. Romanticized by Hemingway and fueled by thousands of enthusiasts, it has become one of the most popular stops on the backpacker's tour of Europe and one of the wildest annual events in the world. There is a whole lot more, however, to San Fermín than just the bulls. It's a weeklong celebration filled with drinking, singing, drinking, dancing, drinking, and sleeping where you fall.

The countdown to San Fermín begins at the stroke of the New Year; every month brings the festival closer and closer, and it can't come soon enough for the eager residents. There are some things about this weeklong insanity-fest that are a little harder for outsiders to swallow than all the wine. First off, this is a religious celebration—held in honor of San Fermín, the patron saint of the city. Swear to God, taking part in all the sinful acts here could actually come in handy later on in purgatory. Second, can you believe that there is actually a strict organization to all this mayhem?

It all starts with a bang at 11am on July 6 in front of city hall, when one of the city's councilmen lights a rocket that explodes high overhead. He then proclaims to the crowd—in Spanish and in Basque—"People of Pamplona, long live San Fermín." After that, hold onto your hat and watch your behind, 'cause this is one ride you can't just get off.

Every day from July 7 through July 14, things begin bright and early. At 6am, roving bands (I use the word loosely) wind through the city streets, banging on anything they can get their hands on to rouse everyone for another day. People begin to stir and prepare for the running of the bulls. What started out as a way of getting bulls to the bullring, by running them from their pens through the streets, has become an event that for some people represents Spain. No one knows when people first began running in front of the bulls—as opposed to the much more traditional (and sane) place *behind* them. Today, no one really cares.

If you are running, here are some guidelines to follow:

Don't run alone. Get someone with experience to be with you the first time.

Don't spend the previous night boozing. Go to bed early and get plenty of sleep.

Watch the whole affair from the sidelines at least once. Get a feel for exactly what you're getting into.

Above all, be just as scared of the other runners as the bulls. Mobs in a panic are just as dangerous as big horned animals.

Worry about finishing, not getting close enough to make out with a bull.

Be on course by 7:30am. After that, it's closed.

At eight o'clock in the morning, a rocket explodes in the air, announcing the opening of the bulls' pen. This is followed by a second burst, which means all the bulls have left their enclosure and are on the course. *El encierro* [see *by foot,* below] is an 800-meter dash in front of, next to, and sometimes even under the bulls. The course is often overrun with runners, whose sheer numbers sometimes block a bull's movement entirely. Be warned: A bull away from the herd is the most dangerous kind. The fact that they get surrounded by maniacs screaming at the top of their lungs only freaks out the poor, scared animals even more. This is when people are most likely to get gored.

A third rocket is fired once all the bulls have reached the bullring, and a fourth and final rocket signifies the end of the day's running, when all the bulls are safely inside their pens.

Each day of the festival is filled with processions, dancing, carnivals, concerts, and, of course, partying (which *never* stops!). Bullfights are held at 6:30pm every day; you can usually find scalpers selling tickets, or you can pick one up the night before the fight (tickets go on sale at 8pm daily). You'll have a choice of two sections, *sol* (sun) or *sombra* (shade). The shade costs more, and the sun is home to the Peñas, the party animals of San Fermín. The *sombra* seats are sold out weeks in advance, so your best bet is to ask for a *sol* seat. These start at 2,500ptas. People who crave shade can usually get a scalped ticket. The festivities continue well into the night, complete with concerts, fireworks, and more processions. People grab any noise-making device they can get their hands on—from trumpets to trashcans—for the *Estruendo de Iruña,* an impromptu parade. They bang away without a care in the world. Wine flows like water and people drop to the wayside along the way. The entire festival finally wraps up on July 14, when all throughout the old town people console each other over the close of another year's festival with the singing of what is basically a sob song, *"Pobre de mi"*—"Poor, poor me, now I must wait another year for San Fermín."

wired

Unfortunately, all the Internet hookups are well outside of the old town. Most are south in Milagrosa, down around the universities. None are all that special—no rocking bars or crazy game places. These are just copy shops with a couple of computers to hook you up with friends and family back home. One such place is **Work Center** *(Tajonar 4; Tel 948/290-133; Buses 1,6, and 9; 8am-10pm daily; 500ptas per hour)*. The friendly staff here will get you surfing on one of the terminals. They also offer fax and copy services if you have any need.

IturNET *(Iturrama 1; Tel 948/252-820; Buses 1 or 2; 10am-2pm/4:30-10pm Mon-Sat; 500ptas per hour)* has a slightly more social environment, but still not enough to draw your attention away from Mom's report on Fido's latest escapades.

During San Fermín, Plaza del Castillo turns into the belly of the beast. Although the festivities spread throughout the city, this plaza is ground zero, with vendors selling food and drink, bands playing, and people attempting to catch a 5-minute nap wherever there's room to lie down.

Café Iruña [see *eats,* below] sits on the edge of the plaza and during warmer weather has tables out front. Unfortunately, it's become something of a local attraction, so this ain't no dollar coffee joint. But one look inside and you'll find paying a little more is worth it. They could film a classic Hemingway novel here: High molded ceilings and elegant decor give the room the feel of a much more romantic era. The cafe stays open pretty late on the weekends, so it's also not a bad spot to catch your breath and re-caffeinate around 2am.

Saunter on over to the green belt on the west side of town if you're looking for some fresh air. All the parks here are spacious, with tree-lined walkways, open, Frisbee-friendly lawns, and welcoming benches. The largest park to the south has the **Ciudadela** (citadel) on its grounds. This pentagonal fortification with star-shaped bulwarks was built in the time of Philip II during the mid-16th century. Today, its walls serve only to keep the noise of the city out. Inside, the grounds are fun to explore. They are full of gardens and hidden sanctuaries, perfect for when you and your...*friend* are feeling a little frisky. The entrance to the Ciudadela is awkwardly located on the busy Avenida Ejército. If you don't enter there, you'll just have to stare at the walls from the rest of the park and wonder what they conceal.

There's no central hangout square for students, although there's a large park, the Parque de la Ciudadela (but biking and skating are prohibited—be warned!). It isn't the ideal place to hang out, however. You'll run into more students in the bars on calle de San Nicolás, or in the cafes along Plaza del Castillo, where they get together in the early evening.

bar scene

Get ready! The old town provides more watering-hole choices than you'll know what to do with. Wander around the old streets and your head will start to spin—and that's before you've even downed a pint. Each block has its own scene. It's kind of broken down by age: On San Gregorio and San Nicolás, adults crowd the streets and raise a ruckus. The bars on Caldereria, San Agustin, and Tejeria attract the 20- to 30-year-old crowd and those wild university students. Jarauta generally gets a younger, very rowdy high school crowd. Everyone comes together in the streets radiating out from Plaza del Castillo, where the different scenes and people totally mix it up in the bars.

Your best bet for a good time are the spots around Plaza del Castillo, where you'll find places like **Café Iruña** [see *eats*, below] and **Sub Suelo** [see *club scene*, below)—and on San Agustin. On the weekends every place on the street is packed, but it's **Txu-Kinderr** *(San Agustin 6-8; No*

five things to talk to a local about

You'll find the people of Pamplona very friendly and open. Striking up a conversation will never be a problem; getting out of it, you're on your own.

1. **San Fermín:** You won't even have to bring this one up. Everyone you meet, from university students to that cute old lady at the market, will ask you one thing when they discover you're from out of town, "Are you staying for San Fermín?" The people here love their festival and love to talk about it.

2. **Hemingway:** This one can be fun. Some of the people here know all about Hemingway and his connection to their town. They know where he hung out and what he ate for breakfast. Then there are those who recognize the name but draw a blank. They're never shy to guess, though: One guy had Hemingway as a rock star.

3. **Basque:** People here are just as Basque as their neighbors in the autonomous Basque country, and they'll let you know it.

4. **La marcha:** Young and old take part every weekend in the city's *marcha*. People here think they're the hardest partiers around.

5. **San Fermín:** Seriously, it's sick. People have San Fermín on the brain here like the rest of the world thinks about sex.

phone; 8pm-midnight daily; Beer 180-200ptas; No credit cards) that really draws the crowds. This bar has an urban feel, with one whole wall completely covered by a great graffiti mural. When the hip-hop comes on you may wish you had a 40 to wave around. It's not all hip-hop, though—reggae and rock get time, selected from a good CD and vinyl collection. The beer and sangria taps flow down to the bar from the ceiling, and there's a rolling-paper dispenser conveniently located over the bar. The casual crowd makes this a lively and fun place to spend some time.

Not far up the street, **Garazi** *(Caldereria 36; No phone; 6pm-3am daily; No credit cards)* is equally inviting. It's got a *huge* CD library that the bartender chooses from, so what you hear depends on who's manning the controls. One hour it's all London, modern underground stuff, the next it's classic rock. The crowd is a mix of artsy, hip, alternative, and prep. Everyone gets along fine, and you'll definitely catch a little *el chocolate* (hash) scent floating in the air.

Almost directly across from Garazi, **Terminal** *(Caldereria 19-21; No phone; 6pm-midnight Sun-Wed, 6pm-4am Thur-Sat; Beers 200ptas, mixed drinks 600ptas; No credit cards)* offers an alternative to the typical dance scene. A mostly twentysomething crowd of hippies, punks, and hipsters packs in under the black lights of this dark and smoky joint, where hash *purros* are said to be liberally rolled and enjoyed. The bar runs back two-thirds of the place before opening up to a small dance floor where dreads dance with spikes. You'll hear modern rock, hip-hop, and the occasional metal tune. The action peaks from around midnight to 3am.

If you're in the mood for something different, there's an unassuming place named simply **Bar** *(Corner of Navarreria and Carmen; No phone; 4pm-whenever daily; No credit cards)*. Home to an older crowd of 30- and 40-year-old fun-loving Spaniards, this bar plays great jazz and swing music, and the folks here are willing to shake their caboose. Just a couple of blocks west of the cathedral, the place is bright, but not that big. The music is loud and the dance space limited, but no one seems to care. Some young blood would do this place good, although I think the old folks could still out-dance the youth.

Over on the other side of the old town, across the Plaza del Castillo and a little north, is Calle Jarauta, where you'll find one of the more crowded and rowdy scenes in town. That's probably because Jarauta sometimes gets overrun with high-schoolers, so things can get a little juvenile. It definitely kicks on weekends, and locals say the scene isn't always so young there. Swing by and see what's up; it'll only take one look to know if it's for you or not. Home to head bangers and angst-ridden teens, **Club Depotivo** *(Jarauta 78; No phone; 4pm-midnight Sun-Thur, 4pm-3am Fri, Sat; No credit cards)* gets mostly an 18- to 24-year-old crowd. Depotivo plays thrash and metal loud enough to make sure you're deaf by 30. Sometimes they mix things up with a little ska. When you can't think straight any longer, let yourself be mesmerized by the really cool wall behind the bar—it looks like a cliff face, complete with little figures scaling it.

LIVE MUSIC SCENE

Pamplona's live music scene doesn't compare with that of some other big cities, but there are a couple of good places to hear a band or see a concert. Turn to the ever-faithful *Disfrutar Pamplona* to find out who and what's playing where. This little guide lists not only who's performing in the bars and clubs, but also gives the scoop on classical concerts and free concerts. How's that for useful?

One of the best places to see a live performance in Pamplona is at your neighborhood Irish pub, **O'Connor's** *(Paseo de Sarasate 13; Tel 948/222-543; 10am-1 or 2am Sun-Thur, till 3 or 4am Fri, Sat, closed Sun mornings; No cover; No credit cards).* It hosts live blues and rock bands downstairs every Thursday and Friday night. The schedule isn't set in stone, but the bands usually go on sometime between 10pm and midnight, and there's never a cover. O'Connor's actually books some decent rock bands, a feat not easily accomplished in this country. The bar staff will tell you they're trying to bring in some genuine Irish music acts, but they've have had a hell of a time tracking any down in these parts; as long as they keep putting up quality bands, we don't think anyone is going to care. The bar itself is a friendly place, and the bartenders are authentically Irish, so if you're in the mood for some English conversation and an inside look at the city, it's a good place to start. Conveniently located about four blocks northeast of the citadel.

If you want something with a little more class, the **Teatro Gayarre** [see *performing arts,* below], not far from the Plaza de Toros, has classical music events—some of which are free. There's no set schedule, so either consult *Disfrutar Pamplona* or head directly to the theater.

CLUB SCENE

In the city that doesn't sleep for days on end during San Fermín, what's the big deal about partying from midnight until 4pm the next afternoon at any other time of year? If that's what you want, it can be done here. The clubs in Pamplona are all outside the old town—in San Juan, Milagrosa, and Iturrama, although San Juan has the biggest scene. The *marcha* works like most others in the country. Get your molars floating in the bars and *puffs* (mini-discos), then find your way to the clubs around 3 or 4am. Be prepared for a little walk from the old town, since the clubs are not exactly centrally located. Don't be afraid to join the steady stream of people heading in the same direction. It will give you a chance to talk to people before you go inside to be deafened by the *thump-thump-thump.*

One *puff* in the old town breaks the boundaries—if it didn't close early, it could be considered a full-on club. **Sub Suelo** *(Plaza del Castillo 44; No phone; 10pm-4am Thur-Sat; No cover; No credit cards)* is actually in the basement of **Café Iruña** [see *eats,* below] and has just as much character as the cafe above. Row upon row of stone archways break up this cavernous space. You'll feel like you're partying in medieval times here—no wild lights and disco balls needed. The crowd is mainly 18- to

Rules of the Game

During San Fermín the only rule is there are no rules. You can pretty much do whatever you want, whenever you want, and nobody is going to do a thing to stop you. This is within reason, of course. The rest of the year, the rules don't get much stricter. Hash is pretty popular year-round here. If you're in town for a weekend you'll catch the scent in almost all the bars along Caldereria, and some bars even have rolling-paper dispensers handy. Feel free to bring your drink with you as you jump from one place to the next, as drinking on the streets is the norm. Calle Jarauta is proof of just how avidly that 18-year-old drinking age is enforced: Wasted and rowdy high schoolers line this street on the weekends. (Yeah, we bet their older brother bought them the beer.)

30-year-old wannabe hipsters and norms. The music, mostly Spanish and Euro dance music, inspires some loose stepping and fanny shaking. The best time to hit this place is around 1-4am.

When you're ready to leave the old town and trek out to parts unknown, follow the crowds out to San Juan. One of the first places you'll come to as you walk along Avenida de Bayona is **Music Club Marengo** *(Bayona s/n; No phone; 10pm-6am Thur-Sat; Cover 500ptas; No credit cards)*, which collects the flow of people stumbling out of the old town. It's an okay scene, but it's better to push on to hipper places.

Four blocks farther down the road brings you to **Reverendos** *(Monasterio de Velate 5; Tel 948/261-593; Midnight-7am Thur-Sat; Cover 1,000ptas)*. You'll know it as soon as you see the round pink building that houses Pamplona's most popular disco; it's *the* place to be. Crowds of beautiful 20- and 30-year-olds gather to dance, bump, and grind together on the lively dance floor. The music starts out kind of weak with a lot of pop and dance, but as the party heats up, it improves. Later in the night, when this place gets bumping, DJs spin hard house and trance. Dress well; no sneakers are allowed here. You'll get one drink with the cover charge.

Hold back those yawns, this party is still getting started. For the after-after-hours party, you have to find **npb** *(corner of Avda. Ejército and Avda. de Pio XII)*, which is hidden around the back of the Edificio Singular building. This is where the people who are still partying at noon the next day come to end a wild night (that doesn't mean you can't spend a Sunday afternoon here even if you did crash the night before). There's no cover, and this small place gets packed with people, mainly twentysome-things who shed their club gear long ago and are down to T-shirts and tank tops. The DJ keeps people fueled by spinning some of the city's best trance and house music, giving everyone the energy to dance. Hash is smoked very liberally all over. Somehow the party goes on until sometime around 5pm, when the last revelers finally drop.

ARTS SCENE

▶▶VISUAL ARTS

For those with any interest in the local arts scene, the streets of Ensanche and the old town will more than fulfill your needs. Here galleries showcase everything from undiscovered locals to national stars. The great diversity makes ducking in and out of galleries a fun way to spend an afternoon. Common to many of these galleries is artwork depicting San Fermín—in photos, painting, sketches, etchings, and more. *Disfrutar Pamplona* publishes a full listing of exhibits (you really gotta get your hands on it!).

In the old town, most of the galleries are small one- or two-room affairs that exhibit an artist for about a month before putting on a new show. **Sala Descalzos 72** *(Descalzos 72; Tel 948/222-008; 11am-1pm/5-8pm Mon-Sat)* features modern paintings, photography, and the random sculpture exhibit from regional artists. The gallery moves things through rapidly—some of the shows here turn over as quickly as every two weeks.

Not far away is **Sala Zapateria 40** *(Zapateria 40; No phone; 6-8:30pm Mon-Fri, noon-2pm Sat and festivals)*, which exhibits a mix of local and national artists and avant-garde photographers. Displays here generally run for three or four weeks.

Also in the old town is **Area Cultural** *(San Gregorio 22, third floor; Tel 948/222-008; 5-8pm Mon-Fri)*, a gallery with a slightly more international edge, featuring work by avant-garde artists from the area and abroad.

Don't overlook Ensanche when tracking down art. After all, the **Escuela de Arte de Pamplona** *(Amaya s/n; No phone; 8am-2pm Mon-Fri)* has its gallery space here. Students and alumni display art here of all media and styles, from modern to traditional. The staff is made up mostly of students, who can be very interesting and informative to talk with.

A little more traditional is **Casa de la Juventud** *(Sanguesa 30; Tel 948/233-512; 11am-2pm/5-10pm Mon-Fri, 10am-2pm/5-9pm Sat, 10am-2pm Sun)*. They stick mainly to contemporary painting and photography exhibits.

▶▶PERFORMING ARTS

The center for performing arts in Pamplona is the **Teatro Gayarre** *(Avda. Carlos III; Tel 948/212-350; Box office hours noon-2pm/5-8pm Tue-Sun; Avg. ticket 2,000ptas; AE, MC, V)*, one block south of the Plaza del Castillo. Here you will find a variety of dance, drama, opera, and musical performances, certainly more than enough to keep you entertained for a couple days while you're in town. Prices, times, and all the rest range widely from event to event; plays generally start at 8pm. Swing by the theater to get the full details; you'll find a schedule posted out front.

Much more informal than the performances at the Teatro Gayarre, but just as entertaining, are the drama and comedy shows at **Escuela Navarra de Teatro** *(San Agustin 5; Performances Fri, Sat, Sun, show times vary; Tickets 800-1,000ptas)*. The performances are all in Spanish, so if you're going to go, you've got to flow with it. Live performance has a way of breaking down the language barrier, anyway. Performance times vary but are usually around 8-10pm. The box office opens one hour before the shows start.

There are plenty of good places to catch a flick if you're not looking for anything too esoteric. There are no good art cinemas in the center, so you'll have to settle for big-name productions. **Saide Carlos III** *(Avda. San Ignacio at Cortes de Navarra; Tel 948/222-228; Show times at 5:30pm, 8pm, and 10:30pm daily; Tickets 700ptas, Mon matinee 500ptas; No credit cards)* has five screens showing mostly Hollywood flicks, some dubbed, others with Spanish subtitles. (If the letters V.O. appear on the movie poster, it means it's dubbed.) There may also be one big Spanish movie thrown into the mix. Visit the theater for a full list of what's playing and when.

gay scene

The gay scene in Pamplona is a lot like the rest of this crazy city: full of contradictions. Because Pamplona is such a religious city, there's a pretty ingrained streak of homophobia here. However, when you ask locals about gay bars and clubs, they don't seem all that fazed and will tell you that the northeast section of the old town around the cathedral is the gay area. Their religion may tell them that homosexuality is a sin, but they don't totally condemn it. People in Pamplona really have no problem mixing with all sorts; for example, you'll see a hippie and a punk rocker sharing a joint in a bar. But while the area around the cathedral may be considered the gay part of town, we only found one exclusively gay club. All the same-sex couples we saw, and there were a few, were out enjoying themselves alongside everyone else. But unfortunately, the outside of one gay club we went by had recently been defaced by not-so-friendly graffiti. So the city's contradictions really do run the gamut—like everywhere in the world.

We'd recommend just heading out and following the party, since all the clubs are gay friendly. **Alakarga** *(Monastario de Vilate s/n; No phone; 9pm-6am Thur-Sat; No credit cards)* is one of the few gay clubs in the city. It's set back from the street in a small shopping plaza, across from where Avenida de Bayona intersects with Monastario de Vilate. Alakarga is fairly small as far as discos go, but we all know size doesn't matter. A mostly male crowd in their thirties and forties dances the night away here: not the wildest scene. If you want something a little better, just head down the street to **Reverendos** [see *club scene*, above].

culture zoo

For a city with a history that extends back more than 2,000 years, you'd expect a bunch of ancient monuments lying around town. Unfortunately, most have long since crumbled, burned, or been destroyed. This means

by foot

Whether you're in town for San Fermín or not, it's worthwhile to stroll down the route that the running of the bulls takes. Outside of mid-July, you'll have to use your imagination as you walk these quiet streets. Try to visualize what it must be like to be surrounded by a mob of loonies with a herd of gigantic horned bulls charging toward your rear.

Start out on the northern edge of the old town by **Parque de Santo Domingo.** Ahhh...what a peaceful little park. Now imagine it packed with thousands of runners peering at a pen full of bulls that are about to be let loose. From there follow **Santo Domingo** uphill (uphill!?! I got bulls on my heels!), back into the city. Continue all the way to **Plaza Consistorial,** where you should take a moment to admire the facade of the City Hall. Pretty, isn't it? This is also the first real turn of *el encierro* and the spot where some bulls are likely to be separated from the herd, turning them into scared, dangerous monsters. From the plaza follow **Mercaderes** west two blocks and hang a sharp right onto **Estafeta.** A lot of bulls don't make that right as well as you did and are sent crashing into the *barrio* ahead. I bet that would make an interesting vantage point; more separated bulls now, too.

You're now halfway through the course, with a long straight-away ahead. Estafeta is a peaceful street, lined with harmless tourist shops, bars, and restaurants. It slopes a little uphill, so take your time as you walk. Notice how uneven these cobblestone streets are. (Aren't you glad you're not in a rush?) You can see the **Plaza de Toros** as you near the end of the street, only a little bit farther, but Ferdinand is catching up. As you cross **Bajada de Labrit** you'll come to the outside of the bullring and a bronze bust of Hemingway. Had this been a real *encierro,* you would have entered the most dangerous part of the course, where the bulls and runners are squeezed together and funneled into the bullring. For now, just hang here to chill with Hemingway and thank him for bringing a little recognition to a great local tradition.

pretty slim pickings on the cultural attraction front. But the city itself is a kind of museum: Just by walking the streets of the old town, you'll encounter buildings of all designs and styles, some with wild facades, and you can get lost for hours strolling these ancient streets. But once you get tired of walking aimlessly, there are a couple of places in town that you can't miss.

The number of churches in Pamplona stands testament to the religious nature of its people. If you're here on a Sunday, you can't help but notice that there are church bells ringing all day long (of course, that could just be your head after a Saturday night here). The Sunday ritual is an ancient one: People get dressed up to go to church and stroll through town.

Catedral *(Navarreria s/n; Tel 948/219-827; 10am-1:30pm/4-7pm Mon-Fri, 10am-1:30pm Sat; 500ptas):* At the heart of Pamplona's religious scene is the city's 14th-century Gothic cathedral. At the time it was built, the cathedral was the second largest in Spain. Some of its luster has since worn off, but it's still worth a visit. As you stand there and take in the place, just consider that this is the final resting place of the mid-18th-century rulers Carlos III from Navarra and his wife, Queen Dona Leonor—good folks who helped to develop Spain's culture and economy. So pay them some respect. The cloister next to the cathedral is peaceful and beautiful. Admission to the cathedral includes entrance to the adjoining museum which, while small, has some religious art pieces from as far back as the 12th century. While you're out at the cathedral, take a short detour by walking straight out of the building (head for trees and green grass) to see the best-preserved part of the old city walls. Follow the narrow Calle del Redin to the ramparts. The view overlooking the plains must have been pretty incredible before the city expanded.

Museo de Navarra *(Cuesta de Santo Domingo s/n; Tel 948/426-492; 10am-2pm/5-7pm Tue-Sat, 11am-2pm Sun; 300ptas, free for students if you say it's for studies):* As long as you're in Pamplona, a stop here is obligatory. A 4-minute trek west of the cathedral, this great museum has well-laid-out exhibits of art and archaeology that include a little bit of everything. In the category of one man's garbage is another man's treasure, there's a fascinating exhibit of things the Romans left behind: column tops, tiled walls, engraved stones, jewelry, and pottery. There are also examples of pre-Roman figure reliefs. A huge, two-story Gothic painting taken from the cathedral makes for a powerful display. The museum's fine art collection includes two floors of Gothic, Renaissance, and Baroque artwork, and one floor dedicated to 20th-century art from Navarra. On the ground floor is a temporary-exhibit room where the museum displays some impressive visiting shows; in the past this has included ceramics by Picasso as well as photos from the Spanish Civil War. This is definitely a good museum to spend some time exploring.

Ayuntamiento *(Plaza Consistorial, north of Plaza del Castillo):* The front of Pamplona's town hall shouldn't be overlooked. Facing out over the Plaza Consistorial, this building's beautiful and festive Baroque facade overlooks where San Fermín officially begins.

modification

Piercings are pretty popular with the younger crowd here. Attitudes in the Basque region tend to be more rebellious than in the rest of Spain anyway, so if you want a fourth or fifth hole in your ear or a new set of doorknockers for your knockers, you won't have any problem getting it done. The best place to head for all of your body modification needs is

Jarauta Rabiosa *(Jarauta 76; No phone; Noon-2/5-8:30pm Mon-Fri; No credit cards).* If the bulls didn't mark you, this place will. It's a piercing studio, tattoo studio, and hair salon all in one, and if you want to get one of the wildest haircuts to be had in Spain, this is your place. After a visit here, you'll stand out in any crowd, getting every turned head, glance, and stare your desperate ego could desire. They give haircuts and dye jobs that leave punks wondering what's going on: If you want the top of your head to look like a soccer ball, they can do it. While they specialize in giving the guys the wacky cuts, they'll be more than happy to hook the ladies up as well. The tattoo and piercing studios are clean and sterile, to ease any doubts you might have. The staff may not look it, but they're professionals who know their trade. Just because it smells like hash in here doesn't mean they were just burning one down. Now come on, where did you want that tattoo?

CITY SPORTS

Pamplona has figured out *the* way to make sure their citizens and guests get a death-defying workout. They've discovered the secret to elevating the heart rate and to inspiring peak performances. No, it's not some new wonder drug...it's a herd of big angry bulls.

So what do the locals do the other 51 weeks of the year? Walk, jog, and bike in the green belt. The lovely parks here have plenty of fairly flat paved walkways, so you can run for hours in preparation for your mad dash out of a bull's way. In **Parque de Antoniuti** you'll find a well-designed skate park by Plaza de Juan XXII. It's got a complete half-pipe and plenty of ramps and grinds to keep the boarders and in-line skaters entertained. Amazingly, they mix without any friction. (People just get along in Pamplona.)

If your training can't stop just because you're on vacation, there's a **Polideportivo** *(Sanguesa s/n; No phone; 9am-2pm/4-9pm daily, closed Sun afternoon; No credit cards)* next to Estadio Larrabide in Milagrosa. Extensive modern facilities include a pool, weight room, and gymnasium. It's open to the public, but you must buy a daily pass. The price varies depending on what you want to use. The people working reception are all really friendly and will help you out.

STUFF

If you have some pesetas burning a hole in your pocket, the stores of Pamplona are as good a place as anywhere to unload them. The streets of the old town hide many alluring stores, while the southwest side of town is saturated with retail shops. Look in **Ensanche** for chic boutiques and department stores.

▶▶**DUDS**

There is an interesting phenomenon in Pamplona. The summer clothing line isn't released, or if it is, it certainly doesn't get any time in store windows. What dominates the displays here as the weather warms up are the San Fermín fashions. *Everything* is red and white, and *every* storefront mannequin seems to be wearing some variation of the festival's traditional white pants and shirt and flowing red belt. Then there are the wilder designs that follow the traditional lead, but take some weird turns; the designers must have experienced flashbacks or something during the creative process. If you want to do San Fermín like a local, you've got to get the traditional get-up. It won't be tough since every store sells them before the festival, and you can pick up the whole uniform for a couple thousand pesetas. Just please don't embarrass us by wearing it before or after the festival!

▶▶TUNES

Your best bet for buying music in the old town is **Planet Rock** *(San Francisco 8; No phone; 9:30am-1:30pm/4:30-7:30pm Mon-Sat)*, right next to the tourist office. It stocks all the current releases as well as the old blasts from your past. The staff here also knows everything about live music performances throughout the city.

▶▶GIFTS

A little too grossed-out to send a bull's tail to your loved ones back home? (Hey, it's good enough for the matador's sweetie.) **Echeve** *(Estafeta 47; Tel 948/222-834; 10:30am-2pm/4:30-8pm Mon-Sat; MC, V)* is the best place to stock up on gifts that aren't quite so violently gotten. It carries a pretty good selection of local crafts such as clothes, carvings, and ceramics. Be sure to pick up a *bota* (leather canteen) so you can have easy access to your vino during San Fermín. You'll find Echeve between the Plaza de Toro and the Plaza del Castillo.

EaTS

Eating is a major pastime in Pamplona. You could eat at a different restaurant every meal of every day for a year and still not come close to covering them all. There is little need to leave the confines of the old town when it comes to food. Indeed, it's actually the destination point for most people. Restaurants, cafes, and tapas bars abound. The greatest concentration, though, lies along San Gregorio and San Nicolás. So when you feel a rumble in your tummy, you'll never have to look far for a good meal.

Lunch is the big meal of the day. This is when the most economical *menú del días* are offered. Come dinnertime, the prices shoot up. More popular for an evening bite are, of course, tapas. People go out for tapas starting at around 9pm and hop from place to place, enjoying a drink while tossing back a few little bites.

During San Fermín and the following couple of weeks, many restaurants in town shut down. Either their owners want to party along with everyone else, or they want to get the hell out of town before the coming of the apocalypse. But don't panic, you won't starve. There are plenty of food stands set up to serve the hordes (of people, that is—the bulls are on their own), especially around Plaza del Castillo.

▶▶CHEAP

Cheap restaurants aren't exactly lurking around every corner here. There are a couple of spots by the Plaza del Castillo that serve *platos combinados* for around 1,000ptas. Tapas bars offer another way to grab a bite at a not too unreasonable price, although there's a catch involved: As you drink your way from place to place, the bill can quickly put a dent in your wallet. Most places charge around 175ptas per tapa, although some of the fancier ones can go for as much as 350ptas. You can always ask how much things are.

San Nicolás is an easy street "to tapa" on. Most of the restaurants lining the street have a bar up front serving tapas, including the popular **Baserri** *(San Nicolás 32; Tel 948/222-021; 1-4pm/8-midnight daily)*, where you can order any number of tapas to go with your beer or wine. There's also a *comedor* in back for those who need more than a few little morsels to fill them up.

Pamplona's veggie restaurant isn't just a refreshing alternative in this carnivorous environment; it also offers its fare at a very earthy price. **Sarasate** *(San Nicolás 21, upstairs; 1:15-4pm Mon-Sat, 9-11pm Fri, Sat; 700-1100ptas per entree)* serves up a variety of vegetarian, and some vegan-friendly, dishes. Its dining room has a nice atmosphere and the service is quite attentive.

▶▶DO-ABLE

The legendary **Café Iruña** *(Plaza del Castillo 44; Tel 948/222-064; 8-1am daily, 8am-3am Fri, Sat; 1,700ptas menú del día)* is a city fixture. Rumor has it that Hemingway haunted this place during his time here. It's certainly easy to imagine Papa sitting in this large, elegant room, whose cathedral ceilings are lavishly engraved with ornate moldings. Considering the elegance of this cafe, it comes as a surprise that the *menú del día* costs only 1,700ptas. Most popular as a cafe and bar throughout the day, the restaurant serves food during lunch and dinner hours. Even if you don't eat a meal here, you should drop by for a cup of coffee or a drink and tapas, just to check the place out. Try not to be a slob, because this place tends to draw an older, more fashionable crowd.

Another option for a good sit-down meal is **Bar Casa Garcia** *(San Gregorio 12; Tel 948/223-893; 1,000-2,000ptas entrees, 1,500ptas menú del día)*. This place has it all: tapas and bar on the ground floor, a nice restaurant on the second floor, and rooms for rent above. Conceivably, you could live here and never leave the building. The restaurant does a fine job of preparing standard Spanish dishes. Take advantage of the inexpensive *menú*—it will completely sate your appetite.

▶▶SPLURGE

Locals in the know swear that **Josetxo** *(Plaza Principe de Vianna 1; Tel 948/222-097; 1-4pm/9-11pm Mon-Sat; 2,200-4,600ptas entrees; V, AE)* is the best restaurant in town. It's a short walk from the old town into Ensanche. Josetxo specializes in Basque cuisine and uses only the freshest ingredients, so the menu is in constant flux. Call ahead on weekends as it has a well-established reputation, and for the love of God, wear something other than jeans.

crashing

With the exception of San Fermín, when the rules dramatically change, finding a place to crash won't be a chore here. You'll want to stay in the old town, and there are plenty of choices. Dirt-cheap places, where all you get is a lumpy mattress in a drafty room for a rock-bottom price, are easy to come by, and so are luxury hotels. And there are plenty of others in between. Generally speaking, the rates at the nicer places go up a little during the late summer and early fall.

During San Fermín, not a room, no matter how ugly, is to be found in town. Locals rent out floor space to those foolish enough to believe they are getting real sleeping quarters. Unless you've reserved a room a year in advance, don't count on a comfortable night's sleep. Rates during San Fermín skyrocket, too; most places as much as triple their rates from July 4-14. Although we won't officially recommend it, if you really want to be a part of the action, your best bet is to join the thousands of others sleeping in the parks. Comfortable it ain't, but your bones will be so weary you won't notice. Be *very* careful, though: Crime skyrockets during San Fermín, so lock your bags at the train station and keep your valuables close by.

▶▶CHEAP

Some of the cheaper rooms to be had are along San Nicolás and San Gregorio. It seems that almost every bar on these two streets has a sign advertising beds for rent. One of the biggest bargains in town is **Fonda Bar 'La Montanesa'** *(San Gregorio 2; Tel 948/224-380; 1,600ptas single, 3,000ptas double, 1,500ptas per person triple; No credit cards)*. This place offers basic, basic rooms with lumpy mattresses. Oh, and did we mention they were basic? Most of the rooms are actually located across the street at number 57, on the fourth and fifth floors. Some have nice balconies overlooking the city's rooftops. The shared bathrooms are not the world's cleanest.

A little nicer is **Camas** *(Nueva 24; Tel 948/227-825; 2,000ptas single, 4,000ptas double; No credit cards)*, about a block from the tourist office. It doesn't advertise itself out front—just a simple sign marked "Camas" to let you know you've reached the place. The rooms lack character, but are functional. There's a washer and dryer in the shared bathroom—but they're off limits to guests.

Another cheap option is **San Nicolas** *(Calle San Nicolás 13; Tel 948/221-319; 2,000ptas per person single or double, shared baths; V, MC, AE)*.

▶▶DO-ABLE

A world of difference marks the do-able options from their cheaper counterparts. Suddenly the mattresses lie flat and there are no drafts in the rooms. You even get your own bathroom and TV! The price jump is severe, though. **Hostal Bearan** *(San Nicolás 25; Tel 948/223-428; 4,500-5,500ptas single, 13,000ptas San Fermín, 5,500-6,500ptas double, 15,000ptas San Fermín; V, AE)*, in the center of the action, is one of the nicer choices. All of its rooms are modern, with hardwood floors and walls painted a soothing salmon shade. They all include a private bath, TV, and phone. See if you can get a room overlooking the street; they have nice little balconies.

Right across the street from the bus station is **Hostal Navarra** *(Tudela 9; Tel 948/225-164; 5,140ptas single, 9,900ptas San Fermín,*

7,000ptas double, 14,500ptas San Fermín; V, MC, AE). The very friendly staff here speaks some English and will make you feel right at home. So will their fresh modern rooms, which come with all the amenities but not a lot of space. The rooms do all have a private bath, TV (with English channels), phone, mini bar, and hair dryer. For a few extra pesetas the hostel staff will also do a load of laundry for you.

Another do-able option is **Habitaciones Mendi** *(Calle De Las Navas De Tolosa 9; Tel 948/225-297; 4,000ptas single, 6,000ptas double; all rooms with private bath; V).*

▶▶SPLURGE

Right on Plaza del Castillo is **La Perla** *(Plaza del Castillo 1; Tel 948/227-706; 10,600-11,500ptas double with full bath, 7,300-7,900ptas without, 31,000ptas San Fermín; V, MC, AE).* The staff here is just waiting to pamper you after putting you up in one of their plush rooms. Most of the rooms come with a full bath, and the few that don't share several nice common bathrooms. All rooms have TVs and phones.

need to know

Currency Exchange There are banks all over the city that will exchange your money. There is a **BBV** bank *(Plaza del Castillo, 8:30am-2:30pm Mon-Fri)* on the northwest corner of the Plaza del Castillo that also has a 24-hour ATM.

Tourist Information The main **tourist office** *(Eslava 1; Tel 948/206-540; 10am-2pm/4-7pm Mon-Fri, 10am-2pm Sat Sept-June 10am-2pm/4-7pm Mon-Sat, 10am-2pm Sun July-Aug; oit.Pamplona@cfnavarra.es)* is on Plaza San Francisco. It has information on everything in town, from places to stay to upcoming events. They'll also book rooms for you here. During San Fermín, they can even tell you where to go to take a shower (Lord knows you need one). English spoken.

Public Transportation Pamplona has a good system of **city buses** *(Tel 948/129-300; 7am-10pm main lines, 10pm-midnight Mon-Fri night lines, 11pm-4am Fri, Sat; 95ptas).* You can pick up a bus map in the tourist office. Twenty lines run throughout the city by day, and nine cover it at night. You won't need a bus if you stick to the old town or Ensanche. In those two areas, a good pair of shoes is your best mode of transportation.

Health and Emergency For all emergencies: *112*. **Hospital de Navarra** *(Irunlarrea s/n; Tel 948/422-100)* can be reached on either the 4-1 or 4-2 bus. It's outside the center in Irunlarrea. During San Fermín the Red Cross sets up stands to provide aid to anyone who needs it. The **National Police** can be reached at 091.

Pharmacies There are *farmacias* all over the city marked by **neon green crosses.** No single one is open 24 hours a day; instead, *farmacias* rotate the all-night responsibility. Each one posts a schedule indicating who will be open on what night. For info on nighttime pharmacies, try the information service line *(Tel 948/222-111).*

Telephones Regional code: *948.*

Airport Aeropurto de Noain *(Tel 948/317-182)* is 6 km (3.5 mil) from the city center and has connections to Madrid and Barcelona. You'll have to get a cab to and from the airport since there's no bus or shuttle service; fare costs about 1,200ptas.

Trains The **Estacion RENFE** *(Plaza de Estacion s/n; Tel 948/130-202)* is across the river, out of the city center. Bus 9 connects it with Paseo Sarasate on the edge of the old town. Pamplona offers plenty of connections with Barcelona, Madrid, San Sebastián, and other cities along the northern coast.

Bus Lines Out of the City The **Estacion de Autobus** *(Oliveto 2; Tel 948/223-854)*, in the Ensanche a block east of the citadel, houses 20 private bus companies that offer connections to almost everywhere around. There are plenty of buses running to Madrid, Barcelona, and San Sebastián. Less frequent buses head to some of the smaller towns in the region.

Laundry The **Lavanderia La Casa de Baños** *(Calle Eslava 9; Tel 948/221-738; 8:30am-8pm Tue-Sun)* is your ticket to clean duds.

Postal The **post office** *(Paseo de Sarasate 9; Tel 948/212-600)* is just outside the old town. They don't offer any specials on mailing wills home before jumping in front of bulls, though.

Internet See *wired*, above.

aragón &
the pyrenees

aragón & the pyrenees

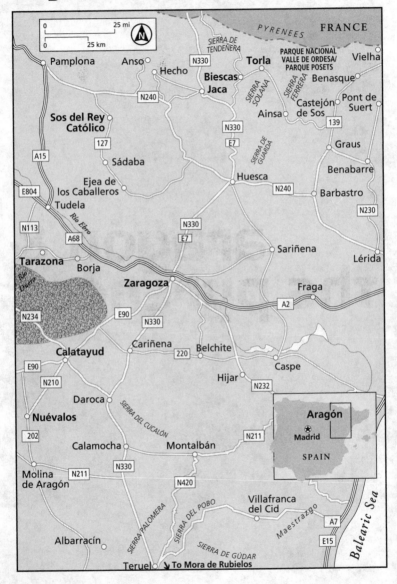

Y ou go to Aragón if you want to get a genuine feel for small-town Spain, or if you want to play in the Pyrenees Mountains. Situated just north of Catalunya, Aragón has nothing that compares to Barcelona when it comes to urbane, European punch, but its local mentality is a lot more "Spanish." There is no local language, and no one in Aragón says that it should secede from the country. Things are a little more laid-back in this province—unless, that is, you're into sports, and then it's a wild ride.

If you're looking for adventure sports in Spain, then you need look no further than Aragón. The towns of **Jaca** and **Benasque** are pretty much dedicated to sending your adrenaline gland into a spasm. There are people who live in these towns whose sole purpose in life is to get your pathetic tourist butt to the top of a mountain—whether to parachute off in the summer, or ski down in the winter. Kayak down sweet mountain streams, ride horseback through valleys that rest beneath limestone peaks, and hike, backpack, and climb your way around jagged cliffs, over quiet mountain creeks, and up to grand summits. It's some of the most beautiful natural scenery in all of Europe, including the awesome **Parque Nacional de Ordesa** and the no less inspiring **Parque Naturel Posets-Maladeta.**

One of the nice things about choosing to do the outdoor thing in Aragón is that you will find plenty of company, and plenty of help. *Multiadventura,* as the Spanish say, is a favorite summer pastime, and loads of French people cross the border to join in on the fun in the summer. Because of the boon, you'll find all kinds of pros who can help you in your various ventures, with a range of guides and places to rent gear, from full-out "hold your hand all the way up" shops to the friendly DIY empowerer.

Even if you're from the big city and your idea of nature consists of the patch of grass growing through a crack in the sidewalk in front of your apartment building, it still might not be a bad idea for you to go to Aragón. One of the fun things about being on vacation is checking out new things, maybe even challenging yourself. If you decide to take the plunge, you'll find all of the big sky, tall mountains, trees, and wildlife you need to pump your blood vessels full of great outdoor juice.

Now, if you are some kind of super-adventurer type, and you've seen the top of Mt. Everest, swum down the Amazon River, wrestled crocodiles in the Australian outback, and outrun lions on an African savannah, then don't bother coming to Aragón. While the beauty is immense, the away-from-humankind component of the area isn't. You are never really a day's hike from civilization, and never, ever more than two. And if you've seen the peaks of the Himalayas, ogling the highest limestone range in Western Europe just doesn't compare. But for those of us who grew up on the fifth floor of some apartment building, or who smoked dope while listening to Pink Floyd in our suburban bedroom after school, the Aragonese Pyrenees might be as much adventure as we can handle.

When you tire of getting wet, sore, and dirty, you can make a brief stopover in **Zaragoza.** It's not the most exciting of towns, but there are plenty of great tapas joints, a majestic basilica, and a true honest-to-God Spanish flavor. You'll hear singing in the streets, and go to bed alone, just like a real Spanish person your age. But there is plenty of fun to be had, and when you're unwinding from a hell of a trip in the Pyrenees, nursing the sore ankle you got from that faulty parachute, and wishing you hadn't slept on that strange itching plant, you don't necessarily need to be workin' it Barcelona-style.

Getting around Aragón ain't that easy, especially if you want to see the cool stuff. You will have to take a few buses, and the rides aren't that much fun. While you do get to see some fantastic scenery, you also are either going up or down a mountain the entire ride. Little baggies are provided for your convenience, but try to keep the noise down while you evacuate your stomach.

As far as the art and architecture of Aragón, it might make an interesting PhD dissertation if you have already exhausted every other region of Spain and the rest of Europe, Asia, Africa....Seriously, there is some good stuff to see in Aragón. The architecture can range from the typical mid- and southern-style Spanish city with Muslim influences, narrow streets, and standard pueblo-style construction, to more open French- and Basque-style wood and stone. Keep your eyes open—the towns are small and if you blink you might miss them.

To get the most out of Aragón, you should choose whether to go to Benasque or Jaca. They might look close on the map, but it's at least a 5-hour bus ride between the two, so unless you want to hike it...just read up on them ahead of time and make a decision. I know that our generation is used to having our MTV and eating it too, but it ain't that way in Spain. And when in Spain, wear tight pants, speak Spanish, and don't get upset if the waiter takes an hour and a half to bring your food.

getting around the region

Getting to Zaragoza from Barcelona or Madrid is trouble-free. Just hop on one of Spain's fast and fancy high-speed trains. Unfortunately, getting around the rest of Aragón is more complicated. There are buses and trains that take you pretty much everywhere you want to go. However, they are generally slow and often take you slightly out of the way due to big mountains and other such Mother Nature–type inconveniences.

Since Zaragoza is the heart of Aragón, you will probably want to start there. You can get RENFE trains all around the region, as well as buses from a number of different private companies.

More specifically, the local RENFE train that leaves from Zaragoza goes to Huesca and Jaca. In Huesca you can catch a bus to Benasque, which has no train station. Be warned, though, that only two buses a day run from Huesca to Benasque, so start this trip early.

If you are in Barcelona and itching for some outdoor adventure but are not interested in Zaragoza, you can take a bus from Barcelona to a town called Barbastro, and from there you catch the connection bus to Benasque.

Also, just so you don't have to learn the hard way, I repeat: Jaca and Benasque look close together on most maps but due to the Pyrenees mountains in between them, you end up taking buses way out of your way, not to mention getting very bus-sick in the process.

TRAVEL TIMES

All times are by road unless indicated by a star

	Zaragoza	Benasque	Jaca	Parque Nacional de Ordesa	Parque Naturel Posets-Maladeta	Madrid
Zaragoza	-	3:25	2:05	2:45	3:40	-
Benasque	3:25	-	2:35	2:45	:15	6:40
Jaca	2:05	2:35	-	1:10	2:50	5:20
Parque Nacional de Ordesa	2:45	2:45	1:10	-	2:15	6:00
Parque Naturel Posets-Maladeta	3:40	:15	2:50	2:15	-	6:55

zaragoza

Zaragoza is a fair-sized city, especially by Spanish standards, with a population of around 600,000 people, more than half the total population of Aragón. The atmosphere is an interesting mix of the metropolitan and the provincial, with big department stores, a bustling commercial district, a decent public transportation system, and a healthy nightlife, as well as back street mom-and-pop bakeries, a handful of small-town open-air markets, and a slow-paced, laid-back attitude in many parts of the city. There aren't the same sophisticated partying options that you might have gotten used to in Barcelona or Madrid.

You won't feel overpowered by foreign tourists in Zaragoza. While people do come from all over the world to check out this city, it is a far less popular destination than other more interesting cities in Spain. You won't want for something to do in Zaragoza, but you may find yourself a little disappointed if you came expecting an urban jungle or an intense immersion in a foreign culture.

In all honesty, there are lots of places higher on our to-do list. If you're only in Spain for a week, or even a month, you probably aren't going to want to spend a lot of time here. The larger, more urban cities will have more draw both party-wise and culture-wise, and there are tons of smaller towns that will give you a better idea of the "authentic" Spanish personality. But if you are planning on visiting a bunch of destinations in Spain, or if you want to see a lot of Aragón and the Pyrenees Mountains and you need a nice stopover city with plenty of modern accommodations and nightlife with a heartbeat, then Zaragoza is your town.

Not that many people speak English in Zaragoza, especially when compared to Madrid or Barcelona; if you took some Spanish in high school or college and want to brush up, you will definitely get the chance here. People here speak an unaccented type of Spanish, and there are no local languages like Basque or Catalan to deal with.

There are a lot of old people out and about in Zaragoza, which is a great change from the U.S., where we tend to closet our old people away in surreal, institutional "communities." You'll also see bunches of young families out for strolls. The twentysomething crowd tends to stick to certain neighborhoods; if you're a student this means the university area, otherwise down at calle de Dr. Cerrada. Young people here aren't as hip as in other parts of Spain, which also means their culture is of the more unfiltered variety. Old cultural norms about sex and drugs die hard here,

five things to talk to a local about

1. **Tom Jones:** He's one of Spain's favorite performers, especially among the young crowd. You will astound and astonish your new Spanish friends by telling them that in the U.S., people don't exactly have the highest regard for this meat-packing marvel.

2. **David Copperfield:** He might be best known for having dated Claudia Schiffer, but his magic doesn't impress many Americans who are not grandparents. On the other hand, Spaniards are dazzled by his powers of illusion, mystery, and magic. Talk to folks about David as much as possible, a good opener being, "How does he do it?"

3. **Zaragoza:** This is always a good topic for people around here. In all of Spain, people are actually more loyal to their city and community than they are to their country. You can also get fun conversations started by asking what the difference is between people in Aragón and Catalunya; we guarantee you'll get an earful.

4. **Soccer:** This one works on almost any European, and people in Zaragoza are no exception to this rule. Just make sure you call it *futbol,* or else no one will know what you are talking about.

5. **Vegetarianism:** The meat-free lifestyle is a big mystery for many Spaniards outside of Barcelona. For diehard country folks, the thought of missing pork at a meal might cause nightmares. Whether you eat flesh or not, as an American you are probably familiar with the arguments, and you'll get some pretty wild looks from the people you talk to about it.

zaragoza

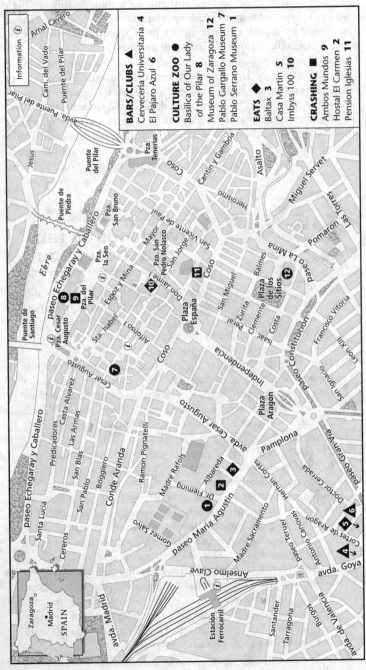

BARS/CLUBS ▲
Cerveceria Universitaria **4**
El Pajaro Azul **6**

CULTURE ZOO ●
Basilica of Our Lady
of the Pilar **8**
Museum of Zaragoza **12**
Pablo Gargallo Museum **7**
Pablo Serrano Museum **1**

EATS ◆
Baltax **3**
Casa Martin **5**
Imbyss 100 **10**

CRASHING ■
Ambos Mundos **9**
Hostal El Carmen **2**
Pension Iglesias **11**

and Zaragoza's youth culture prefers a more classic Spanish format for a good time: drinking, eating tapas, and singing in the streets. This vibe can be felt especially around the Plaza del Pilar, where the outdoor seating is conducive to a little vocal cord stretching and where, if your ears can take it, you can sample some of the musical musings of your new Spanish friends.

neighborhoods

Zaragoza is defined by the **Rio Ebro,** which runs along the old quarter. Everything that you are going to care about is pretty much on the south side of the river, unless some hottie you meet who has his/her own place (a rarity among under-30 Spanish folks) invites you to go "up north."

Most of the good times in this city can be found in the **old quarter** of town. The old quarter is outlined by the former city wall, some of which still remains, but for modern-day reference, it is the area bordered by **Avenida Cesar Augusto** on the western side, and **Calle Coso,** which wraps around the southern and eastern sides. Calle Coso also intersects with **Plaza de España,** a traffic circle filled with crazy Spanish drivers whirling around it at 100 miles an hour. This intersection gets you to **Paseo Independencia,** a long and wide arcade where you can find a bunch of shopping, including the ubiquitous **El Corte Ingles** [see *stuff,* below], the most popular department store in Spain.

There are some cool places worth checking out in the old quarter. In the immediate vicinity of **Calle don Jaime I** you will find a bunch of decent tapas joints. The **Basilica** [see *culture zoo,* below] is on **Plaza del Pilar** [see *hanging out,* below], one of the most happenin' places during the weekends and in the evening. The few tourists who do find themselves in Zaragoza generally end up at this plaza, so if you want to meet fellow travelers, this is the place to be. However, the mix is still predominantly Spanish, as you will hear from their singing as the night progresses. On either side of the Plaza del Pilar, which is really quite big, you'll find a large, modern-looking fountain covered with tons of pigeons. During the day, Moroccan guys hawk their wares and sell big colorful balloons to children. Groups of folks who just went on a guided tour of the Basilica make up a large portion of the daytime crowd in the Plaza del Pilar on the weekends.

Paseo Gran Via, just south of the Paseo Independencia, is one location for bars and restaurants, but more important is **Calle de Dr. Cerrada,** which is off Paseo Gran Via. Dr. Cerrada is a great place for revelers, and the tight design of the streets gives the area a bustling, electric feel, especially during prime party hours.

Another key area to become familiar with is the neighborhood defined by the **University of Zaragoza** and **Plaza San Francisco.** Here you can find plenty of restaurants, bars, and Spanish-style cafeterias to satisfy your hunger or thirst. Mostly populated by students, this area has the feel of a college town. Most of the businesses cater to the needs of students: food, drink, books, etc. You'll find lots of postings for local events, music, and

rules of the game

Zaragoza is a very safe city, and solo women travelers can feel confident in most neighborhoods at night. Of course, common sense should be exercised at all times with sketchy-looking characters, but there is far more danger of being asked to dinner than being harassed. Like elsewhere in Spain, if you are old enough to read this book, you can drink, probably legally. The only curfew is set by Spanish mothers telling their 35-year-old sons and daughters not to forget to go to sleep before the sun rises. There isn't much of a super-late night scene in Zaragoza, and if there is, it's more likely by common agreement of bar owners than by any government action. The drug culture, however, is not as open here as in other cities in Spain.

activities on campus and in the surrounding neighborhood. For face-to-face interactions with Zaragozian youth, this is the best place to be.

Buses are the only form of mass transit in Zaragoza, but taxis are abundant and not too expensive. You can walk around the old quarter and each of the individual neighborhoods, but you're probably better off taking a cab out to the university. Once you get a feel for the super-cheap buses, they are fine, although the map is kind of convoluted.

hanging out

The most obvious hangout spot is the **Plaza del Pilar.** Our choice for people watching, where you can milk a *café con leche* for hours while chatting and watching folks, is the **Café Augusta** (*Plaza del Pilar 8; Tel 976/295-964; 300ptas for a drink; AE, MC, V),* but don't eat the food because it's no good. At the Plaza del Pilar, you will find the most international crowd in all of Zaragoza. You'll also see a wide variety of ages, from young couples and families to older folks. As with some of the less urban parts of Spain, no one does anything alone, so expect to see lots of groups.

A popular spot for young people to meet before a night out or to chill in between classes during the week is the **Plaza San Francisco,** located right at the gates of the University, and occupied almost exclusively by students. You'll find people hanging out on the benches and chatting at the outdoor cafes and bars. If you are interested in meeting Spanish students who are interested in meeting you, go to the **Filologia** building on campus during the day and walk inside. On the big bulletin board there are postings from Spanish students who want to practice their English, and you can get their names and phone numbers. Give 'em a call, and they'll show you their favorite spots and chat you up. This is a great, great way to have a real experience with an actual Spanish person who wasn't paid to be nice to you. With around 40,000 students at the university, the odds are strong that someone will like your pathetic pale ass. University classes finish at the end of July and don't begin again until early October. There are very few late-summer courses, often drawing foreign students, but this is so limited as to have little impact on the city's overall scene. The student hangouts more or less empty out in August and September as young people escape to either the coast or the mountains to avoid the fierce heat.

bar scene

The only things going on in this town in terms of nightlife are tapas joints and bars—traditional, Spanish-style fun. When the people of Aragón say that this city has *"mucha marcha,"* which loosely translates to "big partying," they mean that the people of Zaragoza like to snack and drink. More than in Barcelona or Madrid, your choice of late-night ventures is limited: You either drink, and maybe join in a song or two, or you go home. The international music, hipster, club, fashion, punk, underground, DIY scene hasn't quite penetrated the youth culture of Zaragoza. You can still have a good time, but you just need to chuck your well-worn pretensions at the city gate. Trust us, if you get off the train decked out in your coolest post-eighties punk modster outfit with designer gel-job haircut, striking a pose in Zaragoza won't get you very far. The locals might try to take a picture of you, but they sure as hell won't be familiar with your favorite bands or your idea of a good time. Save your best for Barcelona.

Most of the bars listed here are either along the calle de Dr. Cerrada or in the university area. If you are partying at Dr. Cerrada, just walk from your hostel. If you want to go up to the university, take a cab. As is par for the course in Spain, people wear their best when going out, but as we've mentioned, Zaragoza is not a style capital, so "best" means tight pants. Cheesy Eurotrash and American pop dominate the music selection. Nothin' tops listening to Spanish kids singing along to American Top 40: "I'm a genie-bottle, babe."

Translating the name of **El Pajaro Azul** (*Calle Dr. Cerrada s/n, corner of Paseo de Pamplona; Tel 976/239-383; 5pm-3am daily; 600ptas drinks;*

wired

In addition to the computers at **CHANGE** [see *need to know,* below] you can go to **Ciudad Robot** (*Plaza San Francisco 4; Tel 976/557-312; www.ciudadrobot.com; 500ptas per hour*), where they have ten computers, one TV with video games, and lots of very excited eight-year-old boys. You can send an e-picture back home using their equipment for 200ptas.

FIVE-O

Policing has a different definition in Spain than in the U.S. There is very little chance that you will be harassed or bothered by the police. If you see them at all it will probably be to ask them for directions. More likely than not, you'll just leave on the train and ask yourself, "Were there cops in Zaragoza?"

No credit cards) isn't so tough, considering the giant blue parrot on the sign. The inside is kind of pretty, with a blue and yellow tile floor, and tiny blue and white tiles on the walls. A long bar along the right side is where you'll find drinks, and a big-screen TV in the back corner shows soccer games. Everyone here is young and casually dressed, and the vibe is pretty laid-back and chill. Since this joint doubles as cafe and bar, you can either stop here for an early afternoon drink, or drop by at night when the crowd picks up.

In the university neighborhood, the **Cerveceria Universitaria** *(Plaza San Francisco 17; No phone; 10am-10pm daily; 300ptas drinks; No credit cards)* serves drinks and tapas. The tapas are very good—they're displayed at the long bar, where you can point and click for 500ptas per. There is more seating on the second floor, but you have to carry your drinks up or wait for a server. Outside, a ton of plastic tables and chairs sprawl out under a big green awning. And since you are right on the Plaza San Fran, you can get in some decent people-watching. This place stays busy afternoon, evening, and night, with the crowd largely dominated by students.

LIVE MUSIC SCENE

To tell the truth, this town is not where you want to be if you're interested in catching the latest music, or even if you want to hear some decent jazz. Since Zaragoza is well off the beaten track, there really isn't a local music scene to speak of. The town lacks the kind of atmosphere necessary to nurture young bands to maturity or to draw top-notch musicians from other areas. Therefore, the best way to get a taste of homegrown live music is to listen to the ubiquitous late-night singing of the locals.

For the American unaccustomed to a lot of regular folks singing popular songs, there is something kind of poignant about this Spanish custom. Song is one of the things that binds a society together, and having a data bank of old and new folk songs that everyone learns as a child is a great way to define a living cultural heritage. Hanging out late at night in the Dr. Cerrada area is the best way to check out this great local custom.

CULTURE ZOO

For the most part, your cultural tour of Zaragoza will stimulate your brain the way English cuisine stimulates your taste buds (think blood pudding), but there are also some great finds. The standard must-sees include the immense Basilica, elaborately decorated inside and out, and the Museum of Zaragoza, a rather uninteresting regional collection of art and artifact. Outside the main city center, you'll find two cool sculpture museums dedicated to individual artists who share the same first name, the Pablo Serrano Museum and the Pablo Gargallo Museum. Zaragoza also features two of the most boring museums anywhere, both of which are well worth skipping.

Basilica of Our Lady of the Pilar/Pilar Museum *(Plaza del Pilar; Tel 976/397-497; Basilica 5:45am-9:30pm daily, museum 9am-2pm/4-6pm daily; Free):* Now *this* is worth checking out. There are a bunch of different chapels in the basilica, each with its own saint, artwork, and intricate gold or plaster decoration, as well as a candlelit main altar where the Mass is celebrated. The huge, fantastically intricate gold altarpiece is gorgeous. The sky-high ceiling is a series of domes and arches. At certain times of the day, especially around 11am or noon, you can climb up the tower and get a great panoramic view of the city, including the Río Ebro a few blocks to the north. The museum houses the most valuable offerings to the Virgin of Pilar.

Museum of Zaragoza *(Plaza de los Sitios 6; Tel 976/222-181; 10am-1pm Tue-Sun, closed holidays; 200ptas unless you are an EU citizen):* This city museum, a few blocks east of Plaza de los Sitios, has fine arts, archaeology, ethnology, and ceramics sections. If you are really

chico meets chica

Since everyone in Spain goes home to Mommy, the chances of getting some tender satisfaction are pretty slim most of the time, especially since Zaragoza is significantly more conservative than her sister cities in Spain. However, if Juan likes you, he'll make it known by walking right up to you and barraging you with his terrible English. These guys are totally harmless, and probably don't expect any action—they're just acting their goofiest selves to look cool in front of the American girls.

But things move pretty slowly in this part of the world, so don't expect Zaragoza to be a Roman orgy, or even a Midwestern frat party for that matter. In many parts of non-urban Spain, the tradition is to spend the first 8 years of your post-puberty life in one, or maybe two, relationships and then get married. With a framework like that, the Spanish guard their sons and daughters from your marauding eye with a powerful set of social mores. You'll have better luck in other parts of Spain, where the effects of international culture can be more directly felt.

interested in Spanish art, you will find plenty to satisfy your taste, although the 20th-century collection is very limited. If you get off on old Spanish culture, you should visit the archaeology and ethnological sections.

Pablo Serrano Museum *(Paseo Maria Agustin 20; Tel 976/280-659; 10am-2pm/5-8pm Mon and Wed-Sat, 10am-2pm Sun; Free):* There is a lot of modern sculpture here, as well as opportunity aplenty to get to know the work of an individual artist—if you didn't know who Pablo Serrano was beforehand, you will after a visit to this museum, which houses the work of this funky Aragonese sculptor. The museum lies a few blocks southwest of calle de Ramóny Caial.

Pablo Gargallo Museum *(Plaza de San Felipe 3; Tel 976/392-058; 10am-2pm/5-9pm Tue-Sat, open Sun and holidays in the morning; Free):* The artist's daughter got sick and tired of storing Dad's bronze stuff, so she donated Gargallo's work to the city of Zaragoza and they built this museum. His style is of the abstract variety, and he plays with shape, density, and space in a cool way. Gargallo is big on empty space, and you may see some of Picasso's influence in his work. The museum is in the old town, a 5-minute walk south of Plazadel Pilar.

The Museum of the Forum of Caesaraugusta *(Plaza de la Seo 2; Tel 976/399-752; 10am-1pm/5-8pm Tue-Sat; 400ptas):* This museum is the winner of our "most boring place in the universe" award (just beating out the state of Nebraska...). It's a "permanent exhibition of the remains excavated from the Plaza de la Seo between 1988 and 1989," which prominently features a drain from the time of Tiberius.

The Rosa Molas Museum *(Via Iberica 15; Tel 976/563-238; 10:30am-1:30pm Mon-Fri, 10am-1pm Sat-Sun; Free):* And here's the first runner-up for "the most boring place in the universe," a national museum dedicated to minerals that includes a special collection of rocks from Aragón.

CITY SPORTS

After a few nights at a comfy hostel watching *The Simpsons* dubbed into Spanish while you wait to hit the bars, it might be a good idea to get off your duff and do something that will make you sweat. If you're feelin' the need to get your blood flowing with a nice run or even a long walk, Zaragoza offers a couple of decent options.

The **Parque Primo de Rivera** *(Plaza Princesa, Paseo Fernando El Católico; Bus lines 20, 29, 35, 40, 42, 45; Open during daylight),* a 30-minute walk or 10-minute bus ride southwest of the city center, across from the soccer stadium, is a lush place with lots of fountains, trees, paths, well-tended flowers, and plenty of benches for reading and people-watching. A favorite among the locals, the park is a great way to spend a lazy afternoon, or have a good run while checking out the scenery.

Cutting through a good portion of town, the Rio Ebro is a good place to chat with the local retired folk while they fish. There's a small park on either bank with benches and a path that's perfect for a long walk or jog while looking at the whole of downtown on one side and the pretty river on the other.

You can also make your way to one of the numerous public sport complexes that dot the town, including the **C.D.M Gran Via** *(Calle Domingo Miral s/n; Tel 976/550-849; Bus lines 22, 29, 35, 42),* where you can swim, serve, and shoot hoops.

STUff

The best place to go to burn some cash fast is the Paseo Independencia, located just south of the old quarter, where the fun starts at the Plaza de España and finishes at the Plaza de Aragón. It's basically a wide arcade with big sidewalks and tons of people window-shopping and chatting it up, especially on weekends. Crowding is intensified by the Moroccan guys who spread out their towels and sell cheap watches and other junk on the sidewalks. You'll find your main Spanish-style clothing and shoe stores here, as well as some nondescript bookstores. Also, you need to check out at least one of the outdoor markets or bazaars.

only here

Even if you're only in Zaragoza for a short time, you'll notice that there is something different in the air. There is a kind of quietness in the empty, winding streets of the old city, and a laid-back, almost sedate feeling in the new neighborhoods. This kind of subtle reserve is even present outside the sometimes bustling facade of Paseo Independecia and the Plaza del Pilar. We think it is a touch of old Spain in this growing metropolitan area, a feeling that time continues to crawl beneath the fleeting and consumptive surface of a city still moving from fascist obscurity to capitalist prosperity.

Since every place in Spain has more history than any place in the U.S., it's hard to discern how time feels different in Zaragoza, but if you keep your ears open and chat to some people, you'll understand what we're talking about. Perhaps it's because Zaragoza is still pretty much off the beaten tourist path, or maybe folks in Zaragoza silently resist the superficial pleasure of international pop culture. This is not to say you can't find a McDonald's (in today's world, a city without a McDonald's is like a day without light), but there is still a feeling of distance between the locals and these modern-day transplants.

▶▶DUDS

You can find designer knock-offs of the Spanish variety for somewhat reasonable prices at **Zara's** *(Paseo Independencia s/n; 10am-9pm Mon-Sat; AE, MC, V)*, in the center at the corner of calle Zurita. This famous Spanish clothing store with outlets all across the country (and now in America too) sells more than just clothes for very skinny women—it also sells clothes for very skinny men and children too.

El Corte Ingles *(Paseo Independencia 11; Tel 976/238-644; 10am-9pm Mon-Sat; AE, MC, V)*, near the corner of calle San Miguel in the city center, has clothes as well, but you can get everything else here too, like toasters, armchairs, chess sets, and cell phones. When in a bind, it ain't a bad place to go, although you may feel like you're back in the States at an upscale Wal-Mart.

▶▶BAZAAR

El Rastro *(Plaza Toros; Bus line 25; Sun morning)* is a flea market open for a few hours on Sunday morning. Booths are set up around the Plaza Toros, and you can find all manner of things antique or just old. There's lots of quirky Spanish stuff, as well as a chance to mingle with the shopkeepers and other bargain hunters. If you're feeling tough, you can even do a little haggling, a shopping technique you should try at flea markets in Spain.

At **The Mercadillo** *(Luis Bermejo 3; Bus lines 29, 30, 35, 40, 42, 45; Wed and Sun mornings)*, right outside of the soccer stadium, you can find clothing, jewelry, and other accessories as well as household goods.

Dominated by painting and craftwork, the **Plaza de Santa Cruz Mercado** *(Plaza de Santa Cruz; Sun morning)* is in the old part of town. It's easy to get to and can be fit in as part of your Sunday activities without too much trouble.

EATS

Like any relatively big Spanish city, Zaragoza offers plenty of American fast food, pizzerias, and bad Chinese restaurants. The Aragonese people like their meat, so finding vegetarian joints can be a pain. One of the best dining options is to go bar hopping and sample the various tapas or small snacks. At the tapas bars here, the food is usually under a glass cover on the bar, and you can just point at something that looks good and you'll get a little of it, usually for around 500ptas.

▶▶CHEAP

For a great place to get cheap breakfast, brunch, or early lunch, try **Imbyss 100** *(Calle Don Jaime 39; Tel 976/292-945; 8am-1pm daily; 100-400ptas lunch; No credit cards)*, in the center near the corner of calle Espozimina. Fresh-squeezed orange juice, pastries, sandwiches, croissants, ice cream, coffee, and booze can all be found at this little joint for great prices. It's the equivalent of a diner, but with a small-town Spanish twist; you'll see what we mean when you see the blue decor, tons of mirrors, and big TV. This is where you'll find old men having shots of booze in their espresso at 10am; the waiters don't even have to ask what kind they want.

TO MARKET

The main food market in town, the **Mercat Central** *(Calle Modernist s/n; No phone; 9am-2pm/5-8pm Mon-Fri and on Sat morning)* is located close to Plaza del Pilar and has lots of great fresh food. You'll find everything from dried fruit, cheese, fresh bread, great veggies, fresh cuts of meat, and more seafood than you can shake a stick at, to bloody lamb brains on ice. It's a great way to save a little flow when you are running low, but you won't be able to take full advantage of the deliciousness without a kitchen.

▶▶DO-ABLE

Near the university, **Casa Martin** *(Plaza San Francisco 9; Tel 976/354-809; 2,000ptas dinner; AE, MC, V)* is the nicest place on the Plaza San Francisco. It has both indoor and outdoor seating, and follows a green and white color scheme. If you're getting sick of Spanish *bocadillos* (sandwiches), this is a nice option. They've got a full range of meat and fish dishes that are all very good.

Baltax *(Paseo Maria Agustin 15; Tel 976/228-601; 1,200ptas lunch, 2,500ptas dinner; AE, MC, V)* is a two-in-one joint near Dr. Cerrada, with a cafe and tapas bar in the front and a nice restaurant in the back. The bad modern art on the nasty peach-colored walls doesn't spoil the pizza, pasta, fish, and good meat dishes. You can tell how good the food in the back room is by the way the locals crowd in to get some of it. The front room, lined with booths and benches, serves great seafood tapas.

Near the train station is **La Zanahoria** *(Calle Tarragona 4; Tel 976/358-794; Bus 22 or 35 to train station; All main courses 1,050ptas; fixed-price menu 1,200ptas;1:30-4pm and 9-11:30pm Daily; MC, V)*, which for years has been feeding hungry passengers who arrive to take in the glories of Zaragoza. A favorite with young people, often university students, the kitchen here is known for simple but good-tasting home-cooked meals. The decor is plain but your attention will be focused on your heaping plate of food, most of which comes from the harsh Aragonese countryside itself. On a hot day, the crisp salads and the quiches are ideal, but at night an array of soups, meat, and fish dishes round out the fare.

Everybody's favorite budget restaurant, **Casa Pascualillo** *(Calle Libertad 5; Tel 976/397-203; Main courses 650-1,400ptas, set menu 1,200ptas; Tue-Sun 11am-4pm; Tue-Sat 8-11pm; AE, MC, V)* in El Tubo district, on a small street off calle Méndez Nuñez between Plaza de España and the cathedral. In an old house that has been restored and altered over the years, you can eat tapas and drink wine downstairs, or dine a little more formally at small tables upstairs. The food is not spectacular, but it is fresh, wholesome, and served in generous portions. Nouvelle cuisine here means nothing later than General Franco's era, and you get the standard fish, beef, and poultry dishes served all over Spain.

crashing

Since tourists don't really flock to Zaragoza, finding a place to stay is much easier than it is in other cities in Spain. There are a few nice hotels and hostels, and you can sleep in a pension cheaply as well. The quality is generally good, and they don't try to stick it to you with the prices. It's never a bad idea to call ahead and make reservations, or at least check to see if they've got any vacancies.

▶▶CHEAP

Buzz up to a nice old man who has fashioned some cheap housing out of an extra apartment across the hall at **Pension Iglesias** *(Calle Veroncia 14, floor 2; Tel 976/293-161; 1,600-1,800ptas single; 3,500ptas double with bath; No credit cards)*, just a short walk from Plaza del Pilar. There are only a handful of places, so get there early. You get a small, kind of old but fully functional TV in your room, and it is located on a quiet, skinny side street. The owner is nice and friendly—he even puts on a little apron and cleans every single day—so go easy on him about his taste in art. You'll get a key to the front door, so don't worry about waking the old guy.

down and out

If you've spent your last peseta on that new hot pink top at **Zara's** [see *stuff,* above], fret not, there is plenty of cheap entertainment in good old Zaragoza. Since the **Basilica** [see *culture zoo,* above] is one of the most beautiful in Spain, you should go and hang out there, maybe even for Mass. Regardless of your religious orientation, it will be an interesting cultural immersion exercise; just don't do anything to diss their culture, like make out in the pews. You can also do the step-aerobic walk up to the top of the tower and check out the spectacular view of the city.

If you're just not into churches, then you should hit the **Parque Primo de Rivera** [see *city sports,* above], which is totally free and totally beautiful. Wander around, watch the Spanish families walking around and the teenagers making out on the grass, and get some fresh air. Being out of money can be a chance to clear your head, as any experienced street junkie knows.

Another cheap option is **Fonda La Pena** *(Calle Cinegio 3; Tel 976/299-089; 1,500ptas per person single or double, shared bath; No credit cards).*

▶▶DO-ABLE

Hostal El Carmen *(Paseo Maria Agustin 13; Tel 976/211-100; 2,600ptas single; 4,800ptas double, no bath; No credit cards)* is close to the Dr. Cerrada area, which means that it can be a little bit noisy at night. If your room faces the main street, you get a big window and a balcony, which can be a double-edged sword if you want to get some Z's. You have to buzz in when you first get there, but they'll give you a key to the front door.

Right in the heart of the old quarter, **Ambos Mundos** *(Plaza del Pilar 16; Tel 976/299-704; 4,400ptas double without bath; No credit cards)* has rooms with balconies that look onto the Plaza del Pilar. The rooms, some with private baths, are clean and you can get breakfast, lunch, and dinner right on the premises for a decent price (365ptas for breakfast, 1,300ptas lunch and dinner). The location means you won't waste any time getting out to the sights.

A few others worth trying are **Posada De Las Almas** *(Calle De San Pablo 22; Tel 976/439-700; Fax 976/439-143; 3,800ptas single, 5,600ptas double, all rooms with private bath; V, MC, AE);* **Hostal Estrella** *(Avda. De Clave 27; Tel 976/283-061; 4,000ptas single, 6,500ptas double, all rooms with private bath; No credit cards);* and the fully renovated **Hostal Plaza** *(Plaza del Pilar 14; Tel 976/294-830 or 976/284-839; 3,900ptas single low-season, 4,400ptas single high season, 4,900-6,500ptas double low season, 6,900-7,500ptas double high season).*

If you feel like splurging, try **Via Romana** *(Calle Don Jaime 1; Tel 976/398-215; Fax 976/290-511; 6,600ptas single winter weekends, 7,100ptas single mid-season, 10,600ptas single high season, 8,600ptas double winter weekends, 9,600ptas double mid-season, 15,400ptas double high season; V, MC, AE, DC).*

neeᴅ ᴛo ᴋnow

Currency Exchange There are ATMs and banks everywhere in this city, and they almost always have the best rates. But if you lose your ATM card and need to change cash after the banks close, you're in luck. All you need to do is visit **CHANGE** *(Calle Jardiel 3; Tel 976/399-055; 10am-midnight daily)* where you can exchange money, make money transfers, and pay to use the fax, telephone, or get online. And all of this happens in a room no bigger than your bedroom.

Tourist Information Tourist offices can be found at the train station and a few other locations in the city, but the **main tourist office** *(Plaza del Pilar; Tel 976/201-200; 9:30am-1:30pm/4:30-7:30pm Mon-Sat, 10am-2pm Sun and holidays)* is in the hard-to-miss, smoked-glass cube on the Plaza del Pilar. It has multilingual staff and tons of information. While they can't actually make hotel reservations, they can point you in the right direction.

Public Transportation Zaragoza has only a bus system, **Transportes Urbanos de Zaragoza** *(Tel 976/592-727 for information),* but it can pretty much get you around once you've become familiar with the somewhat complex map you can pick up at the information center. Rides cost ya only 85ptas.

American Express You'll find a travel agent near the Plaza de España: **Viajes Europa** *(Paseo Sagasta 47; Tel 976/383-911; Hours vary)*.

Health and Emergency Emergency: *112;* Police: *092.* For medical problems, get to the **Hospital Miguel Servet** *(Paseo Isabelle la Catolica 1; Tel 976/355-700).*

Pharmacies You can find pharmacies all over town; just look for the big green crosses.

Telephone City code: *976.* Like everywhere else in Spain, you can buy phone cards at the tobacco shops and kiosks.

Airport The **Aeropuerto** *(Ctra. Aeropuerto s/n; Tel 976/712-300)* is about a half-hour cab ride out of the city (which will run you around 2,500ptas).

Trains The **Estacion Portillo** *(Avda. Anselmo Clavé; Tel 976/764-246)* is serviced by bus 21 from Plaza de España. It's about a 10-minute ride, or a 20-minute walk. A taxi will run you about 400ptas.

Buses The red buses of TUZSA *(Tel 976/592-727)* serve all parts of Zaragoza. A one-way passage costs 85ptas, or you can get a pass good for 10 rides for 550ptas. The two most important bus lines are numbers 21 and 33, which split the city between them. You can also pick up a free route map at the tourist office.

Postal The **Correos** *(Paseo Independencia 33; Tel 976/226-952; 8:30am-8:30pm Mon-Fri, 9:30am-2pm Sat)* is cool because there isn't really ever a long line.

Internet See *wired,* above.

Pyrenees

benasque

Unless you've spent your entire life in a cabin next to a bubbling mountain creek in the Colorado Rockies, dreaming of your escape to the big city, you are going to love visiting Benasque. For those of us who *are* city dwellers, and to whom a tree, clean water, and even a breath of air not laden with the smell of garbage and exhaust fumes is a luxury, Benasque is a little bit like heaven.

Benasque is a tiny town; you can circle the entire place on foot in 15 minutes. The gray stone and dark wood buildings are a refreshing change from the typical Aragonese architecture, and an even bigger change from Mediterranean Spanish-style homes. The mountains are not something off in the distance—"in your face" is a more apt description. The Rio Esera runs along one side of town, and you can hear the rumble of the river wherever you go. If you stay at a hostel that's close to the river, you might even have to close the windows to get any sleep.

Benasque is a port of entry into some of the highest mountains of the Aragonese Pyrenees, and while this makes it a hub for Europe's adventure travelers, the 1,000 or so permanent inhabitants have been able to maintain the small-town flavor. People have a tendency to take things slowly; if you want to get along and enjoy yourself, you should do so while you're here. International visitors don't impress the locals, who are sufficiently patient, but not necessarily over-the-top helpful. Also, even though a good part of the economy rests on tourism, fewer locals know English than you would think, so bring your phrasebook.

But you don't come to Benasque for a cultural exchange; you come to Benasque either to prove yourself in the great outdoors or to experience some of the best natural sights this side of the Atlantic. You can visit Benasque year-round and not lack for an exciting and beautiful outdoor adventure. Downhill and cross-country skiing, snowboarding, and cold-weather backpacking are popular winter sports; hiking, biking, kayaking, mountain-climbing, and parachuting provide late spring (June) through early fall (October) fun. The only time Benasque is a ghost town is in the early spring, between peak seasons, when the entire population takes a vacation. Unfortunately, this is when it's at its most beautiful, too. So if you're looking to find the most peace and quiet you've had in years, come in mid-May through mid-June. But if you want to experience some serious outdoor excitement, or just want to hook up with like-minded hikers and outdoorsy people, come in July and August or in the winter months.

Benasque is so close to the outdoors that you can leave your *hostal* and be on a mountain path in 10 minutes. The local ski hill, **Cerler** [see *city sports*, below], features three peaks and 16 lifts and is a mere 6 km (3.5 mi) away. There are a bunch of local outfits that will take you on single or multi-day excursions of your choice, and there are also plenty of resources (like gear rental and car services) for the DIY type. Once in the great outdoors, you'll find lots of great trails, as well as *refugios,* primitive wood structures that allow for overnight stays in the woods.

The best place to meet other travelers is in your hostel or in the local bars. Benasque is way too small to have a plaza where people hang out, but since most of the people who are out in the peak seasons are tourists, you won't lack for international company if that is your desire.

It takes about 2 minutes to learn the geography of the town. The main street is **Avenida de los Tilos,** and the other two arteries are **calle Mayor** and **calle Las Plazas.** You'll find virtually everything on these streets. Because Benasque is such a small town, the numbering of buildings is a little sporadic, but the streets are no longer than a football field, so just look for the signs.

Information about local events can be found in ***Guayente,*** a magazine published every three months and available at local hostels and bars.

bar scene

Nightlife in Benasque consists of hopping between the few local pubs and trading adventure stories and traveling tips with other tourists over a few drinks. The general outdoors-oriented vibe here doesn't stop people from doing a tad bit of partying as well. But if you want to dance the night away, you are pretty much SOL in Benasque. You'll find most bars and restaurants on calle San Marsial, the central street that cuts through town up to the Plaza del Ayuntamiento. Calle Las Plazas and Avenida de los Tilos both have nightlife and food options as well. The hours depend on the season and the mood of the owner. During the peak seasons, places open early and close late. When it's slow, they cut back their hours, sometimes closing altogether during the dead zones between seasons (early spring and late fall).

Cafeteria Araguells *(Avda. de los Tilos; Tel 974/551-619; 9pm-2am daily; Beer 300ptas; No credit cards)* has a long bar, a nice wood exterior, and space for a decent number of people. The vibe during the peak season is touristy, like everywhere in town, but you can meet some interesting folks here and you'll hear English spoken.

The **Pub/Discoteca Chema** *(Calle Las Plazas; Tel 974/551-572; 10pm-2am daily; Beer 400ptas; No credit cards)* isn't really a *discoteca,* but people sometimes dance here. The crowd is generally a little younger and of the international variety. If you have any energy after your all-day hike or ski trip, or you want to numb your sore muscles and stretch them out on the "dance" floor, this isn't a bad bet.

city sports

You can play tennis, soccer, and basketball in town at the **Pabellon de Deportes** *(End of Avda. De Luchon),* but you're wasting your time when you could be parachuting off the top of a mountain. Since you've spent 5 hours defying death and a mean bout of motion sickness on the bus ride into town, you need to find a better way to justify the trip than a rousing game of tennis.

benasque

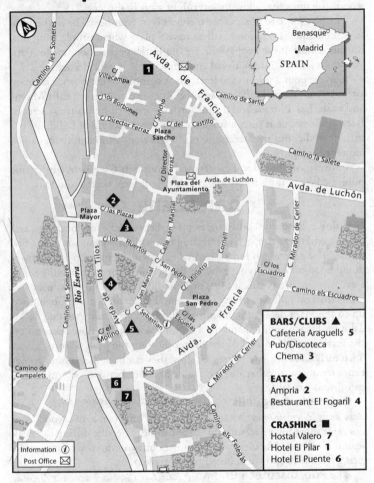

Benasque
•Madrid
SPAIN

BARS/CLUBS ▲
Cafeteria Araguells **5**
Pub/Discoteca
  Chema **3**

EATS ◆
Ampria **2**
Restaurant El Fogaril **4**

CRASHING ■
Hostal Valero **7**
Hotel El Pilar **1**
Hotel El Puente **6**

Information ⓘ
Post Office ✉

    You can find folks all over town who will set you up with gear, a guide, and information about activities in the Benasque area, including the Pyrenees. And since the town is so small, it isn't hard to find a place that will outfit you for your adventure. It makes no difference whether you want to do it yourself or leave it to someone else, as a wide range of services is offered.

    Super DIY types can call **Armand** *(Tel 974/552-094 or 608/998-711; Hours vary; Prices vary; No credit cards)* and ask to go for a ride in his parachute. They call him *el director,* and he boasts 10 years of experience.

    At **Casa de la Montana** *(Avda. de los Tilos; Tel 974/552-094; 10am-1pm/4-7pm, closed Sun; Prices vary; AE, MC, V),* you can find normal outdoor gear like backpacks and boots. They also organize trips in the surrounding area. Stop by and check out the current offerings and prices, which can vary considerably. Rentals are available.

Compania de Guias Valle de Benasque (*Edificio Commercial Barrabes, floor 2, calle Mayor; Tel 974/551-336; Call for hours; lonuevo@guiasbenasque.com; Prices vary; AE, MC, V*) organizes tons of cool trips in the area, and if you want to pay the additional bucks, they can also take you even farther afield (like the Italian Alps). Depending on what you want, you'll be looking to spend somewhere in the neighborhood of 15,000ptas for a three-day trip.

If fishing is your thing, **Danica Guias de Pesca** (*Edificio Batisiellas, Grupo Escarpinosa, floor 1, apartment 6a, Avenida de Francia near calle de los Escuadros; Tel 974/551-378 or 608/735-376; Prices vary; No credit cards*) will take you out to wonderful Pyrenees mountain streams. Rentals and guides are available.

The guys at **Barrabes** (*Edificio Commercial, the beginning of calle Mayor; Tel 974/551-681; 9:30am-2:30pm, 4:30-9pm daily; www.barrabes.com; Prices vary; AE, MC, V*) are serious professionals and can hook you up with everything you need for an intense experience. Mainly an outdoor store, Barrabes hosts adventure sport activities all over Europe—one of the best places being right here in Benasque at the Escuela Espanola de Alta Montana Campalet, which is essentially a ski and rock-climbing school. At the school you can get equipment and info, and sign up for lessons in the winter and guides in the summer.

If you are here during the winter, you are probably here to ski. The **Cerler** (*Cerler; Tel 974/551-111; Open during sunlight; www.cerler.com; 3,500ptas for one day, up to 20,000ptas for seven days; AE, MC, V*) skiing area, just 6 km (3.5 miles) outside of Benasque, is one of the premier downhill skiing facilities in the region. Take a shuttle bus from downtown Benasque to the base of the mountain. There are 16 ski lifts, three big peaks, and three base lodges. This place is awesome. You can sleep on site, but it is expensive. **Edelweiss Cerler** (*Edelweiss s/n; Tel 974/551-242; 7,750-12,600ptas; V*) has all the amenities you could want—TV, VCR, bar, disco, and so on. You'll be paying out the wazoo, though—stay in Benasque if you know what's good for you.

EATS

Ampria (*Calle Las Plazas; Tel 974/551-712; 8pm-1am daily; 2,000ptas; AE, MC, V*) is a medium-sized Basque restaurant with a standout menu, a friendly atmosphere, and a classic wood and stone interior. If your trip itinerary does not include the Basque country, then you should definitely stop here for a taste of Basque cuisine, which is best described as a cross between Spanish and French: rich, fattening, and fabulous.

You'll find **Restaurant El Fogaril** (*Avda. de los Tilos; Tel 974/551-612; 1-4pm/8:30-11pm daily; Tapas 400ptas; AE, MC, V*) on the first floor of the Hotel Ciria. In the back is a three-star splurge, but we recommend going for tapas in the afternoon at the bar in the front, with exposed wood and gray stone walls and wooden booths. They lay the tapas out on the bar, so all you need to do is point at something that looks yummy. There is a big TV, and you can sit and veg in front of it forever (hey, it's what all the local old men do!).

Restaurante Les Arkades *(Calle Ministro Cornel 2; Tel 974/552-092; 1-4pm/8-11pm daily; Fixed-price menu 1,600ptas, main courses 900-1,500ptas; V, MC).* Known for serving one of the best fixed-price menus in the area, this Basque restaurant is sheltered in a house dating back four centuries. Expect a rustic decor of wood and stone. You sit at old wooden tables, often sharing with strangers as though they were family. Stick to the Basque fare and not the array of international dishes put on the menu supposedly to please foreign visitors. Favorite dishes include roasted lamb ribs, deer cooked with flap mushrooms, and a hearty local dish, *Olla Benmasqueza*, a medley of vegetables and meats cooked in a savory stew.

More upmarket than Les Arkades, but worth the splurge, is **La Parrilla** *(Corner of Carretera Francia and Avenida Luchon; Tel 974/551-134; 1-4pm/9-11pm daily, closed last week of Sept; Fixed-price menu 1,700ptas, main courses 1,400-2,000ptas; V, MC).* In the center of town, this is an attractive old restaurant with a rustic decor of wood and stone—everything is rustic in this area. The chefs are Basque experts when rattling those pots and pans. We love their *patata tellena* or stuffed potato. They also have a marvelous way with Basque lamb called *garronets* which is served invariably tender and flavored with fresh herbs. A local river fish is given added zest by the flavor of squid ink, a true Basque favorite.

crashing

During the off-seasons it is pretty cheap to sleep in Benasque, but there isn't much to do. All prices listed below are for peak times, but expect to get a 33 to 50 percent discount if you go off-season.

The 78-room **Hostal Valero** *(Ctra. Anciles; Tel 974/551-061; valero@hoteles-valero.com; www.hoteles-valero.com; 2,500ptas single, 4,500ptas double without bath; AE, MC, V)* is one of the cheapest places in town, but it has lots of perks like a pool, tennis court, and sauna. You can reserve by e-mail, and if you are going during the busy times, you better do it well in advance because this place is the best deal in Benasque. Private baths are available.

Hotel El Pilar *(Ctra. Francia; Tel 974/551-263; elpilar@hotelesvalero. com, www.hoteles-valero.com; 4,500ptas single, 8,100ptas double, private baths; AE, MC, V)* is beautiful for a one-star hotel. Everything inside and outside is made from wood and stone, and you get direct views of the mountain. If you like cows, come here: You can hear the moos and bells from a nearby pasture. The hotel has a pool, tennis court, and dining area, and is across the street from the Red Cross office.

At the **Hotel El Puente** *(San Pedro; Tel 974/551-279; 9,000ptas double; AE, MC, V)* you will pay a little more, but you can get a balcony overlooking the river, a nice bathroom, and a TV and phone in your room. The bus in and out of town stops right outside, so if you feel like crashing as soon as you arrive, this isn't a bad choice.

Other not-too-pricey options include **Pension Barrabes** *(Calle Mayor 5; Tel 974/551-654; 2,000ptas single; 3,900ptas double; shared baths; V, MC, AE)* and **Pension Solana** *(Plaza Mayor 5; Tel 974/551-019; 7,500ptas double; breakfast included; V).*

WiThin 30 minuTES

The **Parque Naturel Posets-Maladeta** [see below] surrounds Benasque. A national park created in 1994, it has some spectacular mountains and views. Many of the peaks that you see from Benasque are part of the park.

need To Know

Currency Exchange There are a handful of banks and ATM machines around the tourist information office and the Plaza del Ayuntamiento.

Tourist Information The clerk at the **main tourist office** *(Calle San Sebastián; Tel 974/551-289; 9:30am-1:30pm/4-8pm daily July-Aug, 10am-2pm/5-8pm Tue-Sat Sept-June)* in the city center does not speak English, but there are plenty of pamphlets in Spanish with cool photos. They don't make hotel reservations, but can provide you with phone numbers and other info.

Public Transportation If you need to get to a distant trailhead, call up **Auto Taxi Benasque** *(Calle de Horno 5; Tel 974/551-157; All hours; Prices vary, expect to pay over 1,000ptas for a decent distance),* or **Excursiones Auto Taxi** *(Calle de Ball Benas; Tel 608/930-450; All hours; 3,000-6,000ptas for tours).*

Health and Emergency Emergency: *Tel 608/536-882.* For all your hospital needs, head to the **Centro Santario** *(Corner of Avenida de Francia and Avenida de Luchon; Tel 974/552-138).* The **Cruz Roja** (Red Cross) is located on Avenida de Francia, right across the street from Hotel El Pilar [see *crashing*, above].

Pharmacies As usual, you will recognize the *farmacias* in town by their **green crosses.**

Buses The **Alta Aragonesa** *(Calle San Pedro; Tel 974/210-700)* bus station is the only way into town unless you have a car. Call for info, or go to the tourist office. The buses run to and from Barbastro, where you can connect to Zaragoza and Barcelona. You can catch the bus on calle San Pedro at either 6:45am or 3pm. Buy tickets (400-600ptas.) on the bus.

Laundry The **Lavandería Ecológica Ardilla** *(Ctra. Francia, Edificio Ball Benas; Tel 974/551-504)* has washers, dryers, and ironing equipment to make your hiking-soiled clothes look like new.

Postal The **Correos** *(Plaza del Ayuntamiento; Tel 974/552-071; 9am-noon Mon-Fri)* will mail your postcards and packages home. Its home, *El Ayuntamiento,* is one of the largest buildings in the town center, almost impossible to miss.

Internet *No hay nada!* (No Internet, sorry.)

jaca

Other guidebooks might say that Jaca ain't nothin' more than a place to prepare yourself for a great hiking trip. While it's true that the main draw here is the nearby **Parque Nacional de Ordesa** [see below] with its many outdoor attractions, you shouldn't miss the opportunity to get to know this quaint little mountain town of 15,000 people.

The non-local crowd in Jaca is mostly of the outdoorsy, L.L. Bean variety, and there's no scarcity of fleece-clad visitors here. Lots of folks from all over Spain and France, as well as a few folks from English-speaking lands, come to hike, bike, camp, and backpack in the staggeringly beautiful Pyrenees Mountains surrounding the town. Jaca is in a valley, and everywhere you turn you get a great mountain view. Some of the taller peaks are snowcapped all year long. Even better, the locals in Jaca are generally friendly and outgoing. If you ask someone for directions, don't be surprised if they walk you to your destination.

The apartment buildings here are of the typical Spanish variety, with balconies and a color scheme that balances nicely with the natural surroundings. You will also see little stucco homes and lots of well-tended rose bushes. Right smack in the middle of town there's an ancient pentagon-shaped fortress called the **Ciudadela** [see *culture zoo*, below]. While Jaca is most lush and beautiful in May and June, the high season for outdoor summer stuff is in July and August, and December and January are the best months for winter sports.

The main drags in Jaca are **calle Mayor** and **Primer Viernes de Mayo.** Running north to south, Primer Viernes de Mayo virtually splits the town into east Jaca and west Jaca. South of the cathedral, calle Mayor runs east to west. The historic core, including the cathedral, lies north of this street. South of calle Mayor is the less intriguing southern district. Dominating the cityscape is the **Ciudadela,** which takes up most of the western sector of Jaca. Nearly all the landmarks of tourist interest lie within walking distance of each other in the central core. This is where you'll find most of the restaurants, the tourist information office [see *need to know*, below], and lots of sporting-goods stores. For other types of fun, you can take in a movie at the two-screen, all-Spanish-language **Cine Astoria** *(Calle de Miral)* or even play a little mini-golf at the **Gran Hotel Miniature Golf,** located above the tourist office (yes, above, as in on the second floor!).

Nightlife in Jaca is extremely limited, as most of the adventurer-types like to get a good night's rest before heading into the hills. But there are a few nice restaurants where you can hang out, have a drink, and chat with some of the other folks who are in town to prepare for an excursion to the Pyrenees. You'll bump into hikers anytime in the spring or summer, although the Spaniards take their holidays here in July and August, and the French and German hikers show up as soon as the weather warms up. At certain times of the day, you'll also run into people who are walking the Camino de Santiago, a 30-day hike across the north of Spain [see **Galicia,** above]. You'll find all details about any cultural events in the two local newspapers, *El Pirineo Aragonez* or *El Diario de Alto Aragón.*

bar scene

The nightlife scene in Jaca consists of one restaurant/bar called the **Pilgrim Café** *(Primer Viernes de Mayo 7; No phone; Hours vary; tapas and a drink for 1,000ptas; No credit cards).* A short walk east of the Ciudadela, it's the perfect place to rejuvenate after the long ride to Jaca or a long day of hiking and adventuring in the mountains. Stepping inside from the very small-town street to such a modern and with-it place can be a little surreal. The surprisingly hip young staff will tend to your needs, and they play a great international list of cool music like Björk. If you go during the right time of year, you'll get to mingle with the hiking crowd and share some stories at the bar. This place is big, with indoor and outdoor seating, lots of exposed wood and natural light, stone tables, and a big circular stone bar in the center. The cafe serves a wide variety of tapas and sandwiches, as well as some great salads (which can be rare in Spain). Order a few drinks and enjoy the scenery while you either recuperate from, or get ready for, some hard traveling.

CULTURE ZOO

While in Jaca, you might as well check out the cathedral and museum, as well as the cool former fortress called the Ciudadela. They are all located basically on top of each other in the northwest section of town, and give you a chance to check out more Spanish architecture.

Catedral/Museo Diocesano *(Calle San Pedro; Tel 974/356-378; Cathedral 8am-2pm/4-9pm daily, museum 11am-1:30pm/4-6:30pm Tue-Sun):* Jaca's cathedral is not as nice as the other 800 cathedrals in Spain, but it gives the town character, and there isn't too much else going on. The Romanesque church was built around 1060. The museum housed in the cloister is known for its splendid collection of 12th- to 15th-century frescoes, many of which were brought here from other churches in the province.

Ciudadela *(Primer Viernes de Mayo; Tel 974/360-443):* This is the castle you dreamed of building in the sand, complete with a cool moat and tall walls. It is an imposing structure that you can see from pretty much anywhere in town. You can't miss it. In the 1600s the Ciudadela was used to protect the town from the French Huguenots. If this isn't the perfect setting for the next Robin Hood-esque movie, then nothing is.

CITY SPORTS

There aren't really any sports in town, unless you count tossing a tennis ball against the cathedral wall, or joining the 10-year-olds kicking a dusty soccer ball around an empty street. However, just hook up with one of the outdoor shops in town and you'll find yourself on an amazing

jaca

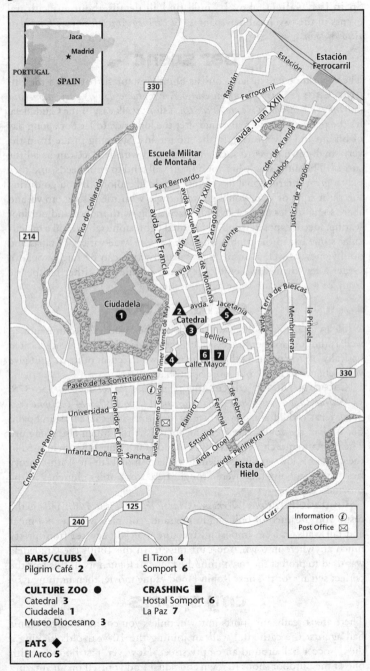

Jaca
Madrid
★
PORTUGAL
SPAIN

330

Estación
Ferrocarril

Rapitán
Ferrocarril
Estación
avda. Juan XXIII
cde. de Aranda
Fondabós
Justicia de Aragón

Escuela Militar
de Montaña

San Bernardo

Prca de Collarada

avda. de Francia

avda. Escuela Militar de Montaña

avda. Juan XXIII

Zaragoza

Levante

avda.

avda.

214

Ciudadela
❶

avda. Terra de Biescas

Membrilleras

la Piñuela

Primer Viernes de Mayo

❷ avda. Jacetania
Catedral ❺
❸
Bellido
❹ ❻ ❼
Calle Mayor

330

Paseo de la Constitución

ⓘ

Universidad

Fernando el Católico

avda. Regimiento Galicia

Ramiro I

Ferrenal

7 de Febrero

Infanta Doña   Sancha

✉

Estudios

avda. Oroel

avda. Perimetral

**Pista de
Hielo**

Cno. Monte Pano

125

240

Gas

Information ⓘ
Post Office ✉

BARS/CLUBS ▲
Pilgrim Café **2**

El Tizon **4**
Somport **6**

CULTURE ZOO ●
Catedral **3**
Ciudadela **1**
Museo Diocesano **3**

CRASHING ■
Hostal Somport **6**
La Paz **7**

EATS ◆
El Arco **5**

excursion. These trips can be tons of fun, and are the only option for those of us who don't travel across Spain with our kayak or horse in tow.

Mountain Travel *(Avda. Regimiento Galicia; Tel 974/355-770; info@mountaintravel.net; Prices vary; AE, MC, V),* a 2-minute walk south of the Ciudadela, offers all kinds of organized trips. You can find their pamphlet, *Aragon Aventura,* which describes all of their excursions in detail (including prices) and gives little bios of their guides, at the information office or right in the store. The store doesn't sell anything but fun, so don't go there to buy clothes. The inside is set up like a travel agency, except with a nice relaxed atmosphere. These guys will take you on small local rafting, hiking, rappelling, caving, and biking adventures. Prices for a simple weekend trip will run you 14,000ptas including gear, a guide, and a place to stay. They'll even get you to the top of Mt. Everest if you have the dough (no joke). It gets more expensive the longer and farther you go, culminating in an Everest trip for a cool $20,000.

Alcorce Pirineos Aventura and Guias de Montana *(Avda. Regimiento Galicia 1; Tel 974/356-437; 10am-1:30pm/5-8:30pm Mon-Sat; alcorce@iname.com, www.alcorceaventura.com; Prices vary; AE, MC, V),* in front of the tourist office, is both an outdoor gear store that sells hiking boots, backpacks, clothes, and fleece (if you forgot yours), and an outfit that organizes trips. While somewhat tamer than Mountain Travel (they mostly limit their excursions to the Jaca area and the Parque Nacional de Ordesa), they have nice day and weekend trips at very reasonable prices. You can hike, cave, ride horses, kayak, raft, climb cliffs, or hydro-speed. A one-hour horse ride costs 2,000ptas, level 2 rafting runs 5,500ptas, and a two-day kayak trip will set you back 12,000ptas.

EATS

If you choose to leave the **Pilgrim Café** [see *bar scene,* above], you can head down the street to **El Tizon** *(Avda. Primer Viernes de Mayo 14; Tel 974/362-780; 1-4pm/8-10:30pm; Dinner menu 1,650ptas; AE, MC, V),* one of the fancier restaurants in town. They have lots of hearty meals for darn cheap, including a range of pastas that cost 500-1,000ptas, as well as tasty fish dishes for around 1,500ptas. The crowd is a mix of locals and tourists.

Somport *(Echegaray 11; Tel 974/363-410; Hours vary by season; 300-400ptas for a sandwich; AE, MC, V)* is on the first floor of **Hostel Somport** [see *crashing,* below] and has cheap but good food, including decent hamburgers, sandwiches, and seafood. Even though it's in a hotel, it comes recommended by the locals.

The only vegetarian restaurant in town is **El Arco** *(Calle San Nicolas 4; Tel 974/364-448; 1:30-4pm/8:30-11pm Mon-Sat; Around 1,500ptas for a meal),* a 2-minute walk southeast of the cathedral. Here, you can get the most fantastic *tortilla patata* (potato omelette) in Spain. It's the next best thing to a home-cooked meal.

crashing

Located on a beautiful little side street a 2-minute walk south of the cathedral, **Hostel Somport** (*Echegaray 11; Tel 974/363-410; 3,000ptas single, 5,500ptas double with bath; AE, MC, V*) is a super-cute, peach-colored building with black wrought-iron railings. The 16 good-sized rooms are nice and clean, and come with a TV, not to mention a restaurant on the first floor [see *eats,* above].

La Paz (*Calle Mayor 41; Tel 974/360-700; 5,000ptas single, 8,000ptas double with bath; AE, MC, V*) is a two-star hotel where you can feel comfortable taking a bath. All rooms have a TV and bathroom, and the sheets are immaculate. There is a rec room with video games and a pool table, and downstairs there's a small bar/cafe where you can have tapas, breakfast, or a drink at night. There are 35 rooms. Prices drop significantly during the off-season.

Other options on the cheap side are **El Arco** (*Calle San Nicolas 4; Tel 974/364-448; 2,000ptas per person single and double, shared bath; No credit cards*) and **Hostal Paris** (*Plaza De San Pedro 5; Tel 974/361-020; 2,500ptas single low season, 2,700ptas single high season, 3,850ptas double low season, 4,200ptas double high season*).

need to know

Currency Exchange You can find **ATMs** around town and at the **Iber-Caja** (*Calle Lacodena Azpeitia; 8:15am-2:30pm Mon-Fri*).

Tourist Information The **main tourist office** (*Calle Regimiento de Galica 2; Tel 974/360-098; 9am-2pm/4:30-7pm Mon-Fri, open weekends depending on the season*), a few blocks south of Paseo de la Constitución, has a couple of English-speaking folks, and you can find out all about local outdoor opportunities here.

Health and Emergency Consorcio Hospitalario de Jaca (*Avda. Rapitan; Tel 974/355-331*) is a 15-minute walk northeast of the Palacio del Congreso, in the vicinity of the train station. From the center of town a local bus marked Hospital stops right in front of the medical facility. Otherwise, the hospital is a 7-minute taxi ride from the center if you have to get there fast.

Pharmacies As always, look for the **green crosses. Farmacia Ortopedia** (*Calle Lacodena Azpeitia; 9am-2pm Mon-Fri*) has a condom dispenser outside.

Trains and Buses About a 10-minute walk from the center of town, the train station, **Estacion de Ferrocarril** (*Calle Estacion; Tel 974/361-332*), is very small. The **bus station** (*Calle La Pinuela; Tel 974/355-060*) is north of town, but more central than the train station. You can get to Jaca by train on the Zaragoza-Huesca-Confranc line, or you can take a bus on the Zaragoza-Huesca line. The bus is slightly more expensive (1,460ptas one-way) because it makes fewer stops than the train. However, there is only one bus per day, while there are frequent trains running all day between 7am and 6:30pm.

Laundry The **Tintoreria Betes** *(Calle San Nicolas 10; 9am-1:30pm/4:30-8pm Mon-Sat)* will do dry cleaning or regular laundry.

Postal The place to get your mail in town, **Correos y Telegrafos** *(Avenida del Regimiento Galicia; 8:30am-2:30pm Mon-Fri, 9:30am-1pm Sat),* is cool because there is never a line.

parque nacional de ordesa

Parque Nacional de Ordesa is filled with high peaks, steep slopes, rivers, canyons, deserts, lush valleys, wild animals, and waterfalls. It covers 15,608 hectares of diverse terrain that includes 1,500 plant species, 65 different types of birds, and 32 mammal species. This is one big-ass, serious national park. If you get a chance to take in the stunning sights and sounds of this fantastic mountain wilderness, you'll never forget it. However, it's no picnic getting around this place and you'll need the proper equipment, guidebooks, and maps (and perhaps, depending on the level of adventure you seek, a real live flesh-and-blood guide), as well as lots of time (a couple of days minimum) to make it worthwhile. There are also a handful of small villages within the park's borders where you can get a glimpse of what Spanish life must have been like a hundred years ago.

The park has a varied and interesting geological history. Starting as a sea basin that filled with silt, the land was pushed up to form mountains, which were shaped by glaciers and many years of erosion. The Monte Perdido range, the biggest limestone range in Western Europe, dominates the scenery. Monte Perdido is also the highest peak in the park at 3,355 meters (11,175 feet). The landscape fluctuates in height from about 750 to 3,000 meters (2,460 to 9,843 feet) at the mountaintops.

You really only want to be here in the late spring, summer, and early fall. The weather will dictate much of your journey. Fortunately, you can call ahead and get weather information *(Tel 906/365-322, information updated daily at 3pm).*

For those who want to take a leisurely day hike, there are probably better locations. The public transportation network doesn't service the park very well, and you'll be hard-pressed to get out to the park, into the woods, and back into town in one day. However, if you are willing to spend a little time, and ready to put up with a fair degree of hassle getting to and fro, the Ordesa National Park can provide you with one of the most rewarding adventures of your holiday.

If you do decide that you want to commit a few days, Ordesa offers opportunities for all levels of hikers. Well-maintained trails traverse the park, although even the easiest are unapologetically rugged and can be challenging for the uninitiated. Altitude gain should not be a hiking problem for most people, and the weather in the summer is still very much Mediterranean, so that shouldn't be a problem either.

The crowd is famously thick in July and August, when lots of folks come from Spain and France to check out the spectacular natural beauty. If you want to feel secluded, plan your trip for another time of year, or else plan to venture deeper into the park.

need to know

Tourist Information The best entrance into the park is through the village of Torla, where a **visitor center** (*Avenida Ordesa 4; Tel 974/486-152; 9am-2pm/3:30-6pm daily Apr-May, 9am-1:30pm/4-7pm daily June, 9am-1pm/3:30-6pm daily July-Aug*) lies near the signposted entrance to the park. It sells maps for 400ptas and offers information about hiking in the park.

Directions and Transportation Again, getting to the park can be difficult. A train runs to the town of Sabinaigo on the Zaragoza-Jaca line, and you can take a bus from there to Torla. This is not ideal, though, as the only train from Jaca to Sabinaigo leaves at 7:36am and arrives at 7:56am, leaving you to wait in dreary Sabinaigo for the 11am bus to Torla. It's better to take the 10:15am bus from Jaca, which gets you to Sabinaigo at 10:45am, in time, if all goes smoothly, for the 11am bus to Torla. From Torla, you can take a shuttle bus up to the park entrance if you are traveling in July and August. Otherwise you must hike about 5.6 km (3.5 mi) to the park entrance, or take a taxi (about 1,800ptas). You can also rent a car from Jaca's one minor agency, **Transpemer** (*Tel 974/360-781; 6,000ptas per day)*; call, and a representative will bring the car to you. It's a considerably better deal than a taxi, which could cost as much as 7,000ptas each way.

Rental We recommend working with one of the two outfits in Jaca, **Mountain Travel** and **Alcorce Pirineos Aventura** [see **Jaca,** above]. Both run reasonably priced trips into the park that include gear, transportation, and an experienced guide.

Crashing There are tons of campsites in the park, as well as *refugios*, which are very primitive buildings where you can sleep—and do very little else. There are far too many to list here, so you'll need to get a guidebook or map to the park at one of the information offices, or talk to the guys in Jaca to plan your itinerary. As for sleeping in the park, there is no need for a camping permit to set up camp under the stars. However, if you stay at one of the organized campsites in Torla or near other small villages within the park, there will be a small fee. The *refugios* are on a first-come, first-serve basis. The majority of them are free and they sleep anywhere from 10 to 100 people. Be aware that although there are many *refugios* in the park, they are spread out. Find a map in advance and plan out your hike so that you know there will be one on or near your trek.

parque naturel posets-maladeta

This 15,000-acre nature park includes the highest peaks in the Pyrenees: the Posets (3,375 meters), Aneto (3,405 meters), and Maladeta (3,354 meters) mountains, each of them covered with glaciers. There's so much to do here you could practically write a book about it: You can ride a horse; jump on a parachute; go mountain cycling, climbing, or trekking; arrange a camping expedition; strap on some skis; go canoeing; do a little bird watching; or try your hand at fishing. Or you may just want to opt for the simplest of choices and take a hike through the park's ample forests of birch, black pine, oak, and fir. If you're lucky, you might even glimpse one of the park's snow partridges, or the famous *Parnasius Apollo Pyrenaica* (that's celebrated butterfly of the Pyrenees to you!).

Posets-Maladeta is a more recent subdivision of the government-protected areas of the Pyrenees National Park, and was created in 1994. The park surrounds the Valley of Benasque, lying on the high plateau of the Esera River basin. Manmade creations, like romantic little Lombard-style churches, blend into a landscape of high mountain peaks, craggy rock surfaces, and small mountain streams and waterfalls. During the late spring and summer it seems like every conceivable surface turns green, while a blanket of pristine snow puts the whole area to sleep in the winter, covering the already peaceful valley in dead quiet. The trails are well kept, but even the easy ones can be a challenge if you haven't strapped on the hiking boots in a while.

The **Cerler** ski area is nearby [see **Benasque,** above], but if you're not into all that namby-pamby ski-lifts-and-cocoa-in-the-lodge crap, some outdoor outfits in Benasque will walk you to the top of one of the mountains in the park and you can ski your way down [see *need to know,* below].

Actually, no matter what your plans are in the park, we'd recommend getting in touch with one of Benasque's excellent outdoor outfits. They can rent or sell you gear, hook you up with a package expedition, provide you with guides—both printed and human—and generally give you the inside scoop. But don't expect that you're going to get all this beauty to yourself—it gets kind of packed here in the summer, and the super peak season is in July and early August.

need to know

Hours/Days Open The park is open year-round. For more information on park activities, contact the Benasque tourist information office *(Tel 974/551-289; 9am-2pm/4-9pm daily July-Aug, 10am-2pm/5-8pm Tue-Fri, 5-9pm Sat, and 9:30am-1:30pm Sun Sept-June).*

Directions and Transportation From anywhere in Benasque, you can hike right into the park. If you want to find the official park entrance, it is on A139, about 10 km (6.2 mi) from the center of town. If you want to get a car or 4x4 to take you up to the woods, either meet a hottie with wheels at a local pub and turn on the charm, or call up one of the services in Benasque (car services, that is) to take you there.

Rental Any of the outdoor outfits in Benasque can help you with all sorts of gear, from skis to tents to climbing ropes [see **Benasque,** above].

Eats If you get hungry while you're on the trail, look in the free pamphlet titled *El placer de aprender,* available at the tourist office in Benasque. You'll find a guide to local mushrooms on the back page. Avoid the ones marked with the skull and crossbones, and enjoy. If you need something more substantial, head down to one of the restaurants in Benasque.

Crashing The **Llanos del Hospital** *(Camino del Hospital s/n; Tel 974/552-012; www.llanosdelhospital.com/frpist.htm; Prices vary by season and package; AE, MC, V)* is a ski area and glorified *refugio* sitting in the center of the park, clearly marked by signs along the main park road. The old stone house sits against a snow-covered mountainside that you've seen in movies like *The Sound of Music,* but never thought really existed. If you're here in the winter looking for a warm place to stay and some organized skiing, this is your best bet. It's also a summer option for those who prefer a bit of luxury to camping under the stars. They offer a number of different package deals that include food and lodging—and skiing, if that's what you came here for. For example, one night of lodging in a room for five to seven people with all meals included will run 5,600ptas per person.

There are tons of spots to camp in the park, as well as *refugios,* which are large, heated stone houses full of bunk beds that can accommodate a whole heap of people. There are far too many to list, and which one you choose to stay at really depends on the shape your trip takes. You'll need to get a guide to the park at the tourist office, or talk to the guys in Benasque to plan your itinerary.

If you decide you want to stay in a *refugio,* you'll need to reserve ahead of time by calling *(Tel 974/552-106).* The cost is 650ptas per person in a bunk bed. Refugios also offer access to a kitchen, where guests can prepare their own food.

catalunya &
the costa
brava

catalunya & the costa brava

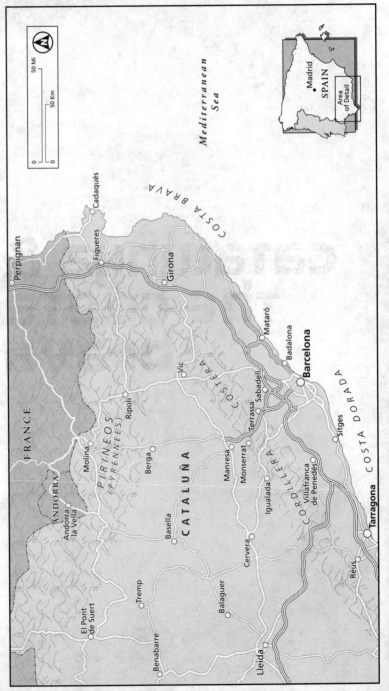

If you have only a limited amount of time in Spain, no one will act surprised if they find out you spent the entire time in Catalunya (which is the Catalan name for this region; its also known as Cataluña in Castilian, usually Catalonia in English). Between the art, architecture, and the drop-dead hipness of Barcelona, the gay culture and great atmosphere of Sitges, and the history of Tarragona, it has everything a poor young visitor could want and so, so much more.

If you are looking to find some edgy underground stuff in a foreign land, look no further than Barcelona. International culture has always felt right at home here. It's only intensified with the post-Olympic tourist boom that has made the city flush and happy. But, amazingly, the tourists don't get in the way of a good time, and the locals seem to dig the international vibe rather than exploit or resent it. According to Spaniards, Barcelona is the most European city in Spain. To the average Spanish person this might not be a compliment. But people in Barcelona strive to be as with-it, modern, and—most importantly—as hip as they can be. That means rad underground record labels and 'zines like *Ozono Kids,* great bars, a live music scene that rivals that of towns three times its size, and young people who are about as knowing as you'll find in Spain.

When the Spanish revolution went down, the anarchist stronghold was Barcelona. The workers took over the factories and a bunch of the rest of the city and made the dream work for a little while, until Franco came in and the fascist fun began. You can still feel a little of the do-your-own-thing energy in the air, and much of the Catholic traditionalism and state-supported conservatism has melted away in this city. It's all about great times and expressing yourself here, and you won't find a more modern and non-provincial atmosphere.

Oddly, for such an anti-colloquial place you'll find lots of local pride, including a local language. *Català* (Catalan) [see *language,* below] is one of the official languages of Barcelona and all of Catalunya. But instead of creating an isolated feel, the pride of the Catalan people is a pride that wants to show itself off, reveling in foreign curiosity (and to a certain extent, the envy of the rest of their countrymen). Catalunya is also the richest area of Spain. Foreign investors feel right at home in Barcelona, and Catalunya is a key banking and financial area. Madrid is still the capital, but the real, non-state money is flowing around in banks and businesses in Catalunya. The combination of wealth, pride, and a certain amount of shame at their countrymen (from Franco to the violent acts of the ETA to the backwater attitudes of some of the more secluded towns) has driven some Catalans to proclaim that Catalunya should be its own country. They aren't rabid about it, and hence no car bombs, but if you meet some Barcelona youth and get invited to dinner with the fam, it just might come up in conversation.

The coolness of **Barcelona** has definitely rubbed off on the smaller towns of Catalunya, to the point where they are each happenin' enough to add to the overall appeal and character of the region. If you want lovely, lovely sun and some great beaches, you'll be visiting the Costa Brava and the town of **Cadaqués,** where Dalí used to live. You can check out his trippy house after you get a nice healthy sunburn. The people are all outgoing, and protective of their town's beauty. That means a minimum of high tower-type buildings that screw up the atmosphere of many coastal villages.

Our runner-up for "most fun place we might just decide to move to," behind the all-powerful Barcelona, is **Girona (Gerona),** a town of only 80,000. Don't be surprised by your urge to gleefully skip through the old quarter with zeal, and expect to take some of your best rolls of film here. The great outdoor party in the La Devesa neighborhood and park, the awesome cultural offerings, and the friendliest, most with-it international

Language

Like several other distinct languages in this country, *Català* (Catalan in Castilian) is experiencing a rebirth after decades of being banned by Franco. This romance language that didn't seem to catch on is a source of great regional pride, and explains much of the people's independent streak. Just imagine all of those angry, frustrated Catalans shaking their fists impotently as France and Spain took over their country.

Catalá is closely related to Castilian Spanish, but also has roots in medieval Provençal. In this chapter we've kept to the *Català* names for towns, since many maps are now in *Català*. Many of the words, in any case, are similar, and you will probably recognize them. When trying to zen the meaning of a *Català* phrase, just imagine you are reading a cross between French and Spanish—Spench!

Some sample *Català* words: Plaça (for plaza), Avinguda (for Avenida), Passeig (for Paseo), Platja (for Playa), and Carrer (for Calle).

locals ever, might help you decide that Girona is where you want to go and raise your babies.

Want Roman ruins? Well have we got the place for you. If Roman ruins were THC, then **Tarragona** would be kind indeed. The nightlife is not as kicking here as it is in the big cities, but if you can't get back on that flight home without taking a picture of a Roman amphitheater for Mom, then you need to be checking out this place. Make sure to dig on the very, very Spanish townspeople and town layout. There's a great old quarter, and more history than you can shake a stick at.

If you are looking for fantastic nightlife, look no further than **Sitges,** probably the most beautiful place in the world in some ways. You'll find people out flaunting their thing, struttin' their stuff, and gettin' their groove on for 24 hours a day during the peak summer season. The hip, trendy, stylish gay and hetero crowd from across Europe flocks here to be at their best. Great beaches and so much tolerance it makes you cry.

So, no matter what your thing, if you are tight and in Spain you need to be in Catalunya for at least a little while. You can practice your Catalan, all the while learning about a culture that will take your brain, juggle it, spin it on one finger, and hand it back to you full of new ideas.

arT In CaTaLunya

What do you want, what do you want, what do you want? If you're a budding, streetwise, overtly trendy hipster who digs on the abstract, the brain crunchy...then check out Miró [see *culture zoo,* Barcelona]. If you prefer to have your little head tickled, touched, and fondled...do Dalí [see *culture zoo,* Cadaqués]. Or if you just like really, really fly buildings that make you think about design and habitats and rue your own uninspired little concrete box...go for Gaudí [see *culture zoo,* Barcelona]. Oh, you want to rethink perspective, dig on the fractured, and familiarize yourself with the revolutionary...find your way back to Picasso [see *culture zoo,* Barcelona].

Catalunya is to art and architecture what Bob Dylan is to singer/songwriters: defining yet revolutionary, in a way that makes some of us bubble up with admiration (against our more cynical natures). You can't get out of Barcelona without becoming cooler and more aware of art, and if you go in with the right attitude, there is no better place to shake up those preconceived notions of space, mind, and the individual.

If anyone ever tainted the water supply of a nice little European city with a whole load of LSD, you might get Barcelona, and it shows in the artwork. There are museums, galleries, public displays of affection, and performance on the streets and in the cafes. Just keep your eyes open and you will see.

The rest of Catalunya is no joke either, with festive atmospheres, film expos [see *festivals,* Sitges], Dalí's old house, museums, ancient cathedrals, Roman ruins, Moor-influenced old quarters, and people feeling that Catalan pride. If you are looking to dig on some of that Mediterranean vibe, and want to experience firsthand the effects of sun, time, and good wine (as well as absinthe, if you can find it) on the brain, just come to Catalunya and see the art and architecture. You might start getting a little creative with those sandcastles you're making on a Costa Brava beach.

If you have any questions about the viability of the modern art and music world, just come to this region where art lives, and is accessed by the people, too. There is no reason to be intimidated when art isn't an excuse for fancy parties, vogue photos, and caviar. In Barcelona, art is a part of life, an excuse from work and drudgery. If you keep your eyes open and your ears to the ground, you'll find that through art, lived as part of their daily lives, the people of Barcelona often transcend the banality of everyday existence with a little sip of the sublime.

getting around the region

Getting around Catalunya isn't too hard. There is a train that runs along the coast, so you can get from point A to point B without too much trouble. The main problem that you will encounter is that no matter where you go, you probably won't want to leave. That is why our biggest

TRAVEL TIMES

All times are by road unless indicated by a star: * = time by train ** = time by fast train	Barcelona	Cadaqués	Figueres	Girona	Sitges	Tarragona	Madrid
Barcelona	-	2:05	1:45*	1:25*	:35	1:20*	7:00** 9:00*
Cadaqués	2:05	-	:40	1:15	2:30	3:00	8:10
Figueres	1:45*	:40	-	:30*	1:55	2:50*	11:20*
Girona	1:25*	1:15	:30	-	1:40	2:15*	10:30*
Sitges	:35	2:30	1:55	1:40	-	:45	6:05
Tarragona	1:20*	3:00	2:50*	2:15*	:45	-	6:20*

pointer for traveling in Catalunya is to give yourself enough time. You won't want to be in and out of Barcelona in a couple of days. If you do limit yourself severely, you will get stuck chasing after tourist traps and being disappointed. Catalunya shines with treasures of culture and fun, but like all good booty this treasure is buried. You don't want to feel like you are missing something the whole time you are in Spain, so give yourself enough time and follow your instincts to the smokin' spots in town.

Getting around Catalunya is fairly easy because of each town's relative proximity to Barcelona and the shorter distances between towns. If you make Barcelona your home base you can take two separate trips, one north of the city and one south.

All of the beach towns north of Barcelona on the Costa Brava are breathtaking, so if you are interested in seeing others you can either take local buses or better yet, rent a car for a day.

To go south of Barcelona take the RENFE train headed for Tortosa. This train makes stops at Sitges, Tarragona, and Port Aventura.

A good itinerary might be to land in Barcelona, either on a plane or train from Madrid, and spend a few days getting used to the city. Don't expect too much initially, you'll need to scope out the area to get a feel. After you've got the Catalunya vibe down, take a one-hour train north to Girona and hang out for a few days, then take another hour ride to Figueres. From there, take an hour-and-10 minute bus ride into Cadaqués to spend some sweet time on a Costa Brava beach. Or you can go one hour south from Barcelona to Sitges on the train, party till your brain falls out, then head to Tarragona (1/2 hour). If you have the time, do both, with a stopover to see your old friend Barcelona.

barcelona

If you took the all-out party power of Parliament's George Clinton and mixed in equal parts of the more refined tastes of Sting, then shook them up and poured them over ice, you'd be pretty close to the trippy, wild, and refined flavors that make Barcelona such a delicious drink. Now, we'll be up front and tell you that Barcelona cannot compete with Madrid when it comes to per-capita party animalism—but who can? A smallish nation like Spain would probably have to admit its entire population into rehab if it had two cities like Madrid. However, Barcelona is gonna give you everything you want: fantastic bars and clubs, a fun and funky local population, more art and culture than Oasis has eyebrow, and a real, live beach.

Want to see the artwork, homes, and architecture of some of this century's greatest artists? Can do. Want to party from Thursday through Monday morning? *Sí, Señorita.* Want to sit around and drink coffee all day and watch the beautiful world pass by? Not a problem. Young folks like ourselves come here from all over Europe for these exact reasons, so maybe the first thing you should know before you drink down the big glass of electric kool-aid that is Barcelona is that you'll be surrounded by travelers and expats. Its location on the Mediterranean and its northern latitude has always kept Barcelona better-connected with Europe than other parts of Spain, so this city has been dealing with travelers of one sort or another for the better part of the last 1,500 years. You're just as likely to meet cool people from, say, Denmark or Australia as a local from B-town (as we like to call Barcelona). Well not just as likely, but it will happen quite a bit. This is not a bad thing. Barcelona is a legitimately international town, so meeting and becoming friends with out-of-towners (as well as people who grew up here but are of an ethnicity other than Spanish) really is part of the authentic local experience. It happens to natives all the time too, especially in the summer when people come pouring into town like Jeep Cherokees and ganga goo-balls into a Phish show. But unlike in Madrid, here international is a lot less likely to equal uncool.

In addition to travelers and expats, Barcelona now deals with its evil twin, the Commercial Tourist. (The difference between a traveler/expat and a tourist put simply: Bob Dylan is to travelers/expats as Billy Joel is to tourists.) Yes, 'twas the summer of 1992 when the Olympics came to town and brought with it a lot of money, a lot of revitalization, and a lot of people in white baseball hats. Some of the results of the XXV Olympiad are not, in our minds, so great. A whole lot of lame commercial venues sprouted up here that are as exciting and fun as a pimple before the prom. But some good things have come out of the age of the Commercial Tourist as well: You can now use your credit card nearly everywhere, and you'll be able to get by more easily with English—not only with the pre-conditioned locals, but also with the Germans, Swiss, and Dutch you'll be tripping over.

And speaking of speaking, remember that the national (or regional, depending on your politics) language here is not Spanish, it's Catalan, a language that is more or less half-Spanish and half-French. If you speak either, you'll probably be able to understand Catalan in the same way that you see things without your glasses: The general shapes and colors will be understood, but you'll miss out on most of the details. Understanding spoken Catalan is not usually something that's gonna happen for the newcomer, but the French or Spanish you learned in high school will help you out some, we hope. Even though Barcelona is in Spain, the locals have a lot of regional pride, and all of the signs, menus, and TV and radio shows are in Catalan. The flip side is that everyone in Barcelona also speaks perfect Spanish. It's totally kosher to address someone in *castellano* (Castilian, aka Spanish) without first asking if they speak it. Catalans are usually sympathetic to foreigners who speak only Spanish because A: that's better than speaking only English, and B: they know that Catalan isn't spoken anywhere else on Earth. We asked many locals to translate Catalan fliers and menus into Spanish for us, and they were all thrilled to translate words like "Tuesday," "free admission," and "happy hour."

The language in Barcelona is not its only distinctive feature—Catalan culture is unique, too. Most notably, the people here are a little more...cool, a bit more savvy. Barcelona will take anything and make it a piece of art: The sidewalks, the buildings, the bicycles; not to mention hair, shoes, and skirts. Authentic Vespa mopeds park alongside beautifully ornate water fountains. The serene streets and buildings of the Barri Gòtic district are only a few steps from the beautiful tile and glasswork of the Modernist architecture along Passeig de Grácia. Most of the streetlights in this town are good-looking, for chrissake! Each step these people take is imbued with a bit of style, and the look in their eyes—if you don't mind our generalizing—reflects an appreciation for the finer things in life. Even if it's just the young folks having coffee, their hipster look is more, well, hip.

So while the rest of the country accuses Barcelona of being too European (read: cold and standoffish), it's only because your new friends here aren't ravenous in-your-face party maniacs. (And we mean that literally: In Madrid people will get so close to you in conversation that your vision blurs, but here the locals—although still as animated and friendly—are slightly less thrilled to death by every passing moment.) Don't get the wrong idea—Barcelona is still a freakin' blast. You and your kind will probably party hard in this young people's town, but the locals don't do it with quite the sense of urgency and dedication that keeps Madrid throbbing till 6am. Barcelona has always had a better business sense than Madrid, and some folks here even seem to be more interested in being clear-headed for work the next day than they are in a sixth rum and Coke. Everything you like about Spain is still here—namely liberal drinking, dancing, and so on—but Barcelona is better-dressed and just a little calmer when it does these things. And despite the wild times you'll experience here, this town still somehow has more of a...homey feel. A lot of the venues are right downtown, and are an easy walk or cab ride from where you're gonna be staying, so you get a neighborhood vibe. Plus, most of the nightspots here host more than one kind of party—places like **Suborn** [see *bar scene,* below], **La Boîte** [see *live music scene,* below], and **Club Apolo** [see *club scene,* below] switch from live music to a DJ after 2am on most nights—so you'll keep coming back to the same spots.

August, by the way, is the worst month to visit Barcelona—tourists are rampant, and many locals literally head for the hills, so your chances of hanging with locals diminishes considerably. And finding a place to stay becomes a real pain in the rump.

So how do you find the cool and keep away from the drool? As in Madrid, the *Guía del Ocio* is also available here (in *castellano* only, but easy to navigate), and it's as all-knowing here as it was there. Barcelona is home to several other very groovy magazines too, most notably *A Barna (aB), Punto H, Micro,* and a very trendy magazine called *b-guided.* All three have a lot of good reading (with articles in both Spanish and Catalan, although *b-guided* is in English and Spanish) about club scenes, fashion, movies, etc. But you'll probably like them best for club and bar "window shopping"—when you see something that looks cool in any of them, look it up in the *Guía* to make sure the event is still on (*A Barna* and *Micro* both come out only monthly).

neighborhoods

Barcelona's most obvious landmark is the Mediterranean Sea, its coastline running from southwest to northeast. The Barcelona you'll want to experience lies largely in the **Ciutat Vella** ("old city"), situated along the southeastern edge of the city close to the Mediterranean. **La Rambla** is the big avenue that splits the Ciutat Vella in two equal halves, with the **El Raval** neighborhood on the southwest and the **Barri Gòtic** on the northeast. You're gonna get a whole lot of La Rambla, friends—it runs from the **Plaça Catalunya** at the north straight down to the **Mirador de Colón** [see *culture zoo*, below] at the edge of the sea (about a 20-minute walk from end to end), and everything you'll be looking for in the **Ciutat Vella** will be conveniently located to one side or the other of it. There's no way to avoid this street, which, like the Spin Doctors, you'll totally love at first, but soon will wish just wasn't around so often.

The cobblestone streets in the Barri Gòtic are narrow and winding; you'll come upon cool little plazas and beautiful hidden buildings. The traditionally bohemian **El Born** neighborhood is also located here (on the northeastern edge of the Barri Gòtic, about a 15-minute walk northeast from the center of La Rambla), along with several great bars and restaurants as well as the **Picasso Museum** [see *culture zoo*, below].

A few minute's walk along the shore to the east of **Mirador de Colón** is the **Maremagnum,** a "waterfront development area" (read: a mall with a boardwalk) spawned by the Olympic-related hoopla. It is remarkably like a North American mall and therefore not really given a lot of air time in this guide. There's a whole lot of Olympic and tourist hype here in general. It's great to walk along the water here, but the restaurants in this area are overpriced, and the only locals you'll meet will be the ones serving you dinner. Maremagnum's also got a whole lot of clubs that offer free admission and a free drink or two—but unless you're really broke, they're best avoided. If you continue walking northeast along the coast for another 5 minutes or so, you'll come to the **Port Olímpic,** which is even more hyped than Maremagnum. The beach begins here, though, and for that reason it is worth checking out.

Other enormous but uninteresting streets that people will direct you to are the east-west **Gran Vía** (runs through **Plaça de Espanya,** and is just a few blocks north of **Plaça de Catalunya**), **Avenida Diagonal** (runs northwest to southeast and cuts the whole city in half, 10 blocks northwest of the **Cuitat Vella**), and **Passeig de Gràcia,** which begins at Plaça de Catalunya and runs north to Avenida Diagonal.

Gràcia, about an hour's walk to the northwest of the Ciutat Vella, is like the Norman Rockwell portrait of Barcelona. It's an idyllic neighborhood with a sense of community distinct from downtown Barcelona. Be sure to check out the **Plaça del Sol,** the centerpiece of the neighborhood, for a relaxing drink among the natives.

East of the Barri Gòtic and El Raval is **L'Eixample** (often divided into **L'Eixample Izquierdo**—the left half—and **L'Eixample Derecho**—the right half), which means "the enlargement," and is nothing more than a big grid of commercial streets that is void of any detectable character—the coolest thing about this area is the octagonal intersections and **La Raspa** [see *hanging out,* below]. The neighborhood of Gràcia was once a separate little village outside the old city walls (erected by the Romans). They were knocked down, however, to make way for the modern streets of L'Eixample.

The **Sants-Montjuïc** neighborhood (**Mont Juïc** is the big mountain in the southwest part of town) is an otherwise unremarkable middle-class city neighborhood at the northwest end of the city. The Plaça de Espanya, at its southeastern corner, is the most important thing about this area. Be sure to check out the fountains here one night [see *down & out,* below]. The **Poble Espanyol** area is notable too, if only for the EPCOT-esque culture park of the same name [see *culture zoo,* below] and a handful of clubs—most notably **La Terrrazza** [see *club scene,* below], and yes, it has three r's.

Parallel/Poble Sec, between El Raval and Mont Juïc, is considered the theater district by the natives but is really more like off-Broadway. The best theaters [see *arts scene,* below] are sprinkled throughout town. Poble Sec is home to **Club Apolo** [see *club scene,* below], and that's about it.

El Raval, bordering the southwest side of La Rambla, used to be the worst part of town, complete with hookers, hard drugs, and a lot of muggers waiting for naive or lost tourists. But, like John Travolta, this neighborhood has experienced a remarkable comeback in recent years. Although first cleaned up by throwing everyone in jail (in preparation for the Olympics), El Raval has since been populated by artists and musicians in need of low rent. Several museums, coffee shops, and thrift shops can be found here, too, but you should still use caution on **L'Arc del Teatre** and points south. This area of El Raval is known as **Barre Xinés,** which, translated literally, means China Town, but in Catalan slang, means red-light district. Since the cleanup, though, the worst that will probably happen to you here is that an aging prostitute might proposition you, but you should still be wary of your wallet, and women should not travel here alone.

Can't figure out why everyone was staring at you as you slid your metro card through the reader to your right? Well, maybe after you've rammed your crotch into an ungiving subway turnstile you'll figure it out. When your breath returns, take a closer look at the card readers and you'll notice that they're on the *left* side of the turnstiles, contrary to every other turnstile in the free world. Once you've made it to the platform, you'll realize that Barcelona's efficient and clean subway system is like the anti-Visa: It's almost never where you want to be. We can only assume that they didn't want to dig up the Ciutat Vella to set up metro stops there, so the stops closest to where you wanna get are on La Rambla and over by the Port Olímpic. You'll find that it's a lot easier to walk to a lot of destinations. But that's cool—the architecture here is beautiful and, if you're here in the summer, the weather isn't as overbearing as it is in towns to the south. One thing to check out, though, is Line 1 (red line) on the metro. This subway train is ONE BIG CAR, man! It's too freaking much!! One big, bendy, tube of a train! Whoooo-hoo!

hanging out

El Café que pone Muebles Navarro (aka **Muebles Navarro, Café Muebles,** etc.) *(Riera Alta 4-6; Tel 607/188-096; Metro to Liceu; 4pm-midnight Tue-Thur, 5pm-2am Fri, Sat, 5pm-midnight Sun; No credit cards)* is an absolute must-see on your quest for cool Barcelona. Like its XL name (which refers to a past life as a table factory), this building's

five things to talk to a local about

1. **Language skills:** The Catalans truly are bilingual. They float in and out of Spanish and Catalan as easily as grandma weaving her 1984 Buick between two lanes on the highway. If you want to get on someone's good side, simply ask "Do you really speak Catalan as well as Spanish?" Then sit back and listen to your new Barcelona friend expound upon his or her mad language skills and those of the community at large.

2. **Madrid vs. Barcelona:** In the Madrid chapter, we told you how the Madrileños consider those in Barcelona to be closed-minded. Here in Barcelona, they'll tell you how in Madrid, they have no sense of fashion, art, or business. Especially business. Catalunya has been an epicenter of trade for the better part of 2,000 years, and the thriving trade of this region has continually been circumvented by political bungles in Madrid.

3. **El Raval:** We've given you a few warnings here and there about the El Raval neighborhood, but ask a local what this (and other) parts of Barcelona were like before the Olympics. If you're lucky, you'll get a tour and hear the story about the police officer who used to stand where L'Arc del Teatre meets La Rambla, warning travelers not to enter that neighborhood.

4. **Cultcha:** Ask a local why Barcelona likes its theater and art so much. The locals here lean toward the philosophical anyway, and a question like this is bound to get them thinking.

5. **More Cultcha:** Ask your local what his or her favorite museum is—maybe they'll take you there. If your new friend doesn't have a favorite, dump him/her quick. Barcelona's got more museums than NASCAR's got bad sunglasses. In the home of some of the last century's most influential artists, everyone ought to have a favorite museum.

physical size will give you vertigo if you've become accustomed to the little tiny bars and cafes (and, let's face it, everything else) of Europe. Texas-sized space between tables, many couches, and authentic NYC cheesecake. For-sale artwork, Barcelona's only poetry slam (in Catalan, Spanish, and occasionally English), plays, and live acoustic music are enjoyed by young folks, 20 to 32, wearing anything from combat boots and lip rings to button-down shirts and hair gel. Very Greenwich Village.

The Jardins Rubio i Lluch *(Metro to Liceu; 10am-sunset Mon-Sat),* at the **Escola Massana** [see *arts scene,* below] would be a cool place to hang out even if it wasn't usually full of art students smoking cigarettes between classes. Plenty of benches, steps, archways, and colorful trees keep you company while you sit and read. Afterward, walk into the *escola* and check out the (usually impressive) works on display in the two-room student gallery. If you're looking to meet María or José de la Arte, keep in mind that their midday break runs from noon till 3.

An *intercambio* (interchange) is when people from different nations get together to practice speaking each other's languages. It's a great way to learn a language and to make friends, too, and not in the least as cheesy as it might sound. As with everything in Spain, these events usually involve a drink. Enter **La Raspa** *(Mallorca 188; No phone; Metro to CLOT; 7pm-2:30am daily; No credit cards)*, a fantastic place to meet people from all over the globe (including worldly Catalans). Although relocated internationals stop by the bar every day of the week, Wednesday at 9:30pm is the official *intercambio* time. If you're a stranger, you'll be greeted by the hostess. Tell her what you'd like to speak, and you'll be brought to a table with like-minded individuals (who come from all walks of coolness, but are always under 35 years of age). Because most people are here to try something different, be prepared to speak Spanish with Swiss, Japanese, and other Americans; the actual Spanish will be trying their luck at the English or French tables. The booze (about 350ptas per beer) helps to make the talk easier and more fun, but the vibe here is unmistakably cerebral.

Impress friends and family back home by telling them about how you saw the sun rise on the Mediterranean Sea. If you don't dig the crowds, continue walking past all the hotel lounge chairs, bar-huts, and other assorted Olympic hoopla until things thin out a bit. Outdoor parties pop up on the beach during the summer months—check the *Guía del Ocio*.

Plaça George Orwell, in the Barri Gòtic, is worth checking out for the name alone. But, as you might have guessed, this *plaça* is anything but Big Brother. You'll find a whole lot of cool bars and restaurants (almost 30 if you count the adjoining streets), and, on Saturdays and Sundays, small markets offering clothes, CDs, etc. There's a big weird-looking Picasso statue and lots of artists and other cool young folks in black sitting around drinking and enjoying a cool night breeze (the sea is only a few minutes away) before hitting the clubs for the night. Occasional drum circles happen here, but it's not a hippie scene. Many locals say that this is the best place to meet young artsy types of all varieties.

The big, tree-lined La Rambla is full of street performers, artisans, outdoor bars and restaurants, gift shops, people from all over the world, and Spain's only sex museum. Begin at **Plaça de Catalunya** at the top of the street and start struttin', baby. You'll wind up at Colón and then the Port Olímpic and then (more importantly) the Mediterranean! Give yourself a good two to three hours so that you can take in the dozens of trinket shops and statue performers [see *only here,* below], along with top-notch architecture-sighting and eating/drinking. All of this is true, by the way, whether you're here at 9am or 3am.

bar scene

Barcelona is a drinker's town. With a rich tradition of spending time with friends and family (and occasionally plotting anti-Madrid revolutions) in pubs, the opportunities for a beer here have evolved into something of an art form. Whether you want small and dark or modern and vibrant, we had a hard time picking out the bars that we liked best. In general, the best bars are in El Raval and El Born. Also check the **Plaça George Orwell** [see *hanging out,* above]. Like Madrid, the bars here stay open till 3 or 4am. The one downside to the B-town bars, however, is that they're not very tapas-centric—unless they're serving actual meals, anything beyond peanuts or chips is simply not part of Catalunya culture. Without further ado, below are some truly great Barcelona bars.

If the starship Enterprise was stuffed into a blender with Deee-lite, you'd get **Dot** *(Nou de Sant Francesc 7; Tel 933/027-026; Metro to Drassanes; 9pm-2:30am Mon-Thur, Sun; 9pm-3am Fri, Sat; No credit cards).* Teleporter-style lights, subtle neon, and Japanese Godzilla movies on the projector TV create a futuristic, edgy look that, incredibly, still somehow exudes "neighborhood pub." In the back room, *el DJ residente,* Professor Angel Dust, spins a good mix of electronica most nights of the week, but never so loud that you can't talk with the young, style-y, and (semi-) international crowd here. The two-room venue becomes too crowded Thursday through Saturday, but the weekdays, honestly, are very right-on. Wear cosmo-black, prep, goth, club...this place is right out of a Levi's ad. Beer costs 300ptas. And you're only seconds away from **Harlem** [see *live music scene,* below].

If Dot is the bar of the future, **Olivia Club** *(Joaquín Costa 39; No phone; Metro to Plaça de Goya; 6pm-2am daily; No credit cards)* is definitely the bar of the past. It's like a movie about your parents' first apartment in the '70s, with a soundtrack by modern Catalan bands who apparently grew up listening to Talking Heads. Olivia, located on the east end of El Raval, is actually somebody's living room during the day—the floor lamps with yellowed shades, the old felt loveseats, and the low coffee tables really do play host to the owner and his guests during off-hours. Beers are cheap at 200ptas, and everything is comfortable. The crowd is artists and an occasional grungy hipster (mid-twenties) who know they've found a good thing here.

Suborn *(Ribera 18; Tel 933/101-100; Metro to Jaume I; 9pm-2:30am Tue-Sat, noon-1:30am Sun, closed Mon; V, MC)* offers DJs, live music, art exhibitions, free movies, and food. But regardless of the event, you can always have a drink—that's why we put it in *bar scene.* Although Suborn's modern, metallic look contrasts with the historically bohemian (and hardwood) El Born neighborhood, this new kid on the block still has a familiar feel, thanks mainly to a kitchen that's run by the mom of one of the owners and the 10 or so terrace tables facing the **Parc de la Ciutadella** [see *great outdoors,* below]. Wednesday and Thursday nights are often the best here. The regulars, who are in their twenties, like their pants corduroy and their hair spiked. The unique hipster sports bar scene that develops here when Barcelona is on the soccer pitch is worth checking out, even if you're not into soccer.

Bar Rosal Café *(Passeig del Born 27; No phone; Metro to Jaume I; 9:30am-3am daily; No credit cards)* is located only 5 minutes from Suborn, but exudes a more classical El Born attitude: small dining room, low lights, and political discussions. Rosal's menu of couscous and other Mediterranean favorites won't win over any critics, but the real allure of this venue is the big-time terrace scene: Nurse your coffee or beer (a mere 150ptas) and enjoy fantastic people-watching as you sit with the local kings and queens of thrift-shop cool.

When you've had enough of the "polished" side of Barcelona, it's time for **Kentucki** *(Arco del Teatro 11; Tel 933/182-878; Metro to Drassanes; 8pm-3am Mon-Sat; No credit cards),* where the dress code and drink prices are so prole that you expect to see Billy Bragg playing "From Red to Blue" in the corner. It's warm and communal, despite a rough Raval facade. Amenities include a working pinball machine (!), a jukebox with only 10 discs (including Cher, early Wailers, and ABBA), and absinthe [see *only here,* below]. Crowded, lively, and young on weekends, with a dominating local crowd. Weeknights are just about the same, after the soccer matches end at 11:30pm and the old men go home. This place is a trip, full of wackos and very real people with good stories to tell.

Plaça del Sol *(in the Grácia neighborhood; Most restaurants open till midnight, bars till 3am)* is the perfect evening place in spring and summer. The scene here is formed by the tables and chairs from the eight or nine bars surrounding the plaza. Although the crowd is older than in other places we liked, the place is hardly uptight (it *is* Spain we're talking about

hambo meets hamba

Barcelona is a whole lot less sexually charged than Madrid, so the rules are pretty much as they are in the States. Buy someone a drink, say "hola," ask for directions or a translation, or "accidentally" brush up against them on the dance floor. Travelers aren't much of a novelty here, so you're gonna get fewer points for uniqueness than you might in more remote parts of Europe, but on the other hand, a local is more likely to know what they're in for when they're talking to somebody wearing a NY Yankees hat. Keep in mind, too, that there's a chance you might actually make it into someone's apartment in Barcelona, because young folks here (many of whom have been travelers just like you) have a better shot than their Madrileño counterparts of moving out of Mom and Dad's and into their own places.

here...). You're guaranteed a real-deal Barcelona neighborhood experience. As always, there are foreigners, too, but at least they're the ones who
live and work here. Wear what you like—you won't stand out for looking
"going-out" good or for wearing sandals and a two-day shadow. Beers
usually cost 300ptas.

LIVE MUSIC SCENE

Barcelona is just as much a greenhouse for music as it is for art. It just
seems to grow and grow here, needing little else besides water, air and
sunlight. Barcelona has a long history as a city with a deep love for jazz.
Consequently, the jazz clubs are the most established and well-known.
However, this hardly means it is the only thing going on. While you'll
definitely want to check out one of the many jazz clubs, also keep your
eye out for flyers and posters advertising other kinds of live music. There
are plenty of shows and local bands here. This city has it all—the only
trouble is much of it is underground. Barcelona and its cosmopolitan self
has an indie-rock music movement going on, many experimental flamenco groups and possibly the most thriving electronic music scene in
Spain. The moral of the story is: If live music is what you want, you can
get it. You may just have to work a little harder for it.

Jamboree *(Plaça Reial 17; Tel 933/017-564; Metro to Drassanes;
10pm-3am daily; www.masimas.com; No credit cards)*, pronounced yam-
boree, is a historic Barcelona jazz mecca in El Raval. Chet Baker, Ella
Fitzgerald, and newcomers like Danilo Pérez have all played this small,
smart venue. As would be expected with the music, the crowd is older
and quieter, but certainly not old and quiet. The stone arches, low
lighting, and little tiny tables will nicely complement a dress or clean
shirt. Entrance is between 1,500 and 1,800ptas, which includes a drink.

There's a gig at the small and comfortable **La Boîte** *(Diagonal 477;
Tel 933/191-789; Metro to Hospital Clínic; 11pm-5:30am daily;
www.masimas.com; No credit cards)* seven nights a week. Although the management at this L'Eixample spot claims to offer an "eclectic" program, a lot
of the music here leans toward jazz. To that end, though, some serious
names have played here, including Jimmy Smith, Lou Donaldson, Elvin
Jones. For whatever reason, this place is a magnet for young couples who
know they're listening to some of the best and behave and dress accordingly.
Cover is usually between 1,000 and 1,500ptas; a gin and tonic goes for
800ptas.

Penúltimo *(Passeig del Borne 19; Tel 933/102-596; Metro to Jaume I;
10pm-2:30am daily; 500-1,000ptas cover; penultimo@hotmail.com; No
credit cards)* is very El Borne—cramped, dark, and small enough that you
can watch the guitarist's fingering, if you want. The clientele consists
mostly of artists in their late twenties who seem to be going somewhere
with their careers and artists in their mid-forties who never got on the
train. The music (which comes from all over Europe and the Americas) is
usually quality and includes everything from Latin funk to pop and
reggae. Skits and poetry readings are also part of the itinerary.

Sidecar *(Heures 4-6, Plaça Reial; Tel 933/021-586; Metro to Drassanes; 10pm-3am Tue-Sun; No credit cards),* pronounced *see-day-car,* is a cornerstone of the Barcelona live music scene, supplying the locals with everything from (you guessed it) jazz to thrash-metal monkeys and most things in between. Unless the band is big (as in FM-radio big), entrance is only 300ptas (which also gets you a ticket for a free beer). Because Sidecar is on the Plaça Reial, right off La Rambla, many a young traveler winds up here. But the locals show up for the ample downstairs music venue, pool table, and chill upstairs (as well as for the saucy international pickup scene).

Although the price is right *(Free Tue-Thur and Sun, only 600ptas Fri, Sat)* for jazz and blues at the **Harlem Jazz Club** *(Comtessa de Sobradiel 8; Tel 933/100-755; Metro to Plaça de L'Angel; 10pm-3am Tue-Sun; No credit cards),* the vinyl floor, dropped ceilings, and cheap photos of sheet music resting on top of piano keys don't exactly give the Harlem feel. But the college-student crowd is cool with that; they're all wearing sneakers and T-shirts anyway. And even though Harlem isn't pretty, the music is usually good, drinks are cheap, and you'll make friends here with more ease than at any other music venue in town.

For even more jazz, check out the **Pipa Club,** in the Teatre Malic [see *arts scene,* below].

cLub scene

The Barcelona club scene can't compete with Madrid's in terms of numbers, but the attitude is still right: Drink late, stay awake by any means possible, and dance, dance, dance. Although both cities warm up around midnight, hit their prime time at about 2am, and only begin to let up around 4:30am, Barcelona is a little less ferocious about the whole thing: There are fewer clubs fighting for your time, and the bouncers are generally more relaxed. B-Town outdoes Madrid, however, in that its 'zines have got it together. *A Barna (aB)* and *Micro* are both published here, both by former students of the **Escola Massana** art school [see *arts scene,* below], and give you the live, ground-level look at what your friends would be wearing, playing, doing, and watching if you had friends in Spain. (Of course there's also the Barcelona edition of the omniscient *Guía del Ocio.*) Keep in mind that the many clubs of the Port Olímpic are often populated by young obnoxious internationals and older businessmen who are looking a little too hard for some monkey business.

There's a great student culture in this town—stay away from the harbor and have a great time with great people at places like Galaxy and Club Apolo and Moog [see below]. Barcelona club prices are usually the same as Madrid (usually 1,200-2,000ptas, including a free drink), and you can find the same range of clubs, from meat market (Port Olímpic) to hipster/sophisticated (Galaxy).

Locals use words like "mythic" and "legendary" when describing **Moog** *(Arc del Teatre 3; Tel 933/017-282; Metro to Drassanes; 11:30pm-5am daily; www.masimas.com; No credit cards),* the El Raval club that is

only here

Barcelona, in itself, is one of a kind. They'd have to paint the parking meters like rainbows and put clown shoes on the cops to make the place any more festive and happy than it already is.

One specific example: the statue performers along La Rambla. These silver and bronze people stand perfectly still until you put some money in their box, and then they move like Disneyland robots. Most of these guys are cool, and each one has his or her gimmick—just be sure to give them money if you're gonna take a picture or video.

Another unique thing (in Spain, at least): absinthe. Yes, absinthe, friends, the legendary, hallucinogenic drink of yore. Is it real? Is it legal? Is it simply anise and a whole lot of talk? Well, we did our best to get the lowdown on this elusive drink. Although the owner of **Marcela** (*Sant Pau 65; No phone; Metro to Liceu; 9pm-3am daily; No credit cards*) claims that only his establishment serves "real" absinthe, a variety of other bars, including **Kentucki** [see *bar scene*, above] and **Bar Patsís** (*Santa Mónica 4, El Raval; No phone; Metro to Sant Antoni; 7:30pm-2:30am daily; No credit cards*) will also serve you something that, if not absinthe, is still pretty lethal. When you buy the absinthe, you get a bottle of water and two sugar cubes with it. Rest a fork over the top of a glass and put a sugar cube on top. Pour a bit of water on the cube so that it slowly dissolves into the absinthe below. When it's done, add a little more water (a glass of absinthe tastes like a handful of black licorice–flavored Altoids) and toss it back, baby. Be careful. The effects (akin to the fringe of a hallucinogenic fever) take a minute or two to kick in. Some people, notably Brazilians, pour a bit of it into a saucer, then mush up the sugar cubes into the absinthe. They do not add water; instead, they light it on fire! (Fire! Fire!) They wait a minute as the potent mixture begins to crystallize, then jab their hand into the blue flames, pull the red-hot glob out quick, and put it in their mouth! The hand won't get burned, but the head might.

home away from home for many of Europe's biggest DJs. But the truth is that the "big" house DJs that spin on weekends don't cut it. Instead, experience the Moog's past glory on Wednesday nights, when an international DJ (who will probably favor hardcore techno) takes the tables. The young crowd fills up the 300-person-capacity dance floor at about 3am. The

barcelona

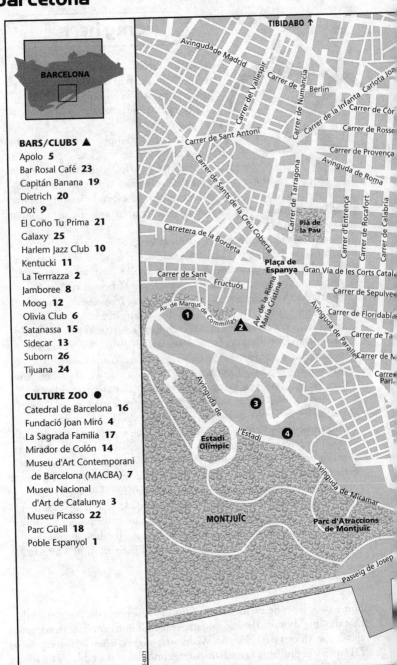

BARCELONA

BARS/CLUBS ▲

Apolo **5**
Bar Rosal Café **23**
Capitán Banana **19**
Dietrich **20**
Dot **9**
El Coño Tu Prima **21**
Galaxy **25**
Harlem Jazz Club **10**
Kentucki **11**
La Terrrazza **2**
Jamboree **8**
Moog **12**
Olivia Club **6**
Satanassa **15**
Sidecar **13**
Suborn **26**
Tijuana **24**

CULTURE ZOO ●

Catedral de Barcelona **16**
Fundació Joan Miró **4**
La Sagrada Familia **17**
Mirador de Colón **14**
Museu d'Art Contemporani
  de Barcelona (MACBA) **7**
Museu Nacional
  d'Art de Catalunya **3**
Museu Picasso **22**
Parc Güell **18**
Poble Espanyol **1**

E-0371

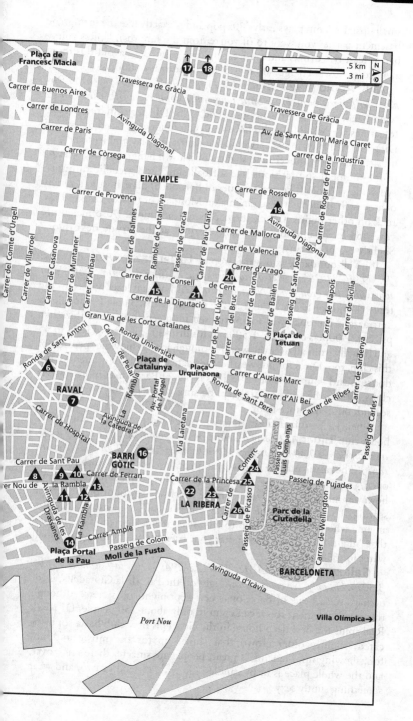

Plaça de Francesc Macia

Carrer de Buenos Aires

Carrer de Londres

Carrer de Paris

Carrer de Còrsega

Travessera de Gràcia

Avinguda Diagonal

17 18

0   .5 km
     .3 mi

N

Travessera de Gràcia

Av. de Sant Antoni Maria Claret

Carrer de la Industria

EIXAMPLE

Carrer de Provença

Carrer de Rossello

19

Avinguda Diagonal

Carrer de Balmes

Ramble de Catalunya

Passeig de Gràcia

Carrer de Pau Claris

Carrer de Mallorca

Carrer de Valencia

Carrer d'Aragó

Carrer de R. de Llúcia

del Bruc

Carrer de Girona

Carrer de Bailén

Passeig de Sant Joan

Carrer de Roger de Flor

Carrer de Napols

Carrer de Sicilia

Carrer del Comte d'Urgell

Carrer de Villarroel

Carrer de Casanova

Carrer de Muntaner

Carrer d'Aribau

Carrer del

Consell

Carrer de la Diputació

15   21

20

de Cent

Plaça de Tetuan

Gran Via de les Corts Catalanes

Carrer de Casp

Plaça de Sardenya

Ronda de Sant Antoni

Carrer de Sant Antoni

Carrer de Pelai

Ronda Universitat

Plaça de Catalunya

Plaça Urquinaona

Plaça de Tetuan

Carrer d'Ausias Marc

Ronda de Sant Pere

Carrer d'Ali Bei

Carrer de Ribes

Passeig de Carles I

6

RAVAL

7

Rambla

Av. Portal de l'Angel

Avinguda de la Catedral

Via Laietana

Carrer de Hospital

BARRI GÒTIC

16

Carrer de Ferran

Carrer de Sant Pau

8   9   10

la Rambla

13

11   12

La Rambla

Carrer de la Princesa

Comerç

24

Passeig de Lluís Companys

Passeig de Pujades

22   23

LA RIBERA

25

Carrer de

26

Passeig de Picasso

Parc de la Ciutadella

Carrer de Wellington

14

Plaça Portal de la Pau

Carrer Ample

Passeig de Colom

Moll de la Fusta

Avinguda d'Icàvia

BARCELONETA

Port Nou

Villa Olímpica →

small upstairs room plays early-'80s pop and is exactly like the fifth-grade basement parties you went to (if you're from the suburbs). Unless you've had at least five drinks and are wearing dark sunglasses, avoid this room at all costs. Cover charge 800 to 1,500ptas, beers for 500ptas.

Club Apolo *(Nou de La Rambla 113; Tel 934/414-001; Metro to Parallel; Midnight-6am Thur-Sun; www.nitsa.com; No credit cards)* hosts Nitsa Club, which is at the opposite end of the DJ spectrum from Moog: It features very good DJs who have small cult followings (kind of like Ani DiFranco had back in '92). Two additional rooms play ambient and pop music. The young movers and shakers of B-town hang out here, wearing of-the-moment sub-fashions like softball shirts and metallic turquoise eye shadow. Apolo (like most venues in Barcelona) plays host to a variety of arts, such as international cinema on Mondays or (disco) salsa and live rock on other nights. Check the papers to learn more. (Also make sure you sample the abundant pinball offerings at the arcade next door.) Slightly out of the way, over in Poble Sec.

If it's all-out dance you want, stop by **La Terrrazza** *(Poble Espanyol; Tel 934/231-285; Metro to Espanya; Midnight-6am Thur-Sun; www.nightsun-group.com; No credit cards)*. Although it loses points for the three r's and for being located in the tourist-centric Poble Espanyol, La Terrrazza is fun once you accept the self-indulgent decor and Ibiza-like prices (2,400ptas entrance! 1,500ptas for drinks!). The crowd is 18 to 35 and literally from all over the world—though locals enjoy the spectacle of this club, too. Dress for hot weather, hot dancing, and hot innuendo, but don't discard your sense of taste: This is one of Barcelona's more upscale clubs. When the sun's coming up, be sure you're getting down on the second, outdoor dance floor.

When La Terrrazza closes, many people head over to the after-after-hours club **Tijuana** *(Passeig Marítim 34; No phone; You'll be taking a cab, trust us; 6am-10:30am Sat-Sun May-Oct only; Cover 2,000ptas; No credit cards)*. The music may be all bass and no brains, but when nothing else is open, you start not to care. The big (1,000-plus people) and dark venue, however, may do less for you than the beachside splendor of the terrace seating. The crowd can be very gay but is usually well-mixed, because anyone who is too hepped-up to fall asleep winds up here. Go once for that "nightlife-in-Spain" story that your friends back home want. Small water for 600ptas.

Galaxy *(Princessa 53; Tel 934/122-294; Metro to Jaume I; 11pm-3:30am Sat only; No credit cards)*, right off the Parc de la Ciutadella, is (or perhaps was...) one of Barcelona's best-kept nightclub secrets. Although this small basement room can cram in only about 250 people, DJ Mark Ryal spins the best deep house in the city. This new club has a sophisticated, slightly older crowd that shows up for the music and not for...showing up. Dancing is great, people are sincere, there's no cover, and the whole place is lit by candles. Go with a friend or two, and wear something subtly sexy.

ARTS SCENE

Unlike Madrid, whose epicenters of art and culture are like islands in a sea of industry and bureaucracy, Barcelona emits artistry and creativity from every street corner. The quarterly Spanish/English guide *b-guided,* which can be picked up at Tribu [see below], will guide you to the city's best secrets in young and on-the-money fashion, art, restaurants, and clubs. Seek out Tribu and this magazine early in your visit, as they will lead you right into the middle of the best this city has to offer. In addition to *b-guided,* the *Guía del Ocio* will open you up to a thunderstorm of theaters, galleries, and cafes that *all* host live music *and* art exhibitions *and* small plays. The city itself (i.e., the government) brings to the party an absurd number of *festivales* dedicated to the arts, which the citizens here eat up. This city has, after all, produced the likes of Picasso, Dalí, Miró, and Gaudí. Most of the best stuff happens in the Ciutat Vella, which is split into two art hemispheres: the torn and frayed El Raval to the west and the philosophical Barri Gòtic (which includes El Born) to the east.

▶▶VISUAL ARTS

Hangar *(Marqués de Santa Isabel 40; Tel 933/084-041; Metro to Poblenou or Bus 40, 42, 71; 9am-2pm/3-6pm Mon-Fri; www.hangar.org)* is an artist-advocacy group that offers dirt-cheap studio space, fantastic connections, and a politically sharp staff. If you're an art student (in video, photography, computer animation, sculpture, acting, painting, or drawing) who will be in Barcelona for awhile, drop by. Although there are no exhibits at Hangar, the staff is well-informed on where the exhibits are. Contact Laia González (she's very friendly) at the above address for more info on how to obtain studio space or otherwise get involved. Hangar is in the northeastern area of the Poble Nou neighborhood and is best reached by any of the buses listed above.

The **Escola Massana** *(Hospital 56; Tel 934/422-000; Metro to Liceu; 10am-1pm/4-6pm Mon-Fri; www.ictnet.es/massana)* is a small school of art and design that offers a similar scene. In addition to the mellow **Jardins Rubio i Lluch** [see *hanging out,* above], the school offers bulletin boards with info on small art exhibitions, a two-room gallery that displays student work, and, of course, real, live Catalan art students! Be sure to study their look—they wear things you won't see elsewhere. Scoping time is prime at about 1pm, the midday break, so plan to be here in El Raval around then.

Near Escola Massana is the small, raw, and urban **Galleria Urania** *(Doctor Dou 19; Tel 934/122-345; Metro to Liceu or Catalunya; 11am-1:30pm/5-8:30pm Tue-Sat; artinproject@mail.cinet.es; V, MC, AE).* Exhibitions include a "fair balance" of up-and-coming folks and more established artists. The management also runs "Art in Project," a program that was created to give art students international exposure via a network of small galleries throughout Europe.

festivals and events

Carnestoltes (carnival) *(February)* includes the castelles, or castles, where Barcelonians pit their strength and balance against each other in attempts to build the tallest human towers. Also freaky *gegantes* (giants) and the freaky-freaky *capgrossos* (fatheads). Watch out for the *capgrossos*—they are among the goddamn freakiest things you ever saw.

A particularly beautiful holiday is the **Día de Sant Jordi** *(April 23),* when lovers exchange gifts. Women will gripe about this holiday (in jest), because tradition dictates that the man buys the woman a rose (for three bucks or so) and the woman lays out the equivalent of 15, 20 or more dollars for the traditional gift of a book for the man. This holiday has not yet been mucked up by the corporate vultures who have ruined Valentine's Day in the States, but book and rose vendors pop up on the streets this day faster than trannie fights on *Jerry Springer.*

The **Día de Sant Joan** *(June 24)* is Barcelona at its best: Bonfires, firecrackers, painted faces, and—of course—the outdoor drinking and revelry that make Spain one of the coolest countries in the world. Midway between Madrid's San Isidro festival and Mardi Gras, this whole affair is very absinthe-friendly.

The **GREC Festival** and **the Marató de L'Espectacle** both take place in July and feature a smorgasbord of theater, dance, and live music with performers from all over the world—neither festival is to be missed [see *arts scene, below*].

The **Festa Major de Grácia** *(Usually third week in Aug)* is another example of Barcelona at its most celebratory. This festival is a little bit tamer than the festival hoopla normally reserved for La Rambla. Featuring lots of outdoor bands on small stages throughout the decorated neighborhood, and lots of kids, fewer drugs, and more drink.

The **Festa de la Mercé** *(Sept 17-24)* is the celebration of Barcelona's patron saint, Our Lady of Mercy. It's another Mardi Gras–type celebration featuring lots of human towers, glorious fireworks, general revelry, and *gegantes.*

The **Fira del Disc de Col.Leccionista** *(Estació de França (França Railway Station); Held annually, usually in mid or late November)* is organized by Catalunya Radio. This annual Record Collectors Trade Fair offers all things vinyl to those who love records. Comb carefully, and you may find a funky Catalan recorded artifact to take home to your turntable.

Just a few blocks to the east is **Serrahima** *(Riera Alta 10; Tel 934/427-205; Metro to Liceu; Noon-2:30pm/5-9pm Tue-Sat; www.logiccontrol.es/serrahima),* which is small like Urania and Tribu [see below], but has nothing to do with students or anything else low-rent. The exhibits here are generally more thought-provoking and mature than in the other, "younger" galleries, with works by established European artists. Like the art, the atmosphere at Serrahima is more refined, but that doesn't make it boring. Take a break from the secondhand clothes in El Raval's stores and the secondhand couches in its cafes and check this out. It will do your head some good.

Once you've had enough of acting academic, get youself over to **Tribu** *(Avinyó 12; Tel 933/186-510; Metro to Liceu; 10:30am-2pm/4:30-8:30pm Mon-Sat; V, MC, AE).* This place is one of our Barcelona favorites. The sparse collection of club fashions that you see when you first walk in is little more than a facade for the squatter-style gallery awaiting you in the rooms beyond. The artists here are local and young, their work is usually weird and disturbing, and the staff is style-y and nice. Exhibits rotate every six weeks, and the majority of artists are from Spain. Tribu also runs a young artists' network but isn't affiliated with the universities.

▶▶PERFORMING ARTS

Realizing that Barcelona freaks on its theater is as easy as walking down La Rambla and checking out all the street performers. Although many productions here are in Catalan, the very best things—the festivals—are presented in several languages (or none at all) because the companies come from all over Europe. A festival here can be anything from a half-dozen companies and a theater that get together for one weekend to a size-12 bugout with 48 continuous hours of fire-eaters, contortionists, comedians, and the weirdest clowns you ever saw. If you're looking to meet theater people, the **Bar Rosal Café** [see *bar scene,* above] or anyplace else in the El Born neighborhood is a safe bet, and **Hangar** [see above] is a great place to get connected to a variety of art scenes.

Although it lasts for only two days in the second week of June, the **Marató de L'Espectacle** *(Mercat de les Flors at calle de Lleida 59; Tel 902/101-212; Metro to Espanya; Most shows at 10pm; No credit cards)* packs in a whole lotta hoopla. Production companies and artists from around the world offer theater, dance, skits, animation, cinema, music, and circ (circus-related performances like fire-eating, etc.). The name fittingly means "marathon of the spectacle"—the good times begin at 10:30pm and don't end till dawn. Locals *love* this event; the inherent weirdness that transpires during these two days is always the talk of the town. Located in the historic and beautiful **Mercat de les Flors** *(Tel 934/261-875),* which began as a flower market for the 1929 World's Fair, it has been bringing Spain's and Europe's best theater groups to Barcelona since 1985.

The **GREC Festival** *(Nearly 50 different venues, information booths at the Plaça de Catalunya; Dial general information at 010 for more info; End of June and all of July; www.grecbcn.com)* is a true juggernaut of theater, dance, and music. Usually about a month after the Marató de L'Espectacle, this five-week event also brings in performers from all over the world. If you're here in the summertime, pick up a free schedule at the big booth in the Plaça de Catalunya. The whole town totally loves this event, and, if you're a fan of dance, theater, or live music, you're guaranteed to be impressed. Try and see at least one show at the beautiful amphitheater at Montjuïc, commonly known as **Teatre Grec.**

Teatre Malic *(Fusina 3; Tel 933/107-035; Metro to Jaume I; Shows at 9pm, 11pm Mon-Sun; Most productions; www.daucom.es/malic; 1,500-2,000ptas; No credit cards)* is a small independent theater in El Born that began as a puppet theater. These days, the 60 seat venue plays host to mainly Spanish and Catalan productions, reserving Mondays and Tuesdays for "alternative" or up-and-coming production companies. It's also home to a pleasant cafe and an extensive collection of entertainment fliers and magazines. On Sundays at 11pm, Teatre Malic becomes the temporary home of the **Pipa Club,** Barcelona's smallest and best jazz bar.

L'Espai de Dansa i Música de la Generalitat *(Travessera de Gràcia 63; Tel 934/143-133; Metro to Provença; No credit cards)* is a small, government-operated theater in the northeast of the city, beyond Avenida Diagonal, that most often plays host to smaller dance companies. Don't expect tame performances, however, just because *el gobierno* is running the show—L'Espai, like so many venues here, dabbles in the avant-garde.

Since 1989, **Sala Beckett** *(Alegre de Dalt 55; Tel 932/845-312; Metro to Joanic; Most shows 9:30pm; salabeckett@ctv.es; No credit cards),* out on the east end of the city, has billed itself as an alternative/experimental venue, a "theater for theater people." Although they offer playwriting courses here, they're less interested in promoting new actors than are many of the other venues in Barcelona or Madrid. Sala Beckett has received the *El Premio Max* award for alternative theater in Spain, but unfortunately, the majority of the performances are in Catalan. The foyer displays a handwritten letter by Samuel Beckett himself, agreeing to allow this theater to use his name and giving it his blessing.

Like the movie theater of the same name in Madrid, the **Filmoteca** *(Avda. de Sarriá 33; Tel 934/107-590; Metro to Hospital Clínic; Shows 5:30pm, 7:30pm, 10pm daily, check the Guía for listings; 400ptas; No credit cards)* here, over in L'Eixample, specializes in the greatest movies you've (probably) never seen. All movies are VO (original versions...you know, subtitled) and are taken from a variety of themes and artists, such as the works of Hitchcock or movies with Fred Astaire. Shows sell out quick because they're so cheap. Pick up the monthly schedule in the foyer and be prepared.

gay scene

"Tolerant" sometimes means separate but equal, like the gay-heavy Chueca district in Madrid. But Barcelona is *so* uninterested in creating labels or judging others, no real "gay district" exists here, and many (but not all) of the "gay" clubs and bars host very mixed crowds, especially on the weekends. If a particular group seems to stand out (like the pierced-and-eyelined at Tu Prima, see below) we note it, but that doesn't mean the whole crowd is wearing collars and combat boots. *Punto H* (it has a big H on the cover) is a great gay fashion/music/nightlife magazine, as is *Shangay Express*. Both are in Spanish.

Been waiting for just the right place to put on that wig and eyeshadow you stowed away in the bottom of your backpack? Or maybe you haven't done laundry in a few weeks and the only thing you have left to wear is the tight leather underwear and dog collar you decided to bring along at the last minute. **Capitán Banana** *(Moiá 1; Tel 932/021-430; Metro to Provença; 12:30am-5am daily; No credit cards)*, is all about transvestites, drag queens, leather, and disco. Like most clubs, it becomes hot and sweaty here at about 2am.

Mezzanine *(Provenza 236; Tel 934/548-798; Metro to Provença or Hospital Clínic; 1-4pm/9pm-midnight Mon-Sat, closed Sun; About 900ptas per entree; V)* is popular with the gay theater crowd (mostly guys from 22 to 32) but is a must for *anyone* who doesn't eat meat. The entrees at this beautiful, *de moda* restaurant and gallery in L'Eixample are all vegan. The menu changes daily, but selections from the juice bar don't and are absolutely worth investigating—the *zumo nocturno*—packs as much energy as a six-pack of Jolt. Art exhibits rotate every two months and are usually by young local painters.

The menu at **El Colibrí** *(Corner of Riera Alta and Erasme de Janer; Tel 934/423-002; Metro to Sant Antoni; 8am-10:30pm Mon-Sat; V, MC, AE)* changes almost daily, usually to accommodate whatever fish seemed best at the market that morning. Although most of the diners here are 25 to 35 and gay, it's not like they're gonna throw you out if you're not. An interesting subset here are professors from the nearby design and literary schools. There's lots of literature on gay and music happenings in town, and drag shows happen once a month (see the posters). Very mellow and relaxing, with plenty of space between tables so that you can kick back.

The lighting at **Dietrich** *(Consell de Cent 255; No phone; Metro to Passeig de Gràcia; 10:30pm-3am daily; No credit cards)* has an odd, gold quality that gives the place a bar-of-the-future kind of feel. Everything is shiny, including the roof of the huge glass atrium in the back corner. Indiscriminate jazz on the hi-fi is quiet enough that you can talk. The entirely gay clientele is professional and ranges in age from 20 up to 50. Spacious and easygoing, Dietrich touts itself as a gay *teatro* cafe, but the drag-queen shows here are not regularly scheduled. Check the *Guía* or *Punto H* for listings. Drinks are about 650ptas.

El Coño Tu Prima *(Consejo de Ciento 294; No phone; Metro Passeig de Gràcia; 11pm-3am daily; No credit cards)* is a big deal, man. As in three floors, Death Star–sized disco balls, huge papier-mâché dragons, big. Tu Prima hosts (local) pop and techno/house DJs (sometimes both in the same night), usually for about a 1,000ptas cover. Mixed crowd (up to age 35) on the weekends, and The Prodigy would fit right in with the leather and pierced set that always seems represented here. Note: Be sure to ask what the name of the bar translates as....

Satanassa *(Aribau 27; Tel 934/510-052; Metro Passeig de Grácia; 10:30pm-3:30am daily; No credit cards)* was, according to the management, the first gay dance club in Barcelona. The crowd becomes more gay during the weekend and is more straight during the week. The bar is adorned with lewd paintings and statues of men and women, but the dance floor vibe is very Detroit: all concrete, dark, and ready to really party (in the let's-get-wasted-and-loud sense). Fashion for the young crowd here is a very weird mix of working-class and drag queen: We guess it just doesn't matter once you've had as much to drink as these people have. The weekday DJ is technically flawless but favors the worst flavors of dance club pop.

CULTURE ZOO

All of Barcelona is a museum—even typically mundane objects like benches and sidewalks have a subtle aesthetic quality here. Although

12 hours in barcelona

1. **La Sagrada Familia:** We've said it so many times, but this tower is the coolest, man. Ken Kesey would've loved this thing. If it doesn't blow your mind, go home—the trains shouldn't be wasting valuable fuel carting your boring ass around the continent.
2. **(Vamos a jugar por...) La Playa:** That is, the beach. It's free, it's fun, and you can drink without fear of the law. Don't spend too much time here, though—there's plenty in this town to see besides the sea.
3. **Galaxy:** The best of the clubs here. It's not real big physically, but its vibe is beautiful. The smaller size makes it easier to start a conversation, make friends, and get treated right when you return [see *club scene*, above].
4. **La Manzana de la Discordia:** This world-famous "Block of Discord" (a 5 minute walk from **Plaça Catalunya** on the **Passeig de Grácia**) is the home of three very modernista houses from three of the top architectural teams of this movement (including, you guessed it, Gaudí). The houses look nothing alike, as each one was meant to push the limits of design. Only five blocks up the same street is another far-out Gaudí creation, the **Casa Milá** (more often known as **La Pedrera**—"The Quarry"). Barcelona, in fact, has as much cool architecture as any city in the world. If you're interested, ask for the walking-tour-of-Barcelona-modernista-architecture brochure at the tourist office underneath **Plaça Catalunya.**

there's no single museum that can match Madrid's Prado, Barcelona has art for every taste, from the historic (and beautiful) cave paintings in the Museu Nacional to the wild architecture of the Sagrada Familia. As with everywhere else in Spain, most museums are inexpensive (all mentioned are around 700ptas) and offer half-off to students with valid ID. The following days are free for all museums: May 18 (International Day of Museums), October 12 (Fiesta Nacional de España), and December 6 (Día de Constitución Española).

If you're trying to kill two museums with one afternoon, we suggest any of the following combinations:

Museu d'Art Contemporani de Barcelona (MACBA) and Centre de Cultura Contemporania de Barcelona (CCCB) are right next to each other in El Raval (and very close to many small galleries and La Escola Massana).

Fundació Joan Miró, Poble Espanyol, and Museu Nacional d'Art de Catalunya are all in the Plaça de Espanya/Montjuïc part of town.

Catedral de Barcelona and Museu Picasso are both in the Ciutat Vella.

5. **Plaça George Orwell:** A great place to have a drink and meet lots of cool young people, all outside [see *hanging out,* above].

6. **Parc Güell:** We've talked about this place almost as much as Gaudí's **La Sagrada Familia.** A great way to get out of the city for a few minutes and collect your thoughts [see *culture zoo,* above].

7. Barcelona's European football team, C.F. Barcelona (or simply Barça), celebrated its 100th season in 1999. Yes, this professional team was scoring goals before the radio was invented. Barcelona's 120,000-seater **Camp Nou** stadium *(Travessera de les Corts 65; Metro to Les Corts or Bus 54, 56, 57, 157, 53N, 15, 75 to Camp Nou; Tickets 2,000-6,000ptas)* is one of the greatest football stadiums in the world, and the red and blue stripes of Barça are recognized everywhere but America as one of history's great teams. Several international games take place here, but you'll also enjoy watching the home team beat the crap out of a lesser Spanish team if it's a league match.

8. **Picasso Museum:** There are a lot of museums here, but the Picasso is cool because it tells the story of a single individual in addition to sharing captivating art. Off-hours are earlier in the morning [see *culture zoo,* above].

Parc Güell and La Sagrada Família aren't really near anything else but are worth special trips.

Museu d'Art Contemporània de Barcelona (MACBA) *(Plaça dels Angels; Tel 934/120-810; Metro to Plaça de Catalunya or Universitat; Noon-8pm Mon, Wed-Fri; 10am-8pm Sat, 10am-3pm Sun):* If you are a modern-art lover you will fall head over heels for this museum. The building's architectural design is art itself, but the painting and sculpture inside are what's really enticing. This museum is dedicated to bringing contemporary art to the masses both national and international and it generally has a photography exhibit going on.

Centre de Cultura Contemporània de Barcelona (CCCB) *(Montalegre 5; Tel 934/811-069; Metro to Catalunya or Plaça Goya; 11am-2pm/4-8pm Tue, Thur, Fri; 11am-9pm Wed, Sat; 11am-7pm Sun, holidays; www.cccb.org):* The CCCB focuses on the trends and technologies that shape modern culture and, by extension, art. The exhibits often explore themes relating to cities and art and the media and art. The CCCB has regular multimedia exhibits.

Poble Espanyol *(Marqués de Comilias, Parc de Montjuïc; Tel 933/257-866; Metro to Espanya or Bus 61 to Poble Espanyol; 9am-8pm Mon; 9am-2am Tue, Wed, Thur; 9am-4am Fri, Sat; 9-midnight Sun; www.poble-espanyol.com):* It's a tourist trap for sure, but you can get some great souvenir shopping done in this "village" in which every region of

down and out

All out of pesetas? Don't let it get you down, you happen to be in one of the trippiest cities on the continent. A great place to visit (even if you do have money) is the magic fountains at **Plaça de Espanya** *(Metro to Plaça de Espanya; 11am-8pm daily May-Oct).* Now don't write off these fountains as something (like the Ice Capades) that only your grandma would like. We assure you that you've never seen water quite like this. The colors are beautiful, the fountain arrangements are so complex they probably require a Cray Supercomputer to run, and the music goes from classical to some Eurotrashed-out Peter Gabriel-ish theme of Barcelona.

If you want to get to know water in a more natural setting, check out the beach, only a 15-minute walk from the base of La Rambla. The occasional topless woman, the Mediterranean Sea, and...well, that's it. But what else do you expect from a beach? Keep in mind that the scene is more tranquil as you move farther from the Port Olímpic.

Spain is represented by miniature versions of their most recognizable attractions.

Fundació Joan Miró *(Parc de Montjuïc; Tel 933/291-908; Bus 16 from Plaça de Espanya; 11am-7pm Tue, Wed, Fri, Sat, 11am-9:30pm Thur, 10:30am-2:30pm Sun, Mon, holidays):* Miró is yet another artist to come out of Spain, one whose work strongly impacted modern art. Miro's paintings, sculptures, and tapestries will put you in a good mood and show how simple forms and shapes and bright colors collaborate to create vitality. His art was designed to stimulate the imagination and this it certainly does. Also while at the museum check out the super-cool Mercury Fountain, given to him by his longtime friend, American sculptor Alexander Calder.

Museu Nacional d'Art de Catalunya *(In the Palau Nacional, Parc de Montjuïc; Tel 934/237-199; Metro to Plaça de Espanya or Bus 9, 27, 30, 38, 56, 57, 65, 91 to same; 10am-7pm Tue, Wed, Fri, Sat; 10am-9pm Thur; 10am-2:30pm Sun)* tells, through art and artifacts, the history of Catalunya. Absolutely worth checking out—learn history while appreciating the art.

Catedral de Barcelona *(Plaça de la Seu; Tel 933/151-554; Metro Jaume 1; Bus 17, 19, 40, 45 to same; Cathedral 8am-1:30pm/4-7:30pm daily, museum 11am-1pm daily):* This place was started in the 13th century, finished in the 15th (the workers must've been union...), and is a primo example of the medieval splendor of Barcelona. Yup, it's an old cathedral all right. At least it's right near La Rambla, so that you can take your picture quick and get on with your day. The museum portion features *La Pietat* by Bermejo.

Museu Picasso *(Montcada 15-19; Tel 933/196-310; Metro Jaume 1; 10am-7:30pm Tue-Sat, holidays, 10am-3pm Sun).* People who are familiar with Picasso and the works that made him famous (i.e., Cubism, Blue and Pink period) might be disappointed by what this museum has to offer. However, if you don't expect to see his masterpieces and instead you are interested in him as a child and an old man, then this place is worth a visit. The gift shop has great Picasso paraphernalia.

Mirador de Colón *(Portal de la Pau; Tel 933/025-224; Metro to Drassanes or Bus 14, 18, 36, 57, 59, 64; 9am-9pm daily late June-Sept; 9:30-8pm Oct-early June):* This tower with a statue of Columbus on top, built in 1888, is one of the landmarks of the city. For 250ptas, you can ascend the tower for a great view of the city and the Mediterranean.

La Sagrada Familia *(Mallorca 401; Tel 934/550-247; Metro to Sagrada Familia; 9am-6pm daily Oct-Feb; 9am-8pm Apr-Aug; 9am-7pm Mar, Sept):* This church is the coolest thing ever. If you see one "sight" in Barcelona, La Sagrada Familia, designed by Gaudí, started in 1882 and still incomplete, has to be it.

Parc Güell *(Tel 934/243-809; Metro to Vallcarca or Bus 24, 25, 31, 74; 10am-6pm daily Nov-Feb; 10am-7pm daily Mar-Oct):* Also designed by Gaudí, this park is a close second to La Sagrada Familia in terms of sheer coolness. Plus it's free! Be sure to take a tour of Gaudí's house (designed by Francesc Berenguer but full of Gaudí-designed furniture) while you're here.

modification

A man has simple criteria for a barbershop: no disco music, no neon or pastel decor, and a barber at least as old as his dad. Oh yeah, and it should cost less than $15 (U.S.) and not take all day. Gentlemen, **Pulequeria Manolo** *(Regomir 17; Tel 933/152-809; Metro to Jaume I; 9am-2pm/4-8pm Mon-Fri, 8:30am-2pm Sat; About 1,200ptas for a cut; No credit cards)* delivers. Manolo himself will cut your hair efficiently, pleasantly, and exactly how you like it (while exchanging pleasantries with every local who walks by the small front door). A great guy, a great haircut, a true cultural experience.

Barcelona isn't exactly the punk or teen-angst capital of the world (What would they rebel against? No drinking age? The international club scene? The sexually permissive cultural norms?), but you still have the opportunity to pierce yourself silly. Several locals directed us to **L'Embruix** *(Boqueria 18; Tel 933/011-163; 10am-2pm/4-8pm Mon-Sat, 10am-8pm July, Aug; No credit cards)* because of their good artistry and cool demeanor. The several women (hence the name, which means "the witches") who run the show will charge you a minimum of 6,000ptas for a tattoo and 4,000ptas for piercings. The actual jewelry is extra (an average ring is 400ptas), as is anesthesia (1,000ptas).

great outdoors

Parc de la Ciutadella *(Metro to Ciutadella; 8am-9pm daily)* near El Born is the main park of the city, where you can jog, rollerblade, and practice yoga amidst green grass, shady trees, fragrant gardens, tranquil ponds, and one hell of a freaky fountain. The Cascada fountain was created with a little help from Gaudí, and man, does it show....The atmosphere here can be more wholesome (especially on weekends) than expected because the city zoo (which features an albino gorilla, poor thing) is located here. Like most big-city parks, Parc de la Ciutadella is safe during daylight hours but should be traversed using common sense at night.

Barcelona by Bicycle *(Esparteria 3; Tel 93/268-21-05; Metro to Juame I; Daily tours 10am-12:30pm Sat, Sun for 2,000ptas, evening tours 10:30pm-midnight Tue, Sat for 5,000ptas)* is a guided bike tour of the Ciutat Vella and Barri Gòtic. Both day and evening tours include a stop for a drink (we love Spain...) in the Barri Gòtic, and the evening tour also includes dinner on the port. Prices include food, booze, and bike. Evening tours require an advance reservation.

Although Barcelona is no slouch as a traveler's destination, most of what it offers only fits into the "oh, that's cool" category. A few attractions and sights, like **La Sagrada Familia** [see *culture zoo,* above] and **Marató de L'Espectacle** [see *arts scene,* above] could be included in the "wow" category, but the beautiful and serene mountains of

rules of the game

The legal drinking age in Barcelona is 16, but who's keeping track? Like everywhere else in Spain, nobody cares about your drinking problem unless you're starting a fight or whizzing in the middle of La Rambla. Drug policies (and practices) are the same here as in Madrid [see *rules of the game*, Madrid]. When staggering out of the bars and clubs, keep in mind that the locals are very courteous to their Ciutat Vella neighbors. Bars like **Kentucki** and (particularly) **Dot** are located in residential neighborhoods where the doormen will ask you to stop shouting if you're too wasted to realize that you are....

Montserrat, a 90-minute train/cable car journey from Barcelona, will probably leave you speechless. The famous monastery of the same name *(9am-6pm daily, shorter hours Nov-Mar)* that sits atop this 4,000-foot wind-carved mountain was established by Benedictine monks in the 9th century. Barcelona and all of Catalunya love this place; they come to see the statue of Catalunya's patron saint, La Moreneta (the Black Madonna), which was supposedly found near the monastery some time in the 12th or 13th century. After arriving at the monastery, you can take a funicular ride *(10am-7pm daily Apr-Oct only, 340ptas)* that will carry you (even) higher (Sly will be with you in spirit), to the top of the mountain. From here, you'll be able to see the Pyrenees Mountains to the north and Mallorca and Ibiza (which is best seen up close) to the east. Montserrat is the religious center of Catalunya, so don't go on a Sunday—you'll grow old waiting in line. Also remember to dress for temperatures that are about a season colder than Barcelona, and wear attire that's respectful of the monks, their monastery, and their religion (no tank tops or miniskirts). The Manresa line of the FGC (suburban) trains leaves five times a day from Plaça d'Espanya. It connects with a cable car that brings you directly to the monastery. Round-trip is 1,800ptas.

STUFF

Portal de L'Angel and the surrounding streets of Calle de la Portaferrissa, Calle de Cucurulla, and Calle Arcs are the places to go for clothes and shoes. Barcelona is much more European that Madrid, and it shows in the fashions. If it's gifts for the family and friends back home that you're looking for, **La Sagrada Familia** and the **Museo Picasso** [see *culture zoo*, above, for both] both have fantastic gift shops that offer better-than-average trinkets and posters for prices that won't keep you from that second glass of absinthe in the evening.

▶▶THRIFT

Mies & Felj *(Riera Baixa 5; Tel 934/420-755; Metro to Liceu; 11am-2pm/4:30-9pm daily; V, AE, MC)* offer the best secondhand butterfly-collar hipster shirts in the whole of Barcelona. They've got some tough competition from the handful of other retro clothing (and vinyl) stores on the same funky little block, but they take plastic here and really outdo the others' selections.

▶▶GIFT

4ART *(Boters 4; Tel 933/011-325; Metro to Liceu; 10:30am-2pm/4:30-8:30pm Mon-Sat; V, AE, MC)* has more prints and frames than Cher's had surgery. In the town that produced so many of this century's greatest painters, you're bound to find a few worthwhile gifts here. Prints start at 1,500ptas. Some artisan-type stuff is also for sale here.

ART Escudellers *(Escudellers 23-25; Tel 934/126-801; Metro to Drassanes; 11am-11pm daily; V, AE, MC)* offers a huge selection of (mainly) ceramic work created by artisans from all over Spain. A lot of expensive items here, but you can buy a lot of cool small things too, like rings, magnets, and coffee mugs. Their late hours are great for last-minute shopping.

▶▶DUDS

System *(Portaferrissa 12; Tel 933/012-526; Metro to Plaça de Catalunya; 10am-2pm/4:30-8:30pm, closed Mon; MC, V)* has six different stores in Barcelona, and all of their clothes are of their own label. Carrer de Portaferrissa, along with Portal de L'Angel, has a million women's clothing stores, but the quality and price at System are better than most. Lots of linen (about 1/3 cheaper than in the U.S.), and not your usual overdose of black and club gear. Very cool in a sexy-professional-mellow-woman kind of way, but not snobby. Few accessories and no shoes.

There are so many shops in Portal de L'Angel and nearby streets that it's easy to miss out on the one or two stores that really outshine the rest of the standard shoe-sellers and disco clothing shops. **Fantasy Shop** *(Comprising two stores that are right down the hall from each other, on the third floor of the Gallerías Gralla Hall, Portaferrissa 25; Tel 934/122-283; Metro to Liceu; 10:30am-8:30pm Mon-Sat; V, MC)* are not to be missed. The simple and elegant jewelry, shoes, and clothes in these little shops cannot be found elsewhere in Barcelona. The staff is great, and you will almost certainly walk away with a purchase of distinction. Most items are for casual wear, with an understated tone of refinement. The two stores are for him and her; his store also has some beautiful rings and bracelets, but the clothing and shoes lean more toward standard-issue club gear.

▶▶BOUND

Laie *(Pau Claris 85; Tel 933/181-739; Metro to Catalunya; Bookstore 10am-9pm Mon-Sat, cafe till 1am; V, MC)* has an overall good-bookstore feel, created by a broad selection of titles (a handful in English), semi-random stacks of books, and a cool staff. Buy your book and head upstairs to the cafe: Meals are served for around 1,000ptas, but you can just grab a cup of coffee and snack and enjoy the poet's atmosphere. Good bulletin board scene, too. A second Laie store is at the **CCCB** [see *culture zoo*, above].

Angel Battle *(Palla 23; Tel 933/015-884; Metro to Liceu; 9am-1:30pm/4-7:30pm Sun-Fri; No credit cards)* is your basic Old Europe hole-in-the-wall bookstore. Used books only, nearly all of them hardcover, and none in English. But this cluttered, dusky store is for people who love old books for their physical beauty—you—half-expect to find Indiana Jones browsing the aged collection for clues on the Holy Grail. The cheapest offerings begin at around 2,500ptas. Angel Battle has also got hundreds of cool prints from Franco's Spain and earlier (very interesting stuff...).

eats

As in most places in Europe, some of the cheapest and most interesting eats are at the markets. Late-night snacks can be purchased right from the news kiosks on La Rambla: Most of this stuff is like overpriced Pringles

wired

El Café de Internet *(Gran Vía de les Corts Catalanes 656; Tel 934/121-915; Metro Passeig de Grácia; 10am-midnight Mon-Wed, 10am-2am Thur-Sat; 1,000ptas per hour, 800ptas per 30 min; No credit cards)* has more than a dozen machines in a low-lit, air-conditioned, pop-rock-playing venue. A half-hour is a little pricey, but the full hour is a deal, so you might as well go for that. These prices are for students only, but the "student" policy is lax here (you look like one, you are one). Buy your drinks and food below and bring them with you upstairs. The international love quotient here is high.

The Interlight Café *(Pau Claris 106; Tel 933/011-180; Metro to Passeig de Grácia; 11am-10pm Mon-Sat, 5-10pm Sun; 700ptas per hour; interlight@bcn.servicom.es, www.gdesigners.com/interlight; No credit cards)* is one of the newer cybercafes in Barcelona and certainly one of the best. The very friendly staff speaks English well, and they serve food and coffee here. The venue itself has more sunlight and air than other e-mail locations. All 16 machines with Word. Printing is occasionally free.

While the name isn't exactly catchy, **E-mail from Spain** *(Ramblas 42/Bacardi 1; Tel 934/817-575; Metro to Drassanes; 10am-8pm Mon-Sat; 1,000ptas per hour, 600ptas per 30 min; No credit cards)* at least has a good location at the foot of La Rambla. The 11 machines here have Word, Excel, and an Adobe-like program that can be used with the in-house scanner. The main room can become unbearably hot in the summer and the pickup scene here is not the same as at Interlight or Café de Internet.

barcelona

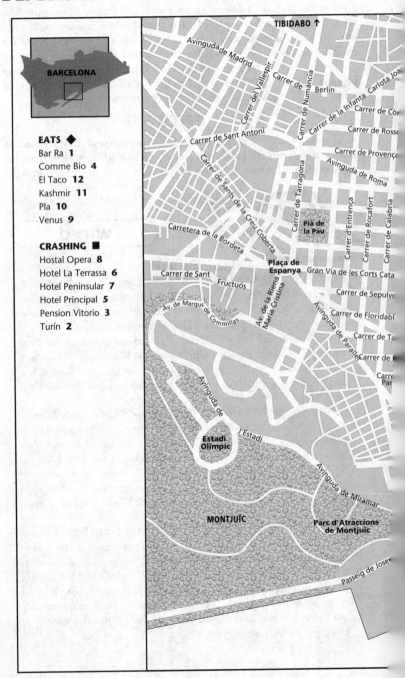

BARCELONA

EATS ◆
Bar Ra **1**
Comme Bio **4**
El Taco **12**
Kashmir **11**
Pla **10**
Venus **9**

CRASHING ■
Hostal Opera **8**
Hotel La Terrassa **6**
Hotel Peninsular **7**
Hotel Principal **5**
Pension Vitorio **3**
Turín **2**

TIBIDABO ↑

Avingudade Madrid

Carrer del Vallespir

Carrer de Numància

Carrer de

Berlin

Carrer de la Infanta Carlota Joa

Carrer de Cör

Carrer de Rosse

Carrer de Sant Antoni

Carrer de Provença

Avinguda de Roma

Carrer de Sants de la Creu Coberta

Carrer de Tarragona

Pla de
la Pau

Carrer d'Entrença

Carrer de Rocafort

Carrer de Calabria

Carretera de la Bordeta

Plaça de
Espanya　Gran Vía de les Corts Cata

Carrer de Sant

Fructuós

Av. de la Riera
Maria Cristina

Carrer de Sepulve

Av. de Marqus de
Commillas

Avinguda de Parallel

Carrer de Floridabl

Carrer de Ta

Carrer de

Carre
Par

Avinguda de

J'Estadi

Estadi
Olímpic

Avinguda de Miramar

MONTJUÏC

Parc d'Atraccions
de Montjuic

Passeig de Jose

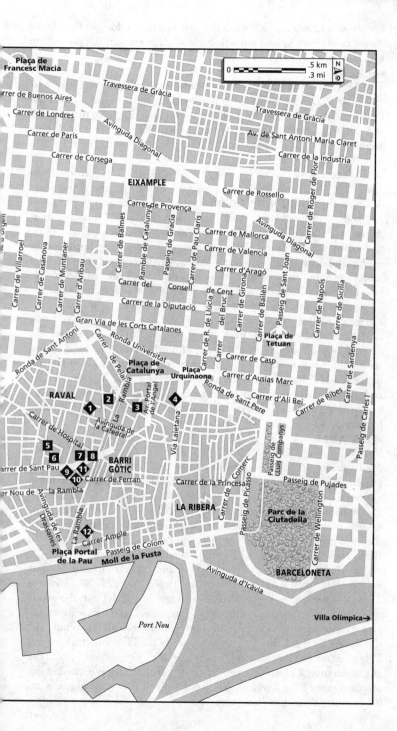

Plaça de Francesc Macia

Travessera de Gràcia

rrer de Buenos Aires

Carrer de Londres

Travessera de Gràcia

Carrer de Paris

Av. de Sant Antoni Maria Claret

Avinguda Diagonal

Carrer de Còrsega

Carrer de la Industria

EIXAMPLE

Carrer de Rossello

Carrer de Provença

Avinguda Diagonal

Carrer de Roger de Flor

Carrer de Balmes

Ramble de Catalunya

Passeig de Gracia

Carrer de Pau Claris

Carrer de Mallorca

Carrer de Villarroel

Carrer de Casanova

Carrer de Muntaner

Carrer d'Aribau

Carrer de Valencia

Carrer del   Consell

de Cent

Carrer d'Aragó

Carrer de R. de Llúcia

del Bruc

Carrer de Girona

Carrer de Bailén

Passeig de Sant Joan

Carrer de Napols

Carrer de Sicilia

Carrer de la Diputació

Gran Via de les Corts Catalanes

Ronda Universitat

Ronda de Sant Antoni

Carrer de Pelai

Rambla

Plaça de Catalunya

Plaça Urquinaona

Av. Portal de l'Angel

Plaça de Tetuan

Carrer   Carrer de Casp

Carrer de Ribes

Passeig de Sardenya

RAVAL

Carrer de Hospital

❶ ❷ ❸ ❹

Avinguda de la Catedral

Via Laietana

Carrer d'Ausias Marc

Ronda de Sant Pere

Carrer d'Ali Bei

Passeig de Carles T

❺ ❻ ❼ ❽ BARRI GÒTIC

rrer de Sant Pau

❾ ⓫ ❿

Carrer de Ferran

Carrer de la Princessa

Passeig de Lluis Companys

er Nou de   la Rambla

Carrer de la Princesso

LA RIBERA

Passeig de Picasso

Passeig de Pujades

Parc de la Ciutadella

Carrer de Wellington

❿

La Rambla

Avinguda de les Drassanes

⓬ Carrer Ample

Passeig de Colom

Plaça Portal de la Pau

Moll de la Fusta

Avinguda d'Icàvia

BARCELONETA

Port Nou

Villa Olímpica→

0   .5 km
     .3 mi

N

and cookies and candy. What's the biggest surprise for food in Barcelona? An ice cream cone at McDonald's. Seriously. They're only 50ptas and are real, true ice cream (as in, delicious).

▶▶CHEAP

The Mercat Sant Josep (*On La Rambla between Carrer de Carme and Carrer de L'Hospital*) is like a big hockey game for the senses. Smell the fresh fruit, the raw meat, the fresh bread. Buy anything from roasted nuts and candy (at about 100ptas) to fresh olives to skinned rabbits and other animals (or not...). The best buy is the *menú del día*—a full meal for 800 to 1,200ptas.

El Taco (*Plaça Duc de Medinaceli 1; Tel 933/186-321; Metro to Drassanes; 8am-1am daily; No credit cards*) is a quick bite and drink place down by the **Mirador de Colón** that sells "grande" soft tacos (about one-and-a-half times larger than a T-Bell soft taco) for 375ptas and margaritas for 350ptas. The *Rajas con Crema de Gambas*, chock-full of shrimp, is recommended. Tropical plants and mellow flamenco-pop music soothe the hip and occasionally semi-famous clientele (whom you never heard of 'cause you're not from Spain). Also caters to the well-dressed, I-want-to-be-a-professional-already students from the nearby architecture school.

Bring the morning paper to **Bar Ra** (*Plaça de la Garduña, behind Carrer de Carme; No phone; Metro to Liceu; 9am-2am daily; No credit cards*) and sit down to muffins, cereal, juices, and bagels. Vegetarian dishes (650ptas) are among the choices for other meals, and the nachos are highly recommended. At night, one of the cooler crowds in B-town hangs at this El Raval spot; dress in your best "you" clothes, be under 30, and you'll fit right in. The outdoor terrace is set in a quiet urban court-yard/parking lot that makes you feel alive and adventurous, even if you're just having a beer.

▶▶DO-ABLE

Venus (*Avinyó 25; Tel 933/011-585; Metro to Liceu; Noon-midnight Mon-Sat; Avg 500ptas per entree; No credit cards*) offers a wide variety of vegetarian dishes along with their standard, delicious menu. In addition to great food, Venus also boasts a fantastic location that is just outside the always-friendly, always-dreddy Plaça George Orwell. Chat with the exceptionally pleasant staff, take a look at the pleasant artwork, and check out the most expansive collection of fliers and free magazines that we saw in Barcelona. The chili is highly recommended for carnivores.

Barcelona is the home of many Indian and Pakistani restaurants, but nobody can touch **Kashmir** (*Sant Pau 39; Tel 934/413-798; Metro to Liceu; 1-5pm/8pm-midnight Wed-Mon, closed Tue; V, MC*) in the goodness-for-the-price category. This small, inexpensive, and delicious restaurant is recommended by locals and is perfect for lunch after checking out the Raval's local galleries and secondhand shops. Tandoori chicken, artfully prepared by Chef Waseem Sarwar, goes for 750ptas. Very busy in the afternoon from 2 to 4. Although relatively safe, Kashmir is located in the roughest part of the Raval neighborhood, so you may want to make it a lunch rather than late-dinner spot.

▶▶**SPLURGE**

Pla *(Bellafila 5; Tel 934/126-552; Metro to Liceu; 9pm-midnight week-days, till 1am weekends, bar till 3am; V, MC)* is so tucked away in the Barri Gòtic's maze of narrow cobblestone streets that most foreigners show up here only when they get lost. The establishment itself is a tall, wide-open-yet-warm-and-intimate space. Hardwood floors, candles, handwritten menus, the ever-mellow Grover Washington, Jr. on the hi-fi, and beautiful artwork combine for a serene, refined atmosphere. The clientele are late-twenty and thirtysomethings who enjoy looking good in black. Appetizers start at 725ptas, entrees at 1,800ptas. The menu of local specialties changes almost daily, but there's usually one vegetarian dish. Reservations necessary on weekends.

Comme Bio *(Via Laietana 28; Tel 933/198-968; Metro Jaime; about 2,500ptas dinner, 1,500ptas lunch; 9am-midnight daily; V, MC, AE)* has been making vegetarian tourists and health-conscious Spaniards happy for 25 years. It is a vegetarian restaurant/health food store that serves up pizzas, pastas, salads, and organic juices and sells not-tested-on-animals products, tofu, soymilk, and tasty desserts from the bakery. This place is a vegetarian's dream, but no one will be able to deny how good the food is and how all-around cool this place is. Definitely have a fruit-juice combo.

crashing

What makes the hostels in Barcelona so much more expensive than those in Madrid? Are we paying for more culture? Or for the nearby beach? Of course the real reason might be that the population of Barcelona nearly doubles with young tourists in the summertime. Well, whatever it is, you'll be hard-pressed to find a double for 2,500ptas or a single for under 1,500ptas. Even though there are a hundred or so hostels in the Ciutat Vella, you won't get a room in one in July or August unless you start looking right around noon, when the management knows exactly who's vacated and who's sticking around another night. If you don't, you'll either wind up on the street or in a really nice hotel that you can't afford. If all else fails, go to the tourist office—they can make reservations for you. One good thing about most hostels in Barcelona is that they'll give you a key to the building, so you don't have to get buzzed in at 6 in the morning and make slurred small talk with the proprietor.

▶▶**CHEAP**

Pension Vitorio *(La Palla 8; Tel 933/020-834; Metro to Liceu; 1,500-2,000ptas single, 2,500-4,000ptas double, 3,500-4,500ptas triple; V, MC)* is in a good, quiet location in a beautiful old neighborhood only 2 minutes' walk from La Rambla and Plaça George Orwell. Singles and triples don't have their own baths, but all rooms come with bare furniture, balconies (Room 202 has three!), and are clean enough for the price.

Alberg Pere Tarrés *(Numancia 149-151; Tel 934/102-309, Fax 934/196-268; Metro to Les Corts; 1,500ptas/bed in a quad, linen additional 250ptas; alberg@peretarres.org; V, MC)* isn't exactly downtown (it's over in the southwest), but we've included it in our list since lodging is so scarce in the Ciutat Vella in the summertime. There's coin-op laundry, a quiet rooftop terrace, a ground-floor terrace with a ping-pong table, and continental breakfast included in the price. A good place to meet and chill with other travelers.

Hotel La Terrassa *(Junta del Comerç 11; Tel 933/025-174, Fax 933/012-188; Metro to Liceu; 2,200-3,400ptas single, 3,600-4,400ptas double, 4,800-5,700ptas triple; V, MC, AE)* is one of the best deals in town. It's in (the good part of) El Raval, and right next to La Rambla and the Barri Gòtic. The second-floor terrace is a great place to meet fellow travelers. Everything is clean, and the day staff speak English.

▶▶**DO-ABLE**

Hotel Principal *(Junta del Comerç 8; Tel 933/188-970; Metro to Liceu; 6,900ptas single, 9,500ptas double, 11,500ptas triple, 13,700ptas quad; hprincip@lix.intercom.es; V, MC)* is on the same quiet street as the Hotel La Terrassa [see above] but will give you a lot more in the way of creature comforts. Big ornate rooms include phone, satellite TV, air conditioning, bath, and continental breakfast. With a small, cozy pub and an actual restaurant, too!

Hostal Opera *(Carrer Sant Pau 20; Tel 933/188-201; Metro Liceu; 3,200-5,000ptas single, 6,000-7,000ptas double; No credit cards)* has 70 rooms, all of which have recently been renovated. If you want clean and comfortable as close to Las Ramblas as possible, this place is a good bet. While the decor is as bland as your freshman dorm room the day you moved in, the Spanish men chatting in the lounge and the new lobby make up for it.

For a lot of character and personality at a good price, try the **Hotel Peninsular** *(Carrer Sant Pau 34; Tel 933/023-138; Metro Liceu; 5,000ptas single, 7,000ptas double; V, MC, AE)*. In one of its many past lives, it was part of a convent, but it's been recently renovated and restored. These days it hosts student groups and a diverse crowd of tourists in its 80 rooms. The hanging plants, black and white tiled floor, glass ceiling, iron railings, relaxing courtyard, and decent continental breakfast all make this place genuinely one of the nicest places to stay in Barcelona.

▶▶**SPLURGE**

Turín *(Pintor Fortuny 9; Tel 933/024-812; Metro to Plaça de Catalunya; 11,600ptas double, 13,450ptas triple; AE, V, MC)* is an island of luxury in the stormy waters of El Raval. The rooms aren't enormous, but they're very comfortable. They all have air conditioning, TV, telephone, and balconies. Although the restaurant below is good, you'll get more local flavor per peseta if you dine elsewhere in the Ciutat Vella.

need to know

Currency Exchange You can exchange money at the **airport,** both **train stations,** and at various locations along **La Rambla;** but a **bank, ATM,** or credit card will always get you the best rates and lowest service charge.

Tourist Information The main tourist office is located underground at the **Plaça de Catalunya** *(Tel 933/043-421; Metro to Catalunya; 9am-9pm daily).* Look for the sign with a big, red *i.* The office has lots of free magazines and fliers, including info on the big discos and bars, and will make hotel reservations for you. You can also get help from the official tourist guys wearing the red vests. They walk along La Rambla until 9pm.

Public Transportation Keep in mind that the metro and buses can't help you out in the ancient and narrow Barri Gòtic, where you'll spend most of your time....A 10-trip T1 pass costs only 825ptas, and it can be used on the Metro and buses throughout Barcelona. The subway shuts down at the ridiculous hour of 11pm on weekdays and 2am on Fridays and Satudays.

American Express There are two offices in Barcelona—one on La Rambla *(Ramblas 74; Tel 933/011-166; Metro Liceu; 9am-midnight daily Apr-Sept, 9am-8:30pm Mon-Fri, 10am-2pm, 3pm-7pm Sat, closed Sun Oct-Mar),* in the center of all the hype and happiness, and the other north of Placa Catalunya *(Passeig de Grácia 101; Tel 93/217-00-70; Metro Diagonal; 9:30am-6pm Mon-Fri; 10am-noon Sat)* in a less touristy neighborhood.

Health and Emergency Emergency: *061;* ambulance: *Tel 061/933-00-20 20;* English-speaking police: **Turisme-Atención** *(La Rambla 43; Tel 933/019-060),* which is located in the heart of the tourist area.

Pharmacies Pharmacies operate here as they do elsewhere in Spain: Every little neighborhood has at least one *farmacia,* marked by **big green neon crosses.** No single one is open 24 hours all the time; instead, *farmacias* rotate the all-night responsibility. Each one posts a schedule of which will be open on what night, as do the major newspapers like *El País.*

Telephone City code: *93;* operator: *1003;* international operator: *1005.* Recent changes in Spain's phone system now require that all local calls within Barcelona be dialed with the 93 prefix.

Airport Aeroport del Prat *(Tel 932/983-838)* is the official name of Barcelona's airport. The **Aerobús** *(5:30am-11:15pm Mon-Fri, 6am-11:20pm Sat, Sun; 475ptas)* leaves from the airport every 15 minutes and arrives at Plaça de Catalunya about 30 minutes later.

Trains RENFE *(Tel 934/900-202)* is Spain's national train line. **Estació Sants** *(Metro to Sants-Estacio)* handles most trains traveling within Spain. If you're leaving for or arriving from France, you'll usually wind up at the **Estació de França** *(Metro to Barceloneta).* Both stations have Metro access, so use it! Get off in the Barri Gòtic (either the Liceu or Plaça de Catalunya stops) and find a hostel there.

Buses Out of the City The main station is **Estació del Nord** *(Alí Bei 80; Tel 93/265-65-08; Metro to Arc de Triomf).*

Boat Transmediterránea *(Moll de Barcelona; Tel 93/295-91-00)* is the major ferry service that operates between Barcelona and the Balearic

Islands (Mallorca, Ibiza, etc.). There's no metro stop close to here, but it's only a 10-minute walk from the Drassanes metro stop (at the base of La Rambla). If you've got a lot of stuff, a taxi would be your best bet.

Bike Rental Biciclot *(Carrer St. Joan de Malta 1; Tel 933/077-475; 9am-2pm/5-8pm Mon-Fri, 10am-2pm Sat; 500ptas/hr, 2000ptas/day; No credit cards)* will get you mobile on a mountain bike or a 10-speed.

Laundry The kind people at **Lavanderia Lamin** *(Robador 13; No phone; Metro to Liceu; 9am-8pm Mon-Sat; 1,000-1,600ptas per machine; No credit cards)* speak English, wash your clothes nice, fold them up, and put your clean garments in a bag. Although the official policy is "next day," you can often pick up your stuff three to four hours after drop-off. Self-service, too.

everywhere else

cadaqués

Dalí is to Cadaqués what Elvis is to Memphis. Their personal fame put their towns on the map, and almost nothing has gone untouched by their influence. Most importantly, you cannot pass through without making a visit to their dripping-with-personality, fantastically elaborate homes.

If you are a diehard Surrealism fan, Cadaqués will give you a greater insight into Salvador Dalí as an artist and as a person. Artists and tourists have been coming here for that reason for years.

Even if dripping clocks, twirly mustaches, and Freudian references don't float your boat, making the trek to Cadaqués is more than worth it. It is one of the most beautiful towns on the Costa Brava. The quaint little village sits inside the Cap de Creus peninsula, and boasts white houses, small tourist shops, a rocky shore, a handful of seafood restaurants, and narrow cobblestone streets. It is surrounded by hills, olive trees, and breathtaking views on all sides. Cadaqués has been able to keep its secluded charm free of big hotels and typical tourist gentrification because the locals voted to keep it big-building-and-train-station-free a few years ago. Folks here are an eclectic mix of tourists of all ages, wealthy families who are lucky enough to own their summer homes here, and funky locals who work in the bars and are waiting for the town to have its rebirth as an artist colony.

When you come into Cadaqués on the bus from Figueres or Barcelona, it will be obvious to you why you took that one- or two-hour bumpy ride. You'll find yourself looking down at a small Spanish pueblo with white-washed buildings that wrap around a small inlet to form a beautiful (and wealthy) cove. It's an enchanting vision.

If you need a break from Dalí, check out the set of paths that line the cliffs of Cadaqués. If you walk along these cliffs at night, the water rumbles and glistens with the lights from the night yachters, and you can pretend that you are stylish and European enough to appreciate the beauty of it.

cadaqués

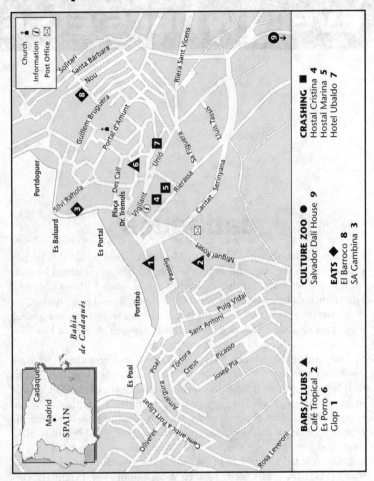

One of the draws of Cadaqués is the really pretty pebble beaches. You can see kids skipping rocks during the day. The color of the water here is, as a rule, fantastic, what you imagine the Caribbean Sea to look like before you go there: turquoise and perfectly clear.

There isn't a ton going on in Cadaqués in terms of big hotels, raging nightlife, or busy metropolitanism. A few older white houses have been converted to *hostales*, there are some fine restaurants and bars with a classy but laid-back vibe, and, of course, touristy little shops where you can find the ubiquitous Dalí paraphernalia. If you're lucky, you might even be able to find some tripped-out Dalí "paraphernalia" to give to your Dead Head friend back home.

If you go to visit the Dalí house, don't forget to take in some of the vibe from the town that inspired the artist. Yeah, a lot has been Spanish-gentrified, but the lack of touristy stuff will give you a chance to check out a more genuine Costa Brava town.

The town's layout is simple enough; there's a network of narrow streets leading to the main square, **Plaça Frederic Rahola,** the main hangin'-out spot in Cadaqués. The best routes into and out of the Frederic Rahola area are along **Avinguda Caritat Serinyana** and **Paseo Passeig.** From the Plaça, it's literally a stone's throw to the resort-style beaches of **Playa El Llane Gran, Playa El Llane Petit,** and **Playa Saconca.**

bar, club, & live music scene

Cadaqués truly is a small town, so if you came for some serious partying you are not going to find it here. However, there are a couple of chill places where you can finish out a good day with a few drinks. And there is something to be said for a relaxed night out in a small pueblo, sipping some good wine or a cold San Migy (the Spanish young person's beer) while soaking in some of the laid-back local attitude. Plus, going to check out the minimal nightlife gives you an excuse to be walking around outside after dark when the house and churches are all lit up.

Best of all, since this is a small town that more or less shuts down by 2am, if you're drunk enough and feeling free, go ahead and take a little moonlight skinny-dip in the sea. It makes a great story, and if the toothless fishermen get an eyeful, more power to ya.

For all of the venues below, there is no public transportation option, unless you hire one of the local drunks to carry your ass home.

You guessed it, **Café Tropical** *(Carrer Miguel Rose 19; Tel 972/258-801; 8pm-3am; Drinks around 600ptas; No credit cards)* serves tropical drinks and exploits palm trees and a Caribbean theme. It occasionally has live music, usually of the Latin variety, including salsa, merengue, etc. Feel free to strike up a conversation at the big pool table, or act your most art-pretentious self while examining and deconstructing the next generation of Dalís hanging on the walls. To boot, you can find a nice balance of tourists and local folks, so if you are jonesing for some English, talk to the Brits, or if you want the authentic, the locals are waiting for your clever wit.

Es Porro *(Carrer Portal de la Font; No phone; Midnight-5am daily; 300ptas for a beer; No credit cards)* yearns to be a combination disco/bar, but definitely leans more toward the bar end of the spectrum. After a few rum and Cokes, when the juices start to flow, folks usually will start busting a slight groove, but don't come here for a raging club atmosphere. In most places in Spain, almost anything where people have room to dance can be considered a disco, so this too is a *discoteca.* The DJ plays a wide variety of music ranging from pop to house, an eclectic if sometimes mind-numbing mix. The ambience is a little flat, same old strobe lights and colored light effects as 10,000 other little places dotted across the country. If Dalí's ghost wandered in, he'd probably run out screaming.

For our money, the best place in town for a good time is **Glop** *(Carrer Passeig Maritim; No phone; 9pm-3am daily; 800ptas for a mixed drink; No* *credit cards).* This place is super-cool. You can sit outdoors on beige couch-like creatures, under a nice white awning, inside on a wooden bench, or at the bar making small talk with one of the cute bartenders. They've been building a bunch of candle mountains for years by plopping a new white candle atop the already voluptuous bunch of melted wax on the tables. These candles are the primary source of lighting. Even cooler, word is that Dalí designed the logo for this joint, and if you get a matchbox you can check out the super-duper-surreal image of this Dalí logo on one side juxtaposed with a '70s airbrushed picture of the owner's wife on the other. Also, the original airbrushed photo sits behind the bar. Sweet! A house band plays older American rock fare, and for a cheesy local band, we must admit they do rock a bit. Anyhow, it's definitely worth the ride.

CULTURE ZOO

The primary draw to Cadaqués is the Dalí house. Ah, Dalí, definitely one of the geniuses of the 20th century. His work was strongly influenced by the predominating movements of the day, including Freud's psycho-analysis, and Surrealism. Dalí brought new ways of looking at the world to bear on his images of humans and landscapes, often lurching from the real, to the hyperreal, to the surreal and back in a single painting. His work has influenced everyone, even if they don't know it, and you can see traces of Dalí in computer-generated art, modern writing, and pretty much anywhere you look if you look hard enough. Dalí had no qualms with self-promotion (minus the much-derided moustache), and he erected museums around the world (Florida, Paris) to promote his work. But going to these museums can offer only so much insight into the char-acter of the artist. By visiting the Dalí house, you get a chance to look at the stuff that Dalí sat in and put on his own walls to please his own eye (and butt for that matter). It offers the chance to get a more unfiltered look at the mind behind the art, rather than just trying to decipher the deep metaphor of the work he designed for the public. Also, for any aspiring artists, writers, or intellectual types, seeing Dalí's house will give you a new perspective on just how weird you need to be to change the world.

Teatre-Museu Salvador Dalí *(Port Lligat—the Dalí house is basi-cally the whole town, which is a 15-minute walk north of Cadaqués on a well-marked; Tel 972/258-063; 10:30am-6pm Mar 13-June 14/Sept 16-Jan 9, entrance into museum permitted until 5:10pm, closed Mon; 10:30am-9pm daily June 15-Sept 15, entrance permitted until 8pm; You need to call ahead and reserve a time for a tour; pllgrups@dali-estate.org; 1,300 ptas; No credit cards).* The house has a sofa made to look like huge red human lips, egg sculptures lining the roof, playfully colored walls, and furnishings that were designed to make you trip without acid. You'd never know from the relatively tame white modern exterior the kinds of deliciously bizarre treats that Dalí put inside his home. Every room holds a surprise—look for windows with such great scenes of the sea that it tricks your eye into thinking you are looking at an idyllic painting.

FESTIVALS

Festival of the Rising Sun *(Jan 1, 7am; Cap de Creus):* On the first day of the new year, folks from around the town get together too early in the morning and do Catalan folk dances to the first sunrise.

Antique Fair *(Last Sunday of every month; Promenade):* A good chance to check out some authentic old Spanish stuff. As always, you can find great deals or terrible rip-offs at these fairs, so keep your eyes open but don't be too free with daddy's dough.

Grand Summer Festival *(Sept, Es Portal Platja):* Folks get together for traditional folk and sailor songs, sailboats, kids' games, and fun in the sun. Kind of a nice way for the locals to say good-bye to the tourist season and look forward to the year's best swimming.

Grand Winter Festival *(Dec 18, various venues in town):* In honor of one of the zillions of this country's saints, the town puts together mountain bike races, dancing, and other fun sporting events.

CITY SPORTS

Since Cadaqués is located in a calm little cove on the Mediterranean, it is a great area for swimming (including the skinny-dipping mentioned above)—right on the main beach or, if you go on a little hike, off one of the paths that follow the sea. There are always boats out—small sailboats and yachts for fun, and small but serious sea-fishing vessels. There are even big crazy boats for ridiculous tourists and old people, where you pay to hear some guy with a bad accent yell about the water. If you are *really* feeling the tourist vibe, try the ones with the glass bottom. *A three-hour tour, a three-hour tour....*

If the weather starts getting rough, just pack in the kayak and rent a scooter or bike to jump around and check out the scenery or pick up high school kids at 3pm. Scuba diving is always a blast, and the cove offers a great opportunity to get some low-impact hours on the Mediterranean.

Located near the water, **Animal Area** *(Platja es Poal; Tel 972/258-027; 9am-1:30pm/4-8:30pm Mon-Sat; Prices vary; AE, MC, V)* is an adventure-sport rental shop that caters to the international crowd, with prices in English and an employee you can talk to. You can get single and double sea kayaks (beware, don't go out on windy days...trust us), rockin' scooters if you have some kind of driver's license, nice mountain bikes, and zodiacs (small motorboats). Prices are pretty decent, and everything but the kayaks rents by hour, day, or week. A kayak for an hour is 1,200ptas, a bike for a day is 2,000ptas, a scooter for a day is 5,900ptas, and a zodiac for a day is 15,000ptas.

Scuba isn't necessarily the best way to get to know a culture, but it can be a damn good time. **Sotamar** *(Avda. Caritat Serinyana 17; Tel 972/258-876; 2 trips per day; Times vary, best to call ahead or stop by; sotamar@intercom.es, www.usuarios.intercom.es/sotamar; 6,000ptas for beginner dive; AE, MC, V)* has lots of options for licensed scuba divers, as well as a nice package deal for the beginner. They'll take you out on their boat with gear and an instructor, and you can get to know the ropes. Make sure they have one of their English teachers available before you take the plunge (unless you like to live *dangerously*). You can also buy a bunch of preppy clothes for the section of your closet designated "weekend yachtwear" (before it was Tommy Hilfiger, it was just plain old preppy nonsense).

EATS

This town is fantastic for seafood. Almost any restaurant will be able to serve you up a really great bucket of mussels or *gambas* (shrimp). If you want to be more experimental when sampling the cuisine, try the *lenguando a la plancha* (which is essentially grilled fish); the locals will be impressed with your knowledge of their regional dishes. **SA Gambina** *(Carrer Nemesio Llorens; Tel 972/258-127; 1-4pm/8-11pm; 1,200ptas lunch menu of the day; AE, MC, V)* redeems itself a bit with the gazpacho, at 500ptas a good deal. This is a nice, typical Spanish restaurant, with white tablecloths, patio with umbrellas, and indoor seating. The mostly Catalan food is kind of mediocre, but the location right next to the beach is key. You will find better paella, so don't bother at 1,600ptas and definitely DO NOT get the dessert; there is a high risk of freezer burn.

At **El Barroco** *(Carrer Nou; Tel 972/258-632; 1-4pm/8-11pm; 2,500ptas for dinner menu; AE, MC, V),* you can get Catalan and French-style food at a slightly higher price. The place has a pleasant ambience, mostly deriving from the ivy growing inside, and the white stucco everywhere, which characterizes the whole town's decor. You can go out to eat on the patio if you want, and be sure to check out the logo, designed by Dalí in 1978.

crashing

A good deal, considering the town, can be found at **Hostal Marina** *(Carrer Riera de St Vincenc 3; Tel 972/28-199; 4,500ptas double no bath, 6,000ptas double with bath (no singles); No credit cards).* Here you'll find normal, plain rooms with two single beds, a bunch of rooms with balconies, and a very friendly old couple that run the place. The location of this two-star *pensión* is very good, right down by the water, and you get a key to the front door so you don't have any weird restrictions. It is also located right next to the information center. One special tip: You won't find any soap in the room, but if you ask the nice owners they will give you really great soap.

Hostal Cristina *(Carrer Riera de St Vincenc 4; Tel 972/258-138; 4,000ptas without bath 6,000ptas with bath; No credit cards)* is located right next to the Hostal Marina—it's a decent Plan B if the Hostal Marina is full. Also close to the beach and info center, but the balconies aren't quite as nice and it doesn't have the same homey feel to it. To top it off, there is no special soap.

If you are looking for something a little nicer, you can upscale it to a genuine hotel at **Hotel Ubaldo** *(Carrer Unio 13; Tel 972/258-125; 5,000-7,500ptas; No credit cards)*. It isn't right on the beach, which is a drag, but it is only a 5 minute walk away. It's very close to the bus station on a nice little winding side street. Rooms have telephones, TVs, and, of course, the private bathrooms are very clean and the beds are comfy.

Other cheap to moderate options include **Fonda Vehi** *(Carrer de l'E-glesia 5; Tel 972/258-470; 2,000ptas single, 4,000ptas double; shared bath; V, MC, AE)*, a block away from **Eglésia de Santa Maria** and **Hostal El Ranxo** *(Avinguda de Caritat Serinyana s/n, Tel 972/258-005; 7,000ptas single, 3,500ptas double, 9,000ptas triple, breakfast and tax included, private baths; V, MC)*, a short walk north from the center of town.

need to know

Currency Exchange ATMs are all over this town, so you won't have any problem changing money here. And since you get the best rates using your credit card or bank account, you might as well just ignore anyone that wants to change your American cash.

Tourist Information The folks at the **tourist information office** *(Carrer Cotxe 2; Tel 972/258-315; 10am-1pm/4-8pm Mon-Sat, 10am-1pm Sun and holidays)* speak a little English and do their best to be helpful.

Health and Emergency Medical assistance *(Carrer Nou; Tel 972/258-807)*, local police *(Carrer Vigilant 2; Tel 972/159-343)*, and fire station *(Carrer Carles Rahola; Tel 972/258-008)*.

Pharmacies The two pharmacies in town are Colomer *(Ctra. Port-Lligat; Tel 972/258-932)* and Moradell *(Plaça Frederic Rahola; Tel 972/258-751)*.

Buses The buses go only to and from Figueres and to and from Barcelona (there are no trains to Cadaqués); the **Sarfa** bus company *(Caritat Serinyana; Tel 972/258-713; 2,200ptas to Barcelona)* runs the whole show. The bus stop is less than a 10-minute walk, along Carrer Unió and Carrer Vigilant, from the center of town.

Bike/Moped Rental See *city sports,* above.

Laundry A good place for laundry or dry cleaning is La Lavanderia *(Carrer de la font Vella; Tel 972/258-489; Prices by kilogram)*. The owner will be understanding about your inability to conquer the metric system and currency conversion.

Postal The **main post office** *(Carrer Rierassa; 9am-2pm)* should be able to handle your postal needs.

figueres

The fastest way from Barcelona to Cadaqués (because the direct bus doesn't run too often) is to take a train to Figueres, then the bus to Cadaqués. Although perhaps not quite as interesting a town as Cadaqués to the Dalí fanatic, Figueres is his birthplace and does have one very essential spot that must be experienced by anyone even remotely interested in the surrealist madman, the **Museu Dalí** *(Plaça Gala-Salvador Dalí 5; Tel 972/511-800; 10:30am-5:45pm Jan-June and Oct-Dec; 9am-7:45pm July-Sept, entrance allowed up to 30 min before closing, closed holidays; 1,000ptas)*. Built on the grounds of the old town theater that originally presented Dalí's paintings, this immensely popular museum houses a number of works from his early years as well as some of the darker, more psychologically trenchant pieces he created later in life. To see Dalí at his most whimsical, yet no less bizarre, check out the *Sala de Mae West,* a living room he modeled in the memory of one of Hollywood's most voluptuous starlets. The various furnishings of the room form her body—two fireplaces for her nostrils, a red sofa for her lips, and so on, a perverse tribute indeed. Dalí was not only a painter but a collector of the works of other artists, and these pieces, which include El Greco's memorable and elongated version of St. Paul, are, likewise, on display. The Museu Dalí was designed and concieved by Dalí himself as kind of a tortuous funhouse and compendium to his crazy, albeit fascinating mind. Although it can be a bit difficult to handle at times (Dalí's notion of beauty can be quite skewed), it's an experience not to be missed.

eats

A world-class gourmet like Dalí might not eat here, but chances are you'll find **La Llesca** *(Carre Mestre Falla 15; Tel 972/675-826; Main courses 500-1,800ptas, fixed-price menu 1,100ptas; 7am-1:30am Mon-Sat, 6pm-2am Sun; MC, V)* most satisfying. Catalan and Spanish regional specialties mix comfortably on the menu at the best food value in town—portions are generous and the food is home-cooked. Closed the second and third week in November.

Another option is **La Pansa** *(Carrer L'Emporada 8; Tel 972/501-072; Main courses 600-1,200ptas, fixed-price menu 1,200ptas; Daily noon-4pm and 8-10pm; MC, V)*. The simple bistro decor is modesty itself, but the reasonably priced food is fresh and satisfying. Thursdays can get a bit crowded with locals hungry for the chef's famed paella. Otherwise, you're treated to some locally caught fish dishes plus a selection of veal, steaks, and other meat dishes. From June to August and during the first 3 weeks of September it closes on Sunday.

crashing

If you have to spend the night in town, a comfortable and, most importantly, affordable option is the **Hostel La Barretina** *(Carrer Lasauca 13; Tel 972/676-412; 3,500ptas single; 6,000ptas double; MC, V)*. The hostel is surprisingly stylish considering its relatively modest prices. You check in at the on-site restaurant downstairs where you can also order breakfast the following morning (not included in the overnight rate). Each room is tastefully and comfortably furnished with air-conditioning,

TV, and phone, along with an immaculate shower-only bathroom. From the rail station head up the left side of La Rambla, walking almost to its end, where you'll come to the junction with Carrer Lasauca.

Other cheap to moderate options include **Habitacions Bartis** (*Carrer de Mendez Nunez 2; Tel 972/50-14-73; 1,800ptas single, 2,900ptas double, same price with or without private bath; No credit cards*), near the train station; **Habitacions Mallol** (*Carrer de Pep Ventura 9; Tel 972/502-283; 2,000ptas single, 3,450ptas double, shared baths; No credit cards*), in the city center a short walk from the Museu Dalí; **Hotel Espana** (*Carrer de la Jonquera 26; Tel 972/500-869; Fax 972/512-022; Open June-Sept; Rooms with bath 5,000ptas, rooms without bath 3,500ptas; V, MC, AE, DC*), in the heart of the city center; and **Hostal La Venta del Toro** (*Carrer de Pep Ventura 5; Tel 972/510-510; 2,000ptas single, 3,500ptas double, shared baths; V, MC*), right next door to Mallol.

need to know

Tourist Office Look for the blue **i** if you need the **main tourist office** (*Plaça del Sol; Tel 972/503-155; 9am-9pm Mon-Sat, 9am-6pm Sun, July, Aug; 9am-3pm/4:30-8pm Mon-Fri, 9:30am-1:30pm Sat, Apr-June; 9am-3pm Mon-Fri the rest of the year*); otherwise, between July and September you can find info booths in front of the bus station and the Museu Dalí.

Trains and Buses The train (*Tel 972/207-093*) and bus (*Tel 972/673-354*) stations are right next to each other at **Plaça Estació.** Trains run all day from Barcelona and take about an hour and a half. Buses run about five times a day from Barcelona and take about 2 hours. The **Sarfa** bus company at the bus station will take you to Cadaqués in a little over an hour. In July and August, there are five buses a day between Cadaqués and Figueres. During the other months, there are only two or three buses per day. If you're dependent on public transportation, it is entirely likely you might end up in Figueres for the night.

girona

With only about 80,000 people, the walled city of Girona (*Gerona* in Castilian) packs quite a punch for such a small town, and is a welcome relief if you've spent a few days frying your brain on the beaches of the Costa Brava. The people are very sophisticated—they'll be into talking with you about interesting topics and will be curious to hear your point of view on their culture. A lot of people know English, so communication is much smoother than in other places in Spain. The old quarter of town is totally beautiful with narrow winding streets that make you feel like you are in a living castle. While the old town is obviously more culturally packed and intimately engaging, the new part of town also carries

girona

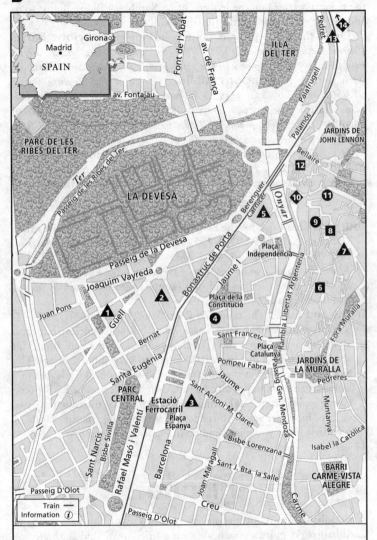

its own special charm. Tree-lined streets, airy, open architecture, and small shops with classy goods come together to make the newer part of Girona a rival to the old.

Located about a 30-minute drive from the coast and an hour's train ride from Barcelona, Girona is a great place to visit for a few days or more. If you spend a little time getting to know the place, I guarantee that you will not want to leave. Girona is kind of like a person that you get along with so well you feel like you've known them forever. And when you leave Girona, you'll feel like you are saying goodbye to an old friend, too.

The standard of living in Girona is very high relative to other Spanish towns. People generally have a little bit more money, are better educated, and have experience traveling. You'll sense that some of the pride and cosmopolitan feel of Barcelona has filtered up to this little city that isn't even really a city. You might find the population more accessible than in other towns, and it's possible that they will show a higher interest in you. At the very least, more people will be looking to practice their English on you. So, if your *Catalá* isn't quite up to speed, fear not: You'll be able to manage better here than in the more provincial pueblos.

While no one would accuse people in Girona of being pushy, they don't subscribe to the same laid-back attitude toward life that you find in many other places in Spain. There is a bit more intensity here, and people seem to have a passion for life that drives them to get the most out of their experiences. There is also a fair amount of Catalan pride in Girona—you'll hear a lot of *Catalá* in the streets, but don't let that intimidate you. Of course everyone knows Castilian (i.e., the Spanish you learned in high school) as well, and some people know English too.

Folks here are all ages but you do get a higher proportion of young people thanks to the **Casa Cultura.** The young people keep the town vibrant, and a few small industries and tourism keep the economy above average for Spain. Ten years ago there wasn't any tourism, but Girona's been slowly making a name for itself. Hang out here long enough and you'll begin to see why it's no small wonder that statistically 90 percent of Spaniards consider themselves happy.

The town of Girona is divided by the **Riu Onyar,** which runs from north to south. On the west side of the river lies the new town, on the east side is the old town, otherwise known as the **Barri Vell.** Bordered by the old city wall, the Barri Vell includes the **Catedral,** the **Cort Reial,** a pleasant street where you can find a bunch of solid restaurants, and an old Jewish neighborhood called **El Call** [see *culture zoo,* below]. The Barri Vell is quaint, beautiful, spectacular, and every other positive adjective known to man. When something is just great in every way, Spanish kids use the expression *"Que guay!"* and that pretty much sums up our opinion of the Barri Vell.

The new part of town, the **Barri del Mercadal,** includes the **Plaça Independencia** as well as the Casa Cultura. The Casa Cultura is a small but famous music conservatory, theater, art gallery, and liberal arts college that contributes to this town's intellectual and creative vibe. The Plaça Independencia, known as the "living room of Girona," shelters a number of pricey restaurants, as well as a few cheap coffee shops excellent for kicking back and doing some good old-fashioned people-watching.

Another cool area is **La Devesa,** which is just northwest of the Barri del Mercadal. This park is a great place to hang in the summertime because everyone drinks outside and the whole place turns into a cool outdoor party. (Nature-lovers may want to take note: This may be the extent of your outdoor activites in Girona—the town does't even have bike rentals. If you're looking for the sporting life, you're going the wrong way; head back to the Costa Brava.) The bars here are called *las-carpas* (which is essentially an outdoor booth selling drinks) by the locals. All of the action here is outdoors and don't be surprised to find live music some nights too. The bars are especially thick on **Passeig de la Devesa.**

In the **Barri de Pedret,** north of the Barri Vell on the eastern side of the river, you can find a bunch of great *discotecas,* live music joints, and bars.

You can do some good people-watching during the afternoon and evenings at the **Plaça Catalunya,** which serves as a transition area between the old and new parts of town. Located literally on a bridge over the river, it's got cafes, Spanish-style *cervercias* (beer halls), ice cream shops, and small restaurants. You'll find people here chatting with friends and sitting outside to soak up the great Mediterranean sun. All age groups are represented.

The Cort Reial is at the beginning of the very old section of the Barri Vell and has a bunch of bars, lots of outdoor seating, and some cool little shops and music stores that can be enjoyed during the day. For the most part, these small shops sell unusual clothing and jewelry that's a little on the expensive side. But if you're enjoying a strong American dollar, go ahead and do some serious American shopping.

In the heart of the Barri Vell, the hills are quite steep; Girona's cathedral is on an especially large hill. There are always groups of Spanish students and international types going into the cathedral to check out the magnificent Gothic architecture. The steps leading up to it can serve as kind of a meeting ground for young tourists, because everyone wandering around the old section of town ends up here sooner or later. If you are in desperate need of some English conversation, just go here and you're sure to chat it up with someone.

Many of the bridges that connect the old quarter with the new over the Riu Onyar are too old and small to accommodate cars. This makes them great places from which to stare out peacefully at the homes along the river, especially at night when things calm down a bit and the glow of the houselights reflects off of the water. You'll find tourists doing the same gazing exercise here, but locals also come to check out the view and get a little tranquility.

bar, club, & live music scene

The nightlife in Girona is substantial for a town of its size. Different establishments cater to different tastes, so you should be able to find something that suits your fancy. People start to hit the streets around midnight and the party continues until 4am or so. A good night might start out in the Barri Vell at Le Bistrot, where you can have some drinks and then wander between bars along the intricate cobblestone streets. Next, move to the Plaça Catalunya where you can meet up with your friends, or watch other people meet up with theirs, then head out to the Barri del Mercadal and toss down a few while checking out the sights and sounds of the outdoor bar L'Imprempta. At this point, unless you are an experienced lush, you'll have some kind of buzz, so take it kind of easy while you stroll over to La Devesa. Bars open at 10pm and close down, depending on how cool both you and the owner are, around 3am. *Discotecas* stay open till about 6am, although some places are known to stay open later, discreetly of course. For nightlife in Girona, just bring ample cash when you go out, because credit card service is sporadic, and when the joint is hopping the bartenders won't have time to deal...he or she might just tell you they don't take *tarjetas*.

Le Bistrot (*Pujada de Sant Domènec 4; Tel 972/218-803; 1-3pm/9-11pm daily; 500ptas beer*) is located in the Barri Vell, and it's one of the classier places around. You can check out the antiques and play Parcheesi with the Catalan-speaking locals. A great way to start your evening out is to stop by early, drop a few, and get some quality cross-cultural time. If you have an aesthetic sense that is finely tuned for digging on the "local" vibe, hanging out here for hours will be a treat.

It is really, really fun to listen to Spanish people hack away at American songs, really. At the **Bar Extrem** (*Carrer Barcelona 179; No phone; 10pm-3am; 400ptas beer*) you will experience exactly what we mean. In the southern part of the Barri del Mercadal, this bar features karaoke 7 days a week and people butcher songs from across the globe. Let me tell you, even though they don't know how to spell "extreme" you are in for an *extreme* time. And you thought the BASE jumping in Benasque was going to be your thrill for the vacation. Well, you were wrong baby, dead wrong.

L'Imprempta (*Carrer Ramon Turro 18; Tel 972/202-131; 10pm-3am; 400ptas beer*) is where locals go before they hit the all-night party over in La Devesa. Located about halfway from Barri Vell, it is a great place to stop and play some pool or foosball, sit on the ample seating, and relax a bit from the staggering 10-minute walk. Enjoy the atmosphere and drink a few while you gear up for the outdoor fun.

Platea (*Carrer Real de Fontclara at the end of the street; Tel 972/227-288; 10pm-3am; 700ptas mixed drinks*) is right next to the Cinema Albeniz. The club is unmarked, so just follow the music or some hip-looking young person right on in. There is live music some nights from 11pm-1am, and then the dancing starts. In its glory days this building was a beautiful theater, and now the bands rock out on the old stage. There is no techno at this club; instead, the bands and DJs play a mix of Spanish Top 40. Don't forget to love Tom Jones as much as the Spanish kids do. Dig on the sweaty 16- to 22-year-old dancing people. Go along with the fun and don't be too snotty to love the bad music—you *are* on vacation.

If you are looking for an *ecstatic* time, go to **La Sala del Cel** *(Carrer Pedret 118; Tel 972/214-664; 11pm-6am; 700ptas)* in the Barri de Pedret. This place is big, this place is sex, this place is (reportedly) drugs, and this place is rock 'n' roll. The crowd moves to the heavy house and techno, and no nice Spanish girls go here.

It's Thursday night and you're looking for something to do? Well then, check out **La Sala de Ball de Girona** *(Carrer Riu Guell 2; Tel 972/215-539; 11pm-6am, but showing up before 1am is* really *uncool; 600-800ptas mixed drinks).* Normally this venue is for older people, but on Thursday nights, when the students are sick of studying and before they go back to *mama* in the *casa* in the pueblo, they come here to dance to salsa or *the techno* or *the pop.* As the night moves on, it gets more crowded, and what the music might lack in quality it makes up for in volume.

CULTURE ZOO

If you took the three best cultural spots in Girona, recorded them, and sent them to your local DJ to spin together, you'd get a pretty solid cut. Unlike places like Tarragona, which weighs you down with Roman ruins, Roman pottery fragments, Roman coins, Roman...you won't get too run-down in Girona on a single theme because you get a great ancient neighborhood with intense history, El Call, the God-fearing architecture of the Catedral, and the *muy divertido* Museu del Cinema.

El Call *(Carrer Sant Llorenc; Tel 972/216-761; callgirona@grn.es— this e-mail address goes to folks at the Patronat Municipal Call de Girona who work to preserve the Call):* The history of the Call, the old Jewish neighborhood, is a history of persecution followed by peace, followed by persecution. Amid the ancient winding streets, it's easy to imagine the lives of the people who lived here, often secluded and hated. Although the Jews of Girona were never really awarded full citizen status, they were a very important part of the local economic and cultural life. There was an independent and thriving Jewish community here for 600 years before the religious rage of Isabella and Ferdinand kicked them out for good in 1492. Walking through these narrow corridors, you get a sense of this history.

Catedral *(Plaça de la Catedral; Tel 972/214-426; 9am-1pm daily, also during the afternoon depending on a very complicated seasonal schedule, which you can obtain from the tourist office. It's likely to be open every day before 2pm, except Sat):* You need to climb up a ton of stairs up a hill to get here, but it is well worth it. This cathedral holds the title for the "widest Gothic nave in the world," and has held it since its construction in the 15th and 16th centuries. Gorgeous stained-glass windows and high vaulted ceilings round out the experience.

only here

The old wall—which once served to protect the city of Girona from the various reli-
gions taking their turn at trying to rule—is
in such great shape that at three points along
the wall, you can still climb up a set of stairs
that takes you to the top. You can more or less
walk around the **Barri Vell** along the top of the wall. An
amazing feature of this town, it is a great way to get to know the old
quarter. From here, you can see the **Catedral,** as well as the smaller
churches and monasteries in town that actually service the majority
of church-going Gironians. You also get a great view of **El Call** from
a totally strange perspective. After walking around the tight, closed
streets, getting lost in the history and charm of this little neighborhood, seeing it from above only increases your appreciation of its
winding corridors and skinny passageways.

The wall breaks about halfway through, so if you want to see the
whole Barri Vell from on high, you need to get up on top at either
end. The best place to start is at the stairs by the **Plaça Catalunya.**
Just walk over from the southeast corner of the plaza to the **Plaça
General Marva,** and you will see the wall and the access point. The
stretch starting here is the longest that you can walk continuously,
winding around half of the old quarter. You can get off at the eastern
end of town at another set of stairs. The other entrance point is on
the northern side of town behind the cathedral.

While strolling along the top, be sure to pretend that you and
your friends are Muslims, warding off the Christian hordes; Christians, warding off the Muslim hordes; or Jews, warding off the Christian monarchs. So many hordes, so little time.

Museu del Cinema *(Carrer Sequia 1; Tel 972/412-777; 10am-8pm
Tue-Sun May-Oct; 10am-6pm Tue-Fri, 10am-8pm Sat, 11am-3pm Sun
Nov-Apr; 500ptas):* Film buffs, don't miss this one. You enter and watch a
little mini-documentary about the history of cinema in your own language. Then you take an elevator up to the top floor and walk down while
looking at and touching various artifacts from the history of the moving
image. You haven't had this much fun in a museum since the first time
you went to the Smithsonian on a class trip.

EATS

For delicious and authentic Catalonian food, try **Restaurante Lle-
gendes** *(Riera Can Camaret 3; Tel 972/220-709; 1-4pm/9-11pm daily;
Entrees about 3,000ptas; AE, MC, V).* It is a bit out of the town's center,

so you may want to take a cab. There is an old Catalan legend about spirits turning into butterflies, and you need to know this to decode the decor. The food is great and comes highly recommended by the locals.

Right in the old quarter, **El Cul de la Lleona** *(Carrer Calderers 8; Tel 972/203-158; 1-4pm/8:30-11pm; Entrees about 2,500ptas; AE, MC, V)* serves up both Moroccan and Spanish favorites—try the couscous dishes and the Catalan salad. The warm colors of the restaurant lend a cozy air to the place, and the food is fantastic. The owner of the place, Jose, is a good guy—don't forget to tell him hello from us.

crashing

There are only a handful of *hostales* in Girona. It would be nice if there were a few more in the Barri Vell like **Hotel Bellmirall,** which with all of its art and romance makes you feel like you are finally sleeping in Spain. In general, though, the town does not have a shortage of places to stay, relative to its size and the number of tourists that come here. You might as well call in advance if you are coming up from Barcelona, but it isn't a necessity as it is in towns along the Costa Brava.

You'll find the **Pensión Llado** *(La Barca 31; Tel 972/210-998; 3,000ptas single, 4,000ptas double; No credit cards)* over the top of a restaurant. If you stop in the restaurant, someone behind the counter will give you keys to a room and the front door and escort you up to take a look and see if it suits you. You will probably decide to stay since all the rooms and bathrooms are generally spacious and clean. It is a little out of the center of town but it is just down the hill from the historic district. You can stop by the restaurant for breakfast before you set out on a day o' adventure or for an afternoon snack before your siesta. This is a good place for the price and its proximity to El Call.

Look for the blue "pension" sign to reach **Pensión Viladomat** *(Ciutadans 5; Tel 972/203-176; 3,200ptas single, 4,500ptas double; No credit cards),* which is on a quiet street in the old quarter. Walk up the stairs and ring the doorbell. A nice old woman will take you up a million stairs to your room. The sheets here are all pretty new and the rooms have recently been painted. Not all of the rooms have bathrooms, but the ones in the hall are better than decent and, overall, this place isn't a bad deal.

If you are treating yourself, try the **Hotel Bellmirall** *(Bellmirall 3; Tel 972/204-009; 5,000ptas single with bath, 8,580ptas double with toilet; No credit cards).* It's essentially a bed and breakfast in an old Spanish house; all the rooms are stone with antique furniture and have windows looking out on the old quarter (singles with a view tend to cost a little more). It is a bit pricey but it all seems worth it when you wake up in the morning and go to the garden for a fresh, filling breakfast of croissants, fruit, and other treats. All over the walls you'll find artwork made by the owner of the house, an accomplished painter. If he's home and you're interested, ask to see his studio and the terrace on the top floors. This place is often full, so call ahead to reserve a room. The woman who runs the hotel speaks English and is glad to help.

Other reasonable options include **Hotel Peninsular** *(Carrer Nou 3, Tel 972/203-800, Fax 972/210-492; 5,600ptas single, 7,700ptas double, private baths; www.tems.com/peninsular, novarahotels@cambrest.es; V, MC, AE)*, on the eastern bank of the Riu Onyar, and **Hostal Gerunda** *(Carrer de Barcelona 34; Tel 972/202-285; 2,100ptas single, 4,100ptas double, shared bath; No credit cards)*, a 5-minute walk from the train station.

need to know

Currency Exchange There are plenty of banks and ATM machines in Girona. Try **La Caixa bank;** there's a branch on Carrer dels Abeuradors off Rambla de la Llibertat and on Carrer Nou, across the river.

Tourist Information The **main tourist office** *(Carrer Rambla Llibertat Argenteria; Tel 972/226-575; 8am-8pm Mon-Fri, 8am-2pm/4-8pm Sat, 9am-2pm Sun)* is right above Plaça Catalunya and right next to the river. The staff here are very helpful and speak very good English.

Public Transportation If you are planning to mainly explore the old quarter you won't need to know the bus system.

Health and Emergency In the case of an emergency where an ambulance is needed contact the *Creu Roja,* the Red Cross *(Tel 972/222-222)*. Otherwise, contact the main hospital, **Hospital Dr. Trueta** *(Carrer Avinguda De Franca 60; Tel 972/202-700)*, which is in north Girona, or the **Policia Municipal** *(Carrer Bacia 4; Tel 972/419-090)*.

Pharmacies As usual, the pharmacies can be spotted by the **big green crosses.** The **Carolina Murtra** *(Carrer Rambla Llibertat 18; Tel 972/200-191)* is one located near the tourist office.

Trains and Buses The **RENFE Estacio del Ferrocarril** *(Tel 972/207-093; 6am-10pm Mon-Sat)* and the **Estacieó d'autobusos** *(Tel 972/212-319; 6am-10pm Mon-Sat)* are both located at Plaça d'Espanya in the newer part of town, about a 20-minute walk to the old center. You can get express trains to France and pretty much anywhere in Spain, as well as local buses and trains around the Costa Brava region.

Postal The **main post office** *(Avda. Ramon Folch 2; Tel 972/203-236; 8:30am-8:30pm Mon-Fri, 9:30am-2pm Sat)* is the place for your missives.

Internet You can use the Internet for free at the library, **Edifici les Aligues** *(Plaça Sant Domenech s/n; Tel 972/418-046; www.udg.es/)*.

SITGES

If you had visited the quaint little fishing village of Sitges 50 years ago, you probably wouldn't have been able to predict that it would turn into a mecca of trendy summertime nightlife and gay culture. In fact, you might have tried to commit anyone who made such a Cassandra-like prediction. But it's all come true, my friends, it's all come true....

This place is no joke. If you're into being cool, having a great time, and hanging with fabulous people, you will love it as much as we do.

sitges

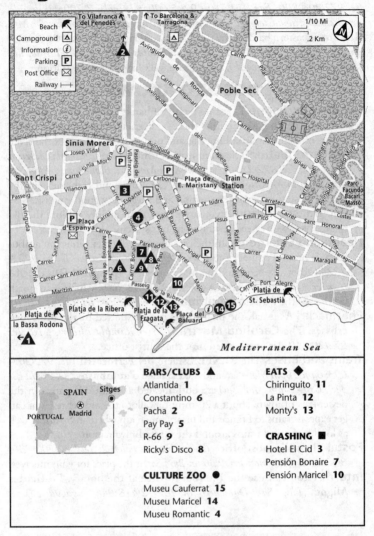

BARS/CLUBS ▲
Atlantida **1**
Constantino **6**
Pacha **2**
Pay Pay **5**
R-66 **9**
Ricky's Disco **8**

CULTURE ZOO ●
Museu Cauferrat **15**
Museu Maricel **14**
Museu Romantic **4**

EATS ◆
Chiringuito **11**
La Pinta **12**
Monty's **13**

CRASHING ■
Hotel El Cid **3**
Pensión Bonaire **7**
Pensión Maricel **10**

Located on the beautiful sand beaches of the Costa Dorada about an hour south of Barcelona, Sitges is jam-packed with summer parties during the peak season, but tourists visit all year round. During July and August, you need to call well in advance if you want to get a bed, because this place turns into a festival like you've never seen. Some say that Sitges rivals Ibiza for party punch, but if you ask us, it takes what is good and beautiful in Ibiza, distills it for impurities, and sells it on the top shelf.

The hipness of Sitges isn't super-high-profile. Instead, it is confident enough to wait for you to figure it out, and too cool to care if you don't. If you know the code, however, you'll be lovin' every minute of it, from the strutting and pedestrian-cruising of **Primero de Mayo,** which turns into **Carrer Marques Montroig**—together called **"La Carrer del Pecado"** by the locals—to the over-the-top and out-of-the-closet **Calle Sant Bonaventure.** When you're in Sitges, you'll never stop marveling at the openness and open-mindedness that sets this town apart from any other place in Spain.

Over the years, Sitges has drawn intellectuals, artists, and writers from all over the world, as well as Spain's own Salvador Dalí and Federico García Lorca. You can feel that vibe in the bars and restaurants, or in simple conversations with shop owners, other travelers, and the locals. The folks who work in tourist-related industries usually know some English, so you can break through the cultural/language barrier and get to know the place from the people who live here. Sitges's economy is almost exclusively reliant on tourism these days, hence the number of locals who work in the industry.

There are no sharp generational lines in Sitges; old folks hang out with young as part of the break-down-the-barriers-that-divide-us feel of the place. Maybe the reason everyone is so friendly and all-inclusive is because they have a special Zen perspective on life, or maybe the 365 (okay, maybe 364) days of straight sun start to erode everybody's Seasonal Affective Disorder.

There are really only two neighborhoods in Sitges, the center of town and all of the residential homes to the west. In the main center of town, you'll find typical Mediterranean architecture, with balconies, yellows, whites, and lots of awnings. The buildings are close together, and the streets have a cozy, familiar air that makes you feel right at home. And even more beautiful than that, nothing here is more than 5 minutes from the beach. You won't wander far from the commercial part of town unless after a heavy night out you get invited back to someone's home. In the area surrounding **Plaça Cap de la Villa** and **Plaça Industria** you'll find everything you're interested in—bars, hostels, restaurants, and shops. If you decide you want to sample the old culture of the city, climb up the steps of the **Parroquial Church** and you'll find two of the town's three museums up on this hill. You can also get a great view of the sea from here.

La Carrer del Pecado, begining at **Carrer de Parellades** and running to **Passeig de la Ribera,** and **Playa Ribera,** is where the largest and most popular bars are located. At night, the area comes alive with travelers and locals alike crowding the bars and bountiful outdoor seating. Lots of laughter can be heard and there is generally a jovial atmosphere. During the day, people have coffee and shop on La Carrer del Pecado, where you can find that rainbow bathing suit you've been searching the world for.

On Carrer Sant Bonaventure, in the city center off **Carrer Espalte,** you'll find most of the gay bars in town. Although it's a pretty small street, it has gained international fame as a meeting place for the rich and stylish gay and hetero crowd of Europe. It gets really crowded here even in the off-season, so prepare to be rubbing more than elbows on this main drag.

The town of Sitges basically opens onto what seem like one big beach, yet for some reason the area is divided into little sub-beaches with different names. They all have decent facilities like bathhouses and showers, as well as sun, sand, and water; however, they all tend to get very crowded when the weather is right. If you're looking for some naked time, walk west along the beach for about half an hour. Just past **Club Atlantida** [see *bar, club, and live music scene,* below], you'll find two popular nude beaches. The first is for heteros and gays alike, the second has a much smaller boob quotient. There is a rumor that lots of heated *conversations* go on in the woods behind the beaches.

hanging out

When people—locals as well as tourists—are getting ready to go out, they meet at either **Plaça Cap de la Villa** or at the **Plaça Industria.** These two plazas are at the intersection of all the streets in the center of town, so they make great places to get together before you hit the night with a wooden stick.

If you want to do some daytime people-watching, Sitges is one of the best places to do it. You can stop at **Hatuey Café and Art Gallery** (*Carrer Sant Francesc 44; Tel 938/945-209; 10am-1pm/4-11pm, hours vary during off-season; 200ptas coffee; V, MC*), a fab place to chill for a bit while sipping on a *café con leche*, snacking on a pastry, or having a beer and a sandwich for lunch. This cafe overflows with a personality all its own. One wall is filled with books from floor to ceiling, while the other walls are painted blue with an elaborate underwater scene including fish and a sunken ship. The ceiling is also blue, but features a mural of clouds and outer space. To top it off, the cafe displays intense photography and the work of local artists.

Mont Roig Café (*Carrer Marques de Montroig 11; Tel 938/948-439; 10am-1pm/4pm-3am; 300ptas; AE, V, MC*) is much bigger than your local Starbucks, much cooler, not to mention much classier. This joint gets really busy in the afternoons and evenings. There are two floors of indoor seating, but if you prefer to be outside you can either sit out in front watching the natives, or you can sit in the more private garden terrace in back. This place has every coffee drink your little caffeine-addicted mind could dream of, all of which go great with the yummy pastries and typical Spanish sandwiches available.

bar, club, & live music scene

The late-night scene is great in Sitges, where a mixed gay and straight crowd hits the streets in search of a good time. The basic plan for the evening is to start out at one of the many bars on Carrer del Pecado or Carrer Sant Bonaventura, then when they close down around 3am, head to a *discoteca*. The clubs in the city center are really just smaller spaces where you are allowed to dance, but you can take a shuttle bus out to either Atlantida or Pacha, where throngs (sometimes in thongs) gyrate and groove to a mix of disco, techno, and house. The focus is on self-expression, inhibition-free fun, and stylish revelry.

Constantino *(Dos de Mayo 15; Tel 938/947-018; 6pm-3am Sun-Thur, 6pm-3:30am Fri-Sat; 300ptas beer; No credit cards)* has a huge sound system that pumps out everything from Shania Twain to hard house and techno. The big disco ball, white fabric-covered ceiling, and pink and green lighting give it a fun post '70s might-be-cheesy-in-America-but-it's-cool-in-Spain vibe. The crowd here is a young, modern, gay/straight bunch. The place gets crowded, so if you want a seat at the long bar or at one of the tables, come early. Join a game of pool at the table in back to make some friends.

If you are looking for someplace where you can indulge in a serious margarita or other larger-than-life tropical drink, then **Pay Pay** *(Marques de Montroig 10; Tel 938/947-733; 6pm-4am daily during peak season, weekends only off-season; 500-800ptas drinks; No credit cards)* is the place for you. Tourists and locals alike must agree, because they've been coming to Pay Pay for over a decade and the place is still going strong. The decorating theme is an Asian tropical mix. The long bar and stools are made from bamboo, the walls are covered with Asian fans, and the huge tanks behind and around the bar are filled with colorful tropical fish. Drink three or four of the huge house specials and you'll be well on your way to a good time.

The Sitges "all-in-one" award goes to **R-66** *(Bonaire 12; Tel 938/945-791; 11pm-4am daily; 500ptas; No credit cards)* for being a bar, *discoteca*, and live music club, all at the same time. Open for more that five years, this place does it all, even providing free dance lessons early in the night for those who want to get in before the crowds and see if they can diversify their moves. The music is generally salsa, merengue, and cha cha, played by a live band or DJ. R-66 is short for Road House 66. Catering to a mix of gay and straight, tourist and local, by 1am the dance energy is high.

At **Ricky's Disco** *(Sant Pau 25; Tel 938/949-681; 11pm-4am, daily; 1,300ptas cover; AE, MC, V)* you can dance right in the center of town. The mixed crowd is fun, and there is always a vibe that screams: dance, dance, dance.

Once the night has worn a bit, and you're ready to hit the big clubs for action on the dance floor, the place to be is...on the bus. Unfortunately, that is the only way to get out to the two big clubs in town. You can catch the bus at the end of Primero de Mayo and Passeig de la Ribera in the center of town. **Atlantida** *(Passeig Maritim; Tel 938/942-677; Midnight-6pm; AE, MC, V)* is a great late-night party on the beach, with a stylishly dressed mixed crowd, hotties making out on the dance floor, and sticky bathroom floors. **Pacha** *(Passeig Sant Didac s/n; Tel 938/942-298; Midnight-6am daily; AE, MC, V)* is the classic European *discoteca* chain that people all over Spain identify by the two red cherries in its logo. If you can't get enough of strobe lights and techno music and sweaty dancing, you won't be disappointed.

gay scene

Talking about a gay scene isn't really relevant when describing Sitges, because Sitges *is* the gay scene. There are places that are a bit more exclusive than others, but generally straight or gay, the people mix. It's as if the flag flying over Sitges isn't just the same old red and yellow Spanish hues, but takes in a few more of the other colors of the rainbow as well.

Gays from all over Europe come to Sitges to vacation, so you can't run a hostel, hotel, restaurant, shop, or bar unless you're gay friendly. Tolerance is practiced so naturally that you come to realize that tolerance is just a lack of prejudice, and not some kind of positive feature of a person or place. The street with the most intense concentration of gay folks is **Carrer Sant Bonaventura.** Everything is packed tight and it's all good. On and around Carrer Sant Bonaventura you can find a number of bookstores and specialty shops where you can buy anything you forgot to pack—educational or raunchy.

culture zoo

Checking out old buildings and museums isn't really where it's at in Sitges, but there are still some nice things to see in between the beach and the bars. The **Museu Cauferrat,** the **Museu Maricel,** and the **Museu Romantic** are all cool places to visit if you have the time. They all have the same hours and entry fee; you can buy a ticket for all three museums for 800ptas, or 400ptas if you're a student, but we don't recommend it (you'd be spending way too much time away from the beach).

The **Museu Cauferrat** *(Carrer Fonollar s/n; Tel 938/940-364; 9:30am-2pm/4-6pm Tue-Fri, 9:30am-7pm Sat, 9:30am-3pm Sun Nov-May; 9:30am-2pm/5-9pm Tue-Sun June-Sept; 500ptas, 50 percent off for students):* This place is the former home of Santiago Rusiñol, one of Sitges's favorite sons. Rusiñol was a modernist Catalan painter and writer who did his best work at the turn of the last century (along with all the other Spanish modernist masters). In the house you can find a few Picassos as well as Rusiñol's work. Also on display are collections of glassware and iron and ceramic art. If you happen to be decorating your kitchen, you might stop by for some ideas.

Museu Maricel *(Carrer Fonollar s/n; 938/940-364; 9:30am-2pm/4-6pm Tue-Fri, 9:30am-7pm Sat, 9:30am-3pm Sun Nov-May; 9:30am-2pm/5-9pm Tue-Sun June-Sept; 500ptas, 50 percent off for students):* Skip the old stuff and go straight to the modern art gallery. The Catalan ceramics are worth a gander, too.

Museu Romantic *(Sant Gaudenci 1; Tel 938/942-969; 9:30am-2pm/4-6pm Tue-Fri, 9:30am-7pm Sat, 9:30am-3pm Sun Nov-May; 9:30am-2pm/5-9pm Tue-Sun, June-Sept; 500ptas, 50 percent off for stu-*

festivals and events

During the second week of October, **Festival Interna-cional de Cinema de Catalonia** *(Avda. Josep Tarradellas 135; Tel 934/193-635; www.sitges.com/cinema)* invites filmmakers from around the world to show off their goods (about 180 films were aired during the 2000 Festival). There are films of different types and from various genres, including shorts, animation, documen-taries, series, and TV movies, but the focus (pun intended) is on fantasy films. Movies are shown at several venues throughout the city, and there are tons of international indie productions. A crowd of over 100,000 comes out to see it.

The week-long ancient pagan festival **Carnaval** *(throughout the city; for more info, call the **tourist office**)* [see *need to know*, below] starts right before Lent, which itself begins on the Monday of the seventh week before Easter and ends on the Friday that is 9 days before Easter, which means it changes every year and you should ask someone. Carnaval is an event that draws about 30,000 party hounds to the Sitges area to partake in the—ummm—carnality. Many small towns and mid-sized cities across Spain do some kind of Carnaval festival, a kind of last-minute, pre-Lenten bash, vaguely akin to Mardi Gras. These festivals can take various forms, from goat killing to a parade to live performances. Sitges boasts probably the most outrageous Carnaval on mainland Spain (the Canary Islands are rumored to have the best), featuring a parade, floats, and tons and tons of parties in the clubs, bars, and restaurants. Bring your feather boa and dive in.

dents): If you're into dolls, this place is for you. It might not come as a sur-prise that Sitges houses one of the best doll collections in Europe. This museum also coolly re-creates what it was like to be stinking rich and living on the Mediterranean a decade ago.

CITY SPORTS

Water sports are all the rage in Sitges. The best windsurfing is offered at **Club de Mar** *(Paseo Marítimo; Tel 938/943-844)*. One hour will run you 1,500ptas; the price goes up to 4,000ptas for 3 hours. There is a remarkable outfit at Sitges called **Sport Nature/Camping El Gar-rofer** *(Tel 938/941-780),* which will hook you up with just about any-thing that floats. Here 15 minutes of waterskiing costs 3,000ptas, or else you can go parasailing for 4,800ptas. Two people can rent a kayak for 2,800ptas an hour; you can also rent a water motorcycle costing 20,000ptas for one hour. When you tire of the beach, the staff will hook you up with a motorbike for a mountain jaunt for 3,500ptas for the day.

EATS

On the boardwalk facing the beach, **Chiringuito** (*Passeig de la Ribera s/n; Tel 938/947-596; 10am-3am daily during the summer; sunup to sundown off-season; 400-800ptas per tapas; No credit cards*) is a great place to watch the "tides." There is indoor and outdoor seating, so depending on how tan you want to get, the choice is yours. The decor is nothing too exciting, just metal chairs and tables and the walls painted white with blue trim, all keeping with the local look. But what it lacks in style it makes up for with the food. This place is open all day so you can enjoy a beer and amazing seafood tapas anytime. They also serve sandwiches and salads, and the mussels are highly recommended. They have a menu in English that may help you choose from all the appealing possibilities.

Part of the Hotel Santa Maria, **La Pinta** (*Passeig de la Ribera 58; Tel 938/940-999; 1-4pm/8-11pm; 1,500ptas lunch menu; AE, MC, V*) is a little fancy, with white tablecloths and waiters in blue vest uniforms, but the portions are considerable and your taste buds won't be disappointed. The hotel itself is nice but pricey—luckily, it is cheaper to eat than it is to sleep. On the lunch menu, you'll find *fideua,* paella with pasta instead of rice—totally Catalan and totally delicious. The rest of the seafood dishes are also reasonably priced. Inside, the place is decked out in things taken from boats and ships, such as giant anchors. Outside, you can sit facing the water and watch real boats sail by.

Because the chef specializes in pastas and salads at **Monty's** (*Passeig de la Ribera 19; Tel 938/110-844; 1-5pm/9pm-12am daily; 1,200ptas; AE, MC, V*), this place is perfect for lunch or a light dinner. There are many vegetarian options, and all the food is super-fresh. The brightly colored chairs in shades of blue, green, and yellow complement the brightly colored art on the walls. From the food to the service to the ambience, everything about this place exudes charm.

crashing

Crashing in Sitges is relatively painless in spring and fall, but if you didn't book in advance, good luck in July and August. Off-season you can show up at the tourist office in the morning, ask for the list of pensions and hotels, and land a place after a few calls. Call one month in advance if you're staying in July and August. If you want a room during the Festival Internacional de Cinema de Catalonia or Carnaval [see *festivals and events,* above] call several months in advance. If you're looking for a single room, try the pensions because few of the hotels offer singles. A word to the wise: You pay a price for coolness here. It's an expensive town by Spanish standards.

One block up from the beach and only a couple of blocks over from the center of the nightlife, **Pensión Bonaire** (*Carrer Bonaire 31; Tel 938/945-326; 4,500ptas single, 6,000ptas double; AE, MC, V*) has basic

wired

PC Web *(Carrer Angel Vidal 2; Tel 938/111-046; www.web@sitgespc.com; 600ptas per hour)*, pretty much the only Internet option in town, has about 20 computers.

furnishings, clean bathrooms, and a great location. The owners who run this hostel are really sweet, have a cute little dog and will stop what they're doing—usually working on their stained glass or watching TV in the kitchen—if you need anything. You can buzz up all day and night, and even if you come home in the wee hours of the morning you need not feel bad; these guys knew how to party back in their day.

Another deal, by Sitges standards, is **Pensión Maricel***(Carrer Raco 13; Tel 938/943-627; maricel@milisa.com, www.milisa.com, 7,000ptas double peak season; AE, MC, V).* The 11 rooms are especially nice, equipped with telephones, radios, and fans. There is also a small Spanish-style breakfast of coffee and toast or cookies included in the price. The bathrooms are a little on the small side, but everything is very clean.

Centrally located, **Hotel El Cid** *(Sant Josep 39; Tel 938/941-842; 8,400ptas double peak season; AE, MC, V)* is slightly higher in quality and comfort and comes with more amenities then the *pensiónes:* Breakfast is included, there is a bar/cafe downstairs, and you can use the safety deposit box. There is a great garden out back and swimming pool if you've tired of swimming in the sea.

And then of coure there is **Pensión Bonanza** *(Plaça Dr. Robert 2; Tel 938/948-121; 4,000-5,000ptas single; 6,000-7,000ptas double; MC, V).* A favorite of Euroboys, this is a place where you can indulge in some serious pillow talk after a day at the beach. The rooms are small and simple but comfortably furnished nonetheless with good beds and a small shower-only bathroom. Each room comes with a TV and phone. Breakfast is not included in the rate, but can be bought at the coffee bar on the ground floor. Closed Dec 15 to Jan 2, when you wouldn't really hit the beach anyway.

For another reasonably priced option try **Hostal Parelladas** *(Carrer de les Parellades 11; Tel 938/940-801; 2,800ptas single with shared bath, 6,000ptas double with private bath; No credit cards),* 50 meters from the beach.

need to know

Currency Exchange Since Sitges is a touristy kind of town, you'll have no problem changing your money. Banks and ATMs abound. There is an actual **Currency Exchange** on Carrer San Pere between calle Bonaire and Carrer San Paul that also has an ATM.

Tourist Information The clerk at the **main tourist office** (*Carrer Sinia Morera 1; Tel 938/984-251; info@sitgestur.com; www.sitgestur.com*) speaks good English. He won't, however, book hotel rooms for you.

Public Transportation Shuttle buses to the big clubs outside town run every night in the summer and on the weekends in the off season. You can catch it at the end of Primero de Mayo and Passeig de la Ribera in the center of town.

Health and Emergency For the police: *Tel 938/117-625.* For medical assistance: *Tel 938/946-426,* and for emergencies: *Tel 938/943-949.* The **Sant Camil Hospital** (*Ctra. Puigmolto; Tel 938/960-025*) is located a bit out of town.

Pharmacies Pharmacies are located all over town. Look for the **red** or **green crosses.**

Trains and Buses The **Estacion RENFE** (*Plaça E. Maristany; Tel 934/900-202*) is less than a 10-minute walk from the beach and the center of town. There are two **bus stations:** (*Carrer Sant Francesc 56; Tel 938/948-383*); and (*Carrer Espana 24; Tel 938/110-550*). The tourist office has the bus schedules and destinations.

Laundry If you have dirty laundry, take it to **Net-I-Sec** (*Carrer Artur Carbonell 8; No phone; Open 24 hours*). It's super-convenient and efficient. The machines already have soap in them and the washers and dryers both take only about 30 minutes. The dry cleaning section has certain hours but the do-it-yourself, easy-as-hell laundry machines are open 24 hours year-round. It is near the train station, costs 700ptas for a load in the wash and 100ptas for 8 minutes in the dryer.

Post Office The **main post office** is right off of Plaça Espanya, **Correros y Telegraphos** (*Carrer Mossen Llopis Pi; Tel 938/941-247; 8:30am-2:30pm Mon-Fri, 9:30am-1pm Sat*).

Internet See *wired,* above.

Tarragona

Tarragona is not a party town. But if you are interested in seeing some of the remains of the biggest party ever—the Roman Empire—Tarragona is a great little place to check out. There are a bunch of well-preserved ruins in a relatively small area. It's easy to spend a day here and see a lot of old Roman ruins, a Catholic cathedral, and other artifacts.

One of the great things about going to Tarragona is that the town has a very distinct Mediterranean flavor that hasn't succumbed to the homogenizing influence of American pop culture as so many other European towns have. In Tarragona, you can still feel a little lost wandering through the old, narrow, winding streets, breaking out in a refreshing sweat as you hike up the hills that help define the character of this little pueblo. The people are unique too: In the post-Franco era, after years of suppression, the Catalonians of Tarragona are reasserting their culture and renaming streets, places, and buildings in their own language. You'll notice a certain sense of clear-headed pride and enthusiasm when you interact with the locals.

The center of all of the fun sightseeing is, of course, the old section of town—which, of course, means that it's glutted with tourists (particularly in the summertime). If you can deal with this, you'll find the stunning **Catedral** [see *culture zoo,* below], the **information center** [see *need to know,* below], and lots of *tchotchke* stores (full of antiques, junktiques, and other not-needed items) here. The decaying city wall forms the border of the old neighborhood and is also worth seeing in and of itself, as a substantial portion of the old Roman-built structure is still standing after all these years. The southern border of the old town is **Rambla Vella,** a street that's blocked from cars so it feels like a big outdoor square. A few blocks south, and parallel to Rambla Vella, stretches **Rambla Nova,** the busy street that forms the commercial center of the city. There are lots of bars, cafes, and small restaurants where you can enjoy a mid-afternoon snack and sangria. All of the nightlife action in this town takes place on one of the two Ramblas, or the three or four streets that connect them.

If you walk up to the top of Rambla Nova, and by up I mean *up* the dramatic incline, you will hit a wall that overlooks the ocean and offers you a spectacular view. If you look to your right, you'll see train tracks that lead to the station, and to the left you will see the smallish but still nice, sandy **Costa Dorada** beaches and the impressive old **Roman Amphitheatre** [see *culture zoo,* below].

There is a bus system, but it isn't really necessary if you just want to take in the old quarter and hang out in the Ramblas. If you want to get a better feel for the whole pueblo, though, you can board the magenta-colored 2 line for 110ptas, and it will take you all through the town, to the train station (which is about one-third of a mile southwest of Rambla Nova), and down to the port. You can also get to the small outdoor market on the 2 line [see *stuff,* below].

If you do take the bus down to the port, you'll be treated to a great view of a bunch of commercial barges. Walk past the commercial area, and you'll find the best seafood restaurants in town, as well as a more evenly balanced blend of locals and tourists. There are also a few clubs down here, though it is not the party central area and the *discotecas* are open only on weekends.

If you want to meet some locals or hang and relax, our favorite spots are the two **Gelateria Italiana Oliver** *(Rambla Nova 6 and 54; Tel 977/235-108 and Tel 977/233-133; 300ptas; No credit cards)* ice cream shops located right on Rambla Nova. You can sit outside under the big umbrellas while sampling delicious ice cream (that Spain isn't exactly famous for) and shooting the breeze Spanish-style, i.e., while waiting for service.

bar, club, & live music scene

Well, there isn't that much to say about the nightlife in Tarragona. It isn't a place to go to have a hedonistic love-fest or try out the drag queen

tarragona

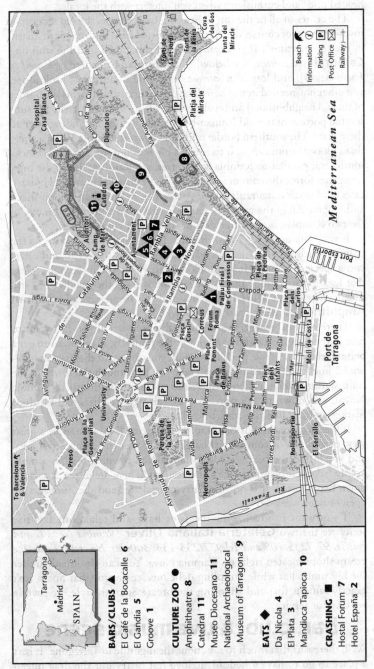

Fort de Sant Jordi
Fort de la Reina
Cova del Gos
Punta del Mirade

Platja del Mirade

Hospital Casa Blanca

Curt de la Cuixa

Diputacio

Mediterranean Sea

Catedral

Camp de Mart

Auditori

Rambla Vella

Rambla Nova

Passeig Maritim Rafael Casanova de Catalunya

Girona

Port Esportiu

Plaça de la Pedrera

Palau Firal i de Congressos

Correus

Plaça Ponent

Plaça de Braus

Plaça dels Infants

Parque de la Ciutat

Necropolis

Rio Francolí

Port de Tarragona

El Serrallo

Poliesportiu

Moll de Costa

To Barcelona & Valencia

University

Plaça de la Generalitat

Preso

Beach
Information ℹ
Parking 🅿
Post Office ✉
Railway ┼┼

SPAIN
Madrid
Tarragona

BARS/CLUBS ▲
El Café de la Bocacalle **6**
El Gandia **5**
Groove **1**

CULTURE ZOO ●
Amphitheatre **8**
Catedral **11**
Museo Diocesano **11**
National Archaeological
Museum of Tarragona **9**

EATS ◆
Da Nicola **4**
El Plata **3**
Mandioca Tapioca **10**

CRASHING ■
Hostal Forum **7**
Hotel España **2**

outfit you bought in Barcelona. All of the real hedonistic stuff went down almost 2,000 years ago when the Romans were in town.

On the other hand, there is still plenty to do for the restless-at-night crowd. The Plaça de la Font is an especially chill environment, with lots of little bars and cafes with outdoor seating and a jovial vibe. If you're into the late-night scene, however, you are pretty much SOL. The town is dead by 3am unless you're a garbage man—er, sanitation engineer.

A pretty cool live music club, **Groove** *(Carrer Cervantes 4; No phone; Check posters for show times and events; 500-700ptas; No credit cards)*, near the Forum Romano, specializes in funk, blues, and jazz. This is basically "what's goin' on" in terms of underground music in Tarragona. The crowd is a fun bunch of twenty- and thirtysomething types who come out to listen to some good music and have a good time.

The tourists sit outside **El Gandia** *(Plaça de la Font; No phone; 2pm-3am daily; 400-800ptas for a drink; No credit cards)* to dig on the Plaça feeling, but inside, check out the funky, sometimes punked-out young Spaniards in their twenties. Offering a wide range of tapas, pastries, beer, liquor, juice, and coffee, El Gandia is decorated to look like a cave, except with lots of washed-out green, blue, and orange. The long bar that runs down the side is an interesting orange, and the walls are lined with photos and some weird art. The music is usually of the homegrown Spanish variety, and can range from flamenco rock to more pop-y fare.

CULTURE ZOO

Old people from all over the world come to check out Tarragona's Catedral as well as the ruins the Romans left, some housed at the Museu Nacional Arqueològic (National Archaeological Museum), and the more impressive and well preserved Amfiteatre (amphitheater). The best way to appreciate these ruins is to imagine *Gladiator*—or *Spartacus,* if you prefer Kirk Douglas to Russell Crowe (can't imagine, but some people might...)—taking place in the Amfiteatre. Then you can truly get a feel for the blood-and sex-drenched aura that surrounds this place. Even 2,000 years hasn't fully sanitized this old town, as long as you use your imagination.

Catedral and **Museo Diocesano** *(Plaça de la Seu; Tel 977/238-685; 10am-1pm/4-7pm Mar 16-Jun 30; 10am-7pm Jul 1-Oct 15; 10 am-12:30pm/3-6pm Oct 16-Nov 15; 10am-2pm Nov 16-Mar 15 (both share the same hours); 300ptas adults, 150ptas students and seniors):* The cathedral, which is right in the old part of town, was built between 1171 and 1331, and its architecture includes both Roman and Gothic styles. Dig on the different types of arches all over the place, as well as the basilica and chapels. This cathedral, for my buck, is one of the best in Spain, and really is breathtaking if you're a sucker for this kind of thing.

The museum was created in 1915 and has tons of artwork and other treasure, the booty that belongs to the Archbishop of Tarragona. Lots of gold, tapestries, and other important stuff. Naked sculptures, too.

only here

Those of you who claim that cheerleading is a sport need to check out the **Consurs de Castells,** which are huge human towers that the men of Tarragona make out of themselves the first Sunday of October on even-numbered years. Basically, hundreds of dudes dress up in white pants, huge black leather belts and red shirts, and pile together in a relatively small space, and then hoist up their fellows. This is quite a sight, and one of the cultural quirks that make this region unique. If you are claustrophobic or have a fear of heights, definitely do not go to this festival. Otherwise, it is a great little insight into the kinds of strange things that people will do when bored. The closest thing you'll find to this in America is at the national cheerleading competition, but trust me, nothing quite compares. While you do miss out on the voyeurism (a la *American Beauty*) that comes with a standard cheerleading competition, it's still a good show.

Amfiteatre *(Parc del Miracle; Tel 977/242-579; 9am-9pm June-Sept; 10am-1:30pm/3:30-5:30pm Oct-Mar; 10am-1:30pm/3:30-5:30pm Apr-May; Free):* After hanging out at the cathedral, you can take a nice stroll down to the amphitheater, which is carved out of a cliff overlooking the Mediterranean and is surrounded by beautiful gardens. If you have some capital, we think it should be turned into the hottest club this side of Ibiza. The Amfiteatre conjures up all kinds of fantasies from Roman times, and is in great shape for being almost 2,000 years old.

Museu Nacional Arqueològic *(Plaça del Rei 5; Tel 977/236-209; mnat@mnat.es, www.mnat.es; 10am-8pm Tue-Sat, 10am-2pm Sun and holidays, closed Mon June-Sept; 10am-1:30pm/4-7pm Tue-Sat, 10am-2pm Sun and holidays, closed Mon Oct-May; 225-400ptas depending on a very complex price structure):* This museum puts the Archbishop's collection to shame when it comes to full-on frontal nudity. It's all about mosaics, ceramics, and sculpture. Each of the rooms has its own specialty, ranging from the mundane ("everyday Roman objects") to very elaborate mosaics. If you studied Latin in high school, and haven't gotten any action since the prom, you would probably love spending an entire year at this museum. For the rest of us, an hour or two in the late afternoon will suffice, if only as a break from the summer heat that the air-conditioned environs of this museum kindly provides.

STUFF

Tarragona offers a few options for the visitor with some money to burn. Ranging from small owner-operated craft shops and antique joints in the old section of town to an outdoor bazaar with all kinds of different booths, you can find some real bargains if you have the time to look.

If you want to bring home a paella pan, you've got a good chance of finding a great deal at the **Mercadet de Sant Quadrat** *(Carrer de Reding; 9am-9pm daily; Corsini stop on the magenta 2 bus; Prices vary),* a bustling outdoor market surrounding a smaller, enclosed food market. You can find heaps of stuff like scarves, jewelry, bathing suits, towels, shoes, sunglasses...you know, normal market fare. The booth people are an eclectic bunch, with Spanish families, young Spanish hippies, and Moroccan folks selling their wares.

At the **Taller de Ceramica** *(Claustre 3; No phone; Hours vary; 700-15,000ptas depending; AE, MC, V)* you can find all kinds of great pots, jewelry, wind chimes, and other homemade ceramic items. Located behind the Catedral, this shop is both a store and the artist's studio. You can even watch her working as you browse through her eye-catching crafts.

EATS

A rare oasis for vegetarians in the pork-infested world of Spain, **Mandioca Tapioca** *(Merceria 34; Tel 977/239-421; 10:30am-1:30pm/4-9pm; 1,200ptas; AE, V, MC)* is located in a pretty little square, **Plaça Forum,** not too far from the Catedral. The pleasant wood decor and paintings of Tarragona on the walls allow for a nice relaxing meal. The place serves a variety of veggie fair—including salads, pastas, and couscous—coined "healthy food" and "food of nature" in the semi-English of the owners. You can also get basic tapas here, as well as various tortillas, for around 500ptas.

You can satisfy your need for pizza or pasta at **Da Nicola** *(Comte de Rius 11; Tel 977/238-001; 10am-1:30pm/4-9pm; Lunch menu 1,300ptas; AE, MC, V).* The inside is pretty classy looking, and the food is pretty high caliber, especially considering the price. You can order a solid pasta for between 800-900ptas and pizza for 750-1,300ptas, depending on how elaborate you want to get. The green-checkered tablecloths at this medium-sized restaurant are vaguely reminiscent of your favorite local Italian place back home, and the staff is very friendly so go ahead and strike up a conversation. A pride flag outside declares Da Nicola a "safe zone." It's around a 5-minute walk southwest of The Catedral.

As Spanish restaurants go, **El Plata** *(Carrer August 20; Tel 977/232-223; 10am-1:30pm/4-9pm; 1,300-1,800ptas; AE, MC, V)* is hyper-typical. You'll find Spanish people (old men drinking booze in the morning and moped-riding young men drinking soda in the afternoon) and Spanish food *(patatas bravas*—tasty Spanish fried potatoes—and *tortillas tenways).* You can choose between inside and outside seating, but no matter where you sit, be sure to sample the *patatas bravas* (400ptas) and some tasty sangria. If you don't know anything about Spanish cuisine and don't have the language skills to ask the waiter, you can point at the pictures on the menu. It's a 5-minute walk south of the cathedral between Rambla Nova and Rambla Vella.

CRASHING

Each room comes with a small TV, telephone, and bathroom at **Hotel España** (*Rambla Nova 49; Tel 977/231-712; 3,000ptas single off-season, 3,300ptas single in-season, 5,500ptas double off-season, 6,000ptas double in-season; AE, MC, V*), a one-star hotel. The balconies give you a sweet view of Rambla Nova, which is nicely lit up at night, and you can even people-watch the folks cruising out to the cafes. The rooms are spacious, and on the sixth floor there is a dining area where they serve a decent breakfast from 8 to 10:30am. The central location keeps you close to the action.

A little more hit-or-miss, quality-wise, the **Hostal Forum** (*Plaça de la Font 37; Tel 977/231-718; 2,500ptas single in-season, 2,000ptas off-season, 4,000ptas double with shower off-season, 5,000ptas in-season; No credit cards*) has about 20 rooms. There is a nice restaurant downstairs, but it's a bit pricey. To inquire about rooms, go into the restaurant and then up the stairs to the staff hangout area. The guys there will walk you up. If you want to spend a bunch of time chilling and drinking at the cool Plaça de la Font, this *hostal* is a great location.

WITHIN 30 MINUTES

If you've been in Spain long enough to miss Disney World and the ubiquitous Six Flags, then buck up and wipe that frown offa yer face, 'cause Universal Studios has plopped down a theme park just for you. Since 1995, Spaniards have been going *loco* for the biggest roller coaster in Europe and the thoroughly inauthentic Mediterranean, Far West (i.e., American Midwest), Polynesian, Mexican, and Chinese "villages" at **Port Aventura** (*Port Aventura; Tel 902/202-220; 10am-8pm Mar 26-June 19; 1pm-midnight June 20-Sept 13; 10am-8pm Sept 14-Jan 11; www.por taventura.es; 4,100ptas adult*)—it's more fun than you can handle, baby.

WIRED

You can get Internet access for free at the **Biblioteca Publica** (*Carrer Fortuny 30; Tel 977/240-544; 10am-1pm Tue-Sat, 3-8:30 Mon-Fri*), located 3 minutes from the train station. Computers are on the second floor, and you have to leave ID at the front desk. Caution: You may have to wait in line.

The best way to arrive is by train on the Barcelona-Sitges-Tarragona line. (Times vary, so check the schedule.) Or head west on N-340 for around 7 km, then follow the signs. In the tradition of great American theme parks, you can't bring in food, but don't fret, there are kilotons of overpriced and mediocre fast food stands. You'll have a great time getting caught up in the excitement of the Spanish clientele.

Four km (2.5 mi) south of Tarragona, you will find the town of **Bonavista,** which has one of the largest open-air markets in Europe. You can find scores of great places to eat, including top-notch tapas joints, and more outdoor market stuff than you can shake a stick at. **The Association de Veins de Bonavista** *(Tel 977/547-913)* is helpful if you need more info. With over 900 booths, this place is an outdoor shopper's dream, and makes a great day trip from Tarragona. Local buses marked Mercadillo and Bonavista make the run to the market on Sunday. The cost of a one-way ticket is 125ptas.

need to know

Currency Exchange As always, ATMs will provide a good rate. There is also a bank, **La Caixa** *(Fortuny 6; 8:15am-2pm Mon-Fri),* right next door to the tourist information center.

Tourist Information The helpful folks at the **tourist office** *(Fortuny 4; Tel 977/233-415; 10am-2pm/4:30-7pm Mon-Fri, 10am-2pm Sat)* speak English and are really nice

Public Transportation The bus line in Tarragona can be helpful, but it isn't really necessary to get around. The main city line is the magenta 2, which pretty much runs to the train station, the port, through Rambla Nova, and by the open-air market and post office. It'll run you 110ptas. You can pick up a bus map from the tourist info office.

Pharmacies As always, the **big green cross** means pharmacy in Spain. There's a **farmacia** *(Carrer Fortuny, 9am-1:30pm/5-8pm Mon-Fri)* close to the tourist office.

Trains and Buses The main train station is **Estació FFCC** *(Plaça Pedrera; Tel 977/240-202).* The bus station is **Terminal de Autobuses** *(Plaça Imperial Tarraco; Tel 977/222-072).* Both places are a walkable mile from the pulse of the town

Postal The primary post office is the **Correus** *(Plaça de Corsini; Tel 977/240-149; 8:30am-8:30pm Mon-Fri, 9:30am-2pm Sat).*

Internet See *wired,* above.

Valencia &
the Balearic
Islands

valencia & the balearic islands

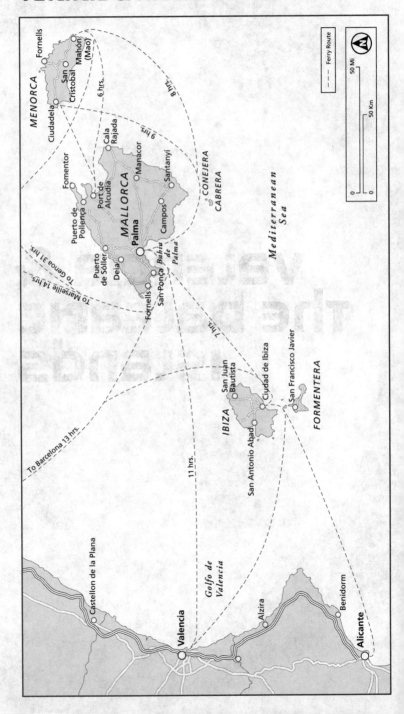

You've decided that even with the limited amount of vacation time you have, you're going to spend some of it in Spain. Who knows why you picked Spain. Maybe it was some Hemingway that you read in high school. Maybe you hate bulls a lot and want to see them get tortured and killed. Maybe you dig on Spanish history, art, and architecture. Maybe you heard a thing or two about passionate, handsome, intelligent men and beautiful, big-eyed, to-die-for women. Or maybe you want to brush up on your Spanish before you take the bilingual exam. If you're coming to Spain for any of these reasons, skip the **Balearic Islands.**

On the other hand, if you decided to come to Spain because you heard about all-night, rage-till-dawn-then-end-up-naked-on-the-beach partying, then come on down to these little islands of horrors, baby.

There is of course another possibility. For those of you who are strangely drawn to this scene, but also want a taste of a slightly more traditional Spain, spend a couple of days in the Communidad de Valencia on the Mediterranean coast before catching a boat or plane out to the islands and giving in to your dark and dirty side. The region's capital, **Valencia,** the third-largest city in Spain, is a modern, thriving, urban center with a rocking nightlife and one of the country's great fiestas, *Las Fallas,* in March. Valencia lacks the great monuments and architecture of other Spanish cities, but it also lacks the gaggles of tourists that are drawn to these attractions. Surrounding the city is the *huerta* (irrigated land), a fertile area known as the garden of Spain, whose most famous products are Valencia oranges.

Valencia's coastline consists of the **Costa del Azahur** to the north of the capital and **Costa Blanca** to the south. Costa Blanca means "White Coast," which is somehow fitting since it's literally filled with white faces—and we're talking *pale.* Brits, Germans, and other Northern Europeans have overrun this stretch of fine beaches, turning it into an overdeveloped concrete eyesore. The Costa del Azahur, the "Orange Blossom Coast," is also pretty well developed, although less dominated by foreigners. It's a big vacation destination in July and August for the Spanish, especially those from Madrid. (If you're looking for Spain's great beaches, you're better off in Andalucía's Cabo de Gata and Costa de la Luz, Catalunya's Costa Brava, [see above for both] or the Balearic Islands.)

The best reason to come to Valencia is for its lively capital, Valencia City. Its citizens are renowned for their party-till-dawn attitude, and the city offers a wealth of cultural activities as well, from art museums to foreign film houses. You can also just kick back at the beach, eat some authentic *paella,* and drink in the streets of the boisterous old quarter El Carme.

If you're in Spain in the middle of March, you should not miss Valencia's great festival, *Las Fallas de San José,* where hundreds of giant papier-mâché sculptures are displayed around town and then burned simultaneously on the last night in a great chaotic catharsis of fire. Another odd festival is *La Tomatina,* the tomato-throwing festival held in the town of Buñol, one day at the end of August. You may have seen highlights from this messy party on "World's Funniest Home Videos" or something. Basically, truckloads of tomatoes are dumped in the middle of the town, and everyone starts pelting each other with as many as they can grab. After an hour, the war is over, so it's not really worth trekking across the country to see. Needless to say, if you do go, bring a change of clothes.

Historically, Valencia and the Balearic Islands followed a pattern similar to that of other Spanish coastal areas. The great Roman road, Via Augusta, which ran all the way to Italy, passed through Valencia. The town of Sagunto was the capital of the area during Roman times, and traces of Roman occupation can still be seen. The Balearics—Forementera in particular—were Roman agricultural centers. Both Valencia and the Islands flourished under the Muslim occupation, until the *Reconquista* by Jaume I of Aragón in 1238. The Christians eventually not only kicked out the Muslims, but tore down all of their temples and architecture, even reconfiguring the streets, which is why modern Valencia and the Balearic Islands lack the Muslim flavor of Andalucía.

Valencia is more culturally connected to Catalunya than to the rest of Spain; Catalán is the preferred language of the region, and is used in the education system, although Castilian Spanish is still more common in day-to-day conversations, especially among young people in the bigger cities. You'll also hear Catalán spoken in the Balearic Islands.

Now, if you're in the Balearic Islands for the party (and you should only be here for the party) then go to **Ibiza**. Of the four islands—Ibiza, Formentera, Mallorca, and Menorca—you'll probably only be interested in Ibiza and Mallorca. Formentera is pretty small, and Menorca is pretty subdued. Ibiza, on the other hand, is the craziest place in the world, with a full complement of drag queens and freak shows, as well as clubs with a bigger summertime population than the state of Montana. Hordes of dazed English college students can attest to this, as can any one of the professional "performers" that work it on stage nightly. Ibiza will knock your socks, shoes, shirt, pants, and probably undies right off.

Once you get to the islands, via plane or ferry, anywhere you go is going to be very expensive. The rich and trendy of Europe have been flooding the islands for the last 50 years, and the influence of all of that tourist cash means your measly budget won't go very far. But if you've got the dough, then do it up.

If you're into a somewhat more low-key nightlife environment, without the party-till-we-die-or-reach-Nirvana atmosphere, you might want to try out **Palma,** on the island of Mallorca. Don't go there expecting the best clubs or nightlife in the world—that's in Ibiza. But you will find traveling terribly easy in Palma, with locals who come from England rather than Spain, tons of good food, great beaches, and lots and lots of tourists. If you like watching older German people turn from scary white to scary red, there is no better place in the world, except perhaps Valencia's Costa Blanca.

getting around

Valencia City is the major transportation hub here, with numerous trains and buses to Barcelona and Madrid, both of which are 4-5 hours away. If you take the high-speed Euromed train, you can be whisked to Barcelona in three hours in extreme comfort. Getting between Valencia and Andalucía can be a little difficult, at least by train. There's no train service directly down the coast as you would expect; instead you have to go inland almost all the way to Madrid. Direct buses to Andalucía are faster, more frequent than trains, and take 7-8 hours. Valencia is also a hopping-off point to the Balearic Islands. Flights are frequent to Ibiza City and Palma de Mallorca; they'll cost between 15,000-25,000ptas, depending on how far in advance you book the flight and the time of year. Between June and September, a fast ferry leaves Valencia City every day for Ibiza City; the

Travel Times

All times are by boat unless indicated by a star:
* = time by train

	Valencia	Ibiza	Palma	Madrid
Valencia	-	7:00 :30	6:00 1:00	3:35*
Ibiza	7:00 :30	-	4:30 :20	1:10 10:35
Palma	6:00 1:00	4:30 :20	-	1:00 9:35

trip takes only three-and-a-half hours. In the off-season, ferries are slower and much less frequent, with usually only one departure a week. Frequent ferries also leave for San Antonio on Ibiza from the town of Denia.

Flying, taking a ferry, or swimming are your only options for getting to the Balearics from mainland Spain. For the time and money, it's probably worth it to fly. However, it can also be part of the overall party experience to take the ferry to Ibiza or Palma and possibly meet other like-minded travelers. Regardless of which mode of transport you choose, you'll want to leave from either Barcelona or Valencia. Once you've arrived, you have the same three options for traveling between Ibiza and Palma.

To get around each individual island, there are a handful of buses, but if you really want to see more than the big cities without wasting a huge amount of time you should look into renting a car or a scooter.

VALENCIA

Life in Spain's third-largest city is lived in the streets. In the daytime, students, shoppers, and businesspeople rush through the city; in the evening cafes and bars fling open their doors and boisterous revelers spill out onto the plazas, alleys, and tree-lined avenues. They call the nightlife here *"La Movida"* ("The Movement"); it's an ambitious and somewhat chaotic way of enjoying life, most sublimely expressed in March during *Las Fallas,* undeniably one of Spain's (and therefore the world's) greatest parties. All this constant motion may be a result of a complex about being the third-largest, but certainly least-known, of Spain's major urban centers. Valencia certainly lacks the fantastic monuments, world-renowned museums, historical ambience, and photo ops of other great Spanish cities. But if you've had enough of Madrid's dust or Barcelona's hipsters, and seen enough tourist attractions and way too many tourists themselves, clean and attractive Valencia can be a breath of fresh air. It makes up for its lack of historical sites by moving forward. The city expects to complete work on its spectacularly modern cultural and learning complex, the City of Arts and Sciences, by the time of this book's publication. Not only does this stand as Valencia's bold step into the 21st century, it's also one of the more ambitious and daring architectural projects Spain has ever seen.

Valencia offers all those things we expect of modern Western urban centers: lively bars, throbbing dance clubs, a modern art museum, a foreign film house, an IMAX theater, a well-paid soccer team, a large university, a thriving gay scene, public gardens, and beaches. It also offers some of Spain's best eats. The surrounding *huerta* (irrigated farmland) rates as one of Europe's great producers of fruits and vegetables—most

valencia

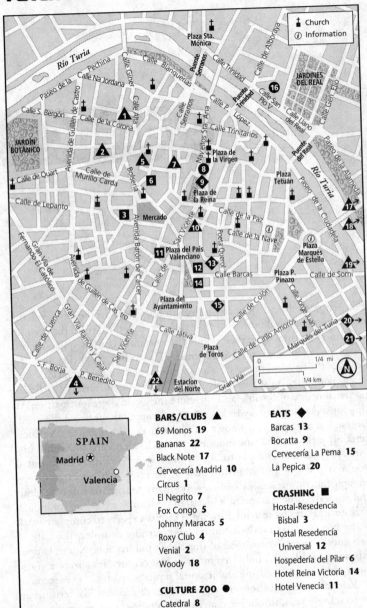

BARS/CLUBS ▲
69 Monos **19**
Bananas **22**
Black Note **17**
Cervecería Madrid **10**
Circus **1**
El Negrito **7**
Fox Congo **5**
Johnny Maracas **5**
Roxy Club **4**
Venial **2**
Woody **18**

CULTURE ZOO ●
Catedral **8**
La Ciudad de las Artes
  y las Ciencias **21**
Museo de Bellas Artes **16**

EATS ◆
Barcas **13**
Bocatta **9**
Cervecería La Pema **15**
La Pepica **20**

CRASHING ■
Hostal-Resedencía
  Bisbal **3**
Hostal Resedencía
  Universal **12**
Hospedería del Pilar **6**
Hotel Reina Victoria **14**
Hotel Venecia **11**

famously, Valencia oranges—and the city is the birthplace and consummate purveyor of *paella,* the divinely inspired rice dish that you'll be tempted to eat at every meal. Try the classic *paella valenciana,* which usually contains chicken, rabbit, green beans, large butter beans, snails, artichokes, and saffron. The *paella* alone is reason to come here, but the real attraction is the opportunity to get off the tourist route and mix with the liberal and lively locals by joining *La Movida.*

Valencia's lack of historical attractions doesn't mean that it sprang up out of nowhere, but rather that war and flood destroyed many of its ancient architectural treasures. In Valencia's most famous battle, the local Christian hero, the legendary soldier of fortune *El Cid,* briefly took the city back from the Muslims in 1094, though after his death in 1099 it was lost again until 1238. In the 20th century, Valencia sided with the leftist Republicans during the Spanish Civil War, and during late 1936-1937 was the base of the eventually futile resistance against the Nationalists.

Today Valencia remains an open, progressive city. Its location on the Mediterranean means good weather and cool breezes all year round. The main disturbance is the noise: Traffic here can be hellish and makes crossing the street a death-defying act. The bilingual locals speak Castilian and their own dialect of Catalán called *valenciano.* Street signs are often posted in *valenciano,* and the locals take pride in their Catalán heritage, but they're not as protective of the language as their northern neighbors in Barcelona. Good old Castilian Spanish will always be understood here, English not so much. While a fair number of foreign students study Spanish in Valencia, they are overwhelmed by the natives and don't stand out like they would in smaller cities.

To navigate yourself through the cultural stew, check out the monthly guide *Que y Donde,* available at newsstands, or, for more up-to-date info, the daily newspaper *Levante,* which has a special supplement on Fridays listing the weekend's events, including what's happening at the dance clubs and information on the notorious "disco train."

neighborhoods

Unlike many places in Spain, Valencia actually has visible street signs to help you find your way around; the only difficulty is that the signs (especially in the rural areas) are often in Catalán, sometimes in Castilian Spanish, and sometimes with both versions. These two versions are usually similar, but be aware that the spelling might be different from what you expect. We try to use the Castilian version here whenever possible; most tourist maps are in Castilian, as well.

The train station, major plazas, old city, and center of nightlife all lie in the city center of Valencia, south of what used to be the ancient **Rio Turia.** Due to flooding problems, the river was diverted further south of the city in the 1950s, and now the Rio Turia has become the **Jardines del Turia,** a park on the dry riverbed. North of the riverbed are the **Jardines de Real** [see *hanging out,* below], the university, and about two

burning down the house

What do you get when you combine 20 tons of fuel, over 300 giant papier-mâché sculptures, 3 million people, and a whole lot of *paella* and beer? It's **Las Fallas de San José** *(March 16-19):* a pyromaniacs dream, a fireman's worst nightmare, and one of the world's great parties. A week of festivities leads up to one night, *La Nit de Foc* ("The Night of Fire"), when the *fallas*—artful, cartoon-like figures made from wood and paper that can be up to 15 meters (50 feet) high—are burned. The whole thing is carefully planned and follows strict traditions, but an unmistakable air of anarchy still takes hold of the streets. Over the course of a year, each neighborhood builds its own *fallas* (or *ninots,* in Catalán), which traditionally satirize local politicians but can also characterize anyone or anything from Evander Holyfield to Monica Lewinsky to the war on drugs. During the week of the fiesta, the *fallas* are displayed in plazas for the whole town (and swarms of tourists) to check out and judge, and everyone eats and drinks from the *casals* (food stands). Everyday at 2pm an official fireworks display, called the *Mascletá,* takes place in Plaza del Ayuntamiento, although since it's the middle of the day it's mostly just for the sake of ear-deafening noise. Fireworks also light up the nighttime skies over Paseo Alameda (did you guess that they like fireworks here?). During the day at Plaza de la Virgen, people make offerings of flowers to *La Virgen de los Desamarados* ("Virgin of the Foresaken")...and no, that sculpture is not burned.

At midnight on the final night, *La Crema de Las Fallas* begins. To the accompaniment of more fireworks and a general, cathartic release of all sanity, the artful sculptures, most of which took a year to make, are set ablaze at 28 different locations around the city. The fire department has the situation fairly under control; they even put special fireproof covers over nearby buildings. The final fires of the night are set to the most revered *fallas* in Plaza del Ayuntamiento. Only one sculpture is spared from the flames: the one that was voted best of the year by the crowds. It's bound for the **Museo Fallero** *(Plaza Monte Olivete 4; Tel 963/525-478; 10am-2pm/4-6pm Mon-Fri, 10am-2pm Sat),* where it will be housed for eternity. You can see these beautiful and humorous salvaged sculptures year-round at the museum, which has *fallas* from as far back as 1934. But it's more fun to watch them burn.

kilometers (1.24 miles) east, the Mediterranean Sea and a long stretch of city beaches.

The train station, despite being called **Estación del Norte,** is actually right in the middle city, south of the old quarter, on **Calle Játiva** (also known as **Xátiva**). If you arrive here you'll be within walking distance of the major neighborhoods for hostels and nightlife. Make sure to notice the entrance to the train station itself; it's one of Valencia's best examples of early-20th-century architecture and is decorated with ceramic tiles depicting oranges, in honor of the city's most famous export. Coming out of the train station, the bullfighting arena, **Plaza de Toros,** will be on your right, and the city center will be straight ahead. Head up **Marqués de Sotelo** for two blocks to get to the heart of Valencia, **Plaza del Ayuntamiento** (also called **Plaza Ajuntament**), a Renaissance plaza with fountains, bus stops, and the impressive 18th-century **Ayuntamiento** (City Hall), which looks like it belongs in France. North of Plaza Ayuntamiento you'll find the **old quarter** (**Ciutat Vella**). From the top of the plaza, two streets fork diagonally. The left is **Plaza del Mercado,** which leads you to the must-see-it-to-believe-it market, **Mercado Central.** To the right is **San Vicente Martir,** which leads to **Plaza de la Reina,** another lively square both by day and night. At the north end of this plaza is the entrance to the **Catedral** [see *culture zoo,* below]. The northern end of the Catedral joins with another impressive church with a much longer name, **Real Basílica de Nuestra Señora de los Descamporados** ("Our Lady of the Forsaken"), which sits on **Plaza de la Virgen** [see *hanging out,* below], a pedestrian square with a statue of a man reclining on a fountain. West of here, the cobblestone alleys of the **Barrio del Carmen,** which everyone calls *El Carme* [see *hanging out,* below], meander off the main street, **Calle Caballeros.** A working-class, starving-artist neighborhood during the day, El Carme is the red-light district at night, but it also draws a wide range of ages and classes for the hippest of bars and discos. North of Calle Caballeros, El Carme gets less popular and funkier, which is fine during the day but can be a bit dodgy at night, especially around **Plaza del Carmen.**

East and south of Plaza de Ayuntamiento lies a pedestrian shopping district with lots of upscale stores and hotels. Further south of here, the wide, tree-lined **Gran Via Marqués del Turia** separates the shopping area from the more upmarket areas of **Gran Via** and **L'Eixampla;** the avenue ends at **Plaza Canovas de Castillo,** another nightlife center just before the riverbed. At least eight traffic/pedestrian bridges around the old city cross the old riverbed, now the Jardines del Turia, a long stretch of gardens and dirt playing fields used for bike riding and pickup soccer games. Just across the riverbed, northwest of Plaza de la Virgen, are the pretty Jardines de Real, a shady public park, and the site of the **Fine Arts Museum.** West of here, the enormously wide **Avenida de Blasco Ibañez** seems to go on forever, and is the main thoroughfare of the **University District** [see *hanging out,* below]; the center of campus is a little bit north

12 hours in valencia

1. Grab a coffee at the cafe in the **IVAM Julio Gonzalez** modern art museum [see *arts scene,* below] and then try to comprehend the 20th century through its exhibits.
2. Take the metro out to *la playa,* get some sun, and then eat the outstanding *paella* at the legendary **La Pepica** [see *eats,* below] on Paseo Neptuno.
3. Cruise the **Mercado Central** [see *to market,* below], one of Europe's biggest food markets, a weird and wondrous feast for all the senses.
4. Catch an IMAX movie at **L'Hemisferic** [see *arts scene,* below]. This futuristic blinking eyeball of glass and metal houses one of the biggest concave movie screens in the world.
5. Climb Miguelete, the octagonal bell tower attached to the **Catedral** [see *culture zoo,* below] and get a 360-degree view of the city's skyline. You can also get your workout climbing the 207 steps up to the top.
6. Experience *La Movida* in El Carme. Nightlife in the old quarter is about movement. Start the night at the boisterous **El Negrito,** move on to the psychedelic **Circus,** and end the night at the thriving gay *discoteca,* **Venial** [see *club scene,* below, for all].
7. Take the disco train to **Bananas** [see *club scene,* below]. On Saturdays, the soul train leaves the city at 1:15am. You can't get back until 6:15am, so you might as well start dancing.

of here. Another 2 kilometers (1 1/4 miles) east of the university area are the long, wide, and crowded city beaches. Walking to the beach is not a good idea, since the neighborhoods near the beach, **Cabanyal** and **Malvarrosa,** are not especially welcoming at any time of day. Take a taxi, bus, or the metro. At the south end of the beaches, the **Port**—which brought Valencia prosperity during the Age of Discovery—hums with commercial activity.

On the eastern edge of the old city, south of the Rio Turia from the port, is the site of the ambitious super-modern cultural complex, **La Ciudad de las Artes y las Ciencias** ("City of Arts and Sciences"), which when completed will house a planetarium, an opera house, a science museum, and an aquarium, and will be the prime attraction of modern Valencia [see *culture zoo,* below].

Getting around the old quarter of Valencia is as easy as putting one foot in front of the other. To explore further reaches of the city, take a taxi at night; during the day, most people take buses, and there's even an underground metro, easy to use but only useful if you're going to specific places outside the city center such as the university area or the beach. Most of the major buses you might need leave from Plaza de Ayuntamiento. The metro is not much help in the old city because the streets there are traffic-clogged, narrow, and easy to get around on foot, but there's a stop at the entrance of the train station (metro stop: Xativa), which is handy for catching metro trains out to the University District and the beach [see *hanging out,* below]. The price depends on how far you're going, but within the city is usually 125ptas; tickets can be purchased at the automatic machines at all stops. All of the tourist offices [see *need to know,* below] have metro and bus maps.

hanging out

Every European city worth its salt has a slightly seedy old neighborhood loaded with funky bars, but not many of them can claim to draw as diverse—and as lively and loud—a crowd as **El Carme.** During the day, this neighborhood masquerades as a fairly quiet, atmospheric, working-class section of town, with some tattoo parlors and record shops. But at night, especially on weekends, its streets fill with a mixed bag of partiers. The main drag, Calle Caballeros, has some of the more cosmopolitan bars, where people really dress up for the evening. Calle Alta heads north from the western end of Calle Caballeros, and draws a younger, more alternative crowd. The further north you get on Calle Alta, the funkier

wired

Two decent websites for scoping out the Valencia scene are *www.valencia.lanetro.com* and *www.gva.es.*

Just checking your e-mail at **Andromeda Cyber-Pub** *(Salamanca 37; Tel 963/353-070; 6pm-2:30am Tue-Sun; 500ptas per hour),* you feel as if you're about to blast off into some Barbarella-esque psychedelic virtual world. You may be disappointed that you only get Hotmail instead. Still this is the future: dark lighting, space-age furniture, electronica, and beer (300ptas) along with your Internet connection. You'll find it in the eastern part of the center city, a few blocks south of Plaza Cánovas del Castillo.

For a more traditional Internet place, and one that's open during the day, go to **Sala Falcons** *(Ribera 8; Tel 963/940-311; 11am-10pm Mon-Thu, 11-3am Fri-Sat, 11am-9pm Sun; 500ptas per hour).* It's centrally located north of the Plaza de Toros and near Plaza del Ayuntamiento.

things get, until it gets a little too funky at Plaza del Carmen, where locals go to buy drugs or women; it should be avoided at night. During the day, it's cool, as it hosts the modern arts center **IVAM Centre del Carme** [see *arts scene,* below].

A lot of daytime activity takes place on **Plaza de la Virgen,** at the eastern edge of El Carme. This long, rectangular space gives a home to students and tourists just chilling and to skateboarders and roller-bladers trying out their schticks. South of here is the larger and more bustling **Plaza de la Reina,** full of folks passing through its bars, shops, and cafes in the afternoons.

For a tranquil hangout in the shade, check out the **Jardines de Real** across the riverbed from the old quarter. You probably have never seen a better maintained public park in a big city, with its sculptured gardens, rose beds, long shady lanes, and duck pond. Benches abound for quiet contemplation or PDA, and you won't even notice that you're right next to a huge avenue.

If you're looking for students, you're going to have to cruise the **University District,** whose main street is the seemingly endless Avenida Blasco Ibañez, northwest of the city center. The city's two colleges and 18 different schools spread out along this street, though the heart of the school lies a few long blocks north of Blasco Ibañez. You'll see lots of students running around between classes. **Plaza Xuquer,** one block north of Blasco Ibañez, makes a good meeting point, with lots of student bars. If you want to reenact your teenage years, you can loll around in front of the 24-hour 7-Eleven mini-mart at the corner of Blasco Ibañez and Gascó Oliag.

The most popular hangouts in summer (which lasts a long time here) are Valencia's beaches, the biggest of which is **Playa de la Malvarrosa.** The water at this wide beach has a less than stellar reputation for swimmability, but you would never know from the ton of people sunning on the nice sand and just jumping quickly in and out of the warm water. It's still a lively beach environment, with people kicking soccer balls around, topless women getting tan in all the right places, and hey, topless men, too! The beachside bars and restaurants can become scenes, especially in the summer. Avoid the neighborhoods a few blocks behind the beach; they're not as inviting as the surf and sand. To get to the beach, you can take a taxi (700ptas), bus 19 from Plaza Ayuntamiento, or the preferred mode of transport, the metro, an underground subway that becomes an above ground streetcar on this side of town. From the city center; take the 3 (red-line) train (destination: Rafelbubunyal) from metro stop Xativa, right in front of the train station Estación del Norte, and get off at Benimaclet. Exit the station and transfer to the streetcar, which is line 4 (blue line, destination: Dr. Lluch), and get off at Eugenia Viñes or whenever you see the beach.

If you're looking to get a good swim in, try **Playa El Saler,** a pretty beach 10 kilometers (6.2 miles) south of Valencia.

bar scene

If you're going to be in Valencia for just a night or two, you'll want to head to El Carme; the bars here will keep you occupied for a good long while. If you're in Valencia for an extended stay, you might want to expand your horizons: On the eastern edge of the old city, Plaza Canovas de Castillo and the streets south of it (on or just off Calle Salamanca) have a lot of upmarket bars, with outdoor tables on tree-lined streets. Despite the upscale environment, drinks usually cost less here than they do in the rough-and-tumble working class El Carme, which just goes to show that you have to pay for authentic bohemia. If it's possible, things actually seem to start later in Valencia than in the rest of Spain. Nothing's really open before 9pm and the action doesn't really get going until 11pm or midnight. Bars generally stay open until 2am on weekdays and 3 or 4am Thursday through Saturday. Look for Valencia's famous cocktail, *agua de Valencia,* usually made with champagne, vodka, Cointreau, and, of course, orange juice.

A great place to start *La Movida* is Plaza Negrito, just south of Calle Caballeros, where you'll find, among other bars, the classic **El Negrito** *(Plaza Negrito 1; Tel 963/91-4233; 5pm-2 or 3am daily).* As many people as there are crowded into this small, classic bar, there are always more chatting it up outside on the plaza. An eclectic selection of music, from Lou Reed to Spanish pop, and an eclectic crowd to match keep things interesting. Young people flock here, but you also may find yourself sitting next to someone your parents' age at one in the morning, and wondering, "Isn't it a little late for them to be out?" Not here. Everyone gets along beautifully, perhaps because they serve that sunshiny cocktail, *agua de Valencia,* which would put a smile on a corpse. Beer will set you back 225ptas.

A more well-heeled crowd heads up to Calle Caballeros for over-the-top theme bars like **Johnny Maracas** *(Calle Caballeros 39; Tel 963/915-206).* The drinks are absurdly expensive here (900ptas cocktails), and the

rules of the game

Although Valencia is a liberal city, it doesn't seem to have quite the hash-fueled nightlife you'll find elsewhere in Spain. The locals are too busy moving around, drinking, dancing, and talking to pass out on the sofa. But hash certainly is smoked here, especially up in El Carme, and of course, always with tobacco, and never with any hassle from the local authorities. El Carme and the center city in general have a fairly large share of prostitution. Guys, don't get so drunk that you mistake a working girl for an extremely friendly local.

crowd is older, more made-up, and trying *really* hard to have fun by dancing to the Cuban-flavored Latin disco beats. Still, this spot is worth a visit if only to check out the men's bathroom: urinals, TV screens, water...we can't really even convey it. If that isn't trippy enough for you, part of the bar is a fish tank.

Next door is the equally done-up **Fox Congo** *(Calle Caballeros 35)*, which has a bouncer—but he's strictly there to open the door for you. The clientele is similarly well-prepared for a night out (read: over-dressed) but the music is more bouncy electronica than Latin. Again, not that we have to remind you: Go check out the bathroom.

To ditch the oldsters, head up Calle Alta from Plaza San Jaime, where a stretch of more down-to-earth student bars has tables outside on the street. If you want something a little more psychedelic, why don't you join the freakin' **Circus** *(Calle Alta 11; No phone; 8pm-2:30am)?* There are no drunk clowns or circus freaks, but the crazy murals and bohemian crowd definitely contribute to the sideshow vibe. This rocker bar plays serious homage to Led Zeppelin, although it sometimes has electronica nights. The tiny upstairs veranda becomes an impromptu dance floor no matter what's playing. A strong beer like Kilkenny on tap will run you mere peanuts (400ptas).

Just north of Plaza Ayuntamiento, **Cervecería Madrid** *(Abadía de San Martin 10; Tel 963/529-671; 9pm-2 or 3am daily)* pulls off a fine balancing act; it's the classiest watering hole in town but doesn't have an ounce of pretension. That combination only comes with age, and this bar has been around a long time. The house specialty, a version of *agua de Valencia,* combines orange juice, vodka, gin, and sugar, and is served in glass pitchers. Downstairs is down-home with a wooden bar and tables, while upstairs puts on a more elegant face, with plush velvet booths and jazz photographs. It's a great place to bring a date and sneak into one of the little nooks. They also have live jazz, usually Tuesday through Thursday.

LIVE MUSIC SCENE

Valencia is a big enough city to attract well-known touring bands and foster a decent underground rock scene. Check out the *Levante* newspaper's Friday supplement for what's on for the week.

The little big names usually play at the diverse and spacious **Roxy Club** *(San Vicente 200; Tel 963/803-852; Hours vary; Cover 1,000ptas),* located south of the train station. Started in 1994 by a group of young music-loving entrepreneurs, this place books all kinds of music, though rock is the most common. Touring punk, ska, and alternative bands play here, along with the best of Valencia's own pop and rock groups. The shows usually start at midnight, with doors opening at 11pm and a standard cover of 1,000ptas. Thursday through Saturday, the action continues after 2:30am with DJ music and dancing; the cover includes one drink.

For jazz, soul, blues, or reggae four or five nights a week, check out the scene at **Black Note** *(Polo y Peyrolón 15; Tel 963/933-663; No cover).*

There's never a cover at this paean to *música negra* (their term, not ours), located halfway between the Jardines del Turia and Avenida Blaso Ibañez. The music starts at 11pm. You can also hear jazz two or three nights a week in the atmospheric **Cervecería Madrid** [see *bar scene,* above].

club scene

Valencia can justly claim to be one of the Spanish capitals of clubbing. It was here that *bacalao,* the distinctively Spanish form of electronica, was first played, though it later became associated with the Barcelona club scene. *Bacalao* literally means "cod," and its bouncy rhythm makes people want to jump up and down like a fish on a hook. It basically sounds like jumpy techno with some Latin flavoring; if you've been in Spain for any length of time you probably recognize it already. Connoisseurs of more rhythmically intricate dance music such as drum 'n' bass or breakbeats might know it better as that "slightly annoying Spanish techno music." Though *valencianos* like to dance to *bacalao* all the time, most of the clubs are open on weekends only, and close very late. There are a couple of dance spots in El Carme, near the University, and near the beach at Playa Malvarossa, but in the summer the biggest *discotecas* are outside of town, where they can play the music as loud and as late as they want.

To get to the most infamous of these clubs, hop on the *discotren* ("disco train") to the *maxi-disco* **Bananas** *(Carretera Valencia-Alicante, El Romaní; Tel 961/781-706; midnight-6am Fri-Sat; Cover 2,000ptas),* situated 16 kilometers (almost 10 miles) south of the city. Check the Friday edition of the daily newspaper *Levante* for current details, but basically it works like this: On Saturdays in the summer, the disco train boogies out of Valencia's main train station, Estación del Norte, at the unholy hour of 1:15am and takes you to the El Romaní station, which is 50 meters (160 feet) from the club. At 6:15am, bright and early, the train returns to Valencia. The ride is free, but the entrance to the club is 2,000ptas. The

boy meets girl

Courtship here runs pretty much the same as it does anywhere else in modern Europe. Ask for directions, compliment someone's choice of piercing, buy them a drink, or pretend you're a travel writer who needs to do "research" (just kidding on that last one). There are not as many *guiris* (foreigners) here as in Madrid or Barcelona, so you might have a better chance of standing out, in both good and bad ways. The locals are proudly modern and independent, so don't think that cute mangled Spanish accent is all it takes to impress them. They want you to be impressed with Valencia and their taste in music.

little town of El Romani consists of Bananas and a few villagers who don't get much sleep on weekend nights. Inside, the club has three main rooms, one each for '80s music, techno, and *bacalao,* as well as the requisite bars, swimming pool, terrace, and general debauchery. Sometimes they import famous Latin American or Spanish DJs. If it sounds a lot like other mega-clubs in Spain, it is. But is it worth the trek? Well, if only for the experience of saying you rode the disco train, it probably is.

If you don't want to leave town to get down on it, head to gay disco **Venial** *(Quart 26; Tel 963/917-356; midnight-6am daily; No cover Sun-Thu, cover 1,500ptas Fri-Sat)* in El Carme. The scene is largely made of up hip young gay men, whose shirts are steadily unbuttoned as the night goes on. But everyone is welcome here: Drag queens, students, nerdy gay men, and lesbians fill out the dance floor, which becomes packed on weekend nights until very late. Groove to the mostly Spanish dance music and try not to be distracted by the crazy light show. There's no cover most of the week, but on Friday and Saturday nights it'll cost 1,500ptas, which includes a free drink. Let it all hang out here, but don't bother showing up before 2am.

In the University District is the very popular **Woody** *(Menéndez y Pelayo 37; Tel 963/618-551; 9:30pm-5am Wed-Sun; Cover varies).* One block north of Avenida Blasco Ibañez, and a couple short blocks west of Avenida de Cataluña, you'll see an imposing metal storefront next to a supermarket. If you go behind the metal doors, you'll find a cavernous moody space with red velvet sofas where students and yuppies bounce to *bacalao.* The bummer is the cover, which can be up to 1,700ptas, depending on the night.

If you're tired of all the *bacalao,* head out to **69 Monos (sobre un cable de acero)** *(Eduardo Boscá 27-29; Tel 963/370-830; midnight-5am Fri-Sat).* An Aussie opened this club to give Valencia an alternative to the Spanish dance music that dominates the city. It features a lot of house music. The full name of the place means "69 Monkeys (on a steel cable)," which gives you some indication that this is not your middle-of-the-road *discoteca.* It's near the beach, Playa Malvarossa, so it's best to take a taxi (700ptas).

arts scene

There are a number of long-standing artistic institutions in Valencia, but the city continues to push for more cutting-edge artistic spaces.

▶▶VISUAL ARTS

The centerpiece of Valencia's modern art scene is the **Instituto Valencia de Arte Moderno (IVAM),** which has two outposts located near each other in the northern part of the old city. **IVAM Centre Julio González** *(Guillem de Castro 118; Tel 963/863-000; 10am-7pm Tue-Sun; 350ptas Tue-Sat, free Sundays)* has a large permanent collection of avant-garde 20th-century sculptures, paintings, drawings, and photographs from Spain and abroad. Temporary exhibits focus on the process of creating art itself, especially within the sphere of

only here

Valencia's oranges are famous worldwide, so *valencianos* take their enjoyment of the perfect little fruit seriously. In the airport and train stations they even have orange juice vending machines. You put in your 100ptas, the refrigerated machine squeezes the oranges into a little plastic cup, and you have fresh, cold OJ. Just add a little vodka and you can start the cocktail hour.

Another local specialty you should try is *horchata*, invented in the little suburb of Alboraya. This thick milky drink, made from something called tiger nuts, is sort of chalky and leaves a weird taste in your mouth. Just think of it as local culture.

To see justice in action, you can watch the **Tribunal de las Aguas** ("The Water Court"), which meets outside the Catedral Thursdays at noon. The farmers from the nearby countryside still settle their irrigation disputes orally, in Catalán, as they've done for hundreds of years.

montages and abstract and pop art, and include contemporary Spanish artists as well. The staff here is perfectly grumpy; checking your coat is like asking them to kill their firstborn, but once you get past them you can wander around all the rooms at your own sweet pace. Stop by the cafe for a coffee, but look at the walls (which have posters of seemingly every one of the museum's major exhibits), not the floor (the dirtiest of any museum cafe we've ever seen).

The main museum's younger, spunkier sibling is **IVAM Centre del Carme** (*Museo 2; 11am-2:30pm/4:30-7pm Tue-Sun*). Although this small center makes its home on Plaza del Carme in an old convent that dates to the 13th century, its focus is contemporary Spanish art, including challenging work by local artists, a lot of which will have you scratching your head, but in a good way. Sculpture, paintings, and stuff placed randomly on the floor get equal billing.

▶▶PERFORMING ARTS

Valencia's main theater, in an attractive building near Plaza del Ayuntamiento, is more than just a playhouse. **Teatro Principal** (*Barcas 15; Tel 963/510-051*) also features ballet, opera, and classical music, but the house specializes in plays by modern Spanish playwrights, usually put on by touring companies. Tickets start at 1,000ptas for most shows.

The **Palau de Música** (*Paseo de la Alameda 30; Tel 963/375-020, 963/995-577 ticketline; www.palauvalencia.com; 8am-11pm Mon-Sat,*

10am-9pm Sun), a modern concert hall stuck in the middle of the old riverbed (now the Jardines de Real), holds classical music concerts two or three nights a week. Valencia's City Orchestra frequently performs here, as do touring international orchestras. They occasionally branch out to more modern music, such as the jazz festival in July, which in the past has drawn legends like Herbie Hancock, McCoy Tyner, and Tony Bennett. Ticket prices start at 1,000ptas.

In an arts center on Plaza del Ayuntamiento you'll find **Filmoteca** *(Edificio Rialto, Plaza del Ayuntamiento 17; Tel 963/512-336; 200ptas)*, which shows classic foreign and Spanish films, as well as the occasional recent American release. Look for *V.O. subt.* in the listings for films in their original language with Spanish subtitles. The price is right: 200ptas for all shows.

For a more intense movie-going experience, there's a 900-square-foot IMAX screen in **L'Hemisferic** *(Avenida Instituto Obrero de Valencia; Tel 902/100-031; 1,100ptas Tue-Thu, 1,000ptas Fri-Sun)* at the **Ciudad de las Artes y de las Ciencias** [see *culture zoo*, below]. Still under construction at this site when we went to press is the **Palacio de las Artes.** When completed, it will have one outdoor and two indoor auditoriums and will be one of Valencia's major venues for opera, plays, and music.

gay scene

Valencia is a large, liberal city, and the gay community here is big and fairly uninhibited, mixing it up with all the other funky goings-on in the El Carme district. The local gay organization, **Lambda** *(Genir 9; Tel 963/912-084)*, is a good source of information on all things queer in Valencia.

The popular gay disco **Venial** [see *club scene*, above] is the established late-night spot in El Carme. A well-dressed male crowd hangs out here, but there's room on the dance floor for drag queens and lesbians as well. Earlier in the evening, a mixed gay crowd descends upon **Café de la Seu** *(Santo Caliz 7; Tel 963/915-715; 8pm-2am, closed Mon)*.

Gay men will want to check out Calle Quart, which has a number of bars, including **Central** *(Quart 57; No phone)* and the very cruisy **La Guerra** *(Quart 47; Tel 963/913-675; 8pm-3am)*. For women, the hotspot is **Donna Donna** *(Portal Valdigna 2; No phone; 6pm-2am Thu-Sun)*.

culture zoo

While Valencia may not have the rich cultural and historical sites of Madrid or Barcelona, there's still plenty to see.

Catedral *(Plaza de la Reina; Tel 963/918-127; 7:30am-1pm/4:30-8:30pm; free)*: Valencia's cathedral was begun in 1262, but it took 200 years just to finish the original structure. Later additions have made it an architecturally confused, albeit interesting, building, with Gothic, Baroque, and Romanesque styles. Admission is free, but you'll be charged 200ptas to climb to the top of the Gothic tower, Miguelete, which offers grand views of the city and surroundings. For 500 years this church has

FIVE THINGS TO TALK TO A LOCAL ABOUT

1. Valencia has a fairly kick-ass **soccer team,** which made it to the 2000 European club championships. Unfortunately, they lost to dreaded Real Madrid in the final, so offer them your condolences.

2. Everyone loves the party of fire called **Las Fallas** [see *burning down the house,* above], and they'll be glad to give you the blow-by-blow rundown of the event and tell you how you haven't experienced Valencia until you've seen it.

3. Swapping *paella* recipes may not sound like your idea of a good time, but you can mine secrets that you can use to take on the Iron Chef or cook authentic Spanish fare for your latest obsession back home.

4. You can either blame Valencia for the repetitive, bouncy, techno music called *bacalao* or open your mind and let them explain its intricate mysteries.

5. The potent local cocktail *agua de Valencia* is made with orange juice and booze, but comes in many varieties; ask which combo they prefer. Or try to explain to them what a "screwdriver" is and why orange juice and vodka has that name. It could take all night.

claimed to be the final resting place of the legendary Holy Grail, the cup used during the Last Supper and chased by everyone from Sir Galahad to Indiana Jones. No one, of course, can accurately confirm or deny the story, but Valencia's cup *has* been dated at 2,000 years old, and although it doesn't radiate beams of light and joy, it's certainly as appropriate a symbol of Christianity as any. You'll find it on display in one of the side chapels.

Museo de Bellas Artes *(San Pio V 9; Tel 963/605-793; 10am-3pm/4-6pm Tue-Sat, 10am-2pm Sun):* Situated next to the Jardines de Real, this small but renowned museum presents its collection of paintings and sculptures, mostly from the golden oldy days, with a smattering of 20th-century work. A Velázquez self-portrait from the 17th century is the best-known work, but the most popular subject is definitely religious suffering. This would be a good place to write a thesis on "Jesus Christ as sex symbol." The one painting you have to see is not by a Spanish artist, but by Dutch artist Hieronymus Bosch, whom the Spanish call "El Bosco." He painted the surreal *Triptico de la Pasion* hundreds of years before the term "surreal" was invented.

La Ciudad de las Artes y las Ciencias: The buzz in Valencia is all about the 90-acre "City of Arts and Sciences" on the southeastern edge of the city at Plaza Monte Olivete; it was 10 years in the making. It hosts four distinct, state-of-the-art venues: **L'Hemisferic,** a giant domed interior that can be used to display IMAX movies on a 900-foot screen or converted into a planetarium; **Palacio de las Artes,** an opera house and performance center [see *arts scene,* above for both]; **Museo de las Ciencias,** an interactive hands-on science museum for kids; and **L'Oceanografic,** an aquarium complex with a series of man-made bodies of water simulating all of the world's oceans. The buildings themselves are works of art. L'Hemisferic, designed by local award-winning architect Santiago Calatrava, resembles a giant glass eye sitting on a reflecting pool. The eye literally blinks when the retractable roof is operated, revealing the "eyeball" of the domed theater itself. The other buildings are equally futuristic, made with glass and steel shaped into organic, shell-like curves that produce an overall sense of weightlessness.

modification

If you're looking to make your body a canvas, try the reputable **X Tattoo** *(Quart 1; Tel 963/914-065; 11am-2pm/5-9am, closed Sun)*. It doesn't have biker ambience, so you won't be talked into getting "Hell on Wheels" put on your arm. It's a modern, mellow place where you can feel comfortable getting that butterfly tattoo on your ankle.

stuff

Valencia is not the place to pick up all the souvenirs you can fit into your suitcase, so you're going to have to buy that *boda* bag with the flamenco dancer on it somewhere else. But other shopping opportunities certainly exist here, mostly centered in big clusters. The high-class shopping district is east of Plaza del Ayuntamiento on pedestrian streets like Sagasta and streets south. In this area, Calle Colón is the million-dollar mile, where the upmarket designers strut their stuff. The unbelievably gargantuan shopping center **Nuevo Centro** *(Avenida Pio XII 2-6; Tel 963/411-642),* just northwest of the old quarter over the riverbed, has every kind of store you would ever need, including a huge Corte Ingles department store. What it doesn't have is character, but 15 million shoppers a year can't be wrong....For more mellow and alternative shopping, cruise El Carme. Unless noted, shops keep fairly uniform hours of 10am-1:30pm/5-8pm Monday through Saturday.

▶▶**CLUB GEAR**

Maybe "street gear" is a better term for what you'll find at **Urban Klan** *(Museo 5; Tel 963/925-599; 10am-1:30pm/5pm-8pm Mon-Sat),* located near IVAM Centre El Carme. It carries a lot of Dickies and Iron Maiden T-shirts for your work and rock needs.

▶▶**TUNES**

Everything a 17-year-old kid needs to live—compact discs, books, computer games, and stereos—can be got at **Fnac** *(Guillem de Castro 9; Edificio San Agustín; 10am-9:30pm Mon-Sat, noon-9:30pm Sun),* a superstore west of the train station. The music selection is Top-40 heavy, and Spanish Top-40 is an odd mix of some forgotten English-language artists (Iron Maiden and Tom Jones) and national heroes who are trying to sound like English-language artists. Fnac is a chain store that has a slightly corporate feel, but it does have those cool listening stations. Local bands often make in-store appearances.

If you're looking for a less generic shopping experience, **Addiction** *(Serranos 1; No phone; 10am-1:30pm/5pm-8pm Mon-Sat)* has a mix of used (1,500ptas) and new (2,500ptas) CDs. This funky little shop in El Carme, near Torres Serranos, doesn't have a huge selection, but you'll find a good assortment of everything from Metallica to Fatboy Slim.

▶▶**BOUND**

The English Book Centre *(Calle de Pascual y Genis 16; 10am-2:30pm/5-8pm Mon-Sat)*, east of Plaza del Ayuntamiento, doesn't carry a lot of books, but what it does stock is in English, so you'll find plenty to choose from. Load up on Hemingway (1,500-2,000 ptas), grab a bottle of wine, and lock yourself in your hotel room for a few days. On second thought, maybe that's not such a good idea.

For books in Spanish, head to **Librería Soriano** *(Játiva 15; No phone; 9:30am-2pm/4:30-9pm Mon-Sat, 10am-2pm Sun)*, a huge bookshop right across from the train station. It's got a good magazine selection too.

EATS

Valencia is famous for its oranges and its *paella*. You can get good *paella* at just about every restaurant in the city, but finding the truly excellent and affordable version takes some time. Be sure to check out the other somewhat exotic *arroces* (rice) dishes, such as *arroz negro,* which is rice with squid ink. If it's oranges you're looking for, go to the **Mercado** [see *to market,* below].

▶▶**CHEAP**

We don't usually trust fast-food chains, but if you're tired of *paella* and tapas, you won't find a better cheap meal in Valencia than at **Bocatta** *(Various locations, including Plaza de la Reina, Plaza del Ayuntamiento; 9-1am; sandwiches 450ptas)*. Okay, so it's sort of like Subway, but the sandwiches here are fresher, with crisp vegetables, and they're served on warm, toasted baguettes instead of soggy roles, for just 450ptas. Also unlike fast food joints in other places, these restaurants are clean, with plenty of seats and a security guard to open the door for you. And they serve beer. If you're afraid you're not getting the "authentic Spanish experience," we can guarantee that you'll find more young attractive *valencianos* here, lingering over their Number Five extra-value meal (695ptas) than in any atmospheric tapas bar.

Speaking of tapas bars, they pop up all over the city, of course. **Barcas** *(Barcas 7; Tel 963/521-233; 7-1am)* is a local favorite and stays open all day, even during siesta. Located just off Plaza del Ayuntamiento, this old-fashioned place draws coffee guzzlers in the morning, businessmen at lunch, and folks just kicking off *La Movida* in the evening. The crowds

TO MARKET

Every Spanish city has an indoor local market, but Valencia's **Mercado Central** *(Plaza del Mercado; 7am-3pm Mon-Fri, 10am-1pm Sat)* is a behemoth. It's reputed to be the second biggest market in Spain, housed in a grand modernist temple dedicated to fresh food. Produce recently picked from the surrounding countryside, including brilliant oranges, of course, makes shopping here a feast for the eyes and taste buds. Walk through the endless stalls of seafood trying to guess the names of sea creatures you never knew existed, and make sure to visit the "eel man," who grabs live squirming eels out of a bucket and chops their heads right off, to the delight (or horror) of onlookers.

mean the tapas—including lots of yummy fishy dishes, small portions of *paella,* and our favorite, *empanadas de átun,* made with spicy tuna—keep moving, so you won't be getting something that's been sitting under the counter all day (although there is something to be said for "aged" tapas—they collect the aromas from all the other food).

▶▶**DO-ABLE**

According to local taste, the best value for *paella* is at **Cervecería La Pema** *(Mosén Fernandes 3; Tel 963/526-650; 12:30-5:30pm/8pm-midnight; entrees 950ptas).* It's located on a little restaurant-filled alley off the shopping district between the train station and Plaza del Ayuntamiento, off of Calle Rufaza. A huge portion of *paella* or *arroz negro* will only run you 950ptas; the outside seating and the sounds of the spirited staff yelling at each other in the kitchen are free.

▶▶**SPLURGE**

Follow in Hemingway's steps at **La Pepica** *(Paseo Neptuno 6 and 8; Tel 963/710-366; metro stop: Eugenia Viñes; 1-5pm/9pm-midnight; entrees 1,200ptas),* located on the beach at the south end of Playa de Levante. Hemingway came here for the *paella,* and today locals and visitors alike flock here for the same reason. The ugly pink tablecloths and old-fashioned service may not be worth the trek, but once you taste the affordable and authentic *paella valenciana* (1,200ptas), brought to your table in a giant sizzling pan, you'll feel your time was well spent.

crashing

Most of budget accommodations cluster around Plaza del Ayuntamiento, with some more worn hostels in the rambling El Carme.

▶▶**CHEAP**

Located right off Plaza del Ayuntamiento, **Hostal Resedencía Universal** *(Barcas 5; Tel 963/515-384; 2,300ptas single, 3,600ptas double, 5,100ptas triple)* occupies three floors, starting with the third floor, which makes the walk up good exercise. The rooms are clean, with cozy beds, closets, sinks, and little balconies, and the shared bathrooms are kept immaculate. An extremely friendly family runs the place, but when they want to clean the room, they really want to clean the room: They'll let you know with a ferocious knock.

Hospedería del Pilar *(Mercado 19; Tel 963/916-600; 2,140ptas single, 3,850ptas double)* gives exercise freaks another good walk-up. A favorite among backpackers, this slightly aging *pension* just across from the Mercado Central has a great location, over 30 well-maintained rooms (some with private showers and toilets), and curt but efficient service.

▶▶**DO-ABLE**

Just east of the Mercado Central you'll find the friendly and funky **Hostal-Resedencia Bisbal** *(Pie de la Cruz 9; Tel 963/917-084; 3,200ptas single, 5,400ptas double)*. With an excellent location near El Carme and the center of the city, this hostel is run by a helpful family that speaks good English. The small rooms are simple but clean, all with private baths. The elevator is a little scary—is it supposed to lurch like that?

For more modern conveniences, try the larger, recently renovated **Hotel Venecia** *(En Lop 5; Tel 963/524-267; 900ptas double without shower; 1,100ptas double with shower)*, right at the top of Plaza del Ayuntamiento. All the rooms have TV, air conditioning, and telephone.

down and out

Valencia offers plenty of cheap ways to pass the time. Head to the beach, take a ride on the metro, see the holy grail at the **Catédral** [see *culture zoo*, above], chill in the lovely **Jardines de Real,** or people watch at **Plaza de la Virgen** [see *hanging out*, above for both]. It also won't cost you a peseta to enter **La Londja de Seda** *(9am-1:30pm/5-7pm Mon-Fri, 9am-1:30pm Sat-Sun)*, a Gothic building that looks like a church but isn't. Located across from the Mercado, this interesting architectural site, featuring spiraling staircases and stained-glass windows, used to house the old silk market. You can also check out the ancient towers that used to be the entryways to Valencia's old city: **Torres de Serrano** in the north and **Torres de Quart** in the west.

▶▶**SPLURGE**

The most glamorous hotel in Valencia, **Hotel Reina Victoria** *(Barcas 4; Tel 963/520-487; 14,000ptas and up double)* has an old-world ambience you can't get at a Holiday Inn. Queen Victoria, Picasso, Dalí, and Lorca have all stayed at this grand neoclassical hotel, built in 1913 and centered right in the heart of town next to the Plaza del Ayuntamiento. It can't compete with more modern commercial hotels for space and high-tech amenities, but if you're going to lay down 100 bucks a night, you want to get some history and atmosphere, not a Stairmaster.

need to know

Currency Exchange Valencia is a major commercial center, so ATMs spill out cash all over the place, especially in Plaza del Ayuntamiento.

Tourist Information If you arrive by train, you'll stumble over the **provincial tourist office** *(Tel 963/528-573; 10am-2:30pm/4:30-7pm Mon-Fri, 10am-2pm Sat)* at the Estación del Norte. The **main city tourist office** *(Tel 963/510-417; 8:30am-2:15pm/4:15-6pm Mon-Fri; 9am-12:45pm Sat)* is at Plaza del Ayuntamiento. A second **provincial tourist office** *(Tel 963/514-907; 10am-2:30pm/4:30-7pm Mon-Fri, 10am-2pm Sat)* is just east of this plaza at Calle Barcas and Poeta Queral. They all have maps of the city, hotel listings, and Internet connection info, but they can't make hotel reservations for you.

Public Transportation The **metro** is mainly designed to shuttle people to the suburbs, but it can be useful in the city for getting to the University District or the beaches. Trains come every ten minutes or so, and tickets (125ptas within the city) can be bought at automated machines in every station. The main stop in the center city is in front of the **Estación del Norte. City buses** (110ptas) leave frequently from Plaza del Ayuntamiento to all parts of the city and generally run until 11pm; a map is available from the city tourist office or at the **EMT Office** *(En Sanz 4; Tel 963/528-399; 8am-3:30pm Mon-Fri).* **Bus 19** takes you from Plaza del Ayuntamiento to the city beaches as well as the port. **Taxis** are especially useful late at night; flag one down on the *avenidas* or the major plazas, or call 963/703-333.

Health and Emergency Emergency: *085;* Police: *091* or *092.* The **national police station** *(Gran Via de Ramon y Cajal 40; Tel 963/510-862)* is southwest of the train station. The **general hospital** *(Tel 963/862-900)* is on Avenida El Cid.

Pharmacies *Farmacias* are located all over the city center; look for the **green neon cross.** If you need something late at night, call the hotline *(Tel 900/161-161)* for the nearest all-hours pharmacy. **Farmacia Gran Via,** located east of the train station at the corner of Gran Via Marqués del Turia and Jorge y Juan, is open 24 hours.

Telephone Pay phones around Valencia usually work more often than in other big cities. All local numbers begin with the **96** prefix. There's also a **telephone office** *(Plaza del Ayuntamiento 24; Tel 96/003; 9am-11pm Mon-Sat)* with booths where you can make long-distance calls.

Airport **Aeropuerto de Manises** *(Tel 963/609-500)*, 15 kilometers (9.3 miles) west of the city, has frequent flights to Madrid, Barcelona, and the Balearic Islands. For tickets, there's an **Iberia Airlines Office** *(Paz 14; Tel 902/400-500; 9am-2pm/4:30-7pm Mon-Fri)* east of Plaza de la Reina in the city center. To get to the city center from the airport, take a **taxi** (1,900ptas) or the hourly **Bus 15** (150ptas).

Trains The train is the best way to reach Valencia; trains arrive at **Estación del Norte** *(Játiva 24; Tel 963/520-202)*, conveniently located in the heart of the city. There are at least ten trips daily to Madrid (5-7 hours) and Barcelona (3-5 hours).

Bus Lines Out of the City The bus station, **Estacío Terminal d'Autobuses** *(Avenida de Menéndez Pidal 15; Tel 963/497-222)*, is a 30-minute walk northwest of the city center, near the Nuevo Central shopping center. You can also take **Bus 8** to and from Plaza del Ayuntamiento.

Boats **Trasmediterránea** *(Estació Maritimo; Tel 963/673-972, 902/454-645 for toll-free reservations; www.trasmediterranea.net)* has ferry service from Valencia's port to the Balearic Islands, including Ibiza city and Palma de Mallorca. They don't run as frequently as you'd like, with only Thursday service to Ibiza (a 6-hour trip), except during the height of summer between June and September. For current departures call ahead or check out the website.

Laundry **Lavandaría Autoservicio El Mercat** *(Mercado 12; Tel 963/912-010; 10am-2pm/4:30-8:30pm Mon-Fri, 10am-2pm Sat)* is located right near Mercado Central.

Postal The main **Correos** *(8am-8:30pm Mon-Fri, 9:30am-2pm Sat)* is on Plaza Ayuntamiento.

Internet See *wired,* above.

Ibiza

Those who appreciate the finer cultural nuances of traveling abroad should not visit Ibiza during the summer months. There *are* a few points of interest that don't involve gin and strobe lights or the sounds of the tide, but they don't do much for you after you've been out all night. The discos and beaches are why everyone's here. But if you like to dance, look good, feel good, and ride excess like a bareback horse, Ibiza will knock your socks off. If Ibiza were a woman, its sunny, beautiful beaches and good-natured locals would probably remind you of Cameron Diaz. But that's during the day. When the sun goes down on this island, Ibiza becomes more like Courtney Love: wild, hard-partying, and looking for almost-scary fun. Imagine the festive feel and colorful clothes of Mardi Gras and put that together with the thumping and theatrical Studio 54—that's what Ibiza is like every day from the middle of July until the end of August. So, if you want to go to Ibiza, go now, because it might kill you (or your career, or your sanity) when you're older. If Ibiza were a water slide, it would be tall, man, real tall. Yup, grab the Baeleric Bull by the horns and dig in your spurs...This is the biggest damn slip and slide of a party you ever saw.

This small island was once best-known for its beautiful beaches and the small artisan communities that grew from a European hippie invasion in the early and mid-1970s. Ibiza still holds true to this character for nine months of the year (and year-round in the inland villages). In the past decade, however, Ibiza has become a giant, fire-breathing Godzilla of a party. Each summer, this island rears its head, thumps it chest, and emits a terrifying war cry in the form of electronic music from the world's greatest DJs. Ibiza is one of the epicenters of modern disco/rave culture, and savvy Europeans and Aussies seek the sounds that came out of this island in the late '80s like your old college roommate sought Dead tapes from the early '70s. Even though most Americans have never heard of Ibiza, European youth recognize this little island as *the* place for summer holiday. How wild are the times here? Basically, if you took the formidable nightlife of Madrid, crushed it up and snorted it, you would be on Ibiza.

Even at its worst, Ibiza is fascinating to watch: Imagine an English Daytona Beach, complete with boorish young English men and their screeching pale girlfriends, both refusing to speak anything other than English to the locals who put up with their antics for three months every summer so that they can live in peace during the other nine months of the year. You'll find a lot of the same type of Germans, Italians, and Spanish, too, but in fewer numbers. At its best, though, Ibiza is a beautiful, almost spiritual fun place that tolerates everything. (The gay community is so predominant here that we hardly gave it its own section in this chapter.) This is the time and place to try something that you think will make you feel good but have never had the balls to try out back home: Dress up! Dance! Talk to strangers! People here want to soak you in and check you out; they want you to *contribute* to the good times, not just watch them.

You'll be doing plenty of watching, though, if you show up here without a lot of money. A week's worth of nightlife will cost you as much as a new Hyundai. Getting into clubs can cost up to US$40, and most hotels double (and sometimes triple!) their prices in July and August. This island will take a toll not only on your wallet, but on your body and brain. For some people, being put on Ibiza is the same as sending a NASA explorer to Mars: They're gonna crash and burn. Despite the tremendous amount of wild, smiling fun that you can have here, we urge you to be just a little careful....

When you're ready to venture out, you'll have no trouble finding sources of info to help you navigate, red-eyed, through this hurricane of discos and sunshine. *DJ Ibiza* gives you the most info on clubs, bars, restaurants, beaches, and markets in the least amount of words, along with short interviews from the big DJs. *Ministry in Ibiza* is like the *Maxim* of this island: funny articles written by a staff that jumps into the whole Ibiza scene head-first. You're sure to get the inside (read: wasted) view of how the club scene operates. Two smaller magazines that we like are *Party San,* which you can pick up at the **Sunset Café** [see *bar scene,* below] and *7.* The websites *www.ibizanight.com* and *www.ibiza hotel.com* give you basic info on the clubs but are more useful for their detailed info on the Disco Bus [see *need to know,* below], restaurants, and—most importantly—reservation information (make your reservations early!). Both sites are in English and Spanish, although the official language of the Baeleric Islands is Catalán, the language of Barcelona. But, between the heavy influence of Spain and England, you'll often be

ibiza

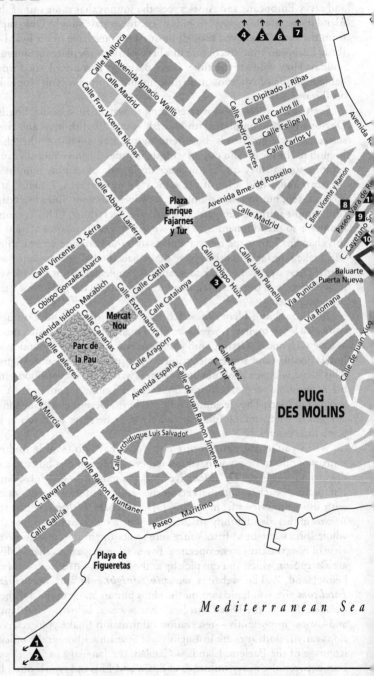

Calle Mallorca

Avenida Ignacio Wallis

Calle Madrid

Calle Fray Vicente Nicolas

Calle Pedro Frances

C. Dipitado J. Ribas

Calle Carlos III

Calle Felipe II

Calle Carlos V

Avenida R...

Calle Abad y Lasierra

Avenida Bme. de Rossello

Plaza Enrique Fajarnes y Tur

Calle Madrid

C. Bme. Vicente y Ramon

Paseo Vara de Re...

Calle Vincente D. Serra

C. Obispo Gonzalez Abarca

Calle Castilla

Calle Extremadura

Calle Catalunya

Calle Obispo Huix

Calle Juan Planells

C. Cayetano S...

Baluarte Puerta Nueva

Via Punica

Avenida Isidoro Macabich

Calle Canarias

Mercat Nou

Calle Aragorn

Via Romana

Calle Baleares

Parc de la Pau

Avenida España

Calle Perez

C. I Tur

Calle de Juan Xico

Calle Murcia

Calle Archiduque Luis Salvador

Calle de Juan Ramon Jimenez

PUIG DES MOLINS

C. Navarra

Calle Ramon Muntaner

Calle Galicia

Paseo Maritimo

Playa de Figueretas

Mediterranean Sea

BARS/CLUBS ▲
Amnesia **25**
Bar Zuka **23**
Bora Bora **1**
Café Mambo **24**
Can Pou Bar **15**
Corazón Negro **21**
Dôme Bar **20**
El Divino **5**
Hype **18**
Pacha **6**
Space **2**
Sunset Café **11**
Teatro Pereyra **13**

EATS ◆
Bar Costa **4**
Bar de Pintxos **14**
Café d'Art **10**
El Faro **22**
El Jardin Bar y Taverna **19**
Mr. Hot Dog **16**
Se Caldera **3**

CRASHING ■
Hotel Montesol **12**
Hostal
  Residencia Parque **9**
Pension La Peña **17**
Tagomago Aparthotel **7**
Vara de Rey **8**

able to speak English (and even German), and you can *always* speak Spanish to any locals you might come across. The mixed-language influence has been so strong that the two big towns—La Ciudad de Ibiza and Sant Antoni—are commonly referred to as Ibiza Town and San Antonio.

neighborhoods

San Antonio is on the west coast, and **Ibiza Town** is on the east. Take note now that San Antonio is the absolute weakest. It is a nightmarish combination of suburban shopping mall, soccer riot, and frat party, where the youngest and most terrible of the tourists come to party. Except for the **Café Mambo** [see *bar scene,* below], it should be avoided at all costs. But a mere half-hour bus ride away, on the other half of the island—and the opposite end of the spectrum—is Ibiza Town, the focal point of the island. Unless otherwise stated, all venues written up in this chapter are located here.

12 hours in ibiza

1. Watch the sunset at **Café Mambo** (or **Sunset Café** right next door) in San Antonio [see *bar scene,* below, for both].
2. A day at either **Las Salinas Beach** by Ibiza Town, **Cala Xarraca Beach** up on the north coast [see *great outdoors,* below, for both], or any of the beaches in Formentera (Illetes, for example) [see *hanging out,* below].
3. Party calisthenics: Warm up on the beach at **Bora Bora** [see *bar scene,* below]. Get your full workout across the street at **Space** [see *club scene,* below], and then cool down at Bora Bora again.
4. Take a scooter ride through the countryside (pack a picnic...).
5. Experience extreme Ibiza by going to *Manumission* at **Privilege** [see *club scene,* below]. Don't forget your latex and whips.
6. Look good and feel good while at Ibiza's traditional party: *Renaissance* at **Pacha.** It's full of smart dressers and a warm, beautiful vibe [see *club scene,* below].
7. Watch the freaks go by in Sa Penya, particularly on Calle de La Virgén. Sock-and-sandaled and sunburnt German tourists, English fashion victims, loudmouth drag queens, and many, many beautiful party people from all over Europe.
8. Spend a couple hours walking around D'Alt Villa, the Old Fortress. Beautiful views of the sea.

Ibiza Town is on the southern end of the island's eastern coast and lays to the south and west of the **Marina.** A small and unremarkable portion of Ibiza Town does curve around to the north of the Marina, but you won't be spending any time there. The **Sa Penya** neighborhood is where the action is—action like you may never have seen before. Dozens of bars, restaurants, street vendors, drag queens, and nationalities converge here and get warmed up for the nightly sacrifice to the disco club gods. During the day, you can find good fashion shopping, pubs, and groceries here. The beginning of Sa Penya is marked by **Plaça d'Antoni Riquer** and the street that runs through it, parallel to the Marina, which is called **Calle de Lluís Tur i Palau** to the west of the Plaça, and **Passeig des Moll** to the east. **Calle de La Virgén** is the most famous of the streets here; it is a long, narrow street that runs parallel to the Marina, from the eastern tip of the city to the equally busy **Calle de Pou,** which begins right at the Marina and runs north to south. Sa Penya continues south for about eight misshapen blocks before it runs into the foot of the elevated **D'Alt Villa** (Old Fortress). Ibiza Town more or less ends at the southern point of the Old Fortress. **Paseo de Vara de Rey** is the other major landmark in Ibiza Town—several hostels, the tourism office [see *need to know,* below], a travel agency, and a few good shops and restaurants are all on this street. Paseo de Vara de Rey is three blocks to the west of D'Alt Vila and runs northeast to southwest. Everything that we've mentioned here can be walked between in 20 minutes or less.

Other villages worthy of a day or half-day trip for some rural relaxation are **Santa Gertrudis** *(to the northwest of Ibiza Town, in the very middle of the island, about a half hour by bus),* **Santa Eularia** *(to the east of Ibiza Town, on the coast, 20 minutes by bus),* and **San Rafael** *(directly between Ibiza Town and San Antonio).* The clubs **Privilege** and **Amnesia** [see *club scene,* below, for both] are both just outside of Ibiza Town. No point on the island of Ibiza is much more than an hour from Ibiza Town by bus, or 90 minutes by scooter. **Playa d'en Bossa** is a mere 15-minute bus ride south of Ibiza Town. This is the one of the most crowded and commercial beaches on the island, but **Space** [see *club scene,* below], **Bora Bora** [see *bar scene,* below], and the **Aguamar waterpark** [see *great outdoors,* below] are all located here.

Remember that Ibiza is ridiculously small. The villages are even smaller. Venues that aren't in Ibiza Town or San Antonio simply have the village listed for the address because all of the stores/bars/etc., are located on one central street. Basic maps and road signs work just fine if you're going to scooter it between beaches and villages, and the buses go to all villages we have named and many beaches. And the clubs themselves (also reachable by bus) are landmarks that every cab driver and local knows. You'd have to work really hard to get lost on this island.

hanging out

You'll have no trouble finding the cool kids on this island, friends. The whole of Ibiza is one big party, but if you really want to "hang out," the beaches are the best for that, especially since all of them are topless (and

fIVE-O

One quick way to lose money here is by handing it over to José Law when he pulls you over for swerving around on your rented scooter. El Hombre isn't really out to get you, but let's face it: If your island were invaded each summer by two million hallucinating British Gen X-ers, you, too, would want to try to control things at least a little bit. Road blocks with breath tests are the newest attempt to keep you and your wasted friends out of harm's way. Take our advice: Use a cab at night.

many are nude) [see *great outdoors,* below]. Hoards of young folk don't really congregate in any of the plazas or squares here. With all the beautiful stretches of sand around, why would they?

Ibiza's best hangout, however, turns out to be difficult to find. Not only are these fabled **full-moon parties** hard to suss out, you also have to accept that they're only going to happen once a month. When they do go down, there will be no fliers, and the Germans and the English won't be able to help you out, but if you make friends with just a few locals, they'll be able to tell you the day and location of one of the island's best events. Drum circles, booze, bonfires, and more on secluded black-sand beaches that are beautiful enough to make you cry.

Calle de Santa Agnes, in San Antonio, is probably the last place you want to hang out, unless you're 16, belligerent, and culturally void: The scene here is vomiting and groping in the streets, 100 percent rude, 100 percent lame. If you want to get some pale English lovin', though, this street is definitely the place. We hung out for 10 minutes and then ran.

bar scene

As you would expect with a Spanish island, Ibiza has a bar for every occasion. Some are for cool beachside drinks, others are for hot late-night action, but the bulk of the bars you'll encounter in Ibiza Town are meant to operate like giant cannons that will blast your wasted ass into the disco stratosphere. Don't try and fight it, either, pal. Keep your chin up, strap on your crash helmet, and head on down to the crowded international big-top mayhem that is the Sa Penya district. It's your job to get there at about 11pm or midnight and to be ready to perform death-defying stunts of fashion and consumption. Among the feather boas, platform shoes, and glitter, you'll notice a fair number of attractive and seemingly coked-up folks who—despite all of their talking—are rather stationary. It's their job to get you into their bar. Here's how it usually goes: A sexy and fast-talking hawker approaches you and says "Hey there, mate. How about tickets for Amnesia tonight?" Be sure that you know where you want to go ahead of time, because they will always try and sell you on the less-attractive events first (e.g., a foam party [see *good clean fun,* below] instead of a hot dance scene that ends with live sex on stage). So having already done your homework, you say, "How abouts tickets for Pacha?" What usually happens next is that you'll agree to go in for a drink. Yes, that's right; if you agree to a couple of (relatively) cheap whiskey-and-cokes, you'll get a big discount or even free admission! What a great system! Don't you wish that getting a driver's license or paying off your student loans was this easy? A good negotiating tactic is to not be shy about sticking it in the camera, baby. As so many of the twentysomething party people here already know, looking sexy and freaky will get you what you want, because the clubs want beautiful people!

Hype *(Calle d'Emile Pou 11A; No phone; 8pm-3am daily; V, MC)* is only one of the very many bars that operate in this way in the Sa Penya district. Drink your way to cheap disco and watch the freak show pass by from the terrace seating.

Bar Zuka *(Calle de la Virgén 75; No phone; 9pm-3am daily; No credit cards)* has candles, an old tile floor, a more-refined-less-hectic vibe (until they break out the tequila later at night), beautifully painted walls, and regular attendance by some of England's biggest DJs. Less queeny and painted-up than the rest of Calle de la Virgén.

When the MTV beach parties grow up, they want to be **Bora Bora** *(Playa d'en Bossa, across the street from Space; No phone; Open all the time—really; No credit cards)*. Drink, dance, and chill while coming down from nearby Space (or while gearing up for it, depending on your schedule and stamina). Along with the party people, there are many unaware beach-goers here who have a dim realization that they are not in the same state as everyone else at the bar. This is a very mellow, very appropriate, very Ibiza way to end a disco marathon: 300ptas for a beer and usually around 500 people.

In addition to alcohol, **Sunset Café** *(Plaza del Parque 3; Tel 971/301-032; 9:30-3am Mon-Sat; No credit cards)* serves tasty chicken sandwiches (500ptas), fresh juice, and "breakfast salads" (garden salads with a lot of fruit) for 500ptas. Good house music with its own DJ from 9pm till 1am.

rules of the game

Despite their overwhelming abundance, drugs are still illegal in Ibiza. However, in traditional Spanish fashion, people don't get busted unless they get violent. So don't. The standard Spanish chill factor applies here as well, but the locals have become less patient with the rowdy English tourist in recent years, so if you do get in a bind, don't go shooting your mouth off. Also be forewarned that most people get a good searching when traveling from Ibiza to another country. Taking the boat between Ibiza and Barcelona/Valencia, however, is a cake walk.

Be sure to say hi to Stephan, the friendly German owner, and whichever hottest-woman-ever happens to be behind the bar with him. Sitting on their pleasant plaza right off the Paseo de Vara de Rey is a great getaway from Ibiza Town nonsense.

Can Pou Bar *(Corner of Lluis Tur i Palau and Montgri; Tel 971/310-875; 8-4am daily; Open in winter; MC, V)* has been a local favorite for over 80 years, except that the customers back then were all fishermen, not disco and clothing store owners. There are a few terrace tables and the inside is comfy (they don't try to cram people in here for the extra buck like many other places). Coffee, juice, small sandwiches, and breakfasts are served. Walls are lined with beautiful artwork that reflects the local temperament. Right on the Marina between Sa Penya and Paseo de Vara de Rey.

Café Mambo *(End of Avenida de Vara de Rey, in San Antonio; No phone; 11-4am daily, kitchen till midnight; MC, V for purchases over 5,000ptas)* is in San Antonio, but nobody's perfect. Listen to mellow ambient music, have a drink, and watch a magnificent sunset over the water from the terrace (a must-see while in Ibiza). The rabid British party monkeys that swarm San Antonio do show up later on, but it's fun to slip slowly from the mellow sunset to that high-energy fiesta while getting sauced on gin-and-tonics. Including the surrounding beach, max capacity is about 2,000 people. 800ptas for a drink.

LIVE MUSIC SCENE

Live music? Yeah, right. Only the most popular DJs on earth spin here on a nightly basis. Save for a handful of German and Dutch expats who live inland, there's not much of a live music scene on this island. If middle-aged Germans covering the Eagles and the Dead is your thing, though, be sure to rush on over to **Teatro Pereyra** *(Corner of Calle Conde Rosellon and Calle Anibal; No phone; 7-4am daily; No credit cards)*. The good times get rolling at 11:30pm. Despite everything, they do get points here for being open 21 hours a day and for having an enormous and beautiful bar. The big round tables can seat about six stools, and capacity is about 300 European preps. Lord knows why they came to Ibiza.

CLUB SCENE

Because they're the big business here, all of the clubs adhere to the same high prices and late schedule. Here's the lowdown (exceptions are noted in the club descriptions):

1. Clubs run from the middle of May until the end of September and are open from midnight till 6 or 8am daily.
2. Prime time is from around 3:30 to 5:30am.
3. Cover is between 6,000 and 10,000ptas! Discount fliers are easy to come by, though, and bring the price down to 4,000 to 6,000ptas [see *bar scene,* above, to learn more].
4. Little bottles of water are around 1,000 ptas, and drinks are 1,500-2,500ptas. Amnesia charges 2,000ptas for water, and the owners might well go straight to hell when they die.

5. The best way to get to all of these clubs is by taxi or Disco Bus [see *need to know,* below].

6. None of the clubs are exclusive at the front door. Instead, they have exclusive rooms within.

7. All of the clubs take at least Visa and MasterCard. They want your money, in any form.

8. Each club holds between 5,000 (Pacha) and 10,000 (Privilege) people at once! They all have smaller rooms tucked away here and there (especially Pacha), so don't get put off if you don't like the feel of the main room. A little exploring will do you nice.

9. The crowds are between 19 and 30 years old. Despite the fashion blitzkrieg here, there are also thousands of preps and dorks and family men running around this island. These folks are more likely to not make it past the bar scene at Sa Penya, though.

English magazines *Ministry* and *DJ Ibiza* will keep you current on the club scene.

Even on Sunday at 4pm, **Space** *(Playa d'en Bossa; 8-6am the next day— how wild is that?; www.space-ibiza.com, www.ibiza-online.com/privilege)* is still insane and happy from the night before. Whoop! This x-tensive club doesn't even open till the others close, so pretty much the whole island congregates here around 8am. A big open-air room with a semitranslucent tarp for the ceiling gives the whole club a sitting-under-a-shady-tree kind of feel. Space ties with Pacha as our favorite club. Best event: *Home,* starting Sunday at 8am.

good clean fun

Amensia and one or two other clubs host the infamous espuma (foam) parties that you've seen on E!, full of scantily clad hotties splashing around and getting it on in six feet of bubbly goodness. Well, color me soaking wet with soap in my eye! Who thought that being buried alive in foam was going to be a good time? Listen. If you're gonna do a foam party, do it right because—no joke—you'll wind up gagging, getting felt up (which might be what you're lookin' for), and slipping and cracking your head in six feet of the stuff. Being prepared, though, can make a foam party a lot more fun. The foam pros show up with backpacks containing goggles, bathing suits, beach sandals or old sneakers, and a towel. They gear up before the foam comes to town (it rains down like one of the Ten Plagues, like the fury of God himself, in terrifyingly enormous quantities), and make sure that they're a good 30 feet from the center of the dance floor.

boy meets girl

Yeah, more like boy meets boy on this island.

Or girl meets boy dressed like girl, or boy meets girl who looks like a boy dressing as a girl, or...whatever. Ibiza is not a place for the shy. The whole point of this island is that you can do whatever you want, baby. Do it loud, do it bright, do it in spandex, and do it topless—you can rest when you get home. When the summer rolls around, the local hippie types will often refer to "the colors returning," referring to the bright clothes, jewelry, and smiles that come to this island each summer. So make sure you play up the part! Believe us, you're gonna be meeting a lot of boys and girls, whether you like it or not. Of course it's easier to make small talk on the beach, but for folks of a more North American or English upbringing, it's hard to talk to someone about the weather when they're half-naked. The gay nightlife here is not a separate entity; it's all swirled together like Jell-O pudding. Our best advice on an island like this is to be safe with whomever you wind up with, because lord knows you'll have the opportunities here. The one thing we don't recommend is buying a lot of drinks for your catch-of-the-night. As the drinks regularly cost as much as US$15, you'll be broke real quick.

Privilege *(10 minutes north of San Rafael; 15 minutes by bus, 10 minutes by cab from Ibiza Town; www.ibiza-online.com/privilege; Closed Tue)* is midgets and strobe lights and 10-foot-drag queens on stilts, people shagging on stage (really), fire-eaters and an enormous swimming pool, and music, and lord knows what else running around all over the place. And you have to pay money for toilet paper! Now *that's* wild. Privilege tends to be more gay than other clubs, particularly for *Manumission* (Mondays), which is also its best event.

Open since 1975, **Pacha** (accent on the second syllable) *(On the Paseo Maritimo, a 20-minute walk southwest of Ibiza Town; www.pacha.com; Open year-round)* is the original Ibiza disco and is considered to be one of the finest nightclubs on planet Earth. Like Sean Connery or your favorite M.I.L.F., Pacha has aged with elegance over the years and hosts a more noticeable contingent of 30- and 40-year-olds (although they are very far from the majority). Pacha is *muy fashion,* as they say here, and the most international (read: not two-thirds English and German) of the clubs. The go-go girls are fly and the dance floor gets hot and grimy (the way you like it, baby), but the drag queens and freak-outs that keep the other clubs churning are usually not here (so don't dress out for Pacha, dress up). Famous people stop by all the time. Best nights: *Renaissance* on Wednesday and *Ministry* on Friday.

If Pacha is the Sean Connery of the clubs, **Amnesia** *(2 minutes south of San Rafael, 15 minutes by bus, 10 minutes by cab from Ibiza Town; www.amnesia.es)*, which was full of hippies and liquid acid in the early '80s, is more like Mick Jagger: past its prime and blissfully unaware of it. Yes, it's as big as an airplane hangar. Yes, it has a retractable roof. Yes it has trees and drag queens and several rooms and dancers and balconies, but big deal—where's the love? Best nights: *Godskitchen* on Tuesday and *Cream* on Thursday.

El Divino *(On the Paseo Maritimo at the Puerto de Ibiza Nueva, across the harbor from Ibiza Town; www.ibiza-online.com/eldevino)* is beautiful (almost opulent) and often semi-exclusive. You can get here by taking the boat that leaves every half hour from the Marina; you can't miss it, it's the one with the flashing lights and the big sign that says "El Divino." The best areas of the enormous and ornate deck on the water are usually roped off for the many VIPs that attend this club. One of the main events, *Miss MoneyPenny,* is basically the prom for a whole lot of English drag queens. *Submission,* on Saturdays, is one of the island's wildest events. Wear your latex and leather and bring a whip, because you're gonna git your freak on tonite! Be prepared for wild costumes, excessive groping, and shagging in the bathrooms. Straight out of a movie—or hell, if you're a Puritan.

gay scene

Gay life here is as prevalent as Britney Spears songs are on FM radio, so we'll just point out that a lot of mostly gay bars are on the Calle de la Virgén and Calle Mayor in Ibiza town. Check out the **Dôme Bar** *(Calle Alfonso XII 3; No phone; 8pm-3am daily; No credit cards)* for some the trendiest and queeniest times on the island. **Corazón Negro** *(Calle de la Virgén 23; No phone; 9pm-4am daily; No credit cards)* is one of dozens of bars in a row that appeal to a more-gay clientele, but, like we said, few things here are strictly one way or the other. One exception, though, is the 95 percent gay, 100 percent nude **Es Cavellet Beach** *(15-minute bus ride south of Ibiza Town, close to the southernmost tip of the island).* Expect bad techno music, a whole lot of drugs, and *a lot* of naked gay men (and some women). Straight girls sometimes stop by for a bit of sightseeing and weird fantasizing.

arts scene

▶▶VISUAL ARTS

Besides functioning as a bookstore, **Libro Azul** *(Village of Santa Gertrudis; Tel 971/197-454; 9:30am-2pm/5-10pm Mon-Fri, till 2pm Wed, Sat; www.libroazul.com; No credit cards)* hosts one or two readings and art expos every month. The art here leans toward the enormous, like sculptures as big as a fridge. The books (many of them secondhand) lean toward the New Age and are in German, English, Spanish, and Catalán.

Sala de Cultura "Sa Nostra" *(Aragó 11; 11am-1:30pm/6:30-9:30pm Mon-Fri, 6:30-9:30pm Sat)* is a quaint little place, with rotating exhibits every two weeks.

Galleria Can Daifa (*Santa Gertrudis; noon-3pm/6-11pm Wed-Fri, noon-8pm Sun*) is more traditional than its neighbor, Libro Azul, but is also run by Germans.

▶▶**PERFORMING ARTS**

All the performance on this island takes place in the clubs: live sex acts, striptease, midgets, stilt freaks, fire eaters, drag queens, go-go girls, aliens, latex—and then there's all the freaks who pay to get in. Just what goes on in the bathrooms during *Manumission* at **Privilege** [see *club scene*, above] is more "performance" than most people will need in a lifetime.

modification

There are dozens of tattoo shops on the island, but they all looked iffy and none of the locals could direct us to one that stood out above the rest. In general, we recommend NOT getting a tattoo while here. That Mitsubishi symbol probably seemed like a good idea at 9am on a Saturday morning when you were still going from the night before, but the significance will be hard to explain later on when you return home and are trying to get a job that does not involve checking IDs.

great outdoors

The Ibiza tourist office claims that this tiny island has something like 56 different beaches!! If you really want to explore them, head to the tourist office [see *need to know*, below] and pick up the free *IBIZA: Playas a la Carta*. This catalog describes each of the 56 beaches and tells you how to get there, too.

To get away from the tourist hype that envelopes the beaches closer to Ibiza Town, try **Las Salinas Beach** (*about seven miles south of Ibiza Town; follow the signs for the airport*), a full-on nudist beach that's less than 15 minutes from Ibiza Town by scooter. The attractive crowds here tend to be a little older (as in over 21), more local, and with more money. This beach is the height of cool in Ibiza.

You'll miss **Cala Xarraca Beach** unless you're looking for the restaurant of the same name. It makes sense, though, because the restaurant is the only thing here besides a few beautiful houses. The beach is more tiny pebbles and shells than sand. Surrounded by rocky cliffs, the water is very clear with tints of blue and doesn't get deep for quite a while. Topless, not a huge beach, but super-cool. Bring goggles and a snorkle for collecting stones in the water. Paddle boats are rented by the restaurant for 950ptas an hour.

The tiny island of **Formentera** is about 10 miles south of Ibiza and features dreamy and unspoilt stretches of white sand that seem to go on forever. Its three beaches, Illetes, Levant, and Es Pujols, all outdo anything on Ibiza; they're prettier and the crowds are cooler. Only 5,000 people are permanent residents on this island, and although that number jumps to 20,000 in the summer, this place is still more chill than a penguin on ice. Boats leave Ibiza Town at least once an hour from 7:45am till 10:30 at night. You'll get to Formentera in about 30

SCOOT OVER

The best way to get away from some of the hype is to rent a scooter. They're cheap and they're a total blast. Try and avoid the temptation to drive your scooters when really f#@!ed up—it's hard to look good when you're picking your teeth and kneecaps up off the pavement. We don't want to sound like Nancy Reagan, but there's really no need to be driving your scooters while blinded by whiskey. The cheapest places to rent are just a little out of the tourist section [see *need to know*, below]. A short cab ride or long walk will reward you with ample savings. A little scooter that maxes out at 40mph can traverse the entire island (east to west) in about 45 minutes. And even during the crowded tourist season, many of the roads are barely populated. Bring a picnic! Find a beach! The locals inland are not likely to speak English; for them, Spanish is a second language.

minutes and will pay about 2,500ptas each way. Contact **Baeleria Lines** *(Calle Aragón 71; Tel 971/310-711; 7:30am-10:30pm daily; V, MC)* for more info.

Ibiza has some of the best diving in the Mediterranean. Unlike you, some people come here specifically for the clear waters and the unique marine life and mysterious shipwrecks that can be found beneath the surface. For a beautiful adventure, contact **Ibiza Diving** *(Puerto Deportivo in the village of Santa Eulária; Tel 971/332-949; www.ibiza-diving.com; 9:30am-1pm/2-6pm daily; MC, V)* or **Figueral** *(Playa de Es Figueral, 45-minute bus ride north of Ibiza Town, on the northeastern coast; Tel 971/335-079; 9am-2pm/4-6:30pm daily; V, MC)*. Instructors at both places speak English. Or get reefed and hit the water slides! Just watch your language around the children. Of Ibiza's two water parks, the **Agualandia** *(near Cap Martinet)* and **Talamanca's Beach** *(15-minute bus ride northeast of Ibiza Town, way on the other side of the harbor; No phone; 10am-6pm daily; No credit cards)* has the better slides. **Aguamar** *(Playa d'en Bossa; Tel 971/396-790; 10:30am-6:30pm daily; No credit cards)*, however, is right next to **Space** [see *club scene*, above] and across the street from **Bora Bora** [see *bar scene*, above].

STUff

Between the influence of the hippies and the already-artistic leanings of the native Ibizan culture, there's plenty of artistry, beautiful pottery, clothes, and jewelry on the island. Make sure that you set aside some

fashion

Platforms, pigtails, and a Stetson will get you real far here. As will pushing yourself to the fashion limits: Dye your hair! Paint your face! Wear just a bathing suit top! The fashion here goes right with the free-wheeling and tripped-out attitude of the island. People might sneer at you if you're walking around in the middle of Iowa with a too-mini leather skirt and a quarter-ounce of glitter on your face, but people here will love it. Everyone wants you to look wild and feel good about it.

money for gifts! If you don't, an empty bottle of Jack Daniels, a mostly-smoked *purro,* and a sunburn are all you'll have to bring back to Mom.

▶▶**MARKET**

If you're asking directions, don't bother translating Hippy Market into *mercadillo de hippi* or something like that. The locals themselves call the fun outdoor markets by their English name, as well. The biggest and best of them takes place in **Es Canar** *(northeast of Santa Eulária, 20-minute bus ride from Ibiza Town; 9:30am-7pm Wed only Apr-Oct; A few of the booths accept credit cards, but don't rely on it here).* Unlike many other outdoor markets, this one has some truly beautiful stuff: great hats and sarongs for the beach, all sorts of handmade wind chimes, instruments, ceramics, fans, and also the requisite T-shirts, bowls, and watches. The market at Es Canar is right in the middle of a hippie village and has been running since the early '70s. Get here by bus (130ptas) or by scooter (30 minutes max). It's easy to spend a few hours among the nearly 400 booths here, so give yourself some time. The bright wooden carvings of Paulo Viheira capture the warm and creative essence of non-disco Ibiza. Although he does have his own studio in Santa Eulalia, you'll have an easier time tracking him down here. Prices range from about US$20 for something the size of a dinner plate to nearly US$300 for enormous carvings that you could windsurf on. Very recommended, and easy to find. Ask any one of the friendly workers at the market.

▶▶**DUDS**

The motto at **Holala!** *(Plaza de Mercado Viejo 12; Tel 971/316-537; 10am-1pm/3-11pm; MC, V)* is "unique clothing for unique people." In sticking to this creed, it has taken used clothing and brought it into the world of high fashion. Written up in nearly every fashion magazine you can think of (including *Elle, Vogue,* and *Cosmopolitan*), there's always something cooking at this trendsetting and semi-famous little shop. It sells everything from old kimonos and military surplus to modern clothing like dickies and Adidas. But bring your wallet—those old 501s don't sell for cheap.

Mapa Mundi *(Plaza de Vila 13, at the base of the Fortress; Tel 971/391-685; 11am-2pm/6pm-midnight Mon-Sat May-Oct; V, M, AE)* is all about the shoes, which are totally unique, not too costly, and make a great gift for Mom, Sis, girlfriends, or yourself. The dresses here are beautiful, but out of the range of most travelers (they begin at 14,000ptas). If Indiana Jones and Stevie Nicks opened a store together, it might look like this place. Beautiful, flowy dresses set in an Old-World setting with maps, old travel trunks, and beautiful tribal-looking jewelry.

▶▶**BOUND**

DK *(Ignacio Wallis 35; 971/ 191-339; 9am-2pm/5-8:30pm Mon-Fri, 9am-2pm Sat, Sun; V, MC)* is a pleasant little bookstore that sells good maps, magazines, stationary, school supplies, and, of course, books. The friendly staff doesn't speak English.

EaTS

Pills and thrills aside, try to avoid too many bellyaches by eating at least one decent meal a day. It will help you go the distance at night, too. It's sad to note that all-night food in Ibiza is only a little more common than an acoustic Happy Mondays song. Although some of the clubs sometimes have a guy in the parking lot vending pretzels and bottled water for a price that would usually get you a case of wine, you really can't count on it. Your best bet is to buy food at a local market (they're everywhere) during the day and stow it away in your hotel room for when you come back at night. Think smart and buy in advance: You'll want chips and bread to soak up some of the booze, probably some boxed juice and bottled water to un-parch your throat and calm your jittery body, and some oranges and bananas for the highs and lows (respectively). Good luck!

▶▶**CHEAP**

The legendary sandwiches of **Bar Costa** *(village of Santa Gertrudis; No phone; 7am-1:30am Wed-Mon, closed Tue; No credit cards)* are worthy of the rep. Plus it's cheap here; a big warm-bread cheese sandwich and a beer are only 450ptas. The mood here is super small-town mellow. Bring a book or newspaper and—if you're lucky—you'll get to talk with the locals about politics, the weather, or the good old days.

El Jardin Bar y Taverna *(Calle Mayor 30-73-28; 10am-midnight Mon-Sat, till 5pm Sun; No credit cards)* is a pleasant little restaurant tucked away within the confines of the D'Alt Villa. Beautiful, calm, and shady, with a whole lot of beautiful purple bougainvillea plants, island music, and umbrellas in your drinks. The atmosphere and desserts are better than the entrees, which run from 500ptas for a salad to 1,375ptas for a steak. Definitely not a hot spot, but that's why we recommend it. Best as a place to sit and have a drink and some ice cream after exploring the old city.

It's not like you need a travel guide to find **Mr. Hot Dog** *(at the Marina; 9:30am-4:30am daily; No credit cards)*, but we've written it up so that you know that you're getting a fair price and good food here. Mr.

Hot Dog will serve you up a big-ass yummy cheeseburger for 450ptas. The French bread and chicken breast is also recommended. Their terrace seating is right in the middle of it all, providing you with some great people-watching.

▶▶**DO-ABLE**

Café d'Art *(Cayetano Soler 9; Tel 971/302-972; 10am-9pm Mon-Sat; V, MC)* has nothing to do with art, but this small old country store sells all kinds of semi-gourmet meats, cheeses, fresh bread, wine, and ready-made tapas. Perfect stuff for a picnic at a quiet beach of your choice, or you can sit outside at the base of the old city and eat at one of the cafe tables.

Bar de Pintxos *(Conde de Rosellon 1; No phone; 11:30am-3:30pm/8pm-2:30am daily; No credit cards)* is a small outdoor cafe away from the hoopla in the harbor, right next to the old city. Pleasant staff and classic Basque tapas. 200ptas for pinchos frios (small uncooked things like salmon on yummy bread) and 800ptas for calamari.

▶▶**SPLURGE**

Se Caldera *(Obispo Padre Huix 19; Tel 971/306-416; 1-4pm/8pm-midnight Sun-Fri, 8pm-midnight Sat; Menu del día 1,800ptas, 2,800-6,400ptas per entree, bottles of wine 1,200-3,800ptas; V, MC, AE)* is the restaurant of choice for locals (even other restaurant owners) of Ibiza Town. Run by the same native Ibizenco couple for 15 years now: The husband cooks, the wife runs the show. All the food is "down-home," specializing in fresher-than-fresh fish. The *menu del día* costs a whopping 1,800ptas, but includes spectacular main dishes like fresh salmon. Located a little away from the port (about a 10-minute walk), so you won't see the sunset or hear the tide with your meal, but you will be treated right and get a great look at the locals in action.

El Faro *(Plaza Sa Riba 1; Tel 971/313-233; noon-3am daily May-Oct; V, AE, M)* is very touristy, very ritzy. Kings, presidents, rock 'n' roll stars, and famous athletes have been eating here regularly for 20 years. Choose from the living fish and lobsters for your dinner. Like Se Caldera, you can pay up to 6,000ptas for paella here, but unlike Se Caldera, the atmosphere here is downright swank. The restaurant is right in front of the water and a little distance from the Sa Penya hoopla a few blocks down. Reservations should be made. The owner's name is Mercedes, which totally makes sense.

crashing

The thing about Ibiza is that there's not a lot of people who are just "passing through": This is their destination. People come to this island for a wild vacation and expect to pay for it. But the prices aren't too, too crazy—it's simply finding a room here that's a big pain. Save yourself a whole lot of headaches by making a reservation for a room before you arrive on the island. A little planning ahead will get you a sweet little room at Vara de Rey or something with a view in Hotel Montesol. For the most up-to-date list of vacancies, check out ***www.ibiza-hotel.com.***

You're a serious addict if you're wasting your time, money, and mind in front of a computer screen in Ibiza when you could be wasting those same things on the beach or at a club. If you need that fix, though, log on at **Centro Internet Eivissa** *(Avenida Ignacio Wallis 39 Bajos; Tel 971/318-161;* www.compre sarial.com/cie; *10am-11pm Mon-Sat, 5-11pm Sun; No credit cards).* Along with 14 PCs, scanners and color printers are also available if you need them, you geek.

▶▶CHEAP

Pension La Peña *(Calle de la Virgén, 76; Tel 971/190-240; 1,500-2,400ptas single, 2,500-3,500ptas double; No credit cards)* has, as far as we can tell, the cheapest rooms in Ibiza Town. The common bathrooms are of questionable character, but many of the rooms (though small and bare) have a beautiful view of the sea. The 10 doubles and three single rooms are rented out almost exclusively to gay guys who want to be near the action that makes the Calle de la Virgén famous.

Another fairly reasonable option is **Sol y Briso** *(Avingunda B.V. 15; Tel 971/310-818; 3,500-5,000ptas double; No credit cards).*

▶▶DO-ABLE

Hostal Residencia Parque *(Calle Vicente Cuervo 3, just south of Paseo Vara de Rey; Tel 971/301-358; 4,000ptas single with shared bathroom, 11,000ptas triple with private bath; V, MC)* has 28 rooms, many with a pleasant view of the park and plaza below. Clean common bath for the singles. Most boarders at this hostel are Spanish. The stately common room has a TV, but there are better places on Ibiza to meet people than in a musty old TV room!

Pray that you can get a room at **Vara de Rey** *(Paseo de Vara de Rey 7; Tel 971/301-376; 5,000ptas single, 8,000ptas double in peak season; V, MC).* The young couple that runs this hostel is beautiful to look at and to talk with. Their artist's touch makes every room a calm and serene haven from Ibiza's madness. Call ahead; many guests have been returning for years. Already a great place to make new friends, since there are only 10 rooms here, things are only going to get more irie when the rooftop terrace is completed in the summer of 2000. Shared bathrooms only, but clean. Great, great people and beautifully painted rooms.

Hotel Montesol *(northeastern end of Paseo de Vara de Rey 2; Tel 971/310-161; 8,100-15,250ptas single/double, 6,500-10,000ptas for the few single/doubles that share bathrooms; V)* has been the hotel in Ibiza Town since 1934. Private baths, phones, air conditioning, and TVs make this place worth the extra bucks. All rooms have great views (of the harbor, old city, or quaint Paseo de Vara de Rey). Big rooms and spacious closets, plus bathtubs! The sophisticated bar here is more fashionable in the off-season.

▶▶**SPLURGE**

Tagomago Aparthotel (*Paseo Maritimo, opposite side of the harbor from Sa Penya, a 5-minute cab ride from there; Tel 971/316-550; www.ibiza-hotel.com/tagomago; 12,000-21,000ptas single/double in June, 21,000-39,000ptas last week of July through Aug; V, MC, AE, Eurocard*) gets jammed with Spanish coeds who have Come to Party. Bright modern rooms with a full kitchen (save cash by cooking!), living room, balcony (view of harbor), air, and TV. If you're smooth, you'll be able to get extra folks on the floor—the staff doesn't really pay attention to who's coming and going. Also, the single beds are big, and can comfortably fit two people. Hotel has cafeteria/bar, currency exchange, and will help you to rent cars and bikes. Just a 1-minute walk to **Pacha** and five to **El Divino.**

need to know

Currency Exchange As always, you will get the best exchange rate at an ATM. Although there aren't many of them right in **Sa Penya,** there are several scattered all around the **Paseo de Vara de Rey** (5-minute walk), particularly at the southwestern end.

Tourist Info Tourist office (*Vara de Rey 13; Tel 971/30-19-00; 9am-1pm/5-8pm Mon-Fri, 10:30am-1:30pm Sat*). A second, smaller tourist office is located right across from where the boats let you off. They won't make hotel reservations for you—like we told you, call hotels in advance.

Public Transportation The only public transportation is the buses. They leave Ibiza Town from the **Bus Stop Bar** (*Isidoro Macabich; No phone; 9am-11pm daily; 250ptas or less per fare; No credit cards*). The service here is slower than Nyquil. Sometimes the woman behind the counter will just close up shop for 20 minutes so she can yap with her friend behind the bar, regardless of the number of people in line. You can always buy a ticket from the actual bus driver, which is recommended, since there are four different bus companies in Ibiza, and it's easy to get confused. Getting back into Ibiza Town is always easy because the buses are the biggest, loudest things to happen to the little villages and beaches to which they travel. Missing one would be like missing a marching band in your backyard.

At night, it's all about the **Disco Bus.** The fare is around 300ptas, and the destinations are every major club and hotel on the island. The Disco Bus hits each location once per hour and runs (like everything else) mid-May through end of September. See ***www.ibizanight.com*** to learn more about the Disco Bus and a whole bunch of other club-related info.

Cabs are available and recommended for club-hopping if you have the extra cash to spare (*Tel 971/307-000*). They're more expensive than they should be, but they're not ripping you off any worse than anyone else on the island. As in the rest of Spain, 100ptas or so is plenty for a tip. Like most of the natives here, the cabbies are mellow and safe people.

American Express AMEX is represented by **Viajes Ibiza Sa** *(Calle Vicente Cuervo 9; Tel 971/311-111; 9am-1:30pm/4:30-8pm Mon-Fri, 9am-1:30pm Sat).*

Health/Emergency Emergencies: *092.* Red Cross 24-hour ambulance service: *Tel 971/390-303.*

Pharmacies The pharmacy on Paseo de Vara de Rey has condoms (preservativos) *(9am-1:30pm/5-9pm Mon-Sat, 5-9pm Sun).* The one in D'Alt Villa is open 24 hours for you and your horny/nauseous/sunburned friends.

Telephone City code: *971;* operator: *1003;* international operator: *1005.* Note that recent changes in Spain's phone system now require that all local calls be dialed with the 971 prefix.

Airport The **airport** *(Tel 971/809-000)* is located southwest of Ibiza Town, just above the southern coast. Buses leaving from the airport will bring you to the Bus Stop Bar in about 15 minutes. They leave by the hour 7:30am-10:30pm and cost 135ptas. **Iberia** *(Passeig de Vara de Rey 15971; Tel 971/302-580)* is the pretty much the only airline that can get you directly to the island.

Boats Trasmediterránea *(Andenes de Puerto Estación Maritimo; Tel 971/312-104; V, MC, AE)* is the main man. Boats from Barcelona, Valencia, and Palma de Mallorca leave all day long. If you arrive by boat, you'll be dropped off right in the middle of it all.

Bike & Moped Rental Valentín Car/Bike *(Avenida Bmé. Vte. Ramón 19; Tel 971/310-822; 8:30am-2pm/3:30-8pm Mon-Fri, 5:30-8pm Sat; 1,500-5,000ptas, 5,000ptas deposit if paying cash; you pay gas; V, MC)* allows you to rent by the day, and has everything from old Vespas to spanking-new 250cc Yamahas. It'll also rent you a good old-fashioned bicycle. **Bravo Rent a Car** *(Avenida de Santa Eulalia; Tel 971/313-901; 8:30am-1:30pm/4-8:30pm daily; 3,500-11,750ptas, 3,000ptas deposit, you pay gas; V, MC, AE)* brings in new cars and bikes each year. In both places, helmets are required for anything bigger than 50cc.

palma

If you want a very, very tourist-friendly experience, then Palma is a good place to start. The population swells with visitors over the summer months, mainly from European countries like Germany, England, and France, but you can also find some Americans and Aussies if you look hard enough. There's plenty of nightlife (although it pales in comparison to what you'll find in club capital Ibiza, just an island-hopper south), as well as good shopping, a degree of history, and some fine beaches. Everyone speaks English—many of the people who run the hostels and other tourist-centric businesses hail from the UK or other English-speaking nations—so you won't have any problems communicating at all. In all of Mallorca, Catalán is the official language, but everyone knows Spanish, too. However, you may have better luck practicing your German.

Palma is the largest city on Mallorca—indeed, in the Balearics—and, if you can overlook the high-rise horror of its bay, it's actually kind of pretty. The city is defined by the sea: For many years Palma was a major shipping port, although now it mostly just ships in tourists, gets some of their money, and ships 'em back home. The architecture in the old quarter of town makes it easy to imagine that you're Blackbeard the pirate, hobbling around on your wooden leg and commenting to the parrot on your shoulder about how the closed-in streets feel like a cramped Greenwich Village apartment, but the shade sure is a great break from the afternoon sun. There's a mix of old, worn-down buildings with rounded edges and plenty of balcony space, and modern, somewhat boring, cheesy hotels. You can also find narrow, winding streets to get lost in, if that's your thing, but it's a small town, so don't expect to be lost for long.

The people of Palma are for the most part a sophisticated lot. They come from all over the world and are at home with people from other countries. If anything, they're a little jaded, less impressed with foreigners than people in other parts of Spain. The positive side of this is that there's a lively art and fashion scene in Palma that's worth checking out.

The nightlife in town ranges from bar-hopping in the old quarter to clubbing out in the Gomila, way out on the western side of the harbor. Both have a certain appeal, but if you're in Palma during the off-season (September through May), you'll probably want to stick to the bars downtown. You can find some decent live offerings, ranging from jazz to flamenco to down-home Spanish rock and roll. There are also some good places to enjoy tapas and suck down a beer, but in all honesty, if it's clubs you want, you should just go to party-mad Ibiza. If you go there before Palma, you'll just be disappointed by the clubs here, and if you go there before Ibiza, you'll just wonder why you wasted your time. However, if you're easing into the whole "traveling in foreign countries" thing, starting at the shallow end of the pool isn't a bad idea. With English spoken everywhere and gaggles of tourists on package tours, it doesn't get too much shallower than Palma.

The package deals, which come complete with a fancy hotel in a prime location near the beach, are huge here. These can be on the pricey side, but will offer a full set of luxuries including great rooms, nice beaches, and food for one big price. The best way to get hooked up with one of these deals is to talk to a travel agent either back home or on the mainland of Spain. If you don't mind a serious Club Med vibe, it isn't a bad way to unwind—with all your needs taken care of from an airport shuttle to someone cleaning your room—but they're a little out of the typical twentysomething's price range.

As you might expect, the youth culture in Palma is really a dabbling of the moneyed youth from around the world. As such, you can expect people to be savvy about the newest trends in fashion and music on the Continent and in the States, but don't expect too much depth. Drugs and sex don't define the moment like they do in Ibiza, but you can get both if you look hard enough.

neighborhoods

The main hangout area is the **Plaça de la Reina,** a smallish little plaza just northeast of the port where you can chill and stare at the little fountain in the middle with a drink. The Plaça de la Reina is conveniently located in the old quarter of town, just around the corner from the scene. You can also meet up at the **Plaça del Rei Joan Carles 1,** just north of Plaça de la Reina at the end of **Passeig D'es Born,** which has a great fountain and some restaurants with local specialties. As the night progresses, you might be able to check out some spontaneous live performances of Spanish drum-and-flute hippie music at the **Plaça Llotja,** located just off the corner of **Avinguda Gabriel Roca** and **Avinguda D'Antoni Maura.** Some of the cooler outdoor restaurants and bars are on this plaza as well.

only here

Only in Palma will you find more tourists per square inch than Spaniards. The feel is so far from authentic that they might as well just have converted the entire island to a big Club Med. Sometimes it feels like they have. Recently, the government of Palma has wised up and is now trying to curb some of the detrimental effects of tourism, blocking off a portion of the island to development, and encouraging a more eco-friendly tourist industry. However, since the economy of the island of Mallorca is based on fleecing foreign people, old habits will die hard.

One great thing about seeing tourists everywhere you look is that you don't have to travel throughout Europe to meet people from different countries. For all the Brits, Germans, French, Americans, and rich Spanish people you can take, just go to Palma.

The winding streets of the old city make car and bus travel difficult, so the best way to get around Palma is by foot. As it is, everything is walkable. If you need to get to the Gomila, just hop in a cab; to get to the beaches, you can take the local buses.

bar, club, and live music scene

The nightlife in Palma can be hopping enough, especially if you're used to those cold northern nights standing by the keg in an empty field waiting for the popular girls to give you the time of day. You can find some decent options for drinking, and if you aren't overly discerning, some fine music as well. While the crowd can be a little weak, sometimes reminding you of a frat party with nicer clothes, you can have a good time if you lose yourself in the moment. Once again, Palma is pretty much dominated by the tourist vibe, so don't bother searching around for the "authentic" place. The touristy places here *are* the authentic joints. You'll also pay more for a drink in Palma than on the mainland, as the constant influx of capital keeps the whole island flush. In general, people dress nicely to go out in this town, so leave the flannel from your grunge days at home.

Café Barcelona *(Calle Dels Apuntadores 5; Tel 971/713-557; 9pm-4am daily; 500ptas beer, 900ptas mixed drinks; usually no cover, but 500-1,500ptas for big names; MC, V)* is a small but popular place a 2-minute walk from the Plaça de la Reina. Go up the stairs and peer through the smoke and dim lighting and you'll find short red-cushioned chairs and a little bar, as well as jazz photos hanging on the peach walls. Opened in 1966, this place claims to be the oldest bar playing live music in Mallorca. The crowd is, as expected, very touristy. There's live music every night of the year, from jazz and blues, which are the staples, to the occasional flamenco artist and even Latin sounds. The crowd mainly comes to listen, so don't go if you're too drunk to keep your mouth shut. Café Barcelona begins to crowd up around 11pm and will stay open past 4am if there's a good jam going. Say hi to David, the friendly English-speaking bartender who has also been doing all the bookings for the last few years.

Walk down Apuntadores, take a right on San Joan and a quick right onto Ma Del Moro and you'll find **Blues Ville** *(Calle Ma des Moro 3; No phone; 10:30pm-4am; 400-500ptas beer, 800-1,000ptas mixed drinks; No credit cards)*, the other good place in town to listen to live music. You'll hear blues, rock, funk, and Latin. With only two somewhat small rooms with low tables, the crowd of locals and tourists (aged 25 to 40) gets pretty thick around show time, usually 12:30am. Wood is the primary element of the decor, but they have some interesting Americana decorations, like vintage ads for Coca-Cola from when there was still some coca in the cola. Bands do their thing on a very small stage in the back room.

boy meets girl

"I'm from America, how about you?"

"Me too. I live in Nebraska."

"Wow, that's too cool. I live in Pennsylvania. Do you go to college?"

"Yeah, at the University of Michigan. How about you?"

"I go to Penn State."

"Wow, that's great."

You get the picture. Since the crowd is all tourists, all the time, people are pretty much out for some booty. What the girl/boyfriend back home doesn't know can't hurt, right?

Because of the lovefest, the hostels can turn into something of a college-dorm environment. So if you plan on getting any sleep, you need to either pick a roommate who's a monk or get a single. And even then, you know, the walls ain't all that thick in Palma....Fortunately, the locals and guests of Palma don't have any weird hang-ups about sexuality, so the cruising scene is a free-for-all. When it's vacation time, people just don't seem to have the same need to surround themselves with barriers.

Just remember to be safe; you don't want to bring any gifts that you didn't pay for back to the main squeeze at home. The word for condom in Spanish is *preservativo.*

Abaco *(San Juan 1; Tel 971/714-939; 9pm-3am daily; Cover 800ptas and up; AE, MC, V)* is an odd bar, and probably worth a visit, if only for one drink. The interior is all decked out with fruit, flowers, and pseudo-historical artifacts like fake broken Greek pottery and faux medieval Spanish swords.

At the **Atlantico** *(Sant Feliu s/n; Tel 971/728-986; 9pm-3am daily; Cover 800ptas and up; MC, V)*, they have fun concocting all kinds of crazy booze and juice combinations. If you want to get looped up real fast, go ahead and try a couple. The crowd is mixed but, again, is heavily international.

If you feel the need to dance and just can't get to Ibiza soon enough, then you can visit the clubs in the Gomila neighborhood, at the intersection of Plaça Gomila and Avinguda Joan Miro. You probably just want to take a cab there, since you'll be decked out in your tightest pants, regardless of your gender, to blend in with the other nighthawks. You'll also be going late unless you want to be hanging around with Dieter and the other Germans who aren't cool enough to know that nobody gets to clubs before midnight.

Two places to try are **El Patio y Olas** *(Schembri 3; Tel 971/402-714; midnight-past 5am; Cover varies by season; No credit cards)*, which is busy and loud, and **Pacha** *(Passeig Maritimo 42; Tel 971/737-788; midnight-5am; Cover 2,500ptas and up; V, MC)*, which is more fun. Located throughout Spain, Pacha clubs are popular for good reason: they consistently deliver lively ambience and good times. The music is of the disco and techno variety.

arts scene

Palma's huge community of artists keeps almost 20 fully functional art galleries going. The exhibitions run the gamut from good to bad, modern to traditional, homegrown to foreign. If you want to spend some time shopping for great art, or just checking out local trends, you'll have ample opportunity. Prices vary, but don't expect to get away with a steal. These folks are used to tourists who are willing to spend a few extra bucks. You can get more information on all of the galleries at the tourist office [see *need to know,* below]

For a quick tour of two very good galleries, walk over to Can Veri, where you'll find the **Centre Cultural Contemporani Pelaires** *(Via Veri 3; Tel 971/720-418; 10am-1:30pm/5-8:30pm Mon-Fri)*, where you can check out impressive paintings from Spain and around the world in their two showrooms. Although there's an eclectic range of artists, don't expect to find the avant-garde. This gallery works with tried and true artists who are more recognized.

The two **Joan Guaita** *(Calle Veri 10; Tel 971/715-989; 10:30am-1:30pm/5-8:30pm Mon-Fri)* galleries, one dedicated to sculpture and the other to different media, are a fun addition to a Centre Cultural Contemporani Pelaires visit. While the work here can be challenging, there's still fun to be had in appreciating the various methods and means to the madness. Check it out and see if you can piece together what the artists are trying to say.

Located right in the old quarter, the **Casal Solleric** *(Passeig d'es Born 27; Tel 971/722-092; 10:30am-1:45pm/5-8:30pm Tue-Sat, mornings only Sun)* has a big exhibition area that houses photography, old paintings, and sculpture. The great old building, finished in 1775, has an impressive interior, as well as a bookstore and cafe for your enjoyment. Relax on a bench in the courtyard and dream about spending the rest of your life contemplating cool art on a Mediterranean island.

CULTUrE ZOO

There are some very interesting cultural sights to see in Palma, especially the cathedral and museum, artist Joan Miró's old house, and a great Gothic castle looking out over the bay. These are the crème de la crème, and you'll want to stick with them unless you have a particular love of old buildings, in which case the tourist office can fill you in with an extensive list of places to visit.

Catedral/Museu *(Mirador 7; Tel 971/714-063; 10am-3pm Mon-Fri, 10am-2pm Sat Nov-Mar, 10am-6pm Mon-Fri, 10am-2pm Sat Apr-Oct; free):* Palma's cathedral, called *La Seu* in Catalán, is constructed in the Gothic style, with tremendous columns that stretch like trees up to the vaulted, sky-like ceiling above. Antoni Gaudí helped renovate some of the interior at the beginning of the 20th century. In the museum, you'll find paintings and artifacts from the Middle Ages.

Fundació Pilar i Joan Miró *(Joan de Saridakis 29; Tel 971/701-420; Bus 3, 21, 22; 10am-7pm Tues-Sat; 10am-5pm Sun; 700ptas):* If you're a fan of modern artist Miró, this old house where he once lived is worth a visit. You can peruse his paintings, drawings, and sculpture, as well as get a feel for the living space of this great artist.

Castell de Bellver *(Parque de Bellver; Tel 971/730-657; Bus 3, 21, 22; 8am-7pm daily Oct-Mar, 8am-8pm daily Apr-Sep; 260 ptas):* The circular shape of this castle, built at the beginning of the 14th century, makes it special among Gothic structures. The museum inside houses a bunch of sculpture. The castle offers an excellent view of Palma and the harbor, making a great destination at the end of a nice long walk around the bay.

modIfICATIOn

Drunken sailors probably started getting tattoos in Palma centuries ago, long before it became a Gen X fad. Well-known among locals who know about such things, **Tatoo** *(Joan Miró 62; Tel 971/450-519; 10am-1:30pm/4-7pm; 6,000ptas and up)* is the best place to join in this hallowed tradition.

CITY SPOrTS

Sport in Palma means hanging on the beach; the most exercise you'll get is turning over on your towel. Actually, you'd have to be crazy *not* to spend as much time as possible on the beautiful beaches, perfect for soaking in the hot sun, as well as warm water. Keep in mind though that during peak season, you're going to have a tough time finding uncrowded beaches anywhere. The water's warmest in July and August, but the beaches are topless all year round.

If you're feeling antsy and you need to stretch your legs, the best place to run to is the **Castell del Bellver** [see *culture zoo,* above]. It's far enough away from the congested city center that at least you'll be breathing some fresh air.

Centrally located and not too crowded, **Ciudad Jardin** is a decent beach if you don't feel like straying too far. Take Bus 15 to find it. Located further from the city, **Illetas** attracts fewer people. Take either Bus 20, 21, or 22. English folks seem to favor **Cala Mayor.** Hop on Bus 21 or 22 to get there. It's one of the best beaches close to the heart of town. Allow for a 30-minute bus ride to reach it, though. The swimming at Palma's beaches is best from June to October. Some Scandinavians or Germans jump into the water in other months, but chances are that you'll find it too cold. There are lots of hotels, fast food joints, and places dispensing beer or wine nearby, and you can rent lounge chairs or umbrellas from the beachside kiosks.

A big beach that gets very, very crowded during peak season and some-times off-peak as well, **Playa El Arenal** (sometimes called Playa Palma) will remain popular as long as watching hundreds of prone, sunburning, topless English lasses is sufficient motivation to get to a beach. Bus 15 or 26 will get you there; it will take about 45 minutes from the center of Palma. This beach has the longest stretch of golden sand on the island, and it's flanked by a bevy of hotels, restaurants, and shops. This is the best-equipped beach on Palma, offering all sorts of water sports, fast food eateries, beer, wine, beach umbrellas, towels—whatever you need or forgot to bring with you. Not too far from Arenal, **Con Pastilla** is another great beach, with fine sand and great water. Take Bus 15, 23, or 26.

If you're interested in getting off the beach and doing some bowling, hit **Inter Bowling** *(Joan Miró 17; Tel 971/738-145; 10am-1:30pm/4-9pm, although hours vary; 550 ptas),* which offers eight alleys of fun.

If you feel like you've "done" Palma and are tired of the beach, what are your options? One is to stretch your legs on a mountain trail out-side the city. There are many possibilities for hiking on the island, but of course you'll have to leave Palma to enjoy them. The low mountain range of Sierra del Tramuntana has some great trails, which are clearly marked on the detailed maps in *20 Hiking Excursions on the Island of Majorca.* Pick it up at the tourist office. All you have to do is tear your-self away from the beach and go for it. If you want more specific infor-mation, you can also call the folks at **Grup Excursionista de Mallorca** *(Can Cavalleria 17; Tel 971/711-314),* the headquarters of the Majorcan Hiking Association.

Another day-trip option is to head for the hamlet of **Valldemossa,** where Chopin and George Sand hung out for one winter. Sprawled along the slope of the Sierra de Tramontana, the village lies to the west of Palma.

During the day, buses leaving from Calle Arxiduc Salvador in Palma reach Valldemossa in about half an hour. The cost is 200ptas each way. For schedules, call 971/490-680.

EATS

You can get all kinds of cuisine in Palma, everything from basic Spanish tapas to very, very expensive sit-down dinners. If you just want to wander around and see what catches your fancy, go to side street Carrer dels Apuntadors in the old quarter, where you'll find the best selection.

A 3-minute walk east of Plaza del Rey Juan Carlos, **Hamburgueseria Alaska** (*Plaça de Mercat; No phone; 10:30am-midnight; 600ptas food and beer; No credit cards*), grills up the rolls real nice, and offer quick service. You can get a real cheap burger, fries, sandwiches, ice cream, and beer. It's an outdoor stand that has some bar stool–style seating as well as a few tables. It's also one of the few places in Palma where you almost feel like you're eating with genuine locals. Almost.

A 3-minute walk south of the Plaça Espanya, **Restaurante del Mercado de El Olivar** (*Plaça de El Olivar; Tel 971/721-162; lunch only 1-3:30pm Mon-Sat; 1,200ptas; No credit cards*) is fantastic, with food that's fresh as you can get and so, so good. The cramped atmosphere only adds to the charm. The restaurant is located within the outdoor food market at Mercado de El Olivar, a good spot to pick up some picnic fixings before you hit the beach.

Located right in the old quarter of town, **Café Brondo** (*Calle Brondo 5; Tel 971/715-567; noon-5pm/8pm-midnight Mon-Sat, closed holidays; 2,000ptas and up; AE, MC, V*) is a short walk to everything. It's a great place to visit, with a very cool, laid-back vibe; the chill servers will be glad to struggle over the menu in your bad Spanish or their bad English. Café Brondo's specialty is a big, delicious salad, but its menu also includes lots of great meat and fish dishes. The interior is wood and mirrors, with dining upstairs if you want to be cool and hang with the locals or chat it up with the bartender. The downstairs offers privacy and quiet.

crashing

If you're visiting during the summer months, you'll need to plan in advance. The hostels that take reservations book up real fast. Those that don't—or do sporadically, which is usually the case—fill up by noon.

WIRED

Palma is home to a great Internet joint: **Cyber Central** (*Calle Soledad 4, basement; Tel 971/712-927; 100ptas per 6 minutes; MC, V*), which offers free coffee.

TALK THE TALK

So you think you know the language, eh? Sure Spanish will help, but if you'd really like to impress the Palma locals, try learning a few of these useful Mallorquin words. What's Mallorquin, you ask? It's a nuanced variation of Spanish that incorporates aspects of French. It may be similar to Español (some of the words are exactly the same), but it is *not* a dialect, at least according to those who speak it.

The Basics

Yes	*si*
no	*no*
please	*per favor*
thank you	*gracies*
hello	*hola*
goodbye	*adeu*
good morning	*bon dia*
good afternoon	*bona tarda*
goodnight	*bona nit*
excuse me	*perdoni*
you're welcome	*de res*
do you speak..?	*parla ..?*
english	*angles*
I don't understand	*no ho entenc*
how much?	*quant es?*
today	*avui*
tomorrow	*dema*

Because Palma is such an amazingly popular place for tourists to go, it can be a real headache finding a place to sleep. The two most popular *hostales* in town are located right in the heart of things on Carrer dels Apuntadors, just down from the Plaça de la Reina.

Cheap and good, **Hostal Apuntadores** *(Calle Apuntadores 8; Tel 971/713-491; apuntadores@ctv.es; 2,600ptas single w/o bath; 4,800ptas double with shower; No credit cards)* attracts an international crowd of travelers that tilts heavily toward backpacker-types. The staff all speak English—they might not even speak any Spanish. The *hostal* has a laid-back, folksy lounge where people can be found at all hours, chewing the fat or munching on some of the American-type snacks available (burgers, sandwiches, etc.). You can also get breakfast whenever they're serving food, usually from 8am to 9pm. The beds are comfortable, and the owners make an effort to renovate something every year, so the place is in pretty good shape. There's a fantastic view of the water and the old part of town

Crashing

hotel	*hotel*
Bed and breakfast	*llit i berenar*
single room	*habitacio senzilla*
double room	*habitacio doble*
one person	*una persona*
one night	*una nit*
reservation	*reservas*
bath	*bany*
shower	*dutxa*
toilet	*toaleta*

Eats & Drinks

pub/bar	*celler*
beer	*cervesa*
wine	*vi*
cafe	*cafe*
breakfast	*berenar*
lunch	*dinar*
dinner	*sopar*
waiter	*cambrer*
waitress	*cambrera*
dessert	*postres*
bill	*cuenta*
water	*aigua*
coffee	*cafe*

from the terrace up top. Unfortunately, due to a conga line that formed on the precipice a few years ago, the terrace is only open till 10pm.

The **Hostal Ritzi** *(Calle Apuntadores 6; Tel 971/714-610; 3,500ptas single w/o bath; 5,500ptas double with shower; No credit cards)* is right next door. The English-speaking staff is friendly, and the atmosphere is jovial and relaxed. The front door locks at 10pm, but you'll have a key, so you don't have to worry about any weird curfew. The crowd is young and international, with backpackers and the rest of us. You'll get some street noise, but that's the price you pay for sleeping in the middle of the fun.

Located on a quiet street in the heart of the old city, the slightly more expensive **Hostal Brondo** *(Calle Brondo s/n; Tel 971/719-043 or 626/952-154; 3,500ptas single w/o bath; 6,000ptas double with shower; No credit cards)* caters mostly to young, 20-30-year-olds who stay for at least a few days. You can get a good night's sleep in one of the simple, clean rooms. You can also rent the apartment on the top level, which can sleep up to five people and includes a kitchen and a TV lounge with a satellite dish. Prices for the apartment range from 8,000ptas to 15,000ptas per night, depending on how many people are in your group.

need To KNOW

Currency Exchange There are exchange shops all over town, but you're better off avoiding them. You'll get a much better rate at the ATM or one of the numerous banks. **Banco Central Hispano** *(Passeig Bom 17; Tel 971/725-146)* is one of the most centrally located banks and has ATMs.

Tourist Information The **tourist office** *(Plaça de la Reina 2; Tel 971/720-251; 9am-1pm/5-8pm Mon-Fri, till 1pm Sat)* is really easy to find. The staff knows a little English, and there are tons of maps and good info.

Public Transportation Palma has a decent public transportation system, but you generally won't need to use it. The few times you need to go somewhere far away, it's easiest to use a taxi. The exception to this rule is getting to the beaches, when the buses are indispensable. Beach-bound buses leave from the Plaza La Reina along Paseo des Born, and fare to the beach will usually run you around 300ptas.

Health and Emergency Emergency: *112;* Police: Tel 971/281-600.

Pharmacies Pharmacies are located all over town and can be identified by a **green cross.** One of the most central pharmacies is **Pharmacy Castaner***(Plaza del Rey Juan Carlos; Tel 971/711-534).*

Airport The **Aeropuerto Son San Juan** *(Tel 971/264-162)* is located about 6 kilometers (about 3 1/2 miles) from town. You can get into the city either by taxi or by taking one of the minivans that drive you to the Plaça de España.

Trains No one takes the dinky, unreliable train that runs between Palma and the town of Inca every hour or so. If you insist, the station is at the Plaça de España.

Bus Lines Out of the City The buses out to the rest of the island are all privatized, with a bunch of different companies that keep sporadic and seasonal schedules. They run out of a station at the Plaça de España. To get a timetable that means something, you'll have to go to the station.

Boat You can get to Palma on the **Trasmediterranea** *(Tel 902/454-645; www.trasmediterranea.es)* or the **Buquebus** *(Estacion Maritima 3, Muelle de Paraires; Tel 902/414-242)* for around the same price. The schedules are always changing, so it's best to call ahead to find out what the most current iteration is.

Bike Rental Check out **Bimont** *(Plaça Progreso 19; Tel 971/731-866; 10am-1pm/4-8pm daily; 1,500ptas for a whole day; No credit cards).* The best place to go biking is along the long and winding El Paseo Marítimo bordering the sea. It has a lane for bikers.

Postal The main office is **Correos y Telegrafos** *(Constitucio 6; Tel 902/197-197; 9am-1:30pm Mon-Fri).*

Internet See *wired,* above.

COSTA DEL SOL

COSTA DEL SOL

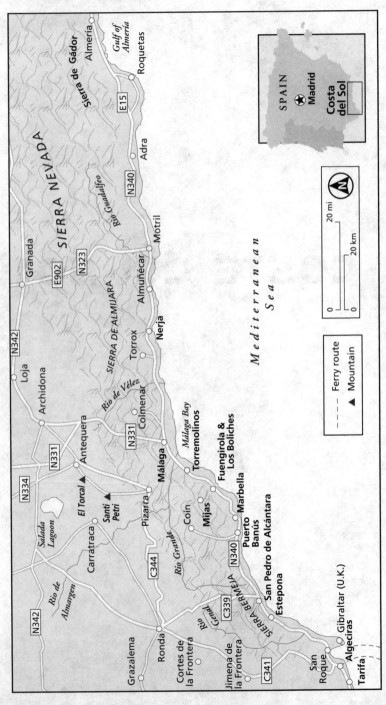

While politically and geographically a part of **Andalucía,** the Costa del Sol shouldn't be included in an Andalucian report card, since it would bring down the region's grade. Much of its charm has been sucked away by concrete high-rises and the droves of British, German, and other Northern Europeans who holiday here. Costa del Sol epitomizes the insane lengths people are willing to go to get near a body of water (which many don't even bother to swim in) and into the sun (which painfully burns them) in order to drink alcohol (which causes them to pass out and get even more sunburnt). And the beaches they flock to aren't even that impressive. They're mostly thin and pebbly. Despite all this, though, there's definitely plenty of sun, beautiful people, and nighttime fun to be found on the Costa del Sol—and there are a few major exceptions to the no-culture rule that seems to be central to the tourist code of conduct here. The chief exception is the capital, **Málaga,** which most sun-seekers bypass. It's a typical modern, liberal, Andalucian city with a ton of young people and a rocking nightlife, some interesting Muslim remains on the hillside, and soon (well, eventually), a museum dedicated to its most famous son, Pablo Picasso.

Once you leave Málaga, the number of actual Spanish people begins to decrease, and the cheese factor increases along with the tourist count. **Torremolinos** is the most infamous example of overdevelopment, poor taste, and pasty-white Northern Europeans on "drinking holiday." It's also strangely fascinating, and you certainly won't have to endure it sober: Wall-to-wall bars and cheap drinks abound. Jet-setters park their yachts in **Marbella,** a ritzy seaside resort where the beaches are too crowded to breathe. In its defense, Marbella does have a charming old quarter, some cheap accommodations, and an amazing number of cool bars that go all night. The small town of **Nerja,** east of Málaga, is the best town on the coast; it retains a laid-back charm despite being a bit too touristy. It also has the prettiest beaches, which draw a lot of international young people. If you're traveling on to Morocco, you might have to slink into the drab port city of **Algeciras.** Near Algeciras is **Gibraltar,** a British-owned colony stuck on a big hunk of limestone rock at the bottom of Spain. If you're just dying for fish 'n' chips, you'll have to take a bus to nearby **La Linea.** In Gibraltar's nature preserve are Europe's only wild primates, Barbary Macaques, sometimes referred to by jaded travelers as "those flea-ridden monkeys."

Until the 1960s, the Costa del Sol followed a historical path similar to that of as the rest of Andalucía: The Muslim era—from roughly the 8th century until 1487, when Málaga fell to the Christians—was followed by an economic boom in the 16th century thanks to trade with the Americas, and then lean years after the loss of Spain's holdings there. The Spanish Civil War of the 20th century was especially hard on liberal Málaga, which was staunchly pro-Republican until the city fell to the Nationalists after air raids in 1937. Heinous acts were committed by both sides. Through most of these tumultuous centuries, the seaside towns outside of Málaga passed the days as quiet little fishing villages. That all changed in the late 1950s and early 1960s, when General Franco saw a gold-mine in the year-round sunshine and blue waters of the Mediterranean. Concrete high-rise hotels sprung up on the Costa del Sol like wildflowers, and sun-starved Northern Europeans followed in packs. By the late 1970s the region had become synonymous with "package tours." More recently, attempts have been made to spruce up the joint (meaning lots of golf courses), to attract more well-heeled travelers and their money.

Today the Costa del Sol has a year-round contingent of British and Scandinavian expats, mostly retired pensioners, while in the summer the beaches and bars are filled with young revelers from all over Europe, even some from Spain. July and August are insane with crowds—especially the beaches and the nightclubs—but if you've come here, you're obviously not trying to "get away from it all" anyway.

TRAVEL TIMES

All times are by road unless indicated by a star:
* = time by train

	Malaga	Marbella	Nerja	Torremolinos	Madrid
Malaga	-	:40	:50	:20	4:15*
Marbella	:40	-	1:15	:30	5:50
Nerja	:50	1:15	-	1:00	5:45
Torremolinos	:20	:30	1:00	-	5:30

Despite the invasion of fish 'n' chips shops and American fast food, you'll still find plenty of tapas bars for your authentic low-budget Spanish eating experience. If you're into fish, they cook up all kinds of sea creatures from simple yet sumptuous *salmón* and *rape* (monkfish), to little slimy things like *boquerones* (anchovies) and *pulpo* (octopus). If you're into Phish, go to Vermont. Beer lovers will be happy to find hearty Northern European beers, including Guinness, at many bars down here, in addition to the inevitable Spanish brands—*Cruz Campo, St. Miguel, Alhambra,* and *Mahou.* Everyone should try some Málaga dessert wine, which is much sweeter than Andalucía's sherry.

getting around costa del sol

Unlike most of Spain, trains won't get you very far on the Costa del Sol. There are plenty of trains to Málaga, approximately four hours from Madrid, and three hours from Sevilla or Granada, but from there you'll have to take a bus or rent a car to get to the beach resorts (the exception is a local train to Torremolinos—see chapter below for details). You won't have to go very far, however; Torremolinos is only 20 minutes west of Málaga, Marbella another 40 minutes, and in the other direction, Nerja is 1 hour from Málaga. Up to 20 buses a day run from Málaga to Marbella, and at least 10 go to Nerja. Renting a car here is less expensive than in many other parts of Spain, due to the increased competition for all those tourist dollars.

málaga

Málaga, the liberal, freewheeling capital of Costa del Sol, lives on its own terms. Unlike most of the nearby beach resorts, which would sell their souls for your tourist dollars, Málaga has a bustling port and a commercial and cultural life that goes on with or without you. Many *guiris* (non-Spanish travelers) use the city as a gateway to the more mellow beach towns on the coast, and some mention getting a "bad vibe" here, mostly because of a well-earned reputation for loud traffic and petty crime. But if you're willing to give Málaga a chance, you'll find out why it is called *la ciudad dónde la vida es arte:* the city where life is art. The monuments may be slightly crumbling, the Picasso Museum might never be completed, but life happens in the vegetarian restaurants, beachside bars, international cinemas, street parties, and rock 'n' roll pubs that keep Málaga rolling year-round.

Malaguenos, the locals who keep the city up until very late at night, are famous for being free-spirited and fun-loving. They're also much hipper—as in more pierced and guitar-carrying—than the rest of their Andalucian neighbors, and frankly not as interested in what you're doing here. They see enough beach-bound Northern Europeans and North Americans to know that the great majority of foreigners are too worried about the state of their tan or where to buy absinthe to care what's going on in the youth culture of Málaga. But if you make the effort to find out, you have a good shot at connecting with local Spanish people.

Málaga is attractive and a little bit dangerous, as all good port cities are. And while life is lived at the normal mellow pace of southern Spain, it is lived with a determination that makes the whole city seem like it's in constant motion. Lingering in a cafe here is not an activity in itself, but a place to plan your next move. Getting oriented in Málaga is not difficult; the main part of town lies just north of the **Mediterranean Sea** between the river on the west and the big green hill (or little mountain) with the castle on it to the east. The major thoroughfare, **Alameda Principal,** runs east from the river **Rio Guadalmedina** to the **Plaza de Marina.** South of here is the marina itself, with cruise liners full of tourists and immense cargo ships being loaded up by giant cranes. North of Alameda Principal is the beehive of activity that is the old quarter of the city. **Calle Marqués de Larios** takes you through to the shopping district and the **Plaza de Constitución,** the center of the old quarter. The similarly named **Calle Molina Lario** also goes north from the marina, to the Catédral before it ends at **Calle Granada.** Calle Granada, the epicenter of alternative living, bends through the old quarter to **Calle San Augustin,** a studenty street filled with little cafes and teterías, which itself ends at the pretty 18th-century **Plaza de Merced.** Here you'll find the **Casa Natal de Picasso** (the birthplace of Pablo Picasso), where in 1891, Málaga's most famous son was born, though his family only stayed in town for the first 10 years of his life [see *picasso's "kid" period,* below]. Just west of here is the **Roman Theater** (its renovation scheduled for completion when the Roman Empire reconquers Europe—in other words, it'll be a few years) and, rambling up the hill, the old Muslim fortress, the **Alcazaba** [see *culture zoo,* below]. A winding stone path leads up the south wall of the Alcazaba to an even older castle that sits on top of the hill, **Castillo de Gibralfaro,** with its brilliant vews of the city and the sea.

Back down the hill, the main road, Alameda Principal, becomes **Paseo del Parque,** a leafy, tree-lined boulevard that offers plenty of shade on those sweltering summer days. At the end of the park is the **Plaza Del General Torrijos** and behind that is the bullfighting ring **Plaza del Toros de la Malagueta.** South of here, when the port ends, the beach **Playa de La Malaguera** begins. It's definitely an urban beach, but the Mediterranean still sparkles, and there's plenty of *chiringuitos,* which is a fancy name for bars on the beach.

Like any big city with high unemployment, Málaga has its share of pickpockets and bag-grabbers, though you're certainly as safe as you would be in most big European cities. As always, watch your gear at the bus and train stations. At night stick to the well-traveled, well-lit areas mentioned above, avoid the pathway up to the Gibralfaro, and you should be fine. Plenty of taxis are available in the center of the city if you have a long walk ahead of you.

hanging out

While Málaga is big, most of the places you'll want to hang out in are in a fairly compact area in the old quarter, but the streets are a twisted labyrinth so plan to get confused. Day and night, life centers, coincidentally or not, around Picasso's childhood playground, Plaza de la Merced. Street performers, young malcontents, and outdoor cafe squatters line this square at all hours.

málaga

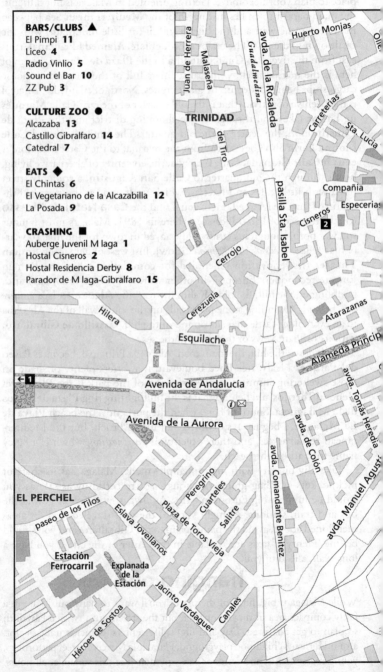

BARS/CLUBS ▲
El Pimpi **11**
Liceo **4**
Radio Vinlio **5**
Sound el Bar **10**
ZZ Pub **3**

CULTURE ZOO ●
Alcazaba **13**
Castillo Gibralfaro **14**
Catedral **7**

EATS ◆
El Chintas **6**
El Vegetariano de la Alcazabilla **12**
La Posada **9**

CRASHING ■
Auberge Juvenil M laga **1**
Hostal Cisneros **2**
Hostal Residencia Derby **8**
Parador de M laga-Gibralfaro **15**

TRINIDAD

EL PERCHEL

Estación
Ferrocarril

Explanada
de la
Estación

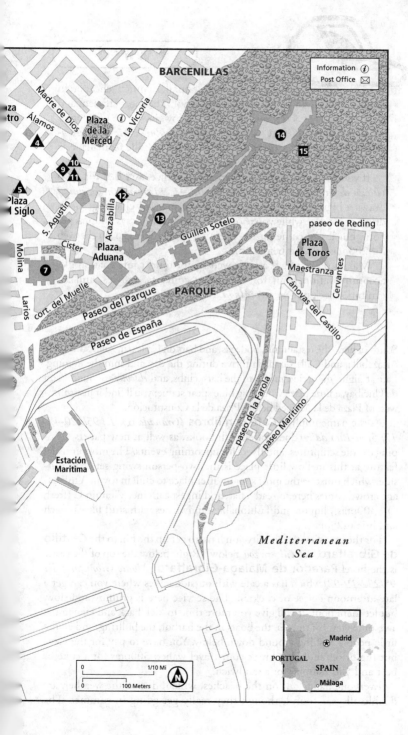

BARCENILLAS

Information (i)
Post Office ✉

Madre de Dios
Álamos
Plaza
tro
Plaza
de la
Merced
La Victoria

4

10
9
11

5
Plaza
l Siglo

S. Agustín
Acazabilla

12

13
Guillen Sotelo

14
15

paseo de Reding

Plaza
de Toros

Cervantes

Molina
Cister
Plaza
Aduana

7

Maestranza

Cánovas del Castillo

Larios
cort. del Muelle
Paseo del Parque
PARQUE

Paseo de España

paseo de la Farola

paseo Marítimo

Estación
Marítima

Mediterranean
Sea

0   1/10 Mi
0   100 Meters

N

Madrid
PORTUGAL
SPAIN
Málaga

WIRED

Checking your e-mail is much cheaper in Málaga than in the rest of the Costa del Sol. The most efficient and modern Internet access available, for the low, low price of 300ptas an hour, is at **rent@net** *(Santiago 8; Noon-midnight Mon-Sat, 4pm-midnight Sun)*. It's located on a side street off of Calle Granada, two blocks south of Plaza de la Merced.

If you want a more social Internet experience, **Art Bar Picasso** *(Plaza de la Merced 20; Tel 95/222-02-41; 11am-midnight daily)* draws a big crowd of internationals surfing and chatting. Get a drink or a coffee while you're online—Internet access is 400ptas per hour, but if you come for the morning special you can do the web for 200ptas an hour before 1pm.

Málaga doesn't have a great website for tourist information like accommodations, but for upcoming concerts, movies, and art exhibits, check out ***www.málaga.lareto.com.***

South of here, the restaurants, bodegas, and bars on Calle San Augustin, Calle Alcazabilla, and Calle Granada thrive during the day and into the evening. Late at night, the action moves to the bars, clubs, and *discotecas* around Plaza de Uncibay, a little plaza with a big blue spear statue; you'll find it just southwest of Plaza de la Merced before Plaza de la Constitución.

As the name implies, **Cafe con libros** *(Granada 63; Tel 95/220-47-17; 5pm-1am daily)* does coffee with books, as well as newspapers, dripping candle sculptures, and flyers for upcoming events. The most unusual feature at this mellow little place is the two-person swing-set chair outside, which must be the most sought-after place to chill in town. A mixed-age crowd comes here to read, chat, and ingest caffeine, Vitamin C (fresh OJ, 300ptas), liquor, and fashionable sandwiches with stuff like spinach and brie (425ptas).

For the best views of the city you have to get up the hill to the **Castillo de Gibralfaro** [see *culture zoo,* below]. Right below the top of the castle is the hotel **Parador de Malaga-Gibralfaro** *(Monte Gibralfaro; Tel 95/222-19-02)* which has a cafe with outside tables where you can get a late-afternoon coffee or cocktail. The service here is grumpy and slow, but let them pout; it will give you more time to kick back and take in the awesome views of the sea, the boats in the harbor, the bullring, and all the little people rushing around down below. You have to pay for the view, but the prices shouldn't break your travel wallet: 300ptas for a coke or beer and 500-800ptas for a sandwich.

Everyone hangs out on the beaches, which, due to the weather, are doable all year round, though they really get going in summer. The beaches are wide and fairly clean, but remember Málaga is a city, not an island, so there are crowds and traffic noise. You might be better off saving your beach days for other, less urban spots on the coast and enjoying the cultural life Málaga offers. If you're in town during the midsummer heat, however, you're either going to have to stay inside where there's AC or go jump in that water. **Playa Malagueta** is the beach closest to the city, just east of the port, and the beginning of a long stretch of beaches along Paseo Maritimo. About 5 kilometers (3.1 miles) east of the center of town stretches **Playas del Palo,** a very popular beach with the locals, who refer to it as the *Ruta de Boqueron,* "the route of the anchovy," because that's the most common *pescaíto* (fried fish) served in the *chiringuitos.* Bus 11 (125ptas) from Paseo del Parque can take you there; ask for 'El Palo'.

bar and live music

A wide variety of bars—many of them unnamed tapas joints—cluster around Plaza de la Merced, Plaza de la Constitución, and Plaza de Uncibay. While there's always something going on, the real scene happens only from Thursday to Saturday, especially in the off-season. Weekend nights in summer are always hopping, and the streets around these plazas become impromptu outdoor pickup and hook-up scenes.

For a true taste of Málaga, try the local wine at the combo old-school/new-school institution **El Pimpi** *(Granada 62; Tel 95/222-89-90).* In a cavernous space away from the street, this place is three floors of authentic bodega atmosphere with flamenco and bullfighting decor and stacked wine barrels. It attracts civilized but raucous groups of students and even more raucous groups of old-timers. You can't create this kind of atmosphere, it happens over time, and even the jazzy disco music they play somehow doesn't seem out of place. Try a glass of the local *fino dulce* (sweet sherry wine), which tastes like potent grape juice. This is a great place to come with big groups because there's plenty of space; each of the three levels—*Casa Cordoba* on the ground floor, *Barra* on the second floor, and *El Palomar,* popular with younger patrons, on the third floor—has the same decor, music, and tapas.

For a pint o' the plain, stumble on over to the huge Irish pub **O'Neill's** *(Luis de Velázquez 3; Tel 95/260-14-60),* north of Plaza de la Constitución. This place seems to support the entire Irish work force in Málaga, as it takes three or four bartenders to work the long, busy bar at all times. The decor is all brand-name Irish stuff, but the crowd is a mix of English-speakers and curious locals. They're not afraid to try silly promotions here, like making all the bartenders dress up like Santa Claus in the middle of summer. Ask Santa for a Guinness, 500pts a pint.

ZZ Pub *(Tejón y Rodríguez 6; Tel 95/244-15-95; 10pm-5am daily)* gives shelter to long beards and twirling guitars on a street that runs up off Plaza de Uncibay. Local bands, cut out of the Tom Petty/Deep Purple mode, perform rock, R&B, and blues here, and while you might not rush out to buy the CD, this dive is so small and spirited you'll feel like you're hanging backstage. The no-cover music happens four or five nights a week at about 11pm or later. When there's no band on, you're bound to hear the Red Hot Chili Peppers on the sound system.

If you like your music a little quieter, seek out the soulful sounds of the nearby **Cantor de Jazz** *(Lazcano 7; Tel 95/227-43-34; 9pm-4am Mon-Sat)*. This shrine to American music presents live jazz one or two nights a week, usually on Friday or Saturday. The yellow stucco walls are plastered with black-and-white photos of musicians, and the bar specializes in cocktails from around the world, *(550-600ptas)*.

For burning down the house, you're going to have to wait till the weekend and stay up late. The clubs and *discotecas* around Plaza de Uncibay don't open until 11pm or midnight and usually only Thursday-Saturday. There are quite a few cheesy neon-signed discos in this neighborhood, some of which can charge absurd cover charges.

A few blocks off Plaza Uncibay and extremely popular with both local and international students, **Liceo** *(Beatas 21; Tel 95/260-24-40; 11pm-5 am Tue-Sat)* has turned a converted old mansion into two floors of wall-to-wall people late at night, with local DJs playing technically sound if not groundbreaking beats. If you get here early you can take advantage of happy hour (11:30pm-12:30am), when beers are only 150ptas.

For a less hectic vibe try **Sound El Bar** *(Granada 36; No phone; 10pm-5am Mon-Sat)*. It draws a young crowd, and though it can be a little too quiet sometimes, there's no cover, so you can always go check it out. A DJ plays Latin-tinged dance music for an international crowd in a small postmodern industrial setting. On Thursday nights, ladies can get free salsa lessons from an Argentine with Richard Simmons energy leading them through the paces.

Desperate measures can sometimes be attractive, which is why we like **Radio Vinilo** *(Denis Belgrano 17; No phone; 11pm-3am Wed-Sat)*. Surrounded by discos, this place attracts people by giving not only free admission but also a free "cocktail." When you go inside to the bar you'll be served a strange orange Kool-Aid-and-booze mix you didn't ask for—that's your complementary cocktail. But it's free, and the plan works: At about 2am, people start pouring onto the tiny dance floor and turn it into a load of sweaty good times. A good signal to leave is when they play the "I Will Survive" re-mix for the third time. Vinilo also has cute girls outside on the streets handing out flyers for their parties, like Wednesday's "El Infierno," a diabolical Halloween experience, if you want to go hell.

ARTS SCENE

Picasso may have abandoned Málaga, but the local arts scene still marches on. Galleries are generally open from 11am to 2pm and again from 6 to 9pm Monday to Friday, with morning hours on Saturday. The organization that fuels much of the scene in Malaga is Fundación Picasso, a foundation dedicated to the famous painter, which not only preserves his memory but organizes exhibits by his contemporaries and his followers. One recent event was a screening of Andy Warhol's cinematic experiments. Most of the happenings take place at **Casa de Natal Picasso**

(Plaza de la Merced; Tel 95/221-50-05; 11am-2pm/5-8pm Mon-Sat, morning hours Sunday; Free admission).

Among other galleries that strut their stuff around Plaza de la Merced is **Galería Pablo Ruiz** *(Granada 44),* which shows works by Spanish artists, mostly modernist but not so far out there that you can't tell what it is. Some is eye-opening stuff, and some is ordinary. Look at the window display to determine if it's your bag.

Galería Alfredo Viña *(Denis Belgrano 19; Tel 95/260-12-29),* a well-respected gallery just off Plaza de Uncibay, hosts changing exhibitions of Spanish art, specializing in figurative paintings.

To see what the kids are up to, check out the **Sala de Arte de la Universidad de Málaga** *(Plaza de la Merced 21; No phone),* a gallery for art students at the local university on the same plaza as Picasso's birth place.

For the performing arts, the place to be is **Teatro Cervantes** *(Ramos Marín; Ticket office: 8am-3pm Mon-Fri; Tel 95/222-41-09; www.teatrocervantes.net).* You can see modern theater, classical and world music, even some of Broadway's greatest hits, in a stately building in the northern part of the center city.

If the latest Cannes hits interest you more, **Albéniz Multicines** *(Calle Alcazabilla 4; Tel 95/221-58-98; 600ptas, 400ptas matinee)* shows indie movies in their original language (with subtitles). This hip theater is located just southeast of Plaza de la Merced, just up from the Alcazaba, and right next to **El Vegetariano de la Alcazabilla** [see *eats,* below], which makes for a double dose of late '90s culture still alive in the new century.

CULTUre ZOO

Málaga struggles against the forces of time, nature, and money to keep up its cultural sites. The excavation of the Roman Theater ruins next to the Alcazaba shows no sign of completion. The transformation of the old Museo de Bellas Artes into the exciting new Museo de Picasso has dragged on a few more years than planned [see *Picasso's "Kid" period,* below], and the Muslim fortresses are slowly crumbling. Even the Catedral is still missing a tower. But the locals love their monuments just the same, and they're the only ones you're going to find on the Costa del Sol—plus they're all cheap or free and rarely crowded—so you should love them, too.

Alcazaba *(Plaza de la Aduana; Tel 95/221-60-03; 9:30am-8pm daily, closed Tuesday; Free admission):* This Muslim palace, originally from the 11th century (although later additions were made in the 20th century), seems to modern eyes more like a fortress than a residence. The double walls, arrow slits, and intentionally confusing passageways are certainly imposing, but home sweet home it ain't. At certain times, the crowds are so thin, or just so spread out over the grounds, that you get a spooky yet exhilarating feeling that you're all alone here with the birds and the ghosts. A museum of archaeology displays artifacts from the oldest known inhabitants of Málaga.

Castillo de Gibralfaro *(Cerro de Gibralfaro; 10am-8pm daily; Free admission):* The south wall of the Alcazaba continues all the way

picasso's "kid" period

Some art critics argue that although the most celebrated artist of the 20th century was born here, Málaga had little or no impact on Picasso's work. Now, we don't claim to be experts, but it seems impossible to believe that the vibrant blue and white light of the city made no impression on the young maestro. What can't be debated is that he was born here, in 1891, in a house on Plaza de la Merced, and that he lived here for the first ten years of life. To honor its native son, Málaga is transforming the **Museo de Bellas Arts** *(Calle San Augustin 8; Tel 95/221-83-82)* into the **Museo Picasso**, thanks to a large donation of his work by his daughter-in-law Christine Ruiz-Picasso. This exciting new project should be a major boost to Málaga's cultural life...and should be ready any year now. The museum was originally set to open in winter 2000, but now it looks like 2001, if they're lucky. If you're coming to Málaga specifically to see this place, call the museum or the tourist office [see *need to know,* below] to find out if it's ready. Picasso-heads can already visit his birthplace, **Casa de Natal Picasso** *(Plaza de la Merced; Tel 95/221-50-05; 11am-2pm/5-8pm Mon-Sat, morning hours Sunday; Free admission),* which displays some of his early work (mostly drawings), and has revolving exhibits of work by other modern artists.

up the hill to this even older castle-fortress. Reach the castle by following a rambling stone footpath that meanders uphill in the shadow of the wall, and drink in the scenic views along the way. You can also take bus 35 up or down the hill from Paseo del Parque (125ptas). The first one goes up the hill at 11am and the last one comes down at 7:20pm. Once there, you can freely roam the multi-level grounds consisting of towers and parapets. The view will make you feel like a Caliph surveying his kingdom.

Catedral *(Plaza Obispo; Tel 95/221-59-17; 10am-12:45pm/4-6:30pm Mon-Sat; 200ptas):* Like many cathedrals in Andalucía, this one took a couple of centuries to build and is therefore a mix of Gothic, Renaissance, and Baroque architectural styles. Only one tower of the planned two was ever finished, which is why the nickname for the church is *La Manquita,* meaning the one-armed. The story goes that the money intended for the other tower was sent to the New World to help the poor colonists defeat the British during the American Revolution. So all Americans must make a one-armed salute, because if it weren't for the sacrifice of this cathedral, you might all be eating fish 'n' chips and getting your knickers in a twist about Oasis breaking up.

STUFF

Málaga's major shopping takes place in the twisted web of cobblestone streets in the centro, and mixes with the cafe and bar scenes. The center point is Plaza de la Constitución and the streets off it, while the closer you get to Plaza de la Merced, the funkier the shops get. There are not a lot of tourist traps, so you might have to buy that matador outfit somewhere else. Shops keep similar hours: 10am-2pm...siesta...5-8pm, Monday through Friday, with morning hours only on Saturday.

EATS

Málaga's food is just as good as you'll find in any other town in Spain...but enough already. The only place you really need to know about is **El Vegetariano de la Alcazabilla** (*Pozo del Rey 5; Tel 95/221-48-58; 1-5pm/9-11pm, Mon-Sat*), which just might be one of the best vegetarian restaurants on the planet. Or maybe it just seems that way because it's such a welcome break from the pig/egg/gazpacho diet you get used to over here. No matter, it's certainly a welcome oasis, and a lot more fun than California-vegetarian restaurants because you can drink beer and taste the food here. You can get simple yet delicious things like vegetarian pâté, spinach pies, soy burgers, brown rice, or all of the above on the combo plate for only 1,150ptas, and you can wash it down with a big drool-inducing Belgian beer (400ptas). They also let people write on the yellow walls with black ink, which probably seemed like a good idea at the time. If you decide to take up the pen, be aware that every life-affirming cliché you can think of ("Life is like an onion..." etc.) has already been written. Try to drag your Spanish friends here because the food seems to scare away all but the most adventurous locals, and draws lots of shiny, healthy Northern Europeans. The restaurant is located right next to **Albéniz Multicines** [see *arts scene,* above], two blocks away from Plaza de la Merced. Don't get it confused with other vegetarian restaurants in the area—this is the original and the best.

If you want to eat higher up on the food chain, go to the tapas temple of grilled meat, **La Posada** (*Granada 33; Tel 95/221-70-69; 1-4pm/6pm-midnight*). Stand at the bar, pick out something fleshy from the display counter, and watch as it's grilled on the giant barbecue built into the back wall of the kitchen. This place also serves one of the more mouthwatering *tortillas españoles* in existence, which includes little chunks of ham. Tapas and beer will only set you back 375ptas, and you can enjoy them with a boisterous, carnivorous crowd of locals.

The best-known restaurant in town is the old-fashioned and historic **El Chinitas** (*Moreno Monroy 4; Tel 95/221-09-72; 1-4pm/8pm-midnight daily*). It might seem a little fancy when you walk in, but you can just head to the bar for classic cheap tapas, most of which you've never heard of. Artists and writers such as García Lorca, whose poem adorns the entrance, used to hang here, but now the crowd consists of former-bohemians-gone-straight who dig the classical music. There will probably also be some other foreigners at the bar trying to decipher the plates on the wall that contain the names of the dishes, like *bacalao* (cod) and *sangre encellobada* (congealed chicken blood). Friendly, enigmatic bartenders will try to explain all this to you. Everything is salty, oily, and tasty—and less than 300ptas for tapas. A couple of other atmospheric tapas places popular with the locals—Bar Orellana and El Candil—can be found on the same street.

crashing

While Málaga has plenty of cultural opportunities and a thriving nightlife, there's a definite lack of cheap quality accommodations. Plenty of hostels in the center of town compete for your pesetas, but most of them have seen better days. "Musty" is the word most often used by travelers.

▶▶CHEAP
Albergue Juvenil Málaga *(Plaza Pio XII; Tel 95/230-85-00; 1,500ptas, 2,000 26 and over; Double rooms only; Shared baths; No curfew; No AC; V, MC)* is one reliable cheap option; unfortunately, it's located 1.5 kilometers (almost a mile) west of town. Bus 18, which runs along Avenida de Andalucía, will take you there.

▶▶DOABLE
Hostal Cisneros *(Cisneros 7; Tel 95/221-26-33; 3,500ptas single, 6,500ptas double)* is one place we can vouch for. Despite its somewhat faded facade, the rooms are well-maintained, almost cozy. It's located just west of Plaza de la Constitución.

Hostal Resedencia Derby *(San Juan de Díos 1; Tel 95/222-13-01; 3,500ptas single, 6,000ptas double; All rooms with private baths; TV in common area; No AC; No credit cards)* deserves its popularity, because even though the rooms are aging, they're clean and have attached bathrooms with sink and shower. A cool balcony in the common area offers a great view of the port and the busy street below. This hostel is located at the bottom of the center city, just off Alameda Principal. Across an alley from McDonald's is a giant imposing door—you have to ring the bell, get buzzed in, and take the elevator to the fourth floor.

▶▶SPLURGE
If you're looking to splurge, you might as well do it at the **Parador de Malaga-Gibralfaro** *(Monte Gibralfaro; Tel 95/222-19-02; 18,000ptas and up, double; V, MC, AE, DC)*. This government-owned hotel is one of the oldest and most traditional paradors in Spain, long known for its supreme panoramic location high on a hill next to the ruins of the Gibralfaro castle. All the rooms come with air conditioning, minibar, TV, phone, and balconies with amazing views of the sea and city below. There is a large swimming pool and a first-class restaurant specializing in Andalusian regional dishes.

need to know

Currency Exchange You can change money at the airport or get cash from any of the ATMs in the center, especially on the two Larios: **Calle Marqués de Larios** or **Calle Molina Lario.**

Tourist Information The multilingual staff at **Junta de Andalucía** *(Pasaje de Chinitas 4; Tel 95/221-34-45; 9am-2pm/4-6pm Mon-Fri, 10am-7pm Sat, 10am-2pm Sun),* off the southeast corner of Plaza de la Constitución, can provide full accommodation lists and detailed maps of the city.

Public Transportation The center city is very walkable, but the local **buses** can be helpful for getting to the beach (bus 11), Castillo Gibralfaro (bus 35), or the youth hostel (bus 18), all of which have stops on Paseo de Parque. There's also a local train, with service to the beach resorts along the coast (including Torremolinos and Fuengirola) and the airport. The **Centro-Alameda** stop is the last one on the line and is located where Alameda Principal hits the river. There's also a stop at the train station [see below].

Health and Emergency Hospital Cruz Roja *(Avda. Jorge Silvela 64; Tel 95/224-05-50).* Police: **Policía Nacional** *(Plaza de la Aduana 1; Tel 95/221-13-02).* Emergency: *061* for medical, *091* for police.

Pharmacies **Neon green crosses** mark the *farmacias,* which can be found all over the center of town. No single one is open 24 hours a day; instead, *farmacias* rotate the all-night responsibility. Each one posts a schedule indicating which will be open on what night.

Airport Aeropuerto de Málaga *(Tel 95/204-88-04)* is 10km (6.2 miles) outside of the city. To get to the city center take the **Cercanías Málaga** local train (140ptas) which leaves approximately every 30 minutes until 11:30pm and will take you the train station or the **Centro-Alameda** stop in the city center.

Trains Málaga's **train station** *(Esplanada de la Estación; Tel 95/236-02-02)* is southwest of the city center. Along with **RENFE** service to major destinations in Spain, there's also a local train, **Cercanías Málaga,** with frequent service to the airport and the beach resorts along the Costa del Sol, such as Torremolinos and Fuengirola. If you're going to Marbella, you can take the local train to Fuengirola (160ptas) and then get a bus the rest of the way. The center of Málaga is a 15- to 20-minute walk from the train station. Make sure you're heading up Cuartales, a street that will take you to the river at Alameda Principal. You can also take the local train from the train station to the center of the city, but you only save about 10 minutes. Late at night, grab a taxi, or **bus 4.**

Bus Lines Out of the City The bus station, **Estacion de Autobuses** *(Plaza de los Tilos; Tel 95/235-00-61),* is right behind the train station, so follow the same rules for getting to the center of the city. Take care of your bags here.

Postal The main **Post Office** *(Avda. de Andalucía 1; Tel 95/235-90-08)* is east of the center city, just across the river on the main thoroughfare.

Internet See *wired,* above.

marbella

Marbella has long been known as the glamour resort of the Costa del Sol, a place for international jet-setters to park their yachts and pay way too much money to drink martinis by the sea. Although recently the nearby port of Puerto Banús has overtaken Marbella as *the* place for the fabulously wealthy, central Marbella is still a very attractive and upscale resort town with a charming old quarter and a lot of rich people. So you might be wondering if there's any room for a humble backpacker on a budget amid all the golf shirts and luxury cars. Surprisingly, there is, due to some good budget hostels and a vibrant nightlife that draws beautiful young people into the hilly cobblestoned streets and the port. This is not wild Spain, nor authentic Spain, but if you just want to chill for a few days, while still having e-mail access and a Versace store, Marbella can be an attractive stop.

There are no trains to Marbella, so you'll be coming by bus or your own wheels. The main highway, N-340, goes right through the center of town, changing names often, but is called **Avenida Ramón y Cajal** in the heart of the city. Buses from the east stop or at least let you out at **La Alameda,** a leafy park on the south side of the street. Get off here, because you'll be on the edge of the old town; otherwise you'll have to go to the bus station, which is on a hill, a 20-minute walk away. The center of the cute little old town is **Plaza de los Naranjos** (Plaza of the Oranges), with some orange trees and the *Ayuntamiento* (City Hall) from the 16th century. Unfortunately, there's not really anywhere to sit here, unless it's at one of the overpriced restaurants whose outdoor tables overwhelm the square. From Plaza de los Naranjos, the old quarter's winding cobblestoned streets are difficult to navigate, but fun to stumble through, so plan to get lost. One street you should find is **Calle Peral,** a couple of blocks northwest, which has two good hostels and some lively bars. From the top of Calle Peral, **Calle Aduar** will take you up toward the official youth hostel and eventually the bus station. Northeast of the Plaza de los

Naranjos are some remains of the ancient Muslim walls, and the small but impressive museum, Museo del Grabado Español Contemporáeno. Down the hill from the old quarter, on the other side of the highway, **Avenida Miguel Cano** leads to the port, Puerto Deportivo, with its boats and late-night bars, and the beaches, **Playa de Venus** and **Playa de la Fontanilla.** The beaches are narrow, with dark sand and not much room for Frisbee, but that doesn't stop the fabulous people from flocking here. The recently refurbished walkway **Avenida Duque de Ahumada,** which becomes **Paseo Maritimo,** is lined with trees, souvenir shops, and restaurants as it ambles along the beach. East of the port a few minutes, and a couple of blocks up from the beach, are more retaurants and bars, mostly drawing an older crowd, on the streets around **Calle Camilo José Cela.** Five kilometers east of Marbella along the "Golden Mile" lies the glitzy port of **Puerto Banús,** where the super-rich dock their yachts. It's a good place to hang out if you're looking to snag an oil magnate, but any character the place has is solely based on money.

While you are bound to hear lots of English spoken here (much of it with a German tourist accent), and your mangled Spanish accent that was so cute in that little farming town certainly won't be a novelty, Marbella is not the sole property of *guiris* (foreigners). Lots of young, well-off-enough-to-hang-out-and-smoke-hash-all-day Spanish people like to vacation here, too.

As with everywhere along the coast in Spain, the weather draws visitors year-round, but the happening part of the year is mid-May to mid-September, especially on weekends. Although Marbella has a few museums [see *culture zoo,* below], you come here more for the beaches than for culture. Some of the art galleries in the ***casco antiguo*** (which seem to open and close with the season) provide a more intriguing view of contemporary art than you are likely to find in any local museum. If Marbella has an artistic treasure, it is the *casco antiguo* itself. A stroll, especially at night, along the old town's cobblestoned streets and whitewashed Andalusian facades with their flowered balconies, is, though hardly the equal of anything in Seville, the most fascinating promenade you can take in Marbella.

Start out from the center at the Plaza de los Naranjos and walk in any direction that intrigues you, perhaps stopping in at a *simpatico* bar to tank up on wine and tapas. These little tapas bars are called *chiringuitos.* You won't run into as many *putas* (prostitutes) or drug pushers as you would have in the legendary '70s and '80s—the old town is now fairly safe at night. In August, expect wall-to-wall people in resort garb (often daring).

the scenes

Standing in the Plaza de los Naranjos at 10 or 11pm on a summer night, feeling the breeze, watching old retired people wander off to bed as restaurants close up, you may ask yourself "How did I get here?" What you don't know is that in tiny alleyways right around the corner, bars that are just opening for the night will soon be absolutely packed with sultry

marabella

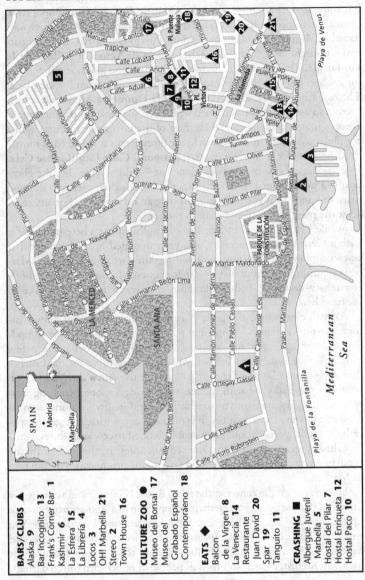

young people ready to party. Three hours later you could very well be out of your head, drinking on the street or down at the port, showing off your limited Spanish skills with the locals. And again you may ask yourself "How did I get *here*?" Well, we'll show you, because for a small town, there's no shortage of unique and atmospheric bars.

For our money, the coolest bar in the old quarter is **Town House** *(Alamo 1; No phone; 10pm-3am/4am)*. This loungy place is one of the few in Marbella that's open seven days a week, year-round, and therefore draws a faithful clientele of locals. In the dead of winter, it might be your only option, and in summer it's a great place to start your night, although the comfy benches, funky (almost tropical) decor, smooth dance music, and well-made cocktails (500ptas) make it difficult to leave. Like all good lounges, it's somewhat hidden away, on the second story of quaint building in the old quarter. From Plaza de los Naranjos, head down Calle Nuevo, then take a left on Calle Alamo. There's usually a sign on the street with an arrow to make your mission easier. You enter into a plant-filled patio with a fountain; take the stairs up to get to the cozy bar. Ask Peter, the friendly owner, for the house special, a mixed shot he calls "apple pie," which tastes just like Mom used to make, only a little more potent. We think it has apple schnapps, cinnamon and something else, but Peter is way too smart to give away the secret recipe.

The coolest evening hang-out near the beach is **Cafe La Librería** *(Sevillano 2; Tel 95/277-60-94; 5pm-12:30am)*. The predominantly local crowd is too busy chatting and laughing and listening to Spanish rock music to peruse the books stacked all around the bar area downstairs. If you're extremely lucky you might get the table in the window and get swallowed up by the fat couch, which surpasses all other bar seats in the known universe. International bottled beers for 300-450ptas.

Once you've got your buzz going, head to the streets. At the top of Calle Peral there's a crazy intersection of bars near Calle Mesóncillo, where the action spills into the street on weekend nights. One of the most popular bars is **Alaska** *(Peral 6; No phone; 9pm-4am)*, right in front of Hostal Pilar. It draws an international crowd as well as fashionable groups of Spanish twentysomethings. Color coordination with other members of your party, whether intentional or not, seems to be popular. You may have to fight your way through the perfumed and cologned crowd to get to the bar, but the real action here is on the street anyway. Pick a bar, but don't feel you have to stay.

A much more chill scene is at the nearby smoking den, **Kashmir** *(Rafina 8; No phone; 10pm-4am Mon-Sat)*. No neon sign marks this spot in a little alley between Calle Aduar and Calle Ancha, but you can't miss the purple paint job or the groups of pierced and dreaded youth sitting in front of the entrance. They feel right at home downing cheap drinks in the grungy but comfortable two floors of candlelit atmosphere filled with smoke that doesn't (seem to) come from ordinary cigarettes. The music is loud but organically groovy.

Another one-stop super shop of bars is on little Calle Pantaleón, on the southwestern edge of Plaza de los Naranjos; just follow the groups of boisterous young people to get here. The three cervecerías on this street only open at 11pm on weekend nights, and don't get crowded until 12:30am. At the top of the street an outdoor bar is set up during the summer. Impromptu dancing is expected and accepted.

Once you're really starting to tie one on, you can move downhill towards the port, but of course since this is Marbella there are more bartenders on the way who will gladly accept your *efectivo* (cash). If you're feeling malcontented or just looking for an alternative to the trendoid bars, check out **La Esfrera** (*Avda. Puerta del mar 4; No phone; Midnight-4am/5am*), located one block east of Avenida del Mar, near the waterfront. This multicolored cave, a real hole-in-the-wall, keeps the beat alive with cool French hip-hop and dancehall. It's gay-friendly, and just overall friendly, in a loud, dark sort of way.

If you're just in the mood to speak nothing but English go to **Bar Incognito** (*Avda. Miguel Cano 15; No phone; 8:30pm-4am, closed Tuesday*), a few short steps away from the beach. Run and frequented by Brits and English-speaking Europeans, they keep the home fires burning by getting you heated as quickly as possible. You get half-priced cocktails until 10pm, but after that you *only* get a free shot with every cocktail. Although you won't find many *Españoles* here, you will find plenty of spirited expats who work in Marbella, getting pissed and taking the piss out of each other.

After midnight, we're gonna let it all hang out...in the port itself. No seafaring atmosphere down here, or bars with names like the Rusty Barnacle—it's all postmodern and chill. They might as well call **Locos** (*Puerto Deportivo; No phone; Midnight-5am, Thur-Sat*) the Bob Marley bar, since photos of the man himself, as well as other politically correct world music legends, adorn the walls. Live cover bands sometimes play here, but don't hold your breath for the next Santana. Jah-maican me crazy, mon.

Across the plaza from Locos, **Stereo** (*Puerto Deportivo; No phone; Midnight-5am Thur-Sat*) has recently become the most happening port spots for the kids. They play some '70s dance music in this lively joint, and there's a tiny dance floor, though most of the patrons are way too baked to get off the window sill. We haven't seen this many pie-eyes since Amsterdam at 4:20pm on April 20. They serve drinks here, too.

For clubbing purposes, you're going to have to leave the center of town. This requires a taxi, plenty of which are waiting for you at the top of Avenida Miguel Cano, next to the Alameda park. "Adjacent to a fancy hotel a few kilometers east of town" doesn't sound like a prime location for a cutting-edge *discoteca*, but if you're picturing a gown and black tie affair, you would be wrong. Open only in summer, the horridly named **OH! Marbella** (*Hotel Don Carlos, Jardines de las Goldondrinas, N-340 km 192; Tel 95/283-11-40; Midnight-6am Wed-Sun, summer only; 1,500ptas cover, sometimes more depending on event*) draws DJs from Madrid and sometimes international DJs on their way to Ibiza. House, techno, breakbeat—whatever's happening that summer also happens here.

Other places to go for dancing are the clubs in Puerto Banús, which you can just call 'Banús' if you're cool. You're going to have to pay out the wazoo for the privilege of dancing with people probably wealthier than you are.

If all this sounds like too much for you, you can join the older, less stony drinking crowd that congregates in the serene tree-lined streets east of the old quarter. **Frank's Corner Bar** *(Camilo José Cela)* is an institution on the corner of Calle Camilo Jose Cela and Gregorio Marañon. It attempts to recreate an American roadhouse rock 'n' roll bar, and has been around long enough that it comes closer than you might expect. Pool tables and an outdoor patio make drinking pints of Murphy's (500ptas) here a pleasant experience, if you can ignore the annoyingly repeated house mix of Spanish pop. A TV here sometimes airs American and international sporting events. Below Frank's is the **Rock Club,** which on some weekend nights becomes a rock club, with a cover charge of 500ptas or more for reasonably adequate live music. Across the street on Gregorio Marañon are two very suave bars with outdoor tables and a Palm Beach vibe: **Atrium** and **Havana,** places to see and be seen.

CULTURE ZOO

Museo del Bonsai *(Parque Arroyo de la Represa, Avda. del Dr. Maíz Viñal; Tel 95/286-29-26; 10am-1:30pm/4-6pm daily):* This shrine to artfully trimmed little trees is one-of-a-kind in Spain and one of the best bonsai collections in Europe. Intricately shaped specimens—from the Chinese "Almez" to local olive trees and Pinsabo Pines, all lovingly cared for by their owner, Miguel Angel García, flourish in a serene, Zen-like setting in a park on the northeast edge of town.

Museo del Grabado Español Contemporáneo (Engraving Museum) *(Hospital Bazan; Tel 95/282-50-35; 10am-2pm/5:30-8:30pm Mon-Fri, 10am-2pm Sun):* Come see some works by Dalí and Picasso that you may not have seen before: this unique museum is dedicated to engravings and etchings only.

The most cutting-edge art gallery in the town center is **Galleria d'Arte Van Gestel,** *(Plaza de los Naranjos 11; Tel 95/277-48-19; Mon-Fri 10am-2pm/5-8:30pm, Sat 10:30am-2pm),* which lies on the heartbeat main square of the old town. Your search for the best contemporary art might also lure you to Puerto Banús, where the best of contemporary artwork, both Spanish and international, is displayed at the **Sammer Gallery,** *(Avenida de Rivera, Las Terrazas de Banús, Local 10-16; Tel 95/281-29-95; Mon-Sat 9am-12:30pm5-9pm, Sun 5-9pm).*

STUFF

Who you're wearing in Marbella is more important than what you're wearing. Loads of European designers have absurdly expensive shops here, many behind the port in Puerto Banús. If you have the cash or just want to window shop, keep in mind that these stores are closed for siesta, between 2 and 6pm, but generally stay open until 10pm on summer evenings. In Marbella's old town, below the Plaza de los Naranjos, is **Gucci** *(Valdes 8).* In Puerto Banús, at the Centro Commercial, you'll find **Versace** *(Benabola 8; Tel 95/281-02-96).* In the same shopping center are other fabulous outlets of Moschino, Boutique 007, and Elite.

If you're looking for club gear with a bit less pretension, try **Metropolis** *(Tetuan 2; 10:30am-2pm/6-10pm Mon-Sat, 6pm-10pm Sun)*. At the bottom of Marbella's old quarter, it carries postmodern outfits and small, medium, and giant platform shoes.

Andalucía is also known for its handicrafts, the best and most reasonably priced of which are displayed at **Ceramica San Nicolas** *(Plaza de la Iglesia 1; Tel 95/277-05-46; 11am-1:30pm/5:30-9:30pm Mon-Sat, Mar-Nov; 11am-1:30pm/5-8pm, Sat 11am-1:30pm, Dec-Feb)*.

EATS

Eating in Marbella can tax your wallet if you randomly walk into restaurants, especially in the old quarter and the waterfront and...just about everywhere. One way to save is to hit the **Spar** supermarket *(Puente Malaga Plaza; 9am-9pm Mon-Sat)* on the eastern edge of the old town.

▶▶CHEAP

Locals and tourists crowd the popular **La Venencia** *(Avda. Miguel Cano; Tel 95/285-79-13; 1pm-2am daily)*, just up from the port, for cheap, good tapas served on the top of barrels, at tables, or at the bar. The *salmon ahumado* (smoked salmon) for 350ptas is awesome, especially when wrapped around the fresh bread. You'll be coming back for more, especially after you see the prices at the nearby restaurants. Vegetarians and animal lovers initially may be appalled by the charred piglet that is sometimes sprawled on top of the bar. It's called atmosphere, people. Or just turn your head away and order one of the salads, which are never as good as the meat in Spain.

If you want to eat with the locals at an old-school Andalucian restaurant, try **Restaurante Juan David** *(Marques de Nájera; Tel 95/286-23-56; 1-10pm Tue-Sun)*. This place doesn't have any decor to speak of—it's just a big room that looks like a cafeteria—but the low prices and humble food draw in big groups and extended families, especially on Sunday afternoons. A *menú* with an appetizer, and a main dish of roast chicken, paella, or spinach tortilla, is only 775ptas.

▶▶DOABLE

If you want to semi-splurge, well then you've got more options than a stalker at an awards show. Check out the menus on the streets north of Plaza de los Naranjos, and window shop your way to a good meal. A reasonably priced yet full-blown dining experience can be found at **Balcon de la Virgen** *(Remedios 2; Tel 95/277-60-92; 7pm-midnight daily, closed Tuesdays off-season)*. Look for the statue of the Virgin Mary above the door. Dishes like ratatouille Malaga-style (695ptas), and Paella (1,250ptas) are carefully prepared and won't break your bankroll, but if you want to go for it, the marinated swordfish, which will set you back 2,000ptas, is where it's at. Nearby, the Argentine *parilla* **Tanguito** *(Buitrago 2; Tel 95/286-3520; 7:00pm-midnight Mon-Sat)* serves highly recommended food in a lovely setting. Grilled meat (1,400ptas and up) is their bread and butter, but they also have grilled corn on the cob

(400ptas) or an *ungrilled* Waldorf salad (900ptas). A rooftop terrace and a bar on the downstairs patio make a visit a unique experience.

▶▶SPLURGE

At least once on your visit you may want to indulge in a place that's a bit decadent and fabu. Our choice is the **Villa Tiberio** (*Carretera de Cádiz, km 178.5; Tel 95/277-17-99; 7:30pm-12:30am Mon-Sat; Main courses 1,800-3,200ptas; AE, DC, MC, V*). Right across from the swankiest hotel on the Costa del Sol, the Marbella Club, this is your chance to check out the jet-setting scene without going broke. In the 1960s this was a private villa known for its notorious parties, a place where Princess Grace might slip away with her young man of the month. Today it serves some of the most creative Northern Italian cuisine along the coast. Try the *funghi fantasia*, a large wild mushroom stuffed with seafood and lobster sauce, and follow it with *pappardella alla Sandro*, those large flat noodles studded with hunks of sweet lobster, a zesty tomato sauce, and lots of garlic. There's no bus, but a taxi from the center of town is 1,000ptas.

crashing

Many backpackers avoid Marbella because it just sounds like it's going to cost a lot of money. It can, but there are also a good number of reasonably priced hostels in the old town. Always reserve in advance or plan your visit to Marbella for early in the summer.

▶▶CHEAP

The official youth hostel, **Albergue Juvenil Marbella** (*Calle Trapiche 2; Tel 95/277-14-91; 1,200ptas, 1,500ptas over 26, 1,500/2,000ptas June-Sept*), is a little bit of a hike (about a 20-minute hike, to be exact). From

wired

Checking your e-mail is expensive in Marbella, but if you need to talk to your friends back home while eating a bagel, try **American Donats & Bagels Cafe** (*Travesia Carlos Mackintosh between Miguel Cano and Avenida del Mar; 850ptas per hour*), which is right on the Alemeda two blocks up from the beach in the center of town. That's their spelling of donuts, not ours. You can excuse them because they are German-owned and they import donuts and bagels all the way from the States. So okay, these not the freshest of bagels, but if you slather them with cream cheese (395ptas total), they're kind of excellent, actually, and as close to New York as you're going to get in Spain. Donuts, 100ptas, coffee 150ptas, and, oh yeah, decent computers, too.

the old quarter, walk up Calle Aduar to the top of the hill, and then continue up the next hill on Calle Trapiche. The hostel has a nice swimming pool, but it's not much of a hangout due to the no-drinking policy. It sometimes overflows with student groups.

The British-run **Hostal del Pilar** *(Mesóncillo 4; Tel 95/282-99-36; 2,000ptas single, 2,500ptas high season)* definitely ranks as a hangout. Not only does it have a bar, but it's about five feet away from a bunch of other bars on Calle Pilar. The rooms are hostel-style, which means you'll be sharing a room with other folks, usually friendly British chaps or chappettes, some of whom seem to have moved in permanently. Communal bathrooms are clean and the staff is either low-key or just bored with your presence, but they'll give you your own keys so you can come and go as you choose.

▶▶**DO-ABLE**

If you want your own room, venture down the street to the welcoming **Hostal Paco** *(Peral 16; Tel 95/277-12-00; 3,700ptas single, 5,700ptas double)*. Nothing spectacular unless you consider good, clean, comfortable rooms with their own bathrooms spectacular, which you very well may at this point. If you're traveling with friends, you might want to go right around the corner and try **Hostal Enriqueta** *(Los Caballeros 18; Tel 95/282-75-52; 7,000ptas double; 9,630ptas triple, 11,770ptas quad, high season)*. It's a step up from hostel territory price-wise, and is only worth the extra money if you're squeezing in three or four people.

need to know

Currency Exchange They want you to spend money here. **ATMs** are located all around town, but the biggest conglomeration lies along **Avenida Ricardo Soriano,** the town's main drag.

Tourist Information: East of the port along the sea front is **Oficina de Turismo** *(Glorieta de la Fontanilla; Tel 95/277-14-42; 9:30am-9pm Mon-Fri, 10am-2pm Sat; turismomarbella@ctv.es)*. This is the home base of the regional tourist office, Junta de la Andalucia, so there's plenty of information on the whole region, as well as local maps...and the people speak English. If you e-mail them in advance they will send you a list of accommodations or anything else you might need, but can't actually make reservations for you. If you come on a Sunday or holiday when it's closed, they usually leave a stack of city maps at the entrance. There's a smaller **tourist office** *(Plaza de los Naranjos 1; Tel 95/282-35-50; 9am-2pm/5-7pm Mon-Fri)* in the old quarter. They also speak English but are no help when it comes to reserving a bed for the night.

Public Transportation To get to the luxury yachts and nightlife of Puerto Banús, grab a bus going west (to your right if you're facing the sea) on Avenida de Ricardo Soriano with destination: *San Pedro.* They come every 15-20 minutes during the day, 125ptas.

Health and Emergency Emergency: *061;* medical, *091;* police, *091.* The public health clinic: **Ambulatorio Leganitos** *(Plaza Leganitos; Tel 95/277-82-24)*.

Pharmacies In the center of the old town is **Farmacía Espejo** (*Plaza de los Naranjos 7; Tel 95/282-71-41; 9:30am-2pm/5-9pm Mon-Fri; 10am-2pm Sat*). A rotating schedule of 24-hour pharmacies is posted here.

Trains and Buses The main **bus station** (*Tel 95/276-44-00*) is on a hill northwest of the old town, with hourly service to Málaga. To get to the center of the city, you have to cross the freeway, go through the roundabout, and walk down Calle Trapiche, to Calle Aduar. It takes about 20 minutes. If you're coming from Málaga, you can take the local train to Fuengirola (160ptas), walk one block to the bus station, and get a bus to Marbella (310ptas). It's a hair-raising ride on the N-340, with frequent high-speed pullovers. Get off the bus at Plaza Alameda in the center of Marbella rather than going up to the bus station.

Bike/Moped Rental **Rainbow Rent a Moto** (*Avda. Severo Ochoa 9; Tel 95/277-16-99*) has a good deal on bikes (1,000ptas a day) and scooters (3,500ptas a day). It's five minutes east of the Marbella center, on the highway.

Postal Correos: (*Jacinto Benavente 26; Tel 95/277-28-98; 8:30am-2:30pm Mon-Fri, 9:30am-1pm Sat*)

Internet See *wired*, above.

nerja

Nerja is the cooler older brother that the gaudier towns on the Costa del Sol want to be like. Located 56 kilometers (35 miles) east of Málaga, it's still fairly mobbed with tourists in the summer, but it feels more like a beach town than a resort town. This is thanks mainly to its geography; rather than one long beach, Nerja consists of a series of picturesque coves, which makes it much more difficult to shove a high-rise on top. The centerpiece of the town is **El Balcón de Europa** (The Balcony of Europe), the site of a former castle and now a brilliant lookout point that juts out into the sea, offering wide vistas up and down the coast. While the views and the beaches bring in a lot of sun-seekers, even more people come here for the nearby **Cuevas de Nerja,** a gigantic prehistoric cave of stalagmite and stalactite, located 3 kilometers (1.9 miles) east of the city.

The road between Nerja and Málaga remains free of the concrete high-rises that blight other coastal resorts, but the more subtly sinister forces of tract housing developments are rapidly overtaking the landscape; it seems part of a conspiracy to make the entire world look like a giant suburb. Fortunately, the town of Nerja has escaped that fate thus far, and while spruced up for the tourists, it retains its Muslim character with crooked alleys and flat-roofed houses. The beaches of Nerja are what you would expect from the Mediterranean but don't always get: wide, a little bit pebbly, but with warm, clear blue water and plenty of corners to explore. A young international crowd hangs out at **Playa de**

nerja

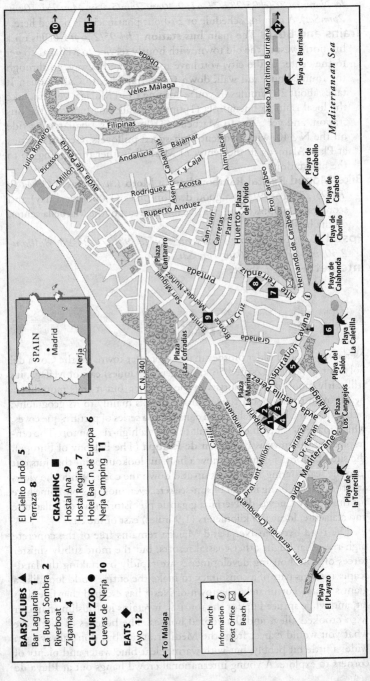

Church ✝
Information ⓘ
Post Office ⊠
Beach ⌇

← To Málaga

Mediterranean Sea

Playa Marítimo Burriana
Playa de Burriana
Playa de Carabeillo
Playa de Carabeo
Playa de Chorillo
Playa de Calahonda
Playa La Caletilla
Playa del Salón
Playa de la Torrecilla
Playa El Playazo

SPAIN
Madrid
Nerja

C.N. 340

Burrian, the longest of the town beaches, a few coves east of the Balcón de Europa. To get there from the center of town, head down **Hernando de Cabrabeo** until the end, then take long set of wooden stairs down to the beach. An older crowd congregates at the **Playa de la Torrecilla** on the west side of town.

The main street in "downtown" Nerja is **Calle Pintada,** which runs all the way from the Balcón de Europa up to the highway, C.N. 340, where you'll find the bus station. At nighttime, everyone heads to the Balcón de Europa to enjoy the views, an ice cream, or a beer. Then the old people go to bed and the young people wonder where all the young people went. To **Calle Tutti Frutti,** of course. That is not a nickname, but the honest-to-God official name of a street in the west side of town that's home to a string of loud music bars. Drinking bars line the street below it, **Calle Antonio Millon,** which stays packed on weekend nights. Despite evidence to the contrary, Nerja does not mean "alley cat," although you will see more stray cats than people slinking through the streets at night. It adds an ominous feeling to this otherwise shiny happy little town.

bar, club, and live music scene

We're not sure what the young folk here say to each other when planning their nights out. "Hey, going to the Frutti?" or "I'll see you at Tutti, okay?" or maybe just "Tutti Frutti?" But you have to go to Calle Tutti Frutti and its more dignified neighbor, Calle Antonio Millon, for nightlife other than playing bingo, drinking in fake Irish pubs with red-faced British men, or watching cats mate.

The bars on Antonio Millon, each within a few steps of the next, are generally open from 9pm to 2am, later on weekends. The prices are a consistent 250ptas for a Spanish beer, 400ptas for international brew, and 500ptas for cocktails. **Riverboat** *(Antonio Millon 1; No phone)* is one of the more tranquil pubs; it attracts a large British clientele, including many who live here year-round. Across the street and a few doors down you'll find **Zigamar** *(Antonio Millon),* the local alternative hangout with a pool table, trippy paintings, good funk music on the turntable, and a dreadlocked crowd.

On Plaza Tutti Frutti itself, directly northeast of Antonio Millon, things don't get started until midnight, and there's plenty of scooter parking and dancing for all. **La Buena Sombra** *(Plaza Tutti Frutti 5; No phone)* has loud pop music and outside tables on the plaza that are packed on weekends. Next door, **Bar Laguardia** *(Calle Tutti Frutti 7; No phone)* is the place for dancing.

CULTURE ZOO

Visitors are attracted to Nerja by the beauty of the little Andalusian village's whitewashed buildings and narrow cobblestone streets, which invite endless wandering and exploration. The town's major landmark is the **Balcón de Europa,** at the southernmost point of the town. The prom-

five things you didn't know about the caves of nerja

1. Hidden for almost three thousand years, the caverns were rediscovered in 1959 by a group of five local boys who were trying to catch bats in a nearby narrow shaft. They felt a draft coming from a section of the shaft that was covered in stalactite, and returned the next day with tools. When they finally made it through to the giant caverns, they found out they weren't the first visitors; prehistoric human skeletons lay next to ceramic bowls. Did we mention this all took place on Halloween night? (Okay, so that last part isn't true.)

2. The caves were opened to the public in 1960 and designated a monument one year later, but it wasn't until 1969 that another passageway was discovered that led to the so-called "Upper and New Galleries." Unfortunately, the human remains and prehistoric cave paintings of animals and fish found here remain off-limits to the public. Did we mention they also found the remains of giant Sasquatch? (Okay, so not really).

3. The different caverns and areas of the caves have all been given cool names such as Hall of the Phantom, the Organ Chapel, the Diverticulum of the Dolphins, the Columns of Hercules, the Passage of the Horse, the Labyrinth, and the Coca-Cola Pavilion. (Okay, so that last one's not true...yet).

4. Every year in July, the Festival of the Nerja Caves brings international performers to the unique concert hall inside the Hall of the Waterfall. Past performers include Yehudi Menuhin, the Russian Ballet, and Poison. (Every rose has its thorn).

5. The Caves of Nerja is the third most visited monument in Spain, after the Alhambra in Granada, and Antonio Banderas's house. (I guess that last one is more of a shrine than a monument).

enade dates from 1885 when it was constructed to honor a visit from King Alfonso XIII.

Cuevas de Nerja (*Carretera de Maro; Tel 95/252-96-35; 10am-2pm/4-6:30pm daily; 750ptas*): The main attraction in Nerja. These awesome prehistoric caverns were inhabited in ancient times until about 2000 B.C., but they remained hidden to modern eyes until 1959. They are anything but undiscovered these days—every hour buses deliver camera-toting tourists and screaming school groups to this full-blown attraction. The caves are made of stalactites and stalagmites, and whether you know the difference or not, you're really in for a treat. A wooden boardwalk leads you through the well-lit caves; don't be surprised to have your picture randomly taken inside (you can buy a print of it when you come out, like at ski slopes and amusement parks). The moderns have also "improved" upon the work of the ancients by building a giant auditorium into one of the largest caverns (some poor Cro-Magnon guy is rolling over in his grave), where occasional concerts occur (call for more information). These touches have a Disney-esque quality, so you have to keep reminding yourself that these are *real,* man. It really is worth the short trip from Nerja. To get there, take one of the hourly buses (105ptas) that leave Nerja until 8:15pm from the main bus stop on C.N. 340. You can buy your bus tickets at the little booth across the highway. From the drop-off point atop the town of Mora, you have to walk up to your left, under a highway overpass, and then up the hill for 5 minutes. To get back to Nerja, the same bus leaves from the entrance to the caves.

EATS

Nerja's international population brings an interesting potpourri of eating options, and makes this a good place to get off your tapas routine and try eating around the world.

El Cielito Lindo *(El Barrio 26; Tel 95/252-17-83; 7pm-midnight daily),* a five-minute walk northwest of the Balcón de Europa, wholeheartedly attempts to recreate Mexico on the Mediterranean. The decor is over-the-top, with sombreros, piñatas, fake peppers; it looks like someone just returned from a spending spree in Tijuana. Authentic Mexican-food lovers must be warned that the veggie burrito consists entirely of corn, onions, cheese, and runny beans, and the salsa that comes with the chips is kind of like spicy tomato sauce. But it's an honest effort, especially if you're tired of tapas, and worth it for the ice cold Pacifico beer (even though they serve it with a lemon, not a lime). Viva la cerveza.

At the handsome Greek restaurant **Terraza** *(Gloria 11; Tel 95/252-67-35; 6:30pm-midnight, closed Tuesday),* a five-minute walk northeast of the Balcón de Europa, you'll get tasty moussaka for 895ptas or "greens del Brian" for 1,350ptas...that's Brian the Greek I guess. The best deal is the take-away gyro sandwich for 600ptas. Grab one and head down to the Balcón de Europa for a killer evening picnic.

For an amazing, authentically Spanish outdoor lunch while at the beach, you must go to the *paella* institution, **Ayo** *(Playa Burriana; Tel 95/252-22-89),* at the far end of Playa Burriana, east of the old town on the Mediterranean. Sweaty cooks whip up all-you-can-eat *paella* (675ptas) every day in huge smoking pans. One of the cooks is Señor Ayo himself, a local legend for more than just his paella. He was among the group of boys who discovered the Caves of Nerja in 1959 (see *sidebar,* this page). Ayo is a can't-miss dude and a can't-miss meal while in town.

crashing

Rooms in Nerja cost considerably more in July and August, and are harder to find.

▶▶CHEAP

The best value in town is **Hostal Ana** *(Calle Cruz 62; Tel 95/252-30-43; 3,000ptas single, 5,000ptas double)*, a newly built *hostal* on the northwest edge of the center. A friendly couple runs this place, and its clean, modern rooms all have AC, TV, and their own bathrooms. It's quiet here at night, but you get your own key to the front door so no need to worry about the hour.

Centrally located just up from the Balcón de Europa, **Hostal Regina** *(Pintada 6; Tel 95/252-36-53; 4,000ptas single, 6,000ptas double; No A/C; TV; Private baths, V, MC)* sits atop a lively restaurant and bar that draw a young international crowd. They only have 10 rooms, so call ahead.

Just past the Cuevas de Nerja is **Nerja Camping** *(C.N. 340 km 297; Tel 95/252-97-14; 600ptas per person, car, and tent)*, a well-groomed camping site that is the cheapest option around. You'll need your own car to get here at night, however; the nearest bus is the one serving the *cuevas;* it stops at Maro, a good mile away. The campsite has pay phones, communal restrooms (open April-September) with showers, and a small snack bar selling basics like bread and milk.

▶▶SPLURGE

You'll pay a lot for the right to stay in the best location in town. **Hotel Balcón de Europa** *(Paseo Balcón de Europa 1; Tel 95/252-08-00; 15,000 and up double)* is not only right on the famous lookout point, it also has its own little private beach below, which seems to take all the fun out of going to the beach, unless you're hiding from something. The hotel is a 1970s pile whose most dramatic feature is its network of private balconies opening onto the Mediterranean. Rooms, mid-sized and furnished with modern pieces, each come with air conditioning, TV, minibar, and phone. Its fourth-floor restaurant, **Azul,** offering panoramic views of the Mediterranean, and beachside restaurant, **Nautico,** both serve international cuisine. The hotel is one of the best equipped in the area, with a sauna, health club, and solarium. Unless you're rolling in dough, though, you're probably better off staying at one of Nerja's many flower-draped, whitewashed houses, which are more moderately priced, if less dramatically located.

need to know

Currency Exchange There are banks with **ATMs** on Calle Pintada and Calle Cavana, both near the **Balcón de Europa.**

Tourist Information Just off the Balcón de Europa you'll find the small, crowded, but very helpful **tourist office** *(Puerta del Mar 2; Tel 95/252-15-31; 10am-2pm/5:30-8pm Mon-Fri, 10am-1pm Sat).*

Health and Emergency The **local police** *(Virgen del Pilar 1; Tel 95/252-15-45)* are on the north side of town, across the highway. For an ambulance, *95/252-09-35*. Though there is no local hospital, there is a small clinic, **Centro de Salud Nerja** *(Calle Carlos Millon, s/n)*, in the center of town.

Pharmacies Your best bet for finding a *farmacia* is **Calle Pintada.** One is located at #33 *(Tel 95/252-57-00; 9:30am-1:30pm, 4:30pm-8pm daily)*.

Buses The bus station is actually just a stop by the side of the C.N. 340 highway at the top of Calle Pintada. There's a little ticket booth with schedules for **Alsina Graells buses** *(Tel 95/252-15-04)* on the north side of the street. There are hourly buses to and from Málaga, but only three a day to Granada.

TORREMOLINOS

If you've ever drunk so much that you threw up repeatedly the next morning, you already have some idea what Torremolinos is like. Its name is synonymous with everything fun or frightening on the **Costa del Sol:** overdevelopment, package tours for beach-seeking Brits and Germans, soccer fans out on the piss, sunburns, cruising gay men, and gaudy *discotecas*. Recently, it's also begun to draw another species: the curiosity-seeking backpacker. Torremolinos is a place that never fails to live up to its infamous and cheesy reputation, yet somehow it attracts even as it repels. If you're an eco-tourist, a teetotaler, or looking for the true heart of Spain, avoid this place like the plague. But if you're a seeker of life experiences, a student of human behavior, or you just like to get drunk for cheap and go to the beach, you might want to try a day and night in Torremolinos...but certainly not any more than that. Like Las Vegas, it's one of those places where if you stay even one minute too long, things start to get ugly.

Torremolinos was once a quiet little fishing village, until the 1960s when dictator Francisco Franco became hell-bent on turning the south of Spain into an international tourist destination. Unappealing concrete high-rise hotels sprung up, and the British followed in their wake, lusting after the cheap accommodations and year-round sunshine. In the 1970s British package tours so overwhelmed the town that it was like a Monty Python skit come to life: "What's the point of being carted around in buses, surrounded by sweaty mindless oafs from Kettering and Boventry in their cloth caps and their cardigans and their transistor radios and their *Sunday Mirrors*, complaining about the tea, 'Oh, they don't make it properly here do they, not like at home'?"...In the '90s Torremolinos attempted to spruce up a bit to draw a more cultured, free-spending crowd—with mixed success. Today, retired pensioners live here in the winter, and in the summer loads of young British, Irish, and other Northern Europeans come to live, work, and drink. Though English seems to be the most common language, Spanish people like the beach, too, and some vacation here as well. And while Torremolinos has none of the things usually associated with modern gay life—such as good taste—it still draws loads of gay men and a few women to its beaches and infamous nightlife super center, La Nogalera. Keep in mind that while there's stuff happening here between May and October, the full Torremolinos experience only happens in July, August, and September.

Torremolinos is small and easily navigable; the next bar or the beach is never more than a few steps away. Walking through the streets here is an experiment in information overload; signs, mostly in English, shout out at you, trying to draw you in to a pub, restaurant, or hotel with enticing names like "Paddy Loco's," or invitations like "Come see Badger, the 'Utter Nutter', at the Red Parrot every Thursday." When you come up from the train station, you'll be at the pedestrian-only center of town, officially called **Avenida Jesús Santos Rein,** but also known as **Plaza Nogalera.** We'll call it Plaza Nogalera because it looks much more like a plaza than an avenue, with a fountain, a carousel, cafes, and bars. On summer nights, partiers parade through here, and groups of high-socked, white-shorted tourists sit at the outdoor tables to people-watch. Many of them aren't shy about it either—they'll actually turn their chairs toward the plaza, as if they were settling in to watch a good television show. Across the little plaza from the train station is the official La Nogalera, a mini-mall of bars, restaurants, and more bars, mostly gay. The address for of all these places is just a number, the street name for all of them is considered La Nogalera. The main pedestrian thoroughfare in town is **Calle San Miguel,** which runs from **Plaza Costa del Sol** down past La Nogalera and eventually to **Camino de la Playa,** the walkway out to the beach. Plaza Costa del Sol sits right in the middle of the N-340 highway. More nightlife takes place on streets that lead from the plaza: **Calle Doña Maria Barabino,** packed with little bars, goes up a hill to **Plaza de la Independencía,** where you'll find the tourist office. **Avenida Palma de Mallorca** contains many of the discotecas.

Torremolinos is built on a slight incline, so if you just go downhill from wherever you are you'll eventually reach the 7 kilometer (4.3 miles) stretch of beaches. They're not spectacular—just good sand and warm sea and a ton of people. In the center of town, below the "thousand steps" walkway (we didn't count but we'll take their word for it), is **Playa de Bajondillo,** which becomes **Playamar** further down to the left. Little palm-covered cabanas attached to "beach clubs" take up much of the sand here, but you can usually find plenty of free space, too. If you're facing the water, to the right of Playa de Bajondillo the beach becomes **Playa de la Carihuela,** which 1.5 kilometers (.93 miles) later brings you to a small fishing village—cleaned up for the tourists— La Carihuela. If any of this sounds confusing, it's really not. After being in the bigger cities of Europe, Torremolinos seems like a miniature golf course: everything is small-scale and easy to find, and everyone speaks English, so you can always ask.

bar, club, and live music scene

Getting drinks in Torremolinos is as easy as falling off a boat. During the day, the bars on the beach have a spring-break feel. In the evening, start your drinking at the outdoor cafes in the center of town. The bars mentioned below are nighttime haunts, generally opening at 9pm and going until 4am, though it's all dependent on the season and how many people are around.

The two bars right across from the metro station on Plaza Nogalera, **Tonic** (La Nogalera 309; No phone) and **Amsterdam** (La Nogalera 311), pull people in early in the game. They're literally wall-to-wall and seem to be the exact same bar; it's a wonder they don't just merge into one. These bars will give you a perfect idea of what to expect from all the other bars in town: outdoor tables, waitresses in skimpy dresses, seedy atmosphere, and cheap drinks. There's a fountain on the plaza right here, and if you're lucky you may see some "bloke on the piss" jump right in it. Remember, this is not Rome, and the cops will be on you in a second if you pull that stunt, though they'll usually just give you a warning if you seem to be having a good time.

things to do in torremolinos when you're dead

Hungover? It's difficult to find anything to do in this town that doesn't involve copious amounts of alcohol and team puking. But if you're a "wee bit delicate" from a long night out, you can go to the beach or rent a bike—or how about a trip to the **Aqua Park** (Cuba 10; Tel 90/211-49-96; 10am-6pm daily, May-Sept; 2025ptas)? It's over 70,000 square meters of water slides and wave pools and good clean fun (except for the urine-soaked kiddie pools). They have gnarly adventures like the Black Hole, Kamikaze, the Twister (on second thought, how rough *was* last night?), and Savage River, as well as more mellow pursuits like mini-golf and hot-dog eating. It's located in the northern part of town, above the N-340. If you're looking for good unclean fun, check out the **Super Sex Shop** (Avda. Los Manantiales, 11, Edificio Tres Torres; Tel 95/237-11-96; 10:30am-1am daily). Coincidentally enough, this place also has things called Kamikaze, the Twister...hmmm. They also have books and movies, and toys, both gay and straight.

On the same plaza, above a restaurant, is **El Open Arms** *(Cauce 10; No phone)*, a bar notable for having the worst karaoke in the history of the world. You might see some 75-year-old German guy belting out "Mack the Knife," a sloppy-drunk group of British girls butchering Madonna, or a frat boy warbling a sentimental version of "American Pie"...not the radio version, either—the whole eight minutes and fifty-two seconds. On second thought, maybe this is the best karaoke ever. Drink specials every night, and beers for 200ptas just might give you the courage to get up there yourself.

There's another pack of bars on Calle Doña Maria Barabino, which connects Plaza de Costa del Sol and Plaza de la Independencía. **New Tina's** *(Doña Maria Barabino 6; No phone)* is determined to get you drunk. If you order a simple beer they'll give you a free shot of schnapps as if you've won something. Young, attractive, British expats work here as bartenders, and the outside tables and the homey cave-like interior are always packed with other young, attractive northern Europeans. Besides a selection of international beers, you can also pick up free passes to the Palladium.

Quick quiz: If you're looking to keep the funk going all night long in Torremolinos, do you try to find the subtle, out-of-the-way hipster club? Hell no, this ain't Barcelona. You go to the loudest, most obnoxious megaplex of a discoteca, one with a swimming pool built in the middle of it: **Palladium** *(Avda. Palma de Mallorca, 36; Tel 95/238-42-89; 11am-6am Thur-Sat)*. This two-story legend-in-its-own-mind also has foosball and a pizzeria, and—oh yeah—dance floors and bars. Go late, when it's crowded with attractive young Spanish folk and drunk Northern Europeans; it's spookily empty before 1:30am. The DJs aren't cutting edge, they're more there to play the well-known crowd-pleasers. But you won't hear just plain old Britney Spears either...you'll get the Britney Spears re-mix! Cover is a silly 1,100ptas but you can get free passes at the bar New Tina's.

gay scene

Gay life in Torremolinos is always described as cruisy, which means the Northern European gay men (and a few women) who come here are looking to have their week of hedonism in paradise before returning to their day jobs. They follow a strict routine: the beach **Playamar** during the day, and the meat market area **La Nogalera,** right in the center of town, at night. So many gay bars have scrunched into La Nogalera's mall-like passageways, who knows where to begin? Olympo or Bacchus? Soho or Manhattan? Don't fret, however, no choice is final—no matter what bar you go into, another one beckons just three steps away. Hours are a fairly consistent 10pm to 5am.

Parthenon [see *bar scene*, above] is the best-known, and is highly recommended for a mixed-ages crowd of beautiful tanned men and their admirers. Next door, **Men's Bar** *(La Nogalera 714; No phone)* draws an in-your-face leather and Levi's crowd. For a slightly more refined atmosphere, try the bar at **Porquoi Pas?** *(La Nogalera 703; No phone).* The best dancing in La Nogalera, and an outside bar, is at **Tension** *(La Nogalera 524).* Late night/early morning, many men actually leave La Nogalera to go to a dance club built underground a few minutes away, **Bronx!** *(Calle de la Cruz, Edificio Centro Jardin).* Look for the stairs going down, which sort of look like you're entering a subway line.

eats

Torremolinos is not an epicenter of authentic Spanish cuisine, it's more of a mish-mash of cultures; you can get fish 'n' chips, bratwurst, or dutch pancakes as easily as tapas. There are plenty of little supermarkets around the center of town, most of which stay open during siesta hours, so you can grab some munchies (Kraft's 'Lunchables' for your protein-fix) to take to the beach.

A definite benefit of the British invasion can be found at one of Spain's few excellent Indian restaurants, **Golden Curry** *(Guetaria, 6; Tel 95/237-48-55; 1-4pm, 7pm-12am daily, closed Friday).* A wide selection of chicken dishes, such as biryani or curry, costs about 900ptas; a vegetable curry, 500ptas. Don't forget to try the mouthwateringly warm garlic nan bread (300ptas) and to talk with the friendly owner who came to the Costa del Sol via London and Calcutta. Outside seating on the patio is available. The restaurant is located on the second floor of a building at the bottom edge of La Nogalera.

If you're determined to get tapas, try **La Bodega** *(San Miguel, 40; Tel 95/238-73-37; 12pm-12am daily).* In the center of town, this lively place draws old local dudes as well as tourists for the reasonably priced and tasty fried fish tapas (200ptas and up).

You can also get good fresh fish tapas at any of the chiringuitos, the beachside bars on Paseo Maritimo. For a healty hangover-helper at the beach, look for the giant orange, which goes by the name **Viva Naranja** *(Paseo Maritimo, no address).* The pleasant man inside of the orange (no, you're not still drunk) will squeeze you fresh orange juice for 250ptas for a normal-sized glass, or 550ptas for a *grande.*

crashing

While drinking in Torremolinos is cheap, sleeping will cost you a bit more than the youth hostels in the big Spanish cities. The good news is that plenty of hotels and hostels do business in the center of town—you can't miss their signs—and you'll get what you're paying for, because they're generally all modern and well-maintained. Prices fluctuate wildly depending on the season. Basically, if you're coming between July and September, you'll pay nearly twice as much as you would in winter. Book ahead in high season.

▶▶**DO-ABLE**

Hotel El Pozo *(Casablanca, 2; Tel 95/238-06-22; 3000ptas single, 5000ptas double, low-season; 4,000ptas single, 8,000ptas July-Sept)* offers the best value for the money. Its location, right between the nightlife center and the beach, appeals to young, fun-seeking Europeans in the summer. The staff is friendly, the rooms are big and airy and all have bathrooms, telephones, and cable TV. There's also a bar in the plant-filled lobby and a billiards table, which makes it a great meeting place.

Whitewashed hostels stack themselves one on top of the other on Calle Peligrino, a little souvenir-stand street just off Playa de Bojondillo.

A good bet is **Hostal Loreto** *(Calle Peligro, 9; Tel 95/237-08-41; 4,000ptas single, 4,500ptas double, 5,500ptas single, 7,000ptas double in high season).* This German-run operation isn't as roomy as Hotel El Pozo, but it's just as clean and well maintained, and the beach is literally steps away. There are also some rooms with communal bathrooms down the hall, which are 1,000ptas cheaper than the prices listed above.

need to know

Currency Exchange They give you no excuse for not spending money here; you can't miss the signs wanting to exchange your currency on **Calle San Miguel,** but you'll get a better rate at the **ATMs** on **Plaza Costa del Sol** or next to the **train station** on Plaza La Nogalera.

Tourist Information The English-speaking **Tourist Information Office** *(Plaza de la Independencia, no address; Tel 95/237-95-12; 10am-2pm Mon-Sat),* just up from Plaza Costa del Sol, is only open four hours each day, maybe because they want to get to the beach, too.

Health and Emergency National Police: *(Tel 95/238-99-99),* Ambulance: *(Tel 95/222-22-22).* There is no hospital in Torremolinos. There is a service clinic, **Ambulatorio de Torremonlinos** *(Calle Pablo Bruno, no address; Tel 95/238-38-38)* in the center. For greater emergencies patients are transferred to the hospital in Málaga.

Trains and Buses The **train station** *(Avenida Jesús Santos Rien/Plaza La Nogalera, no address; Info: Tel 95/238-57-64)* is really just an underground metro station on the local **Malaga Cercanías** line between Malaga and Fuengirola. Malaga is only 25 minutes and 140ptas away and trains leave every half-hour. Go undergound where you see the train symbol on Plaza La Nogalera in the center of town to find the tracks and a timetable. The **bus station** *(Calle Hoyo; no address; Info: Tel 95/238-24-19)* is also in the center of town, one block up from Plaza Costa del Sol.

Bike/Moped Rental At **moto mercardo** *(Plaza de las Communidades Autónomas, s/n; Tel 95/205-26-71; 10am-2pm, 5pm-8pm Mon-Sat),* you can rent a *bike* for 1,500ptas for 24 hours (5,000ptas deposit) so you can keep it with you overnight. If you want to get your motor running, get a little Puegot *scooter* for 3,500ptas a day (10,000ptas deposit) or a crotch rocket Honda Goldwing Gl 1500 SE for 25,000ptas a day, though you'll need a credit card and a driver's license if you're that hard-core. Located right on the beach Playa del Bajondillo.

Postal The main post office is **Correos** *(Avenida Palma de Mallorca 25; Tel 95/238-45-18; 8:30am-8:30pm Mon-Fri, 9:30am-1pm Sat).*

andalucía

andalucía

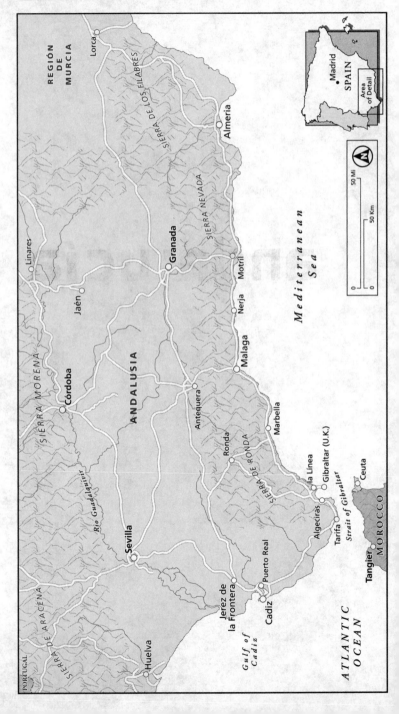

andalucía isn't so much a region as it is a mood, an atmosphere: sensual and exuberant like flamenco; festive, colorful, and tragic like a bullfight. It exudes history, romance, and beauty from every corner (except for the **Costa del Sol,** which has a slightly different thing going and therefore gets its own chapter—see above). Spread over a huge, dramatically diverse terrain, with green terraced farmland, winding rivers, snowcapped mountain peaks, and endless beaches, Andalucía is unified by a uniquely Spanish passion for life. Once the cornerstone of the Western Muslim Empire—which gave it the name "Al-Andalus" and its grand Islamic architecture—Andalucía is also the cultural cradle of the most authentically Spanish of traditional arts: bullfighting, flamenco, tapas, and sherry-making. All of this, along with great weather, relatively inexpensive costs, and a boisterous till-dawn nightlife, make it one of the great world headquarters of hanging out—although you won't be the first one to discover its unique charm. Fortunately, the influx of visitors has not damaged Andalucía's soul (except, again, for the Costa del Sol).

From the incomparably romantic cities of **Sevilla** and **Granada,** to picturesque hilltop villages, to miles of **Mediterranean** coastline, Andalucía is a place that lives up to its advanced billing as "must see," although "must experience" is more accurate. Because it's not about running around from monument to bar with a camera strapped to your eyeball; it's about allowing yourself to be seduced by the distinct rhythm of life here. Wake up late, get a *cafe con leche,* wander around the cobblestoned alleys, see a monument, get some evening tapas, join *"la marcha,"* or disco till the sun comes up. And repeat. Take it easy, because while the cities here never sleep, they definitely siesta. But mellow doesn't mean dull. Andalucía is imbued with an unmistakable sensuality. This is helped by the fact that there are a lot of attractive people walking around, but it's mostly due to the Andalucian outlook on life: an appreciation of beauty with an acute awareness of tragedy. *"Lo que pasa, pasa,"* you'll be reminded, "whatever happens, happens. Life is short. Live everyday to the fullest." The locals instinctively follow all these sayings which we have to constantly remind ourselves to try to live up to.

Geographically, Andalucía is as diverse as anywhere this side of California. It contains Spain's highest peaks, in the **Sierra Nevadas** near Granada, which are covered with snow year round, and also Spain's driest region, in the wild semi-deserts near **Almería.** But most of the region

ON TO MOROCCO

Right across the Strait of Gibraltar, Africa looms. If you're planning to go to Morocco for a day trip or an extended stay, there are two places to get ferries to Tangiers in Andalucía: Algeciras and Tarifa. Algeciras is the major port between Spain and Africa, an uninspiring city with a reputation for drug-smuggling and petty crime. Tarifa is a mellow windsurfing town with an attractive old quarter. Having said all that, we must tell you that Algeciras has a multitude of boat companies making the two-hour trip to Tangiers, with departures on the hour. Tarifa only has one scheduled departure a day, but there are often more, depending on demand. Algeciras also has a train station. But Tarifa is just a 25-minute bus ride from Algeciras, and the bus station in Algeciras is across the street from the train station. Still can't decide? Well, we'll decide for you: Tarifa is a better option if you have time, especially since a night in Tarifa can be a blast and the surroundings are epic; if you're in a hurry, however, you might as well just go to Algeciras, head straight for the port, and jump on one of the boats. Be warned that in summer, the port can be packed with Moroccans returning home for holiday. The prices are around 3,500ptas from Algeciras to Tangiers, and 3,100ptas for the one-hour trip from Tarifa to Tangiers. In recent years, travelers have complained about leaving from Tarifa because the service was sporadic, but Southern Ferries has begun a daily crossing (see **Tarifa** chapter for details), so you can avoid Algeciras altogether. Wherever you leave from, it's best to travel with someone to Tangiers, or try to hookup with someone on the boat, because the crowds and craziness and guides trying to get money off you can be overwhelming if you're not sure where you're going.

consists of rugged green hills topped with white villages, and fertile river valleys where olives (for olive oil) and grapes (for sherry) are among the main crops. Then of course there are the coasts, which can be broken down into distinct regions: **The Costa de la Luz** in the west is green and hilly alongside the colder waters of the **Atlantic;** it stretches from Portugal down to the Strait of Gibraltar, just a stone's throw from Africa. In the east of the province, the little promontory **Cabo de Gata** is mostly undeveloped, with wild beaches and warm Mediterranean waters. In between the two is the touristy and overdeveloped Costa del Sol (see separate chapter).

The highlights of Andalucía are its two magnificent cities, Sevilla and Granada, which both fall into the category of "must see before you die." The capital of the region, Sevilla, meanders along the **Rio Guadalquivir,** and is the seductive epicenter of flamenco and bullfighting. Orange trees, plazas, narrow, cobblestoned streets, one of Europe's biggest cathedrals, and a wandering party-in-the-streets nightlife never fail to live up to expectations. Granada is a dramatic, multicultural city with a vibrant student population, set in the foothills of the snowcapped Sierra Nevada mountains, and dominated by the spectacular Muslim fortress/palace, the Alhambra. (It's so popular, you have to reserve your tickets in advance during the high season, so plan ahead). Gypsies, hippies, backpackers, Moroccan-style teahouses, and fat Middle Eastern sandwiches make Granada always a unique experience, and its surroundings are equally diverse: you could conceivably ski in the morning, go to the beach in the afternoon, and be back at Plaza Nueva in time for the nightlife. While these two historical yet modern cities are the most famous, other less-known Andalucian cities are also fascinating. **Córdoba,** the former capital of Muslim Spain, has a world-renowned *Mezquita* (mosque), with a Christian cathedral stuck in the middle. It also has an attractive old quarter with plant-filled patios, and a small, almost underground alternative culture. On the Costa de la Luz, **Cádiz** is the oldest city in Western Europe, an authentic, atmospheric port city with long stretches of white sand beaches and a never-say-die nightlife. **Jerez (de la Frontera)** literally means "sherry," and it's home to hundreds of bodegas that offer tastings of Spain's ancient wine, produced in nearby vineyards. Today it's a modern city that is also the capital of a couple of other Spanish passions: equestrian sports and motorcycle racing.

Of all of Andalucia's hilltop white villages (*pueblos blancos*)—and there are many—**Ronda** is the most spectacular and the most visited, thanks to its location atop a steep 500-foot gorge. It's also the former hideout of bandits and the birthplace of the rules of modern bullfighting, and it's surrounded by amazingly green hills and wild flowers. Equally impressive and mysterious are the towns that sit in the deep valleys southeast of Granada, like **Las Alpujarras.**

If you're looking for nature or outdoor adventure, head to Andalucía's lesser-known coasts. The Atlantic-side Costa de la Luz has long stretches of uninterrupted beach, plenty of campsites, and quaint fishing villages. On its southern tip, with views of the green hills of Africa, lies the mellow and historical **Tarifa,** the windiest spot in Europe, where "windsurfing is king." The diehard windsurfers turn the town into a little international community, with a vibrant yet laid-back nightlife set in the historic old quarter. Tarifa is also a good place to catch a ferry to Morocco, while avoiding the charmless port of **Algeciras** [see *on to Morocco,* below]. On the southeastern edge of Andalucía, Cabo de Gata offers the wildest and most spectacular beaches in Spain, with red volcanic rocks, steep cliffs, soft sand, and plenty of nude people. The town of **San José** is a super-mellow little beach town that's the best base for exploring Cabo de Gata. It may be hard to believe, but you can also ski and snowboard in Andalucía, at **Solynievein** in the Sierra Nevada, just 30 minutes from the city of Granada. It's the southernmost ski resort in Spain, offering plenty of sunshine, typically Andalucian late, late, nightlife, and decent-to-good snow from November to April. Above the ski resort is the highest road in Europe, which makes a challenging bike ride. Also for mountain bikers and hikers, Las Alpujarras, on the back side of the Sierra Nevada, offers spectacular ascents to the top of Spain's highest peak, **Mulhacén,** as well as paragliding for the truly adventurous. Rockclimbers and people who like heights in general should check out El Chorro river gorge—between Ronda and Málaga (on the Costa del Sol)—a deep ravine with sheer cliffs and a somewhat sketchy footpath. Andalucía also contains over half of the country's environmentally protected lands. The two most dramatic natural parks are the mountainous **Parque Natural Sierra Nevada** and **Parque Natural de Cabo de Gata-Nijar.** In the west of the region is **Parque Nacional de Doñana,** a series of wetlands and an important wildlife refuge. **Parque Natural Los Alcornales,** northeast of Tarifa, is a vast Mediterranean woodland, crucial to many migrating birds. In the northwest of the region is the biggest natural park in Spain, **Parque Natural de Cazorla,** which unfortunately is difficult to explore without your own wheels. All of the parks have some accommodation, whether it be campsites or youth hostels.

The history of Andalucía is, of course, complex, but we'll gladly oversimplify it for you, so you can at least get your bearings straight when looking at a historical attraction. In ancient times, Phoenician traders, Visigoths, and other cultures lost to history came and went without leaving much of a trace. Andalucía then became part of the Roman Empire, which also didn't leave as much here as in other parts of Spain, though there are some Roman ruins in Málaga and Córdoba. The Muslims, who came from Africa in the 8th century, had a huge impact, making Andalucía a center of culture and learning, giving the towns and cities a distinctive maze-like layout, and building great architectural feats such as the Mezquita in Córdoba and Alhambra in Granada. To give just one of countless examples of Muslim Spain's cultural advancement, they added the sixth string to the Arab lute and thus invented the guitar. Where would all you rockers be without that one? Córdoba was the first capital of the empire and one of the leading cities in Europe until the 11th century, when the capital was moved to Sevilla. In the 13th century, the Christians retook Córdoba and Sevilla, leaving Granada as the last stronghold of Muslim Spain. The *Reconquista* (reconquering) ended with the taking of Granada in 1492 by the victorious *Reyes Católicos* (Catholic Kings) Isabella and Ferdinand, who now have a street named after them in every city. In a strange historical coincidence, 1492 was also the year Columbus, having shipped off from Andalucía, discovered the Americas. Andalucía flourished during the Age of Discovery, when trade with the New World brought huge amounts of wealth, particularly to the port cities, and most of all, Sevilla. So if you can't remember dates to save your life, at least remember 1492, as it was the turning point in Andalucía's history. Unfortunately, along with prosperity came religious persecution of

Jews and Arabs during the Spanish Inquisition. Bad karma, infighting, and mismanagement among the nobility led to the loss of colonies in the New World and a serious decline in the fortunes of the region. Andalucía began to come back to life during the Industrial Revolution, but that was quickly squashed by the Spanish Civil War (1936-1939), which divided communities and left deep wounds all across Spain. The Franco Years were lean ones for Andalucía, a trend that was reversed only with the tourism boom that began in the 1960s and continues to this day. While tourism has definitely provided a boost to Andalucía's economy, the region still has one of the highest rates of unemployment in Spain.

If you're looking at some monument in Andalucía, at least try to determine if it's from Muslim Spain, from an architectural trend after the Reconquista, or, as in most cases, a combination of both. The Muslim (also referred to as Moorish, Islamic, Arabic) touches include horseshoe arches, ornately carved wood ceilings, and intricately detailed tiling, usually decorated with verses from the Koran (those pretty patterns you see probably spell out something like "Allah is the only Conquerer"). Other architectural terms you'll hear are *mudejar,* (made by Muslim craftsmen who remained behind after the Reconquista), and *mozarabic,* (Christian elements based on Muslim motifs). In the centuries after the Reconquista, Gothic was big, as seen in many of Andalucía's cathedrals. Later, many Baroque elements were added.

The citizens of Andalucía are justly proud of their home and view tourists with some bewilderment and amusement, although they're generally tolerant and warm to all but the most obnoxious. The idea of young people trotting around the globe is a strange concept to many of them. "Why would I go anywhere else?" is the general attitude, and once you've experienced Andalucía, you'll see their point. Andalucians aren't encouraged to leave their families for any period of time. Even more than the Catholic faith, Andalucians revere the institution of family. Young people live at home until they're married and sometimes long after. Another tradition that has survived subtly in Andalucía is *machismo,* a distinct form of male chauvinism. If you're not spending a long time here, or you're just having too good a time to care, you probably won't even notice it. But isn't it odd how few women you see in tapas bars? That's tradition, baby. Ask your new Andalucian friends (if they seem open-minded) about the male/female dynamic and you're bound to get an earful or else a tight-lipped shaking of the head. These traditions don't necessarily apply to *guiris* (foreigners), who are seen as some other sort of species altogether.

According to legend, *tapas* were invented in Andalucía, near Jerez. The name literally means "cover" or "lid," and the story goes that a bartender started putting a piece of bread over the top of his customers' drinks in order to keep flies and dirt out of the glass. Then, when he started putting a piece of cheese or ham over the bread, customers began flocking and a new cuisine was invented. You'll do a lot of tapas-hopping in bars here if you're trying to live it up and live on the cheap. Preparing pig meat is an art here, so don't be surprised to find cured legs of *jamon* (ham), with hoofs still attached, hanging in every tapas bar in Andalucía. They also serve pig in many other forms, such as *lomo* (pork loin) and *chorizo* (sweet sausages). Seafood is, of course, big on the coast and is very often *frito* (fried). Cold soups such as *gazpacho* or *ajo blanco* (white garlic) are ubiquitous and especially refreshing on hot summer days. In the mountain regions, game such as deer or rabbit is popular, though it tastes a little too gamey for some people. For wine lovers, Andalucía is one of the oldest wine-producing regions in the world, and sherry is its name. The sherry triangle, near Jerez, is where it's produced, and you'll see the locals enjoying a glass with their tapas. The young people mainly stick to the local beer (Cruzcampo and Mahou are the most popular) or mixed drinks, and the tourists drink sangria. Desserts have retained much of their Muslim influence: nutty and sweet rather than chocolaty and decadent; *helado* (ice cream) is also popular. Vegetarians and vegans should be warned: you're not in California anymore. *Tortillas* are usually a safe bet, but they are sometimes what we call "Spanish vegetarian," which means they have bits of ham. Salads and soups are also available at almost all restaurants, though the salads are not remarkable. On the plus side, every Andalucian city and town has a *mercado* with excellent, cheap, fresh fruits and vegetables. Granada is a special treat for vegetarians, due to the omnipresent falafel stands.

The best times to go to Andalucía are spring and fall, although even in winter the weather is comfortable throughout most of the region. July and August are the most popular months and can be somewhat insane: It's hot as all hell, especially in Sevilla and Córdoba, and the whole country seems to head south for the beaches, making the coastal resorts a fun-loving madhouse. Spring is festival time, and Andalucians love their *fiestas,* which is not the same thing as saying they love to party. They do love to drink and dance, but they also revere the traditions behind all of their festivals. *Carnaval* in Cádiz starts off the party season with Andalucia's best street fest, one of the wildest and most unique Mardi Gras celebrations outside of Rio. *Semana Santa,* (the Holy Week before Easter) is a time for solemn religious processions all around Andalucía, the most spectacular and famous being in Sevilla. Three weeks after Easter, they let it all hang out at Sevilla's *Fería,* a week-long blowout where the whole town dresses up in traditional attire and heads out to the nearby fairgrounds. While Sevilla's are the best known, every city and small town has some celebration of *Semana Santa,* and a yearly *fería.* Be aware that hotel prices skyrocket during these events.

getting around andalucía

Andalucía is divided into eight provinces, each with a capital city of the same name: **Sevilla, Córdoba, Cádiz, Málaga, Granada, Jaén, Almería,** and **Huelva.** The major cities and towns are never too far apart from each other; in three hours or less you can always be somewhere uniquely interesting. You will definitely be going to Sevilla and Granada, or else life is not worth living. Plus they're located within good striking distance of all the other spots. From Sevilla, Granada is 4 hours away, Málaga and the Costa del Sol are approximately 3 hours, Cádiz is 2 hours, and Córdoba is 2 hours or less. From Granada, Málaga is 3 hours or less, Almería is 3-1/2 hours, and Las Alpujarras is 3-1/2 hours. You get the picture; you won't be wasting your time in Andalucía on "travel days" but will have time to make it to each town, get settled in, and hit the streets.

Good old trains and buses are the best ways to get around. Trains run frequently between the big cities, which tend to be the provincial capitals. To get into the mountains or out to the coasts you'll need to take buses, which are run by various independent companies, but which are quite comfortable and run on time. (Of the towns covered in this region, the following do not have train service: Tarifa, Las Alpujarras, Sierra Nevada, and Cabo de Gata.) Many travelers claim that Andalucía's buses are not only cheaper than trains, but also more comfortable, which can be true depending on the class of train. You should try to take at least one ride on the superfast **AVE** train, which runs between Madrid and Sevilla, with a stop in Córdoba, at speeds up to 280 kilometers per hour. It's more expensive than other classes of trains (even Europass holders have to pay a 1,500ptas "reservation" charge) but the thing flies, man, and it's like being on an airplane, with free movies and stewardesses. It's so efficient that if it's more than five minutes late you'll get your money back. (Don't count on it.) To explore the nooks and crannies of the region, a rental car can be useful, although in the cities it may be more of hassle than it's worth. Renting a car can be expensive in Andalucía; try getting a car in other major cities in Spain, such as Madrid, Valencia, or Barcelona. Be careful where you park your car in the cities here; on the street is never a good idea as break-ins are frequent. Find a hotel with a private garage or parking lot with an attendant.

▶▶ROUTES

If you've only got a short time, you'll want hit the two biggies: Sevilla and Granada.

If you have more time and want to get outdoors, do Sevilla, then Granada, and from there head either to the Sierra Nevada (30 minutes), Nerja on the Costa del Sol (3 hours), or to get away from it all, Cabo de Gata, via Almería(4 hours).

To hit all the romantic historical cities without ever getting off the train: go from Córdoba down to Sevilla (45 minutes), then to Cádiz (2 hours), up to Ronda, and on to Granada.

For our most highly recommended blend of historical cities and nature, do historical Córdoba, atmospheric Sevilla, the beaches of Cádiz, windy Tarifa, the gorge of Ronda (via Algeciras), sun-drenched Nerja, dramatic Granada, the mysterious hikes of Las Alpujarras, and the wild beaches of Cabo de Gata.

TRAVEL TIMES

All times are by road unless
indicated by a star:
  * = time by train
  ** = time by fast train

	Sevilla	Cadiz	Cordoba	Granada
Sevilla	-	1:45*	:45*	2:55*
Cadiz	1:45*	-	2:45*	3:45*
Cordoba	:45*	2:45*	-	2:20
Granada	2:55*	3:45*	2:20	-
Cabo de Gata	5:30	3:05	5:10	3:00
Jerez de La Frontera	1:10*	:40*	2:00** 2:30*	3:20
Las Alpurjarras	3:40	4:30	3:05	:35
Ronda	3:30*	2:15	2:35	2:30
Sierra Nevada	3:50	4:55	3:30	1:00
Tarifa	2:45	1:45	3:30	3:15

Cabo de Gata	Jerez de La Frontera	Las Alpurjarras	Ronda	Sierra Nevada	Tarifa	Madrid
5:30	1:10*	3:40	3:30*	3:50	2:45	2:30*
3:05	:40*	4:30	2:15	4:55	1:45	4:50*
5:10	2:00** 2:30*	3:05	2:35	3:30	4:00	1:45*
3:00	3:20	:35	2:30	1:00	3:15	5:50** 9:10*
-	6:15	2:25	4:50	1:35	5:15	7:00
6:15	-	4:15	1:50	4:20	1:55	4:15
2:25	4:15	-	3:05	2:25	3:40	4:55
4:50	1:50	3:05	-	3:35	2:00	6:20
1:35	4:20	2:25	3:25	-	4:20	5:10
5:15	1:55	3:40	2:00	4:20	-	7:10

For the all-inclusive tour: First Córdoba, then Sevilla, Jerez, down to Cádiz, down the coast to Tarifa, up to Ronda (via Algeciras), down to Málaga, over to the cheesy Costa del Sol (Marbella, Toremolinos, or Nerja), then up to Granada, over to Las Alpujarras, and down to Cabo de Gata (via Almería). This sounds insane, but none of the trips is more than 3½ hours and many are an hour or less (except for the final leg to Cabo de Gata, which can take 5 hours from Granada but is worth it).

SEVILLA

"Sevilla doesn't have an ambiance. It is ambiance."
—James Michener

Celebrated throughout history in song, poetry, and travel writing as the most romantic of all Spanish cities, you might expect Sevilla to buckle under its own reputation; instead, it is one of those rare places that lives up to its clichés. If Madrid is the sexiest city in Spain and Barcelona the most cultured, Sevilla is the most sensual. But just as the root of attraction is hard to define, Sevilla retains a sense of mystery, of atmosphere, of, dare we say, *ambiance,* that is impossible to miss but even harder to pinpoint. In the tradition of its most famous fictional residents (Don Juan, Carmen, the Barber), the city doesn't blow your mind as much as it seduces (and isn't the seduction the best part anyway?). To put it in simpler terms, if Spain were an amusement park (and some yahoos behave as if it were), Madrid would be the roller coaster and Barcelona the psychedelic funhouse, but Sevilla would definitely be the Tunnel of Love.

The climate here in "the frying pan of Spain" helps create the libido-charging atmosphere; it gets hot, damn hot, especially in late summer, forcing the whole city out onto the streets. If you're getting too fried, do as the locals do and head to the cooler banks of the river. The **Guadalquivir** has always been the lifeblood of Sevilla, allowing it to prosper during the Age of Discovery, when it was the city that launched a thousand ships.

Today Sevilla remains the capital of Andalucía, and the epicenter and caretaker of Spanish tradition. Flamencos are danced and bullfights are

sevilla

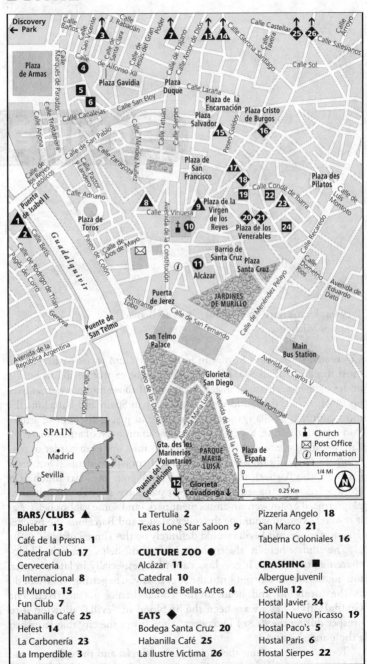

BARS/CLUBS ▲
Bulebar **13**
Café de la Presna **1**
Catedral Club **17**
Cerveceria
  Internacional **8**
El Mundo **15**
Fun Club **7**
Habanilla Café **25**
Hefest **14**
La Carbonería **23**
La Imperdible **3**

La Tertulia **2**
Texas Lone Star Saloon **9**

CULTURE ZOO ●
Alcázar **11**
Catedral **10**
Museo de Bellas Artes **4**

EATS ◆
Bodega Santa Cruz **20**
Habanilla Café **25**
La Ilustre Victima **26**

Pizzeria Angelo **18**
San Marco **21**
Taberna Coloniales **16**

CRASHING ■
Albergue Juvenil
  Sevilla **12**
Hostal Javier **24**
Hostal Nuevo Picasso **19**
Hostal Paco's **5**
Hostal Paris **6**
Hostal Sierpes **22**

held not just as a put-on for the tourists (although they will gladly take your money) but as an essential part of the city's culture. The younger generation proudly accepts the past, but also practices the essential 21st-century arts of DJ-ing, piercing, and Internet-surfing with equal vigor. Despite this infusion of modern European hipsterdom, Sevilla remains the most Spanish of all cities, at least in those images that Spain conjures in our imaginations: cobblestoned streets, Gothic doorways, Moorish arches, whitewashed houses, flower-filled plazas, meandering riverbanks, stone bridges, thumping discotecas, drinking on church steps, big-mustached cops, kids making out at the bus stops, etc. But just as a kick-ass jazz solo relies on its silences as much as the notes that are played (listen to "Sketches of Spain" by Miles Davis), the beauty of Sevilla lies not in the list of all its attributes, but in the spaces between them, in the atmosphere, and in the passion of the people creating it.

five things to talk to a local about

1. **The locals are justly proud of their city,** and beginning any conversation by complimenting the incomparable beauty of the architecture, women, men, sidewalks, lampposts, etc., will get you in like Flynn.
2. **The Sevillana** is the distinctly local form of flamenco dancing, which almost all kids here learn in school at a young age. If you ask to learn a few steps, you'll be surprised to find that no matter how easy the moves seem, the sensual rhythm it requires just might not be in your gene pool.
3. **Sevilla lives for its festivals, Semana Santa and Feria,** and if you miss them, its residents will tell you what a fool you are and give you a play-by-play of the action.
4. **The establishment here is fiercely protective of its right to bullfight,** no matter how outsiders view public displays of animal cruelty. So of course, the rebellious youth love to poke fun at it, because hey, in a place of perfect beauty and perfect weather you've got to have something to rebel against, right? Just don't refer to it as a sport.
5. **Machismo,** that particular Spanish form of male chauvinism, is a touchy subject bound to get the passions flowing and give you a new insight into modern Spain. Be careful who you ask (a group of oldsters watching the bullfight on TV is not a good idea) and if you get a reply such as "What are you talking about?" or "There's no such thing," it's best to drop it.

Like the city itself, *Sevillanos* take some time to get to know; they have a reputation in the rest of Spain for having a bit of an attitude. But once you break the ice with a local (usually a goofy smile or an *Hola* is all it takes) they'll open up like a sports car on the autobahn, and you'll have a hard time getting a word in. And yes, la-de-da-dee, they like to party, but their idea of a good time is not getting piss drunk as quickly as possible. Going out is about being with friends and family, about conversation, rather than yelling movie references back and forth and pounding beers before staggering to the club to get some action. Leave your drinking games at home, and instead bring an opinion.

A buttload of American students studies Spanish here, an estimated 3,000 of them at any one time. If you're a hard-core authenticity seeker who can't stand to play the name game ("You're from New York, you must know my friend Julie!"), you might not be able to leave your hotel room. But Sevilla is just big enough and has a modern enough infrastructure (tourism seems to be the only industry) that it can handle the waves of *extraneros* without losing any of its character. Also, foreign students can be great sources of information, especially if you're having trouble remembering what you learned in 11th-grade Spanish class. They are more than happy to let you in on the coolest spots and show they are not as *guiri* as you are. One warning: Anyone who refers to the city by its English name "Seville" (suh-vill), instead of the poetic *Sevilla* (se-vee-ya) is not to be trusted under any circumstances.

Plenty of written sources exist to help you navigate through all this ambiance. **The Tip,** a free English/Spanish paper for exchange students published on the 15th of every month, is easy to read, and has a decent listing of events, informative articles, and good tips for survival. **El Giraldillo,** in Spanish, is the monthly entertainment bible and also free. These can both be found at many cafes (especially the Internet variety) and tourist offices. **La Util de tu Ciudad,** a university publication with more current music listings, is harder to find; your best bet is to stop by the university or ask someone who looks like a student. The daily newspapers, such as **ABC Sevilla,** also have up-to-date listings.

neighborhoods

True to its seductive nature, Sevilla promises great rewards if you give it time and attention. A good pair of walking shoes will come in handy, too. Geographically flat, it lacks the dramatic first impression of other great cities; it's what stoners might call a "creeper." But in the crooked paths of **Santa Cruz,** the banks of the river Guadalquivir, and the rambling alleys of the **Centro** and **Macarena,** the city finds itself, at times strolling, most often strutting.

To orient yourself, use the Gothic Catedral as your reference point; it's the heart of the city and easily identifiable by its tower, the Giralda, the tallest thing in town, with the spinning gold weathervane on top. To the east lies Santa Cruz, the *judería* (old Jewish quarter), with serpentine cobblestoned streets, flower-filled plazas, and charmingly overpriced restaurants.

People love to explore the barrio Santa Cruz, with its maze of cobblestoned streets and whitewashed houses. Planning a walk here is impossible, since the whole point is to get lost, but make sure you hit **Plaza Santa Cruz,** near the walls of the Alzcazar. This serene, flower-filled plaza with a cross in the middle might be the only one in the barrio not surrounded by restaurants or bars.

For a good riverside walk, start at Alemanes, the street in front of the Catedral, and continue west (across Avenida De La Constitución, where it becomes Vinuesa). This cobblestoned street is radiant in the evening, when the sun sets in front of you, especially if there's a bull-fight on and the whole neighborhood buzzes with anticipation. Veer to your right at Adriano, which will take you right past the Plaza de Toros de La Real Maestranza, one of the world's great living shrines to the *corrida;* it's the Wrigley Field of Spain. If one is taking on a bull [see *performing arts,* below], or if you're just too squeamish, you can still check out the ring, the souvenir shop, and the bullfighting museum for 500ptas any day between 9:30am and 7pm. Calle Adriano ends at the river, so take a right on Paseo de Cristóbal Colón, and then another quick right onto Reyes Católicos. A couple of minutes up on your right you'll find **Iglesia de La Magdalena,** an impressive Baroque church with a cupola that dominates the neighborhood. If you don't know what Baroque is, stay a while longer and stare. Behind the church, find Calle Bailen and dance down it (Spanish speakers will get that joke) to the **Museo De Bellas Artes** [see *culture zoo,* below]. From here head down Alfonso XII to the **Plaza de Armas,** a classy old train station that has been turned into a mall. Circumvent said mall to get to the banks of the old Rio Guadalquivir. Take a right and walk along the river to the **Pasarlela La Cartuja,** a pedestrian bridge that offers brilliant views of the river, especially the modern bridges north that were built for Expo '92. The farthest one, Puente del Alamillo, looks like a gleaming white roller coaster and represents a modern architectural conundrum: a one-way suspension bridge. You also get a good look at some of the weird and wonderful exhibition buildings constructed for Expo '92, including a French rocket ship. Across the river take an immediate left and walk along the banks for about 20 minutes. You'll go past DiscoveryPark to a walkway called Paseo Nuestra Señorita de la O, which eventually turns into Calle Betis in the old maritime quarter, Triana, where sailors docked and flamenco thrived. To get back to the Catedral you can take Puente San Telmo at the end of Betis, giving you a nice view of the old Muslim tower, Torre del Oro, which is said to have been originally lined with gold, although there's no evidence of that anymore.

West of the Catedral, the legendary bullfighting arena, Plaza de Toros de Real Maestranza, makes its home in the lively **Arenal,** which ends at the river Guadalquivir. Across the river you'll find **Triana,** historically the home of sailors leaving for or arriving from the New World. Now highlighted by **Calle del Betis,** the street that runs along the river north from **Puente San Telmo** (that's a bridge) to **Puente Isabella II,** Triana is an essential spot for summertime cruising and boozing. Also on this side of the river are the fairgrounds for April's annual *Feria,* to the south; to the north is **Isla Cartuja,** the site of Expo '92, much of which is now dormant.

North of the Catedral, the main drag **Avenida de La Constitución** takes you to the commercial center of Sevilla, the appropriately named **Centro.** Daytime activity gives the big, tree-lined **Plaza Nueva** its buzz, but if nighttime is the right time, you'll want to head east to **Plaza Salvador** and nearby **Plaza Alfalfa.** North of Plaza Nueva stretches the shopping district, which is centered on the pedestrian-only streets **Calle Sierpes** and **Calle Tetuan;** there are no cars or tricked-out scooters here to interfere with the capitalist machinery of chain stores. If you walk a few minutes further north, along the funkified **Calle Amor de Dios,** you'll end up in the working-class-becoming-artsy-but-still-sketchy-enough-to-be-interesting area around **Alameda de Hércules,** which everyone just calls the "Alameda." They used to call it the "Barrio de Putas," a colorful way of saying red-light district, and you still might see some working girls/boys/?s at night. The east side of Alameda de Hercules, lined with bars, is well-trod and fairly safe, though for some reason a few dark little streets directly east are quite dodgy and should be avoided, especially at night. Stay on Alameda de Hércules or **Calle Dr. Letamendi** and you'll be fine. Further east is the **Macarena,** a classic working-class neighborhood that's quiet at night, but great to stroll through during the day, especially the main drag Feria.

South of the Catedral, wide avenues take you past Universidad de Sevilla and to the very attractive **Parque María Luisa,** with canals you can row through, and couples making out on nearly every bench.

Be forewarned that many maps of Sevilla, including those given out by the tourist offices, have a strange affliction: Due North is not at the top of the map, but somewhere off to the left. Make sure to find the compass on your map and don't end up in the Indies when you're looking for India.

Sevilla is definitely meant to be walked, but if your legs give out from exhaustion or sangria, or it's just too damn late at night, plenty of taxis are available. A small tip, usually 50ptas, is not required but is appreciated.

hanging out

If Andalucía is one of the great world headquarters of hanging out, Sevilla is the plush couch in the CEO's office. If you get a coffee or beer at a cafe, lingering is not only encouraged, it's required. The service is usually quite laid-back, so you may have to beg and plead for your check, but you'll never be asked to leave. So relax, Columbus's remains will still be here tomorrow. The locals already understand this, which is why you'll find them lingering over a 12-ounce Coca-Cola for an hour and a half. Really. The most popular neighborhood for tourists to *tomar algo* is Santa Cruz, for students it's Centro (especially little Plaza Alfalfa), down-to-earth (stony) artist types flock to Alemeda (see *bars* and *eats*, below), and the locals head over to La Macarena or Triana.

An Irish pub, **P O'Flaherty's** *(Arenales 7; Tel 95/421-04-51; 11am-2am)*, lays claim to one of the best locations in Spain, right across from the Catedral. Yes, a pint is expensive, 600ptas, but it is Guinness, which

wired

If you're a technophobe who loses sleep over silly things like the "I love you" virus, you'll be happy to know that the Vatican has nominated a patron saint to protect computers, computer users, and the Internet, and it's none other than Sevilla's own St. Isidore (556-636 A.D.), known to history for his Etymologies, a comprehensive, cross-referenced medieval encyclopedia. So instead of banging your computer screen when it crashes or won't load that funny picture your friend sent you, say a little prayer to Isidore of Sevilla, your direct hyperlink to God.

Isidore would be happy to know that thanks to the influx of Americans and Europeans here, Sevilla has a number of reasonably priced Internet cafes. The most happening, near Plaza Nueva, is **Netsk@fe** *(Carlos Cañal 5; Tel 95/450-20-43; 9am-midnight (or later) Mon-Fri, noon-1am Sat, noon-midnight Sun; 400ptas per hour)*, which, in addition to fast computers, has a bar and a giant-screen TV, usually showing soccer but sometimes movies in their original language. There is nothing authentically Spanish here, but it's a good place to meet other *extrañeros,* and the room in back with the computers is reasonably quiet. Thursday is party night. Break out the microchips, and bring your virus scanner.

Cheaper, with equally fast computers, is **Cibercafe Torre del Oro.net** *(Nuñez De Balboa 3; Tel 95/450-28-09; 9am-1am daily; 300ptas per hour)*, located, logically, on a side street near Torre del Oro. Its computers are actually coin-operated, which may sound Pac-Man-esque, but the system works extremely well; if you just want to check your e-mail quickly, you can drop in 25ptas for 5 minutes.

Good Sevilla websites:
www.sol.com
www.adalunet.com
www.andalucia.com
www.spainnet.co.il

is worth at least two Spanish beers. Plus, the outdoor tables are right in the thick of the action for people-watching, and it's a good place to meet other foreigners as well as locals trying their first stout (*"Que fuerte!"* is the most common reaction).

Alfalfa X *(Plaza Alfalfa 10; Tel 95/421-38-41; Noon-2am daily)* holds its own as the place in the center of town for cappuccino (200ptas), veggie sandwiches (350ptas), and dessert. You can choose the funky interior with the Arabic lamp shades and computers, or the outside tables on the crowded plaza.

For nighttime hanging out, especially in spring, summer, and fall, the place to be is Plaza Salvador. Here young people practice the custom of the *botellón,* which means bring your own bottle and chill outside with your homeys; the church steps are a favorite spot. Or, order a drink to go from one of the bars on the southeast side of the plaza. The friendliest of these joints is the one on the far right, **Los Soportales** *(Pza. Salvador s/n; 8pm-2am),* where 125ptas will get you a beer in a plastic cup and 150ptas will get a *tinto de verano* (red wine with lemon soda). The plaza is packed on weekends with everyone from sketchers to yuppies until about 1am, when the action moves to the nearby bars of Plaza Alfafa or up to the Alameda.

In the summer, when the city is baking, the party moves across the Guadalquivir, especially to Calle Betis. A ton of bars line the esplanade along the river, many with outside tables [see *bar scene,* below]. Just remember, if a bar sells its own T-shirts in the windows, it's probably best to go elsewhere.

bar scene

Bars in Andalucía can be divided into two types, those that serve sangria and those that don't. This is not any type of a judgment, just a fact: If you see sangria, there's a 90 percent chance it's being drunk by a *guir,* such as yourself. That doesn't mean you should avoid sangria—it's undeniably tasty, refreshing, and sucking on the pieces of fruit will get you hiiiiggh. It also means the places that serve it welcome you. Just be aware that you're not the first *extrañero* to enter the premises. Okay, there is actually a third category of bar, those that serve *tinto de verano,* a bastardized sangria made from red wine and *limon,* (lemon soda). It sounds sacrilegious but is actually quite tasty, and these are the bars we like best. It's as if they're saying, "We'll give them what they want, but we're not going to keep a fresh pitcher waiting for them." Bars are usually open from about 8pm in the evening until 2am on weekdays and 4 on weekends. The bars on Calle Betis, however, tend to open later, usually 10pm, and don't really get going until after midnight. Many of the bars on this street are total scenes—just look for the mobs of people pouring out of the places. If you actually want to have a conversation with Spanish people, try the friendly **La Tertulia** *(Betis 13; Tel 95/433-32-85),* which literally means a "social gathering." It's one of the few bars that doesn't serve any kind of coffee or tapas, so you'll get your booze that much faster, beer for 200ptas, cocktails for 700ptas. The music

digamé (tell me)

That's what your bartender will ask you, and he's asking not for your life story but your drink order. Sangria? Well, sure, if you're a *guiri*, but to drink like the locals means drinking beer, and that means the inevitable Cruzcampo. You could just ask for a cerveza, but to sound like you know what you're talking about, ask for a *caña* (a small draft beer), a *tubo* (a taller glass of draft beer), or a *tanque* (an even larger mug of beer, not always available). Mixed drinks are also very popular, especially whiskey with Coca-Cola or *limón*, lemon soda. A good *camarero* (bartender) will put three cubes of ice in a tall glass, pour the booze up to the top of the second cube, and give you the mixer separately. Ask for the brand of liquor you want, but please take our advice and avoid DYC whiskey unless you just really, really enjoy hangovers. The Spanish are also on such familiar terms with Bacardi rum that they call it by its first name, Ron, as in a *Ron y Coca-Cola* (Rum and Coke). Whatever you choose to imbibe, take it slowly because the bar is not closing anytime soon.

tends towards Spanish pop, but feel free to ask the bartender to look for something better on the cable radio hook-up. If anything resembling salsa comes on, impromptu dancing might break out, but never enough to knock the drink from your hand or slow down the conversation.

A few doors down is the refined but still happening **Café de la Prensa** *(Betis 6; Tel 95/433-34-20; 1pm-3am daily)*, with wooden benches, flyers on the wall, and all the Enya you can handle. During the day it's a good place to get a *cortado* (a shot of espresso with milk) and read the paper. At night, young intellectuals killing their brain cells pack the outside tables with the great views across the river. After a long night of drinking on Calle Betis, or just to soak some of it up before heading to the discotecas, it is a tradition to stop by the nameless Churreria at the end of Puente Isabella II for *churros con chocolate.*

In the center of town, right off of little Plaza Alfalfa, a cluster of lively bars on Calle Pérez Galdós offers loud music and kitschy decor. If the level of hipness of a bar is directly related to how difficult it is to find, then **El Mundo** *(Siete Revueltas 5; No phone)* is the coolest bar in Sevilla. To find it from Plaza Alfalfa, go down Calle Pérez Galdós and take your first left, then another quick left onto the crooked alley that zig-zags seven times, which is why it's called Calle Siete Revueltas. At the third zig (or is it a zag?) look to the left for a sign with a red heart (below an ivy-covered balcony). Open the door, enter the dark, narrow bar, and order some-

thing. You are now officially an insider. Flamenco guitar performances
Tuesday nights [see *live music,* below].

If you're tired of the inevitable Cruzcampo, or just want a taste of
home, wherever home is, go to **Cerveceria Internacional** *(Gamazo 3;
Tel 95/421-17-17; 5pm-3am daily),* near Plaza Nueva. This place advertises 15 beers on tap and 200 bottled beers, although we never bothered to
count. If you're from Texas, however, you must go to the **Texas Lone
Star Saloon** *(Placentines 25; Tel 95/421-03-34),* just north of the Catedral, to bring you back home. Well, at least there's a Texas flag and a giant-
screen T.V., though more European soccer matches than American
sporting events (unless it's the Super Bowl) seem to make it onto the tube.
Y'all ready for some *fútbol?* You can down Bass, Bud, and Corona for
500ptas, but no Shinerbock. Even though they dared mess with Texas, this
place gets packed with young foreigners and even some locals at night,
grooving to throbbing pop/dance music that would make Willie Nelson
pee his Wranglers. As of yet, no one has put a shotgun rack on their scooter.

The best places to get irie with the locals are the bars that line up on
the east side of the bohemian Alameda de Hércules, north of the Centro.
Bulebar *(Alameda de Hércules 83; No phone; 4pm-2am Sun-Thu, 4pm-
4am Fri, Sat)* has very chill tables out front, and red velvet couches and
green marble columns inside. It's definitely gay-friendly but draws a
mixed crowd of all types who like cheap beer (125ptas). The music is
mostly Spanish rock, but if you try to ask who you're listening to, instead
of a name, you'll get a comparison like "they're the Spanish Beastie Boys"
or "the Spanish Lou Reed" or "the Spanish Stryper."

It's hard to imagine a bar more mellow than Bulebar, but here it is, right
up the street with the eagle mural on the outside wall, where the Greek letters spell out **Hefest** *(Alameda de Hércules 70).* This is the kind of place
you not only bring your dog to, but also order drinks for it. A dressed-
down, pierced-out, scruffy, and friendly crowd hangs out in this tiny bar
and sometimes moves out to the front patio to, reportedly, roll a little
number (and they ain't talking about the Lotto).

On the northern end of the Alameda, **Habanilla Café** *(Alameda de
Hércules 63; Tel 95/490-27-18; Noon-2am or later)* may appear unassuming

but is in fact a supercenter of funky good times: coffee during the day, tapas in the afternoon, and drinking at night, when the crowds spill out onto the street. A series of little carved heads (don't ask...) holds up the railing of the classic long wooden bar, and a collection of gem stones shimmers above the bar, behind the goateed servers in ironic T-shirts. The scene is fueled by acidic jazz and trippy jam music, and attracts visionary malcontents of all ages, from rockers, to punks, to hippies (and even a few left-over beatniks).

LIVE MUSIC

Sevilla has world-class flamenco. If you want to see some rock 'n' roll...Sevilla has world-class flamenco. If you want to see jazz, blues, reggae...let us repeat: Sevilla has world-class flamenco. If it ain't flamenco, the live music scene here compares to what you'd find at any college watering hole.

Any number of places in town will charge you an arm and both legs for their flamenco show, but there's no reason to give up any appendages when **La Carbonería** *(Levíes 18; Tel 95/421-44-60; 8pm-3:30am Mon-Sat, 8pm-2:30am Sun)* is always free. On the edge of the barrio Santa Cruz, housed in what used to be a coal yard, this venue will always be cool no matter how many tourists tramp through it for the nightly flamenco music and dance performances. These sultry shows begin sometime between 11pm and midnight in the German-beer-hall-style room in the back. In the front room—what New Yorkers would call a "great space," sloping up from the street, with cobblestoned walls and high ceilings—live jazz and/or folk acts go on every night except for Monday and Wednesday, starting at approximately 9pm. They attract a local crowd of music aficionados who actually listen.

The aforementioned **El Mundo** [see *bar scene,* above] also has no-cover flamenco, but just the music; you'll have to do the sensual dancing yourself. Performances are on Tuesday nights sometime after 11pm or whenever the band shows up (you know how flaky flamenco musicians can be). During the show, the price of beer doubles to 400ptas.

For an eclectic mix of live music, the arts center **Sala La Imperdible** *(Plaza San Antonio de Padua 9; Tel 95/438-82-19),* between Alameda de Hércules and the river, has a cafe, **Almacén,** that hosts everything from

RULES OF THE GAME

A cloud of smoke does not envelope Sevilla as it does other Southern European cities, but the young folk do like their *chocolate,* especially in the Alameda, where most anything goes. Drinking is part of life here, but drunkenness is not. The rule is: If you're casual, it's casual. Be aware that hash is always rolled with tobacco, so if you pull out your pipe and load it up, you are suddenly a drug abuser and will be kindly asked to leave the premises.

alternative rock and country western to jazz and electronica. Check your local listings.

Right on the Alameda, the giant **Fun Club** (*Alameda de Hércules 85; Tel 95/421-80-64*) usually comes alive as a late, late night dance spot, but it also gets some live Spanish rock, for example a kick-ass classic rock band that pays tribute to Deep Purple. Any band that knows a song besides "Smoke on the Water" is bowing down at the altar.

club scene

Sevilla doesn't have the throbbing mm-ch-mm-ch-mm-ch dance scene or world-class DJs of other places in Spain. But after inhaling all that ambiance and history, if you just want to put your ass in that puddin', there are opportunities. The bouncers are generally muscle-bound but fair, and if you were lucky enough to be born with breasts, or have a really convincing drag outfit, you won't have to pay a cover. Don't think of going before midnight: Things don't get really cooking until 2am.

Located near Plaza Salvador, **catedral club** (*Cuesta del Rosario 12; Tel 95/422-85-90; Midnight-8am daily*) has no connection whatsoever with the Gothic cathedral of the same name, though the dance floor is only slightly smaller. So please don't go banging on the door of the church at 2am. This is the most popular club with the international set (Americans), and local and guest DJs spin a lot of hip-hop and some house, depending on the night. Consult the free English guide *The Tip*, which usually contains a back-page ad listing the upcoming parties. Everyone pays 1,000ptas unless they're female or they got a free pass beforehand from an Internet cafe or hostel. The scene at 3:30am is studenty, bouncy, sweaty, and black-clad.

Less Americanized and scrappier, in the tradition of its location, **Fun Club** (*Alameda de Hércules 85; Tel 95/421-80-64; Fri, Sat, midnight-8am*) smokes on weekends in the Alameda until very, very late. Go here if you're still dying to try out your "running man" and it's 5am in the morning. The music is also varied and less strictly dance; the house DJs will work in Sublime and the Red Hot Chili Peppers (try your running man now, MC Hammered). A very eclectic crowd hangs out and watches the skate videos on the T.V. screen. Next to the DJ booth, a pair of double doors lead to the chill room, where it's a little quieter for conversation. You can spend a whole night here just watching pie-eyed rookies push as hard as they can on the double doors to try to get back into the main room (pulling works much better.) Cover is 500ptas for *tios,* including a drink; for *tias,* it's *nada.*

ARTS SCENE

Sevilla is much stronger in the performing arts than the visual; probably because the people are just so dramatic. You won't find any strict "artists quarter" with giant studio spaces and young Picassos setting up their

FESTIVALS

"Sevilla lights up for a feast-day as a face lights up for a smile."—Arthur Symons, 1903.

The two spring monster-fiestas, which draw crowds from all over the world, are taken *seriously* in Sevilla.

Semana Santa (April 8-15, 2001), the Holy Week from Palm Sunday to Good Friday, features spectacular religious processions that inch through the streets with music, people in pointed white hoods, and, most importantly, floats with giant recreations of 17th-century images of the Christ and the Virgin Mary. The parades leave from various churches around the city and go right through the center of town, ending at the Catedral, while thousands of onlookers trample (sometimes literally) their way for a closer look. The atmosphere is somewhat solemn and reverent, but this is still Spain, so the bars do a good business as well.

Feria de Abril (April 30-May 6, 2001) is the all-day and all-night blow-out that takes place two weeks after Easter, on the fair-grounds in the Los Remedios district. During the day men in full costume ride horses, and girls from seven to 85 appear in their best flamenco dresses to dance the *sevillana,* the local, joyous form of flamenco. The most prestigious bullfights also take place during this week. Nighttime is for more dancing, eating, and drinking in the hundreds of *casetas,* or tents, each of which is run by a different family or organization and requires an invitation to enter. Except for a few public *casetas,* the event feels like a giant family reunion mixed with a county fair, leaving the visitor to stand around and gape; you might even get a sight of that rare species: drunk Spanish people. Also be warned that all hostels and hotels will double their rates, and that the center of the city becomes a ghost town.

easels on the sidewalk. You will find a wide range of theater, from classical to opera to avant-garde. The Alameda is certainly the place to meet the starving artists.

▶▶VISUAL ARTS

Ceramics have long been a specialty of the Triana neighborhood across the river. *Ceramicas* dot the streets around Calle Rodrigo de Triana, where you'll find hand-painted vases and tiles with the classic Andalucian patterns that you may have marveled over in the Alcazar.

The well-regarded gallery **Rafael Ortíz** *(Mármoles; Tel 95/421-48-74; 11:30am-1:30pm/6-9pm Mon-Sat, closed Monday and Saturday afternoons)* features constantly changing exhibits of established modern Spanish painters. All kinds of styles are represented but mostly within the confines of paint on canvas and sculptural shapes that you can recognize.

▶▶PERFORMING ARTS

The most traditional and spectacular theater in Sevilla takes place at the bullfights at the **Plaza de Toros de la Real Maestranza** *(Paseo Colón 12; Tel 95/422-45-77)*. No, bullfighting is not a sport because the combatants are not equally matched. The *matador* has the advantage of opposable thumbs, a bigger brain, no sedatives, sharp clothes, sharper weapons, and teammates with horses, armor, spears, and other sharp pointy things. The Spanish already know this and that's why the local newspapers cover the *corridas* in the arts and culture section, not on the sports page. Hemingway knew this also, which is why he called bullfighting "a tragedy: the death of the bull, which is played, more or less well, by the bull and the man involved and in which there is danger for the man but certain death for the bull." Just so you have no misconceptions about going to a bullfight, let us repeat: The bull will be tortured and killed, there will be lots of blood, and the animal will be dragged unceremoniously out of the ring by a team of horses. (If it's any consolation, he is taken to the butcher.) But by all means, you must go to truly get under the skin of Spanish tradition. A bullfight in one of the most famous arenas in Spain is a colorful spectacle like no other: a brass band playing, the costumed matador's *machismo* stare, men shaking their heads at less-than-perfect swipes of the cape, and overly made-up, bloodthirsty women chanting "olé," waving their white hankies, throwing roses, jackets, and hats at the matador's feet. There is also the extremely miniscule chance that if the bull puts up a good enough fight or sticks his horn through the matador's leg, he will be spared for breeding purposes. It does happen, if only rarely. So root for the bull, just not too loudly. The action begins at 6:30pm, with usually three matadors each performing twice for a total of six kills. Tickets can be purchased around town but it's best to get them at the official ticket office (entrance at Colon 12, or Adiano 35) on the day of the *corrida,* with prices starting at 3,000ptas for a hot seat in the *sol,* and at least twice that much for a cool seat in the *sombra.* The season runs from Easter to October, with the bullfights taking place on Sundays, except during and around the *Feria de Abril,* when the blood is spilled every day.

Right up the street is a much more civilized venue that shares its name with the gladiator pit: **Teatro de la Maestranza** *(Colón 22; Tel 95/422-*

65-73; Tickets 10am-2pm/5-8pm). An opera house, it also stages other difficult to comprehend arts, such as poetry accompanied by dance, and piano recitals.

Teatro Central *(José Galvez, Isla de la Cartuja s/n; Tel 95/446-07-80; www.teatrocentral.com)* gleams across the river on the Isla Cartuja. A stunning set of interconnected theaters, which can be manipulated into an endless array of seating arrangements, provides space for flamenco, touring theater, dance, and ballet. This is also where people-you-may-have-heard-of play when they come to Sevilla, such as the Bill T. Jones dance company and even Tom Waits (which gives it instant street cred in our minds). Tickets start at around 2,000ptas.

Traditional theater takes place near Parque María Luisa at **Teatro Lope de Vega** *(Avda. María Luisa s/n; Tel 95/459-08-27),* where you may see Shakespeare or new plays by Spanish authors; whatever it is, it's going to be in Spanish. Bring a bilingual friend or one of those ear pieces they wear at the United Nations.

The bar at the eclectic **Sala La Imperdible** *(Plaza San Antonio de Padua 9; Tel 95/438-82-19)* is a hang-out for artistic types. We already mentioned their cutting edge live music, but they also have risk-taking theater from local and touring groups. Much of it is physical comedy, so even if you don't understand everything it might still be worth checking out. Prices are generally 800ptas and up.

To see films in their original language with subtitles (V.O.), check out what's playing at **Avenida Cinco Cines** near Plaza de Armas *(Marques de Parada 15; Tel 95/422-15-48).* **Alameda** *(Alameda de Hércules 9-10; Tel 95/4380-156)* has four theaters with a variety of subtitled movies, and nearby **Cine Cervantes** *(Amor de Dios 33; Tel 95/438-58-10)* has one screen that is *still* probably showing *American Beauty* (the Spanish love to laugh at the American "dream"). All of these theaters are part of the same chain and have the same prices: 650ptas during the week; 700ptas on weekends; 450ptas on "cheap day" (Wednesday) and for *Sesión Golfa,* which literally translates as the "whore session"—don't get excited, that just means the midnight show. Times and descriptions of movies can be viewed in the daily papers or at the chain's excellent website: *www.cinecuidad.com.*

gay scene

Sevilla is sometimes called "The Queen of Spanish Cities" for its cultural offerings, but the young gay life here is not especially queeny. It tends more toward the be-proud-but-don't-flaunt-it variety. Still, gay life does thrive in the Alameda and outwards. No one has of yet opened a gay flamenco bar, where everyone would dress up in gender-bending fashion: men in flamenco dresses and women in matador outfits. We think it's a great idea.

The place to dance the night away is **Itaca** *(Amor de Dios 31; 10pm-5am),* which recently moved from its old digs a few doors down. Action goes late into the night, especially in the "dark room." Use your imagination.

Just up the street is the more campy **El Hombre y El Oso** *(Amor de Dios at Delgado; 10pm-4am),* which literally means "The Man and The

Bear." To find this club walk up Amor de Dios until you see the window with a rainbow flag and a giant stuffed teddy bear above the door.

Though the range and number of gay spots might be a bit limited, gays and lesbians can try out their gay-dar at a bunch of gay-friendly bars and cafes, such as the above-mentioned Habanilla Café and Bulebar on Alameda de Hércules, and La Tertulia on Calle Betis.

CULTURE ZOO

Hopefully we've hammered it into your little heads that Sevilla is about atmosphere, not about hopping from monument to museum. Still, some manmade structures here are worth entering, and the biggies (Catédral and Alcázar) demand to be seen—even if it means losing that important siesta.

Catedral *(Plaza Virgen de los Reyes; Tel 95/421-49-71; 11am-5pm Mon-Sat, 2-6pm Sun; 700ptas, 200ptas students, free on Sun):* Depending on who's doing the measuring, Sevilla's cathedral is one of the three biggest churches in Europe, right up there with St. Peter's in Rome and St. Paul's in London. According to the locals, if you measure cubic centimeters rather than just the area of the floor, it's actually the biggest, although we can't imagine how you'd get a tape measure up in the vaunted Gothic ceiling. Maybe they can just fill all three of them with water and decide once and for all. Anyway, don't get so caught up with the size of the thing (you know who you are) that you miss the stunning stained-glass windows or giant canvases depicting violent scenes from the Bible. You also must make a trip up to the top of La Giralda, the tower that was originally built by the Moors in the 12th century and which the Christians had the good taste not to tear down. You walk up La Giralda on a long series of ramps, apparently put in place for horses, which must have enjoyed the stunning 360-degree vistas of the city without having had to elbow so many gasping-for-breath tourists out of the way.

Alcázar *(Plaza del Triunfo; Tel 95/450-23-23; 9:30am-8pm Tue-Sat, 9:30am-6pm Sun, closed Mon; 700ptas, students free; Tickets sold up to one hour before closing):* Just behind the Catedral is this palace that since the 11th century has housed everyone from ruthless Muslim rulers to ruthless Christian rulers, each one building additions according to the architectural trends of the period. As in all great palaces, you can't help but fantasize about the intrigue, treason, and romance that these walls have witnessed over the years. The backyard is pretty nice, too—an amazingly verdant series of maze-like gardens that stretches as far as the nose can smell. It's a great place to contemplate your own next conquest, whether it be man, woman, or *tortilla*.

Museo de Bellas Artes *(Plaza del Museo 9; Tel 95/422-18-29; 3-8pm Tue, 9am-8pm Wed-Sat, 9am-3pm Sun):* Here you'll discover important religious works by Spanish masters you've probably never heard of, such as Murillo and Zurbarán. Admission is only 250ptas or free with European student ID (or most American ones if you look like a student), and it's worth it for Sala V alone, which has a gorgeous ceiling and giant Murillo canvases depicting religious figures with scary things (like rabid dogs) lurking in the shadows. The Museo can't match any of the major museums of Madrid (its modern art collection is forgettable), but the air conditioning is just as strong on hot summer days.

▶▶**MODIFICATION**

Sevilla offers a couple of one-stop piercing/tattoo super shops for all your self-mutilation needs. In the Alameda, **Sevilla Tattoo** *(Amor de Dios 55; Tel 95/490-73-87; 11am-2pm/5-9pm Mon-Sat)* has been around since 1989, when body art was still something that scared your parents. They have plenty of original designs and a reputation for quality, sanitary work. In the centro, near Plaza Alfalfa, **Downtown New York** *(Pérez Galdós 1; Tel 95/450-10-46)* has more of a clubber aesthetic. Besides piercing

---

12 hours in Sevilla

1. **La Giralda:** The tower attached to the Catedral that's on all the postcards is the highest point in town, so climb to the top, survey your kingdom, and plan your attack.

2. **Get lost in Barrio Santa Cruz:** Some complain that the *judería* (Jewish Quarter) has been a little too well restored, but all the tour groups in the world can't suck the charm out of this place. And you can still get so lost in the cobblestoned maze that you won't even be able to hear German being spoken.

3. **Chill in the Alameda:** The antidote for Santa Cruz is Alameda, the center for alternative living. Get tattooed, buy health food, smoke a *purro*, watch an indie movie...basically just act as if you were at home. Late at night, Fun Club is the *discoteca* you most certainly do not have at home (at least not at 5am).

4. **Tapas:** Sevilla brings cheap bar food to a new level, if you know where to go (see *eats*). Tortillas at Bodega Santa Cruz and ostrich at Taberna Los Coloniales are essential.

5. **Plaza Salvador at night:** B.Y.O.B. and anything else you want to share, and make new *amigos* on the steps of the church.

6. **Calle Betis:** Not a pub crawl, nor *la marcha*, but a bar stroll down the esplanade along the Rio Guadalquivir.

7. **Bullfight:** The pageantry, the drama, the moral conundrum: to root for the matador or the bull?

8. **La Carbonería:** Join the tourists for the spicy flamenco show in the back, or hang with the locals in the front room for live folk or jazz.

and tattoos, you can pick up funky accessories shipped all the way from New Jack City, without the attitude. The friendly staff has the lowdown on the best clubs in town and can point you in the right direction.... Whether you leave with new holes in your body is up to you.

STUff

Every Spanish city seems to have a centrally located shopping district set on pedestrian-only cobblestoned streets, and Sevilla is no exception. On Calle Sierpes, Calle Tetuan, Calle Cuña, and the streets that run between the three, you can find your friendly neighborhood chain stores, like the Body Shop, but also classy local joints that specialize in flamenco dresses and accessories. Even if you're not planning on becoming *that* authentic, it's fun to window shop. Funkier shops and funkier salespeople set themselves up in the Alameda. Wherever you are, remember that siesta thing: The iron gates come down at 2pm and don't go back up until 5.

One place that doesn't close for siesta is the gargantuan department store **El Corte Inglés** *(Plaza Duque 6; Tel 95/422-09-31; 10am-9pm Mon-Sat),* which seems to have everything you would ever need and tons of stuff you won't, kind of like Wal-Mart without the auto parts. Before you disregard this cathedral of capitalism, realize that if you stay long enough in Sevilla you will end up looking here for something you need. If you have a place to cook, it has, hidden in its basement, the biggest and most modern supermarket in town, including a wide selection of local wines. The sports outlet across the plaza has a decent, if pricey, selection of camping supplies.

Plaza de Armas *(Plaza de la Legión s/n; Tel 95/490-82-82; 10am-10pm Mon-Sat)* is a 3-story mall built into a beautiful old train station near the river, north of the Plaza de Toros. Okay, so it's still a mall with upscale outlets, including a Warner Brothers Store (does anyone actually shop there?), but the food court is a happening hang-out for young consumers, especially on rainy days.

▶▶BOUND

One benefit of all the young Americans studying in Sevilla is the easy availability...you think you know where we're going with this but you're wrong...of books in English. Right across from the university, **Librería Vertice** *(San Fernando 33-35; Tel 95/422-97-38; 9:30am-2pm/5-10:30pm Mon-Fri, 11am-2pm Sat)* has a good selection of *Penguin Classics* for 150ptas. These easily fit right into your backpack or even your back pocket, if you want to appear intellectual. If you're trying to practice your Spanish, pick up something in the *Alianza Cien* series of pocket-size books (150ptas), which have short novels or long short stories, in Spanish, by cool modern authors from Kerouac to Borges. The short length and big type will make them much easier to get through than *Don Quixote*. Vertice is also a good place to snag a free local entertainment guide and to meet students of all backgrounds, especially around 6pm when they come pouring out of class.

moda

Despite all the flamenco propaganda you'll get from the tourist offices and picture books, colorful dresses, riding gear, and fans are not in fashion here unless it's the week of *Feria*. Black is more like it, and a lot of wool: wool sweaters, wool skirts, all the way into the unbearable heat of summer. Sevillanos might be a little more fashionable than the rest of Andalucía, but the scene is still certainly a lot more mellow than in Madrid or Barcelona. Here, it's more about how you walk than what you're wearing. Women can wear dresses or skirts, although the painted-on pants that dominate Spain are still the most common. Midwestern university sweatshirts are also very popular...oh wait, that's the American students. In the Alemeda, the crusty look reigns: jeans, rock 'n' roll T-shirts, piercings, and the favorite accessory of all—a dog.

The reliable chain bookstore **Librería Beta** (*Sagasta 16 Tel 95/422-84-95; and Constitución 9; Tel 95/456-28-17; 10am-2pm/5-8:30pm Mon-Fri, till 10:30pm Sat*) sells Spanish novels for around 2,000ptas and travel guides in English (as if you need another one!) for 3,000ptas.

▶▶TUNES

For new and used music and good browsing vibes, go to the Alameda. **Record Sevilla** (*Amor de Dios 27; Tel 95/438-77-02; 10am-2pm/5-9pm Mon-Sat*) carries an eclectic mix of CDs and vinyl, and it's always surprising and sometimes frightening to see who they stock a lot of: King Crimson, The Kelly Family, Soul Asylum, Scatterbrain...who knew? This place has a good punk section, as well as an odd category called *musica negra,* which includes everything from Prince to Sly and the Family Stone to Queen Latifah. They should just call it *musica americana.* Rock T-shirts are also on sale here, and they're almost always playing something hopping on the in-house stereo.

Nearby, the tiny **Discos Pera** (*Dr. Letamendi 5; Tel 95/47-04-87; 10am-2pm/5-9pm Mon-Sat*) has more good music per square inch than anywhere in town, e.g., an LP of Lou Reed's *Transformer.* Old music posters cover every available section of wall, giving you that comforting feeling of being surrounded by guardian angels of good taste as you flip through the crates.

Neither of these stores has a smashing electronic music section, so you may have to go to the more sterile and Top-40 **Sevilla Rock** (*Alfonso XII 1; Tel 95/422-97-38; 10am-1:45pm/5-8:30pm Mon-Sat*), near Corte de Inglés, to find what you were dancing to the night before.

▶▶BAZAAR

El Jeueves, the Thursday flea market on Calle Feria in the Macarnea district, has been a Sevillan tradition for centuries. Some of the second-hand clothes and antiques look as if they've been around about that long, though there are some real finds here, especially if you want *recuerdos* of Andalucía.

The lively Sunday morning market on **Alameda de Hércules** presents an even stranger assortment of items, largely because you don't even have to set up a table here, so anyone with a full closet or tool shed can lay out some stuff in the dirt: tires, chess boards, doorknobs, hand-painted ceramics, comic books, screwdrivers. It's a great place to throw together a modern art piece.

Also on Sunday, **Plaza Alfalfa** becomes an outdoor animal market. If you just can't resist adorable little puppies, kittens, and chirping birds, stay away, because you will want to take one home. If you forgot to bring your alarm clock to Spain, you can also buy a rooster.

EATS

Sevilla is not the kind of place where you can just indiscriminately stumble on unique, tasty, and cheap food; it takes a little bit of research. Almost any bar or restaurant can offer decent tapas such as the humble *tortilla española,* a tuna sandwich, or the inevitable gazpacho. But if you aren't careful you can spend your time in Sevilla eating authentic but uninspired food, and paying 700ptas for a 350ptas ham sandwich. However,

only here

Real Fábrica de Tobacos, now part of the Universidad de Sevilla, used to employ over 10,000 *cigarreras* in the 19th century, the largest female workforce in Spain. In Bizet's opera, Carmen rolled cigars on her thighs here (only Sevilla can make repetitive manual labor sexy).

Isla de Cartuja, which was totally revamped for Expo '92, and then mostly left for dead, has one of strangest collections of structures anywhere, from French space ships and suspension bridges to replicas of Magellan's ships and the stunning Teatro Central. Two theme parks here celebrate Sevilla's role in the exploration of the New World: **Isla Magica,** with your typical roller coasters, water rides, and zones like "Gates of America" and "Fountain of Youth" (but no "Diseased Blankets Pavilion"); and **Discovery Park,** where you can venture into some of the more popular attractions of the Expo, such as a Pavilion of Navigation and a Digital Planetarium.

if you choose wisely, my friend, you can be eating exotic delights at value meal prices. Follow us....

▶▶CHEAP

For an introduction to the most fundamental of tapas, go to **Bodega Santa Cruz** *(Rodrigo Caro 1; Tel 95/421-32-46; 9am-midnight daily)*, right up the street from the Catedral, in the barrio Santa Cruz. It gets packed at lunch and at night with tourists, but they only add to the live-liness of the place. The bartender will keep track of your bill by making chalk marks on the wooden bar in front of you. We love their individu-ally cooked, Frisbee-shaped *tortillas.*

Habanilla Café [see *bar scene,* above] has already been mentioned at least twice in this chapter, but we're not going to stop harping on it until you come here. The menu changes daily, so just look on the chalkboard by the kitchen, where you'll find simple and unique dishes like pork loin with apples, potatoes with creamed spinach, or chicken breast with Roquefort cheese. Tapas portions will only set you back about 225-300ptas.

Nearby, the atmospheric **La Ilustre Victima** *(Dr. Letamendi 35; noon-2am daily)* is another cool bar that also does great food. Rice balls with cheese, and little fried spinach guys with pine nuts are just two of the 300ptas vegetarian tapas available here (strict vegetarians should be aware that sometimes dishes are what we call "Spanish vegetarian," which means they only have ham). They also have shawarma sandwiches for 475ptas, all served in a moody, Moorish red room, accompanied by something Cat Stevens-esque on the stereo.

Centrally located, but just far enough out of the way to avoid the tourist crush, the tradition-rich **Taberna Coloniales** *(Plaza Cristo de Burgos 19; Tel 95/421-41-91; Noon-midnight daily)* does such original and excellent tapas we're afraid to let the secret out. So if you go, don't blow it; just walk casually up to the busy bar and order a tapas of *avestruz* and a beer. What you'll get is ostrich, succulent ostrich, the meat you never knew you liked, as well as mouthwatering puffy potatoes...all for only 325ptas. Another winner is the chicken with almonds for 250ptas. You might like the tapas so much that you'll want to splurge and get a whole order of them (1800ptas) and enjoy sitting at one of the outside tables on the pretty Plaza de San Pedro.

▶▶DO-ABLE

Restaurante San Marco *(Mesón del Moro 6-10; Tel 95/456-43-90; 1:15-4:30pm/8:15pm-12:30am, Tue-Sun)* is part of a locally owned chain, so make sure you go to the right one. This location, built directly into ancient Arab baths in barrio de Santa Cruz, is special not just for its pizza and pastas but also for its dramatic setting. The spiffily dressed waiters might make you think otherwise, but the prices are totally reasonable given the surroundings: pasta for 700ptas and up and pizzas at around 800ptas. This is definitely a place to bring a date, because something about Arab baths just drives people crazy.

Another pizzeria but with a decidedly more low-key vibe is **Pizzeria Angelo** *(Luchana 2; Tel 95/421-61-64),* a pleasant hole in the wall on

down and out

If you're short of pesetas, the best thing to do in Sevilla is to keep walking—there are always new barrios to explore, especially if you haven't been to La Macarena or Triana. Or take a stab at getting through some of the four million documents that record the discovery of the Americas in the Archivo General de Indias; this collection includes letters from Columbus to Queen Isabella ("I found India!"), some of which are displayed in glass cases. Parque María Luisa is also always free and great for strolling, sleeping, rowing, PDA, even architecture appreciation at Plaza de España and Plaza de América.

the edge of Santa Cruz toward Plaza Alfalfa. Tasty vegetarian pizza and salads (from 600-1,000ptas) go well with the pizza-parlor vibe and the oldies music. There's also a takeout window if you just want a slice to go.

▶▶SPLURGE

If you've got money to burn, treat yourself to a full sit-down meal at one of the tapas bars mentioned above, especially Taberna Coloniales, or else go nuts at Restaurante San Marco with a whole bottle of wine, dessert, coffee, etc. The pricier restaurants in Sevilla are fine but they don't have the atmosphere of either of these places.

crashing

Finding a room in Sevilla during the summer can be a pain in your sphincter, and during Semana Santa and Feria it's nearly impossible (even if you're willing to pay the jacked-up rates) unless you've booked weeks in advance. Though the tourist office won't make hotel reservations for you, they will give you an exhaustive list of local crashing options.

A good place to reserve is the friendly **Hostal Paco's** (Pedro del Toro 7; Tel 95/42-21-71-83; 2,500ptas single). The family that owns this centrally located hostel near Plaza Nueva also runs a couple of other hostels if this one is full. Paco's is the simplest, with well-maintained communal showers. Their mini-conglomerate includes the slightly more comfortable **Hostal Paris** (San Pedro Mártir 14; Tel 95/422-98-61; 3,500ptas single, 6,420ptas double), where all the rooms come with air conditioning, telephones, and TVs. (Keep in mind the unwritten rule that you are not allowed to watch TV in Sevilla unless it's a bullfight, or "The Simpsons" dubbed into Spanish.)

The youth hostel, also known as **Albergue Juvenil Sevilla** (Isaac Peral 2; Tel 95/461-31-50; 1,500ptas, 2,000ptas over 26) is a fine establishment—it's just a little bit out of the way. You can take bus 34 from the Tourist Office to get here, or grab a cab. It does have the advantage of having mostly twin rooms, reducing the number of people you wake up when you stumble home in the morning.

If you've just arrived in town without a room and want the most bang for your buck, go to Calle Archeros, in the Santa Cruz. Five ramshackle hostels squeeze into this narrow street and one of them's gotta have a room. One of the friendliest is **Hostal Javier** *(Archeros 16; Tel 95/441-23-25; 6,000ptas doubles with bathroom, 5,000ptas with shared bathroom)*. It's got a comfy, plant-filled patio for a lobby, though make yourself scarce when they want to vacuum or you might lose a limb.

▶▶**DOABLE**

Hostal Neuvo Picasso *(San Gregorio 1; Tel 95/421-08-64; 5,000 singles, 7,500ptas high season, 6,000ptas doubles, 8,500ptas high season)* has the sweetest location, right behind Plaza Triunfo, in a restored house built almost into the walls of the Alcazar, with views of the Catedral. The bright pastel rooms match the bright pastel lobby, and not only do the rooms have AC, but so do the shared bathrooms. Get in now, before they realize what they've got and hike the prices.

If you have a car you might want to park it at **Hostal Sierpes** *(Corral del Ray 22; Tel 95/422-49-48; 4,000ptas singles with shared bathrooms, 6,000ptas doubles)*, which has a garage right across the street. Located in the heart of Santa Cruz, close to the action, it also has its own bar in the lobby, and functional if not spectacular rooms.

need to know

Currency Exchange You'll get the best rate at ATMs, which are all over the center of town, especially on Avenida de la Constitución and in the shopping district. Those old-fashioned exchange booths can be found at the airport and the train station.

Tourist Information The main **Tourist Office** *(Avenida de la Constitución 21; Tel 95/422-14-04; 9am-7pm Mon-Sat, 10am-2pm Sun)*, right around the corner from the Catedral, can get overwhelmed during the high season. If you have patience, however, you can get good info on places to stay, maps, and a helpful free guide to the city called *Welcome&olé*.

Public Transportation Sevilla is very walkable and also traffic-infested, which means you can usually walk almost as fast as the buses that go bumping around the cobblestoned streets. Save yourself the 125ptas and hoof it, unless you're going to the train station or airport (see below).

American Express *(Plaza Nueva 7; Tel 95/421-16-17; 9:30am-1:30pm/4:30-7:30pm Mon-Fri, 10am-1pm Sat)*.

Health and Emergency For major medical emergencies, go to **Hospital Virgen del Rocío** *(Avda. Manuel Siurot s/n; Tel 95/424-81-81)*. For smaller cuts and scrapes there's a **first aid post** just east of the Alcazar on the other side of the road from Jardines de Murrillo *(Menéndez Pelayo at Avda. Málaga; Tel 95/441-17-12)*. The local **police station** is 1km (.62 miles) south of Catedral *(Paseo de las Delicias 15; Tel 95/461-54-40)*.

Pharmacies Neon green crosses mark the *farmacias,* which can be found all over town. No single one is open 24 hours a day; instead, *farmacias* rotate the all-night responsibility. Each one posts a schedule indicating who will be open on what night.

Telephone There are plenty of pay phones around town, most of which accept coins (but won't always give them back) and all of which take telephone cards. You must dial the prefix 95 for any number in Sevilla.

Airport Aeropuerto San Pablo *(Tel 95/467-29-81)* is about 9km (5.6 miles) outside of the city, which is about a 25-minute, 1,200ptas taxi ride. Or for 750ptas you can take an **airport bus** *(Tel 90/221-03-17),* which leaves frequently and will drop you at the Hotel Alfonso XII on Calle San Fernando, behind the Alcazar. You'll most likely be flying on **Iberia** *(Tel 90/133-31-31, toll-free).*

Trains Trains come into the fairly modern **Santa Justa** *(Avda. Kansas City s/n; Tel 95/454-02-02).* To get to the city center, exit the station and head toward your right for about 20-25 minutes. If your bags are too heavy for all that walking, you can get bus 32 (125ptas) to Plaza Encarnación, or vice-versa.

Bus Lines Out of the City Most of the buses you want will arrive at and leave from **Prado de San Sebastián** *(José María Osborne 11; Tel 95/441-71-11),* located near Plaza de España. The exceptions are buses headed to western destinations, including Portugal, which go from the station at Plaza de Armas *(Tel 95/490-80-40).*

Bike Sevilla Mágica *(Calle Miguel de Mañara; Tel 95/456-38-38; 10am-2:00pm/5-8:30 pm),* on a side street between the Alcazar and the tourist office, will rent you pedal power for 1,500ptas for half a day or 2,000ptas for 24 hours.

Laundry There's a notable dearth of places to wash those atmosphere-soaked clothes in Sevilla; the one exception is **AutoServico de Lavandería Sevilla** *(Castelar 3; 9:30am-1:30pm/5-8:30pm Mon-Fri, 9am-2pm Sat; 1,000ptas wash and dry)* located in the Arenal just off Calle Adriano.

Postal The **Correos** is right near the Catedral and the main tourist office *(Avda. de la Constitución 32; Tel 94/421-95-85; 8:30am-8:30pm Mon-Fri, 9:30am-2pm Sat).*

Internet See *wired,* above.

cádiz

The oldest inhabited city in Western Europe, the port of Cádiz bustles with a youthful exuberance and an ancient mariner's soul. Balanced precariously on the tip of a peninsula and surrounded by water, it has that mysterious, slightly seedy atmosphere you can only get in authentic sea towns. It's an ambiance you can actually smell, as the salty air mingles with frying fish, beer, incense, and hash smoke. You half expect a ghost ship to dock in the bay and drunken pirates to pour into the claustrophobically narrow cobblestone streets; like all revelers they would be swallowed up by the thriving nightlife, especially during Cádiz's legendary *Carnaval* [see *festivals and events,* below]. They might also be pleasantly surprised (as you will be too) to find long stretches of clean, wide beaches.

The Phoenicians were the first to discover Cádiz's gifts when they arrived way back in 1100 B.C. They were followed by Visigoths, Carthaginians, Romans, Arabs, and other civilizations you learned about in World History class but can't quite place, all of whom recognized its vital location as a gateway to the *Atlantic*. Columbus embarked on his second journey to the New World from here. Sir Francis Drake raided the harbor and Anglo-Dutch forces sacked the city in the 16th century. Later, Napoleon's armies tried for two years but couldn't capture it. All of this tumult left little of ancient Cádiz, and most of what you see of the *casco antigua* (old town) is from the 18th century, when Cádiz flourished thanks to trade with the Americas. They say, however, that beneath every stone lies a Phoenician or Roman remain.

Though ancient, Cádiz continues to be recharged by constant sunshine and constant motion: fishermen, backpackers, smugglers, shop-

cádız

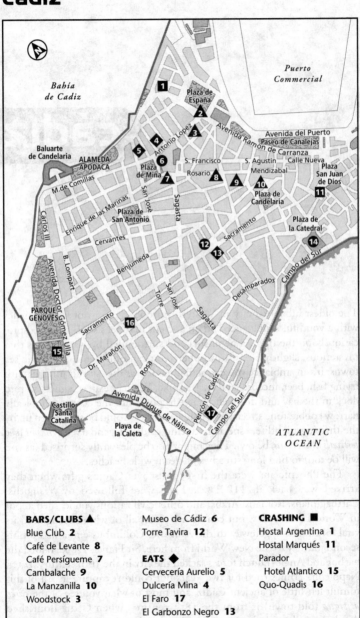

BARS/CLUBS ▲
Blue Club **2**
Café de Levante **8**
Café Persígueme **7**
Cambalache **9**
La Manzanilla **10**
Woodstock **3**

CULTURE ZOO ●
Catedral **14**

Museo de Cádiz **6**
Torre Tavira **12**

EATS ◆
Cervecería Aurelio **5**
Dulcería Mina **4**
El Faro **17**
El Garbonzo Negro **13**

CRASHING ■
Hostal Argentina **1**
Hostal Marqués **11**
Parador
  Hotel Atlantico **15**
Quo-Quadis **16**

pers, stray dogs, and speeding scooters keep the streets alive at all times. *Los gaditanos* (the locals) are liberal, freewheeling, spirited, and known for their sense of humor, so bring a good joke. They're also overwhelmingly young and attractive. In fact, *gaditanos* will tell you over and over that they have the most beautiful women in Spain (the Romans spoke highly of them as well). Of course, every town in Andalucía claims to have the most beautiful women. We think that they're all right, so just agree whole-heartedly, wherever you are, by saying *claro* (of course) or even *claro que si,* which when said with the right tone comes across as "hell yeah!"

This is a beach town, so fashion is even more laid-back than in the rest of southern Spain. Even though there's no surf, surf clothes are always popular and sunglasses are essential. At nighttime the locals just sit their shades up on top of their heads in case they need them. As you would expect from a port city in southern Spain, Moroccan hash, *chocolate,* is readily available here and is smoked with tobacco in plazas and clubs fairly openly. Pot smokers beware; *chocolate* gives a very physical high, so while you may not get paranoia and the giggles, you may get glued to your seat for a good hour.

neighborhoods

Unless you arrive by pirate ship, you'll enter Cádiz by way of a narrow peninsula, with the Bay of Cádiz on your right and the Atlantic Ocean to the left. The old town is like a head stuck on the neck of the penin-sula. If you arrive at the train station you'll be at **Plaza de Sevilla,** directly in front of the **Puerta Comercial** (Commercial Port). Go through the plaza and continue for one block. On your left you'll find **Plaza San Juan Dios,** an important place to remember: It's surrounded by restaurants with outdoor tables for people-watching, and the local tourist office is here (and has an excellent map of the city). And once you leave here, you will get lost. The streets directly behind Plaza San Juan Dios run at all kinds of crazy angles so you might think you're going straight but you're not. One important exception is **Calle Nueva,** a major shopping street that starts at the north end of the plaza. It runs basically straight, but like all long streets in Cádiz it has to change names at least once, so it does after it crosses little **Plaza de San Augustin,** where it becomes **Calle San Francisco.** Parallel to this street is **Calle Mendizabal,** which becomes **Calle Rosario,** where you'll find a lot of cool cafes and bars for hanging out. These parallel streets end at pretty **Plaza San Francisco,** and just past that is **Plaza de Mina,** which is essential for late-night outdoor drinking and talking. A lot of the happening bars are also in the Plaza de Mina area. **Plaza de España,** five blocks to the east, is an even bigger, more *tranquillo* green square, with one important club [see *bar and cafe scene,* below] and also the bus station, next to the port.

Now imagine you are back in Plaza San Juan de Dios (maybe you really *are* still standing there, reading this like the tourist you are...)—there are a couple other key streets that begin near here. **Calle Sacramento** runs

MOTO-CITY

When the tourist office of Andalucía recently polled visiting tourists about the state of the region as a vacation destination, one of the most oft-mentioned menaces was "*motos.*" That's right, the humble scooter: gas-efficient, cheap, easy to park. You will soon learn, however, that scooters, mopeds, and motorcycles in Spain are rarely humble; Not only do the kids go extremely fast through narrow streets, but they saw off the tailpipes and generally trick out their bikes to be AS LOUD AS POSSIBLE. Cádiz has a reputation for being the capital of fast, loud scooters. The noise has been described as a mosquito buzzing inside your ear, or a small yappy dog barking ferociously but futilely. Its menace is often discussed among citizens and politicians in the local press, although no regulations have been set. In defense of the *moto* posse, it should be pointed out that adolescent young men (and older men still stuck there) around the world have the same hormonal instinct to announce their presence with loud machine-made noise. What can you do, it's in the DNA. So if you can't beat 'em, join 'em [see *need to know,* below].

northwest from Plaza San Juan de Dios, taking you near **Plaza de las Flores** and the **Mercado Central,** past the 18th-century watchtower, **Torre Tavira,** and eventually to the **Teatro Falla** and close to the independent youth hostel. You can't fail to notice the **Catedral,** four blocks southeast of Plaza San Juan de Dios; it's the one with the gleaming gold dome, right across the street from the ocean. Surrounding the bewildering center of town is the **waterfront,** which is much easier to navigate; by following the coast, you can take a 45-minute walk around the city for excellent views of the **Bay of Cádiz** and the Atlantic Ocean. Start at the **Alameda Apocado** gardens on the northern edge of Cádiz, very near Plaza Mina and Plaza de España. From here the coastline curves around about half a mile to **Pargue Genoves,** an extremely pretty park right on the water, great for relaxing on a bench beneath a tree. About half a mile further south along the water is the small, urban **Playa de la Caleta,** a pleasant beach given that it's right in the city, very popular with the locals. In the evening it becomes lovers' lane, with kids making out beneath the pier. Continuing along the coast will take you back to the Catedral and Plaza San Juan De Dios.

beaches

Though the **Playa de la Caleta** is nice enough if you don't have the time or desire to leave the city, the best beaches for sun worship are outside of the old town, down the peninsula. **Playa de la Victoria,** about 1 kilometer (.62 miles) down the peninsula, is a wide beach with nice sand and lots of seaside development. **Paseo Marítimo,** a cafe- and bar-lined boulevard running along the beach, is the heart of the summertime beachside party scene. Further down the peninsula, where the hotels and bars stop, lies the more remote **Playa de Cortadura.** You'll be amazed to have a whole stretch of beach to yourself here, while still being able to see the glowing old town shimmering in the sunlight. You can walk down to Playa de la Victoria in about 25-30 minutes, or you can take Bus 1, which runs from Plaza de España down the peninsula one block from the ocean (on a street that changes names many times), and back the same way (120ptas). A good reference point for getting off the bus is the stop for the Hotel Playa Victoria.

bar and cafe scenes

The distinction between bar/cafe/live music joint is even more blurred here than in the rest of Spain. A ton of cafes become bars at night and feature live music, but for some reason every act seems to take place on Thursday at 10pm or 11pm. All the places mentioned here in the old city are near Plaza de Mina and Plaza de España. These plazas and many other smaller ones become their own scenes on weekend nights, with people of all types chillin' like villains.

Our favorite little corner bar is **Woodstock** *(Manuel Rancés y Antonio López; No phone; 9pm-2am Mon-Wed, 9pm-4am Thu-Sat, noon to midnight Sun),* a celebration of peace, love, and beer. Despite the name and the Woodstock festival posters on the wall, the vibe is much more '70s blues, rock, AC/DC, Van Morrison, CCR, so keep your tie-dyes at home and don't stress about the brown acid. It's also a nice respite from the inevitable Cruzcampo or Mahou beer, because you can get Guinness or Caffery's on tap for 300ptas a half-pint, which is twice as expensive as Spanish beer and probably has twice as much alcohol. A worldly crowd fills this place at night and on weekends it spills out onto the street. Inside, guitars hang on the wooden walls, along with notices behind the bar about musical instruments for sale, in case you want to buy an accordion or an equalizer (cash only). There's no street number for this place, but just look for the Bass sign on the corner of Rancés and Antonio Lopez a block up from Plaza de España.

The literary crowd hangs out at **Café de Levante** *(Rosario 35; Tel 95/622-02-27; Noon-midnight daily),* a few blocks west of Plaza de Candelabria. It's sophisticated but mellow in the spirit of a Seattle coffee house, with old movie stills on the walls. It hosts poetry readings by local writers most every Thursday night at about 10pm.

Café Persígueme *(Calle Tinte y Calle Sagasta s/n; Tel 95/622-84-20)* is a suave jazz bar located on a corner just south of Plaza de Mina. It's got the mood right: The place is smoky, with a long, glass bar and funky art deco furniture, but the jazz is usually only of average quality. However, the knowledgeable 25-years-and-up crowd sucking down bottles of Carlsberg (300ptas) appreciates the effort.

Another jazz/blues bar that's more hole-in-the-wall is **Cambalache** *(José del Toro 20; No phone)*, a block away from Café de Levante. The bands play in the back against a brick wall, usually on—you guessed it—Thursday nights. No cover, but beers go up to 300ptas during performances. Good, divey ambiance, and the band may actually have some soul if you're lucky.

To carouse like a wine connoisseur on a backpacker's budget, cleanse your palette and sample some of the local *fino* (a type of sherry) at **La Manzanilla** *(Feduchy 9; Tel 95/628-54-01; Noon-3pm/5-10pm Mon-Sat)*, right next to Plaza de Candelabria. *Manzanilla* comes from the San Lúcar grape-growing region, and bartenders here pour a variety of these fine local sherries from big wooden casks. Because it's from a coastal grape, *manzanilla* is supposed to have a hint of a salty taste, but you have to pretty much be a wine afficianado to notice. If you don't know anything about sherry or just don't care, ask to try one *seca* (dry) and one *dulce* (sweet) and see if you can tell the difference. A glass, accompanied by two olives, is only 125ptas and is served, of course, in a sherry glass with a narrow top in order to give you the full aroma...but of course you knew that already.

In the summer a lot of the party scene moves down the peninsula to Playa de la Victoria, on the oceanside walkway Paseo Marítimo. There are lots of bars here, many of which only exist for one summer and disappear or change names. One we can vouch for is **La Jarra** *(Paseo Marítimo 11; Tel 95/625-82-54)*, a good place to get a *jarra* (a jar of beer) and hang out with the young revelers who come from all over Spain to party on the beaches of Cádiz.

To dance to DJ music you'll most likely have to wait for the weekends unless it's the height of summer. In the old city, located beneath a nondescript storefront on Plaza de España, is the funkified **Blue Club** *(Plaza de España 12; Midnight-6am Thu-Sat)*. Formerly known as the Ajo Club, it's been turned into a stony blue cave, with local DJs playing mostly funky mixes and breakbeats. No cover, but make sure you buy a drink (beer is 300ptas); the *camareras* (bartenders) are friendly and mellow to everyone except freeloaders. It opens at midnight, but no one shows up until 1:30am, and it doesn't start going off until 3am.

Playa de la Victoria supports a pop-oriented club scene in summer. The hot spots seem to change every year so your best bet is to ask a local at Plaza de Mina or any of the other bars we've mentioned.

There is a gay scene in Cádiz, for men and women both, but in the liberal spirit of the town it's mixed with all the other scenes rather than being exclusive. Some gay-friendly spots are **Café de Levante** [see above] and **El Garbonzo Negro** [see *eats,* below].

A gay/straight artsy crowd can be found at **Cenobio** *(Rafael de la Viesca s/n; 5pm-2am daily)*, located in a great space—the lower floor of a noble Cádiz home from the 18th century—and with a medieval vibe. It's on a corner between Plaza de Mina and Plaza de España.

ARTS SCENE

Cádiz is a performing arts town known for its comedic theater; during Carnaval the whole city gets involved [see *festivals & events,* below]. At any other time of year you won't want to miss the tradition-rich **Gran Teatro Falla** *(Plaza de Fragela s/n; Tel 95/622-08-28).* Actually, you'd really have to make an effort to miss it. It's located in a big, beautiful, 19th-century reddish-pink Muslim-influenced building with striped arches above the doorways; it definitely stands out, even in the architectural jumble that has arisen in Cádiz during the last 300 years. Traditional theater (in Spanish, of course), flamenco spectaculars, classical music, and even the occasional pop music concert go down here.

For a funkier scene, check out the alter ego of the traditional Teatro Falla, **Central Lechera** *(Plaza de Arguelles; Tel 95/622-06-28).* This arts center offers modern theater, world music, book readings, just about anything you could imagine, in an informal, postmodern setting just off Plaza de España.

FESTIVALS & EVENTS

If you're in Spain during February/March, you must go to Cádiz's legendary **Carnaval,** a 10-day blow-out that lasts until the weekend past "Fat Tuesday," which signals the end of other Mardi Gras celebrations for the rest of the world. While the great *feria's* of Andalucía, such as Sevilla's, take place on fairgrounds, Cádiz brings the party into the streets. Carnaval is about performance as much as boozing (although there's plenty of that too); masks, face paint, and fancy dress allow the townspeople to invent an identity—usually for a humorous effect. Friends and organizations form *murgas,* which are official groups dressed in a particular theme that perform songs, satirical sketches, and/or dances for the enjoyment of the crowd. Other groups, called *ilegales* because they're not part of the official competition, perform even more outrageous sketches and campy songs. They also give themselves funny names like *El Vigilantes de la Playa* (The Beach Vigilantes). Of course all of this just seems like barely controlled chaos to an inebriated visitor anyway. Finding a place to stay in Cádiz during Carnaval is impossible unless you've booked months in advance. You can try staying in a nearby town, or if you're hard-core you can just stay up partying all night and sleep on the beach during the day.

CULTURE ZOO

Cádiz does not have the big tourist attractions that draw lines of camera hounds, mostly because anything older than the 18th century was sacked by some marauder or another. But just walking through the rambling old town is a feast for the eyes; make sure to look up, or you'll miss the gargoyles, Gothic windows, statues, and other cool stuff.

Torre Tavira *(Marqués del Real Tesoro 10; Tel 95/621-29-10; 10am-8pm June-Sept, 10am-6pm Oct-May; 500ptas):* Smack in the center of the old town, this 18th-century watchtower—named after its first watchman, Antonio Tavira—provides spectacular views of the city. Even cooler, it has a Camera Obscura, one of the few left in the world, which shows beautiful live magnified projections of the city. How does it work? Well, it shows you the city using mirrors and lenses...you see, it's all about the refraction of light...let's explain it another way...the world's first cameras were based on this technology...light travels in rays, you know, so, uh...O.K., let's just say it's one of those things you have to see to understand. Just go. The exhibitions happen every 30 minutes and there are least three or four a day that are narrated in English; ask at the ticket counter for the next one.

Catedral *(Plaza de Catedral; Tel 95/628-61-54; 10am-12:30pm; Free admission, museum 500ptas):* You'll have noticed the glowing gold dome on top of this baroque cathedral. Some of us are happy just catching a glimpse of it; other people need more, so they go inside to see the impressive stone interior, the finely decorated crypt of Cádiz-born composer Manuel de Falla, and even the museum, with paintings by people you've never heard of and will probably forget as soon as you leave. The cathedral itself is free, but take note that it's only open in the mornings.

Museo de Cádiz *(Plaza de Mina; Tel 95/621-22-81; 2:30-8pm Tue, 9am-8pm Wed-Sat, 9:30am-2:30pm Sun; 250ptas, free Sun):* Take a crash course in Cádiz history at the city's museum, which houses works by some people you may have heard of, such as Murillo, Zurbarán, and Rubens, although the real treasures are the archeological finds from 3,000 years of Cádiz history, from Phoenicians to Romans and some folks in between.

EATS

This is a fishy town, and most of it's fresh out of the water, so dinner won't leave you with any strange swellings or hives. You'll also see lots of places with a sign saying *Hay caracoles*, which means yes, they have snails! One of our favorite cheap snacks is the *empanada de atún* (tuna empanada) to go, available from most any bakery for about 125ptas.

▶▶CHEAP

For cheap old-school tapas near Plaza de Mina, try **Cervecería Aurelio** *(Zorilla 1; Tel 95/622-71-22; Noon-4pm/6pm-midnight)*. There's a menu here but it's easier just to crane your neck and try to identify those odd-looking things on display behind the bar. Seafood, as you'd expect, is big here. You can get a little plate of *atún* (tuna), something more exotic like *pulpo* (octopus), or *ortiguillas* (some sort of sea plant) for around

TO MARKET

Cádiz's central market, **Mercardo Abastos** *(Plaza de Libertad 10am-1pm/5:30-8:30pm Mon-Fri, 9am-1:30 Sat)*, is as funky and colorful as the rest of town, with heaps of fish of course, but also fruit and veggies, and an old woman with a bucket of live snails. It's located right next to Plaza de las Flores, a very pretty square with flower stands.

200ptas. The decor is very '70s cafeteria, and the friendly guys behind the bar, with their rumpled shirts, ties, and big mustaches, are straight out of the Beastie Boys' "Sabotage" video.

   El Garbanzo Negro *(Sacramento 18; Tel 95/622-10-90; Call for hours)* is the most pastel place in the known world. Located near Torre Tavira, it actually has pastel paintings on pastel walls, just what you need to put a smile on your face in the morning. Good thing the decor is sunshiny—you'll need it when you learn about breakfast "Andalus," which is toast with olive oil and a coffee for 150ptas. (Toast is really all they eat for breakfast in Andalucía—no donuts, no bagels, no Cinnamon Toast Crunch, so get used to it.) At night, this shiny, happy little cafe becomes a gay-friendly-but-mixed-crowd hang-out for cocktails and seafood-oriented tapas.

   Another good breakfast spot, a block north of Plaza de Mina, is **Dulcería Mina** *(Antonio López 2; 9am-3pm/5-9pm daily)*, which has a much more down-home diner ambiance (e.g., grumpy waitresses in hairnets). The breakfast special of toast, coffee, and fresh-squeezed O.J. for 300ptas is available until noon. The rest of the day, you can get coffee cakes, pastries, and ice cream.

▶▶DO-ABLE

El Faro *(San Félix 15; Tel 95/621-10-68; 1-4:30pm/8:30-midnight daily)*, everyone's favorite restaurant in Cádiz, makes its humble home in the working-class Barrio de la Viña, a few blocks east of Avenida Duque de Najera, which runs along the Playa de la Caleta on the town's west coast. Visitors and locals flock to this temple of seafood where the main courses run from 1,200ptas and up for all kinds of oceanic delights, fried, baked, stewed, etc. If you're on the cheap you can also get reasonably priced tapas at the bar. Be aware that El Faro is closed during the afternoon.

crashing

There are plenty of reasonably priced, funky accommodations in the old town that have the same weather-beaten-but-still-standing charm as the

wired

Cádiz does not have any genuine hipster Internet cafes...yet. But the way things are going, by the time you read this we may all have wireless modems implanted in the fillings of our teeth. For now you'll have to be content with the computers at **enred** *(Sacramento 36; Tel 95/680-81-81; 11am-2pm/6-10pm daily; 500ptas per hour)*, near Torre Tavira. The computers are decently fast, and the staff speaks English, but sometimes it suffers from that Internet menace: nerds! That's right, the species does actually exist in Spain, despite what the movies show us. We all like nerds, just not when they are groups of 13-year-olds playing war games and shouting excitedly at every kill. Of course, they will probably soon be running their own multinational e-businesses, so start sucking up now.

There are a number of informative websites about Cádiz, though they're all in Spanish:
www.infocadiz.com
www.cadiznet.com
www.cádiz.org

rest of the city. Call ahead for rooms during the height of summer and call years in advance if you want to stay during *Carnaval*.

▶▶CHEAP

Quo-Qadis *(Diego Arias 1; Tel 95/622-19-39; 1,000ptas single, 3,200 double, 4,800 triple)* takes hostelry to a whole new level. This independent youth hostel near Teatro Falla is not just a place to sleep (in fact you may not sleep at all) but a center for alternative living. It's got a bar, vegetarian meals in the dining room (including free breakfast), planned excursions, and snorkel rental (1,000ptas); you can even sign up for courses during the summer in things like Spanish, flamenco dancing, and juggling. This whirlwind of activity is choreographed by the friendly English-speaking owner, Enrique, who's also not afraid to shove an extra bunk bed in the already overcrowded dorm rooms, bringing the total to an absurd ten sweaty backpackers. If you're in one of these dorms you'll know what it must have been like to sleep in the galley of one of Columbus's ships, and you won't get a peaceful night's sleep unless you're bombed out of your *calavera* (skull). It is, however, a good place to compare the accents, snores, and odors of different cultures (our own informal survey says Americans from the Pacific Northwest are the snoring champions, somewhere between a grizzly bear and a freight train). If you're traveling with others and sleep is a daily requirement, we recommend reserving one of the double or triple rooms in advance.

▶▶DO-ABLE

If the youth hostel is full, they'll probably send you to **Hostal Argentina** (*Conde O'Reilly 1; Tel 95/622-33-10; 2,500ptas single*). That's awfully nice of them, because this place off of Plaza de España is a sweet deal—the rooms have big beds and little TV sets.

To be closer to the train station and the center of town, try **Hostal Marqués** (*Marques de Cádiz 1; Tel 95/628-58-54; 2,500ptas single, 3,500ptas double*). Located behind Plaza San Juan de Dios, this friendly place offers another good deal. The rooms are clean, with sinks, new closets, and precarious balconies to view the action in the winding streets below. Showers are down the hall and seem to flood the entire bathroom upon use. There are a few other hostels on this street if Marqués is full.

▶▶SPLURGE

Paradors in Andalucía are the government-owned luxury hotels that almost always have the best location in town. **Parador Hotel Atlantico** (*Duque de Nájera 9; Tel 95/622-69-05; 15,000ptas and up single, 18,000ptas and up double*) is no exception. If you've got the cash, you might as well buck up and go for it. This one sits right on the Bay of Cádiz next to Parque Genovés and has its own little beach. The rooms all have private baths and balconies with ocean views.

need to know

Currency exchange There are a few banks with ATMs in the shopping district north of Plaza San Juan de Dios on Calle Nueva, which turns into Calle San Francisco. Banks are open Monday to Friday from 9am to 2pm in summer, and also Saturday 9-2 the rest of the year.

Tourist Information The **local tourist office** (*Plaza San Juan Dios 11; Tel 95/624-10-01; 9am-2pm/5-8pm Mon-Sat*) near the train station has a good map of the city, which you will definitely need. The **regional tourist office** (*Calderón de la Barca 1; Tel 95/621-13-13; 9am-7pm Tue-Fri, 9am-2pm Mon and Sat*), on the corner of Plaza de Mina, has English speakers and good info on excursions outside of the city.

Public Transportation The old city is small enough to walk through, but you might want to take bus 1 from Plaza de España to get to the beaches on the peninsula. You can also take a taxi here from Plaza San Juan de Dios for around 700ptas.

Health and Emergency Medical emergencies: *061*, police: *091* or *092*. For less urgent matters go to the **Comisaría de Policia** (*Avenida de Andalucía 28*).

Trains and Buses The **train station** (*Plaza de Sevilla; Tel 95/625-43-01*) is two blocks east of Plaza San Juan de Dios. Buses are run by **Autobuses Comes** (*Plaza de Hispanidad 1; Tel 95/621-17-63*), which is located next to the port off of Plaza de España.

Bike/Moped Rental If you want to ride like a local, you can rent scooters or bikes from the friendly folks at **Gestatur** (*Antonio López 5; Tel 95/622-41-56*). A *moto* will cost you 3,500ptas for 24 hours, if you live that long. A more gentle *bicicleta* will cost 1,300ptas per day, although roads and traffic are not bike-friendly until you get out to the beach. You also have to leave a deposit, which is 10,000ptas for scooters and 3,000ptas for bikes.

Postal The main **Correos** *(Plaza de Topete s/n; Tel 90/219-71-97)* is in the old city on Plaza de Topete, which also goes by the name Plaza de Flores.

Internet See *wired,* above.

córdoba

Córdoba might be the most underrated city in Andalucía. Sevilla and Granada get all the ink, but Córdoba not only has the Mezquita, a Muslim architectural wonder as awe-inspiring as anything in Spain, but also a happening nightlife that is just underground enough to be off the radar of most foreigners. Many travelers either make Córdoba a day trip, or else do the Mezquita, walk around the old quarter looking at the pretty patios, and then call it a night. You should give Córdoba more of a chance if you want to meet the locals, who are cosmopolitan but also laid-back enough to give this big city (population: 306,000) a small-town vibe.

Historically, Córdoba was anything but small-town. At the end of the last millennium (Y1K!), it was the biggest and most fantastic city in Western Europe, the capital of the Western Muslim Empire, with over 500,000 residents, 1,000 mosques, 600 public baths, and even streetlights (hundreds of years before they went on in those backwaters of London and Paris). While Northern Europe was stuck in the Middle Ages, Córdoba thrived as a cultural center of philosophy, astronomy, religious theory, medicine, and law. The Reconquista, which hit here in 1236, ended all that, but at least the Christians had the good sense not to tear down the Mezquita—they just plopped a cathedral right in the middle of it instead.

Today, Córdoba may not party like it's 999, but if you have your walking shoes you can find not only treasures from its Muslim past, but typical Spanish traditions like tapas and bullfighting, as well as bohemian speakeasies, and even some rock 'n' roll.

Another cool thing about Córdoba is that unlike other big cities in Spain, there is not a big foreign (American) student population, nor as

córdoba

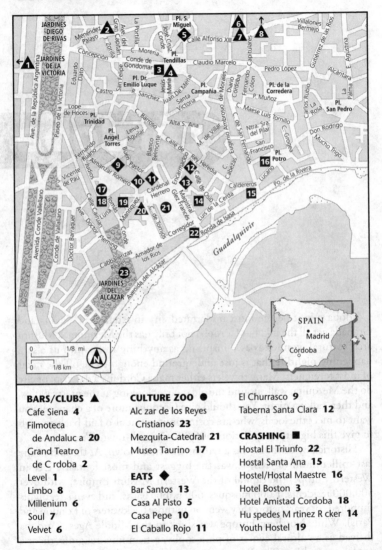

BARS/CLUBS ▲	CULTURE ZOO ●	El Churrasco **9**
Cafe Siena **4**	Alc zar de los Reyes	Taberna Santa Clara **12**
Filmoteca	Cristianos **23**	
de Andaluc a **20**	Mezquita-Catedral **21**	CRASHING ■
Grand Teatro	Museo Taurino **17**	Hostal El Triunfo **22**
de C rdoba **2**		Hostal Santa Ana **15**
Level **1**	EATS ◆	Hostel/Hostal Maestre **16**
Limbo **8**	Bar Santos **13**	Hotel Boston **3**
Millenium **6**	Casa Al Pisto **5**	Hotel Amistad Cordoba **18**
Soul **7**	Casa Pepe **10**	Hu spedes M rtinez R cker **14**
Velvet **6**	El Caballo Rojo **11**	Youth Hostel **19**

big a backpacker contingent. So you're going to have to actually *habla* with the locals if you can find it in your heart to leave the cozy touristy confines of the *judería* (Jewish Quarter). So dust off that *Español,* and don't stress, Cordobeses are laid-back. But don't try to impress them by reeling off your record collection, either; Córdoba is the closest big Andalucían city to Madrid, so the kids know *que pasa* (what's up).

Although Córdoba can feel like a small town, it is a city, and cities have some level of crime. Use caution, avoid parks at night, don't pass out drunk on the street, and you should be fine; your rent-a-car is definitely in more danger than you are. There's plenty of available free parking on the street near the Mezquita for a reason. Breaking into cars is something of an art here, so even if your luggage is locked in the trunk the back window can be broken and the back seat ripped out (trust us on this one). If you have wheels, use one of the available secured parking lots [see *need to know*, below]. If you're on foot, scooters and speeding cars in the old quarter will be the biggest threat to your health [see *walk on the wild side*, below].

neighborhoods

The center of any visit is the **judería,** one of the best-preserved neighborhoods in all of Andalucía, with endless mazes of narrow cobblestoned streets, whitewashed houses, and plant-filled patios. Street signs are virtually nonexistent here, so you will get lost, but if you head downhill toward the river and just follow the tourists you will eventually find the **Mezquita-Catedral** [see *culture zoo*, below] in the southwest corner, a block away from the Guadalquivir river. Inside the Mezquita's walls, you can chill in the **Patio de los Naranjos** (Courtyard of the Orange Trees) during the day free of charge. Behind the Mezquita is **Puente Romano** (Roman Bridge), which is no longer Roman, but is still a nice way to see the river, despite the exhaust fumes from cars. There are innumerable quaint plazas to explore in the *judería*; some of the best known are: **Plaza de Maimonides** (named after the famous 12th-century Jewish theologian), north of the Mezquita; the handsome **Plaza del Potro,** a former trading center a few minutes' walk east of the Mezquita; nearby **Plaza de la Corredera,** directly adjacent to the Mercado, a large square currently undergoing major renovations; and **Plaza de San Pedro,** a 10-minute walk east from the Mezquita, which can get filled with high school kids showing off their scooters in the evenings. Just west of the Mezquita, outside the walls of the *judería,* lies the **Alcázar de los Reyes Cristianos,** another must-see cultural site with impressive gardens [see *culture zoo*, below]. A 20-minute walk north of the Alcázar stretches a mile-long series of public parks that change names from **Jardines de la Victoria** to **Jardines Diego de Rivas** to **Jardines de la Agricultura**—no matter what name they go by, they are all pleasant, shady places to escape from the blistering heat of summer. The verdant green ends at **Avenida de America,** running diagonally along the north side of town, where you'll find the train and bus stations. West of all those parks is the **Ciudad Jardin** (Garden District), a leafy residential neighborhood that has a nightlife area centered around **Plaza Costa del Sol,** frequented by well-to-do locals and their kids. The urban center of Córdoba is north of the walls of the *judería:* **Plaza Tendillas** is a bustling square with a fountain and cafes with outside seating. **Avenida de Gran Capitán,** which runs north-south three blocks west of Plaza Tendillas, is the heart of the shopping district; it's also the site of the **Gran Teatro de Córdoba** [see *live music scene*, below]. Further north is the **El Brillante** suburb, which has

walk on the wild side

If you like danger, stroll the *judería* for a while. The ancient streets are so incredibly narrow and seem left over from an era so different, you'll be amazed to learn that modern killing machines like cars and scooters actually fit through here. They do (just barely) and almost always at high speed, forcing you to leap onto the 6-inch-wide sidewalk (if there is one) and suck in your stomach to avoid being killed. After a few hours of near-misses as you walk/jump through here, you'll be swearing like a Tarrantino character, while the locals, as is their fashion, don't seem to mind. Mothers with strollers calmly swipe up their youngsters and cling to the nearest wall as the side-view mirror of a truck just misses their earlobe, then continue moseying along as if a breeze had passed.

a thriving nightlife in summer. Our favorite nighttime haunts, however, hide themselves along and near **Calle Alfaros,** which runs north-south about a five-minute walk east of Plaza Tendillas.

bar, cafe and live music scene

If you want to hang out in the *judería* and find a little hole-in-the-wall tapas bar, you have plenty of options, but just be warned that your drinking companions are most likely to be middle-aged Northern Europeans. To discover Córdoba's alternative scene you'll have to venture north of the old quarter, but not too far. The cafes and bars around bustling Plaza Tendillas are great for an open-air drink day or night. **Cafe Siena** *(Plaza Tendillas 1)* on the southeastern corner is reputed to be gay-friendly although you won't necessarily find evidence of that. The owner is definitely friendly, however, and you can pass hours at the outside tables drinking beer and snacking on the free olives.

We urge you to explore the bohemian scene around Calle Alfaros, east of Plaza Tendillas, which may not seem like a scene at all if you don't know where you're looking (that's why we're here). It starts one block north of the Roman Ruins, which are easy to locate because of their six big stone columns, lit up at night. Just off the southern end of Calle Alfaros is Calle Alfonso XIII. (Be aware that there's also an Alfonso XII in another part of the city.) A few storefronts up on your left you'll find the bar/cafe *mas guay* (most cool), **Soul** *(Alfonso XIII 3; Tel 95/749-15-80; 9am-3am daily, till 4am Thu-Sat)*. Walking in here you might think you've stepped into a lounge in lower Manhattan: back-lit liquor bottles behind the bar, glass tables, benches made from industrial steel poles, comfy chairs in the chill room to the left, light projections on the wall, framed black and white photos (including the inevitable Audrey Hepburn from

Breakfast at Tiffany's). And while the late-night crowd might give the impression of New York's East Village—dressed in black, pierced—they're definitely more laid-back, friendly, and of mixed ages, though the dominant group is 22-30. During the day you can relax in the air-conditioning with a coffee, while listening to slightly alternative American music like Alanis Morissette or Beck. Most every night of the week there's a DJ humbly hidden behind the bar spinning excellent funk, hip-hop, drum 'n' bass, anything with soul. In accordance with the mellow vibe of the place, it's not a big production; the DJ is here to play good music, not show off his or her scratching skills. And since this is Europe, you've got choices, man: you can get coffee, mixed drinks, beer, or wine at any hour, all for between 200 and 300ptas. And if you're an actor or model you can even get a mineral water or diet soda at 1am without using that "I'm driving" excuse, and no one will look at you funny.

Because its hours are consistent, Soul is the most reliable in the bohemian circuit of venues in this area, which also includes Millennium, Velvet, and Limbo, all of which are a couple of blocks north and keep spottier hours. Generally they're open Mon-Sat, from about 9pm to 3 or 4am. For live music, check out **Millennium** *(Alfaros 33; No phone)*, where you enter into a mellow bar. If you go up the smoke-filled stairs, past the folks sitting here because they're too high to stand up, there's another bar and a small stage that features a lot of local jazz (usually Wednesdays), as well as visiting groups playing funk, Cuban salsa, whatever. The crowd up here gets sweaty and happy during performances, which usually begin at 10pm or later. Right next door is **Velvet** *(Alfaros 31; No phone)*, which, true to its name, is very smooth. Candles on the tables and cushioned benches welcome people who have already been to Soul and Millennium and just want to chill out and talk. Around the corner, just off Calle Alfaros, hides the most underground bar of all, **Limbo** *(Juan Rufo 2; No phone)*, which has no sign whatsoever, and, mysteriously, an address that is actually number 6, but over which a number 2 has been stuck. This speakeasy doesn't require a secret knock to get in— the wooden doors just have to be open. Upon entering you run right into the low-ceilinged, homey bar, where a stereo plays whatever music the bartender feels like putting on; there's also a back room for hanging out that has work by local artists on its walls. You might get some surprised looks from the bohemians when you first enter, as in "How did that *guir* find his way out of the *judería*?", but they'll be glad you made the effort, and will want to talk until very late, when this place finally closes.

In the garden district, the circular Plaza de Costa del Sol draws a younger crowd, which the hipsters of the Soul set refer to as "those kids." Rockers congregate at their no-frills shrine to loud music, **Level** *(Antonio Maura 57; No phone)*, a few blocks east of Plaza Costa del Sol. Legend has it the Pixies played on this tiny stage years ago...imagine the Pixies playing in your basement, except your basement is probably bigger, not as dark, and doesn't serve Heineken. The music here is definitely hit-or-miss; the best shows are probably the punk and metal bands from

Madrid. To find out who's playing, just walk around town—Level must hire a small army to do promotions because their flyers announcing upcoming shows plaster the place. A word of advice that stands for all venues in Spain: just because a band has an evil-sounding name, such as *Los Demonios de Infierno* (The Devils of Hell), does *not* automatically guarantee that they rock. The unhealthy reliance on the electric keyboard is one of the main causes of this affliction.

ARTS SCENE

The arts scene in Córdoba gains a certain authenticity from the fact that it is presented not for the benefit of tourists, but for the Córdobans themselves. The passionate flamenco dances often performed here are said to be a *flamenco puro*—that is, a pure form of the art not bastardized for tourists, as is so often the case in cities such as Madrid. If you speak Spanish, you can see many works by Andalusian playwrights not performed elsewhere

OUT WITH THE OLD, IN WITH THE NEW

In the 16th century, the whole center of the magnificent Mezquita was ripped out and replaced by a cathedral [see *culture zoo*, below]. Even King Charles V, who approved the deconstruction, remarked, "Had I known what this was I would not have given permission to touch the old...you have unmade what was unique in the world." Today, architecture buffs still bitch about the mammoth Christian intrusion on the purity of the Mezquita's "concept." Before you start throwing a fit and taking the Lord's name in vain in front of praying nuns, think of it this way: 1) At least they didn't tear the whole thing down, as they did in other parts of Spain after the Reconquista; 2) There's nothing any of us can do about it now, so chill; 3) There's no better representation of the history of Andalucía under one roof anywhere. Think of it. You've got the grandiose Islamic mosque—which was partially built using materials from the original Visigoth church and local Roman ruins—subjugated, but not eliminated, by the bluntly placed, extravagant Christian cathedral, which was funded by riches from the discovery of the New World. Then there's you, and your fellow gawkers, with your video cameras, pagers, and dental floss, representing modern Andalucía, the tourist Mecca that struggles daily with the balance between tradition and tourism. And that's...one to grow on.

in Spain. While the arts scene here is hardly the equal of Madrid in size or overall quality, there are a few galleries here worth visiting.

▶▶VISUAL ARTS

Al Muk *(Avda. de Aeropuerto 6; Tel. 957/414312; 10am-1pm and 5-9pm Mon-Fri),* west of the cathedral, is one of the most cutting-edge art galleries in Córdoba, and some art lovers and patrons go here twice a month, as they change their exhibitions every 15 days. You see not just paintings, but some of the most avant-garde sculptures being turned out in the ateliers of Andalusia.

Sala Museistica de Caja Sur *(Avda. Rondas de los Tejares 6; Tel. 957/481517; 6-9pm Mon-Sat noon-2pm and 6-9pm Sun),* a 3-minute walk west of the Plaza Colón, is like a prestigious art show. Many of the artists displayed here have works that hang in leading museums. It's highly unlikely that most people will be able to afford any of the art on sale here, but it's one of the best art shows in town. Not just Spanish artists are displayed but international painters as well. On our latest visit, the leading contemporay artists of Peru were showcased.

▶▶PERFORMING ARTS

For civilized acts, turn to the **Gran Teatro de Córdoba** *(Avda. Gran Capitán 3; Tel 95/748-02-37; Ticket office 11am-2pm/5-9pm, Mon-Sat),* a stately 19th-century performing arts institution in the center of town. It features theater, most of it modern and in Spanish, as well as performances in the international languages of ballet, modern dance, and classical and traditional music. Ticket prices start at a very reasonable 800ptas for the nose-bleed seats.

Housed in a stunning old building near the Mezquita, **Filmoteca de Andalucía** *(Medina y Corella 5; Tel 95/747-20-18; **www.cica.es/filmo**, screenings 8:30pm Mon-Thu)* ranks as much more than a cool independent movie theater: It's the essential film organization in Andalucía. Along with a library and an archive, it also puts together a continuous program of obscure and classic movies in their original language with Spanish subtitles. One night might feature a tribute to older directors known only to film geeks, such as Douglas Sirk *(Magnificent Obsession);* another night will honor a more recent filmmaker like John Sayles, Atom Egoyan, or Lars Von Trier. Not only is the setting and programming unique, a ticket costs just 150ptas (don't do the math, we'll tell you: it's less than a buck). Showtime is 8:30 but show up on time, because once the movie starts you won't be allowed in.

CULTURE ZOO

It isn't Seville. It isn't Grenada. Compared to those stellar attractions, though, Córdoba's generally agreed-upon status as the third grandest city in Andalucía is nothing to be ashamed of. Córdoba has a few big three-star attractions, including its Mezquita-Catédral and its Alcázar, but to appreciate the city fully you need to walk through the narrow streets of the old Arab and Jewish quarters to take in the whitewashed Andalusian houses and their flower-filled balconies and patios. They are so lovely that

fESTIVALS

Semana Santa, the holy week between Palm Sunday and Good Friday, is a time for artistic religious processions in much of Andalucía, and Córdoba is no exception. But May is the big festival month in Córdoba, so much so that it's hard to tell when one begins and another ends. **Las Cruces**—when giant crosses of flowers sprout up in plazas all over town—takes place in the first half of May, as does the famous **Los Patios,** which finds proud Cordobeses throwing open their iron gates and showing off their patios to the public. Prizes are awarded for the most elaborate patios. Things really rage at the **Feria de Nuestra Señora Salud,** which happens over ten days at the end of May, sometimes into June. In the beginning of July is the **Festival de Guitarra** *(Tel 95/7480-644; www.guitarracordoba.com)*, an international celebration of the possibilities of the six-string Andalucía introduced to the world. Performances of classical, jazz, blues, and, of course, flamenco, take place at dramatic settings like the Gran Teatro and the Jardines de Alcázar for around 1,200ptas a show. There are also week-long courses in various types of axe-handling, including flamenco and guitar construction. Call or check out the website for more details.

UNESCO made the historic core of Córdoba a World Heritage site. It's fun to get lost—wander at will.

Mezquita-Catedral *(Cardinal Herrero s/n; Tel 95/747-05-12; 10am-7pm daily May-Sept; 10am-6pm Oct-Apr; 900ptas):* Sevilla's Catedral is bigger, Granada's Alhambra is more opulent and more photographed, but for sheer originality, inspired invention, and jaw-dropping awesomeness, we like Córdoba's. You've never seen anything quite like the forest of candy-cane striped arches that dominate its interior and make it one of the most sublime examples of Islamic architecture in the world. It's also the oldest of the three by far; the original mosque was built in the 8th century by the Muslim ruler Abd Al Raman, and the original 11 aisles still remain—you'll see them when you first enter. Later Muslim rulers added on to these, continuing to use red brick and white stone to create the inspired striped pillars, 1,300 in all, of which 800 still remain. The *mirhab,* which functioned as a prayer room, is surrounded by more intricate and colorful arches and domes. Then there's the slightly obnoxious 16th-century cathedral shoved right in the middle of it all (it's not called the Mezquita-Catedral for nothing), an unwelcome intrusion by most accounts [see *out with the old, in with the new,* below]. But the homage to Jesus reveals some impressive work as well, especially the mind-numbingly intricate mahogany choir stalls (try to imagine how long it took to carve those things) and the giant pipe organs (which they should let Stevie Wonder play, just once).

The blessed absence of blinding artificial light inside the building calms everyone except the most fervent picture-takers, who will never grasp it all anyway. The courtyard in front of the Mezquita, Patio de los Naranjos, is a relaxing place to chill after seeing the Mezquita, or any time of day when you're tired of walking.

Alcázar de Los Reyes Cristianos *(Amador de los Rios s/n; Tel 95/742-01-51; 10am-2pm/6-8pm May-Sept, 9:30am-3pm/4:30-6:30pm Oct-Apr, morning hours only Sun, closed Mon; 450ptas):* This fortress was built for military defense, hence the three towers. But it also functioned as a palace in its day; Columbus met with Queen Isabella here to discuss the plans for his little boat ride. You can picture them strolling through the magnificent gardens, and you'll want to relax among the fountains, trimmed hedges, and immense flower gardens. Stop and smell the roses.

Museo Municipal de Arte Táurino *(Plaza Maimónides; Tel 95/720-10-56; 10:30am-2pm/6-8pm Tue-Sat, 9:30am-3pm Sun; 450ptas):* For a complete change of pace, check out this bullfighting museum, which focuses on two homegrown legends of the *corrida,* Manolete and El Cordebés, local boys done good. They even have the ear from the bull that killed Manolete in 1947, and a bloodstained uniform of El Cordebés, who has managed to stay alive so far. If *toredors* are treated like rock stars in Spain, El Cordebés is like The Who: he's always announcing his farewell tour but then keeps coming back for *one* more performance....

STUFF

Shopping, like most things in Cordoba, is available but not shoved down your throat, except at the tourist-hounding stalls around the Mezquita.

The skilled craftspeople in town run an association, **Zoco Artesiana** *(Calle Judios s/n; 10am-8pm Mon-Fri, 10am-2pm Sat, Sun),* where they sell everything from leather, silver, and iron to ceramics with Muslim motifs—all locally made. If you're on a budget you may not be able to afford anything in the shop, but it's still great to hang out in the beautiful courtyard. Not only is there a bar, but some of the artists have workshops on site where you can watch them ply their trade.

Cooking aficionados should not miss **La Tienda del olivo** *(San Fernando 124b; Tel 95/7474-495; 10am-2:30pm/4-7:45pm),* a temple dedicated to olive oil, the grease that runs Mediterranean cooking. Many of them come from the olive groves of Andalucía, and there's a wide range of prices, 600-900ptas being the average. No, they don't have vinegar.

For less expensive local products and more current trends you'll have to go the modern shopping district, which is centered on Plaza Tendillas, Avenida Gran Capitán, and Calle Claudio Marcelo. Everything from surf shops (no, the ocean is not nearby, in case you were wondering) to shoe palaces (but remember you're not in Milan). For music, **Madrid Rock** *(Claudio Marcelo 6; Tel 95/748-20-83; 10am-2pm/5-8:30pm Mon-Sat; V, MC)* is the local outlet of the CD chain store.

Another chain, **El Corte Inglés** *(Ronda de los Tejares 32; Tel 95/747-02-67; 10am-10:30pm Mon-Sat),* is slightly disturbing because it has everything—CDs, books, a supermarket, women's underwear—in one gargantuan building. For a more authentic street-shopping experience, Plaza de Corredera has an outdoor market Monday through Friday with works by local artists and T-shirt peddlers.

EATS

There are plenty of affordable eating options in Córdoba, even in the touristy *judería,* if you stick to tapas. If you're really broke you can get fruit and staples at any of the little family-run mini-stores scattered around the neighborhood, and picnic in any of the innumerable quaint plazas. Some local specialties to try at restaurants are *salmojero* (a vegetable soup with eggs), *ajo blanco* (a thick garlicky soup), and for the more adventurous, *robo del toro* (oxtail soup, a stew made with the tail of a bull or ox).

▶▶CHEAP

Even though **Bar Santos** *(M.G. Frances 3; No phone; 10am-9pm Mon-Sat)* is literally steps away from the Mezquita in the most visited part of town, this little joint is strictly hardcore tapas. That means bullfighting photos on the wall, ham hocks hanging from the ceiling, and no seats. So stand up and get a *cerveza* and *tortilla* (325ptas), because Francisco, the owner, has been crowned Córdoba's "King of the Tortilla," and has the newspaper clippings to prove it. *Bocadillos* (sandwiches) made with tuna (200ptas) or *jamon* (300ptas) are also cheap options; for the latter they'll slice the smoked ham right off the pig's ass.

Another tradition-rich tapas bar, in the center of town just north of Plaza Tendillas, is so nice they named it twice: **Casa Al Pisto** *(Plaza San Miguel 1; Tel 95/729-01-66; Noon-4pm/8pm-midnight Mon-Sat)* is also called **Taberna San Miguel.** Your lunch companions at the bar will be businessmen having a glass of Montilla-Moriles, the local *fino,* a dry pale-yellow wine, and a few tourists enjoying the old tavern atmosphere (more bullfighting pictures). Tapas, including the mouthwatering chorizo, are generally all under 300ptas, or you can get a tall glass of gazpacho.

The restaurant **Casa Pepe** *(Romero 1; Tel 95/720-07-44; 1-4pm/8pm-1am daily)* has a lively nighttime tapas bar attached to it. Tourists easily find their way over to this quaint corner of the old quarter, but despite that, the bar has all the atmosphere you'd expect from a place that's been open since 1928. Try the *ajo blanco* (exactly 184ptas), which is extra garlicky and perfect for dipping the hunks of French bread. The service is curt, but in a kinda cute, showy way. It's located just north of the Mezquita on the corner of Calle Deanes and Calle Romero.

▶▶DO-ABLE

If you're too civilized to stand at a bar and eat, you'll have to pay a little more. One good option to try is the restaurant of the tapas bar we just mentioned, **Casa Pepe,** with entrées ranging from 650 to 2,000ptas.

Taberna Santa Clara *(Osio 2; Tel 95/747-50-36),* hidden on a quiet little street west of the Mezquita, offers a *menú del dia* for 1,300ptas that includes an entrée of *paella* or *robo de toro*. What does the tail of a bull taste like? We could tell you, but then that would ruin the surprise.

▶▶SPLURGE

El Churrasco *(Romero 16; Tel 95/729-08-19; 2-5:30pm/7:45pm-midnight daily)* is a paean to all things meat. You can smell the fat frying as you enter and are seated in either the homey downstairs or classy upstairs. The next thing you notice is the ton of waiters pouring out of the kitchen like clowns out of a clown car—you'll never be lacking for attentive service. They'll start you off with a local *fino*; then you can order typical Cordoban specialties like *robo de toro* (1,200ptas) or the title dish on their menu, *churrasco* (1600ptas), which is scrumptious grilled pork sirloin. Budget travelers be wary that anything they offer you here, including water and the bread wrapped in paper that's sitting at your table, will be added on to your bill.

A delicious meal can be had at the famous **El Caballo Rojo** *(Cardinal Herrero 28; Tel 95/747-53-75; 1-4:30pm/8pm-midnight daily; Entrées 1,500-3,000ptas)*, just across the street from the Mezquita. Downstairs is a verdant patio and modern bar; upstairs is a dining room always packed with out-of-towners. The zesty food (yes, we said zesty) is typical Cordoban fare, but with that little extra Muslim twist: almonds, apples, or currants to bring out the flavor.

crashing

Cordoba doesn't have quite the overwhelming number of backpacker-friendly hostels as other Andalucian cities, so it's a good idea to call ahead in the high season to get one of the choice spots near the Mezquita.

▶▶CHEAP

There cannot be a more excellently located youth hostel in Andalucía than **Albergue Juvenil Córdoba** *(Plaza Judá Levi; Tel 95/729-01-66; 1,500ptas under 26, 2,000ptas over 26)*. It sits in the back of a little plaza in the old quarter, not more than a 1-minute walk from the Mezquita. The rooms are modern and comfortable, with four beds or fewer, and many with their own bathroom.

If you don't like strangers, you have other options. **Huéspedes Martínez Rücker** *(Martínez Rücker 14; Tel 95/747-25-62; 1,750ptas single, 3,500ptas double)* is deservedly popular with backpackers, since it's affordable, friendly, right near the Mezquita, and in a typical Cordoban house with a wrought-iron gate and patio. Call ahead.

▶▶DO-ABLE

The spiffy and friendly **Hostal Santa Ana** *(Luis de la Cerda 25; Tel 95/748-58-37; 1,800ptas single, 5,000ptas double)* is just east of the southern end of the Mezquita. Unfortunately, there's only one single room in this little place, without a bathroom. The doubles not only have bathrooms, but TVs and air conditioning, and if you have a car there's a parking garage available for 1,000ptas per day.

A little farther east, on a side street off of Calle San Fernando, **Hotel Maestre** *(Romero Barros 4/6; Tel 95/747-24-10; 4,500ptas single,*

7,000ptas double) is part of a multiplex of accommodations: a hotel, a hostel, and long-term apartments. **Hostal Maestre** *(Romero Barros 16; Tel 95/747-32-34; 2,500ptas single, 5,000ptas double)* has a charming plant-filled patio when you enter, and big, recently renovated rooms with their own bathrooms, tile floors, and bright paintings. The decor of the rooms in the hotel is very similar; the extra dough wins you a modern lobby, TV, air-conditioning/heating, and a telephone for your room. A parking garage is available for guests of both places.

You'll feel like you've been time-warped into the '70s when you walk into the funky/formal lobby at **Hostal El Triunfo** *(Luis de Cerda 79; Tel 95/747-55-00; 4,000ptas single, 7,000ptas double, 8,400ptas triple)*. There's a wide variety of rooms here, and they're all comfortable and clean with TV and A.C. Nothing can rival its location: right across the street from the Mezquita and one block from the river.

Hotel Boston *(Málaga 2; Tel 95/747-41-76, 3,500ptas single, 5,600ptas double, 6,600ptas triple in low season)* has a different kind of ambiance than the quaint, patioed hostels of the judería. It's in a stately red building right on bustling Plaza Tendillas, but still a short walk from the old quarter. This is one of the taller buildings in town, and unlike other venues in Córdoba, you won't miss the sign for this place. The rooms are comfortable, with little TVs, air-conditioning, and telephones.

▶▶SPLURGE

Hotel Amistad Córdoba *(Plaza Maimónides 3; Tel 95/742-03-35; 14,500ptas single, 18,000ptas double)* is notable for its location. It's so unobtrusively built in two converted mansions on the serene plaza in the *judería* (which also features the bullfighting museum), it almost seems like it belongs here. It's quite a feat to subtly stick a four-star hotel that offers laundry, parking, hair dryers, air conditioning, and the morning paper in amongst the ancient *juderia,* but they pull it off.

need to know

Currency Exchange There is currency exchange at the train station, or else use ATM machines at one of the many banks on Avenida del Gran Capitán.

Tourist Information The main **tourist office** *(Calle Torrijos 10; Tel 95/747-12-35; 9:30am-8pm Mon-Sat, 9am-2pm Sun)* is right next to the Mezquita and gets very crowded. It's also the **Junta de Andalucía,** so they have info on other places in the region. The local **municipal tourist office** is located next to the youth hostel *(Plaza de Judá Levi; Tel 95/720-05-22; 9am-2pm/4:30-6:30pm Mon-Fri, 8:30am-2:30pm Sat, 9am-2pm Sun)*. There is a lodging service *(Tel 95/727-9964)* in the train station that will give you a complete list of local hotels, though they won't make reservations for you.

Public Transportation Cordoba's got buses, but the main part of town is small enough that you can walk everywhere, even to the train and bus stations [see below]. If it's late at night you can also always get a **taxi** *(Tel 95/745-00-00)*.

Health and Emergency For health emergencies dial *061* or go to **University Hospital Reina Sofía** *(Avda. de Mendéndez Pidal; Tel 95/721-71-60)*. For other types of trouble, **Policía Nacional** *(Avenida Dr. Fleming 2; Tel 95/747-75-00)* can be reached in an emergency by dialing *091*.

Trains and Buses The **train station** *(Avenida de América; Tel 95/749-02-02)* is one of the most modern and well-run in Spain, with escalators to take you down to the tracks. Next door is the new **bus station,** completed in 1999, which conveniently conglomerates the various bus companies. When you arrive here, you can easily walk to the city center in 10-15 minutes. Take Avenida de America northeast to Avenida de Cervantes; take a right, and follow Avenida Cervantes south until you hit the *jardines.* You can also take bus 32 (125ptas) to Plaza Tendillas or the *juderia.* To get back to the stations you can get bus 32 behind the Mezquita on Ronda de Isasa, which runs along the river.

Postal To send postcards, go north of Plaza Tendillas to find the **Correos** *(Calle Cruz Conde 15; Tel 95/747-82-67)*.

granada

To Spanglicize a local expression: If you haven't seen Granada, you haven't seen *nada*. Spectacularly set in the foothills of the **Sierra Nevada** mountains, Granada exudes history and romance equal to its geography. If Sevilla is sensual like a winding river, Granada is dramatic and mysterious like a snow-capped mountain peak. Its magnificent hilltop Muslim fortress, the Alhambra, dominates the city, physically, spiritually, and commercially; it brings tourists by the busload, and stands as the most obvious symbol of Granada's close links to its Moorish past. Today, Granada thrives despite—or perhaps because of—a variety of life that would be in opposition anywhere else. While you can't escape the old, it's a youthful town with a huge student population. It's multicultural but distinctly Spanish. It draws both bus-touring camera hounds and budget-seeking backpackers. You can ski in the nearby mountains or swim in the nearby Mediterranean. The Sacromonte caves are full of gypsies and the commercial downtown bustles with businesspeople. This variety means Granada has just about everything a traveler could ask for: nightlife, history, physical beauty, funky people, nearby sporting ops, cheap hostels, and free tapas. That's right, *free food*, and we're not talking pretzels, at just about every bar. What more could you want?

Granada's physical distinctness is largely due to its place in history as the last stronghold of Muslim Spain. When Isabella and Ferdinand conquered the armies of Boabdil, the last Moorish king, in 1492, it signaled the official end of the Moorish Empire in Western Europe. Evidence of the Arab influence can be seen today, most famously in the Alhambra, and in the old Arab quarter, Albaicín, which rambles up the hill directly across from it. Religious persecution of Jews and Arabs, unfortunately, followed the Reconquista, as it did in the rest of Andalucía, helping lead Granada into an economic and moral slump. In the 1830s, interest in Granada's storied past attracted Romantic writers, such as the American Washington Irving, whose *Tales of The Alhambra* brought renewed attention to the crumbling fortress and helped "save" it for future generations. In the 20th century, Granada was one of the first cities to fall during the Spanish Civil War to the Nationalists, who then brutally turned on the liberal elements of society (the most infamous incident being the 1936 murder of Spain's greatest modern poet and dramatist, Federico García Lorca). Now a tourist Mecca, Granada is still politically conservative, but much more tolerant than it used to be of other cultures and alternative lifestyles, and there's a bunch of them here.

12 hours in granada

1,2,3. Alhambra: This really requires about 6 hours, so take at *least* three. Make sure you see the lush gardens of the Generalife, the views from Torre de la Vela, and the sublime detailing of the Palacio de Nazaries.

4. Teterías in "Little Morocco": Go to one of the Arabian-style tea houses on Calderería Nueva or Calderería Vieja, and get a warm soothing cup of something herbal, exotic, or caffeinated as well as an incense buzz.

5. Plaza Trinidad: Cruise the bookstores, get a *café con leche*, get out of the sun, and watch couples argue in this leafy plaza.

6. Mirador San Nicolás: Wind your way through the old Arab quarter, Albaicín, to this look-out point for "the most beautiful sunset in the world" (according to Bill Clinton—and he never lies).

7. Free tapas hop in Plaza Nueva: Order a beer, then get a little plate of free food in any of the atmospheric bars at this international meeting spot.

8. Do the Pedro: To relive your freshman year of college, toss back one of the 120 volatile shots at a chupitería, and cruise the loud pubs of this party strip.

9. Discoteca LLA: Go to this no-cover *discoteca* where attitude takes a backseat to disco fever.

10. Late night shawarma off Calle Elvira: Soak up all those chemicals with some vegetables, sauce, and meat from a rotating spit.

granada

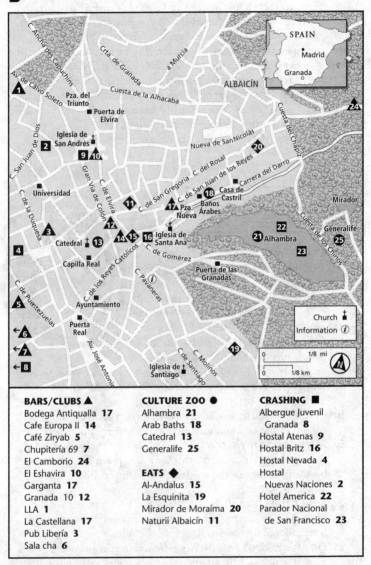

BARS/CLUBS ▲
Bodega Antiqualla **17**
Cafe Europa II **14**
Café Ziryab **5**
Chupitería 69 **7**
El Camborio **24**
El Eshavira **10**
Garganta **17**
Granada 10 **12**
LLA **1**
La Castellana **17**
Pub Libería **3**
Sala cha **6**

CULTURE ZOO ●
Alhambra **21**
Arab Baths **18**
Catedral **13**
Generalife **25**

EATS ◆
Al-Andalus **15**
La Esquinita **19**
Mirador de Moraíma **20**
Naturii Albaicín **11**

CRASHING ■
Albergue Juvenil
  Granada **8**
Hostal Atenas **9**
Hostal Britz **16**
Hostal Nevada **4**
Hostal
  Nuevas Naciones **2**
Hotel America **22**
Parador Nacional
  de San Francisco **23**

There are at least 60,000 university students in Granada, and they keep the downtown buzzing till late, late at night. There's also a sizable gypsy population, much of which lives in somewhat modernized caves dug into the hills of the Sacromonte, doing that gypsy thing that they do, which generally means trying to get money off you. Another element here is European wanna-be gypsies, who are not *gaditano* by blood, but by choice, and have adopted the gypsy traditions of roaming, panpipe playing and trying to get money off you. We like to call these combination gypsy hippies "gyppies." The hip ones are "gypsters," and the ones on trust funds with Northface backpacks can be called "gyuppies." Anyway...there are also the tourists, of course, who do the Alhambra so hard during the day they pass out at 9pm, and there are the American students studying Spanish, 75 percent of whom seem to be young blonde women. Gays and lesbians have also carved a cool little niche here, coming from all over the province for the bars *ambiente*. Life in Granada depends on which group you're hanging with, but, as in the rest of Spain, it generally involves drinking and especially eating. The Arab influence on cuisine here expands the variety of options beyond typical Andalucian fare to exotic treats like falafel and schawarma.

To find out *que pasa* while you're in town, the monthly *Guía del Ocio*, sold at newspaper kiosks, is your best bet. It's in Spanish only, but words like *cine* and *concierto* should be easy to figure out.

neighborhoods

The main geographic feature and tourist destinations of Granada are its two hills, on the north side of town: **La Sabika**—which is more commonly referred to as the Alhambra, because of the imposing Muslim fortress complex of the same name that stands guard atop it—and the **Albaicín,** with the old Arab quarter and, higher up, the gypsy caves of Sacromonte. Between the two hills is the **Rio Darro,** which is just a trickle much of the year. Another river, **Rio Genil,** runs through the southern part of the city, but is not boat-worthy either. García Lorca famously said "only sighs glide on the rivers of Granada." At the foot of the two main hills lies central Granada, which has a 19th-century European flavor, dominated by wide avenues, alleyways, and plazas. You can't see the Alhambra from most of modern Granada, and it seems a world away when you're enveloped in tall buildings, shopping centers, honking traffic, and people rushing around like they're in Manhattan. The two main thoroughfares through the center of Granada are **Gran Vía de colón,** and **Calle Reyes Católicos,** which meet at the **Plaza de Isabel La Católica,** with its statue of Isabella and Cristóbal Colón, also known as Christopher Columbus. Another few short blocks up Reyes Católicos is **Plaza Nueva,** which is not a new plaza at all, but is today the heart of the city. Bars and restaurants with outdoor tables, and a funky international crowd make this *the* meeting place in Granada.

From Plaza Nueva, **Cuesta Gomérez** winds up the hill toward the Alhambra. The lower part of this street teems with hostels and souvenir shops, but once you pass through the **Puerta de las Granadas,** you'll feel as if you've entered into another, more ancient world, despite the tourist overload. Lush groves of cypress and elms hide the Alhambra itself, until you reach its reddish exterior walls. The Alhambra complex includes not only the ornate Palacio Nazaries, but the watchtower, Torre de las Armas, and further up the hill the verdant fountains and gardens of the **Generalife** [see *culture zoo,* below].

only here

The bottom part of the Albaicín, above Calle Elvira, is often referred to as Little Morocco, due to its sights, smells, and *teterías,* Moroccan-style tea houses. The most atmospheric is **Kasbah** *(Calderería Nueva 4; Tel 95/822-79-36),* which serves all manner of teas from all over the world (250ptas) in a super-chill smoking den atmosphere. Plush couches with Arab designs fill up all the little corners, where New-Agers in flowing skirts and dreadlocks, as well as tourists, smoke, sip tea or liquor, and generally mellow out beyond levels previously thought possible. It's open daily from 3pm "until the candles burn out."

The gypsy caves of Sacromonte are probably unlike anything you've seen before, unless you're a gypsy yourself. Some of the lower caves dug into the hillside have modern conveniences like TVs while some of the ones higher up are more sparse. The walls of the caves and the earth itself help to keep the "apartments" warm in the winter and cool in the summer. During the day, the neighborhood can be eerily quiet; it's best to explore with others. In the evening, the music starts, with the gypsies stomping and clapping and playing guitar, the sounds echoing through the hills and drawing fascinated yet frightened tourists for impromptu flamenco "shows" designed to empty your wallet. For a reputable visit at night, try a meal at **Casa Juanillo** *(Camino del Sacromonte 83; Tel 95/822-30-94; 1:30-5pm/8:30pm-midnight, closed Monday)* just up from the Albaicín, with enticing "gypsy" stews, flamenco performances, and a terrace with great views of the Alhambra. Don't miss the Sacromonte omelette, with sweet-bread and brains (probably pig) if you're feeling stupid.

The 11th-century Bañuelos (Arab Baths) in the Albaicín have recently begun offering visitors a chance to actually experience the ritual of hot-tubbing followed by a massage, for 2,000ptas, in some of the best preserved Arab baths in Spain. Call 95/822-99-78 for more information and reservations.

From the Plaza Nueva, **Calle Reyes Catolicos** runs up the opposite hill to **Plaza Santa Ana,** where there is an impressive church, Iglesia de Santa Ana. From there, **Carrera del Darro** heads up the side of the hill along the river, and is the most popular walk in town, with great views of the Alhambra on your right as you go up. At the top of the hill, the road turns sharply to the left and becomes steeper as its name changes to **Cuesta del Chapiz.** This is the top of the Albaicín—below, the old

Muslim quarter spreads out with its tangled web of cobblestoned streets and whitewashed houses, a great place to lose yourself, at least during the day. You have to find **Mirador San Nicolás** (there are signs), the lookout point in the center of the Albaicín, which offers amazing views of the green hill of the Alhambra, the city below, the farming plains, and the Sierra Nevada peaks in the distance. Above the Albaicín, **Camino del Sacromonte** somewhat mysteriously winds farther up the hill, through the gypsy caves of the Sacromonte. Some of the homes in the caves are rudimentary, but others are modernized with TV sets, telephones, house bars, and, at night, discos. While fascinating, Sacromonte is best explored during the day with others.

Another famous street off Plaza Nueva is the weird and wonderful **Calle Elvira,** a narrow pedestrian street that runs along the bottom of the Albaicín, parallel to Gran Vía de colón, and is an essential part of the nightlife. It ends at **Puerto Elvira** (at **Plaza Triunfo**), the old arched entrance to the city, where they used to hang the heads of executed criminals. Not anymore, unfortunately, as there's no death penalty in this backwards country.

Of course, Granada has a cathedral or it would have to leave the country, but unlike in most Spanish cities, it's not blatantly visible, as other buildings of similar size surround it. The **Catedral** sits just off Plaza Isabel La Católica, between Gran Vía de colón and Calle Reyes Católicos. Next door is the **Capilla Real** where the shrunken little bones of Queen Isabella and her husband, Ferdinand, lie [see *culture zoo,* below, for both]. Past the cathedral, to your right as you walk south (and ever so slightly west) on Calle Reyes Católicos, are the busy **Plaza Bib-Rambla** and the leafy **Plaza Trinidad.** Calle Reyes Católicos eventually ends at the commercial center, **Puerta Real,** where you'll find the main *Correos* (Post Office). The street continues as **Calle de Recogidas**; take a right at the McDonald's (we love using the golden arches as orientation points because it annoys people so) to wind your way to **Plaza de Gracia,** a hangout for twentysomethings. One long block farther south is **Calle Pedro Antonio de Alarcón,** the street that every college town must have, where the kids go to get plastered on cheap drinks.

In the western part of the city, the major thoroughfare is **Avenida de la Constitución,** which runs east-west from Plaza del Triumfo to A-92, passing the shooting fountains of **Fuente El Triunfo** one block north of the train station. Out here at the edge of town you'll find the **Ciudad Universitario,** the main campus of the University of Granada. The bus station is a 10-minute ride out of town along **Avenida de Ancha de Capuchinos.** Walking is the preferred mode of transportation in Granada, though taxis are common at night. Local buses can be useful to get to the outskirts of town, and if you're tired of walking, there are microbuses [see *need to know,* below] that go up to the Alhambra and the Albaicín from Plaza Nueva.

While downtown Granada is fairly safe for a big city, always be aware of your surroundings at night. You should definitely avoid the upper parts of the Albaicín and especially Sacromonte at night unless you have a destination and are traveling with others. Especially in Sacromonte, but generally all over Spain, be aware of "diversions," like when someone creates a commotion or drops something in order to bump into you and discretely pick your pocket. The most horrifying, and yet somehow most brilliant, of these schemes we've heard about, is the "baby-toss," wherein a gypsy will throw a childlike doll in your direction, and when your human instinct takes over and you grab it, another cohort is ready to snag your wallet. It would be extremely irresponsible of us to suggest that you drop any flying babies you might come upon...instead, just keep your wits about you as you would anywhere outside of your living room. Don't be paranoid either, because 99 percent of visitors have no problems whatsoever.

hanging out

Plaza Nueva attracts young Spanish hipsters, Eurotrash, American students studying abroad, expats, and people with staring problems. During the day it's mellow, with plenty of tourists eating at the cafes on the plaza and lots of loiterers just loitering, which means smoking cigarettes. Every traveler and a good number of students seem to start their night here at one of the nearby tapas bars, and end their night at one of the Middle Eastern takeout joints that stay open until ridiculous hours for that schawarma, kebab, or falafel fix. Many of these spots are just off of Plaza Nueva on Calle Elvira. You also have a very good chance of being offered a great deal on hash here, though buying on the street is stupid—not stupid like "phat," but stupid like not smart.

Just around the corner from Plaza Nueva, off Calle Elvira, is Caldería Nueva, a funky little street heading up the Albaicín. It feels like a Moroccan alley out of a hippie's fantasy, with little New-Agey jewelry shops, health-food restaurants, *teterías* (teashops), strong whiffs of incense, and more dreadlocks than you can shake a rain stick at.

For a more well-heeled crowed, Campo del Príncipe is a renowned meeting spot, drawing locals 25 years and up and a sprinkling of tourists. Located south of the Alhambra, about 10 minutes from Plaza Nueva, it's lined with wall-to-wall restaurants with outdoor seating. At nighttime the lively conversation from all these spots fills the plaza.

During the day, shoppers, students, and workers spend their siesta on Plaza Bib-Rambla and nearby Plaza Trinidad, both below the cathedral. The former is a square that often features street performers; the latter is lined with bookshops and filled with trees offering shade to couples, lost souls, and men on hot summer days. For a more cosmopolitan, postmodern, and air-conditioned spot near Plaza Trinidad, try **botánico café** *(Málaga 3; Tel 95/827-15-98; 10am-1am Mon-Thu, till 3am Fri, Sat, noon-1am Sun)*, right near the botanic gardens, with a window on Calle Duquesa but an entrance around the corner. When the name of the place is in lowercase letters, you just know it's on the cutting edge. The

wired

Thanks to the wealth of university students and a lot of competition, Internet access in Granada is easy to find and dirt cheap compared to the rest of Spain.

You'll get the deal of the new millennium at **net** *(Santa Escolástica 13; Tel 95/822-69-19; 9am-11pm Mon-Sat, 3-11pm Sun; 150ptas per hour).* That's no misprint: 150 pesetas an hour, which if you've been in the Costa del Sol seems impossibly cheap. This irresistible bargain attracts plenty of foreign students and travelers, but the computers hold up pretty well at this spot just off Plaza Isabel La Católica. The owners also run two cybercafes: one right around the corner at Plaza de los Girones 3, another one behind the cathedral at Buen Suceso 22.

For just a few pesetas more, at **Red Isis** *(Veronic de la Magdelena 1; Tel 95/826-16-67; 10am-midnight Mon-Fri, 3pm-midnight Sun; 10am; 200ptas per hour),* a five-minute walk south of Plaza de Gracia, you'll get slightly faster computers. The library-like atmosphere is broken up only by stony chuckles from foreigners and the yelps of nerdy Spanish pre-teens playing video games.

Useful addresses:
www.granada.org
www.granadainfo.com

drum 'n' bass music and sparse NASA space-age orange decor give one the feeling of lower Manhattan, but the attitude is much more relaxed here. It's open all day, every day, so it's a good place for a snack, cocktail, or meal; after a big night, the strong coffee and *pan con tomate* (toast with tomatoes and olive oil) for 210ptas help to ease in the day. A lot of lesbians congregate here [see *gay scene,* below], but everyone is welcome aboard the spaceship.

To get away from the mobs of foreigners at Plaza Nueva, head over to Plaza De Gracia, which draws a ton of local students and families at night. There's a popular movie theater, a discoteca, some classic inexpensive tapas bars, and one of the few live music spots in town, **Sala Cha** [see *live music scene,* below].

For spring break atmosphere year round, young people head to the raucous **Calle Pedro Antonio de Alarcón,** which is usually just referred to as "Pedro Antoni" or even just "Pedro." As in, "Do you want to do Pedro tonight?" If you do, it's going to be a late night—the action doesn't start until around midnight. Bars pack this strip, especially between Calle Huerta and Calle del Sol, but many of the 17- to 22-year-olds who flock here on weekends just bring their own bottles and drink and smoke on the street. Not surprisingly, then, the streets are kind of dirty, the floors of the bars (with silly names like Pub Ghetto) are littered with cigarette butts and peanut shells, the music is loud and poppy, but if you're willing to ride the Pedro—and drink a lot—it can be a sleazy good time. There is a plethora of randy 17-year-old boys wearing soccer jerseys who haven't learned to hold their liquor, and girls who had to go to their friend's house to change into that skimpy outfit their parents would never let them leave the house in. But this is Spain, and so you'll only get attitude if you're not having enough fun.

bar scene

Tapas are generally free at night in Granada. How does it work? Well, you go to a tapas bar, order a beer or a cocktail, and soon after your drink arrives, a little plate with hot food (usually meat) is set in front of you. Don't be the *guir* who says, "What is this, I didn't order this?" Nor be the one who orders a free tapas without buying a drink. When some places get crowded at night you might have to let the bartender know you're hungry by politely saying "tapas?" or the equivalent when your drink comes. The food ranges from pedestrian potato chips and slices of meat, to little hamburgers, to sublime roasted lamb kebab. You might expect the drinks to be more expensive when they come with free food, but, on the contrary, drinking in Granada is actually slightly cheaper than in other big cities in Spain. What's the catch? The salty food will dehydrate you and cause you to drink more than planned. O.K., so what's the real catch? You can't live on beer and free tapas alone...well, actually you can, because people do it all the time.

Drinking, conversation, dancing, and music also take place in bars in Granada, so don't get confused in your search for food. Not all bars serve tapas—you'll know right away if there are little plates of food in front of everyone at the bar. Some of the liveliest tapas bars are on and around Plaza Nueva; you can hop from one to the next trying to find the best eats. The grungy bars on Pedro Antonio de Alarcón are generally bright, neon-signed pubs more for drinking and impromptu dancing. They open around 11pm and don't get going until midnight. Both of these areas have late-night kebab houses to soak up the booze so you'll never go hungry.

On Plaza Nueva, **Cafe Europa II** *(Elvira 1; No phone; Noon-2am daily)* draws a young lively crowd for coffee during the day, and *cañas* and tapas at night. The small, wood-paneled interior and friendly bartenders pull in locals and travelers; the only downside is the annoying Spanish pop/rock music, but it's never loud enough to overwhelm the conversation. The first free tapas is literally a *ham*-burger, meaning it's a little pork patty inside of a bun. If it's not too busy, you can ask them to prepare a vegetarian tapas. Other nearby tapas spots off Plaza Nueva include the extremely popular **Bodega Antiqualla,** with a takeout window for drinking and eating in the street; **La Castellana,** a bigger place for sitting down, and some of the tastiest free tapas anywhere; and **Garganta,** known for its good tapas but sometimes overrun by American students doing tequila shots.

For a mellow tapas-less bar with a more mixed local crowed, try the bluesy **Pub Libería** *(Duquesa 8; 8pm-1am daily)* off Plaza de la Trinidad. It's got live music on Thursdays at 11pm or later, usually local blues bands, but it's a good hangout at any time to play pool or board games. If you think your Spanish is pretty good, try playing Trivial Pursuit in *Español,* or go for the more universal language of Connect Four. Cocktails from the friendly, grizzled bartender are 550ptas.

The "best tapas in town," according to many locals and our own taste buds, can be had at **Café Ziryab** *(Corner of Calle de Gracia and Veronica de la Magdalena; No phone; 8pm-1am, later on weekends).* Students crowd this spot two blocks up from Plaza de Gracia, drinking and munching on the Mediterranean specialties like hummus, or stuffed peppers, free with your beer (125ptas). Be sure to get a *media ración* (half-portion) of *mousaka* (500ptas), which is a tasty Middle Eastern lamb dish kind of like lasagna. Not a lot of room to sit, but you can always drink and eat at the outside counters.

If you're feeling like a loud, boozy good time and it's after midnight, head to the bar-filled Pedro Antonio. It might not be everybody's scene, as even the Ayuntamiento's official tourism guide admits: "Indeed, but for the urban sprawl of bars and discos to be found on the Calle Pedro Antonio de Alarcón, it would seem that Granada's relaxed atmosphere is compatible with everybody's tastes." The boors among us will want to check out **Chupitería 69 Pedro Antonio** *(Pedro Antonio de Alarcón 69; No phone; 11pm-4am),* which ranks as one of the most "Pedro" of all spots. A *chupito* (literally, a "little suck") is a shot, so a *Chupitería* is a place that only serves shots. One hundred and twenty different kinds of shots (150ptas, listed on the menu above the bar) can be tossed back here, all of them made with cheap generic liquor. Try *Zorro* (vodka, blue liquor, and mint), which is sort of like toothpaste; or a creamy *quickf—k* (cream whiskey, kiwi flavor and grenadine); or guess what's in a *torpedo, Super-Macho* or *orgasmo.* The silliest of all is *Fuego,* a seemingly pointless combination of whisky, vodka, and tequila. Why? For each one you down (or throw up) you get a little coupon, sort of like at an arcade, that you can redeem for exciting prizes. With 14 coupons, you can get a very cool straw cowboy hat, but please don't try to win it on your own, get some help from your amigos. From here you can stumble down to any of the loud music bars in the vicinity, which roll on weekends until morning.

LIVE MUSIC SCENE

The best live music you're going to hear in Granada will probably come from gypsies playing guitar in the streets. The exceptions are the occasional big-name summer concerts put on by **Huerta de San Vicente** *(Tel 98/258-466; www.huertagarcialorca.org),* the foundation that preserves the poet García Lorca's cultural sites [see *Lorca's Granada*]. Recent

rules of the game

Rules? There are no rules in Granada, man!
Okay, despite the hash-smoking you're likely to see and smell on the street, there are a few rules. Don't get so drunk that you start fights, or puke on any national monuments. You can basically be as loud as you want on Pedro Antonio, but in other parts of town try to keep it down. Hash rolled with tobacco is generally accepted in the youth-centered areas of town, just don't flaunt it. And don't buy on the street, no matter how many great offers you get from dudes near Plaza Nueva. Start a conversation, find a friend, and the *purro* will come around to you.

international studs it brought in include Bob Dylan, Lou Reed, Ali-Faka-Touré, and Suzanne Vega, most of whom have performed at the Parque Federico García Lorca, though Sting played the Plaza de Toros. Check the website or posters around town for upcoming events; tickets can be bought at the department store **El Corte Inglés** *(Carrera de Genil 20-22; Tel 90/240-02-22)* or the kiosk on Acera del Casino, both at Puerta Real.

There is one cool jazz bar in town, **El Eshavira** *(Postigo de la Cuna 2; 10pm-4am Mon-Sat).* It must be cool because it's so hard to find, hidden away on a little corner off the north end of Calle Elvira. Take Elvira from Plaza Nueva for a few minutes, until you get to Calle Azacayas, then take a left and you'll see a little alleyway on your right that leads down some steps. The cover charge is 800ptas, kind of pricey for Granada, but it includes a cocktail (normally 600ptas), so it works out alright. The bands play on the second floor, where the hipster crowd sits on wooden benches beneath a sloping roof that looks like it might crumble at any second. Very homey atmosphere, and the jazz, often the Latin variety, is sometimes very good, and always decent, if not for purists. Shows start at about 11pm but many times the band will play sets all night.

Below Plaza de Gracia is **Sala cha** *(Ancha de Gracia 4; No phone; 10:30pm-1am),* a live music bar with an ambitious lineup of performers on Friday and Saturday nights, sometimes too ambitious. The lineup includes everything from Brazilian jazz to blues, from flamenco to Celtic to funk, which waters down the quality of the music. Look for flyers around town, but don't get your heart set on anything in particular because sometimes shows are canceled. No cover is a benefit, so it doesn't hurt to take a chance; beers are 300ptas.

club scene

Granada is famous for many things, but world-class DJs are not among them. Still, this is a university town, so there are always clubbers afoot on weekend nights.

Granada 10 (*Cárcel Baja 10; Tel 95/822-40-01; Midnight-6am Wed-Sat*) is the most well-known and centrally located, but suffers from those two factors. The bouncers will not only charge you 1,000ptas if you're male, they'll hassle you if you're wearing sneakers. You can usually talk your way in eventually, and there are certainly plenty of beautifully made-up people inside, as well as two dance floors and four bars. A little cheesy, yet not cheesy enough to be unique.

A less pretentious, yet pumped-up atmosphere can be found at **LLA** (*Santa Bárbara 3; Tel 95/829-57-68; Midnight-6am Tue-Sat*). This place is definitely cheesy, but in a good way, with no cover charge and mellow bouncers. An orgasm of disco lights on the low ceiling, '70s hits, along with whatever Spanish dance songs are popular that month give this place a no-attitude good vibe. Near the university, it draws students and other revelers who are out way too late to care anymore, so they might as well get down on it. Discoteca LLA (pronounced "yah!") is located right off Avenida de la Constitución, across from Fuente del Triunfo.

For an altogether different experience, try dancing in a cave at **El Camborio** (*Camino Sacromonte, no address; No phone; Noon-6am, Fri,Sat*). It's best to arrive at this outpost in the Sacromonte by taxi rather than by foot. It has no formal address but is easy to find, just 200 meters (220 yards) or so up the Camino Sacromonte from Cuesta de Chapiz. Your taxi driver might know it, too. You can also take the Albaicín microbus [see *need to know*, below], which runs until 2am on weekends. After paying a reasonable 600ptas cover charge, you enter a modern cave dug into the hillside, with a bar and little intimate nooks and crannies. Upstairs, the dance floor on the patio looks out to the lit-up Alhambra—this has to be the best view to be had at any disco, anywhere. The crowd is definitely eclectic, but includes many adventurous twentysomethings.

boy meets girl

Granada doesn't have a huge pickup scene, except of course on Pedro Antonio, where blatantly forward approaches (usually accompanied with a stumble) are commonplace, and Plaza Nueva, which is a big international spot and where a lot of the lines ("What do you think of the Al-*ham*-bra?") are in English. If you want to meet local cuties, and your Spanish is up to it, try around Plaza de Gracia or the late night dance spot LLA. More normal courting happens here: staring, smiling, talking, then "your parents' house, or my hostel?"

ARTS SCENE

▶▶VISUAL ARTS

The line between artist and craftsman gets blurred in Granada. Lacking a genuine modern art scene—most of the young painters head to Barcelona or Madrid—the city instead provides a community for artisans, who work in the tradition of the skilled hands that built the Palacio de Nazaries at the Alhambra. Specialties of the area include pottery, metalwork, leather-embossing, instrument-building, and marquetry—the practice of decorating furniture and other wooden objects with inlaid designs of precious wood, ivory, or mother-of-pearl bone. You can see the results of this work, and other artisans' creations, in the Alcaicería, the market next to the Cathedral, as well as in shops on Cuesta de Gomérez.

Another art that's been perfected in Granada is guitar-making. What, you don't think guitars can be art? You haven't seen the handmade guitars of **Casa Ferrer (Tienda Eduardo Ferrer Castillo)** *(Cuesta de Gomérez 30; Tel 95/822-18-32; 9am-2pm/4:30-8:30pm Mon-Fri, morning hours Sat)*. These ain't your JC Penney Stratocaster rip-offs; these are authentic, sensual, silk-string classical guitars, which hang in every corner of this shop that's been around since 1875. Guitarists, especially of the flamenco ilk, come from all over Spain and the whole of Europe to Cuesta de Gomérez to check out the guitars here and at other shops further down the street. You'll want to touch them all and take one home, but there's no room in your bags and you probably can't afford them anyway (up to 400,000ptas).

▶▶PERFORMING ARTS

Teatro Alhambra *(Molinos 56; Tel 95/822-04-47)* produces well-known modern and classical plays at its playhouse near Campo del Príncipe. It also has a traveling troupe that performs all over Spain. Lots of García Lorca, of course, since this is Granada.

There are not a lot of options for movies in their original language in Granada. If you need your cinematic fix, you might have to watch something dubbed into Spanish at **Multicines Centro** *(Solarillo de Gracia 9; Tel 95/825-29-50; 600ptas)*. On Plaza de Gracia, this movie house shows

FESTIVALS

The big performing arts event in Granada is the Festival Internacional de Música y Danza *(Two weeks in summer; Various venues; Tel 95/827-62-00)*, celebrating orchestral music, often according to a theme, as well as ballet, modern dance, flamenco, and postmodern compositional music. The 2001 festival takes place from June 22 to July 8.

a lot of Hollywood blockbusters a few weeks after they open in the U.S., especially anything with Jim Carrey or George Clooney in it.

gay scene

Granada's gay life does not qualify as in-your-face, but it is definitely active, and for both women and men. Information can be gotten from NOS *(Tel 95/820-06-02),* the local gay and lesbian organization; also check out the website ***www.gaygr.com*** (in Spanish only). One area of activity, mostly local and young, centers around Plaza de La Trinidad, on Calle Duquesa and the streets below it. Another more international gay scene tends toward Calle Darro, near the Arab Baths, naturally. Many of the bars *ambiente* draw a mixed gay/straight crowd.

five things to talk to a local about

1. **García Lorca:** *Granadinos* are justly proud of their world-famous poet/playwright, who was born and, sadly, killed near here. Everyone has a favorite verse—get them to recite it in Spanish, because it always sounds much more beautiful.
2. **Sevilla vs. Granada:** The locals already know their hometown is more historic than Madrid, and more authentically Spanish than Barcelona, but they have a complex about the other great Andalucian city. There's not a right answer, unless you're in Granada, of course.
3. **Rock 'n' roll Pedro Antonio:** The 18- to 22-year-olds who roam around Calle Pedro Antonio de Alarcón on weekend nights are as much into punk and metal as all good hormone-charged kids. Compliment them on their taste in music by saying, *"de puta madre,"* which literally translates as something unprintable, but which in Spanish slang means "really frigging cool." So use it, even if you don't necessarily believe it, as in "Red Hot Chili Peppers...de puta madre!" They'll soon be sharing their beer and funny cigarettes with you.
4. **Skiing vs. Snowboarding:** Even though the mountain is only 30 minutes away, not everyone hits the slopes here. Those who do will undoubtedly have an opinion on the old school or new school way to get down the hill.
5. **School:** With 60,000 college students here, there's a good chance whoever you're talking to is taking classes in something. Maybe English, if you're really, really lucky.

Tic-Tac *(Horno de Haza 19; Tel 95/829-63-66; 7pm-4am daily, till 5am weekends)* is one of the more well-known gay hangouts, mostly men, located three blocks south of Calle Duquesa. Many come to this small and friendly place for coffee or cocktails in the evening, but it really gets going late at night when the music—funk and house—begins pumping.

A mixed crowd, including a lot of hip lesbians, hangs out at **botánico café** [see *hanging out,* above], a cool fusion of cafe, bar, and restaurant.

At **Rincon de San Pedro** *(Carrera del Darro 12; No phone; 5pm-2am daily),* the walls are painted purple for a mixed gay/lesbian/straight/pierced crowd. This funky hangout near the Arab baths goes from the evening until late. On Thursday nights, the *Millennium* dance party starts at 10pm, with a DJ and uninhibited dancing on the small psychedelic dance floor.

CULTURE ZOO

We've got one word for you: Alhambra.

Alhambra *(Palacio Carlos V; Tel 95/822-09-12, Ticket Office Tel 90/222-44-60; 9am-8pm/10pm-midnight Mon-Sat, 9am-6pm/10pm-midnight Sun, Apr-Oct, 9am-5:45pm/8-10pm, Nov-Mar; 1,000ptas):* This is the biggy. It goes without saying that it's a must-see, the most sublime example of Muslim architecture west of Mecca, and one of the world's great remaining architectural treasures. This fortress/palace complex impresses visitors not only with the grandiosity of its hilltop setting, but with the exquisite detailing of its arches, tiles, and fountains. Because it's that awesome, it's incredibly popular and overrun with tourists, so planning a trip here is like scheming to get tickets for that Lionel Ritchie concert you've waited your whole life for. To preserve the Alhambra, the number of visitors allowed on any day is rationed, and many a weary traveler has visited Granada in the spring or summer only to be shut out when the tickets were all snapped up ahead of time. To ensure your place in history, you have to either a) get there really early or b) buy your tickets ahead of time. The ticket office opens at 8:30am so if you haven't planned ahead and it's high season, get there before then. To rest easier, you can buy tickets up to a year in advance by calling and using a credit card, and then picking up your tickets at least 2 hours before your assigned visiting time at the Alhambra. If you're already in Spain, you can stop by any BBV Bank, of which there are over 2,800 branches, to buy a ticket in cash or pick up your prepaid ticket, up to a day in advance. Advance tickets have a 125ptas surcharge, but it's well worth the peace of mind. All tickets will be stamped with a half-hour time slot, which is the time you must enter the Palacio de Nazaries, the most popular part of the Alhambra. You can go to the other parts, the **Alcazaba** (fortress) and the **Generalife** gardens, at any time during the day. Though this all sounds like a big complicated hassle, it's not really—and when you see the number of camera-crazy tourists tramping through the grounds, you'll understand and wish visits were limited even more.

The whole complex, nestled in the trees, a world away from the bustle of modern Granada, can seem overwhelming at first, but if you break it down in your mind into its distinct sections it's easily navigable, though you'll need at least half a day to fully explore it. The Alcazaba, originally built in the 9th century for defensive purposes, is the oldest part of the Alhambra, with towers and fortified walls. You must climb up to the top of the **Torre de la Vela,** a watchtower with amazing views of the Albaicín, Sacromonte, and downtown Granada. Later, 14th-century Muslim rulers expanded the complex by constructing the jewel of the Alhambra, the **Palacio de Nazaries.** This is what people flock here for, and though you must enter during the time specified on your ticket, you can linger as long as you like. You'll first enter into some council chambers, with exquisitely tiled floors, and later move into the living quarters, which for Muslim sultans meant a place to house and utilize their harem. The Patio de los Leones, with a fountain of stone lions, is the most photographed courtyard, and during the high season you'll have to dodge the elbows of amateur architecture fiends as they maneuver for the perfect picture to bore their friends with. You have to just ignore all that, and take a deep breath, stop, and notice all of the intricate details that make the palace special: from the ceiling to the floor, from the arched entryways to the carved stucco walls, artwork covers every inch of space. Next to the Palacio de Nazaries stands a later intrusion on the Alhambra, the 16th-century Renaissance structure, **Palacio de Carlos V.** Behind that is the information and ticket office, and also the rest rooms if all those fountains are affecting your bladder. It's about a 5-minute walk up the hill to the entrance to the Generalife, and on the way you'll pass by a couple of restaurants and hotels, the grandest being the **Parador de San Francisco,** which has to be one of the best located hotels in the world.

The Generalife, with its spectacular gardens and airy palace, used to serve as a summer retreat for Muslim rulers. Water and nature become art forms here, and you can wander the maze-like gardens and linger by the sensual fountains for hours. As you can imagine, this was another key place for harems and sexual intrigue. Make sure you check out the fountains and views from the actual palace itself, and the hill behind it with the *escalera de agua* (stairway of water). The entrance to the Alhambra is a healthy 15- to 20-minute walk uphill from Plaza Nueva, though if you're really lazy you can take city bus 2 or the Alhambra microbus (125ptas) from Plaza Nueva.

After you've seen how the sultans lived, you'll want to see how the other 99 percent of Muslims lived, and where *Granadinos* (locals) still live today, the Albaicín. On the hill opposite the Alhambra, the old Arab quarter's whitewashed houses, churches, tiny plazas, and vistas are essential for exploration [see *by foot,* below].

Catedral *(Gran Vía de colón 5; Tel 95/822-29-59; 10:30am-1:30pm/3:30-8:30pm Mon-Sat, 4-7pm Sun; 350ptas)* and the **Capilla Real (Royal Chapel)** *(Oficios 3; Tel 95/822-78-48; 10:30am-1pm/3-*

lorca's granada

Poet, playwright, and martyr of the Spanish Civil War, Federico García Lorca was born and died near Granada. While he spent much of his artistic life in Madrid and abroad, Granada—and its Muslim past in particular—always captivated him. He wrote, "One should remember Granada as one should remember a sweetheart who has died." He referred to the Reconquista as a "tragedy," a statement that did not sit well with the Catholic church, of course, nor were they too keen about his fascination with gypsies, whom he portrayed in his famous book *Gypsy Ballads*. García Lorca was born in 1898 in the nearby town of Fuentevaqueros in a house that is now the **Casa Museo Federico Garcia Lorca** *(Poeta García Lorca 4; Fuentevaqueros; Tel 95/851-64-53; 10am-2pm/6-7pm).* His family later moved to Granada itself, to the **Huerta San Vicente** *(Virgen Blanca; Tel 95/825-84-66; 10am-1pm/5-8pm May-Sept; 10am-1pm/4-7pm Oct-May; Closed Monday; 300ptas, free Wednesday; www.huertagarcialorca.org),* which is now a cultural center and the home of a foundation that puts on performance arts and music shows throughout the year. It's located in the Parque Federico García Lorca, a 15-minute walk from the center of Granada. Even after he left Granada, Lorca spent nearly every summer at Huerta San Vicente and wrote some of his most famous works here. If you take one of the hourly tours, you can still see his writing desk and the views of the Alhambra that inspired him. While García Lorca took part in the brief cultural renaissance in Granada of the 1920s, the town was still too conservative and provincial for him; most of its inhabitants saw him as "that homosexual poet." García Lorca went to Madrid and hung out in the brightest artistic circles, with friends like

6pm Mon-Sat, 11am-1pm/4-7pm Sun; 350ptas): In the center of modern Granada and next door to each other are the city's most well-known Christian monuments. After the splendors of the Alhambra, or other cathedrals in Europe, the Cathedral kind of just seems like an unnecessarily big church. The exterior facades and doorways are more impressive than the interior and don't cost anything to look at. The 16th-century **Royal Chapel** is slightly more interesting, due to the simple but somber crypt of the most famous Spanish monarchs, Isabella and Ferdinand, who oversaw the Reconquista and Columbus's discovery of the New World in 1492. Notice how little they were, just wee little people. The other coffins in the crypt belong to their daughter Juana *la Loca* (The Crazy), son-in-law Felipe *El Hermoso* (The Beautiful), and grandson Miguel (just Miguel). A small museum houses their art and personal artifacts, the coolest being the crown and scepter of Queen Isabella...if you ever won-

Dalí and Luis Buñuel. But he returned to Granada in 1936, at the age of 38, and would never leave. Spain was at the height of its civil war, and the Fascist Nationalists had taken control of Granada and were instructed to eliminate their enemies. On some trumped-up charges, such as communicating to communists through his piano, García Lorca was arrested and held for three days at the Policía Nacional station, which still stands today at Calle Horno de Haza and Calle Duquesa. The reasons for his arrest are still unclear, and no specific charges against him were ever made public. He was not a member of the Communist Party, although he had communist friends and associates; he was homosexual, and not a fan of the Catholic church; and that was enough. García Lorca saw himself as completely apolitical, and famously said "I am a poet and no one shoots poets." He was wrong. He was taken to the nearby town of Viznar, where he was lined up against the wall and shot to death. His body was never found, though there is a marker just outside the town of Viznar at the Parque García Lorca. His death became a worldwide symbol for all the injustices done during the Spanish Civil War. And with the publication of his later works, such as his renowned play, *The House of Bernada Alba,* and his travelogue of the U.S., *A Poet in New York,* García Lorca became an international literary star as well. During Franco's regime in Spain, however, his work was banned until the 1970s.

dered what a real crown looked like. The Chapel is a quick visit and worth the 350ptas.

great outdoors

The only thing that compares to the variety that you can find in the city of Granada is the multitude of nearby outdoor getaways. The popular ski area **Estación de Esqui Sierra Nevada** is only 30 minutes away, and the Mediterranean Sea at the **Costa Tropical** is only 90 minutes. Every young person here has a story about the day they were going to go skiing, but then got to the bus station and saw it was sunny, so they decided to go the beach instead. It can happen. In fact, you could conceivably ski in the morning, go to the beach in the afternoon, and be drinking beer and eating tapas beneath the shadow of the Alhambra by nightfall. But there's no need to take it that fast.

by foot

The best walks in Granada are up through the Albaicín, which is a tangled web of crooked cobblestone streets and amazing lookout points. Trying to follow any sort of planned route is futile, but we like to try the impossible; even if you don't follow us exactly, it's fun to get lost and you won't stay that way too long. Start at **Plaza Nueva** and walk up the pedestrian-happy **Carrera del Darro,** which runs along the little Rio Darro. You'll see the **Alhambra** looming up to your right, and the **Albaicín** to your left. You'll pass the 11th-century **Arab Baths** *(Carrera del Darro 31; Tel 95/822-23-39)* on your left, which can be visited for free from 10am-2pm Tuesday through Saturday. Continue up the hill where the street becomes **Paseo de los Tristes** (Avenue of the Sad), so called because of the funeral processions that used to wind through here on their way to the cemetery. From the top of this street, you can take an alternate pathway to the right, across the river and up **Cuesta del Rey Chico** to reach the oldest entranceway to the Generalife gardens and the Alhambra. But we're going to head to the left, up the steep hill on **Cuesta de Chapiz,** which climbs to the top of the Albaicín. You'll hit an intersection, with the **Camino de Sacromonte** to your right. We're going to take the left again, onto the little cobblestone street **Cuesta San Augustin.** Take a quick right at the first intersection to get on a parallel street with almost the exact same name, **Caril de San Augustin,** and take a left because you won't be able to go straight. You'll soon hit a little zig-zag, try to go right-left-right, to get onto **Atarazana Cuesta Cabras,** which will take you right below **Mirador San Nicolás**. If you somehow miss this trick, follow the signs for Mirador San Nicolás, because that's where you want to get to. Some call this amazing viewpoint "Mirador de Clinton," because Dollar Bill visited here and proclaimed it "the most beautiful sunset in the world." He's a politician, so he probably says that about every sunset, although he knows the view well from his own days as a European traveler. You can almost picture him as a young Arkansas buck, staring across at the magnificent Alhambra, in awestruck admiration of its beauty and the harems (interns?) those Sultans used to keep. Today, tourists, stoners, kissy-kissy couples, and souvenir-selling old ladies keep the scene lively here. We've gotten you to the best views in town; it's your job to get down the hill.

The mountains of the Sierra Nevada are snowcapped for much of the year, offering good skiing conditions as early as November, often lasting until late May. Europe's highest mountain road passes by the ski resort of **Solynieve** at 2,100 meters. Southeast of Grenada the Sierra Nevada mountains are the highest in Iberia, the highest peak at **Mulhacén** at 3,481 meters. Buses leaving from the station in Grenada will carry you to the Estación de Esqui Sierra Nevada, 35 kilometers away. The **Boral** bus company *(Tel 958/273-100; One-way fare 850ptas)* operates only one bus a day, leaving in the morning and returning in the late afternoon. If you want to spend more time in the area, there are dozens of hotels and restaurants.

Costa Tropical is one of the most up-and-coming beach strips along the Costa Del Sol, lying between Málaga in the west and Motril in the east. This coast is the "beach" for Grenada. The mountains of the Sierra Nevada run right down to the sea, and the coastline here is riddled with little coves for seabathing. Some of the best white sandy beaches lie between the promontories of **Cerro Gordo** and **Punta de la Mona.** Yachts pull into the harbour at **Marina del Este,** and scuba diving and water sports can be arranged at various kiosks along the coast. The best center for beach visits is the relatively unspoiled village of **Salobreña** with its old whitewashed houses beneath a Moorish fortress. The little town opens onto five kilometers of beachfront, riddled with bars and restaurants. Because the mountains protect this coastal strip from winter winds, this is one of mainland Europe's sunniest spots in the cold months. The entire Costa Tropical is about 70 kilometers long, lying 80 kilometers south of Grenada. The **Alsina company** *(Tel 95/825-13-96; One-way fare 800ptas)* runs about 10 to 12 buses a day from the Grenada bus station to the coast.

STUff

Granada offers a wide range of spending opportunities in various quarters of the city: The main pedestrian shopping district is near Plaza Trinidad and Plaza Bib-Rambla; antiques, and just cool, old junk can be found in little rambling shops on Calle Elvira; souvenirs and locally made crafts are sold in the Alcaicería, the market in front of Catedral; incense, natural health-care products, jewelry, '60s attire, and all your modern hippy needs are on Calderería Nueva. To buy anything, check out the six floors of the mega department store **El Corte Inglés** *(Carrera de Genil 20-22; Tel 95/822-32-40; 10am-10pm Mon-Sat)* at Puerta Real. Yeah, it's a big chain store, but where else can you find books, CDs (international rock to local flamenco), beauty supplies, underwear, ATMs, currency exchange, a modern supermarket, local wines, ticket sales for cultural events, shoes, etc., all under one roof? Nowhere. Most shops are open 10am-2pm, and then again from 5-8pm, and closed Sunday.

▶▶DUDS

If you're in the market for hipster Italian fashions and piercings, check out **El Blanco y Nero** *(Duquesa 31; No phone; 10am-2pm/5-9pm Mon-*

fashion

What to wear in Granada depends entirely on where you're hanging out, but to be honest, no one really cares what you look like as long as you don't look too much like an American. Soccer jerseys or rock 'n' roll shirts for boys and crack-clenching tight pants and skimpy tops for the girls on the Pedro. In the center of town, a collared shirt and jeans for men, slightly less tight but still leaving nothing to the imagination pants for the women. Dreadlocks, pachouli oil, armpit-hair, loose, droopy clothes for the gypsters on Calderería Nueva.

Sat), a funky little shop right off Plaza Trinidad and full of beautiful people. Simple shirts and skirts start around 1,000ptas and go up from there, depending on how simple they are.

On the other end of the scale is **Ropero** *(Escuelas 12; Tel 95/828-60-99; 10am-3pm/5-9pm Mon-Sat)*. Next to the *Facultad de Derecho* (law school) off Calle Duquesa, this secondhand clothing shop draws bargain seekers and those looking to look like bargain-seekers. A good place to pick up that leather or jean jacket when the weather starts to get cold.

▶▶BOUND
Bookstores surround Plaza de Trinidad. A particularly big one, **Librería Urbana** *(Tablas 6)*, stocks a lot of textbooks, the latest bestsellers, and a small section of English-language novels. **Atril** *(Duquesa 8)*, a smaller, friendlier store, has new and used books, and a shelf of books in English. Off of Plaza de Gracia, **Metro** *(Calle Gracia 31; Tel 95/826-15-65)* specializes in foreign-language books, and has some good tomes about Spain in English.

▶▶TUNES
Reciclaje *(San Jerónimo 13; Tel 95/829-08-70)* started out as a used bookstore, but it's snuck in crates of used CDs in between all the books. A general hangout for students, especially from the nearby law school.

You'll find a more comprehensive and up-to-date selection at **Krisis Discos** *(Moral de la Magdalena 29; Tel 95/829-08-70)*, which specializes in rock 'n' roll in all its various forms (metal, folk, pop, etc). This is also a good place to get info on upcoming shows. It's located in the center, about a four-minute walk south of Plaza de Gracia.

EATS

A well-known local expression, from the poet Francisco de Acaza, is, "There is no pain in life greater than being a blind man in Granada." While there's some validity to that, being without taste buds in Granada would be total drag, too. It's not known as a purveyor of fine cuisine, but you're not here for champagne wishes and caviar dreams, anyway. You just want something good and cheap, and hopefully not another *jamon y queso* (ham and cheese) sandwich. Granada's links to its Arab past include a healthy appetite for spicy Middle Eastern food, unlike much of Spain where "flavoring" means adding a ton of olive oil and salt.

▶▶CHEAP

We've already told you about all the free tapas in town; Middle Eastern takeout places stand out as the other great cheap eating options. Some call them kebab houses, some call them falafel places, some call it getting a shawarma, but by any name they are essential stops. If you are not familiar with the mysterious wonders of the pita sandwich, here's how it goes: Take a pita, stuff it with fresh vegetables, tahini, spices, and one of the following: chicken or lamb roasted on a spit (shawarma); chicken or lamb grilled on a stick (kebab); fried chick pea balls (falafel). All right, enough with the culinary school lesson....

The most popular place for Middle Eastern food is right on Plaza Nueva at **Al-Andalus** *(Hermosa 6; No phone; Noon-5pm/7pm-1am daily, closed Tuesday)*. It has quality falafel sandwiches for 300ptas and chicken shawarma for 375ptas for takeout as well as more substantial meals. You can eat at the tables outside on the plaza, but it will be slightly more expensive. This joint is busy all the time, especially with the bar traffic in the area at night.

After Al-Andalus closes, the kids still want their shawarma, which is why there's a cornucopia of takeout places just off Plaza Nueva at Calle Calderería Nueva and Calle Calderería Vieja that stay open until 3am on weekends. Everyone has their favorite, but Baraka, which is always packed due its location next to the Granada 10 disco on Calderería Nueva, and El Rincon on Calderería Vieja, get the most kudos.

▶▶DO-ABLE

The Arabian-influenced vegetarian restaurant **Naturii Albaicín** *(Calderería Nueva 10; No phone; 1-4pm/7-11pm daily)*, also in "Little Morocco" near Plaza Nueva, is extremely popular with locals and travelers on the good side of the force. They come for the food, obviously, since the decor is simple, according the strict laws of vegetarianism. The menu changes daily, but includes simply garnished dishes like eggplant stuffed with rice, veggie cous-cous, or veggie paella, all for 700ptas. The combo *menú* for 950ptas includes a salad, bread, and dessert with your entrée. Also available are fresh juices, such as the rejuvenating carrot/apple combo for 300ptas. The flavors here don't exactly explode in your mouth, but you'll certainly feel as if you washed away weeks of unhealthy beer, cheese, and cigarettes after eating here. No alcohol is served, and for some reason no toilet paper is found in the bathroom either, so bring your napkin or blank journal pages with you.

For a much less healthy but more atmospheric eating experience, try **La Esquinita** *(Campo del Príncipe; Tel 95/822-71-06; Noon-5pm/8pm-2am, closed Monday)*, the famous "little corner" on Campo del Príncipe.

If you want to do it cheap, you can stand at the bar with the old men in suits and order drinks, each of which will come with a different plate of tapas; according to custom, they're supposed to get better with each drink, though it depends on your tastes. Somehow, little fried chicken things don't seem as good as a creamy fish empanada. See how far you can go until they serve you the *primera* (the first one) again. For a more civilized experience, sit down and relax at the tables outside on the plaza and get a full meal. Entrées will cost around 1,300ptas. Fried fish is a specialty here, despite the fact that we're in the mountains.

▶▶**SPLURGE**

For spectacular views, take a loved one or a new-found love to **Mirador del Moraima** *(Pianista Garcia Carillo 2; Tel 95/822-82-90; 1:30-3:30pm/8:30-11:30pm, closed Sun)*. With patios and dining rooms overlooking the Alhambra from a beautiful, terraced setting atop the Albaicín, the vista takes precedence over the food. But the chow is pretty good too, hearty Andalucian fare, which means gazpacho and a lot of meat (1,400ptas per entrée) and fish (1,800ptas and up). Very popular, so reservations are recommended.

crashing

Granada is blessed with lots of cheap, decent accommodations. There are so many *pensiones* here, you usually don't even have to reserve a room, but can just sort of walk around until you find one. You should call ahead in the summer, however, in order to snag a good location. The hostels cluster around Plaza Trinidad and near Plaza Nueva, especially on Cuesta de Gomérez. More pricey, comfortable digs are near Gran Vía de colón and, if you're in the market for spectacular surroundings (at a spectacular cost),

down and out

If you're running low on pesetas, don't blame it on Granada, because it's one of the cheaper cities in Western Europe for travelers. Come on, there are free tapas [see *bar scene*, above]. Sure, you have to buy a 150pta beer to get the free grub, but still, it's pretty fine. If you somehow ended up penniless here, try hanging out at Plaza Nueva; there are lots of other broke kids from all over Europe who would be happy to share your misery. Or start walking—there's way too much to see here, especially in the Albaicín. Another cool spot is Fuente de Triunfo, the fountains on Avenida de Constitución. The rows of shooting water are an engineering feat, and you'll be right on the main path for students coming from the University to the center of town, so there will be a lot of eye candy.

up at the Alhambra itself. All hostels and hotels are used to people coming home late, some are just friendlier about it than others. A complete list of hotels can be obtained at the tourist information office [see *need to know,* below].

▶▶**CHEAP**

The official youth hostel, **Albergue Juvenil Granada** *(Calle Ramón y Cajal 2; Tel 95/828-43-06; 1,500ptas, 2,000ptas 26 and over),* has all the official youth hostel amenities—swimming pool, double rooms, institutional attitude—but it's located inconveniently out of the center of the town, although it's very close to the train station.

Very conveniently located is **Hostal Britz** *(Cuesta de Gomérez 1; Tel 95/822-36-52; 2,400ptas single w/o bath, 3,900ptas double w/ bath),* right in the middle of the action at the bottom of the street heading up to the Alhambra, across from Plaza Nueva. Because of its prime location, the owners could keep their 22 rooms full year-round even if they were jerk-faces, but actually they're extremely friendly. There seems to be a lack of adequate lighting throughout this place, but it just adds to the ambience. Unlike most places in Andalucía, the prices here are the same year-round. If this place is full, try one of the other hostels just a few steps away.

Near Plaza Trinidad, **Hostal Nevada** *(Tablas 8; Tel 95/259-223; 2,500ptas single, 3,000ptas double, 5,000ptas triple, 1,000ptas more for in-room bathroom)* stands out among the crowd for being a two-star hostel at one-star prices. The small upstairs rooms have air conditioning and bathrooms, but it costs more to pee inside your own room. The lively owner here is definitely four-star, though he doesn't speak English.

For urban adventure, try **Camping Sierra Nevada** *(Avda. de Madrid 107; Tel 95/815-00-62; Approx 2,100ptas for 2 people with tent and car),* although it's only open from March to October, because it gets chilly here in winter. Located right off the highway just on the other side of the bus station, this is definitely car camping; even if you don't have a car, you'll still be camping near parked cars. Only a 15-minute bus ride from the center of the city, it has a swimming pool and drinking water.

▶▶**DO-ABLE**

Unlike most *hostales* in Granada, **Hostal Nuevas Naciones** *(Placeta de Triviño 1; Tel 95/827-05-03; 2,900ptas single, 4,500ptas double)* has been recently refurbished and is kept so clean that it feels brand-spanking new. The communal bathrooms are big, and the bright rooms are cozy with comfy beds, desks, and closets. The family that runs it is so friendly you'll feel bad about buzzing them awake when you come home late at night. Located right off of Calle San Juan de Dios, near Avenida de la Constitución, it's a 10-minute walk from Plaza Nueva.

More like a hotel than a hostal, **Hostal Atenas** *(Gran Vía de colón 38; Tel 95/827-87-50; 4,500ptas single, 6,700ptas double)* has AC, TV, and bathrooms in all the rooms. The rooms are decorated like your parents' bedroom when you were a kid—a lot of beige—and there's a secure parking garage if you have your own wheels, though it will cost you 1300ptas per day.

▶▶**SPLURGE**

What you'll be paying for to stay at the **Hotel America** *(Real de la Alhambra 53; Tel 95/822-74-71; Closed Dec-Feb; 15,500ptas double)* is not its one-star rooms but its spectacular, 10-star location within the walls of the Alhambra. The rooms are small but quaint; it doesn't really matter because you won't be spending much time there anyway. A serene plant-filled patio is a lovely retreat from sightseeing. There are only 13 rooms, so you have to reserve far, far in advance if you want to be able to walk out your door into history.

If you have the cash, and you can somehow get a room at **Parador Nacional de San Francisco** *(Real de Alhambra; Tel 95/822-14-40; Toll-free from U.S. 800-343-0020; 33,000ptas and up, double)*, the government-run luxury hotel, you will be in one of the best-located accommodations in Spain. Built into the walls of the Alhambra, the building used to be a Muslim mosque before it was converted into a convent after the Reconquista of 1492. Needless to say, the views are awesome and you must reserve far in advance, like a year or something. There are a lot of rich people out there.

need to know

Currency Exchange Banks abound on the two main drags, **Gran Via de Con** and **Calle Reyes Católicos,** and at **Puerto Real.**

Tourist Info The most helpful tourist office, with lots of free maps and an English-speaking staff, is at **Plaza de Mariána Pineda** *(Tel 95/822-59-90; 9am-7pm Mon-Fri, 10am-2pm Sat)*. It's three blocks east of Puerta Real. They won't make hotel reservations for you, but never fear: there is a **Central Reservation system** *(Tel 925/92-02-01)* that will.

Public Transportation Traffic in Granada makes bus travel in the center a slow affair, but city buses can be handy for getting to the train and bus stations (see below). Traffic has recently been restricted on the Albaicín and the Alhambra hills, but the air-conditioned **red microbuses** make loops every 15 minutes in peak season. At Plaza Nueva look for the red mini-van looking things, with either 'Alhambra' or 'Albaicín' as the destination (125ptas). This is a new service, so ask at the tourist office about any route changes. There are plenty of **taxis** available, especially at Plaza Nueva, or call 95/828-06-54.

Health and Emergency Medical: *061*; police: *091*. **Hospital Provincial San Juan De Dios** *(San Juan Dios 15; Tel 95/820-43-00)* is the most centrally located medical facility. **Policia Nacional:** *(Duquesa 15; Tel 95/827-83-00)*.

Pharmacies As in the rest of Spain, *pharmacias* all share 24-hour duty on a rotating basis. Look for the **neon green crosses** in the center of town.

Telephone All numbers in Granada begin with *958;* pay phones don't seem to eat change as fast as in other Spanish cities, but you'll get more time if you buy a *tarjeta telefónica* at any tobacco shop. There's a *Locutorio Público* (public phone center) at Reyes Católicos 55.

Trains The **train station** *(Avenida Andaluces; Tel 95/827-12-72)* is on the western edge of the center, about a 15-minute walk from the major sights and hostels. You can also walk up to Avenida de la Constitución and get **bus 3** to the cathedral, if you're carrying a heavy load.

Bus Lines Out of the City The bus station *(Carretera de Jaén)* is about 3km (1.8 miles) west of the city. The main carrier is **Alsina Graells** *(Tel 95/818-50-10)* with service to most major spots in Spain. If you arrive by bus, get city **bus 3** (125ptas) from right outside the main entrance of the station, which will take you down Avenida de la Constitución, then Gran Vía de Colón to the center, in 15 minutes. The exception for buses leaving Granada are those to Sierra Nevada, which are run by **Bonal** *(Tel 95/827-31-00)* and leave from Paseo Del Violón (see *Sierra Nevada* chapter for details).

Laundry As in the rest of Andalucía, finding a place to wash your clothes is somehow a near impossible task; most everyone lives at home and has their mommy do it. Seek out **Lavanderia Tintoreria Duquesa** *(Duquesa 24; Tel 95/828-06-85; 9:30am-2pm/4:30pm-8:30pm Mon-Sat)* located right off alle San Juan de Dios. For 1,200ptas they'll wash and dry your clothes for pick-up the next day.

Postal The main **Correos** *(Puerta Real; Tel 95/822-48-35)* is a hard-to-miss building at Puerta Real. If you're just mailing a post card (115ptas) go downstairs; the ground floor is for packages.

Internet See *wired,* above.

everywhere else

cabo de gata

Despite what anyone tries to tell you, the most epic beaches in Spain are found here, in Cabo de Gata (The Cape of the Cat), a little piece of desert paradise that juts out into the Mediterranean on the southeastern edge of Almería. In Cabo de Gata those wild cowboy deserts meet the Mediterranean in spectacular fashion: Burnt red volcanic cliffs rush down to meet fine white sand, hidden coves, and a deep blue sea. This area—and in particular the mellow beach town of **San José**—can break your traveling heart because you know you'll have to leave it eventually, and because you know it can't remain undiscovered for too much longer. In fact, quaint San José is already being built up at a fairly rapid pace, with apartments for the Northern Europeans who vacation here. Sitting on the little city beach in town, you can hear the sounds of jackhammers and cranes echoing in the hills. Fortunately, the whole area, including the town of San José, is part of a nature preserve, **Parque Natural de Cabo de Gata-Nijar,** so development is restricted. There are no high-rise hotels or four-lane highways, and the vast majority of the area, including the most spectacular beaches, is currently off-limits to developers. So get here while you can—just don't bring any real-estate moguls with you.

If you have your own wheels you're free to roam much of Cabo de Gata. If not, you're going to have to get a bus from the modern city of **Almería** to the west. Almería is a fine enough place, but it's also hot and noisy and has one of the more unpleasant bus stations in Spain—it's best used as a transfer point to Cabo de Gata. If you get stuck in Almería, there's a nice *hostal*, **Hostal Resedencia de Americano,** right down from the bus station [see *crashing*, below]. There is a booth at the bus station with a helpful lady who seems to know all the bus schedules by heart. Ask her the way to San José, as there are two buses daily. If you just ask to go to 'Cabo de Gata', you might end up on a bus to the town of **San Miguel Cabo de Gata,** which is another nice, mellow fishing village with some tourists, east of San José. San Miguel is the type of place where old fishermen will give you a taste of their octopus and laugh—with you, not at you—as you try to figure out how to eat it. From San Miguel, it's a beautiful 3½-hour walk around the coast, past the southernmost tip of the cape at the Faro de Cabo de Gata lighthouse, to get to San José.

North of San José, the park continues up the coast through more quaint towns, such as **Las Negras,** and more secluded beaches, though you'll need your own wheels to explore.

If you make San José your base for exploring Cabo de Gata—which we most highly recommend because it has the best budget accommodations, bike rental, and beach access—it's easy to get your bearings since it's built like an old Western town. **Calle Correo** is the main drag where you'd have your gunfights; it's also where the bus stop, the supermarket, and the ATM are located. Between this street and the little city beach is the main plaza, simply called **El Plaza,** with the tourist office. At the east end of the city beach is a port, and behind that is a hill where the youth hostel and campsites are located, about a 5-minute walk from the center.

beaches

Life is lived at an almost surreally mellow pace here. Get up in the morning, grab a coffee, rent a bike, get some groceries, and head west down the dirt road to the spectacular beaches of **Playa de los Genoveses** and **Playa de Mónsul.** From town, it's about a 25-minute walk to Genoveses, and another 15-20 minutes past that to Mónsul. If you take a bike, you get to ride on a gravelly, dusty road that should be renamed "The Nutcracker" because you'll be bounced unmercifully with extreme distress to your most sacred parts. But the scene that greets you at the beach, just beyond the fields of cactus and natural palms, makes it all worthwhile: Playa de los Genoveses is a long uninterrupted cove with volcanic outcroppings on either side and a chill international crowd, many of them butt-naked. You'll see beautiful couples who have suntanned every crevice, even where you thought the sun wouldn't shine. Many of the nudies hang out in these little palm-frond-covered bunkers, so if you're thinking of seeing what's under that little shelter, be prepared. Even on the busiest days, there's plenty of room here to get away from it all. Playa de Mónsul is possibly even more visually stunning, with windswept cliffs and a straight line of white beach. It can get uncomfortably windy, however, and seems more of a place for lovers—there are always frisky couples frolicking in the surf.

bar scene

As you'd expect, nighttime in San José is quiet. One cool local bar to check out is **Dagobah** *(Calle Lillemor I; No phone; 9pm-2am),* with a killer CD collection and posters of the Clash, the Specials, and, of course, Yoda. It's a good place to meet the surprisingly hip locals, and bitch about all the tourists (not including yourself, of course...). To get here, head out of town on Calle Correo and take a hard left after the second cupola (which is a rooftop dome, for those of you who are architecturally challenged) and you'll see it. Or just ask someone in town—most of them know where it is. The patio bar at the youth hostel [see *crashing*, below] is another chill place to hang out and drink. If the staff is around they'll gladly pour you something and then sit down and enjoy it with you.

eats

Like everything in San José, eating out is a casual experience. Fresh fish is always a good idea. There's a line of restaurants at the port, usually closed during the off season, and a couple more near the plaza in the center of town. Wandering is encouraged—they are all equally reputable, pick the one that has the best outdoor seat open for you. Among the restaurants at the port, **Dolce Vita Pizzeria** *(Puerto Deportivo 8; Tel 95/038-00-17; noon-3pm/5:30-10:30pm, closed Nov-Feb)* has great gazpacho, pizza, and outdoor seating. For groceries, you can't miss **Super Spar** *(Correo; No phone; 10am-2pm/5-8pm)* in the center of town.

crashing

On the eastern edge of San José, halfway up the hill from the port, is one of the cooler youth hostels you'll ever find, **Albergue Juvenil de San José** *(Montemar; Tel 95/038-03-53; 1,200ptas single, mid-April to Sept only)*. The patio, with a bar and cafe run by the young chill staff, is a postcard-perfect place to hang out mornings and evenings, with flamenco music and even some Tom Waits, as if you weren't relaxed enough. Unfortunately, the building boom has directly affected its location: The two-story building (the limit in San José) under construction across the street will be just tall enough to block the ocean views. It won't shatter the good vibrations here, however, which are only interrupted by the occasional large school group that takes over the bunk rooms. (If you're nice to the staff, they might let you sleep on the roof.)

Near the hostel, at the bottom of the hill, follow the signs to find **Camping Tau** *(Tel 95/038-01-66; 500ptas per person, tent, and car, mid-April to Sept only)*, which is another good budget option.

Hostal Bahia *(Calle Correo; Tel 95/038-03-37; 6,000-8,000ptas double)* is your standard, clean, comfortable Spanish hotel, though it lacks the good vibes of the official youth hostel.

At the other end of the spectrum, **Hotel de San José** *(Calle Correo; Tel 95/038-01-16; www.hotelsanjose.com; 22,000ptas double)* offers luxury in a pristine location on a cliff overlooking the Mediterranean and the town of San Jose.

If for whatever reason you're stuck in Almería, rooms are available at **Hostal Resedencia Americano** *(Avda. de la Estación 6; Tel 95/025-80-11; 3,160ptas single, 5,490ptas double high season)*. Located just a couple blocks from the bus station, its convenience can't be beat, and the owner is a pleasant dude who's seen his share of backpackers.

need to know

Currency Exchange There's a 24-hour ATM in the center of town, at the corner of Calle Correo and Calle de la Plaza.

Tourist Information For such a mellow, friendly town, San José has an uneven **tourist office** *(Calle de la Plaza; Tel 95/038-02-99; 10am-2pm Mon-Sat)*. They very well may not be open during opening hours, for no stated reason, and if you speak to them on the phone they might outright lie to you, such as telling you there's no taxi service in San José, even though there is *(Tel 95/005-62-55)*. They have information on bike rental and other outdoor opportunities, but if you hit them on a bad day, don't worry: The best way to get info here is to ask your waiter, grocery store clerk, or a random person in the street.

Transportation First you have to get to Almería, which is easiest to do by bus, especially if you're coming from the coast. For some reason trains hardly run here, even though it's a big port. From Almería, **Autocares Bernardo** *(Tel 95/025-04-22)* runs two buses every day (except Sunday, when there is no service) to San José. They stop in the center of town on Calle Correo, across from Hostal Bahia. It's a 1-1/2-hour trip, and costs around 350ptas.

Bike/Moped Rental Ask at the tourist office or youth hostel for a list of places that rent bikes. They will probably tell you about **Mountain Bike Aventura** *(Correos 14; Tel 95/038-04-48; 2-8pm daily; 2,000ptas per day)* and **Camping Tau** *(see crashing above; 2,000ptas per day)*.

Jerez de la frontera

Jerez is famous worldwide for its booze and its horses. The state of Kentucky is also famous for its booze and its horses. So Jerez is kind of like Kentucky, right? Not exactly, since the booze isn't Jim Beam, but sherry, and you can't bet on the horses unless you can get odds on equestrian competitions. Jerez is the refined wine capital of Andalucía; its name literally translates as sherry, a type of sweet wine specific to this corner of the world. Its expansive *bodegas* offer tours and free tastings, so cleanse your palette before arriving. If you think of sherry and dancing horses as something rich old people like, you're right, and you also have some idea of the average visitor to Jerez. But if you're imagining a sleepy little wine village overrun by blue-hairs, you'll be surprised to find that today Jerez is a modern city with a population over 200,000. The area is one of the cradles of other Andalucian arts such as bullfighting, tapas, and flamenco, and a large university population keeps the arts of beer drinking and rock 'n' roll alive as well. For all these reasons, Jerez makes a good day trip from Sevilla (1 hour), Cadiz (40 minutes), or a stopover between the two; stay the night if you want to hang with the proud locals. They'll tell you that today Jerez is almost as famous for its shrine to another great Spanish pas-

JEREZ

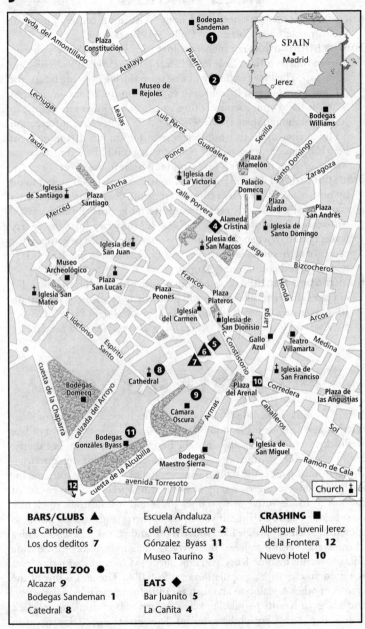

Bodegas Sandeman ■ 1

Plaza Constitución

avda. del Amontillado

Atalaya

Pizarro

SPAIN
• Madrid

• Jerez

Lechugas

Museo de Rejoles ■

2

Lealas

Luis Pérez

3

Sevilla

Bodegas Williams ■

Taxdirt

Ponce

Guadalete

Santo Domingo

Zaragoza

Iglesia de Santiago ✝ ■

Plaza Santiago

Ancha

Merced

calle Porvera

✝ Iglesia de La Victoria

Plaza Mamelón

Palacio Domecq

Plaza Aladro

Plaza San Andrés

Alameda Cristina ◆ 4

✝ Iglesia de Santo Domingo

Larga

Iglesia de San Juan ■✝

Iglesia de San Marcos ✝

Museo Archeológico ■

Plaza San Lucas

Francos

Bizcocheros

✝ Iglesia San Mateo

S. Ildefonso

Espíritu Santo

Plaza Peones

Plaza Plateros

Iglesia del Carmen ✝

Honda

Larga

Arcos

Medina

Iglesia de San Dionisio ✝

Gallo Azul

Teatro Villamarta ■

5

6

▲ 7

C. Consistorio

✝ 8 Cathedral

cuesta de la Chaparra

Bodegas Domecq ■

calzada del Arroyo

9

Cámara Oscura

Armas

Plaza del Arenal

10

Corredera

✝ Iglesia de San Francisco

Plaza de las Angustias

Sol

Bodegas Gonzáles Byass ■ 11

cuesta de la Alcubilla

Bodegas Maestro Sierra ■

✝ Iglesia de San Miguel

Caballeros

Ramón de Cala

12 ↓

cuesta de la Alcubilla

avenida Torresoto

Church ✝

BARS/CLUBS ▲
La Carbonería **6**
Los dos deditos **7**

CULTURE ZOO ●
Alcazar **9**
Bodegas Sandeman **1**
Catedral **8**

Escuela Andaluza
del Arte Ecuestre **2**
Gónzalez Byass **11**
Museo Taurino **3**

EATS ◆
Bar Juanito **5**
La Cañita **4**

CRASHING ■
Albergue Juvenil Jerez
de la Frontera **12**
Nuevo Hotel **10**

sion: motor sports. On second thought, maybe Jerez is like Kentucky, except instead of NASCAR and Harleys they have Formula One and European motorcycle championships. Given that Jerez bills itself as a wine capital, you might be surprised to find no vineyards in or around the city. The grapes are grown closer to the coast in the "sherry triangle" formed by Jerez, Sanlúcar de Barrameda, and El Puerto de Santa Maria. Jerez is home to the biggest and most well-known bodegas where the sherry is aged and bottled. This big city, while thoroughly modernized with shopping malls, wide avenues, and traffic congestion, does have a quaint old quarter and a whole lot of churches.

If you arrive by train or bus, you'll be on the eastern edge of the old city. Walk down **Calle D. Fernandez Herrera** or **Calle Medina,** which run parallel where Medina runs east-west, for about 10-15 minutes to get to the center. A good place to start is the very helpful Tourist Office, three blocks up on **Calle Larga,** which runs parallel to Calle Medina where Medina begins running north-south. They can give you a good map and also tell you which bodegas are offering tours and their opening hours. South of here, through the pedestrian shopping district, is the large modern square **Plaza del Arenal** with benches for relaxing and people-watching on those blazing hot summer days. Immediately southwest lie the three holy sites of Jerez—the Muslim fortress, the Alcazar; the Christian Catedral; and maybe the reason you're in town, the Bodega Gónzalez Byass, maker of the most famous sherry of all, Tío Pepe. A tangle of charming cobblestone streets and grand churches spreads northwest of the Alcazar, a great neighborhood for wandering around. Farther west, flamenco reigns in the **Barrio de Santiago,** where the art of flamenco was originated by *gitanos* (gypsies) and where the flamenco center, Fundación Andaluza de Flamenco, makes its home. Of course, this neighborhood also has lovely cobblestone streets and churches. The northern part of the city center is home to the Museo Taurino (Bullfighting Museum), more sherry bodegas, and the school of equestrian arts, the Real Escuela Andaluza del Arte Ecuestre. **Calle Porvera,** the northern extension of Calle Larga, is one of the prettiest streets in town, with purple-flowered trees in spring, and students imbibing at outside tables. You'll find the **Plaza de Toros** and another young hangout area with a bunch of bars, **La Plaza de Canterbury,** in the northeast section of town. Ten kilometers (6.2 miles) east of town is the *Curcuito de Jerez*, the world-class speedway that hosts major European motorcycle and Formula One races. This is what kids all over Spain dream of as they race their tricked-out scooters through the streets. Check the daily *Diario de Jerez* newspaper for race events and other entertainment information. May means party time in Jerez, thanks to the influx of horse freaks who come into town for the *Feria de Caballo* (Horse Festival), usually the second week of the month. Costumed riders parade on horses and equestrians compete, while mere mortals dance, drink, and listen to music. If you're more of a dog or cat person, this is a good time to stay away, plus you'll save on hotel rooms, which skyrocket in price and shrink in availability at this time.

oh, sherry

Your first taste of sherry might make you grimace: It's definitely an acquired taste, especially if you've been tramping across Europe enjoying the drinkable reds from France, Italy, and central Spain. But keep in mind that the potent potion you're drinking is part of history, one of the true ancient wines. Archaeologists have excavated wine presses dating from the 8th century B.C., when the Phoenicians were near Jerez. The chalky, nutrient-deficient soil of this region makes sherry unique; the English especially go mad for it. They're the ones who bastardized the Muslim name for the town "Scheris" into "sherry." When Sir Francis Drake sacked the city of Cádiz, he looted a mountain of sherry, unintentionally starting the sherry boom in England that made Jerez prosper. That booze-hound William Shakespeare also sang its praises through his great comic character Falstaff, who lauded the 'sherris sack' for improving his wit and warming his blood: "If I had a thousand sons, the first human principle I would teach should be to forswear thin potations, and to addict themselves to Sack." We wouldn't go that far, but we do suggest you at least try a glass or two. Make one an *oloroso*, the darker and older variety, and one a *fino*, a paler, dryer type.

bar scene

There's a big weekend bar scene in the northeast part of the old town near streets like Divina Pastora, and in the mini-mall of bars at Plaza de Canterbury (Nuño de Caña-Circo intersection). But if you're only in Jerez for a night, and you already have a sherry buzz going, you probably just want to stay in the center of town, on the little but happening Plaza de Vargas. It's not labeled well on most maps, but it's just east of Plaza del Arenal, at the end of Calle Pescadería Vieja, next to the *Ayuntamiento* (City Hall). It's dead during the day, but starting at about 9pm on weekends and other party nights it begins to draw crowds and you'll be able to find it *sin problema* (without a problem). Leather jackets and suits recover from work at **La Carbonería** (*Plaza de Vargas s/n; 7pm-2am*), but this suave place loosens up as the night progresses. There's plenty of liquor choices and loud Spanish pop in the dark wood interior. Catty-corner from La Carbonería is the more raucous and friendly **Los dos deditos** (*Plaza de Vargas s/n*), which draws an eclectic crowd of students and older rockers, especially on weekend nights, when it sometimes has live rock or blues music.

CULTURE ZOO

You'll be happy to learn that many of the cultural attractions in Jerez involve drinking. Tourists flock to the hundreds of sherry bodegas that offer tours and tasting, although if you're planning a bender, keep in mind that sherry is potent—it always gives you that little shudder if you take more than a sip—and difficult to down in mass quantities. But if you want to get a nice afternoon buzz, the opportunity certainly exists. Many of the bodegas require advanced reservations, so get a complete rundown from the Tourist Office.

Gónzalez Byass *(Manuel María Gonzáles 12; Tel 95/635-70-00; Tours 10am-5:30pm; 500ptas):* The Disneyland of bodegas. Here, they make the famous Tío Pepe (as they'll be happy to remind you every five minutes). This slick operation runs hourly tours in English. Little trams take you around to the historic bodegas where the sherry ages in American oak casks; there's also a cheesy video presentation—basically a long advertisement—narrated by an actor "playing" Tío Pepe himself—after which you get two free samples in the tasting room, and then are literally corralled into the gift shop. Despite the incessant sales pitch, Gónzalez Byass is still an E-ticket ride. The highlights are the *bodega de la concha*, designed by A.G. Eiffel (who apparently built a tower in France somewhere), and the famous drunk mice scurrying around your feet; there's always a glass of sherry left out for the little rodents, and a miniature ladder for them to climb up for a sip. Classy. This is also one of the few tours you don't need to book in advance and that runs on weekends.

Bodegas Sandeman *(Pizarro 10; Tel 95/63-31-29-95; 10am-4pm Mon-Fri; 500ptas):* If you're more of a fine wine connoisseur than someone who enjoys watching mice get looped, try a tour at this renowned bodega, a few minutes north of the center. The tours here are more refined: You can see the grapes being pressed, learn about the bottling process, and get a complete explanation of the *solera* aging system, as well as three free glasses at the end. They take their sherry seriously here. George Glas Sandeman, the nephew of the Scottish founder of the brand, was once quoted as saying "Bad wine does me no harm. It never gets past my nose." Right on, brother.

Escuela Andaluza del Arte Ecuestre *(Avda. Duque de Abrantes 11; Tel 95/631-96-35):* Next to Sandeman is the epicenter of Andalucian horse culture. This "school of equestrian art" teaches riders to become one with their horse and properly tip their cap to the judges at dressage competitions. Sort of like summer camp meets Jedi training. Monday through Wednesday and Friday from 11am to 1pm you can pay 450ptas to watch the riders train and to visit the stables of the handsome steeds (the horses), who come from the legendary *cartajuno* Arab-Hispano breed, famous for its beauty and intelligence. On Thursdays at noon (and some Tuesdays in summer), there's a full-blown dancing horse show with rider and horse gallivanting in perfect unison to classical music. Seats are 1,500ptas and up, and, this being Jerez, you can get sherry here as well.

Museo Taurino *(Pozo de Olivar 6; Tel 95/632-14-00; 9am-1:30pm Mon-Sat; 400ptas)*: In Jerez, you can even drink at the bullfighting museum. In fact, the air conditioning, vaunted ceiling, and collection of bullfighting memorabilia makes it the best place in town for an early afternoon drink. The entry fee includes a free sherry or *cerveza,* and after you look at the impeccably decorated main room, which focuses more on bullfighting art than artifacts, retire to the beautiful bar area for a round.

Alcazar *(Alemeda Vieja s/n, Tel 95/631-97-98)* and **Catedral:** As of now you can't get drunk inside the 12th-century Alcazar or the 18th-century cathedral, although in the summer a bar sometimes springs up in the plaza between the two. But that doesn't mean you shouldn't check them out, even if you've been in Andalucía long enough that you feel you've seen enough cathedrals and fortresses. The Catedral can only be entered during mass, but it's worth a walk around the outside to see the exterior. Much of the Alcazar is under renovation, but the recently added Camera Obscura is open every day of the year except for Christmas and New Year's, and offers a unique look at the city.

EaTS

Tapas rule in Jerez, and **Bar Juanito** *(Pescadería Vieja 10; Tel 95/633-48-38; 1-5:30pm/8pm-midnight; Closed Mondays in winter, Sundays in summer; Tapas 225-350ptas, meals 1,200ptas and up)* is king. It's located on a fairy-tale little restaurant row that ambles off the northwest side of Plaza del Arenal. The unbeatable selection of over 50 tapas and the warm, boisterous atmosphere draw crowds of locals and tourists to the outside tables and cramped bar. The current owner, Faustino, will be here, chatting it up and overseeing the preparation of specialties such as *fideos de gamba* (shrimp with noodles) and *alacauciles de Trebujena* (grilled artichokes). Tapas are cheap, full meals are doable. Sherry is not only served here, but revered above all else; no other cocktails are available, as they'll proudly tell you.

For a younger crowd and cheaper grub, try **La Cañita** *(Porvera 11; Tel 95/634-19-19; Noon-midnight daily),* north of the city center. The high tables beneath the umbrellas outside collect students and other excitable people for the down-home tapas, fried fish, and beer. A good place to start your bar-hop.

crashing

If you decide to sleep off that wine headache, you can overnight in Jerez for pretty cheap.

The youth hostel, **Albergue Juvenil Jerez de la Frontera** *(Avda. Carreo Blanco 30; Tel 95/634-28-90; 1,200ptas, 1,500ptas over 26, low season; 1,500/2,000ptas high season)* is 2 kilometers (1.2 miles) south of the center of town. You can take bus 9 from the train or bus stations.

To stay in the center, your best bet is 2 blocks off Plaza del Arenal, the comfortably priced **Nuevo Hotel** *(Caballeros, 23; Tel 95/633-16-00; 3,000ptas single, 4,500ptas double in low season; 4,000ptas single, 7,000ptas double in high season; Breakfast 400ptas)*. Well-run by a friendly English-speaking owner, the rooms have heating, private baths, TV, and telephone, and an old hotel feel, despite its name. The street is fairly safe but has some strange activities, like...you know when two people get in a car together but don't go anywhere? Just don't leave valuables in your car, and you should be fine.

need to know

Currency Exchange There are a gaggle of ATMs on Calle Larga near the Tourist Office.

Tourist Information Jerez has a kick-ass **Informacion Turista** *(Larga 39; Tel 95/633-11-50; 9am-2pm/5-8pm Mon-Fri, 9am-2pm Sat, April-Oct; 8am-3pm Mon-Fri, 5-7pm Sat, off-season)*. The English-speaking staff coolly and quickly dispense with sherry-thirsty tourists, offering them maps, hotel listings, and info on the bodega tours.

Health and Emergency Medical emergencies *061;* Police matters *091.* **Hospital de Santa Cruz** *(Avda. de la Cruz Roja s/n; Tel 95/630-74-54)* is on the northeast edge of the old town. **Police station**: *(Plaza del Arroyo s/n; Tel 95/634-21-72)*.

Trains and Buses The train station, **Estacion de Ferrocarril** *(Plaza de la Estacion; Tel 95/634-23-19)*, 1km (.62 miles) east of the city center, is on the extremely well-traveled Sevilla-Cadiz line. Buses arrive right down the street at the **Estacion de Autobus** *(Cartuja; Tel 95/634-52-07)*.

Postal Correos *(Cerrón s/n; Tel 95/634-22-95)* is just east of the southern end of Calle Larga.

las alpujarras (capileira)

Alluring, sacred, and just plain weird, this series of unbelievably green valleys, sprinkled with gleaming white hill towns, lies beneath the southern peaks of the **Sierra Nevada** mountain range and runs to the Mediterranean. Not long ago it was one of the last undiscovered regions of Spain, but it's just too unusually beautiful to have remained so, and now tourism has become its main industry. Despite the increasing number of sightseers, time seems to stand still here, in the craggy peaks, deep ravines, mountain streams, and simple way of life. You're just as likely to see a goat herder tending his flock as a group of German hikers piling out of a bus. Fortunately, the geography of the land and the small size of the villages have remained virtually unchanged, and the air here is so clean and pure, you might need to cut it with something to take it all in. Outdoor lovers should make a point of hiking up Spain's highest peak, **Mulhacén,** through the vast **Barranco de Poqueira,** a series of steep valleys. To get your heart beating even faster, you can mountain bike up and down the challenging hills or hang glide over the deep ravines.

Las Alpujarras's history is as strange as its geography. When Boabdil, the last sultan of the Western Muslim empire, finally relented to the

Christian conquerors in 1492 at Granada, he was awarded the kingdom of Las Alpujarras as sort of a booby prize. He went from Granada to the top of Mulhacén, where legend has it he turned back to look at his former empire and the magnificent Alhambra palace, and wept. It became known to history as "the Moor's Last Sigh," and they say you can still hear it in the running streams of the valleys here. According to legend, his own mother even told Boabdil to "weep like a woman for what you could not defend like a man." Ouch. Boabdil fled Spain soon after, and despite promises to the contrary, the victorious Christians first repressed the Muslim population of the Alpujarras, then eventually expelled and replaced them entirely with Christian settlers in the 16th century. But the Moors definitely left their mark on Las Alpujarras; you can still see it today in the terraced farming techniques used on the hills, and in the distinctive "Berber" style architecture and narrow cobblestone alleyways of the villages.

While there are countless numbers of charming hilltop villages here, the best tourist facilities, the easiest access to the hikes of the Sierra Nevada, and some of the most scenic views can be found in three white towns clinging to the sides of the **Poqueira gorge: Pampaneira, Bubión,** and **Capileira.** They're on the same bus route, about 2½ hours from Granada [see *need to know,* below]. Each town has a year-round population of between 300 to 600 people, and very few modern buildings, so you won't get lost in the towns themselves. The lowest of the villages is Pampaneira, which has an ATM (right where the bus stops) and an official tourist office with an outdoor travel company [see *need to know,* below]. From here you can see the higher villages perched on the cliffs above; it's a steep 25- to 30-minute walk to Bubión but the scenery is amazing: Go to the top of Pampaneira, where there's a little supermarket, and take a left to find the path up the hill. Bubión is the home of two rural tourism organizations that have English speakers [see *need to know,* below]. The lovely Capileira, another 20-minute walk along the paved road, is the second highest village in Spain (the highest is nearby **Trevelez**), and a well-recommended base for exploring the region, because of a couple of good hostels and restaurants, a helpful tourist kiosk (if it's open), and the closest access to hikes up to the peaks of the Sierra Nevada.

In late spring, summer, and early fall you can hike up to the top of the majestic Mulhacén, through the vertical-seeming **Barranco de Poqueira,** part of which is included in the **Parque Natural Sierra Nevada.** If you leave Capileira early enough in the morning you could make it a long, arduous day hike, up and back in about 12-13 hours. A saner option is to overnight at the **Refugio Poqueira** [see *crashing,* below], a shelter run by a mountaineering organization at the base of the mountain; it's about 4 hours from Capileira, and 3 hours from the top of the peak. If you want a shorter but still awesome hike, you can climb up to the base of the mountain near the refugio, and return in 7 hours or so. The weather is usually excellent in the summer, but storms can be ferocious in other seasons, due to the lack of any nearby mountains to soften the blow. Be aware of the weather forecast, and always be prepared for cold conditions in the mountains. While the hiking trails are well worn, despite what anyone tells you, they are not well-marked. They're designated by color and in some guides by number, which gets very confusing, and the wooden trail maps around the towns are weather-beaten and fairly useless. Maps available from the tourist offices are helpful, but not detailed or up-to-date (most of them don't show Refugio Poqueira, but show other refugios that are no longer used). Your best bet is to get *detailed* directions from the tourist offices or other hikers, or ask any local. Ask how to get to Refugio Poqueira or Mulhacén and listen carefully. The geography of the valleys, with lots of vistas and not too many trees, makes it fairly easy to get oriented, so you won't get Blair Witch lost, but you might take unnecessary detours. Any fine details we would give you here would probably just confuse you more...but basically: From Capileira, you want to go uphill out of town, follow the power lines to the power station (45 minutes-1 hour), then head left along the ravine, toward the big snowcapped peaks. (If you go to the right, you'll be on a longer, higher road to the refugio, which goes past the Access Control of the *Parque Natural Sierra Nevada,* where you might have the opportunity to meet a drunk park ranger.) But don't take our word for it—take as many maps as you can get your hands on and ask everyone you see. We can tell you that you'll go through green terraced farms, along freshwater streams, then above the tree-line to the ominous barren peaks; look for mountain goats, boar, hang gliders, and eagles. Toward the top, the landscape becomes bare and a little bit spooky, and you will feel small compared to the depth of the ravine and the height of the mountains. You'll also understand why so many mystics and visionaries reside in the Himalayas and other high places, because when the air starts to get thin and the sun is glaring off the snow, you'll start to see things, too.

bar scene

You certainly don't come to Las Alpujarras to party, but this is Spain so even little Capileira has a couple of interesting spots to chill out after a long day's journey, usually open in summer only. **Muy Buenas Pub** plays good rock music, Joan Jett to Lenny Kravitz, has a pool table upstairs, and beer for 250ptas. It's right off the highway, around the corner from **Hostal Paco Lopez** [see *crashing,* below]. Look for the happy face. Virtually next door is **La Jarilla,** the local *discoteca.* What is a dance club doing way up here, you might ask? Basically giving 14- to 16-year-old boys from the surrounding hills a chance to play foosball and avoid the local girls, and allowing a few Northern European tourists a place to drink late at night on summer weekends.

eats

Two hostels in Capileira have restaurants that specialize in local cuisine. Local cuisine means a lot of stews and game. If you don't mind eating cute furry things, **Hostal Paco Lopez** has a mouthwatering *conejo al horno* (baked rabbit) for 700ptas; **Pension Meson Poqueira** offers a similar menu [see *crashing*, below]. There are no exact hours for the restaurants. They're open when they want to open if anyone is around, and usually stay open until 10 or 10:30pm. Anything with pig is good up here, as they take the curing of their hams very seriously. For those who don't like to eat things that once had skeletons but prefer well-prepared vegetarian options, **Casa Ibero** *(1-3:30pm/8:30-10:30pm, closed Wed and Sun)* is located at the bottom of Capileira (just follow the signs) and has veggie cous-cous (875ptas) or veggie soufflé (975ptas). Keep in mind this is a small town so restaurants shut down earlier than in the big cities in Spain. Each town has a small supermarket where one can buy food for a big hike; they're generally open 9am-2pm and 5-8pm.

crashing

If you're interested in staying in the **Refugio Poqueira** *(Tel 95/834-33-49; 1,100ptas)*, at the base of Mulhacén, call ahead. In Capileira there are two hostels across from each other right in the center of town. **Pension Meson Poqueira** *(Dr. Castilla 6; Tel 95/876-30-48; 2,500ptas single, 4,000ptas double)* seems to be run by one friendly old man who manages to be everywhere at once, until you realize he has a twin brother. Across from the bus stop is the family-run **Hostal Paco Lopez** *(Carretera de la Sierra 5; Tel 95/876-30-11; 2,000ptas single, 3,500ptas double)*, which has clean, if somewhat dark, rooms with their own bathrooms.

need to know

Tourist Information In Pampaneira on the "main drag," **Centro de Visitantes** *(Plaza La Libertand; Tel 95/876-31-27; 10am-3pm daily)* is somewhat helpful and has lots of brochures and displays about the region. The staff speaks some English. In the center of Capileira is a little **information kiosk** run by friendly young local dudes, but the hours depend on who's around (generally 10am-2pm/4-6pm, closed Monday afternoons and Tuesdays).

Directions/Transportation From Granada's bus station, **Alsina Graells** *(Carretera de Jaén; Tel 95/818-54-80)* runs three daily buses to the villages of the Poqueira with stops in Pampaneira (2 hours), Bubión (2 hours 15 minutes), and Capileira (2 hours 25 minutes). Return trips do the same route the other way. If you want to get out of town early, a bus leaves Capileira at the insane hour of 6:20am; otherwise, the next one isn't until late afternoon. Get a schedule from tourist offices in Granada or Pampaneira.

Rental From the tourist office in Pampaneira, **Nevadensis** *(same info as Centro de Visitantes, above)* runs guided trips on horses (4,000ptas a day), on mountain bikes (4,500ptas a day), and by foot (2,300ptas a day). It also offers rock climbing (8,500ptas) and hang gliding (10,000ptas) excursions. Obviously, not all of these activities are available every day, so if you want to get in on the action, plan ahead and call or e-mail them before you arrive *(nevadensis@arraki.es)*. If you just show up, they'll most likely be out doing something adventurous.

If you're in Bubión, and you're really lost, and you don't speak any Spanish, stop by **Rustic Blue** *(Mirador de los Castanos L-9, Tel 95/876-33-81; 10am-2pm/5-8pm Mon-Fri, 11am-2pm Sat)* on the right side of the road right when you get to town. These English speakers set up rural tourism holidays, but they're friendly chaps who can point you in the right direction and answer questions about the region.

ronda

If you're tired of the overdeveloped Costa del Sol, make like an outlaw and head for the hills, where you'll find the postcard-perfect town of Ronda perched atop the awesome **El Tajo gorge.** The barren cliffs, hidden ravines, and caves of the surrounding **Serranía de Ronda mountains** were once a remote outpost for *bandoloeros* (bandits) and smugglers on the wrong side of the law. Today, however, you'll find that Ronda draws a gentler crowd of camera-toting tourists on the run from their day jobs. They come to gape at the gorge, and no matter how jaded you are you can't help but be impressed by the stunning scene of whitewashed houses almost absurdly stuck on sheer cliffs, and the impossibly green hills and grazing sheep in the valleys below. And if you're looking to ditch the crowds or that annoying "traveling companion" who's been following you since Madrid, you can strap on your backpack filled with contraband and ride, drive, hike, or climb around the surrounding hill towns or natural parks. While there are certainly plenty of spots to enjoy the immensity of the scenery, there's no university in Ronda, and therefore it lacks the party-like-a-flamenco-star nightlife or modern cultural offerings of much of Spain. It's more a place to catch a sobering breath of mountain air in between benders.

Geography has defined Ronda's history. It was one of the last frontiers of Muslim occupation, and didn't fall to the Christians until 1284, due to its obvious natural defenses. But advancements in modern transportation spelled the end of Ronda's isolation, and this town in the center of Andalucía is now easily accessible from the Costa del Sol (1 hour), Sevilla (3 hours), and Granada (3 hours). Whichever way you come there's spectacular scenery, and when you arrive in town you'll feel like you've traveled back in time a few centuries. A sense of timelessness, even sorrow, hovers over the ancient gorge and the river that runs through it.

The majestic **El Tajo,** 500 feet deep and 300 feet wide, literally splits the town in two. On the northern side lies the new town, with most of the hotels, restaurants, what little nightlife there is; it's where you'll arrive by bus, train, or via the main highway. The other side of the gorge, connected by picturesque bridges, holds the old Muslim quarter, **La Ciudad.** To orient yourself head straight for **Plaza de España,** the main square in the new town, which sits right on the edge of the gorge. You can cross into the old town via the spectacular bridge **Puente Nuevo,**

ronda

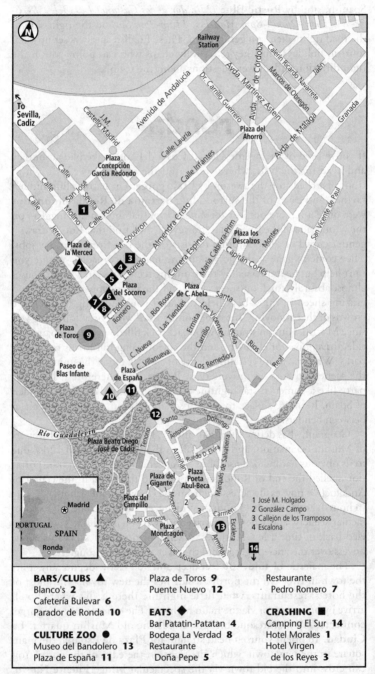

1 José M. Holgado
2 González Campo
3 Callejón de los Tramposos
4 Escalona

BARS/CLUBS ▲
Blanco's **2**
Cafetería Bulevar **6**
Parador de Ronda **10**

CULTURE ZOO ●
Museo del Bandolero **13**
Plaza de España **11**

Plaza de Toros **9**
Puente Nuevo **12**

EATS ◆
Bar Patatin-Patatan **4**
Bodega La Verdad **8**
Restaurante
  Doña Pepe **5**

Restaurante
  Pedro Romero **7**

CRASHING ■
Camping El Sur **14**
Hotel Morales **1**
Hotel Virgen
  de los Reyes **3**

which crosses the El Tajo at its highest point. Across Puente Nuevo, the winding streets and whitewashed houses of La Ciudad invite exploring during the day; and no matter where you walk, you seem to end up back at the gorge. The eastern edge of La Ciudad contains the 13th-century Arab baths, as well as the two older bridges, **Puente Arabe** and **Puente Viejo,** which both offer more great views of the gorge. In the center of the old town stand mankind's creative feats: the **Minarete de San Sebastián**, a 14th-century Muslim tower, and the eclectic church **Santa María la Mayor,** a mixture of Muslim, Gothic, and Baroque architecture. East of the old town is **Plaza Maria Auxiliadora** (also called **Plaza del Campillo**); from here a path that is the starting point for an excellent hike [see *by foot,* below] leads down the side of the cliffs. The most popular and view-laden stroll in town is from Plaza de España in the

by foot: do the gorge

While tourists come by the busload to view Ronda's gorge, not many of them bother to make the beautiful walk down into the valley below, because it's difficult to descend the hill when you have a video camera in one hand and an ice cream cone in the other. For those less encumbered, it's a relatively easy hike, however, and offers the best views of El Tajo, the Puente Nuevo Bridge, and the surrounding Manzanilla tree farms. At Plaza Maria Auxiliadora (also called Plaza del Campillo) in the old city, a stone pathway winds down the hillside and drops you into verdant green hills overflowing with wild flowers in spring. If you head right (east) across the bottom of the ridge toward the center of the gorge, there are a couple of spectacular lookout points. One of the dirt paths along the ridge leads to an old abandoned house, overgrown with weeds and sort of spooky, but offering an amazing view of the magnificent arches of the Puente Nuevo and all the little people looking down from Plaza de España. Continue back down the hill to the bottom of the valley, with views of the gorge and the western side of the cliff faces. Unfortunately, it's illegal to actually hike into the center of the gorge, and you won't find a clear path anyway. Continue north, across the river on a dirt path, and keep going through the picturesque farm country; the road will eventually slope up and lead to the highway just northwest of town, about a 15-minute walk back to the center. You can also try to scramble up the hill to the Hotel Reina Victoria, but there's no well-marked path. The whole route can be done in 2 hours or less, but you'll want to take more time to enjoy the sites and the peace and quiet.

new city all the way around the western lip of the gorge. Start by walking on the footpath around the hotel Parador de Ronda. Continue past the hotel and you'll see the Plaza de Toros on your right, the oldest and one of the most storied bullfighting arenas in Spain. Just past that is the leafy park **Alemeda del Tajo.** Here everyone from old men with funny hats to young kids with dreadlocks seeks refuge in the shade and enjoys the views of the rolling farmed hills in the distance. You can keep going on the little walkway **Paseo de los Ingleses** all the way to the end of the storied Hotel Reina Victoria. Another important plaza in the new town, a block up from the Plaza de Toros, is **Plaza del Socorro,** where you'll find scores of restaurants with outdoor seating, and tapas bars on the side streets. You'll also be surprised to see local kids playing games of soccer on the crowded concrete square. But keep in mind it might be the only place in town where a stray boot of the ball won't send it rolling into the eternity of El Tajo.

bar scene

While Ronda must have rocked in the past, today it's dead at 11:30pm on weekdays. Your best bet is to start at one of the tapas bars near Plaza del Socorro [see *eats,* below], which draw a youthful crowd, and find out if anything's happening.

If you need to keep drinking after that, go to the end of the little alley on Plaza del Socorro beneath the blue neon flashing sign that says **Cafetería Bulevar** *(Plaza del Socorro s/n; 8pm-2am).* Ronda is a small town and this place has that small-town American bar feel. There's a pool table, often surrounded by an international crowd, as well as video games, a slot machine, and a friendly bartender. If that isn't Midwestern enough for you, check out the nut vending machine and order a grilled ham and cheese on white bread to soak up the beer.

A more modern hipster bar claims the spot next to the Hotel Royal. Funky decor, a funky CD collection—James Brown to US3—and beautiful bartenders make the suave little **Blanco's** *(Virgen de la Paz 42; No phone; 9pm-2am Mon-Sat)* seem bigger and grander than it is. You can get bar service at the outside tables across the street next to Alemeda del Tajo. It's very quiet in the off-season, but it makes its money on weekend summer nights, when a well-heeled crowd packs in for cocktails (600ptas) and beer (200ptas).

The best place to grab a drink during the day is the **Parador de Ronda** *(Plaza de España; Tel 95/287-75-00; 11am-5pm daily),* which has the most epic location in town: right on the edge of the gorge off Plaza de España. You probably can't afford to stay here, but you can stomach a coffee or beer at the cafe on the back side of the hotel. Be aware that it closes at 5 in the evening.

CULTURE ZOO

Puente Nuevo bridge: Almost as awesome as the El Tajo gorge itself is this architectural wonder, which crosses the gorge at its highest point.

literary ronda

Ronda's tragic beauty has cast its spell not only on bandits and bullfighters, but on artists and writers as well. Something about the haunting quality of the gorge, the confrontation with eternity, the ominous undertone of the river coming up from below, inspires creativity. The poet Rainer Maria Rilke summered in a room at the Hotel Reina Victoria, and wrote *The Spanish Trilogy* here. There is a statue of Rilke in the gardens of the hotel, with an inscription: "the river in the gorge reflects the ragged lights of the cliff top (and therefore me)/of me and all this, only to give a home/señor for me and my regret." Hemingway came to Ronda frequently, for the bullfights of course, and in *Death in the Afternoon* he called Ronda the perfect place "if you ever go to Spain on a honeymoon or if you ever bolt with anyone." The great actor and filmmaker Orson Welles was another frequent visitor; he also came for the bulls (and, presumably, to eat). Ronda so entranced him that he asked to be buried here when he died. His ashes lie in a well on the property of his friend, the famous bullfighter Antonío Ordóñez (no, you can't go and visit them).

The soaring Roman-influenced stone arches are a brilliant example of man overcoming nature while remaining in harmony with it. The view down into the depths of the gorge from Plaza de España produces a sense of vertigo, not only from the height but from the weight of history. Local legend has it that the architect, Martín de Adehuela, was attempting to engrave the completion date, 1793, on the side of the bridge when he fell to his death. Hemingway fans might recall another chilling gorge tale from his Spanish Civil war classic, *For Whom the Bell Tolls,* when the fascists of a small town were beaten and thrown over the edge of a cliff; a scenario that reputedly is based on actual events at the Plaza de España. In the 19th century, Ronda's most famous son, the great bullfighter Pedro Romero found his wife in bed with another man, stabbed him, then grabbed her and carried her through the streets before dropping her into the gorge. Stories in Ronda tend to be as big as the gorge itself and, in true Spanish fashion, combine a deep understanding of tragedy as well as beauty.

Plaza de Toros (*Virgen de la Paz s/n; Tel 95/287-41-32; 10am-8pm daily June-Sept, 10am-6pm Oct-May; 300ptas):* Another tragic art is that of the *corrida,* and Ronda is renowned as the birthplace of modern bullfighting, which dates to the 18th century. Aficionados should definitely check out the ring here, built in 1785—the oldest major ring in Spain. You can walk around the orange dirt floor of the atmospheric old arena and imagine what it would be like to hear the roar of the crowd, feel the glare of the sun, and see a snarling piece of enraged beef charging at you. Admission also includes a visit to the **Museo Táurino,** a crowded museum primarily dedicated to the legendary Romero family of Ronda, who are credited with inventing the rules of engagement for modern bullfighting in the 18th and 19th centuries. The patriarch of the family, Francisco, had the bright idea of using a cape to attract the bull and the killing sword to finish it off. A few bullfights are still held in the arena, mostly during the Goyesque Corrida in early September when matadors fight—in 19th-century costumes—in honor of Pedro Romero, who was immortalized by Goya in a series of paintings.

Museo del Bandolero *(Calle Armiñán 65; Tel 95/287-77-85; 10am-8pm daily, 10:15am-6pm winter; 350ptas):* If you've ever killed a man just to watch him die, you'll love this outlaw museum. It's a shrine to the bandits and smugglers who once roamed and/or terrorized the surrounding countryside, and the stories and songs that made them folk heroes, much like the outlaws of the old West. There are life-size figures, newspaper accounts, clothes, and weapons of the most famous of these bad-ass dudes, some of whom were chivalrous Robin Hood figures, and some of whom were just sick puppies. A small percentage of the information is translated into English. Piped-in moody folk music accompanies the exhibits and sets the outlaw tone as well as any Johnny Cash song.

EATS

For your hiking sustenance, try **masKom supermarket** *(Molino 36; 9am-9pm Mon-Sat),* a block or two up from the park Alameda de Tajo.

The best places for cheap tapas and youthful atmosphere are just off Plaza del Socorro. Half a block east of the Plaza, the lively **Bar Patatin-Patatan** *(Lorenzo Borrego Gómez 7; No phone; 12:30pm-midnight daily)* is almost always hopping at night. Locals and young foreigners congregate on stools or the comfy booths in back to drink beer and scarf the house specialty, *papas fritas,* a mound of home fries with a variety of dipping sauces. Tapas are 250-300ptas.

If you're searching for the truth, look no further than a side street on the other side of the plaza, at **Bodega La Verdad** *(Pedro Romero 5; No phone; 12:30pm-midnight).* Okay, so you might not find the truth here, but you will find wicked meat and roasted veggies on kebab sticks—whole meals unto themselves—for only 350ptas. Beer is 150ptas in this old-fashioned-looking, boisterous bar attached to the Hotel Hermanos Macias.

Plaza del Socorro itself is filled with outdoor tables catering to an international crowd drinking sangria. Many of these places serve similar menus at similar prices, so much so that you might wonder if there's just a central kitchen in the back where all the restaurants get their food. **Restaurante Doña Pepe** *(Plaza del Socorro 10; Tel 95/28-72-47-77,*

12-3:30pm/5pm-midnight daily) is the most popular, so they must be doing something right. For around 1,500ptas you can get a *menu* with leg of lamb, a member of the partridge family, or other little flying things. Vegetarians have some options as well, such as the omnipresent gazpacho.

Restaurante Pedro Romero *(Virgen de la Paz 18; Tel 95/287-11-10; 12:30-4pm/8-11pm daily; 1,200-2,000ptas)* is not only a restaurant but a bullfighting art museum named after the local legend and one of the most famous matadors of all time. Pedro killed over 5,000 bulls in his career, and the chefs here have probably cooked up at least that many lambs, rabbits, quails, and other mountain food to the aged crowd that flocks here.

crashing

Sleeping in Ronda can be more expensive than you might be used to. Backpackers are certainly welcome, but the tourist facilities here are built with deeper pockets in mind.

Camping El Sur *(Carretera Algeciras KM. 1.5; Tel 95/287-59-39)*, 2km (1.24 miles) southwest of town, offers one cheap option. Getting here is a scenic (depending on the size of your pack) 30-minute walk: Go through the old city and down the hill to the Algeciras highway and continue for 1.5 kilometers (.93 miles). The camp has a restaurant, swimming pool, ping-pong table, and mountain bike rental in a pristine setting.

Hotel Morales *(Sevilla 51; Tel 95/287-15-38; 3,500ptas single, 6,000ptas double high season)* used to be a hostel, but before you complain about the name change and the consequent rise in prices, realize that this is not just an ordinary hotel, but an information supercenter. They call themselves the "friendly hotel" and they mean it; the talkative owner will give you not only a room, but information about sights, hikes around the region, and the only reasonably priced laundry service (1,000ptas) in town. It's located in the center of town, and the rooms are clean and comfortable with their own bathrooms.

Another well-run, functional hotel in the center of town is **Hotel Virgen de los Reyes** *(Lorenzo Borrego Gómez 13; Tel 95/287-11-40; 3,500ptas single, 6,000ptas double)*, with clean rooms, TVs, and in-room bathrooms.

If you got the dough, you gotta go...to **Parador de Ronda** *(Plaza de España s/n; Tel 95/287-75-00; 15,000ptas double)*, the government-run parador that has the most prime location imaginable, right off Plaza España on the edge of the gorge. All the rooms have spectacular views and unnecessary but enjoyable modern comforts such as mini bar, TV, and access to the swimming pool.

need to know

Currency Exchange The best place to find an **ATM** is on **Calle Virgen de la Paz** off of Plaza de España.

Tourist Information Right on Plaza de España is the **tourist information office** *(Plaza de España 1; Tel 95/287-12-72; 9am-2pm/4-7pm*

Mon-Fri, 10am-3pm Sat, Sun). They haven't used the slogan "Ronda is gorge-ous!" but we think they should.

Health and Emergency Help me, Ronda...*061* medical emergency. Ambulance: *Tel 95/387-17-73.* Police station: Plaza Duquesa de Parcent, or dial *092.*

Trains and Buses The train and bus stations are located on the north-western side of the new town. **Estación de Autobuses** *(Plaza Concepción de Garcia Redondo 2; Tel 95/287-26-57).* For trains on the Algeciras/Bobadilla line: **Renfe** *(Avendida de Andalucía; Tel 95/287-16-73).*

Bike/Moped Rental Jesus Rosada *(Tel 95/287-02-21; 10am-2pm/5-8:30pm Mon-Fri, 10am-2pm Sat)* has two locations in the new town, one at the bus station *(Cte Salvador Carrasco L1)* and one that's more central, *(Plaza del Ahorro 1).* They'll rent you well-maintained modern bikes for 1,500ptas per day, 2,500ptas for two days.

Laundry Hotel Morales *(Sevilla 51; Tel 95/287-15-38)* will wash your duds clean for 1,000ptas per load.

Postal The **Correos** *(Calle Virgen de La Paz 18-20)* is across the street from the Plaza de Toros.

sierra nevada (pradollano)

This stunning mountain range southeast of Granada contains Spain's highest peak, **Mulhacén** (3478 meters [11,410 feet]) and its most happening ski resort, **Solynieve (Estación de Esquí Sierra Nevada)** at **Pradollano.** Only 100 kilometers (62 miles) from the Mediterranean Sea, these barren, almost ominous peaks rise seemingly out of nowhere and remain covered with snow year-round. The 1996 World Alpine Ski Championships brought improved roads and facilities, and the skiers have followed, making this formerly quiet resort a mini winter boom town.

Solynieve is the southernmost ski spot in continental Europe and its name literally means "sun and snow." They promise the white stuff from December to April, sometimes later, and sunshiny days 70 percent of the time. In the spring you're likely to see bikinis and shorts as well as more traditional ski/snowboard gear. This raises the question: How good can the skiing be? Better than you would expect, due to the high altitude of the mountain, **Pico del Veleta** (3,396 meters [11,141 feet]), although hardcore downhillers will remind you that "it's not the Alps." The sun can make the slopes icy in the mornings and slushy in the afternoons, but it also means warmer temperatures, which means more comfortable conditions, which means a lot of skiers. There are 19 lifts, including two gondolas, and four on-slope restaurants (with full bar!), but despite the modern infrastructure, it can still get crazy packed and hectic, especially on weekends. But remember, this is Spain, so everyone enjoys themselves, and takes the art of *apres-ski* as seriously as ski.

North American skiers will be surprised at the complete lack of trees up here, and you may feel as if you're skiing on a giant lunar landscape. These wide-open runs with no obstacles are good for beginners, and anyone who doesn't want to pull a Bono. While most of the 34 *pistes* (runs) are for intermediate skiers, there are five "black" runs that will challenge the most radical dudes/dudettes, as well as nearby opportunities for extreme skiing. Pico del Veleta was the first Spanish mountain to allow snowboarding and it's recently added a skate park with a half-pipe for the pierced, shredding crowd. Unlike the orderly lift-lines you might be used to, anarchy reigns here, and people will crowd into the lift areas like they're piling into the Madrid Metro. You might get your skis or board stepped on, or get an inadvertent pole to the shin, but this is Spain, so *no pasa nada,* it's no big deal.

The ski season lasts from late November until May, and snow-making machines will compensate here if mother nature isn't cooperating. There is no shortage of places to rent equipment, sleep, eat, and party in Pradollono [see *need to know,* below]. A gondola, Borreguilles, connects the main skiing area to the town, though at the end of the day you can ski all the way back into town. Other winter activities are available, such as cross-country skiing, dog sledding, ice skating (in **Plaza de Sevilla**), and the rarefied and challenging sport of inner-tubing.

You won't think "quaint Alpine village" when you see Pradollano, nor will the super chic vibe of Aspen come to mind, but you will enjoy this modern, relaxed town. Like all ski resorts, it draws a mixed international crowd of families, young hotties, and ski bums. Unlike most ski towns, the bars are open until ridiculous hours of the morning; you may not think of discos and skiing as going together but somehow they do here. For a more traditional sit-by-the-fire ski lodge atmosphere on the mountain, try **Crescendo** *(bottom of River and Madril ski runs; No phone; 11am-1am).* This multi-leveled *apres-ski* hangout is famous for its combinations of hot liquids (coffee or hot chocolate) and brandy. Later at night, check out the psychedelic **Sticky Fingers,** with its giant murals of Miles Davis and Jimi Hendrix, and then party with the young people who can stay up all night and still ski the next day at **La Chimenea** *(Edificio Primavera 2)* or **El Golpe** *(Edificio Atlas, below Hotel Kenia).* If you can't find these places, just ask around—you're in a very small village. Getting to Pradollano is fairly easy, as it's a 30-minute drive from Granada, and there's daily bus service between here and there [see *need to know,* below]. You can easily return to Granada in the evening for cheaper lodging and free tapas ([ee *Granada* chapter].

If you come in the summer, it's much quieter but still beautiful up here, and there are great opportunities for hiking and mountain biking in the **Parque Natural Sierra Nevada.** In 2000, the World Mountain Bike Championships were held here and you can see why. The road from

Pradollano to the top of Pico del Veleta is the highest road in Europe, so you'll be gasping for breath if you're using pedal power, but the views are amazing and coming back down (partially through the ski runs) is a blast. You can also hike to the top of Pico de Veleta in about 4 hours from the ski resort, and it's another 4 hours to the top of Mulhacén. Cars aren't allowed up here, but if you're on foot or bike, you can spend the night in a *refugio* (mountain shelter) and even continue down the south slope of the Sierra Nevadas to the stunning valleys of Las Alpujarras (see *Las Alpujarras* chapter for details). For more info on the national park, stop by the visitor's center, **Centro de Visitantes El Dornajo** (*Carretera de Sierra Nevada Km 23; Tel 95/834-06-25; 9:30am-2:30pm/4:30-7:30pm daily*), on the highway up from Granada, 10 kilometers (6.2 miles) before the ski resort; the tourist office in Granada (see *Granada*); or the tourist office in Pradollano (see *need to know*, below).

need to know

Contact Information You can reach the **Estación de Esquí** at *95/824-91-11*, and get reports on ski conditions at *95/814-91-19*.

Hours The **Estación de Esquí** is open from 9:30am to 4:30pm daily, plus two extra hours on weekends for night skiing.

Costs Lift tickets are 3,650ptas.

Directions/Transportation The slopes are a 30-minute drive from the city of Granada, on the modern three-lane highway, A-395. Buses from Granada are run by **Bonal** (*Tel 95/827-31-00*) and leave Granada from Paseo Del Violón, just over the Rio Genil via the Puente de la Virgen bridge. Buses leave every weekday morning at 9am, returning at 5pm, with more frequent service during ski season. Tickets can be bought at the departure point from **Bar Ventorillo** (*425ptas one way, 800ptas return*).

Rental The following all offer full equipment rental as well as the possibility of lessons. Expect to pay between 2,200-2,500ptas for a full-day rental. Lessons start at 3,500ptas for one-on-one instruction but can be much cheaper if your round up a group of fellow ski/snowboard virgins. For basic skiing needs and English-language instructors, try **Escuela Internacional de Esquí** (*Plaza de Andalucía, Edificio Enebro 18.196; Tel 95/848-01-42*) in front of the ice skating rink. For snow boarding: **Surfin Snowboard** (*Plaza Pradollano; Tel 95/848-01-25*). For a truly old-school skiing experience try **Telemark** (*Plaza de Andalucia, Edificio Salvia 15; Tel 95/848-11-53*).

Crashing Accommodations can be pricey and difficult to come by during the height of the ski season, so book ahead. The best deal is at the official youth hostel, **Albergue Juvenil Sierra Nevada** (*Estación de Pradollano; Tel 95/848-03-05; 1,500ptas, 2,000ptas 26 and over*). This place can become a total scene at the peak of winter, when skiers and snowboarders from all over Europe play "Quien es Mas Macho?" It also offers ski storage and equipment rental. For a ski package at one of the fancier digs, call the resort's central booking (*Tel 95/824-91-11*).

Tarifa

The mellow old town of Tarifa sits on the southernmost tip of Spain, right across from Morocco, on the narrowest part of the **Strait of Gibraltar,** also known as *la maquina de viento,* 'The Wind Machine'; and you better believe that thing is cranking 365 days a year. The constant strong winds are the first thing you notice here. They make the green hills of the Costa de Luz shimmer like waves and sea foam on the horizon, and make walking two blocks a strenuous exercise, but they don't seem to bother anyone. In fact, many come to Tarifa specifically for the winds; those would be the windsurfers (you can't miss them—windburned and hauling tons of equipment), who have made Tarifa the European Mecca of their sport.

The constant gusts can make lying on the pristine white beaches here a painful experience—you'll get sand in crevices you didn't know existed—but they also work like a cultural filter. The fierce winds and rugged coastline draw the hardy (windsurfers, adventure enthusiasts, bird watchers, mountain bikers, campers, Moroccan-bound backpackers), and filter out the weak (concrete high-rise dwellers, package tourists, soccer hooligans, fast-food restaurants). The wind also makes everyone equal—you're all going to have bad hair days every day—so you can drop your international man/woman of mystery act and just be natural. Smiling at strangers is appropriate here. Even during the March-October high season, when Spanish and European vacationers turn the ancient streets of the old quarter into an international sporting community with a full-blown nightlife, the town retains a laid-back charm that other places only dream of.

Tarifa's bemused seen-it-all attitude is well-earned. The Romans, the Vandals, the Visigoths—these sound like heavy metal bands, but they're actually among the civilizations that have passed through here over the years, though little trace of them is left. The Muslim Tarif ibn Malik led a raid here in 710A.D., endowing the town with its name and opening the doors for Muslim conquerors who gave the old quarter its characteristic tangle of cobblestoned streets. The Christians took control at the end of the 13th century, withstanding many sieges at the Castillo de Guzmán El Bueno, the fortress that still stands on the edge of the old town today. Guzmán was called El Bueno, because during one such invasion, the Moors grabbed his son and threatened to execute him if Guzmán didn't surrender the castle. Guzmán threw the kidnappers his own dagger, saying he would choose "honor without a son, to a son with dishonor." They slit his son's throat, leaving him his honor. Not exactly textbook parenting skills, but Guzmán earned his place in history.

The most recent invaders have been the windsurfers, many from Northern Europe who come here for the ride of their life, and many who stay to set up hotels, bars, and surf shops. Though they are somewhat of a strange breed—not quite surfers, not quite sailors—they are generally

tarifa

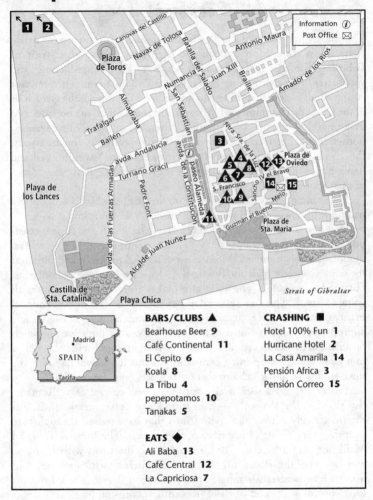

Information ⓘ
Post Office ✉

Plaza de Toros

Canovas del Castillo
Navas de Tolosa
Batalla del Salado
Numancia
San Sebastián
Juan XIII
Braille
Antonio Maura
Amador de los Ríos

Almadraba
Trafalgar
Bailén
avda. Andalucía
Turriano Gracil
Padre Font
avda. de las Fuerzas Armadas
avda. de la Constitución
paseo Alameda
Alcalde Juan Núñez

Ntra-Sra. de la Luz
Sancho IV el Bravo
Melo
Guzmán el Bueno

Playa de los Lances

3

4 **12** **13** Plaza de Oviedo
5 **8**
6 **7**
S. Francisco
14 **15**
10 **9**
11
Plaza de Sta. Maria

Castilla de Sta. Catalina
Playa Chica

Strait of Gibraltar

SPAIN
Madrid
Tarifa

BARS/CLUBS ▲
Bearhouse Beer **9**
Café Continental **11**
El Cepito **6**
Koala **8**
La Tribu **4**
pepepotamos **10**
Tanakas **5**

EATS ◆
Ali Baba **13**
Café Central **12**
La Capriciosa **7**

CRASHING ■
Hotel 100% Fun **1**
Hurricane Hotel **2**
La Casa Amarilla **14**
Pensión Africa **3**
Pensión Correo **15**

very chill, friendly, and respectful of their environment. There are plenty of Spanish who come to vacation here, too, so you won't be entirely surrounded by Germanic languages. Like most warm places, Tarifa does of course get a few yahoos out on the piss in big packs (to protect the weaker ones we guess) but we wouldn't want to mention which country they tend to come from because we wouldn't want to offend anyone, now would we, mate?

Even if you're not into windsurfing or drinking, the **Costa de la Luz** offers plenty of outdoor activities, and guides who'll rent you the stuff or even take you there [see *great outdoors,* below]. And with the recent introduction of more reliable daily ferry service to Tangiers, Morocco, you can skip the uninviting port of Algeciras altogether [see *need to know*, below]. So just let the breeze take you where it may, because in Tarifa you don't have any other choice.

There are no trains to Tarifa (probably the wind again), which may bother you Eurorail nuts, but is actually another bonus because it keeps the area from being mobbed. Whichever direction you come from, the ride will take you through verdant hills, and on a clear day you'll be treated to spectacular views of the green hills of Africa looming across the water. If you take a bus you'll arrive at the Comes bus station, which is really just a little office with a place for buses to pull over on the main thoroughfare **Batalla del Saludo.** Head down this street for two blocks, toward the walls of the old city, and you'll come to the **Puerta de Jerez,** the only remnant of the wall still standing from Muslim times. Enter through here into the top of the old quarter and you'll feel like you've entered a time warp. Savor the view of cobblestoned streets and white-

five things to talk to a local about

1. **Wind:** Instead of just saying, "goddamn, it's windy as hell out there," try distinguishing between the *Levante* (easterly, from the Mediterranean) and the *Poniente* (westerly, from the Atlantic).

2. **Windsurfing:** The best spots; the best sails; the best boards; the best conditions; slalom or waves; the flysurfing experience; the best windsurfers. Any of these topics will prompt a long lecture or, if you're lucky, a heated argument.

3. **The onslaught of windsurfers** in the last 15 years has definitely transformed Tarifa, but has it been for good or evil? Throw out the question to a local. It's interesting to note that before Tarifa became the "Windsurf Capital" of Europe, it was famous for having one of the highest suicide rates in Europe. Chew on that one.

4. **Wind farms:** Outside of Tarifa stretch miles of windmills creating environmentally friendly energy. Spain, along with the Netherlands, is at the forefront of harnessing wind as a viable source of energy for the future, while the superpowered United States is stuck in the nuclear era and showing no signs of changing. Discuss.

5. **For a more cultured exchange,** try discussing the symbolism of Cervantes's windmills in *Don Quixote,* or of Bob Seger's classic rock ballad "Against the Wind."

washed houses stacked below you, the glimpses of Africa in the distance, and, if it's daytime, the extreme quiet (everyone is out at the beach). As you walk down **Nuestra Señora de La Luz** (usually just called **Calle de La Luz**) or any of the ancient streets that head down the hill, you'll begin to notice strange incongruities, like bars with English names, Internet services, windsurf shops among the scrunched buildings. At the bottom of the hill you can't fail to see the "main drag" of the old quarter, which just means there are shops on both sides of the street, **Calle Sancho IV El Bravo.** Even if you don't see a street sign you'll know you're here by the crowd hanging out at the tables outside **Café Central** [see *eats*, below]. This cafe is the essential day and night meeting spot for foreigners, and it's got good food and strong coffee as well. Nearby is the Iglesia de San Mateo, a 15th-century church that they never really got around to finishing.

If you take Sancho IV El Bravo the other way, you'll soon hit the bottom of the old town (it doesn't take long) and the fortress Castillo de Guzmán El Bueno. Part of the castle walls that extend east become the **Miradar del Estrecho,** a great lookout point that offers the best views of Africa you're going to get unless you're in the water. West of the castle takes you beyond the walls of the old town and onto **Paseo Alemeda,** a tree-lined walkway, at the top of which is the Tourist Office. If you go west from the bottom of Paseo Alemeda, around the walls of the old quarter, you'll find the Estación Marítima, where you can get to the ferry to Tangiers, Morocco [see *need to know,* below]. Southwest of the old quarter is the small isthmus leading out to the **Punta de Tarifa,** which is controlled by the Spanish military and is the absolute most southern point of Continental Europe and therefore one of the windier spots in the world. As you're being blown out to sea try to catch a glimpse of the pretty and somewhat sheltered city beach, **Playa Chica,** to your left. To the right stretches the 10-kilometer-long (6.2 miles) beach, **Playa de los Lances.** You'll find some of the best windsurfing here, as well as campgrounds, hotels, and windsurf rental. To get to these facilities you'll have to go back to the old quarter or **Calle Batallo de Saludo** and try to get a ride. There are always plenty of friendly windsurfers who will be glad to give you a lift; you can meet them at Café Central, or any of the number of windsurf shops around town, especially on Batallo de Saludo.

bar, club and Live music scene

During the high season from March until October the old quarter has a lively bar scene; revelers fill the crooked streets, hopping from bar to bar. The old town is compact, so keep moving—another cool spot lies just around the next corner. Things definitely quiet down during the off season, but there's still some action, especially on the weekends. Most of the bars, along with everything else here, keep flexible hours, meaning they open and close when they feel like it, or depending on the crowd and wind conditions.

The Dutch-owned **Café Continental** *(Paseo de la Alemeda s/n; Noon-midnight Sun-Thu, noon-2am Fri, Sat)*, on the edge of the old town, is one of the few places that has live music in Tarifa, and it always has a lively international crowd tipping back a few. Try to snag one of the chairs beneath the palm trees on the plaza. And plan to call home from here; the public phone is inside, which means you won't get blown away by the wind mid-sentence.

You'll only find a place like **Koala** *(Calle de la Luz 5; Tel 95/668-50-03; 11am-2pm/6pm till they decide to close)* in Tarifa. This funky, colorful boutique sells artfully made hippy items like candles, clothes, drums, and jewelry. It also has a tiny little bar, and computers with Internet access (800ptas per hour). To complete the picture, there's a juicer here, too; we highly recommend a screwdriver with fresh-squeezed orange juice to start your night. You get your vitamins at the same time you're killing your brain cells. Talk to the friendly, beautiful couple that owns the place, or just stare at the lava lamps.

Windsurfers take note: **La Tribu** *(Calle de la Luz 7)* is for you. You won't find anyone but *guiris* (foreigners) watching windsurfing videos in the cool dark, wood-paneled room. But if you want to find out the latest wind conditions, argue about the relative merits of a 3.5 sail versus a 6.5 sail, or if you just have a fetish for athletic blond men who practice odd sports, this is the place.

Despite an English name, Irish draft beer (Guinness, 500ptas), German bottled beer (Heineken, 200ptas), and Europop music, **Bearhouse Beer** *(Sancho IV El Bravo 27; 7pm-2am)* draws a mixed-aged crowd of foreigners and Spanish vacationers, including tons of young kids who hang out on the tavern's back terrace on weekend nights. Many of them head across the alley to dance at **pepepotamos** *(Carniceria 4)*. There's some debate over what the name of this bar means, but the best guess is that the original owner of the place was named Pepe and was somewhat girthy in stature, sort of like the large African animal, *el hipopótamo*. This place has a big dance floor and no cover, so it gets packed with bouncy, sweaty Spanish folk and a few foreigners on weekend nights. Not much room to move, but great atmosphere.

El Cepito *(Plaza San Hiscio s/n)* also attracts *Españoles,* but an older, more eclectic type than pepepotamos. The candlelit interior feels like a wine bar that the Red Baron might have strolled into after his plane went down during World War I. They might play James Brown here, they might play flamenco, but they'll keep you guessing.

On the same plaza is the big *discoteca* **Tanakas** *(Plaza San Hiscio; Midnight-6am Fri, Sat)*. It's open every weekend of the year, and you'll know when it's open because there will be three or four bouncers outside, including two in full police uniform, though their main job seems to be opening the door and smiling at you as you enter. The 800ptas cover will earn you a cheesy light show, somewhat decent dance music, and a lot of new friends. At 4am, when most of windsurfers have gone home to rest up, the Spanish will be dancing their asses off on the stairs, on the stage, and in the bathroom.

The great outdoors

"Windsurf is King" in Tarifa as you'll undoubtedly be told, thanks to the challenging winds and—if you're not too busy hanging on for dear life—the amazing views you'll catch of the green hills of Africa. The most popular spots are along the Playa de los Lances, all the way from Tarifa to Punto Polama 10 kilometers away (6.2 miles). The windsurfers who flock here, many world class, will tell you that if the wind isn't blowing one day, it's bound to blow the next. If you've got the skills and the equipment head straight for the beach; you can't miss the sails flapping off the coast at places such as Hurricane and Casa de Porro. The winds can be tough on beginners, but there are plenty of places willing to rent equipment and give you lessons and watch you flail around for a few hours. If you really get the windsurf bug, the places listed below can also give you week-long lessons, by the end of which you'll be riding like a semipro.

Rent boards at **Club Mistral Windsurf School** *(Hurricane Hotel; Tel 95/668-49-19)* for 4,000ptas for 2 hours, 7,000ptas for a full day, and around 28,000ptas for a week. You can also rent a mountain bike or take a guided horse ride along the beach.

100% Fun Factory *(100% Fun Hotel; Tel 95/668-52-77; www.100x100@tnet.es)* is a board shop and factory that rents, sells, and repairs windsurf and *flysurf* equipment. Flysurfing is a relatively new sport, where you surf behind a long kite-like parachute thing. Radical.

A two-hour lesson at **Spinout Fanatic Center** *(Casa de Porro, C.N. 340 Km75; Tel 95/668-08-44; www.tarifaspinout.com; Mar-Oct only)* is about 6,600ptas, or rent a board for a day for 7,000ptas. This place also occasionally organizes windsurf trips to Morocco.

If windsurfing ain't your thing, a panoply of other outdoor action-adventures will get your blood pumping, many of them offered by **Aky-Oaky** *(Batalla del Salado 37; Tel 95/662-71-87; www.akyoaky.com; 10am-2pm/5:30-9:30pm)*. The friendly dudes here will tell you that if you haven't been to see them, you haven't been to Tarifa, and they might be right. They can tell you the best places to hike or ride your mountain bike, and rent you the bikes to do it: 3,000ptas per day for bikes with suspension or 2,000ptas per day if you're just cruising to the beach. They also lead mountain bike trips to stunning waterfalls for 7,500ptas, or, for 8,500ptas, will take you rock-climbing or canyoning, where you put on wetsuits and helmets and hike up a river into a gorge. And to add insult to injury, they're open year-round *and* they all speak English, or at least they'll all try, so go see them, Akyoaky?

If you're more interested in smaller doses of adrenaline, you'll be happy to learn that Tarifa ranks as one of the world's great bird-watching sites. You can see majestic, soaring birds such as eagles and vultures, especially during the fall migration when they rest in Tarifa and wait for the right wind to make it across to Africa, their winter home. Spy these beautiful birds from the excellent lookout point Mirador Del Estrecho, 7 kilometers (4.3 miles) west of Tarifa, or at **Los Alcornocales Natural Park** [see *within 30 minutes,* below]. Migrating whales also attract a lot of attention here. For day-long whale-watching trips, contact the environmental group The Foundation for Information and Research of Marine Mammals **(firmm)** *(Pedro Cortés 3; Tel 95/662-70-08; 4,500ptas)* in the center of town, or **Whale Watch España** *(Edificio Parque Feria, Callao 6; Tel 95/6627-013),* which meets at Café Continental.

eats

Everyone ends up at **Café Central** *(Sancho IV El Bravo 8; No phone; 9am-2am)* at some time, so you might as well go now. The outside tables here are the essential meeting point for *extrañeros* for breakfast, lunch, dinner, and drinks. This also might be the best place in Spain to nurse a hangover (if it's not too windy)—strong coffee, huge omelettes (400ptas), tables in the breezy sunshine, beautiful people, Bob Marley playing on the stereo. What more could you want? A little hair of the dog that bit you? They've got booze, too, including a juice cocktail called *contra la resaca* (the hangover cure).

   Been in Spain a while? Tired of eating pig meat and potatoes? Want something cheap, fresh, healthy, slightly exotic, and tasty? Well that's why God (whichever one you believe in) made **Ali Baba** *(Sancho IV El Bravo 8; No phone; 1:30-4pm/7pm-1am)* and put it right in the center of town next to Café Central. This little takeout joint has falafel sandwiches for 350ptas and kebab sandwiches for 400ptas, which can be eaten messily on the tall outside tables. Remember to thank your local deity. There are a few pizza places in town, but **La Capriciosa** *(San Francisco 5; Tel 95.668-50-40)* draws the youngest, most vibrant crowd. It's tucked back on a little street in the center, with booths in a cave-like room and tasty pies for 500-800ptas.

crashing

Tarifa has plenty of reasonably priced accommodations; your best bets are the hostels in the old quarter, or camping along the highway N-340, west of town.

   A sweet find at the top of the old quarter is the recently opened **Pensión Africa** *(María Antonia Toledo 12; Tel 95/668-02-20; 2,000-3,000ptas single; 3,500-5,000ptas double, depending on season).* It gets its name from its rooftop terrace, which has great views of Africa and the other rooftops of the old quarter, and is one of the best spots in town for kicking back. A tiled floor keeps the whole place cool, and the clean rooms have comfortable beds and understated tropical decor. There's also storage for your windsurfing equipment or bikes, and the place is run by a funky, warm, international couple, Miguel and Eva.

   At the bottom of the old quarter is the aging but effective **Pensión Correo** *(Coronel Moscardó 9; Tel 95/668-02-03; 2,000ptas single, 3,000ptas double, high season).* There are a lot of different rooming options, depending on how many people you have and the time of year, most all with shared bathrooms, in a slightly claustrophobic but well-run house just down from Café Central.

If you have wheels or can score a ride or taxi (800-1,000ptas), camping spots abound on the road between Tarifa and Punto Paloma, along or near Playa de los Lances. The bigger ones are like small villages with swimming pools, restaurants, bars, and washers/dryers. The campsites generally charge the same prices, about 2,500ptas for two people, a tent, and a car, or 2,000ptas if you're on foot.

About 6 kilometers (3.7 miles) out of Tarifa is the extremely popular **Camping Tarifa** (C.N.340, Km 78; Tel 95/668-47-78). Surrounded by a forest of pine trees, filled with windsurfers and families in the high-season, this mega-camp site has an ideal location: just 50 meters (164 feet) from the beach. Eight kilometers (almost 5 miles) out of town is the smaller **Torre de la Peña** (C.N.340, Km 76; Tel 95/668-49-03). Set in the hills across from the beach, it has fewer amenities but also fewer people and is more mellow. Another site with all the bells and whistles—and room for over 1,000 people if necessary—lies further west at Punto Paloma, **Camping Paloma** (C.N. 340, Km 74; Tel 95/668-42-03).

Windsurf fanatics who want to stay near the beach in more comfortable surroundings will want to check out **Hotel 100%Fun** (C.N. 340, Km76; Tel 95/668-00-13; 5,900ptas single, 7,900ptas double, 2,000ptas more July, Aug) and the even more comfortable **Hurricane Hotel** (C.N. 340, Km 76; Tel 95/668-03-29; 16,000-19,000ptas double, July-Sept; 13,000-16,000ptas double in low season). Both of these places have their own swimming pools, windsurfing schools, board rental, and board shops on Playa de los Lances [see outdoor sports, above].

For homier surroundings in the middle of the old town, try the apartments at pretty **La Casa Amarilla** (Sancho IV El Bravo 9; Tel 95/668-19-93; 6,000ptas double, 8,000ptas triple, 10,000ptas quadruple in high-season). It means "the yellow house," and it's right across from Café Central, so you should be able to find it fairly easily. The rooms have little kitchens, and extra beds can be added for 2,000ptas each. To reserve, you will have to pay 20 percent of your bill in advance with a credit card.

WITHIN 30 MINUTES

Do you want to see some Great Tits? You can find them, as well as Long-Tailed Tits, Bee-Eaters, Dartford Warblers, Little Bustards, Royal Owls, buzzards, and other birds, of course, at **Parque Natural Los Alcornales.** This park, with extensive Mediterranean woodlands, especially cork oak trees (alcornales), stretches northwest of Tarifa for 75 kilometers (46.5 miles). Its most notable features, along with its birds, otters, and game, are the deep valleys of subtropical vegetation, remnants of prehistoric Iberia. There are no eye-popping sites here, just rolling, rambling woods, and you'll need a car to really explore the park. Coming from Tarifa, go east for 12 kilometers on C.N. 340 to get to **Huerta Grande Visitors Center** (Tel 95/667-91-61) for more information. There is no camping in the interior of the park.

need to know

Currency Exchange To see firsthand the effect of wind erosion, check out the **ATMs** on **Calle Sanco IV El Bravo** or **Calle de la Luz.** These machines are so rusty you'll be amazed money comes out of them, but it does (if you have any).

Tourist Information At the top of Paseo de la Alemeda, and very friendly and mellow because this is Tarifa, is the **Oficina de Turismo** *(Paseo de la Alemeda s/n; Tel 95/668-09-93; 10:30am-2pm/5-7pm, closed Sat).*

Buses Transporres General Comes *(Batalla de Saludo s/n; Tel 95/668-40-38).* The little office, located 2 blocks north of the old quarter, is only open 9-11am and 1-3pm, but you can always check the schedule for the Cadiz/Algeciras line, which runs hourly, and just pay on the bus. Buses to Algeciras arrive and leave on the same side of the street as the office, while buses to Cadiz are across the street.

Boats Backpackers or daytrippers on their way to Morocco have long been searching for an alternative to the blight that is Algeciras, but until recently Tarifa's ferry service to Tangiers was spotty. The opening of year-round daily service to Tangiers should change all that. In the port behind the old quarter is **Southern Ferries, S.A.** *(Recinto Portuario s/n; Tel 95/662-70-44; 3,000ptas per person, 9,300-12,000 per car depending on size).* There are now scheduled daily departures at 9am to Tangiers (45 minutes), and a return trip at 3pm. They also run departures from Tarifa at 1:30pm and 6:30pm, and returns at 9am and 6:30pm "depending on the demand," which means don't absolutely count on it unless it's the middle of summer. Due to the less-than-reliable history of ferries from Tarifa, we strongly suggest you call ahead to be sure this service is still running at these times.

Postal Oficina de Correos *(Coronel Moscardó; Tel 95/668-42-37)* is right in the middle of the old quarter.

planning your trip

In this chapter, you'll find everything you need to plan your trip, from a sketch of Spain's various regions to tips on when to go and how to get the best airfare.

The regions in brief

Known as much for its tranquil sun-drenched days as its wild, up-till-sunrise nights, Spain faces the Atlantic Ocean and the Bay of Biscay to the north and the Mediterranean Sea to the south and east. Portugal borders on the west, with the Pyrenees separating Spain from France and the rest of Europe. The southern coastline is only a few sea miles from the north coast of Africa. It's difficult to generalize about Spain because it is composed of so many regions—50 provinces in all—each with its own geography, history, and culture.

MADRID & ENVIRONS Set on a high, arid plateau near the geographic center of Iberia, **Madrid** was created by royal decree in the 1600s, long after the much older kingdoms of León, Navarra, Aragón, and Catalunya, and long after the final Moor was ousted by Catholic armies. Since Madrid's birth, all roads within Spain have radiated outward from its precincts, and as the country's most important airline and railway hub, it's likely to be your point of arrival (although many international flights and European trains now arrive in Barcelona as well).

Despite the city's increasingly unpleasant urban sprawl, its paralyzing traffic jams, and its skyrocketing prices, Madrid remains one of Europe's great cities. Take in the Prado, the Thyssen-Bornemisza Museum, and perhaps the Royal Palace. Walk through historic neighborhoods around the Plaza Mayor (but beware of muggers). Devote time to one of the city's greatest pastimes: a round of tapas tasting.

Plan on at least 2 days to explore the city and another 3 for trips to the attractions beyond the capital. Worthy excursions include a view of the Roman aqueduct at **Segovia** and tours through such monuments as **El Escorial.**

EXTREMADURA & CASTILLA LA MANCHA South and west of Madrid, far from the mainstream of urbanized Spain, fascinating Extremadura lives in a time warp where hints of the Middle Ages and ancient Rome crop up unexpectedly beside sun-baked highways. Many of the conquistadors who pillaged native civilizations in the New World came from this hard, granite land.

Perhaps as important as a visit to Madrid is a day trip to the imperial city of **Toledo,** which brims with monuments and paintings by El Greco and is home to one of Spain's greatest cathedrals. After a day or two here, you'll be prepared for the hot, arid landscapes and smoking diesel trucks carrying heavy loads through this western corridor between Madrid and Lisbon. You can see a lot in about 2 days, stopping off at such sites as **Guadalupe,** whose Mudéjar monastery revolves around the medieval cult of the Dark (or Black) Virgin, and **Trujillo,** where many of the monuments were built with gold sent home by native sons like Pizarro, Peru's conqueror. **Cáceres** is a beautiful, fortified city with one foot planted firmly in the Middle Ages, while Zafra displays greater evidence of the Moorish occupation than anywhere in Spain outside of Andalucía.

Heading south and back east from this part of Extremadura, you will see the land change again as you travel through the heart of New Castile and approach the Sierra Morena mountain range, at the doorstep of Andalucía.

OLD CASTILE & LEÓN The proud kingdoms of Castile and León in north-central Iberia are part of the core from which modern Spain developed. Some of their greatest cathedrals and monuments were erected when each was staunchly independent. But León's annexation by Queen Isabella of Castile in 1474 (five years after her politically advantageous but unhappy marriage to Ferdinand of Aragón) irrevocably linked the two regions.

Even Spaniards are sometimes confused about the terms *Old Castile* and *New Castile,* a modern linguistic and governmental concept that includes a territory much larger than the medieval entity known by Isabella and her subjects. Although it's easy to take a train to and from Madrid, we don't recommend you try to see these northern regions' highlights as day trips from Madrid; it's better to treat them as overnight destinations in their own right.

Highlights include **Burgos** (the ancient cradle of Castile), **Salamanca** (a medieval Castilian university town), and **León** (the capital on the northern plains of the district bearing its name and site of one of the most unusual cathedrals in Iberia).

GALICIA & THE CAMINO DE SANTIAGO A true Celtic outpost in northwestern Iberia, Galicia's landscape is often compared to rainy, windswept Ireland. Known for a spectacularly dramatic coastline, the region is wild and relatively underpopulated. If you've got wheels, spend at least 2 days here enjoying some of the most scenic drives in Iberia. Stop at historic and religious sites like **Santiago de Compostela;** trace the ancient Pilgrims' Route—**Camino de Santiago**—and appreciate its contribution to the spread of Romanesque art and architecture across Spain; or visit the ancient Roman outpost of Lugo. Perhaps the region's greatest city is **La Coruña,** the point of embarkation for Spain's tragic Armada, sunk by the English army on its way to invade Britain in the late 16th century.

ASTURIAS & CANTABRIA Positioned on Iberia's north-central coastline, these are the most verdant regions of Spain. In the Middle Ages pilgrims passed through here on their way to **Santiago de Compostela**— a legacy evident from the wealth of Romanesque churches and abbeys in the vicinity. Come for beaches that are rainier, but much less crowded, than those along Spain's southern coasts.

Enjoy such beach resorts as El Sardinero and Laredo, as well as the rugged beauty of **Los Picos de Europa,** a dramatic mountain range that is home to rich colonies of wildlife. Sites of interest include the Caves of Altamira (called "the Sistine Chapel of prehistoric art," although admission is strictly regulated), the pre-Romanesque town of **Oviedo,** and the architecturally important old quarter of Gijón. The region's largest city, **Santander,** lies amid a maze of peninsulas and estuaries favored by boaters. In summer it becomes a major beach resort, although San Sebastián is more fashionable.

PAIS VASCO (THE BASQUE COUNTRY) País Vasco is the native land of Europe's oldest traceable ethnic group, the Basques. The Basque people have been more heavily persecuted than any other group within Spain by Madrid regimes determined to shoehorn their unusual language and culture into that of mainstream Spain. The region of rolling peaks and fertile, sunny valleys hugs the Atlantic coast adjacent to the French border. It also boasts the best regional cuisine in Spain.

Unless you want to spend more time relaxing on the beach, allow 3 or 4 leisurely days for this unusual district. Visit **San Sebastián** (Donostia) for its international glamour and industrial **Bilbao** for the fantastic Frank Gehry–designed branch of the Guggenheim Museum.

NAVARRA Just east of the Pais Vasco lies Navarra. This strategic province, one of the four original Christian kingdoms in Iberia, shares a border, and numerous historical references, with France. One of France's

Renaissance kings, Henri IV "de Navarre," was linked to the province's royal family. Many Navarre customs, and some of its local dialect, reflect the influence of its passionately politicized neighbors, the Basques. Celtic pagans, Romans, Christians, and Arabs have all left architectural reminders of their presence. The province contains nine points where traffic is funneled into and out of Spain, so if you're driving or riding the train from, say, Paris to Madrid, chances are you'll get a fast overview of Navarra. The province's best-known destination is **Pamplona,** the district capital and annual host for the bull-running Fiesta de San Fermín.

ARAGÓN & THE PYRENEES Except for Aragón's association with Ferdinand, the unsavory, often unethical husband of Queen Isabella, few foreign visitors ever thought much about this northeastern quadrant of Iberia. A land of noteworthy Mudéjar architecture and high altitudes that guarantee cool midsummer temperatures, it's also one of the foremost bull-breeding regions of Spain. Foreign visitors also miss a good bet if they overlook getting out and about into the Pyrenees Mountains themselves. Along the border with France, these natural wonders may be experienced by camping or hiking the many trails to be found in the **Parque Nacional de Ordesa** or the nearby **Parque Naturel de Posets-Malada.**

CATALUNYA & THE COSTA BRAVA **Barcelona** is the heart of Catalunya. Its history is older than that of its rival, Madrid, and its streets are filled with Gothic and medieval buildings that Spain's relatively newer capital lacks. During the 1200s it rivaled the trading prowess of such cities as Genoa and Pisa, and it became the Spanish city that most resembled other great cities of Europe. Allow yourself at least 3 days to explore the city, with stops at the Picasso Museum, the Joan Miró foundation, the Gothic quarter, and, a crowning triumph of early *modernista* architecture, the Eixample District, where you'll find many of Antoni Gaudí's signature works. Make time for a stroll along Las Ramblas, one of the most delightful outdoor promenades in Spain.

Don't overlook Catalunya's other attractions, all within easy reach of Barcelona. A short drive to the south is **Sitges,** a stylish beach resort that caters to a diverse clientele ranging from freewheeling nudists and gay party crowds to fun-seeking families. Other destinations are **Tarragona,** one of ancient Rome's district capitals, and **Montserrat,** the "Serrated Mountain," site of one of Europe's best-preserved medieval monasteries.

To the north is the Costa Brava, Spain's other Riviera. A region with a deep sense of medieval history and a topography, that's rockier and more interesting than that of the Costa del Sol. The "Wild Coast" stretches from the resort of Blanes, just north of Barcelona, along 95 miles (153km) of dangerously winding cliff-top roads that bypass peninsulas and sheltered coves on their way to the French border. Despite hordes of Spanish and Northern European midsummer visitors, the Costa Brava resorts still manage to feel less congested and less spoiled than those along the Costa del Sol.

Sun worshippers usually head for the twin beachfront resorts of Lloret de Mar and Tossa de Mar. Travelers interested in the history of 20th-century painting go to **Figueres;** Salvador Dalí was born here in 1904, and a controversial and bizarre museum of his design is devoted exclusively to his surrealist works.

VALENCIA & THE BALEARIC ISLANDS Valencia, the third-largest city in Spain, is rarely visited by foreign tourists because of the heavy industry that surrounds its inner core. More alluring are destinations not far to the south, along the beaches of Costa Blanca. Unless you opt to skip Valencia completely, plan to see the city's cathedral, the exterior of its Palacio de la Generalidad, and as many of its three important museums as you can fit into a 1-day trip.

Valencia, along with Barcelona, should also be remembered as a good jumping off point for the Balearic Islands. "Discovered" by English Romantics in the early 19th century, and long known as a strategic naval outpost in the western Mediterranean, these islands are sunny, subtropical, mountainous, and more verdant than the Costa del Sol. **Palma,** the capital of the island of Majorca, and **Ibiza**—*especially* the superior Ibiza, with its legendary club scene—transform into hedonistic party towns every summer as travelers from around the world drop in to play. Expect an overflow of British and German visitors.

THE COSTA DEL SOL The Costa del Sol sprawls across the southernmost edge of Spain between Algeciras to the west—a few miles from the rocky heights of British-controlled Gibraltar—and Almería to the east. Think traffic jams, suntan oil, sun-bleached high-rises, and near-naked flesh. The beaches here are some of the best in Europe, but this can also be an overly crowded, crime-filled region.

Unless you travel by car or rail from Madrid, chances are you'll arrive by plane via **Málaga,** the district's most historic city. The coast's largest resort town is distinctive, Renaissance-era **Marbella,** the centerpiece of 17 miles of beaches. Today it's a chic hangout for the tanned and wealthy. **Nerja** is just one of the booming resorts that has kept its out-of-the-way, fishing-village feel. The most overcrowded and action-packed resort is **Torremolinos.** One modern development that has managed to remain distinctive is Puerto Banús, a neo-Moorish village curving around a sheltered marina where the wintering rich dock their yachts.

ANDALUCÍA In A.D. 711 Muslim armies swept into Iberia from strongholds in what is now Morocco. Since then, Spain's southernmost district has been enmeshed in the mores, art, and architecture of the Muslim world. During the 900s, *Andalucía* blossomed into a sophisticated society—advanced in philosophy, mathematics, and trading—that far surpassed a feudal Europe still trapped in the Dark Ages. Moorish domination ended completely in 1492, when Granada was captured by the armies of Isabella and Ferdinand, but even today the region offers echoes of this Muslim occupation. Andalucía is a dry district that isn't highly prosperous, despite such economically rejuvenating events as Sevilla's Expo.

The major cities of Andalucía deserve at least a week, with overnights in **Sevilla** (hometown of Carmen, Don Giovanni, and the barber); **Córdoba,** site of the Mezquita, one of history's most versatile religious edifices; and **Cádiz,** the seaport where thousands of ships embarked on their colonization of the New World. Perhaps greatest of all is **Granada,** a town of such impressive artistry that it inspired many of the works by the 20th-century romantic poet Federico García Lorca.

VISITOr InformaTION

The official website for the Spanish tourist office is **www.okspain.org.** See "Spain Online" following this chapter for tips on where to find lots of other help and information on the Internet.

In The United States For information before you go, contact the **Tourist Office of Spain** *(666 Fifth Ave., 35th Floor, New York, NY 10103; Tel 212/265-8822),* which can provide sightseeing information, calendars of events, train and ferry schedules, maps, and much, much more. Elsewhere in the United States, branches of the **Tourist Office of Spain** are located at 8383 Wilshire Blvd., Suite 956, Beverly Hills, CA 90211 *(Tel 323/658-7188);* 845 N. Michigan Ave., Suite 915 E., Chicago, IL 60611 *(Tel 312/642-1992);* and 1221 Brickell Ave., Suite 1850, Miami, FL 33131 *(Tel 305/358-1992).*

In Canada Contact the **Tourist Office of Spain** *(102 Bloor St. W., 34th Floor, Toronto, ON M5S 1M9; Tel 416/961-3131).*

In Great Britain Contact the **Spanish Tourist Office** *(22-23 Manchester Square, London WIM 5AP; Tel 020/74-86-80-77).*

enTry requiremenTS and cusToms

ENTRY REQUIREMENTS

Visas are not needed by U.S., Canadian, Irish, Australian, New Zealand, or British citizens for visits of less than 3 months. You do need a valid passport unless you're a citizen of another EU country (in which case you need only an identity card, although we always recommend you carry a passport anyway). Safeguard your passport in an inconspicuous, inaccessible place like a money belt. If you lose it, visit the nearest consulate of your native country as soon as possible for a replacement. Passport applications are downloadable from the Internet sites listed below.

U.S. CITIZENS If you're applying for a first-time passport, you need to do it in person at one of 13 passport offices throughout the U.S.; a federal, state, or probate court; or a major post office (though not all post offices accept applications; call the number below to find the ones that do). You need to present a certified birth certificate as proof of citizenship, and you better bring along your driver's license, state or military ID, and social security card as well. You also need two identical passport-sized photos (2 in. by 2 in.), taken at any corner photo shop (but not one of those cheapo strip photos from a photo-vending machine).

For those of you over 15, a passport is valid for 10 years and costs $60 ($45 plus a $15 handling fee); for those 15 and under, it's valid for 5 years and costs $40. If you're over 15 and have a valid passport that was issued within the past 12 years, you can renew it by mail and bypass the $15 handling fee. Make sure you allow plenty of time before your trip to apply; processing normally takes 3 weeks but can take longer during busy periods (especially spring). For general information, call the **National Passport Agency** *(Tel 202/647-0518)*. To find your regional passport office, call the **National Passport Information Center** *(Tel 900/225-5674; http://travel.state.gov)*.

CANADIAN CITIZENS You can pick up a passport application at one of 28 regional passport offices or most travel agencies. The passport is valid for 5 years and costs CAN$60. Kids under 16 may be included on a parent's passport but need their own to travel unaccompanied by a parent. Applications, which must be accompanied by two identical passport-sized photographs and proof of Canadian citizenship, are available at travel agencies throughout Canada or from the central **Passport Office, Department of Foreign Affairs and International Trade** *(Ottawa, Ont. K1A 0G3; Tel 800/567-6868; www.dfait-maeci.gc.ca/passport)*. Processing takes 5 to 10 days if you apply in person, or about 3 weeks by mail.

U.K. CITIZENS As a member of the European Union you need only an identity card, not a passport, to travel to other EU countries. But if you already have a passport, it's always best to carry it. To pick up an application for a regular 10-year passport (the Visitor's Passport has been abolished), visit your nearest passport office, major post office, or travel agency. You can also contact the **London Passport Office** *(Tel 017/12-71-30-00; www.open.gov.uk/ukpass/ukpass.htm)*. Passports are £21 for adults and £11 for children under 16.

IRISH CITIZENS You can apply for a 10-year passport (IR£45) at the **Passport Office** *(Setanta Centre, Molesworth Street; Tel 016/711-633; www.irlgov.ie/iveagh/foreignaffairs/services)*. Those under 18 must apply for a 3-year passport (IR£10). You can also apply at 1A South Mall, Cork *(Tel 021/272-525)* or over the counter at most main post offices.

AUSTRALIAN CITIZENS Apply at your local post office or passport office or search the government website *(www.dfat.gov.au/passports)*. Passports for adults are A$126, under 18 A$63.

NEW ZEALAND CITIZENS You can pick up a passport application at any travel agency or Link Centre. For more info, contact the **Passport Office** *(P.O. Box 805, Wellington; Tel 080/022-50-50)*. Passports for adults are NZ$80, under 16 NZ$40.

CUSTOMS

You can take into Spain most personal effects and the following items duty-free: 2 still cameras and 10 rolls of film per camera, tobacco for personal use, 1 liter each of liquor and wine, a Walkman or portable CD player, a tape recorder, a laptop, a bicycle, sports equipment, and fishing gear.

WHAT YOU CAN BRING HOME TO THE U.S. Returning U.S. citizens who have been away for 48 hours or more are allowed to bring back, once every 30 days, $400 worth of merchandise duty-free. You'll be charged a flat rate of 10 percent duty on the next $1,000 worth of purchases. Be sure to have your receipts handy. On gifts, the duty-free limit is $100. You cannot bring fresh foodstuffs into the United States; tinned foods, however, are allowed. For more information, contact the **U.S. Customs Service** *(1301 Constitution Ave., P.O. Box 7407, Washington, DC 20044; Tel 202/927-6724)* and request the free pamphlet *Know Before You Go*. It's also available on the web at *www.customs.ustreas.gov/travel/kbygo.htm.*

WHAT YOU CAN BRING HOME TO THE U.K. Citizens of the United Kingdom who are returning from a European Community (EC) country will go through a separate Customs Exit (called the "Blue Exit") especially for EC travelers. In essence, there is no limit on what you can bring back from an EC country, as long as the items are for personal use (this includes gifts) and you have already paid the necessary duty and tax. However, customs law sets out guidance levels. If you bring in more than these levels, you may be asked to prove that the goods are for your own use. Guidance levels on goods bought in the EC for your own use are 800 cigarettes, 200 cigars, 1 kilogram smoking tobacco, 10 liters of spirits, 90 liters of wine (of this, not more than 60 liters can be sparkling wine), and 110 liters of beer. For more information, contact **HM Customs & Excise** *(Passenger Enquiry Point, 2nd Floor Wayfarer House, Great South West Road, Feltham, Middlesex, TW14 8NP; Tel 020/89-10-37-44; from outside the U.K. Tel 440/20891-03744),* or consult the website at *www.open.gov.uk.*

WHAT YOU CAN BRING HOME TO CANADA For a clear summary of Canadian rules, write for the booklet *I Declare,* issued by **Revenue Canada,** 2265 St. Laurent Blvd., Ottawa K1G 4KE *(Tel 613/993-0534; www.ccra-adrc.gc.ca).* Canada allows its citizens a $750 exemption, and you're allowed to bring back duty-free 200 cigarettes, 2.2 pounds of tobacco, 1.5 liters of liquor, and 50 cigars. In addition, you're allowed to mail gifts to Canada from abroad at the rate of Can$60 a day, provided the gifts are unsolicited and don't contain alcohol or tobacco (write on the package "Unsolicited gift, under $60 value"). All valuables should be declared on the Y-38 form before departure from Canada, including serial numbers of valuables you already own, such as expensive foreign cameras. *Note:* The $750 exemption can be used only once a year and only after an absence of at least 7 days.

WHAT YOU CAN BRING HOME TO AUSTRALIA The duty-free allowance in Australia is A$400 or, for those under 18, A$200. Personal property mailed back from England should be marked "Australian goods returned" to avoid payment of duty. Upon returning to Australia, citizens can bring in 250 cigarettes or 250 grams of loose tobacco and 1,125 milliliters of alcohol. If you're returning with valuable goods you already own, such as foreign-made cameras, you should file form B263. A helpful brochure, available from Australian consulates or customs offices, is *Know Before You Go.* For more information, contact **Australian Customs Services** *(GPO Box 8, Sydney NSW 2001; Tel 029/213-20-00; www.dfat.gov.au).*

WHAT YOU CAN BRING HOME TO NEW ZEALAND The duty-free allowance for New Zealand is NZ$700. Citizens over 17 can bring in 200 cigarettes, 50 cigars, or 250 grams of tobacco (or a mixture of all three if their combined weight doesn't exceed 250 grams); plus 4.5 liters of wine and beer or 1.125 liters of liquor. New Zealand currency does not carry import or export restrictions. Fill out a certificate of export, listing the valuables you are taking out of the country; that way, you can bring them back without paying duty. Most questions are answered in a free pamphlet available at New Zealand consulates and customs offices: *New Zealand Customs Guide for Travellers, Notice no. 4.* For more information, contact **New Zealand Customs** *(50 Anzac Ave., P.O. Box 29, Auckland; Tel 093/596-655; www.customs.govt.nz).*

money honey

CURRENCY
The basic unit of Spanish currency is the peseta (abbreviated pta), currently worth about 6/10 of a cent in U.S. currency. Coins come in 1, 5, 25, 50, 100, 200, and 500 pesetas. Notes are issued in 500, 1,000, 5,000, and 10,000 pesetas.

All world currencies fluctuate, so you should be aware that the amounts appearing in this book are not exact. Currency conversions are presented only to give you a rough idea of the price you'll pay in U.S. dollars. There is no way to predict exactly what the rate of exchange will be when you visit Spain. Check the newspaper or ask at your bank for last-minute quotations.

Be advised that rates of exchange vary, depending on where you convert your money. In general, you'll get the best exchange rate by using your credit card or withdrawing cash from an ATM. Banks also offer competitive rates, but keep in mind that they charge a commission for cashing traveler's checks. You'll get the worst rates of exchange at your hotel, as well as at point-of-entry sites like an airport or train station.

The euro, the new single European currency, became the official currency of Spain and 10 other countries on January 1, 1999, but not in the form of cash. (There are still no euro banknotes or coins in circulation; payment in euros can be made only by check, credit card, or some other bank-related system.)

The Spanish peseta will remain the only currency in Spain for cash transactions until December 21, 2001, when more and more businesses will start posting their prices in euros alongside those in pesetas, which will continue to exist for a while longer. Over a maximum 6-month transition period, peseta banknotes will be withdrawn from circulation.

Although at this time very few, if any, Spanish hotel and restaurant bills are actually paid in euros, there will be an increasing emphasis on the new pan-European currency during the lifetime of this edition.

ATM NETWORKS
PLUS, Cirrus, and other networks connecting automated-teller machines operate in Spain. If your bankcard has been programmed with a PIN, it's likely you can use your card at ATMs abroad to withdraw money directly from your home bank account. Check with your bank to see if your PIN code must be reprogrammed for use in Spain. Before leaving, always determine the frequency limits for withdrawals and what fees, if any, your bank will assess. For **Cirrus** locations abroad, call Tel 800/424-7787; also, Cirrus ATM locations in selected cities are available on Master-Card's Internet site *(www.mastercard.com)*. For **PLUS** use abroad, contact your local bank or check Visa's page on the web *(www.visa.com)*.

TRAVELER'S CHECKS
Traveler's checks are something of an anachronism from the days before the ATM made cash accessible at any time. These days traveler's checks seem less necessary, but some people still prefer the security of knowing they can recover their money if it's stolen.

You can get traveler's checks at almost any bank. American Express offers denominations of $10, $20, $50, $100, $500, and $1,000. You'll pay a service charge ranging from 1-4 percent. You can also get American Express traveler's checks over the phone by calling 800/221-8472; by using this number, Amex gold and platinum cardholders are exempt from the 1 percent fee. AAA members can obtain checks without a fee at most AAA offices.

Visa offers traveler's checks at Citibank locations nationwide, as well as several other banks. The service charge ranges from 1.5-2 percent; checks come in denominations of $20, $50, $100, $500, and $1,000. **MasterCard** also offers traveler's checks. Call 800/223-99-20 for a location near you.

If you opt to carry traveler's checks, be sure to keep a record of their serial numbers, separately from the checks of course, so you're ensured a refund in an emergency.

CREDIT CARDS
Credit cards are invaluable when traveling. They are a safe way to carry money and provide a convenient record of all your expenses. You can also withdraw cash advances from your credit cards at any bank (but you'll start paying hefty interest on the advance the moment you get the cash, and you won't receive frequent-flyer miles on an airline credit card). At

most banks, you don't even need to go to a teller; you can get a cash advance at the ATM if you know your PIN.

Note, however, that at press time some credit card companies were discussing plans to increase fees for foreign currency transactions. Citibank, in particular, was considering adding a whopping 4 percent fee onto the 1-2 percent fee already charged by Visa or MasterCard. Ask your bank about fees before you go.

when to go

CLIMATE

Spring and fall are ideal times to visit nearly all of Spain, with the possible exception of the Atlantic coast, which experiences heavy rains in October and November. May and October are the best months, in terms of both weather and crowds.

In summer it's hot, hot, and hotter still, with the cities in Castile (Madrid) and Andalucía (Sevilla and Córdoba) heating up the most. Madrid has dry heat; the average temperature can hover around 84°F in July and 75° in September. Sevilla has the dubious reputation of being about the hottest part of Spain in July and August, often baking under average temperatures of 93°.

Barcelona, cooler in temperature, is often quite humid. Midsummer temperatures in Majorca often reach 91°. The overcrowded Costa Brava has temperatures around 81° in July and August. The Costa del Sol averages 77° in summer. The coolest spot in Spain is the Atlantic coast from San Sebastián to La Coruña, with temperatures in the 70s in July and August.

August remains the major vacation month in Europe. The traffic from France, the Netherlands, and Germany to Spain becomes a veritable migration, and low-cost hotels along the coastal areas are virtually impossible to find. To compound the problem, many restaurants and shops also decide it's time for a vacation, thereby limiting the visitors' selections for both dining and shopping.

In winter, the coast from Algeciras to Málaga is the most popular, with temperatures reaching a warm 60° to 63°. Madrid gets cold, as low as 34°. Majorca is warmer, usually in the 50s, but it often dips into the 40s. Some mountain resorts can experience extreme cold.

HOLIDAYS

Holidays include January 1 (New Year's Day), January 6 (Feast of the Epiphany), March 19 (Feast of St. Joseph), Good Friday, Easter Monday, May 1 (May Day), June 10 (Corpus Christi), June 29 (Feast of St. Peter and St. Paul), July 25 (Feast of St. James), August 15 (Feast of the Assumption), October 12 (Spain's National Day), November 1 (All Saints' Day), December 8 (Immaculate Conception), and December 25 (Christmas).

No matter how large or small, every city or town in Spain also celebrates its local saint's day. In Madrid it's May 15 (St. Isidro). You'll rarely know what the local holidays are in your next destination in Spain. Try to keep money on hand, because you may arrive in town only to find banks and stores closed. In some cases, intercity bus services are suspended on holidays.

spain calendar of events

The dates given below may not be precise. Sometimes the exact days are not announced until 6 weeks before the actual festival. Check with the National Tourist Office of Spain [see *Visitor Information, Entry Requirements & Customs,* above] if you're planning to attend a specific event. For more options, see the **festivals and events** sidebars throughout the book.

JANUARY

Granda Reconquest Festival, Granada. The whole city celebrates the Christians' victory over the Moors in 1492. The highest tower at the Alhambra is open to the public on January 2. For information, contact the **Tourist Office of Granada** *(Tel 958/226-688).* January 2.

Día de los Reyes (Three Kings Day), throughout Spain. Parades are held around the country on the eve of the Festival of the Epiphany. Various "kings" dispense candy to all the kids. January 6.

Día de San Antonio (St. Anthony's Day), La Puebla, Majorca. Bonfires, dancing, revelers dressed as devils, and other riotous events honor St. Anthony on the eve of his day. January 17.

FEBRUARY

ARCO (Madrid's International Contemporary Art Fair), Madrid. One of the biggest draws on Spain's cultural calendar, this exhibit showcases the best in contemporary art from Europe and America. At the Crystal Pavilion of the Casa de Campo, the exhibition draws galleries from throughout Europe, the Americas, Australia, and Asia, who bring with them the works of regional and internationally known artists. To buy tickets contact **El Corte Ingles** *(Tel 914/188-800)* or **Madrid Rock** *(Tel 915/472-423).* The cost is between 5,000ptas ($30) and 6,000ptas ($36). You can get schedules from the tourist office closer to the event. Dates vary, but usually mid-February.

Bocairente Festival of Christians and Moors, Bocairente (Valencia). Fireworks, colorful costumes, parades, and a reenactment of the struggle between Christians and Moors mark this exuberant festival. A stuffed effigy of Mohammed is blown to bits. *(Tel 962/905-062 for more information.)* February 4-7.

Carnavales de Cádiz, Cádiz. The oldest and best-attended carnival in Spain is a freewheeling event full of costumes, parades, strolling troubadours, and drum beating. *(Tel 956/211-313 for more information.)* Late February or early March.

Madrid Carnaval. The carnival kicks off with a big parade along the Paseo de la Castellana, culminating in a masked ball at the Círculo de Bellas Artes on the following night. Fancy-dress competitions last until February 28, when the festivities end with a tear-jerking "burial of a sardine" at the Fuente de los Pajaritos in the Casa de Campo. This is followed that evening by a concert in the Plaza Mayor. *(Tel 914/293-177 for more information.)* Dates vary.

MARCH

Fallas de Valencia, Valencia. Dating from the 1400s, this fiesta centers around the burning of papier-mâché effigies of winter demons. Burnings are preceded by bullfights, fireworks, and parades. *(Tel 963/510-417 for more information.)* March 13-19.

APRIL

Feria de Sevilla (Sevilla Fair). This is the most celebrated week of revelry in all of Spain, with all-night flamenco dancing, entertainment booths, bullfights, horseback riding, flower-decked coaches, and dancing in the streets. You'll need to reserve a hotel early for this one. For general information and exact festival dates, contact the **Sevilla Office of Tourism** *(Tel 954/221-404)*. April 30-May 7.

Semana Santa (Holy Week), Sevilla. Although many of the country's smaller towns stage similar celebrations (especially notable in Zamora), the festivities in Sevilla are by far the most elaborate. From Palm Sunday until Easter Sunday a series of processions with hooded penitents moves to the piercing wail of the *saeta,* a love song to the Virgin or Christ. *Pasos* (heavy floats) bear images of the Virgin or Christ. Again, make hotel reservations way in advance. Call the **Sevilla Office of Tourism** for details *(Tel 954/221-404)*. April 16-23.

Moros y Cristianos (Moors and Christians), Alcoy, near Alicante. During 3 days every April, the centuries-old battle between the Moors and the Christians is restaged with soldiers in period costumes. Naturally, the Christians who drove the Moors from Spain always win. The simulated fighting takes on almost a circuslike flair, and the costumes worn by the Moors are always absurd and anachronistic. *(Tel 965/200-000 for more information)*. April 23-25.

MAY

Festival de los Patios, Córdoba. At this famous fair residents decorate their patios with cascades of flowers. Visitors wander from patio to patio. *(Tel 957/471-235 for more information.)* May 4-16.

Romería del Rocío (Pilgrimage of the Virgin of the Dew), El Rocío (Huelva). The most famous pilgrimage in Andalucía attracts a million people. Fifty men carry the statue of the Virgin 9 miles to Almonte for consecration. May 14-24.

Fiesta de San Isidro, Madrid. Madrileños run wild with a 10-day celebration honoring their city's patron saint. Food fairs, Castilian folkloric events, street parades, parties, music, dances, bullfights, and other festivities mark the occasion. Make hotel reservations early. Expect crowds and traffic (and beware of pickpockets). For information, write to **Oficina Municipal de Información y Turismo,** Plaza Mayor 3, 28014 Madrid *(Tel 914/293-177)*. May 12-21.

Feria del Caballo (Horse Fair), Jerez de la Frontera. "Horses, wine, women, and song," according to the old Andalucían ditty, make this a stellar event at which some of the greatest horses in the world go on parade. *(Tel 956/331-150 for more information.)* May 14-21.

JUNE

Veranos de la Villa, Madrid. This program presents folkloric dancing, pop music, classical music, zarzuelas, and flamenco at various venues throughout the city. Open-air cinema is a feature in the Parque del Retiro. Ask at the tourist office for complete details (the program changes every summer). Sometimes admission is charged, but often these events are free. Mid-June until the end of August.

Corpus Christi, all over Spain. A major holiday on the Spanish calendar, this event is marked by big processions, especially in Toledo, Málaga, Sevilla, and Granada. June 6.

International Music and Dance Festival, Granada. This prestigious program of dance and music attracts international artists who perform at the Alhambra and other venues. It's a major event on the cultural calendar of Europe. Reserve well in advance. For a complete schedule and tickets, contact **El Festival Internacional de Música y Danza de Granada** *(Tel 958/221-844).* June 20-July 6.

Las Hogueras de San Juan (St. John's Bonfires), Alicante. Bonfires blaze through the night to honor the event, just as they did in Celtic and Roman times. The bonfire signals the launching of 5 days of gala celebrations with fireworks and parades. Business in Alicante comes to a standstill. *(Tel 965/200-000 for more information.)* June 20-24.

Verbena de Sant Joan, Barcelona. This traditional festival occupies all Catalans. Barcelona literally lights up—with fireworks and bonfires—and dances until dawn. The highlight of the festival is the fireworks show at Montjuïc. June 23-24.

JULY

La Rapa das Bestas (The Capture of the Beasts), San Lorenzo de Sabuceno, Galicia. Spain's greatest horse roundup attracts equestrian lovers from throughout Europe. Horses in the verdant hills of northwestern Spain are rounded up, branded, and medically checked before their release into the wild again. For more information, call 986/850-814. July 1-3.

Festival of St. James, Santiago de Compostela. Pomp and ceremony mark this annual pilgrimage to the tomb of St. James the Apostle in Galicia. Galician folklore shows, concerts, parades, and the swinging of the *botafumeiro* (a mammoth incense burner) mark the event. July 15-30.

San Sebastián Jazz Festival, San Sebastián. This festival brings together the jazz greats of the world at the pavilion of the Anoeta Sport Complex. Other programs take place alfresco at the Plaza de Trinidad in the old quarter. The **Office of the San Sebastian Jazz Festival** *(Tel 943/481-179)* can provide schedules and tickets. July 21-26.

Fiesta de San Fermín, Pamplona. Vividly described in Ernest Hemingway's novel *The Sun Also Rises,* the running of the bulls through the streets of Pamplona is the most popular celebration in Spain. It also includes wine tasting, fireworks, and, of course, bullfights. Reserve many months in advance. For more information, such as a list of accommodations, contact the **Office of Tourism,** Duque de Ahumada 3, 31002 Pamplona *(Tel 948/206-540).* July 7-14.

AUGUST

Santander International Festival of Music and Dance, Santander. The repertoire includes classical music, ballet, contemporary dance, chamber music, and recitals. Most performances are staged at the Plaza de la Porticada. For further information, contact **Festival Internacional de Santander** *(Tel 942/210-508)*. Throughout August.

Fiestas of Lavapiés and **La Paloma,** Madrid. These two fiestas begin with the Lavapiés on August 1 and continue through the hectic La Paloma celebration on August 15, the day of the Virgen de la Paloma. Thousands of people race through the narrow streets. Apartment dwellers hurl buckets of cold water onto the crowds below to cool them off. There are children's games, floats, music, flamenco, and zarzuelas, along with street fairs. *(Tel 914/293-177 for more information.)* August 1-15.

The Mystery Play of Elche. This sacred drama is reenacted in the 17th-century Basilica of Santa María in Elche (near Alicante). It represents the Assumption and the Crowning of the Virgin. For tickets, call the **Office of Tourism in Elch**e *(Tel 965/453-831)*. August 11-15.

Feria de Málaga (Málaga Fair). One of the longest summer fairs in southern Europe (generally lasting for 10 days), this celebration kicks off with fireworks displays and is highlighted by a parade of Arabian horses pulling brightly decorated carriages. Participants are dressed in colorful Andalucían garb. Plazas rattle with castanets and wine is dispensed by the gallon. *(Tel 952/213-445 for more information.)* August 11-20.

La Tomatina (Battle of the Tomatoes), Buñol (Valencia). This is one of the most photographed festivals in Spain, growing in popularity every year. Truckloads of tomatoes are shipped into Buñol, where they become vegetable missiles between warring towns and villages. Portable showers are brought in for the cleanup, followed by music for dancing and singing. Last Wednesday in August.

SEPTEMBER

Diada, Barcelona. This is the most significant festival in Catalunya. It celebrates the region's autonomy from the rest of Spain, following years of repression under the dictator Franco. Demonstrations and other flag-waving events take place. The *senyera,* the flag of Catalunya, is everywhere. Not your typical tourist fare, but interesting. September 11.

Fiestas de la Merced, Barcelona. This celebration honors Nostra Senyora de la Merced, the city's patron saint, known for her compassion toward animals. Beginning after dark, and after a mass in the Iglesia de la Merced, a procession of as many as 50 "animals" (humans dressed like tigers, lions, and horses) proceeds with lots of firecrackers and sparklers to the Cathedral of Santa Eulalia, then on to the Plaza de Sant Jaume, and eventually into Las Ramblas, Plaça de Catalunya, and the harborfront. *(Tel 934/784-704 for more information.)* September 24.

International Film Festival, San Sebastián. The premier film festival of Spain takes place in the Basque capital, often at the Victoria Eugenia Theater, a belle époque masterpiece. Retrospectives are often featured, and weeklong screenings are held. *(Tel 943/481-212 for more information.)* September 21-30.

OCTOBER

St. Teresa Week, Avila. Verbenas (carnivals), parades, singing, and dancing honor the patron saint of this walled city. Dates vary.

Autumn Festival, Madrid. Both Spanish and international artists participate in this cultural program, with a series of operatic, ballet, dance, music, and theatrical performances from Strasbourg to Tokyo. This event is a premier attraction, yet tickets are reasonable. Make hotel reservations early. For tickets, contact **Festival de Otoño,** Plaza de España 8, 28008 Madrid *(Tel 915/802- 575).* Late October-late November.

Grape Harvest Festival, Jerez de la Frontera. The major wine festival in Andalucía honors the famous sherry of Jerez, with 5 days of processions, flamenco dancing, bullfights, livestock on parade, and, of course, sherry drinking. *(Tel 956/333-11-50 for more information.)* Mid-October (dates vary).

NOVEMBER

All Saints' Day, all over Spain. This public holiday is reverently celebrated, as relatives and friends lay flowers on the graves of the dead. November 1.

DECEMBER

Día de los Santos Inocentes, all over Spain. This equivalent of April Fools' Day is an excuse for people to do loco things. December 28.

study abroad

Salminter, calle Toro 34-36, 37002 Salamanca *(Tel 923/211-808; Fax 923/260-263),* conducts courses in conversational Spanish, with optional courses in business Spanish, translation techniques, and Spanish culture. Classes contain no more than 10 persons. There are courses of 2 weeks, 1 month, and 3 months at seven progressive levels. The school can arrange housing with Spanish families or in furnished apartments shared with other students.

Another good source of information about courses in Spain is the **American Institute for Foreign Study (AIFS),** 102 Greenwich Ave., Greenwich, CT 06830 *(Tel 800/727-2437 or 203/399-5000).* This organization can set up transportation and arrange for summer courses, with bed and board included. It can help you arrange study programs at either the University of Salamanca, one of Europe's oldest academic centers, or the University of Granada.

The biggest organization dealing with higher education in Europe is the **Institute of International Education (IIE),** 809 United Nations Plaza, New York, NY 10017 *(Tel 212/883-8200; www.iie.org).* A few of its booklets are free, but for $44.95, plus $6 postage, you can purchase the more definitive *Vacation Study Abroad.* To order the book, call 800/445-0443.

One well-recommended clearinghouse for academic programs throughout the world is the **National Registration Center for Study**

Abroad (NRCSA), 823 N. 2nd St., P.O. Box 1393, Milwaukee, WI 53201 *(Tel 414/278-0631; www.nrcsa.com).* The organization maintains language-study programs throughout Europe, including about 10 cities throughout Spain. Most popular are the organization's programs in Sevilla, Salamanca, and Málaga, where language courses last between 4 and 6 hours a day. With lodgings in private homes included as part of the price and part of the experience, tuition begins at around $615 for an intensive 2-week language course. Courses accept participants ages 17-80.

A clearinghouse for information on at least nine different Spain-based language schools is **Lingua Service Worldwide,** 216 E. 45th St., 17th Floor, New York, NY 10017 *(Tel 800/394-5327 or 212/867-1225).* Maintaining information about learning programs in 10 languages in 17 countries outside the United States, it represents organizations devoted to the teaching of Spanish and culture in 11 cities in Spain, including one in the Canary Islands.

For more information about study abroad, contact the **Council on International Educational Exchange (CIEE),** 205 E. 42nd St., New York, NY 10017 *(Tel 800/226-8624 or 212/822-2700; www.council travel.com).*

health & insurance

STAYING HEALTHY

Spain should not pose any major health hazards. The rich cuisine—garlic, olive oil, and wine—may give some travelers mild diarrhea, so take along some antidiarrhea medicine, moderate your eating habits, and even though the water is generally safe, drink mineral water only. Fish and shellfish from the horrendously polluted Mediterranean should only be eaten cooked.

If you are traveling around Spain (particularly southern Spain) over the summer, limit your exposure to the sun, especially during the first few days of your trip and, thereafter, from 11am to 2pm. Use a sunscreen with a high protection factor and apply it liberally.

If you suffer from a chronic illness, consult your doctor before your departure. For conditions like epilepsy, diabetes, or heart problems, wear a **Medic Alert Identification Tag** *(Tel 800/825-3785; www. commed icalert.org),* which will immediately alert doctors to your condition and give them access to your records through Medic Alert's 24-hour hotline. Membership is $35, plus a $15 annual fee.

Pack prescription medications in your carry-on luggage. Carry written prescriptions in generic, not brand-name form, and dispense all prescription medications from their original labeled vials. Also bring along copies of your prescriptions in case you lose your pills or run out.

Contact the **International Association for Medical Assistance to Travelers (IAMAT)** *(Tel 716/754-4883 or 416/652-0137; www.sentex.net/-iamat).* This organization offers tips on travel and health concerns in the countries you'll be visiting and lists many local English-speaking doctors. In Canada, call 519/836-0102.

INSURANCE

There are three kinds of travel insurance: medical, lost luggage, and trip-cancellation coverage.

In most cases, your existing health plan will provide all the medical coverage you need. Be sure to carry your identification card. You should check to see whether you are fully covered when away from home. If you need hospital treatment, most health insurance plans and HMOs cover out-of-country hospital visits and procedures, at least to some extent. (HMOs are least likely to provide such coverage.) However, most make you pay the bills up front at the time of care, and you get a refund after you've returned and filed all the paperwork. Members of **Blue Cross/Blue Shield** can now use their cards at select hospitals in most major cities worldwide. *(Tel 800/810-BLUE or www.bluecares.com for a list of hospitals)*

If you, or your parents', plan won't cover you, look into the **Council on International Education Exchange (CIEE)** described in "Tips for Travelers with Special Needs" [see *Tips for Students,* below] can provide health insurance for students and non-students under 26. For other independent travel health-insurance providers and some resources that combine medical coverage with other travel-related options, see below.

For lost or stolen luggage, your (or, often, your parents') homeowner's or renter's insurance should provide coverage. The airlines are responsible for losses up to $2,500 on domestic flights if they lose your luggage (finally upped in early 2000 from the old 1984 limit of $1,250); if you plan to carry anything more valuable than that, keep it in your carry-on bag.

Trip-cancellation insurance is a good idea if you have paid a large portion of your vacation expenses up front, say by purchasing a charter flight or a tour. Trip-cancellation insurance should cost approximately 6-8 percent of the total value of your vacation. (Don't buy it from your tour operator, though—talk about putting all your eggs in one basket!)

If you do require additional insurance, try one of the companies in these listings. But don't pay for more than you need. If you need only trip-cancellation insurance, don't purchase coverage for lost or stolen property.

Comprehensive insurance programs, covering basically everything from trip cancellation and lost luggage to medical coverage abroad and accidental death, are offered by the following companies: **Access America** *(Tel 800/284-8300),* **Travel Guard International** *(Tel 800/826-1300),* and **Travelex Insurance Services** *(Tel 800/228-9792).* In the United Kingdom, there's **Columbus Travel Insurance** *(Tel 020/7375-00-11 in London; www.columbusdirect.co.uk).* Companies specializing in accident and medical care include **MEDEX International** *(Tel 888/MEDEX-00 or 410/453-6300; Fax 410/453-6301; www.medexassist.com)* and **Travel Assistance International** *(Worldwide Assistance Services; Tel 800/821-2828 or 202/828-5894; Fax 202/828-5896).*

Tips for travelers with special needs

TIPS FOR STUDENTS

The best resource for students is the **Council on International Educational Exchange,** or **CIEE,** 6 Hamilton Place, Boston, MA 02108. It can set you up with an ID card (see below), and its travel branch, **Council Travel Service** *(Tel 800/226-86-24; www.counciltravel.com),* is the biggest student travel agency operation in the world. It can get you discounts on plane tickets, railpasses, and the like. Ask for a list of CTS offices in major cities so you can keep the discounts flowing (and aid lines open) as you travel.

From CIEE you can obtain the student traveler's best friend: the $20 **International Student Identity Card (ISIC).** It's the only officially acceptable form of student identification, good for cut rates on railpasses, plane tickets, and other discounts. It also provides you with basic health and life insurance and a 24-hour help line. If you're no longer a student but are still under 26, you can get a GO 25 card from the same people, also for $20, which will get you the insurance and some of the discounts (but not student admission prices to museums).

In Canada, **Travel CUTS,** 200 Ronson St., Ste. 320, Toronto, ONT M9W 5Z9 *(Tel 800/667-2887 or 416/614-2887, or 020/75-28-61-13 in London; www.travelcuts.com),* offers similar services. **Usit Campus,** 52 Grosvenor Gardens, London SW1W 0AG *(Tel 020/77-30-34-02; www.usitcampus.co.uk),* opposite Victoria Station, is Britain's leading specialist in student and youth travel.

TIPS FOR WOMEN

WomanTraveler *(www.womantraveler.com)* is an excellent woman-authored site guide with listings of women-owned hotels, hostels, etc., plus safe places for women to stay.

There are also some good books out there for the girl on the go. The *Virago Women's Travel Guides* series is excellent but new, and it covers only three cities to date: London, San Francisco, and Amsterdam. *Safety and Security for Women Who Travel,* by Sheila Swan Laufer and Peter Laufer, is well worth picking up.

TIPS FOR GAYS & LESBIANS

In 1978, Spain legalized homosexuality among consenting adults. In April 1995, the parliament of Spain banned discrimination based on sexual orientation. Madrid and Barcelona are the major centers of gay life in Spain, and the most popular resorts for gay travelers are Sitges (south of Barcelona), Torremolinos, and Ibiza.

Besides the resources listed below, gay and lesbian travelers will want to check out our "Gay Scene" write-ups for each location throughout this book. Frommer's *Gay & Lesbian Europe,* packed with sightseeing tips, hotel and restaurant reviews, shopping, and lots of nightlife suggestions for Madrid, Barcelona, Sitges, and Ibiza, is a comprehensive book source.

The **International Gay & Lesbian Travel Association (IGLTA)** *(Tel 800/448-8550 or 954/776-2626; Fax 954/776-3303; www.iglta.org)* links travelers up with the appropriate gay-friendly service organization or tour specialist. With around 1,200 members, it offers quarterly newsletters, marketing mailings, and a membership directory that's updated quarterly. Membership often includes gay or lesbian businesses but is open to individuals for $150 yearly, plus a $100 administration fee for new members. Members are kept informed of gay and gay-friendly hoteliers, tour operators, and airline and cruise-line representatives. Contact the IGLTA for a list of its member agencies, who will be tied into IGLTA's information resources.

General gay and lesbian travel agencies include **Family Abroad** *(Tel 800/999-5500 or 212/459-1800; gay and lesbian)* and **Above and Beyond Tours** *(Tel 800/397-2681; mainly gay men).*

There are also two good, biannual English-language gay guidebooks, both focused on gay men but including information for lesbians as well. You can get the *Spartacus International Gay Guide* or *Odysseus* from most gay and lesbian book stores, or order them from Giovanni's Room *(Tel 215/923-2960)* or A Different Light Bookstore *(Tel 800/343-4002 or 212/989-4850)*. Both lesbians and gays might want to pick up a copy of *Gay Travel A to Z* ($16). The *Ferrari Guides* *(www.q-net.com)* is yet another very good series of gay and lesbian guidebooks.

Out and About, 8 W. 19th St. #401, New York, NY 10011 *(Tel 800/929-2268 or 212/645-6922)*, offers guidebooks and a monthly newsletter packed with good information on the global gay and lesbian scene. A year's subscription to the newsletter costs $49. ***Our World,*** 1104 N. Nova Rd., Suite 251, Daytona Beach, FL 32117 *(Tel 904/441-5367)*, is a slicker monthly magazine promoting and highlighting travel bargains and opportunities. Annual subscription rates are $35 in the United States, $45 outside the United States.

TIPS FOR TRAVELERS WITH DISABILITIES

Because of Spain's many hills and endless flights of stairs, visitors with disabilities may have difficulty getting around the country, but conditions are slowly improving. Newer hotels are more sensitive to the needs of those with disabilities, and the more expensive restaurants, in general, are wheelchair-accessible. (In Madrid, there's even a museum designed for the sightless and sight-impaired called the Museo Tiflológico.) However, since most places have limited, if any, facilities for people with disabilities, you might consider taking an organized tour specifically designed to accommodate travelers with disabilities.

There are more resources out there than ever before. *A World of Options,* a 658-page book of resources for travelers with disabilities, covers everything from biking trips to scuba outfitters. It costs $35 ($30 for members) and is available from Mobility International USA, P.O. Box 10767, Eugene, OR 97440 *(Tel 541/343-1284, voice and TDD; www.miusa.org).* Annual membership for Mobility International is $35, which includes its quarterly newsletter, *Over the Rainbow.*

The **Moss Rehab Hospital** *(Tel 215/456-9600)* has been providing friendly and helpful phone advice and referrals to travelers with disabilities for years through its Travel Information Service *(Tel 215/456-9603; www.mossresourcenet.org).*

You can join the **Society for the Advancement of Travel for the Handicapped (SATH),** 347 Fifth Ave. Suite 610, New York, NY 10016 *(Tel 212/447-7284; Fax 212/725-8253; www.sath.org),* for $45 annually ($30 for seniors and students), to gain access to its vast network of connections in the travel industry. It provides information sheets on travel destinations and referrals to tour operators that specialize in traveling with disabilities. It quarterly magazine, *Open World for Disability and Mature Travel,* is full of good information and resources. A year's subscription is $13 ($21 outside the U.S.).

Travelers with disabilities may also want to consider joining a tour that caters specifically to them. One of the best operators is **Flying Wheels Travel,** 143 West Bridge (P.O. Box 382), Owatonna, MN 55060 *(Tel 800/535-6790).* It offers various escorted tours and cruises, with an emphasis on sports, as well as private tours in minivans with lifts. Other reputable specialized tour operators include **Access Adventures** *(Tel 716/889-9096),* which offers sports-related vacations; **Accessible Journeys** *(Tel 800/TINGLES or 610/521-0339),* for slow walkers and wheelchair travelers; **The Guided Tour** *(Tel 215/782-1370);* and **Directions Unlimited** *(Tel 800/533-5343).*

Vision-impaired travelers should contact the **American Foundation for the Blind,** 11 Penn Plaza, Suite 300, New York, NY 10001 *(Tel 800/232-5463),* for information on traveling with guide dogs.

British travelers with disabilities can contact **RADAR (Royal Association for Disability and Rehabilitation),** Unit 12, City Forum, 250 City Rd., London EC1V 8AF *(Tel 020/72-50-32-22),* for useful annual holiday guides. *Holidays and Travel Abroad* costs £5, *Holidays in the British Isles* goes for £7, and *Long Haul Holidays and Travel* is £5. RADAR also provides holiday information packets on such subjects as sports and outdoor holidays, insurance, and financial arrangements for people with disabilities. Each of these fact sheets is available for £2. All publications can be mailed outside the United Kingdom for a nominal fee.

Another good British service is the **Holiday Care Service,** 2nd Floor Imperial Buildings, Victoria Road, Horley, Surrey RH6 7PZ *(Tel 012/93-77-45-35; Fax 012/93-78-46-47),* which advises on accessible accommodations. Annual membership costs £15 (U.K. residents) and £30 (abroad) and includes a newsletter and access to a free reservations network for hotels throughout Britain and, to a lesser degree, Europe and the rest of the world.

getting there by plane

FROM NORTH AMERICA

Flights from the U.S. east coast to Spain take 6 to 7 hours. The national carrier of Spain, **Iberia Airlines** *(Tel 800/772-4642; www.iberia.com)*, has more routes into and within Spain than any other airline. It offers daily nonstop service to Madrid from New York, Chicago, and Miami. In addition, Iberia has service to Madrid from Toronto (through Montréal) 2 and 3 times a week, depending on the season. Also available are attractive rates on fly-drive packages within Iberia and Europe; they can substantially reduce the cost of both the air ticket and the car rental.

A good money-saver to consider is Iberia's **EuroPass.** Available only to passengers who simultaneously arrange for transatlantic passage on Iberia and a minimum of two additional flights, it allows passage on any flight within Iberia's European or Mediterranean dominion for $250 for the first two flights and $125 for each additional flight. This is especially attractive for passengers wishing to combine trips to Spain with, for example, visits to such far-flung destinations as Cairo, Tel Aviv, Istanbul, Moscow, and Munich. For details, ask Iberia's phone representative. The EuroPass can be purchased as a part of an Iberian Air itinerary from your home country only.

Iberia's main Spain-based competitor is **Air Europa** *(Tel 888/238-7672)*, which offers nonstop service from New York's JFK Airport to Madrid, with continuing service to major cities within Spain. Fares are usually lower than Iberia's.

The latest Spanish airline in the market is **S**panair *(Tel 888/545-5757)*, which is the only airline to service the Washington, D.C., area. Spanair flies directly from Washington's Dulles Airport to Madrid 7 days a week, with services continuing on to many of the main cities in Spain.

American Airlines *(Tel 800/433-7300; www.aa.com)* offers daily nonstop service to Madrid from its massive hub in Miami.

Delta *(Tel 800/241-4141; www.delta-air.com)* runs daily nonstop service from Atlanta (its worldwide hub) and New York (JFK) to both Madrid and Barcelona. Delta's Dream Vacation department offers independent fly-drive packages, land packages, and escorted bus tours.

United Airlines *(Tel 800/538-2929; www.ual.com)* does not fly into Spain directly. It does, however, offer airfares from the United States to Spain with United flying as far as Zurich and then using another carrier to complete the journey. United also offers fly-drive packages and escorted motor coach tours.

Continental Airlines *(Tel 800/231-0856; www.continental.com)* offers daily nonstop flights, depending on the season, to Madrid from New York (Newark).

US Airways *(Tel 800/428-4322; www.usairways.com)* offers daily nonstop service between Philadelphia and Madrid. The carrier also has connecting flights to Philadelphia from more than 50 cities throughout the United States, Canada, and the Bahamas.

FLY FOR LESS: TIPS FOR GETTING THE BEST AIRFARES

Keep your eyes peeled for sales. Check your newspaper for advertised discounts, or call the airlines directly and ask if any promotional rates or special fares are available. You'll almost never see a sale during the peak summer vacation months of July and August or during the Thanksgiving or Christmas seasons, but in the off-season, there have been astoundingly low European fares in the past few years. If you already hold a ticket when a sale breaks, it might even pay to exchange your ticket, which usually incurs a $50 to $75 charge.

Ask the reservations agent lots of questions. If your schedule is flexible, ask if you can secure a cheaper fare by staying an extra day or by flying midweek. Many airlines won't volunteer this information, so you've got to be persistent on the phone.

Consolidators, also known as bucket shops, are a good place to find low fares. Consolidators buy seats in bulk from the airlines and then sell them back to the public at prices below even the airlines' discounted rates. Their small boxed ads usually run in the Sunday travel section at the bottom of the page. Before you pay a consolidator, however, ask for a record locator number and confirm your seat with the airline itself. Be prepared to book your ticket with a different consolidator—there are many to choose from—if the airline can't confirm your reservation. Also be aware that bucket shop tickets are usually nonrefundable or rigged with stiff cancellation penalties, often as high as 50 or 75percent of the ticket price.

Council Travel *(Tel 800/226-8624; www.counciltravel.com)* and **STA Travel** *(Tel 800/781-4040; www.sta.travel.com)* cater especially to young travelers, but their bargain-basement prices are available to people of all ages. **Travel Bargains** *(Tel 800/AIR-FARE; www.1800airfare.com)* was formerly owned by TWA but now offers the deepest discounts on many other airlines with a 4-day advance purchase. Other reliable consolidators include **1-800/FLY-CHEAP** *(www.1800flycheap.com);* **TFI Tours International** *(Tel 800/745-8000 or 212/736-1140),* which serves as a clearinghouse for unused seats; or rebators such as **Travel Avenue** *(Tel 800/333-3335 or 312/876-1116).*

Surf the web for bargains (but always check the lowest published fare before you shop for flights online, so you know if you're getting a deal). See "Spain Online" following this chapter for lots of advice on how to use the Internet to its fullest; it goes into much greater detail than we do here. However, just to mention a couple of sites briefly, good bets include **Arthur Frommer's Budget Travel** *(www.frommers.com),* **Microsoft Expedia** *(www.expedia.com),* **Yahoo's Travel Page** *(www.yahoo.com),* **Travelocity** *(www.travelocity.com),* and **Trip.com** *(www.trip.com).* Several major airlines offer a free e-mail service known as E-Savers, via which they'll send you their best bargain airfares on a regular basis. It's a service for the spontaneously inclined. But the fares are cheap, so it's worth taking a look. See the web addresses given above for each airline.

Consider a charter flight. Discounted fares have pared the number available, but they can still be found. Most charter operators advertise and sell their seats through travel agents, thus making these local professionals your best source of information for available flights. Before deciding to take a charter flight, however, check the restrictions on the ticket: You may be asked to purchase a tour package, to pay in advance, to be amenable if the day of departure is changed, to pay a service charge, to fly on an airline you're not familiar with (this usually is not the case), and to pay harsh penalties if you cancel—and be understanding if the charter doesn't fill up and is canceled up to 10 days before departure. Summer charters fill up more quickly than others and are almost sure to fly, but if you decide on a charter flight, seriously consider cancellation and baggage insurance [see *health & insurance,* above].

Among charter-flight operators is **Council Travel,** a subsidiary of the Council on International Educational Exchange (CIEE), 205 E. 42nd St., New York, NY 10017 *(Tel 212/822-2700).* This outfit can arrange charter seats to most major European cities, including Madrid, on regularly scheduled aircraft. Another big charter operator is **Travac,** 989 Sixth Ave., 16th Floor, New York, NY 10018 *(Tel 800/TRAV-800 or 212/563-3303).*

Be warned: Some charter companies have proven to be unreliable in the past.

FROM THE UNITED KINGDOM
British Airways (BA) *(Tel 034/522-27-47, 020/87-59-55-11 in London)* and Iberia *(Tel 020/78-30-00-11 in London)* are the two major carriers flying between England and Spain. More than a dozen daily flights, on either BA or Iberia, depart from London's Heathrow and Gatwick airports. The Midlands is served by flights from Manchester and Birmingham, two major airports that can also be used by Scottish travelers flying to Spain. There are about 7 flights a day from London to Madrid and back and at least 6 to Barcelona (trip time: 2 to 2-1/2 hours). From either the Madrid airport or the Barcelona airport, you can tap into Iberia's domestic network—flying, for example, to Sevilla or the Costa del Sol. The best air deals on scheduled flights from England are those requiring a Saturday-night stopover.

British newspapers are always full of classified advertisements touting "slashed" fares to Spain. A good source is *Time Out.* London's *Evening Standard* has a daily travel section, and the Sunday editions of most papers are full of charter deals. A travel agent can always advise what the best values are at the time of your intended departure.

Charter flights to specific destinations leave from most British regional airports (for example, Málaga), bypassing the congestion at the Barcelona and Madrid airports. Figure on saving approximately 10-5percent on regularly scheduled flight tickets. But check carefully into the restrictions and terms; read the fine print, especially in regard to cancellation penalties. One recommended company is **Trailfinders** *(Tel 020/79-37-54-00 in London),* which operates charters.

In London there are many bucket shops around Victoria Station and Earls Court that offer cheap fares. Make sure the company you deal with is a member of the IATA, ABTA, or ATOL. These umbrella organizations will help you out if anything goes wrong.

CEEFAX, the British television information service, runs details of package holidays and flights to Europe and beyond. Just switch to your CEEFAX channel and you'll find travel information.

FROM AUSTRALIA From Australia, there are a number of options to fly to Spain. The most popular is **Qantas/British Airways** *(Tel 13-13-13),* which flies daily via Asia and London. Other popular and cheaper options are **Qantas/Luftansa** via Asia and Frankfurt, **Qantas/Air France** via Asia and Paris, and **Alitalia** via Bangkok and Rome. The most direct option is on **Singapore Airlines,** with just one stop in Singapore. Alternatively, there are flights on **Thai Airways** via Bangkok and Rome, but the connections are not always good.

getting there by train

If you're already in Europe, you might want to go to Spain by train, especially if you have a EurailPass. Even without a pass, you'll find that the cost of a train ticket is relatively moderate. Rail passengers who visit from Britain or France should make couchette and sleeper reservations as far in advance as possible, especially during the peak summer season.

Since Spain's rail tracks are of a wider gauge than those used for French trains (except for the TALGO and Trans-Europe-Express trains), you'll probably have to change trains at the border unless you're on an express train (see below). For long journeys on Spanish rails, seat and sleeper reservations are mandatory.

The most comfortable and the fastest trains in Spain are the TER, TALGO, and Electrotren. However, you pay a supplement to ride on these fast trains. Both first- and second-class fares are sold on Spanish trains. Tickets can be purchased in the United States or Canada at the nearest office of Rail Europe or from any reputable travel agent. Confirmation of your reservation takes about a week.

To go from London to Spain by rail, you'll need to change not only the train but also the rail terminus in Paris. In Paris it's worth the extra bucks to purchase a TALGO express or a "Puerta del Sol" express—that way, you can avoid having to change trains once again at the Spanish border. Trip time from London to Paris is about 6 hours; from Paris to Madrid, about 15 hours or so, which includes 2 hours spent in Paris just changing trains and stations. Many different rail passes are available in the United Kingdom for travel in Europe. Call or stop in at **Wasteels** at Victoria Station opposite platform 2, London, SW1V 1JZ *(Tel 020/78-34-70-66).* The staff here can help you find the best option for the trip you're planning.

getting there by bus

Bus travel to Spain is possible but not popular—it's quite slow (service from London will take 24 hours or more). But coach services do operate regularly from major capitals of western Europe and, once in Spain, usually head for Madrid or Barcelona. The major bus lines running from London to Spain are **Eurolines Limited,** 52 Grosvenor Gardens, London SW1W 0AU, UK *(Tel 099/014-32-19 or 020/77-30-82-35),* and **Aerolineas** *(Tel 934/904-000 in Barcelona or 015/82-40-4511 in Britain).*

getting there by car

If you're touring the rest of Europe in a rented car, you might, for an added cost, be allowed to drop off your vehicle in a major city such as Madrid or Barcelona.

Highway approaches to Spain are across France on expressways. The most popular border crossing is near Biarritz, but there are 17 other border stations between Spain and France. If you're planning to visit the north or west of Spain (Galicia), the Hendaye-Irún border is the most convenient frontier crossing. If you're going to Barcelona or Catalunya and along the Levante coast (Valencia), take the expressway in France to Toulouse, then the A-61 to Narbonne, and then the A-9 toward the border crossing at La Junquera. You can also take the RN-20, with a border station at Puigcerdá.

If you're driving from Britain, make sure you have a cross-Channel reservation, as traffic tends to be very heavy, especially in summer.

The major ferry crossings connect Dover and Folkestone with Dunkirk. Newhaven is connected with Dieppe, and the British city of Portsmouth with Roscoff. To take a car on the ferry from Dover to Calais on P&O Stena Lines *(Tel 087/06-00-06-11)* costs £118 ($200.60) and takes 1 hour, 15 minutes. This cost includes the car and two passengers.

One of the fastest crossings is by Hovercraft from Dover to Boulogne or Calais. It costs more than the ferry, but it takes only about half an hour. For reservations and information, call Hoverspeed *(Tel 800/677-8585 for reservations in North America or 087/05-24-0241 in England).* The Hovercraft takes 35 minutes and costs £105-£169 ($178.50-$287.30) for the car and two passengers. The drive from Calais to the border would take about 15 hours.

You can take the Chunnel, the underwater Channel Tunnel linking Britain (Folkestone) and France (Calais) by road and rail. Eurostar tickets, for train service between London and Paris or Brussels, are available through **Rail Europe** *(Tel 800/4-EURAIL for information).* Make reservations for Eurostar by calling 099/030-00-03 in the UK; 014/451-06-02 in Paris, and 800/EUROSTAR in the United States. The tunnel also accommodates passenger cars, charter buses, taxis, and motorcycles, transporting them under the English Channel from Folkestone, England, to Calais, France. It operates 24 hours a day, 365 days a year, running every 15 minutes during peak travel times and at least once an hour at night. Tickets may be purchased at the toll booth at the tunnel's entrance. With "Le Shuttle," gone are the days of weather-related delays, seasickness, and advance reservations.

The cost is £254.20 ($432.15) for the car and up to seven passengers. Once you land, you'll have about a 15-hour drive to Spain.

If you plan to transport a rental car between England and France, check in advance with the rental company about license and insurance requirements and additional drop-off charges. And be aware that many car-rental companies, for insurance reasons, forbid transport of one of their vehicles over the water between England and France.

getting around the country

BY PLANE

Two affiliated airlines operate within Spain: **Iberia** and its smaller cousin, **Aviaco.** (For reservations on either of these airlines, call *Tel 800/772-4642* in the U.S.) By European standards, domestic flights within Spain are relatively inexpensive, and considering the vast distances within the country, flying between distant points sometimes makes sense.

If you plan to travel to a number of cities and regions, Iberia's "Visit Spain" ticket, priced between $240 and $260 ($299 and $349 to include the Canary Islands), depending on the season, can be a good deal. Sold only in conjunction with a transatlantic ticket and valid for any airport within Spain and the Balearic Islands, it requires that you choose up to four different cities in advance, in the order you'll visit them. Restrictions forbid flying immediately back to the city of departure, instead encouraging far-flung visits to widely scattered regions of the peninsula. Only one change within the preset itinerary is permitted once the ticket is issued. The dates and departure times of the actual flights, however, can be determined or changed without penalty once you arrive in Spain. Also, passengers who want to exceed the designated number of stops (four) included within the basic ticket can add additional cities to their itineraries for $50 each. The ticket is valid for up to 60 days after your initial transatlantic arrival in Spain.

BY TRAIN

Spain is crisscrossed with a comprehensive network of rail lines. Hundreds of trains depart every day for points around the country, including the fast TALGO and the newer, faster AVE trains, which reduced rail time between Madrid and Sevilla to only 2-1/2 hours.

If you plan to travel a great deal on the European railroads, it's worth buying a copy of the *Thomas Cook Timetable of European Passenger Railroads.* It's available exclusively in North America from Forsyth Travel Library, 226 Westchester Ave., White Plains, NY 10604 *(Tel 800/FORSYTH)*, at a cost of $27.95, plus $4.95 postage priority airmail in the United States plus $2 (U.S.) for shipments to Canada.

The most economical way to travel in Spain is on the **Spanish State Railways (RENFE).** Most main long-distance connections are served with night express trains having first- and second-class seats as well as beds and bunks. There are also comfortable high-speed daytime trains of the TALGO, TER, and Electrotren types. There is a general fare for these trains; bunks, beds, and certain superior-quality trains cost extra. Nevertheless, the Spanish railway is one of the most economical in Europe; in most cases, this is the best way to go.

RAIL PASSES RENFE, the national railway of Spain, offers the Spain Flexipass, a discounted rail pass. Flexipasses permit a designated number of travel days within a predetermined time block—for example, 3 or 5 days in 1 month or 10 days in 2 months. You must buy these passes in the United States prior to your departure. For more information, consult a travel agent or Rail Europe *(Tel 800/4-EURAIL).*

Iberojet Travel, Inc. offers a computerized link to RENFE with its "instant purchase ticketing." By calling 800/222-8383, travelers can reserve seats for travel between various cities within Spain and on journeys on RENFE to neighboring countries. The network includes access to the **Intercity, Estrella,** and **Tren Hotel** lines, as well as access to the **AVE,** Spain's high-speed network.

The **Eurailpass** is one of Europe's greatest travel bargains, offering unlimited first-class travel in any country in western Europe, except the British Isles (good in Ireland). You must buy these passes in the United States before your departure; call your travel agent or Rail Europe *(Tel 800/4-EURAIL).*

The Eurailpass also entitles you to discounts on some bus and steamship lines. Passes are available for 15 days to as long as 3 months and are strictly nontransferable. If you're under 26, you can purchase a **Eurail Youthpass,** which entitles you to unlimited second-class travel for 15 days, 1 month, or 2 months.

The **Eurail Saverpass** provides discounted 15-day travel for groups of three people traveling continuously together between April and September or two people between October and March. The price of a Saverpass, valid all over Europe, is good for first-class travel only.

The **Eurail Flexipass** allows passengers to visit Europe with more flexibility. It's valid in first class and offers the same privileges as the Eurailpass. However, it provides a number of individual travel days that can be used over a much longer period of consecutive days. That makes it possible to stay in one city and yet not lose a single day of travel. The pass entitles you, within a 2-month period, to 10 or 15 days of travel. With similar qualifications and restrictions, travelers under 26 can purchase a **Eurail Youth Flexipass.** It also allows, within a 2-month period, 10 or 15 days of travel.

The **Europass,** like the Eurailpass, offers the most favorable rates only to buyers who purchase it outside Europe. Europasses can be purchased from any travel agent, or arranged over the phone by dialing *800/4-EURAIL.*

Depending on the fee, the Europass allows unlimited rail travel within and between three and five European countries with shared (contiguous) borders, arranged into several different price tiers. The countries participating in the Europass plan include Italy, France, Germany, Switzerland, and Spain. The terrain covered by the Europass plan is deliberately less broad-based than that honored by the 17 countries within the Eurail network.

If you opt for 5 to 7 days of first-class train travel in three of the above-mentioned countries (Italy plus two contiguous countries on the list), you'll have up to 2 months to complete your travel.

If you opt for 8 to 10 days of travel within any 2-month period, you'll be able to add a fourth country from the above-cited list, and if you opt for 11 to 15 days of travel within any 2-month period, you can travel through all five of the countries while using the pass.

You can reduce costs with this means of transport by sharing your trip with another adult, who will receive a 50-percent discount on each of the above-mentioned fares.

Note: You can add what Europass refers to as an "associate country" (Austria, Benelux, Greece, or Portugal) to the reach of your Europass by paying a surcharge.

BY CAR

A car offers the greatest flexibility while you're touring, even if you're just doing day trips from Madrid. Don't, however, plan to drive in Madrid or Barcelona for city sightseeing; it's too congested. Theoretically, rush hour is Monday to Saturday from 8-10am, 1-2pm, and 4-6pm. In reality, it's always busy.

CAR RENTALS

Many of North America's biggest car-rental companies, including Avis, Budget, and Hertz, maintain offices throughout Spain. Although several Spanish car-rental companies exist, we've gotten lots of letters from readers of previous editions telling us they've had a hard time resolving billing irregularities and insurance claims, so you might want to stick with the U.S.-based rental firms.

Note that tax on car rentals is a whopping 15 percent, so don't forget to factor that into your travel budget. Usually, prepaid rates do not include taxes, which will be collected at the rental kiosk itself. Be sure to ask explicitly what's included when you're quoted a rate.

Avis *(Tel 800/331-1212; www.avis.com)* maintains about 100 branches throughout Spain, including about a dozen in Madrid, eight in Barcelona, a half dozen in Sevilla, and four in Murcia. If you reserve and pay your rental by telephone at least 2 weeks before your departure from North America, you'll qualify for the company's best rate, with unlimited kilometers included. You can usually get competitive rates from **Hertz** *(Tel 800/654-3001; www.hertz.com)* and **Budget** *(Tel 800/472-3325; www.budget.com);* it always pays to comparison shop. Budget doesn't have a drop-off charge if you pick up in one Spanish city and return to another. All three companies require that drivers be at least 21 years of age (at this time, Hertz policy is 21 minimum, Avis is 23, and Budget is 25; check before you go!). To be able to rent a car, you must have a passport and a valid driver's license; you must also have a valid credit card or a prepaid voucher. An international driver's license is not essential, but you might want to present it if you have one; it's available from any North American office of the American Automobile Association (AAA).

Two other agencies of note include **Kemwel Holiday Autos** *(Tel 800/678-0678; www.kemwel.com)* and **Auto Europe** *(Tel 800/223-5555; www.autoeurope.com).*

Internet resources can make comparison shopping easier. **Microsoft Expedia** *(www.expedia.com)* and **Travelocity** *(www.travelocity.com)* help you compare prices and locate car rental bargains from various companies nationwide. They will even make your reservation for you once you've found the best deal [see *Spain Online,* below].

Before you drive off in a rental car, be sure you're insured. Hasty assumptions about your personal auto insurance or a rental agency's additional coverage could end up costing you tens of thousands of dollars—even if you are involved in an accident that was clearly the fault of another driver.

The basic insurance coverage offered by most car-rental companies, known as the Loss/Damage Waiver (LDW) or Collision Damage Waiver (CDW), can cost as much as $20 a day. It usually covers the full value of the vehicle with no deductions if an outside party causes an accident or other damage to the rental car.

Americans who have their own car insurance policies are most likely covered in the United States for loss of or damage to a rental car and liability in case of injury to any other party involved in an accident. Coverage probably doesn't extend outside the United States, however. Be sure to find out whether you are covered in the area you are visiting, whether your policy extends to all persons who will be driving the rental car, how much liability is covered in case an outside party is injured in an accident, and whether the type of vehicle you are renting is included under your contract. (Rental trucks, sports utility vehicles, and luxury vehicles may not be covered.)

Most major credit cards provide some degree of coverage as well—provided they were used to pay for the rental. Terms vary widely, however, so be sure to call your credit card company directly before you rent. If you are uninsured for driving abroad, your credit card provides primary collision coverage as long as you decline the rental agency's insurance. This means that the credit card will cover damage or theft of a rental car for the full cost of the vehicle. If you already have insurance, your credit card will provide secondary coverage—which basically covers your deductible.

Credit cards will *not* cover liability or the cost of injury to an outside party and/or damage to an outside party's vehicle. If you do not hold an insurance policy, or if your policy doesn't cover you outside the United States, you may want to seriously consider purchasing additional liability insurance from your rental company. Be sure to check the terms, however: Some rental agencies cover liability only if the renter is not at fault, and even then, the rental company's obligation varies according to the policy.

DRIVING RULES

Spaniards drive on the right side of the road. Drivers should pass on the left; local drivers sound their horns when passing another car and flash their lights at you if you're driving slowly (slowly for high-speed Spain) in the left lane. Autos coming from the right have the right-of-way.

Spain's express highways are known as *autopistas,* which charge a toll, and *autovías,* which don't. To exit in Spain, follow the *salida* sign, except in Catalunya, where the word to get off is *sortida.* On most express highways, the speed limit is 75 miles per hour (120kmph). On other roads, speed limits range from 56 miles per hour (90kmph) to 62 miles per hour (100kmph). You will see many drivers far exceeding these limits.

The greatest number of accidents in Spain are recorded along the notorious Costa del Sol highway, the Carretera de Cádiz.

If you must drive through a Spanish city, try to avoid morning and evening rush hours. Never park your car facing oncoming traffic, as that is against the law. If you are fined by the highway patrol *(Guardia Civil de Tráfico),* you must pay on the spot. Penalties for drinking and driving are very stiff.

MAPS

For one of the best overviews of the Iberian Peninsula (Spain and Portugal), get a copy of **Michelin** map number 990 (for a folding version) or number 460 (the same map in a spiral-bound version). For more detailed looks at Spain, Michelin has a series of six maps (nos. 441-446), showing specific regions, complete with many minor roads.

For extensive touring, purchase *Mapas de Carreteras-España y Portugal,* published by Almax Editores and available at most leading bookstores in Spain. This cartographic compendium of Spain provides an overview of the country and includes road and street maps of some of its major cities as well.

The **American Automobile Association** *(Tel 800/222-4357)* publishes a regional map of Spain that's available free to members at most AAA offices in the United States. Also available free to members is a guide of approximately 60 pages, *Motoring in Europe,* that gives helpful information about road signs and speed limits, as well as insurance regulations and other relevant matters. Incidentally, the AAA is associated with the **Real Automóvil Club de España,** José Abascal 10, Madrid 28003 *(Tel 915/947-400).* This organization can supply helpful information about road conditions in Spain, including tourist and travel data. It will also provide limited road service, in an emergency, if your car breaks down.

BREAKDOWNS

These can be a serious problem. If you're driving a Spanish-made vehicle, you'll probably be able to find spare parts, if needed. But if you have a foreign-made vehicle, you may be stranded. Have the car checked out before setting out on a long trek through Spain. On a major motorway you'll find strategically placed emergency phone boxes. On secondary roads, call for help by asking the operator to locate the nearest Guardia Civil, which will put you in touch with a garage that can tow you to a repair shop.

As noted above, the Spanish affiliate of AAA can provide limited assistance in the event of a breakdown.

BY BUS

Bus service in Spain is extensive, low-priced, and comfortable enough for short distances. You'll rarely encounter a bus terminal in Spain. The station might be a cafe, a bar, the street in front of a hotel, or simply a spot at an intersection.

A bus may be the cheapest mode of transportation, but it's not really the best option for distances of more than 100 miles. On long hauls, buses are often uncomfortable. Another major drawback might be a lack of toilet facilities, although rest stops are frequent. It's best for 1-day excursions outside a major tourist center such as Madrid. In the rural areas of the country, bus networks are more extensive than the railway system; they go virtually everywhere, connecting every village. In general, a bus ride between two major cities in Spain, such as from Córdoba to Sevilla or Madrid to Barcelona, is about two-thirds the price of a train ride and a few hours faster.

TIPS on accommodations

From castles converted into hotels to basic hostels overlooking the Mediterranean, Spain has some of the most varied accommodations in the world—with equally varied price ranges. After reviewing the basic definitions below, you'll want to check out our listings within each city as well as our comprehensive hostels appendix. Accommodations are broadly classified as follows:

ONE- TO FIVE-STAR HOTELS

The Spanish government rates hotels by according them stars, from one to five, with five being at the high end of the scale. A one- or two-star hotel is relatively inexpensively priced, but there are plenty of other types of accommodations available that may be even less expensive [see below]. *Note:* The government grants stars based on such amenities as elevators, private bathrooms, and air-conditioning. If a hotel is classified as a *residencia,* it means that it serves breakfast (usually) but no other meals.

HOSTALS

Not to be confused with a hostel for students, a *hostal* is a modest hotel without services, where you can save money by carrying your own bags and the like. You'll know it's a hostal if a small *s* follows the capital letter *H* on the blue plaque by the door. A hostal with three stars is about the equivalent of a hotel with two stars.

PENSIONES

These boarding houses are among the least expensive accommodations, but you're required to take either full board (three meals) or half-board, which is breakfast plus lunch or dinner.

CASAS HUESPEDES & FONDAS

These are the cheapest places in Spain and can be recognized by the light-blue plaques at the door displaying *CH* and *F,* respectively. They are invariably basic but respectable establishments.

YOUTH HOSTELS

Spain has about 140 hostels *(albergues de juventil)* [see *hostel appendix.,* below]. In theory, those 25 or under have the first chance at securing a bed for the night, but these places are certainly not limited to young people. Some of them are equipped for persons with disabilities. Most hostels impose an 11pm curfew. For information, contact **Red Española de Alberques Juveniles,** calle José Ortega y Gasset 71, 28006 Madrid *(Tel 915/437-412).*

PARADORS, ALBERGUES, & REFUGIOS

The Spanish government runs a series of unique state-owned inns called paradors *(paradores* in Spanish), which now blanket the country. Deserted castles, monasteries, palaces, and other buildings have been taken over and converted into hotels. Historic and charming though they might be, they are quite expensive and advance reservations are usually necessary. Contact **Paradores de España,** Requeña 3, 28013 Madrid *(Tel 915/166-666).*

The government also operates a type of accommodation known as *albergues:* these are comparable to motels, standing along the roadside and usually built in hotel-scarce sections for the convenience of passing motorists. A client is not allowed to stay in an *albergue* for more than 48 hours, and the management doesn't accept reservations.

In addition, the government runs *refugios,* mostly in remote areas, attracting hunters, fishers, and mountain climbers. Another state-sponsored establishment is the *hostería,* or specialty restaurant, such as the one at Alcalá de Henares, near Madrid. *Hosterías* don't offer rooms; decorated in the style of a particular province, they serve regional dishes at reasonable prices.

fast facts: spain

BUSINESS HOURS Banks are open Monday to Friday 9:30am to 2pm and Saturday 9:30am to 1pm. Most offices are open Monday to Friday 9am to 5 or 5:30pm; the longtime practice of early closings in summer seems to be dying out. In restaurants, lunch is usually 1 to 4pm and dinner 9 to 11:30pm or midnight. There are no set rules for the opening of bars and taverns, many opening at 8am, others at noon; most stay open until 1:30am or later. Major stores are open Monday to Saturday 9:30am to 8pm; smaller establishments, however, often take a siesta, doing business 9:30am to 1:30pm and 4:30 to 8pm. Hours can vary from store to store.

DRUGSTORES To find an open pharmacy outside normal business hours, check the list of stores posted on the door of any drugstore. The law requires drugstores to operate on a rotating system of hours so that there's always a drugstore open somewhere, even Sunday at midnight.

ELECTRICITY Most hotels have 220 volts AC (50 cycles). Some older places have 110 or 125 volts AC. Carry your adapter with you, and always check at your hotel desk before plugging in any electrical appliance. It's best to travel with battery-operated equipment or just buy a new hair dryer in Spain.

EMBASSIES/CONSULATES If you lose your passport, fall seriously ill, get into legal trouble, or have some other serious problem, your embassy or consulate can help. These are the Madrid addresses and hours:

The **United States Embassy,** calle Serrano 75 *(Tel 915/872-200; metro: Núñez de Balboa),* is open Monday to Friday 9am to 6pm. The **Canadian Embassy,** Núñez de Balboa 35 *(Tel 914/233-250; metro: Velázquez),* is open Monday to Friday 8:30am to 5:30pm. The **United Kingdom Embassy,** calle Fernando el Santo 16 *(Tel 913/190-200; metro: Colón),* is open Monday to Friday 9am to 1:30pm and 3 to 6pm. The **Republic of Ireland** has an embassy at Claudio Coello 73 *(Tel 915/763-500; metro: Serrano);* it's open Monday to Friday 9am to 2pm. **The Australian Embassy,** Plaza Diego de Ordas 3, Edificio Santa Engracia 120 *(Tel 914/419-300; metro: Rios Rosas),* is open Monday to Thursday 8:30am to 5pm and Friday 8:30am to 2:15pm. Citizens of **New Zealand** have an embassy at Plaza de la Lealtad 2 *(Tel 915/230-226; metro: Banco de España);* it's open Monday to Friday 9am to 1:30pm and 2:30 to 5:30pm.

EMERGENCIES The national emergency number for Spain (except the Basque country) is Tel 006; in the Basque country it is Tel 088.

LANGUAGE The official language in Spain is Castilian (or Castellano). Although Spanish is spoken in every province of Spain, local tongues reasserted themselves with the restoration of democracy in 1975. After years of being outlawed during the Franco dictatorship, Catalán has returned to Barcelona and Catalunya, even appearing on street signs; this language and its derivatives are also spoken in the Valencia area and in the Balearic Islands, including Majorca (even though natives there will tell you they speak Mallorquín). The Basque language is widely spoken in the Basque region (the northeast, near France), which is seeking independence from Spain. Likewise, the Gallego language, which sounds and looks very much like Portuguese, has enjoyed a renaissance in Galicia (the northwest). Of course, English is spoken in most hotels, restaurants, and shops.

The best overall phrasebook is *Spanish for Travellers* by Berlitz; it has a menu supplement and a 12,500-word glossary of both English and Spanish.

LIQUOR LAWS The legal drinking age is 18. Bars, taverns, and cafeterias usually open at 8am, and many serve alcohol to 1:30am or later. Generally, you can purchase alcoholic beverages in almost any market.

MAIL Airmail letters to the United States and Canada cost 120ptas (70¢) up to 15 grams, and letters to Britain or other EU countries cost 75ptas (45¢) up to 20 grams; letters within Spain cost 35ptas (20¢). Postcards have the same rates as letters. Allow about 8 days for delivery to North America, generally less to the United Kingdom; in some cases, letters take 2 weeks to reach North America. Rates change frequently, so check at your local hotel before mailing anything. As for surface mail to North America, forget it. Chances are you'll be home long before your letter arrives.

POLICE The national emergency number is Tel 006 throughout Spain, except in the Basque country, where it is Tel 088.

REST ROOMS In Spain they're called aseos and servicios or simply lavabos and labeled caballeros for men and damas or señoras for women. If you can't find any, go into a bar, but you should order something.

SAFETY Pickpockets and purse snatchers flourish throughout Spain, particularly in Madrid, Barcelona, Sevilla, and the Costa del Sol. In the wake of so many robberies, visitors have taken to leaving their passports at their hotel. But here's a catch-22 situation: Identification checks are common by Spanish police, who are actually cracking down on illegal immigrants. Police officers or plainclothes agents can stop you at any time of the day or night and demand to see your passport. You can be arrested, as many visitors are, if you can't produce yours. Carry your passport with you, but carefully conceal it on your body, perhaps in a safety belt.

TAXES The internal sales tax (known in Spain as IVA) ranges between 7 and 33 percent, depending on the commodity being sold. Food, wine, and basic necessities are taxed at 7 percent; most goods and services (including car rentals) at 13 percent; luxury items (jewelry, all tobacco, imported liquors) at 33 percent; and hotels at 7 percent.

If you are not a European Union resident and make purchases in Spain worth more than 15,000ptas ($90), you can get a tax refund. To get this refund, you must complete three copies of a form that the store will give you, detailing the nature of your purchase and its value. Citizens of non-EU countries show the purchase and the form to the Spanish Customs Office. The shop is supposed to refund the amount due you. Inquire at the time of purchase how it will do so and discuss in what currency your refund will arrive.

TELEPHONES If you don't speak Spanish, you'll find it easier to telephone from your hotel, but remember that this is often very expensive because hotels impose a surcharge on every operator-assisted call. In some cases it can be as high as 40 percent or more. Note for American travelers: Calling from the U.S. to Europe is generally much cheaper than the other way around, so you can make a legitimate case for friends and family to call you at your hotel rather than you calling them.

On the street, phone booths (known as *cabinas*) have dialing instructions in English; you can make local calls by inserting a 25-peseta coin for 3 minutes. In Spain many smaller establishments, especially bars, discos, and a few informal restaurants, don't have phones. Further, many summer-only bars and discos secure a phone for the season only, then get a new number the next season.

In 1998, all telephone numbers in Spain changed to a 9-digit system instead of the 6- or 7-digit method used previously. Each number is now preceded by its provincial code for local, national, and international calls. For example, when calling to Madrid from Madrid or another province within Spain, telephone customers must dial 911/234-567. Similarly, when calling Valladolid from within or outside the province, dial 979/123-456.

To call Spain from another country, first dial the international long-distance code (011) plus the country code (34), followed by the 9-digit number. Hence, when calling Madrid from the United States, dial (011-34).

To make an international call from Spain, you must dial 07, followed by the country code, the area code, and the telephone number.

The easiest and cheapest way to call home is with a calling card. If necessary, just wait for an English-speaking operator, who will put your call through. You can also call any one of those companies' numbers to make a collect call too; just dial it and wait for the operator.

When in Spain, the access number for an **AT&T** calling card is *Tel 1-800-callATT.* The access number for **Sprint** is *Tel 800/888-0013.*
More information is also available on the Teléfonica website at *www.telefonica.es.*

TIME Spain is 6 hours ahead of Eastern Standard Time in the United States. Daylight savings time is in effect from the last Sunday in March to the last Sunday in September.

TIPPING Don't overtip. The government requires restaurants and hotels to include their service charges—usually 15 percent of the bill. However, that doesn't mean you should skip out of a place without dispensing some extra pesetas. The following are some guidelines:

Your hotel porter should get 75ptas (45¢) per bag and never less than 100ptas (60¢), even if you have only one suitcase. Maids should be given 150ptas (90¢) per day, more if you're generous. Tip doormen 125ptas (75¢) for assisting with baggage and 50ptas (30¢) for calling a cab. In top-ranking hotels the concierge will often submit a separate bill, showing charges for newspapers and other services; if he or she has been particularly helpful, tip extra. For cab drivers, add about 10 percent to the fare as shown on the meter. At airports, such as Barajas in Madrid and major terminals, the porter who handles your luggage will present you with a fixed-charge bill.

In both restaurants and nightclubs, a 15-percent service charge is added to the bill. To that, add another 3-5 percent tip, depending on the quality of the service. Waiters in deluxe restaurants and nightclubs are accustomed to the extra 5 percent, which means you'll end up tipping 20 percent. If that seems excessive, you must remember that the initial service charge reflected in the fixed price is distributed among all the help.

Barbers and hairdressers expect a 10-15 percent tip. Tour guides expect 200ptas ($1.20), although a tip is not mandatory. Theater and bullfight ushers get from 50-75ptas (30¢ to 45¢).

spain online

Travel planning websites

by Lynne Bairstow

WHY BOOK ONLINE?

Online agencies have come a long way over the past few years, now providing tips for finding the best fare and giving suggested dates or times to travel that yield the lowest price if your plans are flexible. Other sites even allow you to establish the price you're willing to pay, and they check the airlines' willingness to accept it. However, in some cases, these sites might not always yield the best price. Unlike a travel agent, for example, they may not have access to charter flights offered by wholesalers.

Online booking sites aren't the only places to reserve airline tickets; all major airlines have their own websites and often offer incentives—bonus frequent-flyer miles or Net-only discounts, for example—when you buy online or buy an e-ticket.

The best of the travel planning sites are now highly personalized; they store your seating preferences, meal preferences, tentative itineraries, and credit card information, allowing you to plan trips or check agendas quickly.

In many cases, booking your trip online can be better than working with a travel agent. It gives you the widest variety of choices, control, and 24-hour convenience of planning your trip when you choose. All you need is some time—and often a little patience—and you're likely to find the fun of online travel research will greatly enhance your trip.

Tips for Staying Secure: More people still look online than book online, partly due to fear of putting their credit card numbers out on the Net.

Secure encryption and increasing experience buying online have removed this fear for most travelers. In some cases, however, it's simply easier to buy from a local travel agent who can deliver your tickets to your door (especially if your travel is last-minute or you have special requests). You can find a flight online and then book it by calling a toll-free number or contacting your travel agent, although this is somewhat less efficient. To be sure you're in secure mode when you book online, look for a little icon of a padlock (in Netscape or Internet Explorer) at the bottom of your web browser.

WHO SHOULD BOOK ONLINE?

Online booking is best for travelers who want to know as much as possible about their options, those who have flexibility in their travel dates and are looking for the best price, and bargain hunters driven by a good value who are open-minded about when they travel.

One of the biggest successes in online travel for both passengers and airlines is the offer of last-minute specials, such as American Airlines' weekend deals or other Internet-only fares you must purchase online. Another advantage is that you can cash in on incentives for booking online, such as rebates or bonus frequent-flyer miles.

Business and other frequent travelers also have found numerous benefits in online booking, as the advances in mobile technology provide them with the ability to check flight status, change plans, or get specific directions from handheld computing devices, mobile phones, and pagers. Some sites will even e-mail or page passengers if their flights are delayed.

Online booking is increasingly able to accommodate complex itineraries, even for international travel. The pace of evolution on the Net is rapid, so you'll probably find additional features and advancements by the time you visit these sites. What the future holds for online travelers is ever-increasing personalization, customization, and reaching out to you.

TRAVEL PLANNING & BOOKING SITES

Below are the websites for the major airlines serving Spain. These sites offer schedules and flight booking, and most have pages where you can sign up for e-mail alerts for weekend deals and other late-breaking bargains.

Air Europa. *www.easyspain.com*
American Airlines. *www.aa.com*
British Airways. *www.british-airways.com*
Continental Airlines. *www.flycontinental.com*
Delta. *www.delta.com*
Iberia. *www.iberia.com*
Qantas. *www.qantas.com*
TWA. *www.twa.com*
United Airlines. *www.ual.com*
US Airways. *www.usairways.com*
Travelocity (incorporates Preview Travel). *www.travelocity.com; www.previewtravel.com; www.frommers.travelocity.com*

Travelocity is Frommer's online travel planning/booking partner. Travelocity uses the SABRE system to offer reservations and tickets for more than 400 airlines, plus reservations and purchase capabilities for more than 45,000 hotels and 50 car-rental companies. An exclusive feature of the SABRE system is its **Low Fare Search Engine,** which automatically searches for the three lowest-priced itineraries based on a traveler's criteria. Last-minute deals and consolidator fares are included in the search. If you book with Travelocity, you can select specific seats for your flights with online seat maps and view diagrams of the most popular commercial aircraft. Its hotel finder provides street-level location maps and photos of selected hotels. With the **Fare Watcher** e-mail feature, you can select up to five routes and receive e-mail notices when the fare changes by $25 or more.

Travelocity's **Destination Guide** includes updated information on some 260 destinations worldwide—supplied by Frommer's.

Note to AOL Users: You can book flights, hotels, rental cars, and cruises on AOL at keyword: Travel. The booking software is provided by Travelocity/Preview Travel and is similar to the Internet site. Use the AOL "Travelers Advantage" program to earn a 5-percent rebate on flights, hotel rooms, and car rentals.

SPECIALTY TRAVEL SITES

Although the sites listed above provide the most comprehensive services, some travelers have specialized needs that are best met by a site catering specifically to them.

For adventure travelers, **GORP** (Great Outdoor Recreation Pages; *www.gorp.com*) has been a standard since its founding in 1995 by outdoor enthusiasts Diane and Bill Greer. Tapping into their own experiences, they created this website that offers unique travel destinations and encourages active participation by fellow GORP visitors through the sophisticated menu of online forums, contests, and discussions.

In the same vein, **iExplore** *(www.iexplore.com)* is a great source for information and for booking adventure and experiential travel, as well as related services and products. The site combines the secure Internet booking functions with hands-on expertise and 24-hour live customer support by seasoned adventure travelers, for those interested in trips off the beaten path. The company is a supporting member of the Ecotourism Society and is committed to environmentally responsible travel worldwide.

Another excellent site for adventure travelers is **Away.com** *(www.away.com),* which features unique vacations for challenging the body, mind, and spirit. Trips may include cycling in the Loire Valley, taking an African safari, or assisting in the excavation of a Mayan ruin. For those without the time for such an extended exotic trip, offbeat weekend getaways are also available. Services include a customer service center staffed with experts to answer calls and e-mails, plus a network of over 1,000 prescreened tour operators. Trips are categorized by cultural, adventure, and green travel. Away.com also offers a Daily Escape e-mail newsletter.

LAST-MINUTE DEALS & OTHER ONLINE BARGAINS

There's nothing airlines hate more than flying with lots of empty seats. The Net has enabled airlines to offer last-minute bargains to entice travelers to fill those seats. Most of them are announced on Tuesday or Wednesday and are valid for travel the following weekend, but some can be booked weeks or months in advance. You can sign up for weekly e-mail alerts at airlines' sites [for their websites, see *Travel Planning & Booking Sites,* above] or check sites that compile lists of these bargains, such as **Smarter Living** or **WebFlyer** [see below]. To make it easier, visit a site that'll round up all the deals and send them in one convenient weekly e-mail. But last-minute deals aren't the only online bargains; other sites can help you find value even if you haven't waited until the eleventh hour. Increasingly popular are services that let you name the price you're willing to pay for an air seat or vacation package and travel auction sites.

Get the Deal Tip: While most people learn about last-minute weekend deals from e-mail dispatches, it can be best to find out precisely when these deals become available. Because the deals are limited, they can vanish within hours—sometimes even minutes—so it pays to log on as soon as they're available. Check the pages devoted to these deals on airlines' web pages to get the info. An example: Southwest's specials are posted at 12:01am Tuesdays (Central time). So if you're looking for a cheap flight, stay up late and check Southwest's site to grab the best new deals.

1travel.com. *www.1travel.com*
Here you'll find deals on domestic and international flights, cruises, hotels, and all-inclusive resorts like Club Med. 1travel.com's **Saving Alert** compiles last-minute air deals so you don't have to scroll through multiple e-mail alerts. A feature called "Drive a little using low-fare airlines" helps map out strategies for using alternate airports to find lower fares. And **Farebeater** searches a database that includes published fares, consolidator bargains, and special deals exclusive to 1travel.com. *Note:* The travel agencies listed by 1travel.com have paid for placement.

Cheap Tickets. *www.cheaptickets.com*
Cheap Tickets has exclusive deals that aren't available through more mainstream channels. One caveat about the Cheap Tickets site is that it'll offer fare quotes for a route and later show this fare isn't valid for your dates of travel; most other websites, such as Expedia, consider your dates of travel before showing what fares are available. Despite its problems, Cheap Tickets can be worth the effort because its fares can be lower than those offered by its competitors.

Bid for Travel. *www.bidfortravel.com*
Bid for Travel is another of the travel auction sites, similar to Priceline [see below], which are growing in popularity. In addition to airfares, Internet users can place a bid for vacation packages and hotels.

Go4less.com. *www.go4less.com*
Specializing in last-minute cruise and package deals, Go4less has some excellent offers. The **Hot Deals** section gives an alphabetical listing by destination of super-discounted packages.

LastMinuteTravel.com. *www.lastminutetravel.com*
Suppliers with excess inventory come to this online agency to distribute unsold airline seats, hotel rooms, cruises, and vacation packages. It's got great deals, but you have to put up with an excess of advertisements and slow-loading graphics.

Moment's Notice. *www.moments-notice.com*
As the name suggests, Moment's Notice specializes in last-minute vacation and cruise deals. You can browse for free, but if you want to purchase a trip you have to join Moment's Notice, which costs $25. Go to **World Wide Hot Deals** for a complete list of special deals in international destinations.

Smarter Living. *www.smarterliving.com*
Best known for its e-mail dispatch of weekend deals on 20 airlines, Smarter Living also keeps you posted about last-minute bargains on everything from Windjammer Cruises to flights to Iceland.

SkyAuction.com. *www.skyauction.com*
This auction site has categories for airfare, travel deals, hotels, and much more.

Travelzoo.com. *www.travelzoo.com*
At this Internet portal, over 150 travel companies post special deals. It features a Top 20 list of the best deals on the site, selected by its editorial staff each Wednesday night. This list is also available via an e-mailing list, free to those who sign up.

WebFlyer. *www.webflyer.com*
WebFlyer is a comprehensive online resource for frequent flyers and also has an excellent listing of last-minute air deals. Click on **Deal Watch** for a roundup of weekend deals on flights, hotels, and rental cars from domestic and international suppliers.

ONLINE TRAVELER'S TOOLBOX
Veteran travelers usually carry some essential items to make their trips easier. The following is a selection of online tools to smooth your journey.

Visa ATM Locator. *www.visa.com/pd/atm*

MasterCard ATM Locator. *www.mastercard.com/atm*
Use these sites to find ATMs in hundreds of cities in the United States and around the world. Both include maps for some locations and both list airport ATM locations, some with maps. *Tip:* You'll usually get a

better exchange rate using ATMs than exchanging traveler's checks at banks, but check in advance to see what kind of fees your bank assesses for using an overseas ATM.

CDC Travel Information. *www.cdc.gov/travel/index.htm*
Health advisories and recommendations for inoculations from the U.S. Centers for Disease Control and Prevention. The CDC site is good for an overview, but it's best to consult your personal physician to get the latest information on required vaccinations or other health precautions.

Net Cafe Guide. *www.netcafeguide.com/mapindex.htm*
Stop here to locate Internet cafes at hundreds of locations around the globe. Catch up on your e-mail, log on to the web, and stay in touch with the home front, usually for just a few dollars per hour [see *Check Your e-Mail*, below].

Universal Currency Converter. *www.xe.net/currency*
Come here to see what your dollar or pound is worth in pesetas.

Mapquest. *www.mapquest.com*
The best of the mapping sites lets you choose a specific address or destination, and in seconds it returns a map and detailed directions. It really is easier than calling, asking, and writing down directions. The site also links to special travel deals and helpful sites.

Tourism Offices Worldwide Directory. *www.towd.com*
This is an extensive listing of tourism offices, some with links to these offices' websites.

Foreign Languages for Travelers. *www.travlang.com*
Here you can learn basic terms in more than 70 languages and click on any underlined phrase to hear what it sounds like. (*Note:* Free audio software and speakers are required.) It also offers hotel and airline finders with excellent prices and a simple system to get the listings you're looking for.

Travelers' Tales. *www.travelerstales.com*
Considered the best in compilations of travel literature, Travelers' Tales is an award-winning series of books grouped by destination (Mexico, Italy, France, China) or by theme (Love & Romance, The Ultimate Journey, Women in the Wild, The Adventure of Food). It's a new kind of travel book that offers a description of a place or type of journey through the experiences of many travelers. It makes for a perfect traveling companion.

Intellicast. *www.intellicast.com*
Here you'll find weather forecasts for all 50 states and cities around the world. Note that temperatures are in Celsius for many international destinations, so don't think you'll need that winter coat for your next trip to Athens.

U.S. Customs Service Traveler Information. *www.customs.ustreas.gov/travel/index.htm*
Wondering what you're allowed to bring in to the United States? Check at this thorough site, which includes maximum allowance and duty fees.

U.S. State Department Travel Warnings. *travel.state.gov/travel-warnings.html*
You'll find reports on places where health concerns or unrest might threaten U.S. travelers. Keep in mind that these warnings can be somewhat dated and conservative. You can also sign up to receive State Department briefings via e-mail.

Web Travel Secrets. *www.web-travel-secrets.com*
If this list leaves you yearning for more travel-oriented sites, Web Travel Secrets offers one of the best compilations around. One section offers advice and tips on how to find the lowest prices for airlines, hotels, and cruises. The other section provides a comprehensive listing of web travel links for airfare deals, airlines, booking engines, cars, cruise lines, discount travel and best deals, general travel resources, hotels and hotel discounters, search engines, and travel magazines and newsletters.

The Weather Channel *www.weather.com*
Weather forecasts for cities around the world.

check your e-mail

You don't have to be out of touch just because you don't carry a laptop while you travel. Web browser–based free e-mail programs make it much easier to stay in e-touch.

With public Internet access available in all of the principal cities and an increasing number of small towns, it shouldn't be difficult for you to log on regularly during your travels. In a few simple steps you can set yourself up to receive messages while overseas from each of your e-mail accounts.

The first step to uninterrupted e-mail access is to set up an account with a freemail provider, if you don't have one already. You can find hints, tips, and a mile-long list of freemail providers at **www.emailaddresses.com.** The advantage of freemail is that all you need to check your mail from anywhere in the world is a terminal with Internet access; since most Internet cafe computers aren't set up to retrieve POP mail, this is the best option. The downside is that most web-based e-mail sites allow a maximum of only 3MB capacity per mail account, which can fill up quickly. Also, message sending and receiving isn't immediate; some messages may be delayed by several hours or even days. Most freemail providers will allow you to configure your account to retrieve mail from multiple POP mail accounts, or you can arrange with your home ISP to have your mail forwarded to the freemail account.

Internet cafes have become ubiquitous, so for a few dollars an hour you'll be able to check your mail and send messages from virtually anywhere in the world. Interestingly, these cafes tend to be more common in very remote areas, where they may offer the best form of access for an entire community, especially if phone lines are difficult to obtain. Many hostels now provide Internet access for residents, as do an increasing number of hotels. If you travel with a laptop, you'll be glad to find that not only hotels but quite a few guesthouses provide a telephone jack in all rooms for dial-up access; many Internet cafes also provide an Ethernet hook-up for travelers who want to surf the Internet from their laptop. See the wired sidebars throughout the book for listings of individual Internet cafes.

The Top Websites for Spain

information updated by matthew garcia

GENERAL GUIDES FOR SPAIN

All About Spain. *www.red2000.com*
Take a region-by-region, city-by-city photo tour of Spain online or check out each city-specific guide to sights, excursions, dining, nightlife, festivals, and the like. This user-friendly site also features an ample travelers' yellow pages with listings of Spain's transportation and tour operators, accommodations, restaurants, job listings, and real estate.

Cyberspain. *www.cyberspain.com*
Whether you want to see some Picassos or get a feel for Spanish *fútbol* fanaticism, this site offers a taste of a colorful Spain. Get a quick flamenco lesson. Peek at the major cities' top tourist attractions. Try out some recipes. One drawback: Cyberspain is short on specifics, such as addresses, phone numbers, and timetables.

Fine Products of Spain. *www.tienda.com*
If you've returned from a visit to Spain and simply cannot forget the taste of chorizo, the smell of Spanish soap, or the beauty of Spanish textiles, you're in luck. Tienda.com is an American site that sells and ships all manner of Spanish products, from foodstuffs (wine, olive oil, cheeses) to painted tiles and cigars.

Tourist Office of Spain. *www.okspain.org*
Stake out a campsite or find out how to see the country from the back of a horse or the seat of a bicycle. The less-rustic traveler can use this guide to make reservations at hotels and villas, explore Spain's culinary possibilities, or plan a cultural vacation.

TuSpain (Your Spain). *tuspain.com*
Appealing to everyone from weekend museum hoppers and summer villa owners to ecotourists and language students, this site has it all. Your Spain covers real estate, arts and culture, news, embassies, residency, education programs, transportation, food and wine, museums, businesses, heritage, and translators. You can even read interviews with foreigners living in Spain.

MADRID

Madrid by All About Spain. *www.red2000.com/spain/madrid*
Along with facts about the history and geography of Spain's capital city, this guide gives basic information on sightseeing, monuments, museums, nightlife, fiestas, cuisine, local folklore, and day trips. The site includes a photo tour and searchable hotel and restaurant directories.

Madridman. *www.madridman.com*
A passionate (bordering on fanatical) American fan of the Spanish city, Madridman is eager to help you plan a trip, offering travel tips, hotel recommendations, transportation facts, photos, museum information, and weather reports. For a multisensory experience, check out the live Madrid radio broadcasts, video clips of Spanish TV shows, audio clips of popular Spanish songs, and video tours.

Museo del Prado. *museoprado.mcu.es*
The art museum's site leads you by the hand on a virtual visit, explaining how to look at a painting, showing samples of Rembrandts and Goyas, and pointing you to the museum's 50 most important works. You can also find out about conferences, guided tours, hours, tickets, and the Prado's history.

Soft Guide Madrid. *www.softguides.com/index-madrid.html*
It's not much to look at, but this vast, easy-to-use site will tell you virtually everything you need to know about Madrid: how to get around, where to stay, what to eat, what to do for fun, where to shop, and so on. Big pluses: detailed city maps, information on local customs, and an ample lodging guide with breakdown of prices.

Web Madrid. *www.webmadrid.com*
This graphics-filled site has weather reports, a restaurant directory, bar and disco listings, an electronic entertainment magazine, and a "Foreign Guide" with all the usual basics on transportation, exchange rates, and tourist offices.

OLD CASTILLA & LEON

Salamanca Guide. *www.guiasalamanca.com/sal.htm*
Although in Spanish only, this barebones guide will give you some quick views of the city, plus information on history, food, and local businesses.

GALICIA

A Coruña. *www.turismocoruna.com*
You'll see the Coruña tower, where Picasso held his first exhibition, on the opening page of this site. Inside you can read up on this beach town's history and sample the many multiperiod art offerings. Look through a list (some with links) of 22 recommended restaurants and their prices and find out how to get two-for-one rates on accommodations. There is a photo gallery and an online map.

Costa da Morte. *www.finisterrae.com*
Romp through more than two dozen coastal villages and see their ancient artifacts, quaint hotels, and sea festivals. In this site's "Tales" section, you can learn about legendary shipwrecks and local figures. Check out the lodgings segment for recommended hotels, restaurants, campsites, and rural inns.

PAIS VASCO (BASQUE COUNTRY) & NAVARRA

Agritourism in Basque Country. *www.encomix.es/nekazal*
For a low-stress and low-cost vacation, take a look at this guide to rural travel in north-central Spain. The site lists accommodations by region, describes the amenities of each establishment, and gives specific prices.

San Sebastián International Film Festival. *www.sansebastianfestival.com*
If you time your visit right, you can catch this annual international film festival in Basque country. The site lists entry requirements, schedules, ticket information, prizes, and so on. There's a section about transportation and lodging as well as a history of the festival.

Sarean: Internet and the Basque Country. *www.cd.sc.ehu.es/Sarean*
Although entirely free of frills, this site virtually overflows with links. The online directory leads to Basque tour guides, individual city and village sites, activities listings, sports clubs, universities, government pages, music, and more.

Hoteles Rurales de Navarra. *www.hotelesruralesnavarra.es*
A view of autumn leaves and waterfalls introduces this guide to rural lodging in Spain's Navarra region. You can make reservations online to stay in a quaint country inn. The site provides photos and a full description of each establishment as well as a brief but appealing guide to each town's attributes.

Sansol. *www.arrakis.es/~melgar*
This little guide to the "most beautiful" village of Sansol shows historic works of art and architecture, plays audio clips of local musicians singing auroras, gives brief history and geography lessons, and provides a chat room.

BARCELONA & CATALUNYA

Barcelona: A Different Point of View. *members.xoom.com/barcy*
A Barcelona native offers a quirky insider's view of the city, sharing historical tidbits and observations alongside photos of oft-overlooked details. The lovely presentation of the site reveals the emotion, the life force, the spirituality, and the sensory pleasures of Barcelona.

Barcelona Prestige. *www.bcn-guide.com*
This online companion to a print guide holds a lot of practical information—price-specific restaurant listings, museum hours, bus and

subway routes, and descriptions of local shops. There's something for the dreamy cybertraveler, too: a photo tour of Barcelona's fabulous monuments.

Poble Espanyol. *www.poble-espanyol.com*
Duck into a little Barcelona attraction. Illustrated with enticing photos, this site guides visitors to the Poble Espanyol district's architecture, galleries, Internet cafes, and convention centers. A calendar lists festivals and other events.

Time Out: Barcelona. *www.timeout.com/barcelona*
As always, *Time Out's* guide is thorough and easily navigable. Along with an entertainment guide, weather reports, online travel booking, and a currency converter, the site provides a wealth of information on accommodations, dining, sightseeing, kids' stuff, gay and lesbian culture, shopping, and more.

Transports Metropolitans de Barcelona. *www.tmb.net/weleng.htm*
If the actual public transportation system in Barcelona is nearly as snazzy as its site, you're in for a treat. Amid chic, color-coded graphics and animated vehicles, you can learn how to navigate the city's bus lines and metro (subway) system, get ticket information, read the latest TMB news, and absorb all sorts of tourist tips.

Castello d'Empuries. *www.castellodempuries.net*
A veritable multimedia extravaganza, this guide to the small Spanish town features numerous video clips, a virtual-reality tour of an ancient church, and interactive maps. Lower-tech travelers can use the events calendar and photo-illustrated text, describing, in detail, Marshes National Park, the bustling Empuriabrava area, and the town's many hotels, restaurants, and tourist attractions.

Catalunya Tourism Guide. *www.travelcat.com*
Click on any Catalunyan town listed in the margin for facts on transportation, news, events, culture, and history. For lodging, check out the guide's recommendations for two- to five-star hotels; links take you right to their sites.

Hoteles Catalonia. *www.hoteles-catalonia.es*
Make reservations online to stay at a hotel in Spain's Catalunya region. This serviceable site lists three- to five-star hotels and their amenities, services, prices, and locations.

Railways of the Autonomous Government of Catalunya. *www.fgc.catalunya.net*
The name is a mouthful, but the site is a simply and attractively designed guide to Catalunya's transportation system. Find maps, ticket information, fares, news, a description of each train line, and customer service.

Tourism Catalonia. *tourism.catalonia.net*
Find out about vacation rentals, farmhouses, hostels, and other accommodations in Spain's Catalunya region. Also see what the area has to offer in the way of festivals and adventure sports. This well-prepared guide's food-and-drink section includes a lesson in Catalán eating habits and a course-by-course description of the local fare. There's also a section on local humor and a glossary of common words and phrases.

VALENCIA & THE COSTA BLANCA

Benidorm. *www.athenea.com/benidorm*
Take a photo tour of Benidorm, a city famous for its beaches, or get the lowdown on lodging, dining, transportation, and travel agencies. If you can't make it to this little corner of Spain, you can still sample Benidorm from home through regional recipes and virtual postcards.

Valencia: A Virtual Trip. *www.upv.es/cv/valbegin.html*
For those who enjoy a walking tour, this site provides a map on which all major sites are marked. It also describes and shows photos of the Mediterranean city's history, festivals, cuisine, nightlife, monuments, museums, sports, business, gardens, shops, hotels, and transportation.

THE BALEARIC ISLANDS

Ciutadella de Menorca. *www.infotelecom.es/ciutadella*
Meander through the burial tombs, caves, and other ancient wonders of the island of Menorca under this site's guidance. A map directs visitors to the island's many beaches. A very good calendar lists cultural events, and special sections show the old town, stone quarries, and signs of urbanization.

Guia de Formentera. *www.guiaformentera.com*
Along with tips on getting to Formentera, this site gives facts on the island's history and geography. For biology buffs, there's a photo-illustrated guide to plant and animal life. Sun worshipers can find a map to the best beaches, complete with a legend deciphering beach signs (a blank sign indicates a nude beach).

Ibiza Hotels. *www.ibiza-hotels.com*
As its name suggests, this site lists hotels in Ibiza and offers online reservation services. Additional perks: You can rent a car, buy a ferry ticket, check the weather report, use the currency converter, and see a virtual-reality panoramic view of the Ibiza harbor.

Ibiza Night. *www.ibizanight.com*
A hint of English-as-a-second-language, coupled with graphics that are equal parts artful and cheesy (a shopping cart on the moon?!), lends an exotic atmosphere to this site's descriptions of Ibiza's art scene, beaches,

fashions, music venues, accommodations, restaurants, and other cultural offerings. For the practical traveler, Ibiza Night lists local public services and emergency phone numbers.

THE COSTA DEL SOL

Absolute Marbella. *www.absolute-marbella.com*
Read the current issue of this Costa del Sol magazine, which includes restaurant reviews, horoscopes, an events calendar, and feature stories. There's also an A-to-Z phone directory of local businesses.

Costa del Sol: Everything Under the Mediterranean Sun. *www.costasol.com*
At this commercial site, you can book a room, hire a car, or find package deals on golf vacations and resort holidays.

Costa Guide. *www.costaguide.com*
This guide's tourist section points visitors to consulates and transportation schedules and provides an online yellow pages listing local shops and services. You can search for a restaurant by cuisine, find out where the good golf courses are, and read a short history of each town on the coast.

Fuengirola: Un Sol de Ciudad. *www.pta.es/fuengirola*
Calling Fuengirola the heart of Costa del Sol, this online brochure introduces the town's cuisine, art, culture, attractions, sports, and famous golf courses. There aren't a lot of details or interactive components, but the site does list hotels and their amenities, bus and train schedules, and useful phone numbers.

Marbella Scene: The Essence and Style of Marbella. *www.marbella scene.com*
A British writer relocated in Marbella shares his impressions of the place "where Europe meets Africa" and recommends his favorite bar, restaurant, hotel, and spots for quiet contemplation. Not much on information, but there are some beautiful photos.

ANDALUCIA

Altur: Travel and Tourism in Andalucia, Spain. *www.altur.com*
Looking for a relaxing sojourn in the countryside of southern Spain? Stop by this site, which directs visitors to beaches and natural areas, rural tourism, culture, and food in the sunny provinces of Sevilla, Granada, Málaga, Córdoba, Cádiz, Almeria, Jaén, and Huelva. You can also reserve hotel rooms and buy train or plane tickets online.

Andalucía: There's Only One. *www.andalucia.org*
There's more than one way to see the region of Andalusia. Each week, this site suggests a new travel route through the area. Better yet, there's a searchable directory of hotels, restaurants, leisure activities, tourist services, and transportation. For an overview of the region's history, geography, and culture, check out the guide's "Touristing in Andalucia" section.

Andalucia.com. *www.andalucia.com*

The Andalucia.com folks provide heaps of information about southern Spain's outdoorsy offerings: camping, hiking, climbing, sailing, hot-air ballooning, bullfighting. For less-adventurous tourists, the site covers museums, festivals, restaurants, flamenco, and the like. There's even a handy village-by-village guide.

Sevilla On Line. *www.sol.com*

Not only can you find a barber in Sevilla with help from this site, but you can also track down business conventions, hotels, bars, restaurants, museums, post offices, and city buses. It also includes a nice listing of fiesta days and other events.

hostel appendix

The source for all hostel listings and hostel-resource information below is the website for Spanish Youth Hostel Network (R.E.A.J., or, Red Española de Albergues Juveniles), a member of the International Youth Hostel Federation: **www.mtas.es/injuve/intercambios/albergues/reaj.html.** The R.E.A.J. is the Spanish link in a chain of approximately 6,000 youth hostels located in over 60 countries; there are 188 hostels in Spain alone. Membership in the R.E.A.J. enables travelers to stay in hostels and take part in hostel activities in Spain and abroad, as well as allows you to make reservations though its main association offices.

Catalunya, Madrid, and Valencia also offer access to the International (or "Central") Booking Network (IBN), which allows users to make reservations in other IBN-linked youth hostels all over the world *(Booking 725ptas (4,36 Euros), Cancellation 725ptas (4,36 Euros))*. The office of Cataluñya also accepts bookings made by phone or fax with a supplement of 725ptas (4,36 Euros).

Website information is subject to error, of course, and is constantly being updated. Please check the site before planning your trip, and even better, contact the individual hostel or one of the main offices directly.

Most of the hostels in Spain are located in areas that offer a wide range of recreational and outdoor sports activities, as well as cultural and environmental pursuits. Accommodations range from the charming and historic to the industrial and more perfunctory. Regardless of the building they are housed in, they are all held to a most respectable standard of service. Some general notes on rates and reservations precede the actual listings, which are offered in alphabetical order by city or town. You can visit the website *www.mtas.es/injuve/intercambios/albergues/reaj.html* to get more specific details about the hostels you are interested in.

Rates:
Youth *(14-25 years):* 500-1,400ptas (3,01-8,41 Euros)

Adult *(26 and over):* 600-1,900ptas (3,61-11,42 Euros)
Note: Rates for hostels in Spain are based on a category designation and may vary by season. Refer to the website **www.mtas.es/injuve/intercambios/albergues/reaj.html,** or check with a regional office or the hostel itself for current rates.

General Hours: Most hostels close around 11pm.

Reservations: Reservations phone numbers for individual hostels are listed when they were available. Besides checking the website above for individual hostels that offer online reservations, you may also call 976/714-797 or contact the main youth hostel association offices or the IBN locations listed above.

YOUTH HOSTEL ASSOCIATIONS

Junta de Andalucia
Inturjoven
calle Virgen de la Victoria 46
41011 Sevilla
Tel: 955/035-815
Fax: 955/035-850
E-mail: edominguez@inturjoven.
   junta-andalucia.es

Diputación General de Aragón
Departmento de Cultura y Turismo
Paseo Mª Agustín 36
50071 Zaragoza
Tel: 976/714-921
Fax: 976/714-049

Principado de Asturias
Instituto Asturiano de Juventud
calle Calvo Sotelo 5
33007 Oviedo
Tel: 985/108-350 or 985/108-355
Fax: 985/108-351

Govern Balear
Xarxa d'installacions de les Illes Balears
calle Jeroni Antich 5 – 3º – C
07003 Palma de Mallorca
Tel: 971/176-093 or 971/176-094
Fax: 971/176-096
Reservations: 902/111-188
E-mail: xib@bitel.es

Gobierno de Canarias
Dirección General de Juventud
Edificio Usos Múltiples II – 3º planta
Profesor Agustín Millares Carló 18
35003 Las Palmas de Gran Canaria
Tel: 928/306-397
Fax: 928/306-324

Gobierno de Canarias
Instituto Canario de Juventud
Leoncio Rodriguez 64º P
Edificio El Cabo
38203 La Laguna (Tenerife)
Tel: 922/630-690
Fax: 922/630-706

Diputación Regional de Cantabria
Dirección General de Juventud
calle Vargas 53 anexo
39010 Santander
Tel: 942/207-406 or 942/207-407
Fax: 942/207-507

Junta de Castilla y León
Consejería de Educación y Cultura
Dirección General de Juventud
Nicolás Salmerón 5
47071 Valladolid
Tel: 983/411-500
Fax: 983/411-570
E-mail: albergues.juveniles@svg.dgdj.
   cec.jcyl.es

Junta Comunidades Castilla la Mancha
Dirección General de Juventud
Plaza de Zocodover 7, 2ª-3ª P
45071 Toledo
Tel: 925/267-440 or 925/267-416
Fax: 925/267-455

Generalitat de Catalunya
Turisme Juvenil de Catalunya, S. A.
calle Rocafort 116-122
08015 Barcelona
Tel: 934/838-363
Fax: 934/838-347

Junta de Extremadura
Dirección General de Juventud
Travesía Rambla Santa Eulalia 1
06800 Mérida (Badajoz)
Tel: 924/381-709 or 924/385-927
Fax: 924/381-507
E-mail: aolmedo@ctv.es
Planintegral@ctv.es

Xunta de Galicia
Subdirección Xeral de Promoción e Actividades
San Caetano s/n
Bloque 3–1°
15771 Santiago de Compostela
Tel: 981/544-855
Fax: 981/545-843

Comunidad de Madrid
Dirección General de Juventud
calle Gran Vía 10-1°
28013 Madrid
Tel: 915/804-202 or 915/804-203
Fax: 915/804-204

C. A. de la Región de Murcia
Dirección General de Juventud
calle Villaleal 1
30001 Murcia
Tel: 968/366-630
Fax: 968/366-620
E-mail: Ana.Albacete@carm.es

Gobierno de la Rioja
Dirección General de Juventud y Deportes
calle Portales 1–1°
26071 Logroño

Tel: 941/291-100 or 941/291-827
Fax: 941/256-120
E-mail: oficina.juventud@larioja.org

Gobierno de Navarra
Instituto Navarro de Deporte y Juventud
calle Arrieta 25
31002 Pamplona
Tel: 948/427-840
Fax: 948/227-469
Reservations: 948/427-878
E-mail: ji.ausin.inigo@cfnavarra.es,
aricosan@cfnavarra.es

Eusko Jaurlaritza-Gobierno Vasco
Kultura Saila/Departamento de Cultura
Gazteria eta Komunitate Ekintzarako
  Zuzendaritza
Dirección de Juventud y Acción
  Comunitaria
calle Donostia-San Sebastian 1
01010 Vitoria-Gasteiz (Araba)
Tel: 945/019-511
Fax: 945/019-535

Generalitat Valenciana
Institut Valencià de la Joventut
calle del Hospital 2
46001 Valencia
Tel: 963/985-920
Fax: 963/985-913
Reservations: 963/985-900
Reservations fax: 963/985-914

CENTRAL BOOKING NETWORK (IBN)
Alicante
Ivaj
Plaza San Cristobal 8-10 1°A7B
03002 Alicante
Tel: 965/141-001
Fax: 965/144-789
E-mail: turivaj@ivaj.gva.es

Barcelona
Mare de Deu de Monserrat
pg. Mare de Deu del Coll 41-51
08023 Barcelona
Tel: 932/105-151
Fax: 932/100-798
E-mail: alberg_barcelona@tujuca.com

Tujuca
carrer rocafort 116-122
08015 Barcelona
Tel: 934/838-363
Fax: 934/838-350
E-mail: atencio_@tujuca.com

Castellón
Ivaj
Orfebre Santalinea 2
12005 Castellón de la Plana
Tel: 964/246-664
Fax: 964/246-662
E-mail: turivaj@ivaj.gva.es

El Masnou
J.M. Batista I Roca
avda. Srs. Cusí i Fortunet 52
08320 El Masnou (Barcelona)
Tel: 935/555-600
Fax: 935/400-552
E-mail: alberg_masnou@tujuca.com

Empuries
Empuries
les coves 41
17130 Empuries (Girona)
Tel: 972/771-200
Fax: 972/771-572
E-mail: alberg_empuries@tujuca.com

Madrid
Tive-Comunidad de Madrid
calle Fernando el Católico 88
28015 Madrid
Tel: 915/437-412
Fax: 915/440-062
E-mail: tive.juventud@comadrid.es

Planoles
Pere Figuera
Ctra. De Nevá, Prat Cap Riu
17535 Planoles (Girona)
Tel: 972/736-177
Fax: 972/736-431
E-mail: alberg_planoles@tujuca.com

Valencia
Turivaj
calle hospital 11
46001 Valencia
Tel: 963/869-700

Fax: 963/869-903
E-mail: turivaj@ivaj.gva.es

HOSTELS
Aguadulce
Albergue Juvenil de Aguadulce
Campillo del Moro s/n
04720 Aguadulce
Tel: 950/340-346
Fax: 950/345-855
Reservations: n/a
E-mail: n/a
# of beds: 210

Aguilas
Albergue Juvenil Calarreona
30880 Aguilas
Tel: 968/413-029
Fax: 968/413-029
Reservations: n/a
E-mail: n/a
# of beds: 82

Alacant
Residencia Juvenil "La Florida"
avda. Orihuela 59
03007 Alacant
Tel: 965/113-044
Fax: 965/282-754
Reservations: 963/985-900
E-mail: n/a
# of beds: 188

Albarracín
Albergue Juvenil "Rosa Brios"
calle Santa María 5
44100 Albarracín
Tel: 978/710-005
Fax: 978/710-005
Reservations: 976/714-797
E-mail: n/a
# of beds: 70

Alborache
Albergue Juvenil Torre D'alborache
Ctra. de Macastre
46369 Alborache
Tel: 962/508-123
Fax: 962/508-020
Reservations: 963/985-900
E-mail: n/a
# of beds: 116

Alburquerque
Albergue Juvenil Castillo de Luna
Castillo s/n
06510 Alburquerque
Tel: 924/400-041
Fax: 924/400-041
Reservations (required): 924/400-041
E-mail: n/a
# of beds: 8

Alcalá de Moncayo
Albergue Juvenil Alcalá de Moncayo
Puerta del Lugar s/n
50591 Alacalá de Moncayo
Tel: 976/646-459
Fax: 976/646-459
Reservations: 976/714-797
E-mail: n/a
# of beds: 86

Alcudia
Albergue Juvenil De Alcudia "La Victoria"
Ctra. Cabo Pinar, km. 4
07400 Alcudia
Tel: 971/545-395
Fax: 971/176-096
Reservations: 902/111-188
E-mail: xib@bitel.es
# of beds: 120

Algeciras
Albergue Juvenil de Algeciras
Ctra. N-340, km. 95
600 Bda. El Pelayo
11205 Algeciras
Tel: 956/679-060
Fax: 956/679-017
Reservations: n/a
E-mail: n/a
# of beds: 100

Almorox
Albergue Juvenil "Ecogranja san Pol"
Camino de Cadalso
45900 Almorox
Tel: 918/623-265 or 915/419-089
Fax: 918/624-065
Reservations (required): 918/623-265
E-mail: n/a
# of beds: 100

Alsasua
Albergue Juvenil Santo Cristo De Otadia
calle Zelai 91
31800 Alsasua
Tel: 948/564-814
Fax: 948/564-973
Group reservations: 948/427-898
E-mail: aalsasua@cfnavarra.es
# of beds: 88

Altafulla
Albergue Juvenil Casa Gran
Placeta 12
43893 Altafulla
Tel: 977/650-779
Fax: 977/650-588
Reservations: 934/838-363
E-mail: alberg_altafulla@tijuca.com
# of beds: 65

Aratores
Albergue Juvenil Aratores "Santa Maria de Aratores"
calle Molino de Aratorés s/n
22860 Aratores
Tel: 974/348-051
Fax: 976/423-019
Reservations: 976/714-797
E-mail: ep.ara1@escolapios.es
# of beds: 60

Arbejal
Albergue Juvenil Arbejal
Ctra. Arbejal
34843 Arbejal
Tel: 979/870-174
Fax: 978/870-174
Reservations: n/a
E-mail: n/a
# of beds: 80

Arriondas
Albergue Juvenil De Arriondas
calle El Barco 12
33540 Arriondas
Tel: 985/840-334
Fax: 985/841-282
Reservations: n/a
E-mail: n/a
# of beds: 12

Auñon
Albergue Juvenil Entrepeñas
Poblado de Entrepeñas
19130 Auñon
Tel: 949/358-415
Fax: 949/222-062
Reservations: 949/222-058
E-mail: n/a
# of beds: 60

Ávila
Albergue Juvenil Duperier
avda. de la Juventud s/n
05003 Avila
Tel: 920/221-716
Fax: 920/221-716
Reservations: n/a
E-mail: n/a
# of beds: 90

Baños de Monte Mayor
Residencia Juvenil Joaquin Sama
calle Calvo Sotelo s/n
10750 Baños de Monte Mayor
Tel: 927/428-003
Fax: n/a
Reservations (required):
    927/428-003
E-mail: n/a
# of beds: 10

Banyoles
Albergue Juvenil "Alberg Banyoles"
Migdia 10
17820 Banyoles
Tel: 972/475-454
Fax: 972/576-747
Reservations: 934/838-363
E-mail: n/a
# of beds: 100

Barbastro
Albergue Juvenil Joaquin
Costa-Barbastro
Plaza de los Pinos 9-13
22300 Barbastro
Tel: 974/313-310
Fax: 974/313-527
Reservations: n/a
E-mail: n/a
# of beds: 96

Barcelona
Albergue Juvenil Hostal de Joves
Pujades 29
08018 Barcelona
Tel: 933/003-104
Fax: 933/003-104
Reservations: 934/838-363
E-mail: n/a
# of beds: 80

Albergue Juvenil Mare de Deu de Monstserrat
pg. Ntra. Sra. del Coll 41-51
08023 Barcelona
Tel: 932/105-151
Fax: 932/100-798
Reservations: 934/838-363
E-mail: alberg_barcelona@tujuca.com
# of beds: 223

Albergue Juvenil Pere Tarres
Numancia 149-151
08029 Barcelona
Tel: 934/102-309
Fax: 934/196-268
Reservations: 934/838-363
E-mail: alberg@peretarres.org
# of beds: 100

Albergue Juvenil Studio
Duquesa de Orleans 56 bis
08034 Barcelona
Tel: 932/050-961
Fax: 932/050-900
Reservations: 934/838-363
E-mail: n/a
# of beds: 60

Barría
Albergue Juvenil Barria
Monasterio-Albergue de Barría
01208 Barria
Tel: 945/317-132
Fax: 945/317-168
Reservations: 945/181-988
E-mail: n/a
# of beds: 200

Bejar
Albergue Juvenil "Llano Alto"
El Castañar
37715 Bejar

Tel: 923/400-702
Fax: 923/400-702
Reservations: 923/404-052
E-mail: n/a
# of beds: 160

Benicarló
Residencia Juvenil Sant Crist Del Mar R.J.
avda. de Yecla 29
12580 Benicarló
Tel: 964/470-500
Fax: 964/460-225
Reservations: 963/985-900
E-mail: luis.burgos@ivaj.m400.gva.es
# of beds: 80

Benicassim
Albergue Juvenil Argentina
avda. Ferrándiz Salvador 40
12560 Benicassim
Tel: 964/300-949
Fax: 964/300-473
Reservations: 963/985-900
E-mail: rosario.espinosa@ivaj.m400.es
# of beds: 140

Bergondo
Albergue Juvenil Marina Española
Corbeiroa-Bergondo
15167 Bergondo
Tel: 981/620-118
Fax: 981/221-336
Reservations: 981/221-954
E-mail: n/a
# of beds: 100

Residencia Juvenil Gandario
15167 Bergondo
Tel: 981/791-005
Fax: n/a
Reservations (required): 981/791-005
E-mail: gandario@teleline.es
# of beds: 300

Biar
Albergue Juvenil Biar
Les Llomes de la Mare de Déu 6
03410 Biar
Tel: 965/810-875
Fax: 965/810-875
Reservations: 965/810-875

E-mail: alberguebiar@ctv.es
# of beds: 80

Biel
Albergue Juvenil Biel
avda. A. de la Mina s/n
50619 Biel
Tel: 976/669-001
Fax: 976/669-001
Reservations: 976/714-797
E-mail: n/a
# of beds: 26

Bijuesca
Albergue Juvenil Bijuesca
calle Virgen III 12
50316 Bijuesca
Fax: n/a
Reservations: n/a
E-mail: ib3100717@ibercaja.public.es
# of beds: 63
Albergue Juvenil Bijuesca
calle Virgen III 12
50316 Bijuesca
Tel: 976/847-292
Fax: n/a
Reservations: 976/714-797
E-mail: ib3100717@ibercaja.public.es
# of beds: 53

Bilbao
Residencia Juvenil "Bilbao Aterpetxea"
Ctra. Basurto Kastrexana 70
48002 Bilbao
Tel: n/a
Fax: 944/275-479
Reservations: 944/270-054
E-mail: aterpe@albergue.bilbao.net
# of beds: 132

Boñar
Albergue Juvenil "Pardomino"
avda. Asturias 13
24850 Boñar
Tel: 987/741-581 or 987/735-510
Fax: 987/741-581
Reservations: n/a
E-mail: n/a
# of beds: 215

Borja

Albergue Juvenil Santuario Misericordia-Borja
Santuario Misericordia
50540 Borja
Tel: 976/867-844
Fax: 976/714-049
Reservations: 976/714-797
E-mail: jjmarti@aragob.es
# of beds: 52

Botaya

Albergue Juvenil Casa del Herrero
calle Unica s/n
22711 Botaya
Tel: 974/359-853 or 976/215-324
Fax: 976/274-414
Reservations: 976/714-797
E-mail: n/a
# of beds: 46

Brañavieja

Albergue Juvenil Alto Campoo
Brañavieja
Tel: 942/779-328 or
    608/309-133
Fax: 942/779-328
Reservations: n/a
E-mail: n/a
# of beds: 42

Burgos

Residencia Juvenil Gil De Siloe
avda. General Vigón s/n
09006 Burgos
Tel: 947/220-362
Fax: 947/220-362
Reservations: n/a
E-mail: n/a
# of beds: 108

Cabrera de Mar

Albergue Juvenil Torre Ametller
Veïnat de Sta. Elena d'agell
08349 Cabrera de Mar
Tel: 937/594-448
Fax: 937/500-495
Reservations: 934/838-363
E-mail: alberg-
    cabrera@tujuca.com
# of beds: 150

Candanchú

Albergue Juvenil Aysa-Candanchú
Puerto de Somport
22889 Candanchú
Tel: 974/373-023
Fax: 974/373-023
Reservations: 976/714-797
E-mail: n/a
# of beds: 40

Canfranc-Estación

Albergue Juvenil Canfranc
Plaza Pilar 2-3
22880 Canfran-Estación
Tel: 974/293-025
Fax: 974/293-040
Reservations: 976/714-797
E-mail: jjmarti@aragob.es
# of beds: 36

Caracenilla

Albergue Juvenil Peñarrubias
calle Consuelo 4
16540 Caracenilla
Tel: 969/272-711
Fax: 969/272-652
Reservations (required):
    969/272-711
E-mail: n/a
# of beds: 30

Carrión de los Condes

Albergue Juvenil Rio Carrión
Plaza Martín Campagnat 1
34120 Carrión de los Condes
Tel: 979/881-063
Fax: 979/881-063
Reservations: n/a
E-mail: n/a
# of beds: 170

Castellbell i el Villar

Albergue Juvenil Viladoms de Baix
Crta. de la Bauma a Vacarisses, km.
    5,150
08296 Castellbell i el Villar
Tel: 938/282-236
Fax: 937/805-299
Reservations: 934/838-363
E-mail: n/a
# of beds: 90

Castelló de la Plana
Albergue Juvenil El Maestrat
avda. Germans Bou 26
12003 Castelló de la Plana
Tel: 964/220-457
Fax: 964/237-600
Reservations: 963/985-900
E-mail: n/a
# of beds: 84

Residencia Juvenil Mare De Déu Del Lledó
calle Orfebres Santalinea 2
12005 Castelló de la Plana
Tel: 964/254-096
Fax: 964/216-677
Reservations: 963/985-900
E-mail: n/a
# of beds: 80

Cercedilla
Albergue Juvenil Alvaro Iglesias
Puerto de Navacerrada
28470 Cercedilla
Tel: 918/523-887
Fax: 918/523-891 or 915/804-215
Reservations (required): 915/804-216
E-mail: n/a
# of beds: 92

Albergue Juvenil "Las Dehesas"
Ctra. Dehesas s/n
28470 Cercedilla
Tel: 918/520-135
Fax: 918/521-836 or 915/804-215
Reservations (required): 915/804-216
E-mail: n/a
# of beds: 72

Albergue Juvenil "Villa Castora"
Ctra. Dehesas s/n
28470 Cercedilla
Tel: 918/520-334
Fax: 918/522-411 or 915/804-215
Reservations (required): 915/804-216
E-mail: n/a
# of beds: 80

Chipiona
Albergue Juvenil de Chipiona
Pinar de la Villa s/n
11550 Chipiona
Tel: 956/371-480
Fax: 956/371-480
Reservations: n/a
E-mail: n/a
# of beds: 216

Ciudad Real
Albergue Juvenil Granja escuela Orea
Ctra. Toledo Aptado 489
13080 Ciudad Real
Tel: 926/690-241
Fax: n/a
Reservations (required): 926/690-241
E-mail: n/a
# of beds: 120

Coma-Ruga
Albergue Juvenil Santa Maria Del Mar
avda. Palfuriana 80
43880 Coma-Ruga
Tel: 977/680-008
Fax: 977/862-959
Reservations: 934/838-363
E-mail: alberg_comaru@tujuca.com
# of beds: 164

Córdoba
Albergue Juvenil de Córdoba
Plaza Judá Leví s/n
14003 Córdoba
Tel: 957/290-166
Fax: 957/290-500
Reservations: n/a
E-mail: n/a
# of beds: 109

Daroca
Albergue Juvenil Daroca
calle Cortes de Aragón 13
50360 Daroca
Tel: 976/800-129 or 976/801-268
Fax: 976/800-362
Reservations: 976/714-797
E-mail: n/a
# of beds: 60

Del Tebere
Albergue Juvenil Mn. Antoni Batlle
avda. Goles de L'Ebre s/n
43580 Del Tebere

Tel: 977/480-136
Fax: 977/481-284
Reservations: 934/838-363
E-mail: alberg_deltebre@tujuca.com
# of beds: 120

Donostia-San Sebastian
Albergue Juvenil La Sirena
Paseo Igeldo 25
20008 Donostia-San Sebastian
Tel: 943/310-268
Fax: 943/214-090
Reservations: 943/310-268
E-mail: n/a
# of beds: 96

Albergue Juvenil Uliamendi
Parque de Ulía, Pº de Ulía 299
20013 Donostia-San Sebastian
Tel: 943/311-293
Fax: 943/214-090
Reservations: 943/310-268
E-mail: n/a
# of beds: 60

Dosrius
Albergue Juvenil Mas Silvestre
calle Veïnat d'en Rimblas
08319 Dosrius
Tel: 937/955-014
Fax: 937/955-199
Reservations: 934/838-363
E-mail: n/a
# of beds: 150

El Bosque
Albergue Juvenil "El Bosque"
Molino de Enmedio s/n
11670 El Bosque
Tel: 956/716-212
Fax: 956/716-258
Reservations: n/a
E-mail: n/a
# of beds: 79

El Masnou
Albergue Juvenil J. M. Batista I Roca
avda. Srs. Cusí i Fotunet
08320 El Masnou
Tel: 935/555-600
Fax: 935/400-552

Reservations: 934/838-363
E-mail: alberg_masnou@tujuca.com
# of beds: 84

El Pueyo de Jaca
Albergue Juvenil Quinta Vista Alegre
Afueras de la Iglesia s/n
22661 El Pueyo de Jaca
Tel: 974/487-045
Fax: 974/487-045
Reservations: 976/714-797
E-mail: n/a
# of beds: 84

El Toboso
Albergue Juvenil el Quijote
avda. Castilla La Mancha 12
45820 El Toboso
Tel: 925/197-398
Fax: 925/197-398
Reservations (required): 925/197-398
E-mail: n/a
# of beds: 50

Empuries
Albergue Juvenil Empuries
Les Coves 41
17130 Empuries
Tel: 972/771-200
Fax: 972/771-572
Reservations: 934/838-363
E-mail: alberg-empuries@tujuca.com
# of beds: 68

Espejo
Albergue Juvenil Espejo
Carretera de Barrio 1
01423 Espejo
Tel: 947/351-150
Fax: n/a
Reservations: 945/181-988
E-mail: n/a
# of beds: 116

Espinosa de los Monteros
Albergue Juvenil Espinosa De Los Monteros
Ctra. de Baranda s/n
09560 Espinosa de los Monteros
Tel: 947/120-449 or 947/143-660
Fax: 947/120-449
Reservations: n/a

E-mail: n/a
# of beds: 60

Estella
Albergue Juvenil Oncineda
Monasterio de Irache s/n
31200 Estella
Tel: 948/555-022
Fax: 948/551-745
Group reservations: 948/427-898
E-mail: oncieda@accesocero.es
# of beds: 125

Ezcaray
Albergue Juvenil Molino Viejo
Camino del Molino Viejo s/n
26280 Ezcaray
Tel: 941/354-142
Fax: n/a
Reservations: 941/291-229 or
    941/201-100
E-mail: n/a
# of beds: 49

Figueres
Albergue Juvenil Tramuntana
Anicet Pagés 2
17600 Figueres
Tel: 972/501-213
Fax: 972/673-808
Reservations: 934/838-363
E-mail: alberg_figueres@tujuca.com
# of beds: 50

Girona
Albergue Juvenil Cerveri de Girona
Dels Ciutadans 9
17004 Girona
Tel: 972/218-003
Fax: 972/212-023
Reservations: 934/838-363
E-mail: alberg_girona@tujuca.com
# of beds: 100

Granada
Albergue Juvenil de Granada
calles Ramón and Cajal 2
18003 Granada
Tel: 958/284-306
Fax: 958/285-285
Reservations: n/a

E-mail: n/a
# of beds: 150

Grañón
Albergue Juvenil "Ermita El Carrasquedo"
Ctra. Nacional 120
26259 Grañón
Tel: 941/746-000
Fax: n/a
Reservations: 941/291-229 or
    941/201-100
E-mail: n/a
# of beds: 40

Hondarribia
Albergue Juvenil Juan Sebastián Elkano
Foroko Igoera z.g.
20280 Hondarribia
Tel: 943/641-550
Fax: 943/640-028
Group reservations: 943/641-550
E-mail: juv.hondarribia@gazteria.
    gipuzkoa.net
# of beds: 200

Huelva
Albergue Juvenil de Huelva
avda. Marchena Colombo 14
21004 Huelva
Tel: 959/253-793
Fax: 959/253-499
Reservations: n/a
E-mail: n/a
# of beds: 128

Jaca
Albergue Juvenil Escuelas Pias-Jaca
avda. Perimetral s/n
22700 Jaca
Tel: 974/360-536
Fax: 974/362-559
Reservations: 976/714-797
E-mail: n/a
# of beds: 150

Jerez
Albergue Juvenil de Jerez de la Frontera
avda. Carrero Blanco 30
11408 Jerez
Tel: 956/143-901
Fax: 956/143-263

Reservations: n/a
E-mail: n/a
# of beds: 120

La Almunia de Doña Godina
Albergue Juvenil Ramón y Cajal
avda. Laviaga Castillo
50100 La Amunia de Doña Godina
Tel: 976/600-833
Fax: 976/600-833
Reservations: 976/714-797
E-mail: n/a
# of beds: 72

La Molina
Albergue Juvenil Mare de Deu de Les Neus
Ctra. de Font Canaleta s/n
17537 La Molina
Tel: 972/892-012
Fax: 972/892-050
Reservations: 934/838-363
E-mail: alberg_lamolina@tujuca.com
# of beds: 148

La Seu d'Urgel
Albergue Juvenil la Valira
Joaquin Viola 57
25700 La Seu d'Urgel
Tel: 973/353-897
Fax: 973/353-874
Reservations: 934/838-363
E-mail: alberg_laseu@tujuca.com
# of beds: 100

La Vecilla
Albergue Juvenil "Santa Catalina"
Finca Santa Catalina
24840 La Vecilla
Tel: 987/741-212
Fax: 987/741-212
Reservations: n/a
E-mail: n/a
# of beds: 80

Las Majadas
Albergue Juvenil Las Callejones
Plaza Mayor 9
16142 Las Majadas
Tel: 969/283-050
Fax: 969/283-121
Reserva tions (required): 969/283-050

E-mail: n/a
# of beds: 45

Layos
Albergue Juvenil El Castillo de Layos
Conde de Mora 14
45123 Layos
Tel: 925/376-585
Fax: 913/572-564
Reservations: 913/572-564
E-mail: layoscam@cempresarial.com
# of beds: 192

Lekarotz (Valle de Baztan)
Albergue Juvenil Valle De Baztan
31795 Lekarotz (Valle de Baztan)
Tel: 948/581-804
Fax: 948/581-838
Group reservations: 948/427-898
E-mail: avbaztan@cfnavarra.es
# of beds: 90

León
Albergue Juvenil "Albergue Municipal De León"
Campos Góticos s/n
24005 León
Tel: 987/259-508 or
 987/255-805
Fax: 987/272-765
Reservations: n/a
E-mail: n/a
# of beds: 96

Albergue Juvenil Miguel De Unamuno
calle San Pelayo 15
24003 León
Tel: 987/233-010
Fax: 987/233-203
Reservations: n/a
E-mail: n/a
# of beds: 60

Residencia Juvenil "Consejo De Europa"
Pº del Parque 2
24005 León
Tel: 987/200-206 or 987/202-969
Fax: n/a
Reservations: n/a
E-mail: n/a
# of beds: 98

Residencia Juvenil Infanta Doña Sancha
Corredera 4
24004 León
Tel: 987/203-414 or 987/203-459
Fax: 987/251-525
Reservations: n/a
E-mail: n/a
# of beds: 124

Les
Albergue Juvenil "Matacabos"
Sant Jaume s/n
25540 Les
Tel: 973/648-048
Fax: 973/648-352
Reservations: 934/838-363
E-mail: n/a
# of beds: 46

L'Espluga de Francoli
Albergue Juvenil Jaume I
Les Masies s/n
43440 L'Espluga de Francoli
Tel: 977/870-356
Fax: 977/870-414
Reservations: 934/838-363
E-mail: alberg-espluga@tujuca.com
# of beds: 160

Llanes
Albergue Juvenil "Juventudes"
calle Celsa Amieva 7
33500 Llanes
Tel: 985/400-770
Fax: 985/400-770
Reservations: n/a
E-mail: n/a
# of beds: 16

Lleida
Albergue Juvenil Sant Anastasi
Rambla d'Aragó 11
25003 Lleida
Tel: 973/266-099
Fax: 973/261-865
Reservations: 934/838-363
E-mail: alberg_lleida@tujuca.com
# of beds: 120

Logroño
Residencia Universitaria
calle Caballero de la Rosa 38

26004 Logroño
Tel: 941/291-145
Fax: 941/256-120
Reservations: n/a
E-mail: n/a
# of beds: 92

Loredo
Albergue Juvenil Loredo
Bajada Playa de Loredo s/n
39140 Loredo
Tel: 942/509-204 or 619/464-221
Fax: n/a
Reservations: n/a
E-mail: n/a
# of beds: 48

Luarca
Albergue Juvenil Fernan Coronas
El Villar s/n
33700 Luarca
Tel: 985/640-676
Fax: 985/640-557
Reservations: n/a
E-mail: n/a
# of beds: 18

Lugo
Albergue Juvenil Hermanos Pedrosa
Pintor Corredoira 2
27002 Lugo
Tel: 982/223-726
Fax: n/a
Reservations: 982/294-352
E-mail: n/a
# of beds: 100

Residencia Juvenil Eijo Garay
Pintor Corredoira 4
27002 Lugo
Tel: 982/220-450
Fax: n/a
Reservations: 982/294-352
E-mail: n/a
# of beds: 100

Madrid
Albergue Juvenil Marcenado—Madrid
Sta. Cruz de Marcenado 28
28015 Madrid
Tel: 915/474-532
Fax: 915/481-196 or 915/804-215

Reservations (required): 915/804-216
E-mail: n/a
# of beds: 72

*Albergue Juvenil Richard Schirrmann—
Madrid*
Casa de Campo
28011 Madrid
Tel: 914/635-699
Fax: 914/644-685 or 915/804-215
Reservations (required): 915/804-216
E-mail: n/a
# of beds: 132

Albergue Juvenil San Fermín — Madrid
avda. de los Fueros 36
28041 Madrid
Tel: 917/920-897
Fax: 917/924-724
Reservations (required):
  917/920-897
E-mail: n/a
# of beds: 60

Manresa
Albergue Juvenil Del Carme
Plaça Milcentenari s/n
08240 Manresa
Tel: 938/750-396
Fax: 938/726-838
Reservations: 934/838-363
E-mail: alberg_manresa@tujuca.com
# of beds: 70

Mazagón
Albergue Juvenil de Mazagón
Cuesta de la Barca s/n
21130 Mazagón
Tel: 959/536-262
Fax: 959/536-201
Reservations: n/a
E-mail: n/a
# of beds: 132

Mieres
Albergue Juvenil De Bustiello
Bustiello
33600 Mieres
Tel: 985/421-318
Fax: 985/421-318
Reservations: n/a

E-mail: n/a
# of beds: 8

Miranda de Ebro
Albergue Juvenil Fernán González
Anduva 82
09200 Miranda de Ebro
Tel: 947/320-932
Fax: 947/320-334
Reservations: n/a
E-mail: n/a
# of beds: 110

Monachil
Albergue Juvenil "Sierra Nevada"
calle Penones 22
18196 Monachil
Tel: 958/480-305
Fax: 958/481-377
Reservations: n/a
E-mail: n/a
# of beds: 214

Mora de Rubielos
Albergue Juvenil Mora de Rubielos
calle Pedro Esteban 28
44400 Mora de Rubielos
Tel: 978/800-311
Fax: n/a
Reservations: n/a
E-mail: n/a
# of beds: 59

Moraira-Teluda
Albergue Juvenil "La Marina"
Camí del Campament 31
03724 Moraira-Teulada
Tel: 966/492-030 or 966/492-044
Fax: 966/491-051
Reservations: n/a
E-mail: n/a
# of beds: 130

Morella
Albergue Juvenil Francesc De Vinatea
Ctra. Morella-Forcall, km. 4,5
12300 Morella
Tel: 964/160-100
Fax: 964/160-977
Reservations: 963/985-900
E-mail: n/a
# of beds: 60

Munilla

Albergue Juvenil Hayedo De Santiago
calle Cipriano Martínez 19
26586 Munilla
Tel: 941/394-213
Fax: n/a
Reservations: 941/291-229 or 941/201-100
E-mail: n/a
# of beds: 55

Navamorcuende

Albergue Juvenil el Chortalillo
Camino de la Tablada s/n
45630 Navamorcuende
Tel: 925/868-256
Fax: 925/808-008
Reservations: 925/811-186
E-mail: n/a
# of beds: 136

Navarredonda de Gredos

Albergue Juvenil Navarredonda de Gredos
Ctra. C-500. km. 41,5
05635 Navarredonda de Gredos
Tel: 920/348-005
Fax: 920/348-005
Reservations: n/a
E-mail: albngredos@dvnet.es
# of beds: 63

Naves

Albergue Juvenil "Rectoria de la Selva"
La Selva Ctra. de Vielha s/n
25286 Naves
Tel: 973/629-92-71
Fax: 937/805-299
Reservations: 934/838-363
E-mail: n/a
# of beds: 111

Olot

Albergue Juvenil Torre Malagrida
pg. de Barcelona 15
17800 Olot
Tel: 972/264-200
Fax: 972/271-896
Reservations: 934/838-363
E-mail: alberg_olot@tujuca.com
# of beds: 76

Orea

Albergue Juvenil El Autillo
Ctra. de Tragacete s/n
Llano Hoz Seca
19311 Orea
Tel: 949/836-470
Fax: 949/836-435
Reservations (required): 949/836-470
E-mail: n/a
# of beds: 60

Ossa De Montiel

Albergue Juvenil Alonso Quinjano
Ctra. de Las Lagunas
13249 Ossa De Montiel
Tel: 926/528-053
Fax: n/a
Reservations: 967/215-012
E-mail: n/a
# of beds: 80

Ourense

Residencia Juvenil Florentino Lopez Cuevillas
A. Pérez Serantes 2
32005 Ourense
Tel: 988/252-412
Fax: n/a
Reservations (required): 988/252-412
E-mail: n/a
# of beds: 60

Oviedo

Albergue Juvenil Ramón Menéndez Pidal
calle Julián Clavería 14
33006 Oviedo
Tel: 985/232-054
Fax: 985/233-393
Reservations: n/a
E-mail: n/a
# of beds: 6/12

Palencia

Residencia Juvenil Escuela De Castilla
avda. San Telmo s/n
34004 Palencia
Tel: 979/721-475
Fax: n/a
Reservations: n/a
E-mail: n/a
# of beds: 65

Residencia Juvenil Victorio Macho
Doctor Fleming s/n
34002 Palencia
Tel: 979/711-676
Fax: n/a
Reservations: n/a
E-mail: n/a
# of beds: 38

Palma de Mallorca
Albergue Juvenil Platja De Palma
Costa Brava 12
Sometines, El Arenal
07610 Palma de Mallorca
Tel: 971/260-892
Fax: 971/176-096
Reservations: 902/111-188
E-mail: albergue.platja.de.
  palma@bitel.es
# of beds: 80

Pamplona
Albergue Juvenil Fuerte Del Principe R.J.
calle Goroabe 36
31005 Pamplona
Tel: 948/291-206
Fax: 948/290-540
Group reservations: 948/427-898
E-mail:
  residencia.fuerte.principe@cfnavarra.es
# of beds: 25

Peñaranda de Bracamonte
Residencia Juvenil Diego De Torres y Villaroel
Severo Ochoa 4
37300 Peñaranda de Bracamonte
Tel: 923/540-988
Fax: n/a
Reservations: n/a
E-mail: n/a
# of beds: 50

Peralta de la Sal
Albergue Juvenil Peralta de la Sal
Plaza Escuelas Pias 1
22513 Peralta de la Sal
Tel: 974/411-031
Fax: 974/411-203
Reservations: 976/714-797
E-mail: n/a
# of beds: 80

Pesquera
Albergue Juvenil Fernandez De Los Rios
39491 Pesquera
Tel: 942/778-614
Fax: n/a
Reservations: n/a
E-mail: n/a
# of beds: 40

Planoles
Albergue Juvenil Per e Figuera
Ctra. de Nevá, Prat Cap Riu
17535 Planoles
Tel: 972/736-177
Fax: 972/736-431
Reservations: 934/838-363
E-mail: alberg_planoles@tujuca.com
# of beds: 170

Platja de Piles
Albergue Juvenil Mar I Vent
Dr. Fleming s/n
46712 Platja de Piles
Tel: 962/831-625
Fax: 962/831-121
Reservations: 963/985-900
E-mail: pascual.gregori@ivaj.m400.gva.es
# of beds: 89

Plentzia
Residencia Juvenil De "A.R. Plentzia"
Ibiltoki 1
48620 Plentzia
Tel: 946/771-866
Fax: 946/773-041
Group reservations: 944/208-746
E-mail: n/a
# of beds: 12

Poble nou del Delta
Albergue Juvenil l'Encanyissada
Plaça del Jardi s/n
43549 Poble nou del Delta
Tel: 977/742-203
Fax: 977/742-709
Reservations: 934/838-363
E-mail: alberg_poblenou@tujuca.com
# of beds: 50

Poo de Llanes
Albergue Juvenil Fonte Del Cai
carretera General

33500 Poo de Llanes
Tel: 985/400-205
Fax: 985/401-019
Reservations: n/a
E-mail: n/a
# of beds: 10

Punta Umbría
Albergue Juvenil "Punta Umbría"
avda. Océano 13
21100 Punta Umbría
Tel: 959/311-650
Fax: 959/314-229
Reservations: n/a
E-mail: n/a
# of beds: 100

Queralbs
Albergue Juvenil Pic de L'Aliga
Nuria
17534 Queralbs
Tel: 972/732-048
Fax: 972/732-043
Reservations: 934/838-363
E-mail: alberg_nuria@tujuca.com
# of beds: 136

Rascafria
Albergue Juvenil "Los Batanes"
Finca los Batanas (Monasterio El Paular)
28740 Rascafria
Tel: 918/691-511
Fax: 918/690-125
Reservations: n/a
E-mail: n/a
# of beds: 122

Ribadesella
Albergue Juvenil Roberto Frassinelli
Ricardo Canga s/n
33560 Ribadesella
Tel: 985/861-380
Fax: 985/861-380
Reservations: n/a
E-mail: n/a
# of beds: 6

Roncesvalles
Albergue Juvenil Roncesvalles/Orreaga
31650 Roncesvalles
Tel: 948/760-302
Fax: 948/760-362

Group reservations: 948/427-898
E-mail: aronces@cfnavarra.es
# of beds: 80

Ruiloba
Albergue Juvenil Gargantia
Bº de la Iglesia s/n
39527 Ruiloba
Tel: 942/720-172 or 608/285-167
Fax: n/a
Reservations: n/a
E-mail: n/a
# of beds: 40

Salamanca
Albergue Juvenil Salamanca
Escoto 13 and 15
37001 Salamanca
Tel: 923/269-141
Fax: 923/214-227
Reservations: n/a
E-mail: esterra@mmteam.interbook.net
# of beds: 65

Salardú
Albergue Juvenil era Garona
Ctra. de Vielha s/n
25598 Salardú
Tel: 973/645-271
Fax: 973/644-136
Reservations: 934/838-363
E-mail: n/a
# of beds: 180

San Juan de Plan
Albergue Juvenil "El Molin" San Juan de Plan
calle Las Callerizas s/n
22367 San Juan de Plan
Tel: 974/506-097 or 974/506-208
Fax: 974/506-208
Reservations: 976/714-797
E-mail: n/a
# of beds: 22

San Lorenzo de el Escorial
Albergue Juvenil el Escorial
Residencia 14
28200 San Lorenzo de el Escorial
Tel: 918/905-924
Fax: 918/900-620 or 915/804-215
Reservations (required): 915/804-216

E-mail: n/a
# of beds: 85

Albergue Juvenil Sta. Maria Buen Aire
Finca La Herrería
28200 San Lorenzo de el Escorial
Tel: 918/903-640
Fax: 918/903-792 or 915/804-215
Reservations (required): 915/804-216
E-mail: n/a
# of beds: 88

San Martin de Castañeda (Lago de Sanabria)
Albergue Juvenil San Martín De Castañeda
Ctra. Lago de Sanabria
49361 San Martín de Castañeda (Lago de Sanabria)
Tel: 980/622-062
Fax: 980/622-053
Reservations: n/a
E-mail: n/a
# of beds: 80

San Pablo de los Montes
Albergue Juvenil Granja Escuela los Baños del Sagrario
Paraje Baños del Sagrario
45120 San Pablo de los Montes
Tel: 925/415-411 or 925/416-057
Fax: 925/415-411
Reservations (required): 925/415-411
E-mail: n/a
# of beds: 250

San Rafael
Albergue Juvenil "El Recreo"
Pinar 1
40410 San Rafael
Tel: 921/171-900
Fax: 921/171-900
Reservations: n/a
E-mail: n/a
# of beds: 72

Albergue Juvenil San Rafael
Pº San Juan
40410 San Rafael
Tel: 921/171-457
Fax: n/a
Reservations: n/a

E-mail: n/a
# of beds: 50

San Vicente del Monte
Albergue Juvenil San Vicente del Monte
39952 San Vicente del Monte
Tel: 942/705-073 or 619/464-193
Fax: n/a
Reservations: n/a
E-mail: n/a
# of beds: 40

Santa Maria de Guia
Residencia Juvenil San Fernando
avda. de la Juventud s/n
35450 Santa Maria de Guia
Tel: 928/550-685
Fax: 928/882-728
Reservations: n/a
E-mail: n/a
# of beds: 70

Santiago de Compostela
Albergue Juvenil Monte do Gozo
Ctra. de Santiago — Aeropuerto km. 3
15820 Santiago de Compostela
Tel: 981/558-942
Fax: 981/562-892
Reservations (required): 981/558-942
E-mail: n/a
# of beds: 300

Segovia
Residencia Juvenil Emperador Teodosio
Pº Conde de Sepúlveda 4
40002 Segovia
Tel: 921/441-111 or 921/441-047
Fax: n/a
Reservations: n/a
E-mail: n/a
# of beds: 118

Seseña Nuevo
Albergue Juvenil Santa Maria del Sagrario
Ctra. de Andalucía, km. 36,200
45224 Seseña Nuevo
Tel: 918/936-152
Fax: 918/936-152
Reservations: 925/267-700
E-mail: n/a
# of beds: 56

Sin
Albergue Juvenil Sin
calle Unica s/n
22366 Sin
Tel: 974/506-212
Fax: n/a
Reservations: 976/714-797
E-mail: n/a
# of beds: 48

Siresa
Albergue Juvenil de Siresa
Reclusa s/n
22790 Siresa
Tel: 976/615-283 or 619/561-004
Fax: 976/615-283
Reservations: 976/714-797
E-mail: n/a
# of beds: 53

Soloranzo
Albergue Juvenil Gerardo Diego
Bº Quintana s/n
39738 Soloranzo
Tel: 942/676-342
Fax: 942/676-342
Reservations: n/a
E-mail: n/a
# of beds: 72

Soncillo
Albergue Juvenil Soncillo
avda. Alejandro Rodriguez de
  Valcarcel
09572 Soncillo
Tel: 947/153-024 or 947/153-080
Fax: n/a
Reservations: n/a
E-mail: n/a
# of beds: 60

Soria
*Residencia Juvenil Antonio
Machado*
Plaza José Antonio 1
42003 Soria
Tel: 975/220-089
Fax: n/a
Reservations: n/a
E-mail: n/a
# of beds: 95

Residencia Juvenil Juan A. Gaya Nuño
calle San Francisco 1
42003 Soria
Tel: 975/221-466
Fax: n/a
Reservations: n/a
E-mail: n/a
# of beds: 105

Soto de Cameros
*Albergue Juvenil Hospital
San José*
San José s/n
26132 Soto de Cameros
Tel: 941/439-033
Fax: 941/256-120
Reservations: 941/291-229 or
  941/201-100
E-mail: n/a
# of beds: 50

Talavera de la Reina
Albergue Juvenil "Talavera"
Ctra. Cervera, km. 3,5
45600 Talavera de la Reina
Tel: 925/709-482
Fax: 925/709-588
Reservations: 925/709-588
E-mail: n/a
# of beds: 186

Tárrega
Albergue Juvenil ca n'Aleix
Plaça del Came 5
25300 Tárrega
Tel: 973/313-053
Fax: 973/500-037
Resevations: 934/838-363
E-mail: alberg_tarrega@tujuca.com
# of beds: 110

Teruel
Albergue Juvenil "Luis Buñuel"
R. Ciudad Escolar s/n
44003 Teruel
Tel: 978/601-712 or
  978/602-223
Fax: 978/605-351
Reservations: 976/714-797
E-mail: n/a
# of beds: 166

Toledo

Residencia Juvenil Castillo San Servando
Castillo San Servando
45006 Toledo
Tel: 925/224-554
Fax: 925/213-954
Reservations: 925/267-700
E-mail: n/a
# of beds: 106

Torrejón el Rubio

Albergue Juvenil Centro de Educación Ambiental "la Dehesa"
Gabriel and Galán 17
10694 Torrejón el Rubio
Tel: 927/455-178
Fax: 927/455-096
Reservations (required): 927/455-178
E-mail: fondotorrejon@sinix.net
# of beds: 30

Tragacete

Albergue Juvenil "San Blas"
16150 Tragacete
Tel: 969/289-131
Fax: 969/178-866
Reservations: 969/178-859
E-mail: n/a
# of beds: 60

Ugena

Albergue Juvenil la Chopera
Camino de Yuncos
45217 Ugena
Tel: 916/414-422 or
   925/592-741
Fax: n/a
Reservations: n/a
E-mail: n/a
# of beds: 20

Uña

Albergue Juvenil "La Cañadilla"
Egido 23
16152 Uña
Tel: 969/281-464
Fax: n/a
Reservations: 969/282-852
E-mail: n/a
# of beds: 30

Uncastillo

Albergue Juvenil De Ayllón
calle Mediavilla 30
50678 Uncastillo
Tel: 976/679-400
Fax: 976/679-497
Reservations: 976/714-797
E-mail: n/a
# of beds: 50

Unicastillo

Albergue Juvenil de Ayllon
calle Mediavilla 30
50678 Unicastillo
Tel: 976/679-400
Fax: 976/679-497
Reservations: n/a
E-mail: n/a
# of beds: 50

Undués de Lerda

Albergue Juvenil Undués de Lerda
Herrería s/n
50689 Undués de Lerda
Tel: 948/888-105 or 689/488-745
Fax: 948/888-105
Reservations: 976/714-797
E-mail: n/a
# of beds: 56

Valdea Vellano de Tera

Albergue Juvenil Valdea Vllano De Tera
calle Soledad s/n
42165 Valdea Vellano de Tera
Tel: 975/273-042
Fax: n/a
Reservations: n/a
E-mail: n/a
# of beds: 70

Valdepeñas

Albergue JuveniL "El Cañaveral"
Ctra. Valdepeñas-San Carlos del Valle,
   km. 6
13300 Valdepeñas
Tel: 926/324-706
Fax: 926/324-708
Reservations (required): 926/324-706
E-mail: n/a
# of beds: 53

Valencia

Albergue Juvenil La Paz
avda.del Puerto 69
46021Valencia
Tel: 963/690-152
Fax: 963/607-002
Reservations: n/a
E-mail: j.badenes@valenciamail.net
# of beds: 110

Valencia de Alcantara

Albergue Juvenil sta ma de Guadalupe
Puerto Roque
10500 Valencia de Alcantara
Tel: 927/584-059
Fax: 927/584-059
Reservations (required):
   927/584-059
E-mail: n/a
# of beds: 10

Valladolid

Albergue Juvenil Rio Esgueva
Pº Cementerio 2
47011 Valladolid
Tel: 983/251-550
Fax: n/a
Reservations: n/a
E-mail: n/a
# of beds: 108

Vic

Albergue Juvenil Canonge Collell
avda. d'Olimpia s/n
08500 Vic
Tel: 938/894-938
Fax: 938/833-062
Reservations: 934/838-363
E-mail: alberg_vic@tujuca.com
# of beds: 156

Vigo

Residencia Juvenil Altamar
Cesareo González 4
36210 Vigo
Tel: 986/290-808
Fax: n/a
Reservations: n/a
E-mail: n/a
# of beds: 80

Villalba de la Sierra

Albergue Juvenil "Casa Flores"
Constitución 44
16140 Villalba de la Sierra
Tel: 969/281-250
Fax: n/a
Reservations (required): 969/281-250
E-mail: n/a
# of beds: 16

Villamanin

Albergue Juvenil Villamanin
Plaza del Ayuntamiento s/n
24680 Villamanin
Tel: 987/598-243
Fax: 987/240-002
Reservations: 987/240-002
E-mail: n/a
# of beds: 56

Villanua

Albergue Juvenil Villanua "Santa M'del Pilar"
Camino de la Selva 18
22870 Villanua
Tel: 974/378-016
Fax: 974/293-040
Reservations: 976/714-797
E-mail: n/a
# of beds: 100

Vitoria-Gasteiz

Albergue Juvenil Carlos Abaitua
Escultor Isaac Díez s/n
01007 Vitoria-Gasteiz
Tel: 945/148-100
Fax: 945/148-100
Reservations: 945/181-988
E-mail: n/a
# of beds: 20/100

Viznar

Albergue Juvenil de Viznar
Camino de Fuente Grande s/n
18179 Viznar
Tel: 958/543-307
Fax: 958/543-448
Reservations: n/a
E-mail: n/a
# of beds: 108

Yeste
Albergue Juvenil "Arroyo de la Sierra"
Valle del Tus
02480 Yeste
Tel: 967/574-227
Fax: 967/301-662
Reservations (required): 967/574-227
E-mail: n/a
# of beds: 50

Zamora
Residencia Juvenil Doña Urraca
calle Villalpando 7
49002 Zamora
Tel: 980/512-671
Fax: 980/512-759
Reservations: n/a
E-mail: n/a
# of beds: 115

Zapillo
Albergue Juvenil de Almería
calle Isla Fuerteventura s/n
04007 Zapillo
Tel: 950/269-788

Fax: 950/271-744
Reservations: n/a
E-mail: n/a
# of beds: 164

Zaragoza
Albergue Juvenil "Baltasar Gracián"
calles Franco and López 4
50005 Zaragoza
Tel: 976/551-387
Fax: 976/553-432
Reservations: 976/714-797
E-mail: n/a
# of beds: 50

Zarautz
Albergue Juvenil Monte Albertia
San Ignacio 25
20800 Zarautz
Tel: 943/132-910
Fax: 943/130-006
Reservations: 943/132-910
E-mail : juv.zarautz@gazteria.
  gipuzkoa.net
# of beds: 182

glossary of useful spanish terms

Most Spaniards are very patient with foreigners who try to speak their language. Although you might encounter several regional languages and dialects in Spain, Castillian (Castellano, or simply Español) is understood everywhere. In Catalunya they speak Catalán (the most widely spoken non-national language in Europe); in the Basque country, they speak Euskerra; in Galicia, you'll hear Gallego. Still, a few words in Castellano will usually get your message across with no problem.

When traveling, it helps a lot to know a few basic phrases, so we've included a list of certain simple phrases in Castillian Spanish for expressing basic needs, followed by some common menu items.

▶▶ENGLISH-CASTILLIAN SPANISH PHRASES

English	Spanish	Pronunciation
Good day	**Buenos días**	*bway*-nohss *dee*-ahss
How are you?	**¿Cómo está?**	*koh*-moh ess-*tah*?
Very well	**Muy bien**	mwee byen
Thank you	**Gracias**	*grah*-see-ahss
You're welcome	**De nada**	day *nah*-dah
Goodbye	**Adios**	ah-*dyohss*
Please	**Por favor**	pohr fah-*vohr*
Yes	**Sí**	see
No	**No**	noh
Excuse me	**Perdóneme**	pehr-*doh*-ney-may
Give me	**Déme**	*day*-may
Where is...?	**¿Dónde está...?**	*dohn*-day ess-*tah*...?

English	Spanish	Pronunciation
the station	**la estación**	lah ess-tah-*seown*
a hotel	**un hotel**	oon oh-*tel*
a gas station	**una gasolinera**	*oon*-uh gah-so-lee-*nay*-rah
a restaurant	**un restaurante**	oon res-tow-*rahn*-tay
the toilet	**el baño**	el *bahn*-yoh
a good doctor	**un buen médico**	oon bwayn *may*-thee-co
the road to...	**el camino a/hacia...**	el cah-*mee*-noh ah/*ah*-see-ah...
To the right	**A la derecha**	ah lah day-*reh*-chuh
To the left	**A la izquierda**	ah lah ees-key-*ehr*-thah
Straight ahead	**Derecho**	day-*reh*-cho
I would like	**Quisiera**	key-see-*ehr*-ah
I want	**Quiero**	*kyehr*-oh
to eat.	**comer**	ko-*mayr*
a room.	**una habitación**	*oon*-nuh ha-bee-tah-*seown*
Do you have...?	**¿Tiene usted?**	tyeh-nay oo-*sted*?
a book.	**un libro**	oon *lee*-bro
a dictionary.	**un diccionario**	oon deek-seown-*ar*-eo
How much is it?	**¿Cuánto cuesta?**	*kwahn*-to *kwess*-tah?
When?	**¿Cuándo?**	*kwahn*-doh?
What?	**¿Qué?**	kay?
There is (Is there...?)	**¿Hay (...?)**	eye...?
What is there?	**¿Qué hay?**	kay eye?
Yesterday	**Ayer**	ah-*yer*
Today	**Hoy**	oy
Tomorrow	**Mañana**	mahn-*yahn*-ah
Good	**Bueno**	*bway*-no
Bad	**Malo**	*mah*-lo
Better (best)	**(Lo) Mejor**	(loh) meh-*hor*
More	**Más**	mahs
Less	**Menos**	*may*-noss
No smoking	**Se prohíbe fumar**	say pro-*hee*-bay foo-*mahr*
Postcard	**Tarjeta postal**	tar-*hay*-ta pohs-*tahl*
Insect repellent	**Rapelente**	rah-pey-*yahn*-te
	contra insectos	*cohn*-trah een-*sehk*-tos

MORE USEFUL PHRASES

English	Spanish	Pronunciation
Do you speak English?	**¿Habla usted inglés?**	*ah*-blah oo-*sted* een-*glays*?
Is there anyone here who speaks English?	**¿Hay alguien aquí qué hable inglés?**	eye *ahl*-ghee-en ah-*key* kay *ah*-blay een-*glays*?
I speak a little Spanish.	**Hablo un poco de español.**	*ah*-blow oon *poh*-koh day ess-pah-*nyol*
I don't understand Spanish very well.	**No (lo) entiendo muy bien el español.**	noh (loh) ehn-tee-*ehn*-do moo-ee bee-ayn el ess-pah-*nyol*
The meal is good.	**Me gusta la comida.**	may *goo*-sta lah koh-*mee*-dah
What time is it?	**¿Qué hora es?**	kay *oar*-ah ess?

May I see your menu?	**¿Puedo ver el menú (la carta)?**	*puay*-tho veyr el *may*-noo (lah *car*-tah)?
The check please.	**La cuenta por favor.**	lah *quayn*-tah pohr fa-*vorh*
What do I owe you?	**¿Cuánto lo debo?**	Kwahn-toh loh *day*-boh?
What did you say?	**¿Cómo?**	*Koh*-moh?
I want (to see)	**Quiero (ver)**	Key-*yehr*-oh vehr
a room	**un cuarto** *or*	oon *kwar*-toh
	una habitación	*oon*-nuh ha-bee-tah-*seown*
for two persons.	**para dos personas**	*pahr*-ah doss pehr-*sohn*-as
with (without) bathroom.	**con (sin) baño**	kohn (seen) *bah*-nyoh
We are staying here	**Nos quedamos aquí**	nohs kay-*dahm*-ohss ah-*key*
only...	***solamente...***	sohl-ah-*mayn*-tay
one night.	**una noche**	oon-ah *noh*-chay
one week.	**una semana**	oon-ah say-*mahn*-ah
We are leaving	**Partimos (Salimos)**	Pahr-*tee*-mohss (Sah-*lee*-mohss)
tomorrow.	**mañana**	mahn-*nyan*-ah
Do you accept	**¿Acepta usted**	Ah-*sayp*-tah oo-*sted* chay
traveler's checks?	**cheques de viajero?**	kays day bee-ah-*hehr*-oh?
Is there a Laundromat	**¿Hay una lavandería**	Eye *oon*-ah lah-*vahn*-day-ree-ah
near here?	**cerca de aquí?**	*sehr*-ka day ah-*key*?
Please send these	**Hágame el favor de**	*Ah*-ga-may el fah-*vhor* day
clothes	**mandar esta ropa**	mahn-*dahr* ays-tah *rho*-pah
to the laundry.	**a la lavandería**	a lah lah-*vahn*-day-ree-ah

NUMBERS

1	**uno**	(*ooh*-noh)
2	**dos**	(dohs)
3	**tres**	(trayss)
4	**cuatro**	(*kwah*-troh)
5	**cinco**	(*seen*-koh)
6	**seis**	(sayss)
7	**siete**	(*syeh*-tay)
8	**ocho**	(*oh*-choh)
9	**nueve**	(*nway*-bay)
10	**diez**	(dee-*ess*)
11	**once**	(*ohn*-say)
12	**doce**	(*doh*-say)
13	**trece**	(*tray*-say)
14	**catorce**	(kah-*tor*-say)
15	**quince**	(*keen*-say)
16	**dieciseis**	(de-*ess*-ee-sayss)
17	**diecisiete**	(de-*ess*-ee-*syeh*-tay)
18	**dieciocho**	(dee-*ess*-ee-*oh*-choh)
19	**diecinueve**	(dee-*ess*-ee-*nway*-bay)
20	**veinte**	(*bayn*-tay)

30	**treinta**	(*trayn*-tah)
40	**cuarenta**	(kwah-*ren*-tah)
50	**cincuenta**	(seen-*kwen*-tah)
60	**sesenta**	(say-*sen*-tah)
70	**setenta**	(say-*ten*-tah)
80	**ochenta**	(oh-*chen*-tah)
90	**noventa**	(noh-*ben*-tah)
100	**cien**	(see-*en*)
200	**doscientos**	(*dos*-se-en-tos)
500	**quinientos**	(keen-ee-*ehn*-tos)
1,000	**mil**	(meal)

TRANSPORTATION TERMS

English	Spanish	Pronunciation
Airport	**Aeropuerto**	Ah-ay-row-*por*-tow
Flight	**Vuelo**	Boo-*ay*-low
Rental car	**Alquila de Autos**	Al-key-lah day ow-tohs
Bus	**Autobús**	ow-toh-*boos*
Bus or truck	**Camión**	ka-mee-*ohn*
Lane	**Carril**	kah-*rreal*
Nonstop	**Directo**	dee-*reck*-toh
Luggage storage area	**Guarda equipaje**	gwar-dah eh-key-*pah*-hay
Arrival gates	**Llegadas**	yay-*gah*-dahs
Originates at this station	**Local**	loh-*kahl*
Originates elsewhere;	**De Paso**	day *pah*-soh
stops if seats available	**Para si hay lugares**	pah-rah *see* aye loo-gahr-*ays*
First class	**Primera**	pree-*mehr*-oh
Second class	**Segunda**	say-*goon*-dah
Baggage claim area	**Recibo de Equipajes**	ray-*see*-boh day eh-key-*pah*-hays
Waiting room	**Sala de Espera**	*Saw*-lah day ess-*pehr*-ah
Toilets	**Aseos**	Ah-say-oos
Ticket window	**Taquilla**	tah-*key*-lah

about the authors

Amanda Buttinger lives on the coast of summer outdoor cafes in the capital of Spain with a Basque star of the stage. She doesn't get hungry for lunch until at least two and has made savoring *café con leche* after the meal and digesting every other moment in life a profession. Along with having a new *sobrin@,* there are plenty of Spanish tapas and wine on the menu in her future. She continues to be seduced by travel writing. Everytime she says it's the last...till they ask her again. In the meantime, she's workin' like she doesn't need the money, lovin' like she's never been hurt, and dancin' like she's under the spotlight.

Arianna Martinez knew when she was a little girl that she would be published by the time she was 21 and while a travel guide isn't quite what she had in mind, she thinks it makes for a good story. She fancies herself full of good stories. Arianna is a student at Purchase College, where she has discovered an unexpected passion for Political Economy. She puts her creative efforts towards the up-and-coming online cultural magazine *the. blowup.com*. Arianna thinks traveling is as necessary as chocolate, appreciates critical and clever discourse, and is excited about the prospect of graduate school. She lives for certain people and certain places that keep her feeling lucky, specifically her sister, her family, her friends, Spain, and NYC. She would note that on her first day of kindergarten she dictated a bio to her teacher that said, "My name is Arianna Martinez. I was born in NYC. I have one sister and a cat. I like to write books and watch TV." Strangely, these things are still relevant. She hopes they will still be relevant 15 years from now, too.

Will Lloyd is biding his time in New York City until he finds a fortune and can spend the rest of his life lost somewhere on the globe. He finds ways to make money for his outing as an assistant editor of documentary films and as a freelance travel writer. His latest endeavor calls upon his great intellect to become a Dive Master in Honduras. He would like to thank his mom and dad and all his friends for supporting him in his crazy adventures.

A recent graduate of SUNY Albany, **Mike Livermore** has never taken a cab for a distance less than 2 miles, and he never will. When you speed around at 50 mph, you miss all the good stuff. However, when you stumble around at 5:00 am....Learning foreign tongues, drinking, smelling, talking about real wine, reading the writings of crazy philosophers, daydreaming, seeing everything and not photographing anything, talking to genuine people, sleeping in strange beds, and engaging in an eternal search for the authentic are a few of Mike's favorite things. While he sometimes gets a little confused as he oscillates between his various personalities as an outdoor addict, a stoic self-denying radical philosopher, a grassroots environmental organizer, and a travel bum, Mike has learned that lunacy is a gift, when you learn to nurture it.

Brian Frank is a graduate of UC Santa Cruz and New York University's Graduate Dramatic Writing Program. He currrently works at a homeless shelter in Northern California. Credit is due to all those who helped him find his way throughout Southern Spain, including Paco in Córdoba, the girls of Granada, Brits in Valencia, Anna in Las Alpujarras and the biggest tio of them all, Tyler in Sevilla.